Visual C++® 6

Mickey Williams, David Bennett, et al.

SAMS

Unleashed

Visual C++ 6 Unleashed

International Standard Book Number: 0-672-31241-7

Library of Congress Catalog Card Number: 98-84584

Printed in the United States of America

First Printing: July, 2000

02   01   00   4   3   2   1

Trademarks

Warning and Disclaimer

ASSOCIATE PUBLISHER
Bradley Jones

ACQUISITIONS EDITOR
Sharon Cox

DEVELOPMENT EDITORS
Kevin Howard
Matt Purcell

MANAGING EDITOR
Charlotte Clapp

PROJECT EDITOR
Dawn Pearson

COPY EDITOR
Fran Blauw

INDEXER
Erika Millen

PROOFREADER
Maryann Steinhart

TECHNICAL EDITORS
Matt Butler
Greg Guntle

TEAM COORDINATOR
Meggo Barthlow

MEDIA DEVELOPER
J.G. Moore

INTERIOR DESIGNER
Gary Adair

COVER DESIGNER
Aren Howell

COPYWRITER
Eric Borgert

PRODUCTION
Gloria Schurick

Contents at a Glance

Contents

About the Authors

Mickey Williams is the author of *Programming Windows 2000 Unleashed* and *Sams Teach Yourself Visual C++ in 24 Hours*. Mickey is the founder of Codev Technologies, a provider of tools and consulting for Win32 development. Mickey is a member of the Association for Computing Machinery and lives in Laguna Hills, California, with his wife and two daughters. Mickey can be reached at `mickey.williams@codevtech.com`.

David Bennett currently develops network management software for Racotek, Inc., which provides software and services for wireless mobile data networks. He has been developing desktop software for the last 16 years in industries ranging from healthcare, to Las Vegas casinos, to the spy business—and has been using Microsoft compilers, APIs, and libraries since the first release of Microsoft C. Along the way, he picked up a B.S. in computer science from Southern Methodist University.

When not stuck behind a keyboard and monitor, David plays rugby for the St. Paul Jazz Pigs, and is still learning to play the guitars he keeps collecting. If you don't run into him on the pitch, in a pub, or in a newsgroup, you might find him on a Quake server near you.

About the Contributors

Chuck Wood is a systems consultant, instructor, and author with more than a decade of experience in developing software. He is the lead author of a number of books including, *Special Edition Using PowerBuilder* from QUE publishing (ISBN 0-7897-0754-3) and *Special Edition Using Watcom SQL* from QUE publishing (ISBN 0-7897-0103-0). He contributed to *Client/Server Unleashed* from Sams Publishing (ISBN 0-672-30726-X), and *Special Edition Using Turbo C++ for Windows* from QUE publishing (ISBN 1-56529-837-3). Chuck develops software in C++, Java, Visual Basic, PowerBuilder, and other languages. Chuck has also spoken internationally on database design, object-oriented design, Java development, and PowerBuilder development, and has taught classes in Electronic Commerce and Web Development at the University of Minnesota and C and C++ at Indiana Vocational Technical College. Chuck has bachelor's degrees in Corporate Finance and Computer Science, and a Masters of Business Administration. He is currently pursuing a Ph.D. in Management Information Systems (M.I.S.) at the University of Minnesota Carlson School of Management.

Andrew J. Indovina is currently a software developer at NetSetGo Inc, located in Rochester, NY. With a Computer Science degree, he has a broad programming background including assembly language, C, C++, Visual Basic, Java, XML, and Active Server Pages. This is his second book with Macmillan publishing.

Jonathan Bates has worked on a whole range of commercial, industrial, and military software development projects woldwide over the past 15 years. He is currently working as a self-employed software design consultant and contract software developer specializing in Visual C++ application development for Windows NT/95 and 98. Jonathan is the author of Practical Visual C++ 6 and the coauthor of Using Visual C++ from QUE publishing. He has also written several technical articles for computing journals on a range of topics.

Vincent (Vinny) W. Mayfield is a Senior Software Engineer and a Microsoft Certified Professional with more than ten years of experience developing software and has spent more than five years developing Windows-based applications with C and C++. Vincent is developing Microsoft Windows–based applications with Visual C++, MFC, and Oracle. Vincent is a co-author of *ActiveX Programming Unleashed*, Sams Publishing.

Ted Neustaedter is a software developer in Vancouver, British Columbia, Canada, and works on a contract basis. His expertise is in the areas of Visual C/C++, Visual Basic, OLE/ActiveX, and ODBC. Send email to ted@neumark.com or visit his Web site at `http://www.neumark.com`.

Mark R. Wrenn is President of SockSoft Corporation (www.socksoft.com), a company specializing in writing software for Windows 95, Windows NT, and the Internet using Visual C++. Mark has more than 15 years of experience as a developer in both the vendor and customer environments. He has led software development teams in the development of both GUI and server software including, most recently, the development of firewall technology for NT. Mark resides in Southern California and is always looking for interesting projects to work on. He can be reached at `mrwrenn@socksoft.com`.

Dedication

For the three people who are always waiting for me to finish something:
René, Ali, and Mackenzie.

—Mickey Williams

Acknowledgments

I'd like to thank a number of people who have helped me get this book finished. If experience is any indication, I'll probably forget a few people, so let me apologize in advance to those of you who don't find your names on this list.

First, I'd like to thank Brad Jones, Sharon Cox, Kevin Howard, Dawn Pearson, and Matt Butler at Sams Publishing.

I'd also like to thank those of you who have worked with me on other projects while I was finishing this book—especially those of you who helped me rearrange schedules to help me get this book finished. In no particular order, thanks to Cherif, Toan, Bruce, and Dennis. At Codev, thanks to Richard and René.

And finally, thanks to Jennie and Mitch for giving me a place to write while in San Diego.

—Mickey Williams

Tell Us What You Think!

As the reader of this book, you are our most important critic and commentator. We value your opinion and want to know what we're doing right, what we could do better, what areas you'd like to see us publish in, and any other words of wisdom you're willing to pass our way.

As an associate publisher for Sams, I welcome your comments. You can fax, email, or write me directly to let me know what you did or didn't like about this book—as well as what we can do to make our books stronger.

Please note that I cannot help you with technical problems related to the topic of this book, and that due to the high volume of mail I receive, I might not be able to reply to every message.

When you write, please be sure to include this book's title and author as well as your name and phone or fax number. I will carefully review your comments and share them with the author and editors who worked on the book.

Fax: 317-581-4770

Email: adv_prog@mcp.com

Mail: Bradley Jones
         Associate Publisher
         Sams Publishing
         201 West 103rd Street
         Indianapolis, IN 46290 USA

Introduction

How to Use This Book

Although you certainly can read this book straight through from beginning to end, each chapter generally stands alone. Most chapters include example programs that illustrate the chapter's topics. If an example program is complex, only selected highlights from the project's source code are presented in the chapter. Full source code for projects is always included on the accompanying CD-ROM.

What You Need to Use This Book

Visual C++ 6 is designed to build programs that run on Windows 95, Windows 98, Windows 2000, or Windows NT. To build and run the examples included in this book and on the CD-ROM, you'll need the following:

- Windows 95, Windows 98, Windows 2000, or Windows NT 4.0
- Visual C++ 6.0
- An adequately equipped computer

Microsoft provides a list of minimum requirements to be able to run Visual C++:

- Pentium class processor, 90 MHz or faster
- 24 megabytes of RAM
- 305 MB free disk space
- CD-ROM
- VGA resolution monitor
- Mouse or compatible pointing device

You should consider this list to be a starting point; Visual C++ performance improves greatly with more RAM and faster processors. In particular, it is not realistic to expect Windows NT to perform adequately with 24 MB of RAM. In addition, installing the *Microsoft Developer Network* (MSDN) or other components increases the amount of disk space required for the installation. My computers are 200 MHz, Pentium Pro or better machines with at least 96 MB of RAM.

And finally, if an example requires a specific operating system (some examples require Windows 2000), it is clearly noted in the text.

What's New in Visual C++ 6.0

Visual C++ offers many new features and improvements over its predecessor, Visual C++ 5.0. The new features covered in this book follow:

- The compiler offers improved support for the ANSI C++ standard. Boolean types are supported, and template support is improved.
- The devclopment system includes new enhancements to MFC, the Microsoft Foundation Class Library. These enhancements include classes for Internet programming and support for new common controls introduced in Internet Explorer 4.0 and Windows 98.
- The Developer Studio Editor is much improved, and it takes advantage of IntelliSense features originally released as part of Visual Basic. These features include statement completion, which greatly improves your efficiency.
- The debugger included with Visual C++ includes a new feature called *Debug and Continue,* which enables you to make small changes while debugging and then immediately continue debugging without restarting the application.
- An improved online help system puts the MSDN in easy reach, just a mouse click away. The online help system automatically uses the latest version of the MSDN Library if it's installed on your computer.

Contacting the Main Author

If you have questions or comments about the material covered in this book, you may contact me at `mickey.williams@codevtech.com`.

Introduction

PART

I

The Visual C++ 6.0 Environment

*by David Bennett
and Mickey Williams*

IN THIS CHAPTER

CHAPTER 1

Although Visual C++ is first and foremost a C++ compiler, it also offers a complete development environment made up of many components that work together to simplify the development process. Many of the features of this environment will be familiar to you; after all, some basic features are ones that any integrated development environment is expected to provide. However, many of the features of the development environment are unique to Visual C++ and might seem a bit foreign at first, but you will soon see that these features can significantly improve your productivity.

In this chapter, you will take a tour of all of the components that make up the Visual C++ Environment. You will examine the Developer Studio and the tools it offers to simplify your development tasks, including the resource editors, Application Wizard, and ClassWizard. You will also take a look at some of the other utilities included with Visual C++ to make your life as a developer a little easier.

For a complete reference on every menu, button, or other widget in the IDE, see the on-line help. I will try to cover the basics and point out some of the most interesting or useful features of the development environment, but won't be rehashing the whole user's guide.

Developer Studio

Visual C++ 6.0 includes the Microsoft Developer Studio Integrated Development Environment (IDE). This environment is the centerpiece of most any interaction you will have with your C++ projects, including source file creation, resource editing, compiling, linking, debugging, and many other useful features.

In the bad old days, all C files, resource files, help files, and everything else had to be created with one or more editors. Then each object or resource had to be compiled with its own flavor of compiler, with its own set of switches and options. Then the whole darn thing had to be linked to create an application. Running and debugging an application involved several other steps and utilities. The only truly integrated development environment at this time was DOS DEBUG—of course, only if you were writing in machine language and entering a byte or so at a time.

Several compiler vendors started making integrated development environments, which allowed editing and compiling source in one application or shell, but still required several other functions to be performed outside of the IDE, not to mention the fact that you had to move in and out of the IDE to debug your application. This switching back and forth could quickly consume a big chunk of your development time.

The Developer Studio included with Visual C++ 6.0 allows you to perform everything you need to do throughout the life of your application, without ever leaving the IDE. Developer Studio also includes several features that will make your development tasks much simpler.

When you first start Microsoft Developer Studio, you should see a screen similar to the one shown in Figure 1.1—although you won't have an open project if this is your first time.

> **Note**
>
> Microsoft Developer Studio should be added to your start menu under Programs, Microsoft Visual Studio 6.0, Microsoft Visual C++ 6.0—or, if you prefer, create a shortcut to:
>
>   Program Files\Microsoft Visual Studio\Common\MSDev98\Bin\MSDEV.EXE
>
> I like to create a shortcut on the taskbar as well as on my desktop.

FIGURE 1.1

Microsoft Developer Studio.

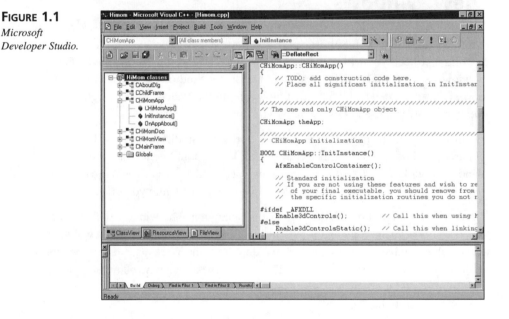

Figure 1.1 shows an example of the windows that you might have open. Unfortunately, production of this book requires standard VGA mode screen shots, so some of the things you see here might appear a bit crowded. If you plan to do much work with Visual C++, you will probably want to use a higher resolution. I find that a 17-inch monitor at 1280×1024 is well worth the cost of the hardware.

> **Tip**
>
> Feel free to try out your own projects in Developer Studio now if you like, but for the rest of this chapter, you might want to install the examples from the CD-ROM and open the HiMom (an MFC version of HelloWorld) example to follow along. You can open an existing workspace by choosing the Open Workspace command from the File menu. (Note that this is different than the Open command on the File menu.) You can open the HiMom example by opening the file `HiMom.dsw`, located in the Chapter 1 `samples` directory on the CD-ROM. Most of the features of Developer Studio are not activated until you have opened a workspace.

View Windows

In addition to the windows for your source files, Developer Studio uses several view windows to present useful information at various stages in project development. When starting a project, you will probably be most interested in the Workspace and Output windows, shown in Figure 1.1. Although Developer Studio also provides separate windows for various debugging information including the Watch, Variables, Registers, Memory, Call Stack, and Disassembly windows.

Each window can be moved around in the workspace in different ways. By default, these windows will dock to an edge of your screen. If you double-click the frame of a docked window, it will undock, and you can freely place it where you like. You can even drag it outside of the Developer Studio window by holding Ctrl while you drag.

However, you might find the docking feature annoying. The window will try to dock when you don't want it to, and it will always float on top of your source windows. You can disable the docking view for each window from the Workspace tab of the Options dialog box found on the Tools menu. This will make the view window act just like a regular source code window, which also means you will no longer be able to drag it outside the Developer Studio frame.

Toolbars

You will notice that several different toolbars are used in Developer Studio. Most of these will normally dock at the top of the window, although you may drag the frame of the toolbar anywhere you like. You can attach the toolbar to any edge of the frame or you can just leave it floating around somewhere.

> **Tip**
>
> If you are unsure about what a tool does, hold the mouse pointer over it and a brief description, or tool tip, will pop up, telling you what the tool does.

Many toolbars are not normally displayed. Sometimes these will pop up at appropriate times—such as the Resource toolbar, when you edit resources. At any time, you can select the toolbars you want to be displayed by right-clicking an empty area of Developer Studio (like an unused portion of the menu bar area). You may also select the toolbars that are displayed from the Toolbars page of the dialog box that is presented by the Customize command on the Tools menu. You may also select which toolbars are displayed by right-clicking in the toolbar area. The New button in the Toolbars dialog box will also allow you to create your own custom toolbars. To add buttons to a toolbar, go to the Commands tab of the Customize dialog box and drag the desired tools from the Commands tab to the new toolbar. You might need to move the Customize dialog box out of the way to see the new toolbar.

The Project Workspace

Working with the Developer Studio is based on working with Project workspaces. These workspaces represent a particular set of projects, which can be anything from a single application, to a function library, to an entire suite of applications. Each workspace may include any number of different projects that you want to group into a single workspace so that you can work closely with each separate project at the same time.

The project workspace (.dsw) file is responsible for maintaining all of the information that defines your workspace and the projects that you have included in it. Each workspace contains one or more projects, with each project using a project (.dsp) file. Previously, you might have used make (.mak) files to maintain projects and the processes involved in creating your applications. Developer Studio 6.0 does not create .mak files by default anymore, although you can force Developer Studio to create a makefile based on current project settings by using the Export Makefile command from the Project menu. This is useful if you are using .mak files to automate your builds outside of Developer Studio.

In addition to makefile-type information about your projects, the project workspace file includes information about the settings you have chosen for Developer Studio itself. This means that whenever you open a project workspace, all of the Developer Studio settings that you had when you last worked with this workspace will be restored. All of the windows that were open before will also be opened and returned to their previous position in the workspace.

You can create a new, empty workspace using the Workspaces tab of the File, New dialog box. However, an empty workspace isn't generally of much use, unless you want to configure a project from scratch. You may create a new workspace whenever you create a new project from the Projects tab of the File, New dialog box. This will present you with several different choices, as shown in Figure 1.2.

FIGURE 1.2

New Projects dialog box.

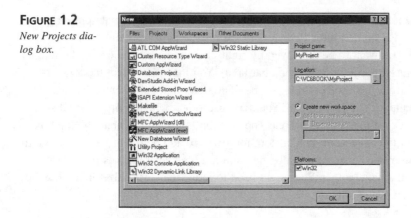

When you create a new project, Visual C++ will set up default build settings for the type of project you specify here. You may also start up one of the Application Wizards from this dialog box. You will see exactly what each of these project types will do for you later in this chapter.

With all of this talk about workspaces, perhaps you would expect that Developer Studio would provide a nice graphical interface to this information. Well, sure enough, it does—the Workspace window.

The Workspace Window

When you open a project workspace you should see the Workspace window. If you do not, it was hidden the last time the workspace was open and can be brought to the foreground by selecting the Workspace command from the View menu or simply by pressing Alt+0. This window provides a roadmap to your projects that allows you to quickly navigate to where you need to go to do the real work of developing your application. You will notice that there are three tabs on the bottom of the window that allow you to view different sorts of information about your projects.

The `FileView`

You will notice immediately that the `FileView` will let you view the list of files in your projects, hence the name. What might not be quite so obvious is the fact that it provides a great deal of functionality designed to help you manage your files and projects. Although many workspaces include only a single project, you will see later that you can add any number of projects to a workspace. The FileView will display each project as a different top-level folder that can be expanded just like any other tree control in Windows. The FileView window for the HiMom example is shown in Figure 1.3.

FIGURE 1.3

FileView *for the*
HiMom *example.*

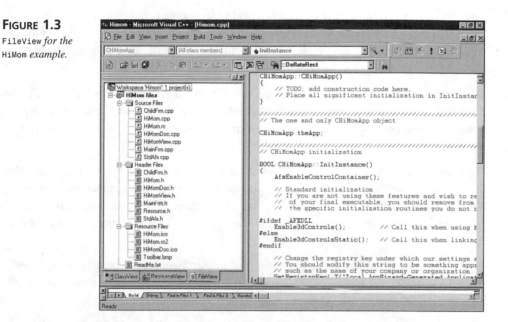

Any files that you create within Developer Studio will be automatically added to your project, so you need to be concerned only with adding files that you have created yourself, outside of Developer Studio. This can include documentation or existing source files that you want to manage as part of your project.

Note that you should not include any of the standard libraries in your project. You should, however, include any libraries that will be built by your project so that the build process can check to see if that library should be rebuilt in order to bring the project up-to-date. Libraries to be included in a project may be specified in the Link tab of the Project Settings dialog box (from the Project, Settings menu command).

FileView allows you to drag and drop files to add them to your project or to move or copy them between your projects. If you want to delete a file from your project, simply select the file and press the Delete key. This will not actually delete the file, but will remove it from your project.

FileView will show an icon next to each filename. These icons can give you additional information about the file. For instance, if the icon has a down arrow on it, this file will be used in building the current configuration. In addition, certain add-on products may alter these icons. For example, if you have a source code control system installed, the icon might have a checkmark to denote that you have the file checked out.

You can open a file for editing by double-clicking it. You can also bring up a context menu by right-clicking the file. This gives you several other options, depending on the type of file you selected. Any version of the context menu will allow you to go to the Project Settings dialog box by selecting the Settings command.

The context menu will allow you to view a file's Properties dialog box, which is different for different file types, but will generally list information about the file, its inputs, outputs, and dependencies. This can be useful in making sure that the files in your project are being put together the way they should.

For source files, the context menu will give you the option to compile that file. Similarly, the context menu for a project will allow you to build the project. You can also use the Set as Active Project command to set it as the default project. For workspaces that contain more than one project, the active project is used whenever you build, execute, or debug.

You may also delete any intermediate files in a project by choosing the Clean command from the project's context menu. This is particularly useful when you see the amount of disk space that even simple projects consume.

> **Tip**
>
> It is a good idea to delete intermediate files from a project before trying to back it up. Some of the intermediate files can become very large, even for small projects.

The `ClassView`

As the name suggests, the `ClassView` displays a tree view of the classes that you have created for your project and allows you to expand the classes to reveal their member functions and variables. The `ClassView` for the `HiMom` application is shown in Figure 1.4.

FIGURE 1.4

ClassView *for*
HiMom *project.*

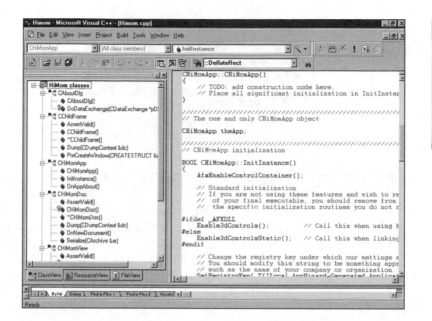

You will notice that each of the class members has one or more icons to the left of it; these give useful information about the member type (data or function) and access class. (Protected members have a key, private members have a padlock, and public members have no access icon.)

You can directly access the source code for your classes by double-clicking the object that you are interested in. Double-clicking a class will immediately open the header file for the class and position the cursor at the start of the class declaration, and double-clicking a member variable will position the cursor on the declaration of the member variable. Double-clicking a member function will take you straight to the function definition, or implementation.

The context menu for a class allows several different choices for you to jump to the more powerful source code browser to examine how a class is used, including direct access to the definitions and references for the class, as well as lists of any base classes and derived classes associated with this class.

The context menu also allows a quick way to add member functions or variables by way of a simple dialog box, shown in Figure 1.5.

FIGURE 1.5

*Add Member
Function dialog
box.*

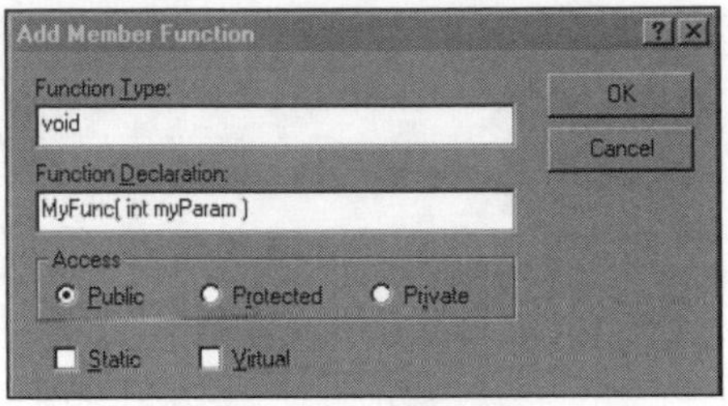

Project Configurations

Visual C++ allows you to work with different build configurations for each project. As long as you are producing the same executable filename (or library), you may select from any number of configurations to determine how the project will be built. Whenever you create a new workspace in Developer Studio, two default configurations will be created for you: one for debug and one for release. The debug configuration will build in many different debugging features that will not be compiled when building release configurations.

You can select a configuration to be the default configuration used for builds from several different places, including the configuration combo box on the Build toolbar, the context menu from FileView, or the Set Active Configuration command from the Build menu. If you want to add or delete configurations, you can do so from the Configurations command from the Build menu.

Project Settings

Each configuration allows you to choose from a wide range of project settings, appropriately handled by the Project Settings dialog box, shown in Figure 1.6. The Project Settings dialog box is started from the Settings command of either the Project menu or the FileView context menu.

You will notice that each of the defined configurations is listed in the Settings For combo box. It seems fairly obvious that if you selected one configuration, you would be working with the settings for that configuration. You can also look at the settings that are common to all configurations by selecting All Configurations from the combo box.

For example, if you selected the All Configurations, you would not see the Output directories on the General page. This is because each of the configurations has different settings for these fields. If you highlighted a single configuration, you would see where the output will go. If you change any settings with All Configurations selected, you will change the settings for *both* projects. This can be very useful, but you should be careful

and have only one configuration selected if you only want to modify one configuration or see all of the settings for a configuration—and not just the settings that two configurations have in common.

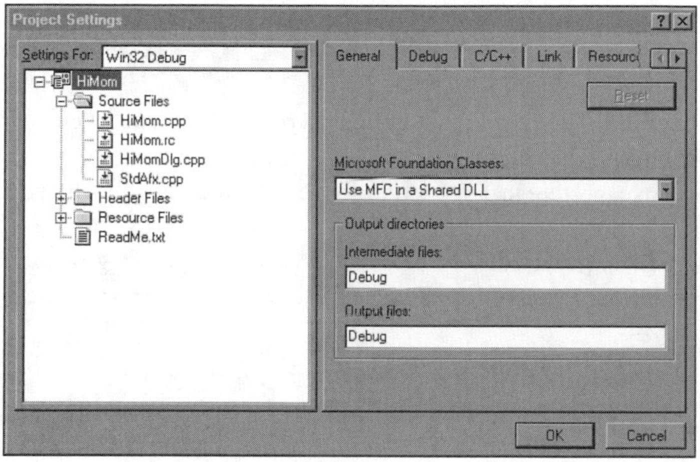

FIGURE 1.6

Project Settings dialog box.

There are about a gazillion options available in the Project Settings dialog box, so the options are grouped into several pages, accessed by the tabs at the top. In addition, several pages, such as the C/C++ page shown in Figure 1.7, have drop-down menus in which you can select several different subpages.

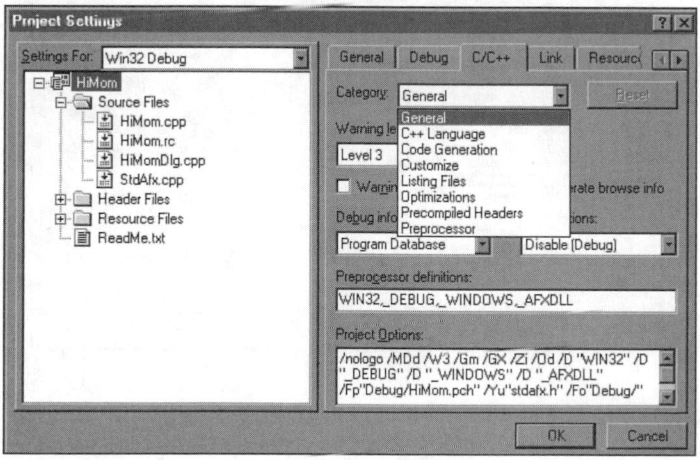

FIGURE 1.7

Drop-down menu in the C/C++ Project Settings page.

It might take a while to find all the various settings, but I think you will find this much easier than trying to keep track of all of the different compiler and linker flags manually. Just remember that you might need to try changing the Category combo box to find the setting you are looking for.

Converting Older Projects

You can use the Open workspace command of the File menu to open project files (or makefiles) from previous versions of Visual C++. When you do this, a warning message will appear suggesting that you save the file to a different name before it performs the conversion. This is generally a good idea if you will still need to use the project from a previous version of Visual C++ (such as when sharing with a group that hasn't upgraded yet) because, once converted, the project file will no longer be usable by older versions of Visual C++.

Working with Multiple Projects

As hinted at earlier, Developer Studio allows you to work with many different projects within the same workspace. This is very handy for working with projects that are closely related. To add a new project to the current workspace, use the File, New command and go to the Project page, as shown in Figure 1.8.

FIGURE 1.8

New Projects page.

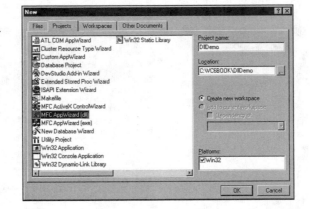

To create a new project and add it to the current workspace, simply click the Add to current workspace radio button and create your new project. If you choose to add the new project to the existing workspace, you also have the option of making the new project a dependency of one of the existing projects in the workspace. This is useful for such things as building a library that is in turn used by an application. When you create the library as a dependency, it will be automatically built for you each time you build the application that depends on it. This can help keeping all of the pieces of a project up-to-date.

Later, you can modify the dependencies that are set up for a workspace by selecting Dependencies from the Project menu. This will allow you to use the Project Dependencies dialog box, as shown in Figure 1.9.

FIGURE 1.9

Project Dependencies dialog box.

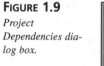

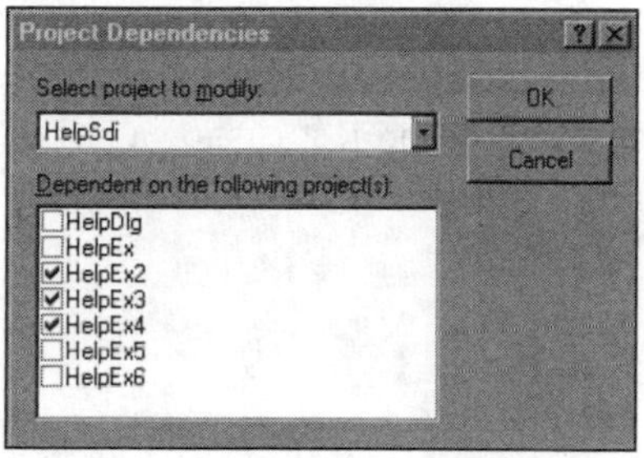

Simply choose one of your projects from the drop-down list at the top and then click the check box next to any of the other projects that are its dependencies.

You will see each of your projects in the Workspace views, and you may easily switch between projects. If you use multiple projects within a workspace, the Batch Build command on the Build menu will allow you to build any number of your projects at once.

Working with Resources

If you have been developing Windows applications for a while, you are probably familiar with resource scripts. These are files that define all of the resources used by your application, including dialog boxes, icons, and menus. In the old days, you often had to move back and forth between your source editor and your resource editor, the C compiler, and the resource compiler. Developer Studio makes this much simpler by providing a visual editor for your resources that is fully integrated with the rest of Developer Studio.

The Resource View

In programming for Windows, you will use several different types of resources. Most of these correspond directly to graphics objects such as bitmaps, cursors, and icons, as well as more complicated types such as menus, toolbars, and dialog box templates. In addition, you will have a string table and version resource, as well as any custom resources you might define.

In the bad old days, all resources were defined in a text resource script (.rc) file. You then had to compile the .rc file with a separate resource compiler and explicitly link your resources to your executable. Visual C++ 6.0 still uses the .rc file, but you will most likely never have to edit it directly. Developer studio allows you to edit your resources graphically, and will automatically take the necessary steps to compile your resource script and link it to your application.

To help you work with resources, Developer Studio provides the ResourceView, which displays information about the various resources included in each project, grouped by resource type. The ResourceView for the HiMom project is shown in Figure 1.10.

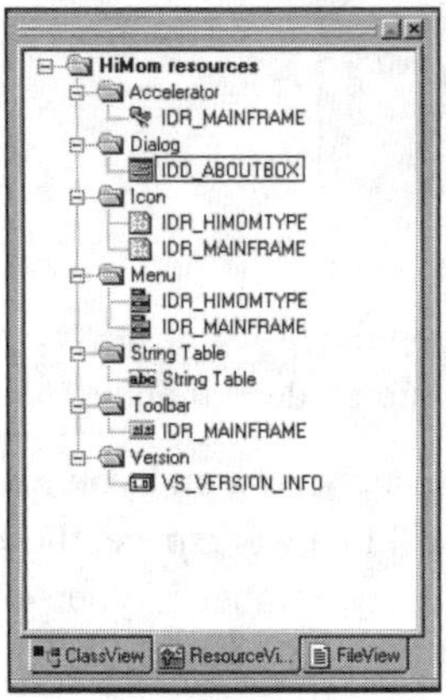

FIGURE 1.10

The Resource view.

If you created a Windows application with AppWizard, a resource script would automatically be created as part of your new project. However, you can also create a new resource script from the Files tab for the New command on the File menu or open existing resource scripts from the Open command on the File menu. Resource script windows support drag and drop, making it quite simple to open an existing resource script from another project and add resources to your current project by just dragging them over.

Like the other Project Workspace views, there is a context menu available by right-clicking in the ResourceView. This allows you to open the selected resource for editing, insert new resources, or import existing resources, among other things. In addition, the context menu gives you access to the Properties page for your resources, as shown in Figure 1.11.

FIGURE 1.11

Resource Proper-
ties dialog box.

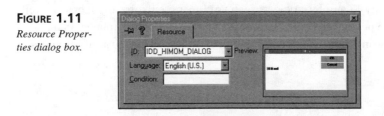

Unlike some property pages, the resource property pages allow you to change some important aspects of your resource, including the ID and language for the resource. In addition, resources such as icons and bitmaps that are stored in files outside of the resource script, allow you to specify the filename for the resource here. The Condition field allows you to enter a precompiler symbol that is used to specify that the resource only be built into your project if the given precompiler symbol is defined.

> **Caution**
>
> The context menu will let you open the binary data for any resource. Although this is useful for custom resource types, be very careful with it. It is very simple to accidentally change a byte in a resource and the window will save your changes without prompting. This can easily make your resource unusable.

Importing Resources

If you have already created resources that exist in separate files, you can add these to the resource script for the current project by importing them. You can add a separate image, icon, or cursor file to your current resource script by clicking the Import button in the Insert | Resource dialog box. This will allow you to browse for the files containing the resources you want to add to the current project.

Managing Resource IDs

Whenever you create a new resource with the Developer Studio, a resource ID is automatically assigned. This means that the symbol you have entered as the resource ID is defined to be a certain value in a header file. Although you might luck out and never have to deal with resource IDs or resource header files directly, The View menu offers two very useful commands: Resource Symbols and Resource Includes. The Resource Symbols command will produce the dialog box shown in Figure 1.12.

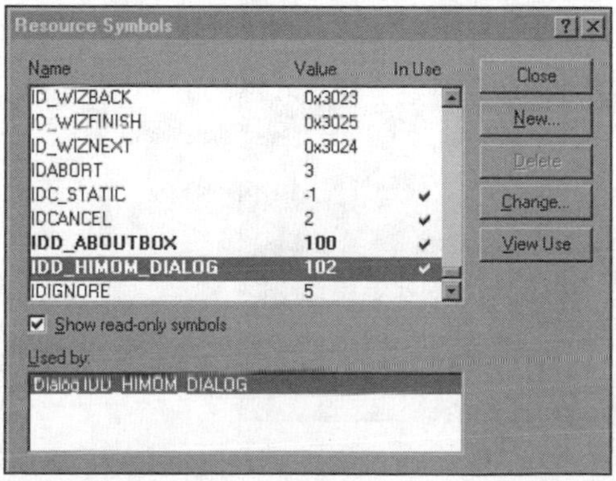

FIGURE 1.12
Resource Symbols dialog box.

Working with Resource Symbols

The Resource Symbols dialog box provides a handy way to work with the symbols that are defined for the currently selected configuration. You will see a list of all of the symbols defined in your project, their values, and whether or not they are currently being used by a resource. If a symbol is in use, the Used by list will show the resources using that symbol. Selecting Show read-only symbols will display predefined windows symbols in a lighter shade along with your symbols.

You can add new symbols by clicking the New button or change values with the Change button. The View Use button will open a window for directly editing the resource that uses the selected ID. To change the value of a symbol that is in use, use the View Use button to open a window for the resource. If you open the properties dialog box for the resource, by right-clicking in the resource and choosing Properties, you can assign a value to the symbol by entering it after the symbol name, like this:

```
IDD_MYDIALOG=111
```

Tip

If you plan to use resource IDs that must be in a consecutive range, as for the ON_COMMAND_RANGE macro, it might be easier to define all of the IDs you plan to use before creating your resources, because the IDs that are automatically assigned are not necessarily consecutive.

Working with Resource Includes

The Resource Includes command from the View menu will display a dialog box like that shown in Figure 1.13. This dialog box allows you to work with the include files that define your resource symbols.

FIGURE 1.13

Resource Includes dialog box.

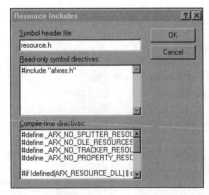

You may change the name of the header file that will contain your resource symbol definitions here. You may also add any #include or #define directives to the header file. This allows you to include additional header files, which can help in group projects. Because none of the Developer Studio tools will modify the #included files, these values are much more likely to remain constant.

Resource Templates

You might have noticed that when you create a new resource, the tree list of resource types available may be expanded, as in Figure 1.14. This provides you with the ability to create resources based on resource templates. This comes in handy whenever you will want to create many different resources that are similar, and can help standardize the look and feel of your applications.

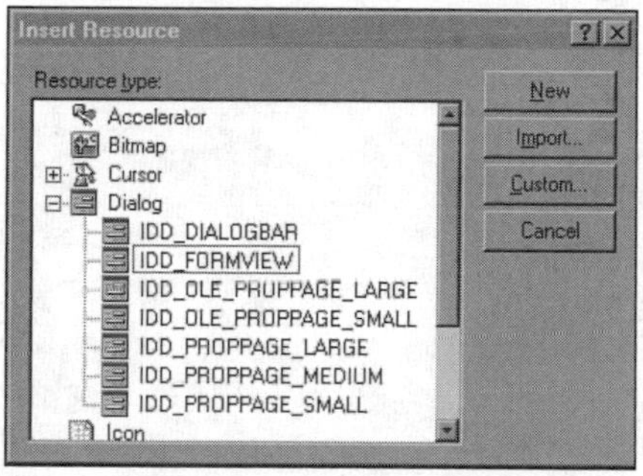

FIGURE 1.14

Creating resources with resource templates.

You can create resources based on the template by selecting the template and clicking New. If you just want a plain, blank dialog boxes, select the dialog box line before clicking New.

With Developer Studio, you can create your own resource templates by choosing Resource Template from the Files tab of the New dialog box displayed by the File | New command. This will open an empty resource script that you can insert resources into. When you are finished, a resource template (.rct) file will be created. When this file is saved in the Microsoft Visual Studio\Common\MSDev98\Template subdirectory with the other templates, Developer Studio will read the template file whenever the Insert Resource dialog box is displayed. If you create a custom resource template and move it into the template subdirectory, you will see that your resources defined in your template are shown among the choices in the Insert Resource dialog box tree. Whenever you create a new resource based on the template, any changes you make to the new resource affect only the new resource and not the template.

Editing Resources

Developer Studio allows you to edit all of your resources with various visual editors that are part of Developer Studio. You can edit any resource by double-clicking it in the ResourceView. In the next few pages, you will be looking at the various resource editors provided by Developer Studio, starting with the Dialog box editor, which you will probably be using most often.

Dialog Boxes

In most applications, dialog boxes provide a large portion of the interface between the user and your application. Dialog boxes allow you to provide an interface to the user for certain sets of information as it is needed, without taking up real estate in your main window. Whenever you open a dialog box resource, you will get a window similar to the one shown in Figure 1.15.

FIGURE 1.15

Dialog Box editor.

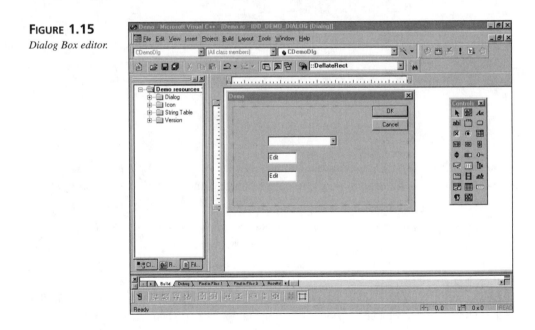

Adding Controls

If you have just created a new dialog box, it's time to make it do something useful. Developer Studio makes this easy. You should notice the controls toolbar floating around your workspace somewhere when you open the dialog box. Each of the icons on the toolbar (with the exception of the pointer in the top left) represents a control that you can add to your dialog box, including any controls that you have added with Component Gallery.

To add a control, select it from the toolbar, click the dialog box, and you have a new control. If you are unsure of what some funny picture on the toolbar represents, just hold the mouse pointer over it. Like other toolbars, this will provide tooltip help that will give a short description of the control.

> **Note**
>
> The Controls toolbar, like the other toolbars, may be docked or hidden altogether. If you don't see it, try using the Toolbars page of the Tools, Customize dialog box to toggle the Controls toolbar on.

When adding a control, it is generally easier to assign its size and location when it is added by dragging a rectangle in your dialog box before releasing the mouse to insert the control. However, if you have already inserted a control, you can easily move it by clicking it and dragging a point within the control to the new location. You can easily resize controls by dragging the resize handles (little boxes) on the border of the selected control.

> **Note**
>
> You can resize either the normal or drop-down size of a combo box by clicking on its drop-down button to toggle which size is shown.

Control Properties

For most controls, you should change their properties after you have placed them in a dialog box. You can edit a control's properties by selecting Properties... from the context menu that you can pull up by right-clicking the control. The Properties dialog box looks similar to the one shown in Figure 1.16.

FIGURE 1.16
Control Properties dialog box.

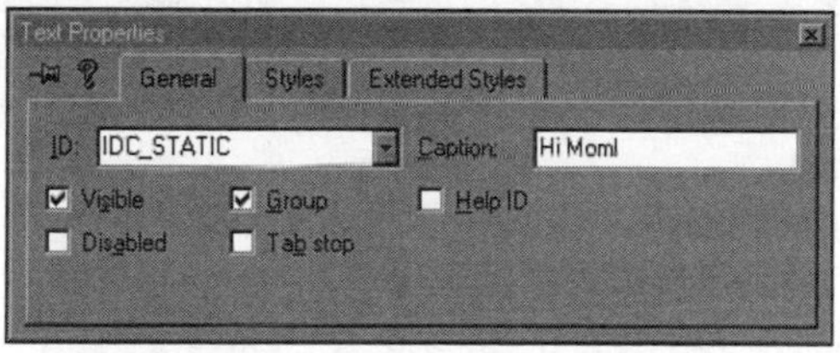

The Properties dialog box will be a bit different for each type of control, but will always allow you to edit the resource ID. Although the ID can be a symbol or a number, you should try to give your resource ID symbol a meaningful name, rather than just a number or the default symbol name. If you want to force your ID to have a certain value, you can specify a value after the resource symbol like this:

```
IDC_MYBUTTON=123
```

For more information about the specifics of the styles and other options on the Properties page, press F1 to bring up context-sensitive help on the current page. You can access the properties of the dialog box itself by double-clicking a blank spot in the dialog box or its title bar.

Laying Out Your Controls

One of the trickiest parts of designing your dialog boxes can be getting everything to line up just right where you want it. The dialog box editor provides several nifty features for dealing with this in the Layout menu. Many of the options in the Layout menu will not be enabled unless you have a certain type of control selected or have several controls selected.

> **Note**
>
> You can select multiple controls by holding the Shift or Control keys while clicking on the controls. The dominant control will be the control last selected.

The Size to Content command in the Layout menu (or F7) is particularly useful with static text and button controls. This will make the control just the right size to contain its text, preventing characters from being clipped off or controls that run over your other controls.

> **Note**
>
> Most of the commands from the Layout menu are also provided by tools in the Dialog Box toolbar.

You might notice a blue, shaded line encircling the contents of your dialog box. If you place any controls in the dialog box so that they touch this margin line, they will be automatically moved whenever you resize your dialog box. Unfortunately, this only works while you are creating your dialog box resource and will not help with resizing at run-time. You may create your own guidelines by dragging in either of the ruler bars at the top or left of your dialog box. By later adjusting these guides, any controls placed on the guide will be moved with it.

Tab Order

Windows allows you to move from control to control within a dialog box by use of the Tab key. This functionality is provided automatically when you create a dialog box in Developer Studio, but you might need to do a few things to tweak it to work just the way you want.

To adjust the tab order of your controls, you can choose the Tab Order command from the Layout menu and click the controls in the order that you want them to be tabbed. If you have a complicated dialog box and only want to change the tab order of a few controls, you can take a little shortcut by holding the Ctrl key down and selecting the last control that tabs properly before selecting the controls that tab incorrectly. Clicking an empty spot in the dialog box, or pressing Enter, will exit the tab order mode.

To prevent a control from being reached using the Tab key, clear the Tab stop checkbox on the control's property page.

Testing Your Dialog Box

You could save your dialog box and rebuild the application to test the layout of your dialog box, but there is a much simpler method of testing things like tab order. The Layout menu provides the Test command (you can also use Ctrl-T or that little switch on the Dialog Box toolbar) that will run your dialog box for you. This test mode ends whenever you exit the dialog box that you are testing.

> **Note**
>
> When you choose Save from the File menu or the ResourceView context menu, the whole resource script file is saved, not just the resource you are working on.

Editing Menus

Double-clicking a menu resource in the ResourceView will open a window like the one shown in Figure 1.17 that allows you to edit your menu resource.

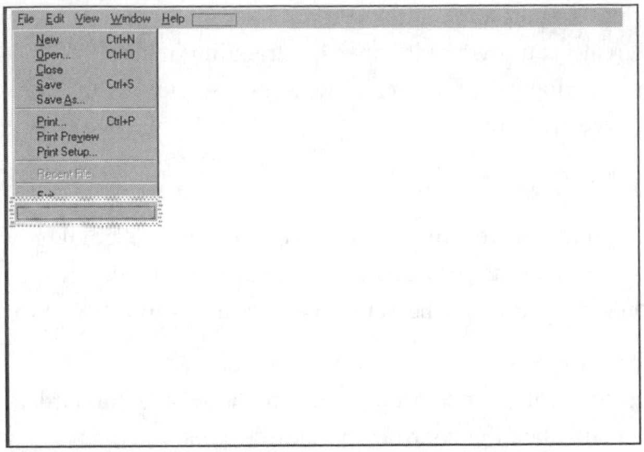

FIGURE 1.17

Menu editor.

To add a new menu item, double-click in the empty space to the right or bottom of the last menu item. This will open the Menu Item Properties dialog box, as shown in Figure 1.18, which lets you enter the menu caption, its associated command ID, and style information. You may freely rearrange your menu items by dragging and dropping.

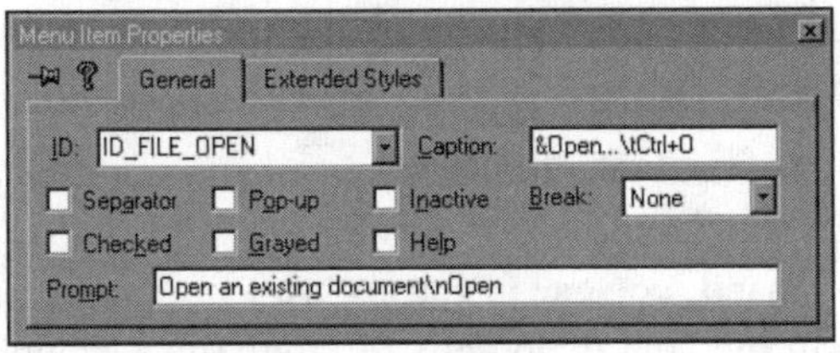

FIGURE 1.18

Menu Item Proper-
ties dialog box.

The Command ID that you enter here will be the command ID that your application will receive when the user selects this menu item.

The Caption is the text that is displayed for the menu item. Placing an ampersand (&) in front of a character will cause that character to become the mnemonic key for that menu item. It is also customary to include text information about accelerators after the caption text, separated by a tab sequence (\t).

The Prompt field is used to enter text that will appear on the status bar when the cursor is on this menu item.

If you choose the Separator style, this will not be a real menu item, but just a separator between menu items. The Checked, Grayed, and Inactive styles determine the initial state of the menu item; these may be changed at runtime. The Help style will cause the menu item to be displayed on the far right of the menu bar, but this convention isn't used as often now as it once was.

By choosing the Pop-up style, you can easily create layers of menus. If you are creating a menu that will be used as a pop-up, you can select the View as Popup option from the right-button context menu to tell the menu editor to display your menu as a pop-up while you are editing it.

Other Resources

Developer Studio also provides visual editors for the other common windows resources, including accelerator tables, bitmaps, icons, cursors, string tables, and toolbars. You may also edit version resources to track various information about the version of your application.

In addition, you may define your own custom resource types that will be bound with your application. Because Developer Studio doesn't "know" how you intend to use these resources, you can only edit these resources in a binary format. You can, however, import existing files into your custom resource.

MFC AppWizard

It has been rumored that in prehistoric days there was but one piece of code ever written and that all projects since were merely the result of cutting and pasting from other projects. This does seem to have the ring of truth every time I cut and paste the same boilerplate code for Windows applications for each new project. Visual C++ makes this task much simpler by providing the MFC Application Wizard, or AppWizard for short.

What MFC AppWizard Can Do for You

MFC AppWizard is really a collection of different Application Wizards that help to do different sorts of projects. (I will generally use AppWizard to refer to any of the Application Wizards and will be more specific when discussing one particular AppWizard.) Each of the AppWizards will guide you through the process of creating a new project, prompting for various option selections along the way.

When you have made all of your choices, MFC will create your project for you. For some types of projects, this can be a tremendous time-saver. For MFC applications, this means creating all of the source, header, resource, help, and project files necessary to create a skeleton for your application. The project created by the MFC AppWizard (exe) will build without any further modifications and has all of the setup for the application features you selected. This can easily reduce half a day's hunting, cutting, and pasting to just a few seconds.

Starting MFC AppWizard

To use MFC AppWizard to help you create a new project, Use the New command from the File menu. The Projects tab of this dialog box, shown in Figure 1.19, will show you a list of all of the available application wizards, including other simple new project types, such as Win32 Application.

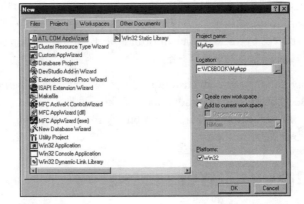

Project Types

The New Project Workspace gives you the opportunity to create several different types of projects, so let's take a brief look at what Visual C++ will do for you when you choose each project type.

ATL COM AppWizard

This is used to create a new project based on the Active Template Library (ATL). This type of project then allows you to add your own COM objects, using ATL.

Cluster Resource Type Wizard

This type of wizard is used to create a workspace that contains two projects that are used with Microsoft Cluster Server (MSCS), part of Windows NT Enterprise Edition.

One of the projects is used to create a resource DLL, which is used by MSCS to manage a resource—typically, a cluster-aware application.

The other project is a Cluster Administrator Extension DLL, which extends the MSCS Cluster Administrator, allowing a user to manage the interaction between MSCS and the resource.

Custom AppWizard

This type of project will allow you to create your very own AppWizard, which may then be used to help you create additional projects.

Database Project

This type of project allows you to test stored SQL procedures directly, without going through the process of creating an ODBC application. This project type is available only in Visual C++ Enterprise Edition.

DevStudio Add-In Wizard

This creates a new skeleton project that may be used to add commands to the Developer Studio environment. This project may include the framework required to add a toolbar to Developer Studio, as well as to handle events that occur within Developer Studio.

Extended Stored Procedure Wizard

This wizard allows you to create a SQL Server extended stored procedure. An extended stored procedure is hosted in a Win32 DLL. This project type is available only in Visual C++ Enterprise Edition.

ISAPI Extension Wizard

This wizard allows you to easily create the framework required to create extensions to Internet Information Server, using the Internet Server API.

Makefile

This project type is used to add a project that works with an external makefile. The project settings will allow you to specify the command line that you want to execute to build this project. By default, this is NMAKE /f myMake.mak. If you have existing makefiles that you want to incorporate into a build from Visual C++, without creating one of the other project types to replace your makefile, you should use this project type.

MFC ActiveX ControlWizard

This AppWizard will help you to create the framework for a project that uses the Microsoft Foundation Classes to implement ActiveX controls. We will be looking at how to implement ActiveX controls in more detail in Chapter 28.

MFC AppWizard (DLL)

This will use the MFC AppWizard for DLLs to create a new dynamic link library project for you. The project created implements the code needed to initialize a DLL that uses MFC, but you will need to add functionality to it.

MFC AppWizard (EXE)

This will start up the MFC AppWizard to help you create the framework for a full-blown MFC Windows application. We will look at this in more detail in Chapter 2, "MFC Class Library Overview," but feel free to try it out if you like. The skeleton application created by AppWizard is a complete application in that it will build and run. You just need to add on the functionality specific to your application.

Utility Project

This project type is a generic container for any types of files or custom build steps you would like to have performed. This type of project is useful as a master project for several subprojects in a workspace.

Win32 Application

The application project uses a very simple wizard that enables you to build three types of generic Win32 applications:

- A simple project with no source files included by default
- A typical generic Win32 project with one C++ source file
- A simple Win32 application that displays Hello World, consisting of resource files and a C++ source file

Each project has the default build settings for a Windows application. These types of projects are useful for creating a Visual C++ 6.0 project for existing applications that you are moving to VC++ 6.0. You will have to add your existing source files to the new project with the Project, Add to Project, Files dialog box.

Win32 Console Application

This project type will create a new project with the build settings appropriate for building console applications. A simple wizard is provided that enables you to build four types of generic console applications:

- An empty project containing no source files. You will need to add your own source files before building this project type.
- A simple project that contains one main source file. When launched, the program immediately exits.
- A simple Hello World project that contains one main source file. When launched, the program displays Hello World and exits.
- A simple project that will support MFC. This project contains a resource file in addition to the main source file.

This type of application does not have a Windows graphical interface, but uses a standard command window. This project type is appropriate for command-line utilities and other applications that do not have a graphical user interface.

Win32 Dynamic Link Library

This project type will create a Win32 DLL. A simple wizard allows you to choose from three types of Win32 DLLs:

- An empty project with no source files. You must add your own source files before building this type of project.
- A simple project with one main source file.
- A project that has one main source file and has examples of how to export symbols, such as classes and variables.

Each Win32 project type will set up the default project settings for creating a Win32 DLL.

Win32 Static Library

This is similar to the Dynamic Link Library option, but the project settings are set to create a standard statically linked library (.lib). A simple wizard allows you to specify if you would like to support pre-compiled headers or MFC in the project.

Other Project Types

You might also see additional project types listed. These are custom AppWizards that you have created, or that were provided by a third-party vendor and optionally loaded with Visual C++.

ClassWizard

In developing C++ applications, you will do a lot of work with your own classes. Developer Studio provides you with the ClassWizard to help in organizing your classes and integrating your classes with Windows. ClassWizard may be started from the View menu or by pressing Ctrl+W. The ClassWizard dialog box is made up of several different tabs, or pages, each of which allows you to work with different aspects of your classes. We will look at each of these tabs in the following sections.

Message Maps

The Message Maps page allows you to work with assigning message handlers to Windows messages that your application will receive. This is really the heart of programming in the Windows event-driven programming model. The Message Maps tab is shown in Figure 1.20.

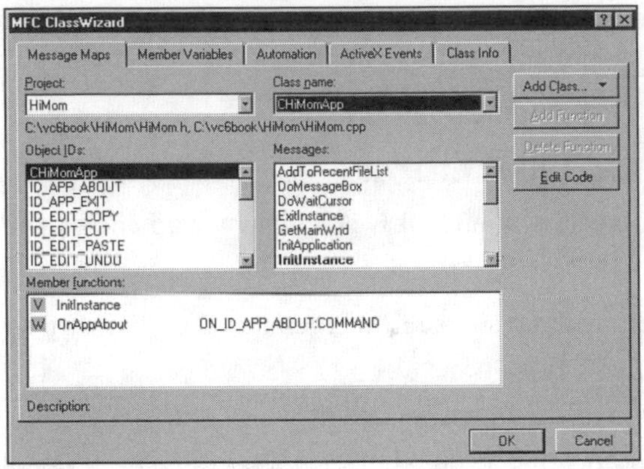

FIGURE 1.20

Class Wizard—
Message Maps.

We will look at the specifics of using Class Wizard to work with message maps in
Chapter 3, "MFC Message Handling Mechanism."

Member Variables

The Member Variables page, shown in Figure 1.21, is used to create member variables of
your class that will be used to work with controls in dialog boxes. Unfortunately, it does
not allow you to work with more general sorts of member variables.

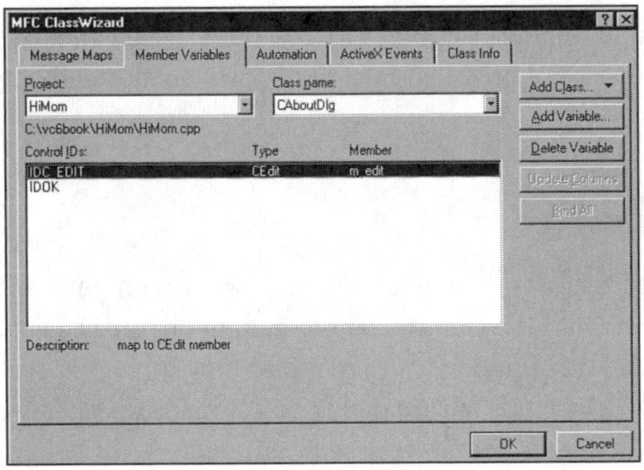

FIGURE 1.21

Class Wizard—
Member Variables.

Automation

The Automation tab, shown in Figure 1.22, helps you work with the methods and properties associated with classes that use Automation.

FIGURE 1.22

*Class Wizard—
Automation.*

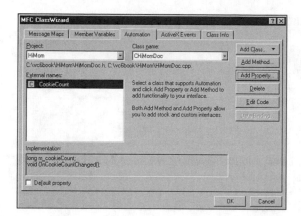

ActiveX Events

The ActiveX Events tab, shown in Figure 1.23, allows you to easily manage the ActiveX events that are supported by your ActiveX classes.

FIGURE 1.23

*Class Wizard—
ActiveX Events.*

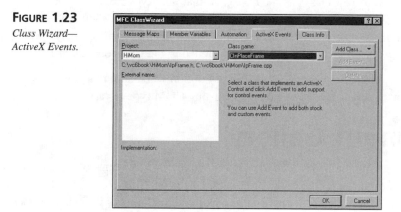

Class Info

The Class Info tab, shown in Figure 1.24, will show you some general information about your classes, including the header and source files that it is defined in, as well as its base class and any resource associated with it.

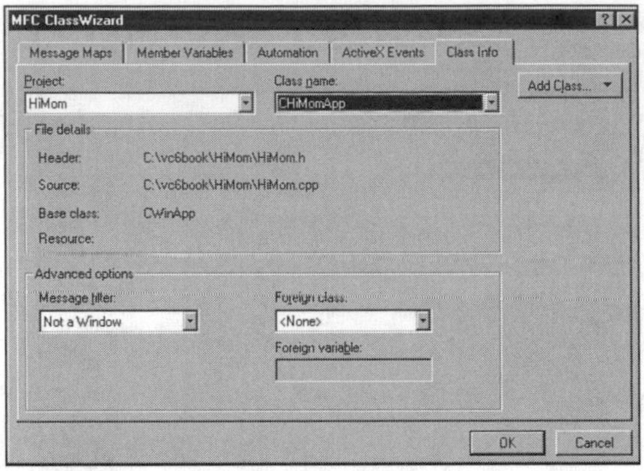

FIGURE 1.24

Class Wizard—
Class Info.

Adding a Class

The Add Class button provides a quick and easy way to create a new class in your project. The New Class dialog box, which is presented when you choose New, allows you to choose the name for your new class and the base class that it derives from. You may select the file to create the class in and specify a particular resource that should be associated with the class. If the base class you choose can support Automation, you may specify options. The new class can also be automatically added to the Component Gallery.

In addition, you may choose the From a Type Library option when adding a new class. This will allow you to create classes based on an existing COM type library.

Component Gallery

Object-oriented programming is intended to promote the reuse of existing software components. To make it even easier to reuse your classes, Developer Studio provides the Component Gallery, which allows you to insert many predefined classes into your project and also provides a handy way to catalog and store your own classes for use in other projects. To start the Component Gallery, as shown in Figure 1.25, choose Components and Controls from the Project, Add to Project menu.

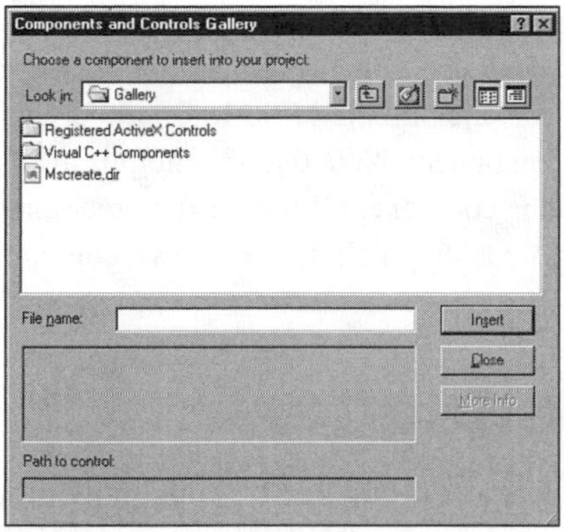

FIGURE 1.25

The Components Gallery.

The components included in the gallery are organized in a directory tree structure. When you first install Visual C++ 6.0, you will see Visual C++ Components, which contains standard Visual C++ components, and Registered ActiveX Controls, which contain any ActiveX controls registered on your machine as top-level directories. You may also add your own controls in their own directory structures. After you open one of these folders, you will see a list of available components, as shown in Figure 1.26.

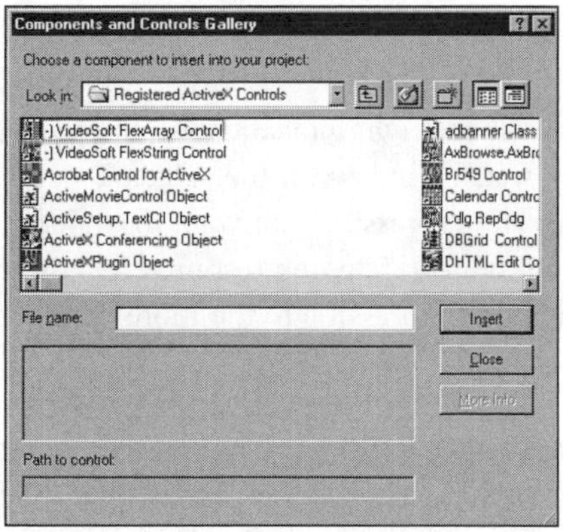

FIGURE 1.26

Visual C++ components.

The predefined components in Component Gallery can be used to add a wide variety of functionality to your applications, ranging from simple controls that can be used in dialog boxes, to ActiveX controls that can add some very complex capabilities to your application with a minimum of effort. Some of the components, such as palette support, add support for functions simply by providing handlers for a few messages.

Many of the components in the gallery might seem a bit cryptic at first glance, but there is a good deal of help available. When you select a component, a short description will appear next in the dialog box. If you click on the More Info button, you will see a much more detailed description of the component. Note that this help is available only if it has been entered by whoever created the component. Most of the predefined components include help, but you might consider adding help for your own components so that others can more easily reuse them.

Integrated Debugger

Developer Studio includes a full-featured debugger for fixing those problems that inevitably manage to slip in. A good reference for the debugger is the online help, and we don't have the space to include it all here, so I will just mention a few things that you may find useful. More information about debugging can be found in Chapter 15, "Debugging and Profiling Strategies."

Looking at Your Data

When you are debugging, you will be concerned with the values represented by the variables in your program. The simplest way to do this in Developer Studio is to point the mouse at the variable in the source code and wait a second or two. A small tip box will appear that displays the current value of the variable.

For a more detailed view, you can use the right mouse button to produce a Context menu, which allows you to open a quick watch window for the selected variable. The quick watch window allows you to enter any expression you want to evaluate in the expression window. However, preprocessor constants (including resource ID constants) are generally not available for evaluation. To add this expression to the more permanent watch window, click the Add Watch button.

Tip

Developer Studio supports drag-and-drop in many situations. For example, you can highlight a variable and drag it to the memory window, which will then automatically display the memory for that variable.

Debugging After Exceptions

At some time or another, you will almost definitely find yourself with an application that will trip over an unhandled exception. This will bring up a dialog box that will allow you to exit altogether or debug the application. You may actually load the debugger to view the current state of your application at the time of the exception, source code and all, even if you were not running your application from Developer Studio at the time!

Command-Line Tools

Despite all of the whiz-bang tools that Developer Studio offers, let's not forget that the heart of Visual C++ is a C++ compiler, a linker, a library utility, a resource compiler, and a build facility. These can all be accessed from the command line directly. Here are the command-line equivalents for these tools:

cl.exe: Compiler

link.exe: Linker

lib.exe: Library utility

implib.exe: Import library utility

nmake.exe: Microsoft's make facility

rc.exe: Resource compiler

If you need to use these utilities directly from the command line, you will find that all of their command-line arguments and options are detailed in the online help.

Other Tools

In addition to Developer Studio, Visual C++ supplies several external utilities that are added to the program group for Visual C++ when it is installed. Several of these are also available from Developer Studio by way of the Tools menu.

> **Tip**
>
> You can add anything else you like to the Tools menu from the Tools page of the dialog box produced by Tools, Customize.

Spy++

Spy++ provides a very detailed view into the goings-on of the Windows operating system. It will allow you to view all processes, threads, and windows on the machine, along with all of the Windows messages that are being sent.

MFC Tracer

This application may be used to enable various levels of debug messages that MFC may send to the Output window of Developer Studio when an application is executing or being debugged.

Register Control

In order to use OLE controls in Win32, the control must be registered with the operating system. Register Control from the Tools menu gives you a convenient method of doing this.

ActiveX Control Test Container

This provides a simple environment that allows you to test your ActiveX controls and how they work when used from a container application.

OLE/COM Object Viewer

This utility provides information about all of the OLE and ActiveX objects that are installed on your system.

Error Lookup

This utility provides a way to easily look up information about the standard error codes that are returned by most Win32 API functions. This might be easier than searching through the various header files used to define errors, although it is a bit slow.

WinDiff

Although WinDiff does not appear in the default Tools menu, it ships with Visual C++ 6.0 as WinDiff.exe. You can find WinDiff in the Common\Tools subdirectory, under the location where Visual C++ was installed. WinDiff allows you to compare two files in a convenient Windows app that is much more user-friendly than other compare or diff tools you might have used from the command line.

Help Workshop

Help Workshop is used to help manage your help projects. Although it is not automatically included in the Tools menu, it is included with Visual C++ 6.0. You will see more information about how to use this tool in Chapter 33, "Adding Windows Help."

Summary

As you have seen, the development environment provided for Visual C++ has come a long way from DOS DEBUG. Everything you need to do to develop applications (in most cases, anyway) can be done from within Developer Studio.

In this chapter, you have seen how to use the Developer Studio environment, including the toolbars and dockable view windows and particularly the project workspace window, which allows you to manage the classes, files, and resources in your application, as well as providing quick access to the online documentation.

You have seen how to create new projects for Visual C++ and the variety of project types and application wizards that are available, as well as how to work with the project settings that build of your application. You have also seen how to create multiple projects into your workspace, including managing dependencies.

In addition, you have seen how Developer Studio provides resource editors for the various Windows resources our projects will use, including dialog boxes, menus, and other resources.

You have also seen a preview of AppWizard and ClassWizard, which are used throughout this book, as well as some of the other tools included with Visual C++.

This chapter has shown you how to get started using the Visual C++ environment, but I obviously haven't shown you everything. I just don't have the time or space. However, with the things I have covered here, you should be able to work with applications. If you're curious about what something does, try it! Play around with a few simple projects and get a feel for the environment. When you're done playing, move on to what goes into your applications.

MFC Programming

PART

II

IN THIS PART

MFC Class Library Overview

by David Bennett
and Mickey Williams

CHAPTER 2

In Chapter 1, "The Visual C++ 6.0 Environment," you looked at Developer Studio and the tools that it provides to help you develop C++ applications for Windows. Now you will get down to business and look at real application development. To help you with this, the Microsoft Foundation Classes (MFC) class library provides an application framework, in addition to the general classes and Win32 API wrapper classes that you expect from a Windows class library.

In this chapter, you will

- Develop a complete application with MFC AppWizard.
- Examine the application architecture used by MFC.
- See how MFC works behind the scenes to make your application run.

The Application Framework

The MFC, as the name suggests, provides a set of reusable classes designed to simplify Windows programming. Like any class library, MFC provides classes for certain basic objects, such as strings, files, and collections, that are used in everyday programming. It also provides classes that wrap common Windows APIs and data structures, such as windows, controls, and device contexts. In addition, MFC provides an application framework, including the classes that make up the application architecture hierarchy.

The application framework helps get your application running by providing program initialization, passing Windows messages to the appropriate places, and cleaning it all up when your application exits. The framework also provides a solid foundation for more advanced features, such as ActiveX and document view processing.

Creating an MFC Application with MFC AppWizard

To kick off your examination of the application framework, you will create the first sample application to illustrate the things that MFC AppWizard can do for you and to provide concrete examples of the MFC application framework.

You will create the HiMom sample included on the CD-ROM, using MFC AppWizard. In a way, this will be a "hello world!" program for MFC, but it also provides much more support for building real applications, so I didn't think HelloWorld would be an appropriate name. (Also, it just so happens that I'd rather say "hi" to my mom than to the rest of the world.) If you would rather use your own application, bear in mind that MFC

AppWizard will name many classes and files based on your application name—if your application name is different, so will the names of your classes and files be different.

Starting MFC AppWizard

To start a new project with Visual C++, you create a new project workspace. To do this, select the New command from the File menu and choose the Projects tab. This will display the New Projects dialog box shown in Figure 2.1.

FIGURE 2.1

The New Projects dialog box.

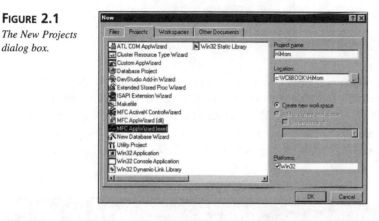

For this example, you use the MFC AppWizard (exe), so make sure it is highlighted in the list box on the left. Next, put the name of your project (HiMom) in the Project name box. Be careful to choose a name here that you can live with; MFC AppWizard will use it to create many class names and filenames and may use some awkward abbreviations. You may also need to be careful about using filenames longer than the 8.3 DOS standard. Long filenames are very useful, and Visual C++ and Win32 operating systems have no problem working with them. However, if you have any tools that support only the 8.3 format, it is *much* easier to adjust the filenames now.

If you don't like the location that MFC AppWizard has picked for your project, you can change it now by entering a new path in the Location box or using the Browse button to pick a new spot. You may also choose whether to create the project as part of a brand new workspace, or as part of the current workspace. If you choose to add the new project to the current workspace, you may create the new project as a dependency of an existing project in the current workspace by checking Dependency of: and selecting a dependent project in the drop-down list. When you are satisfied with your choices, click OK to start MFC AppWizard, which will begin with the wizard page shown in Figure 2.2.

FIGURE 2.2

*MFC AppWizard—
Step 1.*

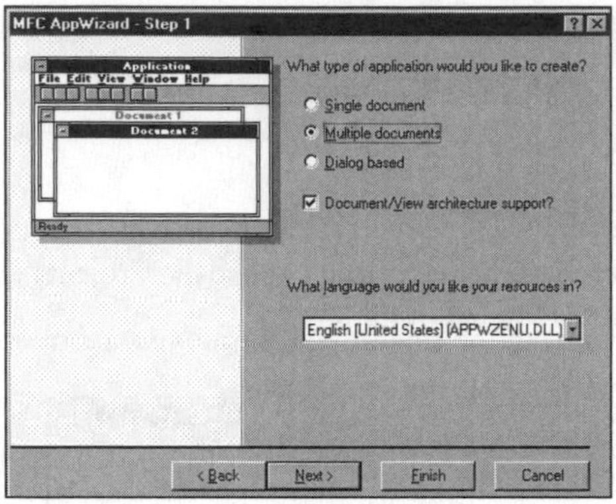

This wizard page allows you to select the type of application you would like to create. For this example, you will use Multiple Documents, which will create an application structure that you may have seen in Word or Excel, where you may view several documents at the same time. For reasons you can well imagine, your sample application will not provide quite as much functionality as MS Word or Excel, but it will allow multiple documents.

> **Note**
>
> In MFC, a document can be any set of data that may be grouped together. Although this can be a word-processing document, it can also be a group of settings for an application, such as a terminal session.

Single document applications are similar, but they allow only one open document at a time. You will learn some other differences in Chapter 4, "The Document View Architecture," where you will start to dig into the document view architecture.

The third choice, Dialog Based applications, does not use the document view architecture at all. These applications are based on a dialog resource. This is useful for small utility applications, but if you plan to implement menus, toolbars, or printing, you should seriously consider using one of the document-based types, because they can implement many of these things for you much easier than you can add these features to dialog-based applications.

By default, single document and multiple document applications are created with Document View support, and the associated checkbox is selected for you automatically. In most cases, you should leave this checkbox selected, since it enables you to take advantage of the built-in Document View architecture offered by MFC.

For an application type other than multiple document, the following steps will be slightly different, but I think you will get the picture. If you do have a question about any step, you can press F1 to bring up help on the current page. This applies not only to MFC AppWizard, but to most other areas of Developer Studio as well.

For this example, you will use English as the language of choice for your resources, but if you want, you may choose any other language offered.

By now, you have probably noticed the row of buttons along the bottom of the dialog box. The Back and Next buttons allow you to navigate between the pages of MFC AppWizard. If you just remembered that you really wanted to change something in a previous step, you can easily go back and change it. When you have entered your selections in a page, click Next to go to the next step. If you know that you want to use the default settings for the rest of the steps, you could click Finish to go straight to the end. For the HiMom sample, you could do this now, because you are going to use only the defaults, but let's take a look at the other options available. The Cancel button enables you to exit MFC AppWizard without creating a new project.

By clicking on the Next button, you can move to the next page, which looks like Figure 2.3.

FIGURE 2.3

MFC AppWizard—Step 2.

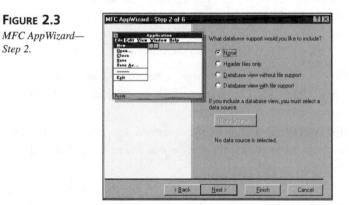

This page allows you to select options for database support in your application. Obviously, if you select None, you will get none (from MFC AppWizard anyway—you can always add things later, but you have to do it manually). The Header Files Only option includes the AFXDB.H header file, which includes simple database support, allowing you to create and use recordsets to work with databases.

The two database view options create a view class for your application based on CRecordView, which gives you a form-based application allowing you to view and update records. The Database View With File Support option supports document serialization. If you choose either of these options, you must also choose a data source. You learn about this in much greater detail in Part V, "Database Programming," so let's go ahead to the next page, shown in Figure 2.4.

FIGURE 2.4

MFC AppWizard—Step 3

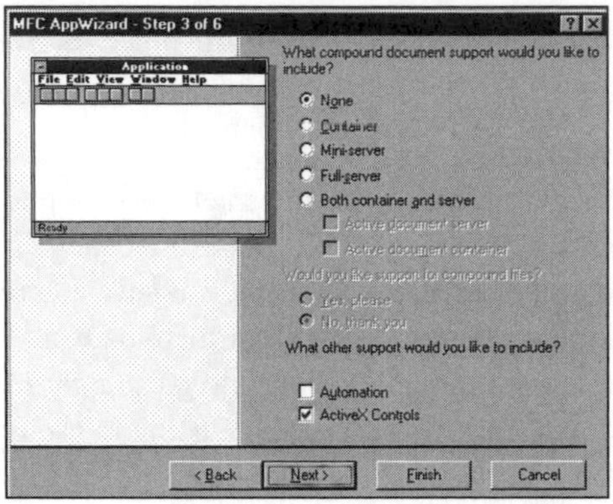

With this page, you can select options that allow your application to support various levels of Object Linking and Embedding (OLE). Once again, if you select None, that's just what you'll get. You have to add OLE support manually if you change your mind after the application is created. You will explore OLE, COM, and ActiveX in much greater detail later, but here's the short version of what the other options mean:

- Container support allows your application to support the embedding of OLE objects. This enables your application to serve as an OLE container just like Word and Excel.

- Mini-server applications can create and manage compound document objects, but they cannot run stand-alone, supporting only objects that are embedded in OLE container applications.

- Full-server applications can also create and manage compound document objects, as well as running stand-alone and supporting both linked and embedded items.

- Select Both Container and Server if you want your application to be able to accept embedded or linked objects into its own documents and be able to create OLE objects for use in container applications.

- If you have selected any of the server options, you can also make your application an ActiveX document server.

- Likewise, if you have selected any of the container options, you can make your application an ActiveX document container.

- If you select support for compound files, MFC will serialize your container appli-cation's documents using the OLE compound-file format. If you choose "No, thank you," it won't.

- You can select Automation to allow automation clients, such as Word, Excel, and the Windows Scripting Host, to access your application.

- If you want to include ActiveX controls in your application, such as those provided in the component gallery, select the ActiveX Controls option.

Step 4, shown in Figure 2.5 allows you to select several advanced features that MFC AppWizard can add for you.

FIGURE 2.5

*MFC AppWizard—
Step 4.*

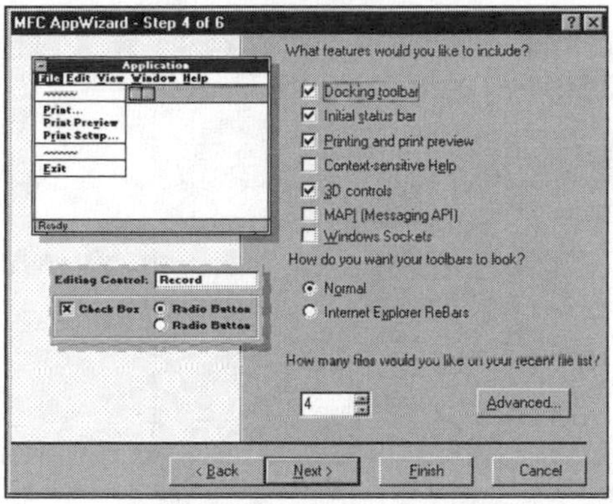

Selecting Docking Toolbar allows the user to move the toolbar from its default location and dock it to the borders of the window.

The Initial Status Bar option provides a status bar, including keyboard state indicators and help for menus and toolbars. This also adds menu commands to hide or display the status bar and toolbar.

The Printing and Print Preview option tells MFC AppWizard to generate code and menu commands to handle printing tasks automatically.

The Context-Sensitive Help option generates help files that you can use to give your users help on specific areas of your application.

If you select 3D Controls, all controls in your application will have that nifty chiseled look.

You can include support for the Windows Open Services Architecture (WOSA) by select-ing the MAPI (Messaging API) option, which allows your application to integrate with mail systems, or the Windows Sockets option, which enables TCP/IP communications.

If you have selected the Docking Toolbar option, you can select the type of toolbar to be used—you can select either a Normal Win32 toolbar, or an Internet Explorer ReBar toolbar.

MFC AppWizard automatically implements a most-recently-used file list for you in the File menu. You may set the number of files here to keep in this list.

The Advanced button allows you to select preferences about document types and window styles for your application.

Step 5, shown in Figure 2.6, allows you to tell MFC AppWizard to include source file comments where appropriate.

FIGURE 2.6

*MFC AppWizard—
Step 5.*

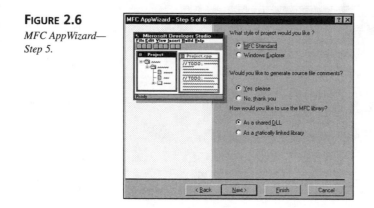

You can also specify the type of project that is to be built. By default, an MFC Standard application is created. Optionally, you can select the Windows Explorer option, which creates a splitter window containing a tree view in the left pane, and a list view in the right pane.

This page also gives you the option to use the shared DLL versions of MFC or the statically linked library. If you know that your application will be the only MFC app running at any given time, you may want to use the static libraries, but it is generally better to use the DLL versions, which can be shared by all applications. Using the DLL versions also reduces the disk and memory requirements of your application's executable file.

Step 6, shown in Figure 2.7 shows the classes that MFC AppWizard will create for you.

If you like, you can change the defaults that MFC AppWizard supplies by selecting the class in the top list and editing the fields below. For many of the classes, options will be

inactive (grayed). In most of these cases, changing the default doesn't make sense anyway—an application class based on anything other than CWinApp just wouldn't work well with MFC.

FIGURE 2.7

MFC AppWizard— Step 6.

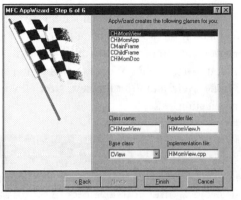

If you don't like the filenames that MFC AppWizard has chosen, you may freely change these (for all but the app class), but you can place only one of the classes in each file.

For MDI applications, you can change only the base class of your view class. You probably will not want to use the base CView class in a real application, but will want to use one of the available derived classes that provide much greater functionality. For more on MFC's view classes, see Chapter 4.

Click Finish here, and you're just about done. MFC AppWizard will display a window like Figure 2.8.

FIGURE 2.8

The New Project Information dialog box.

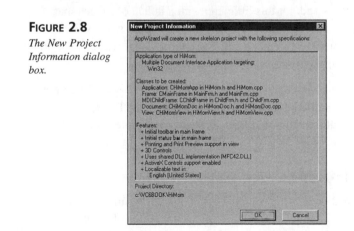

You should review the information presented here to see that it matches the options you selected. If you find that something here doesn't match what you wanted, click Cancel to go back to Step 6. If you are satisfied with your choices, click OK and let MFC AppWizard do the work for you.

You now have a complete Windows application. You can see this for yourself by choosing the `Build HiMom.exe` command from the Build menu to compile and link, then choosing the `Execute HiMom` command from the Build menu to run it. You will notice that many cool functions that you expect from a Windows application have already been implemented for you, such as File, New, and Print Preview. Now all you have to do is the really good stuff to fit your application.

> ### Tip
>
> MFC AppWizard is extremely useful in creating new projects, but it isn't intended to manage your projects after you have clicked on that last OK. If you find yourself wanting to add functionality to an application midway through development, but forgot to choose a few options in MFC AppWizard when you created it, you can use MFC AppWizard to give you some help. If you create a new project with the MFC AppWizard options you used to create your application and then create another with the options you wish to add (or delete), you can use a utility such as WinDiff to see what the new options have added to each of your source and header files.

Getting to Know Your New Application

Okay, so you clicked a few buttons and got this little app with a bunch of menus that don't do anything. What's it got under the hood? Here, you will look at what MFC AppWizard has created for you and how the application framework that was created provides a solid backbone for your application.

If you're like me, your first instinct may be to open a DOS window and start digging through files. Sure, you can still do this, but it really is easier to use the Project Workspace window—I promise. Remember that you can open any source file, usually to just the right place, by double-clicking on the file or class view of the project workspace.

Classes Created by MFC AppWizard

As you may have already noticed, MFC AppWizard has created a handful of classes for you, based on your application's name. These fall into the basic classes of Application classes, Document classes, View classes, and Frame classes. Each class is based on one of the classes in the application architecture hierarchy. (You will almost never use the base classes directly, but will derive your own classes from them.) The HiMom example you just created will implement the classes shown in Table 2.1.

TABLE 2.1   Classes for HiMom

MFC Base Class	Derived Class	Filename
CWinApp	CHiMomApp	HiMom.cpp
CDialog	CAboutDlg	HiMom.cpp
CDocument	CHiMomDoc	HiMomDoc.cpp
CView	CHiMomView	HiMomView.cpp
CFrameWnd	CMainFrame	MainFrm.cpp
CMDIChildWnd	CChildFrame	ChildFrm.cpp

CDocument, CView, and Frame Classes

The classes that you derive from CDocument are intended to hold the data that your application will work with. Your CDocument class will be responsible for reading and writing data files and will serve as a repository for the information that your CView classes will allow the user to view and manipulate. You may choose not to use these classes and the document view architecture, but you will see in Chapter 4, "The Document View Architecture," that these are very useful in helping you implement many functions common to Windows applications.

Classes based on CMainFrame will implement the main frame for your application. (Kinda makes sense, I suppose.) It is this class that will manage the menus, toolbars, and status bars (even the main window itself) for the main window of your application. Classes derived from CChildFrame are used in MDI applications to manage the child windows created for multiple views. Like the main frame, CChildFrame classes can manage menus, toolbars, status bars, and the window for the children of your main frame. You will look at how the document, view, and frame classes work together in Chapter 4, so let's leave it at that for now and move on to the real heart of your MFC application.

The CWinApp Class

Every true MFC application has a class derived from CWinApp. You can see how MFC AppWizard has done this for you by looking at the following sample from HiMom.h:

```
class CHiMomApp : public CWinApp
{
public:
    CHiMomApp();
// Overrides
    // ClassWizard generated virtual function overrides
    //{{AFX_VIRTUAL(CHiMomApp)
    public:
    virtual BOOL InitInstance();
    //}}AFX_VIRTUAL
// Implementation
    //{{AFX_MSG(CHiMomApp)
    afx_msg void OnAppAbout();
        // NOTE: ClassWizard will add and remove member functions here.
        // DO NOT EDIT what you see in these blocks of generated code !
    //}}AFX_MSG
    DECLARE_MESSAGE_MAP()
};
```

The first line shown here is what gives your application the real power of the MFC application framework. This is where the CHiMomApp class is derived from CWinApp. Apart from that, you will notice an awful lot of strange comments. These comments give the ClassWizard landmarks to find the pieces of the code that it manipulates.

> **Caution**
>
> You should notice the DO NOT EDIT warning in the comments. Although it is possible to change or add some things in these sections, it is not generally a good idea. The changes you make here may confuse ClassWizard to the point that you won't be able to use it to help manage your classes. If you feel you must make changes on ClassWizard's turf, it's best to try out ClassWizard right after you make the changes to see whether things still work. You should also realize that ClassWizard may change the code in these sections. If you ever want to use ClassWizard again, by all means *do not delete these comments!*

Just as your Application class derives from CWinApp, CWinApp itself is derived from a chain of other classes in the application architecture hierarchy, including CWinThread, CCmdTarget, and CObject.

The CWinThread Class

One of the major differences between Windows 3.1 and the 32-bit versions of Windows, such as Windows 98 and Windows 2000 is the use of preemptive multitasking. Although Windows 3.1 supports multiple tasks, only one task could be running at one time, and nobody else could run without the running task giving up the processor. Win32 supports true multitasking through the use of threads, which allow more than one thing to be going on at the same time. True, most processors really execute only one instruction stream at a time, but as far as this chapter is concerned, all threads run at the same time.

When your application first starts, it has one—and only one—thread, known as the primary thread. This thread is encapsulated by the CWinApp class that you have derived. This means that a pointer to your CWinApp object is also a pointer to the CWinThread object for the primary thread. Once your application gets going, it can create as many new threads as it wants to manage various tasks.

Note

Even though you may not be using more than one thread, the MFC libraries always expect to link with multithreaded runtime libraries. You should select the appropriate multithreaded libraries in the Build Settings under the C/C++ Code Generation options. (This is not the default for new application workspaces that are not created with MFC AppWizard.)

You learn more about working with threads in Chapter 16, "Multithreading," but for now let's move on to the base class of CWinThread, CCmdTarget.

The CCmdTarget Class

All window classes under MFC that accept user input, including OLE classes, are derived at some level from CCmdTarget. This class is used as a base class for so many other classes because it allows your class to handle Windows messages.

Windows programs are based on an event-driven model. This means that they run in the traditional sense for only a short time at startup, then spend the rest of their lives waiting around for messages, reacting to them, and waiting again for more messages. These messages can be generated by simply moving the mouse, clicking on a button, or selecting a menu command.

In C programs, these messages were generally handled by large switch blocks involving case statements for each message that your application wanted to process. Because the processing of these messages was often dependent on several other variables, most applications ended up with a massive web of nested switch and if blocks.

To remedy this situation, and to allow you to use the power of C++ freely, MFC has implemented message maps to allow your classes to handle Windows messages in a much cleaner fashion. Any class derived from `CCmdTarget` may have its own message map, allowing each class to handle the messages it is interested in however it chooses, while leaving other messages to be handled higher in the class hierarchy.

Working with messages is one of the most important things that you will do in Windows programming (so important that it has its own chapter—Chapter 3, "MFC Message Handling Mechanism"). For now, let's move on to the base class of `CCmdTarget`, `CObject`.

The `CObject` Class

At least as far as MFC is concerned, `CObject` is the mother of all classes (well, most of them anyway). Almost all the classes in MFC are derived from `CObject`—with a few notable exceptions, such as `CString`. Deriving a class from `CObject` provides several very important features, including serialization, runtime type information, and some very important debugging features.

Serialization

Many features of Windows programming with MFC require the capability of serializing the data in your objects. Perhaps the simplest example of this is saving an object to a file. You need to have a way to convert your object to a series of bytes that can be written to disk and brought back later to restore your object to its previous state.

To implement serialization in your classes, you first derive them, either directly or indirectly, from `CObject`. Then you can implement the `Serialize` member function for your class to serialize its data. To see just how to do this, let's start by looking at a few macros MFC provides to help.

The `DECLARE_SERIAL` and `IMPLEMENT_SERIAL` Macros

To help implement serialization in your class, MFC provides a pair of macros: `DECLARE_SERIAL` for use in your class declaration (usually in an h file), and `IMPLEMENT_SERIAL` for use in your class implementation (a cpp file).

The `DECLARE_SERIAL` macro takes only one parameter: the name of your class. Placing this in your class declaration provides prototypes for the serialization functions and some special handling for the insertion operator. You can see how this is used in the following class declaration:

```
Class CEmployee : public CObject
{
public:
    DECLARE_SERIAL(CEmployee)
    void Serialize(CArchive& ar);
private:
    int         m_EmpNo;
    CString     m_Name;
    float       m_Salary;
};
```

Serialize()

Notice that this example declares a Serialize() function, which takes as a parameter a reference to a CArchive object, which provides a context for the serialization. Before calling the Serialize() function, the MFC framework has prepared the CArchive object either to read from or write to objects of your class. You must implement the specific behavior for the Serialize() function in each class that you intend to serialize.

As mentioned previously, the same Serialize() function implements both loading and storing, based on the CArchive context. You can use the CArchive::IsLoading() or CArchive::IsStoring() function to determine the direction of serialization. The implementation for the CEmployee class declared earlier might look like this:

```
IMPLEMENT_SERIAL(CEmployee, CObject, 0x200)
void CEmployee::Serialize(CArchive& ar)
{
    // call base class Serialize() first
    CObject::Serialize(ar);
    // then serialize the data for this class
    if(ar.IsLoading())
    {
        ar >> m_EmpNo;
        ar >> m_Name;
        ar >> m_Salary;
    }
    else
    {
        ar << m_EmpNo;
        ar << m_Name;
        ar << m_Salary;
    }
} // end CEmployee::Serialize
```

There are many interesting things that you should notice in this example, beginning with the use of the IMPLEMENT_SERIAL macro, which takes three parameters: the class name, the base class it is derived from, and a schema number, which you will learn about in just a bit.

Next, you should notice that you call the `Serialize` member of the base class. Every implementation of `Serialize()` must call the `Serialize()` function of the base class to allow it to serialize its data first, before you serialize the data for your class.

Serialization Operators

Notice that the serialization is performed by the overloaded insertion and extraction operators. These are predefined for the `CArchive` class for the following data types:

```
BYTE
WORD
DWORD
LONG
double
float
CObject*
```

The insertion and extraction operators are also defined for any class that implements serialization. You can thank the `DECLARE_SERIAL` and `IMPLEMENT_SERIAL` macros for this. If you need to use any other data types, you have to create your own override functions or use macros or type casts to use the supported types.

Serializing Different Versions

Earlier, you learned that the `IMPLEMENT_SERIAL` macro takes a *schema number* for its third parameter. This can be any number in the valid range of type `UINT`, with the exception of -1, which is reserved for use by MFC. The schema number effectively allows you to embed a version number in your serialized data; if the schema number you specify in `IMPLEMENT_SERIAL` does not match the schema number in the file you are reading, MFC will fail when attempting to read the file. In debug builds, MFC will display a failed assertion dialog box.

If MFC just fails when presented with out-of-date file information, how can it support multiple versions? This is where the `VERSIONABLE_SCHEMA` macro comes in. If you combine your current schema number and the `VERSIONABLE_SCHEMA` macro by using the OR operator (|), your `Serialize()` routine will write your data with the current schema number, but can read any schema. This is handled by use of the `CArchive::GetObjectSchema()` function, as you will see in the following example. Here, you assume that the previous version of `CEmployee` did not implement the `m_Name` member:

```
IMPLEMENT_SERIAL(CEmployee, CObject, VERSIONABLE_SCHEMA|0x200)
void CEmployee::Serialize(CArchive& ar)
```

```
{
    // first, call base class Serialize function
    CObject::Serialize(ar);

    // Now we do our stuff
    if(ar.IsStoring())
    {
        // We are writing our class data,
        //      so we don't care about the schema
        ar << m_EmpNo;
        ar << m_Name;
        ar << m_Salary;
    }
    else
    {
        // we are loading, so check the schema
        UINT nSchema = ar.GetObjectSchema();
        switch(nSchema)
        {
            case 0x100:
                // Old schema, default m_Name
                ar >> m_EmpNo;
                m_Name = ""Dilbert";
                ar >> m_Salary;
                break;
            case 0x200:
                // current version
                ar >> m_EmpNo;
                ar >> m_Name;
                ar >> m_Salary;
                break;
            default:
                // Unknown Version, do nothing
                break;
        } // end switch
    } // end if
} // end CCLient::Serialize()
```

As you can see, you should provide reasonable defaults for data that cannot be retrieved from the archive. On the other hand, you probably should provide some sort of mechanism to report unknown cases to the user, instead of doing nothing, as I did here.

Runtime Type Information

Beginning with version 4.0 of Visual C++, two versions of runtime type information are supported: the ANSI standard C++ typeid() variety and MFC's own, more powerful brand of type identification provided by the CObject class.

2

MFC CLASS
LIBRARY
OVERVIEW

If you want to use the ANSI variety of runtime type information (RTTI), you can enable this in the Project Settings dialog box by selecting the Enable Run-Time Type Information (RTTI) option on the C++ Language page of the C/C++ tab. This allows you to use the C++ `typeid()` operator to get the name of the class.

The MFC version of runtime type information provides backward compatibility with MFC apps that predate ANSI RTTI in Microsoft compilers and provides information for efficient serialization and cross-platform compatibility.

Using MFC Runtime Type Information

To use MFC's runtime type information, you can use the `DECLARE_DYNAMIC` macro, which takes your class name as an argument in your class declaration, and the `IMPLEMENT_DYNAMIC` macro, which takes your class name and its base class in your implementation. These set up the structures that MFC uses to track type information for your classes.

> **Note**
>
> You use only one set of these macros for your `CObject` class. `DECLARE/IMPLEMENT_DYNCREATE` includes `DECLARE/IMPLEMENT_DYNAMIC` functionality, and `DECLARE/IMPLEMENT_SERIAL` encompasses both of these.

`IsKindOf()` and `RUNTIME_CLASS()`

If you have enabled runtime type identification in your classes, you can now verify that any pointer you get is a valid pointer to the class you expect, before your app goes off into the weeds from a faulty pointer. This is done by using the `CObject::IsKindOf()` function, which takes a pointer to a runtime type information structure. This structure can be provided for constant class types by the `RUNTIME_CLASS` macro, taking your class name as a parameter. This example demonstrates this a little better:

```
if(pMyPtr->IsKindOf(RUNTIME_CLASS(CEmployee)))
    DoSomething();
else
    DoError();
```

In this example, if `pMyPtr` points to an object of class `CEmployee` or any class derived from it, `IsKindOf()` returns `TRUE`. If `IsKindOf()` returns `FALSE`, you will probably want to report an error.

STATIC_DOWNCAST and DYNAMIC_DOWNCAST

In addition to the type information available from CObject, MFC provides macros to validate types when you want to cast a pointer to an object to a pointer to a more specific derived class. You can use STATIC_DOWNCAST to check your casting with code like this:

```
CWnd* pWnd;
pButton = STATIC_DOWNCAST(CButton, pWnd);
```

If you are running a debug build and pWnd is not really a pointer to a CButton class object, MFC will assert; otherwise, the cast is performed as normal. In a non-debug build, STATIC_DOWNCAST will always perform the cast without type checking. If you want to do type checking in release builds, you can use the DYNAMIC_DOWNCAST macro, which works the same way in debug and nondebug builds. If the type check fails, or if the pointer is NULL, DYNAMIC_DOWNCAST will return NULL. It is then up to your application to decide what to do.

ASSERT_KINDOF()

If you want to check that a pointer is of the type you want it to be, you could use a line like the following:

```
ASSERT(pMyPtr->IsKindOf(RUNTIME_CLASS(CEmployee)));
```

This may be a bit cumbersome both to type and to read, so MFC provides a shortcut—the ASSERT_KINDOF macro. The following line behaves exactly the same as the previous ASSERT—it just looks neater:

```
ASSERT_KINDOF(CEmployee, pMyPtr);
```

You can probably guess that the first argument is the desired class type and the second is the pointer in question.

Debugging Support

Because CObject is the base class for almost all other classes in the MFC, it serves as a convenient place to stash a few very important debugging features.

AssertValid()

If you want to be able to verify that an object of your class is valid, you can override the AssertValid() member function of CObject. Like many other debug features, this should only be implemented in builds where the preprocessor symbol _DEBUG is defined. To implement an AssertValid() function for your class, the declaration for your class should look like the following:

```
class CMyClass : public CObject
{
// other stuff for your class
public:
#ifdef _DEBUG
    virtual void AssertValid() const;
#endif
};
```

Now you need to implement your `AssertValid()` function. This function should perform a quick check that the elements of your class are in order. Your implementation should look something like this:

```
#ifdef _DEBUG
void CEmployee::AssertValid()
{
    // validate the base class
    CObject::AssertValid();
    // validate this class
    ASSERT(m_EmpNo != 0);
} // end CEmployee::AssertValid()
#endif
```

You should perform all your validity tests with the ASSERT macro (and derivatives like ASSERT_KINDOF). You can use `AssertValid()` in your applications by calling the ASSERT_VALID macro, which takes a pointer to the object to be validated. This macro, like many other debug macros, will not generate any code in non-debug builds, so you won't need to hassle with all those pesky #ifdefs.

The ASSERT Macro

Because I have mentioned asserts several times already, it's about time you look at them in more detail. The ASSERT macro takes any expression that evaluates to a Boolean expression. If this expression is true (nonzero), all is well and the app goes on its merry way. If, however, the expression is false (0), a dialog box like that in Figure 2.9 will appear.

FIGURE 2.9

The Assertion dialog box.

This dialog box gives you three choices. You may choose Abort to stop your app right there; or you can choose Ignore to close the dialog and press on; or you can choose

Retry, which enables you to jump right into the debugger at the point that the ASSERT failed, even if you did not start the application in the debugger. From this point, you can easily use the Call Stack window to figure out just where in your code things went amiss.

Remember that the ASSERT macro does not generate any code in non-debug builds. It will not even evaluate the expression. If you want to have the expression evaluated in release builds, you can use the VERIFY macro instead.

Dump()

Another important debugging feature of the CObject class is the Dump() function. This is useful when you want to spit out information about the current state of your class object periodically, or when you have noticed a problem. Once again, this feature should not be implemented in non-debug builds. To use the Dump() function in your classes, you insert code something like this:

```
class CEmployee : public CObject
{
public:
#ifdef _DEBUG
    virtual void Dump(CDumpContext& dc) const;
#endif
    int m_EmpNo;
    CString m_Name;
    // Other class stuff
} // end class CEmployee
```

Your implementation would include code such as this:

```
#ifdef _DEBUG
void CEmployee::Dump(CDumpContext& dc) const
{
    // first, call base class Dump
    CObject::Dump(dc);
    // then dump this class
    dc << "Employee Number: " << m_EmpNo << "\n"
        << "Employee Name: " << m_Name << "\n";
} // end CEmployee::Dump()
#endif
```

> **Tip**
>
> Remember to use newlines or other whitespace to separate your data; it will make your dump much more readable. It is also a good practice to end your output with a newline to ensure your output doesn't get scrambled with the next object to dump.

If you are running your application under the Visual C++ debugger, MFC will set up the dump context passed to Dump() to send its output to the Output window of the debugger.

The insertion operator for the dump context that is used in the examples is defined for the following types:

```
BYTE
WORD
DWORD
int
UINT
LONG
double
float
CObject*
CObject&
void*
LPCTSTR
LPCWSTR
LPCSTR
```

If the type you want to dump isn't supported, you can generally get by with a simple cast. After all, the data is just going to be converted to a string for output.

The TRACE() Macro

In addition to the Dump() function, your application can write to the debug context with the TRACE() macro provided by MFC. The TRACE() macro works much like printf(). It accepts a string that may include placeholders for other variables, using the same % variables that printf() uses, except TRACE() does not support floating-point variables. The TRACE() macros will, however, support Unicode strings.

With the MFC Tracer application (TRACER.EXE), included in the Tools menu of Developer Studio, you can enable or disable several sorts of trace messages provided by MFC's internals, as well as disable tracing altogether.

If you wish to assign MFC's dump context—and the TRACE() and Dump() output that goes with it—to something other than the debugger's Output window, see the documentation for the CDumpContext and Dumpinit.cpp in the MFC source directory, which declares CDumpContext afxDump. Unfortunately, the details of doing this are beyond the scope of this book.

Putting It All Together

In this chapter, you have taken a look at the classes in the application architecture hierarchy and have seen many of the features these classes have to offer. Now let's take a look at how MFC brings this all together to get your application off and running.

The first thing that your application will do when it begins executing is initialize all the static and global objects in your application. Perhaps the most important global object that will be created is an instance of your CWinApp class. If you have created your app with MFC AppWizard, this is done for you by code like this from HiMom.cpp in the HiMom sample:

```
// The one and only CHiMomApp object
CHiMomApp theApp;
```

The code created by Visual C++ will call the constructor of your CWinApp class just after creating global variables by loading an initialized data segment and constructing a few other objects that MFC uses internally.

You should be aware that the initialization of your application has not been completed when the constructor for your CWinApp (or any other static object) is called. You should avoid doing any serious operations in these constructors, particularly with Windows classes. Simple initialization of your variables (including CString objects) is fine, but you will soon run into trouble if you try to perform operations on other more complicated classes, particularly classes such as CWnd, because the actual window underlying CWnd objects has not been created yet.

WinMain()

Once all the constructors for static objects have run, the runtime library will call MFC's implementation of WinMain(). This function will take care of initializing MFC for you and will then call the InitApplication() and InitInstance() members of your CWinApp class. When these have finished, WinMain() will call the Run() function of your CWinApp class. Normally, this defaults to CWinThread::Run(), which will get the message pump for your application going. At this point, your application will begin to process messages like any good Windows application.

When your application terminates (typically, when a WM_QUIT message is received) MFC will call the ExitInstance() function of your CWinApp class, then the destructors of any static objects, including your CWinApp object. The application then returns control to the operating system and is done.

InitApplication() and InitInstance()

The InitApplication() function is really not necessary for Win32 programming, but is a relic from the good (or bad) days of Win16. In 16-bit windows, two instances of an application could run at the same time, with the InitApplication() code running only when the first instance was started. In Win32, an application that is run twice, it will exist in two totally separate, independent processes. You can place code in InitApplication(), but it is no different than InitInstance() in Win32, except InitApplication() will be called first. If you choose to override the default InitApplication(), you should return TRUE if all is well. If your function returns FALSE, initialization will halt, ending your program.

> **Note**
>
> If you are used to doing all your initialization in WinMain(), you will find that you can still access the information passed in the parameters to WinMain() by way of members of the CWinApp class.
>
> The handle to the executing instance of the application, normally passed to WinMain() as hInstance, is available in CWinApp::m_hInstance or by calling ::AfxGetInstanceHandle(), which can be called from anywhere.
>
> The hPrevInstance parameter to WinMain() is always NULL in Win32 applications, so it is not provided in a member variable.
>
> The lpszCmdLine parameter to WinMain(), which points to the command-line string, may be found in CWinApp::m_lpCmdLine. You will take a closer look at using this in just a bit.
>
> The nCmdShow parameter to WinMain() is available in the m_nCmdShow member. This should be used in your call to ShowWindow().

Your InitInstance() function is where all the serious initialization for your app should occur. If you look at the InitInstance() function created by MFC AppWizard for the HiMom example shown next, you will notice that it does several very important things. Depending on the options you selected in MFC AppWizard, you may see how the wizard initializes things such as OLE, Windows sockets, and 3D controls:

```
BOOL CHiMomApp::InitInstance()
{
    AfxEnableControlContainer();

    // Standard initialization
    // If you are not using these features and wish to reduce the size
```

```
    //  of your final executable, you should remove from the following
    //  the specific initialization routines you do not need.

#ifdef _AFXDLL
    Enable3dControls();          // Call this when using MFC in a shared DLL
#else
    Enable3dControlsStatic(); // Call this when linking to MFC statically
#endif

    // Change the registry key under which our settings are stored.
    // TODO: You should modify this string to be something appropriate
    // such as the name of your company or organization.
    SetRegistryKey(_T("Local AppWizard-Generated Applications"));

    LoadStdProfileSettings();

    // Register the application's document templates.  Document templates
    //serve as the connection between documents, frame windows and views.

    CMultiDocTemplate* pDocTemplate;
    pDocTemplate = new CMultiDocTemplate(
        IDR_HIMOMTYPE,
        RUNTIME_CLASS(CHiMomDoc),
        RUNTIME_CLASS(CChildFrame), // custom MDI child frame
        RUNTIME_CLASS(CHiMomView));
    AddDocTemplate(pDocTemplate);

    // create main MDI Frame window
    CMainFrame* pMainFrame = new CMainFrame;
    if (!pMainFrame->LoadFrame(IDR_MAINFRAME))
        return FALSE;
    m_pMainWnd = pMainFrame;

    // Parse command line for standard shell commands, DDE, file open
    CCommandLineInfo cmdInfo;
    ParseCommandLine(cmdInfo);

    // Dispatch commands specified on the command line
    if (!ProcessShellCommand(cmdInfo))
        return FALSE;

    // The main window has been initialized, so show and update it.
    pMainFrame->ShowWindow(m_nCmdShow);
    pMainFrame->UpdateWindow();

    return TRUE;
}
```

2

MFC CLASS
LIBRARY
OVERVIEW

LoadStdProfileSettings()

You should also notice a call to LoadStdProfileSettings(). This will load some standard data items, including the files on the Most Recently Used list, from either the application's .ini file or from the registry. For now, suffice it to say that the registry allows a hierarchical, secure place to store and retrieve data that was formerly relegated to various .ini files in Win16.

Working with the Command Line

In MFC applications, you can handle command-line information in several ways. Traditional C-style argc and argv processing is available by using the __argc and __argv global variables provided. You may also look at the entire command line provided by m_lpCmdLine. Windows applications, however, can support some special command-line options that are best handled with the methods shown next.

As you can see from the previous example, InitInstance() creates a CCommandLineInfo object and passes it to ParseCommandLine(). This function will then call CCommandLineInfo::ParseParam() for each parameter. ParseParam() will modify the CCommandLineInfo structure based on these parameters. In InitInstance(), the resulting CCommandLineInfo object is then passed to ProcessShellCommand(), which is responsible for carrying out any default actions specified in the command line.

The default implementation of ParseParam() will handle the parameters and the actions detailed in Table 2.2.

TABLE 2.2   Default parameter actions

Parameter	*Action*
(No parameter)	Create new document.
<filename>	Open specified file.
/p <filename>	Print specified file.
/pt <filename> <printer> <driver> <port>	Print file to specified printer.
/dde	Serve a DDE session.
/automation	Start as an Automation server.
/embedding	Prepare to serve an embedded OLE object.

You may use argc, argv processing along with ParseCommandLine() if you want, or you may change the way ParseCommandLine() works by creating your own class derived from CCommandLineInfo and overriding the ParseParam() function.

You may also change your application's behavior by modifying the CCommandLineInfo object before you call ProcessShellCommand(). For example, if you do not want your application to create a new document by default, you can make sure that the m_nShellCommand member of the CCommandLineInfo object is not FileNew before you pass it to ProcessShellCommand(). For more on this, refer to CCommandLineInfo in the Visual C++ online documentation.

Creating the Main Window

The last thing that the MFC AppWizard-generated version of InitInstance does is call ShowWindow() and UpdateWindow() to present the main window of your application, which was created earlier in InitInstance. Like InitApplication(), your InitInstance() call should return FALSE only if something has gone wrong and you want to bail out of your program right there.

The Message Pump

Now that all the initialization for your program has executed, the CWinThread::Run() function will start up the message pump, or message loop, of your application. The message pump will do nothing but wait until it receives a message. At this point, the message is dispatched to a message-handler function, provided by your application or by MFC, that will react to the message. The details of message dispatching are covered in the next chapter.

OnIdle()

When I said that the message pump does nothing but wait around between messages, I stretched the truth just a little. When the message pump finds that the message queue is empty, it will call OnIdle(), which may allow you to do some background processing or update the status of your user interface objects, such as disabling toolbars if needed.

The OnIdle() function will be called repeatedly until it returns FALSE, or until a message is received—at which point, the message is dispatched. When OnIdle() returns FALSE, the message pump will sleep until the next message arrives.

If you choose to implement your own OnIdle() function, you should keep in mind that the message queue for your application (or at least this thread) will not be able to process any messages until OnIdle() returns, because this is a non-preemptive method of multitasking. If you want to do preemptive multitasking, see Chapter 16, "Multithreading."

Also, your implementation of OnIdle() should call the base class implementation, which updates user interface objects and cleans up some internal data structures. With this in mind, the declaration of OnIdle() looks like this:

```
virtual BOOL OnIdle(LONG lCount);
```

The lCount parameter is incremented each time OnIdle() is called and it is set to 0 when new messages are processed.

Summary

In this chapter, you learned how Visual C++ and the MFC class library simplify the process of building Windows applications. The framework provided by MFC provides the basic default behavior used by most applications. Together with MFC AppWizard, the MFC class library enables you to write a simple functioning application with a few mouse clicks.

This chapter also discussed four of the base classes used by MFC: CWinApp, CWinThread, CCmdTarget, and CObject. CWinApp is the base class for your project's application object. CWinThread is the base class for all threads that interact with MFC objects. CCmdTarget is the base class for all classes that handle window messages. The CObject class provides support for persistence, runtime type information, as well as providing enhanced debugging support.

Taken together, the MFC class library and Visual C++ give you a flexible, yet powerful set of tools for building your Windows applications.

MFC Message Handling Mechanism

by David Bennett and Mickey Williams

IN THIS CHAPTER

CHAPTER 3

Windows programs are based on an event-driven programming model. This means that most of the things your application will do are done in response to various Windows messages. If you have done any Windows programming, you already know this. This chapter will show you how to work with MFC to handle messages with C++ classes. In this chapter, you will learn about

- Standard Windows commands handled by the MFC
- How MFC dispatches messages to your application
- Using ClassWizard to handle messages
- Implementing your own message maps

Message Categories

Almost everything that your application will do is based on handling Windows messages. These come in three basic varieties: general Windows messages, control notifications, and commands:

- The Message IDs for Windows messages are generally prefixed by WM_—for example, WM_PAINT or WM_QUIT. These messages, which are handled by windows and views, can represent a wide range of things that happen in your application. Thankfully, MFC provides default handlers for most of these, as you will see. Note that WM_COMMAND messages receive special handling as either control notifications or commands.

- Control notifications are WM_COMMAND messages sent from child windows to their parent window. For example, an edit control will send an EN_CHANGE message to its parent window (usually a dialog box) whenever its content may have changed. Windows messages and control notifications are usually handled by window objects—that is, objects derived from class CWnd.

- Commands are WM_COMMAND messages from menus, buttons (including toolbars), and accelerator keys. Command messages may be handled by a wider array of classes, including documents, document templates, windows, views, and the application itself.

Message Handling in MFC

MFC provides a framework for handling windows messages that can be much easier to work with than the web of switches and ifs that are used in traditional Windows programs to control the handling of messages. This is based on the capability of classes derived from CCmdTarget of having their own message maps. MFC uses the message maps of your classes to decide how any given message should be handled, allowing you to take full advantage of the benefits of the C++ language to encapsulate functionality in your classes so that other classes derived from them don't have to reinvent the wheel.

To further expand on reusability, MFC provides default handlers for a wide range of commands used in most Windows applications. Most of the commands that have default handlers are also included in the default menus generated by AppWizard. The following are menu commands that have default handlers in MFC:

> File menu commands: New, Open, Close, Save, Save As, Page Setup, Print Setup, Print, Print Preview, Exit, and the most recently used files list.

> Edit menu commands: Clear, Clear All, Copy, Cut, Find, Paste, Repeat, Replace, Select All, Undo, and Redo.

> View menu commands: Toolbar and Status Bar.

> Window menu commands: New, Arrange, Cascade, Tile Horizontal, Tile Vertical, and Split.

> Help menu commands: Index, Using Help, and About.

The menus created by AppWizard generate messages for the standard commands defined in AFXRES.H. For example, the File | New menu item generates a message with the command ID of `ID_FILE_NEW`. The other standard commands are similarly named, with `ID_`, the menu name, and the command name.

If you wish to perform one of these standard actions, you can send one of the predefined command messages from anywhere in your application that will be handled by MFC's default handlers. Of course, you can also implement your own handlers for these commands, but you will explore that later. For more information on the default commands, see *Technical Note 22 (TN022)* in the online help.

Message Dispatching

As mentioned in Chapter 2, "MFC Class Library Overview," the Run() function of the CWinThread class provides the message pump for your application. (For now, let's assume there is only one thread in your application. If you want to learn how to use threads to have more than one message pump in your app, see Chapter 16, "Multithreading.") The only function of the message pump is to wait for messages and then send them where they should go to be handled—this is called dispatching the message.

When the message pump receives a Windows message, it identifies the class that should get first crack at handling the message by consulting an internal structure that maps the handles of existing windows to the class responsible for each window. MFC will then check to see whether this targeted class provides an entry for the message in its message map. If an entry is found, the message is passed to the handler, ending the dispatch process. If an entry for the message is not found, MFC will check the message map of the base class for the targeted class, moving farther up the class hierarchy until an entry is found.

For command messages, the search is quite a bit more complicated. When a command is routed to a class, it may allow another class to try to handle it before checking its own message map or routing the command to another command target. In most cases, a command target will route commands in the following order:

1. To the currently active child command target object

2. To itself

3. To other command targets

Table 3.1 lists more specific routing for the usual command target classes. When a class is mentioned in the right side of the table, you should jump to that class on the left side, follow its routing, then go back to where you were to continue the routing.

TABLE 3.1   Standard Command Routing

This Object Type	*Routes Commands in This Order*
MDI Main Frame	1. Active `CMDIChildWnd`
	2. This frame window
	3. Application (`CWinApp`)
MDI child frame	1. Active view
	2. This frame window
SDI Main Frame	1. Active view
	2. This frame window
	3. Application (`CWinApp`)
View	1. This view
	2. Document associated with this view
Document	1. This document
	2. Template associated with this document
Dialog Box	1. This dialog box
	2. Window that owns this dialog
	3. Application (`CWinApp`)

By now, this is as clear as mud, right? The following example will clear things up a bit.

Suppose you add a menu item that will send the ID_MY_COMMAND command message to the MDI main frame of your application:

1. The command is first routed to the main frame, which will check the active child frame first.

2. The child frame will first check the active view, which checks its own message map before routing the command to the associated document.

3. The document will check its own message map before checking the message map of the associated document template.

4. Going back to the child frame's routing, the child frame will check its own message map.

5. Going back to the main frame's routing, the main frame will check its own message map.

6. Ultimately, the message map of the application object is checked, where an entry for your message is found and the appropriate handler is called.

If you find that you must use a different command routing scheme, perhaps to include your own special command target classes, you can do so by overriding the OnCmdMsg() member of CCmdTarget. This may involve overriding OnCmdMsg() for several classes and is beyond the scope of this book; for more information, see Command Routing in the MFC online documentation.

3

MFC MESSAGE
HANDLING
MECHANISM

> **Note**
>
> MFC speeds up this process by using an internal cache of recent message handler search results, avoiding lengthy searches.

I know this all seems horribly complicated, but it will make much more sense when you work with documents and views in the next chapter. In fact, it will seem much simpler even sooner, when you see how you can use ClassWizard to associate messages with the appropriate handler.

Message Handling with ClassWizard

For most all of your message handling tasks, you will find that ClassWizard can be a great help. ClassWizard allows you to map messages to handlers for all your classes that are derived from CCmdTarget, by using the Message Maps page of ClassWizard. Remember that you can always start ClassWizard from the View menu or by pressing Ctrl+W. Selecting the Message Maps tab will present a dialog box that looks like the one in Figure 3.1.

FIGURE 3.1

The ClassWizard
Message Maps
page.

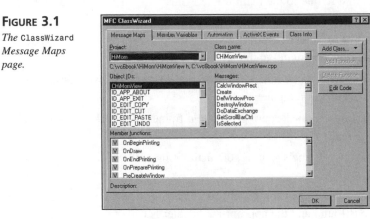

If you have multiple projects in your workspace, you will first need to select the appropriate entry in the Project list. You can then select any of your classes derived from CCmdTarget in the Class name list. This will present you with a list of Object IDs, the Messages those objects may receive, and a list of the member functions already implemented in the Member functions list.

The objects listed in the Object ID's list can be of three different types: the class listed in Class name, menu item objects, and other controls that may send messages to the class you have selected in Class name.

When you select your class name from the top of the Object IDs list, you will see a list of all of the Windows messages that your class is likely to receive, including several functions, such as InitInstance or Create, that aren't really message handlers at all. Nevertheless, ClassWizard will allow you to manage these functions here as well. ClassWizard will display only a certain subset of all available Windows messages, based on the Message filter specified in the Class Info page. This allows you to filter out messages that are not normally handled by certain classes. If you want to handle a message that you don't see listed, try changing the message filter.

Tip

To find out more about a message in the Messages list, highlight the message and press F1 to get help on the specifics of that message and its handler function.

When you select a menu command, such as ID_FILE_OPEN, from the Object IDs list, you will see two entries in the Messages list. To do something when the user selects this command from a menu, select the COMMAND message. The UPDATE_COMMAND_UI message is used to help update the status (checked, grayed, and so forth) of the menu item.

The third type of objects listed in the Object IDs list are controls that may send messages to your class. For simple controls such as buttons, you will receive only a limited set of messages, such as BN_CLICKED and BN_DOUBLECLICKED. For more complicated objects, such as edit controls, you will be able to handle many different control notifications.

Tip

If you want your class to handle notifications from a control that is not listed, make sure that the control is highlighted in a resource editor window before you start ClassWizard.

Once you have selected the message that you want to handle, simply click on the Add Function button to create a handler function. ClassWizard will add a declaration for your handler to the declaration of your class and add a message map entry and skeleton handler function to your class implementation. Alternatively, you can simply double-click the message name to add the message map entry.

All you have to do now is add the code to your handler function. You can go straight to your new handler function implementation by double-clicking in the Member functions list or by clicking the Edit Code button.

Creating Your Own Message Maps

When you create a class with AppWizard or ClassWizard, Visual C++ will produce the code to create a message map for your class. If you create your own CCmdTarget-derived class outside of ClassWizard, you need to create the message map yourself. You should start by adding the following line to the end of your class declaration:

```
DECLARE_MESSAGE_MAP()
```

This macro is defined in AFXWIN.H in the \DevStudio\VC\mfc\include directory. It declares the array that will hold your message map entries and some pointers used to find the message map of the base class. You should be aware, though, that the structures for your class's message map are defined static const. This means that you can have

3

MFC MESSAGE
HANDLING
MECHANISM

only one message map for all objects of your class, not a different map for each object. This also means that you cannot change a class's message map at runtime, at least not with methods that are discussed here. (It can be done with overrides of PreTranslateMessage() or the functions hidden in the message map itself.)

Next, you add a message map to your class implementation. To see how this is done, let's take a look at the message map implementation created for the CHiMomApp class in HiMom.cpp:

```
// CHiMomApp
BEGIN_MESSAGE_MAP(CHiMomApp, CWinApp)
    //{{AFX_MSG_MAP(CHiMomApp)
    ON_COMMAND(ID_APP_ABOUT, OnAppAbout)
        // NOTE - the ClassWizard will add and remove mapping macros here.
        //     DO NOT EDIT what you see in these blocks of generated code!
    //}}AFX_MSG_MAP
    // Standard file based document commands
    ON_COMMAND(ID_FILE_NEW, CWinApp::OnFileNew)
    ON_COMMAND(ID_FILE_OPEN, CWinApp::OnFileOpen)
    // Standard print setup command
    ON_COMMAND(ID_FILE_PRINT_SETUP, CWinApp::OnFilePrintSetup)
END_MESSAGE_MAP()
```

As you can see in this example, message maps are created by a set of macros, beginning with BEGIN_MESSAGE_MAP() and ending with END_MESSAGE_MAP(). To start the definition of your message map, use the BEGIN_MESSAGE_MAP() macro, which takes the name of your class and the name of its base class as parameters.

The BEGIN_MESSAGE_MAP() macro (defined in AFXWIN.H) actually defines the _messageEntries array, leaving the initializer list open, to be filled by additional macros. If you forget to include the END_MESSAGE_MAP() macro, which closes the initializer list, the compiler will become quite lost, so make sure you end your message map with END_MESSAGE_MAP().

Populating the Message Map

In the previous example, you will see a DO NOT EDIT message from ClassWizard. It is a good idea to avoid editing these sections if you don't have to, but you can make changes here. However, you should be aware that changes to these blocks have the potential to confuse ClassWizard so that you cannot edit your class or must regenerate the .clw file, or ClassWizard may just overwrite your new changes. If you make changes to these blocks yourself, try to model your code after other ClassWizard-generated code and check the function of ClassWizard right after making your changes.

That said, you will be populating your message map by using several different macros for different types of messages, including message ranges.

Predefined Windows Message Handlers

For many standard Windows messages, there are predefined message map macros provided in AFXMSG.H. The names for these macros are derived directly from the message ID and they take no parameters. For example, the WM_PAINT message can be mapped by the ON_WM_PAINT() macro. This will map the WM_PAINT message to the OnPaint() function of your class. The other standard Windows messages are implemented in a similar fashion.

Other Windows Messages

For your own user-defined messages, or for windows commands that do not have a default handler, you can use the generic ON_MESSAGE() macro, which takes the message ID and handler function name:

```
ON_MESSAGE( WM_USER+1, OnMyUserMessage)
```

The handler for these messages would be declared like this:

```
afx_msg LRESULT OnMyUserMessage(WPARAM wParam, LPARAM lParam);
```

User-defined messages are generally given values between WM_USER and 0x7FFF. User-defined messages are most useful when sending messages within a single application. If you must send messages between applications, use registered Windows messages, which are discussed later in the section, "Registered Messages."

Command Messages

For command messages, you will use the ON_COMMAND() macro, which takes the command ID (which will be in the wParam of the WM_COMMAND message) and the name of the handler function:

```
ON_COMMAND(ID_FILE_NEW, CWinApp::OnFileNew)
```

The handler function will take no parameters and return void:

```
afx_msg void OnFileNew();
```

Control Notifications

Notifications from controls can be mapped by using the ON_CONTROL() macro, which takes the control ID, the command ID, and the handler function as arguments:

```
ON_CONTROL( BN_CLICKED, IDC_MY_BUTTON, OnMyButtonClicked)
```

The handler for these messages, like command messages, returns void and takes no parameters:

```
afx_msg void OnMyButtonClicked();
```

Command and Control Ranges

There are also macros that will map a handler to messages for a range of commands or controls. This is one of the few areas where you must make your own message map entries, because ClassWizard doesn't handle ranges. Your entries for ranges would look like this:

```
ON_COMMAND_RANGE(TD_MY_FIRST_COMMAND, ID_MY_LAST_COMMAND, myCommandHandler)
ON_CONTROL_RANGE(BN_CLICKED, IDC_FIRST_BUTTON, IDC_LAST_BUTTON, MyButtonHandler)
```

Registered Messages

For message IDs that you have received from the RegisterWindowsMessage() function, you can use ON_REGISTERED_MESSAGE(), which takes the registered message ID and the handler function. The handler again returns void and takes no parameters:

```
afx_msg void OnExplorerRestarted();
```

Registered messages are used to enable multiple programs to exchange window messages without requiring applications to hard-code a specific value for the message. A registered message is defined by calling the RegisterWindowMessage function to determine a unique message number.

Registered messages can't be managed by ClassWizard. You'll need to manually add handlers for all registered messages that your application uses.

Other Message Map Macros

AFXMSG.H also defines many other macros designed to map different special cases of messages that you may find useful in creating your own message maps. For example, the ON_CONTROL() example used above can also be written like this:

```
ON_BN_CLICKED(IDC_MYBUTTON, OnMyButtonClicked)
```

This is actually the syntax that ClassWizard uses when it inserts entries like this, but it results in exactly the same entry in the message map as the ON_CONTROL() macro used above. There are also special macros for handling OLE functions and user interface updates that you will learn about later.

Inside the Message Map

The message map macros DECLARE_MESSAGE_MAP, BEGIN_MESSAGE_MAP, and END_MES-SAGE_MAP are defined in AFXWIN.H. If you are curious, you can find this file in the VC98\MFC\INCLUDE subdirectory under the directory where Visual C++ was installed.

The DECLARE_MESSAGE_MAP macro is declared like this:

```
#ifdef _AFXDLL
#define DECLARE_MESSAGE_MAP() \
private: \
    static const AFX_MSGMAP_ENTRY _messageEntries[]; \
protected: \
    static AFX_DATA const AFX_MSGMAP messageMap; \
    static const AFX_MSGMAP* PASCAL _GetBaseMessageMap(); \
    virtual const AFX_MSGMAP* GetMessageMap() const; \

#else
#define DECLARE_MESSAGE_MAP() \
private: \
    static const AFX_MSGMAP_ENTRY _messageEntries[]; \
protected: \
    static AFX_DATA const AFX_MSGMAP messageMap; \
    virtual const AFX_MSGMAP* GetMessageMap() const; \
#endif
```

In short, `DECLARE_MESSAGE_MAP` defines functions to return the class's message map
(`GetMessageMap()`), and that of its base class (`_GetBaseMessageMap()`), as well as an
`AFX_MSGMAP` structure. This structure consists primarily of an array of `AFX_MSGMAP_ENTRY`
structures (`_messageEntries[]`).

The `BEGIN_MESSAGE_MAP` macro is defined like this:

```
#ifdef _AFXDLL
#define BEGIN_MESSAGE_MAP(theClass, baseClass) \
    const AFX_MSGMAP* PASCAL theClass::_GetBaseMessageMap() \
        { return &baseClass::messageMap; } \
    const AFX_MSGMAP* theClass::GetMessageMap() const \
        { return &theClass::messageMap; } \
    AFX_COMDAT AFX_DATADEF const AFX_MSGMAP theClass::messageMap = \
    { &theClass::_GetBaseMessageMap, &theClass::_messageEntries[0] }; \
    AFX_COMDAT const AFX_MSGMAP_ENTRY theClass::_messageEntries[] = \
    { \

#else
#define BEGIN_MESSAGE_MAP(theClass, baseClass) \
    const AFX_MSGMAP* theClass::GetMessageMap() const \
        { return &theClass::messageMap; } \
    AFX_COMDAT AFX_DATADEF const AFX_MSGMAP theClass::messageMap = \
    { &baseClass::messageMap, &theClass::_messageEntries[0] }; \
    AFX_COMDAT const AFX_MSGMAP_ENTRY theClass::_messageEntries[] = \
    { \
#endif
```

The `BEGIN_MESSAGE_MAP` macro implements the `GetMessageMap()` and
`_GetBaseMessageMap()` functions, then begins initializing the `_messageEntries[]` array.
The initializer list is left without a closing brace, leaving `END_MESSAGE_MAP` to add an
entry that marks the end of the message map and closes the initializer list:

```
#define END_MESSAGE_MAP() \
        {0, 0, 0, 0, AfxSig_end, (AFX_PMSG)0 } \
    }; \
```

Between the BEGIN_MESSAGE_MAP and END_MESSAGE_MAP macros, you use the message
map entry macros, such as ON_COMMAND, which is actually defined like this:

```
#define ON_COMMAND(id, memberFxn) \
    { WM_COMMAND, CN_COMMAND, (WORD)id, (WORD)id, AfxSig_vv,
➥(AFX_PMSG)&memberFxn },
```

The values specified in the message map macros are used to initialize an
AFX_MSGMAP_ENTRY, which looks like this:

```
struct AFX_MSGMAP_ENTRY
{
    UINT nMessage;   // windows message
    UINT nCode;      // control code or WM_NOTIFY code
    UINT nID;        // control ID (or 0 for windows messages)
    UINT nLastID;    // used for entries specifying a range of control id's
    UINT nSig;       // signature type (action) or pointer to message #
    AFX_PMSG pfn;    // routine to call (or special value)
};
```

The first four elements are used by MFC to check whether this message map entry
applies to the Windows message that is being dispatched. The last two elements specify
information about the handler function to be called. pfn is a pointer to the function to
call, and nSig is a special signature type, which MFC uses to specify the return type and
parameters that will be passed to the function specified by pfn.

The values used for nSig are defined in the AfxSig enum type in Afxmsg_.h. This file
also lists the function prototypes that should be used to correspond with each nSig value.

If you are ever unsure of what form a handler function for a given message map macro
should take, you can look up the macro—for example, ON_COMMAND—in Afxmsg_.h, see
that it uses AfxSig_vv, then find the definition of AfxSig_vv to find that your handler
function should return void and take no parameters.

Using ClassWizard to add your handler functions will save you this trouble in most
cases; however, there are certain message map entries that ClassWizard does not support, such as ON_COMMAND_RANGE or ON_THREAD_MESSAGE.

Implementing Handler Functions

When you add handler functions with ClassWizard, your handler function will be created
for you, with the proper parameters and return type. If you create your message map entries and corresponding handler functions yourself, be very careful to declare your handler
function with the parameters and return type that the message map entry expects. Failure
to do so will result in a corrupted stack at some point and can cause big headaches.

PreTranslateMessage()

In most cases, the message pump receives messages and dispatches them by way of message maps, as you saw in the previous example. However, if you find that you need to intercept messages prior to the normal dispatch process, MFC offers a way to do this—the PreTranslateMessage() function.

You can override the PreTranslateMessage() member function in any class derived from CWnd, CWinApp, or CWinThread. The function takes a pointer to an MSG structure and returns a BOOL. If PreTranslateMessage() returns TRUE, MFC will assume that you have handled the message. If it returns FALSE, MFC assumes that you have elected not to handle it and will proceed with its normal dispatch process.

A Common Problem with MFC Message Maps

The MFC message map mechanism is very flexible, and it's well integrated with tools such as MFC AppWizard and ClassWizard. However, a very common mistake made when working with message maps is to attempt to use a message-handling function with the wrong signature. Using a function that has the wrong signature will cause your application's stack to be corrupted—a problem that is very difficult to debug.

Parameters and return values are passed to and from functions on the stack. If the parameter and return value signature don't match the expected values, parts of the stack are overwritten or corrupted. These bugs can be especially difficult to find because they often appear only in Release builds. The fault is masked during Debug builds due to the way the stack frame is managed.

A common mistake is to confuse the signatures on functions used with the ON_COMMAND and ON_MESSAGE macros. Remember that the ON_COMMAND macro expects to use a function with this signature:

```
afx_msg void OnFileNew();
```

The ON_MESSAGE macro expects to see a function with this signature:

```
afx_msg LRESULT OnMyUserMessage(WPARAM wParam, LPARAM lParam);
```

You might think that the C++ compiler would catch errors like this—but it cannot, due to the use of an old-style C++ cast in the ON_COMMAND and similar message handler macros. Knowledge base article Q195032 (available on your MSDN CD-ROM) shows how you can redefine the message handler macros to be type-safe.

Summary

In this chapter, you learned about the event-driven programming model that is central to most Windows applications. Most communication from the operating system to an application takes place via messages, which come in several different flavors. For example, control notification messages are used to notify the owner of a control that an interesting event has occurred. Command messages notify an application that a menu or other command item has been selected. In addition each window receives a large number of messages from the operating system whenever the window needs to be notified of an external event.

The MFC class library simplifies message handling by supplying message maps, which greatly reduce the amount of code that must be written to handle a message. ClassWizard is tightly integrated with the MFC message map architecture, which allows you to add a message-handling function to a specific class in your project with a few mouse clicks.

The Document View Architecture

by David Bennett and Mickey Williams

CHAPTER 4

At some point, you have undoubtedly used a Windows application that works with documents and views, whether or not you called them by these names. The most common example of this is almost any Windows-based word processing application. In this chapter, you will explore how you can use MFC to help you create applications such as the one just described, as well as some that are quite different in appearance but have the same underlying structure. You will learn how to

- Use the document view architecture in MFC.
- Use the view classes provided by MFC.
- Add menus, status bars, toolbars, and splitters to your application.

Examining the Document View Architecture

MFC not only provides a set of classes to help you work with document objects, but it provides a complete architecture that ties the various classes together. In this chapter, you will look at this architecture and what it can do for your applications. I think you will find that the whole of the architecture is much greater than the sum of its parts.

Single Versus Multiple Document Applications

If you have used Windows at all, you should be familiar with applications such as Microsoft Word that enable you to work with several documents within the same application. In Windows terms, these are known as *multiple document interfaces (MDIs)*. In addition to the support the Windows *Software Development Kit (SDK)* provides for MDI, MFC encapsulates MDI in the classes that make up the document view architecture.

The *single document interface (SDI)* is similar to MDI but is designed for simpler applications that work with only one document and one view at any given time. Both MDI and SDI applications can use the document view architecture provided by MFC in much the same way, except the MDI architecture provides an additional level of functionality to deal with multiple documents and views.

Of course, you are not required to use the document view architecture in your applications, and you most likely will have situations in which you don't even want to have a Windows user interface. You can use MFC in your applications without any GUI interface, or you can base your application on a single dialog box. If your application fits in the document view model, however, you will find that creating your application using either the SDI or MDI flavor of the document view architecture can greatly simplify your task of adding features that Windows users have come to expect from all good Windows applications.

Document Classes

Although it doesn't take much imagination to see how a document object would apply to a word processing or spreadsheet application, the concept of a document in MFC also can apply to much more. In general terms, a *document* is any set of data that can be grouped logically. This data may include anything from settings for a terminal session to simulation models to information about your favorite records to just about anything else you might consider writing to a file. In MFC, document objects are derived from the `CDocument` class. In most cases, your application somehow will present the data in your document to the user. This is done by using views.

View Classes

A *view object* is just that—a view of the document. This may be either some direct representation of the document object or some other sort of display related to the data in your document. For example, your document may store settings for some data-acquisition application, and your views will show the data acquired based on those settings. As you might guess, view objects in MFC are derived from the `CView` class. However, you probably will derive your view classes from some of the other classes MFC provides for you that add functionality to the basic `CView` class.

Frames

MFC applications that use the document view architecture use *frames* to contain the views of the application. In SDI applications, the frame that contains the one and only view also serves as the main frame, or main window, of your application. In MDI applications, this functionality is split between the *main frame,* which is the main window for your application, and *child frames,* which provide windows in which each of your views can run. The *frame objects* handle the menus, status bars, and toolbars for your application. The frame objects also receive the command messages generated in your views. In SDI applications, frame windows are derived directly from the `CFrameWnd` class, and MDI main frames and child frames are derived from `CMDIFrameWnd` and `CMDIChildWnd`, respectively.

Document Templates

MFC uses document templates to tie your documents, views, and frames together. As you will see, it is actually the document template that creates new documents and new view windows to display them. Document templates are derived from class `CSingleDocTemplate` for SDI apps and from class `CMultiDocTemplate` for MDI apps.

Creating Your Application

The easiest way to create an application that comes prewired to support the document/view architecture is to use MFC AppWizard to create a project, choosing Single Document or Multiple Documents in Step 1. Although using MFC AppWizard is by no means a requirement for using the document view architecture, it provides you with premade classes for your documents, views, and frames, as well as initializes your document template. Even if you do not use MFC AppWizard to generate your application, you may find that creating a sample application (which takes about 10 seconds) can provide a useful example of how MFC sets things up for working with documents and views.

In any case, developing an application that uses the document view architecture will involve creating your document, view, frame, and document template classes. After you have done this and have properly initialized your objects, your documents and views will pretty much take care of themselves.

Creating Your Document Class

Your document class derives from the `CDocument` class. If you plan to use OLE (which you will explore in Part VI, "MFC Support for COM and ActiveX"), your documents may derive from `COleDocument` or `COleServerDoc` (these classes are themselves derived from `CDocument`). To start, let's look at the following declaration for a document class created with MFC AppWizard, with some of the extra comments generated by the wizard stripped out for clarity:

```
class CMDIAppDoc : public CDocument
{
protected:
    CMDIAppDoc();
    DECLARE_DYNCREATE(CMDIAppDoc)

    // ClassWizard generated virtual function overrides
    //{{AFX_VIRTUAL(CMDIAppDoc)
    public:
    virtual BOOL OnNewDocument();
    virtual void Serialize(CArchive& ar);
    //}}AFX_VIRTUAL

public:
    virtual ~CMDIAppDoc();
#ifdef _DEBUG
    virtual void AssertValid() const;
    virtual void Dump(CDumpContext& dc) const;
#endif
```

```
protected:
    //{{AFX_MSG(CMDIAppDoc)
    //}}AFX_MSG
    DECLARE_MESSAGE_MAP()
};
```

In this example, MFC AppWizard was used to create an MDI project named MDIApp. The code fragment shown here is the class declaration for the document class, derived from CDocument, including the constructor and destructor. Notice that the constructor is protected. This is done because you will never create an instance of a document class directly. Usually, the MFC framework creates documents for you, and the framework only creates new document objects using serialization. It also may seem strange to talk about serialization when you use only the DECLARE_DYNCREATE macro instead of DECLARE_SERIAL. You're only required to use the DECLARE_SERIAL macro if you plan to use polymorphic pointers to your object to access serialization functions. This example calls the Serialize() function directly, which is fully supported by DECLARE_DYNCREATE.

In addition, MFC AppWizard has declared overrides for the OnNewDocument() and Serialize() functions, as well as the AssertValid() and Dump() debug functions. The class declaration also declares an empty message map for the document class.

Document Data

As mentioned previously, your document object will hold the data that is used by your application. When deciding how to structure the data in your document class, you should consider that you will want to support the following operations efficiently:

- Presenting the data to views
- Presenting changes in the data to views
- Storing the data in files
- Presenting the data in pages for printing

It is a good practice to include your document data as member variables of your document class. This allows you to take full advantage of the serialization features provided by MFC and the predefined operations for File New, Open, Save, Save As, and the most recently used files list. After you decide how to represent your data, you implement some of the function overrides discussed in the following sections.

4

THE DOCUMENT VIEW ARCHITECTURE

The Dirty Flag

Users have come to expect that any good Windows app will not let them accidentally do things such as exiting an application without saving their data. To help implement this in your applications, classes derived from CDocument provide a dirty flag to keep track of whether the document has changed since it was last saved. The framework checks this flag before closing a document and prompts the user to save the file.

The dirty flag is cleared when you save or open a document, and it is set for you only when you change an OLE object in your document. Your code is responsible for setting the flag whenever your document changes. This is accomplished by using SetModifiedFlag(), which takes a parameter of TRUE or FALSE. Setting the modified flag to TRUE, which is the default parameter, tells the framework that the document contains changes since the last save. You can query the dirty flag in your application by calling the IsModified() member of CDocument.

Several overrideable functions of CDocument also affect how the framework handles the dirty flag. If you are interested in modifying the default behavior, take a look at CDocument::CanCloseFrame() and CDocument::SaveModified().

Serialize()

Recall that the Serialize() function of your document class is used to implement several functions involving your document and files. Your serialize implementation should look something like the following:

```
void CMyDocument::Serialize(CArchive& ar)
{
    // call base class Serialize() first
    CDocument::Serialize(ar);
    // then serialize the data for this class
    if(ar.IsLoading())
    {
        ar >> m_MyDataVariable;
        // load other data members
    }
    else
    {
        ar << m_MyDataVariable;
        // store other data members
    }
    // Serialize your member objects
    m_MyDataObject.Serialize(ar);
    m_MoreDataObject.Serialize(ar);
} // end CMyDocument::Serialize
```

Remember to call the Serialize() function of the base class first. You also will notice that the serialize functions for the member objects included in the document class are called. This allows the objects to serialize themselves and is included outside of the IsLoading() block, because the Serialize() functions of these classes will have their own check for IsLoading().

OnNewDocument()

The OnNewDocument() function of your document class will be called by the framework whenever the user chooses the New command from the File menu. In MDI applications, a new document object is created, and this function is responsible for initializing it. In SDI applications, the same document object is reused. Your OnNewDocument() function then is responsible for reinitializing the document.

> **Note**
>
> The constructor for your document object is called only once during the lifetime of SDI applications. Any reinitialization code will be run only if it is placed in the OnNewDocument() function.

If you have created your application with the MFC AppWizard, you will see that the default implementation of OnNewDocument() simply defers to the CDocument:: OnNewDocument() function. This function will call the DeleteContents() member function of your class to ensure that the document is empty and will reset the dirty flag of your document. If you choose to override OnNewDocument(), you first should call the base class function:

```
BOOL CMyDoc::OnNewDocument()
{
    if(!CDocument::OnNewDocument())
        return FALSE;
    // Do any other initialization of your document here
    return TRUE;
} // end OnNewDocument()
```

If this function returns FALSE, creation of the new document is aborted. If an exception is thrown during this operation, the ReportSaveLoadException() function, described later in this section, is called.

DeleteContents()

The DeleteContents() member of your document class is called by the default implementation of OnNewDocument() to clear out the data in your document without actually deleting the document object. This is particularly necessary for SDI apps, where the same document object is reused. DeleteContents() also is called just before your document object is destroyed. The default implementation of DeleteContents does nothing, but it can be overridden like this:

```
void CMyDoc::DeleteContents()
{
    // clear data elements
    m_MyCounter = 0;
    // delete dynamic objects created by your document
    delete(m_MyObjectPtr);
    m_MyObjectPtr = NULL;
} // end DeleteContents()
```

You also may want to call this function to implement something like an Edit | Clear All function to clear your document.

OnOpenDocument()

Whenever the user chooses the File | Open command from a menu, the default handler will call the OnOpenDocument() function of your document object. The default implementation opens the file specified in lpszPathName, calls DeleteContents() to clear out the document object, resets the dirty flag for the document, and then calls the Serialize() function to load the new document from the file. Once again, SDI apps will reuse the same document object, and MDI apps will create a new one. If you need to do any initialization of your document that is not provided by the Serialize() function, you can override OnOpenDocument() like this:

```
BOOL CMyDoc::OnOpenDocument(LPCTSTR lpszPathName)
{
    if(!CDocument::OnOpenDocument())
        return FALSE;
    // Perform any additional initialization for your document here
    return TRUE;
} // end OnOpenDocument
```

If this function returns FALSE, the open document operation will fail.

OnSaveDocument()

After the user selects either the Save or Save As command from the File menu, the framework calls the OnSaveDocument() function of your document class. For most applications, the default implementation is adequate. It opens the selected file, calls the Serialize() function to write your document data to the file, and resets the dirty flag.

OnCloseDocument()

The OnCloseDocument() function is called by the framework whenever the user closes a document. The default implementation calls the DeleteContents() member of your document, and then closes the frame windows for all views associated with this document.

ReportSaveLoadException()

If, while saving or loading your document, an exception is thrown that is not handled within your code, the framework calls the ReportSaveLoadException() function, which presents error messages to the user. You can override this function if you want to do any special messaging. You'll learn more about exceptions in Chapter 14, "Error Detection and Exception Handling Techniques."

Accessing Your Document

MFC provides several ways for you to access your document object from within your application. All objects derived from CView are associated with a document object when they are created. You can access the document associated with a view by calling CView::GetDocument(). In addition, you can access the currently active document from any CFrameWnd derivative, including your MDI main frame, by calling CFrameWnd::GetActiveDocument(). If you want to find the active document for your application, you can use the m_pMainWnd member of your CWinApp object like this:

```
pDoc = theApp.m_pMainWnd.GetActiveDocument();
```

Using the View Classes

Now that you have your application's data set up in documents, you need to be able to present the data to the user. You do this by using the view classes, which serve both to present your data to the user and to handle most user input for your data. Remember that you generally will not want to store data in your view—this is what the document is for.

If you want to be able to save settings for your views, you also will want to consider keeping this information in your document. If you want to save settings for your application on a global basis, you should look at loading this data in the InitInstance() function of your application.

MFC provides several view classes that help you implement different general methods of displaying your data and accepting input from the user. All these classes are based on CView, which provides a great deal of the functionality needed to work with views and their associated documents. You probably will not use CView objects directly, however, because they really don't provide much functionality to manage the display. Instead, your views most likely will be based on the CView derivative classes listed in the next sections.

CScrollView

The CScrollView class, as the name suggests, adds scrollbars to your view. Although you still will have to do your own drawing in the view, this class can save you a lot of work by managing window and view-port sizes and managing mapping modes, as well as automatically scrolling when scrollbar messages are received.

Setting Up the Scrollbars

To scroll the display properly in your view, you must tell the scroll view a few things about how to scroll the view. Most important, the view must know something about the total size of your document. In most cases, you will want to add a function to your document class that returns the logical size of your document, preferably in units based on the mapping mode you plan to use for drawing. For more information on mapping modes and drawing in general, see Chapter 6, "Working with Device Contexts and GDI Objects." For now, you will look at how the view classes can help in your drawing efforts.

To tell the view how to set up its scrollbars, you use the `SetScrollSizes()` member of the `CScrollView` class, which takes four parameters. The first parameter is the mapping mode used for the next three parameters. In this section, you use `MM_TEXT`, which maps one logical unit to one pixel. The second parameter is a `SIZE` structure that gives the total size of your document. The third and fourth parameters are also `SIZE` structures that tell the scroll view how far to scroll when scrolling by pages and by lines, respectively. If you omit the third and fourth parameters, the view scrolls by one-tenth of the total size when the user presses the PgUp or PgDn key, and by one-tenth of that when the user presses the arrow keys or clicks the arrows on the scrollbars.

It generally is most convenient to set up your scroll sizes in the `OnUpdate()` and `OnInitialUpdate()` functions of your view class so that the scroll sizes are adjusted any time the underlying document changes. You also should provide a minimum size for your document's view. The following example from the `OnUpdate()` function illustrates how to do this:

```
CSize DocSize = GetDocument()->GetMyDocumentSize();
if(DocSize.cx < 100) DocSize.cx = 100;
if(DocSize.cy < 100) DocSize.cy = 100;
SetScrollSizes(MM_TEXT, DocSize);
```

As an alternative to using scrollbars, you can use the `CScrollView` class to scale the view to show the whole document. You do this by using the `SetScaleToFitSize()` function, which takes one parameter for the total size of the document. If you use this method, you do not need to call `SetScrollSizes()`, although you are free to switch between scale-to-fit and scroll mode by calling these functions.

Drawing with `CScrollView`

You will take an in-depth look at drawing in Chapter 6, but I just want to point out a few things about drawing in a scroll view. Your drawing will be done in the `OnDraw()` member of your view class, but the `CScrollView` class provides an override to `OnPrepareDC()` that sets up the device context for your drawing. The overridden `OnPrepareDC()` function sets the view-port origin in the device context to implement the scroll window. This method works with the mapping mode you specified in your call to `SetScrollSizes()`, so make sure you use the mapping mode with which you intend to draw. If you need to do anything else in `OnPrepareDC()`, you are free to override it, but you should call the base class implementation before doing anything else.

In your `OnDraw()` function, you don't really have to worry about the position of the scrollbars. If you are drawing many things that eventually will be clipped, however, your application is wasting time. You can use the `CWnd::GetUpdateRect()` function to get the rectangle that needs updating to make your drawing code much more efficient by drawing only what needs to be drawn.

If you are interested in the current position of the scrollbars, you can get this by using `GetScrollPosition()` or `GetDeviceScrollPosition()`, which returns a `CPoint` object in logical units or device units, respectively.

`CFormView` and `CRecordView`

Many applications will provide the user with a view similar to what you might see on paper fill-in-the-blank forms. MFC helps you do this and much more with the `CFormView` class. MFC also provides some specialized derivatives of `CFormView` to create forms for working with a database. The class provided for *Open Database Connectivity* (*ODBC*) forms is `CRecordView`; the class for working with *Data Access Objects* (*DAO*) is `CDaoRecordView`. You will look at both these classes in Part V, "Database Programming."

The user interface for a form view is based on a dialog box template, which is created as a modeless child window of your view window. Therefore, you should make sure that your dialog box does not have a border or a caption. You also need to make sure that the constructor for your view is passed the resource ID of the dialog box template it will be using; it will accept either the integer ID or string name for the resource.

Form view classes created by wizards use an initializer list in the implementation of the constructor, like this:

```
MyFormView::MyFormView()
    : CFormView(MyFormView::IDD)
{
    // Constructor code…
```

An enum type, found in the class declaration, is used here to map IDD to the ID of our dialog box template.

Control Views

MFC provides several handy view classes that use a Windows control to interface to the user. These classes include CEditView, CRichEditView, CListView, and CTreeView, which are all derived from the CCtrlView class. You do not use CCtrlView directly for creating view objects, but it does make a good base class for your own control views. As you might guess, each of the derived classes uses the Windows control with a similar name. CEditView uses an Edit control.

Combining the functionality of a control with that of a view in one class presents two issues specific to control views: how to set style bits for a view and how to handle messages in a control. MFC provides solutions to these issues, as shown in the next sections.

Setting Control View Styles

Controls usually are created in dialog box templates, where the Resource Editor gives you easy access to the style bits that dictate how the control will work. You cannot follow this process with control views, however. Instead, you must override the PreCreateWindow() member of your view. If you want to enable buttons in your tree view, for example, you can do something like this:

```
BOOL CMyTreeView::PreCreateWindow(CREATESTRUCT& cs)
{
    if(!CTreeView::PreCreateWindow(cs))
        return FALSE;
    cs.style |= TVS_HASBUTTONS;
    return TRUE;
}
```

You always should call the base class version of PreCreateWindow() first. This action assigns appropriate default values to CREATESTRUCT and, more important, makes sure that MFC loads the appropriate control libraries and registers the correct window classes.

Handling Control Notifications

Control windows generally send notifications to their parent window to make the application aware of what the user is doing. In the case of control views, this means that the frame actually receives these messages. Because it is desirable to contain all the code to manage your view in the view class, MFC provides the concept of *message reflection*.

MFC has altered the message routing code somewhat so that control notifications not handled by the parent (in this case, the frame) can be reflected to the control window itself. If you use ClassWizard to handle your message maps, you will see an equal sign (=) before messages that may be handled by reflection in your view class.

Choosing to handle these messages results in slightly different macros being added to your message map. For example, ON_CONTROL becomes ON_CONTROL_REFLECT. Several control-oriented Windows messages also may be handled with reflection message map macros. For example, WM_HSCROLL may be handled by ON_WM_HSCROLL_REFLECT(). The different message map macros are required because MFC actually uses different message IDs for reflected messages.

Having said that, there are exceptions. All messages commonly used for owner-drawn controls—WM_DRAWITEM, WM_DELETEITEM, WM_COMPARE_ITEM, and WM_MEASUREITEM—are sent with the original message ID and may be handled as normal, without the _REFLECT macros.

CEditView

If you plan to manipulate simple text in your application, CEditView does just that. It uses an Edit control to form the user interface for the view. CEditView does not support different font or color settings, though. For those settings, you use a CRichEditView (discussed later, in the section, "Using CRichEditView"). In addition to wrapping the Edit control, CEditView also adds support for the following command messages:

```
ID_FILE_PRINT
ID_EDIT_CUT
ID_EDIT_COPY
ID_EDIT_PASTE
ID_EDIT_CLEAR
ID_EDIT_UNDO
ID_EDIT_SELECT_ALL
ID_EDIT_FIND
ID_EDIT_REPLACE
ID_EDIT_REPEAT
```

The catch is that the menu items to generate these commands are not implemented automatically; you must add these yourself.

Working with CEditView Data

The CEditView class deviates from the standard document view relationship. Because the view encapsulates an Edit control, which stores its own data, the data for the edit view is not kept in the document, but in the view itself. You therefore must make sure that your application takes great care to synchronize the document and its views (of which you may have several). This also can present a problem when it comes to serializing your document, as the most accurate data may be located in the view rather than the document.

To deal with this, it is generally best to call the Serialize function of your CEditView class in the Serialize function of your document. This writes the text length and actual text from your Edit control. If you want to generate a readable text file, you can use the CEditView::SerializeRaw() function to omit the length information.

You can access a reference to the CEdit control object itself by using the GetEditControl() member of CEditView. Using this member, you can perform any actions normally associated with Edit controls.

> **Tip**
>
> In Windows NT and Windows 2000, you can call CEdit::GetHandle() to access the actual memory used by the Edit control. There is no way to access this memory in Windows 95 or Windows 98.

Using CRichEditView

If you require greater functionality than CEditView, CRichEditView may just do the trick for you. Like the rich edit control on which it is based, views derived from CRichEditView support the Microsoft *Rich Text Format* (*RTF*)—including fonts and colors for your text and allowing the insertion of OLE objects. Because of this functionality, you must include OLE container support in your application.

To support all this functionality, using a rich edit view involves a slightly different architecture than the normal document view setup. First, your document should derive from CRichEditDoc rather than plain old CDocument. This is very important, because CRichEditView and CRichEditDoc work very closely together to support your view. CRichEditView contains the text of the view, and CRichEditDoc contains any OLE objects.

Because of this relationship, you may have only one view associated with a CRichEditDoc object at any given time. However, this relationship also allows the CRichEditDoc::GetView() call to take you directly to the one and only corresponding view.

To serialize your data, simply call CRichTextDoc::Serialize(). If the m_bRTF member is TRUE, this function outputs RTF-formatted text. If m_bRTF is FALSE, the output is just plain text.

> **Note**
>
> You must serialize your `CRichEditDoc` object after all other data, because it reads data until the end-of-file is encountered instead of until a fixed number of bytes is reached.

The `CRichEditView` class provides almost all the functions provided by the `CRichEditControl` class. You also may insert OLE objects into your control with the `CreateClientItem()` function. This works just like the `COleDocument::CreateClientItem()` function, which is covered in Part VI, "MFC Support for COM and ActiveX."

CListView and CTreeView

Although the `CListView` and `CTreeView` classes are very useful, there really isn't much to say about them here. They are basically just wrappers for the list and tree controls and work just like other `CCtrlView` classes.

You probably will want to override the `PreCreateWindow()` function to adjust the style bits to your preference, as well as call `OnInitialUpdate()` to add data to the view.

You can reach the controls contained in the views by calling `CListView::GetListControl()` and `CTreeView::GetTreeControl()`.

Using Document Templates

Document templates provide the framework that MFC uses to bind documents, views, and frames together. In fact, it is the document template that will create new documents and views for your application. Document templates generally come in two flavors: `CSingleDocTemplate` for SDI apps and `CMultiDocTemplate` for MDI apps. You generally won't work with `CSingleDocTemplate` objects as much as the MDI varieties, so you mostly will look at `CMultiDocTemplate` objects here.

Many similarities exist between the two types of templates, however. They are created with the same parameters and perform many of the same operations. The big difference in their operations stems from the fact that MDI applications may have several child frames in the main frame, whereas SDI apps have only one frame.

4

THE DOCUMENT VIEW ARCHITECTURE

The EmpList Sample Project

This section provides code from the EmpList sample project, which is located on the CD-ROM that accompanies this book. EmpList is an MDI project built using MFC AppWizard. EmpList uses two types of views:

- CEmpListView is derived from the CListView class. This view displays a list of names and email addresses in a list view control. This is the application's initial view. You can add and remove items from the view by using the Edit menu.

- CEmpFormView is derived from the CFormView class and displays a list of names and email addresses in a list view control embedded in the form view. Pushbutton controls simplify the task of adding and removing items.

The EmpList project illustrates techniques that are useful when dealing with multiple views for a single document:

- Creating different types of document templates that describe the document view relationships in your application

- Creating a specific type of view on demand

- Synchronizing data between different views

- Optimizing updates between the document and views

Creating a Document Template

Now let's look at how to create a document template. Here is an example of the code from InitInstance() generated by the MFC AppWizard when you create an MDI app:

```
CMultiDocTemplate* pDocTemplate;
pDocTemplate = new CMultiDocTemplate(
    IDR_MYAPPTYPE,
    RUNTIME_CLASS(CMyAppDoc),
    RUNTIME_CLASS(CChildFrame), // custom MDI child frame
    RUNTIME_CLASS(CMyAppView));
AddDocTemplate(pDocTemplate);
```

This code fragment declares a pointer to CMultiDocTemplate and uses new to create a template object on the heap. Template objects should remain in memory for as long as your application exists, even if you do not use the pointers directly after your call to AddDocTemplate(). You don't need to delete the document template; the MFC framework deletes the template at the appropriate time.

The constructor for CMultiDocTemplate is called with four parameters, including a resource ID and class information structures (provided by the RUNTIME_CLASS macro) for your document, frame, and view classes.

After the document template is created, `AddDocTemplate()` is called to register the template with MFC. You'll learn more about what this means later, but let's take a closer look at what the parameters passed to the `CMultiDocTemplate` constructor really mean.

The class information for the document, view, and frame types is used whenever MFC is told to create a new document or view. If you want to use different combinations of these classes in your application, you should create a separate template for each combination.

The first parameter is a *shared resource ID,* and it's really many different parameters in one. In the project that MFC AppWizard will generate, you will notice that both an icon and a menu are created with this ID. When a new frame window is created, it is associated with this icon and menu. You will see the icon in the main frame if you minimize a view window. The menu is attached to the main frame when the view is active.

The shared resource ID allows you to have different menus and icons for different document or view types. If you have defined multiple document templates, you can use the same resource ID for each template or use a different ID for each template. If you do specify a new resource ID but do not define a new menu with this resource ID, the main menu remains the same as the last active view.

The Document String Resource

In addition to being used for icons and menu resources, the resource ID passed to the `CMultiDocTemplate` constructor is the ID of a string resource, which can be edited in the String Table Editor. This string rolls seven different parameters into one, each separated by a newline symbol (\n). From within your application, you can use the `CDocTemplate::GetDocString()` function to access the individual elements. This function takes a `CString` reference, which will hold the returned string, and an index, which is defined by an enum type in `CDocTemplate`. Table 4.1 lists the enum values and their meanings.

TABLE 4.1   Resource String Parameters

enum Value	*Purpose*
`windowTitle`	Name that appears in the application's title bar.
`docName`	Root for the default filename. MFC appends 1,2,3... to this when new documents are created.
`fileNewName`	Name of this document type. If several document types are defined, this is the name that is presented to users when they create a new document. If this portion of the string is blank, it is not available to users.

TABLE 4.1   continued

enum Value	Purpose
filterName	Description of file type and wildcard filter—for example, Dave's files (*.dav)
filterExt	Extension for files of this type. This should have no asterisk (*) but should have a period (.)—for example, .dav.
regFileTypeId	Internal document type used for registration with Windows.
regFileTypeName	Registry document type used by OLE. This is exposed to the user.

Unfortunately, no function is provided to set these values; you must enter them in the String Table Editor in the order listed, separated by the newline character (\n). This means that you cannot change these parameters at runtime. The string resource created by the MFC AppWizard contains the strings entered in the Advanced Settings dialog box of Step 4 of the wizard. The last two parameters are used by OLE servers.

The document string resource always contains a newline character for each item in the enumeration. If a particular value isn't used, several newlines may appear next to each other.

After you create the document template and call AddDocTemplate(), your application is set up to use the default functionality MFC provides for creating new documents and views. Next, you'll see how you can use additional document templates to create multiple views for each document.

Using Multiple Document Templates

As discussed in "Using Document Templates," earlier in this chapter, the document template associates a set of view, frame, and document classes. To use multiple documents or views, you must create a document template for each combination of document view classes you intend to create.

When multiple documents or views are used by an MFC application, it's a good idea to store pointers to the document templates in the application's CWinApp-derived class. For example, in the EmpList project, two document templates are created; pointers to these document template instances are kept in the CEmpListApp class for use later, when a view must be created on demand.

Listing 4.1 contains the relevant portion of the CEmpListApp::InitInstance function. I have removed the code generated by the AppWizard from the listing, but you will find the full source code for the project on the accompanying CD-ROM.

LISTING 4.1   Creating Additional Document Templates for EmpList

```
BOOL CEmpListApp::InitInstance()
{

    // Wizard-generated code omitted...

    m_pListTemplate = new CMultiDocTemplate(IDR_EMPLISTTYPE,
                                RUNTIME_CLASS(CEmpListDoc),
                                RUNTIME_CLASS(CChildFrame),
                                RUNTIME_CLASS(CEmpListView));
    m_pFormTemplate = new CMultiDocTemplate(IDR_EMPFORMTYPE,
                                RUNTIME_CLASS(CEmpListDoc),
                                RUNTIME_CLASS(CChildFrame),
                                RUNTIME_CLASS(CEmpFormView));
    AddDocTemplate(m_pListTemplate);
    AddDocTemplate(m_pFormTemplate);

    return TRUE;
}
```

As discussed earlier, the document template pointers are deleted by the MFC framework when the application is closed. The code in Listing 4.1 causes the MFC framework to use `CEmpListView` as the default view class. By caching the document template pointers, the application can create either type of view on demand.

Creating a Different View for a Document

If your application has a document open and you would like to open a different sort of view to it, you can do so by calling the `CreateNewFrame()` member of a document template that relates the document type to a new view class. The `CreateNewFrame()` function takes a pointer to the existing document object and an optional pointer to an existing frame window. If you use `CreateNewFrame()`, you should be sure to call `CDocTemplate::InitialUpdateFrame()` to initialize the window. This function takes a pointer to the new frame and a pointer to the existing document. You can see an example of this in Listing 4.2, which is taken from the EmpList sample application on the CD-ROM.

4

THE DOCUMENT VIEW ARCHITECTURE

LISTING 4.2   Creating New Views on Demand in EmpList

```
void CMainFrame::OnWindowForm()
{
    CMDIChildWnd* pActiveChild = MDIGetActive();
    if(pActiveChild)
    {
        CDocument* pDoc = pActiveChild->GetActiveDocument();
        if(pDoc)
        {
```

LISTING 4.2   continued

```
            CEmpListApp*  pApp = (CEmpListApp*)AfxGetApp();
            ASSERT_POINTER(pApp, CEmpListApp);
            CDocTemplate* pTemplate;
            CFrameWnd*    pFrame;
            VERIFY(pTemplate = pApp->GetFormTemplate());
            pFrame = pTemplate->CreateNewFrame(pDoc, pActiveChild);
            if(pFrame)
            {
                pTemplate->InitialUpdateFrame(pFrame, pDoc);
            }
        }
    }
}

void CMainFrame::OnWindowList()
{
    CMDIChildWnd* pActiveChild = MDIGetActive();
    if(pActiveChild)
    {
        CDocument* pDoc = pActiveChild->GetActiveDocument();
        if(pDoc)
        {
            CEmpListApp*  pApp = (CEmpListApp*)AfxGetApp();
            ASSERT_POINTER(pApp, CEmpListApp);
            CDocTemplate* pTemplate;
            CFrameWnd*    pFrame;
            VERIFY(pTemplate = pApp->GetListTemplate());
            pFrame = pTemplate->CreateNewFrame(pDoc, pActiveChild);
            if(pFrame)
            {
                pTemplate->InitialUpdateFrame(pFrame, pDoc);
            }
        }
    }
}
```

In Listing 4.2, the GetFormTemplate and GetListTemplate functions are called. These two functions are part of the CEmpListApp class and simply return pointers to the document templates created earlier in Listing 4.1.

The document templates are used to create new views by calling their CreateNewFrame member functions. After the new views are created, the InitialUpdateFrame function is called to force the view to be updated. This update causes the view to synchronize itself with its associated document, keeping all views synchronized.

CDocument::OnChangedViewList()

Whenever a new view is attached to a document, the framework calls the document's OnChangedViewList() function. You can override this function in your application if you need to do anything special when a view is added or deleted from the document's view list. The default implementation of OnChangedViewList() closes the document if no views remain in the document's view list.

UpdateAllViews()

When the data in your document changes, you generally will want to update all the views attached to the document. You can do this by using the UpdateAllViews() function of your document object. UpdateAllViews() takes a pointer to the view that generated the change as its first parameter. This function runs through the document's list of views, calling the OnUpdate() function of each view, with the exception of the view that generated the change. If you want to update all the views, specify NULL as the first parameter to UpdateAllViews().

If you are supporting multiple views, you probably don't want to update every view for each change to the document. It's usually very easy for the active view to update itself without waiting for the change to be reflected through the document class. In the EmpList project, for example, each view is responsible for updating its own user interface when changing the document. Immediately updating the view makes the user interface appear to be more responsive. If the view were to wait for the document to be updated first, the user interface could be noticeably slower in some situations.

Listing 4.3 contains some source code from the EmpList project that is used to add a new employee to the document.

LISTING 4.3 Adding a New Employee in EmpList

```
void CEmpFormView::OnAdd()
{
    CDlgEmp dlg;
    if(dlg.DoModal() == IDOK)
    {
        CEmployee emp;
        emp.m_strEmail = dlg.m_strEmail;
        emp.m_strName = dlg.m_strName;

        // Add the item to the list view control
        int nItem = m_list.GetItemCount();
        AddEmployeeToList(nItem, emp);
        // Add the item to the document
        CEmpListDoc* pDoc = GetDocument();
```

4

THE DOCUMENT
VIEW
ARCHITECTURE

LISTING 4.3   continued

```
        ASSERT_POINTER(pDoc, CEmpListDoc);
        if(pDoc)
            pDoc->SetEmployee(emp, this);
    }
}
```

Note that in Listing 4.3, the view passes a pointer to itself to the document class. The document class uses the view pointer as a parameter when calling UpdateAllViews, preventing the view from being updated.

Optionally, you can pass a long and/or a pointer to a CObject to UpdateAllViews(). These are passed on to the view's OnUpdate() function and can be defined to be anything you want. Generally, you will want to use these if you can somehow optimize your update routines based on the changes that were made.

In EmpList, the update hint consists of a pointer to the structure shown here:

```
enum EmpListHintType{ hintNone, hintRemove, hintAdd };
struct EmpListHint
{
    EmpListHint(EmpListHintType t, int i, CEmployee e)
        : type(t), item(i), emp(e) {};
    EmpListHintType type;
    int             item;
    CEmployee       emp;
};
```

This code enables a view to add or delete any item from the view without requesting more information from the document.

Accessing Views from Your Document

Occasionally, you might want to search through the list of views associated with a document in order to do something with them. If UpdateAllViews() doesn't meet your needs, MFC provides an alternative. Here is an example:

```
void CMyDocument::UpdateSomeViews()
{
    POSITION pos = GetFirstViewPosition();
    while(pos != NULL)
    {
        CView* pView = GetNextView(pos);
        if(myCondition) pView->OnUpdate(NULL, 0, NULL);
    }
} // end UpdateSomeViews()
```

This example declares a POSITION object used to walk through the list of views. The value of pos is set to NULL by the GetNextView function when the end of the list is reached. The call to `GetFirstViewPosition()` sets up the list of views for browsing with the `GetNextView()` call. You then can do whatever you want with the view pointer that is returned. You should note that I used the generic `CView` pointer in this example, however. In the real world, you could cast the return value of `GetNextView()` to your view type, although you need to be careful with this if you support multiple view types for the document.

Working with Frames

Up to this point, you have learned that frames will contain your view windows, but you really haven't looked at what else frames can do. They can do quite a lot for your application. As you will see, frame windows provide the capability to use status bars, toolbars, and splitters. This applies to frame windows in general, regardless of whether you are using the document view architecture, although how this fits with the document view framework is mentioned where appropriate.

Status Bars

Many Windows applications provide useful information about the current state of the application in a status bar at the bottom of the application window. In this section, you will see how you can add this functionality to your own applications.

First, you need an object derived from the `CStatusBar` class. If you have created an MDI or SDI app using the MFC AppWizard, you should notice that `m_wndStatusBar` already has been added as a member of your main frame class. This is a good place to put the status bar object, because it needs to be around as long as the frame window is and should go away when the frame does. Your declaration should look something like this:

```
CStatusBar m_wndStatusBar;
```

Now that you have a `CStatusBar` object, creating the status bar window is a snap. You simply call the `Create()` function of `CStatusBar`, as in this example from the `CMainFrame::OnCreate()` implementation created by the MFC AppWizard:

```
    if (!m_wndStatusBar.Create(this) ||
            !m_wndStatusBar.SetIndicators(indicators,
                sizeof(indicators)/sizeof(UINT)))
    {
        TRACE0("Failed to create status bar\n");
        return -1;        // fail to create
    }
```

The `Create()` function of `CStatusBar` takes a parent window parameter. Because `Create()` is called in the `OnCreate()` member of the frame, this is `this`. If the call to `Create()` is successful, `SetIndicators()` is called to load the text that will be used in the indicators on the right side of the status bar. This takes a pointer to an array of IDs (UINTs) and the number of elements in the array. The indicators array used in the example is defined like this:

```
static UINT indicators[] =
{
    ID_SEPARATOR,               // status line indicator
    ID_INDICATOR_CAPS,
    ID_INDICATOR_NUM,
    ID_INDICATOR_SCRL,
};
```

Each of the values in this array is the resource ID of a string resource that contains the text to be placed in the indicator box when it is toggled on. The first value, ID_SEPARATOR, is a special case. This is used to indicate that you want to use the first pane of the status bar for text—namely, the fly-by help strings that you define when creating menu items and toolbars.

Customizing the Status Bar

You can customize the status bar to display whatever information you want. To do this, begin by adding an entry in the indicators array that is passed to SetIndicators(). If you use 0 for the resource ID, no string will be found, and MFC will create an empty pane with which you can work.

Now you most likely will want to size the pane to fit the data you intend to put into it. To do this, first get some information about the current state of the status bar, then change the areas you care about, and update the status bar with the new settings:

```
m_wndStatusBar.GetPaneInfo(1, nID, nStyle, cxWidth);
m_wndStatusBar.SetPaneInfo(1, nID, nStyle, 50);
```

In this example, the first parameter is the index (0-based) of the pane. Here, a pane is added between the text area and the three indicators used by default. In addition, nID returns the resource ID of a string resource holding the text for the pane, nStyle returns the style bit settings of the pane, and cxWidth returns the width of the pane. You can modify any or all of these before calling SetPaneInfo(). In this case, you simply set the width to a size that is close to what you want. You now can add whatever text you want by using the following:

```
m_wndStatusBar.SetPaneText(1, "Hello");
```

In a real application, taking a guess at the size you want is probably not the best method. You might want to do something like the following example to set the size to exactly what you will need:

```
m_wndStatusBar.GetPaneInfo(1, nID, nStyle, nWidth);
```

```
pDC = m_wndStatusBar.GetDC();
pDC->SelectObject(m_wndStatusBar.GetFont());
pDC->DrawText(_T("Hello"), -1, myRect, DT_CALCRECT);
m_wndStatusBar.ReleaseDC(pDC);
m_wndStatusBar.SetPaneInfo(1, nID, nStyle, myRect.Width());
```

Adding a Toolbar

Chapter 1, " The Visual C++ 6.0 Environment," discusses how to create a toolbar resource. Now you will see how to make it work. First, you need an object derived from class CToolBar. If you asked for it, the MFC AppWizard has already created one for you (as well as the rest of the code you will see here); if not, you just need to add the following line to the declaration of your main frame class:

```
CToolBar m_wndToolBar;
```

The toolbar window is created by code like this from CMainFrame::OnCreate():

```
if (!m_wndToolBar.Create(this) ||
    !m_wndToolBar.LoadToolBar(IDR_MAINFRAME))
{
    TRACE0("Failed to create toolbar\n");
    return -1;     // fail to create
}
```

The call to LoadToolBar() takes the resource ID of a toolbar resource that you created in the Resource Editor (or that the MFC AppWizard created for you).

The Create() call also can take a DWORD with additional style information for the toolbar. This defaults to WS_CHILD|WS_VISIBLE|CBRS_TOP. You may add any of the styles listed in Table 4.2 to affect how your toolbar works.

TABLE 4.2   Toolbar Styles

Style	Effect
CBRS_TOP	Position toolbar at top of window.
CBRS_BOTTOM	Position toolbar at bottom of window.
CBRS_NOALIGN	Control bar is not repositioned when parent is resized.
CBRS_TOOLTIPS	Enable ToolTips.
CBRS_SIZE_DYNAMIC	Make control bar sizeable.
CBRS_SIZE_FIXED	Make control bar a fixed size.
CBRS_FLOATING	Create a floating toolbar.
CBRS_FLYBY	Show fly-by help in the status bar.
CBRS_HIDE_INPLACE	Toolbar is not displayed.

4

THE DOCUMENT VIEW ARCHITECTURE

TABLE 4.2   continued

Style	Effect
CBRS_BORDER_TOP	Create a border for the toolbar on the top.
CBRS_BORDER_LEFT	Create a border for the toolbar on the left.
CBRS_BORDER_RIGHT	Create a border for the toolbar on the right.
CBRS_BORDER_BOTTOM	Create a border for the toolbar on the bottom.

You also can modify these settings later with SetBarStyle(). This can be useful particularly if you want to add a certain feature, such as ToolTips or status bar fly-by help, as in this example, generated by the MFC AppWizard:

```
m_wndToolBar.SetBarStyle(m_wndToolBar.GetBarStyle() |
    CBRS_TOOLTIPS | CBRS_FLYBY | CBRS_DYNAMIC);
```

You should notice that neither ToolTips nor status bar fly-by help is included in the defaults for Create(). The strings for fly-by help and ToolTips are defined in a string resource with the same ID as the command generated by the button—fly-by text first, separated by a newline (\n):

```
"Recall last transaction\nRecall"
```

In addition, you can work with the styles of individual buttons with SetButtonStyle() and GetButtonStyle(), which use the styles in Table 4.3.

TABLE 4.3   Toolbar Button Styles

Style	Effect
TBBS_CHECKED	The button is down (checked).
TBBS_INDETERMINATE	The button state is undetermined.
TBBS_DISABLED	The button is disabled.
TBBS_PRESSED	The button is pressed.
TBBS_CHECKBOX	The button will be a toggle.

Floating and Docking Toolbars

If you want a floating toolbar, you can use the CFrameWnd::FloatControlBar() function, which requires a pointer to the toolbar, and a CPoint that dictates where the toolbar will float. In this example, the toolbar floats in the top-left corner:

```
FloatControlBar( &m_wndToolBar, CPoint(0,0));
```

Optionally, you can specify one of the following alignment styles as a third parameter to dictate the orientation of the toolbar.

    CBRS_ALIGN_TOP

    CBRS_ALIGN_BOTTOM

    CBRS_ALIGN_LEFT

    CBRS_ALIGN_RIGHT

If you want to dock your toolbar to the edges of the frame, you can use something like the following example generated by the MFC AppWizard:

```
m_wndToolBar.EnableDocking(CBRS_ALIGN_ANY);
EnableDocking(CBRS_ALIGN_ANY);
DockControlBar(&m_wndToolBar);
```

Note that you must call `EnableDocking()` for both the toolbar and the frame window. You can enable docking only on certain edges of the frame by using a combination of the following docking flags:

    CBRS_ALIGN_ANY

    CBRS_ALIGN_TOP

    CBRS_ALIGN_BOTTOM

    CBRS_ALIGN_LEFT

    CBRS_ALIGN_RIGHT

The toolbar will dock only to those edges that are enabled for both the toolbar and the frame.

The `DockControlBar()` call tells the toolbar to dock itself. By default, the toolbar tries to dock to the top, left, bottom, and right sides of the frame, in that order. You can specify one of the following as a second parameter to dictate where the toolbar will dock:

    AFX_IDW_DOCKBAR_TOP

    AFX_IDW_DOCKBAR_BOTTOM

    AFX_IDW_DOCKBAR_LEFT

    AFX_IDW_DOCKBAR_RIGHT

More on Working with Menus

In your Windows application, menus undoubtedly will make up a substantial part of your user interface. You looked at how to create menu resources in Chapter 1, and in this chapter, you learned how you can use document templates to assign a menu to a frame window. In this section, you will see how to update the user interface for your menus, implement pop-up menus, and create menus dynamically.

Updating the User Interface

MFC provides mechanisms for automatically updating the status of the command-generating controls of your user interface—namely, menus and toolbar buttons. This is done by implementing handlers for the UPDATE_COMMAND_UI message, which can be done from the ClassWizard when you select a command object. Alternatively, you could add ON_COMMAND_UPDATE_UI macros to your message map by hand:

```
ON_UPDATE_COMMAND_UI(ID_APP_EXIT, OnUpdateAppExit)
```

You then implement a handler function. Here, I have decided that I may want to disable the File | Exit command, so I have created a handler for the UPDATE_COMMAND_UI message:

```
void CMainFrame::OnUpdateAppExit(CCmdUI* pCmdUI)
{
    if(m_bTrapUser)
        pCmdUI->Enable(FALSE);
}
```

The handler is passed a pointer to a CCmdUI object, which should be used for updating the interface item. This will update both the menu item and toolbar button for the given command.

Pop-Up Menus

You may have seen several different applications that use pop-up menus. It has become increasingly popular for applications to generate pop-up menus after the user clicks the right mouse button, such as the context menus found throughout Visual C++.

You actually can add context menu support simply by adding the PopUpMenu component from the component gallery; however, let's look at how you can do this yourself. To create your own pop-up menu, you first should create a menu resource in the Resource Editor, although you will learn how to create menus in your code in just a bit. When you are creating a pop-up menu in the Menu Editor, the caption at the top of your menu will not actually be displayed, so use any placeholder you want.

Next you declare a CMenu object and load it with the resource you created:

```
CMenu myPopupMenu;
myPopupMenu.LoadMenu(IDR_MYPOPUPMENU);
```

Note that you probably will want to do this a bit differently in your application. That is, you may want to declare your CMenu object in your frame class declaration or create it on the heap with the new operator. Now you want to allow the user to use the pop-up menu. This is done best by creating a handler for the WM_CONTEXTMENU message with the

ClassWizard. Then when you want to display your pop-up menu, you should add something like this:

```
void CMainFrame::OnContextMenu(CWnd* pWnd, CPoint point)
{
    POINT curPos;
    GetCursorPos(&curPos);
    CMenu* pSubMenu = myPopupMenu.GetSubMenu(0);
    pSubMenu->TrackPopupMenu(TPM_LEFTALIGN | TPM_LEFTBUTTON,
                        curPos.x, curPos.y, this);
}
```

Here you use `GetSubMenu()` to reach the first submenu that contains your pop-up. You then call `TrackPopupMenu()` to present the menu to the user. This call accepts a few styles—in this case, dictating that the menu's left edge is aligned with the position you give in the second and third parameters, and that the menu will respond to the left mouse button. The last parameter is a pointer to the parent window; here, it is the main frame.

After you call `TrackPopupMenu()`, it handles itself until the user chooses a command from the menu or dismisses it. Commands from pop-up menus can be handled just like any other menu command.

Creating Menus Dynamically

If you want to create the menu used in the previous example within your code, this is actually quite simple. First declare your `CMenu` object as in the example. Then call `CMenu::CreatePopupMenu()` to get a valid Windows menu, and add your menu items to it with `CMenu::AppendMenu()`:

```
m_MyMenu.CreatePopupMenu();
m_MyMenu.AppendMenu(MF_ENABLED, ID_FILE_NEW, _T("&New File"));
m_MyMenu.AppendMenu(MF_ENABLED, ID_FILE_CLOSE, _T("&Close File"));
```

You also may use the `InsertMenu()` function to place menu items anywhere in the menu. You also can dynamically modify the menu for any window by first getting a pointer to the window's `CMenu` object with a call to `CWnd::GetMenu();`.

One advantage of creating your own menus this way is that you no longer have to monkey around with submenus to create the pop-up. In the previous example, you then could replace the call to `TrackPopupMenu()` with something like this:

```
m_MyMenu.TrackPopupMenu(TPM_LEFTALIGN | TPM_LEFTBUTTON,
                    curPos.x, curPos.y, this);
```

4

THE DOCUMENT VIEW ARCHITECTURE

Adding Splitters to Your Application

You probably have seen several applications that provide the capability of splitting the view window into two (or more) different views of the same object. This functionality is supported by MFC and actually can be added by the MFC AppWizard or by inserting the Split Bars component from the Component Gallery. Let's take a look at just how this works.

First, two types of splitters are available: *static* and *dynamic*. If you want to set up your application to have a predefined number of windows in its view, and you do not want the user to be able to define new splits at runtime, you use static splitters. If you want to give the user the capability to split your views at runtime, you use dynamic splitters.

MFC's implementation of splitters, or *split bars,* is based on the CSplitterWnd class. Objects of this class are designed to reside in the frame windows that will hold your views. In SDI apps, this is the main frame; in MDI apps, it is the MDI child frame. You need to add a declaration to your frame class to include a CSplitterWnd object:

```
CSplitterWnd m_wndSplitter;
```

This code is used for both the static and dynamic flavors of splitters. For now, let's look at how to implement dynamic splitters.

Dynamic Splitters

You need to override the OnCreateClient() function of your frame class. OnCreateClient() is called from OnCreate() when your application creates the view that will live in the frame. Your implementation should look something like this example generated by inserting the Split Bars component:

```
BOOL CChildFrame::OnCreateClient(LPCREATESTRUCT lpcs, CCreateContext* pContext)
{
    // CG: The following block was added by the Split Bars component.
    {
        if (!m_wndSplitter.Create(this,
                                  2, 2,
                                  CSize(10, 10),
                                  pContext))
        {
            TRACE0("Failed to create split bar ");
            return FALSE;    // failed to create
        }
        return TRUE;
    }
}
```

Here you see that the `CSplitterWnd::Create()` function is called. The `Create()` function takes several parameters, beginning with the parent window, which will be the frame. The next two parameters dictate the maximum number of rows and columns that may be created. In the current implementation, this limit is 2. If you need more, you have to use static splitters. The next parameter is a `SIZE` structure specifying the minimum size allowed for a pane.

> **Note**
>
> In most cases in MFC, you can use classes such as `CSize` in place of their corresponding structures, such as `SIZE`. To be sure of the acceptable parameter types for a function, see the online help.

The last parameter used in the example is a pointer to a `CCreateContext` object. In most cases, this is simply the pointer that is passed to the `OnCreateClient()` function. Optionally, you can specify styles and a child window ID in the `Create()` function. At this point, your application is all set to go. `OnCreateClient()` is called when the child frame needs to create a view, which then calls `Create()` for the `CSplitterWnd` object, which then creates the actual view based on your document templates.

Creating Different Views

If you want to create a different type of view in the new pane when the user splits the window, you can do so, but you first have to create your own class based on `CSplitterWnd`. In your new class, you have to provide an override for the `CreateView()` function:

```
BOOL CMySplitterWnd::CreateView(int row, int col,
        CRuntimeClass* pViewClass, SIZE sizeInit,
        CCreateContext* pContext)
{
    if(column == 0)
    {
    return CSplitterWnd::CreateView(row, col, pViewClass, sizeInit, pContext);
    }
    else
    {
    return CSplitterWnd::CreateView(row, col, RUNTIME_CLASS(CRightView),
sizeInit, pContext);
    }
} // end CreateView()
```

4

THE DOCUMENT VIEW ARCHITECTURE

In this example, you create a view of type `CRightView` in any panes that are not in column 0 (the leftmost column). You also can create a view based on a new document in a similar fashion, although you have to create your own `CCreateContext` object to pass to the `CreateView()` function. In this object, you can pass a different document template for the new view.

Static Splitters

Working with static splitters is similar to working with dynamic splitters, but some important differences exist. First, you should call `CSplitterWnd::CreateStatic()` instead of `Create()`. You also need to create the views yourself—if you don't, your app will crash. To do this, call `CSplitterWnd::CreateView()` for each pane that you have defined, as in the following example:

```
BOOL CChildFrame::OnCreateClient(LPCREATESTRUCT lpcs, CCreateContext* pContext)
{
    int nCol;

    if (!m_wndSplitter.CreateStatic(this, 1, 3))
    {
        TRACE0("Failed to create split bar ");
        return FALSE;     // failed to create
    }
    for(nCol=0; nCol < 3; nCol++)
    {
        if(!m_wndSplitter.CreateView(0, nCol,
            RUNTIME_CLASS(CMyView),
            CSize(50, 100), pContext))
        {
            TRACE0("Failed to create view ");
            return FALSE;
        }
        return TRUE;
    } // end for
} // end OnCreateClient()
```

This example defines three panes, arranged horizontally, that all use the same view class and document. If you want to use a different view class or document, you can change this, as with the previous example of dynamic splitters.

Adding Drag and Drop to Your Application

Many applications in Windows allow the user to work with files graphically by dragging the files from a drag-and-drop file source, such as Explorer, to the window for an application that can accept the files. This function can be implemented in two ways. The first is with OLE. The second method uses Windows messages to support drag-and-drop.

Enabling Drag and Drop

To enable drag and drop in a window of your application, you use the CWnd::DragAcceptFiles() call to enable the receipt of WM_DROPFILES messages. The single parameter for CWnd::DragAcceptFiles() is a BOOL. You can omit the parameter, because it defaults to TRUE, or you can call it with FALSE to disable drag and drop.

The drag and drop capability can be called from any object derived from CWnd, after its window is created. In the example in this section, you will put a call in the OnCreate() function of the main frame class, after the window is created by the call to CMDIFrameWnd::OnCreate(). This process allows the application to accept files that are dropped anywhere in its main window.

Handling WM_DROPFILES Messages

Next you implement a handler for the WM_DROPFILES message and add an entry to the message map. This is done best with the ClassWizard, which creates a default handler for you. The default handler defers to CMDIFrameWnd::OnDropFiles(), which tries to open a new document view pair for the files that were dragged.

If you want to do something more specific with the dropped files, you can implement your handler for OnDropFiles() something like this:

```
void CMainFrame::OnDropFiles(HDROP hDropInfo)
{
    UINT i;
    UINT nFiles = ::DragQueryFile(hDropInfo, (UINT) -1, NULL, 0);
    for (i = 0; i < nFiles; i++)
    {
        TCHAR szFileName[_MAX_PATH];
        ::DragQueryFile(hDropInfo, i, szFileName, _MAX_PATH);

        ProcessMyFile(szFileName);
    } // end for
    ::DragFinish(hDropInfo);
} // end OnDropFiles()
```

In this example, you can see that you call DragQueryFile() with a second parameter of -1 (0xFFFFFFFF), which returns the number of files that were dropped. You then use this value to loop through all the files, again using DragQueryInfo() to return the full path-name of the file. After you have the filename, you can do with it as you please; just make sure that you call DragFinish() to clean up when you are finished. If you don't do this, your application will leak a bit of memory each time you handle dropped files.

Summary

In this chapter, you looked at the document view architecture used in MFC, as well as how you can use it to easily create very powerful applications. This architecture also helps to ensure that your applications have a similar look and feel, as users will expect from Windows applications.

You also looked at the various view classes that MFC provides, as well as how to implement several other nifty features, such as menus, toolbars, and splitters.

I think that you will agree that using the MFC classes and the document view architecture is a much better way to start off your applications than programming all these features from scratch.

Creating and Using Dialog Boxes

by Jonathan Bates and Mickey Williams

IN THIS CHAPTER

CHAPTER 5

Dialog boxes remain the prime mechanism for detailed data exchange between the application and user.

The MFC libraries provide extensive support for template-based dialog boxes through the CDialog base class.

ClassWizard is an excellent tool for creating dialog box classes and automating the transfer between a dialog box's controls and mapped member variables during dialog box data exchange.

You can only do so much with ClassWizard, however, and often you'll need to get down to the code to gain the full benefits of the dialog box exchange and support mechanisms.

This chapter focuses on some of these advanced techniques to help you exploit the dialog box to its full potential.

Handling Dialog Boxes in MFC

Dialog boxes in MFC usually are based on dialog box templates. These dialog box templates are binary resources held in the structure defined by the Win32 DLGTEMPLATE, DLGITEMTEMPLATE, DLGTEMPLATEEX, and DLGITEMTEMPLATEEX. You can fill these structures with positioning information, size, ID, and style flags required to describe every control on a dialog box.

If these structures were created tediously by hand for every dialog box, user interface software would progress at a snail's pace. Fortunately, the Visual Studio dialog box Template Editor is a powerful tool dedicated to this task.

After you create a dialog box template resource, you can create a CDialog-derived class that uses the template to create the dialog box and then manages the exchange between window controls and your dialog box's member variables.

Creating Dialog Box Template Resources

You can create dialog boxes and add controls by using the Resource Editor, as Figure 5.1 shows.

After you create the dialog box, Visual Studio saves the details in a text format in your project's .rc file. These details provide the source code required for the Resource Compiler to generate the required DLGTEMPLATE and DLGITEMTEMPLATE binary structures.

FIGURE 5.1

Editing a dialog box with Visual Studio's Dialog Box Editor.

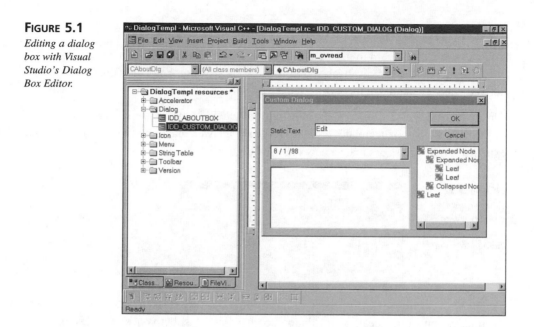

You'll rarely need to edit the `.rc` file directly, because the Resource Editor should solely maintain it. It is interesting to note the code produced after editing a dialog box, however, such as this entry produced for the dialog box shown in Figure 5.1:

```
IDD_CUSTOM_DIALOG DIALOG DISCARDABLE  0, 0, 232, 135
STYLE DS_MODALFRAME | WS_POPUP | WS_CAPTION | WS_SYSMENU
CAPTION "Custom Dialog"
FONT 8, "MS Sans Serif"
BEGIN
    DEFPUSHBUTTON    "OK",IDOK,175,7,50,14
    PUSHBUTTON       "Cancel",IDCANCEL,175,24,50,14
    LTEXT            "Static Text",IDC_STATIC,7,23,44,8
    EDITTEXT         IDC_EDIT1,53,19,97,14,ES_AUTOHSCROLL
    LISTBOX          IDC_LIST1,7,64,147,64,LBS_SORT | LBS_NOINTEGRALHEIGHT |
                     WS_VSCROLL | WS_TABSTOP
    CONTROL          "DateTimePicker1",IDC_DATETIMEPICKER1,"SysDateTimePick32",
                     DTS_RIGHTALIGN | WS_TABSTOP,7,42,146,15
    CONTROL          "Tree1",IDC_TREE1,"SysTreeView32",WS_BORDER | WS_TABSTOP,
                     161,42,64,86
END
```

When you compile the resources, the compiler produces a file with a `.res` extension that holds the binary format of these dialog box templates (and the other resources). This `.res` file then is linked with the program code (`.obj` files) to produce your target `.exe`, `.dll`, or `.lib` file.

5

CREATING AND USING DIALOG BOXES

Creating a `CDialog`-Derived Class

You can use ClassWizard to generate a `CDialog`-derived class by invoking the wizard while the new dialog box is displayed in the Resource Editor. You could create the derived class by hand, but the wizard makes this process much easier.

ClassWizard detects that there is no class currently held in the `.clw` file that uses the ID of the new dialog box template resource. It then displays a dialog box to let you select an existing handler class or create a new one (see Figure 5.2).

Figure 5.2

ClassWizard prompts you to create or select a dialog box handler class.

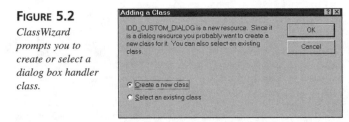

Normally, you would create a new dialog box handler class, but you sometimes may want to select an existing implementation.

If you choose to create a new dialog box handler class, the wizard displays the New Class dialog box, as Figure 5.3 shows.

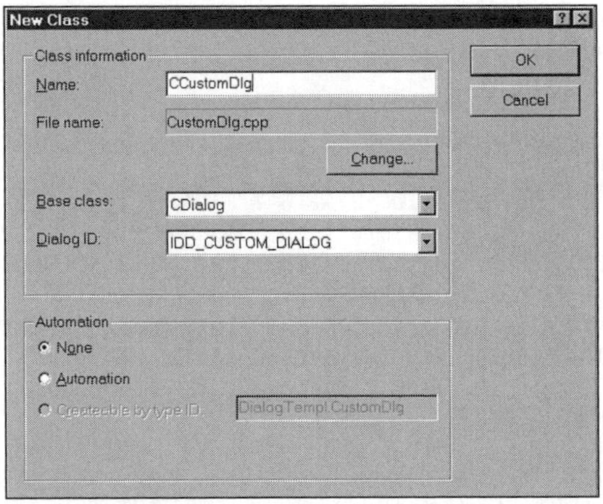

Figure 5.3

The New Class dialog box.

The New Class dialog box lets you change the name of the class. It then generates filenames based on the name you have specified. You can change these autogenerated filenames if they aren't appropriate.

The `CDialog` base class and your dialog box template ID are selected automatically. If your application is *object linking and embedding* (*OLE*)-enabled, you also can specify any OLE automation specific details for the new dialog box.

After you click OK in the New Class dialog box, you see the new dialog box handler class in the ClassView pane. If you examine the new header, you see a minefield of `//{{AFX_...` comments created by ClassWizard. When you subsequently add member variables and functions with ClassWizard, it adds the new code inside the appropriate comment sections.

You'll also notice that the dialog box ID is enumerated as the `IDD` member with a value based on your dialog box template's resource ID, such as this:

```
enum { IDD = IDD_CUSTOM_DIALOG };
```

If you examine the dialog constructor function, you'll see that it passes this ID down to the `CDialog` base class, along with an optional parent-window pointer:

```
CCustomDlg::CCustomDlg(CWnd* pParent /*=NULL*/)
    : CDialog(CCustomDlg::IDD, pParent)
{
  //{{AFX_DATA_INIT(CCustomDlg)
    // NOTE: the ClassWizard will add member initialization here
  //}}AFX_DATA_INIT
}
```

The `//{{AFX_DATA_INIT` section in the constructor implementation is used by ClassWizard to initialize any member variables that you insert using the wizard.

The dialog box class definition also includes a declaration for the `DoDataExchange()` virtual function (covered in more detail later in the section, "The Data Exchange and Validation Mechanism"), and a message map declaration:

```
DECLARE_MESSAGE_MAP()
```

All classes that implement the `DECLARE_MESSAGE_MAP` macro must be derived from the `CCmdTarget` class. The dialog box class is derived from `CCmdTarget` through the `CWnd` class. This is because the dialog box is a window, and your `CDialog`-derived class must process messages from its own window and the various dialog box controls (which are child windows).

Displaying the Dialog Box

At this point, you can create an instance of the dialog box handler class and display the dialog box. Dialog boxes normally are displayed in a modal sense. (Modeless dialog boxes are discussed later in this chapter in "Modeless Dialog Boxes.") When a modal dialog box is displayed, users are unable to interact with any other part of the application until they click OK or Cancel to exit the dialog box.

The CDialog class's DoModal() function initiates the modal process and ends when the EndDialog() member function is called. The default implementation of CDialog calls EndDialog() in response to the user clicking the OK or Cancel button. You can use the integer value returned from DoModal() to find out which button was pressed. This integer actually is returned from the parameter passed to EndDialog(), which by default is IDOK or IDCANCEL in response to the OK or Cancel button.

The following lines show how an object of the CCustomDlg class is constructed and displayed, as well as how the return code determines which button was clicked to close the dialog box:

```
CCustomDlg dlgCustom;
if (dlgCustom.DoModal()==IDOK)
    AfxMessageBox("User Hit OK");
else
    AfxMessageBox("User Hit Cancel");
```

If you do want to use a dialog box template constructed in memory, you should construct a CDialog-derived class calling the constructor with no parameters. Then you can call the InitModalIndirect() function passing a pointer to a DLGTEMPLATE structure in memory, or an HGLOBAL handle to a global memory segment. If the initialization succeeds, InitModalIndirect() returns a TRUE value. You then can call DoModal() as normal to display the modal dialog box.

Warning

If you want to create more than 255 controls in a dialog box, you must add the controls dynamically from within the OnInitDialog() function. The dialog box templates support a maximum of 255 controls.

Dialog Box Coordinates

When you edit a dialog box in the Resource Editor, you'll notice that the coordinates don't correspond to the current screen resolution. Dialog boxes use their own coordinate system based on the size of the font being used in the dialog box. This method helps with the problem of matching the sizes of controls and group boxes to the various font sizes.

When the dialog box is displayed, the control positions and sizes are converted from dialog box units to real-screen units, depending on the size of the font used. Most dialog boxes use the default system font, but you can set different fonts when editing the dialog box, from within your code by calling the CWnd base class's SetFont() function, or by overriding the CDialog class's OnSetFont() function and supplying a pointer to your required dialog box font.

These real-screen units are calculated from the average height and width of the current dialog box font. The real-screen units are one-eighth of the height and one-fourth of the width of the dialog box units.

You can convert between these dialog box units and the real-screen coordinates by passing a RECT structure holding the dialog box coordinates to the MapDialogRect() function. MapDialogRect() then translates these dialog box coordinates into screen coordinates.

> **Tip**
>
> You may find the CWnd base class's ClientToScreen() function useful when manipulating screen coordinates relative to the dialog box. ClientToScreen() converts client coordinates held in a RECT or POINT structure into screen coordinates. The corresponding ScreenToClient() function performs the opposite conversion.

Changing the Input Focus and Default Buttons

When you edit a dialog box template in the Resource Editor, you can set the tab order by pressing Ctrl+D. This action displays sequence numbers above the controls and lets you change the order by clicking on various controls in sequence.

Whenever the user presses the Tab button while the dialog box is displayed, the input focus moves to the next control in this tab order.

A set of member CDialog functions lets you change the current input focus from within your code based on this tab order.

You can set the focus to a specific control after the dialog box is displayed by calling GotoDlgCtrl() and passing a pointer to the control's window. You can find this pointer

by ID by calling `GetDlgItem()`. To set the input focus to the OK button, for example, you could call the following from within your dialog box class (after activation):

```
GotoDlgCtrl(GetDlgItem(IDOK));
```

The `NextDlgCtrl()` and `PrevDlgCtrl()` functions let you move forward and backward through the tab order, setting the input focus to the next or preceding control from the current control with input focus.

Normally the OK button is the default button, so when a user presses the Enter key, the OK button is clicked. You can change this behavior by passing a different button ID to `SetDefID()`. The alternative button then becomes the default clicked when the user presses Enter. The corresponding `GetDefID()` returns the ID of the current default button.

If you are using context-sensitive help, you can set the context help ID for a dialog box by calling `SetHelpID()` and passing the ID that corresponds to the documentation for that dialog box.

Dialog Box Data Exchange and Validation

The controls in a dialog box are specialized windows that store their own copy of the data that the user enters or changes. In the lifetime of a dialog box, you'll normally want to initialize these controls with data from your program, and then save that data back into those variables.

You'll probably also want to validate the values stored in the controls to ensure that they are within acceptable ranges when the user attempts to click OK to exit the dialog box.

Obviously, the first task in this process is to add new member variables to the dialog box handler class that correspond to the controls.

Mapping Member Variables to Controls

You can use ClassWizard to add member variables and provide the mapping for most of the dialog box controls via ClassWizard's Member Variables tab (see Figure 5.4).

The Member Variables tab lists the control IDs of the various controls. You can select an ID and click the Add Variable button to display the Add Member Variable dialog box (see Figure 5.5).

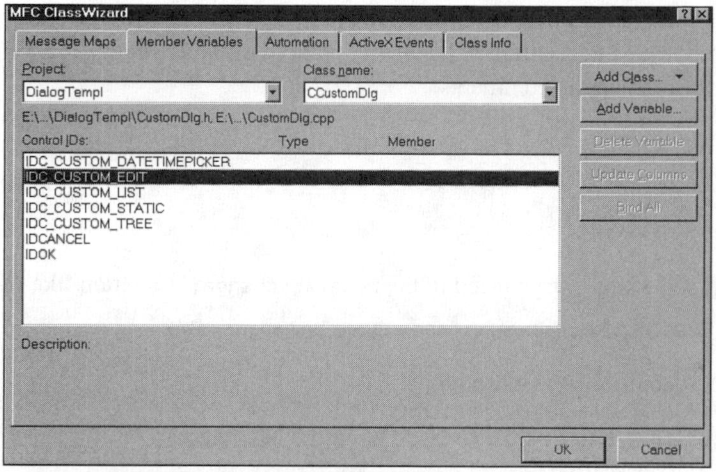

FIGURE 5.4

The ClassWizard Member Variables tab.

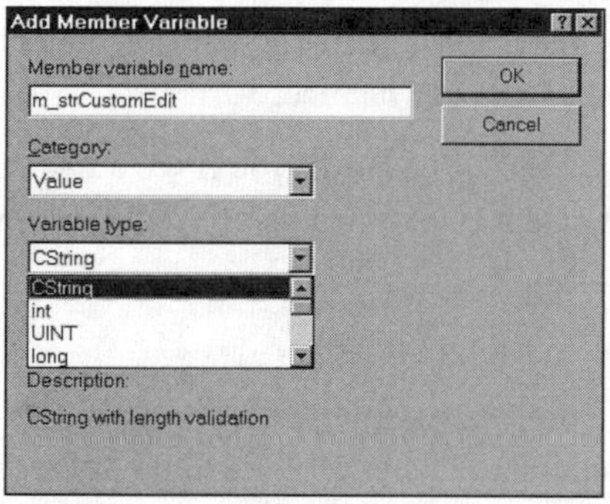

FIGURE 5.5

The Add Member Variable dialog box.

You'll notice that the Add Member Variable dialog box lets you set a category that can be a value or a control, as well as a variable type. The variable types available change depending on your selection in the Category combo box.

If you set the Category combo box to indicate value mapping, the Variable Type combo box lists member variable types that can be used with the type of control being mapped. These values are great for quick and easy value-oriented transfer, but often you'll need to map a control class to the control so that you can manipulate the control's more advanced features.

You can map a number of variables to the same control so that you can perform easy value transfer and allow control handler class mapping concurrently.

5

CREATING AND
USING DIALOG
BOXES

After you add the member variable map, you'll notice that the new member variable is inserted into your dialog box handler class definition between the ClassWizard AFX_DATA-generated comments.

The new variable also initializes your dialog box class's constructor function like this:

```
//{{AFX_DATA_INIT(CCustomDlg)
m_strCustomEdit = _T("");
//}}AFX_DATA_INIT
```

You'll see a new entry placed in the DoDataExchange() function like this:

```
void CCustomDlg::DoDataExchange(CDataExchange* pDX)
{
    CDialog::DoDataExchange(pDX);
    //{{AFX_DATA_MAP(CCustomDlg)
    DDX_Text(pDX, IDC_CUSTOM_EDIT, m_strCustomEdit);
    //}}AFX_DATA_MAP
}
```

The new DDX_Text macro entry automates data transfer between the control identified by IDC_CUSTOM_EDIT and your m_strCustomEdit member variable.

If you were to add a control map for the edit control, you'd see a CEdit member variable entry added to the class definition, and a corresponding DDX_Control macro to map it to the control ID. Consider this example:

```
DDX_Control(pDX, IDC_CUSTOM_EDIT, m_editCustom);
```

If you insert other variable types, you'll see different DDX_ macros used to map the various types of controls to various data types. Table 5.1 lists some of these controls.

TABLE 5.1   Some Common Controls and Their Mapping Classes/Variables

Control	*Mapping Class*	*Allowable Mapped Data Types*
Static	CStatic	CString
Edit	CEdit	CString, DWORD, UINT, int, long
		double, float, BOOL, short
		COleDateTime & ColeCurrency
Button	CButton	None
CheckBox	CButton	BOOL
3-State CheckBox	CButton	int

Control	Mapping Class	Allowable Mapped Data Types
Radio	CButton	int
ListBox	CListBox	CString, int
ComboBox	CComboBox	CString, int
Extended Combo	CComboBoxEx	CString, int
ScrollBar	CScrollBar	int
Spin	CSpinButtonCtrl	None
Progress Bar	CProgressCtrl	None
Slider Control	CSliderCtrl	int
List Control	CListCtrl	None
Tree Control	CTreeCtrl	None
Date Time Picker	CDateTimeCtrl	CTime, COleDateTime
Month Calendar	CMonthCalCtrl	CTime, COleDateTime

You can add some simple validation maps to certain controls, such as Edit controls. Depending on the variable type mapped, the lower section of the Member Variables tab displays a section that lets you specify validation information.

If you map a CString to an Edit control, for example, you can set the validation rules to limit the maximum number of characters allowed in the Edit control. If you map an integer to the Edit control, you can set upper and lower ranges for the entered value.

If you set any of these validation rules, ClassWizard adds DDV_ routines to the DoDataExchange() function to perform validation, like this:

```
DDV_MaxChars(pDX, m_strCustomEdit, 10);
```

Several different DDV_ routines exist for the various types of validation rules, member variables, and control types.

The Data Exchange and Validation Mechanism

The DoDataExchange() function is called several times during the lifetime of a dialog box and performs a variety of tasks. When the dialog box is initialized, this function subclasses any mapped controls through the DDX_Control routine (discussed in more detail later in the section, "Initializing the Dialog Box Controls"). Then it transfers the data held in the member variables to the controls using the DDX_ routines. Finally, after the

5

CREATING AND
USING DIALOG
BOXES

user clicks OK, the data from the controls is validated using DDV_ routines and then transferred back into the member variables using the DDX_ routines again.

You'll notice that the DoDataExchange() function is passed a pointer to a CDataExchange object. This object holds the details that let the DDX routines know whether they should be transferring data to or from the controls. The DDX_ routines then implement the Windows message required to set or retrieve data from the control associated with the given control ID.

When the m_bSaveAndValidate member is set to TRUE, the data exchange should transfer data from the controls to the member variables and perform validation. It is set to FALSE when data from the member variables should be loaded into the controls. You can add your own custom code to DoDataExchange() to transfer data to or from the controls and check the m_bSaveAndValidate member of the CDataExchange object to see whether you should be transferring the data to or from the control.

> **Warning**
>
> When placing code in DoDataExchange(), you should avoid changing the code inside the ClassWizard comment section. Otherwise, ClassWizard may become confused. You can safely add code after the ClassWizard section.

The DDV_ routines check m_bSaveAndValidate and perform the validation if it is set to TRUE. If validation should be performed, the DDV_ macro calls the CDataExchange class's PrepareCtrl() function (or PrepareEditCtrl() for Edit controls), passing the ID of the control to be validated. PrepareCtrl() and PrepareEditCtrl() find the HWND handle of the control associated with the passed ID and store it.

If the validation fails, this window handle is used to reset the focus to the control that caused the validation failure. When failing, the validation macro also calls the Fail() member variable, which throws a CUserException to escape the validation function and display a message box to inform the user as to why the validation failed.

The DDX_ and DDV_ routines can use the m_pDlgWnd member of the CDataExchange object to find the control associated with the specified ID by calling GetDlgItem(). GetDlgItem() is a CWnd function that returns a pointer to a child window of the parent window object (in this case, the dialog box) when passed a control ID. The ID for each of the controls is set in the GWL_ID window value of each control when it is created.

You can use the GetWindowLong() and SetWindowLong() functions to get and change this control ID value for any of the dialog box controls.

You can add your own custom DDX_ and DDV_ routines to handle custom data types. For most circumstances, though, it is easier just to add validation code directly to the DoDataExchange() function to perform the same transfer and validation functions on your custom data type.

Initializing the Dialog Box Controls

Obviously, the DoDataExchange() function must be called initially to load the default values from the mapped member variables into the controls.

This initialization can't be performed until the dialog box is open, because the controls don't exist yet. After the DoModal() function is entered and the dialog box is created, it enters a message loop to wait for interaction from the user. But the first message it receives before the box actually is displayed is a WM_INITDIALOG. This message tells the dialog box handler class that the dialog box and controls have been created but require initialization.

The base class implementation of CDialog handles this message and calls the UpdateData() function passing a FALSE value. UpdateData() is called to set up the starting conditions for a DoDataExchange() call; DoDataExchange() itself is never called directly (except from UpdateData() itself), because UpdateData() initializes the CDataExchange object and also handles the CUserException thrown by a validation rule violation. The FALSE parameter passed from the CDialog class's OnInitDialog() implementation ends up as the m_bSaveAndValidate member passed in the CDataExchange object to DoDataExchange().

In this way, the default OnInitDialog() implementation initializes the controls to their initial settings from the member variables. You can supply your own handler for OnInitDialog() in your derived class to extend to the default functionality.

When you add a handler for the WM_INITDIALOG message through the Add New Windows Message/Event Handler dialog box, your CDialog-derived class gains an OnInitDialog() function that looks like this:

```
BOOL CCustomDlg::OnInitDialog()
{
    CDialog::OnInitDialog();

    // TODO: Add extra initialization here
```

```
    return TRUE;   // return TRUE unless you set the focus to a control
                   // EXCEPTION: OCX Property Pages should return FALSE
}
```

You'll notice that `OnInitDialog()` first calls the base class implementation to initialize the controls. You then can add lines to perform your own specialized initialization. You may want to disable some of the dialog box controls, for example, if you are using the same dialog box in several circumstances. You can do this by passing `FALSE` to the `EnableWindow()` function of any of the control mapping classes (those mapped with `DDX_Control`) like this:

```
m_editCustom.EnableWindow(FALSE);
```

All these mapping classes are derived from `CWnd`, so you can perform any of the `CWnd` operations or any of the more specialized control-specific operations. In this example, `m_editCustom` is a `CEdit` object.

Alternatively, you may want to initialize more sophisticated controls, such as list or tree controls like this list control initialization (where `m_listCustom` is a `CListBox` object):

```
m_listCustom.AddString("Goodbye");
m_listCustom.AddString("Cruel");
m_listCustom.AddString("World");
```

For the examples shown above, ClassWizard generates code to map the `m_listCustom` and `m_editCustom` variables to the edit and list box controls in the dialog box. ClassWizard creates `DDX_Control` maps to initialize the control mapping variables, like this:

```
DDX_Control(pDX, IDC_CUSTOM_LIST, m_listCustom);
DDX_Control(pDX, IDC_CUSTOM_EDIT, m_editCustom);
```

If you don't call the base class implementation of `OnInitDialog()`, you should at least call `UpdateData(FALSE)` before using any of the mapped control classes in `DoDataExchange()`. This is because the first pass of the `DDX_Control` routines also is responsible for initializing the `HWND` member variables of the control mapping classes. If you try to use these mapping classes without setting the `HWND` member, they won't work and will cause an assertion.

You'll also notice that `OnInitDialog()` must return a Boolean value. If you return `TRUE`, Windows sets the input focus to the first control in the dialog box (as defined by the tab order). If you return `FALSE`, you must set the input focus to a specific control yourself from within `OnInitDialog()`.

Retrieving Data from the Controls

You can call UpdateData() passing TRUE to retrieve and validate the current data from the controls. Once again, DoDataExchange() is called from UpdateData()—this time, passing a TRUE value for the m_bSaveAndValidate flag.

UpdateData() returns a TRUE value if the validation succeeded or FALSE if there was a problem validating the data. You can call UpdateData() at any time during the life of the dialog box while the dialog box and controls are active.

UpdateData() often is useful when you are responding to messages from one control (such as a combo box) but want to use the result from that control to update another. By the same token, you may find that UpdateData() is too sweeping and performs validation before the user has completed the whole dialog box or overwrites values in controls or member variables.

For this reason, you occasionally will find that it is best to reserve the use of UpdateData() for initializing and finally closing the dialog box. You can perform more precise data transfers by using the control mapping classes (such as CEdit, CComboBox, CListBox, and so on). The following lines use a CEdit control mapped object (m_editCustom), for example, to retrieve the current contents of an Edit control:

```
CString strText;
m_editCustom.GetWindowText(strText);
```

You also can set the text by using the SetWindowText() function. Each of the control mapping classes has a large range of member functions to exchange and manipulate specific aspects of the control.

Responding to Control Notifications

Often you'll want to receive notifications from the controls. These messages are sent from the control to the parent dialog box after the user performs a specific action, such as changing the selection in a list box.

You can use the Message Maps tab in ClassWizard to insert the message map entries for these notifications. You can select the ID associated with the required control to display the notification messages available from that control. You then can add handler functions for these notifications by clicking Add Function (see Figure 5.6).

When you add the new message handler, a message handler function is generated in your dialog box class along with a message map macro specific to the type of message selected.

Figure 5.6

The Message Maps tab.

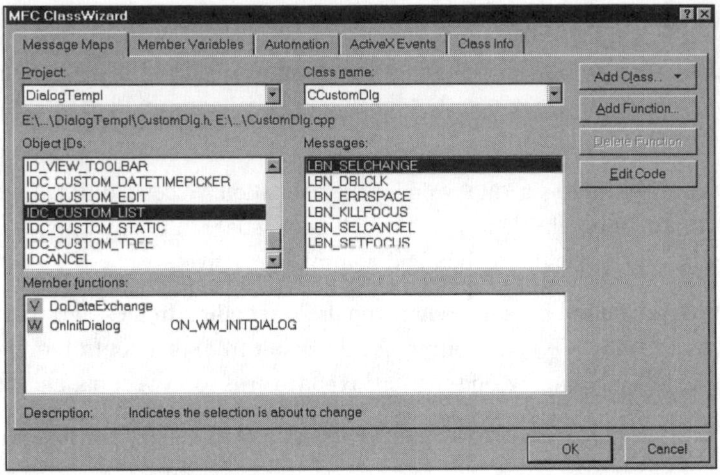

For example, a list box selection changed notification results in the following message map entry:

```
BEGIN_MESSAGE_MAP(CCustomDlg, CDialog)
    //{{AFX_MSG_MAP(CCustomDlg)
    ON_LBN_SELCHANGE(IDC_CUSTOM_LIST, OnSelchangeCustomList)
    //}}AFX_MSG_MAP
END_MESSAGE_MAP()
```

When you click on a valid list box line, the control posts the `LBN_SELCHANGE` notification to the parent dialog box. This message map entry then calls your `OnSelchangeCustomList()` implementation.

Your implementation then can directly manipulate other controls through their control mapping objects. For example, you may want to disable the `Edit` control if the first item in a list box is selected, but enable it otherwise with a notification handler function like this:

```
void CCustomDlg::OnSelchangeCustomList()
{
    BOOL bEnable = (m_listCustom.GetCurSel()==0);
    m_editCustom.EnableWindow(bEnable);
}
```

Your dialog box's message map entries can include all of the messages sent directly to the dialog box itself, such as `WM_SIZE` messages if the dialog box can be resized, or `WM_PAINT` if you want to implement some specialized rendering of your dialog box.

If you don't add specific handlers for these messages, they will be passed down to the CDialog base class (and then the CWnd class) to be handled by the dialog box's default implementations.

Dynamically Mapping Controls

Instead of using ClassWizard to generate member variable control mapping objects and their associated DDX_ routine entries, you may want to just create a local temporary map to a specific control. You can do this by using the GetDlgItem() function and casting the CWnd pointer returned to the specific control mapping class.

To change the text and disable the OK button using a dynamic map, for example, you might add the following code in response to a control notification message:

```
CButton* pOK = (CButton*)GetDlgItem(IDOK);
if (pOK)
{
    pOK->SetWindowText("Not OK");
    pOK->EnableWindow(FALSE);
}
```

If the control ID can't be found, GetDlgItem() returns a NULL value, which you should check; otherwise, you risk a crash caused by calling through a NULL pointer.

You can map any of the control mapping classes to their corresponding controls in this way, and then call any of the control map member functions to send messages that manipulate the control. The corresponding GetDlgCtrlID() function returns the ID associated with any particular control.

Responding to OK and Cancel

When you click OK or Cancel, the framework normally calls CDialog's OnOK() and OnCancel() virtual functions.

The default implementation for OnCancel() is fairly simple and just calls EndDialog() passing IDCANCEL. This closes the dialog box and returns IDCANCEL from the DoModal() function.

The default implementation for OnOk() calls UpdateData(TRUE) to save and validate the information from the dialog box controls. If the validation fails, the dialog box remains open. Otherwise, EndDialog() is called and passed IDOK to close the dialog box.

You can add your own BN_CLICKED handler function for the OK and Cancel buttons to perform specialized validation. If you do this, you normally will want to call UpdateData(TRUE) yourself before your specialized validation to do the standard DoDataExchange() transfer and validation. Then you might perform your own special

`OnOK()` code before calling `EndDialog()` to close the dialog box. If you were to call the base class implementation from your overridden handler function, you might find that you've lost control over when the `UpdateData()` and `EndDialog()` functions are called.

You can call `EndDialog()` at any time during a modal dialog box's lifetime to close the dialog box.

Derived Control Classes in Dialog Boxes

You can extend the functionality of any of the standard control classes by deriving your own classes and then use these extended controls in your dialog box.

This technique can let you subtly (or drastically) modify the behavior of the standard Windows controls. Many third-party software vendors supply libraries full of these extended classes to greatly enhance the control capabilities.

Creating a Derived Control

You can use ClassWizard to create a new class derived from an existing MFC control class by clicking the Add Class button and selecting New to display the New Class dialog box, as shown in Figure 5.7. After entering a name for your new control class, you can set the base class to one of the existing MFC control classes.

After you click OK, a new control class appears in your ClassView. This new class just consists of constructor/destructor functions and a message map derived from the existing MFC class.

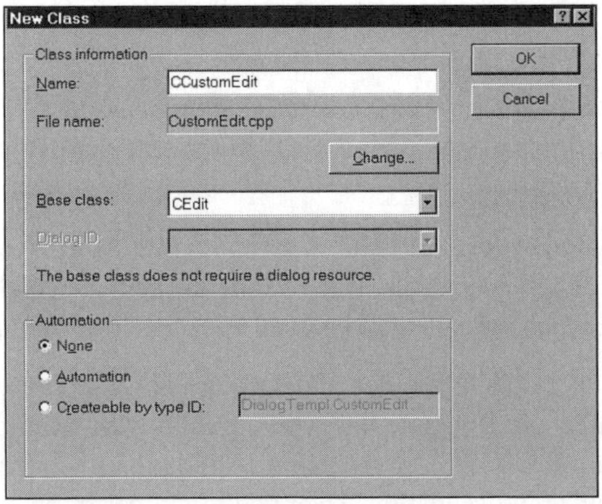

FIGURE 5.7

Deriving your own control class.

You don't have to use ClassWizard to generate this derived control class, but it certainly makes things easier, especially when you incorporate the new control in a dialog box, as you'll see later, in the section, "Using the Derived Control in a Dialog Box."

Instead of deriving your custom control from another MFC control class, you can derive it from CWnd directly and write a new control from scratch. This is a fairly laborious job, however, and you probably would find it more beneficial to create the control as an ActiveX control.

Customizing the Derived Control

You change or extend the default functionality of your new derived class by adding message-handler functions to intercept the Windows messages before they are passed to the base class.

You could create a custom Edit control that converts uppercase letters to lowercase letters, for example. You could add a handler to catch the WM_CHAR messages and change any uppercase characters to lowercase, like this:

```
void CCustomEdit::OnChar(UINT nChar, UINT nRepCnt, UINT nFlags)
{
    if (nChar>='A' && nChar<='Z')
        nChar+=32; // Make it lowercase

    DefWindowProc(WM_CHAR,nChar,MAKELONG(nRepCnt,nFlags));
}
```

If you examine the source code for the MFC control base classes, you'll notice that most call a CWnd function called Default(). This function just calls the DefWindowProc() function passing the details of the last message sent to the window. The DefWindowProc() function then implements the default processing for the Windows message.

Instead of calling the base class CEdit::OnChar() function, the preceding example calls DefWindowProc(), directly passing the modified nChar variable. You'll notice that a corresponding ON_WM_CHAR message-handler macro was added to your derived control's message map, like this:

```
BEGIN_MESSAGE_MAP(CCustomEdit, CEdit)
    //{{AFX_MSG_MAP(CCustomEdit)
    ON_WM_CHAR()
    //}}AFX_MSG_MAP
END_MESSAGE_MAP()
```

This macro is responsible for separating the nRepCnt and nFlags word values from the original LPARAM parameter sent in the WM_CHAR message. The MAKELONG macro merely recombines these values back into a single LPARAM parameter for the DefWindowProc() function.

5

CREATING AND
USING DIALOG
BOXES

You now have a simple customized `CEdit`-derived class that converts all uppercase characters to lowercase. Obviously, this is quite a simple customization, but by catching other Windows messages in this way, you can customize the standard controls beyond recognition.

Using the Derived Control in a Dialog Box

After you derive a custom control, you can use it in a dialog box as a mapped member variable (as you would any standard MFC control). If you used ClassWizard to create the derived control class, you'll find that your new class is available from the list of control variable types in the Add Member Variable dialog box, Figure 5.8 shows.

FIGURE 5.8

Mapping your derived class to a dialog box control.

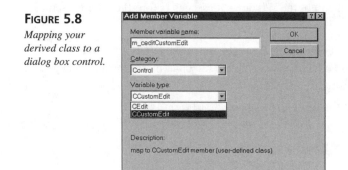

After clicking OK to map the new member variable to your derived class, you'll notice that ClassWizard adds the new member variable to the dialog box's class definition as normal:

```
CCustomEdit    m_ceditCustomEdit;
```

ClassWizard prompts you with a message box to remind you that you must manually add an `#include` for the custom control's class definition before the new member variable declaration. If your new derived class is defined in the `CustomEdit.h` module, for example, you should add the `#include` before your custom dialog box definition:

```
#include "CustomEdit.h"
```

You now should find that when your new dialog box is displayed, the behavior of your new customized control is changed accordingly.

You may not always want to use (or be able to) ClassWizard to map your derived control class to a particular control. If not, you should manually add the member variable declaration for your derived class into the dialog box class definition. You then can call `SubclassDlgItem()` from `OnInitDialog()` to hook your derived control class's message map into the specific Windows control.

The term *subclassing* in this circumstance is different from the object-oriented subclass term and really means *use this class to handle the Windows messages for this control.* This subclassing normally is performed during the first pass of DoDataExchange() from inside a DDX_Control() routine. You must pass the control ID and a valid parent dialog box pointer to SubclassDlgItem().

To manually subclass the new custom edit box (m_ceditCustomEdit), for example, your OnInitDialog() function may look like this:

```
BOOL CCustomDlg::OnInitDialog()
{
    CDialog::OnInitDialog();

    m_ceditCustomEdit.SubclassDlgItem(IDC_CUSTOM_EDIT,this);

    return TRUE;
}
```

> **Warning**
>
> You must call SubclassDlgItem() only after your dialog box and control window have valid window handles. This means placing the subclass call after the call to the OnInitDialog() base class.

If the subclassing succeeds, SubclassDlgItem() returns TRUE. If you already know the HWND handle of the control, you can call SubclassWindow() from the dialog box instead, passing the control's window handle. SubclassWindow() also returns TRUE if the subclassing was successful.

You can add an override for the PreSubclassWindow() virtual function in your derived control class. Your PreSubclassWindow() override is called just before the control's messages are hooked into your derived class's message map. This lets you perform dynamic changes to the subclassing procedure or just some last-minute initialization of your new control-handler class.

You can call UnsubclassWindow() to make the control revert to using the original default (CWnd) handler object.

Modeless Dialog Boxes

So far, you've seen how to create a modal dialog box using the DoModal() function. When a modal dialog box is displayed, the user is unable to interact with any other parts of the application's user interface until the dialog box is closed.

5

CREATING AND
USING DIALOG
BOXES

You may want to display a dialog box like a control palette, for example, or to provide feedback such as coordinates from a drawing operation. To do this, you'll need a modeless dialog box.

Modeless Dialog Box Resource Templates

You should consider a few differences when creating a dialog box template for a modeless dialog box.

First, you may not require OK and Cancel buttons for a modeless dialog box, because these usually are associated with modal operations. The user normally closes a modeless dialog box via the close box (a small x) in the upper-right corner of the dialog box. If you do decide to use OK and Cancel buttons, you must override the default OnOK() and OnCancel() message handlers and create your own that call DestroyWindow(). You must do this because the default functions call EndDialog(), which only closes a dialog box in modal operation.

Second, if you want your dialog box to be visible after creation, you should set the Visible flag in the dialog box's properties (on the More Styles tab). By setting this flag, you create the dialog box with the WS_VISIBLE style. Otherwise, the dialog box is created but remains invisible unless you call the dialog box's ShowWindow() function passing TRUE.

Figure 5.9 shows the Visible property for a modeless dialog box with no OK or Cancel button.

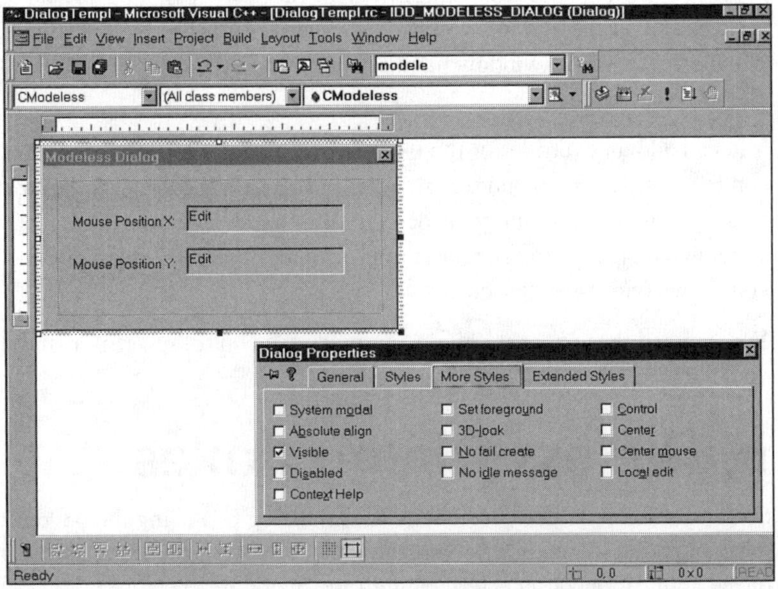

FIGURE 5.9

A typical modeless dialog box template and properties.

Creating and Destroying Modeless Dialog Boxes

You can create a modeless dialog box by using the `Create()` function instead of the `DoModal()` function to display the dialog box.

You should pass the dialog box's template ID (or a resource name) to `Create()` and optionally a pointer to a parent window. If the creation succeeds, `Create()` returns a `TRUE` value and the dialog box is created.

If you haven't specified the `WS_VISIBLE` flag on the dialog box template, nothing is displayed until you call `ShowWindow(TRUE)`. If you have set this flag, the modeless dialog box is displayed immediately.

The `Create()` function returns immediately after the dialog box is created—unlike the `DoModal()`. This has implications for the scope and lifetime of your modeless dialog box class. You should never declare your modeless dialog box as a local function variable as you might with a modal dialog box. If you do, when the function returns, the dialog box's handler object is destroyed, and the modeless dialog box is destroyed immediately by the `CDialog` base class destructor.

Instead, you can allocate the memory dynamically and, depending on your application requirements, track the memory or just let the dialog box delete itself when it is closed.

If you don't track the dialog box, for example, you may create an instance from a menu handler function like this:

```
void CDialogTemplDoc::OnShowdialogDisplaymodeless()
{
   CModeless* pDlgModeless = new CModeless;
   pDlgModeless->Create(CModeless::IDD);
}
```

If you allocate the memory in this way, you must delete it after the dialog box is closed to avoid memory leaks. When the dialog box is closed, the last message sent to your dialog box handler class is `WM_NCDESTROY`. The default implementation of `OnNcDestroy()` then does some housekeeping and finally calls the `PostNcDestroy()` virtual function. You can override this virtual function to delete the C++ `this` pointer to the dialog box object itself.

You can add an override to your `CDialog`-derived class by using the Add Virtual Function dialog box and then adding the `delete` statement like this:

```
void CModeless::PostNcDestroy()
{
    CDialog::PostNcDestroy();

    // Delete Ourselves
    delete this;
}
```

If you want to create the modeless dialog box from a memory-based dialog box template (instead of a resource), you can call the CreateIndirect() function passing a pointer to a DLGTEMPLATE structure or a global memory segment handle to memory containing the structures.

Tracking Modeless Dialog Boxes

The memory-tracking technique in the preceding section is very simplistic and allows the user to create many instances of the modeless dialog box, which probably is undesirable. Also, none of the instances can be destroyed from any objects in your code, because the dialog box object is the only thing that knows where its memory is located.

A more likely scenario is that your document would track the modeless dialog box. To do this, you would add a member variable to your document to track the dialog box so that you can destroy it from the document, and send it messages to provide feedback from other elements of the user interface. You also should place a pointer back to the parent document so that you can inform the document of when the user closes the dialog box.

You could add a pointer to your CDocument-derived class to the modeless dialog box handler class, for example, and initialize it through the constructor like this:

```
CModeless::CModeless(CDialogTemplDoc* pParent)
    : m_pParent(pParent)
{
  Create(CModeless::IDD);
}

void CModeless::PostNcDestroy()
{
  CDialog::PostNcDestroy();
  m_pParent->m_pDlgModeless = NULL;
  delete this;
}
```

You'll notice that the constructor also calls Create() so that the modeless dialog box is created and displayed when the object is constructed, thus simplifying the creation process from the calling object. The PostNcDestroy() function sets its pointer to the modeless dialog box equal to NULL, indicating that the dialog box is dead and gone.

The document then can track the modeless dialog box with its own member pointer and close it from a menu handler, as shown in these lines:

```
CDialogTemplDoc::CDialogTemplDoc() : m_pDlgModeless(NULL)
{
}
```

```
void CDialogTemplDoc::OnShowdialogDisplaymodeless()
{
  if (!m_pDlgModeless) m_pDlgModeless = new CModeless(this);
}

void CDialogTemplDoc::OnShowdialogClosemodeless()
{
  if (m_pDlgModeless) m_pDlgModeless->DestroyWindow();
}
```

This technique also lets you update the controls in the modeless dialog box from other application objects (such as a view to indicate the current mouse position) using dialog box member functions accessible through the document's pointer.

Only one instance of the modeless dialog box can be created at any one time, because the document menu handler function checks the pointer to see whether it already points to a modeless dialog box.

Dialog Bars

A *dialog bar* is a special form of modeless dialog box that encapsulates the functionality of a control bar (like a toolbar or status bar). This bar lets the modeless dialog box dock naturally to the window frames or float with a small frame.

You can create a dialog box template for a dialog bar like that for a normal modeless dialog box. The only difference is that you should set only the WS_CHILD (the Child setting in the Style combo box) and not the WS_VISIBLE flag (visible from the More Styles tab).

You then can construct the dialog bar using the MFC CDialogBar class (inherited from CControlbar) or your own derived class. The default constructor doesn't require any parameters. You normally would embed the CDialogBar object inside a frame window class, such as CMainFrame, as you might a toolbar or status bar.

After you construct the dialog bar, you can call its Create() function to create it. If you've embedded the dialog bar inside a frame window class, you probably will call the Create() function inside the frame's OnCreate() function, just like a toolbar.

The dialog bar's Create() function differs from a modeless dialog box's Create() function and is more like a control bar's Create(). The first parameter is a pointer to the parent window (normally a frame window). The second parameter is the ID of the dialog box template resource that you want to use for the dialog bar (or a resource name string). The third parameter lets you specify a docking/alignment style. This is just like a control bar style and can be a flag value such as CBRS_TOP, CBRS_LEFT, or CBRS_NOALIGN. You should supply an ID for the control bar as the last parameter to uniquely identify the dialog bar.

You can handle the control and messages of a dialog bar as you would a modeless dialog box. Dialog bars let you embed all the normal controls you can use on a dialog box template while letting you dock and reposition the bar like a toolbar.

Summary

It is a rare Visual C++ application programmer who never needs to use dialog boxes. Understanding the intricacies and MFC behavior will help you customize and use the dialog box mechanism.

In this chapter, you learned how to create dialog box templates via the Resource Editor. You also saw how (if necessary) you can create and use memory-based dialog box templates.

You saw how font size affects the dialog box control sizes and position, and how to convert between dialog box coordinates and screen coordinates.

You examined how to use the CDialog class to display ordinary modal dialog boxes and how CDialog exchanges data through the data-exchange mechanism. It is important to understand the sequence of events when initializing a dialog box, updating the individual controls during its lifetime, and then performing validation and data transfer from the controls after the user clicks OK to close it.

You can map simple, value-holding variables to these controls for simple transfer, or you can map control-mapping objects to enjoy all of the sophistication of the Windows controls and their messages via an MFC C++ class specific to the type of control.

You can extend these standard controls with your own derived controls to specialize the functionality offered by the standard controls. Then you can use ClassWizard to add your newly derived control classes to the dialog box.

You saw how the subclassing mechanism attaches your derived class's message map to a control so that it can catch and handle specific messages sent to and from the control.

Modeless dialog boxes let you leave the dialog box open for use while the user works with other parts of your application. This is a handy technique for providing extra floating controls or feedback panels.

Finally, you learned how to use dialog bars, which present an interface similar to a toolbar but offer controls from a dialog box template. These dialog bars allow easier design and positioning of the controls than is possible with an ordinary toolbar.

Working with Device Contexts and GDI Objects

by Jonathan Bates
and Mickey Williams

IN THIS CHAPTER

CHAPTER 6

The *device context,* or *DC*, is the interface between an application that draws graphics and text on a two-dimensional surface and the device drivers and hardware that render those graphics.

Applications can draw with the same *graphics device interface* (*GDI*) functions, regardless of the actual hardware used, to achieve a consistent image to the best capabilities of the device.

The device context also can be interrogated to inform an application of the capabilities and dimensions supported by the device. The device context can use this dimensional information to allow an application to render images in physical coordinate systems, such as inches and millimeters.

Device Contexts in MFC

Device contexts are Win32 objects; they are represented by HDC device-context handles. The MFC provides wrapper classes for the device-context object as the CDC base class, as well as a number of more specialized derived classes.

The basic CDC class is huge and supports all the GDI drawing functions, coordinate mapping functions, clipping functions, font-manipulation and rendering functions, printer-specific functions, path-tracking functions, and metafile-playing functions.

This section briefly covers the various device-context classes and when and how to use and obtain objects of these classes.

The CDC Class

The CDC base class encapsulates all the device-context functionality and drawing functions that use a Win32 HDC object. The actual Win32 device-context handle is accessible via the public m_hDC member. You can retrieve this handle with the device context's GetSafeHdc() function.

You often will be handed a pointer to an initialized CDC object from MFC framework functions, such as CView::OnDraw() and CView::OnBeginPrinting(). These objects are nicely clipped to the dimensions of the window client area so that the results of drawing functions do not appear outside the area of the window.

You also can obtain a pointer to a CDC object for the client area of a window using the CWnd::GetDC() function. If you want a CDC pointer for the entire window area (including the title bar and borders), you can use the CWnd::GetWindowDC() function instead. You can even get a pointer to the entire Windows desktop by calling GetDesktopWindow()->GetWindowDC().

A single Win32 device-context object may be shared among windows of the same registered window class (windows registered with `RegisterClass()`, not to be confused with Object-Oriented classes). The object may be part of a parent window's device context, or it may be private to the specific window.

After you obtain a pointer to the device context, you can perform a number of drawing operations or other device context–specific functions.

If you have obtained the pointer to a window's device context via `GetDC()`, however, you must call `CWnd::ReleaseDC()` on the same `CWnd` object to release that window's device context for other applications to use.

> **Warning**
>
> Some platforms, such as Windows 95, share a limited number of common device contexts among applications. You may be returned a `NULL` pointer if the `GetDC()` operation cannot succeed. You therefore should always call `ReleaseDC()` to alleviate this situation by freeing the device context for other applications.

You also can use the `GetDCEx()` function, which retrieves the device context and lets you pass a flag value to control the clipping of the returned device context.

The `CDC` constructor function constructs an uninitialized device context, where the `m_hDC` member is invalid. You then can initialize it in a number of ways. The `CreateDC()` function lets you initialize the device context for a specific device with a driver and device name. For example, you can create a device context for the screen like this:

```
CDC dc;
dc.CreateDC("Display", NULL, NULL, NULL);
```

Or you could create a device context for a printer like this:

```
CDC dc;
dc.CreateDC(NULL,"Cannon Bubble-Jet BJ330",NULL,NULL);
```

The last parameter lets you pass a `DEVMODE` structure that can be used to set specific initialization defaults. Otherwise, the driver's own defaults are used.

If you just want to retrieve information regarding the capabilities of a device, you can use the `CreateIC()` function and then use the `GetDeviceCaps()` function to retrieve the capabilities of the specified device. The `GetDeviceCaps()` function can be used with any device context, but a device context created with `CreateIC()` is a special cut-down device context that only supplies information about a device and cannot be used for drawing operations.

You can use the `CreateCompatibleDC()` function to create a memory device context compatible with a reference device context supplied as a pointer to a real `CDC` object. The memory device context is a memory-based representation of the actual device. If you pass `NULL` as the reference device context, a memory device context is created that is compatible with the screen.

The most common use of a memory device context is to create an offscreen buffer to perform screen capture copy operations via *bit-blitting* (fast memory copying), or to copy images from the memory device context onto the screen device context.

> **Note**
>
> Memory device contexts created with `CreateCompatibleDC()` are created with a minimum monochrome bitmap. If you want to copy color images between a memory device context and the screen, you must create a compatible memory bitmap.

If you have created a device context (instead of obtaining one via `GetDC()` or using a pointer to a framework device context), you should delete the Win32 device-context object after use by calling the `DeleteDC()` member function.

You also can initialize an uninitialized device context from an `HDC` device-context handle by using the `Attach()` function and passing the `HDC` handle. You can detach the handle by calling the corresponding `Detach()` function, which returns the old `HDC` handle.

If you just want to quickly create and attach a temporary `CDC` object to an `HDC` handle, the `FromHandle()` function allocates and attaches a `CDC` object for you, returning the pointer. You should not keep any references to this object, however, because the object is destroyed automatically the next time your program returns to the application's message loop by a call to `DeleteTempMap()`.

You can find the window associated with a device context by calling the device context's `GetWindow()` function, which returns a `CWnd` pointer to the associated window.

The device context maintains information relating to coordinate mapping modes, clipping rules, and the current GDI objects used for drawing (such as brushes, pens, bitmaps, and palettes). The details of these are discussed in subsequent sections. You can save and restore all these settings by using `SaveDC()` and `RestoreDC()`. When you call `SaveDC()`, an integer is returned identifying the saved instance (or zero, if it fails). You later can pass this integer to `RestoreDC()` to restore those saved defaults.

The `CClientDC` Class

You can use the `CClientDC` class to quickly connect a `CDC` object to a window by passing a pointer to the desired window. This is equivalent to constructing a `CDC` object and attaching an `HDC` handle obtained from a window with the Win32 `::GetDC()` function.

If the constructor succeeds, the `m_hWnd` member variable is initialized with the handle of the window donating the `HDC` handle; otherwise, a `CResourceException` is raised.

When the `CClientDC()` object falls out of scope or is deleted, the Win32 device context object (`HDC`) is released automatically.

For example, you might want to access the client device context of a view window from a view-based menu handler to draw a circle, like this:

```
void CCDCBaseView::OnDrawEllipse()
{
    CClientDC dcClient(this);
    dcClient.Ellipse(0,0,100,100);
}
```

You will notice that the C++ `this` pointer simply is passed to the `CClientDC` constructor to initialize the device context with the view's client device context. After initialization, the circle can be drawn in the view using the `CDC::Ellipse()` function. Finally, the destructor of the `CClientDC` object ensures that the view's `HDC` is released.

The `CPaintDC` Class

A `CPaintDC` object is constructed in response to a `WM_PAINT` message. If you add a handler for this message, you will see that ClassWizard automatically generates an `OnPaint()` handler starting with the following line:

```
CPaintDC dc(this); // device context for painting
```

The `CPaintDC` constructor automatically calls the `BeginPaint()` function for you. The `BeginPaint()` function is responsible for initializing a `PAINTSTRUCT` structure. `PAINTSTRUCT` holds information about the smallest rectangle that needs to be redrawn in response to an invalid portion of a window (usually when one window is moved to reveal a portion of the one behind it).

This process is automated in the constructor so that you can immediately use the device context to redraw the invalid area.

The `PAINTSTRUCT` information is available through the `m_ps` member, and the attached window handle can be found from the `m_hWnd` member.

When the object falls out of scope and its destructor is invoked, the `EndPaint()` function is called to complete the usual `WM_PAINT` procedure and mark the invalid region as valid.

The `CMetaFileDC` Class

A Windows *metafile* is a file that contains a list of GDI drawing instructions required to render an image in a device context. The metafile can be stored on disk, reloaded on another computer with different display capabilities, and redrawn by repeating the drawing instructions to produce a similar image.

You can always play a metafile using the CDC base class's `PlayMetaFile()` and passing a handle to a metafile object. The `CMetaFileDC` class lets you also create and record metafiles, however.

To record a metafile, you should construct a `CMetaFileDC` object. Then call `Create()` or `CreateEnhanced()` to create a simple or enhanced metafile on disk passing a filename and a reference device context for the enhanced metafile.

> **Note**
>
> Enhanced metafiles store palette and size information, so they can be reproduced more accurately on different computers with various display capabilities.

After creating the metafile, you can perform a number of drawing operations in the device context, just as you can in any other device context. The details of these drawing operations are stored in sequence in the metafile as you call each drawing function.

Finally, you should call `CMetaFileDC::Close()` or `CMetaFileDC::CloseEnhanced()` to close the metafile. The close functions return an `HMETAFILE` or `HENHMETAFILE` handle, which can be used by the Win32 metafile manipulation functions, such as `CopyMetaFile()` or `DeleteMetaFile()`.

Brushes and Pens

So far, you have examined the CDC base class and its derivatives and looked at how to obtain and create device contexts in various situations. The main purpose of a device context, however, is to provide a uniform drawing surface for the GDI rendering functions. These rendering functions use two main GDI objects to draw lines and filled areas. Lines are drawn with objects called *pens,* and filled areas are drawn with objects called *brushes.*

These two objects are represented at the Win32 level by the `HPEN` and `HBRUSH` handles. All of the GDI objects, including pens and brushes, are wrapped by the `CGdiObject`

Working with Device Contexts and GDI Objects

CHAPTER 6

151

6

WORKING WITH
DEVICE CONTEXTS
AND GDI OBJECTS

MFC base class. Although the `CGdiObject` is not strictly an abstract base class, you normally would construct one of its derived classes, such as `CPen` or `CBrush`.

`CGdiObject` is responsible for manipulating these handles and provides member functions such as `Attach()` and `Detach()` to attach the object to a GDI handle and detach it after use.

The handle itself is stored in the `m_hObject` member, which you can retrieve by calling the `CGdiObject::GetSafeHandle()` function. A static function (similar to the device contexts) called `FromHandle()` lets you dynamically create a `CGdiObject` for the duration of a Windows message. This object then is deleted by `DeleteTempMap()` when the thread returns to the Windows message loop.

You can find details about the underlying object by using the `GetObject()` function, which fills a structure with the object's attributes. The type of structure filled depends on the type of underlying object. The function itself just takes an `LPVOID` pointer to a buffer to receive the details and the size of the buffer.

The `DeleteObject()` function deletes the underlying GDI object from memory, so you are free to reuse the same `CGdiObject` by calling one of the derived classes' `Create()` functions to create another GDI object.

The `CGdiObject` class is extended by the MFC `CPen` and `CBrush` classes, which greatly simplify creating and manipulating these two drawing objects. This section shows you how these classes are constructed and used.

Pens and the `CPen` Class

Pens are used to draw lines, curves, and the boundaries of filled shapes, such as ellipses, polygons, and chords. You can create pens of various sizes, styles, and colors (even invisible pens for drawing shapes without outlines), and then select a pen into the device context and draw with it. You can select only one pen into a device context at any time. The old pen is swapped out automatically when you select a new pen.

There are two main pen types: cosmetic and geometric. The *cosmetic* pens are simple to create and quick to draw with. The *geometric* pens support more precise world units and let you use complex patterns and hatching effects in ways similar to brushes (described later in this chapter, in the section, "Brushes and the `CBrush` Class").

You can create a variety of pens using the `CPen` constructor. There are two versions of the constructor. You can pass one version of the constructor a set of style flags (as shown in Table 6.1), the pen width, and a `COLORREF` to indicate the color of the new pen.

TABLE 6.1   Simple Pen Styles

Style	Pen Description
PS_SOLID	Draws in a solid color.
PS_NULL	Uses an invisible pen.
PS_DASH	Draws in a dashed style.
PS_DASHDOT	Draws alternating dashes and dots.
PS_DOT	Draws in a dotted style.
PS_INSIDEFRAME	Draws lines inside filled areas.

Note

The PS_DASH, PS_DASHDOT, and PS_DOT styles only work with pens that have a width of 1 pixel; otherwise, they are drawn as solid lines.

The other constructor form lets you supply a pointer to a LOGBRUSH structure to initialize the attributes of a geometric pen. You also can pass an array of DWORD values to specify complex dot and dash patterns. You can use some additional flags to change the *mitering* (how lines are joined) and *end-cap styles* (how lines end). Table 6.2 explains these flags.

TABLE 6.2   Advanced Pen Styles

Style	Pen Description
PS_COSMETIC	Specifies a cosmetic pen.
PS_GEOMETRIC	Specifies a geometric pen.
PS_ALTERNATE	Sets every other pixel (only cosmetic pens).
PS_USERSTYLE	Uses the user-style DWORD array to create the dash-dot pattern.
PS_JOIN_ROUND	Draws round, joined lines.
PS_JOIN_BEVEL	Draws beveled, joined lines.
PS_JOIN_MITER	Draws mitered, joined lines.
PS_ENDCAP_FLAT	Makes the ends of lines flat.
PS_ENDCAP_ROUND	Makes the ends of lines round.
PS_ENDCAP_SQUARE	Makes the ends of lines square.

You also can construct an uninitialized pen by using the default constructor. You then initialize it by using `CreatePen()` and passing the same parameters as the two constructors for the `CPen` class, or by using `CreatePenIndirect()` and passing a pointer to a `LOGPEN` structure that holds the pen-initialization details.

Selecting Pens into the Device Context

After you create a pen, you must select it into a device context in order for the drawing functions to start using that pen. You can select all of the GDI objects by using the device context's overloaded `SelectObject()` function.

The `SelectObject()` function that accepts a `CPen` object returns a pointer to the currently selected `CPen` object. When you select your new object, the current object is deselected automatically. You should save the pointer to this deselected object to reselect it when you finish drawing with your pen.

> **Warning**
>
> You should never let a pen that is currently selected in a device context fall out of scope. You should reselect the original pen into the device context so that you safely can delete your pen after it is out of the device context.

You also can use the device context's `SaveDC()` and `RestoreDC()` functions to reselect the original pens and release your created pen. (Remember that this action also restores all the other GDI objects you have selected.)

Using Stock Pens

The operating system can lend out a number of common GDI objects to applications; these objects are called *stock objects*. These include a white pen, a black pen, and a null pen. You can select these straight into a device context by calling the `CDC::SelectStockObject()` function and passing the `WHITE_PEN`, `BLACK_PEN`, or `NULL_PEN` index values. As usual, the currently selected pen is returned from `SelectStockObject()`.

You also can use the pen's base class `CGdiObject::CreateStockObject()` function, passing the same index values to create a stock `CPen` object.

> **Note**
>
> From Windows NT 5 and Windows 98 onward, you can use a new stock pen object called a DC_PEN. You can change the color of the DC_PEN by using the global ::SetDCPenColor() function, passing the handle of the device context and a COLORREF value. When selected, the DC_PEN draws in the specified color. You also can retrieve this color by calling GetDCPenColor(). At the time of this writing, no equivalent CDC member function exists for this Win32 function.

Drawing with Pens

A number of rendering functions use just pens. Other functions use brushes to fill an area and pens to draw the outline of that area. You also can use the area-filling functions to draw only the outline of a shape by selecting a NULL brush.

The device context stores a current graphics cursor position, and many of the line-drawing functions use their starting point as the current graphics cursor position. You can change this position without drawing a line by using the device context's MoveTo() function. You can find the current graphics position from GetCurrentPosition().

The LineTo() function draws a line from the current position to the specified position and updates the graphics cursor to the specified endpoint.

You can use the Polyline() function to draw a number of lines from coordinates stored in an array of POINT structures, and you can use PolyPolyLine() to draw a number of independent line sections. The PolylineTo() function performs a task similar to Polyline() but also updates the current graphics cursor. You can plot a number of *B[as]ezier splines* (special type of curves) by using the PolyBezier() and PolyBezierTo() functions. The PolyDraw() function lets you draw a number of connected lines and B[as]ezier splines.

You can draw elliptical arcs by using Arc(), ArcTo(), and AngleArc(). You can set the device context's default direction for these arcs to clockwise or counterclockwise by passing AD_CLOCKWISE or AD_COUNTERCLOCKWISE to the device context's SetArcDirection() function. This value also affects the rendering of chords drawn with the Chord() function. You can find the current direction by the flag returned from GetArcDirection().

You can call the area-filling functions to outline the areas with the current pen, as discussed in the following sections about brushes.

The sample OnDraw() function shown in Listing 6.1 draws a number of shapes using different drawing functions in a variety of pens to produce the output shown in Figure 6.1.

Working with Device Contexts and GDI Objects

CHAPTER 6

155

6

WORKING WITH
DEVICE CONTEXTS
AND GDI OBJECTS

LISTING 6.1 An `OnDraw()` Function Using Different Pens to Create Graphics

```cpp
void CPensDemoView::OnDraw(CDC* pDC)
{
    CPen penRed(PS_SOLID,5,RGB(255,0,0));
    CPen penThick(PS_SOLID,10,RGB(0,0,255));
    CPen penDash(PS_DASH,1,RGB(0,128,0));
    CPen penDot(PS_DOT,1,RGB(255,0,255));
    CPen penDashDot(PS_DASHDOT,1,RGB(0,0,0));

    CRect rcClient;
    GetClientRect(&rcClient);
    int nSaved = pDC->SaveDC();
    pDC->SelectStockObject(NULL_BRUSH); // No Area Filling

    for(int i=0;i<rcClient.Height()/6;i++)
    {
        int x=i%3,y=((i%6)/3);
        int w=rcClient.Width()/3, h=rcClient.Height()/2;
        CRect rcDrw(x*w,y*h,x*w+w,y*h+h);
        rcDrw.DeflateRect(CSize(i,i));
        switch(i%6)
        {
            case 0:
                pDC->SelectObject(&penThick);
                pDC->MoveTo(rcDrw.TopLeft());
                pDC->LineTo(rcDrw.BottomRight());
                pDC->MoveTo(rcDrw.right,rcDrw.top);
                pDC->LineTo(rcDrw.left,rcDrw.bottom);
                break;
            case 1:
                pDC->SelectObject(&penRed);
                pDC->Ellipse(rcDrw);
                break;
            case 2:
            {
                POINT pts[] = {
                    {(short)rcDrw.left,(short)rcDrw.bottom},
                    {(short)rcDrw.right,(short)rcDrw.bottom},
                    {(short)rcDrw.left+rcDrw.Width()/2,
                        (short)rcDrw.top},
                    {(short)rcDrw.left,(short)rcDrw.bottom}};
                pDC->SelectObject(&penDash);
                pDC->Polyline(pts,sizeof(pts)/sizeof(POINT));
                break;
            }
            case 3:
                pDC->SelectObject(&penDot);
                pDC->Rectangle(rcDrw);
                break;
```

continues

LISTING 6.1   continued

```
        case 4:
            pDC->SelectObject(&penDashDot);
            pDC->Pie(rcDrw,CPoint(rcDrw.right,rcDrw.top),
                        rcDrw.BottomRight());
            break;
        case 5:
            pDC->SelectStockObject(BLACK_PEN);
            pDC->Chord(rcDrw,rcDrw.TopLeft(),
                        rcDrw.BottomRight());
            break;
        }
    }
    pDC->RestoreDC(nSaved);
}
```

FIGURE 6.1

*Drawing with vari-
ous pen styles.*

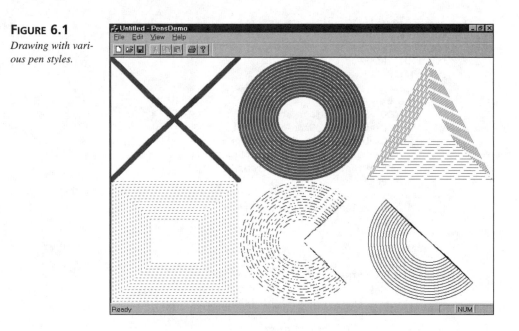

Brushes and the CBrush Class

Whereas pens are used to draw lines, brushes are used to fill areas and shapes. The
CBrush class wraps the GDI brush object and, like other MFC GDI wrapper classes, is
derived from the CGdiObject base class.

You can create brushes that fill an area with a solid color, a pattern from a bitmap, or a
hatching scheme. You can use one of three constructor functions to construct brushes initialized with one of these filling techniques. One form lets you pass a COLORREF value for

a solid-color brush. Another lets you pass a pointer to a `CBitmap` object to create a filling pattern. The third form lets you pass an index describing a hatching technique (as shown in Table 6.3) and a `COLORREF` value to specify the hatching-pattern color.

TABLE 6.3   Brush Hatching-Pattern Flags

Style	*Brush Hatching*
HS_DIAGCROSS	Diagonal crisscross
HS_CROSS	Horizontal crisscross
HS_HORIZONTAL	Horizontal lines
HS_VERTICAL	Vertical lines
HS_FDIAGONAL	Bottom-left to top-right lines
HS_BDIAGONAL	Top-left to bottom-right lines

You can use the default constructor and then one of the creation functions—such as `CreateSolidBrush()`, `CreateHatchBrush()`, or `CreatePatternBrush()`—to create the GDI brush object. The `CreateBrushIndirect()` function lets you initialize and pass a pointer to a `LOGBRUSH` structure to create the brush. You can set the style from a number of flag values to indicate what sort of brush you want with the `lbStyle` member of `LOGBRUSH`. The other members are `lbColor` for the desired color and `lbHatch` to specify any hatching-style flags (remember that the same structure is used with geometric pens).

You can use the `CreateDIBPatternBrush()` creation function to create a patterned brush from a *device-independent bitmap* (*DIB*). You can use a `CreateSysColorbrush()` function to create a brush initialized with one of the current system colors specified by an index value.

Warning

Although Windows NT lets you create patterned brushes using any size of bitmap (bigger or equal to 8×8 pixels), Windows 95/98 can create only 8×8 pixel brushes; larger bitmaps are truncated to the top 8×8 pixels.

Selecting Brushes into the Device Context

You can select a brush into a device context in the same way you would a pen. The device context's `SelectObject()` function has an overload that accepts a pointer to a `CBrush` object and returns the previously selected `CBrush` object.

After you select your new brush, it can use any of the drawing functions that draw filled shapes. As with the pen, you must ensure that the brush is selected out of the device context before it falls out of scope or is deleted.

Using Stock Brushes

You can select a number of stock brushes into a device context with the SelectStockObject() function, as Table 6.4 shows.

TABLE 6.4   Stock Brush Objects

Stock Object Flag	*Brush Description*
WHITE_BRUSH	White
LT_GRAY_BRUSH	Light gray
GRAY_BRUSH	Gray
DKGRAY_BRUSH	Dark gray
BLACK_BRUSH	Black
HOLLOW_BRUSH, NULL_BRUSH	Transparent, like the NULL pen

You also can use the CGdiObject base class's CreateStockObject() function to create a CBrush object initialized from a stock object flag.

Drawing with Brushes

You can use a number of device-context member functions with a brush to draw filled shapes. These shapes are outlined with the currently selected pen.

Some functions, such as FillRect(), let you pass a CBrush object by pointer to draw with that brush. Other functions draw a rectangle from a COLORREF value, such as FillSolidRect(). Most functions, however, use the currently selected brush, such as the Rectangle() function. FillRect(), Rectangle(), and FillSolidRect() all render a filled rectangle from a set of rectangle coordinates. The RoundRect() function lets you draw rectangles with rounded corners.

You can draw filled polygons by using the Polygon() or PolyPolygon() function, which draws a single polygon or number of filled polygons, respectively. These two functions are similar to the Polyline() functions, because they take an array of POINT variables to define the polygon's vertices. When drawing polygons, you can specify one of two filling techniques: *winding* or *alternate.* These techniques affect which areas of a crisscrossing polygon are designated as filled. You can set these modes by using the SetPolyFillMode() function and passing the WINDING or ALTERNATE flag value.

Working with Device Contexts and GDI Objects

CHAPTER 6

159

6

WORKING WITH
DEVICE CONTEXTS
AND GDI OBJECTS

You can draw circles and ellipses using the `Ellipse()` function, pie segments using `Pie()`, and chord sections with the `Chord()` function.

The `FloodFill()` function lets you fill an area bounded by a specified color with the current brush. You can use `ExtFloodFill()` to fill an area bounded by a specific color or fill an area of a specific color with the current brush.

MFC Classes for GDI Operations

Many of the GDI functions use sophisticated MFC helper classes that let you specify coordinates in a two-dimensional coordinate system. These classes also let you manipulate and perform arithmetic operations on sets of coordinates.

The `CPoint`, `CSize`, and `CRect` classes can hold point coordinates, size coordinates, or rectangles, respectively. They wrap `POINT`, `SIZE`, and `RECT` structures and can be cast into each of these structures. Overloaded operator functions accept these structures as parameters, so arithmetic between the various classes can be performed interchangeably.

This section examines these MFC coordinate-manipulation and storage classes in more detail.

The `CPoint` Class

The `CPoint` class wraps a `POINT` structure to hold a single two-dimensional coordinate specified by its x and y member variables. Many of the drawing functions can use `CPoint` objects as parameters.

You can construct a `CPoint` object from two integers specifying the x and y coordinates, another `CPoint` object, a `SIZE` structure, or a `DWORD` value (using the low and high words). You can call the `Offset()` function to add an offset value to move the specified coordinates passing x and y coordinates, another `CPoint` object, or a `SIZE` structure.

Mostly, however, you probably would use the `CPoint`'s operator overloads to add, subtract, or compare two `CPoint` objects. Many of these operators let you specify `POINT`, `SIZE`, or `RECT` structures as parameters and return `SIZE`, `POINT`, or `BOOL` values as appropriate.

Table 6.5 lists the available `CPoint` operator functions.

TABLE 6.5 CPoint Operator Overload Functions

Operator	Description
=	Copies the POINT.
+=	Adds a POINT or SIZE value to the CPoint object.
-=	Subtracts a POINT or SIZE value from the CPoint object.
+	Adds POINT, SIZE, or RECT values.
-	Subtracts POINT, SIZE, or RECT values.
==	Compares for equality with another POINT or CPoint.
!=	Compares for inequality with another POINT or CPoint.

The CSize Class

The CSize class wraps a SIZE structure. This structure stores a two-dimensional size as cx and cy integer members, which are declared as public accessible members. You can construct a CSize object from two integers, a SIZE structure, a POINT structure, or a DWORD value.

You will find that many of the CPoint and CRect functions and operators can take SIZE structure objects as parameters for arithmetic manipulation. Some of the GDI and Windows functions require SIZE structures—usually to specify the size of an object (such as a window).

The CSize class implements the operators listed in Table 6.6.

TABLE 6.6 CSize Operator Overload Functions

Operator	Description
=	Copies the SIZE.
+=	Adds a SIZE value.
-=	Subtracts a SIZE value.
+	Adds POINT, SIZE, or RECT values.
-	Subtracts POINT, SIZE, or RECT values.
==	Compares for equality with another SIZE or CSize object.
!=	Compares for inequality with another SIZE or CSize object.

The CRect Class

CRect is probably the most sophisticated of the coordinate storing classes. CRect wraps a RECT structure that exposes its coordinates as two coordinate pairs. These pairs correspond to the top-left and bottom-right points in a rectangle and are accessible from the RECT structure as the top, left, bottom, and right member integers.

You also can obtain these coordinates as CPoint objects returned by the TopLeft() and BottomRight() functions. The CenterPoint() function is quite useful, because it returns a CPoint object representing the center of the rectangle. You can find the width and height of the rectangle by using the Width() and Height() functions, and you can find the size represented as the CSize object returned from the Size() function.

You can increase and decrease the size of the rectangle by using the InflateRect() and DeflateRect() functions, which are overloaded to take a variety of parameter types. The OffsetRect() function lets you move the position of the rectangle by an amount specified by a SIZE, POINT, or pair of integers.

Intersection, union, and subtraction functions also are provided by IntersectRect(), UnionRect(), and SubtractRect().

- IntersectRect() makes the current CRect object the intersection rectangle of two source rectangles (where they overlap), as shown in Figure 6.2; the resulting CRect object is shaded.

FIGURE 6.2
Determining the intersection of two rectangles.

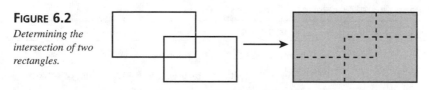

- UnionRect() makes the CRect object the union of two source rectangles (the smallest rectangle that encloses both), as shown in Figure 6.3; the resulting CRect object is shaded.

FIGURE 6.3
Determining the union of two rectangles.

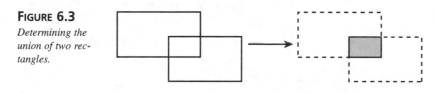

- SubtractRect() sets its first RECT parameter's coordinates to the smallest rectangle that is not intersected by two overlapping rectangles (where the second rectangle encloses the first), as shown in Figure 6.4; the resulting CRect object is shaded.

FIGURE 6.4

Subtracting one rectangle from another.

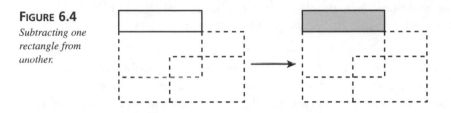

Each of these functions requires that you previously called NormalizeRect(). NormalizeRect() ensures that the top-left point coordinates are lower than the bottom-right coordinates; if they are not, it sets them to be so. You may find that some operations leave the coordinates in a condition where the width or height calculations may give negative results. If this is the case, you can call NormalizeRect() to fix them.

If you are implementing drag and drop or want to perform bounds checking, you will find the PtInRect() member function useful. This returns TRUE if the specified point lies within the rectangle.

Several operator overload functions are available, as Table 6.7 shows.

TABLE 6.7 CRect Operator Overload Functions

Operator	Description
=	Copies the RECT.
+=	Offsets the rectangle by a POINT or SIZE value, or inflates each side by the coordinates of a RECT.
-=	Offsets or deflates the rectangle.
+	Offsets or inflates the rectangle, returning a RECT result.
-	Offsets or deflates the rectangle, returning a RECT result.
&=	Sets the rectangle to the intersection of the rectangle's current value, and another RECT or CRect.
|=	Sets the rectangle to the union of the rectangle's current value, and another RECT or CRect.
&	Returns the intersection.
|	Returns the union.
==	Compares for equality with another RECT or CRect.
!=	Compares for inequality with another RECT or CRect.

The `CRgn` Class and Clipping

The `CRgn` class is another `CgdiObject`-derived GDI object wrapper class that wraps the `HRGN` GDI handle. You can retrieve the `HRGN` handle by casting a `CRgn` object.

Regions are used primarily for clipping; you can select a region into a device context by using the device context's `SelectObject()` or `SelectClipRegion()` function. Thereafter, all GDI-rendering functions performed in the device context are clipped to the specified region.

You can specify complex regions that have overlapped borders, simple regions that do not have overlapping borders, or null regions where there is no specified region data. Many of the functions use and return the type of region specified by the `COMPLEXREGION`, `SIMPLEREGION`, and `NULLREGION` flag values. If an error occurs when combining or selecting regions, the `ERROR` flag is returned.

To create an initialized `CRgn` object, you must construct it by using the default `CRgn` constructor and then use one of the creation functions, such as `CreateRectRgn()` for rectangles, `CreateEllipticRgn()` for ellipses, `CreatePolygonRgn()` for polygons, or `CreateRoundRgn()` for rounded rectangles. Other functions are available that initialize from structures or create multiple polygons.

You can combine two regions by using the `CombineRgn()` function. The two source regions specified by pointers to `CRgn` objects are combined using a logic operation specified by a flag as the last parameter. This flag value can be any one of the following: `RGN_AND`, `RGN_OR`, `RGN_XOR`, `RGN_COPY`, or `RGN_DIFF` (the non-overlapping areas).

By using the `PtInRegion()` or `RectInRegion()` function, you can perform complex bound checking.

You can use the `OffsetRgn()` function to move a region and `CopyRgn()` to copy one region from another. You can test for equivalence between two regions with the `EqualRegion()` function.

Warning

You should bear in mind that regions (especially complex regions) can be fairly memory hungry and are limited to a maximum coordinate displacement of 32,767 pixels. Like other GDI objects, regions can be deleted after you use them by using the `DeleteObject()` function, which is called automatically when a `CRgn` object is deleted.

Working with Fonts

Much of Windows graphical output consists of text in a variety of fonts. Like pens, brushes, and regions, a GDI handle (HFONT) also represents font object instances.

The fonts and their related rendering data for each character make a considerable memory footprint for each instance of a font object. To reduce the overhead of memory and processing time required to load, initialize, and store the details for each instance of a font, Windows uses a font mapper.

Whenever a new font object is created, the font mapper looks for the nearest match of the requested characteristics from the list of installed fonts. It then constructs a font that is as close as possible to the one you have requested.

Fonts and the CFont Class

The MFC CFont class is a wrapper for the HFONT GDI object. To create a font using CFont, you first must construct a CFont object with the default constructor and then call one of the font-creation routines.

The quickest and easiest way to create a font is with CFont's CreatePointFont() function. You can pass a desired point size (in tenths of a point), a typeface name, and optionally a reference device context pointer to create the font. You should pass a pointer to the device context to create an accurate point-size match. Otherwise, the default screen device context is used (which is inaccurate when printing).

You also can use CreatePointFontIndirect() to create a font from the lfHeight member set in a LOGFONT structure.

A much more sophisticated font-creation function is CreateFont(), which lets you specify a huge number of required attributes for the font. These attributes specify the width, height, escapement, orientation, weight, effects, character set, clipping, rendering precision, font family, pitch, and typeface with its 14 parameters. The orientation and escapement attributes are closely related. The orientation attribute refers to the rotation angle of each individual character. The escapement is similar, but refers to the entire line of text. On Windows 95/98, these values must be set to the same value. On Windows NT/2000, these values may be set independently of each other.

Each of these parameters has several associated flag values to hone the type of font required. The font mapper then uses all these attributes to try to find the best matching font for the requested specifications.

You can initialize the LOGFONT structure with these specifications and pass a pointer to the LOGFONT structure to the CreateFontIndirect() function, which then creates a font

Working with Device Contexts and GDI Objects

CHAPTER 6

165

6

WORKING WITH
DEVICE CONTEXTS
AND GDI OBJECTS

and returns a font handle. This creation form is especially useful when you have enumerated the currently installed fonts with one of the font-enumeration functions, such as EnumFonts(). The callback functions for these enumerators are passed a pointer to a LOGFONT structure so that you can create a font object instance directly from it.

After a LOGFONT structure is initialized, you can fill it with the details of a font by using the GetLogFont() function.

The CFont class also has an HFONT operator to retrieve the underlying GDI handle when cast as an HFONT.

Selecting Fonts into the Device Context

As with the other GDI objects, a font must be selected into the device context before you can use it, and the previously selected font is restored after use. You must ensure that the font is not currently selected in a device context when it is deleted.

After the font is selected, it is used whenever any of the text-output functions are called.

Stock Fonts

A number of stock fonts can be selected with the SelectStockObject() function, as Table 6.8 shows.

TABLE 6.8 Stock Font Objects

Stock Object Flag	Font Description
ANSI_FIXED_FONT	ANSI fixed pitch
ANSI_VAR_FONT	ANSI variable pitch
SYSTEM_FONT	Current Windows system font
DEVICE_DEFAULT_FONT	Device's default font
OEM_FIXED_FONT	OEM's fixed-pitch font

Device Context Font Interrogation Functions

The device context has a number of member functions that let you retrieve information regarding the currently selected font.

With variable-pitch fonts, you may need to know about the average and specific widths of characters when rendered in a specific device context. You can use the GetCharWidth() function to fill an array with the widths of individual characters for non-TrueType fonts or GetABCCharWidths() for TrueType fonts.

You can find the average widths, height, and many other specific elements of a font from its TEXTMETRICS structure. The device context's GetOutputTextMetrics() function fills such a structure for you with details of the currently selected font.

You can retrieve the typeface name of the currently selected font by calling the GetTextFace() function and passing a CString object by reference to receive the typeface name.

Kerning pairs specify the width between two characters placed together in a variable-pitch font. These values often may be negative, because characters such as l and i are thin and can be placed close together. The GetKerningPairs() function can fill an array of KERNINGPAIR structures to retrieve this information.

The GetOutlineTextMetrics() function returns an array of OUTLINETEXTMETRICS structures. These structures are full of information about TrueType fonts.

Text-Rendering Functions

Many text-rendering functions are available that perform slightly different jobs in different circumstances. The simplest is TextOut(), which lets you specify an x and y coordinate and a CString holding the text to display.

The device context's text-alignment flags adjust the position of the text relative to the given coordinate. You can adjust these flags by using the SetTextAlign() function and passing a combination of the alignment flags, such as TA_TOP, TA_CENTER, TA_RIGHT, TA_LEFT, TA_BASELINE, and TA_BOTTOM. You can combine this flag value with the TA_NOUPDATECP and TA_UPDATECP to not update or update the current graphic cursor position after the text rendering. The corresponding GetTextAlign() returns the current flag settings.

You can change the color of the rendered text with the device context's SetTextColor() and SetBkColor() functions to set the foreground and background colors to a specified COLORREF value. You can make the background behind the text transparent or opaque by passing the TRANSPARENT or OPAQUE flag to the SetBkMode() function.

The ExtTextOut() function lets you clip text to a specified rectangle by using the ETO_CLIPPED flag. You can supply an array of spacing values to separate the individual character cells to ExtTextOut().

You can use TabbedTextout() to display a text string with embedded tab characters. These tabs then are expanded to positions specified by an array of consecutive tab positions relative to a specified origin.

Working with Device Contexts and GDI Objects

CHAPTER 6

167

6

WORKING WITH
DEVICE CONTEXTS
AND GDI OBJECTS

The `DrawText()` function performs some quite advanced text formatting, such as word wrapping and justification. You can pass a combination of formatting flag values, such as `DT_WORDBREAK`, `DT_LEFT`, `DT_RIGHT`, `DT_TOP`, and `DT_CENTER` (and many others).

You can call the `GrayString()` function to draw grayed text using a specific graying brush and optionally pass a pointer to your own text-rendering function.

You often will want to know the dimensions required by a text string without actually rendering it. You can find these dimensions by using the `GetOutputTextExtent()`, `GetTabbedTextExtent()`, or `GetOutputTabbedTextExtent()` function. These functions use the device context to calculate and return a `CSize` object holding the size required to render the text using the currently selected font and device-context settings.

Creating and Loading Bitmaps

Images are used extensively in Windows; a bitmap instance is another low-level GDI object represented by the `HBITMAP` handle.

Before you can use bitmaps in your application, you generally create a number of bitmap resources that are bound with your `.EXE` or `.DLL` when linked. These bitmaps then are loaded from the current module ready for drawing.

> **Note**
>
> You should not confuse the "loading" terminology used here and expressed by the `LoadBitmap()` function with loading and saving to specific disk files. However, DIBs may be stored in individual disk files. (DIBs are discussed later in this chapter in the "Creating a Device-Independent Bitmap Class" section.) The `LoadBitmap()` function loads bitmap resources only from the application's executable module and *dynamic link libraries* (*DLLs*).

Creating a Bitmap Resource with the Resource Editor

You can create a new bitmap resource from the Insert Resource dialog box in the Visual Studio Resource Editor. You can change the size, the resource ID, and the source bitmap filename from the Bitmap Properties dialog box.

You then can draw the bitmap using the Resource Editor drawing tools, as Figure 6.5 shows.

FIGURE 6.5

Editing a bitmap resource.

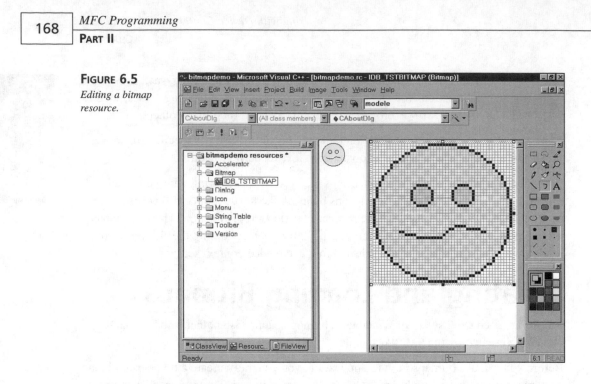

You also can open BMP, JPEG, GIF, and many other common formats and copy and paste the image into a new bitmap.

When you compile the program, the bitmap is bundled into the resulting executable file.

Loading a Bitmap

Before you can use a bitmap, you must load the bitmap resource from the executable file. The CBitmap class is another CgdiObject-derived class, and it wraps the HBITMAP GDI object handle. You can construct a CBitmap object using its default constructor and then load a specific bitmap by calling its LoadBitmap() function, passing a resource ID (or resource name) that identifies the specific bitmap.

If the bitmap is found and loaded from the executable module, LoadBitmap() returns a TRUE value, and the HBITMAP handle is valid. You also can use the LoadMappedBitmap() function to load color-mapped bitmaps and specify a set of COLORMAP structures to define the remapped COLORREF values.

You can load a system stock bitmap with the LoadOEMBitmap() function passing a flag value that loads a few standard bitmaps.

Working with Device Contexts and GDI Objects

CHAPTER 6

169

6

WORKING WITH
DEVICE CONTEXTS
AND GDI OBJECTS

Creating Bitmaps

You can create a bitmap image without an associated resource by using one of the bitmap-creation functions. The `CreateBitmap()` function lets you create a bitmap in memory and specify its width, height, number of bit planes (color planes), number of color bits per pixel, and (optionally) an array of short values to initialize the bitmap image.

> **Warning**
>
> When specifying the color planes or color bits, you should set one or the other to 1; otherwise, you will get a multiple of these values!

The `CreateBitmapIndirect()` function lets you specify these values in a `BITMAP` structure instead of through parameter settings.

You should use the `CreateCompatibleBitmap()` function to create bitmaps that are compatible with specific devices (such as the current display configuration). To do this, you must pass a pointer to a valid device context along with a width and height. This creates a bitmap that has a compatible color depth with a device attached to the device context.

Drawing with Bitmaps

After you create a GDI bitmap object you can draw with it using a memory device context and then copy it to a destination device context. A bitmap is copied to a device using the *Bit Block Transfer* functions. These functions are commonly known as *BitBlt* (pronounced bit-blit) functions. These functions, such as `BitBlt()` and `StretchBlt()` are discussed in the next section.

As you read earlier in this chapter, you can create a compatible memory device context by using the `CreateCompatibleDC()` function.

When a memory device context is created, it is initialized with a monochrome bitmap. You then should select your custom bitmap into the device context (saving the pointer returned to the old bitmap) and perform the copy into the screen device context. After you finish, you must select the original monochrome bitmap back into the device context (thus deselecting your custom bitmap) before deleting the `CBitmap` object or calling `DeleteObject()` to destroy the GDI bitmap object.

Bitmap Copying

After you select a valid bitmap into a memory-based device context, you can use the BitBlt() device-context function to transfer all or part of the image onto a display-based (or printer-based) device context. BitBlt() lets you specify the source device context (your memory DC), the source coordinates to copy from (relative to the memory DC), the destination coordinates (relative to the destination DC), and the width and height describing the area to copy.

You also can specify a raster operation flag that can be used to invert the image during copying, merge the source with the destination image, just copy the source to the destination, or perform a number of other logical operations between the source and destination during the copy.

The StretchBlt() function lets you specify a source width and height, as well as a destination width and height. The image then expands or shrinks to fit the destination width and height. This method provides a fast and easy way to perform zoom operations. You can change the technique used to copy the image area by passing a flag value to the SetStretchBltMode() function. This lets you perform color-averaging stretch copies that give a better image representation (at the expense of speed) or allow a number of different stretching techniques.

You can use the MaskBlt() function to perform an image copy from a source device context through the holes in a mask provided by a monochrome bitmap into the destination device context.

The following code fragment shows how to create a memory device context, load a resource bitmap, and select it into the memory device context. Then you use StretchBlt() to stretch it so that it fills the view.

```
void CBitmapdemoView::OnDraw(CDC* pDC)
{
    // Create a compatible memory device context
    CDC dcMemory;
    dcMemory.CreateCompatibleDC(pDC);

    // Load and select the bitmap resource
    CBitmap bmImage;
    bmImage.LoadBitmap(IDB_TSTBITMAP);
    CBitmap *pbmOriginal = dcMemory.SelectObject(&bmImage);

    CRect rcClient;
    GetClientRect(rcClient);

    pDC->StretchBlt(0,0,rcClient.Width(),rcClient.Height(),
        &dcMemory,0,0,48,48,SRCCOPY);

    pDC->SelectObject(pbmOriginal);
}
```

Creating a Device-Independent Bitmap Class

The bitmaps discussed so far are called *device-dependent bitmaps* because they rely on the current display device context for their palette colors and are dependent on the current display resolution to determine the displayed size.

A *device-independent bitmap* (*DIB*) not only stores the bitmap image but also uses a BITMAPINFO structure to store the color depth, sizing information, and colors. The first part of the structure consists of one of the various header structures followed by an array of RGBQUAD structures that store the colors used in the bitmap. You can create a BITMAPINFO and associate it with a bitmap image to form a DIB.

After you create a DIB, you can transfer it onto different machines and display the same image, represented to the best capabilities of various devices while preserving the original size and colors.

This section shows some of the steps required to create, display, and store a DIB. The sample code builds a DIB class derived from CBitmap to extend the bitmap functionality into a DIB.

Creating a DIB

To create a DIB, you first must initialize a BITMAPINFOHEADER structure or one of its more modern counterparts, such as the BITMAPV5HEADER (which requires Windows NT5 or Windows 98).

> **Warning**
>
> The BITMAPV5HEADER lets you specify advanced compression techniques such as JPEG. To support this capability, you need Windows NT 5 or Windows 98. If your DIB will be used on older platforms, you should use BITMAPV4HEADER for Windows NT 4 or Windows 95, or BITMAPINFOHEADER for older platforms.

You can initialize a number of member variables in the DIB header (BITMAPINFOHEADER structure) to specify the DIB width, height, number of bit planes, bits per pixel, compression technique, pixels per meter in the x and y dimensions, and the actual number of colors used. The more modern versions of the BITMAPINFOHEADER structure (such as BITMAPV5HEADER) offer even more members to specify advanced compression techniques and gamma corrections.

Specifying the pixels per meter provides an important piece of information that lets you render the DIB to the correct size of various devices. By using the information about the resolution of the device, or by using one of the device-context mapping modes (especially the MM_LOMETRIC or MM_HIMETRIC mode), you can render the image to the correct size.

After specifying the header details, you should initialize the RGBQUAD structures that specify each color used in the bitmap. You may want to use the colors from the palette selected in a specific device context by using the SetDIBColorTable() function. This function fills the RGBQUAD array for you from the specified device-context handle.

The following code fragment shows a class definition for a DIB manipulation class:

```
class CDIB : public CObject
{
public:
    CDIB();
    virtual ~CDIB();

    BOOL CreateDIB(DWORD dwWidth,DWORD dwHeight,int nBits);
    BOOL CreateDIBFromBitmap(CDC* pDC);
    void InitializeColors();
    int GetDIBCols() const;
    VOID* GetDIBBitArray() const;
    BOOL CopyDIB(CDC* pDestDC,int x,int y);

public:
    CBitmap             m_bmBitmap;

private:
    LPBITMAPINFO        m_pDIB;
};
```

You will notice that the class uses a BITMAPINFO pointer (m_pDIB) to the buffer containing the DIB and has an embedded device-dependent bitmap (m_bmBitmap) for transferring the image from an existing bitmap resource (discussed in the next section).

You then could implement the CreateDIB() and associated functions to allocate the memory for a DIB and initialize the BITMAPINFO structure, like this:

```
CDIB::CDIB() : m_pDIB(NULL)
{
}

CDIB::~CDIB()
{
    if (m_pDIB) delete m_pDIB;
}

BOOL CDIB::CreateDIB(DWORD dwWidth,DWORD dwHeight,int nBits)
{
    if (m_pDIB) return FALSE;
```

Working with Device Contexts and GDI Objects

CHAPTER 6

173

6

WORKING WITH
DEVICE CONTEXTS
AND GDI OBJECTS

```
const DWORD dwcBihSize = sizeof(BITMAPINFOHEADER);

// Calculate the memory required for the DIB
DWORD dwSize = dwcBihSize +
              (2>>nBits) * sizeof(RGBQUAD) +
              ((nBits * dwWidth) * dwHeight);

m_pDIB = (LPBITMAPINFO)new BYTE[dwSize];
if (!m_pDIB) return FALSE;

m_pDIB->bmiHeader.biSize = dwcBihSize;
m_pDIB->bmiHeader.biWidth = dwWidth;
m_pDIB->bmiHeader.biHeight = dwHeight;
m_pDIB->bmiHeader.biBitCount = nBits;
m_pDIB->bmiHeader.biPlanes = 1;
m_pDIB->bmiHeader.biCompression = BI_RGB;
m_pDIB->bmiHeader.biXPelsPerMeter = 1000;
m_pDIB->bmiHeader.biYPelsPerMeter = 1000;
m_pDIB->bmiHeader.biClrUsed = 0;
m_pDIB->bmiHeader.biClrImportant = 0;

InitializeColors();
return TRUE;
}
```

You will notice that dwSize is calculated from the size of the BITMAPINFOHEADER structure, the size of the RGBQUAD array required for the specified color depth, and the size of the resulting bitmap buffer.

The BITMAPINFOHEADER structure is initialized with dimensions of 1,000×1,000 pixels per meter and uses the specified width, height, and color depth. The compression flag biCompression lets you specify the type of compression used in the DIB image buffer. The BI_RGB flag shown in the code sample indicates that no compression is used.

The colors then could be initialized (all to black) like this:

```
void CDIB::InitializeColors()
{
    if (!m_pDIB) return;
    // This just initializes all colors to black
    LPRGBQUAD lpColors =
        (LPRGBQUAD)(m_pDIB+m_pDIB->bmiHeader.biSize);
    for(int i=0;i<GetDIBCols();i++)
    {
        lpColors[i].rgbRed=0;
        lpColors[i].rgbBlue=0;
        lpColors[i].rgbGreen=0;
        lpColors[i].rgbReserved=0;
    }
}
```

You might want to initialize a specific set of RGBQUAD colors, depending on the requirements of your DIB.

Creating a DIB from a Device-Dependent Bitmap

After you set the color values for the DIB, you can set the pixels for the image directly into a buffer (usually stored immediately after the BITMAPINFO structure) from within your code, or from an existing device-dependent bitmap.

Although it is not necessary, it usually is desirable to keep the bitmap image information directly after the BITMAPINFO structure, as shown earlier in the CreateDIB() implementation.

The following helper functions can help you retrieve the number of colors calculated from the color depth in BITMAPINFOHEADER, a pointer to the bitmap image buffer calculated from the size of the header structure, and the following color value array:

```
int CDIB::GetDIBCols() const
{
    if (!m_pDIB) return 0;
    return (2>>m_pDIB->bmiHeader.biBitCount);
}

VOID* CDIB::GetDIBBitArray() const
{
    if (!m_pDIB) return FALSE;
    return (m_pDIB + m_pDIB->bmiHeader.biSize +
        GetDIBCols() * sizeof(RGBQUAD));
}
```

You can find the size and color-depth information from a device-dependent bitmap by using the CBitmap class's GetBitmap() function. This function fills a BITMAP structure (passed by pointer) with the details about a specific GDI bitmap object.

You then can copy these details along with the extra DIB information into the DIB's BITMAPINFOHEADER to create a DIB with the same width, height, and color depth as the device-dependent bitmap.

The DIB color-value information then can be initialized with the SetDIBColorTable() from a reference device context.

After the DIB header and color values are initialized from the bitmap, it only remains to copy the image bits themselves. The GetDIBits() function can perform this task for you. You just need to pass the DIB information, a reference device context, and the GDI bitmap handle; GetDIBits() then copies the entire image bitmap into your supplied buffer.

If you want to perform the reverse operation of copying a DIB bitmap to a device-dependent bitmap, you can use the corresponding `SetDIBits()` function. You can even create an `HBITMAP` GDI object initialized from a DIB directly by using the global `CreateDIBitmap()` function.

The following implementation for the `CDIB` class's `CreateDIBFromBitmap()` function demonstrates these functions using the device-dependent `m_bmBitmap` member. The `CreateDIBFromBitmap()` function assumes that this `CBitmap` member was initialized previously through a `CreateBitmap()` or `LoadBitmap()`:

```
BOOL CDIB::CreateDIBFromBitmap(CDC* pDC)
{
    if (!pDC) return FALSE;
    HDC hDC = pDC->GetSafeHdc();

    BITMAP bimapInfo;
    m_bmBitmap.GetBitmap(&bimapInfo);
    if (!CreateDIB(bimapInfo.bmWidth,bimapInfo.bmHeight,
        bimapInfo.bmBitsPixel)) return FALSE;

    LPRGBQUAD lpColors =
        (LPRGBQUAD)(m_pDIB+m_pDIB->bmiHeader.biSize);

    SetDIBColorTable(hDC,0,GetDIBCols(),lpColors);

    // This implicitly assumes that the source bitmap
    // is at the 1 pixel per mm resolution
    BOOL bSuccess = (GetDIBits(hDC,(HBITMAP)m_bmBitmap,
        0,bimapInfo.bmHeight,GetDIBBitArray(),
        m_pDIB,DIB_RGB_COLORS) > 0);
    return bSuccess;
}
```

You will notice the `DIB_RGB_COLORS` flag also is passed to the `GetDIBits()` function. You can set this flag to either `DIB_RGB_COLORS` to indicate that the color values are literal RGB values, or `DIB_RGB_PAL` to specify color index positions in the device context's current palette.

You might call the `CreateDIBFromBitmap()` function after loading a resource-based bitmap like this:

```
#include "dib.h"
CDIB g_DIB;

void CBitmapdemoView::OnInitialUpdate()
{
    CView::OnInitialUpdate();
    CClientDC dc(this);
    g_DIB.m_bmBitmap.LoadBitmap(IDB_TSTBITMAP);
    g_DIB.CreateDIBFromBitmap(&dc);
}
```

After calling the `CreateDIBFromBitmap()` function, the embedded DIB will be initialized in the memory pointed at by the `m_pDIB` pointer.

Drawing with a DIB

You can use several GDI functions to draw from a DIB directly into a normal device context. These functions are similar to the device-dependent blit functions you saw earlier.

The global `SetDIBitsToDevice()` function copies the image from a DIB buffer directly to a specified device context at a specified position. You can specify the number of lines to copy, as well as the width, height, and position of the source DIB image. If the operation succeeds, `SetDIBitsToDevice()` returns the number of scan lines copied.

Warning

With the introduction of Windows 98 and Windows NT 5, `SetDIBitsToDevice()` can render JPEG image types. The device-context driver may not support this type, however. If it doesn't, `SetDIBitsToDevice()` returns zero, and `GetLastError()` returns a `GDI_ERROR` value.

You can use `StretchDIBits()` in a way similar to `StretchBlt()` to stretch the DIB bitmap to the required size. This function often is useful when you are trying to preserve the original bitmap size. You can use the DIB's pixels-per-meter values to calculate the correct destination size, as well as a specific mapping mode to draw the image at a specific size.

The following example shows an implementation of the `CopyDIB()` function for the `CDIB` class defined previously. This function uses `StretchDIBits()` to render the DIB into a device context that is provided.

This method maintains the standard size of the DIB by setting the mapping mode to `MM_LOMETRIC`. In this mapping mode, the logical unit size is 0.1 mm, so coordinates specified by the GDI functions will be converted by the device context to represent the correct specified size on the destination device. Therefore the coordinates specified in the destination width and height should be multiplied by 10 so that each DIB pixel represents 1 mm to maintain the 1,000 pixel-per-meter specification:

```
BOOL CDIB::CopyDIB(CDC* pDestDC,int x,int y)
{
    if (!m_pDIB || !pDestDC) return FALSE;
```

```
    int nOldMapMode = pDestDC->SetMapMode(MM_LOMETRIC);
    BOOL bOK = StretchDIBits(pDestDC->GetSafeHdc(),
        x,y,
        m_pDIB->bmiHeader.biWidth * 10,      // Dest Width
        m_pDIB->bmiHeader.biHeight * -10,    // Dest Height
        0,0,
        m_pDIB->bmiHeader.biWidth,           // Source Width
        m_pDIB->bmiHeader.biHeight,          // Source Height
        GetDIBBitArray(),m_pDIB,DIB_RGB_COLORS,SRCCOPY) > 0;

    pDestDC->SetMapMode(nOldMapMode);
    return bOK;
}
```

You could invoke this code from your application's view class in the `OnDraw()` and `OnPrint()` functions, after previously creating the DIB from the loaded bitmap resource (as shown earlier), like this:

```
void CBitmapdemoView::OnPrint(CDC* pDC, CPrintInfo* pInfo)
{
    g_DIB.CopyDIB(pDC,50,-50);
}

void CBitmapdemoView::OnDraw(CDC* pDC)
{
    g_DIB.CopyDIB(pDC,50,-50);
}
```

Regardless of the device context passed to `CopyDIB()` and the ultimate destination device, the DIB should be rendered to the same size and with the same colors to the best capabilities of the device.

> **Warning**
>
> Mapping modes used with display monitors are usually very inaccurate, so the size of a displayed DIB may be physically wrong on a video display.
>
> Printer device contexts provide very accurate physical unit mapping, however, so they should print the image to the correct size.

Summary

In this chapter, you saw how Windows maintains a common interface to applications to produce consistent output across a range of devices, such as screens, printers, and plotters.

You saw how the CDC class wraps an HDC device-context handle and provides member functions for the vast majority of API functions that use the device context.

You learned how device-context objects can be created directly for various devices, such as screens and printers, or obtained directly from windows to give you access to the client or entire rendering area of the window.

You looked at how to use the special CDC-derived classes that are used to get access to client areas, to handle window painting, or to play metafiles.

You saw how to create the basic GDI-rendering objects, such as pens and brushes, to perform a wide range of graphical drawing operations using a variety of line-drawing and area-filling styles and techniques. You also saw how to use the various coordinate storing classes and regions with the drawing functions to perform coordinate manipulation and clipping of the rendered output.

You saw how to draw text in a number of fonts using the various text-drawing functions of the device context. You also looked at how to create fonts, as well as the role of the font mapper in the creation of fonts.

Finally, you learned how to load device-dependent bitmaps from the application's resources or create and use them with memory-device contexts. You examined the limitations of device-dependent bitmaps and how to overcome these limitations with device-independent bitmaps with their additional information structures.

Creating and Using Property Sheets

CHAPTER 7

by Jonathan Bates
and Mickey Williams

IN THIS CHAPTER

Sooner or later, you'll find that a single dialog box doesn't offer enough screen space to display all the controls needed to maintain the properties of a particular object. Or you may find that a complex mass of controls is confusing and unstructured. In these situations, a property sheet provides the ideal solution to this problem by letting you group common sets of controls into individual overlapping pages. The property sheet user can select between these pages by clicking on a titled tab representing each page in a way analogous to those filofaxes so fashionable in the 1980s.

Understanding Property Sheets

From a coding perspective, you should think of a property sheet as a collection of individual modeless dialog boxes (representing each page) held inside a larger modal dialog box.

The property sheet itself is implemented down at Win32 level as a dialog box that contains a tab control (one of the common controls) and a set of controlling buttons, such as OK, Cancel, Apply, and Help. The tab control handles the individual dialog boxes that make up the property sheet pages.

Fortunately the MFC wrapper classes `CPropertySheet` and `CPropertyPage` greatly simplify the creation and operation of a property sheet and its property pages. Visual C++ 6 introduces support for the new Wizard97 style (only supported on NT 5 and Windows 98), which extends standard property sheet classes with the new `CPropertySheetEx` and `CPropertyPageEx` classes. The Wizard97 style specifies new design elements for wizard pages, such as areas for header sections. Information on the Wizard97 specification can be found in the MSDN online help, in the section titled, "Wizard 97". Note that there is a space in the title between Wizard and 97. The documentation from Microsoft is inconsistent in some places, but the true name of the specification appears to be Wizard97 (no spaces), most of the time.

There are two main modes of operation for property sheets. The usual mode lets users select between the various pages via the familiar tab control at the top of the property sheet. Users can implement the changes while keeping the sheet open by clicking the Apply button; or they can click OK or Cancel to end the property sheet in the same way as a modeless dialog box.

Another mode is the Wizard style, where users navigate from the start of a sequence of pages to the end using Next and Back buttons. When they reach the end of the sequence, they can implement the changes they've specified by clicking Finish or cancel them by clicking Cancel at any point in the sequence.

The rest of this chapter discusses how you can implement property sheets for both these modes via the MFC wrapper classes.

Creating a Property Sheet

The MFC wrapper classes `CPropertySheet` and `CPropertyPage` simplify the process of creating and displaying a property sheet and its pages. The `CPropertySheet` sheet class is derived directly from the `CWnd` class, although it has a lot in common with a normal `CDialog` class with a `DoModal()` function orchestrating the property sheet's modal life-time. However, the `CPropertyPage` class, used for creating each property page, is derived directly from `CDialog` and acts largely like a modeless dialog box would.

By deriving your own classes from these two MFC base classes, you can extend the specific functionality required for your application. Like dialog boxes, each property page needs a dialog box template resource to define the user interface and layout of controls for that page. Creating this template is usually the first step when building a property sheet, because you then can use ClassWizard to automatically create your derived classes based on those templates, as the following sections show.

Creating the Property Page Resources

There is little difference between dialog box template resources used in property pages and those used in normal dialog boxes. You can use the Resource Editor's Insert Resource dialog box to add a property page specific template by selecting the `IDD_PROPPAGE_LARGE`, `IDD_PROPPAGE_MEDIUM`, or `IDD_PROPPAGE_SMALL` standard option in the Resource Type list (see Figure 7.1).

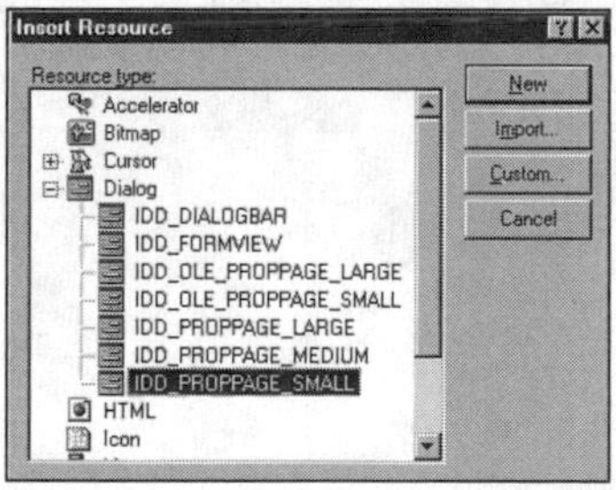

FIGURE 7.1

Inserting a standard property page dialog box template.

After inserting the property page dialog box template, you can resize it as required. You should bear in mind, however, that the final size of the property sheet will be based on the largest property page it contains.

The initial difference from the usual dialog box template that you'll notice is that there are no OK or Cancel buttons; these buttons are added automatically to the property sheet and shouldn't exist on the individual pages. If you examine the Styles tab of the Dialog Properties dialog box for the new template, you'll notice that Style is set to Child and Border is set to Thin, as shown in Figure 7.2.

7

CREATING AND USING PROPERTY SHEETS

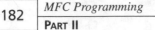

FIGURE 7.2

The property page template Style and Border settings.

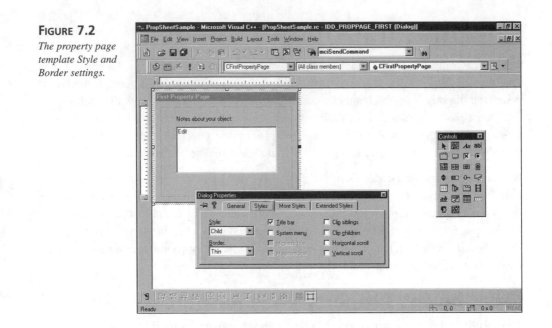

The More Styles tab reveals that the Disabled style also should be set for a property page.

FIGURE 7.3

The property page template Disabled *flag.*

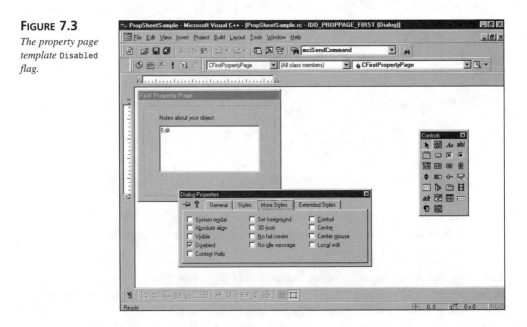

As with a normal dialog box, you should set the resource ID and the caption as appropriate to your application, as shown in Figure 7.4. Your property page caption appears on the tab for that specific page when the property sheet is displayed.

FIGURE 7.4

The property page template resource ID and caption.

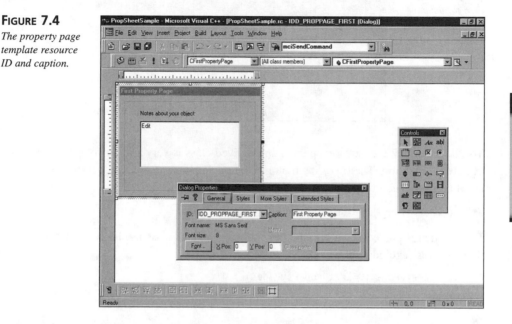

You can add controls to the property page resource template in exactly the same way as you would an ordinary dialog box. You can repeat the same process for each property page you want to include in your property sheet. Each property page must be assigned a unique resource ID, because they are each individual dialog boxes in their own right.

Creating `CPropertyPage`-Derived Classes

For each property page you want to display, you need to create a class derived from the `CPropertyPage` base class to implement your application-specific functionality. You can use ClassWizard to create this class quickly and easily, just as you would for a normal dialog box. If you invoke ClassWizard with the dialog box template resource selected, ClassWizard detects the new resource and offers the option of creating a new class or selecting from an existing implementation. If you decide to create a new class, the New Class dialog box then lets you specify a specific name for your new class. You must remember to change the Base Class combo box from the default `CDialog` setting to `CPropertyPage`, as shown in Figure 7.5.

FIGURE 7.5

Creating a
CPropertyPage-
*derived handler
class for the prop-
erty page.*

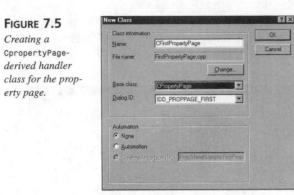

You'll notice that the new CPropertyPage-derived class is very similar to a direct CDialog derivation. The ID of the dialog box template resource is enumerated as the familiar IDD value in the class definition like this:

```
enum { IDD = IDD_PROPPAGE_FIRST };
```

The ID then is passed down into the CPropertyPage base class by the constructor function like this (excluding the ClassWizard lines):

```
CFirstPropertyPage::CFirstPropertyPage() :
        CPropertyPage(CFirstPropertyPage::IDD)
{
}
```

You'll also notice that, like a dialog box, the property page has a DoDataExchange() function so that you can exchange data between the controls and mapped member variables with the usual DDX macro entries. You also can validate that data using the normal DDV macros, which you easily can generate by using the ClassWizard Member Variables tab.

A message map lets you handle messages from dialog controls and notifications from the parent tab control and property sheet. Again, these message map entries have the usual ClassWizard comment placeholders to let you add handler functions from the Message Maps tab.

At this point, you can add mapping variables and event handlers for the various property page controls in the same way as you would for a dialog box. You can repeat the same process of adding a property page handler class for each of the property pages in your property sheet as if they were individual dialog boxes.

Creating a CPropertySheet-Derived Class

After you create a CPropertyPage-derived class to handle each page in the property sheet, you can create a new class to extend the CPropertySheet functionality to cope with your application-specific purpose and tie together the individual property pages.

It isn't strictly necessary to derive a new class from `CPropertySheet`, because the `CPropertySheet` base class has all of the functionality needed to display and tie together the various properties pages. For most applications, however, the various pages probably will maintain different attributes of the same object. The Resource Editor's Dialog Properties property sheet describes dialog box attributes, for example. Therefore, you'll probably want to embed the target object (or a pointer to it) inside the property sheet class. That way, each of the property pages can access the same target object via their parent property sheet.

Again, you can use ClassWizard to generate the `CPropertySheet` class just by setting the `Base` class control to `CPropertySheet` and entering a specific name for your new class.

If you take a look at the new class definition, you'll see that it includes a couple of very similar constructor functions and a message map. The two constructors arc defined like this:

```
CSampleSheet(UINT nIDCaption, CWnd* pParentWnd = NULL,
                                UINT iSelectPage = 0);
CSampleSheet(LPCTSTR pszCaption, CWnd* pParentWnd = NULL,

                                UINT iSelectPage = 0);
```

The only difference between the two constructors is that the first needs a resource for a string table resource, but the second takes a pointer to a string to specify the required caption. By overriding the default zero value in the `iSelectPage` parameter, you can make a property page other than the first display initially.

Now that you have a `CPropertySheet`-derived class and some `CPropertyPage`-derived classes, you have all the elements needed to construct and display a property page object.

Adding the Property Pages

After constructing a `CPropertySheet`-derived object, you can use its `AddPage()` function to add the `CPropertyPage`-derived objects. After the pages are added, the whole sheet can be displayed like a modal dialog box by calling the `CPropertySheet`'s `DoModal()` function, as in this example:

```
#include "FirstPropertyPage.h"
#include "SecondPropertyPage.h"
// ...
void CPropSheetSampleDoc::OnPropertysheetDisplay()
{
    CSampleSheet psSample("Sample Property Sheet");
    psSample.AddPage(new CFirstPropertyPage);
    psSample.AddPage(new CSecondPropertyPage);
    if (psSample.DoModal()==IDOK)
    {
```

```
        AfxMessageBox("Retrieve data from property sheet");
    }
    delete psSample.GetPage(0);
    delete psSample.GetPage(1);
}
```

After the sample property sheet is constructed, two property page objects are instantiated and added. The DoModal() call returns IDOK if the OK button was clicked just as it would for a dialog box.

You'll also notice that the GetPage() function is used to return the pointer to the property page objects.

Adding the pages outside the property sheet gives you some flexibility as to which pages should be added. However, you could call AddPage() to add the property pages inside the property sheet's constructor function (as embedded objects). This solution may be more elegant for situations where the pages used in the property are always the same and the property sheet is instantiated in several places.

In this situation, you can embed the property sheet objects in your derived CPropertySheet class, like this class-definition fragment:

```
protected:
    CFirstPropertyPage m_pageFirst;
    CSecondPropertyPage m_pageSecond;
```

Your property sheet constructor would be modified to add the two member property pages:

```
CSampleSheet::CSampleSheet(LPCTSTR pszCaption,
    CWnd* pParentWnd, UINT iSelectPage)
    :CPropertySheet(pszCaption, pParentWnd, iSelectPage)
{
    AddPage(&m_pageFirst);
    AddPage(&m_pageSecond);
}
```

The greatly simplified code required to display the property sheet now is like this:

```
CSampleSheet psSample("Sample Property Sheet");
if (psSample.DoModal()==IDOK) AfxMessageBox("Ok");
```

> **Warning**
>
> Windows 95 allows a maximum of 16,384 property pages in a property sheet.

If you need to create an array of property sheets, you can break the construction process down into two steps by using the `Construct()` function, which has parameters identical to the constructor. For example, the following lines create two property sheets and then set the caption in two stages. Afterward, you can call `DoModal()` to display the property sheets as normal:

```
CSampleSheet arpsSample[2];
arpsSample.Construct("Sheet 1");
arpsSample.Construct("Sheet 2");
```

Creating a Modeless Property Sheet

You can create a modeless property sheet simply by calling the `CPropertySheet`'s `Create()` function rather than its `DoModal()` function. A modeless property sheet is created without the OK, Cancel, and Apply buttons, but it may be closed using the sheet's system menu or close button. If you need these buttons on a modeless dialog box, you'll need to override the `CPropertySheet`'s `OnCreate()` function and add the buttons manually.

Another consideration is the scope of the property sheet object. Unlike a modal property sheet, your property sheet can't be declared as a local variable to a function. This is because the `Create()` function returns immediately, leaving the modeless property sheet open for use. If it were defined as a local variable, the property sheet object would be destroyed as soon as the invoking function returns.

So as with modeless dialog boxes, a modeless property sheet object should be created with the C++ new operator and tracked by a pointer embedded in a holding class responsible for deleting the allocated property sheet object after its window is closed.

Alternatively, you may want to make the property sheet responsible for its own tracking by overriding the `PostNcDestroy()` virtual function (called when the property sheet window is being closed) and delete the C++ this pointer to free the property sheet memory.

You can force a modeless property sheet window to close from within your code by calling its `DestroyWindow()` function.

The following code fragment illustrates these concepts:

```
CPropSheetSampleDoc::CPropSheetSampleDoc() : m_pPSSample(NULL)
{
}

CPropSheetSampleDoc::~CPropSheetSampleDoc()
{
    if (m_pPSSample) delete m_pPSSample;
}
```

```
void CPropSheetSampleDoc::OnPropertysheetDisplay()
{
    if (m_pPSSample==NULL)
    {
        m_pPSSample = new CSampleSheet("Modeless Property Sheet");
        m_pPSSample->Create(AfxGetMainWnd());
    }
}

void CPropSheetSampleDoc::OnPropertysheetClose()
{
    if (m_pPSSample)
    {
        m_pPSSample->DestroyWindow();
        delete m_pPSSample;
        m_pPSSample = NULL;
    }
}
```

This code assumes that the property pages are created inside the property sheet's con-structor and that the m_pPSSample property sheet pointer is declared in the document class definition like this:

```
CSampleSheet* m_pPSSample;
```

The OnPropertysheetDisplay() function is a menu handler function that allows the user to create the modeless property sheet. The modeless property sheet is created as a child of the application's main window by the Create() call if the object doesn't already exist.

The OnPropertysheetClose() function is another menu handler function that demon-strates how the property sheet can be closed from within the code with a call to DestroyWindow().

Responding to Property Sheet Messages

A host of messages are transmitted around a property sheet during its lifetime. These messages are essentially the glue that holds together the various pages, header control, and parent property sheet window.

The pages themselves act like a series of independent dialog boxes, but a set of activation messages also is sent from the header control to indicate when each page is becoming active or inactive.

Another set of messages is sent to the pages after the OK, Apply, or Cancel button is clicked.

Initializing the Property Pages

After the property sheet has been displayed, the first message that is sent to the initial property page is the WM_INITDIALOG message. You can trap this message in your CPropertyPage-derived class in a normal OnInitDialog() handler function.

Just like a normal dialog box, your property page window and controls are active after the call to the base class CPropertyPage:: OnInitDialog() handler function. At this point, you can call window-based functions on any of your subclassed control-mapping objects (such as those added by ClassWizard), such as EnableWindow(). You also can subclass your own controls inside the OnInitDialog() handler.

As discussed earlier, the WM_INITDIALOG message is sent only once to a property page when it is first displayed. This means that any pages in the property sheet that haven't yet been displayed will not perform OnInitDialog(). Any attempt to access these uninitialized controls—for example, from the property sheet object or a different page object—will cause an assertion.

This only-on-demand initialization of property pages makes for fast and efficient property sheets that need to initialize only the pages that actually are selected by the user.

Property Page Activation and Deactivation

Whenever a particular property page is activated (either for the first time or on subsequent reselection), it is sent a PSN_SETACTIVE notification message from the header control. This notification is handled in the CPropertyPage base class, which then calls the OnSetActive() virtual function. You can provide an override for OnSetActive() in your derived class to perform any initialization required when that page is about to be redisplayed. Your override function should return a TRUE value if the page was initialized successfully, or FALSE if the page was not initialized successfully.

The base class implementation of OnSetActive() calls UpdateData(FALSE) so that your overridden DoDataExchange() function is called to transfer data from your mapped member variables into the page's controls.

When the user then selects a different page, the currently active page is sent the PSN_KILLACTIVE notification, which the CPropertyPage base class translates into a call to the OnKillActive() virtual function. You can stop the new page selection at this point by returning a FALSE value from your own OnKillActive() override function.

The base class implementation of OnKillActive() calls UpdateData(TRUE); this calls through the DoDataExchange() function in save and validate mode. By adding DDX_ and DDV_ macros to your derived class's DoDataExchange() function, you can transfer any

7

CREATING AND
USING PROPERTY
SHEETS

data from the controls to your mapped member variables and perform validation specific to your property page. You can add any additional validation not performed in the DoDataExchange() function to OnKillActive() itself. You must remember to display a message box to inform users why the validation may have failed and their new page was not made active (or risk very irate users).

> **Tip**
>
> You can use the Member Variables tab of ClassWizard to generate DDX_ and DDV_ macros to map and validate most dialog box template controls.

Handling Messages from OK, Apply, and Cancel Buttons

After the property sheet's OK button is clicked, an OnOK() virtual function is called for each of those property pages that have been displayed during the lifetime of the property sheet. Your property pages should override OnOK() to perform any OK handling specific to that page (and that page only). After all of the OnOK() functions have been called and returned in each of the property pages, the property sheet will be closed.

If you want to conditionally stop the property sheet from closing after OK is clicked, you should return a FALSE value from your OnKillActive() overridden function. OnKillActive() is called for the currently active property page just before the OnOK() functions are called.

A corresponding virtual function, OnCancel(), is called in the same way after the Cancel button is clicked. However, the OnKillActive() function isn't called before OnCancel() so that the user can always close the property sheet (unless you explicitly disable the Cancel button). The OnCancel() function actually is called by another virtual function— OnReset(). If you override OnReset() and don't call the base class function, OnCancel() isn't performed. OnReset() is called in response to the PSN_RESET notification.

You can prevent the user from closing the property sheet via Cancel by adding an override for OnQueryCancel() that is called just before the OnCancel() function. By returning FALSE from OnQueryCancel(), you can stop the cancellation from proceeding, but a TRUE value lets the cancellation continue as normal.

The Apply button works differently from OK and Cancel. Apply means *apply those changes without closing the property sheet.* For example, users may want to change the color of a background window and see whether they like it without dismissing the property sheet and still being able to cancel the change. When the property sheet is opened, the Apply button is disabled. Whenever a setting in one of the property pages is changed, you should call that page's SetModified() function, passing a TRUE value. This indicates that the page has been modified, and the Apply button will stay enabled while at least one page is set as modified. You can pass FALSE to SetModified() to reset the page's modified flag.

After the Apply button is clicked, a PSN_APPLY notification is sent to the property pages. This is routed by the base class to call the OnApply() virtual function for each of the initialized property pages (even if their modified flag isn't set). You can return a FALSE value from your OnApply() override to stop the changes from proceeding (and inform the user). Otherwise, you should apply the current changes to your application objects. Remember that the user may want to cancel those changes before closing the property sheet, however, so the original settings also should be preserved.

If you can't preserve the original settings, you can call the CancelToClose() member function of CPropertyPage after applying your changes. After calling this function, the OK button caption is changed to Close, and the Cancel button is disabled to indicate that the changes are irrevocable.

If you don't add an override for OnApply() to your derived property page class, the base class implementation calls the OnOK() virtual function and resets the modified flag in each of the property pages.

You can simulate clicking one of these buttons from within your code by calling the CPropertySheet's PressButton() function from your derived property sheet object. The PressButton() function can be passed PSBTN_OK, PSBTN_CANCEL, or PSBTN_APPLYNOW to simulate the OK, Cancel, or Apply button, respectively. This function passes a PSM_PRESSBUTTON message to the property sheet.

You also can close the property sheet by calling the CPropertySheet's EndDialog() function, which actually posts a PSM_PRESSBUTTON message with a PSBTN_CANCEL value to the property sheet to close it.

> **Warning**
>
> A modeless property sheet doesn't normally have these buttons and so won't respond to these messages in the same way.

7

CREATING AND USING PROPERTY SHEETS

Sending Messages Between Property Pages

You can send user-defined messages between the active property pages of a property sheet by calling the pages' QuerySiblings() member function. This sends a PSM_QUERYSIBLINGS message to each of the other property pages in turn, until one of the pages returns a non-zero value. Like other user-defined messages, PSM_QUERYSIBLINGS lets you pass two values, a WPARAM and a LPARAM, which can be passed in the two parameters of the QuerySiblings() function.

Suppose that you have a property sheet with two property pages. You want the second page to request the result of a multiplication from the first page.

The following code implemented in a button message handler in the second property page initiates the interpage communication:

```
void CSecondPropertyPage::OnMakeChange()
{
    SetModified();
    int a = 123, b = 456;
    LRESULT lRes = QuerySiblings(a,b);
    CString strAnswer;
    strAnswer.Format("Result of %d * %d = %d",a,b,lRes);
    AfxMessageBox(strAnswer);

    // Save Changes...
}
```

The call is made to QuerySiblings() on line 5, passing the two operands for the multiplication request. The result, lRes, which is returned from the query to the second page, then is displayed in the message box in line 8.

The following code implemented in the first property page shows the corresponding message map entry and handler function for the query:

```
BEGIN_MESSAGE_MAP(CFirstPropertyPage, CPropertyPage)
    //{{AFX_MSG_MAP(CFirstPropertyPage)
        // NOTE: the ClassWizard will add message map macros here
    //}}AFX_MSG_MAP
    ON_MESSAGE(PSM_QUERYSIBLINGS,OnQuerySiblings)
END_MESSAGE_MAP()
 8: LRESULT CFirstPropertyPage::OnQuerySiblings(WPARAM wParam,LPARAM lParam)
{
    AfxMessageBox("Got the message, Calculating!");
    return wParam * lParam;
}
```

Notice the message map entry for the PSM_QUERYSIBLINGS message. Its corresponding handler function merely displays a message box and returns the result of the multiplication.

Customizing the Standard Property Sheet

A number of `CPropertySheet` member functions let you change the standard property sheet appearance, and few functions can radically change the standard functionality (such as setting the Wizard mode, which is discussed in a following section).

You would normally set the property sheet title in the constructor, but you can use the `SetTitle()` member function to change this title. `SetTitle()` requires two parameters. The first is a pointer to the new caption, and the second lets you optionally pass a `PSH_PROPTITLE` flag to prefix your title with the text "Properties for".

When the tabs of a property sheet can't all be displayed along one line, the default action is to stack them to produce rows of tabs, as Figure 7.6 shows.

FIGURE 7.6

A property sheet with stacked tabs.

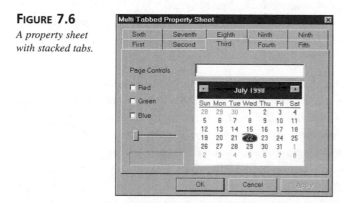

You can change this behavior by calling the property sheet's `EnableStackedTabs()` function and passing a `FALSE` value. This action displays all the tabs along the same line and adds two scroll arrows to let the user scroll through the tabs, as Figure 7.7 shows.

FIGURE 7.7

A property sheet with scrollable tabs.

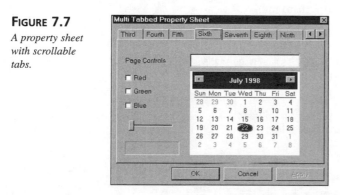

Property Page Management

You can add a page at any time during the life of a property sheet, even after it has been displayed (although this obviously is easier with a modeless property sheet). The tab control is updated automatically after you call AddPage() so that the user can select it. Similarly, you can use RemovePage() and pass a zero-based page index number or a pointer to a specific page to remove that page.

If you find the zero-based index for a specific page, you can use the GetPageIndex() function to return the index by passing the function a pointer to one of the sheet's CPropertyPage objects. The corresponding GetPage() function returns a pointer to the CPropertyPage object specified by an index value.

You can find the number of pages a property sheet holds, which is returned from the sheet's GetPageCount() function.

The current active page number is returned from GetActiveIndex(). If you'd prefer a pointer to the active page, you can find this directly by calling GetActivePage(). The corresponding SetActivePage() lets you set a new active page specified by a zero-based index or a pointer to the desired page.

You can access and change the property sheet's tab control using the GetTabControl() function. This function returns a CTabCtrl pointer to the sheet's tab control object. Using this pointer, you can manipulate the full functionality of the tab control to add images to the tabs via SetImageList(). You can call GetTabControl() only after the property sheet window is opened, and the tab control is guaranteed to exist. This means that you can't call GetTabControl() before calling DoModal(), since the property sheet isn't created except during the call to DoModal(). Fortunately, an OnInitDialog() override in the CPropertySheet class comes to the rescue, providing an excellent place to manipulate the tab control before the window is displayed.

For example, the following property sheet OnInitDialog() override adds an image to each tab from an image list (of 8×8 pixel images) held as a bitmap in IDB_IMAGE_LIST:

```
BOOL CImagePropertySheet::OnInitDialog()
{
    BOOL bResult = CPropertySheet::OnInitDialog();

    m_ImageList.Create(IDB_IMAGE_LIST,8,8,RGB(255,255,255));
    CTabCtrl* pTabCtrl = GetTabControl();
    if (pTabCtrl)
    {
        pTabCtrl->SetImageList(&m_ImageList);
        for(int i=0;i<pTabCtrl->GetItemCount();i++)
        {
```

```
        TCITEM tcItem;
        tcItem.mask = TCIF_IMAGE;
        tcItem.iImage = i;
        pTabCtrl->SetItem(i,&tcItem);
      }
    }
    return bResult;
}
```

The `m_ImageList` member in this listing is defined as a `CImageList` object in the `CImagePropertySheet` class definition. The example iterates through the tabs, setting one of the images against each tab.

Creating a Wizard Mode Property Sheet

Wizards are property sheets with Back and Next buttons instead of tabs to allow users to sequentially traverse the property pages. You'll usually see these buttons used in installation and configuration tasks where users can proceed to the next step only after they've successfully completed the current page.

Turning a normal property sheet into a wizard is simple. Just one call to the property sheet's `SetWizardMode()` function is required before the sheet is displayed, and instantly the property sheet is transformed into a wizard (see Figure 7.8)!

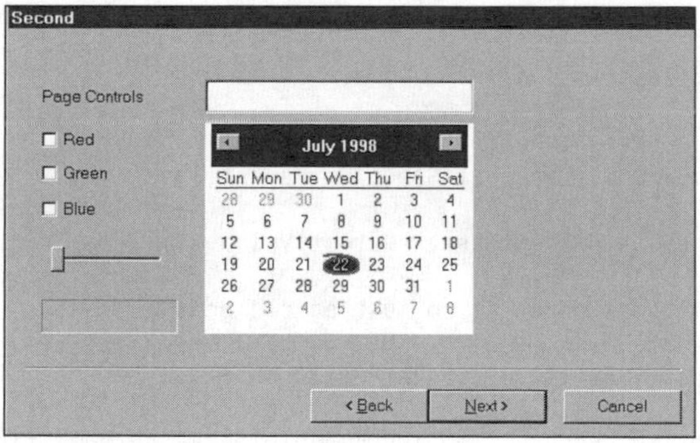

FIGURE 7.8

A Wizard mode property sheet.

7

CREATING AND USING PROPERTY SHEETS

You'll probably want to disable some of the buttons at various stages, and display a Finish button on the last property page. The property sheet's `SetWizardButtons()` function lets you do just that. You can pass and combine a set of flag values to specify the required customization, as Table 7.1 shows.

Table 7.1   Flag Values for Customizing the Wizard Buttons

Flag Value	Description
PSWIZB_NEXT	Enable the Next> button.
PSWIZB_BACK	Enable the <Back button.
PSWIZB_DISABLEDFINISH	Show a disabled Finish button instead of the Next> button.
PSWIZB_FINISH	Show the Finish button instead of the Next> button.

You must call SetWizardButtons() only after the property sheet has been displayed, because it manipulates the property sheet buttons directly. The OnSetActive() virtual function in the property sheet is a good candidate for calling SetWizardButtons(). You can use the window's GetParent() function to get to the property sheet object from a property page and access SetWizardButtons() through the pointer (after casting it) returned from GetParent().

The following code fragment demonstrates these principles by overriding OnSetActive() in a derived CPropertyPage class. The example assumes that the same class (or base class) will be used to implement all the property pages in a property sheet. If this is true, the same function can test the current page to check whether it is at the start or the end of a wizard sequence. At the start, it disables the <Back button; at the end, it displays the Finish button:

```
BOOL CWizProppage::OnSetActive()
{
    CPropertySheet* pParentSheet
        = STATIC_DOWNCAST(CPropertySheet,GetParent());

    const int nPageNo = pParentSheet->GetActiveIndex();

    // Is this the first page, if so just enable next
    if (nPageNo == 0)
        pParentSheet->SetWizardButtons(PSWIZB_NEXT);

    // Is this the last page, if so just enable back and show finish
    if (nPageNo == pParentSheet->GetPageCount()-1)
        pParentSheet->SetWizardButtons(PSWIZB_BACK|PSWIZB_FINISH);

    return CPropertyPage::OnSetActive();
}
```

You can further customize the Finish button by changing its caption with a call to SetFinishText() and passing it a pointer to the required caption text. SetFinishText() also has the effect of removing the <Back button, so that only the button with your text and the Cancel button are displayed.

Using the New `CPropertySheetEx` and `CPropertyPageEx` Classes

The Visual C++ 6 MFC provides two new property sheet and page classes: `CPropertySheetEx` and `CPropertyPageEx`. These are introduced to support the new features included with Windows NT 5 and Windows 98 (and will only work properly on these platforms). The new features let you set a background bitmap in a property sheet and let property pages display both titles and subtitles. At the time of writing, however, these features are available only for wizard-style property sheets.

> **Warning**
>
> Executables using the new Wizard97 style with its background and header bitmaps and property pages with header and subtitle lines will operate correctly only under Windows NT 5 and Windows 98 onward.

`CPropertySheetEx` extends `CPropertySheet`, and the only real difference is the additional constructor parameters. The first three parameters—the caption, parent window, and initial page—arc identical. The next three (optional) parameters let you specify an `HBITMAP` handle for the background bitmap, an `HPALETTE` handle for the bitmap's palette, and an `HBITMAP` handle for the property sheet's header section. You can pass a `NULL` value to any of these parameters if the parameter isn't required.

There is a corresponding `Construct()` function with parameters identical to the constructors for vectoring property sheets, and an `AddPage()` function that takes a pointer to the new `CPropertyPageEx` pages.

You can access the `CPropertySheetEx` class's `m_psh` member to change the Win32 `PROPSHEETHEADER` structure directly. You must add the `PSH_WIZARD97` flag value to the `dwFlags` member of this structure before displaying the property sheet to use any of the new features.

A set of associated flag values lets you tailor the specific details of the new wizard look (see Table 7.2). These flags can be combined with a logical `OR` to add or remove certain presentational aspects of the Wizard97 property sheet style.

TABLE 7.2   Flag Values for Customizing the Wizard97 Property Sheet

Flag Value	Description
PSH_WIZARD97	Sets the Wizard97 mode. You must always set this flag if you want to use the new wizard features.
PSH_WATERMARK	The watermark (background) bitmap style should be used.
PSH_USEHBMWATERMARK	Used with PSH_WATERMARK to specify that the hbmWatermark bitmap handle is used instead of using the pszbmWatermark string pointer to specify the watermark bitmap.
PSH_USEPLWATERMARK	Uses the supplied hplWatermark palette handle rather than the default palette.
PSH_STRETCHWATERMARK	By default, the background image is tiled over the property sheet area. You can set this flag to stretch the bitmap to cover the property sheet.
PSH_HEADER	You should set this flag to use a bitmap in the property sheet header section.
PSH_USEHBMHEADER	Used with PSH_HEADER to specify that the hbmHeader bitmap handle is used instead of using the pszbmHeader string pointer to specify the header bitmap.
PSH_USEPAGELANG	You should set this flag if you want the property sheet language settings to inherit from the first property page's resource template.

The new CPropertyPageEx lets you specify both a title and subtitle for each property page, as well as the normal caption. The CPropertyPageEx class extends CPropertyPage and just supplies constructor functions to support the new features.

The CPropertyPageEx constructor lets you specify a resource dialog box template ID, a string resource ID for a caption, another ID for the header title, and an ID for a subtitle. You can let all but the first parameter (the dialog box template) default to zero if you don't need specific features.

As you'd expect by now, there is a corresponding Construct() function with identical parameters to allow for arrays of property pages.

You can access the m_psp PROPSHEETPAGE structure member to add some new flag values to the property page structure's dwFlags member. These flags are used with the Wizard97 property page style to customize the appearance of each property page. Table 7.3 lists the new flag values, which can be combined with a logical OR.

TABLE 7.3   Flag Values for Customizing the Wizard97 Property Page

Flag Value	Description
PSP_HIDEHEADER	Hides the header section of the property page (when in Wizard97 mode). The property sheet background bitmap then is used to fill the entire property sheet.
PSP_USEHEADERTITLE	Displays the header text line.
PSP_USEHEADERSUBTITLE	Displays the subtitle line.

The last two flags, PSP_USEHEADERTITLE and PSP_USEHEADERSUBTITLE, are set when you pass the title and subtitle resource IDs to the property sheet constructor function. However, you may want to set the PSP_HIDEHEADER flag to display a banner page in the property sheet's background watermark bitmap.

The following code lines show how two bitmap resources can be loaded and then displayed in the body and header sections of the property sheet (note that CBitmap pointers are cast into HBITMAP handles by their HBITMAP overloaded operator). Two property pages are constructed and added to the property sheet; the only difference is that one has the PSP_HIDEHEADER flag set. To simplify the code, only the base classes are used. In a real piece of code, however, you probably would want to derive your own classes from the CPropertySheetEx and CPropertyPageEx classes.

```
CBitmap bmHeader;
CBitmap bmBackground;
bmHeader.LoadBitmap(IDB_HEADER);
bmBackground.LoadBitmap(IDB_BACKGROUND);
CPropertySheetEx pex("New Property Sheet",
    NULL,0,bmBackground,NULL,bmHeader);
CPropertyPageEx* pNewPage =
    new CPropertyPageEx(IDD_PROPPAGE_FIRST,
        IDS_PAGE_CAPTION1,IDS_HEADER_TITLE1,
            IDS_SUBTITLE1);
pNewPage->m_psp.dwFlags |= PSP_HIDEHEADER;
pex.AddPage(pNewPage);
CPropertyPageEx* pNewPage1 =
    new CPropertyPageEx(IDD_PROPPAGE_FIRST,
        IDS_PAGE_CAPTION1,IDS_HEADER_TITLE1,
            IDS_SUBTITLE1);
pex.AddPage(pNewPage1);
pex.m_psh.dwFlags |= PSH_WIZARD97;
pex.DoModal();
```

When run, this code displays the first property page without the header, with the property sheet background bitmap (IDB_BACKGROUND) filling the wizard dialog box, as Figure 7.9 shows.

FIGURE 7.9

FIGURE 7.9

A Wizard97 property page with the header hidden.

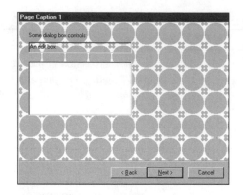

The second page is displayed with the new header style, showing the caption, header line, and subtitle line (see Figure 7.10).

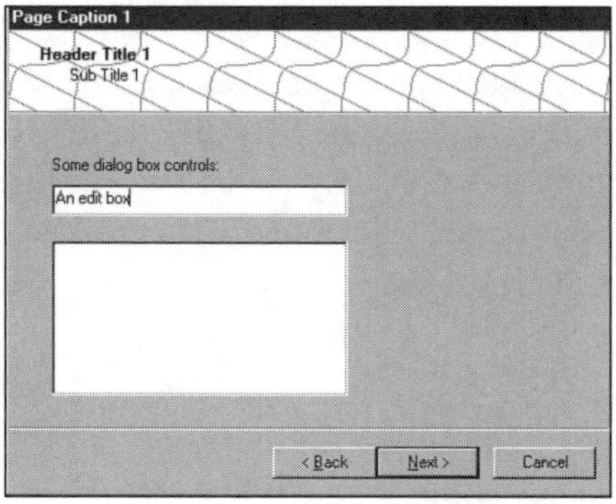

FIGURE 7.10

A Wizard97 property page showing the header and subtitle lines.

Adding Help Buttons and Help Support

You can add a Help button to a property sheet by adding the PSP_HASHELP flag value to each property page that will support help. You should combine the PSP_HASHELP flag with the current dwFlags set in the page's m_psp PROPSHEETPAGE structure before displaying the property sheet. For example, you could add a line like this to the property page constructor:

```
m_psp.dwFlags |= PSP_HASHELP;
```

The Help button then is added to the property sheet and is enabled for each page that sets the PSP_HASHELP flag; otherwise, the button is disabled.

Alternatively, if you are dynamically adding pages after the property sheet has been displayed, you can ensure that the Help button is added by setting the PSH_HASHELP flag in the property sheet's m_psh.dwFlags member. The Help button then will be displayed when the property sheet window is created, even though no current property pages implement help support.

After you add the Help button, you can add a handler for the `ID_HELP` command message notification sent whenever the user clicks the Help button. ClassWizard doesn't automate this command message handler, so you must add the message map and handler function manually:

```
BEGIN_MESSAGE_MAP(CMyPropertyPage,CPropertyPage)
ON_COMMAND(ID_HELP,OnHelp)
END_MESSAGE_MAP

void CMyPropertyPage::OnHelp()
{
AfxMessageBox(IDS_HELP_RESPONSE);
}
```

Instead of displaying the message box as shown here, you normally would invoke your application's helper application.

Users can access context-sensitive help from the property sheet by pressing the F1 key. This generates a `WM_HELPINFO` message that can be handled by an `OnHelpInfo()` handler added to the property sheet or one of the property pages.

> **Tip**
>
> You can use ClassWizard to generate an `OnHelpInfo()` handler function in response to the `WM_HELPINFO` message.

If you want to make the Help button use the same handler function as the context-sensitive F1 help, you can add an `OnHelp()` handler function to the property sheet class and add code to send a `WM_COMMANDHELP` message to the active property page using `SendMessage()`, like this:

```
#include "afxpriv.h"
void CSampleSheet::OnHelp()
{
    SendMessage(WM_COMMANDHELP);
}
```

> **Note**
>
> The `afxpriv.h` header file must be included to provide the definition of the `WM_COMMANDHELP` message.

When the active property sheet receives this message, its own OnHelpInfo() handler function is called in response to a WM_HELPINFO message generated in response to WM_COMMANDHELP. By using this technique, you don't have to implement an OnHelp() handler in each of the property pages, and the standard framework OnHelpInfo() handler automatically invokes your application's helper application.

Understanding the Win32 Sequence of Events

This section gives a brief overview of the structure and sequence of events down at the Win32 level. Unless you like a challenge and have loads of spare time, you won't actually need to implement a property sheet using the direct API calls and structures. Instead, you will use the MFC (or Active Template Library) wrapper classes (discussed in the previous sections), which greatly simplify the process. However, it is worth a brief discussion of these events to understand the processes underlying the wrapper classes.

Before the property sheet is displayed, each page is added to a PROPSHEETHEADER structure in memory as a pointer to a PROPSHEETPAGE structure and corresponding window handle.

When the property sheet is displayed initially, the first page is displayed and sent a WM_INITDIALOG message. If the user then selects another page, the first page is hidden and the new dialog box is displayed and sent a WM_INITDIALOG message. If the user then reselects a previously displayed (but now hidden) page, the reselected page is redisplayed, but no WM_INITDIALOG message is sent.

This sequence of events sent by Windows indicates that each of the dialog boxes comprising the pages of the property sheet is modeless, with the overall modality controlled by the parent property sheet itself.

Except for the initial page, the dialog boxes for each page are never created unless the user specifically selects the tab for that page. However, once created, the individual dialog boxes stay created until the property sheet itself is destroyed. The created dialog boxes are merely hidden when their tab isn't currently active. You can see this in action by using the Visual Studio Spy++ IDE tool to study the window's hierarchy while a property sheet (such as the Internet control panel applet) is displayed.

Obviously, there will be times when you'll need to validate the details on a particular page before allowing the user to select another page. You can perform this validation from the currently active page when the tab control sends it a `PSN_KILLACTIVE` notification message. To keep the current page active, you can set a `TRUE` message result value in response to the notification. Alternatively, a `FALSE` message result allows the selection to continue resulting in a `PSN_SETACTIVE` notification being sent to the newly activated page. You can use the `PSN_SETACTIVE` notification to initialize or reinitialize any controls in the newly activated tab.

After a user clicks the OK or Apply property sheet button, a `PSN_APPLY` message is sent to each of the property pages to let you take whatever appropriate action is required for each page. When the OK or Cancel button is pressed, the property sheet is closed and all the property page and property sheet windows are destroyed. However, the convention is that Apply should implement the changes specified by the modified control settings without closing the property sheet.

Summary

In this chapter, you learned how to build sophisticated tabbed property sheets that let you group and present dialog box templates as individual selectable pages.

Property sheets are an invaluable tool for developers who want to build an easy-to-use but complex user interface. These sheets let you hide and package many of the controls that might otherwise overwhelm users if all the controls were presented on a single dialog box.

You can dynamically add or remove property pages to further customize the property sheet presentation and share common pages while presenting other, more specialized pages when applicable. The Visual Studio Dialog Editor makes good use of this technique; the control properties property sheet shows the same General and Extended Styles pages for all controls, but the Styles page is more specific to the type of control being edited.

You should use the various property sheet messages to control page selection and perform tasks such as validation before allowing users to move off the current page. You can let users apply their changes to your application to provide instant feedback on the impact of those changes without losing the interface, so that they can revert to the old settings or make changes if needed.

Modeless property sheets let you keep the pages displayed while users interact with other parts of your application's user interface. This can give users an extra control mechanism or a feedback mechanism to provide detailed information about the objects they click on and interrogate.

7

CREATING AND
USING PROPERTY
SHEETS

You can use the wizard form of a property sheet to help guide users through a series of forms and required fields when trying to configure parts of an application or install various software components.

The new Wizard97 background and header bitmaps let you present a better-looking interface with clearer titles and subtitles on each of the pages.

Working with the File System

*by Jonathan Bates
and Mickey Williams*

IN THIS CHAPTER

CHAPTER 8

Modern operating systems such as Windows provide a huge variety of services and features. However, if you were to ask what services comprise the core function of an operating system, providing a file system would surely be near the top of the list.

The dual requirements of file-system evolution and backward compatibility have littered the Windows operating system variants with a spectrum of old and new file systems.

To ensure that you can exploit the best file-system features and still maintain compatibility across the various platforms, you should be aware of these differences and their implications on the behavior of file and device I/O functions.

File System Overview

Put simply, a file system turns a vast homogenous array of bits in a storage medium into a highly organized hierarchical structure more akin to the human mode of categorically oriented thinking.

A file system also must be fast and efficient, making good use of the underlying technology to provide rapid responses to user requests to retrieve and store data.

Each file system occupies a storage device such as a floppy disk or CD-ROM drive, or an area on a hard drive called a *volume*. These volumes are labeled with drive names such as A:, B:, C:, D:, and so on.

File systems have evolved to offer many more advanced features, such as long filenames, file security via permissions and ownership, network volume mapping, virtual files, and file/directory compression.

This evolution has led to a number of file-system types. Windows NT supports the largest set of file-system types, providing support for both the latest innovative file systems and the older, simpler types. Windows 98 supports the next-largest set, with Windows 95 and Windows 3.11 bringing up the rear.

Things became more confusing as support for some file-system types was dropped in later versions of the operating system (for example, HPFS was dropped in NT 4.0).

The following sections clarify the various file-system types and operating-system versions that support them.

The FAT File System

The *file allocation table* (*FAT*) file system is the simplest of all the file systems and is supported by all Windows operating systems.

The FAT file system (also known as *FAT-16*) is a leftover from the MS-DOS operating system. As its name suggests, the FAT file system merely stores a table (and a backup table) of all the files and their positions on the disk. The table is stored at the beginning of a disk volume and must be updated whenever files are added or modified. New data is just allocated to slots large enough to contain it, which leads to high fragmentation.

This simplicity leads to poor performance and limited robustness. The maximum size of a FAT file system is 4GB under Windows NT, but performance is seriously degraded for file systems larger than 2GB.

> **Note**
>
> The FAT file system originally was limited to 32MB partitions, until MS-DOS 4 increased the size of the FAT entries.

The basic FAT filenames are limited to eight characters, followed by a dot, and then a three-letter suffix. All lowercase letters in filenames are converted to uppercase letters when stored. Longer filenames are truncated and made unique by conversion to a six-character name, followed by a tilde and an autogenerated number to preserve uniqueness.

FAT file systems support only the very basic file attributes (such as read-only, archive, hidden, and system). No security attributes or permissions can be assigned to files on a FAT file system.

It is unusual for modern Windows versions to create pure FAT file systems for their main hard drive partitions. But older systems (including early versions of Windows 95) still may use and preserve FAT file systems. Also, floppy disks still use FAT (protected mode), because it is the common denominator for file interchange and has a small footprint for small volume sizes (such as the common 1.44MB floppy disk standard).

Protected-Mode FAT

Windows NT 3.5 and Windows 95 (and subsequent versions) use a clever trick to preserve long filenames by using several FAT entries to encode each file with a longer filename. These clever tricks are known as the *protected-mode FAT* and allow filenames of up to 256 characters.

These additional entries are marked with the hidden attribute, so they are invisible when you are browsing the directory entries. This system lets MS-DOS applications see the 8.3 component as normal, but more modern Windows versions can preserve longer names.

8

WORKING WITH THE FILE SYSTEM

The FAT-32 File System

Originally, Windows 95 used the pure FAT file system (FAT-16). This system was very inefficient for the more common larger disk volumes, however, because even a 1-byte file had to consume 32KB of disk space as the cluster size increased.

The FAT-32 file system was introduced with *Operating System Release 2* (*OSR2*) of Windows 95. That system liberates lots of disk space tied up in those large clusters by reducing the cluster size to 4KB (for up to 8GB disk volumes). Unfortunately, the change in cluster size made it difficult for existing Windows 95 users to take advantage of OSR2, as it required a new installation, and could not be applied as an upgrade.

The other big advantage of FAT-32 is the capability to support much larger disk volumes, up to a limit of 2TB (terabytes) or 2,048GB.

Windows 98 supports both FAT-16 and FAT-32 file systems. FAT-16 is used by default, but FAT-32 can deliver more disk space and better performance.

The HPFS File System

The *High-Performance File System* (*HPFS*) originated from the OS/2 operating system. It allowed access to larger disk volumes than FAT and filenames of up to 254 characters (and double-byte character sets, such as Unicode, in filenames).

HPFS also allowed flexible attribute information with a block of up to 64KB available for user-defined attributes, but it didn't offer integrated file system–level security.

HPFS provided a large performance increase over the FAT file systems, but performance degraded with larger volume sizes.

Support for HPFS was dropped from Windows NT 4.0 onward, and previous versions of Windows NT didn't support security permissions for HPFS. Windows 95 and 98 do not support HPFS.

The NTFS File System

The *New Technology File System* (*NTFS*) was designed with Windows NT to fully support the sophisticated NT security model at a low level (however, lack of file encryption makes this fairly pointless, because the volume can be interrogated freely from other operating systems).

Filenames can contain up to 255 characters and preserve case (although they are not case-sensitive).

The theoretical volume size for NTFS exceeds any existing hardware, allowing volumes of up to 16EB (Exabytes). 16 Exabytes is 2^{64} bytes, or 18,446,744,073,709,551,616 bytes.

NTFS is fast and gives a good scalable performance for file systems with volume sizes of more than 400MB.

Windows 95 and Windows 98 do not support NTFS, but Windows NT (obviously) does.

The CDFS File System

The *Compact Disk File System* (*CDFS*) is based on the ISO 9660 Standard (but extends it to allow long and double-byte filenames). To applications, the CDFS file system appears similar to a FAT file system.

Windows 95/98, Windows NT 3.5, and subsequent versions support CDFS.

Networked File Systems and Mapped Volumes

The (modern) Windows family of operating systems (95/98 and NT) was designed with networked file-system sharing from the ground up. Applications can specify filenames that conform to the *Universal Naming Convention* (*UNC*), which includes the name of the host machine, the requested volume on that machine, and the path and filename of the target file.

The hostname starts with two backslash characters (\\). The rest of the name then is separated by single backslashes, as in an ordinary pathname.

For example, the UNC name \\thehost\c\thefile.cpp means *find the file called* thefile.cpp *on the volume labeled* c *on the machine called* thehost.

This name is submitted to the *Multiple Universal Name Convention Provider* (*MUP*), which attempts to resolve the name and hand the file-access request over to a network redirector (RDR).

The RDR then contacts the host machine and passes the I/O request to the remote networked host machine to handle. The host machine then passes the request to the file system for the specified volume, which then sends any return data back to the calling machine.

You can map one of these UNC names to a virtual volume on your local machine (as you can in Windows Explorer with the Tools/Map Network Drive option).

This mapping assigns a local volume letter to the UNC name and establishes a connection to the remote host machine specified. After this connection is established, your applications can specify the volume name and destination filename without needing the full UNC name. This capability lets applications treat the remote volume as if it were just another local storage device, which is very useful for older UNC-unaware applications.

Suppose that you map \\thehost\c\ as X. You then could access thefile.cpp from your application as simply X:thefile.cpp. Because UNC naming allows subdirectory naming, you also can specify subdirectories to map, which then appear as complete volumes in their own right.

However, for operating systems such as Windows 95 and 98 (which have little in-built security), allowing such freedom of access to a networked machine would have dreadful security implications. Therefore, your local machine can access only remote volumes that have been marked explicitly for sharing by a remote machine. (You can mark these volumes for sharing by using the Sharing context menu option from Windows Explorer.)

Because the host machine implements the actual file-system access, networking allows interaction between normally incompatible file systems and platforms. Windows 95 and 98 operating systems can't access NTFS volumes located on the local machine. However, they can access files on a Windows NT NTFS via shared file systems, because the actual file-system access is performed by the Windows NT host machine.

The DFS File System

A *distributed file system* (*DFS*) extends the concept of networked file systems and file mapping so that remote volumes can be mounted on a local file system transparently as subdirectories.

Other operating systems, such as UNIX, have had this design philosophy from their inception. Windows, however, has evolved from the MS-DOS drive name world and was forced by backward-compatibility issues to accept volume mapping by drive letter.

Windows NT Server addresses the problems that drive-letter mapping imposes (such as running out of letters in big networked file systems) by supporting DFS.

Windows NT Workstation and Windows 95/98 platforms can access files over a DFS but only via a Windows NT Server.

DFS provides an excellent mechanism for large organizations to simplify the administration, backup, and virus scanning of a large number of individual PCs by mounting each PC as a subdirectory of an organization-wide network.

File System Compression

Both Windows NT and Windows 95/98 support volume compression, although the technique used differs. Windows 95/98 uses a special format called *DriveSpace,* whereas Windows NT lets you set a compression attribute against each folder to compress that folder.

Unfortunately, Windows NT cannot access Windows 95/98 FAT file systems that have been compressed with the DriveSpace format (except via network access).

This inability can cause problems on dual-boot machines, so you should avoid compression in these cases.

Compression techniques also carry a performance penalty, depending on the type of compression and the file being accessed.

Disk Quotas

NTFS 5 and later versions (with Windows NT 5.0) will support a technique called *disk quotas.* This means that administrators will be able to assign specific limits to the amount of disk space available to individual users.

Write functions may fail when users reach their own quota limits, even though sufficient disk space exists on the volume as a whole.

Differences in Functions Among File Systems

The various capabilities and drawbacks of all these different file-system types have implications that reach right down to individual operating system function calls. If you are designing an application that must work on a variety of platforms, you must be aware of these differences and respond to various return and error codes as appropriate.

Large parts of the *Application Programming Interface (API)* are ignored by lack of file system support, especially in the sophisticated areas of NT security.

Determining the File System and Drive Types

You can determine the file-system type for a volume from within your code by using the GetVolumeInformation() Win32 API function. You can pass the name of a file system's root directory to this function, along with pointers to various buffers, to retrieve lots of information regarding the file system's capabilities and type.

You also can find details about the type of device a particular root path belongs to by passing the root path name to GetDriveType(). The value returned indicates whether the drive is a network drive, a CD-ROM drive, a fixed disk, or another type of technology.

Win32 File Objects

The basic low-level file-manipulation and device I/O functions provided by the Win32 API are CreateFile(), ReadFile(), WriteFile(), SetFilePointer(), LockFile(), UnlockFile(), and CloseHandle(). There are many more, but these probably are the most commonly used.

These functions manipulate a Win32 file object referenced by a Win32 HANDLE type. The object can be of various types, such as these:

- Simple disk (or RAM disk) file
- Directory (disk directory)
- Disk drive (physical floppy disk or hard drive accessed as raw data)
- Sequential communications device, such as a serial or parallel port
- Console object that simulates a simple ANSI-style text terminal
- Named pipe (an *interprocess communication* or *IPC* mechanism that allows one process to efficiently send data to another via shared memory)
- Mailslot (another IPC mechanism that lets one process send data to a number of other processes simultaneously)

Basic File I/O

CreateFile() is used to both create new files and open existing files, and it returns a Win32 HANDLE to the open file.

The first parameter to CreateFile() is the filename, which can be a UNC filename and pathname or the name of a device, such as COM1: or LPT1:.

The size of this filename is limited under Windows 95 and Windows 98 to the maximum size defined by MAX_PATH (which is set to 260 characters). Under Windows NT, however, you can prefix the pathname with the characters \\?\ to bypass this limitation.

The second parameter lets you specify the requested access mode, which can be 0 if you only want to determine the attributes of the file. Or, this parameter can be a combination of GENERIC_READ and GENERIC_WRITE for read and write access.

The third parameter lets you specify how you want to share the file with other applications. If you want exclusive access, you can pass a NULL value. Otherwise, FILE_SHARE_READ or FILE_SHARE_WRITE indicates that you will let other applications have read or write access to the file.

The fourth parameter to `CreateFile()` lets you specify security attributes by passing a pointer to a `SECURITY_ATTRIBUTES` structure. These attributes are available only under Windows NT, and you normally would pass a `NULL` to this parameter to gain the same (default) attributes as the calling process. If your application spawns other processes and then wants to inherit this file handle, however, you should set the `bInheritHandle` member of this structure to `TRUE`. Otherwise, the child process will not be able to use the file. This restriction on inheritance also applies to Windows 95 and Windows 98.

The fifth parameter lets you specify how you want to open the file. You can pass any of the values from Table 8.1.

TABLE 8.1   File Open/Creation Flags Used with `CreateFile()`

Flag Value	*Description*
OPEN_EXISTING	Opens an existing file or device and returns an error if the specified name doesn't exist.
OPEN_ALWAYS	If the file doesn't exist, the function creates it as if you had passed the CREATE_NEW flag.
TRUNCATE_EXISTING	Opens an existing file and wipes out the contents so that the file becomes a zero-length file.
CREATE_NEW	Creates a new file but returns an error if the file already exists.
CREATE_ALWAYS	Creates a new file, regardless of any existing file with the same name.

The sixth parameter lets you set and combine specific file attributes, such as hidden, archive, and read-only. Normally, you would use the `FILE_ATTRIBUTE_NORMAL` flag value.

You also can set a large number of flags in this parameter that change the way the subsequent file read and write functions work, as in the following ways:

- Data is written immediately without waiting for a write cache to be flushed.
- No buffering is performed.
- A special asynchronous mode called *overlapping* may be set where read and write requests can return immediately, even though the data hasn't been read or written, to allow the calling program to perform some other processing after issuing the request. (This topic is discussed later in this chapter, in the section, "Asynchronous I/O.")
- The file is deleted when closed.
- The file is tagged as a random-access or sequential-access file, enabling the operating system to optimize access to the file.

8

WORKING WITH
THE FILE SYSTEM

The seventh parameter lets you specify the handle of a template file that can be used to set the file attributes of a file being created. This functionality isn't supported on Windows 95, however, and returns an unsupported error code.

If CreateFile() successfully creates the file, a valid HANDLE to that Win32 file object is returned; otherwise, INVALID_HANDLE_VALUE is returned. You can use the GetLastError() function to find out what went wrong and return an appropriate error code, as with all the file I/O functions.

You then can use the HANDLE value for subsequent ReadFile() and WriteFile() operations. The parameters for ReadFile() and WriteFile() indicate a buffer to store or read the data from, the number of bytes to write or read, and a pointer to a DWORD value to store the number of bytes successfully read or written. There is also a pointer to an OVERLAPPED structure for overlapped I/O (discussed later in this chapter, in the section, "Asynchronous I/O"). You can pass NULL for this parameter for normal blocking I/O (waiting for the function to complete). These functions return a simple Boolean value to indicate success (TRUE) or failure (FALSE).

You can reposition the current file position with the SetFilePointer() function. You can pass an amount to move by, as well as a flag value or FILE_BEGIN, FILE_CURRENT, or FILE_END to indicate that the amount is relative to the start, current position, or end of the file.

This function lets you specify 64-bit amounts to move by. Normally (for files smaller than 4GB), you'd only use the second parameter to specify the low 32-bit value and pass zero to the third parameter. However, if you have truly huge files, you can pass the high-order 32-bit word in the third parameter to access 2^{64} bytes of data!

If a call to SetFilePointer() fails, a value of (DWORD)-1 is returned.

You can lock and unlock sections of a file using the LockFile() and UnlockFile() functions. These functions also let you specify two 64-bit numbers for the byte position to lock from and the size of the locked region. A Boolean return code indicates success or failure.

Finally, you can close the file with a call to the CloseHandle() function.

You can copy files by passing the source and destination filenames to the CopyFile() function, or you can rename them with the MoveFile() function.

The following listing illustrates these various file-handling functions with a program that uses a Win32 file object to calculate prime numbers (unusually getting faster with the higher primes!):

LISTING 8.1 File Handling Functions

```cpp
#include "stdafx.h"
#include "windows.h"
#include "iostream.h"

const DWORD dwPrimes = 50000;          // Primes to 50,000

DWORD TestPrimes(HANDLE hFile);
DWORD DisplayError(LPSTR strError);

int main(int argc, char* argv[])
{
    HANDLE hPrimes = CreateFile(
            "Primes",                      // Filename
            GENERIC_READ|GENERIC_WRITE,    // Read & Write
            NULL,                          // No Sharing
            NULL,                          // Default Security
            CREATE_ALWAYS,                 // Create it
            FILE_FLAG_DELETE_ON_CLOSE,     // Delete afterwards
            NULL);                         // No template
    if (hPrimes == INVALID_HANDLE_VALUE)
        return DisplayError("Creating");
    // Set the file size to the max number of primes
    char buf[100];
    memset(buf,0,sizeof(buf));
    DWORD dwBytesWritten;
    while(WriteFile(hPrimes,&buf,sizeof(buf),
            &dwBytesWritten,NULL))
        if (GetFileSize(hPrimes,NULL)>dwPrimes) break;
    TestPrimes(hPrimes);
    return CloseHandle(hPrimes); // Close the file
}

DWORD TestPrimes(HANDLE hFile)
{
    DWORD dwBytesRead,dwBytesWritten,dwTestPrime = 2;
    do
    {
        BOOL bFillMode = FALSE;
        DWORD dwPos = dwTestPrime;
        while(dwPos<dwPrimes)
        {
            if (SetFilePointer(hFile,dwPos,0,
                    FILE_BEGIN)==(DWORD)-1)
                return DisplayError("Positioning");

            if (!bFillMode) // Is it a prime?
            {
                BYTE byteTestByte;
                if (!ReadFile(hFile,&byteTestByte,1,
```

continues

LISTING 8.1 continued

```
                            &dwBytesRead,NULL))
                    return DisplayError("Reading");

            if (byteTestByte == 0) // Yes!
            {
                cout << dwPos << ";" << flush;
                bFillMode = TRUE;

                // Backup a byte
                if (SetFilePointer(hFile,-1,0,
                    FILE_CURRENT)==(DWORD)-1)
                    return DisplayError("Positioning");
            }
        }
        if (bFillMode) // Remove all the factors
        {
            BYTE byteFill = 1;
            if (!WriteFile(hFile,&byteFill,1,
                    &dwBytesWritten,NULL))
                return DisplayError("Writing");
        }
        dwPos+=dwTestPrime;
        }
    } while(dwTestPrime++ < dwPrimes);
    return 0;
}

DWORD DisplayError(LPSTR strError)
{
    DWORD dwError = GetLastError();
    cout << "An error occurred when " << strError
        << ", Errno = " << dwError;
    return dwError;
}
```

Asynchronous I/O

Asynchronous I/O under Windows is curiously termed *overlapped I/O*. Fundamentally, these terms refer to the capability to start a read or write request, and then return from the read or write function immediately without waiting for the request to finish. Given that I/O usually involves considerable waiting, asynchronous I/O can speed up a program by allowing it to perform some other processing while the I/O request is handled in the background. After your program has performed some other processing, it can check to see whether the I/O request has completed and process the I/O or continue with other jobs.

Some single-threaded programs may need to perform asynchronous operations so that they don't block while waiting for input (such as characters from a serial port or keyboard).

> **Warning**
>
> Windows 95 doesn't support asynchronous I/O operation for disk files and consoles, although other objects—such as serial ports, network sockets, and anonymous pipes—are supported.

You can indicate that you want to perform an asynchronous I/O operation on a Win32 file object by passing the `FILE_FLAG_OVERLAPPED` value to the sixth parameter of the `CreateFile` function used to open the object. You then must provide a pointer to an `OVERLAPPED` structure for subsequent read and write operations.

The `OVERLAPPED` structure then is filled with internal information about the request when you call `ReadFile()` or `WriteFile()`. The `ReadFile()` or `WriteFile()` function returns immediately, and your program can perform other tasks. The functions return a `FALSE` value, indicating that an error occurred, with `GetLastError()` returning an `ERROR_IO_PENDING` value. This is a normal return code for asynchronous operations and just indicates that the operation is in progress.

You then can periodically check whether the operation has completed by using the `HasOverlappedIoCompleted()` macro, passing it a pointer to the `OVERLAPPED` structure.

You should ensure that the memory for this structure doesn't fall out of scope or become deleted before the function returns. Otherwise, a nasty crash or a blocked I/O situation can occur.

You can set the `Offset` and `OffsetHigh DWORD` members of the `OVERLAPPED` structure to specify a start position for a disk file transfer. You also can set the `hEvent` member to a manual-reset synchronization event handle that will be set to the signaled state when the operation has been completed. This lets you use the `WaitForSingleObject()` or `WaitForMultipleObjects()` function to wait for the I/O to complete.

You can find more details about an asynchronous operation using the `GetOverlappedResult()` function. This function needs the handle of the file object, a pointer to the `OVERLAPPED` structure, as input. It then can return the number of bytes transferred so far into a pointer to a `DWORD` passed as the third parameter. The fourth parameter is a Boolean value that you can use to make the function wait until the I/O operation is completed by passing `TRUE`. Otherwise, a `FALSE` value causes `GetOverlappedResult()` to return immediately, even though the I/O hasn't completed.

8

WORKING WITH THE FILE SYSTEM

If an error occurs during the I/O operation, GetOverlappedResult() returns a FALSE value, and GetLastError() shows the reason for failure. However, this return code also may be ERROR_IO_PENDING if the operation is still in progress.

> **Note**
>
> On Windows 95 and Windows 98, the hEvent member of the OVERLAPPED structure must be set if you want GetOverlappedResult() to wait for completion. This isn't strictly necessary on Windows NT but is preferable to distinguish between multiple asynchronous requests and provide compatibility with the other platforms.

If you want to supply callback functions to be called when the I/O operation completes, you can use the ReadFileEx() and WriteFileEx() functions. These functions let you pass a pointer to an application CALLBACK function that will be passed any error codes, the number of bytes transferred, and a pointer to the OVERLAPPED structure after the I/O request completes.

You can find a sample listing of asynchronous overlapped I/O in the "Asynchronous Communications" section later in this chapter.

> **Warning**
>
> ReadFileEx() and WriteFileEx() call the callback function only when running on Windows 98 or Windows NT (not Windows 95).

You can cancel an asynchronous I/O operation in progress by using the CancelIo() function and passing it the file object handle.

Compatibility I/O

The Windows operating systems support a range of I/O styles that provide compatibility with other operating systems—principally, UNIX and DOS.

These functions can make it easier to port simple UNIX applications and old C-style, text-based applications onto Windows platforms. For simple batch-file processing jobs, these functions can be easier to use than the sophisticated Win32 functions.

All these functions ultimately make calls down to the Win32 functions discussed in previous chapters.

Low-Level I/O

The term *low-level I/O* is a misnomer, because the real Windows Win32 API low-level
I/O functions are the CreateFile(), ReadFile(), and WriteFile() functions. However,
the low-level I/O functions refer to the C-style low-level I/O functions inherited from the
UNIX world.

The basic handle for these low-level functions is called a *file descriptor* and consists of
an integer value. Three predefined standard handles always are available that always have
the values 0, 1, and 2.

> **Warning**
>
> Although these file functions will inevitably use the Win32 subsystem I/O, there
> is no direct compatibility between low-level file handles and Win32 file object
> handles.

These handles are available only from console applications and run from an MS-DOS
shell window. By default, the standard input descriptor (0) is the keyboard, the output
descriptor (1) is the display, and the error descriptor (2) also sends output to the display.

However, these file descriptors can be redirected by using the MS-DOS shell's pipe (|)
and redirection symbols (< and >). This redirection provides a powerful tool to concate-
nate the input and output of programs.

For example, consider this familiar MS-DOS command:

```
DIR | MORE
```

What this really means is that the output handle (1) of the DIR command becomes the
input handle (0) of the MORE command.

The following SORT command redirects the input file descriptor (0) to read a file rather
than the keyboard, and the output file descriptor (1) is sent to a file rather than the display:

```
SORT < INPUT.TXT > SORTED.TXT
```

The shell is responsible for hooking these file handles to the appropriate input or output
file or device and passing them to the command when it starts.

Your low-level I/O program can read and write to these handles using the _read() and
_write() functions.

For example, the following console application garbles the input from the descriptor (0) by incrementing all the characters with an ASCII code over 32 and then writes the result to the output descriptor (1):

```
#include "stdafx.h"
#include "io.h"
int main(int argc, char* argv[])
{
    char szChr;
    while(_read(0,&szChr,1))
    {
        if (szChr>32) szChr++;
        _write(1,&szChr,1);
    }
    return 0;
}
```

You can run this code from the MS-DOS command line, piping the output of DIR into the standard input file descriptor, like this:

```
DIR | GARBLE
```

You can create or open files with low-level I/O using the _creat() and _open() functions. The _creat() function requires a filename and a flag to indicate the file read and write permissions. You can combine the _S_IREAD and _S_IWRITE flag values to indicate these permissions. The _open() function requires a filename and a combination of the following flag values for its second parameter, as Table 8.2 shows.

TABLE 8.2   File Open/Creation Flags Used for the _open Function.

Flag Value	Description
_O_CREAT	Create and open for writing.
_O_APPEND	Open the file for appending.
_O_RDONLY	Open for read only.
_O_WRONLY	Open for write only.
_O_RDWR	Open for reading and writing.
_O_BINARY	Don't perform text conversions.
_O_TEXT	Perform text conversions.
_O_TRUNC	Open and truncate the file.

The optional third parameter lets you specify the _S_IREAD and _S_IWRITE flag values as in the _creat() function. Both _creat() and _open() return a file handle integer for use in subsequent functions, or a –1 value if the file couldn't be opened.

You can position the file using the `_lseek()` function passing the file handle, the offset position, and the origin flag in a similar way to the Win32 `SetFilePointer()` function. The origin flags are `SEEK_SET`, `SEEK_CUR`, and `SEEK_END` to indicate that the file seek should be relative to the start, current, or end file position. You can find the current file position by using the `_tell()` function.

You should use `_close()` to finally close the file. The following example illustrates these functions by creating a file containing a text string, closing it, and then reopening it to read the text string backward and write the output to the console.

```
#include "stdafx.h"
#include "io.h"
#include "fcntl.h"
#include "sys\stat.h"
#include "string.h"
int main(int argc, char* argv[])
{
    // Create a file, setting read and write permissions
    int hFile = _creat("test.txt",_S_IWRITE|_S_IREAD);

    // Write some text to a file
    char* pszTxt = "This is my test text\n";
    _write(hFile,pszTxt,strlen(pszTxt));
    _close(hFile);

    // Re-open the file for reading
    hFile = _open("test.txt",_O_RDONLY);

    // Copy it backwards to the console
    _lseek(hFile,0L,SEEK_END);
    int nLen = _tell(hFile)-1;
    char szBuf;
    while(nLen>=0)
    {
        _lseek(hFile,nLen—,SEEK_SET);
        _read(hFile,&szBuf,1);
        _write(1,&szBuf,1);
    }
    return _close(hFile);
}
```

Stream I/O

The stream I/O functions provide compatibility for C-style I/O. These functions access a handle in the form of pointers to FILE structures called *streams*. These structures themselves encapsulate the low-level file descriptor handle as the `_file` member of the FILE structure. The stream I/O functions use the low-level functions (which in turn use the Win32 functions) but provide extended capabilities and built-in buffering.

The standard input, standard output, and standard error file descriptors are mapped to the stdin, stdout, and stderr streams. These streams are just predefined pointers to FILE structures that map to the low-level standard 0, 1, and 2 handles. Therefore, you can use these standard streams for redirected and piped input and output.

You can use a host of stream functions to provide fairly sophisticated buffered file control. The familiar printf() function, for example, is just a special case of fprintf() that always sends its output to stdout.

You can open files using _fopen() to pass a filename and character string indicating the type of access, such as r for reading, w for writing, and r+ for reading and writing. If successful, a pointer to a FILE structure is returned and can be used for subsequent operations. You can find the low-level file descriptor by using the _fileno() function, and you can use an existing descriptor to open a stream via the _fdopen() function.

Other useful functions are _fread(), fgets(), fgetc(), and _fscanf() for reading in various ways; and the corresponding fwrite(), fputs(), fputc(), and fprintf() for writing.

You can position the file using _fseek() and find the position using _ftell(). The _fflush() function flushes any unwritten output, and _fclose() closes the stream.

The IOStream Classes

Similar to the way the Microsoft Foundation Classes wrap much of the underlying Win32 functionality, the IOStream classes are C++ classes that wrap the stream functionality.

The ios class is the base class for the other I/O stream classes and contains a number of common member functions for status testing and buffer manipulation. This class also contains a number of enumerated flag values for manipulating the input and output stream data.

The istream class extends the ios class to provide a number of reading and repositioning functions, such as get(), read(), peek(), putback(), seekg(), and tellg(). You can use the istream class directly, or derive your own classes from istream to add your application-specific functionality.

A corresponding ostream extends the ios class to provide writing-oriented functions such as put(), write(), flush(), seekp(), and tellp(). Once again, you can inherit your own classes from this class to extend the write-only–oriented functionality offered by ostream.

Using the sometimes-frowned-upon (but more widely accepted) practice of multiple inheritance, the `iostream` class combines the `istream` and `ostream` classes to give you a read- and write-capable class.

Before you use this jungle of classes, you'll notice that the constructors require a pointer to a `streambuf`-derived class. These classes provide the connection to the file, standard I/O channel, or character array in memory via the `filebuf`, `stdiobuf`, or `strstreambuf` subclasses. You must construct an object from one of these three classes (or a derivative) and then pass the pointer to a constructor of a class derived from `iostream` in order to initialize the manipulator object.

Instead of deriving from or using the `istream`, `ostream`, and `iostream` classes directly, you probably would want to use one of the more specific alternatives, such as `fstream`, `stdiostream`, and `strstream`, which derive from `iostream`. You could use `fstream` for file I/O, `stdiostream` for standard-stream I/O, or `strstream` for character buffer manipulation. The big advantage of using these classes is that their constructor functions automatically create the `filebuf`, `stdiobuf`, or `strstreambuf` objects required, thus letting you create one-stop–shop objects.

If all this sounds like a lot of hard work, you're right—it is—but you should remember there are a lot of clever member functions of each of these classes that comprise a very sophisticated suite of file and character-manipulation classes.

Like the low-level and stream I/O on which they are based, three corresponding standard predefined objects let you manipulate the standard input, output, and error channels, as Table 8.3 shows.

8

WORKING WITH
THE FILE SYSTEM

TABLE 8.3   IOStream Objects and Their Related Streams

Object Descriptor	Class Type	Stream	File
cin	istream	stdin	0
cout	ostream	stdout	1
cerr	ostream	stderr	2

These `cin`, `cout`, and `cerr` objects actually are created as objects of `istream_withassign` and `ostream_withassign`, which are classes that allow the objects to be assigned to other types of `istream` and `ostream` objects for piping and redirection to other program output or disk files.

There is also a `clog` object that is similar to `cerr` but is fully buffered, whereas `cerr` is flushed immediately when data is assigned to it.

This example shows how to perform the equivalent text scrambling with a console application, as in the low-level I/O section earlier, but it uses cin and cout:

```
#include "stdafx.h"
#include "iostream.h"
int main(int argc, char* argv[])
{
    char szChr;
    cin.flags(0);
    while(cin >> szChr)
    {
        if (szChr>32) szChr++;
        cout << szChr;
    }
    return 0;
}
```

You'll notice that the cin.flags(0) is used to remove some rather unpleasant text-filtering flags from the input channel. The overloaded >> operator is used to read a character into the szChr single-character buffer, and the << operator writes it out after manipulation.

Serial Communications

Handling serial port I/O presents special problems because of the many different hardware-specific settings, the need for timeouts, and bidirectional asynchronous data transfer.

Parallel ports are a similar communications resource, and although they generally are used in more unidirectional applications (such as printers), they still must provide bidirectional asynchronous transfer.

The following sections discuss some of the aspects of serial data transfer.

Opening and Configuring Serial Ports

You can open a serial port device using the CreateFile() function by specifying a filename that refers to the specific port, such as COM1 or COM2.

When you open a serial port, it is opened automatically for exclusive access, so you should pass a zero for the CreateFile()'s third parameter and OPEN_EXISTING for the open mode (fifth parameter). You can add a combination of the special file mode flags to indicate overlapped I/O or any special buffering requirements, as normal.

If the serial port opens successfully, a Win32 file object handle is returned. Otherwise, INVALID_HANDLE_VALUE is returned. The following example opens the port named by m_strPort for overlapped I/O and doesn't perform any buffering:

```
m_hCommPort = CreateFile(m_strPort,GENERIC_READ | GENERIC_WRITE,
0, NULL, OPEN_EXISTING,
FILE_ATTRIBUTE_NORMAL | FILE_FLAG_OVERLAPPED |
FILE_FLAG_NO_BUFFERING,NULL);
if (m_hCommPort == INVALID_HANDLE_VALUE) return FALSE;
```

After you open a serial port, you must set the many flags required to configure the device. These flags are held in a *device control block* (*DCB*) structure. You can either fill in the entire DCB structure or use one of the helper functions to fill in some of the details. The GetCommState() function fills in a DCB structure with the current settings from the hardware, and you can use a corresponding SetCommState() function to specify the new settings from a DCB structure.

You can use BuildCommDCB() to set some (but not all) of the settings from a command string, as shown here:

```
"baud = 9600 parity = N data = 8 stop =1"
```

The following example turns off all flow control (such as XON/XOFF, CTS/RTS, and DSR/DTR) and sets the baud rate, data bits, and parity settings from the m_strBaud command string:

```
DCB dcb;
memset(&dcb,0,sizeof(dcb));
dcb.DCBlength=sizeof(dcb);
GetCommState(m_hCommPort,&dcb);
if (!BuildCommDCB((LPCTSTR)m_strBaud,&dcb))
{
    TRACE("Unable to build Comm Port config = '%s', err = %d\n",
(LPCTSTR)m_strBaud,GetLastError());
    return FALSE;
}

// Common settings
dcb.fOutxCtsFlow = FALSE;
dcb.fOutxDsrFlow = FALSE;
dcb.fDtrControl = DTR_CONTROL_DISABLE;
dcb.fDtrControl = FALSE;
dcb.fDsrSensitivity = FALSE;
dcb.fOutX = FALSE;
dcb.fInX = FALSE;
dcb.fNull = FALSE;
dcb.fRtsControl = RTS_CONTROL_DISABLE;
dcb.fAbortOnError = FALSE;
if (!SetCommState(m_hCommPort,&dcb))
{
    TRACE("Unable to set Comm Port config = '%s', err = %d\n",
(LPCTSTR)m_strBaud,GetLastError());
    return FALSE;
}
```

8

WORKING WITH THE FILE SYSTEM

You also can find the default communication settings by calling the
GetDefaultCommConfig() function, which fills a COMMCONFIG structure. This structure
holds a DCB structure and a number of application-specific values. To change these settings, you can pass a COMMCONFIG structure with your customized settings to
SetDefaultCommConfig().

Asynchronous Communications

After configuring the serial port, you can start transferring data via ReadFile() and
WriteFile() functions. However, you should remember that if you haven't specified the
FILE_FLAG_OVERLAPPED flag in the CreateFile() flags parameter, ReadFile() will
block waiting for input. This probably is good if your program spawns another thread
that specifically waits for incoming serial port characters, but not if you want to issue a
ReadFile() and periodically check to see whether any characters have arrived.

If you have specified the FILE_FLAG_OVERLAPPED flag, however, you must provide pointers to OVERLAPPED structures for the read and write functions and handle the asynchronous I/O.

The following example demonstrates asynchronous overlapped I/O. This console application issues a read request and then writes a string with the current time to the console. It
then waits for either five seconds or for completion of the read request. If five seconds
pass with no received characters, the loop repeats and writes the time again. If a character is received, a string is printed in response.

LISTING 8.2   Asynchronous Overlapped I/O

```
#include "windows.h"
#include "time.h"
#include "string.h"
#include "stdio.h"

BOOL SetCommDefaults(HANDLE hSerial);

int main(int argc, char* argv[])
{
    HANDLE hSerial = CreateFile("COM2",
GENERIC_READ | GENERIC_WRITE,0,NULL,OPEN_EXISTING,
        FILE_ATTRIBUTE_NORMAL | FILE_FLAG_OVERLAPPED |
FILE_FLAG_NO_BUFFERING,NULL);
    if (hSerial == INVALID_HANDLE_VALUE) return GetLastError();
    SetCommDefaults(hSerial);

    HANDLE hReadEvent = CreateEvent(NULL,TRUE,FALSE,"RxEvent");
```

```
OVERLAPPED ovRead;
OVERLAPPED ovWrite;
memset(&ovRead,0,sizeof(ovRead));
memset(&ovWrite,0,sizeof(ovWrite));

ovRead.hEvent = hReadEvent;

char szRxChar = 0;
DWORD dwBytesRead = 0;
DWORD dwBytesWritten = 0;

while(szRxChar != 'q')
{
    // Check if a read is outstanding
    if (HasOverlappedIoCompleted(&ovRead))
    {
        // Issue a serial port read
        if (!ReadFile(hSerial,&szRxChar,1,
                &dwBytesRead,&ovRead))
        {
            DWORD dwErr = GetLastError();
            if (dwErr!=ERROR_IO_PENDING)
                return dwErr;
        }
    }

    // Write the time out to the serial port
    time_t t_time = time(0);
    char buf[50];
    sprintf(buf,"Time is %s\n\r",ctime(&t_time));
    if (HasOverlappedIoCompleted(&ovWrite))
    {
        WriteFile(hSerial,buf,strlen(buf),
                &dwBytesWritten,&ovWrite);
    }

    // ... Do some other processing

    // Wait 5 seconds for serial input
    if (!(HasOverlappedIoCompleted(&ovRead)))
        WaitForSingleObject(hReadEvent,5000);

    // Check if serial input has arrived
    if (GetOverlappedResult(hSerial,&ovRead,
            &dwBytesRead,FALSE))
    {
        // Wait for the write
        GetOverlappedResult(hSerial,&ovWrite,
            &dwBytesWritten,TRUE);
```

8

WORKING WITH
THE FILE SYSTEM

```
            // Display a response to input
            sprintf(buf,"You pressed the '%c' key\n\r",
                szRxChar);
            WriteFile(hSerial,buf,strlen(buf),
                    &dwBytesWritten,&ovWrite);
        }

    }

    CloseHandle(hSerial);
    CloseHandle(hReadEvent);
    return 0;
}

BOOL SetCommDefaults(HANDLE hSerial)
{
    DCB dcb;
    memset(&dcb,0,sizeof(dcb));
    dcb.DCBlength=sizeof(dcb);
    if (!GetCommState(hSerial,&dcb))
        return FALSE;
    dcb.BaudRate=9600;
    dcb.ByteSize=8;
    dcb.Parity=0;
    dcb.StopBits=ONESTOPBIT;
    if (!SetCommState(hSerial,&dcb))
        return FALSE;
    return TRUE;
}
```

You'll notice that CreateFile() specifies the FILE_FLAG_OVERLAPPED flag for asynchronous I/O. A manual reset event (hReadEvent) is created to signal when incoming serial characters have been read by the overlapped ReadFile() function.

After ReadFile() is called, it returns immediately, and other processing such as the WriteFile() can be performed before finally waiting in the WaitForSingleObject() function for a signal from the read event. This wait has a timeout of five seconds, so if no characters are read, the loop is repeated. GetOverlappedResult() is used to check whether characters are received, and a WriteFile() response is issued to any incoming characters.

Setting Communication Timeouts

At times, you'll probably need to set up various types of timeouts, especially when implementing protocol-driven data transfers.

The SetCommTimeouts() function can help you simplify timeout implementation. The function requires a pointer to a COMMTIMEOUTS structure that contains a number of DWORD members that let you set timeouts in milliseconds, as well as multipliers for those timeouts.

The ReadIntervalTimeout member lets you set the maximum allowable time between reading two characters. If the timeout is exceeded, the ReadFile() operation is completed. You can set this member to zero to indicate that you don't want to use interval timeouts. Alternatively, you can set it to MAXDWORD and set the ReadTotalTimeoutMultiplier and ReadTotalTimeoutConstant members to zero to indicate that the ReadFile() should return immediately.

You can use the ReadTotalTimeoutMultiplier to specify a total timeout for the read operation. This millisecond value is multiplied by the total characters to be read to calculate an overall ReadFile() timeout. The ReadTotalTimeoutConstant value is added to the calculation to let you add a constant to the overall timeout duration. If you don't want to set an overall timeout, you can set these values to zero.

Two corresponding members—WriteTotalTimeoutMultiplier and WriteTotalTimeoutConstant—are used to calculate an overall timeout value for WriteFile() operations.

You can find the current timeout settings using the GetCommTimeout() function, which fills a passed COMMTIMEOUTS structure. The aptly named BuildCommDCBAndTimeouts() does just what it says and lets you set both the DCB settings and timeouts in one go.

The GetCommProperties() function can fill a COMMPROP structure with details about specific driver settings, such as buffer sizes and maximum supported baud rates.

Communication Events

You can set an event mask to enable reporting of various types of communication events. The SetCommMask() function lets you specify a number of flag values, such as EV_BREAK, EV_RXCHAR, or EV_CTS (break signal, received character, and clear-to-send signal).

After you set an event mask, you can use the WaitCommEvent() function to wait for one of those events to occur. This can be a useful way of waiting for received characters before issuing a ReadFile(). The WaitCommEvent() function lets you pass a pointer to a DWORD variable to store the actual event received, as well as a pointer to an OVERLAPPED structure to let you issue asynchronous WaitCommEvent() operations that can be tested and completed using the GetOverlappedResult() function.

You can get the current mask settings by calling the corresponding GetCommMask() function.

If you want to issue special communication events, you can use a number of special functions, such as SetCommBreak(), ClearCommBreak(), and EscapeCommFunction().

8

WORKING WITH
THE FILE SYSTEM

You can purge any pending input or output characters by calling the `PurgeComm()` function. If any hardware errors are detected, you can retrieve the details with `ClearCommError()`; the error condition is reset so that the device can continue.

Using Consoles

Consoles are special types of windows that emulate (and extend) the old 80×25 character DOS-style scrolling text display. An application can have only one attached console at any time, because the application's standard input and output channels are attached to the console.

You probably have seen the console in action when running the MS-DOS command prompt. This console lets you change the font size and screen buffer size, as well as modify the display to full-screen text mode. The console also provides limited cut-and-paste editing support.

The console uses selectable 8-bit code pages to display ANSI character set and national variants. You also can set attributes to show background and foreground colors.

Allocating a Console

Your application can start the console window simply by calling the `AllocConsole()` function. It can detach itself from the console by calling `FreeConsole()`.

You can attach Win32 handles by calling `CreateFile()` and passing either `CONIN$` or `CONOUT$` as the filename and using the `OPEN_EXISTING` flag for the open mode parameter. Alternatively, the `GetStdHandle()` function returns the input, output, or error handles when `GetStdHandle()` is passed `STD_INPUT_HANDLE`, `STD_OUTPUT_HANDLE`, or `STD_ERROR_HANDLE`, respectively. Or, you can redirect the standard handles of a console window by using the corresponding `SetStdHandle()` function.

Console I/O

After the console window is open and attached, you can use low-level, streams-based, or Win32 I/O (covered earlier in this chapter) to communicate with it.

Alternatively, a set of console-specific functions—such as `ReadConsole()` and `WriteConsole()`—can read characters from the keyboard and write character strings to the console window. You can use `PeekConsoleInput()` to read characters from the input buffer without removing them so that subsequent `ReadConsole()` functions retrieve the same "peeked at" characters.

You can call `SetConsoleTextAttribute()` to set the default color attributes of characters subsequently written to the console by passing combined attribute flags, such as `BACK-GROUND_GREEN`, `FOREGROUND_RED`, and `FOREGROUND_INTENSITY`. These flags let you set eight foreground and background colors, each with two levels of brightness, giving 16 overall colors.

You can reposition the console's cursor by using the `SetConsoleCursorPosition()` function and passing the column (X) and row (Y) `SHORT` coordinates in a `COORD` structure. You can change your cursor's size and visibility with the `SetConsoleCursorInfo()` function after setting the `dwSize` and `bVisible` members of the `CONSOLE_CURSOR_INFO` structure. The `SetConsoleCursorPosition()` and `SetConsoleCursorInfo()` counterparts fill the appropriate structures to return the current settings.

You can change the input and output code pages with the `SetConsoleCP()` and `SetConsoleOutputCP()` functions. These change the way keyboard characters are mapped for input and display characters are shown for output.

You can simulate special keyboard events, such as Ctrl+Break and Ctrl+C keys (specified by the `CTRL_BREAK_EVENT` and `CTRL_C_EVENT` flags), by using the `GenerateConsoleCtrlEvent()` function. These events—whether generated by the user or from your code—can be handled by your supplied handler function. Your handler function must be registered with a call to `SetConsoleCtrlHandler()`, which can add a chain of event-handler functions.

Customizing the Console Buffers and Display

You can use a range of functions to set scrollable display buffers that are larger than the current display size. You can change the size of the window using the `SetConsoleWindowInfo()` function. You can find the largest possible size from `GetLargestConsoleWindowSize()` and the current settings from `GetConsoleWindowInfo()`.

You can set the scrollable buffer larger than the visible console region. You can set this buffer size using `SetConsoleScreenBufferSize()` and passing a `COORD` structure holding the new number of rows and columns for the screen buffer. The `ScrollConsoleScreenBuffer()` function then lets you scroll the visible region from within your code to display various parts of the text buffer.

You can customize the title bar of your console window with a call to `SetConsoleTitle()` passing a pointer to the new text string.

Summary

The evolution of the Windows operating system has spawned and supported many file-system types to provide backward (and sideward) compatibility and to provide advanced security and performance (in Windows NT).

Although this evolution is healthy, it does mean that as a software developer, you must be aware of the potential differences in file I/O functions across operating systems and file systems.

The fundamental Win32 file-handling functions are powerful and flexible tools for manipulating normal disk files and I/O devices with a common set of API tools. You can use overlapped (or asynchronous) I/O to improve the performance of your application and to let the operating system implement multithreaded I/O requests instead of having to spawn new threads to handle blocking I/O.

You can use the Win32 synchronization objects with the I/O API functions to provide flexible and efficient waiting and signaling support for your I/O problems. These synchronization objects are particularly useful when dealing with relatively slow communications devices, such as serial ports.

Handling the complex hardware functionality of communication resources can be safely and easily delegated to the operating system. This leaves you with the more pleasant task of implementing your specific application requirements instead of delving down to the device level, as often was required in previous platforms.

The low-level I/O, stream-based I/O, and C++ IOStream classes provide compatibility with other operating systems such as UNIX and DOS. They also can simplify the implementation of file handling and simple text-based applications.

You can use the console window to help provide an emulation of old scrolling terminals and DOS consoles while gaining larger-than-screen-size scrolling buffer support and an ANSI-compatible text-mode display.

Using Serialization with File and Archive Objects

by Mickey Williams

In This Chapter

Serialization is the method used by MFC to store an object to a file or another type of storage. The MFC serialization architecture uses three classes (all are discussed in this chapter):

- The CFile class models a Win32 file I/O object. Some differences exist between Win32 file objects and MFC CFile file objects; these differences are discussed in this chapter.

- CObject provides a common framework for objects to serialize themselves—a property known as *persistence*.

- CArchive handles the serialization of a CObject instance to a CFile object.

This chapter also discusses how you can use the CFile class without using the full MFC Document/View architecture.

File I/O Differences Between MFC and Win32

Win32 and the MFC class library approach application input and output in different ways:

- When using Win32 file I/O functions, you create a file handle and manipulate the file handle with functions such as ReadFile and WriteFile. If there is an error in a Win32 file I/O function, these functions return FALSE, and you must call the Win32 GetLastError function to determine the specific cause of the error.

- When using MFC file I/O, input and output are performed in a more object-oriented manner using the CFile and CArchive classes. If an error occurs, a C++ exception is raised that contains detailed error information.

Using Basic Win32 File I/O

In a Win32 program, file I/O requires a file handle, which is a variable of type HANDLE. No matter what specific type of file I/O you are using, whether it's dealing with disk files, sockets, pipes, or some other Win32 I/O type, you always start by creating a HANDLE. After you open a file handle, the actual input and output are performed with the WriteFile and ReadFile functions. (Enhanced versions of these functions also exist that are used exclusively on Windows NT.) Listing 9.1 provides a short C++ example of a typical Win32 console-mode application named FileCopy to demonstrate how Win32 file I/O is used. FileCopy is a naive implementation of the Win32 CopyFile function.

LISTING 9.1 Using Win32 Functions to Copy a File

```c
#include <windows.h>

char g_szSource[_MAX_PATH];
char g_szDest[_MAX_PATH];
bool fetchParameters(int argc, char* argv[]);

int main(int argc, char* argv[])
{
    char szMsg[_MAX_PATH + 128];
    if(!fetchParameters(argc, argv))
        return 0;
    HANDLE hRead = CreateFile(g_szSource, GENERIC_READ,
                              FILE_SHARE_READ, NULL,
                              OPEN_EXISTING,
                              FILE_ATTRIBUTE_NORMAL, 0);
    if(hRead == INVALID_HANDLE_VALUE)
    {
        wsprintf(szMsg, "Can't open file: %s", (char*)g_szSource);
        MessageBox(NULL, szMsg, argv[0], MB_ICONHAND);
        return 0;
    }
    HANDLE hWrite = CreateFile(g_szDest, GENERIC_WRITE,
                               0, NULL,
                               CREATE_ALWAYS,
                               FILE_ATTRIBUTE_NORMAL, 0);
    if(hWrite == INVALID_HANDLE_VALUE)
    {
        wsprintf(szMsg, "Can't open file: %s", (char*)g_szDest);
        MessageBox(NULL, szMsg, argv[0], MB_ICONHAND);
        CloseHandle(hRead);
        return 0;
    }
    BOOL fRead = FALSE;
    BOOL fWrite = FALSE;
    DWORD dwRead = 0;
    DWORD dwWrite = 0;
    BYTE buff[4096];
    do
    {
        fRead = ReadFile(hRead, buff, sizeof(buff), &dwRead, 0);
        if(fRead && dwRead)
        {
            fWrite = WriteFile(hWrite, buff, dwRead, &dwWrite, 0);
        }
    }while(fRead && dwRead && fWrite && dwWrite);
    CloseHandle(hRead);
    CloseHandle(hWrite);
    return 0;
}
```

9

USING
SERIALIZATION

continues

LISTING 9.1 continued

```cpp
bool fetchParameters(int argc, char* argv[])
{
    if(argc != 3)
    {
        char szMsg[128] = "Usage: FileCopy Source Dest";
        MessageBox(NULL, szMsg, argv[0], MB_ICONHAND);
        return false;
    }
    lstrcpyn(g_szSource, argv[1], _MAX_PATH);
    lstrcpyn(g_szDest, argv[2], _MAX_PATH);
    return true;
}
```

You can compile the example program in Listing 9.1 by creating a Win32 Console Application project, or by using the following command-line (assuming the source file is saved as main.cpp):

```
cl /FeFileCopy.exe filecopy.cpp user32.lib
```

The FileCopy program accepts two filenames as parameters:

```
FileCopy sourcefile destfile
```

FileCopy reads up to 4,096 bytes from the source file into a buffer and copies the contents of the buffer into the destination file. Most of the source code shown in Listing 9.1 is devoted to parameter validation and error checking, even though the error checking is very basic—no information is provided about the specific type of error that occurred.

Using Basic MFC File I/O

The MFC class library uses the CFile class to represent a file I/O object. Listing 9.2 contains the MFCCopy program, a console-mode application that uses MFC for file I/O. Like the FileCopy program in the preceding section, MFCCopy copies the contents of a file from one location to another. Unlike FileCopy, MFCCopy takes advantage of the object-oriented nature of the CFile class and reduces the amount of code that must be written.

LISTING 9.2 A Console-Mode Program That Uses MFC File I/O

```cpp
#include <afx.h>
#include <afxwin.h>

char g_szSource[_MAX_PATH];
char g_szDest[_MAX_PATH];
bool fetchParameters(int argc, char* argv[]);

int main(int argc, char* argv[])
```

```
{
    AfxWinInit(::GetModuleHandle(NULL), NULL,
               ::GetCommandLine(), 0);
    if(!fetchParameters(argc, argv))
        return 0;
    try
    {
        DWORD dwRead;
        CFile fileSrc(g_szSource, CFile::modeRead);
        CFile fileDest(g_szDest, CFile::modeCreate|CFile::modeWrite);
        BYTE buff[4096];
        while((dwRead = fileSrc.Read(&buff, sizeof(buff))) != 0)
        {
            fileDest.Write(&buff, dwRead);
        }
        // CFile destructors will close the files.
    }
    catch(CFileException* pe)
    {
        char szMsg[256];
        pe->GetErrorMessage(szMsg, sizeof(szMsg));
        MessageBox(NULL, szMsg, argv[0], MB_ICONHAND);
        pe->Delete();
    }
    return 0;
}

bool fetchParameters(int argc, char* argv[])
{
    if(argc != 3)
    {
        char szMsg[128] = "Usage: MFCCopy Source Dest";
        MessageBox(NULL, szMsg, argv[0], MB_ICONHAND);
        return false;
    }
    lstrcpyn(g_szSource, argv[1], _MAX_PATH);
    lstrcpyn(g_szDest, argv[2], _MAX_PATH);
    return true;

}
```

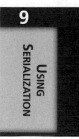

9

USING
SERIALIZATION

Compare the MFCCopy source in Listing 9.2 to the source code for FileCopy in Listing 9.1. One difference in the MFCCopy project is that the CFile class greatly simplifies how you open a disk file; you can specify the name of the file as a parameter to the object's constructor. Another difference is the use of C++ exception handling—all errors are reported as exceptions. MFCCopy actually has more functionality than FileCopy, with fewer lines of code. MFCCopy displays an accurate error message for all types of file I/O errors, for example. The CFile class is discussed in more detail in the next section, "Working with the CFile Class."

The MFCCopy project is located on the CD-ROM included with this book. To create the MFCCopy project from scratch, create a Win32 console-mode application using AppWizard. When the wizard for the type of console-mode application prompts you, select the An Empty Project radio button. After adding the source code from Listing 9.2 to the project, modify the build settings so that the MFC class library is included with the project. Choose Settings from the Project menu. After the Project Settings dialog box appears, select the General tab. You can use the General tab to change the current MFC build settings for the project. Select one of the settings that includes MFC and build the project.

Alternatively, you can save Listing 9.2 as main.cpp, and use the following command-line to create the MFCCopy executable:

```
cl /GX /MT /FeMFCCopy.exe main.cpp user32.lib
```

Working with the `CFile` Class

CFile is used as a base class for all MFC file classes. As Figure 9.1 shows, the MFC class library lets you choose from six file classes.

FIGURE 9.1
CFile *and other*
MFC file classes.

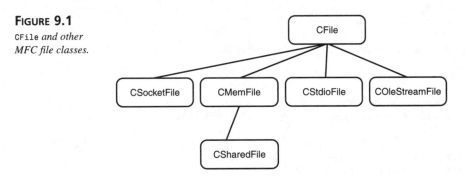

CFile is a general file class, and the other classes are used for more specialized types of files:

- CStdioFile wraps a standard C stream file handle like the standard output handle with a CFile-derived class.
- CMemFile manages a file that is hosted in memory rather than on disk.
- CSharedFile allows for files to be shared in memory.
- COleStreamFile provides CFile access to *Component Object Model* (COM) compound files.
- CSocketFile wraps a Windows socket with a CFile-derived class.

Opening Files

There are two ways to open a file using `CFile`:

- The simplest method is to pass the name of the file to be opened as a parameter to the constructor, as was done in Listing 9.2.

- Alternatively, you can create a `CFile` instance using the default constructor and explicitly open a file using the `Open` member function.

If you open the file during construction, you must use C++ exception handling to handle error conditions. If you don't handle exceptions with this type of construction and an error occurs, your program will be terminated due to the unhandled exception.

The standard pattern for opening a `CFile` during construction and handling any exceptions looks like this:

```
try
{
    CFile myFile("C:\"MyFile", CFile::modeRead);
    // use file here
}
catch(CFileException* pe)
{
    char szMsg[256];
    pe->GetErrorMessage(szMsg, sizeof(szMsg));
    MessageBox(NULL, szMsg, argv[0], MB_ICONHAND);
    pe->Delete();
}
```

The second parameter passed to the `CFile` constructor is used to hold one or more flags that indicate how the file will be opened. Multiple flags are combined using the C++ or symbol, `|`. The most commonly used values follow:

- `modeRead` opens the file for reading only.
- `modeWrite` opens the file for writing only.
- `modeReadWrite` opens the file for both reading and writing.
- `modeCreate` creates the file if it doesn't already exist. If the file exists, the current file is erased, unless `modeNoTruncate` is used.
- `shareDenyNone` gives other processes read and write access to the file.
- `shareDenyWrite` prevents other processes from writing to the file.
- `shareDenyRead` prevents other processes from reading the file.
- `shareExclusive` prevents other processes from writing to or reading the file.

Other mode flags are used to control inheritance of the underlying file handle and to prevent an existing file from being truncated. Check the documentation for `CFile` for details.

9

USING SERIALIZATION

To open a file explicitly, use the `CFile::Open` member function, passing the filename and file open flags as parameters:

```
CFile file;
BOOL bOpened = file.open("C:\MyFile", CFile::modeRead);
if(bOpened == FALSE)
{
    // Handle error
}
```

You should use the `CFile` constructor that accepts a filename only when you are fairly certain that the file can be opened. If you aren't sure whether the file will be opened successfully, it usually is easier to handle errors by using `CFile::Open`, which doesn't raise exceptions.

The `CFile::Close` member function is used to explicitly close an open `CFile`. When an instance of `CFile` is destroyed, the `CFile` destructor checks and closes any open files.

Reading and Writing from a `CFile` Object

Reading and writing to MFC `CFile` instances is much simpler than using the Win32 alternatives. To read from a `CFile` instance, the `Read` member function is used:

```
try
{
    BYTE buff[4096];
    CFile myFile("C:\MyFile", CFile::modeRead);
    DWORD dwRead = myFile.Read(&buff, sizeof(buff));
}
catch(CFileException* pe)
{
    // Handle exception ...
    pe->Delete(); // Free exception instance
}
```

Read takes two parameters:

- The address of a buffer to be filled
- The maximum number of bytes that can be stored in the buffer

The Read member function returns the number of bytes read from the `CFile`. If an error occurs, an exception is raised.

To write to a `CFile` instance, use the `Write` member function:

```
try
{
    CFile myFile("C:\MyFile",  CFile::modeCreate|CFile::modeWrite);
    fileDest.Write(&buff, dwBytesToWrite);
```

```
}
catch(CFileException* pe)
{
    // Handle exception ...
    pe->Delete(); // Free exception instance
}
```

Write takes two parameters:

- The address of a buffer to be written to the CFile instance
- The number of bytes to be written to the file

Write has no return value; if an error occurs, an exception is raised.

You must handle exceptions with the Read and Write member functions. If you don't and an error occurs, your program will be terminated.

Using the CArchive and CObject Classes

When you serialize an object, it is always serialized through an archive rather than directly to a file. You use two MFC classes to serialize objects to an archive:

- CArchive is almost always a file and is the object that other persistent objects are serialized to or from.
- CObject defines all of the interfaces used to serialize objects to or from a CArchive object.

Objects are serialized in one of two ways. As a rule of thumb, if an object is derived from CObject, that object's Serialize member function is called in the following way:

```
myObject.Serialize(ar);
```

If the object is not derived from CObject (such as a CRect object, for example), you should use the insertion operator in the following way:

```
ar << rcWnd;
```

This insertion operator is overloaded in the same way it is for cout, cin, and cerr, which were used extensively in the first part of this book for console-mode input and output.

Using the CObject Class

You must use the CObject class for all classes that use the MFC class library's built-in support for serialization. The CObject class contains virtual functions that are used during serialization. In addition, the CArchive class is declared as a "friend" class for CObject, giving it access to private and protected member variables.

9

USING
SERIALIZATION

The most commonly used virtual function in `CObject` is `Serialize`, which is called to serialize or deserialize the object from a `CArchive` object. This function is declared as virtual so that any persistent object can be called through a pointer to `CObject` in the following way:

```
CObject* pObj = GetNextObject();
pObj->Serialize(ar);
```

As discussed later in the section "Using the Serialization Macros," when you're deriving a persistent class from `CObject`, you must use two macros to help implement the serialization functions.

Using the `CArchive` Class

You use the `CArchive` class to model a generic storage object. In most cases, a `CArchive` object is attached to a disk file. In some cases, however, the object might be connected to an object that only seems to be a file, such as a memory location or another type of storage.

When a `CArchive` object is created, it is defined as used for either input or output but never both. You can use the `IsStoring` and `IsLoading` functions to determine whether a `CArchive` object is used for input or output, as Listing 9.3 shows.

LISTING 9.3 Using the `CArchive::IsStoring` Function to Determine the Serialization Direction

```
CMyObject:Serialize( CArchive& ar )
{
    if( ar.IsStoring() )
        // Write object state to ar
    else
        // Read object state from ar
}
```

Understanding Serialization in MFC

Serialization is the way that classes derived from `CDocument` store and retrieve data from an archive, which is usually associated with an instance of `CFile`. Serialization is the process of storing the state of an object for the purpose of loading it at another time. The property of an object to be stored and loaded is sometimes called *persistence,* which also is defined as the capability of an object to remember its state between executions. Figure 9.2 shows the interaction between a serialized object and an archive.

9

USING
SERIALIZATION

FIGURE 9.2
Serializing an object to and from an archive.

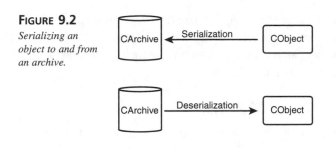

When an object is serialized, information about the type of object is written to storage, along with information and data about the object. When an object is deserialized, the same process happens in reverse, and the object is loaded and created from the input stream.

Using serialization to store objects is much more flexible than writing specialized functions that store data in a fixed format. Objects that are persistent are capable of storing themselves instead of relying on an external function to read and write them to disk. This capability makes a persistent object much easier to reuse, because the object is more self-contained.

Persistent objects also help you easily write programs that are saved to storage. An object that is serialized might be made up of many smaller objects that also are serialized. Because individual objects often are stored in a collection, serializing the collection also serializes all objects contained in the collection.

Using the Insertion and Extraction Operators

The MFC class library overloads the insertion and extraction operators for many commonly used classes and basic types. You often use the insertion operator << to serialize or store data to the CArchive object. You use the extraction operator >> to deserialize or load data from a CArchive object.

These operators are defined for all basic C++ types, as well as a few commonly used classes not derived from CObject, such as the CString, CRect, and CTime classes. The insertion and extraction operators return a reference to a CArchive object, enabling them to be chained together in the following way:

```
archive << m_nFoo << m_rcClient << m_szName;
```

When used with classes that are derived from CObject, the insertion and extraction operators allocate the memory storage required to contain an object and then call the object's Serialize member function. If you do not need to allocate storage, you should call the Serialize member function directly.

As a rule of thumb, if you know the type of the object when it is deserialized, call the Serialize function directly. In addition, you must always call Serialize exclusively. If you use Serialize to load or store an object, you must not use the insertion and extraction operators at any other time with that object.

Using the Serialization Macros

You must use two macros when creating a persistent class based on CObject. Use the DECLARE_SERIAL macro in the class declaration file and the IMPLEMENT_SERIAL macro in the class implementation file.

Declaring a Persistent Class

The DECLARE_SERIAL macro takes a single parameter: the name of the class to be serialized. A good place to put this macro is on the first line of the class declaration, where it serves as a reminder that the class can be serialized. Listing 9.4 provides an example of a class that can be serialized. Save this source code in a file named Users.h.

LISTING 9.4   The CUser Class Declaration

```
#pragma once
class CUser : public CObject
{
    DECLARE_SERIAL(CUser);
public:
    // Constructors
    CUser();
    CUser(const CString& strName, const CString& strAddr);
    // Attributes
    void Set(const CString& strName, const CString& strAddr);
    CString GetName() const;
    CString GetAddr() const;
    // Operations
    virtual void Serialize(CArchive& ar);
    // Implementation
private:
    // The user's name
    CString m_strName;
    // The user's e-mail address
    CString m_strAddr;
};
```

Defining a Persistent Class

The IMPLEMENT_SERIAL macro takes three parameters and usually is placed before any member functions are defined for a persistent class. The parameters for IMPLEMENT_SERIAL follow:

- The class to be serialized
- The immediate base class of the class being serialized
- The schema or version number

The *schema number* is a version number for the class layout used when you're serializing and deserializing objects. If the schema number of the data being loaded does not match the schema number of the object reading the file, the program throws an exception. The schema number should be incremented when changes are made that affect serialization, such as adding a class member or changing the serialization order.

Listing 9.5 provides the member functions for the CUser class, including the IMPLE-MENT_SERIAL macro. Save this source code in a file named Users.cpp.

LISTING 9.5   The CUser Member Functions

```
#include "stdafx.h"
#include "Users.h"

IMPLEMENT_SERIAL(CUser, CObject, 1);
CUser::CUser() { }
CUser::CUser(const CString& strName, const CString& strAddr)
{
    Set(strName, strAddr);
}
void CUser::Set(const CString& strName, const CString& strAddr)
{
    m_strName = strName;
    m_strAddr = strAddr;
}
CString CUser::GetName() const
{
    return m_strName;
}
CString CUser::GetAddr() const
{
    return m_strAddr;

}
```

9

USING
SERIALIZATION

Overriding the Serialize Function

Every persistent class must implement a Serialize member function, which is called in order to serialize or deserialize an object. The single parameter for Serialize is the CArchive object used for loading or storing the object. Listing 9.6 shows the version of Serialize used by the CUser class; add this function to the Users.cpp source file.

LISTING 9.6   The `CUser::Serialize` Member Function

```
void CUser::Serialize(CArchive& ar)
{
    if(ar.IsLoading())
    {
        ar >> m_strName >> m_strAddr;
    }
    else
    {
        ar << m_strName << m_strAddr;
    }
}
```

Creating a Serialized Collection

You can serialize most MFC collection classes, enabling large amounts of information to be stored and retrieved easily. You can serialize a `CArray` collection by calling its `Serialize` member function, for example. As with the other MFC template-based collection classes, you cannot use the insertion and extraction operators with `CArray`.

By default, the template-based collection classes perform a bitwise write when serializing a collection and a bitwise read when deserializing an archive. This means that the data stored in the collection is written bit by bit to the archive.

Bitwise serialization is a problem when you use collections to store pointers to objects. The `Customers` project uses the `CArray` class to store a collection of `CUser` objects, for example. The declaration of the `CArray` member follows:

```
CArray<CUser*, CUser*&>    m_setOfUsers;
```

Because the `m_setOfUsers` collection stores `CUser` pointers, storing the collection using a bitwise write would store only the current addresses of the contained objects. This information would become useless when the archive is deserialized.

Most of the time, you need to implement a helper function to assist in serializing a template-based collection. Helper functions do not belong to a class; they are global functions that are overloaded based on the function signature. The helper function used when serializing a template is `SerializeElements`. Figure 9.3 shows how you call the `SerializeElements` function to help serialize items stored in a collection.

FIGURE 9.3

The SerializeElements helper function.

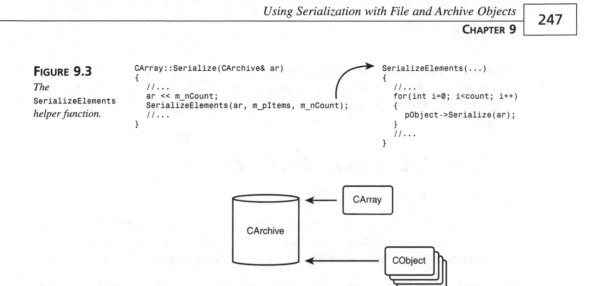

```
CArray::Serialize(CArchive& ar)
{
    //...
    ar << m_nCount;
    SerializeElements(ar, m_pItems, m_nCount);
    //...
}
```

```
SerializeElements(...)
{
    //...
    for(int i=0; i<count; i++)
    {
        pObject->Serialize(ar);
    }
    //...
}
```

Listing 9.7 provides a version of SerializeElements used with collections of CUser objects. This function is used later in the chapter, in the section, "Modifying the Document Class."

LISTING 9.7   The SerializeElements Function

```
void AFXAPI SerializeElements( CArchive&    ar,
                               CUser**      pUser,
                               int          nCount )
{
    for( int i = 0; i < nCount; i++, pUser++ )
    {
        if( ar.IsStoring() )
        {
            (*pUser)->Serialize(ar);
        }
        else
        {
            CUser* pNewUser = new CUser;
            pNewUser->Serialize(ar);
            *pUser = pNewUser;
        }
    }
}
```

The SerializeOElements function has three parameters:

- A pointer to a CArchive object, as with Serialize.
- The address of an object stored in the collection. In this example, pointers to CUser are stored in a CArray, so the parameter is a pointer to a CUser pointer.
- The number of elements to be serialized.

9

USING SERIALIZATION

In Listing 9.7, when you're serializing objects to the archive, each CUser object is written individually to the archive. When you're deserializing objects, a new CUser object is created, and that object is deserialized from the archive. The collection stores a pointer to the new object.

Using Serialization with Document/View

The Document/View architecture uses serialization to save or open documents. When a document is saved or loaded, the MFC framework in cooperation with the application's document class creates a CArchive object and serializes the document to or from storage.

The CDocument member functions required to perform serialization in a Document/View application are mapped onto the New, Open, Save, and Save As commands available from the File menu. These member functions take care of creating or opening a document, tracking the modification status of a document, and serializing it to storage.

When a document is loaded, a CArchive object is created for reading, and the archive is deserialized into the document. When a document is saved, a CArchive object is created for writing, and the document is written to the archive. At other times, the CDocument class tracks the current modification status of the document's data. If the document has been updated, the user is prompted to save the document before closing it.

The routines CArchive uses for reading and writing to storage are highly optimized and provide excellent performance, even when you're serializing many small data objects. In most cases, it is difficult to match both the performance and ease of use that you get from using the built-in serialization support offered for Document/View applications.

How Are Document/View Applications Serialized?

As you know, data stored in a Document/View application is contained by a class derived from CDocument. This class is responsible for controlling the serialization of all data contained by the document class. This includes tracking modifications to the document so that the program can display a warning before the user closes an unsaved document.

A document's life cycle includes five phases:

- Creating a new document
- Modifying the document

- Storing or serializing the document
- Closing the document
- Loading or deserializing the document

Creating a Document

Multiple-document interface (*MDI*) and *single-document interface* (*SDI*) applications create their documents differently. An MDI application creates a new CDocument class for every open document, whereas an SDI program reuses a single document.

Both SDI and MDI applications call the OnNewDocument function to initialize a document object. The default version of OnNewDocument calls the DeleteContents function to reset any data contained by the document. AppWizard supplies a DeleteContents function for your document class when a project is created. Most applications can just add code to DeleteContents instead of overriding OnNewDocument.

Tracking Modifications to a Document

To determine whether a document object can be closed, the MFC framework calls IsModified, a virtual function that is part of the CDocument class. If the document has unsaved changes, the IsDocument function returns TRUE. Although this function can be overridden in any class derived from CDocument, you usually should use the default behavior.

You can use the IsModified function to test whether a document has been serialized:

```
if( IsModified() == TRUE )
{
    AfxMessageBox("Save File Now?");
}
```

The IsModified function tests the value of a modification flag, or *dirty bit,* which is set when changes are made to the document and cleared when the document is saved or loaded. Classes that are derived from CDocument must update the status of the modification flag when the data contained by the document changes. You use the SetModifiedFlag function to clear or set the modification status of a document:

```
SetModifiedFlag(FALSE);
```

The SetModifiedFlag function has a single parameter: Pass TRUE to mark the document as dirty or changed, and pass FALSE to mark the document as clean or unchanged. The parameter has a default value of TRUE, so to mark the document as changed, you can call the function with no parameters:

```
SetModifiedFlag();
```

9

USING
SERIALIZATION

In most cases, you call `SetModifedFlag` only when marking a document as changed. The MFC Document/View framework takes care of resetting the modification flag after the document is serialized.

Storing a Document

When the user saves a document by choosing Save from the File menu, the `CWinApp::OnFileSave` function is called. This function is almost never overridden; it's a good idea to leave it alone, because it calls the `CDocument::OnOpenDocument` function to serialize the document's data. The default version of `OnOpenDocument` creates a `CArchive` object and passes it to the document's `Serialize` member function. Usually, you serialize the data contained in the document. After the document's data has been serialized, the dirty bit is cleared, marking the document as unmodified. Figure 9.4 shows the steps involved in storing a document.

FIGURE 9.4

The major functions called when you store a document.

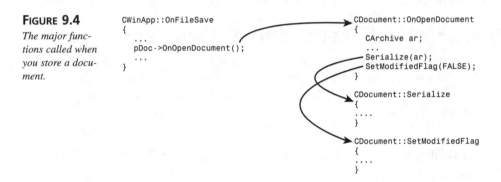

The default version of `OnOpenDocument` is sufficient for most applications. However, if your application stores data in a different way (for example, in several smaller files or in a database), you should override `OnOpenDocument`.

When the user chooses Save As from the File menu, a common file dialog box collects filename information. After the user selects a filename, the program calls the same `CDocument` functions, and the serialization process works as described previously.

Closing a Document

When the user closes a document, the MFC Document/View framework calls the document object's `OnCloseDocument` member function, as Figure 9.5 shows. The default version of this function checks the document to make sure that no unsaved changes are lost by calling the `IsModified` function. If the user did not modify the document object, `DeleteContents` is called to free the data stored by the document, and all views for the document are closed.

FIGURE 9.5

The major functions called when you close a document.

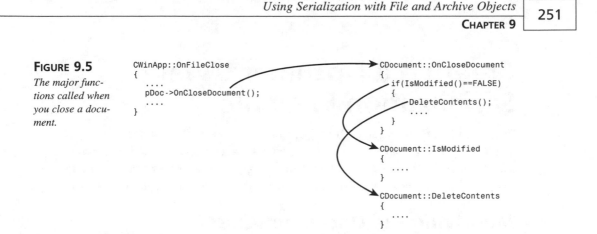

If the user made changes to the document, the program displays a message box that asks the user whether the document's unsaved changes should be saved. If the user elects to save the document, the `Serialize` function is called. The document then is closed by calling `DeleteContents` and closing all views for the document.

Loading a Document

When you're loading a document, the MFC framework calls the document object's `OnOpenDocument` function. The default version of this function calls the `DeleteContents` member function and then calls `Serialize` to load or deserialize the archive. The default version of `OnOpenDocument`, shown in Figure 9.6, is sufficient for almost any application.

FIGURE 9.6

The major functions called when you open a document.

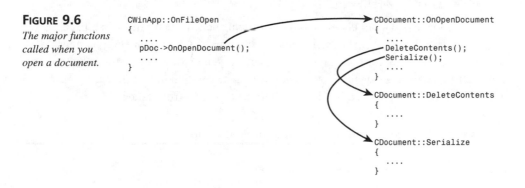

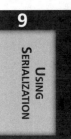

9

USING SERIALIZATION

Creating a Document/View Serialization Example

Using AppWizard, create an MDI project named `Customers`. This project uses serialization to store a very simple list of customer names and email addresses, using the persistent `CUser` class created earlier in this chapter. Copy the source files created earlier, `Users.cpp` and `Users.h`, into the project directory and add `Users.cpp` to the project.

Modifying the Document Class

The document class has one new data member—a `CArray` object that stores a collection of `CUser` pointers representing a customer list. The document class also has two member functions used to get access to the array of `CUser` pointers. Add declarations for `m_setOfUsers` and two member functions to the `CCustomersDoc` class, as Listing 9.8 shows.

LISTING 9.8   Adding a `CArray` Member Variable to the `CCustomersDoc` Class

```
// Attributes
public:
    int     GetCount() const;
    CUser* GetUser(int nUser) const;
protected:
    CArray<CUser*, CUser*&> m_setOfUsers;
```

You should make two other changes to the `CustomersDoc.h` header file. First, because the `CArray` template `m_setOfUsers` is declared in terms of `CUser` pointers, you must add an `#include` statement for the `Users.h` file. Second, you use a version of the `SerializeElements` helper function, so you need a declaration of that global function. Add the source code provided in Listing 9.9 to the top of `CustomersDoc.h`.

LISTING 9.9   Changes to the `CustomersDoc.h` Header File

```
#include "Users.h"
void AFXAPI SerializeElements( CArchive& ar,
                               CUser**   pUser,
                               int       nCount );
```

Because the `CCustomerDoc` class contains a `CArray` member variable, the template collection declarations must be included in the project. Add an `#include` statement to the bottom of the `StdAfx.h` file:

```
#include "afxtempl.h"
```

Creating a Dialog Box

The dialog box used to enter data for the Customers example is similar to dialog boxes created for previous examples. Create a dialog box that contains two Edit controls, as Figure 9.7 shows.

FIGURE 9.7

The dialog box used in the Customers *sample project.*

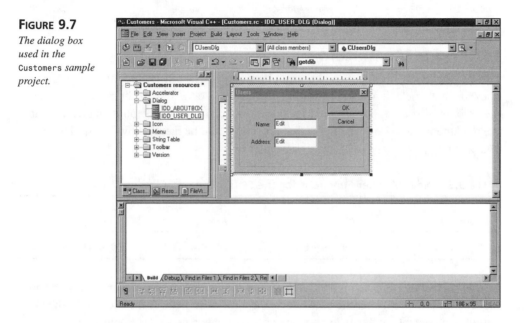

Give the new dialog box a resource ID of IDD_USER_DLG. The two Edit controls are used to add usernames and email addresses to a document contained by the CCustomerDoc class. Use the values in Table 9.1 for the two Edit controls.

TABLE 9.1 Edit Controls Contained in the IDD_USER_DLG Dialog Box

Edit Control	Resource ID
Name	IDC_EDIT_NAME
Address	IDC_EDIT_ADDR

Using ClassWizard, add a class named CUsersDlg to handle the new dialog box. Add two CString variables to the class using the values in Table 9.2.

9

USING
SERIALIZATION

TABLE 9.2 New `CString` Member Variables for the `CUsersDlg` Class

Resource ID Type	Name	Category	Variable
IDC_EDIT_NAME	m_strName	Value	CString
IDC_EDIT_ADDR	m_strAddr	Value	CString

Adding a Menu Item

Use the values in Table 9.3 to add a menu item and message-handling function to the `CCustomersDoc` class. Add the new menu item, Add User..., to the Edit menu. To reduce the amount of source code required for this example, handle the menu item directly with the document class. However, the dialog box also could be handled by a view class or `CMainFrame`.

TABLE 9.3 New Member Functions for the `CCustomersDoc` Class

Menu ID	Caption	Event	Function Name
ID_EDIT_USER	Add User...	COMMAND	OnEditUser

Listing 9.10 contains the complete source code for the `OnEditUser` function, which handles the message sent after the user selects the new menu item. If the user clicks the OK button, the contents of the dialog box are used to create a new `CUser` object, and a pointer to the new object is added to the `m_setOfUsers` collection. The `SetModifiedFlag` function is called to mark the document as changed. Add the source code provided in Listing 9.10 to the `CCustomersDoc::OnEditUser` member function.

LISTING 9.10 Adding a New `CUser` Object to the Document Class

```
void CCustomersDoc::OnEditUser()
{
    CUsersDlg    dlg;

    if(dlg.DoModal() == IDOK)
    {
        CUser*  pUser = new CUser(dlg.m_strName, dlg.m_strAddr);

        m_setOfUsers.Add(pUser);
        UpdateAllViews(NULL);
        SetModifiedFlag();
    }
}
```

Add the source code provided in Listing 9.10 to the `CustomersDoc.cpp` source file. These functions provide access to the data contained by the document. The view class, `CCustomerView`, calls the two `CCustomersDoc` member functions provided in Listing 9.11 when updating the view window.

LISTING 9.11   Document Class Member Functions Used for Data Access

```
int CCustomersDoc::GetCount() const
{
    return m_setOfUsers.GetSize();
}

CUser* CCustomersDoc::GetUser(int nUser) const
{
    CUser* pUser = 0;
    if(nUser < m_setOfUsers.GetSize())
        pUser = m_setOfUsers.GetAt(nUser);
    return pUser;
}
```

Every document needs a `Serialize` member function. The `CCustomersDoc` class has only one data member, so its `Serialize` function deals only with m_setOfUsers, as Listing 9.12 shows. Add this source code to the `CCustomersDoc::Serialize` member function.

LISTING 9.12   Serializing the Contents of the Document Class

```
void CCustomersDoc::Serialize(CArchive& ar)
{
    m_setOfUsers.Serialize(ar);
}
```

As discussed earlier in the chapter, the `CArray` class uses the `SerializeElements` helper function when the collection is serialized. Add the `SerializeElements` function provided in Listing 9.7 to the `CustomersDoc.cpp` source file.

Add an `#include` statement to the `CustomersDoc.cpp` file so that the `CCustomersDoc` class can have access to declarations of classes used by `CCustomersDoc`. Add the source code from Listing 9.13 near the top of the `CustomersDoc.cpp` file, just after the other `#include` statements.

LISTING 9.13   include Statements Used by the `CCustomersDoc` Class

```
#include "Users.h"
#include "UsersDlg.h"
```

9

USING
SERIALIZATION

Modifying the View

The view class, CCustomersView, displays the current contents of the document. When the document is updated, the view is repainted and displays the updated contents. You must update two functions in the CCustomersView class: OnDraw and OnUpdate.

AppWizard creates a skeleton version of the CCustomersView::OnDraw function. Add the source code from Listing 9.14 to OnDraw so that the current document contents are displayed in the view. Because this is not a scrolling view, a limited number of items from the document can be displayed.

LISTING 9.14   Using OnDraw to Display the Current Document's Contents

```
void CCustomersView::OnDraw(CDC* pDC)
{
    CCustomersDoc* pDoc = GetDocument();
    ASSERT_VALID(pDoc);
    // Calculate the space required for a single
    // line of text, including the inter-line area.
    TEXTMETRIC  tm;
    pDC->GetTextMetrics(&tm);
    int nLineHeight = tm.tmHeight + tm.tmExternalLeading;
    CPoint  ptText(0, 0);
    for(int nIndex = 0; nIndex < pDoc->GetCount(); nIndex++)
    {
        CString strOut;
        CUser* pUser = pDoc->GetUser(nIndex);
        szOut.Format("User = %s, email = %s",
                        pUser->GetName(),
                        pUser->GetAddr());
        pDC->TextOut(ptText.x, ptText.y, szOut);
        ptText.y += nLineHeight;
    }
}
```

As with most documents, the CCustomersDoc class calls UpdateAllViews when it is updated. The MFC framework then calls the OnUpdate function for each view connected to the document.

Add a message-handling function for CCustomersView::OnUpdate and add the source code from Listing 9.15 to it. The OnUpdate function invalidates the view, resulting in the view being redrawn with the updated contents.

LISTING 9.15   Invalidating the View During OnUpdate

```
void CCustomersView::OnUpdate( CView* pSender,
                               LPARAM lHint,
                               CObject* pHint)
```

```
{
    InvalidateRect( NULL );
}
```

Add an #include statement to the CustomersView.cpp file so that the view can use the
CUser class. Add the #include statement below the other #include statements in
CustomersView.cpp.

```
#include "Users.h"
```

Compile and run the Customers project. Add names to the project by choosing Add User
from the Edit menu. Figure 9.8 shows an example of the Customers project after adding
a few names.

FIGURE 9.8

The Customers
project after
adding a few
names.

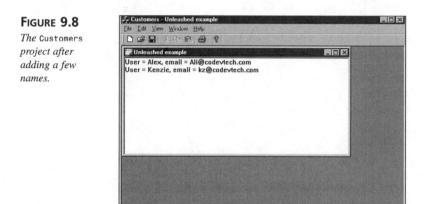

Serialize the contents of the document by saving it to a file, and close the document. You
can reload the document by opening the file.

Summary

In this chapter, you learned about serialization and persistence, and how they are implemented by MFC. You also learned about the classes that are used by MFC to implement
persistence and file I/O: CObject, CFile, and CArchive.

This chapter also discussed how the Document/View architecture uses persistence, and
an example project was created to demonstrate how MFC-based projects easily can serialize their data to disk.

Internet Programming with MFC

IN THIS PART

CHAPTER 10

MFC and the Internet Server API (ISAPI)

by David Bennett
and Andrew J. Indovina

IN THIS CHAPTER

In this chapter, you will look at the *Internet Server (IS) Application Programming Interface (API)*, which you can use to create your own custom enhancements to ISAPI-compliant *Hypertext Transfer Protocol (HTTP)* servers, such as the one included with Microsoft's *Internet Information Server (IIS)*. You look at both the C APIs that are included in ISAPI and the *Microsoft Foundation Classes (MFCs)* that are provided to encapsulate these functions.

ISAPI enables you to create two sorts of extensions to a Web server. The first is called an *Internet Server Extension Application,* or *ISA*. You will see how to implement a DLL that can be called by the Web server on behalf of a client to provide custom functionality similar to *Common Gateway Interface (CGI)* scripts. However, ISAs, which are loaded as a *dynamic link library (DLL)* into the server's memory address space, are more efficient than CGI scripts, which are separate executables that must be started each time a request is made for the script.

The second sort of extension you can create is an *ISAPI filter,* which can be called by the Web server to assist in handling various events in the processing of an HTTP request, ranging from the reading and writing of raw data to the output of log file entries. You can use ISAPI filters to add any number of different sorts of functionality to a Web server, including custom authentication, compression, encryption, and logging schemes.

In this chapter, you will explore version 4.0 of ISAPI, which is included with Visual C++ 6.0.

Developing a Server Extension Application

To get things started, let's look at how to create an Internet Server Extension Application (ISA), which is not really a standalone application but a DLL that can be loaded by the Web server to process requests more efficiently than CGI scripts. You will see the entry points that your DLL must export in order to be an ISA, as well as how your extensions communicate with the client and the server.

To install an ISA on your server, you need only copy the ISA DLL to a directory that is accessible by the HTTP server. The functions of this extension then can be accessed by a client with a request something like this:

```
http://scripts/myISA.dll?SendList?param1=3
```

ISA Entry Points

The DLLs that you develop with ISAPI will interact with the HTTP server by way of three entry points that your DLL exports. The first of these, GetExtensionVersion(), is called by the server when it first loads the extension DLL, and it is used to report the version of ISAPI supported by the ISA. You may also choose to implement and export a TerminateExtension() function, which will be called before the extension DLL is unloaded, although this is not required. The final entry point that you must implement is HttpExtensionProc(), which will be called by the server to process requests to the ISA.

> **Note**
>
> Because the Web server supports concurrent threads, your ISA functions may be called by several different threads at the same time. To make sure that your ISA is thread-safe, take a look at the mechanisms taught in Chapter 16, "Multi-threading."

GetExtensionVersion()

Your extension DLL must export a GetExtensionVersion() function. This will be called by the server when it first loads your DLL, and it is intended to be used to report version information about your DLL to the server; however, you may also choose to do any other initialization that your DLL requires in this function.

Other than any initialization specific to your extension, the code for GetExtensionVersion() is fairly generic. You can pass a description of your ISA and the version of ISAPI that it supports back to the server. Most implementations will look something like this:

```
BOOL WINAPI GetExtensionVersion( HSE_VERSION_INFO *pVer)
{
    pVer->dwExtensionVersion = MAKELONG( HSE_VERSION_MINOR, HSE_VERSION_MAJOR);
    strncpy(pVer->lpszExtensionDesc, "A Description of Your ISA Here",
            HSE_MAX_EXT_DLL_NAME_LEN);
    return TRUE;
}
```

If something goes wrong in any additional initialization that you perform in GetExtensionVersion(), you can return FALSE, which will abort the loading of your extension.

10

MFC AND THE INTERNET SERVER API (ISAPI)

> **Note**
>
> Your ISA is like any other DLL in that you can specify an entry point to be called
> when loading the DLL. You also can use this entry point (usually `DllMain()`
> function) to perform any necessary initialization for your ISA.

TerminateExtension()

Your ISA also may export an implementation of the `TerminateExtension()` function,
although this is not required. This function is called whenever the server wants to unload
the extension DLL and may be useful for cleaning up any dynamic structures or extra
threads that you started in `GetExtensionVersion()`. Here is the prototype for
`TerminateExtension()`:

```
BOOL WINAPI TerminateExtension(DWORD dwFlags);
```

The `dwFlags` parameter will receive one of two values: When `dwFlags` is
`HSE_TERM_ADVISORY_UNLOAD`, the server would like to unload your DLL to tidy up a bit.
If you don't want to let the server unload your DLL, you can return `FALSE`. Otherwise,
returning `TRUE` will allow the server to unload the DLL. On the other hand, if `dwFlags` is
`HSE_TERM_MUST_UNLOAD`, your DLL is about to be unloaded whether or not you like it, so
if you need to clean up, you'd better do it now.

HttpExtensionProc()

In most cases, the bulk of the code for your ISA will be in the `HttpExtensionProc()`
function, which is called by the server for each request to the ISA. The following is the
prototype for this function:

```
DWORD HttpExtensionProc(LPEXTENSION_CONTROL_BLOCK *lpEcb);
```

At first glance, the prototype for `HttpExtensionProc()` looks quite simple, although the
`EXTENSION_CONTROL_BLOCK` (ECB) structure is a bit complicated—it provides many different fields that are passed into your DLL, as well as several different fields that are
returned to the server.

In addition, the ECB contains pointers to several different utility functions, provided by
the server, that your DLL can use in processing the request. It is these functions that
allow your ISA to receive additional information from the client and to send information
back to the client.

You will be looking at the ECB in greater detail in just a bit, but for now, let's take a
look at a simple example to see how the basics of the `HttpExtensionProc()` entry point

work. The following implementation will return a very simple HTML page to the client for any requests made to the ISA:

```c
#include <httpext.h>
#include <stdio.h>
#include <wininet.h>
DWORD WINAPI HttpExtensionProc( EXTENSION_CONTROL_BLOCK *pECB)
{
    BOOL bRc;
    char strStatus[100] = "200 OK";
    DWORD dwMsgLen;
    DWORD dwError;
    char retBuf[1000];

    sprintf(retBuf, "<FONT COLOR=BLUE SIZE=4>Hi Mom!</FONT>\r\n");
    // Send HTTP headers back to the client
    bRc = pECB->ServerSupportFunction( pECB->ConnID,
                                       HSE_REQ_SEND_RESPONSE_HEADER,
                                       strStatus,
                                       NULL,
                                       (LPDWORD) "Content-Type:
text/html\r\n\r\n");
    if(!bRc)
    {
        // An error occurred
        dwError = GetLastError();
        pECB->dwHttpStatusCode = HTTP_STATUS_SERVER_ERROR;
        return(HSE_STATUS_ERROR);
    }

    // Send response data to client
    dwMsgLen = strlen(retBuf);
    bRc = pECB->WriteClient(pECB->ConnID, retBuf, &dwMsgLen, HSE_IO_SYNC);
    if(bRc == FALSE)
    {
        dwError = GetLastError();
        // Do something with the error code...
        pECB->dwHttpStatusCode = HTTP_STATUS_SERVER_ERROR;
        return(HSE_STATUS_ERROR);
    }

    return(HSE_STATUS_SUCCESS);
} // end HttpExtensionProc
```

> **Note**
>
> Your ISA files should include `httpext.h`, although you will not need to link with any special libraries—all the ISAPI-specific functions you will use are passed via pointers from the Web server.

In this example, you use two of the callback functions provided by the Web server via pointers in the ECB. You use ServerSupportFunction() to send the HTTP headers for the response to the client, and then use WriteClient() to send the body of an HTML page that is returned to the client. You will look at both these functions in greater detail later in this chapter.

The return values for HttpExtensionProc() are used to tell the server about the status of the request and whether it can free up its resources for the session:

HSE_STATUS_SUCCESS—The operation completed successfully and the server can free up any resources for the session.

HSE_STATUS_ERROR—An error occurred in processing. The server can close the connection and free its resources.

HSE_STATUS_PENDING—The ISA has queued the request and will notify the server when it is finished processing.

HSE_STATUS_SUCCESS_AND_KEEP_CONN—The operation has completed successfully, but the server should keep the connection open, provided it supports persistent connections.

You also can specify additional information about the status of a request handled by your ISA by setting the value of the dwHttpStatusCode field of the ECB to one of the following values (defined in WinInet.h) before returning from HttpExtensionProc():

HTTP_STATUS_BAD_REQUEST

HTTP_STATUS_AUTH_REQUIRED

HTTP_STATUS_FORBIDDEN

HTTP_STATUS_NOT_FOUND

HTTP_STATUS_SERVER_ERROR

HTTP_STATUS_NOT_IMPLEMENTED

The Extension Control Block

The HTTP server passes requests to your extension DLL by passing a pointer to an EXTENSION_CONTROL_BLOCK (ECB) structure, which contains information about the request to your ISA. This structure also allows you to pass certain information back to the server and provides pointers to a set of helper functions that can be used to communicate with the client. Here is the structure:

```
typedef struct _EXTENSION_CONTROL_BLOCK {
    DWORD     cbSize;
    DWORD     dwVersion;
    HCONN     ConnID;
    DWORD     dwHttpStatusCode;
```

```
CHAR        lpszLogData[HSE_LOG_BUFFER_LEN];
LPSTR       lpszMethod;
LPSTR       lpszQueryString;
LPSTR       lpszPathInfo;
LPSTR       lpszPathTranslated;
DWORD       cbTotalBytes;
DWORD       cbAvailable;
LPBYTE      lpbData;
LPSTR       lpszContentType;
BOOL (WINAPI * GetServerVariable) ( HCONN       hConn,
                                    LPSTR       lpszVariableName,
                                    LPVOID      lpvBuffer,
                                    LPDWORD     lpdwSize );
BOOL (WINAPI * WriteClient)  ( HCONN      ConnID,
                              LPVOID      Buffer,
                              LPDWORD     lpdwBytes,
                              DWORD       dwReserved );
BOOL (WINAPI * ReadClient)   ( HCONN      ConnID,
                              LPVOID      lpvBuffer,
                              LPDWORD     lpdwSize );
BOOL (WINAPI * ServerSupportFunction)( HCONN       hConn,
                                       DWORD       dwHSERRequest,
                                       LPVOID      lpvBuffer,
                                       LPDWORD     lpdwSize,
                                       LPDWORD     lpdwDataType );
} EXTENSION_CONTROL_BLOCK, *LPEXTENSION_CONTROL_BLOCK;
```

General Request Parameters

The first group of fields in the ECB is used to send information from the server about the request. The cbSize field is used to give the total size of the structure, and dwVersion will hold the version of ISAPI that is being used. In addition, the server will pass a value in connID that can be used to identify the connection to the client making the request. connID should not be modified by your DLL but will be used in calls to the helper functions, as you will soon see.

Query Information

The ECB also passes pointers to four null-terminated strings that give information specific to the client request. The string at lpszMethod gives the HTTP method that was requested, such as GET or PUT. Any additional information passed for a query is provided in lpszQueryString. If a path was specified in the client request, it will be passed via lpszPathInfo. In addition, the HTTP server will translate the path to a directory on the local server, which is passed in lpszPathTranslated.

GetServerVariable()

Many other variables are available from the server via the GetServerVariable() function pointer passed in the ECB. Here is the prototype for GetServerVariable():

```
BOOL (WINAPI * GetServerVariable) ( HCONN hConn,
                                    LPSTR lpszVariableName,
                                    LPVOID lpvBuffer,
                                    LPDWORD lpdwSize );
```

This function takes the connection ID (as passed in the ConnID field of the ECB) and one of the following constants used to select a value to retrieve (several of these values also are available directly from the ECB):

AUTH_TYPE—Type of authentication being used (for example, basic). If this is empty, no authentication is used.

CONTENT_LENGTH—Number of bytes expected from the client.

CONTENT_TYPE—Content type of the information received in a POST request.

GATEWAY_INTERFACE—The revision identification value of the CGI specification to which the server complies.

PATH_INFO—Additional path information passed by the client from the URL—after the ISA name but before the query string.

PATH_TRANSLATED—Path information after translation by the server.

QUERY_STRING—The query string information after the ? in the request URL.

REMOTE_ADDR—IP address of the client.

REMOTE_HOST—Hostname of the client.

REMOTE_USER—Username of the client. This is empty if the user is anonymous.

UNMAPPED_REMOTE_USER—Username before any ISAPI filters map the request to an NT user account.

REQUEST_METHOD—The HTTP request method, or verb.

SCRIPT_NAME—The name of the script being executed (the name of your ISA).

SERVER_NAME—The server's hostname or IP address.

SERVER_PORT—The TCP port on which the request was received.

SERVER_PORT_SECURE—A string containing 0 or 1. If the request is on a secure port, this will be 1.

SERVER_PROTOCOL—The HTTP version of the protocol being used (for example, HTTP/1.0).

SERVER_SOFTWARE—The name and version of the Web server software.

HTTP_ACCEPT—HTTP accept headers (for example, text/html, image/*).

URL—Base portion of the *uniform resource locator* (*URL*).

ALL_HTTP—Any additional HTTP headers that have not been parsed into other variables returned into one of the listed variables.

If the call to GetServerVariable() is successful, it will return TRUE and the requested data will be copied to lpvBuffer, with the length returned at lpdwSizeofBuffer. If the buffer passed in lpdwSizeofBuffer is too small for the returned value, the function will return FALSE, and a subsequent call to GetLastError() will return ERROR_INSUFFI-CIENT_BUFFER. The following example shows the use of GetServerVariable() to retrieve the server name:

```
lSize = sizeof(strServerName);
bRc = pECB->GetServerVariable(pECB->ConnID, "SERVER_NAME",
          strServerName, &lSize);

if(!bRc)
    dwError = GetLastError();
```

Additional Request Data

A client request may include a block of data. If additional data is sent, the total amount of data sent will be passed to HttpExtensionProc() in the cbTotalBytes field. The first block of the actual data also is passed to your DLL in a buffer at lpbData. The length of the data available at lpbData is passed in the cbAvailable field of the ECB.

If more data has been sent by the client (that is, if cbTotalBytes is greater than cbAvailable), the rest of the data may be retrieved from the client by using the ReadClient() callback function, which is accessed via a pointer passed in the ECB. Here is the prototype for ReadClient():

```
BOOL (WINAPI * ReadClient)  ( HCONN     ConnID,
                              LPVOID    lpvBuffer,
                              LPDWORD   lpdwSize );
```

When calling ReadClient(), you should pass the connection ID (from the ECB ConnID field) in hConn, a pointer to your receive buffer in lpvBuffer, and a pointer to the size of your buffer in lpdwSize. If the data is read successfully, ReadClient() will return TRUE, the data will be copied to lpvBuffer, and the actual size of the data read will be returned at lpdwSize. If an error occurs, ReadClient() will return FALSE, and you should call GetLastError() for a specific error code.

ServerSupportFunction()

The next callback function you will look at, ServerSupportFunction(), gives your ISA access to many different functions that the server can perform for you, ranging from sending HTTP headers, to setting up asynchronous I/O, to transmitting files. Here is the prototype for ServerSupportFunction():

```
BOOL (WINAPI * ServerSupportFunction)( HCONN hConn, DWORD dwHSERequest,
    LPVOID lpvBuffer, LPDWORD lpdwSize, LPDWORD lpdwDataType);
```

10

**MFC AND THE
INTERNET SERVER
API (ISAPI)**

The hConn parameter should be passed the connection ID from the ConnID field of the ECB. The actual function that is performed by ServerSupportFunction() and how the remaining parameters are used are determined by the value of dwHSERequest, which can have one of the values in the following sections.

HSE_REQ_REFRESH_ISAPI_ACL

HSE_REQ_REFRESH_ISAPI_ACL causes the IIS to reprocess the discretionary access control list (DACL) for a particular ISAPI extension's DLL. This function can also be used to reprocess another extension's DACL, if security permissions allow.

HSE_REQ_IS_KEEP_CONN

HSE_REQ_IS_KEEP_CONN can determine the Keep-Alive status of the active connection.

HSE_REQ_GET_IMPERSONATION_TOKEN

HSE_REQ_GET_IMPERSONATION_TOKEN allows the retrieval of a handle to the impersonation token that the request is implementing.

HSE_REQ_ABORTIVE_CLOSE

HSE_REQ_ABORTIVE_CLOSE will request to the IIS to use an abortive shutdown sequence when closing the TCP/IP connection socket. It generally performs a cleaner and elegant close.

HSE_REQ_GET_CERT_INFO_EX

HSE_REQ_GET_CERT_INFO_EX will specify the certificate context for the first certificate in the certificate chain of the client.

HSE_REQ_SEND_URL_REDIRECT_RESP

A URL redirect (302) message is sent to the client. You should pass the new URL string in lpvBuffer, and its size should be passed in lpdwSize.

HSE_REQ_SEND_URL

HSE_REQ_SEND_URL sends data to the client, based on a URL that specifies data local to the server. The null-terminated URL string is passed by lpvBuffer, and a pointer to its length should be passed in lpdwSize.

HSE_REQ_SEND_RESPONSE_HEADER

HSE_REQ_SEND_RESPONSE_HEADER sends an HTTP server response to the client. lpvBuffer should point to an HTTP status string—for example, 200 OK. You also may append additional HTTP headers to the response by passing a pointer to a null-terminated string in the lpdwDataType parameter.

This function is being deprecated for a future version of IIS. The preferred function to use is `HSE_REQ_SEND_RESPONSE_HEADER_EX`.

HSE_REQ_SEND_RESPONSE_HEADER_EX

This is the same as `HST_REQ_SEND_RESPONSE_HEADER` but more advanced. You can use this function to send a complete HTTP response header to the client browser, including the server version, message time, HTTP status, and MIME version. Also, when used with `HST_SEND_HEADER_EX`, this support function can set the lengths of the header and status strings, as well as specify that the connection should be kept open.

HSE_REQ_MAP_URL_TO_PATH

`HSE_REQ_MAP_URL_TO_PATH` translates a logical path to a physical path on the server. The logical path is passed in a buffer at `lpvBuffer`, and a pointer to the length of the buffer is passed in `lpdwSize`. Upon return, the translated path is written at `lpvBuffer`, and the `DWORD` at `lpdwSize` is updated to hold the size of the string returned.

This function is being deprecated for a future version of IIS. The preferred function to use is `HSE_REQ_MAP_URL_TO_PATH_EX`.

HSE_REQ_MAP_URL_TO_PATH_EX

`HSE_REQ_MAP_URL_TO_PATH_EX` is an improved version of `HSE_REQ_MAP_URL_TO_PATH`. This function enables you to map a logical URL path to a physical one. This permits the ability to collect different types of attributes related to the physical path.

HSE_REQ_DONE_WITH_SESSION

`HSE_REQ_DONE_WITH_SESSION` is used to tell the server when the ISA is finished with a session. You will look at how this is used when you look at asynchronous operations.

HSE_REQ_IO_COMPLETION

`HSE_REQ_IO_COMPLETION` sets up a callback function for the completion of asynchronous operations. You will look at this in more detail in just a bit.

HSE_REQ_TRANSMIT_FILE

`HSE_REQ_TRANSMIT_FILE` tells the server to transmit a file to the client. `lpvBuffer` points to an `HSE_TF_INFO` structure. (See the section "Sending Files," later in this chapter.)

HSE_REQ_GET_SSPI_INFO

`HSE_REQ_GET_SSPI_INFO` retrieves information about a secure connection. `lpvBuffer` receives the context handle, and `*lpdwDataType` receives the credential handle.

HSE_APPEND_LOG_PARAMETER

HSE_APPEND_LOG_PARAMETER can be used to write custom log strings to the log record. The log string will be obtained from lpvBuffer and be appended to the log.

HSE_REQ_ASYNC_READ_CLIENT

Use HSE_REQ_ASYNC_READ_CLIENT to attempt to read from the client asynchronously. When the read has completed, the ISA will call a specified callback function that you must set using the ServerSupportFunction request HSE_REQ_IO_COMPLETION.

HSE_REQ_CLOSE_CONNECTION

HSE_REQ_CLOSE_CONNECTION sends a request to close the current client socket connection. It will perform this action even if there is an asynchronous read pending. Upon using this function, you have to wait for the ISA to call the asynchronous I/O function before ending the session with HSE_REQ_DONE_WITH_SESSION. HSE_REQ_CLOSE_CONNECTION will close the client socket connection immediately, but because ISA has to deal with threads in the thread pool, it takes a small amount of time for the connection to be removed completely.

Important: After you use the HSE_REQ_CLOSE_CONNECTION server support function to close a connection, you must wait for IIS to call the asynchronous I/O function (specified by HSE_REQ_IO_COMPLETION) before you end the session with HSE_REQ_DONE_WITH_SESSION. HSE_REQ_CLOSE_CONNECTION closes the client socket connection immediately, but IIS takes a small amount of time to handle the threads in the thread pool before the connection can be removed completely.

WriteClient()

The WriteClient() function pointer provided in the ECB is used to send a block of data to the client that made the request to your ISA. In many cases, this will be HTML data, although it could be any other data you want to send to the client. The following is the prototype for WriteClient():

```
BOOL WriteClient( HCONN ConnID, LPVOID Buffer,
    LPDWORD lpdwBytes, DWORD dwReserved);
```

You should pass the value from the ConnID field of the ECB for the ConnID parameter. The value passed in Buffer should point to your data, and lpdwBytes should point to a DWORD with the length of the data to send. The dwReserved field can be used to specify how the call should complete. If dwReserved is HSE_IO_SYNC, the call will complete synchronously, blocking until it is finished. If dwReserved is set to HSE_IO_ASYNC, the call will return immediately, and the operation will complete asynchronously. You will look at asynchronous operations in the next section.

If `WriteClient()` completes successfully, it will return `TRUE`, and the `DWORD` at `lpdwBytes` will be updated to reflect the actual number of bytes sent. If an error occurs, `WriteClient()` will return `FALSE`, and you should call `GetLastError()` for a specific error code. The following example shows how you can send data (in this case, a null-terminated string of HTML) to the client:

```
// Send response data to client
dwMsgLen = strlen(retBuf);
bRc = pECB->WriteClient(pECB->ConnID, retBuf, &dwMsgLen, HSE_IO_SYNC);
if(bRc == FALSE)
{
    dwError = GetLastError();
    // Do something with the error code...
    pECB->dwHttpStatusCode = HTTP_STATUS_SERVER_ERROR;
    return(HSE_STATUS_ERROR);
}
```

Sending Files

In addition to the `WriteClient()` callback function, you can send a file to the client by calling `ServerSupportFunction()`, with `dwHSERequest` set to `HSE_REQ_TRANSMIT_FILE`. This will use the WinSock `TransmitFile()` function to send a file more quickly than `WriteClient()`.

> **Note**
>
> You also can send a file to the client by calling `ServerSupportFunction()` with `HSE_REQ_SEND_URL`, provided the server can access the file by a URL.

When calling `ServerSupportFunction()`, you should set `dwHSERequest` to `HSE_REQ_TRANSMIT_FILE`, and `lpvBuffer` should point to an `HSE_TF_INFO` structure, shown in the following:

```
typedef struct _HSE_TF_INFO  {
    PFN_HSE_IO_COMPLETION   pfnHseIO;
    PVOID   pContext;
    HANDLE hFile;
    LPCSTR pszStatusCode;
    DWORD  BytesToWrite;
    DWORD  Offset;
    PVOID  pHead;
    DWORD  HeadLength;
    PVOID  pTail;
    DWORD  TailLength;
    DWORD  dwFlags;
} HSE_TF_INFO, * LPHSE_TF_INFO;
```

The pfnHseIO and pContext fields are used to pass a callback function and context value to be used when the operation completes. If these values are not specified, the values set by a call to ServerSupportFunction(), using HSE_REQ_IO_COMPLETION, will be used. However, if values are passed in the pfnHseIO and pContext fields, these will override those set using HSE_REQ_IO_COMPLETION for the duration of this operation. You will see exactly how these are used in the next section.

> **Note**
>
> The HSE_REQ_TRANSMIT_FILE operation always completes asynchronously.

The file handle passed in hFile must have been previously opened with CreateFile(), using the FILE_FLAG_SEQUENTIAL_SCAN and FILE_FLAG_OVERLAPPED flags.

You should specify the number of bytes to send in the BytesToWrite field (0 will send the whole file) and also may specify a beginning offset from the start of the file in Offset.

Optionally, you can have the server attach HTTP headers to your file by specifying the HSE_IO_SEND_HEADER flag in the dwFlags field. This will build an HTTP header for the status code string specified in the pszStatusCode field—for example, 200 OK. If you use this option, you should not also use the HSE_REQ_SEND_HEADERS operation of ServerSupportFunction() to send headers.

You also can specify additional data blocks to be sent before and after the data from the file by setting pHead and pTail to point to appropriate buffers and specifying the lengths of the data in HeadLength and TailLength.

You also may include HSE_IO_DISCONNECT_AFTER_SEND in the dwFlags field, which tells the server to disconnect the client connection when the file transfer is complete. If you do not specify this flag, you need to notify the server when you are finished with the session by calling ServerSupportFunction() with HSE_REQ_DONE_WITH_SESSION.

Asynchronous Operations

ISAPI supports asynchronous completion for the WriteClient() function and the HSE_REQ_TRANSMIT_FILE operation provided by ServerSupportFunction(). Both of these functions can complete asynchronously by calling a callback function that you specify by calling ServerSupportFunction() for the HSE_REQ_IO_COMPLETION operation. This enables you to specify a callback function in the lpvBuffer parameter and a context value in `lpdwDataType` to be used in subsequent asynchronous operations. The code to set up a callback function would look something like this:

```
BOOL bRc;
bRc = pECB->ServerSupportFunction(pECB->ConnID,HSE_REQ_IO_COMPLETION,
                                  MyCompletionFunc, NULL, (DWORD *)0x123);
```

> **Note**
>
> If you call `ServerSupportFunction()` using `HSE_REQ_IO_COMPLETION` and differ-ent values for the callback function and context values, the previous values will be replaced.

Your ISA now can begin asynchronous operations with either the `WriteClient()` func-tion or `ServerSupportFunction()`, with a `dwHSERequest` value of `HSE_REQ_TRANSMIT_FILE`.

> **Note**
>
> You can have only one asynchronous operation pending for each session.

After you have initiated an asynchronous operation from within your `HttpExtensionProc()` callback, you can return a status of `HSE_STATUS_PENDING` from your `HttpExtensionProc()` function. After the operation completes, you should call `ServerSupportFunction()` with a `dwHSERequest` of `HSE_DONE_WITH_SESSION` to notify the server that you are finished with the session.

The I/O Completion Callback

The callback function that is installed with the previous code should have the following prototype:

```
VOID WINAPI MyIoCompletionFunc(EXTENSION_CONTROL_BLOCK * pECB,
    PVOID pContext, DWORD cbIO, DWORD dwError );
```

Whenever an asynchronous operation completes, the server will make a call to the call-back function that is installed. The server will pass a pointer to the ECB (`pECB`) for the session that started the I/O operation, the context value (`pContext`) that was passed with `HSE_REQ_IO_COMPLETION` (or the `HSE_TF_INFO` structure), the number of bytes transferred (`cbIO`), and an error code (`dwError`).

Your callback function then can do any additional processing that is necessary. You also can initiate an additional asynchronous operation. When you are finished with all the processing for the session, you should call `ServerSupportFunction()` with a `dwHSERequest` value of `HSE_DONE_WITH_SESSION` so that the server can close the connection and free the resources it has allocated for the session.

The following example shows a callback function that simply tells the server that you are finished with a session when the asynchronous operation completes:

```
VOID WINAPI MyCompletionFunc(EXTENSION_CONTROL_BLOCK *pECB,
                             PVOID pContext, DWORD cbIO, DWORD dwError)
{
    pECB->ServerSupportFunction(pECB->ConnID, HSE_REQ_DONE_WITH_SESSION,
                             NULL, NULL, NULL);
} // end MyCompletionFunc
```

Writing to the Server Log

Your ISA can send data to the server's log file by writing a string to the buffer pointed to by the `lpszLogData` field of the ECB. `lpszLogData` points to a buffer of size `HSE_LOG_BUFFER_LEN`. If you write a null-terminated string to this buffer, the string will be written to the server's log file when you return from `HttpExtensionProc()`. The following example shows how you can use this to append your own string to the entry the server writes to the log for a request:

```
// Add Entry to Log File
strcpy(pECB->lpszLogData, "My Additional Log Text.");
```

Exception Handling in ISAs

ISAPI extension DLLs gain a significant performance advantage over CGI scripts, because they are part of the Web server's process and do not require additional process startup time. However, this also introduces the potential for additional problems. In many cases, if your ISA produces a GPF or crashes for some other reason, the whole server will crash.

Because of this, you should be careful to handle any exceptions that may arise from your ISA. You should enclose any potentially risky code with the __try/__except mechanism. It's not a bad idea to enclose the entire body of each of your callback functions in a __try block. This way, problems that arise in your ISA will not affect the rest of the Web server.

You should take the same precautions for ISAPI filter DLLs, which you will look at later.

Debugging Your ISA

Your Internet server extension can be debugged just like any other DLL. However, some extra setup is required to run the Web server as a standalone executable for debugging rather than as a service.

> **Note**
>
> This section discusses specifically the Microsoft HTTP server, shipped with the MS *Internet Information Server* (*IIS*), although other servers that support ISAPI should behave similarly.

First of all, you need to have access to a server for debugging—trying to do debugging on a production server usually doesn't go over very well.

Second, you need to stop all three of the IIS services. Even though you will be using only the HTTP service, you also must stop the Gopher and FTP services. You can do this from the Services applet in the Control Panel or with the Internet Service Manager that was installed with IIS. In Windows 2000, this can be found in the Administrative Tools folder under the Control Panel.

Next, you need to specify the executable for the debug session in the debug settings for your ISA project. This should be the full path to the IIS server, which generally is something like this:

```
c:\winnt\system32\inetsrv\inetinfo.exe
```

You also must specify the following in the program arguments:

```
-e W3Svc
```

Now, when you start debugging your ISA project, the Internet Information Server will be started, and any breakpoints that you have set for your ISA will halt execution and allow you to debug the code in your ISA DLL.

> **Note**
>
> These steps for debugging an ISAPI extension application also apply to debugging ISAPI filters, which you will see later in this chapter.

10

MFC AND THE
INTERNET SERVER
API (ISAPI)

Converting from CGI to ISAPI

If you have existing CGI scripts that you want to convert to ISAPI extension DLLs, you can use the following basic steps.

First of all, you convert your CGI executable to an ISA DLL. For the most part, the main() function of your CGI executable can simply be pasted into the HttpExtensionProc() of the ISA project, with the additional changes listed later. You also need to add a GetExtensionVersion() entry point.

Extension DLLs must be thread-safe, whereas CGI scripts generally do not need to be. You should make sure that any critical sections or shared data are properly protected.

CGI scripts receive data from the client by reading from stdin. In an ISA, this should be changed to read data from the lpbData buffer passed in the ECB and by using the ReadClient() function.

Various information from the server is passed to CGI scripts through environment variables, which are read with getenv(). For an ISA, you should replace these calls with calls to GetServerVariable().

CGI scripts send data back to the client by writing to stdout. In most cases, this should be replaced with calls to WriteClient() in ISA applications, although there are some special cases.

When sending completion status, instead of writing Status: NNN ... to stdout, you should use the HSE_REQ_SEND_RESPONSE_HEADER operation of ServerSupportFunction() or WriteClient().

Also, when sending a redirect response, instead of writing either the Location: or URI: header to stdout, you should use ServerSupportFunction() with the HSE_REQ_SEND_URL operation for local URLs, or the HSE_REQ_SEND_URL_REDIRECT_RESP operation for remote (or unknown) URLs.

ISAPI Filters

In addition to the ISAPI server extensions you already have seen, ISAPI also enables you to create extension DLLs that act as filters, processing various HTTP events either before or after the server has processed a request. You can use these filters to provide your own custom authentication, encryption, compression, or logging functions, as well as many other filtering operations.

Installing a Filter

For the Microsoft *Internet Information Server* (*IIS*), the filters that are used are specified in the Registry under the following value:

```
HKEY_LOCAL_MACHINE\System\CurrentControlSet\Services\W3Svc
➥\Parameters\Filter DLLs
```

This value is a comma-separated list of the filters that will currently be used by the server. The filters are processed in order of their priority, as you will see. In the event of a tie in priority, the filters will be processed in the order in which they are listed in the Registry.

> **Tip**
>
> When adding or removing filters from the list, be careful not to disturb the existing entries.

ISAPI Filter Architecture

Like the extension DLLs you saw earlier, ISAPI filters are DLLs that are loaded into the Web server's process. Filter DLLs communicate with the server by way of a pair of entry points that are exported by the filter DLL.

The first of these entry points is `GetFilterVersion()`, which is called when your filter DLL is loaded, allowing your filter to report its supported version and to register for the events that it wants to handle.

When an event that your filter has registered for occurs, the second entry point, `HttpFilterProc()`, will be called. This function should perform its processing on the event before passing control back to the server. At this point, your filter may decide whether the event also should be handled by other filters in the current filter chain.

GetFilterVersion()

When the Web server loads a filter DLL, it will call the `GetFilterVersion()` function that is exported by your DLL. This function should have the following prototype:

```
BOOL WINAPI GetFilterVersion( PHTTP_FILTER_VERSION pVer);
```

The single parameter is a pointer to an `HTTP_FILTER_VERSION` structure, which looks like this:

```
typedef struct _HTTP_FILTER_VERSION
{
    [in] DWORD      dwServerFilterVersion;
```

10

```
    [out] DWORD     dwFilterVersion;
    [out] CHAR      lpszFilterDesc[SF_MAX_FILTER_DESC_LEN+1];
    DWORD     dwFlags;
} HTTP_FILTER_VERSION, *PHTTP_FILTER_VERSION;
```

When `GetFilterVersion()` is called, the server will pass its version in the `dwServerFilterVersion` field. You should pass the version that your filter is using back to the server in the `dwFilterVersion` field. For the current version of ISAPI, you can use the `HTTP_FILTER_REVISION` constant. You also can write a short ASCII string description of your filter in the buffer passed at `lpszFilterDesc`.

The real meat of this function is what you return in the `dwFlags` parameter. This value includes a combination (bitwise-OR) of the following flags, which specify which events your filter is interested in processing:

> `SF_NOTIFY_READ_RAW_DATA` allows the filter to process incoming data from the client, including headers.
>
> `SF_NOTIFY_SEND_RAW_DATA` allows the filter to process data that is being sent back to the client.
>
> `SF_NOTIFY_PREPROC_HEADERS` allows the filter to access the HTTP headers after they have been preprocessed by the server.
>
> `SF_NOTIFY_AUTHENTICATION` allows the filter to be involved in the user-authentication process.
>
> `SF_NOTIFY_URL_MAP` allows the filter to participate in the mapping of a URL to a physical path.
>
> `SF_NOTIFY_SEND_RESPONSE` allows the filter to process a response after the request has been processed by the ISAPI and before headers are sent back to the client.
>
> `SF_NOTIFY_LOG` allows the filter to be involved in the process of writing to the server log.
>
> `SF_NOTIFY_END_OF_NET_SESSION` tells the filter when the server is closing a session with a client.
>
> `SF_NOTIFY_END_OF_REQUEST` tells the filter when the server is at the end of a request.
>
> `SF_NOTIFY_ACCESS_DENIED` allows the server to process `401 Access Denied` responses before they are sent to the client.

The following flags also should be included to specify whether you are interested in events on only secure connections, nonsecure connections, or both:

> `SF_NOTIFY_SECURE_PORT`—The filter will receive notifications only for events on secure ports.
>
> `SF_NOTIFY_NONSECURE_PORT`—The filter will receive notifications only for events on nonsecure ports.

You use the last set of flags that can be included in the dwFlags field to set the priority of your filter in relation to the other filters present on the system:

SF_NOTIFY_ORDER_DEFAULT—The filter will have the default priority. This should be used for most filters.

SF_NOTIFY_ORDER_LOW—The filter will be processed at a lower priority. This is useful for filters that don't care when they are notified—for example, for logging events.

SF_NOTIFY_ORDER_MEDIUM—The filter will have a medium priority.

SF_NOTIFY_ORDER_HIGH—The filter will have a high priority, receiving notifications before filters of lower priority.

> **Tip**
>
> When requesting notifications, you should request only those that you need to process. Requesting additional notifications that are not necessary can affect the performance of the server.

You also may include any additional initialization code for your filter in the GetFilterVersion() function. (You also could implement a DllMain().) If all goes well, and your filter has initialized properly, you should return TRUE from GetFilterVersion(). If you return FALSE, the filter will not be loaded.

TerminateFilter()

Before unloading your filter, it is recommended that you call the TerminateFilter() function. This function should have the following prototype:

```
BOOL WINAPI TerminateFilter( DWORD dwFlags);
```

This filter enables you to free up any allocated or locked resources before you unload your filter. This filter is considered optional but is strongly recommended for the sake of releasing resources. Before calling this function, you should make sure that all attachments to system resources have been closed.

HttpFilterProc()

After your filter is loaded and has registered for the notifications that it wants to receive, the server will make a call to your HttpFilterProc() whenever one of the requested events occurs.

> **Note**
>
> If an event is handled by another filter with a higher priority, your filter will not be notified if the higher-priority filter chooses not to pass the event on down the filter chain.

In this section, you will take a quick look at the basics of implementing HttpFilterProc(). In the following sections, you will take a closer look at more of the specifics of certain operations.

The prototype for your HttpFilterProc() should look something like this:

```
DWORD WINAPI HttpFilterProc(PHTTP_FILTER_CONTEXT pfc,
    DWORD notificationType, VOID *pvNotification);
```

Your filter is passed an HTTP_FILTER_CONTEXT structure via pfc. This structure provides information about the request, as well as pointers to several utility functions, as you will see in just a bit. The type of event that generated the notification is passed in notificationType. This may include any of the SF_NOTIFY_... values that were used in the GetFilterVersion() call. The value of notificationType also determines how the pvNotification pointer is used. You will look at the specifics of handling each notification type in the following sections.

Your implementation of HttpFilterProc() should perform a switch on the value passed in notificationType, doing whatever processing is necessary, and then should return one of the following values:

SF_STATUS_REQ_FINISHED—The filter has satisfied the client's request, and the server should tear down the connection.

SF_STATUS_REQ_FINISHED_KEEP_CONN—The filter has satisfied the client's request, but the server should keep the connection open.

SF_STATUS_REQ_NEXT_NOTIFICATION—The next filter in the chain should be allowed to process the event.

SF_STATUS_REQ_HANDLED_NOTIFICATION—This filter has handled the event, and no other filters should be notified.

SF_STATUS_REQ_ERROR—An error has occurred. The server will call GetLastError() and forward the error to the client.

SF_STATUS_REQ_READ_NEXT—This should be returned only when filtering on the SF_NOTIFY_READ_RAW_DATA event for stream filters that are negotiating session parameters.

The following example shows the complete implementation of a simple filter, which just adds a bit of graffiti to the Web server's log file:

```c
#include <windows.h>
#include <stdio.h>
#include <httpfilt.h>
BOOL WINAPI GetFilterVersion( PHTTP_FILTER_VERSION pVer)
{
    pVer->dwFilterVersion = HTTP_FILTER_REVISION;
    strcpy(pVer->lpszFilterDesc, "My Sample Extension");
    pVer->dwFlags =
        SF_NOTIFY_SECURE_PORT |      // Notify for both port types
        SF_NOTIFY_NONSECURE_PORT |
        SF_NOTIFY_LOG |              // Notify when writing log
        SF_NOTIFY_ORDER_LOW;        // Filter at low priority
    return TRUE;
}
DWORD WINAPI HttpFilterProc( PHTTP_FILTER_CONTEXT pfc,
                             DWORD notificationType,
                             VOID *pvNotification)
{
    PHTTP_FILTER_LOG pLog;
    char *pBuf;

    switch(notificationType)
    {
        case SF_NOTIFY_LOG:
            // This is the only case we are interested in
            // We will modify the server name to show we were here
            pLog = (PHTTP_FILTER_LOG) pvNotification;
            // Allocate new memory for the new string
            // The server will deallocate this when the request ends
            pBuf = (char *) pfc->AllocMem(pfc, 100, 0);
            // Write to our new string
            sprintf(pBuf, "Server: [%s] Logged with MyFilt",
                        pLog->pszServerName);

            // Replace the server name pointer
            pLog->pszServerName = pBuf;

            break;
        default:
            // We should not receive any other notifications
            // Since we only registered for SF_NOTIFY_LOG
            break;
    }
    // Tell the server to call the next filter
    return(SF_STATUS_REQ_NEXT_NOTIFICATION);
} // end HttpExtensionProc
```

Although this filter may not be horribly practical, it does show the basic structure of a filter, including the processing for the `SF_NOTIFY_LOG` notification and the use of the `AllocMem()` function, which you will learn about later.

The `HTTP_FILTER_CONTEXT` Structure

Much of the interaction between your filter and the Web server is done through the `HTTP_FILTER_CONTEXT` structure that is passed in the call to `HttpFilterProc()`:

```
typedef struct _HTTP_FILTER_CONTEXT
{
    DWORD     cbSize;
    DWORD     Revision;
    PVOID     ServerContext;
    DWORD     ulReserved;
    BOOL      fIsSecurePort;
    PVOID     pFilterContext;
BOOL    (WINAPI * GetServerVariable) (
    struct _HTTP_FILTER_CONTEXT *    pfc,
    LPSTR      lpszVariableName,
    LPVOID     lpvBuffer,
    LPDWORD    lpdwSize);
BOOL    (WINAPI * AddResponseHeaders) (
    struct _HTTP_FILTER_CONTEXT *    pfc,
    LPSTR      lpszHeaders,
    DWORD      dwReserved);
BOOL    (WINAPI * WriteClient)  (
    struct _HTTP_FILTER_CONTEXT *    pfc,
    LPVOID     Buffer,
    LPDWORD    lpdwBytes,
    DWORD      dwReserved);
VOID *     (WINAPI * AllocMem) (
    struct _HTTP_FILTER_CONTEXT *    pfc,
    DWORD      cbSize,
    DWORD      dwReserved);
BOOL    (WINAPI * ServerSupportFunction) (
    struct _HTTP_FILTER_CONTEXT *    pfc,
    enum SF_REQ_TYPE    sfReq,
    PVOID      pData,
    DWORD      ul1,
    DWORD      ul2);
} HTTP_FILTER_CONTEXT, *PHTTP_FILTER_CONTEXT;
```

The `cbSize` field gives the size of this structure, and the `Revision` field gives the version of ISAPI being used. The `ServerContext` and `ulReserved` fields are reserved for use by the Web server—keep yer grubbies off. If the notification is for a secure connection, `fIsSecurePort` will be `TRUE`; otherwise, it will be `FALSE`.

If your filter wants to store any context information for this request, you can assign a context value (usually a pointer to a structure) to the `pFilterContext` field. If you store a value here, it also will be given to subsequent notifications that your filter receives in processing this request.

If you do allocate memory to store data for a request, you should free the memory when the `SF_NOTIFY_END_OF_NET_SESSION` notification is received (or whenever you know that you are finished with the data). You also should look at the `AllocMem()` function later in this section.

The remainder of the `HTTP_FILTER_CONTEXT` structure includes pointers to various utility functions the server provides to your filter.

GetServerVariable()

The `GetServerVariable()` function pointer passed to your filter DLL is not quite the same as the `GetServerVariable()` function that you saw for ISAPI extensions. This version takes a pointer to the `HTTP_FILTER_CONTEXT` structure, which is passed to your `HttpFilterProc()` function instead of an `HCONN`. However, the variables that are available via this function and the way it uses the other parameters are the same as the `GetServerVariable()` function you saw earlier in this chapter.

AddResponseHeaders()

The `AddResponseHeaders()` function pointer passed to `HttpFilterProc()` can be used to attach additional HTTP headers to the response sent to the client. Here is the prototype for `AddResponseHeaders()`:

```
BOOL (WINAPI * AddResponseHeaders) (PHTTP_FILTER_CONTEXT pfc,
    LPSTR lpszHeaders, DWORD dwReserved);
```

This function takes a pointer to the filter context (`pfc`), which is passed to your `HttpFilterProc()` function, and a pointer to a null-terminated string containing the additional HTTP headers. `dwReserved` is reserved for future expansion.

WriteClient()

Like the `WriteClient()` callback that you saw for ISAPI applications, this function enables you to send data directly to the client. The following is the prototype for `WriteClient()`:

```
BOOL (WINAPI * WriteClient) (PHTTP_FILTER_CONTEXT pfc,
    LPVOID buffer, LPDWORD lpdwBytes, DWORD dwReserved);
```

When calling `WriteClient()`, you should pass the pointer to the filter context (as passed to your `HttpFilterProc()` function) in `pfc`, a pointer to the data to send in `buffer`, and a pointer to the length of the data in `lpdwBytes`. The `dwReserved` parameter currently is not used.

10

MFC AND THE INTERNET SERVER API (ISAPI)

> **Note**
>
> The `WriteClient()` function provided for ISAPI filters currently does not support asynchronous I/O.

AllocMem()

If your filter needs to allocate memory when working with a request, you may find the `AllocMem()` function handy. This will allocate a block of memory that automatically is deallocated when the server is done with a request and tears down the connection. The prototype for `AllocMem()` follows:

```
VOID * (WINAPI * AllocMem) (PHTTP_FILTER_CONTEXT pfc,
    DWORD cbSize, DWORD dwReserved);
```

Once again, `pfc` takes the pointer to the filter context, as passed to `HttpFilterProc()`, and `dwReserved` currently is not used. Upon successful completion, `AllocMem()` will return a pointer to a new block of memory of the size specified in `cbSize`.

ServerSupportFunction()

Like the `ServerSupportFunction()` that you saw for ISAPI applications, this function provides a variety of different utility functions to your filter. The following is the prototype for `ServerSupportFunction()`:

```
BOOL (WINAPI * ServerSupportFunction) (struct _HTTP_FILTER_CONTEXT *pfc,
    enum SF_REQ_TYPE sfReq, PVOID pData, DWORD ul1, DWORD ul2);
```

The operation performed is determined by the value of `sfReq`, which may have one of the following values:

`SF_REQ_NORMALIZE_URL`

This function is used to normalize the URL. Normalization involves changes such as decoding hex codes, internationalization coversions, and removing illegal characters.

`SF_REQ_DISABLE_NOTIFICATIONS`

This option is used to disable specific notification types for the ISAPI filter. It remains disabled for the remaining lifetime of the request.

`SF_REQ_GET_PROPERTY`

This option is used to retrieve IIS properties defined in `SF_PROPERTY_IIS`.

`SF_REQ_SEND_RESPONSE_HEADER`

This option sends a complete HTTP response header to the client. You may choose to specify a status string—for example, `401 Access Denied`—in a string pointed to by `pData`. You also may specify additional headers, such as the content type, to append in a string pointed to by `ul1`. This string should include a terminating carriage return/linefeed (`\r\n`).

`SF_REQ_ADD_HEADERS_ON_DENIAL`

This option enables you to specify additional headers that will be sent to the client in the event that the server denies the HTTP request. The additional headers are passed in a string pointed to by `pData`. This string should include a terminating cr/lf (`\r\n`).

`SF_REQ_SET_NEXT_READ_SIZE`

For raw data filters that return `SF_STATUS_READ_NEXT` from `HttpFilterProc()`, you can use this option to specify the number of bytes to read in the next read. The number of bytes to read is passed in `ul1`.

`SF_REQ_SET_PROXY_INFO`

You can use this option to specify that a request is a proxy request. You should set `ul1` to `1`.

`SF_REQ_GET_CONNID`

This option returns the connection ID that is passed to ISAPI applications for this request. You can use this value to coordinate operations between your ISAPI applications and filters. `pData` should point to a `DWORD` that will receive the connection ID. This option is not supported in ISAPI 4.0 or higher.

> **Tip**
>
> If you are developing an ISAPI filter that works closely with an ISAPI extension application, you can include both sets of entry points in the same DLL.

Handling Filter Notifications

In this section, you will look at the different notifications that can be received by an ISAPI filter and the data that is passed with each type of notification.

SF_NOTIFY_READ_RAW_DATA

This notification is sent to your filter whenever the server is receiving raw data from the client. The `pvNotification` parameter of `HttpFilterProc()` will point to an `HTTP_FILTER_RAW_DATA` structure:

```
typedef struct _HTTP_FILTER_RAW_DATA
{
    PVOID        pvInData;
    DWORD        cbInData;
    DWORD        cbInBuffer;
    DWORD        dwReserved;
} HTTP_FILTER_RAW_DATA, *PHTTP_FILTER_RAW_DATA;
```

The pvInData field points to a buffer containing the raw data, and the length of the data is passed in the cbInData field. This will include both HTTP headers and additional data. The total size of this buffer is passed in cbInBuffer.

SF_NOTIFY_SEND_RAW_DATA

This notification is sent to your filter when the server is sending data back to the client. The pvNotification parameter of HttpFilterProc() will point to an HTTP_FILTER_RAW_DATA structure, as you saw previously, which refers to the outgoing data.

SF_NOTIFY_PREPROC_HEADERS

This notification is sent to your filter when a request is received from a client. The pvNotification parameter of HttpFilterProc() will point to an HTTP_FILTER_ PREPROC_HEADERS structure, which includes pointers to utility functions that can be used to manipulate the headers for a request. These utility functions are discussed in the following sections.

GetHeader()

The first of these functions is GetHeader():

```
BOOL (WINAPI * GetHeader) (PHTTP_FILTER_CONTEXT pfc,
    LPSTR lpszName, LPVOID lpvBuffer, LPDWORD lpdwSize);
```

This function enables you to retrieve the header with the name you specify in a string at lpszName. This name should include the trailing colon—for example, Content-Type:. You also may specify the special values of method, url, or version to retrieve portions of the HTTP request line.

If a header is found for the name passed in lpszName, it will be returned in a buffer at lpvBuffer.

SetHeader()

The second of the utility functions is SetHeader(), which you can use to change the value of a header or even delete an existing header:

```
BOOL (WINAPI * SetHeader) (PHTTP_FILTER_CONTEXT pfc,
    LPSTR lpszName, LPSTR lpszValue);
```

This function enables you to specify a new value for the header named in the string at `lpszName`. The new value for the header is passed in a string at `lpszValue`. If this string is empty, the specified header will be deleted.

AddHeader()

You can use the third utility function, `AddHeader()`, to add additional headers:

```
BOOL (WINAPI * SetHeader) (PHTTP_FILTER_CONTEXT pfc,
    LPSTR lpszName, LPSTR lpszValue);
```

The name of the new header is specified in a string at `lpszName`, and the value of the new header is passed in a string at `lpszValue`.

SF_NOTIFY_AUTHENTICATION

This notification is sent to your filter when the server is about to authenticate a user making a request. The pvNotification parameter of `HttpFilterProc()` will point to an `HTTP_FILTER_AUTHENT` structure:

```
typedef struct _HTTP_FILTER_AUTHENT
{
    CHAR * pszUser;
    DWORD  cbUserBuff;
    CHAR * pszPassword;
    DWORD  cbPasswordBuff;
} HTTP_FILTER_AUTHENT, *PHTTP_FILTER_AUTHENT;
```

This structure contains pointers to the username (pszUser) and password (pszPassword) for the user being authenticated. If the user is anonymous, these strings will be empty. The cbUserBuff and cbPasswordBuff fields give the total size of the buffers holding the username and password. Your filter can change the contents of these buffers, provided they are not overflowed. These buffers will be at least SF_MAX_USERNAME and SF_MAX_PASSWORD bytes long, respectively.

SF_NOTIFY_URL_MAP

This notification is sent when the server is attempting to map a URL to a physical path. The lpvNotification parameter of `HttpFilterProc()` will point to an `HTTP_FILTER_URL_MAP` structure:

```
typedef struct _HTTP_FILTER_URL_MAP
{
    const CHAR * pszURL;
    CHAR *       pszPhysicalPath;
    DWORD        cbPathBuff;
} HTTP_FILTER_URL_MAP, *PHTTP_FILTER_URL_MAP;
```

The requested URL is passed in the string at pszURL, and the physical path that it is being mapped to is given at pszPhysicalPath. Your filter may change the string at pszPhysicalPath, provided you do not go over the size of the buffer given in cbPathBuf.

SF_NOTIFY_LOG

This notification is passed to your filter when the server is about to write an entry to its log file. The lpvNotification parameter of HttpFilterProc() is passed a pointer to an HTTP_FILTER_LOG structure:

```
typedef struct _HTTP_FILTER_LOG
{
    const CHAR * pszClientHostName;
    const CHAR * pszClientUserName;
    const CHAR * pszServerName;
    const CHAR * pszOperation;
    const CHAR * pszTarget;
    const CHAR * pszParameters;
    DWORD  dwHttpStatus;
    DWORD  dwWin32Status;
} HTTP_FILTER_LOG, *PHTTP_FILTER_LOG;
```

The pointers in this structure refer to the client's hostname, username, and server name, as well as the operation, target, and parameters for the HTTP request. In addition, dwHttpStatus holds the HTTP status of the request, and dwWin32Status holds any Win32 error code.

You cannot modify the contents of the strings passed by the HTTP_FILTER_LOG structure, although you can replace the values of the pointers. If you change the pointer values, you should assign them to new buffers that are allocated with the AllocMem() function provided by the HTTP_FILTER_CONTEXT structure so that the memory can be released properly when the session is closed.

SF_NOTIFY_END_OF_NET_SESSION

This notification is sent to your filter when the server is disconnecting a session. No specific data are associated with this notification, although it is a good place to clean up any information you have stored about a request in progress.

SF_NOTIFY_ACCESS_DENIED

When a request has been denied by the server, your filter will receive this notification. The lpvNotification parameter of HttpFilterProc() will be passed a pointer to an HTTP_FILTER_ACCESS_DENIED structure:

```
typedef struct _HTTP_FILTER_ACCESS_DENIED
{
```

```
    const CHAR * pszURL;
    const CHAR * pszPhysicalPath;
    DWORD         dwReason;
} HTTP_FILTER_ACCESS_DENIED, *PHTTP_FILTER_ACCESS_DENIED;
```

This structure includes the requested URL at `pszURL` and the physical path it was mapped to at `pszPhysicalPath`. The `dwReason` field contains a bitmap that specifies why the request was denied. This can include the following values:

`SF_DENIED_LOGON`—Logon failed.

`SF_DENIED_RESOURCE`—The *Access Control List* (*ACL*) for the resource did not allow the operation.

`SF_DENIED_FILTER`—An ISAPI filter denied the request.

`SF_DENIED_APPLICATION`—An ISAPI application or a CGI script denied the request.

`SF_DENIED_BY_CONFIG`—This flag may be included with the others if the server's configuration did not allow the request.

ISAPI Support in MFC

Visual C++ 6.0 also provides support for ISAPI extension applications and filters using MFCs that encapsulate the ISAPI you saw earlier in this chapter. The classes provided by MFC to work with ISAPI include the following:

`CHttpServer`—Base class for deriving your ISAs

`CHttpServerContext`—Encapsulates the context for each client request

`CHtmlStream`—Class for managing HTML responses

`CHttpFilter`—Base class for deriving ISAPI filters

`CHttpFilterContext`—Wrapper for the `HTTP_FILTER_CONTEXT` structure

In addition, MFC defines a set of macros that enables you to define a parse map to map requests to your ISA to specific functions in your implementation. Visual C++ also provides an Application Wizard for creating ISAs and ISAPI filters that use the MFC ISAPI classes.

Creating ISAPI DLLs with AppWizard

Visual C++ 6.0 provides an Application Wizard you can use to generate the skeleton of an ISAPI filter or ISA. In fact, you can use it to create both a filter and an ISA in the same DLL project. To use the ISAPI AppWizard, choose File, New and choose the ISAPI Extension Wizard from the Projects page. You also need to select a name and location for your new project.

The first step in the ISAPI Extension Wizard enables you to choose whether you want to create a filter object or a server extension object (ISA). This dialog box also enables you to choose names for your classes and descriptions for your filter or ISA, as well as to select whether to use MFC as a DLL or as a statically linked library.

If you are only creating a server extension, you can click Finish to see a short summary of the project that the wizard will create for you. Just click OK in this dialog box, and the wizard creates the skeleton of a server extension for you.

If you are creating a filter object, clicking Next presents a second dialog box that enables you to set up the priority for your filter and the types of connections and specific notifications it is interested in handling. These options correspond directly to the flags that are returned in the `GetFilterVersion()` function that you saw earlier.

> **Note**
>
> The ISAPI Extension Wizard enables you to create both a filter and a server extension in the same DLL project. This capability can be quite useful if your filter and ISA will interact with each other directly.

After you create the framework for your DLL with the ISAPI Extension Wizard, you are ready to start adapting the MFC classes that it creates to suit the needs of your specific implementation. In the following sections, you will look at each of the classes that MFC provides to help in working with ISAPI.

CHttpServer

An MFC ISA will have one—and only one—object derived from `CHttpServer`. This class encapsulates both the `GetExtensionVersion()` and `HttpExtensionProc()` entry points that you saw earlier. In addition, it provides several other methods that can simplify the processing of client requests, and the `CHttpServer` class enables you to create `CHtmlStream` objects that can be used for building responses.

Your ISA should create one instance of your class derived from `CHttpServer`. You can specify a delimiter character used to separate command parameters in requests for your ISA, although the default (&) generally should be used.

CHttpServer::GetExtensionVersion()

The `CHttpServer` class provides a member function that is identical to the `GetExtensionVersion()` function you saw earlier, which reports version information back to the server when the ISA is first loaded. You also can use this function to perform the initialization of your ISA.

CHttpServer::HttpExtensionProc()

The CHttpServer class also implements a member function that is exported as the HttpExtensionProc() you saw earlier. This function is called once for each client request that is received. The default implementation of this function will create a new CHttpServerContext object for the request, parse the request, call the CHttpServer::InitInstance() member function, and call CHttpServer::CallFunction() to use a parse map to route the client request to a function in your ISA. It also will use the CHttpServer::OnParseError() function to generate HTML responses to handle various errors that may occur.

Tip

The current implementation of CHttpServer::HttpExtensionProc() handles only the GET and POST HTTP commands. If your ISA needs to handle other commands, you need to override this function. For hints, you might want to look at the source for CHttpServer::HttpExtensionProc() in ISAPI.CPP in the MFC source directory.

InitInstance()

The InitInstance() member of CHttpServer is called by the default implementation of CHttpServer::HttpExtensionProc() each time a new request is received. You can override this function in your class derived from CHttpServer to perform any initialization for each request. Any initialization that should be performed only once, when the DLL is first loaded, should not appear in InitInstance() but should be placed somewhere else—in the GetExtensionVersion() member function, for example.

CallFunction()

The CallFunction() member of CHttpServer is called by the default implementation of CHttpServer::HttpExtensionProc() to map the command in the client request URL to a specific function in your ISA. The default implementation of this function uses a parse map (similar to message maps) to choose the appropriate function to call, based on command information from the ECB structure. If you want to perform your own custom mapping of commands to implementation functions, you can override this function—in which case, you will not need to implement a parse map.

Parse Maps

MFC provides a set of macros for defining a parse map in your ISA. The parse map is a structure, similar to MFC message maps, that is used by the CallFunction() method to map a client request to a function that will handle the request. You should define one—and only one—parse map in each of your MFC ISA DLLs.

A parse map begins with the `BEGIN_PARSE_MAP` macro, which takes parameters for the class defining the map and its base class (usually `CHttpServer`), and ends with the `END_PARSE_MAP` macro, which takes the name of the class defining the map.

Between the begin and end macros, you can add entries for specific commands with the `ON_PARSE_COMMAND` macro, which takes parameters for the name of a member function, the class name that the member function belongs to, and a list of constants representing the parameters to be passed to the handler function. The following are the constants used to represent the available argument types:

> `ITS_PSTR`—A pointer to a string
>
> `ITS_I2`—A two-byte integer (short)
>
> `ITS_I4`—A four-byte integer (long)
>
> `ITS_R4`—A float
>
> `ITS_R8`—A double
>
> `ITS_EMPTY`—Handler takes no additional arguments (The third parameter to `ON_PARSE_COMMAND` cannot be blank, so this acts as a placeholder.)

To illustrate how this works, let's take a look at an example parse map, which will map the command `myFunc1` to `CMyIsa::myFunc1()` and `myFunc2` to `CMyIsa::myFunc2()`:

```
BEGIN_PARSE_MAP(CMyIsa, CHttpServer)
    ON_PARSE_COMMAND(myFunc1, CMyIsa, ITS_I2 ITS_PSTR)
    ON_PARSE_COMMAND_PARAMS("param1 param2=default")
    ON_PARSE_COMMAND(myFunc2, CMyIsa, ITS_I4)
    ON_PARSE_COMMAND_PARAMS("myIndex=123")
    DEFAULT_PARSE_COMMAND(myFunc1, CMyIsa)
END_PARSE_MAP(CMyIsa)
```

> **Tip**
>
> In mapping client request commands to handler functions, the command string passed by the client must match the name of the handler function. For example, if the client requests the `DoSomething` command, this will map to `CMyIsa::DoSomething()`. If you want to map commands to functions with names other than the command string, you can do so, but you need to add your own entries to the parse map, without using the `ON_PARSE_COMMAND` macro. Or, you could override the `CallFunction()` method altogether. For hints on how to do this, see `afxisapi.h` for the definition of `ON_PARSE_COMMAND`.

The ON_PARSE_COMMAND_PARAMS macro, used in the example, specifies the names of the parameters for the command in the ON_PARSE_COMMAND immediately preceding it. This macro also is used to assign default values to the parameters; if a default value is not assigned in the parse map, the client must supply a value, or the call will fail. In the example, when the client requests the myFunc1 command, it must specify a parameter named param1. If the client does not specify a param2 parameter, it will default to an empty string.

The example also shows the use for the DEFAULT_PARSE_COMMAND macro, which specifies a handler function (and its class) for cases where the client does not include a command in the request.

Handler Functions

The handler functions specified in the ON_PARSE_COMMAND macros should be members of your CHttpServer-derived class. They also should all return void and take a pointer to a CHttpServerContext object as their first parameter. They also should take additional parameters, as specified in the ON_PARSE_COMMAND macro.

For example, consider the following parse map entry:

```
ON_PARSE_COMMAND(foo, CMyIsa, ITS_I4 ITS_PSTR)
```

The prototype for the handler function should look like this:

```
void CMyIsa::foo(CHttpServerContext* pCtxt, int nParam1, LPTSTR pszParam2);
```

OnParseError()

The OnParseError() member of CHttpServer is called by MFC to create an HTML response for the client based on a set of error codes. If you want to generate your own custom error messages, you can override this member function.

ConstructStream()

MFC will call the ConstructStream() method of CHttpServer to create a new CHtmlStream object. If you want to modify the default behavior, you can override this function.

StartContent()

You can use this function to insert the <Body> and <HTML> tags into an HTML stream to be returned to the client.

EndContent()

You can use this function to insert the </Body> and </HTML> tags into an HTML stream to be returned to the client.

WriteTitle()

This function will insert the title string returned by GetTitle() (surrounded by <Title> and </Title>) into an HTML string to be returned to the client.

GetTitle()

This function is called by MFC to retrieve a title to add to the HTML page to be returned to the client. You can override this function to supply a title other than the default.

AddHeader()

You can call this function to add additional headers to the HTML stream to be returned to the client.

CHttpServerContext

The default implementation of CHttpServer::HttpExtensionProc() will create a new CHttpServerContext object each time it is called to process a new client request. This class encapsulates the ECB structure that you saw earlier, which is available directly via the m_pECB member. The m_pStream member also provides direct access to the CHtmlStream object that will be returned to the client.

This class implements member functions that correspond directly to the GetServerVariable(), ReadClient(), WriteClient(), and ServerSupportFunction() functions that are passed in the ECB, as you saw earlier.

In addition, CHttpServerContext overloads the insertion operator (<<) to write data to the CHtmlStream object associated with the CHttpServerContext object.

CHtmlStream

The CHtmlStream class provides an abstraction for writing HTML data to a temporary memory file before it is sent back to the client. CHtmlStream objects are created by the default implementation of CHttpServer::ConstructStream(), which is called by the default implementation of CHttpServer::CallFunction() to create a new HTML stream to associate with the CHttpServerContext object for a client request. CallFunction() also calls CHtmlStream::InitStream(), which you may override, to initialize the new stream.

You can retrieve the size of the stream file by calling the GetStreamSize() method or by accessing the m_nStreamSize member directly.

CHtmlStream provides the Write() method to enable you to write data to the stream, as well as an overload of the insertion operator (<<) that performs the same function.

Several other members of CHtmlStream also can be used to more closely control the memory used by the stream. Many of these functions can be overridden in classes you derive from CHtmlStream if you are interested in changing the way CHtmlStream deals with memory.

CHttpFilter

MFC provides the CHttpFilter class to encapsulate the functionality required for implementing an ISAPI filter. It will export GetFilterVersion() and HttpFilterProc() entry points, which call CHttpFilter member functions of the same name. For each MFC ISAPI filter, one—and only one—CHttpFilter object should be created. As you will see in just a bit, multiple CHttpFilterContext objects will be created by the CHttpFilter—one for each notification that is received.

CHttpFilter::GetFilterVersion() corresponds directly to the GetFilterVersion() function that you saw earlier. You should override this function in your class derived from CHttpFilter to specify the priority of your filter and the events it wants to process.

You also may override CHttpFilter::HttpFilterProc() to implement your event handlers, although the default implementation will create a new CHttpFilterContext object for you and call one of the other member functions of CHttpFilter, which you can override to handle each specific event. Here are the member functions that are called, with the events that generate calls to them:

SF_NOTIFY_READ_RAW_DATA	OnReadRawData()
SF_NOTIFY_SEND_RAW_DATA	OnSendRawData()
SF_NOTIFY_PREPROC_HEADERS	OnPreprocHeaders()
SF_NOTIFY_AUTHENTICATION	OnAuthentication()
SF_NOTIFY_URL_MAP	OnUrlMap()
SF_NOTIFY_LOG	OnLog()
SF_NOTIFY_END_OF_NET_SESSION	OnEndOfNetSession()

The implementation of these functions is very similar to the handling for the event notifications that you saw earlier.

CHttpFilterContext

A new CHttpFilterContext object is created by MFC whenever a new notification is received. This object provides your filter with information about the notification and also provides mechanisms for your filter to communicate with the server, as well as the client making the request. This class encapsulates the HTTP_FILTER_CONTEXT structure that you saw earlier. You can directly access this structure via the m_pFC member of CHttpFilterContext.

The `CHttpFilterContext` class provides member functions that correspond directly to the `GetServerVariable()`, `AddResponseHeaders()`, `WriteClient()`, `ServerSupportFunction()`, and `AllocMem()` functions that you saw earlier during the discussion of the C version of ISAPI for creating filters.

The Internet Service Manager API

So far in this chapter, you have learned how the ISAPI enables you to add extension applications and filters to the HTTP server. However, the Internet Server API also provides an interface, known as the *Internet Service Manager API* (*ISMAPI*). This enables you to create your own Internet servers that you can manage with the Internet Service Manager application, which you use to start, stop, or pause Internet services on the local machine or across the network.

ISMAPI enables you to create a configuration DLL for your new Internet service. The Internet Service Manager then can be configured to load your configuration DLL to allow the user to control your Internet service from within the Internet Service Manager. The ISMAPI defines the entry points that your configuration DLL should export, allowing the user to discover servers on the network, change the state of your service, configure a server, and get information about servers and services on the network. For more on the ISMAPI, see the online documentation.

Summary

In this chapter, you learned how you can use the *Internet Server API* (*ISAPI*) to create both Internet Server Extension Applications (ISAs) and ISAPI filters, which you can use to add functionality to ISAPI-compliant HTTP servers, such as that supplied with Microsoft's Internet Information Server.

You looked at creating an ISA extension DLL, which can process requests made directly by a client, and the entry points that are exported by an ISA DLL, including `GetExtensionVersion()`, `TerminateExtension()`, and `HttpExtensionProc()`—the real workhorse function of an ISA.

You also took a look at the information provided to your ISA by the server in the `EXTEN-SION_CONTROL_BLOCK` structure, which also provides pointers to utility functions such as `GetServerVariable()`, `WriteClient()`, `ReadClient()`, and `ServerSupportFunction()`.

Next, you saw how to create an ISAPI filter DLL, which you can use to perform special processing for many different events in the process of handling an HTTP request. You learned how the `GetFilterVersion()` and `HttpFilterProc()` functions can be implemented and exported for use by the Web server, as well as the `HTTP_FILTER_CONTEXT` structure, which is used to pass information about a request and to provide utility functions for your filter, including `GetServerVariable()`, `AddResponseHeaders()`, `WriteClient()`, `AllocMem()`, and `ServerSupportFunction()`.

In addition, you took a look at the MFCs that are provided to encapsulate ISAPI, including the `CHttpServer`, `CHttpServerContext`, and `CHtmlStream` classes, which are used to create ISAs using parse maps, as well as the `CHttpFilter` and `CHttpFilterContext` classes, which can be used to implement ISAPI filters. You also saw how to use the ISAPI Extension Wizard to create a framework for applications using these MFCs.

The WinInet API

*by David Bennett
and Andrew J. Indovina*

IN THIS CHAPTER

CHAPTER 11

Visual C++ 6.0 includes the Windows Internet Extensions API, known as WinInet. This includes both a set of C functions and an MFC class hierarchy that enables your applications to add connectivity to Internet servers without having to worry about the specifics of the underlying protocols, such as *File Transfer Protocol* (*FTP*), *Hypertext Transfer Protocol* (*HTTP*), or Gopher.

The WinInet APIs enable you to connect to Internet servers, search for files, and retrieve files. You also can send files to the server or even open a file in place on the server. For many operations, you can use synchronous, blocking calls, or you may use the asynchronous completion mechanisms provided by WinInet.

Using the WinInet C API

Before we get into the meat of the WinInet C API, let's take a look at some of the basic concepts used throughout the WinInet functions, such as the handle hierarchy with which the API functions work. You also will look at how the WinInet functions handle error codes and buffer passing, as well as how asynchronous operations are implemented, before moving on to the specific functions of the WinInet API used for FTP, HTTP, and Gopher communications.

Handles

Most of the WinInet functions use a special sort of handle, HINTERNET. This handle type is used to represent Internet sessions, individual connections, and the results of various open or find calls.

These handles are similar to the file handles used in other Win32 functions, although they are not interchangeable with base Win32 handles. You cannot use an HINTERNET handle in calls such as ReadFile(), for example, and you cannot use a handle returned from CreateFile() in calls to InternetReadFile().

One difference between the HINTERNET handles and other Win32 handles is the fact that Internet handles are arranged in a tree hierarchy. The session handle returned by InternetOpen() is the root of the tree, and connection handles returned from InternetConnect() branch from that root. The handles to individual files and search results then make up the leaves of the tree.

Handles can inherit attributes, such as the asynchronous mode settings, from the handle from which they were derived. You can take advantage of the hierarchy to close the handles for a whole branch of the tree in a single call to InternetCloseHandle()[md]if you close an Internet handle, any handles descended from it also will be closed.

Each HINTERNET handle can have many different options associated with it, depending on the specific type of handle. You can access these options with the InternetQueryOption() and InternetSetOption() functions. You use these functions to access information such as the specific type of handle, timeout settings, callback and context values, buffer sizes, and many other settings.

Error Handling

The functions that make up the WinInet API handle errors the same way the general Win32 functions do. The return value of the function tells whether the call was successful—functions that return a BOOL return FALSE when an error occurs, and functions that return an HINTERNET return NULL when an error occurs or a valid handle if the function succeeded.

In the event that a function fails, more specific error information is available by way of a call to GetLastError(). In addition, if GetLastError() returns ERROR_INTERNET_EXTENDED_ERROR, you can retrieve more information about failed operations with FTP or Gopher servers with a call to InternetGetLastResponseInfo().

For HTTP operations, you also can use the InternetErrorDlg() function to display a dialog box that explains errors to users and enables them to select several choices on how to handle the errors.

Passing Buffer Parameters

Many of the WinInet API functions return variable-length strings by way of a pointer (lpszBuffer) and the buffer length (lpdwBufferLength). If the buffer size passed is too small to hold the returned string (or the pointer is NULL), the function fails, and GetLastError() returns ERROR_INSUFFICIENT_BUFFER. The value at lpdwBufferLength, however, is updated to reflect the total space needed, including the NULL terminator. You can use this value to allocate a new buffer and repeat the call. Note that when the call completes successfully, the value at lpdwBufferLength does not include the NULL terminator in its count.

Asynchronous I/O

By default, the WinInet API functions operate synchronously. This is convenient when you want to create a separate thread for each operation. In cases where you don't want a separate thread for each call, however, it is useful to handle request completion asynchronously, particularly for operations that may take an indeterminate amount of time to complete.

To enable asynchronous operation, you set the INTERNET_FLAG_ASYNC flag in a call to InternetOpen(). Any calls made on the returned session handle, or any handles derived from it, then may complete asynchronously. In addition, you must specify a callback function and a nonzero context value in order for a call to complete asynchronously.

A callback function is attached to a handle with a call to InternetSetStatusCallback(). This callback function then may be inherited by any handle derived from the handle passed to InternetSetStatusCallback(). The callback function is called by both synchronous and asynchronous functions to report the status of an operation. You will look at the callback function in more detail in "Adding a Callback Function" later in this chapter.

A context value may be passed to many of the WinInet functions. This may be used to identify the operation that has generated a call to the callback function. If you specify a context value of 0 to any function, it will operate synchronously, even if the INTERNET_FLAG_ASYNC flag is set.

When calling functions that may complete asynchronously, you always should check the return value, because it is possible that the operation will complete immediately. If an operation will complete asynchronously, the original function call will fail, and GetLastError() will return ERROR_IO_PENDING, which simply signifies that the operation will call the callback function when it completes.

General Internet Functions

Many functions in the WinInet API are used for any sort of Internet connection, such as beginning a session, enabling asynchronous I/O, and manipulating URLs. Here, you will take a look at these general functions before moving on to the protocol-specific elements of the WinInet API.

Beginning a WinInet Session

Before using most of the WinInet functions, you must open a new session with a call to InternetOpen(), which initializes the WinInet library and returns a session handle that will be the root of the handle hierarchy for the rest of your operations within that session. The following is the prototype for InternetOpen():

```
HINTERNET InternetOpen(LPCTSTR lpszAgent, DWORD dwAccessType,
    LPCTSTR lpszProxyName, LPCSTR lpszProxyBypass, DWORD dwFlags);
```

InternetOpen() enables you to specify how this session will use a proxy server. The dwAccessType parameter may specify INTERNET_OPEN_TYPE_DIRECT to resolve all addresses locally, INTERNET_OPEN_TYPE_PROXY to send requests to the proxy server, or

INTERNET_OPEN_TYPE_PRECONFIG to retrieve proxy configuration information from the Registry. In cases where you are using a proxy server, its name is passed in lpszProxyName, although this can be NULL to read proxy information from the Registry.

You also can specify a list of addresses that will be resolved locally in the lpszProxyBypass string. Requests for any address contained in this string will not be forwarded to the proxy server but will be resolved locally.

You may specify the INTERNET_FLAG_OFFLINE flag in dwFlags to specify that all download requests for this session be handled by the persistent cache. If a requested file is not in the cache, operations to access it will fail.

You also may specify the INTERNET_FLAG_ASYNC flag to enable asynchronous operations for this session handle, as well as any handles derived from it.

The INTERNET_FLAG_FROM_CACHE flag returns all requested items from the cache alone. If the item is not found in the cache, an error such as ERROR_FILE_NOT_FOUND (or whatever is most appropriate) is returned. The function InternetOpen uses this flag.

When you are finished with a session, you should close the session handle with a call to InternetCloseHandle(). This also closes any handles that have been derived from the session handle.

Setting Handle Options

If you want to use certain options for all the Internet handles that you will be using in this session, it is easiest to set the options on the session handle. Any handles that are derived from the session handle, such as connection handles created by InternetConnect(), will inherit the options from the session handle. In addition, you could set options for a connection handle, which will be inherited by any handles derived from that connection handle. Note however, that only new handles derived from the modified handle will inherit the new settings. Handles that already have been created will maintain their current settings.

You set specific option settings for an Internet handle with a call to the InternetSetOption() function:

```
BOOL InternetSetOption(HINTERNET hInternet, DWORD dwOption,
    LPVOID lpBuffer, DWORD dwBufferLength);
```

The handle to be modified is passed in hInternet. The buffer passed by lpBuffer, and its length passed in dwBufferLength, are used to pass in data for the specific option that is to be set. You specify the option to set by the value dwOption, and you can use one of the following values:

INTERNET_OPTION_ASYNC_PRIORITY is the priority for an asynchronous download (not currently implemented).

INTERNET_OPTION_CALLBACK is the address of the callback function for this handle.

INTERNET_OPTION_CONNECT_BACKOFF is the delay value, in milliseconds, to wait between connection retries.

INTERNET_OPTION_CONNECT_RETRIES is the number of times to retry a connection request.

INTERNET_OPTION_CONNECT_TIMEOUT is the timeout value, in milliseconds, for connection requests.

INTERNET_OPTION_CONTEXT_VALUE is the context value to be used with this handle.

INTERNET_OPTION_CONTROL_RECEIVE_TIMEOUT is the timeout value, in milliseconds, for receiving control information for FTP sessions.

INTERNET_OPTION_CONTROL_SEND_TIMEOUT is the timeout value, in milliseconds, for sending control information for FTP.

INTERNET_OPTION_DATA_RECEIVE_TIMEOUT is the timeout value, in milliseconds, for receiving data.

INTERNET_OPTION_DATA_SEND_TIMEOUT is the timeout value, in milliseconds, for sending data.

INTERNET_OPTION_PASSWORD is the password for handles created with InternetConnect().

INTERNET_OPTION_PROXY is proxy information for this handle or for global proxy information if hInternet is NULL. lpBuffer should point to an INTERNET_PROXY_INFO structure.

INTERNET_OPTION_READ_BUFFER_SIZE is the size, in bytes, of the buffer for reading data.

INTERNET_OPTION_REFRESH allows options for this handle to be reloaded from the Registry.

INTERNET_OPTION_USER_AGENT is the user agent string to use for HTTP requests.

INTERNET_OPTION_USERNAME is the username for handles created with InternetConnect().

INTERNET_OPTION_WRITE_BUFFER_SIZE is the size, in bytes, of the buffer for writing data.

Note that this is just a partial list, for there are over 50 internet options available.

You also can set the options for a handle with the InternetSetOptionEx() function, which takes an additional dwFlags parameter. You may set the flags to ISO_GLOBAL to modify the settings globally or to ISO_REGISTRY to modify the settings in the Registry.

Querying Handle Options

You can query the current settings for a handle's options with the
InternetQueryOption() function:

```
BOOL InternetQueryOption(HINTERNET hInternet, DWORD dwOption,
    LPVOID lpBuffer, LPDWORD lpdwBufferLength);
```

This function works much like InternetSetOption() and enables you to query all the
options listed previously. In addition, you can query several additional values that are not
set with InternetSetOption():

INTERNET_OPTION_ASYNC is not yet implemented.

INTERNET_OPTION_CACHE_STREAM_HANDLE returns the file handle used for writing
cached data.

INTERNET_OPTION_DATAFILE_NAME returns the filename for the file backing a
download.

INTERNET_OPTION_EXTENDED_ERROR returns the actual Winsock error code from the
last error.

INTERNET_OPTION_HANDLE_TYPE returns one of the following constants, indicating
the type of handle:

INTERNET_HANDLE_TYPE_CONNECT_FTP

INTERNET_HANDLE_TYPE_CONNECT_GOPHER

INTERNET_HANDLE_TYPE_CONNECT_HTTP

INTERNET_HANDLE_TYPE_FILE_REQUEST

INTERNET_HANDLE_TYPE_FTP_FILE

INTERNET_HANDLE_TYPE_FTP_FILE_HTML

INTERNET_HANDLE_TYPE_FTP_FIND

INTERNET_HANDLE_TYPE_FTP_FIND_HTML

INTERNET_HANDLE_TYPE_GOPHER_FILE

INTERNET_HANDLE_TYPE_GOPHER_FILE_HTML

INTERNET_HANDLE_TYPE_GOPHER_FIND

INTERNET_HANDLE_TYPE_GOPHER_FIND_HTML

INTERNET_HANDLE_TYPE_HTTP_REQUEST

INTERNET_HANDLE_TYPE_INTERNET

INTERNET_OPTION_KEEP_CONNECTION returns one of the following constants indicating this handle's use of persistent connections:

INTERNET_KEEP_ALIVE_DISABLED

INTERNET_KEEP_ALIVE_ENABLED

INTERNET_KEEP_ALIVE_UNKNOWN

INTERNET_OPTION_OFFLINE_MODE is not yet implemented.

INTERNET_OPTION_PARENT_HANDLE returns the handle from which this handle was derived.

INTERNET_OPTION_REFRESH returns TRUE if the handle's settings may be reloaded from the Registry.

INTERNET_OPTION_REQUEST_FLAGS returns flags concerning the current download. Currently, only a request flag value of INTERNET_REQFLAG_FROM_CACHE is supported, indicating that the request is being satisfied from the cache.

INTERNET_OPTION_SECURITY_CERTIFICATE returns a formatted string containing the certificate for an SSL/PCT server.

INTERNET_OPTION_SECURITY_CERTIFICATE_STRUCT returns an INTERNET_CERTIFICATE_INFO structure containing the certificate for SSL/PCT servers.

INTERNET_OPTION_SECURITY_FLAGS returns a combination of the following security flags:

SECURITY_FLAG_40BIT

SECURITY_FLAG_56BIT

SECURITY_FLAG_128BIT

SECURITY_FLAGE_FORTEZZA

SECURITY_FLAG_IETFSSL4

SECURITY_FLAG_IGNORE_CERT_CN_INVALID

SECURITY_FLAG_IGNORE_CERT_DATE_INVALID

SECURITY_FLAG_IGNORE_REDIRECT_TO_HTTP

SECURITY_FLAG_IGNORE_REDIRECT_TO_HTTPS

SECURITY_FLAG_IGNORE_REVOCATION

SECURITY_FLAG_IGNORE_UNKNOWN_CA

SECURITY_FLAG_IGNORE_WRONG_USAGESECURITY_FLAG_STRENGTH_MEDIUM

SECURITY_FLAG_STRENGTH_STRONG

SECURITY_FLAG_STRENGTH_WEAK

SECURITY_FLAG_NORMALBITNESS

SECURITY_FLAG_PCT

SECURITY_FLAG_PCT4

SECURITY_FLAG_SECURE

SECURITY_FLAG_SSL

SECURITY_FLAG_SSL3

SECURITY_FLAG_UNKNOWNBIT

INTERNET_OPTION_SECURITY_KEY_BITNESS returns the size of the encryption key in bits.

INTERNET_OPTION_URL returns the URL of a download.

INTERNET_OPTION_VERSION returns an INTERNET_VERSION_INFO structure containing the version of WinInet.dll.

Verifying Internet Connectivity

If your application is capable of operating with or without an Internet connection, you may want to use the InternetAttemptConnect() function, which attempts to connect to the Internet. If this returns ERROR_SUCCESS, the connection was successful and your application should be able to access information on the Internet. If any other error is returned, the connection could not be established and your application should respond appropriately, perhaps operating in an offline mode.

Connecting to a Server

For most cases, in order to communicate with an FTP, HTTP, or Gopher server, you first must establish a connection, although you will see that InternetOpenUrl() does not require you to create a session explicitly before retrieving files. Establishing a connection is done with the InternetConnect() function, which returns a handle (HINTERNET) for the connection. The new connection handle is derived from a session handle created by InternetOpen() and inherits the attributes of the session handle, like the asynchronous mode.

For the FTP protocol, InternetConnect() establishes a genuine connection to the server, although for protocols such as Gopher and HTTP, the actual connection is not established until a specific request is made. The connection represented by the handle returned by InternetConnect() is a sort of "virtual connection" and can be used to store configuration information for the connection.

The prototype for InternetConnect() follows:

```
HINTERNET InternetConnect(HINTERNET hInternet, LPCTSTR lpszServerName,
    INTERNET_PORT nServerPort, LPCTSTR lpszUsername, LPCTSTR lpszPassword,
    DWORD dwService, DWORD dwFlags, DWORD dwContext);
```

The handle passed in hInternet comes from a call to InternetOpen(), and the lpszServerName and nServerPort parameters refer to the desired server. You can specify a value of INTERNET_INVALID_PORT_NUMBER to use the default port for the requested service, or you may use one of the following constants:

INTERNET_DEFAULT_FTP_PORT

INTERNET_DEFAULT_GOPHER_PORT

```
INTERNET_DEFAULT_HTTP_PORT
INTERNET_DEFAULT_HTTPS_PORT
INTERNET_DEFAULT_SOCKS_PORT
```

The optional lpszUsername and lpszPassword parameters may be required to connect to servers that require a login.

The dwService parameter specifies the service to which to connect. This can be one of the following constants:

```
INTERNET_SERVICE_FTP
INTERNET_SERVICE_GOPHER
INTERNET_SERVICE_HTTP
```

The dwFlags parameter is used to specify options for the service. Currently, only the INTERNET_CONNECT_FLAG_PASSIVE flag is implemented, which specifies the use of passive mode for FTP connections.

If an error occurs in InternetConnect(), it returns NULL, and you can call GetLastError() or InternetGetLastResponseInfo() for more details on the error. If the connection is established successfully, InternetConnect() returns a valid connection handle, which can be used in the protocol-specific functions that you will explore soon.

Adding a Callback Function

InternetConnect(), like many other functions that you will look at in this chapter, can be used asynchronously. To do this, the INTERNET_FLAG_ASYNC flag must have been set when the session handle was created by InternetOpen(). You also must assign a context value and have a callback function assigned to the handle. A callback function is attached to a handle with the InternetSetStatusCallback() function:

```
INTERNET_STATUS_CALLBACK InternetSetStatusCallback(
    HINTERNET hInternet, INTERNET_STATUS_CALLBACK lpfnInternetCallback);
```

The hInternet parameter specifies the handle that will use the callback function specified in lpfnInternetCallback. Any handles that are derived from this handle—after the callback is attached—also will use this callback function.

The callback function specified in lpfnInternetCallback should have the following prototype:

```
void CALLBACK myCallback(HINTERNET hInternet, DWORD dwContext,
                DWORD dwInternetStatus, LPVOID lpvStatusInformation,
                DWORD dwStatusInformationLength);
```

When the callback function is called to report the status of an asynchronous operation, the hInternet and dwContext parameters give the Internet handle and context value used in the operation, and the reason for calling the function is given in dwInternetStatus. The data returned through lpvStatusInformation (of length dwStatusInformationLength) is dependent on the reason for the callback, given in dwInternetStatus. The following are possible values for dwInternetStatus:

INTERNET_STATE_BUSY—Indicates network requests are being made.

INTERNET_STATE_CONNECTED—Indicates the current connection state.

INTERNET_STATE_DISCONNECTED—Indicates the connection is disconnected.

INTERNET_STATE_DISCONNECTED_BY_USER—Indicates the connection is disconnected by user request.

INTERNET_STATE_IDLE—Indicates no network requests are being made.

INTERNET_STATUS_DETECTING_PROXY—Notifies the application that a Proxy has been detected.

INTERNET_STATUS_HANDLE_CLOSING—The handle in hInternet has been closed.

INTERNET_STATUS_HANDLE_CREATED—A new handle has been created by InternetConnect(). This occurs before the connection is established.

INTERNET_STATUS_CLOSING_CONNECTION—The connection to the server is closing. lpvStatusInformation will be NULL.

INTERNET_STATUS_CTL_RESPONSE_RECEIVED—Is not currently implemented.

INTERNET_STATUS_CONNECTED_TO_SERVER—The connection to the server at the address specified in the SOCKADDR structure at lpvStatusInformation was successful.

INTERNET_STATUS_CONNECTING_TO_SERVER—Connecting to the server specified by the SOCKADDR structure at lpvStatusInformation.

INTERNET_STATUS_CONNECTION_CLOSED—The connection closed successfully. lpvStatusInformation will be NULL.

INTERNET_STATUS_INTERMEDIATE_RESPONSE—An intermediate status code (100 level) was received.

INTERNET_STATUS_NAME_RESOLVED—The name contained in lpvStatusInformation was resolved successfully.

INTERNET_STATUS_PREFETCH—Not currently implemented.

INTERNET_STATUS_RECEIVING_RESPONSE—Waiting to receive a response. lpvStatusInformation will be NULL.

INTERNET_STATUS_REDIRECT—An HTTP request is about to be redirected to a new URL. lpvStatusInformation points to the new URL string.

INTERNET_STATUS_REQUEST_COMPLETE—An asynchronous operation has completed. lpvStatusInformation points to an INTERNET_ASYNC_RESULT structure containing the dwResult and dwError fields. dwResult contains the value that was returned from the operation, and dwError contains the error code for the operation.

INTERNET_STATUS_REQUEST_SENT—The request was sent successfully. lpvStatusInformation points to a DWORD holding the number of bytes sent.

INTERNET_STATUS_RESOLVING_NAME—The name being resolved is contained in lpvStatusInformation.

INTERNET_STATUS_RESPONSE_RECEIVED—A response was received successfully. lpvStatusInformation points to a DWORD holding the number of bytes received.

INTERNET_STATUS_SENDING_REQUEST—A request is being sent to the server. lpvStatusInformation will be NULL.

INTERNET_STATUS_STATE_CHANGE—Indicates a move between a secure and non-secure server.

INTERNET_STATUS_USER_INPUT_REQUIRED— Indicates the request requires user input.

In many cases, your application may be concerned only with handling the completion of asynchronous operations, specified by a call to the callback function with a value of INTERNET_STATUS_REQUEST_COMPLETE passed in dwInternetStatus, although some operations may generate many other calls to the callback function. A call to InternetConnect(), for example, may generate a dozen or so different calls to the callback function. Because your callback may be called many times, you should try to minimize the operations performed within the callback. Spending excessive time in the callback, like displaying a dialog box, may cause some operations to time out before the callback returns.

Working with URLs

The WinInet API provides several functions that can be useful in simplifying the processing of URLs. You can parse a URL into its various components with InternetCrackUrl(), and you can use InternetCreateUrl() to create a URL string from the individual components. You can use the InternetCanonicalizeUrl() function to convert a URL to canonical form, as well as to convert any unsafe characters into escape sequences. You also can merge a base URL and a relative URL into a single URL string with InternetCombineUrl().

Basic File Operations

For many WinInet functions, you need to explicitly establish a connection (using InternetConnect()) before using the protocol-specific functions. However, the WinInet

API does provide a simple method for retrieving data from an FTP, HTTP, or Gopher server in a somewhat generic manner using the InternetOpenUrl() function:

```
HINTERNET InternetOpenUrl(HINTERNET hInternetSession,
    LPCTSTR lpszUrl, LPCTSTR lpszHeaders, DWORD dwHeadersLength,
    DWORD dwFlags, DWORD dwContext);
```

Each call to InternetOpenUrl() establishes its own connection, so you do not need to create one explicitly with a call to InternetConnect(). However, you do need to pass a valid session handle returned from InternetOpen() in hInternetSession.

InternetOpenUrl() returns an Internet handle for the file requested by the URL string passed by lpszUrl. If this completes successfully, you can use this handle in calls to functions such as InternetReadFile(), as you will see shortly.

For HTTP requests, you can specify a pointer to an additional header string in the lpszHeaders. The length of this string should be passed in dwHeadersLength, although you can pass a length of -1 if the header's string is null-terminated—InternetOpenUrl() then figures out the length of the header's string.

The following are option flags that may be included in dwFlags:

> INTERNET_FLAG_DONT_CACHE means do not cache the data. The preferred method to use is INTERNET_FLAG_NO_CACHE_WRITE.
>
> INTERNET_FLAG_EXISTING_CONNECT attempts to use an existing connection if possible.
>
> INTERNET_FLAG_NO_CACHE_WRITE means do not cache the data.
>
> INTERNET_FLAG_RAW_DATA returns raw data (FIND_DATA structures). Otherwise, directories are returned in HTML formatting.
>
> INTERNET_FLAG_RELOAD reloads the file from the network, even if it is cached locally.
>
> INTERNET_FLAG_SECURE requests use of the Secure Sockets Layer or PCT for HTTP requests.

Querying Data Availability

If InternetOpenUrl() completes successfully, it returns an Internet file handle. You can check to see how much data is available for this file handle by calling InternetQueryDataAvailable(), which also can be used with the file handles returned by the protocol-specific functions that you will see later.

The InternetQueryDataAvailable() function takes an Internet file handle and a pointer to a DWORD where the number of bytes available will be written. Currently, the dwFlags and dwContext parameters must be 0:

```
BOOL InternetQueryDataAvailable(HINTERNET hFile,
    LPDWORD lpdwNumberOfBytesAvailable,
    DWORD dwFlags, DWORD dwContext);
```

`InternetQueryDataAvailable()` returns the amount of data that can be read immediately by a call to `InternetReadFile()`. If the end-of-file has not been reached and no data is immediately available for reading, this function blocks until data is available.

Reading Data

You can read data from a file handle with `InternetReadFile()`. This can be used for handles returned from `InternetOpenUrl()`, as well as handles returned from protocol-specific functions such as `FtpOpenFile()`, `GopherOpenFile()`, or `HttpOpenRequest()`. The following is the prototype for `InternetReadFile()`:

```
BOOL InternetReadFile(HINTERNET hFile, LPVOID lpBuffer,
    DWORD dwNumberOfBytesToRead, LPDWORD lpNumberOfBytesRead);
```

`InternetReadFile()` attempts to read the number of bytes specified in `dwNumberOfBytesToRead` into the buffer at `lpBuffer`. Upon completion, the `DWORD` at `lpNumberOfBytesRead` contains the number of bytes actually read. If there is not enough data currently available to satisfy the request, it blocks until enough data is received. The only time the actual number of bytes requested will be less than the number requested is when the end-of-file has been reached.

Moving the File Pointer

You can move the file pointer for calls to `InternetReadFile()` by calling the `InternetSetFilePointer()` function:

```
BOOL InternetSetFilePointer(HINTERNET hFile, LONG lDistanceToMove,
    PVOID pReserved, DWORD dwMoveMethod, DWORD dwContext);
```

The file handle passed in `hFile` can be any file handle returned from calls such as `InternetOpenUrl()` or `FtpOpenFile()`, with the exception that caching must be enabled for the handle—that is, it must not have been created with the `INTERNET_FLAG_DONT_CACHE` or `INTERNET_FLAG_NO_CACHE_WRITE` option.

The `lDistanceToMove` parameter specifies the number of bytes to move the file pointer from a location specified by `dwMoveMethod`, which can have the following values:

> `FILE_BEGIN` moves from the beginning of the file.
>
> `FILE_CURRENT` moves from the current position.
>
> `FILE_END` moves from the end-of-file.

Positive values of lDistanceToMove move forward in the file, and negative values move backward.

Currently, pReserved and dwContext must be 0. This operation always completes synchronously, although subsequent calls to InternetReadFile() may complete asynchronously.

Writing to Internet Files

For Internet file handles that have been opened with InternetOpenUrl(), as well as other functions such as FtpOpenFile(), you can write data to a file with the InternetWriteFile() function:

```
BOOL InternetWriteFile(HINTERNET hFile, LPCVOID lpBuffer,
    DWORD dwNumberOfBytesToWrite, LPDWORD lpdwNumberOfBytesWritten);
```

This function will write the number of bytes in dwNumberOfBytesToWrite from lpBuffer to the file specified by hFile. On completion, the DWORD at lpdwNumberOfBytesWritten will contain the actual number of bytes written.

Note that the transfer may not be completed until you call InternetCloseHandle() to close the file handle and flush its buffers.

FTP Client Functions

The following functions are provided by the WinInet API to work with connections to an FTP server. The connection handle (hFtpSession) used in these calls is obtained by a call to InternetConnect(), as you saw earlier.

The Current Directory

You can retrieve the current directory for an FTP connection by calling FtpGetCurrentDirectory():

```
BOOL FtpGetCurrentDirectory(HINTERNET hFtpSession,
    LPCTSTR lpszCurrentDirectory, LPDWORD lpdwCurrentDirectory);
```

The lpdwCurrentDirectory parameter should point to a DWORD containing the size of the buffer at lpszCurrentDirectory, which will receive a null-terminated ASCII string containing the absolute path to the current directory. A buffer of size MAX_PATH is sufficient for all pathnames.

You can set the current directory for an FTP connection with the FtpSetCurrentDirectory() function:

```
BOOL FtpSetCurrentDirectory(HINTERNET hFtpSession,
    LPCTSTR lpszDirectory);
```

lpszDirectory points to a null-terminated ASCII string containing either an absolute or relative path to the new current directory.

> **Tip**
>
> For the Ftp functions listed in this section, you can use either forward (/) or backward (\) slashes in your path strings. FtpSetCurrentDirectory() will translate these to the appropriate character for the server.

Creating and Removing Directories

You can create a new directory on the FTP server with the FtpCreateDirectory() function:

```
BOOL FtpCreateDirectory(HINTERNET hFtpSession,
    LPCTSTR lpszDirectory);
```

You can specify either an absolute path or a path relative to the current directory in the null-terminated string passed by lpszDirectory.

You can remove a directory from the FTP server with the FtpRemoveDirectory() function:

```
BOOL FtpRemoveDirectory(HINTERNET hFtpSession,
    LPCTSTR lpszDirectory);
```

lpszDirectory points to a null-terminated string containing either an absolute path or a path relative to the current directory for the directory to be removed.

Finding Files

You can begin a search for a file or a general listing of files on an FTP server with the FtpFindFirstFile() function:

```
HINTERNET FtpFindFirstFile(HINTERNET hFtpSession, LPCTSTR lpszSearchFile,
    LPWIN32_FIND_DATA lpFindFileData, DWORD dwFlags, DWORD dwContext);
```

You can specify a valid directory or filename in the null-terminated string at lpszSearchFile. Additionally, you may specify a NULL or empty string to begin retrieving a listing of files in the current directory.

Information about the first file found is returned in a WIN32_FIND_DATA structure at lpFindFileData.

To retrieve information on additional files found, you can call `InternetFindNextFile()`:

```
BOOL InternetFindNextFile(HINTERNET hFind, LPVOID lpvFindData);
```

The `hFind` parameter gives the find handle returned by `FtpFindFirstFile()`, and a `WIN32_FIND_DATA` structure is returned via `lpvFindData` with information on the next file in the listing.

If no more matching files are found, `InternetFindNextFile()` returns `FALSE`, and a call to `GetLastError()` returns `ERROR_NO_MORE_FILES`.

The nature of the FTP protocol dictates that only one find handle be open at any given time for any particular FTP connection handle. Thus, you must call `InternetCloseHandle()` to close one find handle before starting a new search. You also cannot begin a search with `FtpFindFirstFile()` while there is an open file handle returned by `FtpOpenFile()`.

Retrieving a File

You can copy files from the FTP server to a local drive with the `FtpGetFile()` function:

```
BOOL FtpGetFile(HINTERNET hFtpSession, LPCSTR lpszRemoteFile,
    LPCSTR lpszNewFile, BOOL fFailIfExists,
    DWORD dwFlagsAndAttributes, DWORD dwFlags,
    DWORD dwContext);
```

Null-terminated strings containing the source and destination filenames are passed in `lpszRemoteFile` and `lpszNewFile`. You can specify a value of `TRUE` for `fFailIfExists` to cancel the operation if a local file with the name passed in `lpszNewFile` already exists.

The `dwFlagsAndAttributes` parameter contains flags for the file attributes of the new file. These can be any of the file attribute flags used with the Win32 `CreateFile()` function.

The `dwFlags` parameter may contain the following flags, which control the transfer mode, as well as several other flags that control the caching operation:

> `FTP_TRANSFER_TYPE_ASCII` performs an ASCII transfer, converting control and formatting information to local formats, such as replacing newlines with carriage return/linefeed pairs.
>
> `FTP_TRANSFER_TYPE_BINARY` transfers the file in binary mode; no changes are made to the data. This is the default.
>
> `FTP_TRANSFER_TYPE_UNKNOWN` defaults to `FTP_TRANSFER_TYPE_BINARY`.
>
> `INTERNET_FLAGE_TRANSFER_ASCII` transfers the file in ASCII format.
>
> `INTERNET_FLAGE_TRANSFER_BINARY` transfers the file in binary format.

Sending a File

You can copy a file from a local drive to the FTP server with the `FtpPutFile()` function:

```
BOOL FtpPutFile(HINTERNET hFtpSession, LPCTSTR lpszLocalFile,
    LPCTSTR lpszNewRemoteFile, DWORD dwFlags, DWORD dwContext);
```

`lpszLocalFile` and `lpszNewRemoteFile` point to null-terminated strings containing the local and remote filenames, respectively. The `dwFlags` parameter may specify one of the transfer type constants used in `FtpGetFile()`.

Opening a File on the FTP Server

The WinInet API enables you to access a file in place on the FTP server, which can be useful when you want to read or write data using memory buffers rather than a local file. You also can have more control over the progress of a file transfer by handling the read or write operations manually. You can open a file for reading or writing in-place on the FTP server with a call to `FtpOpenFile()`:

```
HINTERNET FtpOpenFile(HINTERNET hFtpSession, LPCSTR lpszFileName,
    DWORD fdwAccess, DWORD dwFlags, DWORD dwContext);
```

The `hFtpSession` parameter should be a handle returned by `InternetConnect()`. The name of the file is passed in `lpszFileName()`.

To open the file for reading, you should specify `GENERIC_READ` in `fdwAccess`. For writing, you should set `fdwAccess` to `GENERIC_WRITE`. You cannot use both for a given handle.

You can use the `dwFlags` parameter to specify the transfer mode for the file by using either `FTP_FLAG_TRANSFER_ASCII` or `FTP_FLAG_TRANSFER_BINARY`. In addition, you may specify other flags that dictate how caching will be used with this file.

`FtpOpenFile()` returns a handle to the file on the server, which can be used in calls such as `InternetReadFile()` or `InternetWriteFile()`.

When you are finished with this handle, you should call `InternetCloseHandle()` to release the handle. This is particularly important, because the FTP protocol allows only one file transfer at a time for a given connection. Because of this, most other FTP functions that you call while a file handle is open will fail with an error code of `ERROR_FTP_TRANSFER_IN_PROGRESS`.

Other FTP File Operations

You can delete a file on the FTP server with `FtpDeleteFile()`:

```
BOOL FtpDeleteFile(HINTERNET hFtpSession, LPCTSTR lpszFileName);
```

You also can rename files on the FTP server with `FtpRenameFile()`:

```
BOOL FtpRenameFile(HINTERNET hFtpSession,
    LPCTSTR lpszExisting, LPCTSTR lpszNew);
```

HTTP Client Functions

As you saw earlier, you can use `InternetOpenUrl()` to make simple HTTP requests to retrieve files; however, for more complicated operations, you need to use the HTTP-specific functions that you will look at here. These functions require an `HINTERNET` parameter, which is a connection handle returned from `InternetConnect()`.

In this section, you will see how to use the WinInet HTTP functions to create a request, send it to the server, and retrieve the results. You also will look at some special functions used to work with cookies and the persistent cache.

HTTP Requests

Several steps are involved in sending an HTTP request and retrieving its results. To start with, a new request is created with `HttpOpenRequest()`. You then can modify the headers for the request with `HttpAddRequestHeaders()` before sending the request to the server with `HttpSendRequest()`.

Creating an HTTP Request

A new HTTP request is created by calling `HttpOpenRequest()`:

```
HINTERNET HttpOpenRequest(HINTERNET hHttpSession, LPCTSTR lpszVerb,
    LPCTSTR lpszObjectName, LPCTSTR lpszVersion,
    LPCTSTR lpszReferer, LPCTSTR FAR * lpszAcceptTypes,
    DWORD dwFlags, DWORD dwContext);
```

The handle passed in `hHttpSession` is returned by a call to `InternetConnect()`.

The two most important elements of an HTTP request are the object to act on, passed in `lpszObjectName`, and the verb to use, passed in `lpszVerb`, which specifies the action the server should perform on the object.

The string containing the object name, which is passed by `lpszObjectName`, generally contains a filename to retrieve.

The `lpszVerb` parameter points to a string containing the verb to use for the request. You can specify a `NULL` pointer here to use the `GET` default verb, or you can pass a pointer to a string for the following verbs:

> `GET` retrieves data.
>
> `HEAD` retrieves server response headers.

POST sends information for the server to act on.

PUT sends information for the server to store.

DELETE removes a resource from the server.

LINK establishes a link between URLs.

If you are using a version of HTTP other than 1.0, you may specify that version in a string at lpszVersion. If this value is NULL, the default of HTTP/1.0 is used.

The lpszAcceptTypes parameter is used to specify the type of information that the client application will accept. lpszAcceptTypes is a pointer to a null-terminated array of pointers to strings containing data types that will be accepted, such as image/jpeg or audio/*. If lpszAcceptTypes is NULL, the request will use text/* to accept only text files.

You also may choose to specify the URL of a referring page in lpszReferer, a context value for asynchronous I/O in dwContext, or other options for the call in dwFlags. HttpOpenRequest() accepts the same flags you saw for InternetOpenUrl() earlier.

Upon successful completion, HttpOpenRequest() returns an HINTERNET handle for the request. This handle then is passed to calls such as HttpAddRequestHeaders(), HttpSendRequest(), and HttpQueryInfo().

Request Headers

HTTP requests can have a variety of different headers attached to them to clarify just how a particular request is to be satisfied. You can use the WinInet HttpAddRequestHeaders() function to add headers, as well as to modify or remove existing headers:

```
BOOL HttpAddRequestHeaders(HINTERNET hHttpRequest, LPCTSTR lpszHeaders,
    DWORD dwHeadersLength, DWORD dwModifiers);
```

The operation performed by HttpAddRequestHeaders() is specified by the value passed in dwModifiers, which can have a combination of the following values:

HTTP_ADDREQ_FLAG_REPLACE replaces an existing header. If the new header value is empty, this removes an existing header.

HTTP_ADDREQ_FLAG_ADD, when used with _REPLACE, adds the header if it does not already exist.

HTTP_ADDREQ_FLAG_ADD_IF_NEW adds a header only if it does not already exist.

HTTP_ADDREQ_FLAG_COALESCE combines headers with the same name into a single header.

`HTTP_ADDREQ_FLAG_COALESCE_WITH_COMMA` uses a comma to combine headers with the same name.

`HTTP_ADDREQ_FLAG_COALESCE_WITH_SEMICOLON` uses a semicolon to combine headers of the same name.

The headers to be added are passed in `lpszHeaders`, which points to a string containing individual headers separated by a `CR/LF` pair. The length of this string is passed in `dwHeadersLength`, which may be `-1L` if the `lpszHeaders` string is null-terminated.

Sending an HTTP Request

An HTTP request, as specified by an `HINTERNET` created by `HttpOpenRequest()`, is sent to the server with a call to `HttpSendRequest()`:

```
BOOL HttpSendRequest(HINTERNET hHttpRequest, LPCTSTR lpszHeaders,
    DWORD dwHeadersLength, LPVOID lpOptional, DWORD dwOptionalLength);
```

`HttpSendRequest()` enables you to specify any additional headers to send with the request in `lpszHeaders`, with the length of the string in `dwHeadersLength`.

You also can specify any additional data to be sent immediately after the request headers by passing a pointer to the data in `lpOptional` and its length in `dwOptionalLength`. This normally is used only with the `POST` and `PUT` operations, which send data to the server.

`HttpSendRequest()` will send the request to the server and read the status code and response headers from the server. You can access the information in the response headers with `HttpQueryInfo()`. You can read the body of any data returned by using the `InternetReadFile()` function.

Handling `HttpSendRequest()` Errors

If `HttpSendRequest()` completes successfully, it returns `TRUE`; otherwise, it returns `FALSE`, and you should call `GetLastError()` to retrieve the specific error code. In addition, the WinInet API provides a special function for dealing with errors in `HttpSendRequest()`: `InternetErrorDlg()`. You also can use it to detect errors in the response headers that do not result in failure of the `HttpSendRequest()` call. It presents a dialog box to the user, detailing the error and requesting input about how to handle the error.

The prototype for `InternetErrorDlg()` follows:

```
DWORD InternetErrorDlg(HWND hWnd, HINTERNET hInternet,
    DWORD dwError, DWORD dwFlags, LPVOID *lppvData);
```

The `hWnd` parameter gives the parent of the dialog box to be created, and the handle in `hInternet` is the handle of the HTTP request, as returned from `HttpOpenRequest()` and used in the `HttpSendRequest()` call.

The dwError parameter specifies the error that should be handled by the dialog box. This can have the following values:

ERROR_INTERNET_HTTP_TO_HTTPS_ON_REDIR notifies the user of a zone crossing between nonsecure and secure sites.

ERROR_INTERNET_INCORRECT_PASSWORD displays a dialog box prompting for username and password.

ERROR_INTERNET_INVALID_CA notifies the user that a certificate for an SSL site was not found.

ERROR_INTERNET_POST_IS_NON_SECURE displays a warning about posting data on a nonsecure connection.

ERROR_INTERNET_SEC_CERT_CN_INVALID displays the certificate with an invalid common name and enables the user to select a certificate to respond to a server request.

ERROR_INTERNET_SEC_CERT_DATE_INVALID notifies the user of an expired SSL certificate.

The dwFlags parameter specifies what action the function will take in handling an error. The following values are supported:

FLAGS_ERROR_UI_FILTER_FOR_ERRORS indicates that the response headers received from the server will be scanned for errors.

FLAGS_ERROR_UI_FLAGS_CHANGE_OPTIONS indicates that the user's choices from the dialog box may result in changes to the options of the request handle passed in hInternet.

FLAGS_ERROR_UI_FLAGS_GENERATE_DATA indicates that the function will query the handle in hInternet for any needed information.

FLAGS_ERROR_UI_SERIALIZE_DIALOGS indicates that on a password cache entry, authentication dialog boxes are serialized.

The function of the lppvData parameter has not yet been defined, so a value of NULL should be passed.

Retrieving Response Information

You can access information that the server sends back to a client application in the response headers by using the HttpQueryInfo() function:

```
BOOL HttpQueryInfo(HINTERNET hHttpRequest, DWORD dwInfoLevel,
    LPVOID lpvBuffer, LPDWORD lpdwBufferLength, LPDWORD lpdwIndex);
```

The hHttpRequest parameter should be a handle returned from HttpOpenRequest().

The `dwInfoLevel` parameter specifies what information to return and how to return it. This value is formed by combining one of these indexes with one of the flags in this list:

HTTP_QUERY_ACCEPT

HTTP_QUERY_ACCEPT_CHARSET

HTTP_QUERY_ACCEPT_ENCODING

HTTP_QUERY_ACCEPT_LANGUAGE

HTTP_QUERY_ACCEPT_RANGES

HTTP_QUERY_AGE

HTTP_QUERY_ALLOW

HTTP_QUERY_AUTHORIZATION

HTTP_QUERY_CACHE_CONTROLHTTP_QUERY_CONNECTION

HTTP_QUERY_CONTENT_BASE

HTTP_QUERY_CONTENT_DESCRIPTION

HTTP_QUERY_CONTENT_DISPOSTIONHTTP_QUERY_CONTENT_ENDCODING

HTTP_QUERY_CONTENT_ID

HTTP_QUERY_CONTENT_LANGUAGE

HTTP_QUERY_CONTENT_LENGTH

HTTP_QUERY_CONTENT_LOCATION

HTTP_QUERY_CONTENT_MDS

HTTP_QUERY_CONTENT_RANGEHTTP_QUERY_CONTENT_TRANSFER_ENCODING

HTTP_QUERY_CONTENT_TYPE

HTTP_QUERY_COST

HTTP_QUERY_CUSTOM

HTTP_QUERY_DATE

HTTP_QUERY_DERIVED_FROM

HTTP_QUERY_ECHO_HEADERS

HTTP_QUERY_ECHO_HEADERS_CRLF

HTTP_QUERY_ECHO_REPLY

HTTP_QUERY_ECHO_REQUEST

HTTP_QUERY_ETAG

HTTP_QUERY_EXPECT

HTTP_QUERY_EXPIRES

HTTP_QUERY_FORWARDEDHTTP_QUERY_FROM

HTTP_QUERY_HOST

```
HTTP_QUERY_IF_MATCH
HTTP_QUERY_IF_MODIFIED_SINCE
HTTP_QUERY_IF_NONE_MATCH
HTTP_QUERY_IF_RANGE
HTTP_QUERY_IF_UNMODIFIED_SINCE
HTTP_QUERY_LANGUAGE
HTTP_QUERY_LAST_MODIFIED
HTTP_QUERY_LINK
HTTP_QUERY_LOCATION
HTTP_QUERY_MAX
HTTP_QUERY_MAX_FORWARDS
HTTP_QUERY_MESSAGE_ID
HTTP_QUERY_MIME_VERSION
HTTP_QUERY_ORIG_URI
HTTP_QUERY_PRAGMA
HTTP_QUERY_PROXY_AUTHENTICATE
HTTP_QUERY_PROXY_CONNECTION
HTTP_QUERY_PUBLIC
HTTP_QUERY_RANGE
HTTP_QUERY_RAW_HEADERS
HTTP_QUERY_RAW_HEADERS_CRLF
HTTP_QUERY_REFERER
HTTP_QUERY_REQUEST_METHOD
HTTP_QUERY_RETRY_AFTER
HTTP_QUERY_SERVER
HTTP_QUERY_SET_COOKIE
HTTP_QUERY_STATUS_CODE
HTTP_QUERY_STATUS_TEXT
HTTP_QUERY_TITLE
HTTP_QUERY_TRANSFER_ENCODING
HTTP_QUERY_UNLESS_MODIFIED_SINCE
HTTP_QUERY_UPGRADE
HTTP_QUERY_URI
HTTP_QUERY_USER_AGENT
```

```
HTTP_QUERY_VARY
HTTP_QUERY_VERSION
HTTP_QUERY_VIA
HTTP_QUERY_WARNING
HTTP_QUERY_WWW_AUTHENTICATE
HTTP_QUERY_WWW_LINK
```

The indexes listed can be combined with one of the following flags, which specify how the requested data will be returned:

`HTTP_QUERY_CUSTOM` enables you to specify a custom header to search for in `lpvBuffer`. If the header is found, its value is returned in `lpvBuffer`.

`HTTP_QUERY_FLAG_COALESCE` indicates that headers of the same name will be combined in the returned data.

`HTTP_QUERY_FLAG_NUMBER` indicates that the requested data will be returned as a `DWORD`.

`HTTP_QUERY_FLAG_REQUEST_HEADERS` is used to query the headers used for the request, rather than the response headers.

`HTTP_QUERY_FLAG_SYSTEMTIME` can be used to return date and time values as `SYSTEMTIME` structures, rather than strings.

The information that is returned is written at `lpvBuffer`, and its length is written at `lpdwBufferLength`.

The `lpdwIndex` parameter is used to return information on multiple headers with the same name. On calling `HttpQueryInfo()`, you can specify the 0-based index of the header to retrieve in the `DWORD` at `lpdwIndex`. Upon return, the value at `lpdwIndex` is set to the index of the next matching header, or `ERROR_HTTP_HEADER_NOT_FOUND` if no more matching headers are found.

Getting Your Hands in the Cookie Jar

Many Internet applications use *cookies,* which can store on the local machine bits of data associated with a particular URL. In most cases, cookies are used to maintain state information for HTTP sessions. Cookies are stored in the `windows\cookies` directory on Win95 or the `winnt\cookies` directory on WinNT.

You can add a new cookie to the local system with the `InternetSetCookie()` function:

```
BOOL InternetSetCookie(LPCSTR lpszUrlName,
    LPCSTR lpszCookieName, LPCSTR lpszCookieData);
```

This function takes pointers to three null-terminated strings: `lpszUrlName` points to the URL with which to associate the cookie, `lpszCookieName` points to the name of the cookie, and `lpszCookieData` points to the string that will be saved for the new cookie.

> **Note**
>
> Because no `HINTERNET`s are involved, the cookie functions do not require that you call `InternetOpen()` before using them.

You can retrieve data stored in a cookie for a given URL, or its parent URLs, by calling `InternetGetCookie()`:

```
BOOL InternetGetCookie(LPCSTR lpszUrlName, LPCSTR lpszCookieName,
    LPSTR lpszCookieData, LPDWORD  lpdwSize);
```

This function tries to find a cookie named in `lpszCookieName` that is associated with the URL in `lpszUrlName` or its parent URLs and returns any data found at `lpszCookieData` and its length at `lpdwSize`.

Working with the Cache

Many of the WinInet functions you have looked at so far in this chapter can use the persistent cache to store received data to disk, depending on certain flags. This capability enables applications such as browsers to retrieve frequently accessed data more efficiently than having to download it each time.

The WinInet API provides the following functions, which enable you to work with the cache more directly from within your applications:

`CommitUrlCacheEntry()` saves data to the cache.

`CreateUrlCacheEntry()` creates an entry in the cache.

`CreateUrlCacheGroup()` creates a group in the cache.

`DeleteUrlCacheEntry()` deletes a file from the cache.

`DeleteUrlCacheGroup()` deletes a group from the cache.

`FindCloseUrlCache()` closes a search handle created by `FindFirstUrlCacheEntry()`.

`FindFirstUrlCacheEntry()` begins a search of cache entries.

`FindFirstUrlCacheEntryEx()` is an extended version of above.

`FindNextUrlCacheEntry()` retrieves individual cache entries.

`FindNextUrlCacheEntryEx()` is an extended version of above.

`FreeUrlCacheSpace()` frees cache space.

`FtpCommand()` sends an FTP command to the FTP server.

`FtpCreateDirectory()` creates a new directory on the FTP server.

`FtpDeleteFile()` deletes a file on the FTP server.

`FtpFindFirstFile()` searches directory specified on FTP server.

`FtpGetCurrentDirectory()` returns the current directory on the FTP server.

`FtpGetFile()` retrieves a file from the FTP server, creating a new local file in the process.

`FtpOpenFile()` opens a file on the FTP server.

`FtpPutFile()` stores a file on the FTP server.

`FtpRemoveDirectory()` deletes a given directory on the FTP server.

`FtpRenameFile()` renames a file on the FTP server.

`FtpSetCurrentDirectory()` sets the current working directory to a new directory.

`GetUrlCacheConfigInfo()` retrieves configuration information about the cache.

`GetUrlCacheEntryInfo()` retrieves information about a cache entry.

`GetUrlCacheEntryInfoEx()` extended version of above.

`HttpAddRequestHeaders()` adds a new HTTP request header to the HTTP request handle.

`HttpEndRequest()` ends the HTTP request that was released by HttpSendRequestEx.

`HttpOpenRequest()` creates a new HTTP request handle.

`HttpQueryInfo()` returns header information from an HTTP request.

`HttpSendRequest()` sends a request to the HTTP server.

`HttpSendRequestEx()` extended version of above, but allows chunked transfers.

`InternetAttemptConnect()` makes an attempt to connect to the Internet.

`InternetAutoDial()` forces the modem to automatically dial when a connection to the Internet is made.

`InternetAutoDialHangup()` disconnects an Automatic-dialup session.

`InternetCanonicalizeUrl()` canonicalizes the URL.

`InternetCloseHandle()` closes an internet handle.

`InternetCombineUrl()` combines a base and a relative URL to a single URL.

`InternetConnect()` connects to the Internet, opening an FTP, HTTP session, or Gopher session.

`InternetCrackUrl()` cracks a URL into the component parts.

`InternetCreateUrl()` creates a URL from the component parts.

`InternetDial()` utilizes a modem to create an Internet connection.

`InternetErrorDlg()` displays a dialog box for Internet errors.

`InternetFindNextFile()` continues a file search on an FTP site or Gopher site.

`InternetGetConnectedState()` returns the connected state.

`InternetGetCookie()` gets a cookie from a specified URL.

`InternetGetLastResponseInfo()` gets the last Internet function error description.

`InternetGoOnline()` prompts the user before connecting to a URL, thus getting permission.

`InternetHangup()` forces the modem to hang up.

`InternetLockRequestFile()` allows the user to lock a file that is being used.

`InternetInitializeAutoProxyDLL()` is not supported.

`InternetOpen()` initializes an application to use the Internet functions.

`InternetOpenUrl()` begins reading a complete HTTP, FTP, or Gopher URL.

`InternetQueryDataAvailable()` sends a query to the server to determine how much data is currently available.

`InternetQueryOption()` queries an Internet option on the specified handle.

`InternetReadFile()` reads data from an opened handle.

`InternetSetCookie()` creates a cookie from the specified URL.

`InternetSetFilePointer()` sets a file position for `InternetReadFile()`.

`InternetSetOption()` sets an Internet option.

`InternetSetOptionEx()` is not currently implemented.

`InternetSetStatusCallback()` sets up a callback function.

`InternetTimeFromSystemTime()` formats a date and time based on the HTTP version 1.0 specification.

`InternetTimeToSystemTime()` converts an HTTP time/date string to a SYSTEMTIME structure.

`InternetUnlockRequestFile()` unlocks a locked file

`InternetWriteFile()` writes data to an Internet file that is open.

`ReadUrlCacheEntryStream()` reads cached data from a stream opened with `RetrieveUrlCacheEntryStream()`.

`RetrieveUrlCacheEntryFile()` retrieves cache data as a file.

`RetrieveUrlCacheEntryStream()` opens a stream for data from the cache.

`SetUrlCacheConfigInfo()` sets cache configuration information.

`SetUrlCacheEntryGroup()` sets information in a cache group.

`SetUrlCacheEntryInfo()` sets information in a cache entry.

UnlockUrlCacheEntryFile() unlocks a cache file locked with
RetrieveUrlCacheEntryFile().

UnlockUrlCacheEntryStream() releases a stream locked by
RetreiveUrlCacheEntryStream().

Gopher Client Functions

The WinInet API also provides functions that your client applications can use to retrieve
information from Gopher servers. The Gopher protocol was developed at the University
of Minnesota to provide an ASCII-based system for browsing a series of menus to locate
various resources on a network.

The WinInet Gopher functions require the use of a Gopher connection handle that was
created with a call to InternetConnect().

To access objects on a Gopher server, a special ASCII string known as a *Gopher locator*
is used. This string is similar to the URL strings used in HTTP requests. You can create a
locator string with a call to GopherCreateLocator(). You also can retrieve specific information about a locator string with the GopherGetLocatorType() function.

To find Gopher resources on a server, you can start a query with
GopherFindFirstFile() and retrieve individual entries with the InternetFindNext()
function, as you saw earlier for FTP connections.

You can request information from the server about a Gopher object with a call to
GopherGetAttributes(). To retrieve a file from the server, you can use
GopherOpenFile() to open a file handle, which then can be used in calls to
InternetReadFile().

MFC WinInet Classes

In addition to the Win32 Internet Extension C API that you saw previously, MFC provides the WinInet classes that encapsulate this functionality into a set of classes that you
can use to easily add Internet functionality to your C++ applications.

These classes add some additional functionality to the WinInet C API, including buffered
I/O, default parameters, exception handling, and automatic cleanup of handles and connections.

Figure 11.1 shows the relationship of the classes that make up the MFC WinInet classes.

FIGURE 11.1

MFC WinInet classes.

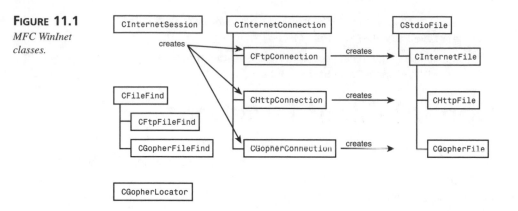

CInternetSession

Any application that is going to use the WinInet classes first needs to have a CInternetSession object. This object is used to create and initialize an Internet session and may be used to handle a connection to a proxy server. Often, if your application will maintain an Internet session for the duration of the application, it is most convenient to make your CInternetSession object a member of your CWinApp object.

Connection Classes

For many Internet operations, you also need to open a connection to a server. MFC uses the CInternetConnection class to represent a connection to a server, as well as a class derived from CInternetConnection for each specific protocol. These include CFtpConnection, CGopherConnection, and CHttpConnection. These objects are created by member functions of CInternetSession.

File Classes

To help your application work with the files used in various Internet protocols, MFC provides several new Internet file classes derived from CInternetFile. These include CInternetFile itself for FTP files, CHttpFile for HTTP files, and CGopherFile for Gopher files. As you will see, these objects are returned from CInternetSession::OpenURL() or the protocol-specific function CFtpConnection::OpenFile(), CGopherConnection::OpenFile(), or CHttpConnection::OpenRequest().

CInternetException

Many of the member functions for the WinInet classes may throw an exception in the event of errors. In most cases, a CInternetException is thrown. For more on handling these exceptions, see Chapter 14, "Error Detection and Exception Handling Techniques." In your applications, you can generate a `CInternetException` with a call to `::AfxThrowInternetException()`.

Using `CInternetSession`

The `CInternetSession` class provides a context for all the other operations that will be performed using the WinInet classes. In this section, you'll look at how to create a `CInternetSession` and how to use it to perform simple file retrieval. You'll also see how the WinInet classes enable you to handle asynchronous operations.

Creating a Session

To establish an Internet session in MFC, you need only construct a new `CInternetSession` object—although you may want to derive your own class from `CInternetSession`, as you will see in the discussion about asynchronous I/O. The constructor for `CInternetSession` takes a fair number of parameters, although you will notice that all these have reasonable default values provided. The following is the constructor for `CInternetSession`:

```
CInternetSession( LPCTSTR pstrAgent = NULL, DWORD dwContext = 1,
    DWORD dwAccessType = PRE_CONFIG_INTERNET_ACCESS,
    LPCTSTR pstrProxyName = NULL, LPCTSTR pstrProxyBypass = NULL,
    DWORD dwFlags = 0 );
```

You can use the `pstrAgent` parameter to specify the name of your application, which may be used, in turn, to identify your application to servers for certain protocols. By default, this is `NULL`—in which case, MFC will get the application name with a call to `AfxGetAppName()`.

`dwContext` specifies a context value that will be used for asynchronous operations on this `CInternetSession` and any objects created by it.

The `dwAccessType` parameter tells MFC how to connect to the network. You can use `INTERNET_OPEN_TYPE_DIRECT` to connect directly, or `INTERNET_OPEN_TYPE_PROXY` to connect through a proxy server. The default, `INTERNET_OPEN_TYPE_PRECONFIG`, will access the network as configured in the Registry.

If you are using proxy access, you also need to specify the name of the proxy server in `pstrProxyName`. In addition, you may specify a list of server addresses that should be accessed directly, without using the proxy server, in `pstrProxyBypass`.

The `dwFlags` parameter enables you to specify several options for how your Internet session will behave. You can specify `INTERNET_FLAG_DONT_CACHE` to tell the framework not to cache data, or you may specify `INTERNET_FLAG_OFFLINE` to tell the framework to access only data that is currently in the cache—attempts to access data not in the cache will return an error. In addition, you may specify the `INTERNET_FLAG_ASYNC` flag to enable asynchronous operations for the session.

Retrieving a File

After an Internet session is established, you can begin retrieving files with calls to `CInternetSession::OpenURL()`. Note that you do not need to establish a connection explicitly before using this function; it will create its own session if necessary.

`OpenURL()` uses the `InternetOpenURL()` Win32 API function and has the same limitations: You can only retrieve data, and you cannot manipulate data on the server. For operations requiring this sort of interaction, you need to open a connection, as you will see later.

`OpenURL()` takes a URL string and returns a pointer to an object of a type appropriate for the file specified in the URL. Table 22.1 lists the types of URLs currently supported, with the types of pointers returned by `OpenURL()`.

TABLE 22.1 URL Types and Associated File Classes

URL Type	`OpenURL()` *Return Type*
`http:\\`	`CHttpFile*`
`ftp://`	`CFtpFile*`
`gopher:\\`	`CGopherFile*`
`file://`	`CStdioFile*`

Note that the `CStdioFile` object may be used just like any other `CStdioFile`, as shown in Chapter 14.

The following is the prototype for `CInternetSession::OpenURL()`:

```
CStdioFile* OpenURL( LPCTSTR pstrURL, DWORD dwContext = 1, DWORD dwFlags = 0,
    LPCTSTR pstrHeaders = NULL, DWORD dwHeadersLength = 0 );
```

The first parameter, *pstrURL*, points to the URL string for the file to retrieve. The *dwContext* parameter is used for asynchronous operations, as you will see soon.

`OpenURL()` also supports several flags, as passed in `dwFlags`, that you can use to alter the behavior of `OpenURL()`. `INTERNET_FLAG_RELOAD` forces the framework to reload the file from the network, even if it is found in the cache. `INTERNET_FLAG_DONT_CACHE` prevents the framework from saving the file in the cache.

The `INTERNET_OPEN_FLAG_USE_EXISTING_CONNECT` flag tells the framework to try to use an existing connection to retrieve the file, rather than opening a new connection for each call to `OpenURL()`.

For FTP applications, you also can specify `INTERNET_FLAG_PASSIVE` to use passive FTP semantics.

Applications requesting files using HTTP may specify the `INTERNET_FLAG_SECURE` flag to use secure transactions, either with *Secure Sockets Layer* (*SSL*) or PCT. In addition, HTTP requests may include additional RFC822, MIME, or HTTP headers, as specified with `pstrHeaders` and `dwHeadersLength`.

The following example shows how an application can create an Internet session and use `OpenURL()` to retrieve a file using HTTP:

```
#include <AfxInet.h>
    // Create Session Object
    CInternetSession mySession;

    CHttpFile *pHttpFile;
    CString tmpStr;
    char inBuf[10000];
    UINT nBytesRead;
    try
    {
        // Open HTTP file
        pHttpFile =(CHttpFile *) mySession.OpenURL("http://www.racotek.com");
    }
    catch (CInternetException)
    {
        AfxMessageBox("Received Exception from OpenURL()");
        // Handle exception
    }
    if(pHttpFile == NULL)
        AfxMessageBox("Error in OpenURL");
    else
    {
        // Read from file
        nBytesRead = pFile->Read(inBuf, sizeof(inBuf));
        tmpStr.Format("Read %d bytes", nBytesRead);
        AfxMessageBox(tmpStr);
    }
```

Note that, although this example shows how you can handle the `CInternetException` that may be thrown by `OpenURL()`, it doesn't do any real error handling. In addition, your application probably will want to use a more robust and efficient buffer mechanism than the simple large array I have used here.

OpenURL() can be used in a similar fashion for other protocols, such as Gopher, FTP, or local files. Just make sure to use the appropriate file object (CGopherFile, CInternetFile, or CStdioFile).

If you are unsure of the type of service for an HINTERNET, you can use CInternetSession::ServiceTypeFromHandle() to determine whether the handle is to be used with FTP, HTTP, Gopher, or local files.

Establishing a Connection

For applications that need to perform more interactive operations with a server, you need to establish a connection. In MFC, a connection is represented by a class derived from CInternetConnection, including CFtpConnection, CHttpConnection, and CGopherConnection. You can create a new connection object by calling one of the Get-connection methods of class CInternetSession. These include GetFtpConnection(), GetHttpConnection(), and GetGopherConnection(). You will see examples of each of these in the next sections.

Asynchronous Operations with CInternetSession

The MFC WinInet classes enable you to take advantage of the asynchronous mechanism that the WinInet C API provides for monitoring the status of operations in progress. The callback function you saw earlier in the C API is implemented as an overrideable member function of CInternetSession. Thus, if you want to use the WinInet classes asynchronously, you first must derive your own class from CInternetSession, overriding the OnStatusCallback() member function. Here is the prototype for this callback function:

```
virtual void OnStatusCallback( DWORD dwContext, DWORD dwInternetStatus,
    LPVOID lpvStatusInformation, DWORD dwStatusInformationLength);
```

When this function is called, it receives the context value for the operation that generated the call in dwContext. For some functions, such as CInternetSession::GetFtpConnection(), this is the context value that was passed to the object's constructor; other functions, such as CInternetSession::OpenURL(), enable you to specify a context value for that operation.

The reason why the callback function was called is passed in dwInternetStatus, and additional information may be supplied in lpvStatusInformation and dwStatusInformationLength. The value of dwInternetStatus and the information passed in lpvStatusInformation is the same as that returned by the C API callback function you saw earlier.

To use asynchronous operations with an object of your new CInternetSession class, you must pass a value of INTERNET_FLAG_ASYNC in the dwFlags parameter of the constructor for your new class. In addition, you must specify a non-zero context value for the operations that you want to complete asynchronously.

> **Note**
>
> As of January 1997, many of the MFC WinInet methods *require* a non-zero context value, implying that they cannot be used in a synchronous manner. In many cases, a context value of 0 (or NULL) will cause an ASSERT or will cause the function to fail.

The last step in enabling asynchronous operations is a call to `CInternetSession::EnableStatusCallback()`, which takes a single BOOL parameter. If this is TRUE (the default), the callback function will be enabled. You can disable asynchronous operation by calling `EnableStatusCallback()` with a parameter of FALSE.

After asynchronous operation is enabled, any calls that are made with a non-zero context value may complete asynchronously—the function will return "failure" (FALSE or NULL), and a subsequent call to `GetLastError()` will return ERROR_IO_PENDING. Various events in the processing of the request then will generate calls to `OnStatusCallback()`. When the operation is complete, `OnStatusCallback()` is called with a status of INTERNET_STATUS_REQUEST_COMPLETE.

Other `CInternetSession` Members

The `CInternetSession` class encapsulates the session handle used earlier in the WinInet C API. As with the session handle, you can manipulate various options for the `CInternetSession` with the `QueryOption()` and `SetOption()` member functions, which are very similar to the C API functions `::InternetQueryOption()` and `::InternetSetOption()`.

You can use the `GetContext()` member of `CInternetSession` to retrieve the context value that was assigned to the session.

`CInternetSession::Close()` should be called when you are finished with a session.

You also can retrieve the actual HINTERNET handle for the session by using the HINTERNET operator provided by the `CInternetSession` class.

Working with FTP

To establish an FTP connection, you can use `CInternetSession::GetFtpSession()`, which returns a pointer to a new `CFtpConnection` object. `GetFtpSession()` enables you to specify the server and port to connect to, the username and password to use, and a flag for active or passive mode. However, you can use the default for many of these parameters.

After you have established the FTP connection, most of the operations your application will need to perform are accessed by way of the member functions of `CFtpConnection`. When you are finished with the connection, you should call `CFtpConnection::Close()` to close the connection.

FTP Directories

`CFtpConnection` enables you to work with the current directory on the FTP server by way of its `GetCurrentDirectory()` and `SetCurrentDirectory()` member functions. In addition, you can retrieve the current server directory as a URL by calling `CFtpConnection::GetCurrentDirectoryAsURL()`.

You also can create a directory on the server with `CFtpConnection::CreateDirectory()` or remove a directory with `CFtpConnectionRemoveDirectory()`.

Finding Files

To help locate files on an FTP server, MFC provides the `CFtpFileFind` class, which is derived from `CFileFind`. To create a new `CFtpFileFind` object, you first must create a valid `CFtpConnection`. The constructor for `CFtpFileFind` then takes a pointer to the `CFtpConnection` and an optional context value.

After you have created the `CFtpFileFind` object, you can use its member functions to search for files. To begin a search, you can call `CFtpFileFind::FindFile()`, which takes parameters for the filename to find and a set of flags. You may use the flags to specify how the find is to operate. For example, you may specify `INTERNET_FLAG_RELOAD` to force the find to get the most current data from the server, rather than using cached data. You may specify a `NULL` pointer to the filename (the default) to browse all files in the current directory.

To find the next file that matches the search string, you can use `CFtpFileFind::FindNextFile()`. For example, if you specified a `NULL` pointer to the filename in `FindFile()`, you can walk through the whole directory by making calls to `FindNextFile()` until it returns `FALSE`. If you have read the entire directory, a call to `GetLastError()` will return `ERROR_NO_MORE_FILES`; other return values indicate a more substantial error.

After a successful call to `FindFile()` or `FindNextFile()`, you can call `CFtpFileFind::GetFileURL()` to return a `CString` that contains the URL for the found file.

In addition, you can use the member functions of `CFindFile`, from which `CFtpFindFile` is derived, to get information about the current file. `CFindFile` implements methods such as `GetLength()` and `GetFileName()` to retrieve information about the file, as well as many others that can be used to retrieve information about a file's attributes.

FTP Files

You can copy a file from the FTP server to the local machine with `CFtpConnection::GetFile()`. This function enables you to specify the local and remote filenames, as well as several other parameters to specify the attributes of the new file, what to do if this file already exists, a context value for asynchronous I/O, and the transfer mode. Fortunately, the default transfer mode is `FTP_TRANSFER_TYPE_BINARY`, rather than the default for many command-line FTP utilities; thus, you have to work harder if you want to mangle your `.exe` files by adding carriage returns.

Similarly, the `CFtpConnection::PutFile()` method enables you to transfer a file from the local machine to the server. However, `PutFile()` enables you to specify only the two filenames: transfer mode and context value. The attributes of the new file are left up to the FTP server.

You also can open a file in place on the server using the `CFtpConnection::OpenFile()` method, which returns a pointer to a `CInternetFile` object. You then may use the `CInternetFile::Read()` or `CInternetFile::Write()` method to read from or write to the file.

`OpenFile()` is useful for instances when your application wants to create a file on the server from data in memory rather than from a local disk file, or when you want to read a file directly into memory rather than into a disk file. `OpenFile()` also may be useful in cases where you want to be able to control the progress of a file transfer more closely—for example, to display the status to the user.

`CFtpConnection` also provides the `Remove()` method for removing files from the FTP server and the `Rename()` method for renaming files on the server.

Working with HTTP

In this section, you will explore the MFC WinInet classes that are used for working with HTTP, starting with the `CHttpConnection` class and including the `CHttpFile` class.

HTTP Connections

MFC provides the `CHttpConnection` class to represent connections to an HTTP server. A new connection is established by calling `CInternetSession::GetHttpConnection()`, which enables you to specify the server and port to connect to, as well as a username and password. In many cases, you need only specify the server name—the defaults for the other parameters usually are sufficient. The following is the prototype for GetHttpConnection():

```
CHttpConnection* GetHttpConnection( LPCTSTR pstrServer,
    INTERNET_PORT nPort = INTERNET_INVALID PORT NUMBER,
    LPCTSTR pstrUserName = NULL, LPCTSTR pstrPassword = NULL );
```

HTTP Files

To work with files from an HTTP server, you will be working with CHttpFile objects. As you saw earlier, you can create a CHttpFile object with CInternetSession::OpenURL(), although here you will see how you can implement greater functionality by creating a CHttpFile object from a connection you have explicitly created with a call to CHttpConnection::OpenRequest(). You also will take a look at the various member functions of CHttpFile you can use to build requests, send them to the server, and retrieve their results.

Creating a New CHttpFile

After you have created a CHttpConnection with CInternetSession::GetHttpConnection(), you can create a CHttpFile from this connection by calling CHttpConnection::OpenRequest():

```
CHttpFile* OpenRequest( LPCTSTR pstrVerb, LPCTSTR pstrObjectName,
    LPCTSTR pstrReferer = NULL, DWORD dwContext = 1,
    LPCTSTR* pstrAcceptTypes = NULL, LPCTSTR pstrVersion = NULL,
    DWORD dwFlags = INTERNET_FLAG_EXISTING_CONNECT );
```

The pstrVerb parameter specifies the verb to use for the request. If this pointer is NULL, GET is used. In addition, you may specify the verb as an int, using one of the following constants:

```
HTTP_VERB_DELETE
HTTP_VERB_GET
HTTP_VERB_HEAD
HTTP_VERB_LINK
HTTP_VERB_POST
HTTP_VERB_PUT
HTTP_VERB_UNLINK
```

pstrObjectName points to a string containing the target object of the specified verb. In most cases, this is a filename, executable module, or search specifier. You can parse the object name, as well as several other elements from a URL, with ::AfxParseURL().

The additional parameters enable you to specify the referring page, the type of data to accept, the version of HTTP to use, a context value, and a set of flags, which give options for things such as cache usage.

Adding HTTP Headers

You can add additional headers to the request contained in the CHttpFile by calling CHttpFile::AddRequestHeader(), which enables you to specify a header string as either a CString or a C string and its length, and a set of option flags for the header operation. You saw the possible flag values in the discussion of the ::HttpAddRequestHeaders() function.

Sending the Request

After you have added all the desired headers to the request, it is forwarded to the server with a call to CHttpFile::SendRequest(), which enables you to specify additional headers to send (as a CString or character array), as well as any optional data that will be sent for operations such as POST or PUT.

After the request has been sent successfully, you can call CHttpFile::QueryInfoStatusCode() to return the status of the request by updating a DWORD at an address you pass. The status may have many different specific values, but these are grouped into the following ranges:

- 200-299: Success
- 300-399: Information
- 400-499: Request Error
- 500-599: Server Error

If the request has completed successfully, you can read the data returned from the server by using the Read() method of CHttpFile.

Working with Gopher

In this section, you will look at the MFC WinInet classes that are used to work with Gopher servers, including CGopherConnection, CGopherLocator, CGopherFileFind, and CGopherFile.

Gopher Connections

A connection to a Gopher server is represented by the CGopherConnection class. You create a new CGopherConnection by calling CInternetSession::GetGopherConnection():

```
CGopherConnection* GetGopherConnection( LPCTSTR pstrServer,
    LPCTSTR pstrUserName = NULL, LPCTSTR pstrPassword = NULL,
    INTERNET_PORT nPort = INTERNET_INVALID_PORT_NUMBER);
```

This function is passed the name of the Gopher server and optional username and password strings. You also can specify a port on the Gopher server if the server uses a port other than the default.

Gopher Locators

Like the URLs used for locating HTTP files, the Gopher protocol uses locator strings to access files. In the MFC WinInet classes, the locator string is encapsulated by objects of class CGopherLocator, which are created by calls to CGopherConnection::CreateLocator(). This enables you to create a CGopherLocator from the individual components of the locator string or from a complete locator string. The locator object then can be used in calls to CGopherFileFind::FindFile() and CGopherConnection::OpenFile().

Finding Gopher Files

The MFC WinInet classes include the CGopherFileFind class to help you find files on a Gopher server. Unlike many of the other WinInet classes, a new CGopherFileFind object is not created by a member function of CInternetSession or a connection class; however, you must pass a pointer to a valid CGopherConnection object in the constructor for CGopherFileFind:

```
CGopherFileFind( CGopherConnection* pConnection, DWORD dwContext = 1 );
```

To begin a search of a Gopher server, you use the CGopherFileFind::FindFile() function, which enables you to begin a search for a particular filename string. There are two versions of FindFile(). The first allows a reference to a CGopherLocator parameter, which will receive the results of the first file found. The second version requires that you use CGopherFileFind::GetLocator() to retrieve the results.

Regardless of which version of FindFile() you used to begin the query, you can retrieve additional results by calling CGopherFileFind::FindNextFile() to find the next file and CGopherFileFind::GetLocator() to retrieve the locator for the found file. When no more files are found, FindNextFile() returns FALSE and GetLastError() returns ERROR_NO_MORE_FILES.

Working with Gopher Files

To retrieve data from a Gopher server, you use the `CGopherFile` class. `CGopherFile` objects are created by a call to `CGopherConnection::OpenFile()`, which takes a reference to a `CGopherLocator` as a parameter. The `CGopherLocator`, which specifies the file to open, is returned by `CGopherConnection::CreateLocator()` or `CGopherFileFind::GetLocator()`.

If `CGopherConnection::OpenFile()` completes successfully, you can use the returned `CGopherFile` to read the data in the file by calling `CGopherFile::Read()`. You also can use the other member functions of `CInternetFile` (the base class for `CGopherFile`) to work with the file, although the Gopher protocol does not allow you to write data to the server.

Summary

In this chapter, you explored how to use both the WinInet C API and the MFC WinInet classes to add Internet functionality to your applications, without having to know the details of the underlying protocols, such as FTP, HTTP, or Gopher.

You saw how the WinInet C API uses a hierarchy of special handles of type `HINTERNET` to manage Internet sessions, connections, and files, as well as the functions used to work with these handles, such as `InternetOpen()`, `InternetConnect()`, and `InternetOpenUrl()`.

You also took a look at the MFC WinInet class hierarchy, including `CInternetSession`, `CInternetConnection`, and `CInternetFile`, as well as the protocol-specific classes derived from these, such as `CFtpConnection` and `CHttpFile`.

CHAPTER 12

MFC HTML Support

by Mickey Williams

IN THIS CHAPTER

One of the new features introduced in Visual C++ 6 is support for writing applications that support Dynamic HTML. In this chapter, you will learn about:

- How the WebBrowser ActiveX control can be used in a dialog box resource
- How MFC classes can be used to write an application that acts as a browser
- How you can navigate to special folder locations, such as the Control Panel

The CD-ROM that accompanies this book includes two example programs: WebCtl demonstrates how the WebBrowser ActiveX control can be used in a dialog box, and WWWTest demonstrates how the MFC `CHtmlView` class is used.

Understanding Dynamic HTML

Dynamic HTML, also known as DHTML, is an acronym for Dynamic Hypertext Markup Language. Dynamic HTML is an updated scripting language based on the older HTML, or Hypertext Markup Language. Both languages, DHTML and HTML, have standards that are specified by the W3C, a standards body that defines various Web standards.

> **Note**
>
> Recent versions of the most popular Web Browsers support DHTML. However, different browser versions from different suppliers have a tendency to interpret DHTML differently. For the purposes of this chapter, the DHTML examples will work correctly with Internet Explorer 4.0 or later.

As Dynamic HTML is a superset of HTML, Visual C++ 6 and MFC will support both HTML and DHTML pages. Dynamic HTML adds new capabilities to HTML pages, enabling pages that are more interactive than typical HTML pages. Listing 12.1 contains an example of a simple DHTML page. This code can be found on the CD-ROM as `Dynamic.htm`.

LISTING 12.1 A Simple DHTML Page

```
<HTML>
<HEAD>
<TITLE>Visual C++ Unleashed Chapter 12</TITLE>

<STYLE>
UL                  { cursor:hand; color:black}
UL LI               { display:none; font:12pt; list-style:circle;
                      color:green; cursor:default; text-indent:20px;}
```

```
UL.showList LI        { display:block; }
UL.defaultStyles LI   { display:none; cursor:default}
</STYLE>
</HEAD>

<BODY>

<H2>An Expanding DHTML List (Click Items to Expand)</H2>

<UL onclick        = "this.className='showList';"
    ondblclick     = "this.className='defaultStyles';"
    onmouseover    = "this.style.color='red';"
    onmouseout     = "this.style.color='black'"
    onselectstart  = "event.returnValue=false;" >Favorite C++ Keywords
    <LI>class
    <LI>template
    <LI>new
</UL>

<UL onclick        = "this.className='showList';"
    ondblclick     = "this.className='defaultStyles';"
    onmouseover    = "this.style.color='red';"
    onmouseout     = "this.style.color='black'"
    onselectstart  = "event.returnValue=false;">Favorite MFC Classes
    <LI>CWnd
    <LI>CArchive
    <LI>CFormView
    <LI>CHTMLView
</UL>


</BODY>
</HTML>
```

As shown in Listing 12.1, a DHTML page is composed of a number of elements delimited by tags in angle brackets. Some of the elements, such as <body> and </body>, are mandatory. Other elements, such as the elements that define text formatting are optional.

When viewed using Internet Explorer, the DHTML source shown in Listing 12.1 creates the page shown in Figure 12.1. Clicking on either of the visible lines causes hidden subitems to be displayed. To collapse the list, double-click on the item.

FIGURE 12.1

*Using Internet
Explorer to view a
DHTML page.*

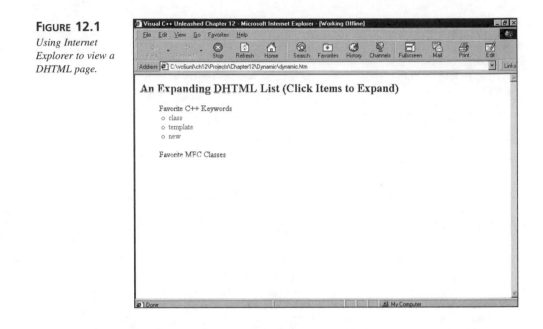

FIGURE 12.1

*Using Internet
Explorer to view a
DHTML page.*

You can use DHTML to create documents that are more interactive than static HTML pages. A DHTML page can have many of the same features as an application, such as buttons and other controls. DHTML documents also have a well-defined model that can be used to manage the page, and allow interaction based on events generated by the page.

Notice that there is no JavaScript or VBScript code in Listing 12.1. All of the effects are managed in DHTML script. There are several dynamic effects occurring on this page:

- When the mouse moves over a list, the list is highlighted in red.
- When the mouse moves away from a list, the list is redrawn in black.
- When a list is clicked, the hidden list items are displayed.
- When a list is double-clicked, the list items are hidden.

This is just a small sample of the interactive effects that can be achieved using DHTML. A full discussion of DHTML is beyond the scope of this book, but a great place to get started is the Microsoft Site Builder Workshop, which can be found at `http://msdn.microsoft.com`.

Using the Win32 WebBrowser ActiveX Control

Writing your own control or component that parses Dynamic HTML would be a daunting task. Fortunately, you don't have to. You can use the support that's already built into Internet Explorer.

One way that you can leverage Internet Explorer in your applications is to use the WebBrowser ActiveX control. The WebBrowser control encapsulates most of the interesting functionality found in a typical web browser, including

- Navigation, both via hyperlink clicks and programmatically to a location named by a specified Uniform Resource Locator, also known as a URL
- Viewing and printing of Web pages
- History and favorite lists
- Security settings for loading and executing specific types of content

The WebBrowser control is implemented as an ActiveX control that is easily added to dialog box resources, enabling you to use the control in dialog boxes and form views. The COM interfaces exposed by the WebBrowser ActiveX control are derived from `IDispatch`, making it easy to use the control with a variety of clients, including applications built using MFC.

Many popular applications use the WebBrowser ActiveX control to implement portions of their user interface. Microsoft Money, Microsoft Outlook, and the HTML Help viewer are just three examples of non-browser applications that use the WebBrowser ActiveX control. There are also a large number of more traditional browsing and editing applications that use the WebBrowser control, such as the AOL browser and the HoTMetaL Pro HTML editor.

The WebBrowser Control Architecture

The WebBrowser control is hosted inside MSHTML.DLL, one of the DLLs distributed as part of Internet Explorer. When Internet Explorer is updated, the functionality provided by the WebBrowser control is also updated. However, an update of the Internet Explorer browser will not break any applications using the WebBrowser ActiveX control, as the interfaces between the control and the application do not change.

> **Note**
>
> The interfaces used by the WebBrowser ActiveX control won't change, due to basic rules that govern how ActiveX controls work. If you're unfamiliar with ActiveX controls, you may want to read Chapter 24, "Overview of COM and Active Technologies" for more information.

The interfaces used when interacting with the WebBrowser control are defined in ExDisp.IDL, the interface definition file for Internet Explorer components. This file is located in the Visual C++ include directory, which by default is located in the \VC98\Include subdirectory under the location where Visual C++ was installed.

The interface used to control the WebBrowser control is `IWebBrowser2`, which is derived from `IWebBrowserApp`. `IWebBrowserApp` is derived from `IWebBrowser`, an older interface introduced with Internet Explorer 3.0. In turn, `IWebBrowser` is derived from `IDispatch`, the interface used to implement all Automation interfaces in COM.

When a WebBrowser control is added to your project, a wrapper class named `CWebBrowser2` is created. This class is used to manage interaction with the WebBrowser control.

WebBrowser Control Properties and Methods

The `IWebBrowser2` interface has a large number of properties and methods, which are documented in the online help. Some of the most commonly used properties are described in Table 12.1.

TABLE 12.1   Commonly Used Properties

Property	*Description*
Document	A pointer to the active Document interface
LocationName	The name of the current browser location
LocationURL	The path to the current browser location
Visible	Determines if the browser is visible
StatusBar	Determines if the status bar is visible or hidden
StatusText	The text displayed on the status bar

Additional properties can be found in the online documentation, or by reading ExDisp.IDL.

When MFC is used to access control properties, accessor functions are created for each property. Two functions are created for properties that can be both read and written; one function is used to read the property, the other function is used to write to the property. For example, the read-only Document property is managed by just one CWebBrowser2 member function:

```
LPDISPATCH CWebBrowser2::GetDocument()
```

The Visible property can be read and written, and so it's managed by two functions:

```
BOOL CWebBrowser2::GetVisible()
void CWebBrowser2::SetVisible(BOOL bNewValue)
```

The functions exposed by the CWebBrowser2 class are slightly abstracted from the raw IDL that you would see in ExDisp.IDL. This simplifies the work that is required to use these interfaces in an MFC program. For example, the Visible property actually has a type of VARIANT_BOOL, a VARIANT type which is awkward to use in a C++ program. The MFC accessor functions enable you to use the more convenient BOOL variable type.

There are also a large number of methods exposed by the WebBrowser control. These functions are used to perform actions such as navigating to a new location and reloading the current page. The most commonly used methods are listed in Table 12.2.

TABLE 12.2   Commonly Used WebBrowser Methods

Method	Description
GoBack	Navigates to the previous location in the history list
GoForward	Navigates to the next location in the history list
GoHome	Navigates to the home URL
Navigate	Loads a specific URL
Navigate2	Loads a specific URL or special folder
Refresh	Forces the current location to be reloaded

Additional methods can be found in the online documentation, or by reading ExDisp.IDL.

The first two methods in Table 12.2 work in conjunction with the history list, and have no parameters. The history list maintains the list of recently visited locations, and these functions enable a user to scroll forward and backward through this list of URLs.

Navigate and Navigate2 are relatively complex methods that allow you to specify where the WebBrowser should navigate, as well as how the navigation is to be carried out. Navigate2 extends the Navigate method by allowing special folders, such as Desktop or My Computer to be loaded.

The MFC wrapper around the Navigate method is declared as:

```
void CWebBrowser2::Navigate(LPCTSTR URL,
                            VARIANT* Flags,
                            VARIANT* TargetFrameName,
                            VARIANT* PostData,
                            VARIANT* Headers);
```

The Navigate method has five parameters:

- A URL specifying the location to be loaded.
- The address of a VARIANT containing navigation flags, if any. Possible values for this parameter are discussed below.
- The address of a VARIANT containing the name of an HTML frame that serves as the navigation target. To load the document into the current frame, pass an empty VARIANT for this parameter.
- The address of a VARIANT containing HTML POST data associated with the navigation; this data will be sent to the server. In most cases, an empty VARIANT is passed for this parameter.
- The address of a VARIANT containing any optional header information to be sent to the server. In most cases, an empty VARIANT is passed for this parameter.

The following navigation flags can be passed for the second parameter to Navigate or Navigate2:

- navOpenInNewWindow specifies that the location should be opened in a new instance of Internet Explorer.
- navNoHistory specifies that the new location should not be added to the history list.
- navAllowAutoSearch specifies that an automatic search is to be performed if the location can't be found. Autosearch works by appending common root domains, such as COM, EDU, and GOV to the requested URL. If the location still isn't found, the URL is passed to a search engine defined in the system registry.
- navBrowserBar specifies that the current Internet Explorer browser bar should be used to navigate to the desired URL.

A VARIANT initialized to VT_EMPTY may be passed for any of the last four parameters. The proper way to initialize a VARIANT as empty is to use the VariantInit function:

```
VARIANT varEmpty;
VariantInit(&varEmpty);
```

Alternatively, you can use the COleVariant class, which automatically initializes a variant for you:

```
COleVariant varEmpty;  // ctor initializes variant as empty
```

More information about handling variants can be found in Chapter 24.

An example of a function that uses the `Navigate` function is shown below:

```
void CWebCtlDlg::OnGotoHelp()
{
    COleVariant varEmpty;
    // m_wb is an instance of the WebBrowser control
    m_wb.Navigate("http:\\www.codevtech.com\\help.htm",
                  &varEmpty,
                  &varEmpty,
                  &varEmpty,
                  &varEmpty);
}
```

As discussed earlier, the `Navigate2` method enables navigation to special folder locations, such as `My Computer`. The MFC wrapper for `Navigate2` differs slightly from `Navigate`:

```
void CWebBrowser2::Navigate2(VARIANT* URL,
                             VARIANT* Flags,
                             VARIANT* TargetFrameName,
                             VARIANT* PostData,
                             VARIANT* Headers);
```

As you can see above, the parameter list for `Navigate2` is slightly different than `Navigate`. The first parameter is the address of a `VARIANT`, which enables you to pass information about special folders in the form of a pointer to an item identifier list, also known as a `PIDL`, in addition to basic URL strings. The remaining parameters for `Navigate2` are identical to the parameters used by `Navigate`.

In order to navigate to a special folder location, you must first create an `ITEMIDLIST` structure, then pack the structure into a `VARIANT` containing a safe array, and then pass the `VARIANT` address to the `Navigate2` function. In order to perform these steps, you need to perform some grungy low-level work using the `ITEMIDLIST`, `SAFEARRAY`, and `VARIANT` structures. The steps required are shown later in this chapter, in the WebCtl project.

WebBrowser Events

The WebBrowser control notifies its container when something interesting happens by sending the container an event. Events generated by the WebBrowser control are conveyed through the `DWebBrowserEvents2` interface. Commonly used events are listed in Table 12.3.

TABLE 12.3   Commonly Used WebBrowser Events

Event	Description
DownloadBegin	A download is beginning.
DownloadComplete	A download has been completed.
BeforeNavigate2	Navigation is about to occur, possibly due to reasons other than the Navigate2 function being called.
NavigateComplete2	Navigation has been completed, and at least part of the document has been downloaded.
DocumentComplete	The document has been completely loaded.

Additional events can be found in the online documentation or by reading ExDisp.IDL.

An Example Project Using the WebBrowser Control

As an example of how a WebBrowser ActiveX control can be embedded into a dialog box, the CD-ROM that accompanies this book includes WebCtl, a dialog box-based MFC project that uses a WebBrowser ActiveX control in its main dialog box. The WebCtl project navigates to the Microsoft Visual C++ Web page, and allows the user to navigate to any linked page. The WebCtl application also displays the control panel folder, enabling a user to launch control panel applets.

The full WebCtl project can be found on the CD-ROM that accompanies this book.

Adding the WebBrowser ActiveX Control to an MFC Project

The first step in using the WebBrowser ActiveX control in a project is to add it to the Tool Palette that's displayed when editing dialog box resources. After the control has been added to the tool palette, you can drag it on to your dialog box resources just like any other control.

In Chapter 24, you'll see how to take advantage of the components and controls included with Visual C++. Right now, we're only interested in the WebBrowser control.

Select Project, Add to Project, Components and Controls… from the menu. The Components and Controls dialog box will be displayed, as shown in Figure 12.2.

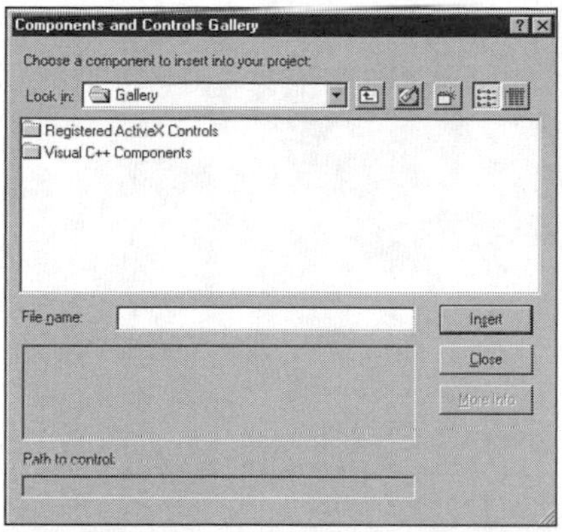

FIGURE 12.2

The Components and Controls dialog box.

Click on the folder labeled Registered ActiveX Controls. This will display all of the ActiveX controls that are available for your use, as shown in Figure 12.3.

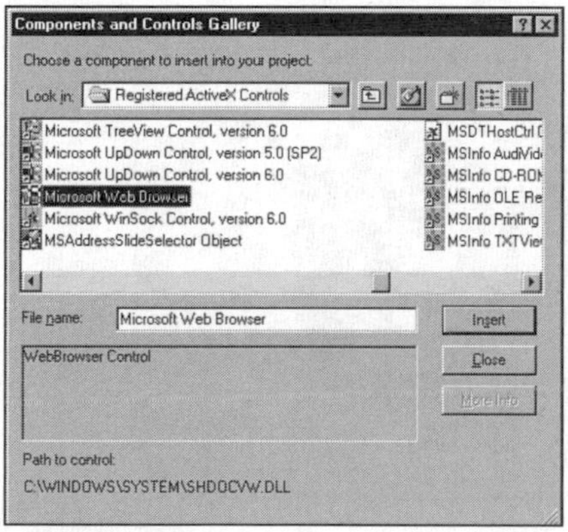

FIGURE 12.3

The available ActiveX controls are listed in the Components and Controls dialog box.

Click on the icon labeled Microsoft WebBrowser and then click the Insert button. Click the OK button on the confirmation dialog. The type library for the WebBrowser control will be read, and you will be asked to confirm the addition of the CWebBrowser2 class to your project—click OK to add the class to your project, then click the Close button to close the dialog box.

After the WebBrowser control is added to your project, an icon will be added to the Control Palette, as shown in Figure 12.4.

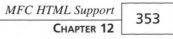

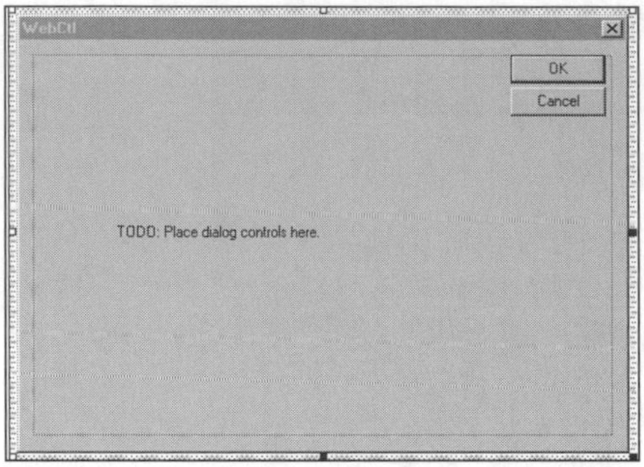

FIGURE 12.4

The Control Palette with a WebBrowser icon.

After adding the WebBrowser control to the project, it can be placed on a dialog box resource just like any other control. You can use drag and drop, or you can select the control and drag a rectangle on the dialog box. Figure 12.5 shows the main dialog box used by the WebCtl project after adding the WebBrowser control and other controls.

FIGURE 12.5

The main dialog box used by the WebCtl project.

The controls used in the dialog box are listed in Table 12.4.

TABLE 12.4 Controls Used in the Main WebCtl Dialog Box

Control	Resource ID
WebBrowser control	IDC_WEB_BROWSER
Control Panel button	IDC_CTL_PANEL

Use ClassWizard to associate a `CWebCtlDlg` member variable with the WebBrowser control, using the values from Table 12.5.

TABLE 12.5 CWebCtlDlg Member Variables

Control Variable	Category	Type	Member Variable
IDC_WEB_BROWSER	Control	CWebBrowser2	m_wb

Modify the CWebCtlDlg::OnCtlPanel function as shown in Listing 12.2, which navigates to the special folder location for the Windows Control Panel.

LISTING 12.2 Navigating to a Special Folder Location Using the WebBrowser Control

```
void CWebCtlDlg::OnCtlPanel()
{
    LPITEMIDLIST pidl;
    COleVariant  varEmpty;
    COleVariant  varPidl;
    // Retrieve the control panel's folder PIDL
    HRESULT      hr = SHGetSpecialFolderLocation(NULL,
                                                 CSIDL_CONTROLS,
                                                 &pidl);

    if(FAILED(hr))
    {
        AfxMessageBox("ShGetSpecialFolderLocation Failed");
        return;
    }

    // Stuff the PIDL into a VARIANT
    VARIANT      varTemp;
    hr = PidlToVariant(pidl, &varTemp);
    if(SUCCEEDED(hr))
    {
        // Attach the VARIANT to a COleVariant
        varPidl.Attach(varTemp);
        // Go to the special folder location
        m_wb.Navigate2(varPidl,
                       &varEmpty,
                       &varEmpty,
                       &varEmpty,
                       &varEmpty);
    }
    else
    {
        AfxMessageBox("PidlToVariant Failed");
    }
    // Free the PIDL
    CoTaskMemFree(pidl);
    VariantClear(&varPidl);
}
```

12

MFC HTML SUPPORT

In Listing 12.2, the OnCtlPanel function passes a PIDL to the Navigate2 function in order to display the control panel folder. First, the PIDL is loaded using the SHGetSpecialFolderLocation function. Next, the PidlToVariant helper function is used to stuff the PIDL into a VARIANT; the source code for this function is provided in the next listing.

Next, the VARIANT is attached to an instance of COleVariant, and passed to the Navigate2 member function. Before returning from the function, the PIDL is freed using the CoTaskMemFree function.

Two helper functions are used to stuff the PIDL into a VARIANT. These functions are shown in Listing 12.3. Add the functions to the top of the WebCtlDlg.cpp file, before any CWebCtlDlg functions.

LISTING 12.3   Helper Functions Used to Manipulate PIDLs.

```
// Calculate the length of the PIDL. Unfortunately, there isn't
// an API call to do this - you must walk the PIDL to calculate
// the size.
UINT GetPidlLength(LPITEMIDLIST pidl)
{
    ASSERT_POINTER(pidl, ITEMIDLIST);
    UINT cbPidl = sizeof(pidl->mkid.cb);
    while(pidl && pidl->mkid.cb)
    {
        cbPidl += pidl->mkid.cb;
        // Walk to next item
        BYTE* ptr = reinterpret_cast<BYTE*>(pidl);
        ptr += pidl->mkid.cb;
        pidl = reinterpret_cast<LPITEMIDLIST>(ptr);
    }
    ASSERT(cbPidl > 0);
    return cbPidl;
}

HRESULT PidlToVariant(LPITEMIDLIST pidl, LPVARIANT var)
{
    ASSERT_POINTER(pidl, ITEMIDLIST);
    ASSERT_POINTER(var, VARIANT);
    if(!pidl || !var)
        return E_POINTER;

    VariantInit(var);

    UINT cbPidl = GetPidlLength(pidl);
    LPSAFEARRAY psa = SafeArrayCreateVector(VT_UI1, 0, cbPidl);
    if(psa)
    {
```

```
          MoveMemory(psa->pvData, pidl, cbPidl);
          var->vt = VT_UI1|VT_ARRAY;
          var->parray = psa;
          return NOERROR;
      }
      return E_OUTOFMEMORY;
}
```

There are two functions in Listing 12.3. Taken together the GetPidlLength and PidlToVariant functions take a PIDL as input, and copy the PIDL into a SAFEARRAY consisting of an array of bytes. The SAFEARRAY is then copied into a VARIANT.

The GetPidlLength function walks the internal structure of an ITEMIDLIST structure, and determines the size of the structure. As PIDLs can be a list of individual items, the function must calculate the length of each item in the list. The final item in the PIDL will consist of an item with a length of 0.

The PidlToVariant function calls GetPidlLength to determine the size of the PIDL. It then allocates the SAFEARRAY and copies the PIDL into it. The SAFEARRAY is then copied into the VARIANT structure.

Add the contents of Listing 12.4 to the end of the CWebCtl::OnInitDialog function. These lines of code load the Visual C++ Web page at Microsoft.

LISTING 12.4 Code Added to the CWebCtl::OnInitDialog Function

```
BOOL CWebCtlDlg::OnInitDialog()
    CDialog::OnInitDialog();
    // Existing code omitted
    .
    .
    .
    // TODO: Add extra initialization here
    COleVariant varEmpty;
    m_wb.Navigate("http://msdn.microsoft.com/visualc",
                  &varEmpty,
                  &varEmpty,
                  &varEmpty,
                  &varEmpty);
    return TRUE;
}
```

Build and run the WebCtl project. When the project runs, the Microsoft Visual C++ page is initially displayed. If you click on the Control Panel button, the Control Panel is displayed.

12

MFC HTML
SUPPORT

The `CHtmlView` Class

The `CHtmlView` class simplifies using the WebBrowser control in MFC view classes. `CHtmlView` encapsulates an instance of the WebBrowser control, and uses it for the view's user interface. In many ways, `CHtmlView` is much easier to use than the WebBrowser control:

- The `CHtmlView` class hides the WebBrowser control behind another layer of abstraction, allowing functions to use more intuitive parameters.
- Functions in the `CHtmlView` class take advantage of C++ features such as overloading and optional parameters, simplifying your code.
- You can leverage standard Document/View events, such as `OnInitialUpdate`.
- You can easily create multiple instances of your class derived from `CHtmlView`.

The disadvantages of using `CHtmlView` are that it is most useful when your application fits into the Document/View model, and that some standard Document/View methods don't work as expected (see note).

> **Note**
>
> The `CHtmlView` class uses the Microsoft WebBrowser control to implement its browser functionality. Printing of DHTML pages is delegated to the WebBrowser control, bypassing the normal printing functionality offered by `CView` subclasses. This means that many of the functions that handle printing are not called for classes derived from `CHtmlView`.

Navigating with `CHtmlView`

`CHtmlView` includes wrappers for WebBrowser navigation functions, including `Navigate` and `Navigate2`. As was discussed earlier, the `Navigate2` function can be used to load special folders, such as the Control Panel, in addition to HTML content specified by an URL.

The `CHtmlView::Navigate` function differs slightly from the `Navigate` function supplied by the WebBrowser control:

```
void Navigate(LPCTSTR URL,
              DWORD   dwFlags = 0,
              LPCTSTR lpszTargetFrameName = NULL,
              LPCTSTR lpszHeaders = NULL,
              LPVOID  lpvPostData = NULL,
              DWORD   dwPostDataLen = 0);
```

There are a few differences between the `CHtmlView::Navigate` function and the WebBrowser control's version of Navigate. The first thing you might notice is that `CHtmlView::Navigate` has six parameters instead of five:

- The URL to be loaded
- An optional navigation flag
- An optional target frame for the navigation
- An optional string of header information to be sent to the server
- An optional buffer of information to be sent as part of an HTTP POST command
- The size of the previous parameter, in bytes

Another difference is that the fourth and fifth parameters are reversed. Also, none of the parameters are passed as `VARIANT` or `COleVariant`, rather they are passed as easier to use C++ types, such as `DWORD` or `LPCTSTR`. This simplifies the work required to use this function in `CHtmlView`.

In many cases, you can take advantage of the default parameters offered by the `Navigate` function. Typically, you only need to provide the first parameter:

```
Navigate("http:://msdn.microsoft.com");
```

There are three overloaded versions of the `Navigate2` function. The first version is used to load a special folder location:

```
void Navigate2(LPITEMIDLIST pIDL,
               DWORD dwFlags = 0,
               LPCTSTR lpszTargetFrameName = NULL);
```

This version of the function has three parameters:

- The address of an `ITEMIDLIST` structure that refers to a folder location
- A browser navigation flag, as with other versions of `Navigate` discussed earlier in this chapter
- A string specifying the target HTML frame for the navigation, or `NULL` if the current frame is to be used

The second version is used to navigate to a URL:

```
void Navigate2(LPCTSTR lpszURL,
               DWORD   dwFlags = 0,
               LPCTSTR lpszTargetFrameName = NULL,
               LPCTSTR lpszHeaders = NULL,
               LPVOID  lpvPostData = NULL,
               DWORD   dwPostDataLen = 0);
```

This version of the function has exactly the same parameters as the CHtmlView::Navigate function discussed earlier.

The third version is used when performing an HTTP POST command, and allows you to pass a CByteArray as the POST data:

```
void Navigate2(LPCTSTR     lpszURL,
               DWORD       dwFlags,
               CByteArray& baPostedData,
               LPCTSTR     lpszTargetFrameName = NULL,
               LPCTSTR     lpszHeader = NULL);
```

Just to keep things interesting, this version of Navigate2 has different parameter ordering than other versions of Navigate2 offered by CHtmlView:

- The URL to be loaded
- Navigation flags, if any
- A CByteArray containing the POST data
- The target HTML frame, or NULL to use the current frame
- An optional string of header information to be sent to the server

Note that this version of Navigate2 doesn't require the size of the POST data to be passed as a parameter—that information is contained in the CByteArray parameter.

As with the Navigate function, many of the parameters used with Navigate2 are optional. For example, you can navigate to a special folder just by passing the appropriate PIDL to Navigate2:

```
LPITEMIDLIST pidl;
// Retrieve the control panel's folder PIDL
HRESULT hr = SHGetSpecialFolderLocation(NULL, CSIDL_CONTROLS, &pidl);
if(SUCCEDED(hr))
{
    Navigate2(pidl);
}
```

Other Useful CHtmlView Functions

The CHtmlView class includes member functions that wrap WebBrowser control navigation functions. In addition to Navigate and Navigate2, the following are commonly used member functions:

- GoBack is used to navigate to the previous location in the history list.
- GoHome is used to navigate to the home URL.
- GoForward is used to navigate to the next location in the history list.
- Stop is used to halt the download of a URL.

- `Refresh` is used to reload the current URL.

- `LoadFromResource` is used to load a document that has been stored as a resource.

- `Navigate`, discussed earlier, is used to navigate to a specific URL.

- `Navigate2`, also discussed earlier, is used to navigate to a specific URL or special folder, such as `Desktop`, or `My Computer`.

Except for the `Navigate` and `Navigate2` functions, the functions listed above have no parameters. For example, to reload the current page, you can simply call the `Refresh` function:

```
void CMyHtmlView::OnViewRefresh()
{
    Refresh();
}
```

Adding Dynamic HTML to Your Programs

So, where do you find a DHTML document to use in your application? There are three ways to introduce DHTML into your program:

- A Dynamic HTML document can be embedded in your program's resource file, just like other resources such as dialog boxes, icons, and menus.

- A Dynamic HTML document can be loaded from a file on the local computer.

- The document can be downloaded from a remote location on the Internet or other network.

If your program uses a specific Dynamic HTML document that must be available at all times, store it as an HTML resource.

Using MFC and Dynamic HTML

As an example of using the `CHtmlView` class, the CD-ROM that accompanies this book includes WWWTest, an example SDI project built using MFC AppWizard. The initial project was built just like any other SDI project, with the following exception:

1. In AppWizard step six, select the View class in the Class list box, in this case, `CWWWTestView`.

2. Select `CHtmlView` from the Base Class combo box; this changes the base class of the view class to `CHtmlView` instead of `CView`.

3. Click the Finish button to end the AppWizard process and display the New Project Information dialog box.

4. Click OK to generate the code for the WWWTest project.

12

MFC HTML
SUPPORT

Simple Navigation Using `CHtmlView`

When the WWWTest project is generated by MFC AppWizard, a default implementation of the `OnInitialUpdate` function in the `CWWWTestView` class is provided, as shown in Listing 12.5. This function will navigate to the Microsoft Visual C++ home page, and display the page in the view.

LISTING 12.5   Navigating to an Internet HTML Document

```
void CWWWTestView::OnInitialUpdate()
{
    CHtmlView::OnInitialUpdate();
    Navigate2(_T("http://www.microsoft.com/visualc/"),NULL,NULL);
}
```

If you're building the project from scratch, you can build the initial project and run it without making any changes. By default, the program will attempt to load the Visual C++ web page over the Internet. Once loaded, you can use the page to begin navigating throughout the Microsoft Web site, just as if you were using Internet Explorer or any other browser.

Navigating to a Source File

You can also use classes derived from `CHtmlView` to interact with Dynamic HTML documents located on a local hard drive. To navigate to a file on the local machine, pass an URL referring to the file to the `Navigate` or `Navigate2` functions.

Listing 12.6. contains a Dynamic HTML page that includes a button control. When the button is clicked, some of the text on the page is hidden. This page is included on the CD-ROM that accompanies this book as Simple.htm in the WWWTest project directory.

LISTING 12.6   An Interactive Dynamic HTML Page

```
<html>
<body>

This example uses DHTML to hide text that has the span attribute.

<!— Define the button control -->
<p>
    <button style="cursor:hand"
        onclick="onOffToggle(document.all.toggledLine);"
        onmouseover="onEnterHighlight(this);"
        onmouseout="onExitHighlight(this);"
    >DHTML Toggle
    </button>
```

```
</p>

Click the button to hide the blue text below.<br>

<!— Define a span as the first part of a line of text -->
<span style="color:blue" id=toggledLine>
        Should I stay or should I go?
</span>

I'm staying no matter what!<br>

<script>
<!— onOffToggle: toggles an element's display property -->
function onOffToggle(theElement)
{
    if(theElement.style.display == "none"){
        theElement.style.display = "";
    }else{
        theElement.style.display = "none";
    }
}

<!— onEnterHighlight: highlights an element -->
function onEnterHighlight(theElement)
{
    thcElement.style.color = 'red';
}

<!— onExitHighlight: clears highlight from an element -->
function onExitHighlight(theElement)
{
    theElement.style.color = 'black';
}

</script>

</body>
</html>
```

To modify the WWWTest project so that `Simple.htm` is loaded when its view is initially displayed, replace the `OnInitialUpdate` function in `CWWWTestView` with the function provided in Listing 12.7. Before executing the program, copy the Simple.htm file to the C:\ directory.

LISTING 12.7   Navigating to a Dynamic HTML Document on the Local Machine

```
void CWWWTestView::OnInitialUpdate()
{
    CHtmlView::OnInitialUpdate();
    Navigate2("c:\\Simple.htm");
}
```

Build and run the WWWTest project. Figure 12.6 shows the WWWTest project displaying the Simple.htm page.

FIGURE 12.6

Displaying a Dynamic HTML page in an MFC application.

Navigating to the User's Home Page

In addition to the navigation capabilities discussed earlier, the CHtmlView class allows you easy access to configuration information used by Internet Explorer. For example, you can navigate to the home page defined by the user by calling the CHtmlView::GoHome member function.

To enable WWWTest to navigate to the predefined home page, you must first add a new menu item to the WWWTest project. Add a menu item to the View menu, using the values from Table 12.7.

TABLE 12.7   A New Menu Item for the View Menu

Menu ID	Caption	Event	Function Name
ID_VIEW_HOME	&Home	COMMAND	OnViewHome

Use the values from Table 12.7 to add a menu handling function to the CWWWTestView class named OnViewHome. Add the source code from Listing 12.8 to the OnViewHome function.

LISTING 12.8   Navigating to the User's Home Page

```
void CWWWTestView::OnViewHome()
{
    GoHome();
}
```

Build and run the WWWTest project. Navigate to the user's home page by selecting View|Home from the WWWTest menu.

Using a Dynamic HTML Resource

As discussed earlier, a Dynamic HTML document can be stored as one of your application's resources. Storing a page as a resource often makes it easier to use in your application because you can refer to the resource by a symbol name instead of providing a path or location.

You add an HTML resource to a project much like any other resource:

1. Right-click the resource tree and select Insert from the shortcut menu. An Insert Resource dialog box will be displayed.

2. Select HTML as the resource type and click New to close the dialog box.

3. A blank HTML document will be added to the resource tree, and the document will be opened for editing.

To modify a property for an HTML resource such as the Resource ID, right-click anywhere in the HTML document while it's loaded in the editor, and select Properties from the shortcut menu.

Add a new HTML resource to the WWWTest project, using the steps outlined previously. Name the resource IDR_VISUALC_LINKS. Add the source code from Listing 12.9 to the resource.

LISTING 12.9 An HTML Page That Displays Useful Links for Visual C++ Programming

```html
<html>
<body>

<h3>Useful Visual C++ Programming Links</h3>
<br>

<ul>

<li><a href="http://msdn.microsoft.com/developer">
        Microsoft Developer's Network
    </a>
<li><a href="http://msdn.microsoft.com/visualc">
        Microsoft Visual C++ Start Page
    </a>
<li><a href="http://www.mcp.com">
        Macmillan Computer Publishing
    </a>
<li><a href="http://www.numega.com">
```

continues

12

MFC HTML
SUPPORT

LISTING 12.9   continued

```
        NuMega Technologies
    </a>
<li><a href="http://www.vcdj.com">
        Visual C++ Developer's Journal
    </a>
<li><a href="http://www.codevtech.com">
        Codev Technologies
    </a>

</ul>

</body>
</html>
```

To enable WWWTest to load the HTML resource, you must first add another menu item to the WWWTest project. Add a new menu item to the View menu, using the values from Table 12.8.

TABLE 12.8   A New Menu Item for the View Menu

Menu ID	Caption	Event	Function Name
ID_VIEW_LINKS	&Links	COMMAND	OnViewLinks

Use the values from Table 12.8 to add a menu handling function to the CWWWTestView class named OnViewLinks. Add the source code from Listing 12.10 to the OnViewLinks function.

LISTING 12.10   Navigating to a Dynamic HTML Resource

```
void CWWWTestView::OnViewLinks()
{
    LoadFromResource(IDR_VISUALC_LINKS);
}
```

Build and run the WWWTest project. The contents of the HTML resource can be displayed by selecting View|Links from the WWWTest menu, as shown in Figure 12.7.

FIGURE 12.7

The WWWTest project displaying an HTML resource.

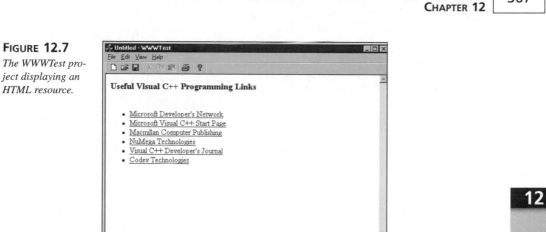

Summary

This chapter discussed how Dynamic HTML can be used with Visual C++ and MFC to create applications that take advantage of the Internet. There are two ways that you can use Visual C++ to leverage Internet Explorer and make use of Dynamic HTML: The WebBrowser ActiveX control, and the CHtmlView class—both of these approaches were discussed in this chapter.

Two example projects were presented: The WebCtl project used a WebBrowser control in a dialog box to navigate to the Microsoft Web site, and also to display the Control Panel on the local machine. The WWWTest project used the CHtmlView class to display a Dynamic HTML page stored as a program resource.

Advanced Programming Topics

PART IV

IN THIS PART

CHAPTER 13

Using the Standard C++ Library

by Andrew J. Indovina

IN THIS CHAPTER

In this chapter, you will look at the Standard C++ Library for Visual C++. This library is made up of C++ language itself and its own standard library.

The standard library contains the *Standard Template Library* (*STL*). This library is a collection of common data structures. In the past, programmers would have to develop their own data structure if the one they needed was not available.

The STL consists of a common set of generic data structures, called *containers*. Also included in the STL are *algorithms*, which are applied to the containers to process their data. To connect algorithms with containers, *iterators* are used. Each of these topics is covered in more depth throughout the chapter.

Finally, you will see how to use STL with MFC and ATL.

Standard C++ Library

Listed below are the main elements of the Standard C++ Library:

- **Language support.** Supplies common type definitions used throughout the entire library. Such common type definitions include functions supporting the starting and ending of C++ programs, dynamic memory allocation support, and other runtime support.

- **Diagnostics.** Contains a global variable for error number codes, components for reporting various types of exceptional conditions, and components for documenting program assertions.

- **General utilities.** Contains memory management components from the C library. Contains components used by the Standard Template Library. Contains dynamic memory management utilities and function objects.

- **Strings.** Contains components for string manipulation, including manipulation sequences of characters. The library provides a class template that defines the basic properties of strings. The types `string` and `wstring` are provided as predefined template instantiations.

- **Localization.** Contains internationalization support for character classification and string collation. Such classifications and collations are date/time formatting, message retrieval, monetary, numeric, and parsing.

- **Standard Template Library (STL).** A library of such components as containers, algorithms, and iterators. The purpose of this library is to provide a standard software library with no loss of performance.

- **Numerics.** Contains components for numeric arrays, generalized numeric algorithms, and complex number types, as well as components to perform seminumerical operations.

- **Input/Output.** Contains components for the declaration of base I/O stream classes, file streams, I/O streams, stream buffering, stream formatting, and predefined I/O stream objects.

- **Standard C Library.** The Standard C++ Library also incorporates the Standard C Library.

Standard Template Library (STL)

The STL consists of several kinds of components; the most important are containers, algorithms, and iterators. The main purpose of the STL was to establish a standard software library without loss of performance.

Why templates? The main advantage of templates is that they allow the use of types as parameters when creating classes. Developers therefore can create the desired class by specifying the proper parameters. In other words, data structures and functions will behave exactly the same, regardless of the data type. Sorting a collection of numbers or a collection of characters is done exactly the same: The language knows how to implement the proper method for each (number sort or character sort) by the parameter that was sent. This is hidden from the developer and allows for generic programming.

A container manages the storage and processing of data. You can think of it as an object that holds other objects. Containers are implemented by template classes to allow them to hold different kinds of data in an easy manner. The STL contains the most common containers that programmers find useful when handling common programming tasks.

Iterators provide methods to traverse the contents of a container and are used to access individual elements in a container. Similar to pointers, iterators can be incremented to point to the next element, and they can be dereferenced to obtain the value of the element to which it points. Iterators allow algorithms and containers to connect and create the bond that enables them to work together.

Algorithms allow functions to be performed on the containers. They are not container-specific or members of the containers; instead, they are standalone functions that are general in nature. The algorithms may be used on containers you create yourself or C++ arrays. Algorithms are represented by template functions.

Containers

A *container* is a data structure that manages a collection of elements. The container itself is responsible for the allocation and deallocation of its elements, as well as methods for adding and deleting elements. Containers most typically contain constructors and destructors as well.

The containers supplied in the STL consist of two categories: *sequence* and *associative*. Sequence containers store elements in sequential order, like a C++ array (which is, in fact, a container). Sequence containers are List, Deque, and Vector. Associative containers are not sequential and use keys to access data. The keys usually are strings or numeric. The associative containers consist of Map, Multimap, Multiset, and Set.

Sequence Containers

Sequence containers store elements in sequential order. It is a linear arrangement where every element in the container is related to the other elements by its position. The containers Vector, List, and Deque are sequence containers.

The Vector Container

The Vector container takes care of the shortcomings of the C++ array. Unlike the C++ array, the vector is an expandable array: It doesn't have to specify its size at compile time. It is very fast and efficient at inserting and removing elements at the end of the array and is quick at random access, but it is slow at inserting or deleting elements from the middle. Table 13.1 lists the member functions and type definitions of the Vector container.

TABLE 13.1 The Vector Container: Member Functions and Type Definitions

Function	Definition
allocator_type	Type definition for template.
assign	Assignment function for sequences.
at	Returns a reference to the element of the controlled sequence.
back	Returns a reference to the last element of the controlled sequence. The last element must be non-empty.
begin	Returns a random-access iterator that points to the first element of the sequence.
capacity	Returns a value equal to the storage currently allocated to hold the controlled sequence. This value will be at least as large as size().
clear	Calls erase(), begin(), and end().
const_iterator	Type definition for constant random-access iterator for the sequence.
const_reference	Type definition for a constant reference to an element for the sequence.

Function	*Definition*
const_reverse_iterator	Type definition for a constant reverse iterator for the sequence.
difference_type	Signed integer type defines an object that can represent the difference between the addresses of any two elements of the sequence.
empty	Returns True for an empty sequence.
end	Returns a random-access iterator that points just beyond the end of the sequence.
erase	Function that can remove the element of the sequence pointed to by it or remove a range of elements.
front	Returns the first element of a sequence. The first element must be non-empty.
get_allocator	Returns allocator.
insert	Inserts an element, a repetition of elements, or the sequence. When inserting a single element, the iterator of the element is returned.
iterator	Type definition that can serve as a random-access iterator for the sequence.
max_size	Returns the length of the largest sequence the object can use.
operator[]	Returns a reference to the element of the sequence at the declared position.
pop_back	Removes the last element of the sequence. The last value must be empty.
push_back	Inserts an element at the end of the sequence.
rbegin	Returns a reverse iterator that points just beyond the end of the sequence.
reference	Type definition for an object that can be a reference to an element of the sequence.
rend	Returns a reverse iterator that points to the first element of the sequence.
reserve	Ensures the storage currently allocated to hold the controlled sequence. The size of the storage is returned.
resize	Ensures the storage currently allocated to hold the controlled sequence. If the size of the sequence must be increased, it adds the number of elements specified.

continues

13

USING THE
STANDARD C++
LIBRARY

TABLE 13.1 continued

Function	Definition
reverse_iterator	Type definition that can serve as a reverse iterator for the sequence.
size	Returns the length of the sequence.
size_type	Type definition that describes an object that can represent the length of a sequence.
swap	Swaps two sequences.
value_type	Type definition for value_type.
vector	Constructor for the vector template class. It can specify an empty sequence, a repetition of elements, or a copy of another sequence.

A code example of the common Vector functions follows. The functions represented in this code are back, empty, erase, pop_back, push_back, Operator[], size, and swap.

LISTING 13.1 Common Vector Operations

```
//Common Vector Operations
//
// Member Functions: push_back, pop_back, size, Operator[]
//                   swap, empty, back, insert, erase

#include <iostream>
#include <vector>

using namespace std ;

typedef vector<int> INTVECTOR;

//Main
void main(){

INTVECTOR VectorSet1;        //Declare 4 vectors of integer
INTVECTOR VectorSet2(3) ;

// Iterator is used to loop through the vector.
INTVECTOR::iterator MyIterator;

//Insert Elements using push_back
VectorSet1.push_back(1);
VectorSet1.push_back(2);
VectorSet1.push_back(3);
```

```
//Insert Elements using Operator[]
VectorSet2[0] = 10;
VectorSet2[1] = 11;
VectorSet2[2] = 12;

//Print Vector Size
cout << "The Size of VectorSet1 is: " << VectorSet1.size() << endl << endl;

// print VectorsSet1 contents
cout << "Contents of VectorSet1:" << endl;
   for(MyIterator = VectorSet1.begin();
    MyIterator != VectorSet1.end();
    MyIterator++)
   cout << *MyIterator << endl;
cout << endl;

// print VectorsSet2 contents
cout << "Contents of VectorSet2:" << endl;
    for(MyIterator = VectorSet2.begin();
    MyIterator != VectorSet2.end();
    MyIterator++)
cout << *MyIterator << endl;
cout << endl;

//Swap VectorSet1 with VectorSet2
VectorSet1.swap(VectorSet2);

// print VectorsSet1 contents
cout << "Contents of VectorSet1 after Swap:" << endl;
   for(MyIterator = VectorSet1.begin();
    MyIterator != VectorSet1.end();
    MyIterator++)
cout << *MyIterator << endl;
cout << endl;

// print last element in VectorSet1
cout << "Last element in VectorSet1: " << VectorSet1.back() << endl;

//Empty out vector1
while( !VectorSet1.empty() )
{
cout << "Popping element " << VectorSet1.back() << endl;
VectorSet1.pop_back();
}
cout << endl;

cout << "Contents of VectorSet1:" << endl;
    for(MyIterator = VectorSet1.begin();
    MyIterator != VectorSet1.end();
    MyIterator++)
```

continues

LISTING 13.1   continued

```
    cout << *MyIterator << endl;
cout << endl;

//Insert number 44
VectorSet2.insert(VectorSet2.begin() + 1, 44);
// print VectorsSet2 contents after insert
    cout << "Contents of VectorSet2 after insert:" << endl;
    for(MyIterator = VectorSet2.begin();
    MyIterator != VectorSet2.end();
    MyIterator++)
cout << *MyIterator << endl;
cout << endl;

//Erase number 44
  VectorSet2.erase(VectorSet2.begin() + 1);
// print VectorsSet2 contents after erase
cout << "Contents of VectorSet2 after erase:" << endl;
    for(MyIterator = VectorSet2.begin();
    MyIterator != VectorSet2.end();
    MyIterator++)
cout << *MyIterator << endl;
cout << endl;

} //END
```

The output of this code follows:

```
The Size of VectorSet1 is: 3

Contents of VectorSet1:
1
2
3

Contents of VectorSet2:
10
11
12

Contents of VectorSet1 after Swap:
10
11
12

Last element in VectorSet1: 12
Popping element 12
Popping element 11
Popping element 10
```

```
Contents of VectorSet1:

Contents of VectorSet2 after insert:
1
44
2
3

Contents of VectorSet2 after erase:
1
2
3
```

The List Container

The `List` container allows the quick addition and removal of elements anywhere in the list. This is kind of like the linked-list version of the `Vector` container. Though quick to access either end, it is slow at random access. Table 13.2 lists the member functions and type definitions of the `List` container.

TABLE 13.2 The List Container: Member Functions and Type Definitions

Function	Description
`allocator_type`	Type definition for template.
`assign`	Assignment function for sequences.
`at`	Returns a reference to the element of the controlled sequence.
`back`	Returns a reference to the last element of the controlled sequence. The last element must be non-empty.
`begin`	Returns a random-access iterator that points to the first element of the sequence.
`clear`	Calls `erase()`, `begin()`, and `end()`.
`const_iterator`	Type definition for constant random-access iterator for the sequence.
`const_reference`	Type definition for a constant reference to an element for the sequence.
`const_reverse_iterator`	Type definition for a constant reverse iterator for the sequence.
`difference_type`	Signed integer type defines an object that can represent the difference between the addresses of any two elements of the sequence.
`empty`	Returns `True` for an empty sequence.

continues

13

TABLE 13.2 continued

Function	Description
end	Returns a random-access iterator that points just beyond the end of the sequence.
erase	Function that can remove the element of the sequence pointed to by it or remove a range of elements.
front	Returns the first element of a sequence. The first element must be non-empty.
get_allocator	Returns allocator.
insert	Inserts an element, a repetition of elements, or the sequence. When inserting a single element, the iterator of the element is returned.
iterator	Type definition that can serve as a random-access iterator for the sequence.
list	Constructor for the list template class. It can specify an empty sequence, a repetition of elements, or a copy of another sequence.
max_size	Returns the length of the largest sequence that the object can use.
merge	Merges two sequences.
operator[]	Returns a reference to the element of the sequence at the declared position.
pop_back	Removes the last element of the sequence. The last value must be empty.
pop_front	Removes the first element of the sequence. The first value must be non-empty.
push_back	Inserts an element at the end of the sequence.
push_front	Removes an element from the front of the sequence.
rbegin	Returns a reverse iterator that points just beyond the end of the sequence.
reference	Type definition for an object that can be a reference to an element of the sequence.
remove	Removes elements from the sequence.
remove_if	Removes elements from the sequence based on a condition.
rend	Returns a reverse iterator that points to the first element of the sequence.

Function	Description
resize	Ensures the storage currently allocated to hold the controlled sequence. If the size of the sequence must be increased, it adds the number of elements specified.
reverse	Reverses the order of the elements in a sequence.
reverse_iterator	Type definition that can serve as a reverse iterator for the sequence.
size	Returns the length of the sequence.
size_type	Type definition that describes an object that can represent the length of a sequence.
sort	Orders the elements of the sequence by a determined predicate.
splice	Performs splice operations on the elements in the sequence.
swap	Swaps two sequences.
value_type	Type definition for value_type.
unique	Removes duplicate elements that equal the desired value.

The following example demonstrates three functions that are unique to List: merge(), reverse(), and unique().

LISTING 13.2   Common Vector Operations 2

```
//Common Vector Operations
//
// Member Functions: merge, reverse, and unique

#include <iostream>
#include <list>
#include <string>

using namespace std ;

typedef list<string> LISTSTR;

//Main
void main(){

LISTSTR List1;
LISTSTR List2;

LISTSTR::iterator MyIterator;
```

continues

13

USING THE
STANDARD C++
LIBRARY

LISTING 13.2   continued

```cpp
List1.push_back("1");
List1.push_back("2");
List1.push_back("3");

List2.push_back("3");
List2.push_back("4");
List2.push_back("5");

// print VectorsSet1 contents
cout << "Contents of List1:" << endl;
    for(MyIterator = List1.begin();
    MyIterator != List1.end();
    MyIterator++)
cout << *MyIterator << endl;
cout << endl;

//Merge Both lists
List1.merge(List2);

// print VectorsSet1 contents
cout << "Contents of List1 after merge:" << endl;
    for(MyIterator = List1.begin();
    MyIterator != List1.end();
MyIterator++)
        cout << *MyIterator << endl;
cout << endl;

//Reverse List1
    List1.reverse();

// print VectorsSet1 contents
cout << "Contents of List1 after reverse:" << endl;
    for(MyIterator = List1.begin();
    MyIterator != List1.end();
MyIterator++)
        cout << *MyIterator << endl;
cout << endl;

//remove duplicates List1
    List1.unique();

// print VectorsSet1 contents
cout << "Contents of List1 after unique:" << endl;
    for(MyIterator = List1.begin();
    MyIterator != List1.end();
MyIterator++)
   cout << *MyIterator << endl;
cout << endl;
} //END
```

Unless you specify -GX when compiling, you will receive numerous warnings upon compiling the program. The results of this program are pretty obvious, as shown here:

```
Contents of List1:
1
2
3

Contents of List1 after merge:
1
2
3
3
4
5

Contents of List after reverse:
5
4
3
3
2
1

Contents of List1 after unique:
5
4
3
2
1
```

The Deque Container

The third sequence container is the Deque (double-ended queue). The Deque is actually like a stack and queue combined. Like a stack, all the input and output takes place at the top of the stack (LIFO). In a queue, all data goes in the front and comes out the back (FIFO). With the Deque container, these attributes are combined so that elements can be inserted or deleted at either end. This makes it quite flexible and thus is used as the basis for stacks and queues. Table 13.3 lists the member functions and type definitions of the Deque container.

TABLE 13.3 The Deque Container: Member Functions and Type Definitions

Function	Description
allocator_type	Type definition for template.
assign	Assignment function for sequences.

continues

TABLE 13.3 continued

Function	Description
at	Returns a reference to the element of the controlled sequence.
back	Returns a reference to the last element of the controlled sequence. The last element must be non-empty.
begin	Returns a random-access iterator that points to the first element of the sequence.
clear	Calls erase(), begin(), and end().
const_iterator	Type definition for constant random-access iterator for the sequence.
const_reference	Type definition for a constant reference to an element for the sequence.
const_reverse_iterator	Type definition for a constant reverse iterator for the sequence.
difference_type	Signed integer type defines an object that can represent the difference between the addresses of any two elements of the sequence.
empty	Returns True for an empty sequence.
end	Returns a random-access iterator that points just beyond the end of the sequence.
erase	Function that can remove the element of the sequence pointed to by it or remove a range of elements.
front	Returns the first element of a sequence. The first element must be non-empty.
get_allocator	Returns allocator.
insert	Inserts an element, a repetition of elements, or the sequence. When inserting a single element, the iterator of the element is returned.
iterator	Type definition that can serve as a random-access iterator for the sequence.
list	Constructor for the list template class. It can specify an empty sequence, a repetition of elements, or a copy of another sequence.
max_size	Returns the length of the largest sequence the object can use.
merge	Merges two sequences.

Function	Description
operator[]	Used to reference elements directly.
pop_back	Removes the last element of the sequence. The last value must be empty.
pop_front	Removes the first element of the sequence. The first value must be non-empty.
push_back	Inserts an element at the end of the sequence.
push_front	Inserts an element at the beginning of the sequence.
rbegin	Returns a reverse iterator that points just beyond the end of the sequence.
reference	Type definition for an object that can be a reference to an element of the sequence.
rend	Returns a reverse iterator that points to the first element of the sequence.
resize	Ensures the storage currently allocated to hold the controlled sequence. If the size of the sequence must be increased, it adds the number of elements specified.
reverse	Reverses the order of the elements in a sequence.
reverse_iterator	Type definition that can serve as a reverse iterator for the sequence.
size	Returns the length of the sequence.
size_type	Type definition that describes an object that can represent the length of a sequence.
swap	Swaps two sequences.
value_type	Type definition for value_type.

An example of a Deque container, supporting push_front, pop_front, and front(), follows:

LISTING 13.3   Deque Example

```
//Deque example
//
// Member Functions: push_back, push_front
//

#include <iostream>
#include <deque>
```

continues

13

USING THE
STANDARD C++
LIBRARY

LISTING 13.3   continued

```
using namespace std ;

typedef deque<int> INTDEQUE;

//Main
void main(){

INTDEQUE::iterator MyIterator;
INTDEQUE  deque1;

deque1.push_back(2);
deque1.push_front(1);
deque1.push_back(3);


// print deque contents
cout << "Contents of deque1:" << endl;
for(MyIterator = deque1.begin();
    MyIterator != deque1.end();
    MyIterator++)
cout << *MyIterator << endl;
cout << endl;

} //END
```

Unless you specify `-GX` when compiling, you will receive numerous warnings upon compiling the program. The results of this program are pretty obvious, as shown here:

```
Contents of deque1:
1
2
3
```

Note the manner of how the elements were placed in the Deque and the final results.

Associative Containers

Associative containers use keys to access data and are not sequential. The keys typically are numeric or strings. The keys are used automatically by the container to arrange the stored elements in a specific order.

There are two types of associative containers in the STL: *sets* and *maps*. A set only stores the key without the associated values. A map associates a key with a value. This value can be any type of object.

Both types of containers only allow one key per given value. It is a one-to-one relationship. However, if the need arises for multiple keys per value, the Multiset and Multimap containers are the ones to use.

Table 13.4 lists the member functions and type definitions of Map, Multimap, Set, and Multiset containers. All apply except for the respective constructors and those otherwise noted.

TABLE 13.4 Map, Multimap, Set, and Multiset Containers: Member Functions and Type Definitions

Function	Description
allocator_type	Type definition for template.
begin	Returns a bidirectional iterator that points to the first element of the sequence.
clear	Calls erase(), begin(), and end().
const_iterator	Type definition for a constant bidirectional iterator for the sequence.
const_reference	Type definition for a constant reference to an element for the sequence.
const_reverse_iterator	Type definition for a constant reverse bidirectional iterator for the sequence.
count	Returns the number of elements of a given range.
difference_type	Signed integer type defines an object that can represent the difference between the addresses of any two elements of the sequence.
empty	Returns True for an empty sequence.
end	Returns a bidirectional iterator that points just beyond the end of the sequence.
equal range	Returns a pair of iterators such that the first one is equal to a given lower bound, and the second is equal to a given upper bound.
erase	Function that can remove the element of the sequence pointed to by it or remove a range of elements.
find	Returns an interator to the first element it finds matching a given value. If no match is found, the iterator is equal to end().
get_allocator	Returns allocator.
insert	Inserts an element, a repetition of elements, or the sequence. When inserting a single element, the iterator of the element is returned.

continues

13

USING THE STANDARD C++ LIBRARY

TABLE 13.4   continued

Function	Description
iterator	Type definition that can serve as a bidirectional iterator for the sequence.
key_comp	Determines the order of elements in a sequence.
key_compare	Compares two sort keys to determine the relative order of any two elements in the sequence.
key_type	Type definition for the sort key object in each element of the sequence.
lower_bound	Returns an iterator that designates the lower bound of a given element value. If no element is found, end() is returned.
map	Constructor for the Map object.
max_size	Returns the length of the largest sequence the object can use.
multimap	Constructor for the Multimap object.
multiset	Constructor for Multiset.
operator[]	Returns a reference to the element of the sequence at the declared position. Applies to Map object only.
rbegin	Returns a reverse bidirectional iterator that points just beyond the end of the sequence.
reference	Type definition for an object that can be a reference to an element of the sequence.
referent type	Type definition of referent.
rend	Returns a reverse bidirectional iterator that points to the first element of the sequence.
reverse_iterator	Type definition that can serve as a reverse iterator for the sequence.
set	Constructor for Set.
size	Returns the length of the sequence.
size_type	Type definition that describes an object that can represent the length of a sequence.
swap	Swaps two sequences.
upper_bound	Returns an iterator that designates the upper bound of a given element value. If no element is found, end() is returned.

Function	Description
`value_comp`	Returns the order of elements in a sequence.
`value_compare`	Compares the sort keys of two elements to determine their relative order in the sequence.
`value_type`	Type definition for `value_type`.

A program example that puts some of this knowledge to work follows. It is quite simple and self-explanatory, but it demonstrates the basics of working with the `Vector` container class.

LISTING 13.4   Vector Program Example

```
// Vector program example
//
// Functions:
//     vector::push_back
//     vector::pop_back
//     vector::begin
//     vector::end
//     vector::iterator

#include <iostream>
#include <vector>

using namespace std ;

typedef vector<int> INTVECTOR;

void main(){

    INTVECTOR MyVector;

// Iterator is used to loop through the vector.
 INTVECTOR::iterator MyIterator;

// MyVector will contain [ 1, 2, 3 ]
MyVector.push_back(1) ;

MyVector.push_back(2) ;

MyVector.push_back(3) ;

// Erase element 3 in vector.
   MyVector.pop_back();
// MyVector will contain [ 1, 2 ] at this point
```

continues

LISTING 13.4   continued

```
MyVector.push_back(4) ;
// MyVector now contains [ 1, 2, 4 ]

// Print contents of MyVector. Shows [1, 2, 4]
    cout << "Results = " ;

for (MyIterator = MyVector.begin();
MyIterator != MyVector.end();
        MyIterator++)
 {
   cout << *MyIterator;
   if (MyIterator != MyVector.end()-1) cout << ", ";
 }
 cout << endl ;
}
Results = 1, 2, 4
```

Iterators

Iterators provide access to containers in a pointer-like manner. You use them to access the elements in a container. The three major classes of iterators are *forward, bidirectional,* and *random access*. A forward iterator provides for one-directional forward movement only, which can be accomplished using ++. Bidirectional iterators can traverse in both directions, using ++ and --. A random-access iterator can move both forward and backward, and jump to an arbitrary position.

Also, two other categories of iterators exist: *input iterators* and *output iterators*. The input iterator can be an intermediate to an input device to read sequential data items and place them into a container. An output iterator can be an intermediate to an output device and write the elements from a container to the device.

Note that the values for the forward, bidirectional, and random-access iterators can be stored in memory for later retrieval. The values for the input iterator and the output iterator cannot be stored, because they would be referencing input and output devices respectively, where the values that are received would not apply.

Algorithms

STL *algorithms* are functions that perform operations to the items in one or more containers. These algorithm functions are standalone template functions. Because they are so general, they can be applied to ordinary C++ arrays or containers you create yourself.

Algorithms are written to work on iterators, not components. They are parameterized by iterator types and unattached from the containers they operate on. Thus, all containers of the same iterator category can use the same algorithms. Table 13.5 describes the available algorithms.

TABLE 13.5 STL Algorithms

Algorithm	Description
adjacent_find	Locates consecutive pairs of matching elements. A predicate version of the function exists.
binary_search	Returns True if a given value resides within a given range. A predicate version of this function exists.
copy	Copies objects from one range to another.
copy_backward	Copies objects from one range to another, with the destination range receiving the elements in reverse order.
count	Returns the number of occurrences of a given value within a sequence.
count_if	Returns the number of elements that satisfy a predicate.
equal	Returns True if objects in two ranges are equal. A predicate version of this function exists.
equal_range	Returns a pair that can be inserted in a sequence, and then preserves the ordering of the sequence. A predicate version of this function exists.
fill	Fills all objects within a range of a given value.
fill_n	Fills objects to each n in a range from the first object to the nth object.
find	Returns an iterator to the first object matching a given value.
find_end	Finds the last occurrence of a subsequence.
find_first_of	Finds the first element equal to a given value. A predicate version of this function exists.
find_if	Returns an iterator to the first object for which the predicate equals True.
for_each	Applies a designated operation to each element in a container. It cannot change the contents of each container.
generate	Fills all objects within a range with a value generated by the function.

continues

13

USING THE
STANDARD C++
LIBRARY

TABLE 13.5 continued

Algorithm	Description
generate_n	Fills all objects from the first element to the nth element within a range with a value generated by the function.
includes	Returns True if every object of one range is in every object of another range. A predicate version of this function exists.
inplace_merge	Merges two sorted subsequences into a single sorted sequence. A predicate version of this function exists.
iter_swap	Swaps to elements by their two iterators.
lexicographical_compare	Returns True if the sequence of the first range is lexicographically less than the sequence of the second range.
lower_bound	Returns the lower bound of a given range.
make_heap	Creates a heap out of a given range of values. A predicate exists for this function.
max	Returns the largest value of two given objects.
max_element	Returns the iterator of the largest element of two given objects. A predicate exists for this function.
merge	Merges two ranges into a third range. A predicate version of the function exists.
min	Returns the smallest value of two given objects.
min_element	Returns the iterator of the smallest element of two given objects. A predicate exists for this function.
mismatch	Returns the first pair of corresponding objects that are not equal. A predicate version of this function exists.
next_permutation	Changes the order of a sequence to the next lexicographic permutation.
nth_element	Partitions elements in a sequence by the given nth element.
partial_sort	Sorts only the middle to the beginning of a range. The remaining elements of the range (middle to end) remain in an undefined order.
partial_sort_copy	Sorts only the middle to the beginning of a range and copies the resulting partial sort to another sequence.
partition	Returns the first element for which the predicate returns False. This algorithm arranges elements in a range, with the elements that returned True for the predicate at the beginning of the sequence.

Algorithm	Description
pop_heap	Removes an element from the heap.
prev_permutation	Changes the order of a sequence to the previous lexicographic permutation.
push_heap	Inserts an element into the heap.
random_shuffle	Shuffles the elements in random order. A predicate function exists.
remove	Removes all elements from a sequence that match a given value.
remove_copy	Copies the elements of a sequence to another sequence, removing any elements that match the given value.
remove_copy_if	Copies the elements of a sequence to another sequence, removing any elements that satisfy a predicate.
remove_if	Removes all elements of a sequence that satisfy a predicate.
replace	Replaces all elements of a sequence that match a given value to a new given value.
replace_copy	Copies all elements of a sequence that match a given value to a new given value
replace_copy_if	Replaces all elements from a sequence that satisfy a predicate with a given value.
replace_if	Replaces all elements of a sequence that satisfy a predicate to a new given value.
reverse	Reverses the order of objects in a range.
reverse_copy	Copies one range to another, reversing the order.
rotate	Rotates the items in a sequence by n positions.
rotate_copy	Rotates the items in a sequence by n positions, and copies the results to another sequence of the same size.
search	Returns the start position of the match if the second range exists in the first. A predicate function exists.
search_n	Returns the start position of the match if the second range exists in the first to the nth object. A predicate function exists.
set_difference	Determines differences of elements from two ranges, with the results sorted. A predicate version of this function exists, determining the order of the results.

continues

TABLE 13.5   continued

Algorithm	Description
set_intersection	Determines the intersection of elements from two ranges, with the results sorted. A predicate version of this function exists, determining the order of the results.
set_symmetric_difference	Determines the symmetric difference of elements from two ranges, with the results sorted. A predicate version of this function exists, determining the order of the results.
set_union	Determines the union of elements from two ranges, with the results sorted. A predicate version of this function exists, determining the order of the results.
sort	Sorts elements within a range. A predicate version of this function exists.
sort_heap	Sorts elements within a heap. A predicate version of this function exists.
stable_partition	Partitions a sequence into two groups. The first group is the group of elements that satisfy the predicate. The second group consists of the elements that did not satisfy the predicate.
stable_sort	Sorts the elements in a sequence, preserving the relative order for equal elements.
swap	Swaps two elements.
swap_ranges	Swaps two elements from two ranges.
transform	Transforms objects from one range into new objects in a second range.
unique	Removes all objects but the first one of equal value. A predicate version of this function exists.
unique_copy	Copies objects from one range to another, but only ones of unique values.
upper_bound	Returns the lower bound of a given range.

After examining these functions, you may have noticed that the functions mention the term *predicate,* especially the functions ending in _if.

A predicate is simply another parameter that is included in the calling of the function. A predicate is a power option simply because it enables the developer to write a separate function. This function is applied against every object in the range, and the results are processed as the _if algorithm dictates. The replace_if example later in this chapter demonstrates the use of a predicate.

A few of the most common algorithms are covered in the following sections.

count()

The count() algorithm counts the number of elements that contain a particular value. The function call requires the beginning and ending ranges of the search, plus the value that is to be matched. The following code shows an example:

LISTING 13.5 Count Example

```
// Count program example

#include <iostream>
#include <vector>
#include <algorithm>

using namespace std ;

typedef vector<int> INTVECTOR;

void main(){

    int total_count = 0 ;

    INTVECTOR MyVector;

// MyVector will contain [ 1, 2, 2, 3 ]
    MyVector.push_back(1) ;

    MyVector.push_back(2) ;

    MyVector.push_back(2) ;
    MyVector.push_back(3) ;

    //Get total count of 1s
    total_count = count(MyVector.begin(), MyVector.end(), 1);

     cout << "Total Count of 1s = " << total_count << endl;

    //Get total count of 1s
    total_count = count(MyVector.begin(), MyVector.end(), 2);

     cout << "Total Count of 2s = " << total_count << endl;

//Get total count of 3s
  total_count = count(MyVector.begin(), MyVector.end(), 3);

  cout << "Total Count of 3s = " << total_count << endl;

} //END
```

The output of this program follows:

```
Total Count of 1s = 1
Total Count of 2s = 2
Total Count of 3s = 1
```

find()

The find() algorithm does pretty much what it says, returning the position of the first element it finds that matches the desired value. The following listing is an example of finding values using vectors:

LISTING 13.6   Find Example

```
// Find program example

#include <iostream>
#include <vector>
#include <algorithm>

using namespace std ;

typedef vector<int> INTVECTOR;

void main(){

int *location ;    // stores the position of the first
                   // matching element.

INTVECTOR MyVector;

// MyVector will contain [ 8, 6, 7, 5 ]
   MyVector.push_back(8) ;
   MyVector.push_back(6) ;
   MyVector.push_back(7) ;
   MyVector.push_back(5) ;

//Get Position of number 8 - Should return 0
  location = find (MyVector.begin(), MyVector.end(), 8);

  cout << "Position of 8 is " << location - MyVector.end()
➥ + MyVector.size() << endl;

//Get Position of number 6 - Should return 1
  location = find (MyVector.begin(), MyVector.end(), 6);

  cout << "Position of 6 is " << location - MyVector.end()
➥ + MyVector.size() << endl;
```

```
//Get Position of number 7 - Should return 2
  location = find (MyVector.begin(), MyVector.end(), 7);

  cout << "Position of 7 is " << location - MyVector.end()
➥ + MyVector.size() << endl;

//Get Position of number 5 - Should return 3
  location = find (MyVector.begin(), MyVector.end(), 5);

  cout << "Position of 5 is " << location - MyVector.end()
➥ + MyVector.size() << endl;

} //END
```

The output of this program follows:

```
Position of 8 is 0
Position of 6 is 1
Position of 7 is 2
Position of 5 is 3
```

Notice how `MyVector.size` was used to quickly get the number of elements from the container.

for_each()

The `for_each()` algorithm enables you to use the values of every item of an object in a relatively easy way. The actual object values themselves cannot be changed, but the resulting values can be obtained for other use. The function that accesses their values and works with them is supplied by the developer.

The following listing takes a list of vector numbers and calls a function to display their value doubled:

LISTING 13.7   For Each Example

```
// for_each program example
//
// Functions:

#include <iostream>
#include <vector>
#include <algorithm>

using namespace std ;

typedef vector<int> INTVECTOR;

// Function to print out vector values
```

continues

LISTING 13.7   continued

```
void unchanged_value(int vector_value)
{
    cout << vector_value << endl;
}

// Function to print out vector values * 2
void double_value(int vector_value)
{
  cout << vector_value * 2 << endl;
}

//Main
void main(){

    INTVECTOR Numbers(5) ;          //Declare 5 vectors of integer

//Set values of Numbers vectors
    Numbers[0] = 0;
    Numbers[1] = 1;
    Numbers[2] = 2;
    Numbers[3] = 3;
    Numbers[4] = 4;

  cout << "Numbers unchanged:" << endl;
  for_each(Numbers.begin(), Numbers.end(), unchanged_value);

  cout << endl;

  cout << "Numbers doubled:" << endl;
  for_each(Numbers.begin(), Numbers.end(), double_value) ;

} //END
```

The output of this program follows:

```
Numbers unchanged:
0
1
2
3
4

Numbers doubled:
0
2
4
6
8
```

merge()

The merge() algorithm takes two objects and merges their values into a third object. To do this successfully with vectors, the destination container must have its elements initialized. The following listing merges two number vectors into a destination vector and displays the results:

LISTING 13.8   Merge Example

```
// merge program example
//
// Functions:

#include <iostream>
#include <vector>
#include <algorithm>

using namespace std ;

typedef vector<int> INTVECTOR;


//Main
void main(){

INTVECTOR Set1(6) ;        //Declare 5 vectors of integer
INTVECTOR Set2(3) ;        //Declare 5 vectors of integer
INTVECTOR Destination(9) ; //Declare 8 vectors of integer
// Iterator is used to loop through the vector.
INTVECTOR::iterator MyIterator;


//Set values of Set1
    Set1[0] = 0;
    Set1[1] = 1;
    Set1[2] = 2;
    Set1[3] = 4;
    Set1[4] = 6;
    Set1[5] = 8;

//Set values of Set2
    Set2[0] = 1;
    Set2[1] = 3;
    Set2[2] = 6;

// Initialize vector Destination
   for(int i = 0; i < 9; i++)
        Destination[i] = 0;
```

continues

Listing 13.8   continued

```
    merge(Set1.begin(), Set1.end(), Set2.begin(),
➥Set2.end(), Destination.begin());

// print content of NumbersDeque
cout << "Merged Results = { " ;
  for(MyIterator = Destination.begin();
    MyIterator != Destination.end();
    MyIterator++)
    cout << *MyIterator << " " ;     cout << " }\n" << endl ;

} //END
```

The output of this program follows:

```
Merged Results = { 0 1 1 2 3 4 6 6 8 }
```

sort()

The sort() algorithm simply sorts a set of objects. The following listing displays the code to achieve the results of a sorted numeric vector:

Listing 13.9   Sort Example

```
//Sort program example
//
// Functions:

#include <iostream>
#include <vector>
#include <algorithm>

using namespace std ;

typedef vector<int> INTVECTOR;


//Main
void main(){

INTVECTOR SortSet(7 ) ;          //Declare 7 vectors of integer

// Iterator is used to loop through the vector.
INTVECTOR::iterator MyIterator;


//Set values of SortSet
SortSet[0] = 10;
```

```
SortSet[1] = -1;
SortSet[2] = 6;
SortSet[3] = 0;
SortSet[4] = -10;
SortSet[5] = 1;
SortSet[6] = -6;

sort(SortSet.begin(), SortSet.end());

// print content of SortSet
cout << "Sorted Results = { " ;
for(MyIterator = SortSet.begin();
    MyIterator != SortSet.end();
    MyIterator++)
    cout << *MyIterator << " " ;    cout << " }\n" << endl ;

} //END
```

The output of this program follows:

```
Sorted Results = { -10 -6 -1 0 1 6 10 }
```

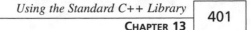

swap()

The swap() algorithm swaps two elements of a set. All that is needed are the two positions of the elements. The following listing demonstrates the swap with a numeric vector:

LISTING 13.10   Swap Example

```
//swap program example
//
// Functions:

#include <iostream>
#include <vector>
#include <algorithm>

using namespace std ;

typedef vector<int> INTVECTOR;


//Main
void main(){

INTVECTOR SwapSet(5) ;        //Declare 5 vectors of integer

// Iterator is used to loop through the vector.
   INTVECTOR::iterator MyIterator;
```

continues

LISTING 13.10   continued

```
//Set values of SwapSet
    SwapSet[0] = 1111;
    SwapSet[1] = 222;
    SwapSet[2] = 555;
    SwapSet[3] = 222;
    SwapSet[4] = 6666;

// print content of SwapSet
cout << "Contents before Swap = { " ;
    for(MyIterator = SwapSet.begin();
    MyIterator != SwapSet.end();
    MyIterator++)
    cout << *MyIterator << " " ;    cout << " }\n" << endl ;

swap(SwapSet[0], SwapSet[4]);

// print content of SwapSet
cout << "Contents after Swap = { " ;
    for(MyIterator = SwapSet.begin();
    MyIterator != SwapSet.end();
    MyIterator++)
    cout << *MyIterator << " " ;    cout << " }\n" << endl ;

} //END
```

The output of this program follows:

```
Contents before Swap = { 1111 222 555 222 6666 }
Contents after Swap = { 6666 222 555 222 1111 }
```

Using _if: The `replace_if ()` Algorithm

The `replace_if` function is a special type of algorithm. Whenever you see an `_if` at the end of an algorithm, it signals that it can use a function. This extra function is called a *predicate*.

The listing below demonstrates the use of `replace_if` function:

LISTING 13.11   Replace If Example

```
//replace_if program example
//
// Functions:

#include <iostream>
#include <vector>
#include <algorithm>
#include <functional>
```

```
using namespace std ;

typedef vector<int> INTVECTOR;


//Main
void main(){

INTVECTOR ReplaceSet(7) ;           //Declare 7 vectors of integer

// Iterator is used to loop through the vector.
    INTVECTOR::iterator MyIterator;

//Set values of ReplaceSet
    ReplaceSet[0] = 5;
    ReplaceSet[1] = 7;
    ReplaceSet[2] = 4;
    ReplaceSet[3] = 3;
    ReplaceSet[4] = 6;
    ReplaceSet[5] = 1;
    ReplaceSet[6] = 0;

// print content of ReplaceSet
cout << "Contents before Replace_If = { " ;
    for(MyIterator = ReplaceSet.begin();
    MyIterator != ReplaceSet.end();
    MyIterator++)
    cout << *MyIterator << " " ;    cout << " }\n" << endl ;

replace_if(ReplaceSet.begin(),ReplaceSet.end(),bind2nd(less<int>(), 5), 0 ) ;

// print content of ReplaceSet
cout << "Contents after Replace_If = { " ;
    for(MyIterator = ReplaceSet.begin();
    MyIterator != ReplaceSet.end();
    MyIterator++)
    cout << *MyIterator << " " ;    cout << " }\n" << endl ;

} //END
```

The output of this program follows:

```
Contents before Replace_If = { 5  7 4 3 6 1 0 }
Contents after Replace_If = { 5 7 0 0 6 0 0 }
```

The previous examples should get you started on how to use the algorithms with the STL. As you can see from Table 13.5, many more algorithms exist.

Reverse Iterator

In this section, you will examine the *reverse iterator*. This iterator gives you the capability to iterate through a container backward. You might think that to iterate backward, all you would have to do is perform the following code:

```
// print vectors in reverse order
cout << "Contents reverse in order:" << endl;
   for(MyIterator = SetToReverse.end();
   MyIterator != SetToReverse.begin();
   MyIterator—)
   cout << *MyIterator << endl;
```

This code will not work with a forward iterator. Forward iterators only support the ++ operator and can only progress forward.

Declaring a reverse iterator looks like this:

```
INTVECTOR::reverse_iterator MyReverseIterator;
```

You also must use the member functions rbegin() and rend() when using a reverse iterator. You cannot use these functions with a forward iterator. When using rbegin(), the reverse iterator is starting at the end of the container. The iterator also must be incremented.

The following example shows a forward iterator and a reverse iterator operating on the same set of vectors:

```
//reverse iterator program example
//
// Functions:

#include <iostream>
#include <vector>
#include <algorithm>
#include <functional>

using namespace std ;

typedef vector<int> INTVECTOR;

//Main
void main(){

INTVECTOR SetToReverse(4) ;          //Declare 4 vectors of integer

// Iterator is used to loop through the vector.
INTVECTOR::iterator MyIterator;
INTVECTOR::reverse_iterator MyReverseIterator;
```

```
//Set values of SetToReverse
    SetToReverse[0] = 0;
SetToReverse[1] = 1;
SetToReverse[2] = 2;
SetToReverse[3] = 3;

// print vectors in forward order
cout << "Contents iterated in order:" << endl;
   for(MyIterator = SetToReverse.begin();
    MyIterator != SetToReverse.end();
    MyIterator++)
   cout << *MyIterator << endl;
   cout << endl ;

// print vectors in reverse order
cout << "Contents iterated in reverse:" << endl;
   for(MyReverseIterator = SetToReverse.rbegin();
    MyReverseIterator != SetToReverse.rend();
    MyReverseIterator++)
   cout << *MyReverseIterator << endl;
   cout << endl ;

} //END
```

The output of this program follows:

```
Contents iterated in order:
0
1
2
3

Contents iterated in reverse:
3
2
1
0
```

Remember: Even though the reverse iterator is starting at the end of the container, use ++
to iterate through it backward.

Using STL with MFC and ATL

This section will briefly introduce how to use STL with MFC and introduce the Active
Template Library (ATL).

Using STL with MFC

The MFC Library is a set of more than 100 classes. All of the classes are tested and optimized, and the MFC Library contains data structure classes similar to STL—such as arrays, lists, and string lists. MFC is quite sufficient when compared to STL, and when it comes down to it, you probably won't come to a point where you have to have STL. When you are using MFC, however, the advantage of a lightweight program is lost, because you must bring along the DLL with distribution. So, what advantage is there in using STL with MFC?

Using STL with MFC enables easier traversal through MFC window containers. Thus, you want to use STL with MFC to help simplify MFC use and expand its use with the STL algorithms.

Introduction to ATL

ATL stands for *Active Template Library*. This library is designed to provide a way to create COM components in a fast and easy manner, and they leave only a small memory footprint. With ATL, you can create COM objects, Automation Server controls, and Active X controls, as well as provide built-in support for fundamental COM interfaces. ATL is an excellent partner to STL in that ATL has no provisions for data structures and algorithms, and STL fits that bill nicely.

Remember that template libraries are distributed as source code, which is a major advantage compared to function libraries. Because ATL is a template library, it only has to include the source needed in the executable, unlike MFC.

ATL Versus MFC

Which one should you use with STL? In short, use ATL to create a COM component when all of the built-in functionality of MFC is not necessary. When the component that is being created is nonvisual, ATL is most likely the better choice. ATL implementation results in faster components that use much less memory and do not carry the excess luggage of DLLs.

Summary

In this chapter, you took a look at the Standard C++ Library. You examined the two major components of the library: the C++ language itself and the *Standard Template Library* (*STL*).

You learned that the STL is a generic container class library. You then examined its main components—containers, iterators, and algorithms. The containers manage the storage and processing of data, and they are implemented by template containers. The iterators are used to traverse the containers, and algorithms create the bond between the containers. The algorithms are standalone functions and are not member-specific.

You learned to think of a container as an object that holds other objects. Containers are implemented by template classes to enable them to hold different kinds of data in an easy manner. The STL contains the most common containers that programmers find useful when handling common programming tasks.

This chapter also showed you how iterators provide methods to traverse the contents of a container and are used to access individual elements in a container. Iterators are similar to pointers and can be incremented to point to the next element; iterators can be dereferenced to obtain the value of the element they point to. Iterators allow algorithms and containers to connect and create the bond that enables them to work together.

Next, you examined how algorithms enable you to perform functions on the containers. They are not container-specific or members of the containers but standalone functions that are general in nature. You saw that you can use the algorithms on containers you create yourself or C++ arrays. Algorithms are represented by template functions. In this chapter, you looked at a well-rounded group of examples using the containers, iterators, and algorithms.

You also were introduced to the *Active Template Library (ATL)*, which you use to create very lightweight COM objects, Automation Server controls, and Active X controls. ATL objects do not require a DLL or static library upon distribution (unlike MFC) and leave a small memory footprint. ATL has no provisions for data structures or algorithms, which makes it an excellent partner with STL.

Finally, you looked at using STL with MFC and ATL. You saw that using MFC with STL is advantageous only if you want to traverse the MFC class libraries using the STL generic method and you want to apply the generic algorithms with MFC. ATL is an excellent partner to STL in that ATL has no provisions for data structures and algorithms, and STL fits that bill nicely.

CHAPTER 14

Error Detection and Exception Handling Techniques

by Andrew J. Indovina

IN THIS CHAPTER

Exceptions are generated when an unexpected event occurs and causes your program to execute abnormally, disrupting its capability to proceed normally, if at all. These events are caused by hardware or software exceptions.

In this chapter, you will look at the three mechanisms of exception handling that Visual C++ 6.0 supports:

- *Structured exception handling (SEH)* used mainly in C programs for Windows NT
- C++ exception handling
- MFC exception handling

In this chapter, you'll examine the basic concepts behind structured exception handling and its use. You'll look at the basic concepts that will be the building blocks for C++ exception handling and MFC exception handling.

C++ exception handling is exception handling using classes and objects. You'll see the advantages it has over the C-based SEH.

MFC exception handling is exception handling for the Microsoft Foundation Classes library. The previous method for MFC exception handling, MFC macros, is covered. You'll see how to perform MFC exception handling with the C++ method.

All the mechanisms discussed in this chapter accomplish the same goal: to deal with hardware and software exceptions.

You'll see what exactly a hardware and software exception is and how to capture it using keywords such as TRY, THROW, and CATCH.

Every mechanism discussed in this chapter is trying to accomplish the same thing: keeping your program running when critical errors occur.

Structured Exception Handling

Structured exception handling is a way to handle exceptions within a program. It is a mechanism for handling both hardware and software exceptions. An *exception* is an event (most likely, an error) that occurs while the program is running. To prevent (or at least try to prevent) the program from crashing, the event may be captured, processed, reported, and hopefully handled properly so that the program can continue in a workable state. If exceptions are handled successfully, it allows for consistent reliable applications.

Note that although you can use SEH with C++, C++ exception handling should be used for C++, and MFC exception handling should be used for MFC programs. The SEH covered in this chapter is designed mainly for C programs written for Windows NT or Windows 95.

There are two types of exceptions: *hardware exceptions* and *software exceptions.* Hardware exceptions are triggered by the CPU. These exceptions usually are caused by illegal operations such as dividing by zero, floating-point overflow, disk read errors, null pointer accesses, array subscript range errors, and out-of-bounds memory addressing. Software exceptions always result from the operating system or the programs themselves, such as array subscript range errors, null pointer accesses, or invalid parameter specified.

Structured exception handling manages both hardware exceptions and software exceptions in the same manner. This makes it easier to handle exceptions, because either exception can be handled in the same manner. The advantage of this capability is that code used for recovery can remain the same without having to satisfy two different types of exceptions.

The Microsoft C/C++ Optimizing Compiler supports three major keywords to help use SEH:

__try	Identifies a guarded body of code
__except	Identifies an exception handler
__finally	Identifies a termination handler

The Structured Exception Method

The old way of handling exceptions was to pass error codes. A function would detect an error and pass that error to its calling function. This error then would be passed around until it reached a function that could properly handle it. What made this method weak was that the whole function would fail if there was a break in the series of function calls; therefore, the error code was unable to surface, and the error could never be handled properly.

Structured exception handling is different and more reliable in that once an exception handler is installed, the exception can be handled regardless of how many other functions are called.

The structure for the exception handlers follows:

```
__try {

guarded-code-block-1

}

__except ( filter ) {

guarded-code-block-2

}
```

The statements that would exist in guarded-code-block-1 would be executed unconditionally. The exception handler defined by the filter and guarded-code-block-2 becomes the current exception handler.

If an exception occurs while guarded-code-block-1 is being executed, control is given to the current exception handler.

```
__try {
  int number1 = 0;
  int number2 = 0;
  number1 = 100 / number2;    //This is the exception to be handled.
  }
__except( GetExceptionCode() == STATUS_INTEGER_DIVIDE_BY_ZERO )
  {
  printf( "Error: Divide By Zero!");
  }
```

One limitation on using exception handlers is that you cannot use a goto statement to jump into a __try code block. The block must always be entered through the normal flow of control. You may jump out of a __try statement block, however.

A Look at Software Exceptions

You raise software exceptions by calling the RaiseException function. Keep in mind that you may treat any condition as an exception by reporting the condition to the RaiseException function. You can flag any type of runtime error this way.

To perform exception reporting with software errors, you must do the following:

1. Define the exception code for the event.
2. Call the RaiseException function when the error is detected.
3. Use exception-handling filters for the defined exception codes.

You can find the format for exception codes in the WINERROR.H header file. When defining your own exception code, make sure to set the third-most-significant bit to 1.

Setting the fourth-most-significant bits is a little more involved. Bits 31 to 30 define the basic status of the code. Bit 00 = success, 11 = error, 01 = informational, and 10 = warning. Bit 29 is the client bit and should be set to 1 for user-defined codes. Bit 28 is a reserved bit and should be set to 0.

Defined exception codes that do not conflict with the exceptions codes of Windows NT may look like the following:

```
#define STATUS_BAD_ERROR_01 0xE0000001
```

```
#define STATUS_BAD_ERROR_01 0xE0000001
```

```
#define STATUS_BAD_ERROR_01 0xE0000001
```

Testing your defined exception is quite simple and may look like the following:

```
__try {
      //Guarded code is goes here
      }
__except (GetExceptionCode() == STATUS_BAD_ERROR_01) ||
         GetExceptionCode() == STATUS_BAD_ERROR_02) ||
         GetExceptionCode() == STATUS_BAD_ERROR_03))
```

A Look at Hardware Exceptions

Hardware exceptions make up the majority of the standard exceptions. The hardware exceptions that Windows NT recognizes follow:

STANDARD_ACCESS_VIOLATION—Reading or writing to an invalid/inaccessible memory location.

STATUS_BREAKPOINT—A hardware-defined breakpoint is being encountered. Used by debuggers only.

STATUS_DATATYPE_MISALIGNMENT—Reading or writing to data at an improperly aligned address.

STATUS_FLOATING_DIVIDE_BY_ZERO—Dividing floating-point type by 0.

STATUS_FLOATING_OVERFLOW—The range of the maximum exponent of a floating point is being exceeded.

STATUS_FLOATING_RESERVED_OPERAND—Using a reserved floating-point format.

STATUS_FLOATING_UNDERFLOW—The range of the lowest negative exponent of the floating point is being exceeded.

STATUS_ILLEGAL_INSTRUCTION—An instruction code that is undefined is trying to be executed.

STATUS_INTEGER_DIVIDE_BY_ZERO—Dividing integer type by 0.

STATUS_INTEGER_OVERFLOW—The range of the integer is being exceeded.

STATUS_PRIVILEGED_INSTRUCTION—An instruction not allowed in the current machine mode is trying to be executed.

STATUS_SINGLE_STEP—One instruction at a time is being executed (single-step mode). Used by debuggers only.

14

ERROR DETECTION
AND EXCEPTION
HANDLING

Most of the exceptions in the preceding list are intended to be handled by debuggers, low-level code, or the operating system itself. The only types of code you should be handling are the integer and floating-point errors. The most likely line of action for the other exceptions is to ignore the exceptions and evaluate them to zero. By not doing so, lower-level mechanisms may not respond to the exception error as they should.

Structured Exception Handling Functions

The following functions are used in SEH:

AbnormalTermination

GetExceptionCode

GetExceptionInformation

RaiseException

SetUnhandledExceptionFilter

UnhandledExceptionFilter

You'll examine these functions in the following sections.

AbnormalTermination

The AbnormalTermination function returns zero if the __try block terminated normally and nonzero if the __try block terminated abnormally. This function can be called only from within a __finally block of a termination handler.

GetExceptionCode

The GetExceptionCode function returns a code that identifies the type of exception that occurred. This function may be called only from an exception-handler block of an exception handler or from within the filter expression.

Here is a list of GetExceptionCode return values:

EXCEPTION_ACCESS_VIOLATION—The thread tried to read from or write to a virtual address that it does not have access to.

EXCEPTION_ARRAY_BOUNDS_EXCEEDED—The thread tried to access an out-of-bounds array element.

EXCEPTION_BREAKPOINT—A breakpoint occurred.

EXCEPTION_DATATYPE_MISALIGNMENT—The tread tried to read or write data on hardware that is misaligned.

EXCEPTION_FLT_DENORMAL_OPERAND—An operand in a floating-point value is too small to be represented as a standard floating-point value.

EXCEPTION_FLT_DIVIDE_BY_ZERO—The thread attempted to divide a floating-point value by a divisor of zero.

EXCEPTION_FLT_INEXACT_RESULT—The resulting floating-point operation cannot be represented exactly as a decimal fraction.

EXCEPTION_FLT_INVALID_OPERATION—Returned for every floating-point exception not met by any floating-point exceptions listed here.

EXCEPTION_FLT_OVERFLOW—The exponent of a floating-point operation is larger than allowed by the corresponding type.

EXCEPTION_FLT_STACK_CHECK—The stack underflowed or overflowed by a floating-point operation.

EXCEPTION_FLT_UNDERFLOW—The exponent of a floating-point operation is smaller than allowed by the corresponding type.

EXCEPTION_INT_DIVIDE_BY_ZERO—The thread attempted to divide an integer value by a divisor of zero.

EXCEPTION_INT_OVERFLOW—The resulting integer value was too large to store, resulting in the carry out of the most significant bit.

EXCEPTION_NONCONTINUABLE_EXCEPTION—The thread tried to continue executing after a noncontinuable exception occurred.

EXCEPTION_PRIV_INSTRUCTION—The thread tried to execute an instruction not permitted in the current machine mode.

EXCEPTION_SINGLE_STEP—A trace trap signaled that one instruction was executed.

These return values can be passed as a parameter to a filter function.

GetExceptionInformation

The GetExceptionInformation function returns a machine-independent description of an exception, as well as information about the machine state that existed for the thread when the exception occurred.

The return value is a pointer to the structure EXCEPTION_POINTERS. This structure contains pointers to two other structures: EXCEPTION_RECORD and CONTEXT. EXCEPTION_RECORD contains a description of the exception. The CONTEXT structure contains the machine-state information.

RaiseException

The RaiseException function handles private application-defined exceptions that are software-generated.

When an exception is raised, the exception dispatcher goes through the following steps:

1. If the process is being debugged, the process's debugger is notified.

2. If the process is not being debugged or the debugger cannot handle the exception, the system searches the stack frames of thread where the exception occurred for a frame-based exception handler. The current stack frame is searched first, and then the previous stack frames are searched.

3. If no frame-based handler is found, or the frame-based handler cannot handle the exception, a second attempt is made to notify the process's debugger.

4. If the debugger cannot handle the exception, or the process is not being debugged, the system provides default handling based on the exception type. The default action of most exceptions is to call the ExitProcess function.

The ExitProcess Function

The ExitProcess function terminates a process as well as all its threads. It is the preferred way of ending a processing, because it provides a clean ending of a process.

SetUnhandledExceptionFilter

The SetUnhandledExceptionFilter function allows an application to replace the top-level exception handler that Win32 places at the beginning of each process and thread.

This filter function takes a single parameter type of LPEXCEPTION_POINTERS and returns a value of type LONG. The following list describes the SetUnhandledExceptionFilter return values:

> EXCEPTION CONTINUE EXECUTION—Indicates to continue execution from the point of exception
>
> EXCEPTION CONTINUE SEARCH—Indicates to proceed with normal execution
>
> EXCEPTION_EXECUTE HANDLER—Usually indicates the termination of a process

UnhandledExceptionFilter

If the process is being debugged, the UnhandledExceptionFilter function sends unhandled exceptions to the debugger. If the process is not being debugged, the function displays an Application Error message box and executes the exception handler.

The UnhandledExceptionFilter function returns two values:

> EXCEPTION_CONTINUE_SEARCH—The exception is passed to the application's debugger.
>
> EXCEPTION_EXECUTE_HANDLER—Control is returned to the exception handler.

Remember that SEH is used mainly for C programs, not C++. Although you can use SEH for C++, the next section shows a better method.

C++ Exception Handling

C++ exception handling enables you to use an object-oriented approach to handling exception errors created by C++ classes. You should use C++ exception handling rather than structured exception handling. Remember that SEH was designed to work with C, not C++. Although you may use SEH for C++, C++ exception handling is a better alternative, resulting in more portable and flexible code.

Using C++ Exceptions

C++ exceptions deal with the relationship of an application and a class member. When the application calls the class member and an error occurs, the class member informs the application of the error. The class member has done what is known as *throwing an exception*. The application takes this exception and handles it in a block of code called the *catch block* or the *exception handler*. It is in this block of code that the error can be dealt with and the program allowed to recover from this error. Taking a few steps back, the code that originally called the class member had to be included in a *try block*. The try block makes it possible to return the exception errors to the catch block. It is a guarded body of code that signifies what code is to return exception errors if they occur. Remember that code that does not interact with the class does not have to be in a try block.

To see whether C++ exception handling is enabled in your project, open the Project Settings dialog box. Select the C/C++ tab. Set the category to C++ Language. Check the Enable Exception Handling check box. You also may use the /GX compiler option.

The C++ Exception Structure

The skeletal structure for C++ exception handling follows:

```
class AnyClass          // a class used for this example
  {
    public:
    class AnyError     // exception class
       {
       }
    void AnyClassFunction()   // member function
       {
       // Check for error.
       // If there is one, then
       throw(AnyError);
       }
  };

void main()             //application
  {
  try                   // try block
     {
       AnyClass Object;
       Object.AnyClassFunction();
     }
  catch (AnyClass::AnyError)
     {
     // perform processing on the error
     }
  }
```

14

ERROR DETECTION
AND EXCEPTION
HANDLING

If an error occurs in AnyClass, the AnyClassFunction throws an exception. When an exception occurs, the keyword throw is used, followed by the constructor class:

```
throw(AnyError);
```

Notice in the main() part of the program that any interaction with the class is guarded by the try statement:

```
try             // try block
{
  AnyClass Object;
  Object.AnyClassFunction();
}
```

If an error is detected, an error is thrown and captured in the catch block:

```
catch (AnyClass::AnyError)
{
// perform processing on the error
}
```

An Exception Example

Code for a complete working example of handling an exception follows, using try, catch, and throw keywords. The exception that will be handled is the classic divide-by-zero error that has surely crashed everyone's program at one time or another.

The program consists of two parts: the class and application. Take a look at this example:

```
//Divide by Zero example
//Demonstration of exception handling
#include <iostream.h>

class DivNumbers
{
public:
   class DivError          //Exception class
   {

   };

   DivNumbers()            //Class constructor
   {

   }

   int PerformDivide(int number1, int number2)
   {
   if (number2 == 0)      //Check if divisor is going to be zero
     throw DivError();    //If true, throw the exception error

     return number1 / number2;
```

```
    }
};

void main()
{
DivNumbers MyDivide;
int result = 0;

try
    {

    result = MyDivide.PerformDivide(10,5);
    cout << result << endl;

    result = MyDivide.PerformDivide(10,10);
    cout << result << endl;

     result = MyDivide.PerformDivide(10,0);     //Error causing code
     cout << result << endl;
     }

catch(DivNumbers::DivError)
{
    cout << "Divide by Zero Error encountered!" << endl;
}

cout << "End of Dividing Numbers." << endl;

}
```

The output follows:

```
2
1
Divide by Zero Error encountered!
End of Dividing Numbers.
```

Let's take a look at exactly what the code is doing.

First, the class `DivNumbers` is declared. The public class exception `DivError` is created:

```
class DivError         //Exception class
    {

    };
```

This class exception is empty, and that is okay. We just need the capability to throw the error at this point, so it just has to be declared. Code may be entered in this routine to gain more information about the error that has occurred.

Next, the `throw` command is inserted into the routine that performs the function that needs monitoring. In this case, it is the member function `int PerformDivide`.

```
int PerformDivide(int number1, int number2)
    {
    if (number2 == 0)     //Check if divisor is going to be zero
      throw DivError();   //If true, throw the exception error

      return number1 / number2;
    }
```

The logic in this function is simple to follow. The variable number2 will cause all the trouble, so a check is performed to see whether it equals zero. If the function ever receives a zero to divide with, the exception error is thrown with this command:

```
throw DivError();
```

The empty exception class DivError is thrown. Now our catch routine will catch this exception. Once caught, the code in our catch block will be executed:

```
catch(DivNumbers::DivError)
{
    cout << "Divide by Zero Error encountered!" << endl;
}
```

The program will print out this message, and processing will continue on, down to the last line of code.

```
cout << "End of Dividing Numbers." << endl;
```

The control of the program continues on to the bottom of the application body without crashing the program. The exception handler also may redirect the program flow to different parts of the program if there is no way to recover from the error.

Multiple Exception Handling

A class can have many exceptions—not just one, as the preceding example shows.

Divide by zero is a nice and simple exception error that every programmer can relate to, so we'll stick with this as well as an unsigned integer check (when an unsigned integer operation results in a negative value). The code will be modified just a bit to allow for different errors to be detected and captured.

```
//Multiple Exception example
//Demonstration of multiple exception handling
#include <iostream.h>

class NumberProcesses
{
public:
class DivError                 //Exception class
{
```

```
};

class DivFloatError          //Exception class
{

};

class UnsignedIntegerError   //Exception class
{

};

NumberProcesses()            //Class constructor
{
}

int PerformDivide(int number1, int number2)
{
if (number2 == 0)            //Check if divisor is going to be zero
throw DivError();            //If true, throw the exception error

return number1 / number2;
}

float PerformFloatDivide(float number1, float number2)
{
if (number2 == 0.0)          //Check if divisor is going to be zero
throw DivFloatError();       //If true, throw the exception error
return number1 / number2;
}

unsigned int PerformUnsignedSubtraction(int number1, int number2)
{
if (number1 - number2 < 0)       //Check if divisor is going to be zero
throw UnsignedIntegerError();    //If true, throw the exception error

return number1 - number2;
}


};

void main()
{
NumberProcesses MyNumbers;
int result = 0;
int unsigned_result = 0;
float float_result = 0.0;

//try block code for Integer operations
try
{
```

```
    cout << "TEST: Integer Divide by Zero" << endl;

result = MyNumbers.PerformDivide(10,5);
cout << result << endl;

result = MyNumbers.PerformDivide(10,10);
cout << result << endl;

result = MyNumbers.PerformDivide(10,0);    //Error causing code
cout << result << endl;
}

//catch for Integer must immediately follow try block
catch(NumberProcesses::DivError)
{
cout << "Integer Divide by Zero Error encountered!" << endl << endl;
}

//try block code for Float operations
try
{
cout << "TEST: Float Divide by Zero" << endl;
float_result = MyNumbers.PerformFloatDivide(10.0,5.5);
cout << float_result << endl;

float_result = MyNumbers.PerformFloatDivide(10.0,9.5);
cout << float_result << endl;

float_result = MyNumbers.PerformFloatDivide(10.0,0.0);    //Error causing code
cout << float_result << endl;
}

//catch for Float must immediately follow try block
catch(NumberProcesses::DivFloatError)
{
cout << "Float Divide by Zero Error encountered!" << endl << endl;
}

//try block code for Unsigned Integer operations
try
{
cout << "TEST: Unsigned Integer" << endl;
unsigned_result = MyNumbers.PerformUnsignedSubtraction(5,4);
cout << unsigned_result << endl;

unsigned_result = MyNumbers.PerformUnsignedSubtraction(5,5);
cout << unsigned_result << endl;

unsigned_result = MyNumbers.PerformUnsignedSubtraction(5,6);
cout << unsigned_result << endl;
}
```

```
//catch for Unsigned Integer must immediately follow try block
catch(NumberProcesses::UnsignedIntegerError)
{
cout << "Unsigned Integer Error encountered!" << endl << endl;
}
cout << "End of Processing Numbers." << endl;
}
```

The output of this program follows:

```
TEST: Integer Divide By Zero
2
1
Integer Divide By Zero Error Encountered!

Test: Float Divide By Zero
1.81818
1.05263
Float Divide By Zero Error Encountered!

Test: Unsigned Integer
1
0
Unsigned Integer Error Encountered!

End of Processing Numbers.
```

Note that the constructor used for each `try` block must immediately follow the corresponding `try` block. This example performs the same test as the preceding example—dividing integers by zero. Then a similar test is performed for floating-point numbers. Finally, the exception error for checking whether an unsigned integer function results in a negative number occurs. Three separate exception classes are created and called by three separate `throw` statements.

Using Arguments with Exceptions

At times, you may need the exception error to return specific information on what caused the exception error, such as which function called the class member to cause the exception. Other such information may involve displaying the values passed to the class member, or possibly a combination of both. This section covers a method to pass such information to make the exception messages more flexible and informative. You can accomplish this by using arguments with exceptions.

The following program example focuses on the unsigned integer exception. Now whenever an exception is thrown, the function name that caused the exception to be thrown is indicated.

```
//Multiple Exception example
//Demonstration of multiple exception handling
#include <iostream.h>
```

```cpp
#include <string.h>

class NumberProcesses
{
public:


class UnsignedIntegerError              //Exception class
{
public:
    char calling_function[80];        //String to hold function name
    int result_value1;                //First number used for subtraction
    int result_value2;                //Second number used for subtraction
        UnsignedIntegerError(char* function_name, int number1, int number2)
        {
         strcpy(calling_function, function_name);  //Assignments
         result_value1 = number1;
         result_value2 = number2;
        };

NumberProcesses()                      //Class constructor
{
}

unsigned int PerformUnsignedSubtraction(int number1, int number2)
{
if (number1 - number2 < 0)     //Check if divisor is going to be zero
    throw UnsignedIntegerError("PerformUnsignedSubtraction", number1, number2);
//If true, throw the exception error

return number1 - number2;
}

};

void main()
{
NumberProcesses MyNumbers;
int unsigned_result = 0;


//try block code for Unsigned Integer operations
try
{
cout << "TEST: Unsigned Integer" << endl;
unsigned_result = MyNumbers.PerformUnsignedSubtraction(5,4);
cout << unsigned_result << endl;

unsigned_result = MyNumbers.PerformUnsignedSubtraction(5,5);
cout << unsigned_result << endl;
```

```
unsigned_result = MyNumbers.PerformUnsignedSubtraction(5,6);
cout << unsigned_result << endl;
}

//catch for Unsigned Integer must immediately follow try block
catch(NumberProcesses::UnsignedIntegerError ExceptionObject)
➡// Declare object ExceptionObject
{
cout << endl << "Unsigned Integer Error encountered!" << endl << endl;
cout << "Function: " << ExceptionObject.calling_function << endl;
cout << "Trying to subtract the following numbers:" << endl;
    cout << ExceptionObject.result_value1 << " - "
➡<< ExceptionObject.result_value2 << endl;
cout << "Result must always be positive for this function." << endl << endl;
}
cout << "End of Processing Numbers." << endl;
}
```

The output of this program looks like this:

```
TEST: Unsigned Integer
1
0

Unsigned Integer Error Occurred!

Function: PerformUnsignedSubtraction
Trying to subtract the following numbers:
5 - 6
Result must always be positive for this function.

End of Processing Numbers.
```

Let's take a look at how the exception class looks for `UnsignedIntegerError`:

```
class UnsignedIntegerError               //Exception class
{
public:
    char calling_function[80];        //String to hold function name
    int result_value1;                //First number used for subtraction
    int result_value2;                //Second number used for subtraction
        UnsignedIntegerError(char* function_name, int number1, int number2)
        {
         strcpy(calling_function, function_name);   //Assignments
         result_value1 = number1;
         result_value2 = number2;
        };

};
```

Essentially the exception class now has public variables defined. These variables will hold the data you want to report to the user. Declared here is a string variable to hold the name of the function that caused the error. The other two variables will hold the values being sent to the operation.

The throw statement now looks like this:

```
throw UnsignedIntegerError("PerformUnsignedSubtraction", number1, number2);
```

It has been expanded to pass all three values to the exception class. Note that the first parameter is the name of the function with the throw statement. (Of course, this string can hold any value you want, but it pays to be informative.)

The final step is to obtain the information on what the exception has caught. The catch statement looks like this:

```
catch(NumberProcesses::UnsignedIntegerError ExceptionObject)
➥// Declare object ExceptionObject
{
cout << endl << "Unsigned Integer Error encountered!" << endl << endl;
cout << "Function: " << ExceptionObject.calling_function << endl;
cout << "Trying to subtract the following numbers:" << endl;
    cout << ExceptionObject.result_value1 << " - "
➥<< ExceptionObject.result_value2 << endl;
cout << "Result must always be positive for this function." << endl << endl;
}
```

This statement has evolved into something a little more involved. The first statement declares an exception object (appropriately titled ExceptionObject):

```
catch(NumberProcesses::UnsignedIntegerError ExceptionObject)   // Declare object
```

This makes it simple to reference the values that reside in the exception. Just remember that this method is totally customizable, and using arguments with exceptions is a very powerful tool.

Exception-Handling Overhead

There is cost of performance and size using the C++ exception handling mechanism. It may increase the size of the resulting executable and slow down the run speed of the program. This is one of the reasons why exceptions should be used only to signal unusual or show-stopping program events. They should be used only where necessary. Sometimes displaying an error message to the user may be enough, instead of throwing an exception.

The /GX compiler option enables C++ exception handling. You can turn off exception handling by using the /GX- option.

MFC Error and Exception Handling

This section introduces the exception-handling mechanisms available in MFC. The two available mechanisms are

- C++ exceptions (available only in MFC 3.0 or later)
- MFC exception macros (available in MFC 1.0 and later)

MFC exception macros should be used only if they already reside in existing code. Better yet, when dealing with an older program using MFC exception macros, use C++ exceptions along with the macros.

MFC Exception Macros

MFC versions lower than 3.0 did not support the C++ exception mechanism. MFC provided macros to deal with exceptions. The macros are TRY, CATCH, and THROW. In contrast, the C++ exception keyword equivalents are try, catch, and throw.

Here is a list of the MFC exception macros:

```
AND_CATCH
AND_CATCH_ALL
CATCH
CATCH_ALL
END_CATCH
END_CATCH_ALL
THROW
THROW_LAST
TRY
```

THROW

This macro throws the exception to the CATCH block. The program execution is interrupted. If a CATCH block is specified, program control goes to the CATCH block. If not, control is passed to an MFC library module to print an error message and exit.

THROW_LAST

This macro throws a locally created exception. The macro sends the exception back to the next CATCH block. Usually when an exception that was just caught is thrown, it goes out of scope, thus being deleted. THROW_LAST passes the exception correct to the next CATCH handler.

TRY

You use this macro to set up a TRY block, which signifies the block of code where the throwing of exceptions occurs. The exceptions are processed in the CATCH and AND_CATCH blocks. The TRY block is ended with an END_CATCH or END_CATCH_ALL macro.

CATCH

This macro defines a block of code that catches the first exception thrown by a preceding TRY block. The TRY block should end with END_CATCH.

AND_CATCH

You use this macro to catch additional exceptional types thrown from a preceding TRY block. Use the CATCH macro to catch the first exception type, and then use AND_CATCH for every other exception type. The TRY block should end with END_CATCH.

AND_CATCH_ALL

This macro catches additional exception types thrown by a preceding TRY block. Use the CATCH macro to catch the first exception type, and then use AND_CATCH_ALL for all other exception types. The TRY block should end with END_CATCH_ALL.

END_CATCH

This macro signifies the end of the last CATCH or AND_CATCH block.

END_CATCH_ALL

Signifies the end of the last CATCH_ALL or AND_CATCH_ALL block.

Here are some possible program skeletons using these macros:

```
TRY
    {

    }
    CATCH()
    {

    }
    AND_CATCH()
    {

    }
    END_CATCH
```

and

```
TRY
```

```
{

}
CATCH_ALL()
{

    THROW_LAST();
}
END_CATCH_ALL
```

This should give you an idea of how these macros go together.

Here is a list of MFC exception-throwing functions:

>   AfxThrowArchiveException
>
>   AfxThrowFileException
>
>   AfxThrowMemoryException
>
>   AfxThrowNotSupportedException
>
>   AfxThrowResourceException
>
>   AfxThrowUserException

These functions are explained in the following sections.

AfxThrowArchiveException

This function throws an archive exception by specifying an integer that indicates the reason for the exception stored in its m_cause member. Here are the enumerators that can be returned:

> CArchiveException::badClass—Tried to read an object into an object of the wrong type.
>
> CArchiveException::badIndex—File format is invalid.
>
> CArchiveException::badSchema—Tried to read an object with a different version of the class.
>
> CArchiveException::endOfFile—The end of the file was reached.
>
> CArchiveException::generic—Error unspecified.
>
> CArchiveException::none—No error occurred.
>
> CArchiveException::readOnly—Tried to write to an archive opened for reading.
>
> CArchiveException::writeOnly—Tried to write to an archive opened for reading.

14

ERROR DETECTION
AND EXCEPTION
HANDLING

AfxThrowFileException

This function throws a file exception by specifying an integer that indicates the reason for the exception. The developer is responsible for determining the cause of the error based on the operating-system error code. Here are the possible enumerators that can be returned:

CFileException::accessDenied—Access to the specified file is denied.

CFileException::badPath—The path is invalid.

CFileException::badSeek—An error occurred while trying to set the file pointer.

CFileException::directoryFull—There are no more directory entries.

CFileException::diskFull—The disk is full.

CFileException::endOfFile—The end-of-file was reached.

CFileException::fileNotFound—The file was not found where specified.

CFileException::generic—Error unspecified.

CFileException::hardIO—A hardware error occurred.

CFileException::invalidFile—The file handle is invalid.

CFileException::lockViolation—A locked region is trying to be locked again.

CFileException::none—No error occurred.

CFileException::removeCurrentDir—The current directory could not be removed.

CFileException::sharingViolation—A shared region is locked, or the program SHARE.EXE is not loaded.

CFileException::tooManyOpenFiles—The number of files currently open is too many.

AfxThrowMemoryException

This function throws a memory exception. This function should be called when using memory allocators, such as GlobalAlloc and malloc functions.

AfxThrowNotSupportedException

This function throws an exception when an unsupported feature is requested.

AfxThrowResource

This function throws a resource exception.

AfxThrowResourceException

This function throws a resource exception when an unsupported feature is requested.

AfxThrowUserException

This function throws an exception to stop an end-user operation. `AfxMessageBox` normally calls this function after it reports an error to the user. The MFC OLE exception functions follow:

```
AfxThrowOleDispatchException
AfxThrowOleException
```

AfxThrowOleDispatchException

This function throws an exception within an OLE automation.

AfxThrowOleException

This function throws an exception and creates an object of type `COleException`. The MFC termination function is `AfxAbort`.

AfxAbort

This function is called internally by the MFC member function when a fatal error occurs. This is the default termination for MFC. `AfxAbort` usually is called by MFC when an exception occurs that cannot be handled. `AfxAbort` can be called by the developer when an error is encountered that makes recovery impossible.

Using MFC Exception Macros with C ++ Exception Handling

You can use MFC exception macros and C++ exception keywords in the same program. Again, it is advisable to do this only when MFC exception macros already exist in the program. Always use C++ exception handling to handle exceptions.

Note, however, that you cannot use MFC macros together with C++ exception keywords in the same block. The reason is that the macros automatically delete exception objects when their scope is lost. Caught C++ exception keywords in a `catch` block have to be explicitly deleted. When MFC macros and C++ exception keywords are mixed, memory leaks can arise if an exception object is not deleted; or, when an exception is deleted twice.

14

ERROR DETECTION
AND EXCEPTION
HANDLING

The Advantages of Converting from MFC Exception Macros

It is almost never necessary to convert from MFC exception macros, because they are compatible with even the latest version of MFC. In fact, MFC macros can coincide with C++ exception handling, but there are advantages to converting.

One advantage is that the code that uses C++ exception handling compiles slightly smaller EXEs and COMs. Another reason to convert is that C++ exception-handling keywords are much more versatile: They can handle exceptions of all data types (that can be copied). The macros can handle only exceptions of the class CException and classes derived from it.

With C++ exception handling, the caught exception is deleted only by explicit instruction. Macros delete the caught exception when the exception goes out of scope.

Converting Code from MFC Macros to C++ Exception Handling

Perform the following steps to convert code from macros to C++ exception keywords:

1. Find every occurrence of the MFC macros THROW, THROW_LAST, TRY, CATCH, AND_CATCH, and END_CATCH.
2. Replace each THROW with throw.
3. Replace each THROW_LAST with throw.
4. Replace each TRY with try.
5. Replace each CATCH with catch.
6. Replace each AND_CATCH with catch.
7. Delete each END_CATCH.
8. Modify each macro argument so that it forms a valid C++ exception declaration.
9. Modify each catch block so that it deletes exception objects where necessary.

Not too difficult, really. The only step that may require more explanation is number 8. Consider this example:

```
CATCH( CException, e )
```

to

```
catch( CException* e )
```

Predefined Exceptions for MFC

Here is a list of predefined exceptions to use the MFC. Each of these exceptions is derived from the base class CException. You can use these with C++ exceptions directly or with the MFC exception macros.

CArchiveException—A serialization exception condition. These are constructed and thrown from inside CArchive member functions.

CDAOException—An exception condition from the MFC database classes based on *data access objects (DAOs)*.

CDBException—An exception condition coming from the database classes.

CFileException—A file-related exception condition. These objects are constructed and thrown in CFile member functions and in member functions of derived classes.

CInternetException—An exception condition coming from the Internet classes.

CMemoryException—A memory exception that signifies an out-of-memory condition. Memory exceptions are thrown new.

CNotSupportedException—An exception that results from a request of a feature not supported.

COleDispatchException—Handles exceptions specific to the OLE IDispatch interface.

COleException—An exception condition from an OLE operation.

CResourceException—Generated when a resource cannot be found or allocated.

CUserException—Thrown to stop an end-user operation in the same manner as covered in the earlier section on C++ exception handling, using the throw/catch exception mechanism.

Using **CFileException**

For a quick introduction, take a look at the following code fragment, which uses CFileException:

```
//Try Block
try
{
  CFile fileNotOpen
    fileNotOpen.SeekToBegin();
}
catch(CFileException* e)  //Catch the file exceptions
{
 if (e->m_cause == CFileException::fileNotFound)
    AfxMessageBox("The File has not been opened.");
 e->Delete();
}
```

The try block guards the code to perform file operations. When a CException is raised, the catch block will catch the thrown exception and create the exception class object e. Note that this is very similar to C++ exception examples in the earlier section. Object e now points to any exception that was created. If this exception is equal to fileNotFound, a message appears telling the user that The File has not been opened. The final statement deletes the exception class object.

It is important to delete the exception class objects when you are finished with them. Unlike C++ exception handling, this is not taken care of automatically.

There are a few cause codes besides CFileException:

CFileException::accessDenied

CFileException::badpath

CFileException::badseek

CFileException::directoryFull

CFileException::diskFull

CFileException::endOfFile

CFileException::fileNotFound

CFileException::generic

CFileException::hardIO

CFileException::invalidFile

CFileException::lockViolation

CFileException::none

CFileException::removeCurrentDir

CFileException::sharingViolation

CFileException::tooManyOpenFiles

You can trigger this exception by calling the AfxThrowFileException() function. The function can take three parameters: The first one is required, and the other two are optional.

The first parameter, `cause`, is a cause code for the exception (listed earlier). It is this code that is placed in the m_cause member in the `catch` group.

The second parameter, `lOsError`, is used to specify an operating system error code. The third parameter is `strFileName`. It gets placed in the m_strFileName member string variable and holds the filename of the file that was being accessed when the error occurred.

Using CMemoryException

The `CMemoryException` exception is raised when the program simply can no longer allocate any more memory. Recovering from such an error is difficult and unlikely. The memory allocation functions C++ uses will trigger this exception.

This exception can be triggered by calling this function:

```
AfxThrowMemoryException()
```

Using CResourceCollection

The `CResourceCollection` exception is raised when the application can't allocate or find the requested system resources.

This exception can be triggered by calling the `AfxThrowResourceException()` function.

Using CArchiveException

The `CArchiveException` object represents a serialization exception condition. The class includes a public data member that contains the cause of the exception.

The m_cause member of the `CArchiveException` class holds the archive-specific cause codes, as listed here:

> `CArchiveException::badClass`
>
> `CArchiveException::badIndex`
>
> `CArchiveException::badSchema`
>
> `CArchiveException::endOfFile`
>
> `CArchiveException::generic`
>
> `CArchiveException::none`
>
> `CArchiveException::readOnly`
>
> `CArchiveException::writeOnly`

Using CDaoException

The `CDaoException` is used for DAO-based database access.

You can throw this exception by calling the AfxThrowDaoexception() function. This function has two optional parameters: nAfxDaoError and an OLE scode value. The nAfxDaoError is a DAO error code specific to DAO. The errors it returns are always specific to the DAO itself. The OLE scode value comes from a DAO-based OLE call.

The nAfxDaoError codes can be any from the following list:

```
AFX_DAO_ERROR_DFX_BIND

AFX_DAO_ERROR_ENGINE_INITIALIZATION

AFX_DAO_ERROR_OBJECT_NOT_OPEN

NO_AFX_DAO_ERROR
```

Using OLE Exceptions: COleException and COleDispatchException

There are two OLE exception errors: COleException and COleDispatchException.

The COleException error normally is used for server-side or OLE-specific operations. You can trigger this exception by calling the AfxThrowOleException() function, passing an OLE scode value. This value then is stored in the m_sc member of the exception.

The COleDispatchException class is used in conjunction with OLE IDISPATCH interfaces and is thrown by the AfxThrowOleDispatchException() function. There are two forms to this function.

The first form has three parameters—the first two required, the last one optional. The first parameter is a wCodeWORD value that is an application-specific error code. The second parameter is an lpszDescription string pointer to represent the verbal string for describing the error. The last parameter is a help context ID.

The second form has three parameters as well. The first parameter is a wCodeWORD value that is an application-specific error code. The second parameter is nDescriptionID for a UINT resource code, which represents a verbal string describing the error. The last parameter is a help context ID.

Both forms are nearly identical—the difference is the second parameter.

Using NotSupportedException

The CNotSupportedException object is generated when a request is made for an unsupported feature. You can trigger this exception by calling the AfxThrowNotSupportedException() function.

Using `CUserException`

You use the `CUserException` class to generate exception objects for application-specific applications.

You can trigger this exception by calling the `AfxThrowNotSupportedException()` function.

Summary

In this chapter, you examined structured exception handling. You saw what exceptions are and how to handle them so that they will not force your program to come to a crashing halt. You also learned the difference between hardware exceptions and software exceptions.

Although you learned that SEH is not really intended to be used with C++ but with C, the SEH concepts carry over to what you can use with C++: C++ exception handling.

You saw how to use C++ exception handling to deal with the relationship of an application and a class member. You learned about throwing an exception and catching one.

You also looked at how to guard your code with `try` and then how to call exception code in the `catch` block after the exception is thrown. Using these keywords, you were able to recover sample programs from exception errors.

After checking out a few examples, you looked at the capabilities of multiple exception handling—how the same class can handle more than one exception. You then looked at using arguments with exceptions. You created an example that passes arguments to the class member so that the exception error can return specific information, such as the function name that caused the error and what values contributed to the exception.

You also looked at MFC error and exception handling. You briefly examined MFC macros. MFC macros were the original way to handle exception errors in early MFC versions. For MFC 3.0 and later, you can use the C++ exception mechanism.

Although all later versions of MFC support macros, it is recommended to use the C++ exception mechanism, and to use macros only to support older programs that previously used them.

Finally, you learned about MFC exception handling, which is C++ exception handling with the MFC predefined exceptions. You were briefly introduced to each predefined exception, and you explored how to generate custom exception classes.

14

**ERROR DETECTION
AND EXCEPTION
HANDLING**

CHAPTER 15

Debugging and Profiling Strategies

by Andrew J. Indovina

In this chapter, you will look at debugging and profiling strategies. Debugging C++ applications can be a very involved process and much more complicated than fixing an incorrect variable assignment.

C++ provides powerful tools to assist in detecting, reporting, and correcting errors.

First, you'll explore the techniques for debugging an MFC application. You'll check out the TRACER utility and touch base with the older error-checking tools—the MFC macros.

Next, you'll look at using the DevStudio *Integrated Development Environment* (*IDE*) debugger. You'll explore some of the features, such as stepping through code while the program is running, one line at a time. You will see how to set breakpoints and step into and over instructions.

You'll learn to use the various view windows, to view variable contents, and to change their values on-the-fly to check for results.

You'll also see how to use the Source Browser tool to inspect code in great detail.

Beyond that, the Dr. Watson log files are briefly discussed. You'll explore the nature of these logs, how to prepare your machine to generate the logs, and what information the logs provide.

Also, you will take a look at the concept of attaching to running processes for debug purposes.

Finally, you will briefly examine profiling and using the profiling tools for code analysis. With these tools, you will be able to determine which areas of code are working efficiently and which ones are hurting the performance of your program. You will learn about PREP, PROFILE, and PLIST. You will see how to run the profiling application from the IDE, as well as from the more advantageous command line.

We will just scratch the surface for most of these applications and tools, because most of them are very powerful and are beyond the scope of this book. Entire books are dedicated to debugging applications.

The purpose of this chapter is to introduce you to what is available and to give you enough information to implement some of the techniques that are covered.

MFC Support for Debugging

You can debug the *Microsoft Foundation Class* (*MFC*) Library applications in a variety of ways. Some of the features MFC contains to help diagnose program problems are the

ASSERT and TRACE macros, the AssertValid and Dump member functions, the CMemoryState class (used to detect memory leaks) and the AfxEnableMemoryTracking and AfxDebugBreak global functions.

When developing your C++ programs, you probably have noticed that you can choose between building a Win32 debug version of the program or a Win32 release. Generally, when you are developing a program involving MFC, you want to detect bugs throughout development, build a Win32 debug version, and link it with the debug version of MFC. When the program is complete and bug-free, a Win32 release version is built and linked with the release version of MFC.

Techniques for Debugging Your MFC Application

Make sure the debugger is positioned onscreen so that it doesn't overlap the program. Otherwise, the debugger might obscure the program being debugged.

From the TRACER application, select the Multiple Application Debugging option when debugging an application and one or more DLLs. This way, the name of the application that generated the error will appear in a prefix.

The Multiple Application Debugger option also is useful in tracking the order of events.

Remember that you can hard code breakpoints into the application by using the following statement:

```
DebugBreak();
```

Or, you can use this statement, which is more appropriate for MFC applications:

```
AfxDebugBreak();
```

Just be sure to remove these statements when building the Win32 release version.

AfxDump

AfxDump is a pointer to an object derived from the CObject class. You should call this function while in the debugger. Doing so dumps the state of an object while debugging. AfxDump should not be called directly by the program. The program should call the Dump member function of the appropriate object instead.

AfxDump is available in the debug version of MFC only.

The `TRACER.EXE` Utility

Included on the Tools menu of Developer Studio is the MFC Tracer application. From this window, you can enable or disable several sorts of trace messages, as well as disable tracing altogether. Note that trace output is available only while using the debugger.

You can set the following options with `TRACER`:

- Database Tracing
- Enable Tracing
- Internet Client Tracing
- Main Message Dispatch
- Main Message Pump
- Multiple Application Debugging
- OLE Tracing
- `WM_COMMAND` Dispatch

MFC Diagnostic Features

Many diagnostic features are included with the debug version of the MFC Library. All the features in the following list are included in all the classes derived from `CObject`. Remember that before you can use any of the MFC diagnostic features, you must enable diagnostic tracing by setting the `afxTraceEnabled` flag, and the `afxTraceFlags` must have a set level of detail. The simplest way to set these flags is to use the `TRACER.EXE` utility.

Trace Output—You can trace debugging output to evaluate argument validity. See the next section, "The `TRACE` Macro," for more information.

Check Program Assumptions—Use the `ASSERT` macro to check program assumptions. See the section "The `ASSERT` Macro," later in this chapter, for more information.

`ASSERT_VALID` Macro—You can perform a runtime check of an object's internal consistency. See the section "The `ASSERT_VALID` Macro," later in this chapter, for more information.

Track Memory Allocations—Use the `DEBUG_NEW` macro to show where objects were allocated. This topic is covered later in this chapter.

Detect Memory Leaks—You can use memory diagnostics to detect memory leaks. This topic is covered later in this chapter.

Use Object Dumps—You can use the `Dump` member function to dump object contents.

The TRACE Macro

The TRACE macro is active only in the debug version of MFC. You can build a release version of the program to deactivate all TRACE calls in the program.

The TRACE macro can handle a wide range of arguments and works similarly to `printf`. The following block of code demonstrates the TRACE macro:

```
// example for TRACE
int integer1 = 1;
char characters[] = "two";
float float1 = 3.3;

TRACE( "Integer = %d\n",integer1);
TRACE( "String = %s", characters);
TRACE( "Float = %f\n", float1);

// The Output would be:
// 'Integer = 1'
// 'String = two'
// 'Float = 3.3'
```

The TRACE macro is limited to sending up to 512 characters at one time. If this limit is exceeded, it causes an ASSERT.

Other TRACE Macros

Another group of TRACE macros is available. These macros are very useful when debugging Unicode, because the _T macro is not required.

Here are the additional TRACE macros:

TRACE0	Takes a format string (only) and can be used for simple text messages that are dumped to afxDump
TRACE1	Takes a format string and one argument (one variable, which is dumped to afxDump)
TRACE2	Takes a format string and two arguments (two variables, which are dumped to afxDump)
TRACE3	Takes a format string and three arguments (three variables, which are dumped to afxDump)

The ASSERT Macro

You use the ASSERT macro to check assumptions made by the functions in the program. The most common use of the ASSERT macro is to locate program errors during development.

15

DEBUGGING AND
PROFILING
STRATEGIES

The ASSERT macro catches errors only when using the debug version of MFC. It automatically is turned off and produces no code when the program is rebuilt with the release version of MFC.

This example shows how you can use the ASSERT clause:

```
int FunctionResult = AnyFunction(x);
ASSERT (FunctionResult < 0);
```

If the argument expression is false (0), the program is halted and the developer is alerted. Nothing happens if the argument is true (not zero).

If the argument is false, a message box appears with the following text:

```
assertion failed in file <name> in line <num>
Abort Retry Ignore
```

where <name> is the name of the source file and <num> is the line number of the assertion that failed.

Choosing Abort terminates program execution. Choosing Ignore continues the program. Choosing Retry breaks into the debugger. Neither Abort nor Ignore activates a debugger.

The ASSERT_VALID Macro

You use the ASSERT_VALID macro to test the validity of an object's internal state. ASSERT_VALID calls the AssertValid member function of the object passed as its argument.

The macro validates the pointer of the object, checks it against NULL, and calls the object's own AssertValid member functions. An alert message is displayed similar to ASSERT if any of the tests fail.

This function is available only in the debug version of MFC.

Using DEBUG_NEW to Track Memory Allocation

To assist you in keeping track of memory being allocated, the macro DEBUG_NEW is supplied with the debug version of MFC. You can use DEBUG_NEW anywhere in the code where you normally would use the new operator.

When a debug version of a program is compiled, the DEBUG_NEW macro keeps track of the filename and line number for every object it allocates. Then, when the object is dumped by DumpAllObjectsSince, each object allocated with DEBUG_NEW shows the file and line number and where it was allocated. This makes it simple to pinpoint the sources of memory leaks.

When the release version of the program is compiled, all DEBUG_NEW statements are transformed into a new operation.

First, define the macro in the source files that will have new replaced with DEBUG_NEW, as shown here:

```
#define new DEBUG_NEW
```

Now new can be used for all heap allocations. The preprocessor will substitute DEBUG_NEW when the code is compiled. In the Win32 debug version, DEBUG_NEW will create debugging information for each heap block. When the code is built with the release version, DEBUG_NEW will be replaced with a standard memory allocation (most likely, new).

Detecting Memory Leaks

Memory leaks can occur when accidentally using memory that already has been allocated, or when memory is allocated on the heap and never deallocated for reuse. Programs that run for lengths of time can really compound any of the problems mentioned earlier.

In the past, memory leaks were difficult to detect. MFC comes to the rescue by providing classes and functions you can use to detect memory leaks at the development stage. Essentially, these classes and functions take a snapshot of all memory blocks before and after a set of chosen operations. By comparing the results, it is easy to see whether all the allocated memory has been deallocated.

The set of operations can range from a single line of code to an entire program.

Using the DevStudio IDE Debugger

Before you begin to debug your program, remember that there are two main compiler configurations: Debug and Release mode. You can see the modes in the upper-left corner of the Project Settings dialog box (Alt+F7), and you can toggle between the modes there.

You can select from three choices after clicking the 'Settings For' drop-down box: Win32 Release, Win32 Debug, and All Configurations. The choice selected in this box when the program is built determines the mode in which it is built. Building the project with All Configurations selected builds both a Win32 release and a Win32 debug version.

Both the debug and release configurations are supplied whenever a new project is created. You can debug code only in Debug mode.

15

DEBUGGING AND
PROFILING
STRATEGIES

Compiler Warning Levels

On the C++ tab of the Project Settings dialog box, a Warning Level drop-down box offers various levels of warnings:

NONE	No warnings
Level 1	Returns only the most severe warnings
Level 2	Returns less-severe warnings but ignores the most common ones
Level 3	Returns most general warnings (default setting)
Level 4	Extremely sensitive; returns the most warnings

Debug Info Settings

The Debug Info settings follow:

NONE	No debugging data is generated; used mainly for Release modes
Line Numbers Only	Creates line numbers to reference functions and global variables
C7 Compatible	Produces debugging information compatible with Microsoft C 7.0
Program Database	Creates a file with a `.pdb` extension that holds the maximum level of debugging information
Program Database for	Generates a `.pdb` file with the maximum
Edit and Continue	level of debugging information that can be used with the Edit and Continue feature

Using the Source Browser Tool

The Source Browser tool is an excellent tool for inspecting source code in great detail. You must enable the Generate Browse Info setting to use this tool. The check box is located in the Project Settings dialog box (Alt+F7), on the C++ tab, below the Optimizations drop-down box. The first time this runs for a project, it pops up a message box saying

```
Browse information is not available for this project. Do you want your build
settings altered (if necessary) and your project rebuilt to generate browse
information?
```

Click Yes to continue.

After you confirm that you want the build settings altered, the Browse dialog box appears. Here, you can enter an identifier for it to browse for. The identifier can be one of the following:

- Class name
- Function name
- Global variable
- Local variable
- Structure name

The Select Query box shows the options for displaying information about the identifier:

- **Definitions and References**—Selecting this option displays in the Source Browser all the files that reference the identifier. It specifies for which file the identifier is defined and for which files it is used.

  Line numbers are displayed beside each filename in each file. You can select the lines by double-clicking the entry to load the code into the Developer Studio Editor.

- **File Outline**—Displays in the Source Browser all classes, data, functions, and macros that are defined by a file identifier.

- **Base Classes and Members**—Returns the full hierarchy of the classes. Each variable and member function is displayed for each found class. The identifier entered should be a class.

- **Derived Classes and Members**—Shows all derived classes from a class identifier.

- **Call Graph**—Displays all the functions that are called by the identifier.

- **Callers Graph**—Returns all functions that call the identifier.

Breakpoints and Single-Stepping

Using breakpoints is an excellent method of debugging. Combined with *single-stepping* (stepping through the code one line at a time), this method is very effective at pinpointing exactly where a problem occurs.

You can set a breakpoint at any line of code in the program. After the program is started, it stops at the line of code that has the breakpoint and does not execute it unless you single step forward or continue running the program.

To add a breakpoint, select the line of code in which you want the breakpoint to appear. Then press F9, or click the hand icon on the Build minibar. A red dot appears next to the selected line of code. To remove a breakpoint, press F9 or click the hand while your cursor is positioned in the line of code.

15

DEBUGGING AND
PROFILING
STRATEGIES

A more involved way to add breakpoints is to select the Breakpoints option from the Edit menu. A Breakpoints dialog box appears, showing all current breakpoints that exist in the code. This box gives you the option to remove all breakpoints.

You can have multiple breakpoints throughout your program.

When the program is stopped at a breakpoint, you can view the contents of any variables by moving the mouse pointer over the variable text. Dragging any variable into the Watch window reveals more information on the variable.

A few options are available for traversing the program after it has stopped. The following sections examine these options.

Apply Code Changes

If program changes were made while debugging the program, this option allows the code to be recompiled. The shortcut key is Alt+F10. This is a new feature in Visual C++ 6.0.

Break Execution

Stops the program from running.

Go

Continues on with running the program after the program has been stopped by a breakpoint. The shortcut key is F5.

Restart

The program is restarted to the very beginning. The cursor stops at the first line of code to be executed. The shortcut key is Ctrl+Shift+F5.

Run to Cursor

Continues on with running the program and stops at the cursor position. The cursor position becomes a breakpoint when this program is run. The shortcut key is Ctrl+F10.

Step Into

The current line will be executed. The cursor can be followed inside function call one step at a time. The shortcut key is F11.

Step Over

The current line will be executed. If the cursor encounters a function call, it runs the function call at normal speed and returns the cursor to the position after the function. The shortcut key is F10.

Step Out

The program will run the function in which the cursor currently resides at normal speed. The program will stop again when it returns from the function. The shortcut key is Shift+F11.

Stop Debugging

Stops the debugger. The shortcut key is Shift+F5.

Debugger Windows

The DevStudio IDE comes with quite a few useful windows to assist in debugging. A few of the important ones are covered here.

Variables Window

The Variables window provides a quick-and-easy view to variables involved in the debugged program.

There are three window tabs:

- **Auto**—Displays variables on the current line of code and the previous statement. Also displays return values from functions.
- **Locals**—Displays the local variables of the function that currently is being debugged.
- **This**—Displays the object pointed to by this. The routine currently at the clientside debugger is the this object.

A Context box also exists in the Variables window. This box enables you to select a context to specify the scope of the variables being displayed. A drop-down list displays the current call stack.

Although you can expand and collapse the variables display, you cannot add variables to this box (unlike the Watch window).

A powerful feature of the Context box is that it enables you to enter new values into any local variable that is not a constant. With this capability, you can perform on-the-fly value testing, as well as fix a value that crashed the program.

To modify the value of a local variable, do the following:

1. Select the Auto tab or Locals tab in the Variables window.
2. Choose the line of code containing the local variable that needs to be changed.
3. Double-click the value, or move to the insertion point with the Tab key.
4. Enter the new value and press Return.

Note that string variables cannot be lengthened and must be changed one character at a time.

Watch Window

You can use the Watch window to specify local or global variables that are to be monitored while the program is being debugged. The Watch window, like the Variables window, can change the values of local variables.

The Watch window contains four tabs: Watch1, Watch2, Watch3, and Watch4. Each tab can display a specified list of variables.

To add a variable to the Watch window, follow these steps:

1. Open the Watch window through the View menu.
2. Select a tab for the variable.
3. Enter the variable name into the Name column on the tab.
4. Press Return.

To view type information for a variable, right-click on a selected variable in the Watch window and choose Properties. Or, choose Properties from the View menu.

To remove a variable from the Watch window, do the following:

1. Select the line with the variable you want to remove.
2. Press the Delete key.

To modify the value of a variable, double-click the value in the Watch window. Or, you can tab down to the value and press Return. You cannot modify date/time, image, or text data types.

QuickWatch Window

You use the QuickWatch window to quickly find the values of SQL variables and parameters. You also can use the QuickWatch window to add a variable to the Watch window or to modify the value of a local variable. The same restrictions apply for changing values that apply for the Watch window.

Registers Window

The Registers window displays the contents of the CPU Registers, floating-point stack, and flags. You can use the Registers window to add Registers to the Watch window. You also can change Register and flag values during a debug session.

To view the value in a Register, open the Registers window. Any Register values that have changed recently appear in red.

To change the value of a Register, select the Register value you want to change and type the new value followed by Return.

Table 15.1 lists the Register flags and the set values for Intelx86 processors.

TABLE 15.1   Register Window Flags

Flag	*Set*
Overflow	O = 1
Direction	D = 1
Interrupt	I = 1
Sign	S = 1
Zero	Z = 1
Auxiliary carry	A = 1
Parity	P = 1
Carry	C = 1

Call Stack Window

The Call Stack window displays the stack of function calls that are still active. Whenever a function is called, it is pushed onto the stack. Whenever a function returns, it is popped off the stack.

The top of the Call Stack window displays the current function being executed; the bottom of the window displays previous function calls. The window also displays the parameter types and values for each function call.

Disassembly Window

The Disassembly window displays code instructions in disassembled form. You can set the breakpoint on any instruction and step through the code just like regular code.

The Disassembly window is extremely useful for stepping through code that contains multiple instructions separated by semicolons—for example,

```
a = 1; b = 2, c = 3;
```

The regular debugger treats this line of code as one step through the code. The Disassembly window treats the line one instruction at a time. Stepping through and viewing code one instruction at a time is very beneficial when dealing with optimized code.

15

DEBUGGING AND PROFILING STRATEGIES

Memory Window

You use the Memory window to view large amounts of data that are not fully displayed in the Watch and Variables windows. Such data includes buffers, large strings, and other large data objects.

Note that the default is to display numbers in decimal format.

Using Spy++

Spy++ is a Win32-based utility that gives a graphical view of the system's processes, threads, windows, and window messages. You can view the parent-child window relationships, as well as the flag settings and window positions.

Spy++ is a read-only program, which means that Spy++ does not change how the program runs or behaves, other than slowing down execution.

Spy++ has four views; these are discussed in the following sections.

Tree View

The Tree view displays a tree of all windows and controls in the system. One of the tools of this view is the Window Finder tool. You can use this tool to locate disabled child windows and discern which window to highlight if there are many child windows that overlap each other.

Within Tree view, you can locate a specific window, given the handle, caption, class, or a combination of the caption and class. You also can specify the direction of the search. If a window is found, it is highlighted in the Windows view.

Messages View

The Messages view views the message stream associated with each window. Message views also can capture messages from a thread or process. This view is helpful when you want to look at messages sent to windows owned by a specific thread or process. The initialization messages can be captured this way.

You can start or stop the message log and search through it using criteria such as the handle, message ID, or type.

Processes View

You use the Processes view to examine a specific system process. Processes are identified by module names, or they are designated as "system processes."

Note that Windows supports multiple processes, where each process can have one or more threads. Each thread then can have one or more associated top-level windows, and the window at the top level can have its own set of windows.

To search for a specific process, the process ID or module string is used as a search criterion. If a match is found, it is highlighted in the View window. To find all processes owned by a module, just enter the module name in the Module box, leaving the Process box blank.

Threads View

The Threads view displays all the threads with associated windows.

You can search for a specific thread by using its module string or thread ID as a search criterion. To find all threads owned by a module, enter the module name in the Module box, leaving the Thread box blank.

A full exploration of the Spy++ program is beyond the scope of this chapter, but you briefly looked at its strong points here. Spy++ is a vast and versatile tool that gives you a graphical view of the system's messages, processes, threads, and window structure.

Using the OLE-COM Object Viewer

The OLE-COM Object Viewer is an application supplied with Visual C++ that displays the COM objects installed on your computer and the interfaces they support. You can use this Object Viewer to view type libraries, which can be quite interesting as well as helpful.

Using the Process Viewer

The Process Viewer lists all the processes currently running on a computer. You can sort and select these processes to view all the threads that stem from each selected process.

Performing Remote Debugging

To perform remote debugging, the Remote Debug Monitor is implemented. The Remote Debug Monitor is a small program that sits on the target computer, which communicates with the debugger and controls the execution of the program being debugged.

To install the Remote Debug Monitor on the target computer, do the following:

1. Copy the following files to the target computer:

15

DEBUGGING AND
PROFILING
STRATEGIES

```
msvcmon.exe
msvcrt.dll
tln0t.dll
dm.dll
msvcp60.dll
msdis110.dll
```

`psapi.dll` is required only for Windows NT.

If you are using Windows 95/98, move the `msvcrt.dll` file to the Windows `System` directory and restart the computer.

On a Win32 computer, use these files:

```
msvcmon.exe
tlw3com.dll
dmw3.dll
```

The files can be located in the `...\Microsoft Visual Studio\Common\ MSDev98\bin` subdirectory.

2. Set up a shared directory that can be viewed by both the remote machine and the local machine. The project should reside on the local machine.

3. Load the project into the Visual C++ development environment.

4. Open the Project Setting dialog box (Alt+F7). Then set the following options:
   - Executable for Debug Session—Enter the name and path of the executable as the local machine references it.
   - Additional DLLs—Enter the name and path of any DLLs as the local machine sees them.
   - Remote Executable Path—Enter the name and path of the executable as the remote computer sees it.
   - File Name— Enter the name of the file.
   - Working Directory—Should be blank.

5. Start `msvcmon.exe` on the remote machine to start the debugger. Click the Connect button to start the connection. (To start the debugger on Win32s platform, click the Visual C++ Debug Monitor icon from the Win32s program group.)

6. On the host computer, choose Debugger Remote Connection from the Build menu. Choose Network (TCP/IP) and then Settings. Enter the remote machine name or the IP address (password is not needed).

7. You now can begin debugging.

If a sharable directory cannot be made, copy the executable and any needed DLLs to the remote computer. The executables and DLLs must remain exactly the same all the time throughout the debugging process. Whenever they change on one machine, they must be copied to the other.

All the other steps remain the same.

Troubleshooting

If the development environment can't find the executable, make sure that you give the correct directories for the correct computers.

Because Visual C++ 5.0 supports only TCP/IP connection, check for the correct machine name and proper network connection with TCP/IP available.

Attaching to Running Processes

There may be instances when parts of the application you are working on are running in separate processes or even on different machines.

The Attach to Process option attaches the debugger to a running process. This enables you to break into the process and perform debugging operations as you normally would.

To attach to a running process, perform these steps:

1. In DevStudio, choose Build, Start Debug, Attach Process. If the process you need to connect to is a system process, select the Show System Processes option.

2. Select the process from the list of running processes.

3. In DevStudio, choose Build, Start Debug, Attach Process.

4. If the process you need to connect to is a system process, select the Show System Processes option.

5. Choose a running process from the Processes list. This list displays all processes currently running on the local machine that can be debugged.

6. Select a process by highlighting it and clicking OK, or by double-clicking the process.

7. To detach from a running process, choose Stop Debugging from the Debug menu.

No project or file has to be open to run the Attach to Process tool. Notice the Show System Processes check box in the window. Checking this box will do exactly what it says.

The Attach to Process dialog box displays three fields: Process, Process ID, and Title (of the process). Clicking on the column names sorts the fields by the chosen field. Clicking and holding on a field separator expands the field for ease of reading.

Note that you must close and reopen the Process dialog box in order to refresh the list.

15

DEBUGGING AND
PROFILING
STRATEGIES

Using Dr. Watson Logs

Dr. Watson is a tool that helps diagnose system faults. It takes a snapshot of your system when a system fault occurs. Dr. Watson intercepts the software fault(s), identifies the software that faulted, and offers a detailed description of the cause (sometimes). Sometimes Dr. Watson can diagnose the problem complete with a solution. This is the tool used by Microsoft Technical Support to evaluate system problems.

The Dr. Watson application is not loaded by default. To start Dr. Watson automatically on Startup, create a shortcut and place it in the Startup group. The application executable is located at \Windows\DrWatson.exe.

Running Dr. Watson

Double-clicking on the Dr. Watson executable starts Dr. Watson. It then runs in the background and generates a DRWATSON.LOG file in the Windows directory. Dr. Watson monitors window activity and stores it in a log file. This file will contain any important information about any errors that occurred in a Windows session.

The Dr. Watson log file is an appending list of errors that have occurred in Windows. Thus, the file could possibly contain information from the following:

- Current session and application
- Previous execution of the application
- Errors from another application

Given this information, it probably is best to rename the log file before starting to debug the application. This ensures that the file contains information resulting from the application alone.

A program that will be run while Dr. Watson is running in the background follows. The program will crash when it tries to divide two numbers by zero. The Dr. Watson log file has been deleted so that it can create a new one.

```
//Dr. Watson Example
//
//Divide By Zero
//

#include <iostream>

void main ()
{
int x = 0;
int y = 0;
int z = 0;
```

```
x = 10;
y = 0;
z = x / y;

} //End
```

When the program is run, it crashes as expected. Opening the log file, the results indicate a division by zero was attempted.

Definitely the most useful part of the log file is the `stack dump` section. This section helps you determine the sequence of functions called and which function caused the General Protection Fault. Dr Watson also shows the exact assembler instruction where the failure occurred and indicates the module information as well.

Profiling Your Application

Profiling your application enables you to determine which areas of your code are working efficiently. To accomplish this, you must use the profiler. The profiler is an analysis tool used to examine the runtime behavior of your programs. This analysis tool produces feedback exposing sections of code that are taking a long time to execute or are not being executed at all.

Remember that profiling is a tuning process, not a one-shot deal. The intention of this tool is to make your programs run better. It is not meant to find bugs or to be used for debugging purposes.

The main reasons for using the profiler follow:

- To determine whether an algorithm is effective
- To determine whether a function is too few or too many times (with respect to the problem domain)
- To determine whether a piece of code is being covered by the software testing procedures

The first reason represents a timing issue. The second represents a counting issue, and the third represents a coverage issue.

You can use two types of profiling to analyze code:

- `FunctionProfiling` locates code that is inefficient. `FunctionProfiling` generally is faster, because there is usually less information to collect.
- `LineProfiling` checks how many times each line is executed, plus the ones that are not executed at all. You use `LineProfiling` to verify the validity of an algorithm.

15

Building the Project for Function Profiling

Before you use the profiler, you must build the project with profiling enabled. To enable profiling, do the following:

1. From the menu bar, choose Project, Settings.
2. Select the Link tab.
3. From the Category drop-down list box, select General.
4. Click the check mark in the Enable Profiling check box to enable the option.
5. Click OK.
6. Build the project.

Note that incremental linking is turned off when enabling the Enable Profiling check box. Clear the Enable Profiling option to reenable incremental linking.

Line Profiling

There are two types of line profiling:

- *Line counting* shows how many times each line was executed.
- *Line coverage* shows which lines were executed at least once.

Line profiling uses the debugging information from the .EXE file of the application to trigger the profiler.

To implement line profiling when building the project, follow these steps:

1. From the menu bar, choose Project, Settings.
2. Select the Link tab.
3. From the Category drop-down list box, select General.
4. Enable the Enable Profiling check box.
5. Click OK.
6. Build the project.
7. From the menu bar, choose Project, Settings.
8. Select the Link tab.
9. From the Category drop-down list box, select General.
10. Enable the Enable Profiling check box.
11. Enable the Generate Debug Info check box.
12. Select the C/C++ tab.
13. In the Category drop-down list box, select General.

14. In the Debug Info drop-down list box, select Program Database or Line Numbers Only.

15. Click OK.

16. Build the project.

After the build is complete, the project is ready to be profiled.

Profiling with PREP, PROFILE, and PLIST

Profiling consists of three separate programs:

- PREP
- PROFILE
- PLIST

The IDE runs all these programs for you after you choose the standard option from the Profile dialog box. The arguments are passed automatically from the PREP program.

Using batch files to run these programs enables you to get the most out of profiling. These files give you more options and control over profiling the applications. You can run the batch files from the command prompt or the Profile dialog box. PLIST output is routed to the output window when using the Profile dialog box. You can redirect the command-line output, such as to a file or to an output device.

The PREP program always is called twice, because there are two phases that are performed when profiling. The first phase is done before the actual profiling is done, and the second phase is done after the profiling.

To transfer information between profiling steps, three files are implemented: `.PBI`, `.PBO`, and `.PBT`.

`.PBI` is the file extension for the *profiler batch input* file. This file provides condensed information to the profiler. The first time the profiler is run on a program, the `.PBI` file is generated by the PREP program.

`.PBO` is the file extension for the *profiler batch output* file. This file is used as an intermediate file used by the profiler. Its function is to transfer information between profiling steps.

The `.PBT` (profiler) file is generated by the PREP program and is used as input to the PLIST program. With this file, the PLIST program generates a profile of the source code.

All these files are intermediate files used by the profiler to transfer information and data between profiling steps.

A profiler batch file might look like the following:

```
PREP /OM /FT /EXC test.lib %1
if errorlevel == 1 goto done
PROFILE %1 %2 %3 %4 %5 %6 %7 %8 %9
if errorlevel == 1 goto done
PREP /M %1
if errorlevel == 1 goto done
PLIST /SC %1 >%1.lst
:done
```

The batch file options will make more sense after you examine each of the programs.

PREP

The PREP program has two phases during a normal profiling operation. In phase 1, it reads an executable file and creates .PBT and .PBI files.

Phase 2 consists of reading .PBT and .PBO files, and then writing a new .PBT file for PLIST.

The syntax for PREP follows:

```
PREP [options][programname1][programname2...programnameN]
```

The command line is read from left to right. Table 15.2 provides a list of PREP options. Note that since the command is read from left to right, the rightmost options override the contradictory options to the left. None of the options are case-sensitive, and all must be prefixed by a forward slash or a dash. Options are separated by spaces.

TABLE 15.2   PREP Options

Option	Phase	Description
/?	1 & 2	Provides information on PREP options.
/AT	1	Retrieves attribution data for function timing and counting. Function attribution reports which function called another function.
/CB	1	Used with function timing, enables you to set the calibrated overhead of profiler calls in case the function timing calls have varied because of calibrated overhead values. The calibrated overhead is displayed in default PLIST output.
/EXC	1	Excludes a specified module from the profile.
/EXCALL	1	Excludes all modules from the profile.

Option	Phase	Description
/FC	1	Designates function count profiling.
/FT	1	Designates function timing profiling.
/FV	1	Designates function coverage profiling.
/H	1 & 2	Provides information on PREP options
/INC	1	Includes the profile. Used in conjunction with /EXCALL.
/IO *filename*	2	Merges an existing PROFILE output file (.PBO). Up to eight .PBO files can be merged at one time.
/IT *filename*	2	Merges an existing PREP phase 1 output file (.PBT). Up to eight .PBT files can be merged at one time. Files from different profiling methods cannot be merged.
/LC	1	Selects line count profiling.
/LV	1	Selects line coverage profiling.
/M *filename*	2	Substitutes for the /IT, /IO, and /OT options.
/NOLOGO	1 & 2	Suppresses the PREP copyright message.
/OI *filename*	1	Creates a .PBI file. If the filename is not specified, the output file is *programname1*.PBI.
/OM	1	Creates a self-profiling file with _LL or _XE function coverage, counting, and timing. This option makes profiling faster.
/OT *filename*	1 & 2	Specifies the output .PBT file. If the filename is not specified, the output file is *programname1*.PBT.
/SF *function*	1	Starts profiling with function, where the function name must correspond to an entry in the .MAP file.
/STACK *dpt*	1	Sets the stack depth (*dpt*).

To specify individual library, object, and application source files, use the /INC and /EXC options.

To specify line numbers with source files, you would use syntax such as the following:

```
/EXCALL /INC example.cpp(12-40,50-80)
```

The following syntax specifies all line numbers from 80 on:

```
/EXCALL /INC example.cpp(80-0).
```

Only lines 12 to 40 and 50 to 80 are included from the file example.cpp.

If you need to specify all the lines in a module, you can specify the .OBJ file as the following:

```
/EXCALL /INC example.obj
/EXCALL /INC test.cpp(50-0)
```

PROFILE

The PROFILE program profiles an application and stores the results in a .PBO file. PROFILE is used after a .PBI file is created with PREP.

The syntax for PREP follows:

```
PROFILE [options] programname [programargs]
```

The command line is read from left to right. Table 15.3 provides a list of PROFILE options. Note that because the command is read from left to right, the rightmost options override the contradictory options to the left. None of the options are case sensitive, and all must be prefixed by a forward slash or a dash. Options are separated by spaces.

If a .PBO filename is not specified on the command line, the base name of the .PBI file with a .PBO extension is used. If neither a .PBI nor a .PBO file is specified, a program name with .PBI and .PBO extensions is used.

TABLE 15.3   PROFILE Options

Option	Description
/?	Provides information on PREP options.
/A	Appends any redirect error messages to an existing file. If the /E option is used without the /A option, the file gets overwritten. This option is valid only with the /E option.
/A	Appends any redirect error messages to an existing file. If the /E option is used without the /A option, the file gets overwritten. This option is valid only with the /E option.
/E	Sends profiler error messages to filename.
/H	Provides information on PREP options.
/I *filename*	Specifies a .PBI file to be read. This file is created by PREP.
/IT *filename*	Merges an existing PREP phase 1 output.

Option	Description
/NOLOGO	Suppresses the PROFILE copyright message.
/OI *filename*	Creates a .PBI file. If the filename is not specified, the output file is *programname1*.PBI.
/O	Specifies a .PBO file to be created. The PREP utility is used to merge with other .PBO files or to create a .PBT file to use with PLIST.
/X	Returns the exit code of the program being profiled.

On the PROFILE command line, the filename of the program that is to be profiled must be designated. If no extension is given, the PROFILE assumes the .EXE extension. The program filename can be followed with command-line arguments.

PLIST

The PLIST program converts the results from a .PBT file into a formatted text file.

The syntax for PLIST follows:

```
PLIST [options] inputfile
```

The command line is read from left to right. Table 15.4 provides a list of PLIST options. Note that because the command is read from left to right, the rightmost options override the contradictory options to the left. None of the options are case-sensitive, and all must be prefixed by a forward slash or a dash. Options are separated by spaces.

The results of PLIST are sent to STDOUT by default. You can use the greater-than (>) character to redirect the output to a file or device.

TABLE 15.4 PLIST Options

Option	Description
/?	Provides information on PLIST options.
/C *count*	Designates the minimum hit count to appear in the listing.
/D *directory*	Specifies an additional directory for PLIST to search for source files. To specify more than one directory, use multiple /D options on the command line. You should use this option when PLIST cannot find a source file.
/F	Lists full paths in a tab-delimited file.
/FLAT	Displays function attribution with no indentation when using function attribution.
/H	Provides information on PLIST options.

continues

TABLE 15.4 continued

Option	Description
/INDENT	Displays function attribution information in indented form when using function attribution. If /FLAT or /TAB is not specified, this is the default option.
/L	List mangled function names.
/NOLOGO	Suppresses the PROFILE copyright message.
/PL *length*	Sets the length of the page for output, where *length* is equal to the number of lines. If *length* is zero, page breaks are suppressed. Other than zero, *length* can be from 15 to 255. The default of *length* is 0 (zero).
/PW *width*	Sets the width of the page for output. The width is equal to the number of characters. Width must range between 1 and 511, inclusive. The width default is 511.
/SC	Sorts output by counts in descending order.
/SL	Sorts output in the order in which lines appear in the file. This option is available only for line profiling. This option is the default setting.
/SLS	Causes line count profile output to be printed in coverage format.
/SN	Sorts output in alphabetical order by the function name. /SNS. Sorts output in alphabetical order by the function name and displays function timing and function counting information in function coverage format.
/ST	Sorts output by time in descending order.
/STC	Sorts output function+child time. /T. Creates a tab-delimited database from the .PBT file to be exported into other applications. All other options, including sort options, are overridden when this option is used.
/TAB *indent*	Sets the tab width for indentation when using function attribution.
/TRACE	Print execution trace if available.

You must run PLIST in the same directory in which the profiled program was compiled.

If a PLIST variable is not specified, default values for PLIST are supplied. The default used depends on the profile type.

Table 15.5 shows the default values used when the PLIST environment variable is not specified.

TABLE 15.5 Default Values Used with PLIST

Profile Type	Sort Option	Hit Count Option
Function timing	/ST	/C 1
Function counting	/SC	/C 1
Function coverage	/SN	/C 0
Line counting	/SL	/C 0
Line coverage	/SLS	/C 0

Summary

In this chapter, you were introduced to MFC support for debugging and debugging techniques used for MFC. Here you learned about the TRACER.EXE utility and briefly examined AfxDump. You looked at the MFC diagnostic features, such as Trace Output, Check Program Assumptions, the ASSERT_VALID macro, Track Memory Allocations, Detect Memory Leaks, and Use Object Dumps.

You also examined the DevStudio IDE debugger. You learned about the two main compiler configurations, Debug and Release mode, and saw how each builds executables that are customized to each of the configurations. An executable built in the Debug mode was slow but contained debugger information and thus could easily be debugged. The Release mode build was fast but not suited for debugging. You saw how to build the same project with both configurations.

Further on, you saw the characteristics of compiler warning messages and how to set them. You also learned that the Source Browser tool is a great tool for inspecting source code in detail.

Each of the debugger windows was discussed, and you saw how to watch variables using the Variables window and the Watch window. You also examined the role of each of the following: the Call Stack window, Disassembly window, Registers window, QuickWatch window, and Memory window.

Spy++ and its features were introduced, as well as its many views and characteristics.

You saw how to attach to running processes within DevStudio to perform debugging.

You took a look at the Dr. Watson utility, and you saw the best way to set it up to capture and diagnose program and system crashes.

Many methods of debugging and the tools to use with Visual C++ 6.0 were covered here. You now should have enough information to debug your applications more effectively using any of the techniques covered in this chapter.

CHAPTER 16

Multithreading

*by David Bennett
and Mickey Williams*

IN THIS CHAPTER

The Win32 operating systems support multiple processes, which are given their own memory address space. In addition, Win32 supports multiple threads within a process. When any application (or process) starts, it has one primary thread. The application then may start up additional threads, which execute independently. All threads share the one memory space of the process in which they are created.

In this chapter, you will see how you can create your own multithreaded applications with MFC, as well as perform these tasks:

- Enable multithreading in your applications.
- Create worker threads for background processing.
- Create user-interface threads.
- Synchronize your threads.

Win32 Processes, Threads, and Synchronization

A process is started by the operating system when an application is launched. The process owns the memory, resources, and threads of execution that are associated with a running instance of an executable program. When the process is started, one thread is initially associated with that process. As long as one thread continues to be associated with the process, the process continues to run.

Understanding Threads

A *thread* is the smallest schedulable unit of execution in a Windows application. A thread always is associated with a particular process—after the thread is started, it never runs in the context of another process. Although many simple applications use only a single thread, it's not uncommon for more complex applications to use multiple threads over the lifetime of the process.

Threads are scheduled according to their priority. Within a particular priority level, threads are scheduled in a circular (or round-robin) fashion. For example, if three threads are running at priority level 7, and these threads never yield, they will each get the same amount of execution time from the operating system.

The thread with the highest priority level is always running, assuming that it is not waiting for a resource to become available or for an event to occur. A maximum of one thread per system processor is allowed to be in the running state—all other threads are either *waiting* or are marked as *ready*. The ready state indicates that the thread is capable of running but is waiting to be scheduled to run.

After a thread begins to run, it continues to run until one of the following actions occur:

- The thread exceeds its maximum execution time, known as a *quantum*. If a thread exceeds its quantum, the thread is placed in the waiting state, and the operating system schedules a new thread to run.

- A higher-priority thread becomes runnable. If a low-priority thread is running, and a thread with higher priority becomes runnable (for example, because a resource becomes available), the lower-priority thread immediately is interrupted, and the higher-priority thread begins executing.

- The running thread yields by waiting for an event or object.

When a thread is prevented from running because its priority is lower than other threads in the system, it is said to be *starved*. Threads that run at lower priorities occasionally are given a "boost" in their priority in order to prevent deadlock.

The Need for Synchronization

After you introduce multiple threads into an application, you must plan for problems that simply don't exist in single-threaded programming. For example, the simple act of reading and writing to a global variable must be synchronized properly. Consider this innocent-looking code fragment:

```
int g_nQueuedRequests = 0;
void QueueRequest(void)
{
    ++g_nQueuedRequests;
    DoSomethingToQueueRequest();
}
void SatisfyRequest(void)
{
    —g_nQueuedRequests;
    DoSomethingToHandleRequestFromQueue()
}
```

This fragment contains two functions that write to the same variable. In a multithreaded application, it would be very easy to have two threads attempt to modify the variable simultaneously, which would cause the value for the variable to be corrupted. Two basic scenarios exist:

- On multiprocessor machines, it's possible for two or more processors to attempt to access the variable at exactly the same time. If your code does not use synchronization primitives from the operating system, a fault definitely will occur.

- On uniprocessor machines, multiple threads don't actually execute at the same time—they only appear to do so. It is possible for a thread to be interrupted at any time. Because several machine instructions are required to update the value of a variable, it is possible for a thread to be interrupted in the middle of modifying the value of a variable, allowing another thread to corrupt it.

As illustrated by the preceding code fragment, synchronization is required for all types of data in your application. If it's possible for multiple threads to update a variable, you must provide some sort of synchronization for access.

The simplest types of synchronization primitives are used to manipulate or test the values of 32-bit scalar variables. The following Win32 functions are guaranteed to be atomic and thread safe, even when used with multiple processors:

- `InterlockedIncrement` increments a 32-bit variable and returns the new value.
- `InterlockedDecrement` decrements a 32-bit variable and returns its value.
- `InterlockedExchange` changes the value of a 32-bit variable to a new value and returns the previous value.
- `InterlockedExchangeAdd` increments the value of a 32-bit variable by a specified amount and returns the previous value.
- `InterlockedExchangePointer` changes the value of a 32-bit variable to a new value and returns the previous value. In 64-bit versions of Windows 2000, the parameters to this function are 64-bit values.
- `InterlockedCompareExchange` conditionally sets the value of a 32-bit variable to a new value and returns the previous value.
- `InterlockedCompareExchangePointer` conditionally sets the value of a 32-bit variable to a new value and returns the previous value. In 64-bit versions of Windows 2000, the parameters to this function are 64-bit values.

Variables passed to these functions must be aligned on 32-bit boundaries (64-bit parameters must be aligned on a 64-bit boundary).

Using Multiple Threads in Your Application

If you have created an MFC application with AppWizard, your application already is set up to handle multiple threads. If not, you have to be certain to link with the multi-threaded libraries, which you can set up in the C/C++ | Code Generation page of the Project Settings dialog box. This is generally a good thing to do anyway, because there are few situations in which your application will require the single-threaded libraries; you also need to use the multithreaded varieties if you plan to use MFC.

MFC Objects and Threads

As discussed earlier, when an application has multiple threads running at the same priority level, the order in which they are executed is somewhat random. Because of this, you must take special care to ensure that two different threads are not attempting to modify certain objects at the same time. You will see how to do this later, in the section, "Thread Synchronization"; for now, keep in mind that *individual* MFC objects may not be used by multiple threads simultaneously. If two threads access the same CString object at exactly the same time, for example, the results are unpredictable at best.

If you will be using MFC objects in your threads, you must create the thread by using the CWinThread class, as you will see here. Threads that are created without using a CWinThread object will not properly initialize the internal variables that MFC needs to work with multiple threads. For example, if you create a thread directly with the C runtime library _beginthreadex() function, the resulting thread will not be able to use MFC objects or other MFC functions.

In addition, although threads share the same memory space, they do not share the same structures that MFC uses to map C++ objects to Windows handles. In general, this means that a thread may access only handle-based MFC objects (such as instances of classes derived from CWnd) created in that thread. There are, however, ways around this that you will look at later, in the section, "Using User-Interface Threads."

Types of Threads

MFC implements two types of threads. Although both types use the same underlying Win32 API thread mechanisms and both use CWinThread, they are different in the way that MFC adds functionality to the thread.

If you are interested in creating a thread that simply goes off on its own and does something, such as background calculations, without interfacing with the user, you use what MFC calls a *worker thread*. These threads are based on CWinThread, but you do not need to explicitly create a CWinThread object, because a call to the AfxBeginThread() function creates one for you.

If, on the other hand, you want to create a thread that deals with parts of a user interface, you create a user-interface thread. MFC adds a message pump to these threads, providing a message loop that is separate from the main message loop of your application's CWinApp object. Actually, CWinApp is itself a prime example of a user-interface thread, because it is derived from CWinThread. Just as MFC derives CWinApp from CWinThread, you create your own class derived from CWinThread to implement user-interface threads.

Using Worker Threads

Worker threads are handy for any time you want to do something such as calculations or background printing. Worker threads also are useful when you need to wait on an event to occur, such as receiving data from another application, without forcing the user to wait. Let's face it—most users are not known for their patience.

Creating a worker thread is relatively simple; the hard part comes later, when you need to make sure that your thread plays well with others—but more on that later, in the section, "Thread Synchronization." To get a worker thread up and running, you implement a function that will be run in the thread, and then create the thread with AfxBeginThread(). Although you may choose to create your own CWinThread-based class, this is not necessary for worker threads.

Starting the Thread

An MFC thread, whether a worker or user-interface thread, is started with a call to AfxBeginThread(). This function is overloaded to handle the creation of the two flavors of threads, but for now, let's look at the variety used to create worker threads. Here is the prototype for this function:

```
CWinThread* AfxBeginThread( AFX_THREADPROC pfnThreadProc,
        LPVOID pParam, int nPriority = THREAD_PRIORITY_NORMAL,
        UINT nStackSize = 0, DWORD dwCreateFlags = 0,
        LPSECURITY_ATTRIBUTES lpSecurityAttrs = NULL );
```

The first parameter is a pointer to the function that will run inside the thread. As you will soon see, this function can take a single parameter, which is passed as the second parameter. Generally, this is a pointer to a data structure of some sort.

Each thread also may have its own priority. This parameter may be set to any of the values accepted by SetThreadPriority(), which is discussed later.

Because each thread executes independently, it must have its own stack to keep track of function calls and the like. The size of the stack may be specified in the call to AfxBeginThread().

In most cases, you probably will want your thread to start doing its thing right off the bat. However, you may specify the CREATE_SUSPENDED flag in the dwCreateFlags parameter to create a thread that is suspended upon creation. This thread will not begin executing until ResumeThread() is called.

Optionally, you may specify a SECURITY_ATTRIBUTES structure to specify security parameters to be used with the thread.

AfxBeginThread() returns a pointer to the newly created CWinThread object. You squirrel this away somewhere so that you can work with the member functions of CWinThread later.

When you call AfxBeginThread(), it creates a new CWinThread object for you and calls its CreateThread() member function. At this point, unless you have specified CREATE_SUSPENDED, your new thread begins to execute the function you specified, and the thread that called AfxBeginThread() goes on its merry way.

The new thread continues to execute the function specified until that function returns, or until you call AfxEndThread() from within the thread. The thread also terminates if the process it is running in terminates.

Implementing a Thread Function

The sole purpose in life for a worker bee is to make honey. The sole purpose in life for a worker thread is to run its thread function, or *controlling function,* as Microsoft calls it in its documentation. In general, when the thread starts, this function starts. When the function dies, the thread dies.

First, your thread function should have a prototype that looks like this:

```
UINT MyThreadProc(LPVOID pParam);
```

All thread functions take a single 32-bit argument. Although you could pass a single value here, such as an int, it generally is more useful to pass a pointer to a structure or other object that can hold more information. This structure also may be used to return information to the rest of your application.

You could use the following simple thread function to encrypt a string, for example:

```
UINT MyThreadProc(LPVOID pParam)
{
    if(pParam == NULL)
        AfxEndThread(MY_NULL_POINTER_ERROR);
    char *pStr = (char *)pParam;
    while(*pStr)
        *pStr++ ^= 0xA5;

    return 0;
}
```

You could use this function in a thread created like this:

```
AfxBeginThread(MyThreadProc, pMySecretString);
```

After the thread is created, it starts executing until it either discovers that the pointer passed to it is null, or it finishes with the string. In either case, whether the function calls

AfxEndThread() or simply returns, the function stops executing, its stack and other resources are deallocated, and the CWinThread object is deleted.

Accessing a Thread's Return Code

The exit code specified when the function returns or calls AfxEndThread() may be accessed by other threads in your application with a call to ::GetExitCodeThread(), which takes a handle to the thread and a pointer to a DWORD that will receive the exit code. The handle to the thread is contained in the m_hThread member of CWinThread, so it should be no problem to pass this to ::GetExitCodeThread(), right?

Well, there's a catch: By default, the CWinThread object is deleted as soon as the function returns or calls AfxEndThread(). You can get around this in one of two ways.

First, you can set the m_bAutoDelete member of CWinThread to FALSE, which prevents MFC from deleting the object automatically. You then can access the m_hThread member after the thread terminates. However, you now are responsible for deleting the CWinThread object.

Alternatively, you can use ::DuplicateHandle() to create a copy of the m_hThread member after the thread is created. You must be certain that you copy the handle before the thread terminates, however. The only way to be absolutely certain of this is to specify CREATE_SUSPENDED when the thread is created, copy the handle, then call ResumeThread() to start the thread. As you can see, this process gets to be a bit involved; thus, it generally is preferable to change the m_bAutoDelete member.

The exit code value returned by GetExitCodeThread() contains STILL_ACTIVE if the thread is still running, or if the thread has terminated, the return code that the thread passed when it returned or called AfxEndThread(). Note that STILL_ACTIVE is defined as 0x103 (259 decimal), so avoid using this as a return code from your thread.

Using User-Interface Threads

User-interface threads are similar to worker threads, because they use the same mechanisms provided by the operating system to manage the new thread. User-interface threads provide additional functionality from MFC, however, that enables you to use them to handle user-interface objects, such as dialog boxes or windows. To use this functionality, you have to do a bit more work than you did with worker threads, but this is still much simpler than using the Win32 API directly to set up a new thread to handle windows messages.

Creating the Thread

To create a user-interface thread, you use a slightly different version of the `AfxBeginThread()` function. The version used to create user-interface threads takes a pointer to a `CRuntimeClass` object for your thread class. MFC creates this for you with the `RUNTIME_CLASS` macro:

```
AfxBeginThread(RUNTIME_CLASS(CMyThread));
```

If you want to keep track of the MFC object for your thread, use this:

```
(CMyThread*) pMyThread = (CMyThread*) AfxBeginThread(RUNTIME_CLASS(CMyThread));
```

Keeping a pointer to the MFC thread object enables you to access the member data and functions of your thread class from other threads.

Additionally, you may specify a priority, stack size, and security attributes, as well as the `CREATE_SUSPENDED` flag for the new thread in the call to `AfxBeginThread()`.

Creating a Thread Class

As mentioned earlier, you derive your own class from `CWinThread` to create an MFC user-interface thread. The class you derive from `CWinThread` must include its own override for `InitInstance()`, but you may choose whether to override several other functions or use the defaults provided by `CWinThread`. You also need to make sure that you use the `DECLARE_DYNCREATE` and `IMPLEMENT_DYNCREATE` macros in the declaration and implementation of your thread class.

Initializing New Threads

Whenever a new thread is created from your thread class by calling `AfxBeginThread()`, MFC calls the `InitInstance()` function of your thread class. This is the one function that you must override in your thread class. In general, you will want to do any initialization of your thread here, as well as allocate any dynamic memory you know you will need.

All that your `InitInstance()` function really must do, however, is return TRUE so that MFC knows the initialization succeeded and that it should proceed. If something goes wrong in `InitInstance()`, such as memory-allocation failures, you should return FALSE. In this case, execution of the thread stops and the thread is destroyed.

If this thread is designed to handle a window, this is a good place to create the window. You then should set the `m_pMainWnd` member of `CWinThread` to a pointer to the window you have created, which enables the message dispatch system of `CWinThread` to manage messages from this window exclusively.

> **Note**
>
> If you create an MFC window object in a thread, that MFC object cannot be used in another thread, but the handle to the underlying window can. If you want to work with the window in another thread using an MFC object, the second thread should create a new MFC object and then call `Attach()` to attach the new object to the window handle passed from the first thread.

If you have allocated memory in your `InitInstance()` function or done anything else in the thread that needs cleaning up, you also should override the `ExitInstance()` member of `CWinThread` in your thread class. This is called whenever your thread terminates, including cases where `InitInstance()` returns `FALSE`.

In addition, you can override the `OnIdle()` member to perform tasks when the message queue is empty, as you saw in Chapter 3, "MFC Message Handling Mechanism." Your thread class also can override `ProcessWndProcException()`, which is called to handle exceptions that have not been handled elsewhere. The default implementation handles only those exceptions caused by the `WM_CREATE` or `WM_PAINT` messages.

Handling Messages in Threads

The default implementation of `CWinThread::Run()` provides a message pump for your new thread. You can override this function to do anything else you want your thread to do, although most user-interface threads will simply use the default implementation of `CWinThread::Run()`.

In addition, you may override the `PreTranslateMessage()` function if you want to intercept messages before the message pump dispatches them, although most messages can be handled in the message map.

Your thread class may implement a message map just as for any other class derived from `CCmdTarget`, as you saw in Chapter 3. However, you also may use a special message map macro, `ON_THREAD_MESSAGE`, to handle messages that are sent directly to the thread rather than to a given window. You can send messages directly to a thread with `CwinThread::PostThreadMessage()`, as shown here:

```
pMyThread->PostThreadMessage(WM_USER+1, myWParam, myLParam);
```

This is similar to the `::PostThreadMessage()` API call, which takes an additional parameter—the thread identifier.

Note that the first parameter specifies the message to post. This example uses WM_USER+1, which gives a valid user-defined message ID. To then handle the message you posted, the message map for your thread would look something like this:

```
BEGIN_MESSAGE_MAP(CMyThread, CWinThread)
    //{{AFX_MSG_MAP(CMyThread)
    // NOTE - the ClassWizard will add and remove mapping macros here.
    //}}AFX_MSG_MAP
    ON_THREAD_MESSAGE(WM_USER+1, HandleThreadMessage)
END_MESSAGE_MAP()
```

This message map results in messages being sent directly to your thread, which have the command ID WM_USER+1, to be handled by the HandleThreadMessage() member of your thread class. The handler for your thread message looks like this:

```
afx_msg void CMyThread::HandleThreadMessage(WPARAM wParam, LPARAM lParam)
{
    PostQuitMessage(MY_THREAD_RECEIVED_END_MESSAGE);
}
```

In this case, you decide to use the WM_USER+1 message to tell the thread to exit, although you may choose to implement more elaborate handlers that use the wParam and lParam values that are passed from PostThreadMessage().

Terminating Threads

A thread can terminate in several ways. Normally, a thread ends when the thread function it is running returns. For worker threads, this process is pretty straightforward. For user-interface threads, however, you generally don't deal with the thread function directly.

The Run() member of CWinThread is actually the thread function that MFC uses by default to implement a message pump for the thread. This function exits after receiving a WM_QUIT message, which a thread may send to itself with a call to PostQuitMessage(), as in the previous example.

Additionally, if your user-interface thread manages an MFC window, as set in the m_pMainWnd member, MFC calls PostQuitMessage() for you when the main window is destroyed. In either case, user-interface threads call ExitInstance() before actually terminating.

The Win32 API provides the TerminateThread() function, but using this method can have some very dire consequences. Unlike the previous methods of terminating threads gracefully, TerminateThread() stops the thread dead in its tracks, without any provisions for cleaning up allocated memory. More important, the thread that is terminated in this way may be interrupted in the middle of several different transactions (such as device driver communications or heap management), which leaves the system in an inde-terminate state. In Windows 95 and Windows 98, this method equates to almost certain doom for the whole system, whereas Windows NT should be able to at least save the rest of the processes.

If you need to terminate a thread from outside that thread, try to use some form of com-munication to tell the thread to terminate itself gracefully. The messages used in the pre-vious example work well for this, although you also could use some global flag or one of the synchronization objects, which are covered later, in the section, "Thread Synchronization."

Thread Local Storage

In some cases, you use several different threads running the same thread function. You may be developing a *dynamic link library (DLL)*, for example, that handles connections to outside processes, and you want to create a new thread for each connection. Although you still should be careful to use the proper synchronization objects to protect global resources, the Win32 API also provides a mechanism to provide storage that is local to a thread.

Providing for storage on a thread-by-thread basis is generally necessary only if you are developing libraries that may be called by multiple threads, and each thread requires its own dynamic storage. For the threads created here, you easily could allocate memory within a thread and store the pointer in a variable local to the thread function of a worker thread or a member of your CWinThread class. Because threads have their own stack, variables local to the thread function are thread local. Likewise, an instance of CWinThread has its own set of data members that are thread local.

Allocating a TLS Index

To use *thread local storage (TLS)*, you first must allocate a TLS index with a call to TlsAlloc(). This function takes no parameters and returns a DWORD, which is the new TLS index. This index then can be used by any threads in the process in a call to TlsSetValue() or TlsGetValue() to access an LPVOID pointer that is local to that thread. When all threads are finished with a given TLS index, the index may be deallocated with TlsFree().

Using Thread Local Storage

This may all seem a bit confusing, so let's look at a more concrete example. Suppose that you are creating a DLL that requires some of its own dynamic memory. Let's also allow the calling process to call the same functions with different threads to work with differ-ent connections.

When a process first attaches to the DLL, `TlsAlloc()` is called to allocate an index you will use to store the connection data pointers for each thread. The index is stored in a place where it can be accessed by the functions that need it (that is, globally).

When each thread attaches to the DLL, your DLL code allocates a block of memory to hold data for this connection. You then can use the TLS index you stored earlier in a call to `TlsSetValue()` to save a pointer to the new data.

Whenever a thread needs to access the connection data, it first should call `TlsGetValue()` with the TLS index you stored. This call returns the pointer that was saved with `TlsSetValue()` for this thread. The pointer then can be used freely.

When a process detaches from the DLL, you should call `TlsFree()` to free the TLS index.

If you find that you require more than one pointer to thread local storage, simply allocate a second index with `TlsAlloc()`. All systems are guaranteed to support at least 64 TLS indexes per process, although you can use the `TLS_MINIMUM_AVAILABLE` constant to see the actual minimum.

Thread Synchronization

Many developers, when they first learn how to create multiple threads in an application, have a tendency to go overboard and try to use a separate thread for everything an application does. This is not generally a good practice. Not only is it more work to create all those threads, but the effort involved in making sure that all threads cooperate may easily increase exponentially with the number of threads.

I don't mean to scare you away from using threads: They are extremely useful—even necessary—in many situations. Creating a multithreaded application that works correctly is not a trivial task, however. You must give very careful consideration to how your threads will communicate with each other and how they will keep from stomping on each other's data.

You must keep in mind that threads in Win32 may (and will) be preempted by the operating system. That is, any thread may be stopped right where it is and another thread allowed to run for a while. Thus, it is safest to assume that all threads are running simultaneously. Even though only one thread at a time actually is using a CPU, there is no way to know when or where a thread will be preempted, or what other threads will do before the original thread resumes execution. On machines with multiple processors, this is not just a safe assumption—several threads actually are running at the same time.

Potential Pitfalls

For an example of how problems can occur, suppose that you have a linked list that uses pointers to dynamically allocated memory. Also assume that you have thread A, which adds items to a list, and thread B, which deletes items from a list. If thread B is in the middle of deleting an item from a list when the thread is preempted, and then thread A tries to add an item, thread A is likely to run into an item that is only half deleted, perhaps involving pointers off into the boonies.

It is not hard to see that this process can cause real problems. This sort of problem is much more difficult to debug, because the problems are dependent on the timing of when threads are preempted. Dealing with bugs that cannot be duplicated makes ditch digging suddenly seem like a much more viable career option.

A similar, but perhaps less obvious, problem can arise even with simple data types. Suppose that one of your threads uses code such as this:

```
if(nCount == 0)
    nCount++;
```

It is quite possible, if not inevitable, that the thread will be interrupted between testing nCount and incrementing it. This provides a window of opportunity for other threads to modify nCount, perhaps setting it to something other than 0. However, when the thread containing this code resumes, it will increment nCount anyway.

It is certainly much more enjoyable to spend the time to design your applications to avoid these problems than it is to try to find the cause of one of these "gotchas" after you have 100,000 lines of code running at sites around the world.

Now that you've seen just how multithreaded applications can go astray, let's see how you can use MFC's thread-synchronization mechanisms to help your threads play well with others.

CCriticalSection

In places where you know that your threads will be dealing with things that only one thread at a time should be accessing, you can use critical sections to ensure that only one thread can access certain pieces of code at the same time.

To use MFC's critical sections, you first need to create a CCriticalSection object. Because the constructor takes no arguments, this step is trivial.

Next, before a thread in your application needs to enter a critical section of the code, it should call the Lock() member of your CCriticalSection object. If no other threads have the critical section locked, Lock() locks the critical section and returns, allowing the calling thread to continue into the critical section and manipulate data as it sees fit. If a second thread tries to lock the same critical section object, the `Lock()` call blocks the thread until the critical section is available. This occurs when the first thread calls `Unlock()`, allowing other threads to access the critical section.

> **Note**
>
> The `Lock()` function will accept a timeout parameter, but it simply ignores that parameter.

`CCriticalSection` provides a simple, lightweight mechanism to limit access to critical sections in your code; however, it does have its limitations.

First, using the `CCriticalSection` object is purely voluntary on the part of the developer. If you don't use the critical section properly, it won't do anything to protect your data. It is your responsibility to correctly and consistently use critical sections to control access to all data that might be corrupted by simultaneous access by multiple threads. You are responsible for calling `Lock()` before each bit of code that might cause problems. You also need to make certain to call `Unlock()` when you are finished working with the sensitive data; otherwise, the other processes will wait forever on the `Lock()` call.

Second, `CCriticalSection` objects are valid only within a process; you cannot use them to protect memory or other resources shared between processes. For this, you need to use one of the beefier classes, such as `CMutex`.

Finally, the performance advantage gained with critical sections tends to be reduced when many threads are contending for a single critical section. Also, critical sections incur slight additional overhead when used on multiprocessor machines.

CMutex

The MFC `CMutex` class is similar to `CCriticalSection` in that you can use it to provide mutually exclusive access to certain sections of your code. Like critical sections, `CMutex` objects work to protect your data only if you use them, although you can use them between different processes. Only one thread may own a given mutex at a given time; all others will block on a call to `Lock()` until the owning thread releases ownership.

First, you create a `CMutex` object. The prototype for its constructor looks like this:

```
CMutex( BOOL bInitiallyOwn = FALSE,
    LPCTSTR lpszName = NULL,
    LPSECURITY_ATTRIBUTES lpsaAttribute = NULL );
```

The first parameter enables you to specify the ownership of the mutex when it is created. It often is useful to declare a mutex object as a member of a class representing data that needs to be protected from simultaneous access by multiple threads. In cases like this, you can initialize the mutex and lock it while the protected data is initialized; then, you can unlock the mutex when it is safe for other threads to start accessing the data.

In addition, you may specify a name for your mutex. This is not necessary if the mutex will be used in only one process, but it is the only way you will be able to share a mutex between processes.

Under Windows NT, you may specify the security attributes for the mutex in the last parameter. Windows 95 and Windows 98 simply ignore this parameter.

You use the Lock() and Unlock() functions in much the same way you use the calls for critical sections, except that Lock() uses the timeout value passed as a parameter. If the mutex is unavailable when Lock() is called, the call blocks for the specified number of milliseconds, waiting for the mutex to become available, at which time Lock() returns TRUE. If the timeout time elapses before the mutex becomes available, Lock() returns FALSE, and your code should react accordingly.

To share a mutex between two processes, you should create a CMutex object in each process, making certain to use the same name in the call to the constructor. The first thread to call the constructor actually creates the operating system mutex, as well as the CMutex object.

The next thread to call CMutex() creates a CMutex object corresponding to the mutex object that already was created with the same name. If the bInitallyOwn parameter is set to TRUE, the call to CMutex() does not return until the mutex becomes available. You can take advantage of this fact to create a CMutex only when you are ready to wait on it, although you will not be able to specify a timeout value using this method.

CSemaphore

Semaphore objects are similar to mutexes, except instead of providing access to a single thread, you may create semaphores that allow access only to a limited number of threads simultaneously. Semaphores are based on a counter that they keep. When a thread is granted access to the semaphore, this count is decremented. If the count is 0, threads requesting access have to wait until a thread releases the semaphore, thereby incrementing the semaphore count.

The prototype of the constructor for CSemaphore objects looks like this:

```
CSemaphore( LONG lInitialCount = 1,
    LONG lMaxCount = 1,
```

```
LPCTSTR pstrName = NULL,
LPSECURITY_ATTRIBUTES lpsaAttributes = NULL );
```

The pstrName and lpsaAttributes parameters work just as they did in CMutex, but you have not seen the first two parameters before. These parameters specify an initial value for the semaphore's counter, as well as a maximum value for the counter. The default values of 1 and 1 create a semaphore that is essentially the same as a mutex, because only one thread may be granted access to the semaphore at any one time. You need to modify these parameters when the semaphore is created to allow more than one thread to have access to the semaphore.

The Lock() and Unlock() functions of CSemaphore work the same as those for CMutex, except that CSemaphore may allow a fixed number of concurrent accesses, and CMutex allows only one.

CEvent

Although the previous synchronization objects provide a method of protecting various resources or sections of your code, occasionally, you will want your program to wait for some event to occur instead of waiting for a resource to become available. This method is useful when waiting to receive packets from a network or waiting for a thread to signal that it has completed some task.

To allow you to signal events, Win32 provides the aptly named event object, which MFC encapsulates in the CEvent class. An event object is always in one of two states: signaled or unsignaled (or set or reset). It is common to create an event object in its unsignaled state, and then set it to signaled when an event occurs.

Creation of a CEvent object begins with a call to its constructor:

```
CEvent( BOOL bInitiallyOwn = FALSE,
    BOOL bManualReset = FALSE,
    LPCTSTR lpszName = NULL,
    LPSECURITY_ATTRIBUTES lpsaAttribute = NULL );
```

This is very similar to the constructor for the other CSyncObject-derived objects you have seen so far. The parameters passed to the constructor include a name for the object, which may be used by other processes, and a pointer to a security attributes structure. Although an event is not really owned by any one thread (as a mutex is), the bInitiallyOwn parameter enables you to set the initial value of the event. If this value is FALSE, the event initially is unsignaled; if TRUE, the event is set to signaled on creation.

The bManualReset parameter is a bit more interesting, because it dictates how the event object behaves. In general, if this parameter is TRUE, the event must be reset manually by your code after it is signaled. If this is FALSE, the event object resets itself. You will see how this works a bit more clearly as you learn how to manipulate the event.

As you can with other CSyncObjects, you can wait on an event with the Lock() member, which enables you to specify a timeout value. If the wait times out, Lock() returns FALSE. If the event is signaled before the timeout, Lock() returns TRUE.

Signaling an Event

As mentioned previously, an event can be signaled when it is first created, but this generally is not done. To signal an event, you can call SetEvent().

If bManualReset for the event is FALSE, only one thread that is waiting on the event can proceed (by returning TRUE from the thread's call to Lock()). The event then is reset before any other threads will return from Lock(). If no threads are waiting on the event when SetEvent() is called, the event remains signaled until one thread is given a lock on it. The event then is set to unsignaled automatically.

If, on the other hand, bManualReset is TRUE, all threads that are waiting on the event are allowed to continue (Lock() returns TRUE). The event is not reset automatically, so any subsequent calls to Lock() for the event do not have to wait, but return TRUE. To manually reset the event, you can call ResetEvent(), thus making any further calls to Lock() the event wait until the event is signaled again.

In addition, the PulseEvent() member of CEvent may be used to signal an event. If bManualReset is TRUE, all threads that currently are waiting for the event acquire a lock, and the event is reset automatically.

If bManualReset is FALSE, one waiting thread can acquire a lock before the event is reset. Note that if no threads currently are waiting on the event, the event is reset immediately. Unlike SetEvent(), PulseEvent() does not keep the event signaled until a thread acquires the lock.

CSingleLock

MFC provides classes that can simplify access to the synchronization objects discussed previously. These classes include CMultipleLock, which allows threads to wait for combinations of objects (as you will see next), and CSingleLock, which you can use to work with single synchronization objects.

In most cases, you will not really need to use CSingleLock, despite the Microsoft documentation that says you must. The Lock() and Unlock() functions work just like the Lock() and Unlock() calls in the underlying CSyncObjects.

The difference is that `CSingleLock` can provide the `IsLocked()` function, which can tell you whether your thread will be able to acquire a lock without actually locking the object. Keep in mind that the state of a sync object may change between a call to `IsLocked()` and the actual `Lock()` call.

Microsoft also justifies the `CSingleLock` class as an excuse to be sloppy in your coding habits. If a `CSingleLock` object falls out of scope and is destroyed, the destructor calls `Unlock()` for you.

As you probably can guess, I am not sold on the `CSingleLock` class. It provides very little useful functionality for the extra code it requires and just muddles your source code. On the other hand, the `CMultiLock` class is extremely useful, if not essential, in writing complex multithreaded applications.

CMultiLock

In complex multithreaded applications, you often will need to acquire several different shared resources to perform an operation, or you may want to wait for one of several different events to be signaled. With what you have seen so far in this chapter, you can do such things in your applications, but it isn't easy.

To help you work with multiple synchronization objects, MFC provides the `CMultipleLock` class, which can greatly simplify operations, such as waiting for several different resources or a set of different events. The prototype for the `CMultiLock` constructor shows that it accepts an array of `CSyncObject` pointers and the size of the array:

```
CMultiLock( CSyncObject* ppObjects[ ],
            DWORD dwCount,
            BOOL bInitialLock = FALSE );
```

In addition, you may specify `bInitialLock` to acquire a lock on the objects specified in the `ppObjects` array when the `CMultiLock` is created. However, you probably will want to hold off on any locking until later, when `Lock()` allows some other special capabilities.

CMultiLock::Lock()

Although you may be interested in using the `IsLocked()` member to query the status of an individual object handled with the `CMultiLock`, the real purpose for `CMultiLock` is its `Lock()` function, as shown in this prototype:

```
DWORD Lock( DWORD dwTimeOut = INFINITE,
            BOOL bWaitForAll = TRUE,
            DWORD dwWakeMask = 0 );
```

The timeout parameter should seem familiar by now. Like the other Lock() calls you have seen, this call can be used to specify a maximum time to wait for a lock (in milliseconds). You can use the special value of INFINITE to wait until you shut down the machine to install the latest, greatest Win32 operating system.

If the bWaitForAll parameter is TRUE, Lock() does not return successfully until all the objects handled in CMultiLock are available. This is useful when you need to lock several resources at one time, and it can go a long way toward preventing deadlocks. If bWaitForAll is FALSE, Lock() returns whenever any one object is locked. This is handy when waiting for several different events, and you want to wait for any one to occur, but don't expect all of them to occur.

In addition to the sync objects specified in the constructor for CMultiLock—the Lock() function—can use the dwWakeMask parameter to specify several Windows messages that cause Lock() to return.

Although your thread will not receive any messages while it is blocked in a call to Lock(), MFC checks the messages that have been sent to your thread to see whether the Lock() should return.

Table 16.1 lists the flags you may specify in dwWakeMask.

TABLE 16.1   dwWakeMask Flags

Flag	*Message Type That Will Interrupt* Lock()
QS_ALLEVENTS	Any message, other than those covered by QS_SENDMESSAGE
QS_ALLINPUT	Any message at all
QS_HOTKEY	A WM_HOTKEY message
QS_INPUT	A user input message (either QS_KEY or QS_MOUSE)
QS_KEY	A keyboard message; includes WM_KEYUP, WM_KEYDOWN, WM_SYSKEYUP, and WM_SYSKEYDOWN
QS_MOUSE	Any mouse movement or button message, such as WM_MOUSEMOVE, WM_LBUTTONDOWN, WM_RBUTTONUP, and so on
QS_MOUSEBUTTON	A mouse button message, such as WM_LBUTTONDOWN, WM_RBUTTONUP, and so on
QS_MOUSEMOVE	A WM_MOUSEMOVE message
QS_PAINT	WM_PAINT or related messages, such as WM_NCPAINT
QS_POSTMESSAGE	Any posted message not included in the preceding categories.
QS_SENDMESSAGE	Any message sent by another thread or application
QS_TIMER	A WM_TIMER message

Okay, so Lock() can return for 101 reasons, but how do you know what caused the return?

CMultiLock::Lock() Return Values

To see what caused Lock() to stop waiting, look at the DWORD that Lock() returns.

If Lock() returns a value between WAIT_OBJECT_0 and WAIT_OBJECT_0 + (dwCount -1), one of the sync objects specified has been locked. You can get the index by subtracting WAIT_OBJECT_0 from the return value. Of course, this is if bWaitForAll is FALSE. If bWaitForAll is TRUE, a value in this range signifies that all the requested sync objects have been locked.

If Lock() returns WAIT_OBJECT_0 + dwCount, a message specified in dwWakeMask is available on the message queue. (Note that the dwCount I use here refers to the number of objects specified in the CMultiLock constructor.)

If Lock() returns a value between WAIT_ABANDONED_0 and WAIT_ABANDONED_0 + (dwCount - 1), one of the objects has been abandoned. This occurs when a process that owns the thread that owns a sync object has died without first releasing the sync object. If bWaitForAll is TRUE, you receive this return value, but not until all other objects specified in CMultiLock are locked or abandoned.

Finally, if Lock() returns WAIT_TIMEOUT, you probably can guess that the timeout time has expired.

Cleaning Up

When you are finished with the sync objects you have locked, you should call Unlock() to unlock all objects used by CMultiLock. Although Unlock() is called for you when CMultiLock is destroyed, it is a good practice to call Unlock() explicitly, as soon as you are finished with the resources protected by sync objects.

Creating a New Process

In some very large applications, you may want to create new processes that include their own memory space and are independent of the process that created them. To do this, you can use CreateProcess().

In short, CreateProcess() takes a filename for an executable file that will be run in the new process. CreateProcess() also takes 27 other parameters, however, either directly or indirectly. Because CreateProcess() seldom is used by the majority of Win32 applications, you won't look at the details of it here. If you do need to do this, however, you will be relieved to know that most of the parameters to CreateProcess() have reasonable default values.

Summary

In this chapter, you looked at many of the nuts and bolts used to construct a multithreaded application in MFC. It now is up to you, the developer, to make sure that your application uses these tools and threads properly, including proper thread synchronization.

You learned how to set up your application to use threads, as well as how to create worker threads to do background processing without holding up other threads in your application.

You also explored how to create user-interface threads that can manage windows independently, as well as the details of creating a class to initialize your user-interface thread and to handle messages it receives.

In addition, you learned how threads can use their own thread local storage, as well as how to synchronize your threads to share common resources or use events to notify your threads when interesting things happen.

CHAPTER 17

Using Scripting and Other Tools to Automate the Visual C++ IDE

by Mickey Williams

IN THIS CHAPTER

Developer Studio is an open environment that you can customize to meet your own development needs. Using VBScript macros and Developer Studio add-ins, you can automate repetitive tasks and add features and commands to Developer Studio. This chapter discusses two ways you can extend Developer Studio:

- You can create VBScript macros that run inside Developer Studio. These macros can appear on toolbars and menus, and can be executed from the command line.

- You can create Developer Studio add-ins that create new commands, toolbars, and menu items. Like macros, add-ins can be executed from the command line. In addition, add-ins are compiled into a *dynamic link library* (DLL) and therefore offer better performance.

In this chapter, you will create a VBScript macro and look at the sample macros shipped with Visual C++. You also will create an add-in that displays information about source files in a Visual C++ project.

The Developer Studio Object Model

The macros used with Visual C++ projects use an object model that is exposed by Developer Studio. Developer Studio exposes two types of objects:

- Singular objects—each representing a single object such as an application, a breakpoint, or a window

- Collections of objects, such as the breakpoints that exist in a project or the set of windows that are currently open

Both types of objects can have properties, events, and methods associated with them. Methods and properties are used to set or collect data from the object. Events are sent from the object as a notification that something interesting has occurred inside the object.

The Objects Exposed in Developer Studio

Figure 17.1 shows the objects that make up the Developer Studio object model.

FIGURE 17.1

The Developer Studio object model.

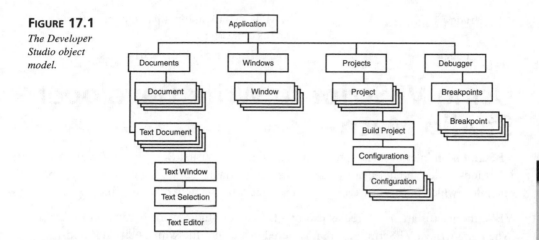

The following objects are included in the Developer Studio object model:

`Application`	The Developer Studio application.
`Breakpoint`	Represents a debugging breakpoint.
`Breakpoints`	A collection that contains all of the breakpoints.
`BuildProject`	A project that contains build information.
`Configuration`	An object that represents the settings used to build a project.
`Configurations`	A collection of all `Configuration` objects in a project.
`Debugger`	Used to interact with a process being debugged in Developer Studio.
`Document`	An open document.
`Documents`	A collection of open `Document` objects; also includes `TextDocument` objects.
`Project`	A group of related files; the files share at least one `Configuration` object.
`Projects`	A collection of `Project` objects in the current Developer Studio workspace.
`TextDocument`	An open text file.
`TextEditor`	The Developer Studio text editor.
`TextSelection`	Represents the currently selected text in a `TextDocument`.
`TextWindow`	A window that contains an open text file.

| Window | A MDI client window that contains a `Document` or `TextDocument`. |
| `Windows` | The collection of all open windows. |

Using VBScript to Write Developer Studio Macros

VBScript is an interpreted scripting language similar to Visual Basic. Like Visual Basic, it has loose rules about declaring subroutines and variable names. Unlike C++, it is not compiled, which means that each line is executed with the help of an interpreter.

VBScript macros are not stored as part of a Developer Studio workspace or project. When you write a VBScript macro, it is stored in a macro file with a DSM extension.

Declaring Variables

VBScript does not automatically require you to declare variables. This opens up a hole that makes it very easy to create new variables simply by misspelling an existing variable, thus introducing a bug that can be very difficult to fix.

You can change VBScript's default behavior so that it requires variables to be defined by changing the declaration mode to explicit. Insert this line at the top of your VBScript source file:

```
option explicit
```

It's a very good idea to use explicit declarations, because it will prevent a common source of bugs in scripting languages.

To declare a variable, use the dim keyword:

```
dim strName
```

Unlike variable declarations in C++, you don't specify the type of the variable—just its name. All VBScript variables have the VARIANT type.

VBScript Subroutines

The VBScript equivalent of a C++ function is a *subroutine*. A subroutine always begins with the sub keyword, followed by the name of the subroutine and a pair of parentheses:

```
sub PrintName()
```

Any formal parameters used with the function are included within the parentheses, much as they are in a C++ function:

Using Scripting and Other Tools to Automate the Visual C++ IDE

CHAPTER 17

493

17

USING SCRIPTING
AND OTHER
TOOLS

```
sub PrintNameAndAge(strName, ByVal nAge, ByRef strErr)
```

There are two differences in the way that formal parameters are declared for a VBScript subroutine when compared to a C++ function:

- The parameter name doesn't include a type.
- The parameter name sometimes is preceded by the ByVal or ByRef keyword.

Prefixing a parameter with ByVal indicates that the parameter is passed by value, just like in C++. If ByRef is used, the parameter is passed by reference, which is the same thing as using a C++ reference parameter. If no prefix is used, ByVal is assumed as the default.

Following the declaration of the subroutine is the body of the function, which consists of zero or more statements. For example, the following subroutine displays a message box:

```
sub dispMsg()
    MsgBox("Hello")
end sub
```

The end of the subroutine is marked by an end sub statement:

```
end sub
```

When this line is encountered, the subroutine is completed, and flow of control returns to the caller.

You can exit a subroutine from inside the subroutine body with the exit sub statement:

```
exit sub
```

When exit sub is encountered, the subroutine is exited, and the flow of control is returned to the caller.

Using Functions in VBScript

VBScript also includes functions that are exactly like subroutines, except that they return a value to the caller. A function looks very much like a subroutine, as Listing 17.1 shows.

LISTING 17.1   A VBScript Function That Returns an Age

```
function GetAge(strName)
    if strName = "Zaphod" then
        GetAge = 42
    elseif strName = "Ford" then
        GetAge = 420
    end if
end function
```

Creating a VBScript Macro

There are two steps to creating a VBScript macro. First create a new macro file, and then add a macro to it. To create a new macro file, follow these steps:

1. Choose Macros from the Tools menu. The Macros dialog box appears.
2. Click the Options button to expand the Macros dialog box.
3. Click the New File button. The New Macro File dialog box appears.
4. Enter a name and description for the new macro file. For this example, enter Unleashed as the macro file name.
5. Click OK.

To add a macro to the Unleashed macro file, click the Edit button, and enter a description for the new macro. For this example, enter numberLines as the macro name, and click OK. Developer Studio opens the macro file and creates a skeleton of the new macro for you. Edit the macro file so that it looks like the source code shown in Listing 17.2. The accompanying CD-ROM also contains the UNLEASHED.DSM macro.

LISTING 17.2   A Macro That Adds Line Numbers to a Source File

```
option explicit
dim dsSelect
sub SelectNextLine()
    ' Selecting a line selects the entire line - including the
    ' carriage return. This can lead to skipping one line, so
    ' this function moves down one line, then up one line, to
    ' prevent this problem from occurring.
    ActiveDocument.Selection.SelectLine
    ActiveDocument.Selection.LineDown
    ActiveDocument.Selection.LineUp
    ActiveDocument.Selection.StartOfLine
end sub

sub numberLines()
    ' Line numbers that contain absolute line numbers. For example
    ' line 25 in the file is always line 25, even if a subset of
    ' the file is selected.
    dim lineFileCurrent 'The current file's line number
    dim lineFileEnd     'The last line in the file to be written
    ' Line numbers that are relative to the selected text. For
    ' example, line 25 might be referred to by a different number
    ' if a subset of the file is selected.
    dim lineFileWrite   'The current line number to be written
    dim CurrText

    if ActiveDocument.type <> "Text" Then
        MsgBox("The active file is not a source file.")
```

```
    else
        lineFileWrite = 1
        lineFileEnd = ActiveDocument.Selection.BottomLine
        lineFileCurrent = ActiveDocument.Selection.TopLine

        ActiveDocument.Selection.GoToLine lineFileCurrent, dsSelect
        do
            CurrText = ActiveDocument.Selection
            ActiveDocument.Selection = cstr(lineFileWrite) + ": " + CurrText
            lineFileWrite = lineFileWrite + 1
            lineFileCurrent = lineFileCurrent + 1
            if lineFileCurrent > lineFileEnd then
                exit do
            end if
            SelectNextLine()
        loop

    end if

end sub
```

To test the `numberLines` macro, open a source file and select a box of text such as a function. Next, open the Macros dialog box and double-click on the `numberLines` macro in the list box. Every line in the block of selected text will be prefixed with a line number, like this:

```
1: int getAnswer()
2: {
3:     doSomethingForALongTime();
4:     return 42;
5: }
```

Removing a Developer Studio Macro File

There is no obvious way to remove a macro file once it has been loaded into Developer Studio. You can enable or disable the macro through the Macro dialog box, but if you really want to remove the macro, you must edit the Registry.

You should attempt the following steps only if you are comfortable editing Registry entries. You can easily render your machine inoperable if you make a mistake in the following steps. *You always should back up your Registry before modifying it in any way.*

Macro filenames are stored at

`HKEY_CURRENT_USER/Software/Microsoft/DevStudio/6.0/Macros`

Developer Studio queries the value of this key to determine which macro files to load. By removing value entries from this key, you can trim the number of macro files loaded by Developer Studio.

Example Macros Included with Visual C++

Visual C++ includes sample macros that illustrate how you can interact with the Developer Studio object model. The sample macros include the following:

- `CloseExceptActive` closes all of the open editor windows except the currently active window.
- `CommentOut` can be used to comment out a block of text.
- `ToggleCommentStyle` is used to swap comment styles between `/*` and `//` formats.

The sample macro file is named `SAMPLE.DSM` and is located in the `Common\MSDev98\Macros` subdirectory under the Visual Studio installation directory.

The sample macros are not loaded by default—you must load the macro file manually at least once. To load the sample macro file for the first time, follow these steps:

1. Choose Customize from the Developer Studio Tools menu. The Customize dialog box appears.
2. Select the Add-ins and Macro Files tab. One of the items displayed on this property page is a list of the currently loaded macro files.
3. Click the Browse button; a standard File Open common dialog box appears. Navigate to the `Common\MSDev98\Macros` subdirectory and select the `SAMPLES.DSM` macro file. If this file is already loaded, you only need to check the associated checkbox to enable the macros.

After the macro file is loaded, you can run individual macros by choosing Macros from the Tools menu. You also can add macros to the toolbar for easy access, as described later in the section "Adding a VBScript Macro to the Toolbar."

Debugging a Visual Studio Macro

There are two ways to debug Visual Studio macros:

- Add output statements to your macro so that your macro can print out information as it executes.
- Add message boxes to your macro so that execution stops while a message is displayed.

Neither of these two options are as sophisticated as the debugger included with Visual Studio. Because macros are generally fairly small, they usually require very little debugging.

Adding a VBScript Macro to the Toolbar

To add a VBScript macro to the toolbar, follow these steps:

1. Load the macro file, if it isn't currently loaded.

2. Choose Customize from the Tools menu.

3. Select the Commands tab, and select Macros from the Categories drop-down list. A list box of all the macros available for use appears.

4. Drag and drop the macro name to the toolbar that will contain the macro's button. The Button Appearance dialog box appears so that you can select the text or image that is displayed for the macro.

5. Select an image for the macro and click OK.

To remove a toolbar item, open the Customize dialog box and drag the item from the toolbar.

Writing Developer Studio Add-Ins

A Developer Studio add-in is a COM object that enhances the Developer Studio environment. An add-in has access to the same Developer Studio object model used by the VBScript macros discussed in the first part of this chapter. As you can with a macro, you can use an add-in to implement commands that are accessible via the toolbar, a menu item, or the command line. The main advantage of add-ins over macros is that an add-in is compiled and therefore offers improved performance over a macro.

All Developer Studio add-ins are in-process COM objects implemented in DLLs. The DLL must be placed in the Common\MSDev98\AddIns subdirectory, where it is discovered by Developer Studio when the compiler is launched. Add-ins can be written in Visual Basic or Visual C++, but because this is a book about Visual C++, we'll use C++ for our example.

Using the Developer Studio Add-In Wizard

The simplest way to write an add-in using Visual C++ is to use the Developer Studio Add-In Wizard. This wizard creates a project that includes the necessary source files and resources used to create the skeleton of a Developer Studio add-in.

To use the Developer Studio Add-In Wizard, open the New dialog box by pressing Ctrl+N or choosing New from the File menu. Figure 17.2 shows the New dialog box.

FIGURE **17.2**

Selecting the Add-In Wizard in the New dialog box.

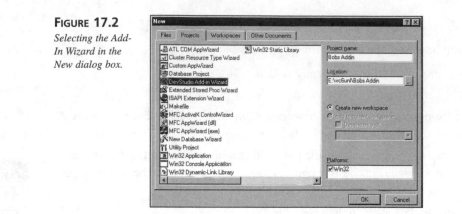

As shown in Figure 17.2, you must select DevStudio Add-In Wizard as the project type. After supplying a project name and clicking OK, you see the one-page Developer Studio Add-In Wizard (see Figure 17.3).

FIGURE **17.3**

The Developer Studio Add-In Wizard.

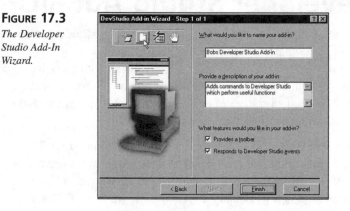

You can specify the following information in the wizard:

- The name of the add-in. This name will be displayed to the user in the Add-ins and Macros property page in the Developer Studio Options dialog box. By default, the name of the add-in is "*[project name]* Developer Studio Add-in", where *[project name]* is the name of your add-in project.

- A description of the add-in. This description also will be displayed in the Options dialog box.

- Whether your add-in includes a toolbar. If your add-in will be accessible through a toolbar, make sure you enable this check box.

- Whether your add-in should be notified of Developer Studio events. If your add-in should be notified about Developer Studio events, such as loading and unloading files or projects, be sure to enable this check box.

As with most projects created using Developer Studio wizards, you can immediately compile the add-in and use it in Developer Studio. To make your add-in useful, you generally need to perform the following actions:

- Modify the toolbar icon, if your add-in is displayed on the toolbar.
- Add command-handling code for your add-in.
- Add event-handling code if your add-in responds to Developer Studio events.

These steps are discussed in the following sections.

The Developer Studio Add-in Architecture

An add-in created with the Developer Studio Add-In Wizard supports two interfaces:

- IDSAddIn is exposed by the add-in to enable connecting and disconnecting from Developer Studio.
- ICommands is exposed by the add-in to enable Developer Studio to invoke commands in the add-in.

If the add-in responds to events from Developer Studio, two additional interfaces are supported:

- IApplicationEvents is exposed by the add-in to receive application events from Developer Studio. Examples of these events include opening and closing documents and workspaces.
- IDebuggerEvents is exposed by the add-in to receive events when breakpoints are hit during a debugging session.

The add-in project consists of both ATL and MFC code. The COM interfaces are supported using ATL, while MFC is used for the DLL framework and user interface. The Add-In Wizard creates three main classes for the project:

- CCommands is an ATL class that implements a COM object derived from the ICommands interface. You add functionality to this class to implement commands for your add-in.
- CDCAddIn is an ATL class that implements a COM object derived from the IDSAddIn class. This COM object manages the connection with Developer Studio.
- C<projectName>App is an MFC class derived from CWinApp that provides the basic framework for the DLL code.

If your add-in responds to Developer Studio events, two nested classes are placed in the
CCommands class:

- XApplicationEvents is an ATL class that implements the IApplicationEvents
  interface. If you're interested in handling Developer Studio events, this is the place
  to add your code.

- XDebuggerEvents is an ATL class that implements the IDebuggerEvents interface.
  This is the class that will contain any code you write that interacts with the
  dcbugger.

The main COM interface exposed by Developer Studio is IApplication. If your add-in
is created by the wizard, a pointer to this interface is available as the
CCommands::m_pApplication member variable.

Adding Command-Handling Code

Each command in an add-in has a corresponding function in the add-in's ICommands
interface. If the name of your add-in is Bobs File Counter, for example, the ICommands
interface includes a function named BobsFileCounterCommandMethod.

Developer Studio imposes a few user-interface restrictions on your add-in:

- Your add-in cannot display any modeless dialog boxes or views.

- Before displaying a modal dialog box, your add-in must disable any modeless dialog boxes by calling the IApplication::EnableModeless member function, passing a parameter value of VARIANT_FALSE.

- After displaying a modal dialog box, your add-in must re-enable modeless dialog
  boxes by calling the IApplication::EnableModeless member function, passing a
  parameter value of VARIANT_TRUE.

The Developer Studio object model is available to your add-in, just as with a VBScript
macro. Listing 17.3 shows a typical command handler. This command handler displays a
modal message box that contains the number of currently open files in Developer Studio.

LISTING 17.3   A Simple Command Handler for a Developer Studio Add-In

```
STDMETHODIMP CCommands::BobsLineCounterCommandMethod()
{
    AFX_MANAGE_STATE(AfxGetStaticModuleState());

    // Retrieve the Documents collection Automation interface
    CComPtr<IDispatch> pDocsDisp;
    VERIFY_OK(m_pApplication->get_Documents(&pDocsDisp));
    // Query for the vtable interface
```

```
    CComQIPtr<IDocuments, &IID_IDocuments> pDocs(pDocsDisp);
    if(!pDocs) return E_FAIL;

    // Get the total number of open documents.
    long docCount;
    VERIFY_OK(pDocs->get_Count(&docCount));

    // Format a message to be displayed to the user
    TCHAR szMsg[48];
    if(docCount != 1)
        wsprintf(szMsg, _T("There are %d open documents"), docCount);
    else
        wsprintf(szMsg, _T("There is one open document"));

    // Disable modeless dialog boxes, and display the message
    // to the user.
    VERIFY_OK(m_pApplication->EnableModeless(VARIANT_FALSE));
    MessageBox(NULL, szMsg, "XSourceInfo", MB_OK | MB_ICONINFORMATION);
    VERIFY_OK(m_pApplication->EnableModeless(VARIANT_TRUE));
    return S_OK;
}
```

Listing 17.3 begins by calling the AFX_MANAGE_STATE macro. You must call this macro in DLL entry points that are exported by DLLs using MFC. For more information about AFX_MANAGE_STATE, see Technical Note 58, "MFC Module State Implementation," in the MSDN Library.

After the AFX_MANAGE_STATE macro is called, the number of open documents is retrieved. This process consists of several actions:

- The m_pApplication interface pointer is used to get the pointer to the Automation interface of the documents collection. This pointer is stored in an instance of CComPtr, an ATL wrapper class for COM interface pointers.

- The ATL CComQIPtr class is used to query for the IDocument interface. CComQIPtr is another ATL smart pointer class that automatically queries for a specific interface. Both CComPtr and CComQIPtr are discussed in more detail in Chapter 29, "ATL Architecture."

- Finally, the number of active documents is retrieved by calling the IDocuments::get_Count function.

Note that before displaying the modal message box dialog, modeless dialog boxes are disabled by calling the EnableModeless function. After the message box is dismissed by the user, EnableModeless is called again to re-enable modeless dialog boxes in Developer Studio.

In Listing 17.3, all functions that return an HRESULT are tested using the VERIFY_OK macro. In debug builds, this macro verifies that the function returns S_OK. If the function returns a different HRESULT value, a debug trace is created. In release builds, this macro has no effect.

A more complete example of an add-in is presented later in this chapter in the section "The SourceInfo Add-In."

Handling Developer Studio Events

In order to enable add-ins to be fully integrated into Developer Studio, the add-in architecture provides for events to be sent from the IDE to an add-in when specific events occur. These events include opening documents, starting project builds, and hitting a debugger breakpoint. There are two types of events: Application events are reported through the IApplicationEvents interface, and Debugger events are reported through the IDebuggerEvents interface.

The following Developer Studio events are provided to add-ins that support the IApplicationEvents interface:

Event	Sent ...
BeforeBuildStart	As a build starts.
BuildFinish	When a build ends. The number of warnings and errors is passed as parameters with the event.
BeforeApplicationShutDown	As Developer Studio is shut down.
DocumentOpen	When a document is opened in Developer Studio. A pointer to the document's IDispatch interface is passed as a parameter with the event.
BeforeDocumentClose	Just before a document is closed. A pointer to the document's IDispatch interface is passed as a parameter with the event.
DocumentSave	After a document is saved. A pointer to the document's IDispatch interface is passed as a parameter with the event.
NewDocument	After a new document is created. A pointer to the document's IDispatch interface is passed as a parameter with the event.
WindowActivate	After a window has become active. A pointer to the window's IDispatch interface is passed as a parameter with the event.

Event	*Sent ...*
`WindowDeactivate`	After a window has been deactivated. A pointer to the window's `IDispatch` interface is passed as a parameter with the event.
`WorkspaceOpen`	When a workspace is opened in Developer Studio.
`WorkspaceClose`	When a workspace is closed in Developer Studio.
`NewWorkspace`	When a new workspace is created in Developer Studio.

In addition to the preceding events, add-ins that implement the `IDebuggerEvents` can receive the following event generated by the Developer Studio debugger:

`IDebuggerEvents`   Sent after a breakpoint is hit. A pointer to the breakpoint's `IDispatch` interface is passed as a parameter with the event.

In order for your add-in to be notified of Developer Studio events, you must select the Responds to Developer Studio events option offered by the Add-In Wizard when your project is created. The wizard inserts the necessary code into your project and provides skeleton implementations for each of the Developer Studio events.

These events are used by add-ins that need to update their internal state when specific events occur. An add-in that tracks the status of project builds, for example, would provide a meaningful implementation for the `BuildFinish` event.

The default implementation provided by the Add-In Wizard simply returns `S_OK` for each event. As Listing 17.4 shows, events are handled in two nested classes enclosed in the `CCommands` class. The `XApplicationEvents` class handles application events, and the `XDebuggerEvents` class handles the debugger event.

LISTING 17.4   An Example of the Skeleton Event-Handling Code Provided By the Add-In Wizard

```
HRESULT CCommands::XApplicationEvents::BeforeApplicationShutDown()
{
    AFX_MANAGE_STATE(AfxGetStaticModuleState());
    return S_OK;
}
```

Event-handling functions have the same restrictions as the command-handling functions discussed in the previous section. You must use the `AFX_MANAGE_STATE` macro, you cannot use modeless dialog boxes or views, and you must disable Developer Studio's modeless dialog boxes before displaying any of your own modal dialog boxes.

The SourceInfo Add-In

As an example of a Developer Studio add-in, the CD-ROM that accompanies this book includes SourceInfo—an add-in that displays information about source files currently open in Developer studio.

The following pseudocode shows the algorithm used by the add-in:

```
For each open file
    if the file is a text file
        increase the file counter
        count the number of lines in the file
        add the number of lines to the line counter
        count the number of semicolons
        add the number of semicolons to the semicolon counter
    end if
end for
Report the number of files, lines, and semicolons
```

The SourceInfo add-in was created using the Developer Studio Add-In Wizard. Figure 17.4 shows the wizard page used to create the SourceInfo add-in.

FIGURE 17.4

The Developer Studio Add-In Wizard used to create the SourceInfo add-in.

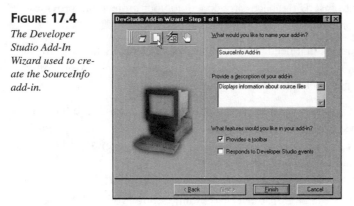

The SourceInfo add-in was created using the following options:

- **Name:** SourceInfo Add-in
- **Description:** Displays information about source files
- **Provides a Toolbar:** Checked
- **Responds to Developer Studio Events:** Unchecked

As with other wizard-created projects, the SourceInfo project has basic functionality right away. To make SourceInfo really useful, you need to perform three steps:

1. Create a dialog box to be used to display source information to the user.

2. Modify the command-handling code to perform the steps outlined in the pseudocode earlier in this section.

3. Modify the toolbar icon associated with the add-in.

Adding the Source Information Dialog Box to the Project

The IDD_SOURCEINFO dialog box was added to the project to display information about open source files. Figure 17.5 shows the IDD_SOURCEINFO dialog box.

FIGURE 17.5

The IDD_SOURCE-INFO *dialog box resource.*

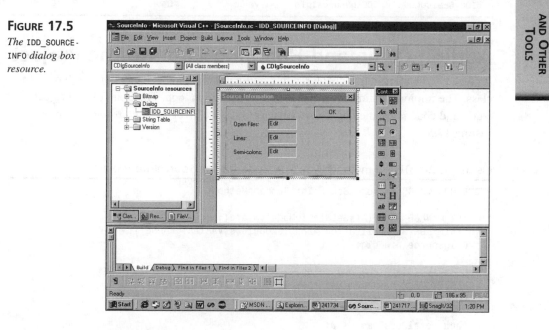

In addition to the OK button, which is added automatically to the dialog box, the IDD_SOURCEINFO dialog box has six controls. Three of the new controls are static text controls, and three controls are edit controls. Table 17.1 lists the properties of the edit controls. Each of the controls also has the read-only property.

TABLE 17.1   Edit Control Properties

Name	Resource ID
Open Files	IDC_FILES
Lines	IDC_LINES
Semicolons	IDC_SEMICOLONS

The IDD_SOURCEINFO dialog box is managed by the CDlgSourceInfo class. Each of the edit controls is associated with a member variable in the CDlgSourceInfo class, as Table 17.2 shows.

TABLE 17.2 Edit Control Properties

Resource ID	Class	Category	Type	Variable[sr] Name
IDC_FILES	CDlgSourceInfo	Value	DWORD	m_dwFiles
IDC_LINES	CDlgSourceInfo	Value	DWORD	m_dwLines
IDC_SEMICOLONS	CDlgSourceInfo	Value	DWORD	m_dwSemiColons

Adding Command-Handling Code to the Project

As discussed earlier in this chapter, command-handling code is located in the CCommands class. The implementation file for this class is commands.cpp. The SourceInfo project's command code is handled by the CCommands::SourceInfoCommandMethod shown in Listing 17.5.

LISTING 17.5 The Command-Handling Code for the SourceInfo Project

```
STDMETHODIMP CCommands::SourceInfoCommandMethod()
{
    AFX_MANAGE_STATE(AfxGetStaticModuleState());
    VERIFY_OK(m_pApplication->EnableModeless(VARIANT_FALSE));
    CDlgSourceInfo dlg;

    CComPtr<IDispatch> pDocsDisp;
    VERIFY_OK(m_pApplication->get_Documents(&pDocsDisp));
    CComQIPtr<IDocuments, &IID_IDocuments> pDocs(pDocsDisp);

    long totalDocsRead  = 0;
    long totalLineCount = 0;
    long totalSemiCount = 0;

    // The number of documents in the collection includes
    // non-text documents.
    long docCount;
    VERIFY_OK(pDocs->get_Count(&docCount));

    // The documents collection is 1-based, rather than the
    // traditional 0-based.
    for(long ndxDoc = 1 ; ndxDoc <= docCount ; ndxDoc++)
    {
        CComVariant         varItemNum = ndxDoc;
```

```
CComPtr<IDispatch> pDocDisp;
VERIFY_OK(pDocs->Item(varItemNum, &pDocDisp));
CComQIPtr<ITextDocument, &IID_ITextDocument> pTextDoc(pDocDisp);

if(!pTextDoc) continue;

CComVariant  varMove = dsMove;
CComVariant  varSearchOpt = dsMatchForward;
CComBSTR     bstrSearch(";");
VARIANT_BOOL vbool = VARIANT_TRUE;
long         lineCount = 0;

CComPtr<IDispatch> pSelDisp;
VERIFY_OK(pTextDoc->get_Selection(&pSelDisp));
CComQIPtr<ITextSelection, &IID_ITextSelection> pSel(pSelDisp);

totalDocsRead++;

// Count lines in file...
VERIFY_OK(pSel->EndOfDocument(varMove));
VERIFY_OK(pSel->get_BottomLine(&lineCount));
totalLineCount += lineCount;

// Move the selection to the top of the file
VERIFY_OK(pSel->StartOfDocument(varMove));

// Count the number of semicolons in the file...
long prevLine = -1;
long prevCol = -1;
while(1)
{
    pSel->FindText(bstrSearch, varSearchOpt, &vbool);
    if(vbool != VARIANT_FALSE)
    {
        // If the new selection hasn't moved down the file
        // break out of the search.
        long currentLine;
        long currentCol;
        pSel->get_CurrentLine(&currentLine);
        pSel->get_CurrentColumn(&currentCol);

        if(currentLine < prevLine) break;
        if((currentLine == prevLine)&&(currentCol <= prevCol)) break;

        prevLine = currentLine;
        prevCol  = currentCol;
        totalSemiCount++;
    }
    else
    {
```

17

USING SCRIPTING
AND OTHER
TOOLS

continues

LISTING 17.5   continued

```
                break;
            }
        }
    }

    dlg.m_dwFiles = totalDocsRead;
    dlg.m_dwLines = totalLineCount;
    dlg.m_dwSemiColons = totalSemiCount;
    dlg.DoModal();

    VERIFY_OK(m_pApplication->EnableModeless(VARIANT_TRUE));
    return S_OK;
}
```

The code provided in Listing 17.5 uses the CDlgProjInfo class to display project information. To compile the commands.cpp file, the following line must be added just after the
existing #include directives at the top of the file:

```
#include "dlgprojinfo.h"
```

The source code in Listing 17.5 follows the pseudocode presented earlier in this chapter.
The Developer Studio IDocuments interface is used to iterate over the collection of files
opened in Developer Studio. Next, the ITextDocument interface is queried for. If this
interface cannot be retrieved for an open document, the document isn't a source file; for
example, open resource files are not capable of returning ITextDocument interface pointers. Next, the number of lines and semicolons in the document is calculated. Finally, after
all documents have tested, the totals for all open source files are displayed to the user.

Modifying the Toolbar

The SourceInfo add-in toolbar icon is modified to make it more easily recognizable
among other Developer Studio toolbar icons. Figure 17.6 shows the bitmap for the new
toolbar icons.

Note that two bitmaps are used for the toolbar—one for large 32×32–pixel buttons and
one for 16×16–pixel buttons.

FIGURE 17.6

The toolbar icons used for the SourceInfo Developer Studio add-in.

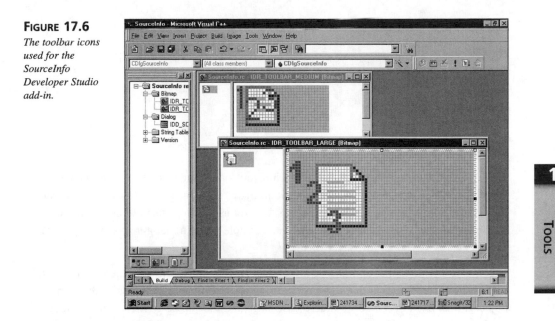

Using the SourceInfo Add-in

To begin using the SourceInfo add-in, you must compile the SourceInfo project and then copy the add-in to the `Common\MSDev98\AddIns` subdirectory under the Visual Studio installation directory.

Like the macro files discussed in the first half of this chapter, add-ins are not loaded automatically. You must specify that the add-in is to be loaded by following these steps:

1. Choose Customize from the Developer Studio Tools menu. The Customize dialog box appears.

2. Select the Add-Ins and Macro Files tab. One of the items displayed on this property page is a list of the currently loaded add-ins and macro files.

3. Add-ins and macros that are loaded by Developer Studio have a check mark next to their icon in the list box. Click on the check box next to the SourceInfo icon to mark the add-in to be loaded.

4. Click the Close button to exit the Customize dialog box. The SourceInfo toolbar appears inside Developer Studio.

Open one or more source files and click the SourceInfo icon. The SourceInfo dialog box appears, along with information about open source files. Figure 17.7 shows an example of the Source Information dialog box.

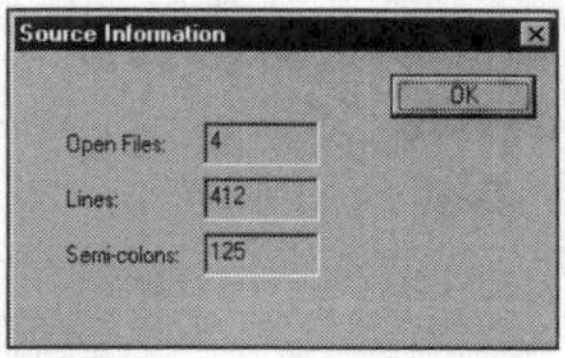

FIGURE 17.7

The SourceInfo Developer Studio add-in.

Summary

This chapter showed you two ways to extend Developer Studio. First, you looked at how Developer Studio macros use VBScript to automate repetitive tasks. You learned about the object model used by VBScript macros, as well as the steps used to create and use VBScript macros. VBScript is a powerful and simple scripting language that is very useful, especially if you know Visual Basic.

Second, you learned that another way to extend Developer Studio is to create an add-in. Add-ins are COM objects that are written in Visual C++ and have access to the same object model used by VBScript macros. Because add-ins can be written in a language you're familiar with (C++), you may find it easier to write an add-in than a macro. Add-ins also offer better performance than macros.

Database Programming

PART

V

IN THIS PART

Creating Custom AppWizards

*by David Bennett
and Mickey Williams*

In This Chapter

CHAPTER 18

In Part II, "MFC Programming," you saw how you, as a developer, can use the Application Wizards of Visual C++ to quickly and easily create skeleton applications that you can customize by making selections in a series of steps.

In this chapter, you will see just how easy it is to create your own custom AppWizards with the Custom AppWizard Application Wizard. You also will see how the parts of your custom AppWizard work together to generate new projects, and how you can further customize your AppWizard by changing templates and modifying the executable code for your AppWizard.

How Do AppWizards Work?

Before we get into the nuts and bolts of creating your own AppWizards, let's step back and take a look at just how AppWizards work in general. Although you probably have used an AppWizard more than once, you might not know what's going on behind the scenes to create your new project.

When you start one of the Application Wizards from the Projects tab of the New File dialog box, Developer Studio calls a special *dynamic link library (DLL)* to handle the dialog boxes for each step of the AppWizard. Each AppWizard has its own special DLL that handles these step dialog boxes. Custom AppWizard DLLs are given the extension .AWX.

When you finish with the AppWizard step dialog boxes, the AppWizard creates the new project from a set of special template files. These template files include the framework for the source code, as well as other things, such as binary resources for your new application. The settings chosen in the step dialog boxes are used in processing the template file to create the new application files, enabling the template to be customized according to the user's selections.

You will look at this process in greater detail and how you can customize it in the following sections.

Creating a Custom AppWizard

Creating a new custom AppWizard project involves the following basic steps:

1. Create a new custom AppWizard project with Application Wizard.
2. Modify and/or add new template files to your custom AppWizard project.
3. Create the dialog boxes for the steps of your AppWizard.
4. Add any other custom modifications to the AppWizard code.
5. Build the custom AppWizard project.
6. Start creating applications with your new AppWizard.

This process enables you to spend as little or as much effort as you want, depending on the level of customization you want to add to your new AppWizard.

Starting a New AppWizard Project

To begin a new custom AppWizard project, choose File | New in Developer Studio.

On the Projects tab of the New dialog box, assign a project name and a location for the new project. You also can choose to create a new workspace for the project or add the project to an existing workspace. Then select Custom AppWizard from the list on the left and click OK. The custom AppWizard appears, presenting you with some options for your new AppWizard project.

In the dialog box for step 1, you can choose the name of your AppWizard as it will appear in the New Project dialog box, as well as the number of custom steps you want to add.

The most important part of this dialog box is choosing a starting point for your new AppWizard. You may choose to create your new AppWizard based on an existing project, based on a standard MFC AppWizard, or from scratch, by implementing your own custom steps.

Creating an AppWizard from an Existing Project

The first option you have is to create a new AppWizard from an existing project. This option takes an existing project that you already have set up and creates an AppWizard project that will generate projects identical to the existing project you selected. The difference is that your project will be given the name you assigned in the New Project dialog box. This name also is inserted into other appropriate places in the project created by this AppWizard, such as filenames and the names of the classes that are generated.

If you choose this option, you can build your AppWizard project without any further modification, although you also can make additional changes. Building your new AppWizard project as-is creates a new AppWizard and automatically adds it to the available choices in the New Project dialog box. You then can use this wizard to create new projects based on the original project you used to create your AppWizard.

Creating an AppWizard from a Standard MFC AppWizard

The second option is to create a custom AppWizard using the standard MFC AppWizard steps. This option enables you to use one of the standard MFC AppWizards as a starting point for your custom AppWizard. This option creates a new project for a custom AppWizard that is identical to the standard MFC AppWizard (other than the fact that it has a different name in the New Project dialog box). You can choose to leave the project as-is, but you probably will want to customize it a bit, as you will see later.

When you choose to create a custom AppWizard based on the MFC AppWizard, you also can choose to add your own custom steps to the wizard. At this point, you should enter the number of custom steps you intend to add; this creates the skeleton for your custom steps. You will look at implementing custom steps later in this chapter in the section "Creating Step Dialog Boxes."

If you choose this option, you should click Next to move on to step 2. In this dialog box, you can choose to base your new custom AppWizard on either the standard MFC executable AppWizard or the standard MFC DLL AppWizard. You also can select which languages your custom AppWizard will support. This choice will affect how certain resources are created by your new wizard, as you will see later.

Creating a Custom AppWizard with Your Own Custom Steps

The third option is to create a custom AppWizard project using your own custom steps. This option creates a bare-bones framework for your AppWizard project, but you will need to add all of the meat yourself. You will look at this process in the next sections.

Components of a Custom AppWizard Project

When you finish with the Custom AppWizard, you have the basic skeleton of a new AppWizard project created for you. This project consists of two basic types of files: source files for your special AppWizard DLL and template files.

The files located in the `Source Files` and `Header Files` folders of the new project are used to create the DLL the AppWizard uses to present the step dialog boxes, and to control the creation of a new project. The Help Files folder also contains files for adding help to your new AppWizard.

Template files are used to provide the new AppWizard with the structure of a new application. These files include resource templates, as well as text templates, which are both located in the `Template Files` folder. The `Template Files` folder also contains two special template files: `newproj.inf` and `confirm.inf`.

You will look at how all these files work together to create a new AppWizard in the following sections.

Template Files

Several types of template files go into creating a new AppWizard. These include the special template files `newproj.inf` and `confirm.inf`, which play a key role in the creation of a new project, as well as text templates and custom resource templates, which make up the building blocks of the new application.

The `newproj.inf` Template File

Your AppWizard uses the `newproj.inf` template file to control how the files of a new project are created from the template files contained in your AppWizard project. This file contains a set of statements that govern how a new project is created, as well as additional directives that can be used for controlling the processing of the file. Here is an example of `newproj.inf` that was created by the custom AppWizard from an existing project:

```
$$// newproj.inf = template for list of template files
$$//  format is 'sourceResName' \t 'destFileName'
$$//    The source res name may be preceded by any combination
$$//         of '=', '-', '!', '?', ':', '#', and/or '*'
$$//       '=' => the resource is binary
$$//       '-' => the file should not be added to the project
$$//               (all files are added to the project by default)
$$//       '!' => the file should be marked exclude from build
$$//       '?' => the file should be treated as a help file
$$//       ':' => the file should be treated as a resource
$$//       '#' => the file should be treated as a template (implies '!')
$$//       '*' => bypass the custom AppWizard's resources when loading
$$//                   if name starts with / => create new subdir

/res

ROOT.CLW    $$root$$.clw
README.TXT  ReadMe.txt
ROOT.H      $$root$$.h
ROOT.CPP    $$root$$.cpp
DIALOG.H    $$root$$Dlg.h
DIALOG.CPP  $$root$$Dlg.cpp
STDAFX.H    StdAfx.h
STDAFX.CPP  StdAfx.cpp
:ROOT.RC2   res\$$root$$.rc2
=:ROOT.ICO  res\$$root$$.ico
RESOURCE.H  resource.h
ROOT.RC     $$root$$.rc
```

18

CREATING
CUSTOM
APPWIZARDS

Statements in `newproj.inf`

The `newproj.inf` file includes several types of statements. These are comments, directory-creation statements, and file-creation statements.

You can add comments to the file by beginning a line with `$$//`. Any text on the remainder of the line is ignored and is used only for readability. The comment characters must be on the very beginning of the line. If you begin a line with one of the other directives, however, you can add a comment to the end of the line simply by adding `//` before the comment text.

You can have the AppWizard create a new subdirectory of the new project simply by adding the new directory name to a line in `newproj.inf`, as in this line from the preceding code example:

```
/res
```

The remainder of the statements in the example are used to create files in the new project, based on the templates contained in your AppWizard project. These statements consist of the name of the source template to be used and the destination for the new file. Take the following statement, for example:

```
README.TXT   ReadMe.txt
```

This statement takes the template named `README.TXT` and processes it, writing the output to a new file named `ReadMe.txt` in the new project. You also may use macros in the names of the destination files, as in the following line:

```
ROOT.CPP   $$root$$.cpp
```

This code creates a new file with a name based on the `$$root$$` macro, which resolves to the name of the project. You will look at the other macros that are available, and how they are used, in the next section.

You also may add one or more of several modifiers to the beginning of a line containing a file-creation statement. These modifiers are listed in the opening comments of the `newproj.inf` file and are described further in Table 18.1.

TABLE 18.1 Template Name Modifiers

Modifier	Description
=	Copies the template verbatim, without any processing. Generally is used for binary resources, such as `.ico` or `.bmp` files.
+	Adds the file to the makefile for the project. Used for source files, such as `.CPP` or `.ODL` files.

Modifier	Description
*	Tells AppWizard to use a standard AppWizard template instead of a custom template specific to your custom AppWizard. In most cases, you won't need this modifier, because if your AppWizard doesn't find a template in your custom AppWizard directory, it tries to grab a standard template.
-	Does not add the file to the project, although it does copy it to the project directory.
!	Marks the file to be excluded from the build.
?	Handles the file as a Help file and adds it to the `Help Files` folder of the new project.
:	Treats the file as a resource file and adds it to the `Resource Files` folder of the new project.
#	Treats the file as a template and adds it to the `Template Files` folder of the new project.

Macros in Template Files

Earlier, you saw a little coverage on the use of macros, such as $$root$$, in template files. You use macros to represent variable values in your template files. In general, these macros are set based on the user's selections in the AppWizard step dialog boxes. You can use two types of macros: *text* macros and *Boolean* macros. Text macros, such as the root macro, evaluate to text values that can be inserted in your templates. Boolean macros, such as those used in conditionals, simply evaluate to Boolean values.

You may use macros in the destination filenames in newproj.inf as you saw earlier by enclosing the macro name in $$, as in the following statement:

```
ROOT.CPP  $$root$$.cpp
```

Similarly, you also may use macro names in any other places in your template text by using the $$ delimiters.

You also will see that you can use macros as parameters to directives, such as conditional directives. When you use macros as parameters to directives, however, you should use them without the $$ delimiters.

You can use several standard macros in your templates. You also may define your own macros, as you will see in the following sections.

Standard Macros

You can set many standard macros by using the standard MFC AppWizard, based on the user's selections in the standard MFC AppWizard step dialog boxes. Some of the more common standard macros are discussed in this section.

The following macros are set according to the user's selections in the New Project dialog box:

FULL_DIR_PATH: Gives the full path to the new project's directory.

ROOT: Gives the project name (all uppercase).

root: Gives the project name (all lowercase).

Root: Gives the project name (case as entered).

SAFE_ROOT: Gives the project name, removing any characters that are not allowed in preprocessor or C/C++ symbols.

TARGET_INTEL: Set to TRUE if the Intel platform is targeted. Similar macros are set for other platforms.

VERBOSE: Set to TRUE if the user chooses to generate a ReadMe.txt file and include source file comments.

In addition, many other standard macros are defined if you are using the standard MFC AppWizard steps. For more information on these macros, see the online documentation.

User-Defined Macros

In addition to the standard macros shown earlier in this chapter, your custom AppWizard can define its own macros to reflect user choices from the custom AppWizard step dialog boxes.

You define your own macros by adding an entry to your AppWizard's dictionary. The dictionary is a mapping of class CMapStringToString, which is a member variable of the CCustomappWiz class in your custom AppWizard's DLL code.

Any custom macros you add to your AppWizard's dictionary may be used in your templates, just like any of the standard macros.

Directives in Template Files

You also may include several different directives in your newproj.inf file, as well as other text template files. You use these directives mostly to control the processing of the template file, based on the user's selections in the AppWizard steps.

Conditional Directives

You may add conditional directives to your template to selectively include or exclude certain statements. You can use a simple conditional with the $$IF and $$ENDIF directives, as shown here:

```
$$IF(VERBOSE)
readme.txt ReadMe.txt
$$ENDIF
```

In the preceding example, if the VERBOSE macro is set, a ReadMe.txt file is added to the new project. Otherwise, ReadMe.txt is not created in the new project. You also may add more complex conditionals using the $$ELIF and $$ELSE directives, as in the following example:

```
$$IF(PROJTYPE_DLL)
dllroot.clw $$root$$.clw
$$ELIF(PROJTYPE_DLG)
dlgroot.clw $$root$$.clw
$$ELSE
root.clw    $$root$$.clw
$$ENDIF //DLG, DLL
```

Loops

You may repeat a block of statements a certain number of times by using the $$BEGINLOOP directive, which takes a single macro parameter that should indicate the number of times to execute the loop. The end of the loop is indicated with the $$ENDLOOP directive.

$$INCLUDE

You may include additional template files with the $$INCLUDE directive, which takes a macro parameter that should evaluate to the name of a custom template. The text from this custom template then is read into the current file, much like standard C/C++ #include processing.

The Default Language

You may create custom template files that are language-dependent by appending the three-letter code to the name of the template file, such as TEMPLATE_DEU.RC. You may tell the AppWizard to search for templates for a particular language by using the $$SET_DEFAULT_LANG directive, which specifies a macro that evaluates to a three-letter language code. This value is used when searching for template files from your own custom AppWizard directory or from the standard AppWizard templates.

The `confirm.inf` Template File

When the user completes the step dialog boxes for an AppWizard, the New Project Information dialog box appears, prompting for final approval to create the new project. The text your AppWizard displays in this dialog box is described in the `confirm.inf` template.

The `confirm.inf` template file can use conditional directives and text macros, as shown previously, to define the text that will be presented. The resulting text should summarize the options the user selected in the step dialog boxes. The text also can contain additional information about the project to be created, including things such as new classes.

To get a taste of what this file looks like, take a look at the portion of the `confirm.inf` file shown here:

```
$$// confirm.inf = the text emitted to the confirmation dialog for
$$//    this configuration
$$IF(PROJTYPE_DLL)
$$IF(EXTDLL)
Creating MFC Extension DLL (using a shared copy of MFC) $$Root$$.dll targeting:
$$ELSE //!EXTDLL
$$IF(MFCDLL)
Creating Regular DLL (using a shared copy of MFC) $$Root$$.dll targeting:
$$ELSE //!MFCDLL
Creating Regular DLL (using MFC statically linked) $$Root$$.dll targeting:
$$ENDIF //MFCDLL
$$ENDIF //EXTDLL
$$IF(TARGET_INTEL)
        Win32
$$ELIF(TARGET_MIPS)
        Win32 (MIPS)
$$ELIF(TARGET_ALPHA)
        Win32 (ALPHA)
$$ENDIF //INTEL&MIPS&ALPHA
$$IF(TARGET_68KMAC)
        Macintosh
$$ENDIF
$$IF(TARGET_POWERMAC)
        Power Macintosh
$$ENDIF

Main source code in: $$Root$$.h and $$Root$$.cpp
$$IF(AUTOMATION || SOCKETS)

Features:
$$IF(AUTOMATION)
    + OLE Automation support enabled
$$ENDIF
```

```
$$IF(SOCKETS)
   + Windows Sockets Support
$$ENDIF //SOCKETS
$$ENDIF //AUTOMATION || SOCKETS
...
```

This is just a snippet of the file created for you if you choose to begin with one of the standard MFC AppWizards. If you are creating your AppWizard project based on an existing project or based on your own custom steps, you will need to start from scratch when creating this template.

Text Templates

Your custom AppWizard uses text templates to provide the basis for creating text files in the new projects it creates. These templates are used for any type of text files, including .cpp or .h source code files, as well as other text file types, such as .rc, .rc2, .odl, .rtf, and even .clw.

It is perfectly acceptable to simply add a regular .cpp file as a template for a .cpp file to create in the new project. However, you might want to add to the customization done by your AppWizard by adding conditional processing or text macros within your text templates. You can use the macros and directives that you saw earlier in your text templates, as well as in .INF files.

Macros commonly are used in source code comments, as well as in the names of include files and new classes that are used, as shown in this example:

```
// $$root$$Dlg.cpp : implementation file
//

#include "stdafx.h"
#include "$$root$$.h"
#include "$$root$$Dlg.h"
$$IF(VERBOSE)
    // Add your source code comments in these blocks.
$$ENDIF
$$IF(OLE_INIT)
struct InitOle {
    InitOle()  { ::CoInitialize(NULL); }
    ~InitOle() { ::CoUninitialize();   }
} _init_InitOle_;
$$ENDIF
```

You can edit these template files in Developer Studio by double-clicking the filename in the Template Files folder in the Workspace window.

18

CREATING
CUSTOM
APPWIZARDS

> **Note**
>
> For .rc files, Developer Studio tries to open the file as a resource script that points to existing resource files. These resource files will not exist in your AppWizard project, however—only in the projects it creates. Thus, you generally will see a warning box if you try to open .rc files. You can click the Edit Code button to edit the text of these files.

Binary Resource Templates

Binary resource templates are used by your custom AppWizard in creating new files that do not contain plain text, such as bitmap (.bmp) or icon (.ico) files. These template files are handled a bit differently than text templates, and because they can contain any binary data, they cannot contain the directives or macros you have seen in other templates.

Although binary resource templates are simple resource files, they are stored in your AppWizard project differently than the resources that are used to build your AppWizard DLL, such as any bitmaps used in your custom step dialog boxes.

Creating Binary Templates

To add a new binary template to your custom AppWizard project, you first need to create the file to be used. In most cases, as for icon files, you simply create a new icon in the Developer Studio's Resource Editor. After you create the file you want to use, you can add it to your project with the following steps:

1. Copy the file to your project's Template directory.
2. Choose Resource from the Insert menu.
3. Select the type of resource and click Import.
4. In the Import Resource dialog box, select the file from the Template directory, select Custom from the Open As list, and click Import.
5. In the Resource Type dialog box, select TEMPLATE from the Resource Type list and click OK.

Your custom resource template now is added to your AppWizard project. You can edit most common resource file types from within Developer Studio simply by double-clicking the filename in the Template Files folder of the Workspace window. Of course, if you are using your own types of custom binary files, Developer Studio might not know how to edit them.

Programming Your AppWizard DLL

When you created your custom AppWizard project, files were created in the Source Files and Header Files folders of your AppWizard project and are used to build the DLL for your custom AppWizard. In many cases, you will never need to touch these source files; you can do a great deal of customization simply by editing the template files for your AppWizard. If you are creating your own step dialog boxes or adding your own macros, however, you will need to make some modifications to this code.

Defining Macros

If you are changing anything in the source for your AppWizard DLL, you most likely will want to add your own macros that can be used in parsing the template files for new projects. This is particularly necessary if you will be creating your own step dialog boxes, because you will need some way of conveying the user's selections from your dialog boxes to the template parsing operations.

When you created your custom AppWizard project, the AppWizard created several classes for your project. One of the most important is the class derived from CCustomAppWiz, which is named according to your project name but ends in AppWiz.

To add your own macros, you need to add entries to the m_Dictionary member of the one and only object derived from CCustomAppWiz. m_Dictionary is a collection of type CMapStringToString, which contains mappings from macro name to macro text value. Generally, macros are added to the dictionary in the OnDismiss() member of your step dialog box classes.

To see how to add macros to the dictionary, look at the following example, which comes from a custom AppWizard project named MyCust (thus, the class names have MyCust in them). Your class names will be different. The member variables used in the following code, such as m_SetOption and m_DocTitle, are values that were retrieved from the user through the step dialog box.

```
BOOL CCustom1Dlg::OnDismiss()
{
    if (!UpdateData(TRUE))
        return FALSE;

    else
    {
        if (m_SetOption)
        {
```

```
        // Set value of existing macro
        MyCustaw.m_Dictionary["VERBOSE"]="Yes";

        // Add our own Boolean Macro
        MyCustaw.m_Dictionary["MYOPTION"]="Yes";
    }
    else
    {
        // Remove our option macro
        MyCustaw.m_Dictionary.RemoveKey("MYOPTION");
    }

    // Set one of our text macro values
    MyCustaw.m_Dictionary["MY_DOC_TITLE"]=m_DocTitle;

    return TRUE;
    } // end else
} // end OnDismiss
```

Creating Step Dialog Boxes

If you chose to add a number of your own custom steps when you created your custom AppWizard project, you will notice that a class for each of your dialog steps was created for you. These classes are named something like CCustom1Dlg and are derived from CAppWizStepDlg, which is in turn derived from good ole CDialog. You also should notice that dialog box templates for each of your steps were added to your custom AppWizard project.

You can develop the dialog boxes for your step dialog boxes by setting up the dialog box templates and adding code to the step dialog classes, just as you would for any other CDialog. The additional thing you generally will want to do is add code to the OnDismiss() member of your step dialog classes to add macros to the dictionary.

You might want to add even greater customization in other places in your AppWizard DLL code, but we cannot cover them all here. For more information, see *Creating Custom AppWizards* in the *Visual C++ User's Guide* in the online help.

Building a Custom AppWizard

When you created your custom AppWizard project with the Custom AppWizard Wizard, all the project settings for your project were set to create a new AppWizard. In general, you shouldn't need to modify any of these settings, other than adding template files to the project.

When you build a custom AppWizard project, the code for your custom AppWizard is compiled to build an AppWizard DLL, which is given the extension .AWX. This file also is copied to Developer Studio's `Template` directory, which is located in the following subdirectory (assuming a default installation):

```
C:\Program Files\Microsoft Visual Studio\Common\MSDev98\Template
```

If your project was built successfully, you will notice that you now may use the new AppWizard by selecting it from the New Project dialog box, just as you would use any other AppWizard.

Debugging a Custom AppWizard

To debug your custom AppWizard project, because it is a DLL, you will need to specify the executable to use for debugging, just as you would for any other DLL. You do this by enabling the Executable for Debug Session check box on the Debug tab of the Build Settings dialog box.

For debugging custom AppWizards, you should specify the executable for Developer Studio itself, which usually is installed to a path similar to this:

```
C:\Program Files\Microsoft Visual Studio\Common\MSDev98\Bin\MSDEV.EXE
```

After you set this path, starting the debugger on your custom AppWizard project starts up a second instance of Developer Studio. You can use the first instance of Developer Studio to set breakpoints in your DLL and perform other debugging tasks. In the second instance of Developer Studio, you need to create a new project using your custom AppWizard. Creating the new project executes your custom AppWizard code, enabling you to debug your code.

Summary

One of the most important features of the Visual C++ 6.0 Developer Studio is the introduction of Application Wizards, which greatly simplify the task of creating new projects by already including all of the boilerplate skeleton needed for the new project, enabling you to spend more time on the important areas of your projects.

In this chapter, you learned how to extend this feature even further by creating your own AppWizards, which can be tailored to create new projects that come with your own custom features preinstalled.

18

CREATING CUSTOM APPWIZARDS

You learned that there are three different ways to create a custom AppWizard: You can start with an existing project, you can extend an existing AppWizard, or you can create a new AppWizard from scratch.

You also learned about the different files, templates, and macros used when creating AppWizard. The `newproj.inf` and `confirm.inf` template files are used to provide feedback to the user. Other text and binary template files are used to create the files used in a new project.

Finally, you learned how to compile, install, and debug a custom AppWizard.

Database Overview

by David Bennett
and Chuck Wood

CHAPTER 19

Most corporate and commercial Visual C++ development involves database access. Database access ranges from single-user databases used in small businesses or corporate departments, such as Microsoft Access, to a much more complex distributed or multi-tiered database server system, such as Oracle. Whatever sort of database you are using, from simple local text files to corporate mainframe systems, Visual C++ includes interfaces that allow you to work with the database from your C++ applications. The next few chapters look at these interfaces in greater detail. This chapter gives an overview of the database interfaces available with Visual C++ 6, including each of the following:

- OLE DB
- The MFC database classes
- Open Database Connectivity (ODBC) 4.0
- ActiveX data objects (ADO)

In addition, because all the interfaces that this chapter discusses use Structured Query Language (SQL) as the primary command and query language for working with the databases, you will also take a look at the basics of SQL.

ODBC 4.0

The Open Database Connectivity, or ODBC, API is perhaps the most widely used database interface for windows applications today. ODBC provides a standard interface to a wide range of different sorts of data sources, ranging from simple text files to full-blown database server systems.

ODBC allows access to database features available in a common API, which can greatly simplify database application development if you plan to support a number of different databases. Instead of having to add special code for the proprietary interface used for each database, you can simply code for the ODBC API. Special ODBC drivers provide any necessary translation between the ODBC API and the proprietary interface used to actually communicate with the database.

You should note, however, that there are many features that can differ significantly from one ODBC driver to another. Thus, although ODBC takes a big step in the right direction toward standard database access, you might find that you will need to add some code to your applications that must do things a bit differently for different database types.

Chapter 20, "ODBC Programming" takes a look at the latest version of ODBC, ODBC 4.0. The ODBC 4.0 C API is best suited for C or C++ applications that need to have fairly direct control of a complete set of features on a wide number of different databases. If you are building MFC applications, it might be simpler to use the MFC database classes, although these generalized classes don't give you as much control of your database interactions as ODBC does. In fact, you might often need to use some native ODBC calls in conjunction with the MFC database classes to perform some types of operations.

OLE DB and ATL's Database Classes

OLE DB is Microsoft's new database interface based on the Component Object Model (COM). This interface provides a great deal of flexibility, allowing you to access a wide range of different types of data sources, including just about any sort of data that can be represented in a tabular form, from Excel spreadsheets to special data acquisition hardware. OLE DB also provides the mechanisms that allow you to create OLE DB data source providers to meet the needs of your particular application. In addition to ODBC drivers, many databases, such as Oracle, Informix, and Microsoft SQL Server, either provide their own OLE DB drivers or have OLE DB drivers available from some other source.

Version 6 of Visual C++ allows the developer to use wizards to quickly develop OLE DB applications. Rather than being forced into using numerous COM interfaces and difficult coding, OLE DB development in Version 6 is quite simplified and should soon become the standard for Visual C++ database applications. MFC has added classes that allow easy OLE DB access. Furthermore, the ActiveX Template Libraries (ATL) use OLE DB to generate quick database applications that are smaller and run faster than equivalent MFC applications.

> **Note**
>
> In previous versions of Visual C++, the OLE DB interface was quite complicated to use. OLE DB developers were either forced to write a good deal more code to work directly with the OLE DB interface, or to develop OLE DB applications using ActiveX Data Objects (ADO), which provided a simpler interface to OLE DB data sources. Although ADO provided an easier interface, it was quite difficult to use.
>
> In version 6, all that has changed. Visual C++ now contains wizards that allow easy access to OLE DB. This allows developers to write faster database applications in a fraction of the time it took to develop ADO applications or pre-VC6 OLE DB applications. Now, most Visual C++ developers will code straight OLE DB rather than ADO that is used so often in other languages.

19

DATABASE
OVERVIEW

ActiveX Data Objects (ADO)

ADO is intended to replace the Data Access Objects (DAO) and Remote Data Objects (RDO) in non-Visual C++ languages. ADO provides a general interface to any OLE DB data source.

Because the objects used in ADO are COM objects, they are easily used from a wide range of programming environments, including Visual Basic (VB), Visual Basic for Applications (VBA), VBScript, and JavaScript, as well as Visual C++. However, whereas database developers using Visual C++ 5 and previous VC++ versions tended to use ADO to access OLE DB data sources, ADO is somewhat obsolete in Visual C++ version 6 because it is now so much easier to develop OLE DB applications without the overhead (or bother) of coding ADO calls. Still, many Visual C++ developers are trained in ADO and will continue using it, whereas other developers may need to perform maintenance on older Visual C++ ADO applications.

MFC's Database Classes

The Microsoft Foundation Classes provide a set of classes that encapsulate the ODBC API and make it a bit simpler to use in C++ applications. However, this simplicity comes with the cost of giving up a bit of the finer control provided by using the ODBC API directly. The Microsoft Foundation Classes also provide a set of classes that encapsulate the Data Access Objects (DAO) interface. The DAO classes are quite similar to the ODBC classes but also have some fairly significant differences.

Of the database interfaces discussed in this book, the MFC database classes are one of the simplest to use, particularly if you are performing only some of the more common simple database operations. The MFC classes also provide some very simple mechanisms for integrating your data into graphical applications, as you will see in Chapter 26, "Active Containers."

> **Note**
>
> MFC is easy to use, easy to work with, and has evolved as Visual C++ has evolved through multiple upgrades. However, Visual C++ version 6 allows ATL applications to be built. These ATL applications are smaller, faster, and every bit as robust as their MFC counterparts. Although MFC will continue to be the choice of database developers, many developers are viewing ATL as the next step in database development.

Structured Query Language

SQL (Structured Query Language) is a common language found in almost all databases. SQL is a relatively simple language, yet it is powerful enough to perform almost any operations you would need to do with a database. SQL was designed to give developers a common method for updating and retrieving data from tables on a database. SQL allows you to access your database from Visual C++ through OLE DB or ODBC. There are many concepts and commands common to most SQL implementations and the most commonly used SQL commands are standard across databases.

All the database interfaces in the next four chapters allow you to use SQL within the framework of the database interface, so let's take a quick look at the basics of the SQL language. This section looks at a generic version of the SQL grammar, which can be used with OLE DB, ODBC, and the other interfaces you will be working with.

> **Caution**
>
> Note that almost every database provides its own dialect of SQL that can use slightly different syntax or support a slightly different set of features, so the grammar that you see here might not work with the query tools provided by your favorite database.
>
> Most databases are highly compliant with the ANSI SQL standard, but some may fall short of full compliance. If you run into problems, check out your database's documentation to see how your database implements its SQL command syntax.

The following sections look at the three basic groups of SQL statements. Data Definition Language (DDL) is used to set up the structure of the database, and Data Control Language (DCL) is used to work with user permissions for certain objects. Finally, and most importantly, Data Manipulation Language (DML) is used to do everything else, including adding and modifying data as well as performing queries. These languages are all a part of SQL and aren't really separate languages, although most applications will use only statements from one of the three available groups.

Data Definition Language

Data Definition Language is the portion of SQL used for defining the structure of the database and creating objects within the database. DDL uses the following three different SQL commands to work with objects in the database:

CREATE: Creates a new object

ALTER: Modifies an existing object

DROP: Removes an object

These commands are used to work with several types of objects in the database, including tables, indexes, and views.

> **Note**
>
> Most programmers aren't allowed to dynamically change the contents of their databases, and database administration usually is done through a program, rather than through a CASE tool. Because of this, many DDL commands, such as CREATE TABLE, are not covered. They can be found in your database documentation.

Tables

Tables are the most commonly used objects in relational databases. They hold the actual data in rows (records) and columns (fields). In many user applications, the tables that you need have already been created for you, whereas other situations require that you create your own tables.

SQL Data Types

Tables are constructed of columns that contain several types of data, so before moving on to the specifics of creating a table, let's look at the available data types for columns.

The SQL data types that you will look at here are grouped according to ODBC SQL conformance levels, although most implementations don't adhere strictly to the conformance-level specifications. Most drivers will support the minimum conformance level, but you should check your system's documentation to see if any others are supported.

The following types are supported by SQL at the minimum conformance level:

CHAR(n): A fixed-length character string of n characters.

VARCHAR(n): A variable length character string with a maximum length of n.

LONG VARCHAR: A variable length character string with no specified maximum length.

DECIMAL(p,s) or NUMERIC(p,s): These are equivalent and define a floating-point value with a precision of p decimal places and a scale of s places to the right of the decimal point.

SMALLINT: A 2-byte integer.

INTEGER: A 4-byte integer.

REAL: A 4-byte, floating-point value.

FLOAT or DOUBLE PRECISION: These are equivalent types that specify an 8-byte, floating-point value.

In addition, the extended conformance level specifies the following types, although support for these can vary widely between different databases:

BIT: A single bit.

TINYINT: A 1-byte integer.

BIGINT: An 8-byte integer.

BINARY(*n*): A fixed-length binary field of *n* bytes.

VARBINARY(*n*): A variable-length binary field with a maximum length of *n* bytes.

LONG VARBINARY: A variable-length binary field with no specified maximum length.

DATE: A date value.

TIME A time value.

TIMESTAMP: A value containing both time and date.

Procedures

Procedures are extremely useful functions that are stored inside a database. The general format for a procedure is:

```
CREATE PROC MyProcedure [optional variable list] AS
    SQL statements go here
```

For example, to create a routine that returns all the employees from a department, you would write the following MS SQL SERVER procedure:

```
CREATE PROC GetDepartment @department varchar (10) AS
    SELECT EmpId, EmpName, Salary
    FROM Employee
    WHERE Dept = @department
```

Procedures can perform a series of any Data Manipulation Language commands. In addition to standard SQL, procedures support decision construct equivalent to an `if` or `switch` statement, and looping constructs equivalent to a `while` statement. Procedures have several benefits over SQL code:

- Procedures can be written to optimize SQL.
- Procedures are pre-interpreted, which makes them faster than creating SQL and sending it to the database to be interpreted.

19

DATABASE
OVERVIEW

- Procedures perform the work at the server, thereby reducing network traffic.
- Procedures allow modular reuse of pretested SQL code. This enforces consistency, improves performance, and reduces programmer error.
- Procedures can automate complex logic, allowing complex operations to be examined only once.

Procedures are executed using either the CALL or EXECUTE command, depending on the database. CALL and EXECUTE are Data Manipulation Language commands that allow the user to execute the procedure. The following command calls the GetDepartment procedure and passes it a string for the MIS department:

```
CALL GetDepartment 'MIS'
```

In addition, many database, such as *Sybase* and *Microsoft SQL Server,* allow execution with or without the EXECUTE statement:

```
EXECUTE GetDepartment 'MIS'
```

```
GetDepartment 'MIS'
```

Triggers

Triggers are special procedures that are executed automatically if an event occurs in the database. For example, if you want an audit trail to automatically generate an audit trail record every time payroll is updated, you could do this by using an *MS SQL Server* trigger:

```
CREATE TRIGGER auditPayroll
ON Employee
FOR Update
AS
INSERT INTO auditTable /* Audit table sets the date automatically */
    (EmpId,
    EmpName,
    Salary,
    Dept)
SELECT
    (EmpId,
    EmpName,
    Salary,
    Dept)
FROM deleted
```

In this code, deleted is a reserved word in MS SQL Server that indicates the record that existed before the SQL statement. Conversely, the inserted keyword is used for the record that exists after the SQL statement. Most databases allow you to capture both previous and new information.

This audit table example shows how useful triggers can be. Without any additional collaborative programming effort, every database call made to change the contents of a table is tracked. This information can be viewed by personnel to reduce fraudulent behavior, or can be used by system administrators to back up data on a row-by-row basis for important tables.

Database Projects

Visual Studio 6.0 includes the ability to create database projects. A database project is a type of CASE tool that allows easy administration of a database.

To start a database project, you need to define or create an ODBC database. Then, inside Visual Studio, you need to create a database project by clicking File, New and choosing Database Project, as shown in Figure 19.1

FIGURE 19.1

Database Projects are used to help administer a database from within Visual Studio.

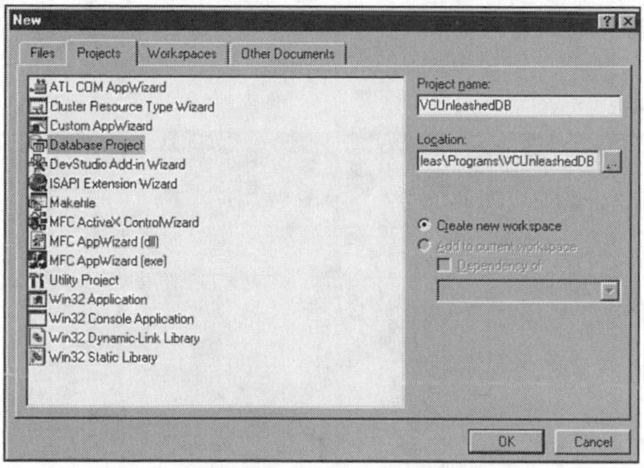

Next, you must choose which ODBC database you want to administer (see Figure 19.2). Most of the time, you will use a Machine Data Source that has been previously defined through the ODBC setup in the control panel.

continues

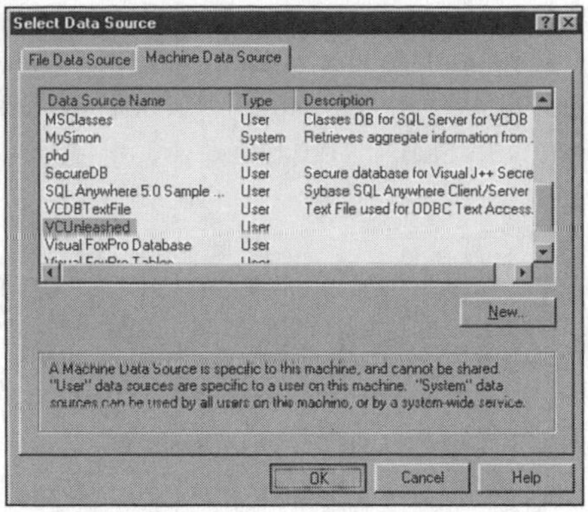

FIGURE 19.2

Visual Studio database projects can administer any ODBC database.

After you choose your database, a database project is created. You can use the database project like the one shown in Figure 19.3 to create tables, procedures (if supported), triggers (if supported), and to test SQL.

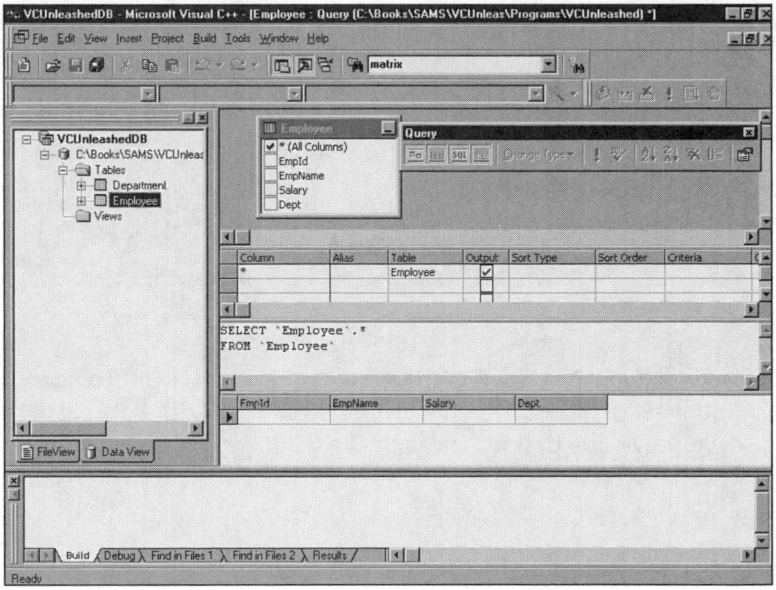

FIGURE 19.3

Database projects can perform a myriad of database tasks for database administration or database development.

Data Control Language

Most database developers will probably not be overly concerned with the security of individual objects within their database. (That's the Database Administrator's job.) However, for those developers who need to handle security programmatically, the Data Control Language must be used to maintain security within a Visual C++ program. Data Control Language is the segment of the SQL language that allows you to work with user privileges for objects in the database. DCL uses the following two SQL commands to work with objects in the database:

GRANT: Gives authority for a user or group to access or update a table, view, or procedure.

REVOKE: Removes authority that has been previously granted to a user or a group.

This section reviews the use of GRANT and REVOKE.

> **Note**
>
> Smaller databases, such as Microsoft Access, may not allow security administration outside of their environment. For example, Microsoft Access handles all security management through their menu structure, and doesn't allow GRANT and REVOKE commands.

Granting Privileges

The SQL language allows you to grant certain privileges on a particular object to a set of users. The privileges that can be granted are listed here:

SELECT: Allows the user to query data.

INSERT: Allows the user to add new rows.

DELETE: Allows the user to delete rows.

EXECUTE: Allows the user to execute procedures.

UPDATE: Allows the user to modify existing rows.

REFERENCES: This privilege is required if a user will be modifying a table that has referential integrity constraints that refer to columns in another table. The user must have the REFERENCES privilege on the columns used in the constraint.

Privileges for a certain object are granted with a GRANT statement, such as the following:

```
GRANT SELECT ON Employee TO PUBLIC
```

The preceding example makes use of the PUBLIC keyword to grant the SELECT privilege on the Employee table to all users. You can also grant several privileges to several users in a single statement, as shown in the following code line. You cannot, however, grant privileges to multiple objects in the same statement.

```
GRANT SELECT, INSERT ON Employee TO Bob, Doug
```

Some databases allow security at the column level. For the UPDATE and REFERENCES privileges, you can grant access to specific columns, as in the following example, which allows Bob and Doug to update only the Salary and Dept columns.

```
GRANT UPDATE (Salary, Dept) ON Employee TO Bob, Doug
```

You can grant EXECUTE privileges to users to give them the rights to execute a stored procedure. The syntax to grant Bob and Doug access to execute the GetDepartment procedure is as follows:

```
GRANT EXECUTE ON GetDepartment TO Bob, Doug
```

Tip

Procedures can bypass much security. For example, although Bob and Doug were able to execute the GetDepartment procedure, they still had no access to individual employee records. Procedures are a good way to supplement security by giving individuals or groups access to limited information within a database.

Revoking Privileges

You can revoke privileges for database objects by using REVOKE statements, which use syntax similar to the GRANT statements shown earlier in this chapter. For example, if you used the following statement to grant privileges:

```
GRANT SELECT ON Royalties TO Ed, Alex, Michal, Dave
```

you could revoke a user's privileges to the Royalties table with a statement like this:

```
REVOKE SELECT ON Royalties FROM Dave
```

You can also add CASCADE or RESTRICT modifiers to your REVOKE statements. If you want to revoke a user's privileges for a certain table, it would also make sense to revoke the user's privileges on any views that require access to that table. The CASCADE modifier will do this for you. On the other hand, the RESTRICT modifier will prevent you from revoking a privilege that is required according to other privileges the user has been granted.

Using Roles

Usually developers don't grant or revoke privileges to users on-the-fly. A better way to grant privileges is to create *roles* or *user groups* that are granted privileges.

For example, say Bob and Doug were in the payroll department. Only members of the payroll department are allowed to update employee information. Rather than trying to manage every single member of the payroll department, you could instead create a "payroll role." In Oracle, this is accomplished through the Oracle SQL syntax:

```
CREATE ROLE payroll
```

After creating the role, you grant permissions to the role:

```
GRANT SELECT, UPDATE, INSERT, DELETE ON Employee TO payroll
```

After granting permission, you assign the individual to the group. In Oracle, this is accomplished through assigning a user to the default role. The following Oracle syntax assigns Bob to the payroll role:

```
ALTER USER Bob DEFAULT ROLE payroll
```

Roles are handled differently in almost every database. For example, Sybase has an sp_role stored procedure that controls roles. If your job requires that you handle database security, check your database documentation for information on how to handle roles or user groups. You'll be glad you did.

Data Manipulation Language

In the previous sections, you looked at the parts of SQL used to set up your databases. Now you come to the juicy bits where you actually get your hands on the data and look at the real meat of SQL—Data Manipulation Language (DML). DML consists of the following basic types of statements:

SELECT: Queries the database.

INSERT: Inserts data into a table.

DELETE: Deletes data from a table.

UPDATE: Changes data in a table.

You can probably guess what each of these statements do, but let's look at the specifics of each in the following sections.

SELECT Statements

SELECT is the command that lets you read from your tables. It is one of the most complex SQL commands. Its format is the following:

```
SELECT { DISTINCT } | select-list |     *     |
FROM table_list
{ WHERE condition }
{ GROUP BY column_name}
{ HAVING condition }
{ ORDER BY  field_list {DESC }}
```

The components of the SQL SELECT command are as follows:

- DISTINCT: If DISTINCT is specified, all duplicate rows are eliminated. Any rows that have information that isn't exactly duplicated by another row is returned.

- select-list: The select-list is the list of column names you want selected, separated by commas. An asterisk (*) in the place of the select-list will cause all columns to be selected.

> **Caution**
>
> Although coding an * for your select-list is much easier than typing every column in a table, if columns are added, deleted, or change order, the SQL inside your Visual C++ program will no longer work. It's better to code in all of the field names.

- FROM table_list: The FROM clause lists the tables to SELECT data from.
- WHERE condition. The WHERE clause eliminates rows from the result that don't meet some condition.
- GROUP BY column_list: The GROUP BY clause groups together multiple rows from the database, based on unique values found in your column_list. GROUP BY is necessary for aggregate functions, like SUM, COUNT, and AVG.
- HAVING condition: The HAVING clause must be accompanied by a GROUP BY clause. The condition of the HAVING clause eliminates rows from the result, much like the WHERE clause. Unlike the WHERE clause, the HAVING clause can use aggregate functions, for example, HAVING AVG(Salary) > 20000.
- ORDER BY field_list {DESC}: The ORDER BY clause allows you to arrange the resulting columns of SELECT in a certain order, defined by field_list. The field_list can either be column names or numbers indicating their position in the SELECT statement. The order is ascending unless DESC is specified.

Some SQL SELECT examples are shown in Table 19.1.

TABLE 19.1 SQL SELECT Examples

SQL SELECT *Statement*	*Description*
SELECT * FROM Employee ORDER BY Salary, EmpName	This selects all columns and rows from the Employee table. Results are sorted by Salary, and then by employee name.
SELECT EmpName, Salary FROM Employee WHERE Salary > 20000 ORDER BY 2	This selects the name and salary for all employees whose salary is greater than $20,000. The results are sorted by Salary (column 2).
SELECT Dept, SUM(salary) FROM Employee GROUP BY Dept HAVING COUNT(*) > 10	This sums the salaries by department for those departments with more than 10 employees.

SELECT Employee.EmpName,
    Department.DeptName
FROM   Employee, Department
WHERE Employee.Salary
    >= 20000
  AND Employee.Dept =
    Department.Dept
	This joins the Employee and Department tables by department code (Dept) and then selects the employee name and department name for all employees making a salary of $20,000 or more.

Expressions

In place of individual column names, you can also use numerical expressions involving multiple columns combined with the following arithmetic operators: +, -, /, *. Expressions can be used in the select-list, as in the following example:

```
SELECT PartNum, PartCost + ExtraCost FROM Parts
```

The WHERE clause can also include expressions, as in the following example:

```
SELECT PartNum FROM Parts WHERE (ExtraCost / PartCost) > .25
```

The LIKE Predicate

In addition to the comparison operators, SQL offers a special comparison operator for character strings. The LIKE predicate allows you to select rows based on a string that matches a certain pattern. In the matching pattern, you can include any normal characters, as well as the special characters % and _. You can attempt to match any string of

19

DATABASE OVERVIEW

characters of any length with % or any single character with _. For example, to select any rows that contain `Database` in the `Title` field, you can use a query like the following:

```
SELECT ChapterNum FROM Chapters WHERE Title LIKE '%Database%'
```

You could also search for titles that have `ata` starting at the second character position with the following statement:

```
SELECT ChapterNum FROM Chapters WHERE Title LIKE '_ata%'
```

The IN Predicate

You can also use the `IN` predicate to simplify some of your `WHERE` clauses that are used to select rows with a value that belongs to a certain set of values. For example, look at the following query:

```
SELECT EmpNum FROM Employee
    WHERE Dept = 'MIS' OR Dept = 'HR' OR Dept = 'Sales'
```

This could be simplified by using the `IN` predicate, as in the following query:

```
SELECT EmpNum FROM Employee WHERE Dept IN ('MIS', 'HR', 'Sales')
```

You can negate the `IN` predicate, as in the following example, which selects all employees who aren't in the listed departments:

```
SELECT EmpNum FROM Employee WHERE Dept IN ('MIS', 'HR', 'Sales')
```

The BETWEEN Predicate

In many cases, you will need to select rows based on column values that fall into a certain range. For example, you could execute a query like the following:

```
SELECT EmpNum FROM Employee WHERE Salary > 20000 AND Salary < 30000
```

This query could be simplified by using the `BETWEEN` predicate, as in the following example:

```
SELECT EmpNum FROM Employee WHERE Salary BETWEEN 20000 AND 30000
```

Like the other comparison operators, you can apply `BETWEEN` to non-numeric columns, as in the following example:

```
SELECT EmpNum FROM Employee WHERE Name BETWEEN 'Andersen' AND 'Baker'
```

You can also negate the `BETWEEN` predicate by adding the `NOT` modifier to select rows that don't fall into the given range.

Aggregate Functions

In many cases, you will want to compute values based on all the rows returned in the result set, such as the total for a column in all the returned rows. These sorts of computations can be done with the aggregate functions shown here:

AVG: Mean average of the column values

COUNT: Number of rows returned

MAX: Maximum value for the column in the result set

MIN: Minimum value for the column in the result set

SUM: Total of all values for this column in the result set

Perhaps the most common use of aggregation is used in retrieving the number of rows returned by a given query, as in the following example, which returns the number of rows in the Employee table:

```
SELECT COUNT(*) FROM Employee
```

If you use COUNT(*), all the rows in the query will be counted. However, if you specify a column name, only rows for which the column value is non-null will be counted. For example, if the Dept column was NULL in one or more rows, the following query would return only the number of rows containing a value for Dept:

```
SELECT COUNT(Dept) FROM Employee
```

In many cases, you will want to use aggregate functions on certain groups of rows in the result set. This can easily be done by adding a GROUP BY clause, which can specify the column used to group the rows that are included in aggregate computations. The following example will generate a list of department codes, followed by the total of the salaries for each department:

```
SELECT Dept, SUM(Salary) FROM Employee GROUP BY Dept
```

Earlier, you saw how the WHERE clause is used to filter the rows that are returned in a query. In a similar fashion, you can restrict the rows returned using aggregation by adding a HAVING clause, as in the following example, which will return only salary totals for departments that have a total salary of less than $200,000:

```
SELECT Dept, SUM(Salary) FROM Employee
    GROUP BY Dept
    HAVING SUM(Salary) < 200000
```

In more complicated queries, it can be a bit confusing to see how various WHERE and HAVING clauses work with each other to produce the end result. When working with aggregation, keep in mind that processing is done in the following order:

19

DATABASE
OVERVIEW

1. All rows that meet the WHERE clause are selected.

2. Aggregate values are computed.

3. The rows resulting from aggregation are filtered by the HAVING clause.

ODBC SQL Literal Values

In some of the previous examples, you have seen the use of simple literal, or constant, values in the SQL statements. For numeric values, whether integral or floating-point, you need only use the decimal representation. For strings, you simply enclose the string in single quotes. You can also use NULL as a literal when setting a column to a NULL value.

> **Tip**
>
> Literals can be tricky. Here are some pointers:
>
> - Be sure to use single, rather than double, quotes around your literals in the SQL statements you use in your C++ code. Double quotes are reserved for column names.
>
> - There are many different date formats for different databases. However, the one format that seems to work across databases is 'yyyy-mm-dd' in single quotes.
>
> - Similarly, there are many different time formats for different databases. The format you most often can use is 'hh:mm:ss.ffffff' where .ffffff is the fraction of a second.

SQL Functions

Databases provide a myriad of functions that allow developers to easily process data. Although each database is different, there are some database functions that seem common to most databases. Table 19.2 defines popular string functions, Table 19.3 defines some popular numeric functions, and Table 19.4 defines some popular date and time functions.

TABLE 19.2   Popular String SQL Functions

String SQL Function	Description
ASCII(string_exp)	Returns the ASCII value of the first character in the string.
CHAR(code)	Returns the length of the string in characters.
LCASE(string_exp)	Returns string_exp converted to all lowercase.
LEFT(string_exp, count)	Returns the leftmost count characters of string_exp.

String SQL Function	*Description*
LENGTH(string_exp)	Returns the length of string_exp in characters.
LOCATE(string_exp1, string_exp2 [, start])	Returns the starting position of the first occurrence of string_exp1 within string_exp2. Optionally, you can specify a start value to begin searching in string_exp2 at character number start.
LTRIM(string_exp)	Returns string_exp with any leading blanks removed.
RIGHT(string_exp, count)	Returns the rightmost count characters in string_exp.
RTRIM(string_exp)	Returns string_exp with any trailing blanks removed.
SOUNDEX(string_exp)	Returns a character string that represents the sound of string_exp.
SUBSTRING(string_exp, start, length)	Returns a string made up of length characters taken from string_exp, starting at start.
UCASE(string_exp)	Returns string_exp converted to all uppercase.

TABLE 19.3   Popular Numeric SQL Functions

Numeric SQL Function	*Description*
ABS(numeric_exp)	Returns the absolute value of numeric_exp.
ACOS(float_exp)	Returns the arccosine of float_exp in radians.
ASIN(float_exp)	Returns the arcsine of float_exp in radians.
ATAN(float_exp)	Returns the arctangent of float_exp in radians.
CEILING(numeric_exp)	Returns the smallest integer greater than or equal to numeric_exp.
COS(float_exp)	Returns the cosine of float_exp, where float_exp gives an angle in radians.
COT(float_exp)	Returns the cotangent of float_exp, where float_exp gives an angle in radians.
DEGREES(numeric_exp)	Returns the angle given in radians in numeric_exp to degrees.
EXP(float_exp)	Returns the exponential value of float_exp.
FLOOR(numeric_exp)	Returns the largest integer less than or equal to numeric_exp.

19

DATABASE
OVERVIEW

continues

TABLE 19.3 continued

Numeric SQL Function	Description
LOG(float_exp)	Returns the natural logarithm of float_exp.
LOG10(float_exp)	Returns the base-10 logarithm of float_exp.
MOD(i1, i2)	Returns the modulus (remainder) of i1 divided by i2.
PI()	Returns the constant pi (3.14159265...).
POWER(num1, num2)	Returns num1 raised to the power of num2.
RADIANS(numeric_exp)	Returns the angle given in degrees in numeric_exp to radians.
RAND([seed])	Returns a random, floating-point value. Optionally, you may specify a seed value.
ROUND(num, [decimal])	Returns the value of a rounded numeric expression. You can optionally provide a decimal argument to specify the decimal places to the right of the decimal point. You can provide a negative decimal argument to round to a certain number of decimal places to the left of the decimal point.
SIGN(numeric_exp)	Returns -1 if numeric_exp is less than 0, 1 if it is greater than 0, or 0 if numeric_exp is equal to 0.
SQRT(num)	Returns the square root of a number.
TAN(float_exp)	Returns the tangent of the angle given in radians in float_exp.
TRUNCATE(num, [decimal])	Returns the value of a numeric expression truncated to a given decimal place (default 0). You can provide a negative decimal argument to round to a certain number of decimal places to the left of the decimal point.

TABLE 19.4 Popular Date and Time SQL Functions

Date/Time SQL Function	Description
CURRENT_DATE()	Returns the current date.
CURRENT_TIME()	Returns the current local time.
CURRENT_TIMESTAMP()	Returns the current time and date in a timestamp format. You may specify a precision, in seconds, in timestamp precision.
CURDATE()	Returns the current date.
CURTIME()	Returns the current time.
DATE(string_exp)	Converts a string in 'yyyy-mm-dd' format into a date.

DAYNAME(date_exp)	Returns a character string containing the day of the week for date_exp in the data source's local language.
DAYOFMONTH(date_exp)	Returns the number of the day of the month for the date in date_exp.
DAYOFWEEK(date_exp)	Returns the day of the week as an integer from 1 to 7, with 1 being Sunday.
DAYOFYEAR(date_exp)	Returns the day of the year in the range 1-366.
HOUR(time_exp)	Returns the hour from time_exp in the range 0–23.
MINUTE(time_exp)	Returns the minute from time_exp in the range 0–59.
MONTH(time_exp)	Returns the month from time_exp in the range 1–12.
MONTHNAME(date_exp)	Returns the name of the month in date_exp.
NOW()	Returns a timestamp for the current time and date.
QUARTER(date_exp)	Returns the quarter for date_exp, in the range 1–4. 1 denotes the quarter from January 1 to March 31.
SECOND(time_exp)	Returns the second from time_exp in the range 0–59.
WEEK(date_exp)	Returns the week of the year for date_exp in the range 1–53.
YEAR(date_exp)	Returns the year from date_exp.

Joins

One of the more important operations performed with relational databases is the *join*, which returns rows of data that are gathered from two or more different tables that are joined in the processing of the query. Joins are even more important if you are working with databases that are thoroughly normalized.

> **Note**
>
> *Normalization* is a process that, more or less, involves structuring the database in order to give the database certain properties and ensure that certain types of operations are performed successfully. To go into any more depth, I would need to talk about more general database theory than I have space for here. If you want to read more about normalization, relations, and the umpteenth normal form, consult a general relational database text.

19

DATABASE
OVERVIEW

To perform a join, select columns from more than one table. For example, assume that you have a Parts table that lists information about parts, including a description, and a separate Prices table that lists pricing information for the parts. The following query would perform a join on these two tables:

```
SELECT Description, Price FROM Parts, Prices
```

However, you might be surprised at the results. The preceding example will return the Cartesian product of the two tables, which is a fancy name for all the possible combinations of the rows in the Parts table and the rows in the Prices table. In most cases, this isn't a useful result.

To narrow the set of returned rows to something more useful, you will need to add a WHERE clause. One of the most common cases is when you have a common identifier in both tables. For example, if both the Prices and Parts tables included a PartNum column, you could generate rows that match a part's description to its price with the following query:

```
SELECT Description, Price FROM Parts, Prices
    WHERE Parts.PartNum = Prices.PartNum
```

> **Note**
>
> You will notice that in the preceding WHERE clause, you used Parts.PartNum and Prices.PartNum instead of just PartNum. This is often necessary in joins to distinguish the PartNum column of one table from the column of the same name in another table, although it isn't necessary if ambiguous column names aren't involved. You can also resolve ambiguity of column names in the select-list with the same syntax.

> **Note**
>
> All SQL database support joins with WHERE. However, many databases, like Microsoft Access, aren't necessarily optimized for WHERE clauses and prefer the INNER JOIN clause:
>
> ```
> SELECT Description, Price
> FROM Parts INNER JOIN Prices ON Parts.PartNum = Prices.PartNum
> ```

Correlation Names

To help simplify some of your queries, SQL allows you to use *table aliases* (also known as *correlation names*), which can reduce the verbosity of your queries and are necessary for some more complicated queries that you will see later. For example, if you had the following query:

```
SELECT MyFirstTable.Name, MyFirstTable.Num, MySecondTable.Date,
    MySecondTable.Time FROM MyFirstTable, MySecondTable
    WHERE MyFirstTable.Id = MySecondTable.Id
```

it could be simplified by using the table aliases f, for MyFirstTable, and s, for MySecondTable, as in the following:

```
SELECT f.Name, f.Num, s.Date, s.Time
    FROM MyFirstTable f, MySecondTable s,
    WHERE f.Id = s.Id
```

In this case, the use of table aliases doesn't affect the meaning of the query in any way; it merely simplifies the notation. However, in more complicated queries, you might find yourself selecting from the same table more than once, as when using subqueries. In these cases, table aliases are essential for specifying exactly which table you are using.

Outer Joins

The syntax for joins you have seen so far performs an inner join, which might not generate the full Cartesian product of the joined tables. For example, if you created a join with the following query:

```
SELECT * FROM Employee, Department
    WHERE Employee.DeptNum = Department.DeptNum
```

the database would process this statement by collecting all the rows present in the Employee table that match those with the rows in the Department table. This result doesn't include results for which no corresponding entry exists in the Employee table. It also won't return any rows for which a matching entry isn't found in the Department table. To create a query that will return rows that don't include a matching row in one of the tables, you will need to use an outer join.

For example, suppose you wanted to select rows for each employee, including those who have not been assigned to a department yet. You can do so by using an outer join like the following:

```
SELECT * FROM
    Employee LEFT OUTER JOIN Department ON
    Employee.DeptNum = Department.DeptNum
```

In the preceding example, you used a LEFT OUTER JOIN, which ensures that all rows of the left table (Employee) will be represented in the result set. You could also use a RIGHT OUTER JOIN to ensure that all rows in the right table are represented, or a FULL OUTER JOIN, which ensures that all rows from both tables are represented, whether or not a matching row appears in the other table.

> **Note**
>
> Outer joins are implemented differently in almost every database. Assume you want to continue our example of selecting all employees including those who have not yet been assigned to a department. In Oracle, a (+) operator is used to indicate an outer join. That syntax would appear as follows:
>
> ```
> SELECT * FROM
>     Employee,
>     Department
> WHERE Employee.DeptNum = Department.DeptNum (+)
> ```
>
> In this Oracle example, the (+) sign appears immediately after the column that can contain a NULL value or be nonexistent.
>
> Sybase and MS SQL Server can implement outer joins using the * operator added to the side of the WHERE clause where you want all your records:
>
> ```
> SELECT * FROM
>     Employee,
>     Department
> WHERE Employee.DeptNum =* Department.DeptNum
> ```
>
> Check out your database documentation for the proper outer join syntax.

Subqueries

In the WHERE clause examples that you have seen so far, you have done comparisons on literal values or comparing two columns, or Boolean combinations of these. However, it is also possible to retrieve information used in a WHERE clause by executing another query, known as a *subquery*.

The first case in which a subquery could be used is with an EXISTS (or NOT EXISTS) predicate. Suppose you wanted to select a list of departments that had no employees assigned to them. You could do so with the following query:

```
SELECT DeptName FROM Department
    WHERE NOT EXISTS (SELECT * FROM Employee)
```

This will return the name of all departments for which the department number isn't found in any of the records in the Employee table.

You could also select a list of departments that have at least one particularly well-paid employee with a query like the following:

```
SELECT DeptName FROM Department d
    WHERE EXISTS
        (SELECT * FROM Employee e
        WHERE e.Salary > 100000 AND d.DeptNum = e.DeptNum)
```

The second case in which subqueries are useful is when using the IN or NOT IN predicates. For example, you could return a list of all the departments that currently have personnel assigned to them by using a query like the following:

```
SELECT DeptName FROM Department
    WHERE DeptNum IN (SELECT DeptNum FROM Employee)
```

The third case in which subqueries are often used involve comparisons that use the ANY or ALL keywords. For example, if you kept separate tables for employees and executives, and wanted to select a list of executives who were paid more than all the regular employees (taken individually, not totaled), you could use the following query:

```
SELECT Ex.Name FROM Executives Ex
    WHERE Ex.Salary > ALL
        (SELECT Emp.Salary FROM Employee Emp)
```

Similarly, you could use the ANY modifier to select a list of executives for which at least one regular employee was better paid with the following query:

```
SELECT Ex.Name FROM Executives Ex
    WHERE Ex.Salary < ANY
        (SELECT Emp.Salary FROM Employee Emp)
```

Union Queries

SQL allows you to generate a single result set from two independent queries by combining them with the UNION keyword. By default, duplicate rows are removed from the result set, although you can disable this by using UNION ALL instead of UNION. Also, you may choose to sort the end result by specifying an ORDER BY clause, which must come after the last query in the union.

For example, you could generate a list of employees in the MIS and SALES departments with the following query:

```
SELECT * FROM Employee WHERE Dept = 'MIS'
UNION
SELECT * FROM Employee WHERE Dept = 'SALES'
```

Of course, there are several other ways that you could more efficiently generate the same results as this query, but this shows a simple example of how UNION works.

INSERT Statements

INSERT puts additional rows into a table. Its format is the following:

```
INSERT INTO table_name {(column_list)}
| VALUES (values_list)    | SELECT command        |
```

The parts of the INSERT command are as follows:

- table_name: This is where you are going to insert new rows. It can be as fully qualified as your database allows.

- column_list: This is a list of columns that you are going to fill with your INSERT. If omitted, the INSERT command assumes all fields will be entered in the order they appear on your table.

Caution

Although column_list isn't required in an INSERT command, you should be careful about omitting it. If you try to save some typing by not adding it and someone later adds fields to your table, your SQL statement may no longer work.

- values_list: This is a list of values (either constants or host variables) that you want to insert.

- SELECT_command: This is a SELECT command that returns values in the same order as the column_list.

Some examples of the INSERT command are shown in Table 19.5.

TABLE 19.5 SQL INSERT Examples

SQL INSERT Statement	Description
INSERT INTO Employee (EmpName, Salary) VALUES ('Joe Schmoe', 50000);	This inserts a row into the Employee table containing the name and salary. Any of the variables that aren't listed (such as Dept) are give a NULL value unless a default is specified.

```
INSERT INTO Employee
VALUES (123, 'Joe Schmoe',
    50000, 'MIS')
```

If you are adding values for each of the columns, omit the column-list and simply assign values for each of the columns, in the order they appear in the table.

```
INSERT INTO FormerEmployee
    (EmpId, EmpName, Reason)
  SELECT EmpId, EmpName,
        'Outsourced'
  FROM Employees
  WHERE Dept = 'MIS'
```

In addition, instead of using the VALUES clause used previously, you could insert rows based on the values returned by a SELECT statement. For example, if your company spun off its MIS department to an outsourcing firm, you could add new records in the FormerEmployee table with a statement like the one in this example.

DELETE Statements

The DELETE command is used to delete existing rows from a table. Its format is as follows:

```
DELETE FROM table_name
{WHERE search_condition}
```

The table_name is the name of the table in which you can delete rows. The search_condition in the WHERE clause is the same as in the SELECT statement.

Some examples of the DELETE statement are shown in Table 19.6.

TABLE 19.6   SQL DELETE Examples

SQL DELETE Statement	Description
DELETE FROM Employee	This deletes all rows from the Employee table.
DELETE FROM Employee WHERE EmpId = 456	This deletes all rows from the table whose EmpID is equal to 456.

19

DATABASE
OVERVIEW

> **Caution**
>
> The DELETE statement is very powerful. Without a WHERE clause, it will delete *all* the rows from a table, often without warning. In most cases, you will want to add a WHERE clause to restrict the number of rows deleted.

UPDATE Statements

The UPDATE command is used to update existing rows on a table with new data. Its format is as follows:

```
UPDATE table_name
SET   column_name1 = expression1,
column_name2 = expression2,...
WHERE condition;
```

The table_name is the name of the table you want to update. The condition in the WHERE clause is the same as in the SELECT statement. The column_name is a name of a column, and expression is the constant or host variable whose value will be placed inside the column.

Some examples of the UPDATE statement are shown in Table 19.7.

TABLE 19.7 SQL UPDATE Examples

SQL UPDATE *Statement*	*Description*
UPDATE Employee SET Salary = Salary + 100	This gives every employee a $100 raise.

UPDATE Employee
    SET Salary = Salary + 100,
      dept = NULL
    WHERE dept = 'Payroll'
	You can use UPDATE to update more than one column at a time or even set a column to NULL. In this example, you give all employees a $100 raise and take away their department assignment if they are in the payroll department.

Summary

This chapter took a brief look at the database interfaces used with Visual C++. This should give you an idea of which of the following chapters will be most useful for you in developing your particular applications. To recap:

- Visual C++ programmers usually use OLE DB and ODBC to access databases from inside a Visual C++ program.

- Although ADO is used in other languages to access OLE DB data sources, new applications written in Visual C++ 6 should concentrate on the pure OLE DB interface rather than the ADO interface.

- Most relational database packages use a variant of SQL (Structured Query Language) to manipulate data inside a database. SQL consists of the Data Definition Language (DDL), the Data Control Language (DCL), and the Data Manipulation Language (DML).

- You usually handle most DDL and DCL calls outside of your Visual C++ program. The new Database Project Wizard included with Visual Studio is a good way to administer databases.

- The DML consists of `SELECT` statements, which query a database, and `INSERT`, `UPDATE`, and `DELETE` statements that change data inside database tables.

19

DATABASE
OVERVIEW

CHAPTER 20

ODBC Programming

by David Bennett and Chuck Wood

The Open Database Connectivity (ODBC) library is provided with Visual C++ to allow your applications to connect to a wide variety of different databases. It provides a common programming interface for accessing databases ranging from simple ASCII files to much more complex mainframe databases. ODBC uses Structured Query Language (SQL) to access all the data sources it supports, including data sources such as text files, which aren't traditionally accessed with SQL.

In addition to Windows platforms, the ODBC library is also being implemented on various other platforms, including UNIX, so the ODBC API can be a valuable tool for producing platform-independent applications. ODBC also standardizes the SQL grammar that is used by your applications—if the data source you are using uses a different dialect of SQL for its native operations, ODBC will perform the necessary translation for you. This can be a great help in developing database-independent applications.

However, this doesn't mean that just because you use ODBC your apps will work anywhere. Developing truly platform-independent applications can require a great deal of additional development work, not to mention testing.

In this chapter, you will explore ODBC version 3, which started shipping with Visual C++ 5.0. Version 3 has changed many of the names of functions and data types that were found in ODBC version 2, although the structure of the API is basically the same. Many of the changes found in ODBC 3 were made to ensure that the Microsoft ODBC API conforms with the Call-Level Interface (CLI) specifications from X/Open and ISO/IEC for database APIs.

> **Tip**
>
> Although previous versions of Visual C++ included help files, Visual Studio 6.0 has all the help contained in the Microsoft Developer's Network. You can look there if you need help with ODBC.

 The source code and project for the code found in this chapter can be found on the CD in the ODBCTest directory.

ODBC Architecture

ODBC applications can use the ODBC API to access data from a variety of different data sources. Each of the different data source types is supported by an ODBC driver specific to that type of data source—it is the driver that implements the meat of the ODBC API functions and performs the actual communication with the database.

The ODBC environment helps you manage connections to different data sources by providing the Driver Manager, which is implemented in `ODBC32.dll`. Your application need only link to the driver manager, which handles the ODBC API calls and passes them off to the appropriate driver. The driver manager also provides certain translations, such as converting between ODBC version 3 and 2 if the application and driver support different versions. Both the interface between your application and the Driver Manager, and the interface between the Driver Manager and individual drivers, use the same ODBC API.

The driver manager will load the appropriate driver when your app tries to connect to a data source of that type, so you don't need to worry about keeping track of separate driver DLLs for each data source type.

Figure 20.1 illustrates how the ODBC functions. An ODBC application makes ODBC database calls to the ODBC Driver Manager. The Driver Manager translates the ODBC call to the appropriate database call provided by the individual database (or data source).

Figure 20.1

Various components of the ODBC environment work together to provide flexible database access for your applications.

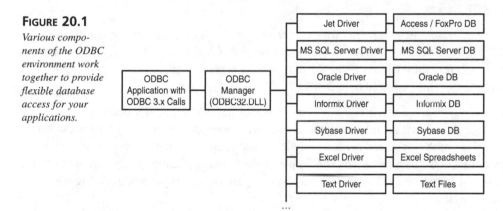

The figure illustrates how your application can use the ODBC API to access a variety of different data sources by linking to a single library—the driver manager.

ODBC Drivers

ODBC allows your applications to access different databases by using different drivers for each database. You can use ODBC to access any database for which a driver is supplied. Visual C++ 6.0 provides drivers for the following databases, although many other drivers are available either from Microsoft or from other database vendors:

- Microsoft SQL Server
- Oracle

- Microsoft Access
- Microsoft FoxPro
- Microsoft Visual FoxPro
- Microsoft Excel
- dBASE
- Paradox
- Text Files

In some cases, the database driver itself will manipulate the data, as is the case with text file drivers. This sort of driver is known as a *single-tier driver*.

In other cases, you may be using *multiple-tier drivers,* in which the database driver uses a database's proprietary client software to communicate to the actual database server. This is most often the case with traditional RDBMS systems, such as Oracle, Informix, or SQL Server.

Each of these drivers supports slightly different levels of functionality. Obviously, an RDBMS such as SQL Server or Oracle can support a wider variety of operations than plain old text files. Likewise, the drivers for these types of data sources support more of the functionality provided by ODBC.

In general, each ODBC driver conforms to one of three levels of conformance: the Core API level, and extension levels 1 and 2. However, many drivers may not implement some functions of their claimed conformance level, and most will implement several higher-level functions. In general, you should plan to test your application with each of the drivers that it may use, because there may be many subtle (or not so subtle) differences between drivers.

Core API Conformance

Core API conformance provides a minimum of ODBC functionality, including connecting to a database, executing SQL statements, and accessing the results of a query. This level also includes limited capabilities for cataloging a database and retrieving error information.

Extension Level 1 Conformance

Extension level 1 includes additional features, giving your applications more complete access to the schema of a database, supporting transactions and stored procedures, and supporting scrollable cursors.

Extension Level 2 Conformance

Extension level 2 provides additional features that are generally found only in complete client-server database implementations, such as more detailed access to the data dictionary, bookmark support, access to special columns, and additional optimization capabilities.

SQL Grammar Conformance

ODBC drivers must support a standard minimum SQL grammar. However, each driver may support a different set of extensions to this minimum standard. ODBC defines conformance levels based on the SQL-92 Entry, Intermediate, and Full levels, as well as the FIPS 127-2 Transitional level. In many cases, as you will see later in this chapter, advanced functionality can be provided via escape sequences, which are standardized in the ODBC API—the driver will translate these as needed for a particular data source.

ODBC Driver Manager

The ODBC Driver Manager provides several very useful features to your application. First, as you saw earlier, the Driver Manager takes care of loading individual drivers as needed (when your application tries to connect to a data source). It also maintains a table of the functions in that driver, based on the connection handle, so that any subsequent ODBC API calls you make are routed to the correct driver. The Driver Manager also provides several functions that aren't provided by drivers, allowing your application to see which drivers and data sources are available on the local system. In addition, the Driver Manager will do some preliminary error checking on many calls before passing them off to the appropriate driver.

Data Sources

In ODBC, a data source is just that—a source of data. It can be an individual file-based database used in desktop database applications, such as MS Access or FoxPro, or it can be a full-blown Relational Database Management System (RDBMS), such as Informix, Oracle, or SQL Server. It can even be a non-relational source of data, such as a text file or an Excel spreadsheet. The concept of a data source allows all the nitty-gritty details of a connection to be hidden from the user, who only selects a data source from a list of data source names and doesn't worry about network addresses or specific file locations. Data sources are made available on the local machine by using the *ODBC Data Source Administrator,* or they may be added programmatically.

ODBC Data Source Administrator

Your ODBC application connects to an ODBC data source, rather than directly to any particular database. The ODBC data sources available to applications on the local machine are configured with the ODBC Administrator application, which can be found in the Control Panel by clicking on the icon labeled 32-bit ODBC. This will open the tabbed dialog shown in Figure 20.2.

FIGURE 20.2

ODBC Data Source Administrator.

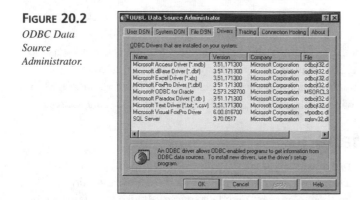

The ODBC Drivers tab lists the drivers that are currently installed on the local machine. The data sources that are configured are shown on the User DSN, System DSN, and File DSN tabs:

- The User DSN tab lists data sources that are configured on the local machine for the current user.

- The System DSN tab lists data sources that can be used by any user on the local machine.

- The File DSN tab lists file data sources, which store all the information needed to make a connection in a .DSN file and may be accessed by any user on any machine that has access to the file (and has the appropriate drivers installed).

Tip

At one time, File DSNs were rarely utilized. However, File DSNs are a good way to control ODBC access without forcing the user or the server administrator to implement a User or System DSN. If you are distributing an executable, or placing ActiveX programs on a Web site and can't get to your Web server, try using a File DSN for your file access.

- The Tracing tab allows you to specify log file tracing options for ODBC.
- The About tab gives information about the current version of ODBC components installed on the local machine.

Adding a Data Source

Before using an ODBC application, you must add the data sources that it will be using. You can add a data source to any of the DSN tabs by clicking on the Add button, which will present you with a dialog to choose the driver to use. Depending on the sort of database driver you choose, you will be presented with additional dialogs prompting for things such as the database name, server address, or other default settings for this data source.

ODBC Installation and Setup Programming

In addition to the utilities such as the Data Source Administrator, the ODBC SDK provides functions that you can use in your own installation and configuration utilities. This goes beyond the scope of this chapter, but is documented in the *ODBC 3 SDK Programmer's Reference*.

ODBC API Basics

Before you get into the various functions provided by the ODBC API, let's look at a few key concepts used throughout the API. In this section, you will look at allocating various handles that are used by ODBC, data types used in ODBC, and how ODBC passes error information to your application.

ODBC Handles

The ODBC API introduces new handle types that are used to reference information about your app's ODBC environment, specific database connections, SQL statements, and Descriptors. In ODBC 3, each of these handle types is allocated with a single function— SQLAllocHandle()—and freed with a single function—SQLFreeHandle().

The SQLAllocHandle() function allocates the internal structures for the various handle types:

```
SQLRETURN SQLAllocHandle(SQL_SMALLINT HandleType, SQLHANDLE InputHandle,
    SQLHANDLE * OutputHandlePtr);
```

> **Note**
>
> In ODBC 3, the `SQLAllocHandle()` function replaces the ODBC 2
> `SQLAllocConnect()`, `SQLAllocEnv()`, and `SQLAllocStmt()` functions, although
> these are still supported by the driver manager, which maps them to
> `SQLAllocHandle()`.

The `HandleType` parameter can be one of the following values:

```
SQL_HANDLE_ENV
SQL_HANDLE_DBC
SQL_HANDLE_STMT
SQL_HANDLE_DESC
```

These values determine which sort of handle is being allocated. You will look at specific examples of allocating each type when you learn about allocating environment, connection, statement, and descriptor handles.

The `InputHandle` specifies the handle from which the new handle is derived. For example, a connection handle is allocated based on an environment handle. An environment handle, however, isn't derived from another handle, so `InputHandle` should be set to `SQL_NULL_HANDLE`.

The `OutputHandlePtr` should point to the new handle that is to be allocated.

If the new handle is successfully allocated, `SQlAllocHandle()` will return `SQL_SUCCESS`; otherwise, it will return `SQL_ERROR`. You will look at how to handle ODBC errors in just a bit.

When you are finished with a particular ODBC handle in your application, you should free the structures associated with the handle by calling `SQLFreeHandle()`, which takes the type of handle to free and the actual handle that is to be freed.

> **Note**
>
> The `SQLFreeHandle()` function replaces the ODBC 2 functions
> `SQLFreeConnect()`, `SQLFreeEnv()`, and `SQLFreeStmt()`. The driver manager will
> map these calls to `SQLFreeHandle()`.

ODBC Data Types

ODBC defines many different standard data types that are used in ODBC applications. There are C data types, which are used in your application code, and SQL data types, which are used to describe the type of data that is used within a data source. Many of the ODBC calls that move data from the application to the data source, or vice versa, can automatically perform conversion between many of these types.

Some of the most common C data types defined in ODBC are listed in Table 20.1, although there are many others described in the *ODBC 3 Programmer's Reference*. The C type identifier is a constant used to represent the type, the ODBC typedef gives the type you should use in declaring this type of variable, and the C type shows what the preprocessor will resolve this to.

TABLE 20.1   ODBC C Data Types

C Type Identifier	ODBC C Typedef	C Type
SQL_C_CHAR	SQLCHAR *	unsigned char *
SQL_C_SSHORT	SQLSMALLINT	short int
SQL_C_USHORT	SQLUSMALLINT	unsigned short int
SQL_C_SLONG	SQLINTEGER	long int
SQL_C_ULONG	SQLUINTEGER	unsigned long int
SQL_C_FLOAT	SQLREAL	float
SQL_C_DOUBLE	SQLDOUBLE	double
SQL_C_BIT	SQLCHAR	unsigned char
SQL_C_STINYINT	SQLSCHAR	signed char
SQL_C_UTINYINT	SQLCHAR	unsigned char
SQL_C_SBIGINT	SQLBIGINT	_int64
SQL_C_UBIGINT	SQLUBIGINT	unsigned _int64
SQL_C_BINARY	SQLCHAR *	unsigned char *
SQL_C_VARBOOKMARK	SQLCHAR *	unsigned char *

ODBC uses SQL data types to describe the data types that are stored in the database. Table 20.2 shows some of the more common types, listing the constant SQL type identifier that is used in your apps and an example SQL definition for the type. For a complete listing, see the *ODBC 3 Programmer's Reference*.

TABLE 20.2   ODBC SQL Data Types

SQL Type Identifier	Sample SQL Definition
SQL_CHAR	CHAR(n)
SQL_VARCHAR	VARCHAR(n)
SQL_LONGVARCHAR	LONG VARCHAR
SQL_DECIMAL	DECIMAL(p,s)
SQL_NUMERIC	NUMERIC(p,s)
SQL_SMALLINT	SMALLINT
SQL_INTEGER	INTEGER
SQL_REAL	REAL
SQL_FLOAT	FLOAT(p)
SQL_DOUBLE	DOUBLE PRECISION
SQL_BIT	BIT
TINYINT	TINYINT
SQL_BIGINT	BIGINT
SQL_BINARY	BINARY(n)
SQL_VARBINARY	VARBINARY(n)
SQL_LONGVARBINARY	LONG VARBINARY
SQL_TYPE_DATE	DATE
SQL_TYPE_TIME	TIME(p)

Creating ODBC Applications

In this section, you will be looking at how to create an ODBC application using the ODBC API directly. In the next chapter, you will see how you can use the MFC database classes and AppWizard to help you create database applications.

Most ODBC applications will perform the following basic steps:

1. Allocate the ODBC environment and connection handles.
2. Write a function to handle errors using environment handles.
3. Connect to a data source.
4. Execute SQL statements or retrieve query results.
5. Disconnect from the data source.
6. Free the ODBC environment.

In this section, you will learn how to connect and disconnect to and from the database, and how to write an ODBC error handling routine. Later in the chapter, executing SQL and retrieving query results will be covered in more detail.

> **Note**
>
> When creating an application that uses the ODBC C API, you include <sqlext.h> (which will also include sql.h) and link to ODBC32.LIB.

Allocating and Freeing ODBC Handles

Before using any other ODBC functions, you must first allocate the ODBC environment, which initializes some of the internal structures and handles used by ODBC. To do this, you must first allocate a variable of type SQLHENV, which will serve as a handle to your ODBC environment. This handle is then initialized with the SQLAllocHandle() function that you saw previously.

To allocate the ODBC environment, HandleType should be set to SQL_HANDLE_ENV, and OutputHandlePtr should point to the environment handle to be allocated. InputHandle should be set to SQL_NULL_HANDLE because the environment isn't derived from another handle. You will see an example of this when you look at SQLConnect() later.

You should only allocate one environment for an application. The same environment can, however, be used for multiple threads and multiple data source connections.

When you are finished with ODBC in your application, you should free the ODBC environment with a call to SQLFreeHandle(), passing a HandleType of SQL_HANDLE_ENV and the environment handle you have allocated.

Setting Your Application's ODBC Version

The ODBC driver manager is designed to support version 2 drivers and applications, as well as newer ODBC 3 components. Depending on the version of ODBC that your application is using, certain functions will behave differently. This requires that your application specify which version of the ODBC API it is using before you go on to allocate connection handles.

Setting the version of ODBC that your application is using is done by calling SQLSetEnvAttr() to set the SQL_ATTR_ODBC_VERSION environment attribute to SQL_OV_ODBC3. You can see an example of this when you connect to a data source.

Allocating a Connection Handle

Next, you allocate a connection handle for each data source that you intend to use. This is also done with the `SQLAllocHandle()` function that you saw previously—`HandleType` is set to `SQL_HANDLE_DBC`, and you should pass the previously allocated environment handle in `InputHandle`. A pointer to the connection handle to be allocated should be passed in `OutputHandlePtr`.

After you have allocated a connection handle, you can attach the returned connection handle to a data source with the `SQLConnect...` functions that you will see next.

When you are finished with a connection, you should free the connection with a call to `SQLFreeHandle()`.

Connection Options

The ODBC API allows you to set many different options associated with a connection handle by calling `SQLSetConnectAttr()`:

```
SQLRETURN SQLSetConnectAttr(SQLHDBC ConnectionHandle, SQLINTEGER Attribute,
    SQLPOINTER ValuePtr, SQLINTEGER StringLength);
```

You should pass a previously allocated `SQLHDBC` in `ConnectionHandle`, although, depending on the attribute set, it doesn't need to be connected to a data source yet. The value passed in `Attribute` determines the option to be set and may include the values listed next, as well as others that may be defined later. You will look at several of these options in more detail later in this chapter:

`SQL_ATTR_ACCESS_MODE` sets read-only mode.

`SQL_ATTR_ASYNC_ENABLE` enables asynchronous operations (more on this later).

`SQL_ATTR_AUTO_IPD` enables automatic population of the IPD after a call to `SQLPrepare()`.

`SQL_ATTR_AUTOCOMMIT` sets auto-commit mode for transaction processing.

`SQL_ATTR_CURRENT_CATALOG` sets the catalog (also called database or qualifier) for the current connection. This is generally something like a specific database name.

`SQL_ATTR_LOGIN_TIMEOUT` sets the timeout value for establishing a connection to a data source.

`SQL_ATTR_CONNECTION_TIMEOUT` sets the timeout value for operations on a connection, other than login or query execution.

`SQL_ATTR_METADATA` determines how string arguments are used in catalog functions.

`SQL_ATTR_ODBC_CURSORS` specifies the type of cursor support that is used.

`SQL_ATTR_PACKET_SIZE` sets the size of the network packets used.

`SQL_ATTR_QUIET_MODE` disables dialogs from the driver or sets the parent window for any dialogs.

`SQL_ATTR_TRACE` enables tracing for the driver manager.

`SQL_ATTR_TRACEFILE` sets the name of the trace file.

`SQL_ATTR_TRANSLATE_LIB` sets the name of a DLL to use for translation between a driver and a data source.

`SQL_ATTR_TRANSLATE_OPTION` sets an option value specific to the translation DLL being used.

`SQL_ATTR_TXN_ISOLATION` sets the level of transaction isolation in use.

The `ValuePtr` and `StringLength` parameters should contain information specific to the option being set.

You can retrieve the current settings for any of these options with a call to `SQLGetConnectAttr()`.

Starting Development on an ODBC Program

Now that you've seen how to allocate the ODBC environment, you are ready to start writing an ODBC program. This section contains simple steps that you can follow that will write an MFC program that uses ODBC calls to connect to an ODBC database. Later in this chapter, more code will be added to each section.

Step 1

Start a new `MFC AppWizard (exe)` project. As you can see in Figure 20.3, a new project called ODBCTest is created using MFC. (This same project will be used throughout this chapter.) Click OK and choose Single Document in step 1 of 6. Click Next.

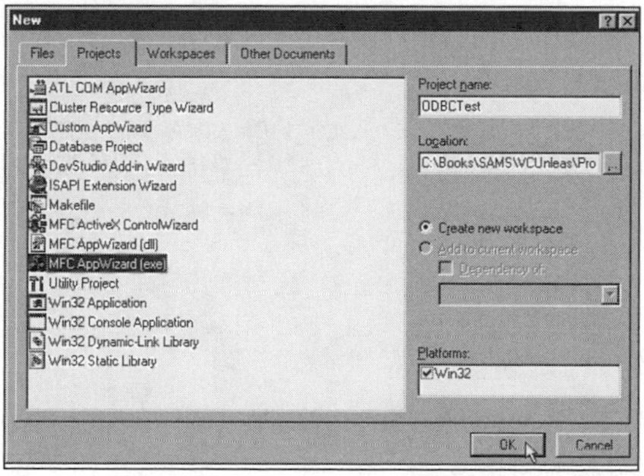

FIGURE 20.3
The MFC AppWizard is a great way to generate database applications.

Step 2

In step 2 of 6 choose Header Files Only, as shown in Figure 20.4. This will allow database support without including any prewritten MFC database code. Click Next, and accept the defaults in step 3 of 6. Click Next, and turn off the Printing and print preview in step 4 of 6. You can accept the rest of the defaults, so you can click Finish here. Click OK when the New Project Information dialog box appears. Your application will then be generated by the MFC AppWizard.

FIGURE 20.4

You can support OLE DB and ODBC by choosing Header Files Only inside your MFC AppWizard.

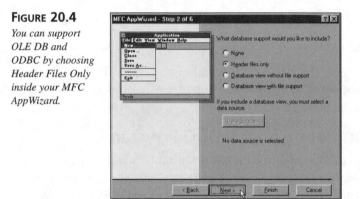

Step 3

In the header file for your view (ODBCTestView.h), add handle variables for the environment and the connection, and add a function prototype for setting up the database. New code needed to do this is shown in gray below:

```
// ODBCTestView.h: interface of the CODBCTestView class
//
/////////////////////////////////////////////////////////////////////////////

#if
!defined(AFX_ODBCTESTVIEW_H__6807EBC2_A9E9_11D3_994A_C4720EBCE741__INCLUDED_)
#define AFX_ODBCTESTVIEW_H__6807EBC2_A9E9_11D3_994A_C4720EBCE741__INCLUDED_

#if _MSC_VER > 1000
#pragma once
#endif // _MSC_VER > 1000

class CODBCTestView : public CView
{
protected: // create from serialization only
    CODBCTestView();
    DECLARE_DYNCREATE(CODBCTestView)
```

```
//////////////////////////////////////////////////
//    Added by Chuck Wood
  SQLHANDLE hOdbcEnv; //ODBC Environment handle
  SQLHANDLE hDbConn;  //ODBC Connection handle
  void setUpODBC();    //Set up the ODBC environment
//////////////////////////////////////////////////
```

```
// Attributes
public:
    CODBCTestDoc* GetDocument();
```

Step 4

In the constructor for your view in your view's source file (ODBCTestView.cpp), call your
(soon-to-be-written) setUpODBC function, as shown below in gray:

```
CODBCTestView::CODBCTestView()
{


    setUpODBC();    //Added by Chuck Wood to set up to ODBC Connection


}
```

Step 5

Finally, at the bottom of your view source file (ODBCTestView.cpp), write a setUpODBC
function, as shown here:

```
// setUpODBC function written by Chuck Wood to allocate ODBC variables
void CODBCTestView::setUpODBC() {
        SQLRETURN sr;                              //Return code for your ODBC calls
// Allocate Environment
        sr = SQLAllocHandle(SQL_HANDLE_ENV, SQL_NULL_HANDLE, &hOdbcEnv);
        if(sr != SQL_SUCCESS && sr != SQL_SUCCESS_WITH_INFO)
                MessageBox("Error in Allocating Environment.");
// Set the App's ODBC Version
        sr = SQLSetEnvAttr(hOdbcEnv, SQL_ATTR_ODBC_VERSION,
        (SQLPOINTER)SQL_OV_ODBC3, SQL_IS_INTEGER);
        if(sr != SQL_SUCCESS && sr != SQL_SUCCESS_WITH_INFO)
                MessageBox("Error in Setting ODBC Version.");
// Allocate Connection
        sr = SQLAllocHandle(SQL_HANDLE_DBC, hOdbcEnv, &hDbConn);
        if(sr != SQL_SUCCESS && sr != SQL_SUCCESS_WITH_INFO)
                MessageBox("Error in Allocating Connection.");
```

20

ODBC PROGRAMMING

```
// Set Connect Timeout
        sr = SQLSetConnectAttr(hDbConn, SQL_ATTR_LOGIN_TIMEOUT, (void*)5, 0);
        if(sr != SQL_SUCCESS && sr != SQL_SUCCESS_WITH_INFO)
                MessageBox("Error in Setting Login Timeout.");
}
```

Step 6

Somewhere, you must free the handles that you've allocated using the `SQLFreeHandle()`
function. This is done in the view's destructor in your view source file
(`ODBCTestView.cpp`):

```
CODBCTestView::~CODBCTestView() {
    if (hDbConn != SQL_NULL_HANDLE)  {
```

```
        //Free connection
        SQLFreeHandle(SQL_HANDLE_DBC, hDbConn);
    }
    if (hOdbcEnv != SQL_NULL_HANDLE)
        //Free environment
        SQLFreeHandle(SQL_HANDLE_ENV, hOdbcEnv);
}
```

When you run your program, you should see the MFC View display. If everything
works, there should be no message that displays.

ODBC Error Handling

The ODBC API provides two levels of diagnostic information about calls to the API. At
the first level, each function returns a `SQLRETURN` value, which will contain a small set of
values indicating the general success or failure of an operation. You've already seen
some error handling with the `SQLRETURN` variable in the previous code example. At the
second level, each function call also generates at least one diagnostic record. These diagnostic records give specific information about any errors that occurred, or other information about the operation.

SQLRETURN Values

All the ODBC functions return a `SQLRETURN` (`signed short`) value, which will receive a
value indicating the success or failure of a function. If a call is completed successfully, it
will return either `SQL_SUCCESS` or `SQL_SUCCESS_WITH_INFO`, which is used to notify your
application that additional information about the operation can be retrieved by calling
`SQLGetDiagRec()`. `SQL_SUCCESS_WITH_INFO` is often used to pass warning messages to

your application. These diagnostic records are useful both for debugging your application and for deciding how to handle certain situations at runtime.

> **Tip**
>
> Because there are two success codes, you should be careful not to simply check for a SQLRETURN value of SQL_SUCCESS, but also check the SQLRETURN for a SQL_SUCCESS_WITH_INFO value.

Currently, all error return codes are defined to be less than 0, although there are some other positive return codes that don't necessarily indicate successful completion. These include SQL_NO_DATA (called SQL_NO_DATA_FOUND in ODBC 2), which is returned when an operation completes successfully, but there is no data to be had; SQL_STILL_EXECUTING, which is used with asynchronous operations; and SQL_NEED_DATA, which is used to indicate that the function needs additional data to complete.

In most cases, if an error occurs in an ODBC function, it will return SQL_ERROR (or SQL_INVALID_HANDLE if things are really wrong).

Diagnostic Records

Each of the ODBC API functions can generate a set of diagnostic records that reflect information about the performance of the operation. These diagnostic records are stored in the structures associated with the ODBC handle that generated the error. For instance, if an error occurs when calling SQLExecDirect(), the statement handle that was used will contain the diagnostic records, whereas errors in something like SQLConnect() will be stored in the connection handle that was used.

The diagnostic records generated by a function can be accessed from the handle until another call is made that uses that handle.

All ODBC calls will return at least a header record and may contain many additional status records. These records consist of a predefined set of fields, as well as others that may be defined by the particular driver you are using.

SQLGetDiagField()

You can retrieve the value of a particular field from a diagnostic record by using the SQLGetDiagField() function:

```
SQLRETURN SQLGetDiagField(SQLSMALLINT HandleType, SQLHANDLE Handle,
    SQLSMALLINT RecNumber, SQLSMALLINT DiagIdentifier, SQLPOINTER DiagInfoPtr,
    SQLSMALLINT BufferLength, SQLSMALLINT * StringLengthPtr);
```

20

ODBC PROGRAMMING

> **Note**
>
> In ODBC 3, `SQLGetDiagField()` and `SQLGetDiagRec()` replace `SQLError()`.

The `Handle` and `HandleType` parameters are used to specify the handle to retrieve records from and its type.

The `RecNumber` field is used to specify the record to retrieve. To retrieve information from the header record, this field should be set to 0. You can retrieve the total number of additional status records available for a handle by retrieving the `SQL_DIAG_NUMBER` field from record 0.

The `DiagIdentifier` parameter specifies which field to return. This may be one of the fields that is predefined in the ODBC API or any additional fields that may be added by specific drivers. The following are some of the most common fields (note that the header record and status records contain different fields):

Header Record Fields

> `SQL_DIAG_NUMBER`—Number of status records available
>
> `SQL_DIAG_RETURN_CODE`—The return code for the previous function call

Status Record Fields

> `SQL_DIAG_SQLSTATE`—A five-character SQLSTATE code (see SQLSTATEs)
>
> `SQL_DIAG_MESSAGE_TEXT`—A plaintext message about the error or warning
>
> `SQL_DIAG_NATIVE`—The native error code from the driver or data source
>
> `SQL_DIAG_COLUMN_NUMBER`—The column (if any) associated with this record
>
> `SQL_DIAG_ROW_NUMBER`—The row (if any) associated with this record

For details on the other fields available in diagnostic records, see the online documentation for `SQLGetDiagField()`.

The information for the requested field is returned in the buffer at `DiagInfoPtr`, and the length of the data is returned at `StringLengthPtr`.

SQLSTATES

There are a great number of possible values for SQLSTATE codes that can be returned in the `SQL_DIAG_SQLSTATE` field, many of which may have a variety of different meanings, depending on the driver you are using. Because of this, you should be careful in how you use the SQLSTATE codes in your programming logic if you intend to use a variety of drivers.

However, in most cases, the following SQLSTATEs can be safely used in your programming logic because they are generally implemented in the same way in most drivers and can be useful in controlling program flow:

01004—Data truncated

01S02—Option value changed

HY008—Operation canceled

HYC00—Optional feature not implemented

HYT00—Timeout expired

For a complete listing of possible SQLSTATEs, see Appendix A of the *ODBC 3 Programmer's Guide*, included in the online documentation. In addition, the SQLSTATEs that can be returned for each function are listed in the online documentation for that function.

SQLGetDiagRec()

In addition to the SQLGetDiagField() function shown previously, ODBC 3 provides the SQLGetDiagRec() function, which will retrieve some of the most commonly used fields from a status record in one fell swoop. This function will return the SQLSTATE, the native error code, and the diagnostic message text that is contained in status records. However, to access the header record, you must use SQLGetDiagField().

Writing an ODBC Error Handling Routine

One of the most common routines to write for ODBC programs is a routine that handles all ODBC errors. With such a routine, it's easy to add error handling to your ODBC database. Furthermore, writing an error routine is simple when armed with the knowledge found in this section. As we continue with our same ODBCTest example, add an error prototype to the view header file (ODBCTestView.h) as shown in gray in the following code:

```
protected: // create from serialization only
        CODBCTestView();
        DECLARE_DYNCREATE(CODBCTestView)

////////////////////////////////////////////////////////////////////////
//      Added by Chuck Wood
        SQLHANDLE hOdbcEnv;                     //ODBC Environment handle
        SQLHANDLE hDbConn;                      //ODBC Connection handle
        void setUpODBC();                       //Set up the ODBC environment

        void displayODBCError (SQLRETURN sr, char *inMessage = NULL);
➥//Display error
```

20

ODBC PROGRAMMING

//

Then, at the bottom of your view's source file (`ODBCTestView.cpp`) write the
`displayODBCError` routine using the `SQLGetDiagRec` function to retrieve error information:

```
// displayODBCError function written by Chuck Wood
// to display ODBC Errors
void CODBCTestView::displayODBCError (SQLRETURN sr,
                  char *inMessage) {
    if(sr != SQL_SUCCESS && sr != SQL_SUCCESS_WITH_INFO) {
        SQLCHAR SqlState[6];
        SQLINTEGER NativeError;
        SQLCHAR ErrMsg[SQL_MAX_MESSAGE_LENGTH];
        int i = 1;
        char message[512];
        strcpy (message, "");
        if (inMessage) {
            strcpy(message, inMessage);
            strcat(message, " - ");
        }
        sprintf(message, "%sError in SQLConnect(): %d.",
                message, sr);
        MessageBox(message);
        while(SQLGetDiagRec(SQL_HANDLE_DBC, hDbConn, i,
                SqlState, &NativeError,
                ErrMsg, sizeof(ErrMsg), NULL)
                != SQL_NO_DATA) {
            sprintf(message,
    "Diag: %d, SQLSTATE: %s NativeError: %d ErrMsg: %s",
                i++, SqlState, NativeError, ErrMsg);
            MessageBox(message);
        }
    }
}
```

Now when a `SQLRETURN` code returns an error, you can call this function to display the
error with minimal coding overhead.

Connecting to a Data Source

After you allocate a connection handle with `SQLAllocConnect()`, you must connect the
handle to a data source before you can start operating on that data source. ODBC provides three functions that can be used for this. `SQLConnect()` provides the most direct
method of connecting from your code, and `SQLDriverConnect()` presents a dialog to the
user to choose a data source. The third connect function, `SQLBrowseConnect()`, can be
used to browse available data sources, while prompting for any additional information
that may be required.

> **Caution**
>
> Before using any of the code examples to connect to a database, you need to define an ODBC User DSN or ODBC System DSN named "VCUnleashed" using the ODBC Data Source Administrator. The procedure for this is shown earlier in this chapter in the section entitled "ODBC Data Source Administrator," and an Access database, VCUnleashed.mdb, is included on the CD that can be used with these examples.

SQLConnect()

The first of the connection functions that you will look at is `SQLConnect()`. This function provides you with the most direct programmatic control of the connection, although if you want to allow the user to choose data sources at runtime, you need to code the user interface for selecting data sources yourself. That said, let's look at how it works. The prototype for `SQLConnect()` is shown in the following:

```
SQLRETURN SQLConnect(SQLHDBC ConnectionHandle, SQLCHAR* ServerName,
    SQLSMALLINT NameLength1, SQLCHAR* UserName, SQLSMALLINT NameLength2,
    SQLCHAR* Authentication, SQLSMALLINT NameLength3);
```

When calling `SQLConnect()`, `ConnectionHandle` should be a connection handle that was previously allocated with `SQLAllocConnection()`. The remaining parameters are used to pass strings for the data source name (`ServerName`), user ID (`UserName`), and password (`Authentication`). For many data sources, such as text files, that are on the local machine, you don't need to specify a user ID or password, and you can pass NULL pointers for `UserName` and `Authentication`.

> **Note**
>
> All string parameters that are passed as inputs to ODBC functions will consist of a pointer to the string and a separate parameter for its length, which is used to support languages that require this. For C/C++ applications, you should pass a pointer to a null-terminated string and set the length parameter to SQL_NTS (Null-Terminated String).

When you call `SQLConnect()` or one of the other connect functions, the ODBC driver manager will load the requested driver if it isn't already loaded and will connect to the requested data source. If an error occurs, `SQLConnect()` will return `SQL_ERROR` (or `SQL_INVALID_HANDLE`), and you should call `SQLGetDiagRec()` to retrieve specific information about the error(s).

Writing a Program to Connect to a Database

This section shows how you can use `SQLConnect()` to connect to a data source named `"VCUnleashed"`:

1. Find some way to call a connection routine. In my example, I added a menu named Connect With SQLConnect. I then used the ClassWizard to create an `OnViewConnectwithsqlconnect` function that is called every time this menu option is selected.

2. After you have defined a function that is called to connect to the database, you need to code the function in your view's source file (`ODBCTestView.cpp`). The code needed to connect to the `VCUnleashed` database is shown in gray:

```
void CODBCTestView::OnViewConnectwithsqlconnect()   {
```

```
// Function for connecting to the database written by Chuck Wood
    SQLRETURN sr;                        //Return code for your ODBC calls
    char szDSN[] = "VCUnleashed";        //ODBC name
    char szUID[] = "";                   //User ID
    char szAuthStr[] = "";               //Password
// Connect to Data Source
    sr = SQLConnect(hDbConn, (UCHAR *)szDSN, SQL_NTS,
                    (UCHAR *)szUID, SQL_NTS,
                    (UCHAR *) szAuthStr, SQL_NTS);
    if(sr != SQL_SUCCESS && sr != SQL_SUCCESS_WITH_INFO)
        displayODBCError(sr, "Error in OnViewConnectwithsqlconnect");
    else
        MessageBox("Connected OK");
```

```
}
```

The previous code example shows how to use the `SQLConnect` function, and how to call the `displayODBCError` function written in the last section if an error occurs.

Tip

You should disconnect from the data source when you are finished with it by calling `SQLDisconnect()`, and then de-allocate the connection handle with a call to `SQLFreeHandle()`. In this example, this is done in the view's destructor in the view source file (`ODBCTestView.cpp`):`CODBCTestView::~CODBCTestView() {`

```
if (hDbConn != SQL_NULL_HANDLE) {
    //Disconnect from database
    SQLDisconnect(hDbConn);
    //Free connection
    SQLFreeHandle(SQL_HANDLE_DBC, hDbConn);
}
```

```
    if (hOdbcEnv != SQL_NULL_HANDLE)
        //Free environment
        SQLFreeHandle(SQL_HANDLE_ENV, hOdbcEnv);
}
```

SQLDriverConnect()

The next of the connect functions that you will look at is `SQLDriverConnect()`, which opens a dialog to the user for selecting a data source. `SQLDriverConnect()` can also be used to pass additional connection parameters that aren't supported by the `SQLConnect()` function. Here is the prototype for `SQLDriverConnect()`:

```
SQLRETURN SQLDriverConnect(SQLHDBC ConnectionHandle, SQLHWND WindowHandle,
    SQLCHAR * InConnectionString, SQLSMALLINT StringLength1,
    SQLCHAR * OutConnectionString, SQLSMALLINT BufferLength,
    SQLSMALLINT * StringLength2Ptr, SQLUSMALLINT DriverCompletion);
```

`ConnectionHandle` should be passed a connection handle that was previously allocated with `SQLAllocHandle()`, and `WindowHandle` may be passed the window handle for the parent of any dialog boxes that may be created.

The `InConnectionString` parameter points to a connection string that is passed into `SQLDriverConnect()`, consisting of a series of attribute keywords and their values. For example, to connect to a data source named `SalesData` for user `JohnDoe` with a password of `JaneDoe`, you might pass a string like the following:

```
"DSN=SalesData;UID=JohnDoe;PWD=JaneDoe"
```

The `DSN`, `UID`, and `PWD` attribute keywords are defined by ODBC, although individual drivers may support many additional keywords.

The value that you pass for `DriverCompletion` determines whether a dialog is presented to the user for selecting a data source. If you set `DriverCompletion` to `SQL_DRIVER_NOPROMPT`, no dialog will be presented. If `InConnectionString` includes incorrect or insufficient information, `SQLDriverConnect()` will return `SQL_ERROR`.

On the other hand, if you specify `SQL_DRIVER_PROMPT`, a dialog will always be presented to the user—the attributes passed in `InConnectionString` are used only as initial values in the dialog.

If you specify SQL_DRIVER_COMPLETE or SQL_DRIVER_COMPLETE_REQUIRED, a dialog is presented to the user only if the attributes passed in InConnectionString are insufficient to connect to a data source. If you have specified SQL_DRIVER_COMPLETE_REQUIRED, only the controls for required information will be enabled in the dialog.

When a connection to a data source is established, SQLDriverConnect() will return the actual connection string that was used in OutConnectionString. This can be used to determine the options that the user has selected from a dialog.

SQLBrowseConnect()

The last of the connection functions is SQLBrowseConnect(), which provides an iterative method for your application to browse available data sources. Note that this function doesn't provide the user interface for browsing, as SQLDriverConnect() does. SQLBrowseConnect() is generally available only for client-server database systems and isn't usually supported for local databases, such as MS Access. Here is the prototype for SQLBrowseConnect():

```
SQLRETURN SQLBrowseConnect(SQLHDBC ConnectionHandle, SQLCHAR *
➥InConnectionString,
    SQLSMALLINT StringLength1, SQLCHAR * OutConnectionString,
    SQLSMALLINT BufferLength, SQLSMALLINT * StringLength2Ptr);
```

When calling SQLBrowseConnect(), you should first pass in a connection string in InConnectionString similar to that used in SQLDriverConnect(). If the information in this string is sufficient to connect to a data source, SQLBrowseConnect() will return SQL_SUCCESS or SQL_SUCCESS_WITH_INFO, and your connection is all set to go.

If additional information is required, SQLBrowseConnect() will return SQL_NEED_DATA. Even more specific information is returned in OutConnectionString.

In general, attributes that must be specified are of the following format: *KEYWORD*:*PROMPT*=?;, where *KEYWORD* is an attribute name, such as UID, and *PROMPT* is a string suitable for prompting the user. (You don't need to use the prompt string when building InConnectionString.) In addition, some attributes returned in OutConnectionString will present a list of possible choices in the following format:

KEYWORD:*PROMPT*={*CHOICE1*, *CHOICE2*, *CHOICE3*};

For example, if you call SQLBrowseConnect() with InConnectionString of DSN=MyRDBMS, it may return SQL_NEED_DATA with OutConnectionString receiving DSN=MyRDBMS;UID:User Name=?;DATABASE:Database={EmpDB, InventoryDB, AccountsDB}.

You then should be able to call SQLBrowseConnect() again with InConnectionString of
DSN=MyRDBMS;UID=JohnDoe;DATABASE=EmpDB. If all goes well, SQLBrowseConnect() will
return SQL_SUCCESS or SQL_SUCCESS_WITH_INFO and your connection is ready for executing SQL statements against the data source.

SQLDataSources()

If you want to code your own browsing function, you can retrieve the available data
sources by calling SQLDataSources():

```
SQLRETURN SQLDataSources(SQLHENV EnvironmentHandle, SQLUSMALLINT fDirection,
    SQLCHAR * ServerName, SQLSMALLINT BufferLength1, SQLSMALLINT *
➡NameLength1Ptr,
    SQLCHAR * Description, SQLSMALLINT BufferLength2, SQLSMALLINT *
➡NameLength2Ptr);
```

To list all the available data sources, you should call SQLDataSources() with
fDirection set to SQL_FETCH_FIRST. This will return the data source name in the buffer
at ServerName and its description at Description. In most cases, you can set the
NameLength1 and NameLength2 parameters to NULL because you usually don't need to
receive the length of the null-terminated strings that are returned.

To retrieve the name and description for the remaining data sources, you should call
SQLDataSources(), with fDirection set to SQL_FETCH_NEXT, until it returns
SQL_NO_DATA_FOUND, which indicates that all entries have been read. By adding the following function at the bottom of your view source file, adding the appropriate function
prototype in the view class definition in the view header file, and adding a function call
in the instructor, you can display a list of data sources like the one shown in Figure 20.5.

```
// Function to list the data sources written by Chuck Wood
void CODBCTestView::listDataSources() {
    UWORD fDirection = SQL_FETCH_FIRST;
    SQLRETURN sr;
    SQLCHAR szDSN[SQL_MAX_DSN_LENGTH+1];
    SQLCHAR szDescription[100];
    char message[4096];
    strcpy (message, "");          //Initialize message
    do {
        sr = SQLDataSources(hOdbcEnv, fDirection,
            (UCHAR *)szDSN, sizeof(szDSN), NULL,
            (UCHAR *)szDescription,
            sizeof(szDescription), NULL);
        if(sr != SQL_SUCCESS
            && sr != SQL_SUCCESS_WITH_INFO)
            sprintf(message,
                "%s\nSQLDataSources returns: %d\n",
                message, sr);
```

```
        else
            sprintf(message, "%sDSN: [%s] Desc: [%s]\n",
                    message, szDSN, szDescription);
        fDirection = SQL_FETCH_NEXT;
    } while(sr == SQL_SUCCESS || sr == SQL_SUCCESS_WITH_INFO);
    MessageBox(message);
}
```

FIGURE 20.5

Output from the
listDataSources()
function

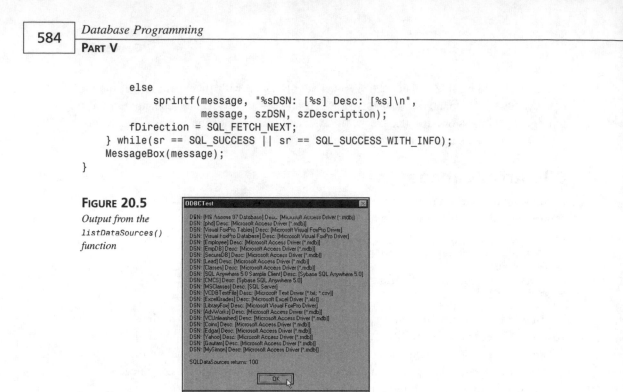

Retrieving Connection Information

In addition to the connection options, you can access a wide range of information about
the ODBC driver and data source associated with an SQLHDBC by using the
SQLGetInfo() function:

```
SQLRETURN SQLGetInfo( SQLHDBC ConnectionHandle, SQLUSMALLINT InfoType,
    SQLPOINTER InfoValuePtr, SQLSMALLINT BufferLength, SQLSMALLINT *
StringLengthPtr);
```

When calling SQLGetInfo(), ConnectionHandle should be a connection handle that was
previously attached to a data source. The InfoType parameter is used to specify which
piece of information is to be retrieved. For more on the specific values supported, see the
online documentation for SQLGetInfo(). For now, let's say that just about anything you
might want to know about a driver or a data source is available via this function, including information on conformance levels, support for various functions, and data types
supported.

Depending on the value you pass for InfoType, the data returned at InfoValuePtr may
take several different formats, including null-terminated strings, 16-bit integers, or 32-bit
values. You should set BufferLength to the maximum size of the buffer at
InfoValuePtr. On return, the value at StringLengthPtr will contain the actual length of
the data returned.

Executing SQL Statements

After you have successfully connected to a data source, it is time to get down to the real work of manipulating the data. This is done by executing Structured Query Language statements against the connected data source. For more on the syntax of SQL, see Chapter 19, "Database Overview."

In the following sections, you will look at how statement handles are used to execute SQL against a data source, including the use of SQLExecDirect() for direct executions, and the SQLPrepare() and SQLExecute() functions, which can be used to prepare a SQL statement in a separate step, which can then be executed multiple times.

Statement Handles

Before executing a statement, you must allocate a statement handle, which provides a data structure for ODBC to keep track of the SQL statement to be executed and the results it will return. Allocating a statement is done with the SQLAllocHandle() function that you saw earlier—HandleType should be set to SQL_HANDLE_STMT, InputHandle should receive a previously allocated connection handle, and OutputHandle should point to a new handle of type SQLHSTMT that will be initialized. You can see an example of this in the next section where you see how to use the statement handle and SQLExecDirect() to execute SQL statements.

The SQLSetStmtAttr() and SQLGetStmtAttr() functions allow you to set and retrieve options for a statement handle in the same way that SQLSetConnectAttr() and SQLGetConnectAttr() work with options for connection handles. You will look at some of the specific options for statements later in this chapter.

When you are finished with a statement handle, you should de-allocate it by calling SQLFreeHandle(), with HandleType set to SQL_HANDLE_STMT.

SQLExecDirect()

As the name suggests, SQLExecDirect() is the most direct (and easiest) method of executing an SQL statement against an ODBC data source. For statements that will be executed only once, this is also the fastest method of submitting SQL statements. The following is the prototype for SQLExecDirect():

```
SQLRETURN SQLExecDirect(SQLHSTMT StatementHandle, SQLCHAR* StatementText,
    SQLINTEGER TextLength);
```

This function simply takes a null-terminated string containing an SQL statement (StatementText) and executes it on the data source connected to the statement handle in

`StatementHandle`. (Remember that, for C/C++ applications, length parameters like `TextLength` should be set to `SQL_NTS`.)

If `SQLExecDirect()` returns `SQL_SUCCESS`, the statement was successfully executed against the data source. In some cases, where the statement was successful, but something abnormal occurred, it will return `SQL_SUCCESS_WITH_INFO`. In this case, or if `SQLExecDirect()` returns `SQL_ERROR`, you can retrieve additional information by calling `SQLGetDiagRec()`.

For most implementations, it's best to have a function that handles all SQL commands. In the ODBCTest example, menu items were added to add "Insert Chuck Wood" and "Delete Chuck Wood" options. These commands are designed to insert and delete a record into an `Employee` table. The following steps show the use of `SQLExecDirect()` to perform a simple `INSERT` and a simple `DELETE` by using a standard SQL routine:

1. Add a function prototype inside your view header file (`ODBCTestView.h`), as shown below in gray:

```
class CODBCTestView : public CView
{
protected: // create from serialization only
        CODBCTestView();
        DECLARE_DYNCREATE(CODBCTestView)

/////////////////////////////////////////////////////////////////////////////
//      Added by Chuck Wood
        SQLHANDLE hOdbcEnv;                       //ODBC Environment handle
        SQLHANDLE hDbConn;                        //ODBC Connection handle
        void setUpODBC();                         //Set up the ODBC environment
        void displayODBCError (SQLRETURN sr, char *inMessage = NULL);
➥//Display error


        void executeSQL (SQLCHAR *SQL); //Execute an SQL string


/////////////////////////////////////////////////////////////////////////////
```

2. Inside the view source file (`ODBCTestView.h`), write the routine using the `SQLExecDirect` function:

```
void CODBCTestView::executeSQL (SQLCHAR *SQL) {
        SQLRETURN sr;                             //Return code for your ODBC
➥calls
        SQLHSTMT hstmt;
// Allocate new Statement Handle based on previous connection
        sr = SQLAllocHandle(SQL_HANDLE_STMT, hDbConn, &hstmt);
        if(sr != SQL_SUCCESS && sr != SQL_SUCCESS_WITH_INFO) {
```

```
                char message[200];
                sprintf (message, "Error Allocating Handle: %d\n", sr);
                MessageBox(message);
        }
        sr = SQLExecDirect(hstmt, SQL, SQL_NTS);
        if(sr != SQL_SUCCESS && sr != SQL_SUCCESS_WITH_INFO) {
                char message[200];
                sprintf (message, "Error in SQLExecDirect. SQL was:\n\n%s\n\n",
➥SQL);
                displayODBCError(sr, message);
        }
        SQLFreeHandle(SQL_HANDLE_STMT, hstmt);
}
```

3. Add the "Insert Chuck Wood" and "Delete Chuck Wood" menu options, and use the ClassWizard to generate these functions. Then simply call the executeSQL function with the appropriate SQL string, as shown by the following lines in gray:

```
void CODBCTestView::OnViewInsertchuckwood() {
```

```
    executeSQL((SQLCHAR *)
        "INSERT INTO Employee (EmpName, Salary, Dept) VALUES ('Chuck Wood',
        ➥120000, 'IS')");
```

```
}
void CODBCTestView::OnViewDeletechuckwood() {
```

```
    executeSQL((SQLCHAR *)
      "DELETE FROM Employee WHERE EmpName ='Chuck Wood'");
```

```
}
```

Prepared SQL Statements

In addition to the SQLExecDirect() method that you saw previously, ODBC also allows you to prepare SQL statements in a separate step before executing them. This can be a much more efficient way to do things if you will be executing the same statement many times. You parse the SQL only once and can then execute the statement many different times, without the parsing overhead. This technique is particularly useful when combined with statement parameters, which you will see later.

The `SQLPrepare()` function is used to prepare an SQL statement for execution:

```
SQLRETURN SQLPrepare(SQLHSTMT StatementHandle, SQLCHAR * StatementText,
    SQLINTEGER TextLength);
```

This function takes a `StatementHandle` previously allocated with `AllocHandle()` and a pointer to a null-terminated string that contains the `StatementText`. Remember that in C/C++ apps, you should pass `SQL_NTS` for parameters like `TextLength`.

When a statement is prepared, the ODBC standard SQL grammar that is passed to `SQLPrepare()` is translated to the native SQL dialect for the data source. You can retrieve this native translation by calling `SQLNativeSql()`.

SQLExecute()

After the statement is prepared by `SQLPrepare()`, you can execute the statement by calling `SQLExecute()` with the statement handle that was passed to `SQLPrepare()`.

Although you can gain some performance advantages by preparing static SQL statements that will be executed several times, prepared statements are most useful when you use parameters with them, as you will see in the next section. You will also take a look at an example after you look at parameters.

Working with Parameters

So far, you have seen how to execute SQL statements based on a relatively static string. You have also seen how to use `SQLPrepare()` to create an SQL statement that can be executed many different times—but often, you don't want to execute exactly the same statement many times. It would be convenient if you could use the same general statement many times, with different values each time. Well, it turns out that ODBC lets you do just this by allowing the use of parameters in your SQL statements.

For example, you could use `SQLPrepare()` to prepare the following SQL statement:

```
"SELECT * FROM Employees WHERE empNo = ?;"
```

The question mark (?) in this statement serves as a placeholder, or marker, for statement parameter. Parameters can be used to pass values into an SQL statement, as in this `SELECT` example. They may also be used to return output values in a procedure call. Values are assigned to the parameter at runtime by binding a variable to the parameter with `SQLBindParameter()`.

SQLBindParameter()

The `SQLBindParameter()` function allows you to bind a buffer in memory to a given parameter marker, before the statement is executed. Its prototype is shown here:

```
SQLRETURN SQLBindParameter(SQLHSTMT StatementHandle, SQLUSMALLINT
ParameterNumber,
    SQLSMALLINT InputOutputType, SQLSMALLINT ValueType, SQLSMALLINT
ParameterType,
    SQLUINTEGER ColumnSize, SQLSMALLINT DecimalDigits, SQLPOINTER
ParameterValuePtr,
    SQLINTEGER BufferLength, SQLINTEGER * StrLen_or_IndPtr);
```

The `StatementHandle` parameter refers to the statement handle that you are using to execute the SQL statement.

The parameters in an SQL statement are numbered from left to right, starting with 1. You can call `SQLBindParameter()` for each parameter, with the appropriate value for `ParameterNumber`.

The `InputOutputType` parameter specifies how the parameter is used. For SQL statements that don't call procedures, such as `SELECT` or `INSERT` statements, this will be `SQL_PARAM_INPUT`. For procedure parameters, you can also use parameters of type `SQL_PARAM_OUTPUT` and `SQL_PARAM_INPUT_OUTPUT`.

The `ValueType` parameter is used to specify the C type of the variable that is being bound—`SQL_C_SLONG`—and the `ParameterType` argument specifies the SQL type only of the parameter—`SQL_INTEGER`. These parameters specify how ODBC will perform any conversion of the data. For more on ODBC data types, see the earlier section on ODBC data types.

The `ColumnSize` and `DecimalDigits` parameters are used to specify the size of the SQL parameter and its precision. These parameters are used only for certain values of `ParameterType` where they are applicable.

The `ParameterValuePtr` parameter points to the buffer in your application that holds the value to be substituted in the SQL statement, and `BufferLength` is used to pass the length of the buffer for binary or character parameters.

The buffer at `StrLen_or_IndPtr` is used to specify information about the data passed in `ParameterValuePtr`. The value in this buffer can have one of the following values:

- The length of the parameter at `ParameterValuePtr`.
- `SQL_NTS`—The buffer holds a null-terminated string.
- `SQL_NULL_DATA`—The buffer holds a `NULL` value.
- `SQL_DEFAULT_PARAM`—A procedure should use a default parameter value.
- `SQL_LEN_DATA_AT_EXEC`—Used to pass parameter data with `SQLPutData()`.

For output parameters, this buffer will also receive one of these values after the statement is executed. A menu option, "Test Prepared Insert" was added to the ODBCTest example,

20

ODBC PROGRAMMING

and the Class Wizard was used to create a new function in the source file
(ODBCTestView.cpp) called CODBCTestView::OnViewTestpreparedinsert that is executed when the new menu option is selected. The following added code shows how you
can prepare a statement to add "Joe Schmoe" to the Employee database:

```
void CODBCTestView::OnViewTestpreparedinsert() {
```

```
//Code added by Chuck Wood
//REMEMBER TO CLICK CONNECT FIRST
    SQLRETURN sr;
    SQLHSTMT hstmt;
    SQLCHAR SQL[200] =
        "INSERT INTO Employee (EmpName, Salary, Dept) VALUES (?, ?, ?)";
    char name[] = "Joe Schmoe";
    double salary = 69584.23;
    char department[] = "Accounting";
    SQLINTEGER nameLength = SQL_NTS;
    SQLINTEGER salaryLength = sizeof(salary);
    SQLINTEGER deptLength = SQL_NTS;
    // Allocate a new statement handle
    sr = SQLAllocHandle(SQL_HANDLE_STMT, hDbConn, &hstmt);
    // Prepare statement
    if(sr != SQL_SUCCESS && sr != SQL_SUCCESS_WITH_INFO)
        displayODBCError(sr,
 "Error in SQLAllocHandle in OnViewTestpreparedinsert");
    sr = SQLPrepare(hstmt, SQL, SQL_NTS);
    if(sr != SQL_SUCCESS && sr != SQL_SUCCESS_WITH_INFO)
        displayODBCError(sr,
 "Error in SQLPrepare in OnViewTestpreparedinsert");
    // Bind Parameters
    sr = SQLBindParameter(hstmt, 1, SQL_PARAM_INPUT,
        SQL_C_CHAR, SQL_CHAR, 0, 0,
        name, sizeof(name), &nameLength);
    if(sr != SQL_SUCCESS && sr != SQL_SUCCESS_WITH_INFO)
        displayODBCError(sr,
         "Error in Binding 1 in OnViewTestpreparedinsert");
    sr = SQLBindParameter(hstmt, 2, SQL_PARAM_INPUT,
        SQL_C_DOUBLE, SQL_DOUBLE, 0, 0,
        &salary, sizeof(salary), &salaryLength);
    if(sr != SQL_SUCCESS && sr != SQL_SUCCESS_WITH_INFO)
        displayODBCError(sr,
         "Error in Binding 2 in OnViewTestpreparedinsert");
    sr = SQLBindParameter(hstmt, 3, SQL_PARAM_INPUT,
        SQL_C_CHAR, SQL_CHAR, 0, 0,
        department, sizeof(department), &deptLength);
    if(sr != SQL_SUCCESS && sr != SQL_SUCCESS_WITH_INFO)
        displayODBCError(sr,
         "Error in Binding 3 in OnViewTestpreparedinsert");
```

```
    // Execute statement with parameters
    sr = SQLExecute(hstmt);
    if(sr != SQL_SUCCESS && sr != SQL_SUCCESS_WITH_INFO)
        displayODBCError(sr,
 "Error in SQLExecute in OnViewTestpreparedinsert");
    SQLFreeHandle(SQL_HANDLE_STMT, hstmt);
```

Parameter Arrays

In the previous example, you passed one set of parameter values for each call to
SQLExecute(). Although this can add some efficiency to your code, you can gain even
more in terms of both network overhead and data source execution time by passing an
entire array of parameters to a single SQLExecute() call. Unfortunately, like many other
advanced features of ODBC, this may not be supported by all drivers.

To pass arrays of parameters, you set the SQL_ATTR_PARAMSET_SIZE statement attribute to
the length of your parameter array(s). You should also set the SQL_ATTR_PARAM_
STATUS_PTR attribute to point to an array to receive the status for the result of each set of
parameters.

Row-Wise Binding

In the previous example, you used column-wise binding to bind a separate buffer for
each parameter, although you can also simplify your code somewhat by binding parameters by row. This allows you to define a structure that will hold all your parameters for a
statement. You can then pass an array of these structures when calling SQLExecute().

To use row-wise binding, you set the SQL_ATTR_PARAM_BIND_TYPE statement attribute to
the size of the structure you have defined to hold the parameters. You will then bind each
parameter individually, binding to the address of the corresponding structure field for the
first element of the array. This is very similar to the row-wise binding that you will see
for column data later in this chapter.

Passing Parameter Data at Execution Time

Earlier, when you explored SQLBindParameter(), you saw that you could pass a value of
SQL_DATA_AT_EXEC in the indicator array specified by StrLen_or_IndPtr. This allows
you to pass data for lengthy parameters at the time the statement is executed. This can be
useful for values that are too long to store in conventional parameter buffers.

To pass parameter data at execution time, you bind the desired parameters with the
SQL_DATA_AT_EXEC flag set in the indicator array, and then call SQLExecute(), which will
return SQL_NEED_DATA if data is required for parameters.

You will then call SQLParamData() to retrieve information about the required parameter data. If parameter data is required, SQLParamData() will return SQL_NEED_DATA, and the parameter number that is required will be returned in the buffer at ValuePtrPtr.

> **Note**
>
> ODBC drivers aren't required to ask for required parameter data in any particular order, so don't assume they will be requested in numerical order.

You can then call SQLPutData() to pass the data for the parameter. This may be called several times to pass long data values.

You then should call SQLParamData() again to see whether any additional parameter data is required. After all required data has been sent, SQLParamData() will execute the statement and return SQL_SUCCESS or SQL_SUCCESS_WITH_INFO, provided the statement executed without error.

Parameter Information

In cases where your application code doesn't know ahead of time about the parameters required for a particular SQL statement, you can use the SQLNumParams() function to retrieve the number of parameters required and can then call SQLDescribeParam() to retrieve specifics about each parameter.

Working with Result Sets

Okay, so you can send SQL to the database with SQLExecDirect() or SQLExecute(), but how do you get your hands on the data the SQL returns? In this section, you will look at how to work with the data (called the result set) returned by calls like SQLExecDirect().

The result set returned by a query is like a temporary table—it includes rows of columns. Rows are retrieved from the result set using cursors, which come in several different flavors. The default cursor used in ODBC is a forward-only cursor, which allows you to access the rows in the result set only one row at a time. Furthermore, if you want to back up in the result set, you close the cursor and start over at the first row. You look at the forward-only cursor first because it is supported in all drivers. You look at other cursor types, which can be used to access more than one row at a time, later on in this chapter.

In most cases, the best way to retrieve data from a result set is to bind the columns of the result set to specific memory locations ahead of time. Then, when you call SQLFetch(), the data for each column is copied into the memory location that you have bound for that

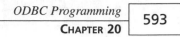

column. You will also see how you can use SQLGetData() to retrieve one column at a time from the current row, after it has been fetched.

Binding Columns

There are two ways to access the data from individual rows of a result set. The first involves binding a column to a location in memory with SQLBindCol() before calling SQLFetch(), at which point the data from the row will be copied into the assigned locations. The second method, which you will see in just a bit, involves calling SQLGetData() to copy a column's data into a memory location after the call to SQLFetch().

SQLBindCol()

To assign the memory location that a column's data should be copied to when a row is fetched, you use the SQLBindCol() function:

```
SQLRETURN SQLBindCol( SQLHSTMT StatementHandle, SQLUSMALLINT ColumnNumber,
    SQLSMALLINT TargetType, SQLPOINTER TargetValuePtr, SQLINTEGER BufferLength,
    SQLINTEGER * StrLen_or_IndPtr);
```

The StatementHandle parameter should be the statement handle on which you are performing SQLExecDirect() and SQLFetch().

The ColumnNumber parameter specifies the number of the column to bind, starting with 1 and numbering left to right (column 0 is used for retrieving bookmarks, as you will see later).

The TargetType parameter is used to specify the desired C data type (for example, SQL_C_CHAR) that the data will be returned as. You saw the available data types in the beginning of this chapter.

When SQLFetch() is called to fetch the next row in the result set, ODBC will attempt to convert the data for each bound column from SQL format to the type specified by the TargetType parameter of SQLBindCol(). This may include some rather elaborate conversions, such as converting a numeric value into an ASCII string or converting character strings into various numeric formats.

If errors occur in the conversion process, or if certain events such as data truncation occur, SQLFetch() will return SQL_ERROR or SQL_SUCCESS_WITH_INFO, and the specific conversion errors (or warnings) can be retrieved with SQLGetDiagRec().

Remember that SQLGetDiagRec() should be called repeatedly until it returns SQL_NO_DATA_FOUND. This allows you to retrieve multiple errors for the same call to SQLFetch().

The TargetValuePtr parameter is a pointer to the location in memory where you want ODBC to place the data, and BufferLength should be passed the maximum size of this data buffer. (For strings, you should include space for the null terminator.)

The memory location at StrLen_or_IndPtr will receive the length of the actual data returned for the bound column each time SQLFetch() is called. In the event a column's data is NULL, this value will be set to SQL_NULL_DATA.

SQLFetch()

To access each row of the result set, including the first row, you call the SQLFetch() function:

```
SQLRETURN SQLFetch(SQLHSTMT StatementHandle);
```

This function simply makes the next row in the result set the current row. It will also copy the data from any bound columns into the memory locations assigned with SQLBindCol(). When there are no more rows available, a call to SQLFetch() will return SQL_NO_DATA_FOUND.

The best method of getting the number of rows in a result set is simply scrolling through them with SQLFetch() until no more are found. You can retrieve the count of rows in a result set with SQLRowCount(), but this isn't supported in all drivers.

The menu resource and the ClassWizard were used to develop a "Fetch Results" menu option. The following example shows the use of SQLExecDirect(), SQLBindCol(), and SQLFetch() to retrieve a single row of data:

```
void CODBCTestView::OnViewFetchresults() {
```

```
//Code added by Chuck Wood
SQLRETURN sr;
SQLHSTMT hstmt;
SQLCHAR SQL[] =
    "SELECT EmpName, Salary, Dept FROM Employee";
// Column Date Variables
struct {
    SQLCHAR name[51];
    double salary;
    SQLCHAR dept[11];
    SQLINTEGER nameLength;
    SQLINTEGER salaryLength;
    SQLINTEGER deptLength;
} row;
char message[4096];
```

```
    strcpy (message, "Fetch Results:\n"); //Initialize
    // Allocate Statement Handle
    sr = SQLAllocHandle(SQL_HANDLE_STMT, hDbConn, &hstmt);
    if(sr != SQL_SUCCESS && sr != SQL_SUCCESS_WITH_INFO)
        displayODBCError(sr,
 "Error in allocating statement in OnViewfetchresults");
    // Execute SQL statement
    sr = SQLExecDirect(hstmt, SQL, SQL_NTS);
    if(sr != SQL_SUCCESS && sr != SQL_SUCCESS_WITH_INFO)
        displayODBCError(sr,
 "Error executing statement in OnViewfetchresults");
    // Bind each column
    sr = SQLBindCol(hstmt, 1, SQL_C_CHAR,
        row.name, sizeof(row.name), &row.nameLength);
    if(sr != SQL_SUCCESS && sr != SQL_SUCCESS_WITH_INFO)
        displayODBCError(sr,
        "Error in Binding 1 in OnViewfetchresults");
    sr = SQLBindCol(hstmt, 2, SQL_C_DOUBLE,
     &row.salary, sizeof(row.salary), &row.salaryLength);
    if(sr != SQL_SUCCESS && sr != SQL_SUCCESS_WITH_INFO)
        displayODBCError(sr,
        "Error in Binding 2 in OnViewfetchresults");
    sr = SQLBindCol(hstmt, 3, SQL_C_CHAR,
        row.dept, sizeof(row.dept), &row.deptLength);
    if(sr != SQL_SUCCESS && sr != SQL_SUCCESS_WITH_INFO)
        displayODBCError(sr,
        "Error in Binding 3 in OnViewfetchresults");
    // Start fetching records
    while (SQLFetch(hstmt) == SQL_SUCCESS) {
        sprintf(message,
        "%s\tName: %s \tSalary: %g \t Department: %s\n",
        message,
        row.name, row.salary, row.dept);
    }
    MessageBox(message);
    SQLFreeHandle(SQL_HANDLE_STMT, hstmt);
```

Figure 20.6 shows the output from the `OnViewFetchresults()` function.

FIGURE 20.6

`SQLFETCH` *allows you to process multiple results from an SQL query.*

ODBCTest

Fetch Results:
Name: Chuck Wood   Salary: 120000   Department: IS
Name: Joe Schmoe   Salary: 69584.2   Department: Accounting

OK

Multiple Result Sets

It is possible for a single call to SQLExecute() to generate several different result sets, as is the case when you execute a batch of SQL statements or call a procedure that returns multiple result sets. After you are finished with the current result set, you can call SQLMoreResults() to move on to the next result set. Generally, you will then want to rebind columns and fetch rows from the new result set with SQLFetch().

Closing the Cursor

When you call a function that creates a result set, such as SQLExecute(), a cursor is opened for you. When you are finished working with a result set, you should close the cursor that was used to fetch the data by calling SQLCloseCursor().

Reusing Statement Handles

You could allocate a separate statement handle for every SQL statement that your application will execute, although it is often neater (and saves overhead) if you can reuse your statement handles for multiple operations.

Before you can use a statement handle for a new operation, you should first free the parameter and result set bindings that were used for the previous operation by calling SQLFreeStmt(), with the SQL_UNBIND option to free any column bindings and the SQL_RESET_PARAMS option to free any parameter bindings. You can then use the statement handle for a new operation, as if it were newly allocated, although you should make sure that the statement attributes are correct for the new operation.

SQLGetData()

ODBCalso offers an alternative to using SQLBindCol() to bind columns to memory locations before calling SQLFetch(). You can call SQLGetData() to retrieve a single column's data, after the current row has been selected with SQLFetch(). This function provides the same sort of data conversion that is set up with SQLBindCol().

In most cases, your application should either bind all columns or retrieve all columns with SQLGetData(). Depending on the driver you are using, there may be some rather strict limitations on support for mixing bound columns and SQLGetData(). For instance, many drivers don't allow you to call SQLGetData() for bound columns, and any columns that you intend to use SQLGetData() on must come after the last bound column.

Here is the prototype for SQLGetData():

```
SQLRETURN SQLGetData( SQLHSTMT StatementHandle, SQLUSMALLINT ColumnNumber,
    SQLSMALLINT TargetType, SQLPOINTER TargetValuePtr,
    SQLINTEGER BufferLength, SQLINTEGER * StrLen_or_IndPtr);
```

The parameters used for SQLGetData() are identical to those used for SQLBindCol(). The only difference is when the actual data transfer takes place. When using SQLBindCol(), the data is transferred each time you call SQLFetch(), whereas SQLGetData() is a one-time affair, retrieving the data from a row after it is selected with SQLFetch().

For columns that contain large character-, binary-, or driver-specific data, you can use multiple calls to SQLGetData() to retrieve the information. On the first call to SQLGetData(), ODBC will move up to BufferLength bytes into the buffer at TargetValuePtr. If there is still more data to retrieve, the call to SQLGetData() will return SQL_SUCCESS_WITH_INFO, and a subsequent call to SQLGetDiagRec() will show a SQLSTATE of 01004 (data truncated). You can then make additional calls to SQLGetData() with the same column number to retrieve additional blocks of the data in the column. When all the data has been retrieved, SQLGetData() will return SQL_SUCCESS.

In addition, you can use SQLGetData() to retrieve information from result sets that may have a variable number of columns. In this case, you may find the functions in the next section useful in determining information about the columns in the result set.

Column Information

Although it is generally a good idea for your database application to know what sort of data it will be retrieving ahead of time, you may find cases, such as a general database browser app, where the application doesn't know which columns will be returned in a result set at compile time. You can retrieve the number of columns in a result set by calling SQLNumResultCols() and can get specific information about each column with SQLDescribeCol() and SQLColAttribute().

SQLDescribeCol()

After you know how many columns there are, you can call SQLDescribeCol() for each column:

```
SQLRETURN SQLDescribeCol(SQLHSTMT StatementHandle, SQLSMALLINT ColumnNumber,
    SQLCHAR * ColumnName, SQLSMALLINT BufferLength, SQLSMALLINT * NameLengthPtr,
    SQLSMALLINT * DataTypePtr, SQLUINTEGER * ColumnSizePtr,
    SQLSMALLINT * DecimalDigitsPtr, SQLSMALLINT * NullablePtr);
```

This will return the column name at ColumnName and the length of this string at NameLengthPtr. The length of the buffer at ColumnName should be passed in BufferLength.

The SQL data type of the column is returned at DataTypePtr. This value will be one of the constants, such as SQL_CHAR, that you saw in the earlier section on ODBC data types.

20

ODBC PROGRAMMING

The precision and scale of the column are returned at `ColumnSizePtr` and `DecimalDigitsPtr`, respectively.

The value returned at `NullablePtr` indicates whether the column allows `NULL` values. This will be one of the following values:

> `SQL_NO_NULLS`—`NULL` values aren't allowed.
>
> `SQL_NULLABLE`—`NULL` values are allowed.
>
> `SQL_NULLABLE_UNKNOWN`—indicates the driver cannot determine whether `NULL` values are allowed.

SQLColAttribute()

You can also retrieve various attributes of a result set column by calling `SQLColAttribute()`, which allows you to get at information such as the format, case-sensitivity, display size, owner, precision, or update permission of a column.

Retrieving More Than One Row at a Time

Earlier in this chapter, you saw how to access a result set one row at a time by calling `SQLFetch()` to access each row. You can also fetch a group of rows, or rowset, at the same time by using the `SQLFetchScroll()` function instead of `SQLFetch()`. This is done by using cursors. In this section, you will be looking at block cursors, which enable you to retrieve groups of rows at a time, as well as scrollable cursors, which allow additional navigation within the result set. (In most cases, a scrollable cursor is a block cursor with additional functionality.)

Earlier, when you were retrieving one row at a time, you were also using a cursor, but it was a special single-row, forward-only case of a nonscrollable block cursor.

Block Cursors

Earlier in this chapter, you saw how to retrieve a single row. As you might guess, this is generally not the most efficient way to retrieve large amounts of data—in addition to the overhead of a greater number of function calls, there can be a great deal more network overhead involved in requesting rows individually. To make your apps more efficient, you can use a block cursor, which retrieves a block of rows, or rowset, in a single request. You will see how to use block cursors soon.

Scrollable Cursors

With block cursors and forward-only cursors, to return to a row in a previous rowset, you must close the cursor and start again from the top. Scrollable cursors allow your application to more easily navigate in any direction in a rowset. However, this additional functionality can introduce some significant additional overhead. In general, if you simply need to retrieve all the data in a rowset for report generation, block cursors are best. If you need to provide more flexible scrolling ability, such as in interactive applications, go ahead and use scrollable cursors.

The ODBC Cursor Library

For database drivers that support cursors, the ODBC SDK provides a cursor library (ODBCCR32.DLL) that implements blocks, static cursors, and positioned updates and deletes. The cursor library sits between the application and the driver that actually connects to the data source. The cursor library may be distributed with your applications and is enabled by setting the SQL_ATTR_ODBC_CURSORS attribute on a connection before connecting to the data source.

Using Block Cursors

Using block cursors to retrieve data from a result set is similar to retrieving one row at a time, although there are a few extra things you must do. To use block cursors, your application should do the following:

1. Set the number of rows to be retrieved in each rowset.
2. Bind columns to memory locations.
3. Call SQLFetchScroll() to retrieve each rowset.

> **Note**
>
> In ODBC 3, SQLFetchScroll() replaces SQLExtendedFetch(). In addition, SQLFetch() has been enhanced to support block cursors.

Setting the Size of a Rowset

The size of the rowset returned by calls to SQLFetchScroll() is set by calling SQLSetStmtOption() to set the SQL_ATTR_ROW_ARRAY_SIZE option to the number of rows you want to receive in a rowset. By setting this attribute to a value greater than one, you tell ODBC to use a block cursor.

Binding Columns for a Rowset

If you are using SQLFetchScroll() to retrieve more than one row at a time, you can set up column-wise binding, as you saw with SQLFetch(), or you can use row-wise binding, which binds rows to a structure holding all the columns.

Column-Wise Binding

By default, a statement handle is set to use column-wise binding, as you saw earlier. The one difference when binding columns for use with block cursors, is that instead of defining a single variable to receive data for a single row and column, the buffer pointer you specify in SQLBindCol() should point to an array of buffers that is long enough to receive a whole rowset worth of data for that column.

Row-Wise Binding

In addition, it is often useful to bind a rowset to memory in a row-wise fashion when using block cursors. This presents the data to your application as a single array of a structure that contains all the columns of the rowset, rather than a separate variable for each column. Row-wise binding may also provide greater efficiency, depending on the driver you are using.

To implement row-wise binding, you must do the following:

1. Define a structure to hold a single row's data. This structure should have a field for each column to be bound, as well as a field containing the length of each column.

2. Allocate an array of this structure. The allocated array should contain as many elements as the size of your rowset. You should also include an additional element if your application will append new rows of data or search for key values.

3. Enable row-wise binding for the statement handle. This is done by calling SQLSetStmtAttr() twice, once with Attribute set to SQL_ATTR_ROW_BIND_TYPE and ValuePtr set to the size of the structure you have defined to receive the data, and once with Attribute set to SQL_ATTR_ROW_ARRAY_SIZE and ValuePtr set the number of elements in the array you will be using.

4. Call SQLBindCol() for each column to be bound. When calling SQLBindCol(), the TargetValuePtr parameter should point to the data field corresponding to the column in the first element of the array, and StrLen_or_IndPtr should point to the corresponding size field in the first element (element 0) of the array.

5. Change the original SQLFETCH code to use an array structure rather than a non-array structure.

The following gray lines below show how you can alter the previous SQLFETCH example to use row-wise binding:

```
void CODBCTestView::OnViewRowwisefetch() {
    //Code added by Chuck Wood
    SQLRETURN sr;
    SQLHSTMT hstmt;
    SQLCHAR SQL[] =
        "SELECT EmpName, Salary, Dept FROM Employee";
    // Column Date Variables
    struct {
        SQLCHAR name[51];
        double salary;
        SQLCHAR dept[11];
        SQLINTEGER nameLength;
        SQLINTEGER salaryLength;
        SQLINTEGER deptLength;


    } row [2];    //Make this an array


    char message[4096];
    strcpy (message,
        "Rowwise Fetch Results:\n"); //Initialize message
    // Allocate Statement Handle
    sr = SQLAllocHandle(SQL_HANDLE_STMT, hDbConn, &hstmt);
    if(sr != SQL_SUCCESS && sr != SQL_SUCCESS_WITH_INFO)
        displayODBCError(sr,
 "Error in allocating statement in OnViewRowwisefetch");
    // Execute SQL statement
    sr = SQLExecDirect(hstmt, SQL, SQL_NTS);
    if(sr != SQL_SUCCESS && sr != SQL_SUCCESS_WITH_INFO)
        displayODBCError(sr,
 "Error executing statement in OnViewRowwisefetch");


    // Set the number of rows to retrieve
    sr = SQLSetStmtAttr(hstmt, SQL_ATTR_ROW_ARRAY_SIZE,
        (void *) 2, SQL_IS_INTEGER);
    if(sr != SQL_SUCCESS && sr != SQL_SUCCESS_WITH_INFO)
        displayODBCError(sr,
 "Error in array size in OnViewRowwisefetch");
    // Set the size of the structure for each row.
    sr = SQLSetStmtAttr(hstmt, SQL_ATTR_ROW_BIND_TYPE,
        (void *) sizeof(row[0]), SQL_IS_INTEGER);
    if(sr != SQL_SUCCESS && sr != SQL_SUCCESS_WITH_INFO)
        displayODBCError(sr,
 "Error in setting bind type in OnViewRowwisefetch");
```

20

**ODBC
PROGRAMMING**

```
// Bind each column
sr = SQLBindCol(hstmt, 1, SQL_C_CHAR,
```

```
   row[0].name, sizeof(row[0].name), &row[0].nameLength);
```

```
if(sr != SQL_SUCCESS && sr != SQL_SUCCESS_WITH_INFO)
    displayODBCError(sr,
        "Error in Binding 1 in OnViewRowwisefetch");
sr = SQLBindCol(hstmt, 2, SQL_C_DOUBLE,
```

```
   &row[0].salary, sizeof(row[0].salary),
   &row[0].salaryLength);
```

```
if(sr != SQL_SUCCESS && sr != SQL_SUCCESS_WITH_INFO)
    displayODBCError(sr,
        "Error in Binding 2 in OnViewRowwisefetch");
sr = SQLBindCol(hstmt, 3, SQL_C_CHAR,
```

```
   row[0].dept, sizeof(row[0].dept), &row[0].deptLength);
```

```
if(sr != SQL_SUCCESS && sr != SQL_SUCCESS_WITH_INFO)
    displayODBCError(sr,
        "Error in Binding 3 in OnViewRowwisefetch");
// Start fetching records
SQLFetch(hstmt);
```

```
for (int loop = 0; loop < 2; loop++) {
```

```
    sprintf(message,
     "%s\tName: %s \tSalary: %g \t Department: %s\n",
     message,
```

```
       row[loop].name, row[loop].salary, row[loop].dept);
```

```
    }
    MessageBox(message);
    SQLFreeHandle(SQL_HANDLE_STMT, hstmt);
}
```

Calling `SQLFetch()` for Block Cursors

After you have your bindings set up, and have set the desired length for the rowset, you can start retrieving rowsets by calling the `SQLFetch()` function, as you saw previously. The difference is that if you have specified a rowset size of greater than one, more than one row will be retrieved.

Row Status Information

In ODBC 2, the `SQLExtendedFetch()` function took additional parameters for returning an array of row status values, and a count of rows returned. In ODBC 3, you can specify a location that will receive the number of rows retrieved by `SQLFetchScroll()` by setting the `SQL_ATTR_ROWS_FETCHED_PTR` statement attribute to point to the location to receive the number of rows.

In addition, you can specify a value of the `SQL_ATTR_ROW_STATUS_PTR` statement attribute to point to an array of `SQLUSMALLINT`s that will receive one of the following values for each row in the rowset. These values reflect the state of the row because it was last retrieved from the data source:

`SQL_ROW_SUCCESS`—The row is unchanged.

`SQL_ROW_SUCCESS_WITH_INFO`—The row was fetched successfully, but generated a warning that can be retrieved with `SQLGetDiagRec()`.

`SQL_ROW_UPDATED`—The row has been updated.

`SQL_ROW_DELETED`—The row has been deleted.

`SQL_ROW_ADDED`—The row has been added.

`SQL_ROW_ERROR`—The row could not be retrieved due to error.

`SQL_ROW_NOROW`—No row was retrieved for this position in the rowset.

Block Cursors and Single-Row Functions

If you are using a block cursor, you take an extra step before using functions such as `SQLGetData()` that operate on a single current row. You set the current row pointer by calling `SQLSetPos()` with the `SQL_POSITION` option.

Using Scrollable Cursors

In addition to the block cursor operations that you saw previously, many drivers support scrollable cursors, which allow you to use `SQLFetchScroll()` to move freely around in the result set, without having to start over at the beginning.

When you fetch a new rowset with a scrollable cursor, the new rowset may also include changes that have been made to the result set because it was first selected from the data source. ODBC provides four different types of scrollable cursors—each can detect different sorts of changes in the result set:

- *Static cursors* are the simplest because they don't reflect any changes to the result set once it has been retrieved from the data source.

- *Dynamic cursors,* on the other hand, reflect all changes to the result set, including any changes that may be made by other users of the database.

- *Keyset-driven cursors* generally detect any changes to the values of the rows that were initially selected in the result set, although they may not detect any new rows that are added or any changes to the ordering of the rows in the result set. This type of cursor builds a keyset containing the key for each row in the result set. This is used to determine whether any of the rows in the result set have changed.

- *Mixed cursors* are a combination of keyset-driven and dynamic cursors. They generally will detect only changes to the values for the rows within the current keyset, but will detect any changes when you fetch a rowset outside of the current keyset.

In any case, changes to the result set are detected only when a new rowset is fetched with a call to `SQLFetchScroll()`. Furthermore, the detection of changes may also be affected by the current transaction isolation level, which you will look at when you talk about transactions.

Cursor Support

The following items returned by `SQLGetInfo()` give information about the level of cursor support provided by the current driver:

`SQL_CURSOR_SENSITIVITY` indicates whether a cursor can detect changes made outside of this cursor—for example, by other users.

`SQL_SCROLL_OPTIONS` indicates only the types of cursors supported (forward-only, static, keyset-driven, dynamic, mixed).

`SQL_DYNAMIC_CURSOR_ATTRIBUTES1`, `SQL_FORWARD_ONLY_CURSOR_ATTRIBUTES1`, `SQL_KEYSET_CURSOR_ATTRIBUTES1`, and `SQL_STATIC_CURSOR_ATTRIBUTES1` return a bitmap of the fetch type values that may be used in `SQLFetchScroll()` for the given cursor type.

`SQL_KEYSET_CURSOR_ATTRIBUTES2` and `SQL_STATIC_CURSOR_ATTRIBUTES2` indicate whether the cursor can detect its own updates, deletes, and inserts.

Setting the Cursor Type

Before executing a statement that returns a result set, you can set the type of cursor that will be used by setting the `SQL_ATTR_CURSOR_TYPE` statement attribute. In addition, for keyset-driven and mixed cursors, you can set the size of the keyset used by setting the SQL_ATTR_KEYSET_SIZE statement attribute. By default, this attribute is set to 0, in which case the keyset size will be set to the size of the entire result set. To use a mixed cursor, you can specify a value for the keyset size that is smaller than the size of the result set.

As an alternative to setting the SQL_ATTR_CURSOR_TYPE attribute explicitly, you can allow ODBC to select a cursor type based on the values you set for the SQL_ATTR_ CONCURRENCY, SQL_ATTR_CURSOR_SCROLLABLE, or SQL_ATTR_CURSOR_SENSITIVITY attributes. Any time you make a change to one of these four attributes, the other three settings may be changed by the driver to reflect the currently selected cursor type.

Calling `SQLFetchScroll()`

To retrieve a new rowset from the result set using a scrollable cursor, you should use the SQLFetchScroll() function, which allows you to move to random locations within the result set. The following is the prototype for SQLFetchScroll():

```
SQLRETURN SQLFetchScroll(SQLHSTMT StatementHandle, SQLSMALLINT FetchOrientation,
    SQLINTEGER FetchOffset);
```

The FetchOrientation parameter specifies how to move through the result set to find the next rowset to retrieve. This may be set to one of these values:

SQL_FETCH_FIRST retrieves the first rowset in the result set.

SQL_FETCH_NEXT retrieves the next rowset in the result set. (If the cursor is positioned before the first row, this is equivalent to SQL_FETCH_FIRST.)

SQL_FETCH_LAST retrieves the last rowset in the result set.

SQL_FETCH_PRIOR retrieves the previous rowset in the result set.

SQL_FETCH_ABSOLUTE retrieves the rowset starting with the row specified in FetchOffset. You can specify a negative value for FetchOffset to retrieve the rowset, starting with the row a given number of rows from the end of the result set.

SQL_FETCH_RELATIVE retrieves the rowset beginning with the row FetchOffset rows from the start of the current rowset. This may include negative values to move backwards.

SQL_FETCH_BOOKMARK retrieves the rowset beginning with the row specified by a bookmark value passed in FetchOffset.

Other than the ability to move at will through the result set, this function works just like SQLFetch()—the rowset that is retrieved will be moved into memory locations, as specified in SQLBindCol() calls.

Using Bookmarks

Many ODBC drivers support the use of bookmarks to directly access a given row in a result set, as you saw in SQLFetchScroll() with the SQL_FETCH_BOOKMARK option.

20

ODBC PROGRAMMING

You can determine what level of support the current driver offers for bookmarks by calling SQLGetInfo() with the SQL_BOOKMARK_PERSISTENCE option.

To use bookmarks, you should use SQLSetStmtAttr() to set the SQL_ATTR_USE_BOOK-MARK attribute to SQL_UB_VARIABLE before executing the SQL statement that generates the result set.

ODBC 3 uses only variable length bookmarks, which will be of different sizes for different drivers. After you have retrieved a result set with bookmarks enabled, you can call SQLColAttribute() for the SQL_DESC_OCTET_LENGTH field for column 0 to find the length needed to hold a bookmark.

You can retrieve the bookmark for a given row by either binding column 0 of the result set or using SQLGetData() to retrieve column 0 from a row. These bookmarks can then be used in subsequent calls such as SQLFetchScroll(). Bookmarks are also used to perform updates, deletions, and fetches by bookmark with the SQLBulkOperations() function, which you will see later.

Inserting, Updating, and Deleting Rows

To insert, update, or delete rows from a data source, you can always simply execute SQL statements to manipulate the rows. This must be supported by all ODBC drivers, and is the best way to perform updates or deletes if you simply want to change a set of rows. However, if you are writing an app that provides more flexible user interaction with the data, this may get to be complicated.

To help simplify applications that involve dynamic user interaction with the data, ODBC allows you to update and delete rows, based on a result set that you have already retrieved. However, these positioned updates or deletions aren't supported by all drivers.

In addition, you can perform bulk operations with the SQLBulkOperations() function, which can be used to insert new rows or perform updates, deletions, and fetches based on bookmarks. You will look at this function shortly.

Positioned Updates and Deletions

First of all, you can retrieve a particular result set by executing a SQL query that uses the FOR UPDATE OF clause:

```
SELECT Col1, Col2 FROM myTable FOR UPDATE OF Col1, Col2;
```

This will retrieve the desired rows and tell the data source that you may be altering the data in these rows.

> **Note**
>
> To use positioned updates or deletions, you must set the cursor concurrency type of the cursor used in this statement because the default is read-only. (See "Cursor Concurrency Types," later in this chapter.)

You also name the cursor that is used for this result set by calling `SQLSetCursorName()`. All cursors have a name, but if you don't name it explicitly, it will be assigned a fairly unwieldy name generated by the driver. You can retrieve the current cursor name by calling `SQLGetCursorName()`.

Next, you call `SQLFetch()` or `SQLFetchScroll()` to find the row on which you want to operate. You then make the row you want to modify the current row by calling `SQLSetPos()` with the `SQL_POSITION` option.

Next, you use a second statement handle to execute an UPDATE or DELETE statement that uses the `WHERE CURRENT OF` clause, as in the following examples:

```
"UPDATE MyTable SET MyCol = 123 WHERE CURRENT OF myCursorName"
"DELETE FROM MyTable WHERE CURRENT OF myCursorName"
```

where `myCursorName` is the name that you assigned to the cursor used to retrieve the initial result set. This will perform the update on the current row, as you specified with `SQLSetPos()`.

For updating columns with long data fields, you can use the `SQLPutData()` function, which can be used to add data one piece at a time, much like the `SQLGetData()` function.

> **Tip**
>
> Some drivers allow you to update a result set without using multiple SQL statements by using the `SQLSetPos()` function for updates or deletions. If you want to use this function, check out your database documentation to see if it's available and how it works.

SQLBulkOperations()

Beginning with version 3, the ODBC API also allows you to perform insertions, updates, deletions, and fetches *en masse* with the `SQLBulkOperations()` function:

```
SQLRETURN SQLBulkOperations(SQLHSTMT StatementHandle, SQLUSMALLINT Operation);
```

This function takes the statement handle that you want to operate on and one of the following values for `Operation`:

```
SQL_ADD
SQL_UPDATE_BY_BOOKMARK
SQL_DELETE_BY_BOOKMARK
SQL_FETCH_BY_BOOKMARK
```

In the next sections, you will see how to use `SQLBulkOperations()` for each of these operations.

> **Caution**
>
> Some databases, like MS Access, don't support bulk operations. MS Access supports bulk operations in a pass-through query mode only. If you need to speed up your database with bulk operations, you'll need to update your database from MS Access to a more robust database, such as MS SQL Server or Oracle.

Inserting with `SQLBulkOperations()`

To insert new rows, you first execute a query that returns a result set for the table you want to add rows to.

Next, you use `SQLBindCol()` to bind arrays of data to the columns of the result set. You must also set the value of `SQL_ATTR_ROW_ARRAY_SIZE` to the length of these arrays by calling `SQLSetStmtAttr()`.

You can then call `SQLBulkOperations()` with an `Operation` of `SQL_ADD` to insert new rows, containing the data in the bound columns. If you have set the `SQL_ATTR_ARRAY_STATUS_PTR` statement attribute, this array will receive the status of the insert operation for each row. The following function was implemented by the menu resource and the ClassWizard. The code inside the function shows how bulk operations work:

```
void CODBCTestView::OnViewBulkinsert() {
```

```
    SQLRETURN sr;
    SQLHSTMT hstmt;
SQLCHAR SQL[] = "SELECT EmpName, Salary, Dept FROM Employee";
    struct rowTag {
            SQLCHAR name[51];
```

```
                double salary;
                SQLCHAR dept[11];
                SQLINTEGER nameLength;
                SQLINTEGER salaryLength;
                SQLINTEGER deptLength;
        } row [7];
        // Allocate Statement Handle
        sr = SQLAllocHandle(SQL_HANDLE_STMT, hDbConn, &hstmt);
        if(sr != SQL_SUCCESS && sr != SQL_SUCCESS_WITH_INFO)
                displayODBCError(sr, "Error in allocating statement in
➥OnViewBulkinsert");
        // Execute SQL statement to open cursor
        sr = SQLExecDirect(hstmt, SQL, SQL_NTS);
        if(sr != SQL_SUCCESS && sr != SQL_SUCCESS_WITH_INFO)
                displayODBCError(sr, "Error executing statement in
➥OnViewBulkinsert");
        //SET STATEMENT ATTRIBUTES
        // Set the cursor type.
        sr = SQLSetStmtAttr(hstmt, SQL_ATTR_CURSOR_TYPE,
                (void*) SQL_CURSOR_DYNAMIC, SQL_IS_UINTEGER);
        if(sr != SQL_SUCCESS && sr != SQL_SUCCESS_WITH_INFO)
                displayODBCError(sr, "Error in setting cursor type in
➥OnViewBulkinsert");
        // Lock out other users.
        sr = SQLSetStmtAttr(hstmt, SQL_ATTR_CONCURRENCY,
                (void*) SQL_CONCUR_LOCK, SQL_IS_UINTEGER);
        if(sr != SQL_SUCCESS && sr != SQL_SUCCESS_WITH_INFO)
                displayODBCError(sr, "Error in setting locking in
➥OnViewBulkinsert");
        // Set the number of rows to process
        sr = SQLSetStmtAttr(hstmt, SQL_ATTR_ROW_ARRAY_SIZE,
                (void *) 7, SQL_IS_INTEGER);
        if(sr != SQL_SUCCESS && sr != SQL_SUCCESS_WITH_INFO)
                displayODBCError(sr, "Error in array size in OnViewBulkinsert");
        // Set the size of the structure for each row.
        sr = SQLSetStmtAttr(hstmt, SQL_ATTR_ROW_BIND_TYPE,
                (void *) sizeof(row[0]), SQL_IS_INTEGER);
        if(sr != SQL_SUCCESS && sr != SQL_SUCCESS_WITH_INFO)
                displayODBCError(sr, "Error in setting bind type in
➥OnViewBulkinsert");
    // Bind each column
    sr = SQLBindCol(hstmt, 1, SQL_C_CHAR, row[0].name, sizeof(row[0].name),
        ➥&row[0].nameLength);
        if(sr != SQL_SUCCESS && sr != SQL_SUCCESS_WITH_INFO)
                displayODBCError(sr, "Error in Binding 1 in OnViewBulkinsert");
    sr = SQLBindCol(hstmt, 2, SQL_C_DOUBLE, &row[0].salary,
sizeof(row[0].salary),
    ➥&row[0].salaryLength);
        if(sr != SQL_SUCCESS && sr != SQL_SUCCESS_WITH_INFO)
```

```
                displayODBCError(sr, "Error in Binding 2 in OnViewBulkinsert");
    sr = SQLBindCol(hstmt, 3, SQL_C_CHAR, row[0].dept, sizeof(row[0].dept),
➥&row[0].deptLength);
        if(sr != SQL_SUCCESS && sr != SQL_SUCCESS_WITH_INFO)
                displayODBCError(sr, "Error in Binding 3 in OnViewBulkinsert");
// Hire the Gilligan's Island crew
// at the same salary for the IS department
        strcpy((char *) row[0].name, "Gilligan");
        strcpy((char *) row[1].name, "Skipper");
        strcpy((char *) row[2].name, "Mr. Howe");
        strcpy((char *) row[3].name, "Mrs. Howe");
        strcpy((char *) row[4].name, "Ginger");
        strcpy((char *) row[5].name, "Professor");
        strcpy((char *) row[6].name, "Mary Ann");
        for(int loop=0; loop < 7; loop++) {
                row[loop].salary = 50000;
                strcpy((char *) row[loop].dept, "IS");
                row[loop].nameLength = SQL_NTS;
                row[loop].salaryLength =
                        sizeof(row[0].salary);
                row[loop].deptLength = SQL_NTS;
        }
        // Add new rows to the database
        sr = SQLBulkOperations(hstmt, SQL_ADD);
        if(sr != SQL_SUCCESS && sr != SQL_SUCCESS_WITH_INFO)
                displayODBCError(sr, "Error in bulk insert");
```

```
}
```

Updating with `SQLBulkOperations()`

Except for inserting new rows, the other operations supported by `SQLBulkOperations()` all use bookmarks to specify the rows that will be manipulated. Thus, you must set the `SQL_ATTR_USE_BOOKMARKS` statement attribute to `SQL_UB_VARIABLE` before executing a query that returns the initial result set with which you will be working.

Next, to update rows, you bind the columns you want to update with `SQLBindCol()`. You should also bind column 0 to an array that will hold bookmarks.

You then fill the bookmark array with the bookmarks for the rows that you want to update and update the other corresponding bound arrays for the row data. You should also set the `SQL_ATTR_ROW_ARRAY_SIZE` statement attribute to the number of rows (and corresponding bookmark array entries) that you want to update.

You can then call `SQLBulkOperations()` with an `Operation` of `SQL_UPDATE_BY_BOOK-MARK` to update the rows with the data in the bound arrays. If you have set the

SQL_ATTR_ROW_STATUS_PTR statement attribute, this array will contain the status of each of the updates.

Deleting with SQLBulkOperations()

Deleting rows with SQLBulkOperations() is very similar to updating rows. You execute a statement that returns an appropriate result set (with bookmarks enabled), bind column 0 to an array that you fill with the bookmarks for rows to be deleted, set the SQL_ATTR_ROW_ARRAY_SIZE statement attribute to the number of bookmark entries, and call SQLBulkOperations() with an Operation of SQL_DELETE_BY_BOOKMARK.

Fetching with SQLBulkOperations()

Fetching by bookmark is also very similar to the update and delete operations shown previously. You should simply bind columns for the data you want to retrieve, including column 0, which you fill with bookmarks for the rows to fetch.

You then set the number of rows to fetch by setting the SQL_ATTR_ROW_ARRAY_SIZE statement attribute and call SQLBulkOperations() with SQL_FETCH_BY_BOOKMARK.

Asynchronous Operations

Previously, you looked at features of ODBC that are used to support asynchronous operations. Basically, ODBC provides a mechanism that allows you to return from a call such as SQLExecute() immediately and then occasionally poll to see whether the operation has completed yet.

This mechanism is provided for single-threaded operating systems, such as Win3.1, and isn't appropriate for use in the Win32 environment, which allows you to start a new thread for blocking calls that may take an arbitrary period of time to complete.

Unfortunately, ODBC 3 doesn't provide for true asynchronous operations (overlapped I/O) in the Win32 environment.

Transactions

In many cases, it is necessary to have several different SQL statements operate together as a single transaction—that is, if one of the operations in a transaction fails, none of the other operations should affect the database. For example, if you are processing a sales order, you will want to update both your shipping table and your billing table. If one of these updates fails, and the other is entered into the database, you could easily end up billing for things that were never sent, or worse yet, shipping free stuff. Although creative use of this feature may have some beneficial effects on your short-term revenues, it's probably not a good career move.

20

ODBC PROGRAMMING

> **Note**
>
> In SQL, to group a set of statements together in a transaction, you could use COMMIT and ROLLBACK statements. However, in ODBC this is highly discouraged, and in fact can leave the driver quite confused about the current state of a transaction. Instead, you should use the SQLEndTran() function for commits and rollbacks.

ODBC Commit Modes

In ODBC, transactions are handled in one of two different ways, depending on the current commit mode of the connection. The connection can be set to either auto-commit mode (the default) or manual-commit mode. The commit mode for a connection is set by calling SQLSetConnectAttr() for the SQL_ATTR_AUTOCOMMIT option.

Auto-Commit Mode

The default mode for a new connection is auto-commit, which is supported by all drivers. In this mode, each statement operates as a separate transaction, the driver will take care of committing each operation on the database automatically, and you really don't have to worry about transaction processing at all.

If you submit a batch of SQL statements in a single SQLExecute() call, ODBC doesn't define whether this is treated as a single transaction or whether each statement is a separate transaction. If you want to send a batch as a transaction, use manual-commit mode.

Manual-Commit Mode

In cases where you want to ensure that multiple SQL statements can be performed as a transaction, you should always use manual-commit mode, which requires your application to explicitly end a transaction with a call to SQLEndTran().

Once again, this isn't supported by all drivers. You can check on the current driver's transaction support by calling SQLGetInfo() for the SQL_TXN_CAPABLE option. In addition, the SQL_MULTIPLE_ACTIVE_TXN option will tell you whether you can have multiple transactions pending at the same time.

To make use of multiple active transactions, you must have multiple connections because only one transaction is ever in progress for each connection.

Your application doesn't need to explicitly begin a transaction. The driver will begin one automatically when the connection is made, when you switch to manual-commit mode, or when the previous transaction is completed.

You will, however, complete each transaction with a call to SQLEndTran():

```
SQLRETURN SQLEndTran(SQLSMALLINT HandleType, SQLHANDLE Handle,  SQLSMALLINT
➥CompletionType);
```

In most cases, you will set HandleType to SQL_HANDLE_DBC and pass the current connection handle in Handle. This will end the transaction on the current connection handle. In addition, you may also specify SQL_HANDLE_ENV and pass your environment handle. This will end the current transactions for all connections associated with this environment. This doesn't, however, combine the transactions for all connections into a single atomic operation.

The CompletionType parameter specifies how to complete the transaction. If this is set to SQL_COMMIT, any changes made in this transaction are written to the database, whereas a value of SQL_ROLLBACK will cause any changes made in this transaction to be rolled back, as if they never occurred at all.

> **Note**
>
> If you switch back to auto-commit mode from manual-commit mode, the transaction in progress will be committed.

When you end a transaction with SQLEndTran(), different drivers may choose to close any open cursors for the connection, as well as closing the access plans for these cursors. To find the behavior that the current driver supports, you can call SQLGetInfo() for the SQL_CURSOR_COMMIT_BEHAVIOR and SQL_CURSOR_ROLLBACK_BEHAVIOR options.

Transaction Isolation Levels

When you are working with a data source that may have multiple transactions active at one time (from within your application or from other users) you should be concerned with the transaction isolation level, which determines how concurrent transactions may interact with each other. In general, this interaction is described by which of the following—generally undesirable—conditions may occur:

- *Dirty reads* involve an operation that reads data that isn't yet committed, and may eventually be rolled back.
- *Nonrepeatable reads* occur when a transaction reads the same row twice, but may receive different data because another transaction has changed something.
- Phantoms occur when a row has been changed to match a query, but it was not selected in an initial query.

You set the current transaction isolation level for a connection by calling `SQLSetConnectAttr()` for the `SQL_ATTR_TXN_ISOLATION` option. This can be set to one of the following values:

`SQL_TXN_READ_UNCOMMITTED`—Any of the above inconsistencies may occur.

`SQL_TXT_READ_COMMITTED`—Dirty reads are prevented.

`SQL_TXN_REPEATABLE_READ[md]`Dirty reads and nonrepeatable reads are prevented.

`SQL_TXN_SERIALIZABLE`—All of the above anomalies are prevented.

Once again, not all ODBC drivers are created equal—you can determine the isolation modes that are supported by calling `SQLGetInfo()` for the `SQL_TXN_ISOLATION_OPTION`. You can also retrieve the default level by using the `SQL_DEFAULT_TXN_ISOLATION` option.

> **Note**
>
> Regardless of the transaction isolation level, all transactions will be able to see any changes that have been made from within that transaction.

Although higher isolation levels can prevent some inconsistencies in the data, they may also introduce a greater amount of overhead, thus affecting your application's performance—and that of other apps that use the same data source. When choosing an isolation level to use, you should weigh this performance cost against the potentials for data inconsistency.

Cursor Concurrency Types

It is in the nature of higher isolation levels to limit inconsistencies in the data by limiting the concurrency of the data source—that is, how multiple operations may occur on the data source simultaneously. You can optimize the concurrency of your application's operations by setting the concurrency type of the cursor that is used with a statement handle.

This is done by calling `SQLSetStmtAttr()` for the `SQL_ATTR_CONCURRENCY` option, which can have the following values:

`SQL_CONCUR_READ_ONLY` indicates the cursor is read-only.

`SQL_CONCUR_LOCK` uses the lowest level of locking sufficient to ensure that a row may be updated.

`SQL_CONCUR_ROWVER` uses optimistic concurrency control, based on row version.

`SQL_CONCUR_VALUES` uses optimistic concurrency control, using values.

You can determine the available options for the current driver by calling `SQLGetInfo()` for the `SQL_SCROLL_CONCURRENCY` option.

The following example uses the menu resource and the ClassWizard to generate menu functions that control transactions. The code added to the four menu options to turn transactions on, turn transactions off, commit, and rollback are defined in gray below:

```
void CODBCTestView::OnViewUsetransactions() {

    SQLRETURN sr = SQLSetConnectAttr(hDbConn, SQL_ATTR_AUTOCOMMIT,
            (void*)SQL_AUTOCOMMIT_OFF , SQL_IS_UINTEGER);
    if(sr != SQL_SUCCESS && sr != SQL_SUCCESS_WITH_INFO)
            displayODBCError(sr, "Error in using transactions");

}
void CODBCTestView::OnViewUseautocommit() {

    SQLRETURN sr = SQLSetConnectAttr(hDbConn, SQL_ATTR_AUTOCOMMIT,
            (void*)SQL_AUTOCOMMIT_ON , SQL_IS_UINTEGER);
    if(sr != SQL_SUCCESS && sr != SQL_SUCCESS_WITH_INFO)
            displayODBCError(sr, "Error in turning transactions off");

}
void CODBCTestView::OnViewCommit() {

    SQLRETURN sr = SQLEndTran(SQL_HANDLE_DBC, hDbConn, SQL_COMMIT);
    if(sr != SQL_SUCCESS && sr != SQL_SUCCESS_WITH_INFO)
            displayODBCError(sr, "Error in commit");

}
void CODBCTestView::OnViewRollback() {

    SQLRETURN sr = SQLEndTran(SQL_HANDLE_DBC, hDbConn, SQL_ROLLBACK);
    if(sr != SQL_SUCCESS && sr != SQL_SUCCESS_WITH_INFO)
            displayODBCError(sr, "Error in rollback");

}
```

If you start using manual transactions, you can perform several inserts from the ODBCTest application, and then either commit them or roll them back.

Catalog Functions

In most cases, when you are developing a database application, you should already know about the structure of the database. However, for certain browser-type applications or administrative tools, your app may not know much about the data source until runtime. You can retrieve information about the structure (catalog, schema, and so forth) of a database with the following functions provided by ODBC:

SQLTables() returns information about the tables in a database.

SQLColumns() returns the names of the columns in a table.

SQLSpecialColumns() returns information about the columns that uniquely identify a row, and any columns that are automatically updated when the row is updated (rowids).

SQLPrimaryKeys() returns the columns that make up a table's primary key.

SQLForeignKeys() returns the columns in a table that refer to the primary key of another table, as well as the columns in other tables that refer to this column's primary key.

SQLProcedures() returns a list of procedures available on this data source.

SQLProcedureColumns() returns information about the parameters for a procedure, as well as info about its result set.

SQLTablePrivileges() returns information about the privileges associated with tables in the database.

SQLColumnPrivileges() returns a list of columns and the privileges associated with them for a given table.

SQLStatistics() returns a set of statistics for a table and its associated indexes.

Summary

In this chapter, you took the whirlwind tour of the ODBC 3 API. To recap:

- The ODBC API can be used to provide a standard interface to a wide variety of different data sources, ranging from simple text files to full-featured RDBMSs.

- Setting up ODBC requires the use of handles for the ODBC environment, data source connections, and SQL statements, as well as ODBC error reporting routines.

- Most connections to ODBC databases use SQLConnect().

- The easiest and fastest way to execute a single statement is with SQLExecuteDirect(), although a SQLPrepare() and SQLExecute() combination is optimal for repeating the same SQL statement again and again.

- Parameters can be sent to an application by using a ? placeholder.
- Data is retrieved from an ODBC database by binding program variables to the columns in a result set, both one row at a time and in groups of rows. Cursor behavior can be defined using ODBC functions.
- Database data can be manipulated using INSERT, UPDATE, or DELETE and an SQLExecuteDirect command, or by using positioned updates and deletes.
- Some databases support bulk operations. These operations can speed up large-scale data manipulation, such as inserting thousands of rows.

In the next chapter, you will explore how MFC has encapsulated the ODBC API, providing a simple C++ interface to ODBC.

CHAPTER 21

MFC Database Classes

*by David Bennett
and Chuck Wood*

IN THIS CHAPTER

The *Microsoft Foundation Classes* (MFC) encompass several classes that you can use to provide a simpler C++ interface to databases. These classes are particularly useful when quickly generating applications that present a simple, consistent interface to the user.

MFC provides classes for using the *open database connectivity* (ODBC) API to interface with ODBC datasources, as well as classes for working with *object linking and embedding databases* (OLE DB) and *Data Access Objects* (DAO) to work with desktop databases. In this chapter, you will look at the ODBC classes specifically, although the OLE DB and DAO classes are very similar. You can find more information on the DAO classes and OLE DB classes in the online documentation. In addition, OLE DB database classes are covered more extensively in the next chapter.

In this chapter, you'll explore the three main classes MFC provides for database access: CDatabase (manages a connection to a datasource), CRecordset (manages a set of rows returned from the database), and CRecordView (simplifies the display of data from CRecordset objects).

After you take a look at these classes that make up the building blocks of MFC database applications, you will see how you can use the AppWizard to set up an application to use the MFC ODBC classes.

Using the AppWizard to Generate MFC Classes

Before delving into the specifics of MFC ODBC database classes, this section shows seven simple steps you can use to quickly and easily generate an ODBC database application using the MFC AppWizard.

Step 1

Start a new Visual C++ project by choosing File, New. Choose MFC AppWizard (exe), enter a project name, and click OK. The MFC AppWizard appears. In Step 1 of the AppWizard, choose Single Document and click Next.

Step 2

In Step 2 of the AppWizard, you are asked what type of database support you would like. You have four options:

- **None**—Gives no database support. This is the default.
- **Header Files Only**—Includes only the header files for the MFC database classes and adds build settings to link with the MFC database libraries. It does not define any database classes for you.

- **Database View without File Support**—Generates database classes for you to modify to make a customized database application.
- **Database View with File Support**—Generates database classes for you and provides support for document serialization and the File menu options associated with document files, such as the Open, Close, Save, and Save As File menu options.

You must choose a datasource to be used with these classes by clicking the Data Source button. A dialog box appears; choose a datasource and set the type of recordset to use. You also are prompted for specific tables, views, and stored procedures in the datasource to use for the recordset and record view classes.

Select the Database View with File Support option, and click the Data Source button.

Step 3

The Database Options dialog box now should be open. Here, you choose what type of database support (ODBC, OLE DB, or DAO) you want to include in your application, the name of the datasource, and the recordset type. Possible ODBC recordset types follow:

- **Snapshot**—"Takes a picture" of the results of a query or SELECT statement when the class is first called. Any changes to the database made while your application is running are not reflected in your application.
- **Dynaset**—Constantly resynchronizes the recordset so that any updates or deletions of other users (or other applications) are reflected in your dataset.

> **Note**
>
> The Table option is not available with ODBC. This option is only used when you have a choice between a table and an SQL query, as in OLE DB. OLE DB is discussed in Chapter 22, "Using OLE DB."

In Figure 21.1, I selected an ODBC database and chose a Dynaset Recordset type.

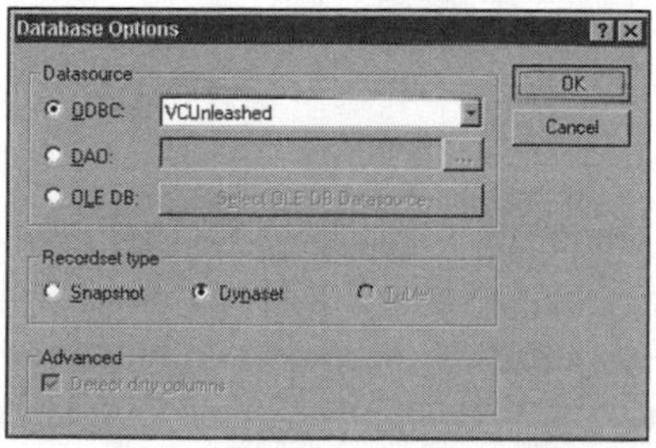

FIGURE 21.1

With the MFC AppWizard, you can create database applications with a variety of datasource types and recordset types.

Step 4

After you choose a valid ODBC datasource, the AppWizard displays a list of tables inside that datasource. Here, you can choose one or more tables or views (or, in MS Access, queries) that you want to use in your database application. In Figure 21.2, the Employee table is chosen as the source for the data in this application.

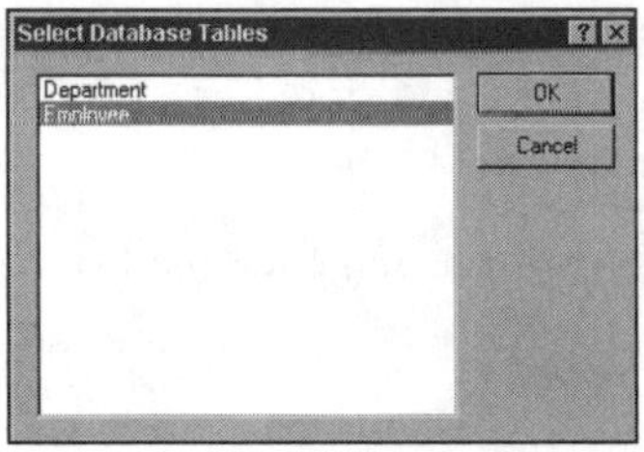

FIGURE 21.2

You must choose the table or tables that will serve as datasources for your AppWizard application.

Step 5

Click Next twice until the MFC AppWizard (Step 4 of 6 dialog box) opens. Deselect Printing and Print Preview. Click Finish. If you've been following this example, a New Project Information dialog box opens with information similar to the information shown in Figure 21.3. Click OK to generate your application.

FIGURE 21.3

The New Project Information dialog box displays the options you chose when developing your MFC AppWizard application.

Step 6

Now that you have an application with database support, you need to display that information. In Figure 21.4, you see a sample dialog box that was created with two edit boxes to hold information from the Employee table. These two dialog boxes are named IDC_EMPNAME and IDC_DEPTCODE and hold the employee name and department code.

Figure 21.4

You need to build dialog box fields to hold the results from your database application.

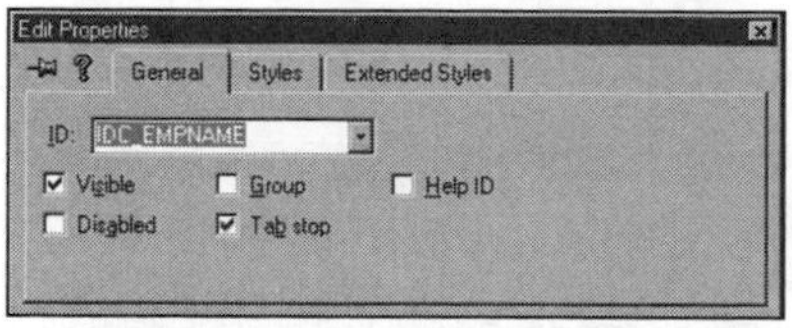

Step 7

In this final step, you need to use the ClassWizard to link your database variables to your dialog box edit boxes. First, open the ClassWizard by choosing View, ClassWizard. Then select the Member Variables tab, as shown in Figure 21.5. The edit boxes you added to your view's dialog box should be displayed.

Figure 21.5

The ClassWizard Member Variables tab shows the controls added to your view's dialog box.

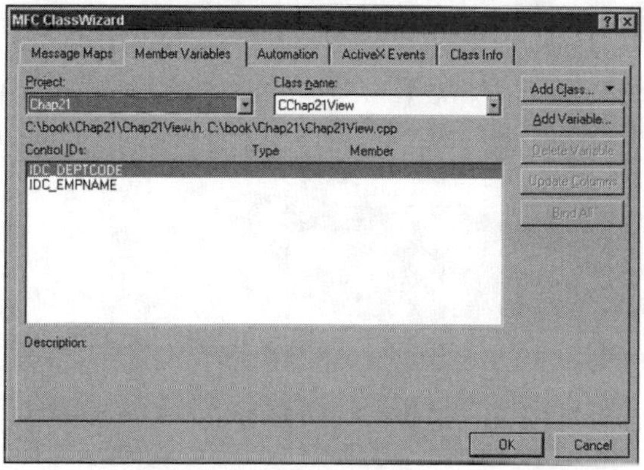

Double-click each variable. Alternatively, highlight each variable and click the Add Variable button. The Add Member Variable dialog box opens, as shown in Figure 21.6. Here, choose the appropriate database variable from the drop-down Member Variable Name list and click OK.

Figure 21.6

Adding database member variables to the dialog box edit boxes.

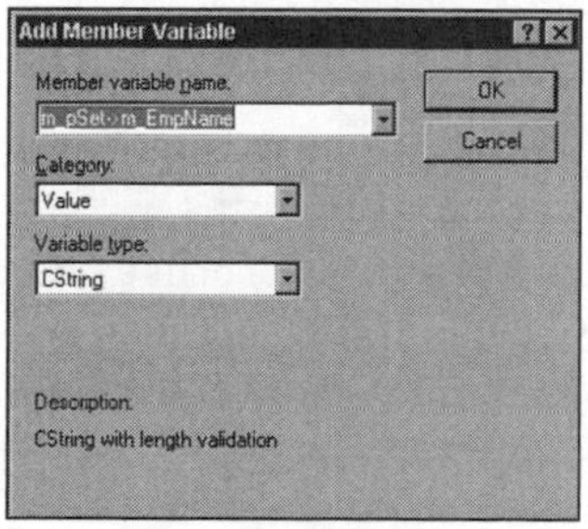

The ClassWizard Member Variables tab appears (see Figure 21.7).

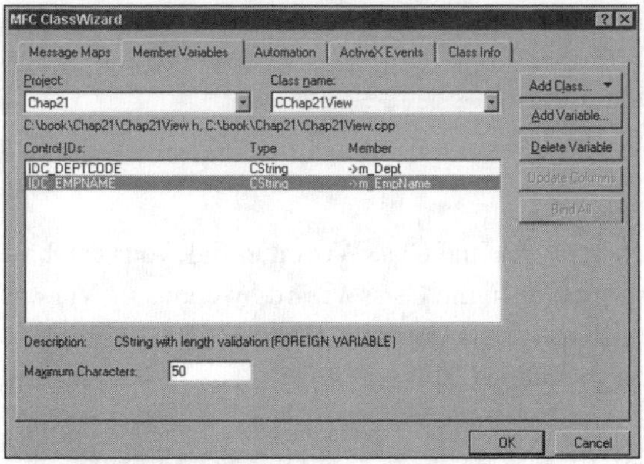

FIGURE 21.7

The ClassWizard displays the data-base variables linked to the dialog box edit boxes.

Now you're finished. When you build your application, you can see a database application that queries the database and allows updates to the data, as shown in Figure 21.8.

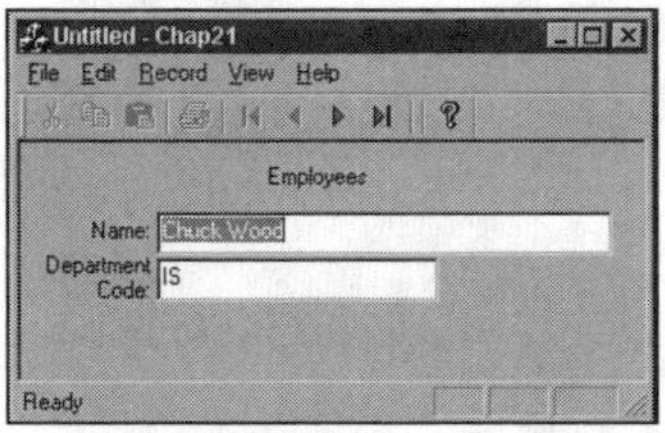

FIGURE 21.8

Simple database applications are easy to build using the MFC AppWizard.

Although the MFC AppWizard is a great tool for quick ODBC database development, eventually database developers will need to make modifications to their database applications. These modifications require an understanding of the MFC ODBC classes. The rest of this chapter describes the MFC ODBC classes that were generated by the MFC AppWizard.

The `CRecordset` Class

You use `CRecordset` to encapsulate queries of the database, as well as to add, update, or delete rows. The MFC AppWizard generates a derived `CRecordset` class and instantiates it with a pointer named m_pSet that can be used to invoke any `CRecordset` functionality. In our example, a new class derived from `CRecordSet` is defined in the `Chap21Set.h` header file, as shown in gray in the following code:

21

```
// Chap21Set.h : interface of the CChap21Set class
//
/////////////////////////////////////////////////////////////////////

#if !defined(AFX_CHAP21SET_H__FCC314EE_AF89_11D3_9447_9FD0F70EAABB__INCLUDED_)
#define AFX_CHAP21SET_H__FCC314EE_AF89_11D3_9447_9FD0F70EAABB__INCLUDED_

#if _MSC_VER > 1000
#pragma once
#endif // _MSC_VER > 1000
```

```
class CChap21Set : public CRecordset
```

```
{
```

You will almost never use CRecordset objects without deriving your own class, because the CRecordset class provides a framework for your own derived classes to use member variables to receive the data from rows returned by the database.

Record Field Exchange

The MFC framework can move data back and forth between the database and the member variables of your CRecordset by using record field exchange, which works very much like the dialog data exchange mechanism you saw in Chapter 5, "Creating and Using Dialog Boxes."

The exchange is set up by implementing the DoFieldExchange() function for your CRecordset class. Like the CDialog::DoDataExchange() function, the bulk of your implementation will use a set of macros that MFC provides for defining record field exchange. Like the DFX_ macros, MFC provides a range of different RFX_ macros for different data types. Table 21.1 shows the available RFX_ macros and the data types for the member variables with which they are used.

TABLE 21.1 Record Field Exchange Macros

RFX *Macro*	*Member Variable Type*
RFX_Binary()	CByteArray
RFX_Bool()	BOOL
RFX_Byte()	int
RFX_Date()	CTime

continues

TABLE 21.1   continued

RFX *Macro*	*Member Variable Type*
RFX_Double()	double
RFX_Int()	int
RFX_Long()	LONG
RFX_LongBinary()	CLongBinary
RFX_Single()	float
RFX_Text()	CString

Each of the macros listed in the table takes three parameters: the CFieldExchange pointer passed to DoFieldExchange(), the name of the database field, and the member variable to hold the data for that field. The DoFieldExchange() function from our example (in Chap21Set.cpp) should help illustrate how these are used:

```
void CChap21Set::DoFieldExchange(CFieldExchange* pFX) {
    //{{AFX_FIELD_MAP(CChap21Set)
    pFX->SetFieldType(CFieldExchange::outputColumn);
    RFX_Long(pFX, _T("[EmpId]"), m_EmpId);
    RFX_Text(pFX, _T("[EmpName]"), m_EmpName);
    RFX_Text(pFX, _T("[Salary]"), m_Salary);
    RFX_Text(pFX, _T("[Dept]"), m_Dept);
    //}}AFX_FIELD_MAP
}
```

After you set up your DoFieldExchange() function, the member variables of your recordset class are updated automatically to hold the values for the current row when you fetch a new row. The data from the member variables also is used automatically when you add new records or update existing records, as you will see later in the "Changing Data in a Recordset" section.

GetFieldValue()

As an alternative to record field exchange, you can always call CRecordset::GetFieldValue(), which enables you to retrieve the value of any field in the current row, even if you have not defined a member variable for the column or set up record field exchange. You can use this function to retrieve the value for a column based on its index or the column name. You can retrieve values as a CString or a CDBVariant object, which enables you to handle many different types of data using a single data type.

> **Tip**
>
> You can retrieve the entire SQL string that was used to select records by calling
> `CRecordset::GetSQL()`. Also, if you are unsure of the name of the table
> retrieved, you can get this by calling `CRecordset::GetTableName()`. In addition,
> you can get the total number of fields returned by calling `CRecordset::`
> `GetODBCFieldCount()`, and you can retrieve information about each field by
> calling `CRecordset::GetODBCFieldInfo()`.

Refreshing the Recordset

If you want to refresh the recordset, you can call `CRecordset::Requery()`. This goes out
and retrieves the data from the database again, including any changes that were made
since the recordset was opened. If you are using a snapshot recordset, this is the only
way to get at any changes made to the data by other users. Also, a dynaset recordset will
not report any INSERTs until a `Requery()` is called.

> **Caution**
>
> Like many other functions, `Requery()` is not supported by all ODBC drivers. You
> can call `CRecordset::CanRestart()` to find out whether the current driver sup-
> ports this.
>
> If your driver does not support requeries, you can refresh your query by calling
> a `CRecordset::Close()` followed by a `CRecordset::Open()`. Check out the
> MSDN documentation to see how this is done.

Moving About in the Recordset

The member variables you defined in your `CRecordset` class to hold column data are
only intended to hold one value at a time. To access the data for the rows in the recordset, move to a specific row in the recordset. The `CRecordset` class provides several
methods that make moving around the recordset quite simple, starting with
`CRecordset::MoveNext()`.

Moving Forward

`MoveNext()` takes no parameters and simply moves on to the next row in the recordset,
updating the member variables of the recordset along the way. Note that calling `Move()`

after you have scrolled to the last record throws an exception. To prevent this, you should call `IsEOF()` to find out whether you are at the end of the recordset before calling `Move()`.

> **Note**
>
> The first row is selected automatically when the recordset is opened, so the recordset member variables reflect the first row without a call to `MoveNext()`.

The following example shows the use of `MoveNext()` to trace through the rows in the recordset. Note that exception handling has been removed to simplify the example, but your applications should be prepared to catch any exceptions that may be thrown:

```
do {
    m_pSet->MoveNext();
}
while(!m_pSet->IsEOF());
```

Scrolling

If your recordset uses a forward-only cursor, you'll have to make do with just the `MoveNext()` function. If your driver supports scrolling, however, you have several other options. You can check whether the recordset supports scrolling by calling `CRecordset::CanScroll()`.

The `MoveFirst()` and `MoveLast()` methods move to the first and last record in the recordset. You also can move to any specific row by calling `SetAbsolutePosition()`, which takes a zero-based index into the recordset.

Additionally, the `MovePrev()` member moves to the previous row. Calling `MovePrev()` when you are already at the beginning of the recordset generates an exception, so it is a good idea to call `IsBOF()` to check whether you are at the beginning of the recordset before calling `MovePrev()`.

Using Bookmarks

You can navigate to specific rows in the recordset by using bookmarks, provided your ODBC driver supports them. You can determine whether bookmarks are supported by calling `CanBookmark()`. You can call the `GetBookmark()` member to retrieve a bookmark for the current row in the recordset. You then can return to that specific row later by passing the bookmark value to `SetBookmark()`.

CRecordset::Move()

Each of the previous navigation functions is supported by the more generic Move() function, which you can use to move a number of rows forward or backward from the current row. Here is the prototype for Move():

```
virtual void Move( long nRows, WORD wFetchType = SQL_FETCH_RELATIVE );
```

The nRows parameter takes the number of rows to move—positive values are used to move forward, and negative values may be used to move backward.

You may omit the wFetchType parameter and simply use the SQL_FETCH_RELATIVE default, or you may specify one of the following values:

- SQL_FETCH_ABSOLUTE—Fetches the nRowth row in the recordset.
- SQL_FETCH_BOOKMARK—Fetches the row specified by a bookmark value passed in nRows.
- SQL_FETCH_FIRST—Fetches the first row in the recordset.
- SQL_FETCH_LAST—Fetches the last row in the recordset.
- SQL_FETCH_NEXT—Fetches the next row.
- SQL_FETCH_PRIOR—Fetches the previous row.
- SQL_FETCH_RELATIVE—Fetches the row nRows from the current row.

If an error occurs in the Move() operation, it throws an exception; otherwise, the current row is set to the new row, and the member variables of the recordset are updated to hold the data for the new row.

Changing Data in a Recordset

In most cases, if your application is to do any real work, it eventually modifies the data in the database. This may consist of adding new rows to tables, deleting rows, or updating the data in an existing row. Because deleting a row is the simplest of these operations, let's start with that.

Deleting a Row

To delete a row from a datasource, you simply open the recordset and call Move() or MoveNext() until the row you want to delete is the current row; then call CRecordset::Delete(). This removes the current row from the database and sets the recordset's member variables to NULL values. You call a Move function to move to another valid row.

> **Tip**
>
> You can check to see whether the current row has been deleted by calling the `IsDeleted()` member of `CRecordset`.

Adding a New Row

Before adding a new row, you should be certain that you have not opened the recordset as read-only. You can easily check this by calling `CRecordset::CanAppend()` to see whether you can add records using this recordset.

Adding a new row involves three steps. First, call `CRecordset::AddNew()` to create a new empty row. Then set the member variables of the recordset to the values you want to place in the new row. Finally, call `CRecordset::Update()` to add the new row to the database. The following example illustrates this process:

```
if(m_pSet->CanAppend()) {
    m_pSet->AddNew();
    strcpy(m_pSet->m_EmpName, "George Washington");
    strcpy(m_pSet->m_Dept, "Executive");
    m_pSet->m_Salary = 100000;
    if(m_pSet->Update())
        TRACE("Row Added OK\n");
    else
        TRACE("Row Not Added\n");
} // end if CanAppend()
```

If you are using a dynaset, the new row appears as the last row in the recordset. If you are using a snapshot, however, you call `Requery()` to update the recordset to include the new row.

Editing an Existing Row

Updating is one of the most complex database update methods in the MFC ODBC API. Fortunately, the AppWizard generates code that allows updates. However, you need to understand the `Update()` function for more complex update operations within a record-set.

Like adding a new row, editing an existing row requires three steps. First, call `CRecordset::Edit()` to begin the update process for the current row. Next, change the values of the member variables of the recordset. When you call `CRecordset::Update()`, these changes are transferred to the database. If you choose not to update the row after you have called `Edit()`, you can cancel the update by calling `CancelUpdate()`.

The following example shows how you can use Edit() and Update() to modify the current existing row in the database:

```
if(m_pSet->CanUpdate()) {
    m_pSet->Edit();
    strcpy(m_pSet->m_EmpName, "George Washington");
    strcpy(m_pSet->m_Dept, "Executive");
    m_pSet->m_Salary = 100000;
    if(m_pSet->Update())
        TRACE("Row Added OK\n");
    else
        TRACE("Row Not Added\n");
} // end if CanAppend()
```

Working with NULL Values

If you want to set a field in the row to a NULL value, you should first check to see whether a NULL value is acceptable for that field by calling IsFieldNullable(). You then can set the field to a NULL value by calling SetFieldNull(). You also can check to see whether a field currently is set to a NULL value by calling IsFieldNull().

Row Locking

When updating rows, you have a choice of how the framework will lock rows that are being updated. *Optimistic* locking locks the row only during the processing of the Update() call, and *pessimistic* locking locks the row when you call Edit() and does not release it until after you call Update(). You can set the locking mode by calling CRecordset::SetLockingMode() after you have opened the recordset, but before any calls to Edit().

Using Statement Parameters

In many cases, you will want to execute some queries that are very similar, but with a few variable values. For example, suppose that you want to derive a CRecordset class that retrieves a set of employee records that fall within a certain salary range. Instead of deriving a separate class for each range you might want to deal with, you can create one class that uses statement parameters to modify the query at runtime.

To use parameters, you can add parameter placeholders to the SQL strings that make up the query for your recordset. Most often, you will parameterize the m_strFilter string, although you also may use parameters in the m_strSort string or in the SQL string passed to Open(). For the salary range example in this chapter, you might want to use a value of m_strFilter, such as the following:

```
m_strFilter = "WHERE Salary >= ? AND Salary <= ?";
```

This statement uses two parameters—MFC will substitute real values for the ? in the SQL whenever you call Open() or Requery() for the recordset. To implement the parameters, you add member variables to your recordset class for each parameter and set the m_nParams member of CRecordset to the number of parameters you will be using.

Next, you modify the DoFieldExchange() member of your recordset to move values between your parameter member variables and the SQL statement sent to the database. You add a call to CFieldExchange::SetFieldType() to set the field type to CFieldExchange::param and then add RFX macros for each of your parameters. The RFX macros for your parameters must appear in the order of the placeholders used in the SQL statement. The parameter name given in the RFX macro is not used for parameter matching, so you can choose any arbitrary name you want.

The following example helps illustrate adding parameters to DoFieldExchange():

```
void CChap21Set::DoFieldExchange(CFieldExchange* pFX)
{
    //{{AFX_FIELD_MAP(CChap21Set)
    pFX->SetFieldType(CFieldExchange::outputColumn);
    RFX_Long(pFX, _T("[EmpId]"), m_EmpId);
    RFX_Text(pFX, _T("[EmpName]"), m_EmpName);
    RFX_Text(pFX, _T("[Salary]"), m_Salary);
    RFX_Text(pFX, _T("[Dept]"), m_Dept);
    //}}AFX_FIELD_MAP
    pFX->SetFieldType(CFieldExchange::param);
    RFX_Text(pFX, "myFirstParam", m_strParamOne);
    RFX_Long(pFX, _"mySecondParam", m_nParamTwo);
}
```

The CRecordView Class

The CRecordView class is basically a form view, with several enhancements that make it easier to display data from a recordset. The CRecordView class enables you to use dialog data exchange to display data directly in a dialog box from the recordset. It also provides default implementations for moving to the first, last, next, or previous records in the recordset. In our example, a derived CRecordView class, CChap21View, is generated automatically by the MFC AppWizard in Chap21View.h.

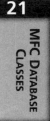

Dialog Data Exchange with `CRecordView`

The `CRecordView` class supports a slightly modified version of the dialog data exchange mechanism that you saw in Chapter 5. The difference is that instead of moving data between controls and member variables in the view class, you can move data between the view controls and the column data member variables of the `CRecordset` associated with the view class.

This is done by using special `DDX_Field` and `DDV_MaxChars` functions in your implementation of `DoDataExchange()`. This is most easily set up using ClassWizard, as you saw earlier in the chapter. The following code from our example in `Chap21View.h` shows the format of the `DoDataExchange()` function:

```
void CChap21View::DoDataExchange(CDataExchange* pDX) {
    CRecordView::DoDataExchange(pDX);
    //{{AFX_DATA_MAP(CChap21View)
    DDX_FieldText(pDX, IDC_DEPTCODE, m_pSet->m_Dept, m_pSet);
    DDV_MaxChars(pDX, m_pSet->m_Dept, 10);
    DDX_FieldText(pDX, IDC_EMPNAME, m_pSet->m_EmpName, m_pSet);
    DDV_MaxChars(pDX, m_pSet->m_EmpName, 50);
    //}}AFX_DATA_MAP
}
```

OnGetRecordset()

The `OnGetRecordset()` member of `CRecordView` is called by the framework to retrieve a pointer to the `CRecordset` associated with the view. The framework calls `OnGetRecordset()` on the initial update of the view, as well as on successive updates. The default implementation supplied by ClassWizard returns the pointer stored in `CRecordView::m_pSet` and creates a new object of the associated recordset class for you, if necessary. You can provide your own implementation of this function if you want to add any special processing to the creation of the recordset.

`CRecordView::OnMove()`

The `OnMove()` member of `CRecordview()` provides a handy way to move your view to a new row in the recordset. It calls the `Move()` member of the associated `CRecordset` and updates the display to show the new row. `OnMove()` also automatically updates the database if the current row has been modified in the record view.

`OnMove()` takes only one parameter, specifying where to move. This can be one of the following constants:

    ID_RECORD_FIRST
    ID_RECORD_LAST

```
ID_RECORD_NEXT
ID_RECORD_PREV
```

When moving around the recordset, you may find the IsOnFirstRecord() and IsOnLastRecord() members of CRecordView useful. These return TRUE if the view currently is positioned on the first or last row of the recordset.

The CDatabase Class

The MFC CDatabase class is used to encapsulate your application's dealings with a connection to the database. This may be a connection to a database server over the network, or it may just be used to keep track of your settings for a desktop database on the local machine. In most cases, the methods associated with CDatabase correspond directly to the functions of the ODBC C API that work with connection handles.

You can retrieve the CDatabase class associated with your CRecordset class by using the m_pSet->m_pDatabase CRecordset class variable.

Executing SQL Statements with CDatabase

For general queries that return resultsets, it usually is easier to use the CRecordset class, which you will look at next. However, you can execute SQL statements that do not return resultsets without using a CRecordset. You do this by calling CDatabase::ExecuteSQL(),:

```
void ExecuteSQL( LPCSTR lpszSQL );
```

This function simply takes a SQL string passed in lpszSQL and executes it against the current datasource. Notice that ExecuteSQL() does not return a value. If something goes wrong (for example, the SQL statement fails), a CDBException is thrown. Your application needs to catch these in order to determine whether the statement did not execute properly.

OnSetOptions()

When you call ExecuteSQL(), the MFC framework makes a call to the OnSetOptions() member of CDatabase before it sends the SQL statement to the database. This allows the CDatabase object to set up any options that are required before executing SQL statements.

In the default implementation, this function simply sets the SQL_QUERY_TIMEOUT option for the statement handle that will be used for the operation to the value that was specified with a call to CDatabase::SetQueryTimeout(). You can add any other options you may need by deriving your own class from `CDatabase` and overriding the `OnSetOptions()` member function, which is passed the statement handle that MFC will use to execute the statement.

Tip

The `CDatabase` class provides an additional, undocumented, virtual function, which gives your class the opportunity to bind parameters to a statement executed with `ExecuteSQL()`. To use this function, you derive your own class from `CDatabase` and override the `BindParameters()` function:

```
void CDatabase::BindParameters(HSTMT hstmt);
```

To actually bind parameters, you use the ODBC C API, as shown in the preceding chapter. When doing these sorts of things, it is very useful to take a look at the source code for the MFC database classes, included with Visual C++ in `DBCORE.CPP`.

Transactions with `CDatabase`

The `CDatabase` class also is responsible for managing transactions for the database connection. Transactions enable you to execute a series of SQL statements as a single operation. If one of the operations in a transaction fails, the rest of the operations in the transaction also can be undone.

This feature is most useful when you need to make several different, but related, changes to a database. If you are entering a sales order, for example, you may want to update both your Shipping table and your Billing table. If you update one of these and the other update fails, you can expect a few extra customer service calls.

Note

Not all ODBC drivers support transactions. You can find out whether the current driver supports transactions by calling `CDatabase::CanTransact()`.

To begin a transaction using the MFC ODBC classes, call `CDatabase::BeginTrans()`. You then can execute the operations that make up the transaction by calling `CDatabase::ExecuteSQL()` or by using `CRecordset` objects derived from this `CDatabase`.

> **Caution**
>
> For some ODBC drivers, calling `BeginTrans()` when `CRecordset` objects already have been opened can cause problems with `Rollback()` processing. To avoid difficulties, it is best to call `BeginTrans()` first, and then open the recordsets that will be used for the transaction.

A transaction can end in one of two ways. If all of the operations were successful and you want to go through with the transaction, you should call `CDatabase::CommitTrans()`. If an error has occurred, and you want to cancel the transaction, you should call `CDatabase::Rollback()`, which will undo all the operations performed with this `CDatabase` (and any derived recordsets) since the call to `BeginTrans()`.

This example shows a simple transaction involving a row insertion made by calling `ExecuteSQL()`:

```
try {
    m_pSet->m_pDatabase->BeginTrans();
    m_pSet->m_pDatabase->ExecuteSQL(
        "INSERT INTO Employee VALUES ('Joe Beancounter', 'Accounting', 80000)");
    m_pSet->m_pDatabase->CommitTrans())
        TRACE("Transaction Commited\n");
    else
        TRACE("Error in CommitTrans\n");
}
catch(CDBException *pEx) {
    pEx->ReportError();
    m_pSet->m_pDatabase->Rollback();
}
```

Effects of Transactions on `CRecordsets`

Ending a transaction on a `CDatabase` object can have different effects on the `CRecordsets` that are created from it, depending on the ODBC driver that you are using. Calling `CRecordset::GetCursorCommitBehavior()` and `CDatabase::RollbackBehavior()` enables you to find out how your driver affects `CRecordsets` when you call `CommitTrans()` or `Rollback()`. Both of these functions will return one of the following values:

> `SQL_CB_CLOSE`—The cursors for any `CRecordsets` are closed. If you want to use them after completing a transaction, call `CRecordset::Requery()`.
>
> `SQL_CB_DELETE`—Any cursors for `CRecordsets` associated with this `CDatabase` are deleted. You should call `CRecordset::Close()` and reopen the `CRecordset` if you need to use it again.
>
> `SQL_CB_PRESERVE`—The `CRecordsets` built from this `CDatabase` are not affected, and your app can continue to use them in their current state.

Using the ODBC API Directly

For some applications, the MFC database classes may not give you quite enough control over the database interaction. If you need to do anything not directly supported by the MFC classes, you can call the ODBC C API directly. Of course, to call the ODBC API, you need ODBC handles. Well, it just so happens that you can get the ODBC connection handle from the m_hdbc member of CDatabase. You also can get statement handles from the m_hstmt member of the CRecordset class.

You may freely mix ODBC C API calls with use of the MFC database classes in your applications. However, you may want to take a look at the source code for the MFC classes to see how the MFC member functions use the ODBC API.

Exception Handling

The MFC database classes report most errors by throwing exceptions rather than returning error codes. For errors specific to database operations, a CDBException object is thrown, although other exception types, such as CMemoryException, also may be thrown.

When handling an exception, you can simply use the CException::ReportError() function to alert the user to the exception, or you may do more extensive error processing based on the member variables of the CDBException. These include m_nRetCode, which gives the ODBC SQLRETURN value that was generated; m_strError, which holds a string with text describing the error; and m_strStateNativeOrigin, which holds a string containing the SQLSTATE, native error, and error message string, including the ODBC component that generated the error.

Bulk Row Operations

Up until now, you have been looking at how to use the CRecordset class to retrieve the data for a single row at a time, which may not always be the most efficient way of doing things. You can often make your applications more efficient and easier to program by fetching a group of rows (rowset) all at once using *bulk record field exchange* (Bulk RFX).

> **Note**
>
> When using Bulk RFX, many of the CRecordset functions are not supported and will throw exceptions. Most notably, this includes AddNew(), Edit(), Delete(), and Update(). Currently, MFC does not support bulk additions, updates, or deletions.

When using Bulk RFX, the member variables of your recordset class should be pointers to the type of data expected. The following shows the declaration of a recordset class for use with Bulk RFX:

```
class CMyBulkSet : public CRecordset
{
public:
    CMyBulkSet(CDatabase* pDatabase = NULL);
    DECLARE_DYNAMIC(CMyBulkSet)
// Field/Param Data
    Cstring m_EmpName;
    Cstring m_Dept;
    Cstring m_Salary;
// Length buffer pointers
    long* m_EmpNameLen;
    long* m_DeptLen;
    long* m_SalaryLen;
// Overrides
    public:
    virtual CString GetDefaultConnect();    // Default connection string
    virtual CString GetDefaultSQL();    // Default SQL for Recordset
    virtual void DoBulkFieldExchange(CFieldExchange* pFX);  // RFX support
// Implementation
#ifdef _DEBUG
    virtual void AssertValid() const;
    virtual void Dump(CDumpContext& dc) const;
#endif
};
```

The constructor for this class should look something like the following:

```
CMyBulkSet::CMyBulkSet(CDatabase* pDatabase)
    : CRecordset(pDatabase)
{
    m_EmpName = NULL;
    m_Dept = NULL;
    m_Salary = NULL;

    m_EmpNameLen = NULL;
    m_DeptLen = NULL;
    m_SalaryLen = NULL;
    m_nFields = 3;
    m_nDefaultType = dynaset;
}
```

Opening a CRecordset for Bulk RFX

To enable bulk row fetching for your CRecordset, you specify the CRecordset::
useMultiRowFetch flag in the options parameter of CRecordset::Open(). You probably will also want to specify the number of rows to be retrieved in each rowset by calling

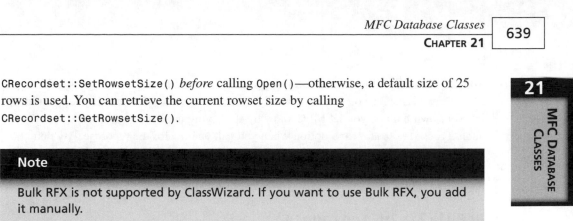

CRecordset::SetRowsetSize() *before* calling Open()—otherwise, a default size of 25 rows is used. You can retrieve the current rowset size by calling CRecordset::GetRowsetSize().

> **Note**
>
> Bulk RFX is not supported by ClassWizard. If you want to use Bulk RFX, you add it manually.

The following example shows how to open a recordset for Bulk RFX, for which MFC will allocate data buffers:

```
// Allocate new recordset
CMyBulkSet* pBulkSet = new CMyBulkSet(m_pDatabase);
// Open Recordset, catching exceptions
try {
    // Set Number of rows in rowset
    pBulkSet->SetRowsetSize(5);

    // Open recordset with dynamic cursor
    bRc - pBulkSet->Open(CRecordset::dynamic,
            "SELECT EmpName, Dept, Salary FROM Employee",
            CRecordset::useMultiRowFetch);
    if(bRc)
        TRACE("Recordset Opened OK\n");
    else
        TRACE("Recordset Not Opened\n");
}
catch(CMemoryException *pEx) {
    pEx->ReportError();
}
catch(CDBException *pEx) {
    pEx->ReportError();
    TRACE("RetCode: %d strError: [%s] strState: [%s]\n",
        pEx->m_nRetCode, pEx->m_strError,
        pEx->m_strStateNativeOrigin);
}
```

Implementing Bulk Record Field Exchange

When fetching rows in bulk, you will use bulk record field exchange, which is similar to regular RFX, with the exception that it retrieves up to the number of rows in the rowset and places the data into array members of your recordset. For each column, you also want to allocate an array of longs that will receive the length of each field returned.

You can manually allocate these arrays, just as you would for RFX column variables as you saw earlier, or you can have MFC allocate the memory for you. If you are allocating your own buffers, you let MFC know by specifying the CRecordset:: userAllocMultiRowBuffers option when you call Open() for the recordset. By default, MFC allocates the memory for you. If you choose to let MFC allocate the arrays, you should declare your member variables as pointers to the appropriate type and initialize them to NULL.

DoBulkFieldExchange()

If you have enabled Bulk RFX, MFC calls the DoBulkFieldExchange() member of your recordset class instead of DoFieldExchange(). You will want to implement this function in your recordset class to move data from the database into the member arrays of your class. The implementation of DoBulkFieldExchange() is very similar to that of DoFieldExchange(), except that you should use the Bulk RFX macros. Instead of using RFX_Int(), for example, you should use RFX_Int_Bulk(). In addition, some of the bulk functions, such as RFX_Text_Bulk(), take a fifth parameter for the maximum allowable buffer size.

The only difference in the bulk macros is that they take a fourth parameter—the address of an array of longs that will receive the length of each field returned. This array will hold SQL_NULL_DATA for any field that has a NULL value. You should make sure that the pointer to the column data points to an array of variables, rather than the single variable used in plain RFX.

The following example shows an implementation of DoBulkFieldExchange():

```
void CMyBulkSet::DoBulkFieldExchange(CFieldExchange* pFX)
{
    pFX->SetFieldType(CFieldExchange::outputColumn);
    RFX_Long_Bulk(pFX, _T("[EmpName]"), &m_Num, &m_EmpNameLen);
    RFX_Text_Bulk(pFX, _T("[Dept]"), &m_Title, &m_DeptLen, 50);
    RFX_Long_Bulk(pFX, _T("[Salary]"), &m_Pages, &m_SalaryLen);
}
```

Fetching Bulk Records

When you call Open() with the CRecordset::useMultiRowFetch option set, the first rowset is fetched from the datasource and copied into the member variables. To retrieve the next complete rowset, you can call MoveNext(). You also may call Move() to fetch a new rowset; however, you should be aware that the parameter to Move specifies the number of rows to move, not the number of rowset blocks. If your rowset size is 10, for example, Open() fetches the first 10 rows, a call to MoveNext() fetches the next 10 (rows 11 to 20), and a call to Move(5) fetches rows 6 to 15.

You can retrieve the number of rows actually fetched in any call to Open(), Move(), or MoveNext() by calling CRecordset::GetRowsFetched(). You can get the status for an individual row by calling CRecordset::GetRowStatus(), which tells you things such as whether the row was successfully retrieved or whether an error occurred. This function also tells you whether the row has been updated, deleted, or added since the last fetch.

In addition, you can refresh the data and status for the current rowset by calling CRecordset::RefreshRowset().

The following example shows how you can use MoveNext() to dump the data returned by a recordset using Bulk RFX:

```
do {
    for(int i=0;i<5;i++) {
        if(pBulkSet->GetRowStatus(i+1) == SQL_ROW_SUCCESS)
            TRACE("Num: %d Title: [%s] Pages: %d\n",
                *(pBulkSet->m_Num + i),
                pBulkSet->m_Title + i*50,
                *(pBulkSet->m_Pages + i));
        else
            TRACE("No Row Fetched\n");
    }
    // Get Next rowset
    pBulkSet->MoveNext();
}
while(!pBulkSet->IsEOF());
```

CheckRowsetError()

When you call any of the cursor navigation functions, including Open(), Requery(), Move(), or MoveNext(), the MFC framework calls CRecordset::CheckRowsetError() to process any errors that may occur. If your application needs to do any special error processing, you can override this function.

Using Single-Row Functions

For functions such as CRecordset::GetFieldValue(), which work on a single row, you set the current row within the rowset. This is done with the SetRowsetCursorPosition() member of CRecordset.

Summary

In this chapter, you explored MFC's support for database operations in your applications.

You learned that most developers will use the AppWizard to begin their MFC ODBC development. It's easy, relatively bug-free, and allows faster development of applications.

You examined the basic classes that MFC provides for working with ODBC data-sources—CDatabase, CRecordset, and CRecordView.

You learned that you can use CDatabase functions to execute SQL statements against the datasource, including transactions. You can use the CRecordset class to provide a simple way to move data from rows in the database back and forth between member variables of the recordset by using record field exchange. You saw that, in addition to using record-sets to select rows from a database, you can use recordsets to add, delete, and update rows in the database.

You also looked at how to use the CRecordView class to provide a convenient interface between the user and the data in a recordset, including a special case of dialog data exchange that supports the member variables of an associated recordset.

Finally, you learned that for efficiency, bulk operations are supported in the MFC ODBC API. This chapter showed you how to implement this feature.

Using OLE DB

CHAPTER 22

*by David Bennett
and Chuck Wood*

This chapter takes a look at one of Microsoft's newest additions to its set of database APIs: OLE DB, which is intended to replace the older Data Access Objects (DAO) and Remote Data Objects (RDO) APIs. OLE DB provides an extremely flexible Component Object Model (COM) interface between data providers and data consumers. In Visual C++ 5.0, this flexibility can make things a bit complicated at times. However, Visual C++ 6.0 added OLE DB functionality to the MFC and ATL AppWizards, making OLE DB development quite easy.

OLE DB is scalable and has functionality that goes beyond the scope of this chapter. This chapter looks at OLE DB development in Visual C++, specifically in the area of OLE DB rowsets, commands, error trapping, and sessions. Also included in this chapter is a step-by-step development process that shows you just how easy OLE DB development has become in version 6.

OLE DB Architecture

The OLE DB architecture defines two basic classes of applications, although there can be a wide range of different sorts of applications in each class, ranging from the most primitive to the very complex RDBMS systems:

> *Providers* are applications that expose data sources in a tabular format. OLE DB providers expose the rowset COM interfaces of OLE DB and can range from simple providers that expose a single table of data to more complicated, distributed database or Online Analytical Processing (OLAP) systems. The most popular provider is the ODBC OLE DB provider. This provider accesses ODBC data through an OLE DB provider, enabling ODBC data sources to be used in an OLE DB application.
>
> *Consumers* are applications that use the OLE DB interfaces to manipulate the data stored in a data provider. User applications, such as the ones developed in this chapter, fall into the consumer class.

Figure 22.1 shows how the classes of OLE DB applications fit together to make up the OLE DB architecture.

FIGURE 22.1
OLE DB architecture.

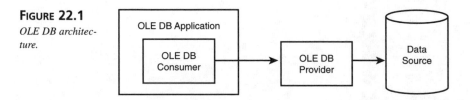

Developing an OLE DB Application

OLE DB development used to be quite difficult. Many OLE DB developers were forced to use the slower ActiveX Data Objects (ADO) interface to access OLE DB data sources simply because of the development time and training required to use OLE DB.

Visual C++ 6.0 changed all that. Now, OLE DB consumers can be developed using either the MFC or the ATL AppWizards. ATL executables, new to version 6, are quite smaller than corresponding MFC applications and tend to run more quickly. MFC may be slightly easier to develop, but MFC uses the same ATL classes developed in the ATL AppWizard to access OLE DB data.

This section takes you through a development process to add OLE DB functionality to an existing ATL application.

> **Note**
>
> The code for this chapter assumes a working dialog box is already set up. To follow the code found in this chapter, you can begin with Chap22Start and add the code as indicated. Chap22Start contains all the dialog box controls and menu items necessary to navigate through the functionality in this chapter. Chap22Final contains the finished code example that is created in this chapter, in case you need to see a fully functional example.
>
> This chapter assumes an ODBC database named VCUnleashed is set up on your machine, with an Employee table and Department table that contain specific columns. A sample database can be found on the CD.
>
> Finally, an error is captured and displayed whenever this program tries to go beyond the start or the end of the recordset and when a record is deleted. This error is the result of trying to update an invalid row. The error was left to illustrate the error handling routine described in this chapter.

Adding an ATL OLE DB Consumer Object

To follow this example, begin a new ATL COM EXE project. Create a dialog box to contain database column information and a menu to aid in navigation. This will usually take some time; if you want to see an example or skip this step, the starting configuration for this example is contained in the Chap22Start directory.

After you've set up a new ATL COM EXE application, click on Insert, New ATL Object from the Visual Studio menu. This opens the ATL Object Wizard dialog box. Select Data Access under Category and choose Consumer, as shown in Figure 22.2.

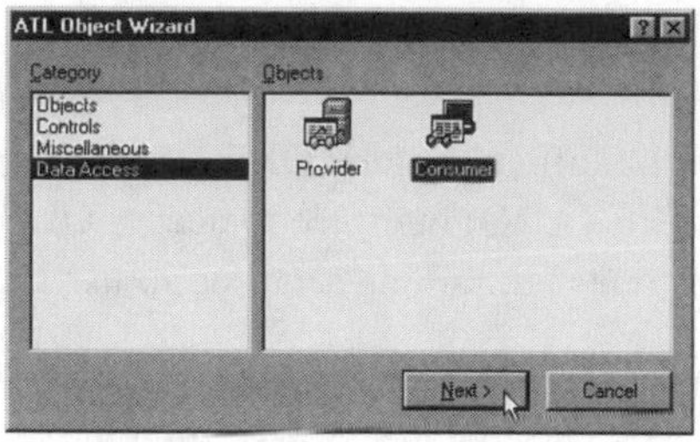

FIGURE 22.2

The ATL Object Wizard makes it easy to create a new OLE DB Consumer.

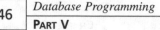

Click Next. The ATL Object Wizard Properties dialog box opens. Immediately click the Select Datasource button, as shown in Figure 22.3.

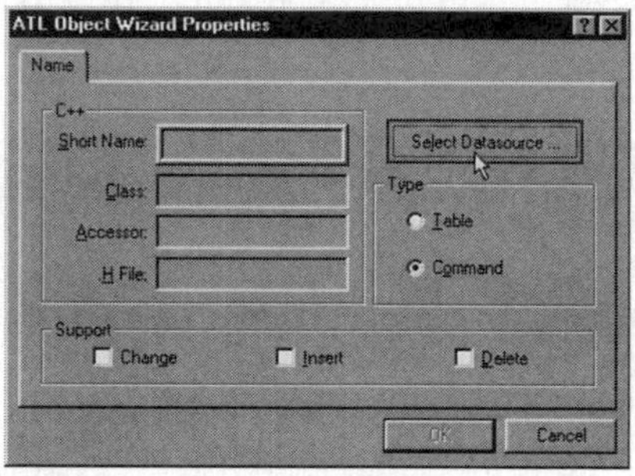

FIGURE 22.3

The ATL Object Wizard enables you to add properties or select data sources for your OLE DB Consumer.

After clicking the Select Datasource button, the Data Link Properties dialog box opens. Here, you select which OLE DB provider you want to write a consumer for. Usually, the choice is the ever-popular `Microsoft OLE DB Provider for ODBC Drivers`, as shown in Figure 22.4.

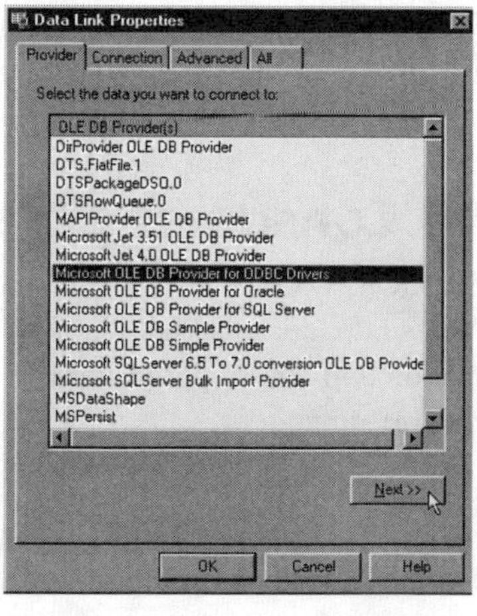

FIGURE 22.4

The Microsoft OLE DB Provider for ODBC Drivers enables you to access any ODBC data source as if it were an OLE DB data source.

When you click the Next button or the Connection tab, the Data Link Properties dialog box enables you to choose the name of your data source, as well as to enter username, password, and catalog information, if appropriate. For this example, VCUnleashed was chosen as the ODBC data source.

When you click OK, a list of tables available in that data source opens inside the Select Database Table dialog box. In Figure 22.5, the Employee table was chosen. When you choose which table or tables you want to access with your OLE DB consumer, click OK.

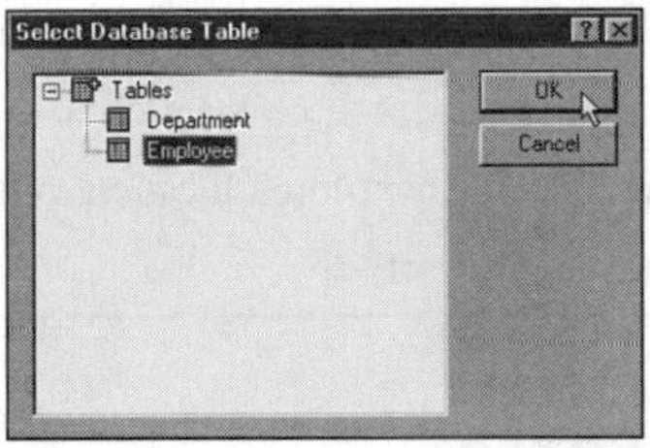

FIGURE 22.5
The Select Database Table dialog box enables you to choose the table for your OLE DB data source.

When you return to the ATL Wizard Properties dialog box, you can see that the names of your header file, class, and OLE DB accessor are filled in. Choose whether you want Table or Command for your data source (usually Command) and whether you want change, insert, and delete capabilities added to your OLE DB rowset (you usually do). When you're finished, click OK. A new OLE DB consumer is then generated and placed inside your Visual C++ project.

Consumer Components

Now your ATL project has a newly generated OLE DB consumer class. For many applications, you won't need to change this project. However, in this application, you need to make some changes to the consumer. This section describes the components and the changes that were made, and why.

CRowset

The main goal of an OLE DB consumer is to allow the developer to access OLE DB data in a rowset format. The CRowset class contains functionality similar to the CRecordset class in the MFC ODBC library. Table 22.1 shows some popular methods contained within the CRowset class. For a more complete list, check out the MSDN documentation.

TABLE 22.1 Popular CRowset Methods

Method	Description
Close	Releases a rowset
Delete	Deletes rows from the rowset
GetData	Retrieves data from the rowset's copy of the row
Insert	Creates and inserts a new row
MoveFirst	Repositions the next-fetch location to the first record
MoveLast	Repositions the next-fetch location to the last record
MoveNext	Increments the next-fetch location to the next record
MovePrev	Decrements the next-fetch location to the last record
SetData	Updates the rowset

CAccessor and CAccessorRowset

In order to work with the data in a rowset, you generally want to use accessor objects. *Accessors* are used to tell OLE DB about the structure of your client application's buffers, which are used either to hold column data from a rowset or values for command parameters.

The CAccessor class is an ATL template class. All accessors created by Visual C++ are derived from CAccessor. In our example, the accessor that is used to build our rowset is based on the CEmployeeAccessor class, which contains four components:

- The accessor should contain the data definition for your rowset. Usually, the ATL Object Wizard generates the data definition. In our example, the employee name, salary, and department are all declared. This enables the rowset to store information that it retrieves into the accessor. The data definition used for the accessor is shown in gray:

```
class CEmployeeAccessor
{
public:
//Autoincrement fields interfere with the Update function.
//Therefore, all references to EmpID have been removed
//from this program by Chuck Wood

    TCHAR m_EmpName[51];
        DB_NUMERIC m_Salary;
        TCHAR m_Dept[11];
```

> **Note**
>
> Notice that the EmpID is left off the accessor data definition because the EmpID is an autoincrement field. Any updates or inserts to an autoincrement field cause database errors.
>
> The ATL Wizard automatically puts all the table columns in the class. If you started working with the Chap22Start project, be sure to delete all references to EmpID. Chap22Final shows how it looks when you're finished.

- The BEGIN_COLUMN_MAP and COLUMN_ENTRY macros enable you to bind database columns to the columns defined in the data definition. In the next code snippet, three columns use COLUMN_ENTRY macros to link columns generated by SQL to C++ class variables:

```
BEGIN_COLUMN_MAP(CEmployeeAccessor)
    COLUMN_ENTRY(1, m_EmpName)
    COLUMN_ENTRY_PS(2, 19, 4, m_Salary)
    COLUMN_ENTRY(3, m_Dept)
END_COLUMN_MAP()
```

> **Note**
>
> Again, notice that the EmpID is left off the column map. When a column is removed, you must be careful to renumber the ordinal (first parameter) of the COLUMN_ENTRY to correspond to columns from a SELECT statement. If you started with the Chap22Start project, you will need to remove the EmpID reference yourself.

- The DEFINE_COMMAND macro enables you to assign a default command for your accessor. In our example, a SELECT statement is issued that selects three columns from the Employee table:

```
DEFINE_COMMAND(CEmployeeAccessor, _T(" \
    SELECT \
        EmpName, \
        Salary, \
        Dept \
        FROM Employee"))
```

- Finally, for convenience, the ALT Object Wizard generates a ClearRecord function that clears data from the accessor. This is useful when creating new blank records for insertion:

```
void ClearRecord()
{
    memset(this, 0, sizeof(*this));
}
```

`CAccessorRowset` encapsulates a rowset and its associated accessors in a single class. By such encapsulation, the developer can access any `CRowset` or `CAccessor` method or variable. The `CAccessorRowset` class is inherited by the `CRowset` and `CAccessor` classes, and is the parent class to the `CCommand` class and the `CTable` class. Figure 22.6 shows the structure of the five main OLE DB classes and how they relate to each other through inheritance.

FIGURE 22.6

The five main OLE DB classes are strongly inter-related.

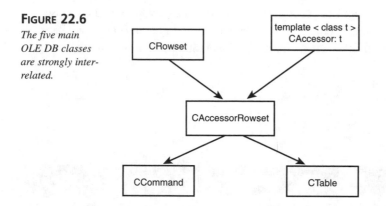

As you can see in Figure 22.6, the `CAccessor` class is inherited from a base class that is defined with a template. (`CEmployeeAccessor` in our example.) This base class enables the `CAccessor` class to not only contain accessor functionality, but also to contain the data definition and `SELECT` statements that are used by the rowset.

CCommand

The `CCommand` class is inherited from the `CAccessorRowset` class. The `CCommand` class is hardly ever instantiated, but rather serves as an ancestor for other classes that can then define how their OLE DB consumer functions.

The `CCommand` class is inherited from a `CAccessorRowset` that is built from a `CRowset` class (`CAccessor`) and the superclass of the `CAccessor` class used for this application's data definition (`CEmployeeAccessor`):

```
class CEmployee : public CCommand<CAccessor<CEmployeeAccessor> >
```

The `CCommand` class has two main functions:

- Data source and session variables are declared and used. The data source contains properties that are used to define the OLE DB connection. The session variable (m_session) contains methods that can control transactions or issue new commands. In the following function, the OLE DB driver for ODBC data sources (MSDASQL) and the VCUnleashed data source are used:

```
HRESULT OpenDataSource() {
    HRESULT hr;
    CDataSource db;
    CDBPropSet dbinit(DBPROPSET_DBINIT);
    dbinit.AddProperty(DBPROP_AUTH_PERSIST_SENSITIVE_AUTHINFO,
false);
    dbinit.AddProperty(DBPROP_INIT_DATASOURCE,
OLESTR("VCUnleashed"));
    dbinit.AddProperty(DBPROP_INIT_PROMPT, (short)4);
    dbinit.AddProperty(DBPROP_INIT_LCID, (long)1033);
    hr = db.Open(_T("MSDASQL"), &dbinit);
    if (FAILED(hr))
        return hr;
    return m_session.Open(db);
}
CSession m_session;
```

- A rowset is created using properties defined by the developer. Notice in bold in the next block of code that new properties can be added. In this case, DBPROP_CANFETCHBACKWARDS enables backward scrolling so that the MovePrev() function will work:

```
HRESULT OpenRowset() {
    // Set properties for open
    CDBPropSet propset(DBPROPSET_ROWSET);
    propset.AddProperty(DBPROP_IRowsetChange, true);
    propset.AddProperty(DBPROP_UPDATABILITY,
        DBPROPVAL_UP_CHANGE | DBPROPVAL_UP_INSERT |
        DBPROPVAL_UP_DELETE );

    //Property added by Chuck Wood
    propset.AddProperty(DBPROP_CANFETCHBACKWARDS, true);

    // Use a NULL to access the default SQL defined
    // in the DEFINE_COMMAND macro in the accessor
    return CCommand<CAccessor<CEmployeeAccessor> >

                    ::Open(m_session, NULL, &propset);

}
```

The CCommand class builds a CAccessorRowset based on an SQL command. In the Open() statement, a NULL is passed where an SQL command should go. The NULL instructs CCommand to use the default SQL found in the DEFINE_COMMAND macro in the accessor.

Data Source Properties

For some providers, you might be able to use the default properties of the provider and move right on to initializing the provider. However, in most cases, you should specify one or more properties before initializing the provider.

Properties for a data source object are divided into two property sets: The DBPROPSET_DBINIT property set contains properties that can be set before the data source is initialized, and the DBPROPSET_DATASOURCE property set contains properties that can be set after the data source is initialized.

The DBPROPSET_DBINIT property set contains the following individual properties:

- DBPROP_INIT_DATASOURCE specifies the name of the data source to connect to.
- DBPROP_AUTH_USERID specifies the user ID that is used to connect to the data source.
- DBPROP_AUTH_PASSWORD specifies the password to be used when connecting to the data source.
- DBPROP_INIT_HWND specifies the window handle to be used as a parent of any dialogs that the data source might need to present to the user, prompting for additional information.
- DBPROP_INIT_MODE specifies the access permissions for the data source. This can be used to set options such as read-only mode.
- DBPROP_INIT_PROMPT specifies whether the user will be prompted for additional initialization information. This can be set to one of the following values:
  - DBPROMPT_PROMPT, in which the provider always prompts the user for initialization information.
  - DBPROMPT_COMPLETE prompts the user only if additional information is required.
  - DBPROMPT_COMPLETEREQUIRED prompts the user only if additional information is required, and the user is allowed to enter only the missing required information.
  - DBPROMPT_NOPROMPT does not prompt the user.
- DBPROP_INIT_TIMEOUT specifies the number of seconds to wait for initialization to complete.
- DBPROP_AUTH_CACHE_AUTHINFO is used to tell the provider whether it is allowed to cache sensitive information, such as passwords.
- DBPROP_AUTH_ENCRYPT_PASSWORD is used to determine whether the password must be encrypted when it is sent to the data source.

- DBPROP_AUTH_INTEGRATED is a string used to specify the authentication service that will be used to authenticate the user.
- DBPROP_AUTH_MASK_PASSWORD specifies that the password will be masked when sent to the data source. This provides a weaker form of encryption than DBPROP_AUTH_ENCRYPT_PASSWORD.
- DBPROP_AUTH_PERSIST_ENCRYPTED specifies that the data source object will persist authentication information in encrypted form.
- DBPROP_AUTH_PERSIST_SENSITIVE_AUTHINFO allows the data source to persist authentication information.
- DBPROP_INIT_IMPERSONATION_LEVEL specifies the level of impersonation that the server can use when impersonating the client.
- DBPROP_INIT_LCID specifies the preferred locale for text that is returned to the consumer.
- DBPROP_INIT_LOCATION specifies the location (such as server name) of the data source.
- DBPROP_INIT_PROTECTION_LEVEL specifies the level of authentication protection in communications between the client and the server.
- DBPROP_INIT_PROVIDERSTRING is used to specify a provider-specific string containing additional connection information.

In addition, you can use the DBPROPSET_DATASOURCE property set to set the DBPROP_CURRENTCATALOG property, which determines which catalog or database is to be used within the data source. For more detail on the acceptable values for the properties listed here, see the OLE DB specification.

CCommand Properties

The properties that you can define for a property set are as follows:

- DBPROP_ABORTPRESERVE determines whether the rowset is preserved after an aborted transaction.
- DBPROP_APPENDONLY is used to create a rowset that is used only for appending new rows.
- DBPROP_BLOCKINGSTORAGEOBJECTS determines whether using storage objects will block other rowset methods.
- DBPROP_BOOKMARKS determines whether the rowset supports bookmarks.
- DBPROP_BOOKMARKSKIPPED determines whether bookmarks for inaccessible rows can be passed to IRowsetLocate::GetRowsAt().
- DBPROP_BOOKMARKTYPE specifies the type of bookmark used.
- DBPROP_CACHEDEFERRED determines whether the consumer will cache column data.

- `DBPROP_CANFETCHBACKWARDS` determines whether the rowset can fetch backwards.

- `DBPROP_CANHOLDROWS` determines whether the rowset will cache rows or transfer them immediately.

- `DBPROP_CANSCROLLBACKWARDS` determines whether the rowset can scroll backwards.

- `DBPROP_CHANGEINSERTEDROWS` determines whether the rowset allows updates to newly inserted rows.

- `DBPROP_COLUMNRESTRICT` determines whether access rights arc determined on a column-by-column basis.

- `DBPROP_COMMANDTIMEOUT` indicates the number of seconds before a command times out.

- `DBPROP_COMMITPRESERVE` determines whether the rowset is preserved after a transaction is committed.

- `DBPROP_DEFERRED` determines whether the rowset will fetch the data for a row immediately or defer until an accessor is used on the columns.

- `DBPROP_DELAYSTORAGEOBJECTS` determines whether storage objects are used in delayed update mode.

- `DBPROP_IColumnsRowset` provides more detailed information about the columns in a rowset.

- `DBPROP_IConnectionPointContainer` provides an interface for creating connection points for receiving COM notifications.

- `DBPROP_IRowsetChange` is used to insert, delete, and update rows in the rowset.

- `DBPROP_IRowsetIdentity` is used to compare two row handles.

- `DBPROP_IRowsetLocate` is used to perform scrolling within a rowset.

- `DBPROP_IRowsetResynch` is used to resynchronize the rowset data to the data source.

- `DBPROP_IRowsetScroll` is used to perform approximate scrolling within the rowset.

- `DBPROP_IRowsetUpdate` is used to work with delayed updates.

- `DBPROP_ISupportErrorInfo` is used for advanced error reporting with OLE DB error objects.

> **Note**
>
> If you are accessing all the columns inside a table and using only one table, the `CTable` class is almost identical to the `CCommand` class. The main difference is that, instead of using a SQL command to build a `CAccessorRowset`, the `CTable` class uses a table definition. Most developers stick with the `CCommand` class because of its flexibility.

Using a Consumer

After creating a consumer, you need to use it to interact with the user. In our example, all the user interaction is handled through the CChap22Dialog class in the Chap22Dialog header file (Chap22Dialog.h). This section shows the code you write to effectively interact with an OLE DB consumer.

Opening and Closing a Rowset

The first step to using a consumer is to include the header file for the consumer .h in the class that needs OLE DB support:

```
//Added by Chuck Wood for OLE DB header file support
#include "Employee.h"
```

Next, you need a class variable to contain the CRowset information. In this example, the CEmployee class, inherited from CCommand, is defined using the m_Set variable at the beginning of the class definition, as shown in gray:

```
class CChap22Dialog :
    public CAxDialogImpl<CChap22Dialog>
{
public:
```

```
    CEmployee m_Set;      //Added by Chuck Wood for DB support
```

After being defined, the rowset can be opened and closed. In the CChap22Dialog constructor and destructor, the rowset is opened and closed, as shown by the lines of code in bold:

```
CChap22Dialog() {
```

```
    m_Set.Open();
```

```
    DoModal();
}
~CChap22Dialog() {
```

```
    m_Set.Close();
```

```
}
```

Updating and Inserting into Rowsets

OLE DB has two routines for updating the database. The first, CRowset.SetData(), is used to update an existing rowset from the class variables defined in the CAccessor (CEmployeeAccessor). The second, CRowset.Insert(), inserts a new row into the rowset and the database using variables defined in the CAccessor. Unlike ODBC, there is no AddNew() function or edit mode. Instead, the programmer usually controls whether an add is in progress and issues the appropriate command depending on whether an insert or update is needed. The following steps can be implemented to handle inserting and deleting inside an ATL program:

1. Declare a Boolean flag used to indicate whether an insert is in progress. In the constructor, set this flag to FALSE. These commands are shown in gray:

```
BOOL m_bInserting;      //Added by Chuck Wood for insert support

CChap22Dialog() {
    m_Set.Open();


    m_bInserting = FALSE;


    DoModal();
}
```

2. The MFC contains an UpdateData() routine used for displaying information from an ODBC recordset to the dialog box and for taking information from the dialog box and updating a recordset. Similar functionality would be useful in an ATL application. The UpdateData() function shown next checks a saveChanges flag to see whether you want to save changes from the dialog box (TRUE, the default) or display contents of the rowset to the dialog box (FALSE). The insert and update functionality is shown in gray:

```
//Functions written by Chuck Wood to aid in database support
void UpdateData(BOOL saveChanges=TRUE) {
    //Written by Chuck Wood for Visual C++ Unleashed
    //Mimics the MFC UpdateData function
    char salaryHolder[25];
    if (saveChanges) {
        GetDlgItemText(IDC_EMPNAME, m_Set.m_EmpName, 51);
        GetDlgItemText(IDC_DEPT, m_Set.m_Dept, 11);
        GetDlgItemText(IDC_SALARY, salaryHolder, 25);
        //Currency conversions (DB_NUMERIC) are a real pain
        double salary = atof(salaryHolder);
        //Adjust salary for scale
        salary *= pow(10, m_Set.m_Salary.scale);
        //Initialize val array to zero
```

```
        for (int loop = 0; loop < 16; loop++) {
            //initialize salary in DB to zero
            m_Set.m_Salary.val[loop] = 0;
        }
        for (loop = 0; salary > 0; loop++) {
            //Adjust hexadecimal power
            double trunc = floor(salary / (16*16));
            m_Set.m_Salary.val[loop] = salary - (trunc*16*16);
            salary = trunc;
        }
        HRESULT hr = 0;

        if (m_bInserting) {
            hr = m_Set.Insert();            //Add new row
        }
        else {
            hr = m_Set.SetData();        //Update row
        }

        m_bInserting = FALSE;
        if (FAILED(hr)) {
            showErrors();
        }
    }
    else {
        //Write data from the database to the dialog box
        SetDlgItemText(IDC_EMPNAME, m_Set.m_EmpName);
        SetDlgItemText(IDC_DEPT, m_Set.m_Dept);
//Currency conversions (DB_NUMERIC) are a real pain
        double salary = 0;      //Initialize salary
        for (int loop = 0; loop < 16; loop++) {
            //Adjust hexadecimal power
            double power = pow(16, loop*2);
            salary += (m_Set.m_Salary.val[loop] * power);
        }
        salary /= pow(10.0, m_Set.m_Salary.scale);
        sprintf (salaryHolder, "%.2f", salary);
        SetDlgItemText(IDC_SALARY, salaryHolder);
    }
}
```

Now the update functionality can be accessed from anywhere in the program. For instance, when the dialog box is closed, an UpdateData() can be called to make sure any final updates are recorded:

```
LRESULT OnCancel(WORD wNotifyCode, WORD wID, HWND hWndCtl, BOOL&
bHandled)
{

    UpdateData();

    EndDialog(wID);
    return 0;
}
```

22

USING OLE DB

Those Annoying Currency Fields

Currency fields are extremely complex for OLE DB. OLE DB uses a *precision/scale* macro, COLUMN_ENTRY_PS, to store the currency:

```
COLUMN_ENTRY_PS(2, 19, 4, m_Salary)
```

This results in a DB_NUMERIC structure to store salary information:

```
DB_NUMERIC m_Salary;
```

The DB_NUMERIC structure is defined as follows:

```
typedef struct tagDB_NUMERIC {
  BYTE precision;
  BYTE scale;
  BYTE sign;
  BYTE val[16];
} DB_NUMERIC;
```

The actual value of the number is stored in the val member. The number is stored in reverse-byte order, and then the number of decimal places is controlled by the scale. Microsoft Access stores currency with four decimal places.

For example, suppose you had a (base-10) salary of 120,000.12. With a scale of 4, the number would be converted to an integer, 1200001200. In hexadecimal, this would be equal to 478690B0. Because each byte holds two hexadecimal digits, the value stored in the val member would be

val Array Elements when 120,000.12 Is Stored as a Scale 4

Val Array	Hex Value	Decimal Value
val[0]	B0	176
val[1]	90	144
val[2]	86	134
val[3]	47	071
val[4]-val[15]	00	000

Notice how the hexadecimal values are stored in reverse order.

To convert such a structure to decimal requires some programming. First, you should include the cmath header file:

```
#include <cmath> //Added by Chuck Wood for pow() support
```

To convert from a DB_NUMERIC structure to a double type, you need to use a loop. Convert each byte of the val array to the appropriate number by multiplying by a power of 16. Then add each byte's adjusted value to the salary. Finally, divide by the scale. The routine to handle the conversion can be seen in the following:

```
//Currency conversions (DB_NUMERIC) are a real pain
double salary = 0;     //Initialize salary
for (int loop = 0; loop < 16; loop++) {
    //Adjust hexadecimal power
    double power = pow(16, loop*2);
    salary += (m_Set.m_Salary.val[loop] * power);
}
salary /= pow(10.0, m_Set.m_Salary.scale);
```

To convert from a double to a DB_NUMERIC, you need to perform the following steps:

1. Multiply the salary by the appropriate scale:

   ```
   //Adjust salary for scale
   salary *= pow(10, m_Set.m_Salary.scale);
   ```

2. Initialize the val array to contain zero in each element:

   ```
   //Initialize val array to zero
   for (int loop = 0; loop < 16; loop++) {
       //initialize salary in DB to zero
       m_Set.m_Salary.val[loop] = 0;
   }
   ```

3. In a loop, subtract each two-digit hexadecimal number, and then remove two digits from the salary until the salary is equal to zero:

   ```
   for (loop = 0; salary > 0; loop++) {
       //Adjust hexadecimal power
       double trunc = floor(salary / (16*16));
       m_Set.m_Salary.val[loop] = salary - (trunc*16*16);
       salary = trunc;
   }
   ```

Conversions to and from DB_NUMERIC fields to double types are cumbersome, but these conversions enable effective processing of special database types, such as the Currency type.

3. Finally, write an insert routine. This routine is called when the user requests a new record. It updates any changes that the user has made in the dialog box using the UpdateData() routine and then calls an insertRecord() function to set up an insert:

```
RESULT OnInsert(WORD wNotifyCode, WORD wID, HWND hWndCtl, BOOL&
bHandled) {
    UpdateData();     //Update database
    insertRecord();     //Set up an insert
    return 0;
}
```

The `insertRecord()` function clears the dialog box fields using the ATL Object Wizard–generated `ClearRecord` function. It then displays the blank fields using a `UpdateData(FALSE)` call and sets the insert flag:

```
Lvoid insertRecord() {      //Set up inserting
    m_Set.ClearRecord();    //Clear dialog box fields
    UpdateData(FALSE);      //Clear window
    m_bInserting = TRUE;    //Initialize add flag
}
```

> **Note**
>
> Unlike ODBC, OLE DB has no edit modes, so the `OnInsert()` and `insertRecord()` functions don't actually do any inserting. Rather, they set up the user to insert a new record, and the `UpdateData()` routine handles the actual updates and inserts when the user is finished typing information for the new record.

Navigating Through a Rowset

Navigating through a rowset involves using the `CRowset.MoveFirst()`, `CRowset.MovePrev()`, `CRowset.MoveNext()`, and `CRowset.MoveLast()` functions. Each of these functions is called through menu routines that enable the user to navigate through the rowset.

The `OnFirst` routine is split into two functions. The menu function updates the current record and then calls the `firstRecord()` function to display the first record:

```
//The rest of this class added by Chuck Wood for OLE DB functionality
LRESULT OnFirst(WORD wNotifyCode, WORD wID, HWND hWndCtl, BOOL& bHandled)
{
    UpdateData();      //Update database
    firstRecord();
    return 0;
}
void firstRecord() {      //Go to the first record
    if (m_Set.MoveFirst() == S_OK) {
        UpdateData(FALSE);      //Display record
    }
    else {
        showMessage("No records found. Inserting new Record");
        insertRecord();
    }
}
```

The reason the `OnFirst()` function is split into two functions is because the `OnInitDialog()` routine needs to display the first record without updating any existing records:

```
LRESULT OnInitDialog(UINT uMsg, WPARAM wParam, LPARAM lParam, BOOL&
bHandled)
{

    firstRecord();      //Display first record

    return 1;   // Let the system set the focus
}
```

The rest of the navigation functions don't need to be split:

```
LRESULT OnPrev(WORD wNotifyCode, WORD wID, HWND hWndCtl, BOOL& bHandled) {
    showMessage("");
    UpdateData();       //Update database
    if (m_Set.MovePrev() == S_OK) {
        UpdateData(FALSE);      //Display record
    }
    else {
        showMessage("No previous records found");
        OnFirst(wNotifyCode, wID, hWndCtl, bHandled);
    }
    return 0;
}
LRESULT OnNext(WORD wNotifyCode, WORD wID, HWND hWndCtl, BOOL& bHandled) {
    showMessage("");
    UpdateData();       //Update database
    if (m_Set.MoveNext() == S_OK) {
        UpdateData(FALSE);      //Display record
    }
    else {
        showMessage("No more records found");
        OnLast(wNotifyCode, wID, hWndCtl, bHandled);
    }
    return 0;
}
LRESULT OnLast(WORD wNotifyCode, WORD wID, HWND hWndCtl, BOOL& bHandled) {
    UpdateData();       //Update database
    if (m_Set.MoveLast() == S_OK) {
        UpdateData(FALSE);      //Display record
    }
    else {
        showMessage("No records found. Inserting new Record");
        insertRecord();
    }
    return 0;
}
```

Deleting Rows from a Rowset

Deleting rows from a rowset (and, hence, from a database table) is always problematic.
Unless transactions are used, there is no way to undo a delete. Make sure that the user

didn't accidentally press the delete option and that there really is a record present to delete, and not a newly inserted record soon to be deleted. The following steps can be used for a delete:

1. Make sure the user really wants a delete:

```
if (MessageBox("Are you sure you want to delete?",
        "Confirm Delete",
        MB_YESNO) != IDYES) {
    return 0;                 // Get outta here
}
```

2. Make sure that an actual record exists to be deleted. If you are in the middle of an insert and you issue a delete, the newly inserted record won't be deleted, but rather *the last record viewed before the insert will be deleted*. This could cause some serious problems for the user:

```
if (m_bInserting) {
    m_bInserting = FALSE;     //Just reset flag, ...
    UpdateData(FALSE);    // display current record, ...
    return 0;             // and get outta here
}
```

3. Delete the record using the `CRowset.Delete()` method:

```
m_Set.Delete();
```

4. Now that the current row is deleted, it is no longer valid. Try moving to a different row, or if there are no more rows, inserting a new record using the `insertRecord()` function:

```
    if (FAILED(m_Set.MoveNext())) {
        if (FAILED(m_Set.MoveLast())) {
            insertRecord();
            return 0;
        }
    }
    UpdateData(FALSE);      //Display record
```

These steps can be seen in the `OnDelete()` function that is called when the user chooses the delete menu option:

```
LRESULT OnDelete(WORD wNotifyCode, WORD wID, HWND hWndCtl, BOOL& bHandled)
{
    showMessage("");
    if (MessageBox("Are you sure you want to delete?",
            "Confirm Delete",
            MB_YESNO) != IDYES) {
        return 0;                 // Get outta here
    }
    //See if you can just cancel add
    if (m_bInserting) {
        m_bInserting = FALSE;     //Just reset flag, ...
```

```
        UpdateData(FALSE);    // display current record, ...
        return 0;             // and get outta here
    }
    if (FAILED(m_Set.Delete())) {
        //Delete failed.  Display messages.
        MessageBox("Could not delete record", "Database Error");
        showMessage("Could not delete record");
        return 0;             // Get outta here
    }
    //Find a new record
    if (FAILED(m_Set.MoveNext())) {
        if (FAILED(m_Set.MoveLast())) {
            insertRecord();
            return 0;
        }
    }
    UpdateData(FALSE);        //Display record
    return 0;
}
```

Now you're finished with this OLE DB application. If you've been following the example, your application should open a dialog box similar to the one seen in Figure 22.7.

FIGURE 22.7

It's easy to create OLE DB applications using the ATL AppWizard and the ATL Object Wizard.

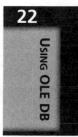

Catching OLE DB Errors

Database errors are generated by the database engine. These errors often give the developer more insight into any potential problems still present in an application.

The main class for processing multiple database errors is the CDBErrorInfo class. This class provides support for one or more OLE DB error records that are returned to the user. To use this class, perform the following steps:

1. Call CDBErrorInfo.GetErrorRecords() to retrieve the number of OLE DB database errors:

   ```
   ULONG numErrors = 0;
   CDBErrorInfo errorInfo;
   errorInfo.GetErrorRecords(m_Set.m_spCommand, IID_ICommandPrepare,
   &numErrors);
   ```

2. If the number of errors is successfully retrieved, retrieve error information into an IErrorInfo interface using the CDBErrorInfo.GetErrorInfo() function in a loop. Use the IErrorInfo.GetDescription() method to retrieve each error message:

```
BSTR sDescription = NULL;
IErrorInfo *pErrorInfo = NULL;
LCID lcid = GetUserDefaultLCID();
for (ULONG loop = 0; loop < numErrors; loop++) {
      errorInfo.GetErrorInfo(loop, lcid, &pErrorInfo);
      pErrorInfo->GetDescription(&sDescription);
}
```

These steps can be viewed in the showErrors function:

```
void showErrors() {
    CDBErrorInfo errorInfo;
    IErrorInfo *pErrorInfo = NULL;
    ULONG numErrors = 0;
    if (FAILED(errorInfo.GetErrorRecords(m_Set.m_spCommand,
IID_ICommandPrepare, &numErrors))) {
        MessageBox("Error information was not retrievable", "Database
Error");
        return;
    }
    if (FAILED(GetErrorInfo(0, &pErrorInfo))) {
        MessageBox("Error information was not retrievable", "Database
Error");
        return;
    }
    char message[4096];
    strcpy (message, "");
    LCID lcid = GetUserDefaultLCID();
    for (ULONG loop = 0; loop < numErrors; loop++) {
        if (FAILED(errorInfo.GetErrorInfo(loop, lcid, &pErrorInfo))) {
            continue;
        }
        BSTR sDescription = NULL;
        pErrorInfo->GetDescription(&sDescription);
        sprintf(message, "%s%S", message, sDescription);
        SysFreeString(sDescription);    //Clean up
        pErrorInfo->Release();
    }
    MessageBox(message, "Database Error");
}
```

This function is handy for collecting errors for any failed database operation. Simply use the FAILED macro to test the HRESULT of any database operation and show the errors if a failure occurs:

```
HRESULT hr = {some database operation}
if (FAILED(hr)) {
    showErrors();
}
```

> **Note**
>
> The example still has some errors that are used to show error functionality. When the user scrolls past all valid records, UpdateData() is still called, resulting in an Invalid Row Handle error. The showError routine retrieves this error and displays it, as shown in Figure 22.8.

FIGURE 22.8
The showErrors
*routine is
designed to dis-
play one or more
OLE DB database
errors.*

Retrieving Column Information

After you have created a rowset object, you can retrieve information about the columns in the rowset, including the column IDs, data types, updatability, and other info. This capability is especially important if you don't quite know the column names or types, as you may not with a SELECT * command. This section describes how to retrieve column information from a recordset.

GetColumnInfo()

You can call the GetColumnInfo() method to retrieve information about the columns in the rowset. The prototype for GetColumnInfo() is shown here:

```
HRESULT GetColumnInfo (ULONG * pcColumns, DBCOLUMNINFO ** prgInfo,
                       OLECHAR ** ppStringsBuffer);
```

GetColumnInfo() returns the number of columns included in the rowset at pcColumns. In addition, it returns a pointer to an array of DBCOLUMNINFO structures—one for each column—at prgInfo, and returns a pointer to a buffer containing all string values associated with the columns (such as column names) at ppStringsBuffer. Both these buffers are allocated by OLE DB and should be freed with a call to IMalloc::Free() when you are finished with them.

DBCOLUMNINFO

When GetColumnInfo() is called, a pointer to an array of DBCOLUMNINFO structures is returned at prgInfo. This array includes a DBCOLUMNINFO structure for each column in the rowset, possibly including a bookmark column.

> **Note**
>
> A bookmark column is always returned, regardless of whether bookmarks were requested or how the rowset was created. Your applications should be prepared to handle these, even if that means simply ignoring the bookmark column.

The DBCOLUMNINFO structure returned from GetColumnInfo() is shown here:

```
typedef struct tagDBCOLUMNINFO {
    LPOLESTR      pwszName;
    ITypeInfo *   pTypeInfo;
    ULONG         iOrdinal;
    DBCOLUMNFLAGS dwFlags;
    ULONG         ulColumnSize;
    DBTYPE        wType;
    BYTE          bPrecision;
    BYTE          bScale;
    DBID          columnid;
} DBCOLUMNINFO;
```

The pwszName field points to a string containing the column name. The memory for this string is allocated by OLE DB in the block of memory specified by the pointer returned in ppStringsBuffer when GetColumnInfo() is called. This way, you can access each of the column names simply by using the pwszName pointer, but you need only call IMalloc::Free() for the one pointer returned in ppStringsBuffer.

In the current release, pTypeInfo is reserved and should always return NULL, whereas the iOrdinal field returns the ordinal for the column. The bookmark column is column 0, and the others are numbered in order, starting with 1. The column ID for the column is returned in the columnid field.

The dwFlags field contains a bitmap that describes the characteristics of the column and can contain a combination of the following values:

- DBCOLUMNFLAGS_CACHEDEFERRED is set if the column's data is cached, as determined by setting the DBPROP_CACHEDEFERRED property for the rowset.
- DBCOLUMNFLAGS_ISBOOKMARK is set if the column contains a bookmark.
- DBCOLUMNFLAGS_ISFIXEDLENGTH is set if all values for this column are the same length.
- DBCOLUMNFLAGS_ISLONG is set if the column contains long data, which is best retrieved by using one of the storage interfaces, although you can also retrieve the data with IRowset::GetData().
- DBCOLUMNFLAGS_ISNULLABLE is set if you are allowed to set the column to NULL.

- DBCOLUMNFLAGS_ISROWID is set if the column contains a rowid, which is used only to identify the row and cannot be written to.

- DBCOLUMNFLAGS_ISROWVER is set if this column is used only for a provider-specific versioning scheme.

- DBCOLUMNFLAGS_MAYBENULL is set if the column can return a NULL value. In certain cases, such as with outer joins, this attribute can be different than DBCOLUMN-FLAGS_ISNULLABLE.

- DBCOLUMNFLAGS_MAYDEFER is set if the data is not fetched from the data source until it is retrieved with a call to IRowset::GetData(). You can set this attribute by setting the DBPROP_DEFERRED property in the rowset property group.

- DBCOLUMNFLAGS_WRITE is set if the column can be written to by calling IRowsetChange::SetData().

- DBCOLUMNFLAGS_WRITEUNKNOWN is set if it is not known whether the column can be written.

The ulColumnSize field contains the maximum length of the column's data. For columns of type DBTYPE_STR or DBTYPE_WSTR, this is given in characters (which are 2 bytes). For columns of type DBTYPE_BYTES, the maximum length is given in bytes. If there is not a maximum length, ulColumnSize is set to 0xFFFFFFFF.

The wType field gives the type of the column data, and the bPrecision field gives the maximum precision for columns with numeric data types. If the column does not hold a numeric value, bPrecision is set to 0xFFFFFFFF. In addition, the bScale field gives the number of digits to the right of the decimal point.

GetColumnsRowset()

In addition to GetColumnInfo(), you can retrieve more complete information about the columns in a rowset by calling GetColumnsRowset(). GetColumnsRowset() returns a rowset object, which can contain a wide variety of optional information about the columns, as well as the information returned by GetColumnInfo(). However, not all providers implement this functionality.

Using Transactions

As with ODBC transactions, OLE DB transactions can be used to control updates to a database and to erase recent changes, if needed. To enable transactions, you use the CSession class of your CCommand. For CCommand objects generated by the ATL Object Wizard, a CSession class variable, m_session, is defined for you. To enable a transaction for a rowset, simply invoke the CSession.StartTransaction() method:

```
CEmployee m_Set;
m_Set.m_session.StartTransaction();
```

To commit a transaction, use the `CSession.Commit()` method:

```
m_Set.m_session.Commit();
```

To roll back a transaction, use the `CSession.Abort()` method:

```
m_Set.m_session.Abort();
```

Using Enumerators

OLE DB enumerators are special rowsets that list all available OLE DB providers. It used to be quite difficult to write enumerators, but Visual C++ provides a `CEnumerator` class that enables your application to view a list of all of the available data sources, as well as other available enumerators. This class provides a mechanism to search through all available data sources.

To use the `CEnumerator` class, simply instantiate it. The `CEnumerator` class is inherited from `CRowset` and therefore contains all the navigation capabilities (`MoveFirst`, `MoveNext`, and so forth) of traditional rowsets. Instead of accessing database data, the `CEnumerator` class accesses OLE DB provider data. The following `OnEnumerate()` function shows how to display all the OLE DB providers using the `CEnumerator` class:

```
LRESULT OnEnumerate(WORD wNotifyCode, WORD wID, HWND hWndCtl, BOOL&
bHandled) {
    char message[4096];
    CEnumerator dbEnum;           //Declare Enumerator
    dbEnum.Open();
    HRESULT hr = dbEnum.MoveFirst();
    strcpy (message, "");
    while (hr == S_OK) {
        sprintf(message, "%s%-60S \t%S\n", message, dbEnum.m_szName,
dbEnum.m_szDescription);
        hr = dbEnum.MoveNext();
    }
    MessageBox(message, "Enumerated OLE DB Providers");
    dbEnum.Close();
    return 0;
}
```

The output from the `OnEnumerate()` function can be viewed in Figure 22.9.

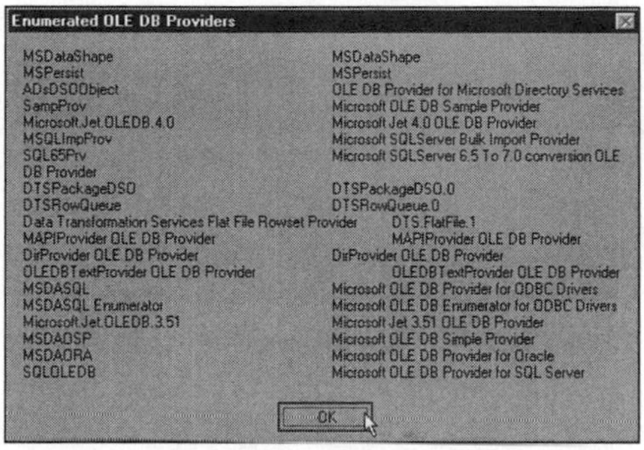

FIGURE 22.9

It's easy to retrieve a list of all OLE DB enumerators using the CEnumerator *class.*

Summary

OLE DB programming used to be for only those developers willing to spend an inordinate amount of time learning the OLE DB techniques and coordinating their programming efforts. Many programmers were forced to adopt the easier but slower ADO in order to access OLE DB data sources. Visual C++ 6.0 changed all that. Although other languages still must rely on ADO, Visual C++ developers can now access OLE DB directly with help from the Active Template Library (ATL). This chapter shows you how.

Tip

For a deep look into OLE DB, check out *OLE DB and ODBC Developer's Guide* by Chuck Wood (M&T Books, ISBN 0-7645-3308-8).

To recap:

- When developing OLE DB applications, you should start with the ATL COM AppWizard and then use the ATL Object Wizard to insert OLE DB functionality into your application.

- The CRowset class contains the needed functionality to navigate around and update your rowset.

- The CAccessor class enables you to define the variables that will be bound to your CRowset class.

- The CCommand class ties the CRowset and CAccessor functionality together for easy OLE DB access through one ATL class.

- The CSession class contains a member variable, m_session, inside the ATL-generated CCommand class that enables you to manipulate transactions for your rowset.

- A special CRowset, CEnumerator, lists the available OLE DB providers in a CRowset format.

Programming with ADO

CHAPTER 23

by David Bennett
and Chuck Wood

This chapter takes a look at ActiveX Data Objects, or ADO, Microsoft's object-oriented interface to OLE DB data sources. ADO was originally conceived in version 5 to replace the Data Access Objects (DAO) and Remote Data Objects (RDO) interfaces, providing both a wider array of features and a higher degree of flexibility. In Visual C++ 6.0, direct OLE DB access has replaced ADO as the primary method of OLE DB data source access. However, there are many developers still using ADO, and many legacy Visual C++ applications that rely on ADO to access databases.

ADO provides a specification for a set of objects that can be used to work with data from many different sorts of applications. Like OLE DB, ADO is based on the Component Object Model (COM), which provides objects that are available from a wide range of programming languages, including Visual Basic, Visual Basic for Applications (VBA), Visual J++, VBScript, and JavaScript applications. ADO can also be quite useful in server or middle-tier applications, particularly when used with Microsoft's Active Server Pages.

> **Warning**
>
> ADO is relatively new and is used extensively in other Microsoft development languages. However, for Visual C++ developers, you should try using pure OLE DB. Version 6.0 made it incredibly easy; it's faster, and most new developers will want to use the AppWizard to create OLE DB applications instead of hand-coding ADO applications.

ADO Objects

The ADO interface is based on a collection of objects that is considerably simpler to use than the OLE DB objects in the last chapter. Although the structure of the objects in ADO is similar to OLE DB, ADO objects are not as dependent on the object hierarchy. In most cases, you can simply create and use only the objects you need to work with, and not worry about creating many other "parent" objects that you don't really care to do anything with.

The following object classes make up the bulk of the ADO interface:

ADOConnection is used to represent a connection to a data source and to handle some commands and transactions.

ADOCommand is used to work with commands sent to the data source.

ADORecordset is used to work with a tabular set of data, including fetching and modifying data.

ADOField is used to represent information about a column in a recordset, including the values for the column, and other information.

ADOParameter is used to pass data to and from commands that are sent to the data source.

ADOProperty is used to manipulate specific properties of the other objects used in ADO.

ADOError is used to retrieve more specific information about errors that might occur.

This chapter explores each of these objects in greater detail in the next few sections and then takes a look at how to use ADO within applications.

Connection Objects

ADO uses Connection objects to represent an individual connection to an OLE DB datasource. Of course, if you are also using MSDASQL, this OLE DB datasource might also correspond to an ODBC datasource.

Any operation performed on a datasource requires a Connection object, although you don't necessarily need to create it yourself. In many cases, you can simply let ADO create a connection used by command or recordset objects. However, you can also perform many operations by using just the Connection object, such as executing SQL that updates database tables. Connection objects are also used to create a single connection that is used by several other objects, which can be useful for optimizing your application. Connection objects are also used to manage transactions in ADO.

To declare a Connection instance, use Visual C++'s smart CComPTR pointer and the CoCreateInstance() function:

```
//ADO header files Added by Chuck Wood for ADO support
#include <adoid.h>
#include <adoint.h>
#include <comdef.h>
//...
CcomPtr<ADOConnection> m_pConn;
//...
CoCreateInstance(CLSID_CADOConnection, NULL,
    CLSCTX_INPROC_SERVER, IID_IADOConnection,
    (LPVOID *) &m_pConn);
```

After creating a Connection variable, you can connect to the database using the ADOConnection.Open() method:

```
m_pConn->Open((CComBSTR) "VCUnleashed",
    (CComBSTR) "",
    (CComBSTR) "",
    adOpenUnspecified));
```

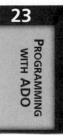

23

PROGRAMMING
WITH ADO

ADOConnection Properties

All ADO Connection objects have the following properties, although specific implementations offer additional properties:

Attributes is used to describe certain characteristics of the connection.

CommandTimeout contains the timeout value to be used for executing commands. This value is also used for other command objects using this connection, although the command objects can override this value by setting their own command timeout.

ConnectionString contains information that is used to connect to the data source. This can include the provider, datasource, user, password, or filename of the datasource.

ConnectionTimeout is the timeout value that is used when attempting to establish a connection.

DefaultDatabase is the default database, or catalog, that is used within the datasource.

IsolationLevel is the isolation level that is used with transactions on this connection.

Mode indicates the read/write and sharing permissions for the connection.

Provider is used to specify the provider that will be used. This defaults to MSDASQL, which is the ODBC provider.

Version specifies the version of the ADO implementation.

Connection objects also contain a Properties collection, which is used to work with certain characteristics of the connection, and an ADOErrors collection, which contains information about any errors or warnings generated by an operation on the connection.

ADOConnection Methods

All ADO connections also support the following methods, although additional methods might also be provided:

Open is used to open a connection to a datasource.

Close is used to close a datasource connection and its dependent objects.

Execute executes a command against the connected datasource. In most cases, this is an SQL query.

BeginTrans begins a transaction on the connection.

CommitTrans commits the current transaction.

RollbackTrans rolls back any changes made in the current transaction.

ADOCommand Objects

ADOCommand objects are used to represent specific commands that will be executed against the datasource. Command objects are used to keep track of parameters associated with the command, and other settings. You can create a command using an existing connection, or you can have ADO create a new connection for use with the new command.

ADOCommand Properties

All ADOCommand objects have the following properties:

> ActiveConnection is used to specify the connection that is to be used with the command. You set this to an existing Connection object or you specify a connection string for a new connection to be used with the command.
>
> CommandText contains the text of the command, usually an SQL statement.
>
> CommandTimeout contains the timeout value that is used for this command.
>
> CommandType specifies the type of the command, which can be a text command—such as a complete SQL statement—a table name, or a stored procedure.
>
> Prepared specifies whether the command will be prepared prior to the first execution.

ADOCommand objects also include an ADOParameters collection, which is used to work with values passed between the Command object and procedure calls or parameterized commands, and an ADOProperties collection containing specific characteristics of the command.

ADOCommand Methods

All ADOCommand objects also support the following methods:

> CreateParameter is used to create a new Parameter object for use with the command.
>
> Execute executes the command against the data source.

ADORecordset Objects

ADORecordset objects provide most of your interactions with the data. They are used to contain a set of records returned from the datasource. You can open a recordset directly by calling its Open() method, or you can generate a recordset by calling Execute() on a Connection or Command object.

The Recordset object represents all the rows returned from the data source, although you might work with only one row at a time—the current row. The data in a row is manipulated by working with the Field objects contained in the recordset's Fields collection.

ADORecordset Properties

All ADORecordset objects have the following properties. Most of these can be used to set or retrieve information about the current state of the recordset, and setting others can perform operations, such as scrolling, on the recordset:

AbsolutePage is used to move the current row to the start of a specified page of rows. The number of rows in a page is set in the PageSize property.

AbsolutePosition is used to make a row at the specified absolute position the current row.

ActiveConnection is used to specify the connection that is to be used for the recordset. This can reference an existing connection, or you can pass a connection string for a new connection that will be created for this recordset.

BOF is true if the recordset is currently positioned before the first row.

EOF is true if the recordset is positioned after the last row.

Bookmark contains the bookmark for the current row.

CacheSize specifies the number of rows of data that will be cached in local memory.

CursorType specifies the type of cursor that is used with this recordset. The cursor can be a forward-only, keyset, static, or dynamic cursor.

EditMode indicates whether the current row has been modified since being fetched, or whether it is a new row that has not yet been written to the data source.

Filter specifies a filter for the rows that will be visible in the recordset. This can specify a SQL WHERE clause, an array of bookmarks, or a constant enabling you to view only pending, affected, or fetched records.

LockType specifies the locking mechanism used when the provider opens the rows in the recordset.

MaxRecords can be used to specify the maximum number of rows that will be returned in a recordset.

PageCount indicates how many pages of rows are present in the recordset, based on the PageSize property.

PageSize specifies the number of rows in a page. This is used in conjunction with the PageCount and AbsolutePage properties.

RecordCount indicates the number of rows currently in the recordset.

Source specifies where the data in the recordset comes from. This can be a Command object, SQL statement, stored procedure, or table name.

Status indicates the status of the current row after a batch update or other bulk operations.

ADORecordset Methods

ADORecordset objects also expose the following methods:

AddNew is used to create a new row in the recordset.

CancelBatch cancels a batch update in progress.

CancelUpdate cancels any changes made to the current row.

Clone creates a new recordset that is a duplicate of the current recordset.

Close closes the recordset.

Delete deletes one or more records from the recordset.

GetRows is used to fetch a block of rows into an array.

Move sets the current row of the recordset.

MoveFirst makes the first row of the recordset the current row.

MoveLast makes the last row of the recordset the current row.

MoveNext positions the recordset on the next row.

MovePrevious positions the recordset on the previous row.

NextRecordset is used to move to the next recordset returned by compound queries. This clears the recordset and returns the data for the next recordset generated.

Open is used to open a recordset directly, rather than as a result of methods from other objects, such as Commands or Connections.

Requery refreshes the data in the recordset by re-executing the query that generated it.

Resync updates the data for any rows in the recordset with the most current data from the datasource. However, this does not return any new rows, as Requery does.

Supports is used to determine whether the recordset supports a variety of different operations, including bookmarks, modifying the data, and batch updates, among other things.

Update is used to submit any changes made to the current row to the datasource.

UpdateBatch submits any changes made in the current batch update to the datasource.

23

PROGRAMMING
WITH ADO

ADOFields Collections and ADOField Objects

Recordset objects contain a collection of field objects used to work with the individual columns of the rowset. Each column that is returned in the recordset has an associated ADOField object in this collection. The Field object gives you access to column metadata, such as the column name and data type, and the actual value for the column in the current row.

ADOFields Collection Members

The ADOFields collection includes a Count property, which gives the number of individual Field objects in the collection, and an Item property, which is used to retrieve individual Field objects. In addition, the Fields collection includes a Refresh method, although this has no real effect on the Fields collection.

ADOField Object Properties

Each of the individual ADOField objects has the following properties:

ActualSize indicates the actual length of the data for the current row's value.

Attributes contains a group of settings for this column, including its updatability, nullability, and other information.

DefinedSize indicates the maximum size allotted for a value of this column.

Name indicates the name of the column. You can access individual fields in the collection either by this name or by their ordinal value.

NumericScale indicates how many places to the right of the decimal point are used to represent this value.

OriginalValue contains the original value of the column as it was last fetched from the data source, prior to any changes you have made.

Precision indicates the maximum number of digits used to represent the value for numerical columns.

Type gives the type of data used for values in this column.

UnderlyingValue reflects the current value of the column in the datasource. This can differ from the Value and OriginalValue properties because of changes made by other applications since the row was originally fetched.

Value contains a VARIANT holding the current data value for this column of the current row in the recordset.

ADOField Object Methods

Each ADOField object also implements the following methods:

> AppendChunk is used to add portions of long data objects to the datasource, enabling you to work with blocks of data smaller than the entire value.
>
> GetChunk is used to retrieve large data objects in smaller, more manageable pieces.

ADOParameter Objects and the ADOParameters Collection

ADOCommand objects contain an ADOParameters collection, which contains all the parameters associated with the command. Each of the individual ADOParameter objects is used to contain information about a parameter that is passed into the command text at runtime, or returned from a procedure executed in a command. New ADOParameter objects are created with the CreateParameter() method of a ADOCommand object.

ADOParameters Collection Members

The ADOParameters collection includes a Count property, which gives the number of individual Parameter objects in the collection, and an Item property, which is used to retrieve individual ADOParameter objects. You can add new ADOParameter objects to the collection with the Append() method or delete them from the collection with the Delete() method. In addition, the Refresh() method can be used to gather information from the provider about parameters used in procedures or parameterized commands.

ADOParameter Object Properties

Each of the ADOParameter objects in the ADOParameters collection of a command has the following properties, although some properties might not be available for certain providers:

> Attributes contains a combination of several bit flags that indicate whether the parameter accepts signed, nullable, and/or long data values.
>
> Direction indicates whether the parameter is used for input, output, or both.
>
> Name contains the name of the parameter.
>
> NumericScale is used to determine the number of places to the right of the decimal that are used for numeric parameters.
>
> Precision indicates the total number of digits used to represent a value for the parameter.

Size contains the maximum size of the parameter value in bytes or characters.

Type specifies the data type for the parameter's value.

Value contains the actual value assigned to the parameter.

ADOParameter Object Methods

The only method provided by ADOParameter objects is AppendChunk(), which is used to append data to large text or binary parameter values.

ADOProperty Objects and ADOProperties Collections

ADOConnection, ADOCommand, ADORecordset, and ADOField objects all include a ADOProperties collection, which is used to hold the individual ADOProperty objects associated with the object. ADOProperty objects are used to represent individual option settings or other characteristics of an ADO object that are not handled by the built-in properties of the object. Although each of the ADO objects can support different sorts of properties, they are all manipulated by using the standard ADOProperty object.

ADOProperties Collection Members

The ADOProperties collection includes the Count property, which gives the number of ADOProperty objects in the collection, and the Item property, which is used to access individual ADOProperty objects in the collection. In addition, the ADOProperties collection supports the Refresh method, which can be used to retrieve information for certain dynamic properties exposed by the provider, although this has no effect for properties that we will see here.

ADOProperty Object Properties

An ADOProperty object is relatively simple. It does not expose any methods and has only the following properties:

Attributes indicates the characteristics of the property, including whether it is supported, required, or optional. This also includes the read/write permissions for the property.

Name contains the name of the property.

Type indicates the data type used for values of this property.

Value contains the actual value of the property.

Writing a Visual C++ ADO Application

In this section, a C++ ADO application is developed. This application will show the basic functionality needed for ADO recordsets.

Step 1—Creating Connections and Recordsets ADO Objects

Connections and recordsets are the heart of ADO. A connection provides a link to a database and enables commands to execute, and a recordset uses a connection to retrieve table data for displaying and updating.

> **Note**
>
> All the code for this chapter is contained in the `Chap23Dialog.h` file in the `Chap23Final` directory. If you want to add the code yourself as an exercise, use the `Chap23Dialog.h` file in the `Chap23Start` directory.
>
> The `Chap23xxxxx` directories use an Active Template Library (ATL) program with the dialog box and menu structure already set up because these concepts are covered elsewhere in the book.

To access ADO commands, you need to include two ADO header files, `adoid.h` and `adoint.h`, at the top of your header file (`Chap23Dialog.h`) as follows:

```
//ADO header files Added by Chuck Wood for ADO support
#include <adoid.h>
#include <adoint.h>
```

> **Tip**
>
> In addition to the two ADO files, it's often beneficial to include `comdef.h` to add support for COM objects, such as COM error processing.

Now you must create ADO COM variables that can be used to store connection information and recordset information. The best way to do this is to use `CComPtr` smart pointers. These pointers automatically do all your COM garbage collection for you so that you don't need to call routines that close the COM object. These COM smart pointers are shown in gray:

```
class CChap23Dialog :
    public CAxDialogImpl<CChap23Dialog>
{
private:

//////////////////////////////////////////////////////////
//Added by Chuck Wood for ADO support
//ADO Connection and recordset variables
    CComPtr<ADORecordset> m_pSet;
    CComPtr<ADOConnection> m_pConn;

//////////////////////////////////////////////////////////
public:
```

Because ADO is a COM interface, your application needs to initialize the COM environment for each ADO construct you use. In this case, you need to initialize the connection and the recordset with a call to CoCreateInstance(). The ADO initialization is done inside the dialog box constructor before the DoModal command is issued, as shown in gray:

```
CChap23Dialog() {

    //Create a new connection
    CoCreateInstance(CLSID_CADOConnection, NULL,
        CLSCTX_INPROC_SERVER, IID_IADOConnection,
        (LPVOID *) &m_pConn);
    //Create a new recordset
    CoCreateInstance(CLSID_CADORecordset, NULL,
        CLSCTX_INPROC_SERVER, IID_IADORecordset,
        (LPVOID *) &m_pSet);

    //Open Dialog box
    DoModal();
}
```

Step 2—Connecting to a Database Through ADO

After creating the database connection COM instance, you can use it to connect to a database through the ADOConnection.Open() method, as shown in the CChap23Dialog constructor:

```
CChap23Dialog() {
    //Create a new connection
    CoCreateInstance(CLSID_CADOConnection, NULL,
        CLSCTX_INPROC_SERVER, IID_IADOConnection,
        (LPVOID *) &m_pConn);
    //Create a new recordset
```

```
CoCreateInstance(CLSID_CADORecordset, NULL,
    CLSCTX_INPROC_SERVER, IID_IADORecordset,
    (LPVOID *) &m_pSet);
```

```
//Connect to the database
if (FAILED(m_pConn->Open(
        (CComBSTR) "VCUnleashed", //ODBC Name
        (CComBSTR) "",     // User ID
        (CComBSTR) "",     // Password
        adOpenUnspecified))) {
    MessageBox("Could not open connection to VCUnleashed", "DB Error");
    m_pConn = NULL;
    return;
}
```

```
//Open Dialog box
DoModal();
}
```

> **Note**
>
> In this example, only the adOpenUnspecified property was used. In most cases, this is the only property you will need. However, ADO supports many other properties. Check out the MSDN documentation to see all the properties you can use.

23

PROGRAMMING
WITH ADO

Step 3—Opening an ADO Recordset

Now you are ready to access your ADO database connection to connect to a database. First, you must declare fields that can hold a single row of your recordset. In the example in gray, I've declared three variables to hold the employee name, department, and salary:

```
/////////////////////////////////////////////////////////////////////////////
//Added by Chuck Wood for ADO support
```

```
//database fields
    char m_EmpName[51];
    char m_Dept[11];
    double m_Salary;
```

```
//ADO Connection and recordset variables
    CComPtr<ADORecordset> m_pSet;
    CComPtr<ADOConnection> m_pConn;
```

Next, you call the ADORecordset.Open() method, as shown in gray, to issue your SELECT (or CALL) statement, your open connection, and your options used in creating the recordset:

```
CChap23Dialog() {
    //Create a new connection
    CoCreateInstance(CLSID_CADOConnection, NULL,
        CLSCTX_INPROC_SERVER, IID_IADOConnection,
        (LPVOID *) &m_pConn);
    //Create a new recordset
    CoCreateInstance(CLSID_CADORecordset, NULL,
        CLSCTX_INPROC_SERVER, IID_IADORecordset,
        (LPVOID *) &m_pSet);
    //Connect to the database
    if (FAILED(m_pConn->Open(
            (CComBSTR) "VCUnleashed", //ODBC Name
            (CComBSTR) "",     //
            (CComBSTR) "",
            adOpenUnspecified))) {
        MessageBox("Could not open connection to VCUnleashed", "DB Error");
        m_pConn = NULL;
        return;
    }

    //Open a new recordset
    if (FAILED(m_pSet->Open(CComVariant((CComBSTR)
    "SELECT EmpName, Dept, Salary FROM Employee"),
            CComVariant(m_pConn),
            adOpenKeyset, adLockOptimistic, adCmdText))) {
        MessageBox("Could not open a recordset", "DB Error");
        m_pSet = NULL;
        return;
    }

    //Open Dialog box
    DoModal();
}
```

> **Note**
>
> In this example, a specific cursor type (adOpenKeyset), locking type
> (adLockOptimistic), and option (adCmdText) were used. Although these choices
> seem to be the most popular, ADO supports many other properties. Check out
> the MSDN documentation to see all the properties you can use for a recordset.

Step 4—Closing the Connection and Recordset

It's important to close the connection and recordset after opening them. Although the
COM smart pointers "garbage-collect" the memory used by the COM interface, the database itself might be corrupted or left either unusable or less efficient if not specifically
closed by the application. In the following code, you see how the recordset (m_pSet) and
the connection (m_pConn) are closed in the destructor for the CChap23Dialog class:

```
~CChap23Dialog() {
    //Added by Chuck Wood to close the connection and recordset
    if (m_pSet != NULL) {
        m_pSet->Close();
    }
    if (m_pConn != NULL) {
        m_pConn->Close();
    }
}
```

Step 5—Writing an `UpdateData` Routine for ADO

MFC enables you to call an `UpdateData` routine that enables you to either update the database with information in the dialog box or update the dialog box with information from the table. In this section, a new `UpdateData` routine is written to function with ADO.

Step 5a—Retrieving Recordset Field Information

Before writing the `UpdateData()` routine, you need to understand how to retrieve recordset information. This involves three steps:

1. Retrieve the `ADOFields` collection object from the recordset using the `ADORecordset.get_Fields()` method:

   ```
   CComPtr<ADOFields> pFields = NULL;
   m_pSet->get_Fields(&pFields);
   ```

2. Retrieve each `ADOField` from the `ADOFields` collection using the `ADOFields.get_Item()` method:

   ```
   CComPtr<ADOField> pEmpName = NULL;
   pFields->get_Item(CComVariant(0), &pEmpName);
   ```

3. Finally, retrieve information from each `ADOField` and store it in a `CComVariant` using the `ADOField.get_Value()` method:

   ```
   CComVariant dbValue;      //Variant holder for db values
   //Get the value of EmpName
   pEmpName->get_Value(&dbValue);
   //Store EmpName and get the value of Dept
   sprintf(m_EmpName, "%S", dbValue.bstrVal);
   ```

This functionality can be viewed in the `retrieveRecordsetFields()` function:

```
HRESULT retrieveRecordsetFields() {
    //Written by Chuck Wood for Visual C++ Unleashed
    //Retrieves recordset information
    HRESULT hr;            //Returns error
    CComPtr<ADOFields> pFields = NULL;
    CComPtr<ADOField> pEmpName = NULL;
```

```
CComPtr<ADOField> pDept = NULL;
CComPtr<ADOField> pSalary = NULL;
//Get fields
hr = m_pSet->get_Fields(&pFields);
//Get individual fields
if (!FAILED(hr))     //Get EmpName (field 0)
    hr = pFields->get_Item(CComVariant(0), &pEmpName);
if (!FAILED(hr))     //Get Dept (field 1)
    hr = pFields->get_Item(CComVariant(1), &pDept);
if (!FAILED(hr))     //Get Salary (field 2)
    hr = pFields->get_Item(CComVariant(2), &pSalary);
if (FAILED(hr))      //Return if error
    return hr;
//Put values in individual fields
CComVariant dbValue;     //Variant holder for db values
//Get the value of EmpName
hr = pEmpName->get_Value(&dbValue);
if (!FAILED(hr)) {
    //Store EmpName and get the value of Dept
    sprintf(m_EmpName, "%S", dbValue.bstrVal);
    hr = pDept->get_Value(&dbValue);
}
if (!FAILED(hr)) {
    //Store dept and get the value of Salary
    sprintf(m_Dept, "%S", dbValue.bstrVal);
    hr = pSalary->get_Value(&dbValue);
}
if (!FAILED(hr)) { //Store salary
    //Currency is stored a little weird.  Check out MSDN.
    m_Salary = (double) dbValue.cyVal.int64 / 10000.0;
}
return hr;
}
```

> **Note**
>
> Some providers enable you to cache any changes made to the recordset locally and send them to the data source in one batch. This is known as *batch update mode*. If batch update mode is not supported, you will always be working in *immediate update mode*. You can determine whether the provider you are using supports batch update mode by calling the Supports() method of the recordset, with CursorOptions set to adUpdateBatch. To send the batch of updates to the datasource, you need to call the UpdateBatch() method of the recordset:
>
> ```
> HRESULT UpdateBatch ( enum AffectEnum AffectRecords );
> ```
>
> The AffectEnum parameter is used to determine which records will be updated in the datasource. This can be set to one of the following constants:

> adAffectCurrent sends changes for only the current row.
>
> adAffectGroup sends changes for all modified records that satisfy the Filter property.
>
> adAffectAll sends all pending changes to the data source.
>
> If batch updates interest you, check out the MSDN documentation for more information.

Step 5b—Updating Recordset Field Information

An UpdateData() method must not only retrieve information from the recordset, but also must allow updates to the database from the current dialog box. To update recordset information, you must perform the following steps:

1. Retrieve the ADOFields collection object from the recordset using the ADORecordset.get_Fields() method:

   ```
   CComPtr<ADOFields> pFields = NULL;
   m_pSet->get_Fields(&pFields);
   ```

2. Retrieve each ADOField from the ADOFields collection using the ADOFields.get_Item() method:

   ```
   CComPtr<ADOField> pEmpName = NULL;
   pFields->get_Item(CComVariant(0), &pEmpName);
   ```

3. Store information in each ADOField using the ADOField.put_Value() method:

   ```
   pEmpName->put_Value(CComVariant(m_EmpName));
   ```

4. Update the recordset using the ADORecordset.Update() method. This requires a variant parameter, but you can pass "null variants" by creating a variant with VT_ERROR for the vt member and DISP_E_PARAMNOTFOUND for the scode member:

   ```
   //Initialize nullVariant
   VARIANT nullVariant;
   nullVariant.vt = VT_ERROR;
   nullVariant.scode = DISP_E_PARAMNOTFOUND;
   //Perform update
   m_pSet->Update(nullVariant, nullVariant);
   ```

This functionality can be viewed in the updateRecordset() function:

```
HRESULT updateRecordset() {
    //Written by Chuck Wood for Visual C++ Unleashed
    //Updates the database with values in the class variables
    HRESULT hr;          //Returns error
    CComPtr<ADOFields> pFields = NULL;
    CComPtr<ADOField> pEmpName = NULL;
```

23

PROGRAMMING
WITH ADO

```
        CComPtr<ADOField> pDept = NULL;
        CComPtr<ADOField> pSalary = NULL;
        //Get fields
        hr = m_pSet->get_Fields(&pFields);
        //Get individual fields
        if (!FAILED(hr))     //Get EmpName (field 0)
            hr = pFields->get_Item(CComVariant(0), &pEmpName);
        if (!FAILED(hr))     //Get Dept (field 1)
            hr = pFields->get_Item(CComVariant(1), &pDept);
        if (!FAILED(hr))     //Get Salary (field 2)
            hr = pFields->get_Item(CComVariant(2), &pSalary);
        //Put values in individual fields
        if (!FAILED(hr))     //Set the value of EmpName
            hr = pEmpName->put_Value(CComVariant(m_EmpName));
        if (!FAILED(hr))     //Set the value of Dept
            hr = pDept->put_Value(CComVariant(m_Dept));
        if (!FAILED(hr))     //Set the value of Salary
            hr = pSalary->put_Value(CComVariant(m_Salary));
        //Update database
        if (!FAILED(hr)) {
            //Initialize nullVariant
            VARIANT nullVariant;
            nullVariant.vt = VT_ERROR;
            nullVariant.scode = DISP_E_PARAMNOTFOUND;
            //Perform update
            hr = m_pSet->Update(nullVariant, nullVariant);
        }
        return hr;
}
```

Step 5c—Pulling It Together in One `UpdateData()` Routine

At last you are ready to write the `UpdateData` function. You can use the `GetDlgItemText()` and `SetDlgItemText()` to retrieve or display, respectively, information to and from the dialog box.

Tip

You can also use the `ADORecordset.get_EditMode()`, `ADORecordset.get_BOF()`, and `ADORecordset.get_EOF()` methods to make sure that you are not trying to retrieve information from an invalid row in the recordset.

You can call the `retrieveRecordsetFields()` and the `updateRecordset()` functions as appropriate to query or update information in the class variables. Here is the completed `UpdateData()` function:

```
void UpdateData(BOOL saveChanges=TRUE) {
```

```
//Written by Chuck Wood for Visual C++ Unleashed
//Mimics the MFC UpdateData function
if (saveChanges) {
    //Write data from the dialog box to the database
    VARIANT_BOOL vb;
    //Check to see whether recordset is positioned at BOF
    m_pSet->get_BOF(&vb);
    if (vb) return;
    //Check to see whether recordset is positioned at EOF
    m_pSet->get_EOF(&vb);
    if (vb) return;
    //Check to see whether current record is deleted
    EditModeEnum eme;
    m_pSet->get_EditMode(&eme);
    if (eme == adEditDelete) return;
    //Continue with update
    char salaryHolder[25];
    GetDlgItemText(IDC_EMPNAME, m_EmpName, 51);
    GetDlgItemText(IDC_DEPT, m_Dept, 11);
    GetDlgItemText(IDC_SALARY, salaryHolder, 25);
    m_Salary = atof(salaryHolder);
    if (FAILED(updateRecordset())) {
        showMessage ("Update failed");
        MessageBox("Could not update employee table","Update error");
    }
}
else {
    //Write data from the database to the dialog box
    if (FAILED(retrieveRecordsetFields())) {
        showMessage ("Display fields failed");
        MessageBox("Could not retrieve information from the  employee
table","Query error");
    }
    else {
        char salaryHolder[25];
        sprintf(salaryHolder, "%.2f", m_Salary);
        SetDlgItemText(IDC_EMPNAME, m_EmpName);
        SetDlgItemText(IDC_DEPT, m_Dept);
        SetDlgItemText(IDC_SALARY, salaryHolder);
    }
}
}
```

Now you can control database or dialog box updates simply by calling the UpdateData()
function as you would with MFC. In the following code, you can see that the
UpdateData() function is called before allowing the dialog box to close:

```
LRESULT OnCancel(WORD wNotifyCode, WORD wID, HWND hWndCtl, BOOL& bHandled)
{
    UpdateData();       //Added by Chuck Wood to update the database
    EndDialog(wID);
    return 0;
}
```

Step 6—Navigating Through a Recordset

Writing the UpdateData function was a little time-consuming, but it sure makes it worth it when navigating through a recordset. The four move functions—MoveFirst(), MovePrevious(), MoveNext(), and MoveLast()—are used to scroll through an ADO recordset. In our example, each move function is called a menu function. This enables the user to control navigation through the recordset. Use the following steps for each move function:

1. Update the current information in case any changes are made using the UpdateData() function.

2. Scroll to the appropriate position in the database indicated by the user.

3. Display new information in the dialog box using the UpdateData(FALSE) function.

The move functions are shown in the following code. Basic error trapping is added to display relevant information to the user:

```
//ADO Move functionality added by Chuck Wood
LRESULT OnFirst(WORD wNotifyCode, WORD wID, HWND hWndCtl, BOOL& bHandled) {
    VARIANT_BOOL vb;
    UpdateData();
    m_pSet->MoveFirst();
    m_pSet->get_BOF(&vb);
    if (vb) {
        showMessage("No records found");
    }
    else {
        UpdateData(FALSE);
    }
    return 0;
}
LRESULT OnPrev(WORD wNotifyCode, WORD wID, HWND hWndCtl, BOOL& bHandled) {
    VARIANT_BOOL vb;
    showMessage("");
    UpdateData();
    m_pSet->MovePrevious();
    m_pSet->get_BOF(&vb);
    if (vb) {
        showMessage("No previous records found");
        return OnFirst(wNotifyCode, wID, hWndCtl, bHandled);
    }
    else {
        UpdateData(FALSE);
    }
    return 0;
}
LRESULT OnNext(WORD wNotifyCode, WORD wID, HWND hWndCtl, BOOL& bHandled) {
    VARIANT_BOOL vb;
```

```
    showMessage("");
    UpdateData();
    m_pSet->MoveNext();
    m_pSet->get_EOF(&vb);
    if (vb) {
        showMessage("No more records found");
        return OnLast(wNotifyCode, wID, hWndCtl, bHandled);
    }
    else {
        UpdateData(FALSE);
    }
    return 0;
}
LRESULT OnLast(WORD wNotifyCode, WORD wID, HWND hWndCtl, BOOL& bHandled) {
    VARIANT_BOOL vb;
    UpdateData();
    m_pSet->MoveLast();
    m_pSet->get_EOF(&vb);
    if (vb) {
        showMessage("No records found");
    }
    else {
        UpdateData(FALSE);
    }
    return 0;
}
```

Step 7—Inserting into the Recordset

ADO inserts involve simply calling the `ADORecordset.AddNew()` method. After this method is called, a new row is added to the recordset, and an `ADORecordset.Update()` method call updates the database with the new record. Any move away from the newly created row in the recordset aborts the add, and a call to the `ADORecordset.CancelUpdate()` method also cancels the insert.

In a recordset browser such as the one in our example, inserting a new record involves three steps:

1. Update the current record with a call to the `UpdateData()` function.
2. Clear the dialog box fields by using the `SetDlgItemText()` function.
3. Call the `ADORecordset.AddNew()` method.

The implementation for these steps can be seen in the following code:

```
LRESULT OnInsert(WORD wNotifyCode, WORD wID, HWND hWndCtl, BOOL& bHandled) {
    UpdateData();
    //Clear dialog box fields
    SetDlgItemText(IDC_EMPNAME, "");
```

```
        SetDlgItemText(IDC_DEPT, "");
        SetDlgItemText(IDC_SALARY, "");
        //Initialize nullVariant
        VARIANT nullVariant;
        nullVariant.vt = VT_ERROR;
        nullVariant.scode = DISP_E_PARAMNOTFOUND;
        HRESULT hr = m_pSet->AddNew(nullVariant, nullVariant);
        if (FAILED(hr)) {
            MessageBox("Cannot insert a new record", "Database Error");
            showMessage("Cannot insert a new record");
            return OnLast(wNotifyCode, wID, hWndCtl, bHandled);
        }
        return 0;
}
```

Step 8—Deleting from the Recordset

You need to be careful when deleting rows from a database. Often, the user might have
hit the delete menu option by accident. Also, the user might often be deleting a new
record before the `ADORecordset.Update()` is called. Deletes involve several steps:

1. Check to make sure that a delete is desired.

2. Check to make sure that you aren't in the middle of an `AddNew` command. If you
   are, simply cancel the add.

3. Delete the current record.

4. Now that the current record is deleted, you need to move the record pointer off the
   deleted record. I usually try the following steps:

   a. Go to the next record.

   b. If there is no next record, go to the last record.

   c. If there are no more records, start a new add.

The following `OnDelete()` function implements these steps:

```
LRESULT OnDelete(WORD wNotifyCode, WORD wID, HWND hWndCtl, BOOL& bHandled) {
    showMessage("");
    if (MessageBox("Are you sure you want to delete?",
            "Confirm Delete",
            MB_YESNO) != IDYES) {
        return 0;
    }
    EditModeEnum eme;
    m_pSet->get_EditMode(&eme);
    if (eme == adEditAdd) {     //Just cancel add
        m_pSet->CancelUpdate();
    }
    else if (FAILED(m_pSet->Delete(adAffectCurrent))) {
```

```
        MessageBox("Could not delete record", "Database Error");
        showMessage("Could not delete record");
    }
    if (FAILED(m_pSet->MoveNext())) {
        if (FAILED(m_pSet->MoveLast())) {
            return OnInsert(wNotifyCode, wID, hWndCtl, bHandled);
        }
    }
    UpdateData(FALSE);
    return 0;
}
```

After implementing these eight steps, you should have a fully functional database application, as shown in Figure 23.1.

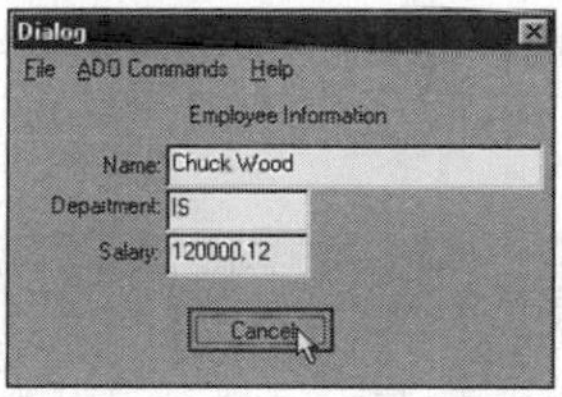

FIGURE 23.1

Database applications can be easily created using ADO, although OLE DB is even easier and preferred.

Processing ADO Errors

ADO enables you to work with a wide range of different database components, including ADO implementations, OLE DB providers, ODBC drivers, and the database systems themselves. Partly because of this, and partly because ADO is a new technology and still has a few bugs, errors caused by ADO operations can be reported in several ways. Errors from particular calls can be reported by way of C++ exceptions, HRESULT return values, and/or in the ADOErrors collection of an ADOConnection object. You should be prepared to handle error information from all these sources, particularly while developing new applications.

You've already seen some error handling by using the HRESULT that is returned by ADO calls. In addition, ADOConnection objects contain an ADOErrors collection, which contains ADOError objects that give specific information about any errors that might have occurred on the connection for a single operation. In most cases, ADOError objects are generated only when errors are returned by the database system, not when procedural errors occur in ADO. Any given operation can generate any number of different ADOError objects, including errors that contain information about warnings that were generated. Whenever a new operation generates an error, the ADOErrors collection is cleared before the errors from the new operation are added.

ADO HRESULT Values, FAILED, and SUCCEEDED

In addition to handling any C++ exceptions that might be thrown, your applications should also check the HRESULT code that is returned from ADO operations, as shown in the previous example. Generally, these codes are defined in winerror.h, but there are also several other header files in which these error codes are defined, depending on the component that generated the error. When developing new applications, you might find yourself searching these header files often to find the cause of an error. You should also be aware that these error codes are usually defined in hex, although some header files define HRESULT values using decimal notation.

The FAILED() and SUCCEEDED() macros discussed in Chapter 22, "Using OLE DB," enable easy error handling. Although these macros don't give detailed descriptions of the error that occurred, they enable a developer to quickly and efficiently trap any errors that occur.

> **Tip**
>
> For a compilation of most of the HRESULT codes that can be returned by ADO, see Microsoft knowledge base article Q168354, which condenses the definitions found in several header files. It also lists hex and decimal representations.

ADOErrors Collection Members

The ADOErrors collection contains a Count property, which gives the number of ADOError objects currently in the collection, and an Item property, which is used to access the individual ADOError objects. The ADOErrors collection also supports the Clear() method, which is used to remove any ADOError objects currently in the collection.

Error Object Properties

Error objects do not expose any methods, but do include the following properties that give additional information about specific errors:

Description provides a text description of the error that is suitable for display to the user.

HelpContext returns a context ID that can be used to access a specific topic in a Windows help file that is relevant to the error.

HelpFile returns a fully qualified path to a Windows help file that can contain help for the specific error.

NativeError contains a database-specific Long value that is returned from the provider.

Number returns a numeric value that indicates the specific error that occurred.

Source returns a string indicating the component that generated the error—for example, ADODB.Connection or SQL Server.

SQLState returns a five-character string containing an ANSI standard SQLSTATE value for the specific error.

ADO C++ Exceptions

Most errors that occur in ADO applications as a result of programming errors, such as bad parameters and such, will generate a C++ exception of some sort. In most cases, an exception of class _com_error will be thrown. However, your application should be prepared to handle other sorts of exceptions.

To handle the exceptions that might be thrown by ADO operations, you should execute your ADO operations within a try block and provide a catch block for an object of type _com_error. This class is used to return errors from the classes that are created by the #import directive, as well as the COM support classes. The _com_error class encapsulates any HRESULT values that might be generated and any IErrorInfo object that might be generated by the underlying OLE DB provider.

The _com_error class provides several member functions that can be used to extract information about an error, including the following:

Error() returns the HRESULT associated with an error.

ErrorMessage() returns a text string describing the HRESULT value.

Description() retrieves a text string describing the error.

Source() returns the name of the component that generated the error.

HelpContext() retrieves a Windows help context value that applies to the error.

HelpFile() retrieves the path to a Windows help file that applies to the error.

GUID() returns the GUID of the COM interface that generated the error.

The following destructor from our example shows how you can use C++ exception handling to deal with exceptions thrown by ADO. This example traps any errors that might occur when closing an ADOConnection or ADORecordset:

```
~CChap23Dialog() {
//Added by Chuck Wood to close the connection and recordset
    try {
        if (m_pSet != NULL) {
            m_pSet->Close();
        }
```

23

PROGRAMMING
WITH ADO

```
        if (m_pConn != NULL) {
            m_pConn->Close();
        }
    }
    catch (_com_error &ce) {
        char message[1024];
        strcpy (message, "_com_error exception thrown\n");
        sprintf (message, "%sHRESULT = 0x%08lx\n",
                message, ce.Error());
        sprintf (message, "%sHRESULT description: %s\n",
                message, ce.ErrorMessage());
        sprintf (message, "%sDescription: %S\n",
                message, ce.Description());
        sprintf (message, "%sSource: %S\n",
                message, ce.Source());
        MessageBox(message, "Close Error Occurred");
    }
    catch (...) {
        MessageBox("Unknown error has occurred",
                "Close Error Occurred");
    }
}
```

The Errors Collection

The last of the error-reporting mechanisms that we look at here is the ADOErrors collection of the ADO Connection object, which can contain multiple ADOError objects for the last ADO operation on the connection. In most cases, the errors (or warnings) reported in the ADOErrors collection are generated by the database, whereas errors that are generated in other components, such as ADODB, are reported via exception or HRESULT.

> **Warning**
>
> For many ADO errors, the ADOErrors collection might not be filled in, so you should be sure to check the other error reporting mechanisms shown previously.

The ADOErrors collection is contained only in the ADOConnection object, and not in other objects, such as the ADORecordset. Thus, you need to check the ADOErrors collection of the ADOConnection object that is being used for a particular operation. You can access the connection for an ADOCommand or ADORecordset object by using its ActiveConnection property.

ADO clears the ADOErrors collection before each operation, so the errors in the collection refer to only the last operation. You can check the number of ADOError objects in the collection by retrieving the Count property. The individual ADOError objects are then retrieved via the Item property.

The ADOError object provides several properties that you can use to gather more information about the error, including the following:

Description provides a text description of the error that is suitable for display to the user.

NativeError contains a database-specific Long value that is returned from the provider.

Number returns a numeric value that indicates the specific error that occurred.

Source returns a string indicating the component that generated the error—for example, ADODB.Connection or SQL Server.

SQLState returns a five-character string containing an ANSI standard SQLSTATE value for the specific error.

HelpContext returns a context ID that can be used to access a specific topic in a Windows help file that is relevant to the error.

HelpFile returns a fully qualified path to a Windows help file that might contain help for the specific error.

The following example displays a message box containing output based on the ADOError objects in the ADOErrors collection:

```
void showError() {
    //ADO Error Function written by Chuck Wood
    long nCount;
    char message[4096];
    CComPtr<ADOError> pError = NULL;
    CComPtr<ADOErrors> pErrors = NULL;
    m_pConn->get_Errors(&pErrors);
    pErrors->get_Count(&nCount);
    strcpy (message, "");
    for(int i = 0; i < nCount; i++ ) {
        long number = 0;
        BSTR string;
        // Retrieve individual error object
        pErrors->get_Item(CComVariant(i), &pError );
        // Add to error message
        sprintf(message, "%s\nError %d of %d) ", message, i+1, nCount );
        pError->get_Number(&number);
        sprintf(message, "%s\tNumber       \t= %ld", message, number);
        pError->get_Source(&string);
        sprintf(message, "%s\tSource       \t= %S", message, string);
        pError->get_Description(&string);
        sprintf(message, "%s\tDescription \t= %S", message, string);
        pError->get_HelpFile(&string);
        sprintf(message, "%s\tHelpFile     \t= %S", message, string);
        pError->get_HelpContext(&number);
        sprintf(message, "%s\tHelpContext \t= %ld", message, number);
        pError->get_SQLState(&string);
```

23

PROGRAMMING WITH ADO

```
        sprintf(message, "%s\tSQLState    \t= %s", message, string);
        pError->get_NativeError(&number);
        sprintf(message, "%s\tNativeError \t= %ld", message, number);
    } // end for
    MessageBox(message, "ADO error list");
}
```

Enhanced ADO Recordset Functionality

In our example, we used basic ADO functionality that you should use in most of your ADO applications. However, ADO enables some advanced functionality that might be useful to you while developing your ADO application. This section covers some of this advanced functionality.

Limiting the Rows in a Recordset

You can limit the total number of records that will be returned into a recordset by setting the MaxRecords property of the recordset before calling its Open() method. Furthermore, you can set the number of rows that are cached locally in the recordset (as opposed to being kept in a cursor on the database server) by setting the CacheSize property of the recordset to the number of rows that you want to hold locally. Again, this property should be set before calling Open(). The value of the CacheSize property will not affect how your application code must be written—but, depending on your network environment, it can have a substantial effect on your app's overall performance.

Filtering Rows in the Recordset

When opening a recordset, you specified a command or query that generates a set of rows. You can limit the set of rows returned by setting the recordset's Filter property. The Filter property is basically an extension to the query (or table name, which generates a simple SQL query) given in the Source parameter of Open(). The string in Filter contains a WHERE clause used to limit the query contained in the source. Note, however, that the string you add to Filter should not contain the actual WHERE keyword. The value of the Filter property is also limited because you can use column names that are contained in the recordset only.

You also can set the value of the Filter property to one of the following constants, which limits the contents of the recordset to rows with a certain status:

adFilterNone cancels the current value of Filter and restores the contents of the recordset to the full result of the original query.

adFilterPendingRecords, in batch update mode, can be used to select only those rows that have changed but not yet been updated in the database.

adFilterAffectedRecords selects only rows that were affected by the last Delete(), Resync(), UpdateBatch(), or CancelBatch() operation.

adFilterFetchedRecords limits the rows in the recordset to those that are currently contained in the local cache.

You can also set the Filter property to an array of bookmark values, which limits the rows in the recordset to those referenced in the bookmark array.

> **Note**
>
> Rows that are excluded by the Filter property are still contained in the recordset, but you will not be able to view them until you change the Filter property to make them visible again.

Refreshing the Recordset

After you have opened a Recordset object, you can call its Requery() method to repeat the query and return a new result set. This is useful in situations wherein you suspect the underlying data in the database might have changed. Requery() will toss out all the rows currently in the recordset and execute the query again, using the current values of the Source and Filter properties.

Similarly, you can resynchronize the data in the recordset with the data in the datasource by calling the Resync() method of the recordset. This is different than the Requery() method because Resync() updates only the rows currently in the recordset, rather than executing the whole query again. The prototype for Requery() as generated by #import, is shown here:

```
HRESULT Resync ( enum AffectEnum AffectRecords );
```

You can pass any of the following values in the AffectRecords parameter:

adAffectCurrent refreshes only the current record.

adAffectGroup refreshes only the rows that satisfy the current Filter property.

adAffectAll refreshes all the rows contained in the recordset, including those that do not satisfy the current Filter setting.

Move()

There are four move commands (MoveFirst, MovePrevious, MoveNext, MoveLast) that were incorporated into our example. The ADO Recordset object also provides the

`Move()` function, which gives a more flexible function for moving around in the record-set. The prototype for the `Move()` function, as generated by `#import`, is shown here:

```
HRESULT Move (
    long NumRecords,
    const _variant_t & Start = vtMissing );
```

The `NumRecords` parameter specifies the number of records that the current record pointer will move. If you pass a positive value of `numRecords`, the pointer moves forward. If you pass a negative value, the current row pointer moves backward. If you do not pass a `Start` parameter, the current row pointer moves from the current row. However, you can pass a bookmark value in `Start`. The current row is then moved `NumRecords` number of rows from the row specified by the bookmark.

If you attempt to move past the last row, `EOF` is set to `True`. Similarly, `BOF` is set to `True` if you attempt to move backward past the first row.

Absolute Positioning

ADO `Recordset` objects also enable you to set the current row to an absolute position within the recordset by setting the `AbsolutePosition` property of the recordset to the number of the desired current rows. The rows in the recordset are numbered from one to the number of rows in the recordset.

> **Note**
>
> If you delete records from the recordset or requery or reopen the recordset, the `AbsolutePosition` of a given record can change.

Scrolling by Pages

The ADO `Recordset` object also enables you to scroll through the recordset by pages. This is very useful in applications in which you are displaying data to the user by pages. To use page scrolling, you first need to set the `PageSize` property of the recordset to the number of rows that you would like to see in a page. You can then find the number of pages contained in the recordset by looking at the `PageCount` property. To set the current row to the first row in a logical page, simply set the `AbsolutePage` property to the number of the page that you want to position the current row on. Like absolute rows, pages are numbered starting with one.

Using Bookmarks

If the recordset that you are using supports bookmarks—as indicated by a call to `Recordset.Supports()`—you can use bookmark values to make a particular row the current row. You can retrieve the bookmark value for the current row by reading the Bookmark property of the recordset. If you save this value somewhere, you can later set the Bookmark property of the recordset to this value to again make the row indicated by the bookmark the current row.

Executing Commands

You can execute simple commands by using the Execute() method of the ADOConnection object, whose prototype is shown here:

```
HRESULT Execute(
    BSTR CommandText,
    VARIANT *RecordsAffected,
    long Options,
    ADORecordset *pSet);
```

The text of the command, which is generally an SQL command, is passed in the CommandText parameter. You can also pass the address of a VARIANT in RecordsAffected. Upon completion, the long value in the VARIANT at RecordsAffected contains the number of rows that were affected by the command. In addition to SQL commands, you can pass a table name or stored procedure in CommandText. The Options parameter is used to specify the type of command that is passed in CommandText. Options can be passed one of the following values:

adCmdText—CommandText is a text (usually SQL) command.

adCmdTable—CommandText is a table name.

adCmdStoredProc—CommandText is a stored procedure.

For commands that generate a result set, Execute() stores a pointer to a recordset containing the results of the command in the pSet parameter. You can use this recordset to retrieve the results of the command.

The following executeSQL function shows how to execute a simple command using the Execute() method of the ADOConnection object:

```
CComPtr<ADORecordset> executeSQL(BSTR SQL) {
    //Execute function written by Chuck Wood
    //Executes SQL and returns any recordset that's formed
    CComPtr<ADORecordset> pSet;
    VARIANT recAffected;
    m_pConn->Execute(SQL, &recAffected, adCmdText, &pSet);
    return pSet;
}
```

23

PROGRAMMING
WITH ADO

Transactions

Transactions enable you to perform several different operations on a database that are executed as a single, atomic operation. This is very useful in cases in which you want to update several tables, but only if all the updates are performed successfully. Transactions can help you avoid the ill effects of partially completed operations if one of the updates should fail.

To begin a transaction on a connection, call its `ADOConnection.BeginTrans()` method, which takes no parameters. You can then perform any changes to the datasource that you want to be a part of the transaction.

If all goes well and you want to save all the changes to the database, you should call the connection's `ADOConnection.CommitTrans()` method. If something goes wrong or you just change your mind, you can call `ADOConnection.RollbackTrans()`, which will undo any changes since the call to `ADOConnection.BeginTrans()`.

After you call `ADOConnection.CommitTrans()` or `ADOConnection.RollbackTrans()` to end a transaction, ADO might not automatically start a new transaction for you. This is controlled by setting the `Attributes` property of the `ADOConnection`. If you include `adXactCommitRetaining` in `Attributes`, a new transaction will be started for you after a call to `ADOConnection.CommitTrans()`. Similarly, including `adXactAbortRetaining` starts a new transaction after a call to `ADOConnection.RollbackTrans()`.

Summary

This chapter took a look at ActiveX Data Objects. ADO provides a common interface that can be used in a wide variety of different programming environments, including Visual C++, Visual Basic, VBScript, and JavaScript. ADO also enables you to access a wide variety of different OLE DB data sources. To recap:

- If you're developing new database applications, try using straight OLE DB instead of ADO. In Visual C++ 6.0, it's faster and easier.

- Various objects make up the ADO interface, including connections and recordsets, as well as several other classes that are used by these objects.

- You can perform basic database operations with ADO including connecting to a data source, forming a recordset, and executing commands.

MFC Support for COM and ActiveX

PART
VI

Overview of COM and Active Technologies

*by Vincent Mayfield
and Mickey Williams*

IN THIS CHAPTER

This chapter will discuss COM, OLE, and Active Technologies. These are the technologies that comprise Microsoft's component strategy, and they are the interprocess communication methods of choice when building applications for Windows. COM is the basic component plumbing that provides services for COM, OLE, and other Active Technologies. OLE is Microsoft's GUI-centric component strategy for enabling desktop applications to work together seamlessly. This chapter introduces COM and OLE, and also takes a look at ActiveX controls and other Active Technologies from Microsoft.

COM, OLE, and Active Technology History in a Nutshell

In 1991, Microsoft introduced a new specification called OLE 1.0. The acronym stood for *Object Linking and Embedding*. OLE 1.0 was basically a way of handling compound documents. A *compound document* is a way of storing data in multiple formats—such as text, graphics, video, and sound—in a single document. At the time, *object-oriented* was the new programming buzzword, and the OLE 1.0 specification was a move to a more object-oriented paradigm. Furthermore, OLE 1.0 was an effort to move toward a more document-centric approach, instead of an applications-centric approach. Unfortunately, OLE 1.0 was coldly received by software developers. Very few independent software vendors (ISVs) and corporations raced to embrace OLE 1.0 and OLE-enable their applications. This reluctance to deploy OLE 1.0 in applications was due mainly to the fact that OLE 1.0 was very complex and had a steep learning curve. Unlike today's COM, OLE 1.0 was not language-agnostic—applications had to be coded using C. Further, the original OLE specification failed to scale well, and it was inefficient when working with large data items. OLE 1.0 was based on the DDE protocol and required data to be copied into RAM, often at inappropriate times—editing a large bitmap stored in a disk file would often result in three copies of the file loaded into RAM or on disk simultaneously.

Fortunately, Microsoft continued to strive to improve OLE. In 1993, Microsoft released the OLE 2.0 specification, which encompassed more than just compound documents; it sported an entire architecture of object-based services that could be extended, customized, and enhanced. The foundation of this services architecture was the Component Object Model (COM). The services available through this architecture are as follows:

- OLE clipboard extensions
- Drag and drop
- Embedding
- In-place activation

- Linking
- Monikers (persistent naming)
- Automation
- ActiveX controls
- OLE and Active documents
- Structured storage
- Uniform Data Transfer (UDT)

From a programmatic view, OLE is a series of services built on top of each other, as shown in Figure 24.1. These services form an architecture of interdependent building blocks built on the COM foundation.

FIGURE 24.1

The foundation of OLE is COM, with each successive service built on the technologies of the others.

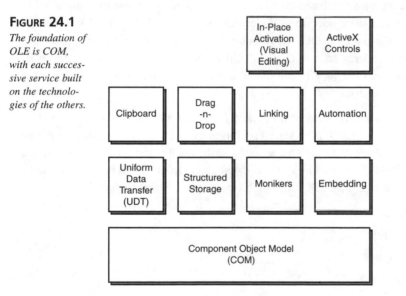

| In-Place Activation (Visual Editing) | ActiveX Controls |
| | |

| Clipboard | Drag -n- Drop | Linking | Automation |

| Uniform Data Transfer (UDT) | Structured Storage | Monikers | Embedding |

| Component Object Model (COM) |

The release of OLE had such an impact on standard ways of computing that it received two prestigious industry awards: a Technical Excellence award from *PC Magazine* and the MVP award for software innovation from *PC/Computing*. Adding to the success of OLE was a new and improved programming interface. Developers could now move to OLE-enabled applications much more easily. The OLE services incorporate many of the principles embodied in object-oriented programming: encapsulation, polymorphism, and an object-based architecture. Further adding to the success of OLE was the release in February 1993 of Visual C++ 1.0 with the Microsoft Foundation Class (MFC) Library version 2.0. MFC had wrapped the OLE API in a C++ class library, thus making it much easier for programmers to use the OLE services architecture.

> **Note**
>
> Don't let the ease-of-use of the MFC Library fool you. OLE programming is very difficult to master. However, I recommend that beginning COM, OLE, and ActiveX programmers use MFC. MFC provides a framework to get you up and programming very quickly.

Today, OLE is no longer the acronym for object linking and embedding. That term is now obsolete. Microsoft refers to it as simply OLE, pronounced "O-lay." Notice that there is no version number attached to OLE any more. Beginning with the technologies introduced with OLE 2.0, OLE is an extensible architecture, and it can be enhanced and extended without changing its basic foundation. A testimonial to this capability is OLE controls. OLE controls were not part of the original release of OLE 2.0. OLE controls were not added to the available OLE services until almost a year after the original release. In fact, objects created with OLE 1.0 still work and interact with modern OLE applications. However, their functionality is limited to the original 1.0 specification, so there is no need for versions.

In March 1996, Microsoft announced the ActiveX technologies, which included optimizations to COM and OLE that improved performance over the Internet and corporate intranets. The technology that made the largest splash was the new ActiveX control specification, which enabled controls used in a distributed environment to be smaller and easier to deploy. At the time, ActiveX was a grab bag of goodies that included:

- ActiveX documents
- ActiveX controls
- ActiveX Scripting
- ActiveX Hyperlinks

Recently, Microsoft has renamed many of these technologies, and only ActiveX controls maintain ActiveX as part of their name. The term Active Technologies is now used to describe many things that were once grouped under the ActiveX umbrella.

The end result of all of this naming and renaming is that today COM, OLE, and ActiveX are terms that tend to mean different things to different people. As you can see in Figure 24.1, COM is the foundation of Microsoft's entire component object strategy. In general, this book will use the following terms:

- *COM* will be used to refer to the basic plumbing that is used to enable objects to communicate with each other.

- *OLE* is a user-centric technology that is primarily concerned with enabling end-users to work with tools such as Word, Visio, and Excel. Drag and Drop, Linking, and Embedding all fall under OLE.

- *Active Technologies* will be used when referring to developer-centric technologies such as Active Documents and Active Scripting.

- *ActiveX Controls* will be used only when referring to controls that are used in a visual development environment, such as Visual C++.

> **Note**
>
> Even with the near constant renaming of anything associated with Microsoft's component strategy, there are still inconsistencies. For example, OLE is generally reserved for user-centric technologies, such as OLE Drag and Drop. For some reason, the newest data access strategy is called—you guessed it—OLE DB. Although it has nothing to do with user interaction, it still incorporates OLE as part of its name.

COM and OLE from the Eyes of the End User

Although many software engineers forget it, the end user is the main reason for our existence as software developers. Because the end user is the main reason software is developed, this section will view OLE from the user's eyes. This will help you grasp the benefits and the available services of COM, OLE, and Active Technologies. The end user's view is simple, less technical, and very understandable. I firmly believe that users decide in the first ten minutes of using an application whether they like it. This sets the stage for all further experiences using that application. Therefore, an application's intuitiveness, appearance, ease of use, capability of performing work or entertainment, and performance are of paramount importance.

24

OVERVIEW OF COM AND ACTIVE TECHNOLOGIES

> **Note**
>
> Always keep in mind that the "devil-spawned end user," as the cartoon character Dilbert by Scott Adams would say, is the main reason for our existence as software engineers. The best software engineers never forget this and always tackle every programming endeavor with the end user in mind.

Microsoft—and Apple before it—knew that a large portion of the software had to have a human-to-machine interface. This is why Windows and the Macintosh each have a standard interface—not only from a user's perspective, but also from a programmer's perspective.

Users interact with COM, OLE, and Active Technologies in three ways:

- Documents, including OLE Documents and the newer Active Documents
- Automation, formerly known as OLE Automation
- ActiveX controls and COM objects

Many of the COM, OLE, and Active Technologies are hidden from the end user. For example, a typical end user has no idea that an ActiveX control is being used. Nor is he likely to know that a particular document is an Active Document launched from a compound file instead of a normal text file. However, the end user is likely to be aware of the ease of use that occurs when using a specific application or opening a specific document.

As a computer professional, I am sure you have seen or worked with Microsoft Word or Excel. Microsoft Word is the classic example of an application that creates OLE documents. In other words, Word is an *OLE document server*. This chapter is not going to outline the functionality of Word, but merely point out the features of COM and OLE that are used by it and similar applications. However, do not be deceived; OLE document servers are not always classic word processors. Think of OLE containers and servers as pieces of Velcro. You have two pieces: the hook side (the document server) and the pile side (the document container).

The first feature of OLE documents is a common user model. This simply means that the user interface (UI) features used to access OLE documents are similar from application to application. The common user model features document-centricity and takes advantage of OLE's integrated data capabilities.

> **Note**
>
> OLE user-interface design guidelines are well documented in *The Windows Interface Guidelines for Software Design*: An Application Design Guide (Microsoft Press, 1995).

One of these integrated data capabilities is called *linking and embedding*. Data objects of different types, created from other applications, can be embedded or linked into an application's OLE document. This enables the user to manipulate the object in the host application without returning to the creating application. The object is simply edited in place, hence the term *in-place editing*. The user interface is modified in the host application with menus, toolbars, and context menus from the application that created the object.

In Figure 24.2, take note of the two kinds of data—text and an embedded Visio drawing. Note also the toolbars and menu.

FIGURE 24.2

A Microsoft Word document with embedded text and graphics.

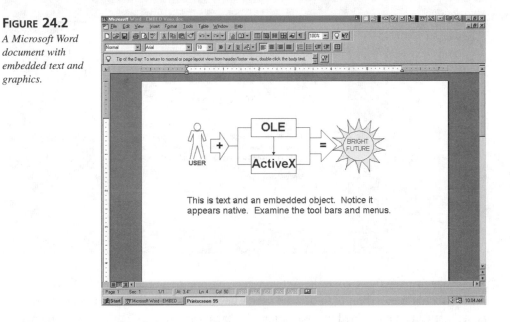

If you double-click the Visio Drawing, the Word application changes, and new user interface objects are added to Word from Visio (see Figure 24.3). Notice that the Word user interface performs a metamorphosis and now has the Visio toolbars, floating dialog boxes, and menu items, as well as the Visio drawing and rulers. The user can then edit this drawing object without switching applications. In addition, these objects can be dragged and dropped between and within applications.

These features are implemented in the same way from application to application. Thus, there is a smaller learning curve for users when they get new applications, because the applications function similarly and have a common user model.

The next level of visibility to the user is Automation. Automation enables the user to access and modify objects through properties and methods, using a high-level language such as Visual Basic for Applications (VBA), VBScript, or JavaScript. This enables the user to customize objects and the interactivity between objects to perform operations the way the user defines. Microsoft Excel spreadsheets are the classic Automation objects. The user can create Excel spreadsheets that update a Microsoft Graph object or update information in a Microsoft Access database.

24

OVERVIEW OF
COM AND ACTIVE
TECHNOLOGIES

FIGURE 24.3

A Microsoft Word document with the Visio drawing activated for in-place editing.

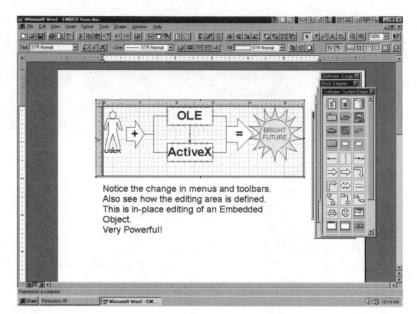

This leads us to ActiveX controls. ActiveX controls are the last area of COM, OLE, and Active Technology visibility to the end user. They are self-contained, reusable components that can be embedded in applications. To the users, they are nothing more than a control that takes their input and passes it to the application that contains it. However, some ActiveX controls are static in nature, such as a picture control. ActiveX controls are also Automation Servers that can have properties set at both compile time and runtime, and ActiveX controls typically have methods that can perform certain operations. The difference between an ActiveX control and Automation Server is that an ActiveX control is a self-contained component.

ActiveX controls also take advantage of two-way communication between the control and the container. This enables an ActiveX control to have an even more special ability beyond simple Automation: It can initiate events that are sent to the control's container.

ActiveX controls also expose properties and methods that may be manipulated. An example of a property might be the date value or the background color in the Microsoft MonthView control shown in Figure 24.4. A method might be a function that changes the date value or the background color. To clarify an event, the MonthView control might have an event fired, when the user clicks a day, that lets the container know that a day has been clicked. These properties, methods, and events make ActiveX controls powerful. They give the programmer and the end user a wide range of functionality, as shown in Figure 24.4.

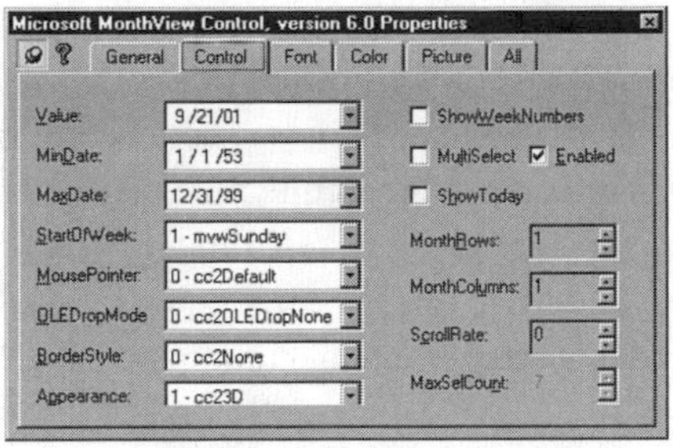

FIGURE 24.4

Properties, methods, and events of the Microsoft MonthView control during development in the Visual C++ Developer Studio.

In future sections, you will discover that ActiveX controls have had a very profound impact in the area of application development (see Figure 24.5), because they are ready-made, self-contained components. From the end user's perspective, they provide increased functionality and lower software costs.

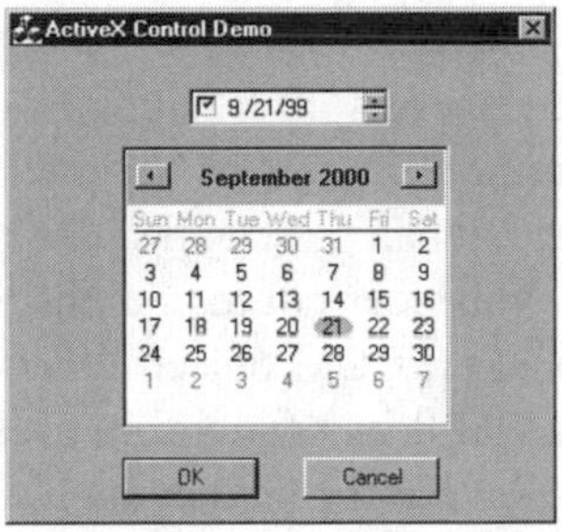

FIGURE 24.5

Two ActiveX controls embedded in an application. The Microsoft Date and Time Picker control is located above the Microsoft MonthView control. These controls come with Visual C++.

COM, OLE, and Active Technologies from a Programmer's View

This section presents COM, OLE, and Active Technologies from a programmatic view. For each service, you will be given a description of the technology and a programmer's view of the interfaces to these technologies. In addition, you will learn the MFC classes that support each technology. Pay particular attention to understanding what each topic does and where it fits into the architecture. Some of the technologies will be discussed in detail in later chapters.

Notice these are the same technologies the end user sees. However, the end user's view is a visual one, and the programmer's view is of a set of interfaces that must be mastered to provide the visual representation the end user sees. These sections are intended to give you an overview of Microsoft's entire component architecture. The specifics of implementation are left to later chapters. You are going to see, though, that Visual C++ and MFC do a lot of the work for you. The MFC implementation of COM, OLE, and the other Active Technologies is a kinder, gentler implementation.

Component Object Model (COM)

When Microsoft designed OLE, it was designed with object-oriented programming in mind. COM objects are much like instantiated C++ classes or an ADA package. In fact, COM was designed with C++ programmers in mind. It supports encapsulation, polymorphism, and reusability. However, COM was also designed to be compatible at the binary level and therefore has differences from a C++ object. As a programmer, you are aware that compiled programming languages such as C, C++, PASCAL, and ADA are machine-dependent. As a binary object, a COM object concerns itself with how it interfaces with other objects. When not used in the environment of its creator, an interface is exposed that can be seen in the non-native environment. It can be seen because it is a binary object and therefore not machine-dependent. This does not require the host environment or an interacting object to know anything about the COM object. When the object is created in the womb of its mother application, COM does not concern itself with how that object interacts within it. This interaction is between the mother application and the child object. When the object interacts with the rest of the world, however, COM is concerned about how to interface with that object. It is important to note that COM is not a programming language; it is a binary standard that enables software components to interact with each other as objects. COM is not specific to any particular programming language. COM can work with any language that can support the binary layout of a COM object. It is a programming model to facilitate the programmability of this standard.

COM objects consist of two types of items: *properties* and *methods*. Properties are the data members, and methods are member functions. COM objects each have a common interface. No matter what they do, COM objects all have to implement the IUnknown interface. This interface is the main interface for all others and is the base class from which all other COM interfaces are derived. The IUnknown interface has the following member functions:

- ULONG AddRef(void)
- ULONG Release(void)
- HRESULT QueryInterface(REFIID id, void **ipv)

Each object implements a *vtable*. A vtable is nothing more than an array of pointers to member functions implemented in the object (see Figure 24.6). This vtable is shared between all the instances of the object also maintaining the private data of each object. A client application evokes an instance of the interface and gets a pointer to a pointer that points to the vtable. Each time a new interface to the object is instantiated, the reference count of objects is incremented with AddRef(). Conversely, each time a reference is destroyed, the reference counter is decremented with Release(). Once the reference count is zero, the object can be destroyed. In order to see what interfaces an object supports, you can use QueryInterface().

FIGURE 24.6

This interface maps into a vtable.

Common Access To Objects

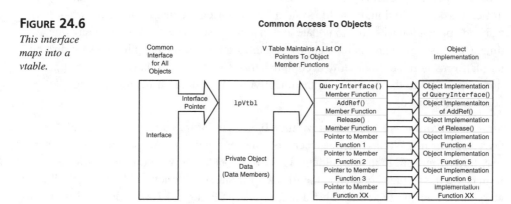

COM objects are never directly accessed. COM objects are always accessed through a pointer to an interface exposed by the object. The QueryInterface(REFIID riid, void **ipv) function takes a reference to an interface identifier (riid) and a void pointer. The REFIID is a 128-bit unique ID that identifies the interface you are retrieving. Notice the double indirection on the pointer: **ipv. The ipv pointer is where the pointer to the interface you are trying to retrieve is stored. Consider this code fragment:

```
IAnyInterface* pAny = NULL;
HRESULT hr = pUnknown->QueryInterface(IID_IAnyInterface, (void**)&pAny);
if(SUCCEEDED(hr))
{
    pAny->DoAnyObjectWork();
    pAny->Release();
}
```

pUnknown is a pointer to the object's IUnknown interface. DoAnyObjectWork() is the member function you want to use to perform some work. You access that function through the pointer to that object's interface pAny.

Visual C++ and MFC encapsulates this IUnknown implementation through the use of *interface maps,* which are much the same as the message maps used to map the windows messages. It is a much easier implementation to understand. Visual C++ and MFC encapsulate much of the work involved in this through the wizards implemented in Visual C++ and the OLE classes implemented in the MFC Class Library. You will learn more about the Visual C++ and MFC implementations in Chapters 25–33.

Structured Storage

Most computing platforms today have different file systems, making sharing data a very difficult task. In addition, these file systems arose during the mainframe days when only a single application was able to update and in some cases access that data at any one time. COM is built with interoperability and integration between applications on dissimilar platforms in mind. In order to accomplish this, COM needs to have multiple applications write data to the same file on the underlying file system. Structured Storage addresses this need.

Structured Storage is a file system within a file. Think of it as a hierarchical tree of storages and streams. Within this tree, each node has one and only one parent, but each node may have from zero to many children. Think of it as like the Windows 95 Explorer. The folders are the storage nodes, and the files are the streams. Structured Storage provides an organization chart of data within a file, as seen in Figure 24.7. In addition, this organization of data is not limited to files, but includes memory and databases.

FIGURE 24.7

Structured Storage is a hierarchical tree of storages and streams.

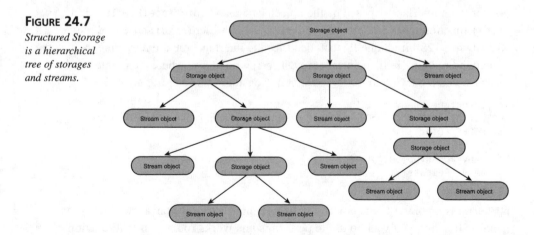

Stream objects contain data, much like files in a traditional file system. This data can be either native data or data from other outside objects. Storage objects are compatible at the binary level; thus, in theory, they are compatible across platforms that support COM and OLE. However, you know that there are minute differences between the various platforms. Notice in Figure 24.7 the tree of the Structured Storage object. The definition of the tree is dependent on how the object's creator defined the storage of the object.

Structured Storage objects are manipulated using the following OLE interfaces:

- `IPersistStorage`
- `IStorage`
- `IStream`

`IStorage`,as the name implies, manipulates storage objects and `IStream` manipulates streams. Rarely would you want to manipulate stream or storage objects individually. More than likely, you would want to manipulate the Persistent Storage object with the `IPersistStorage`. *Persistent Storage* is data that will continue to exist even after an object is destroyed—for example, if you want to allow the user to define the color of an object such as a text label. You would persistently store that object's foreground and background colors. The next time the object was created you could read in from Persistent Storage the colors previously chosen by the end user. You could then apply those attributes to the object and thus maintain the user's preferences. `IPersistStorage` enables you to do this by performing the following operations:

- `IsDirty`
- `InitNew`
- `Load`
- `Save`
- `SaveCompleted`
- `HandsOffStorage`

A great way to see what Structured Storage looks like is with a utility that comes with Visual C++ 6 called DocFile Viewer. DocFile Viewer is added automatically to the Windows Start menu, in the Visual Studio 6.0 Tools folder. DocFile Viewer enables you to look at a compound file, also known as an OLE document. Compound files used for OLE documents are the most common implementation of Structured storage. Figure 24.8 shows an example of DocFile Viewer. (This is the Word document with an embedded Visio drawing object shown in Figure 24.2.)

24

OVERVIEW OF
COM AND ACTIVE
TECHNOLOGIES

FIGURE 24.8

*DocFile Viewer
shows the hierar-
chical tree of a
Structured Storage
object.*

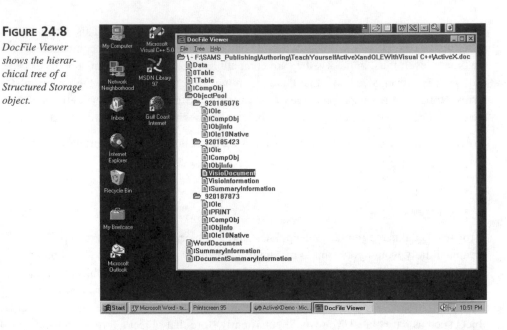

If you double-click a stream object, you can see its binary contents (see Figure 24.9).

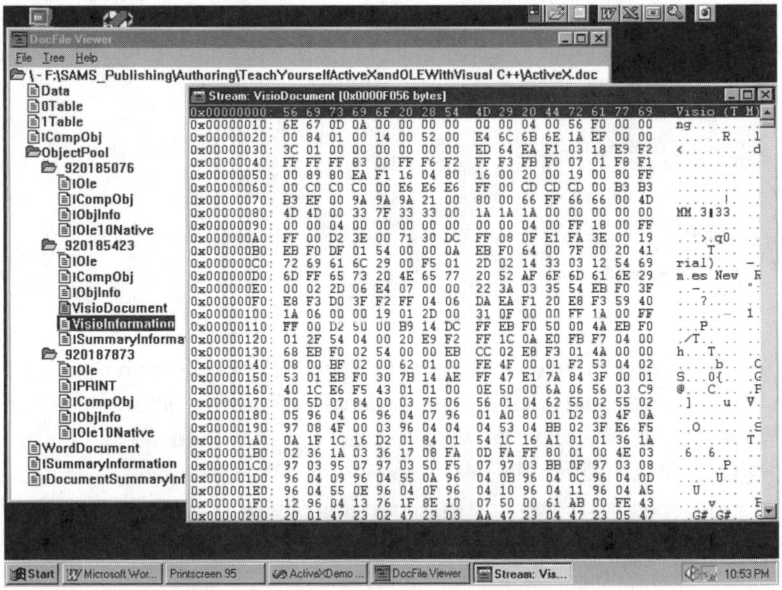

FIGURE 24.9

*The binary con-
tents of a stream
object.*

MFC provides an encapsulation of `IPersistStorage` and `IStorage` through an easy-to-use class called `COleDocument`. In addition, to aid in the manipulation of storages and streams, MFC provides `COleStreamFile`. OLE documents and their extension Active documents will be covered in Chapter 25, "Active Documents." It is important to note that compound documents are not only used for OLE documents and Active documents, but any file type that uses Structured Storage to store its data.

Monikers (Persistent Naming)

Monikers are a way of referencing a piece of data or object in an object-based system such as COM. The original use for monikers was in OLE linking. When an object is linked, a moniker is stored that knows how to get to that native data. For example, if you link a sound file into a Word document, the WAV file is not stored natively in that document. A moniker is created that can intelligently find the WAV file object. Think of a moniker as a map to where X marks the spot. However, a moniker is more than just a name—a moniker is a COM object.

To use a moniker to locate and bind to an object, you must use the `IMoniker` interface and call `IMoniker::BindToObject`. By using the intelligent persistent name of that object, the `IMoniker` interface negotiates the location of that object and returns a pointer to the interface of that object's type. If the COM object is currently running, the moniker will return a pointer to the currently running object. If the COM object is inactive, the moniker handles activating the object, and returning a pointer to the specific instance named by the moniker. The moniker itself can then be released. Think of it as similar to de-referencing a pointer in C or C++ to locate a piece of data. Remember that monikers are persistent. `IMoniker` is derived from `IPersistStream`, and thus it can serialize itself into a stream. This gives it persistence. There are eight basic types of monikers:

- File monikers
- Item monikers
- Anti-monikers
- Pointer monikers
- Class monikers
- Asynchronous monikers
- URL monikers
- Composite monikers

24

OVERVIEW OF
COM AND ACTIVE
TECHNOLOGIES

File Monikers

File monikers store a filename persistently. In binding the text filename to an object that has been persisted to a file, a pointer to the activated object's interface is returned so that you can manipulate that object.

Item Monikers

Item monikers point to a specific place inside an instance of a COM object, such as a paragraph or a portion of an embedded video. An item moniker is always used in a composite moniker. For example, an item moniker is often composed with a file moniker to form a composite moniker that refers to a specific item within a file.

Anti-Monikers

An anti-moniker is the inverse of another moniker. When an anti-moniker is applied to a moniker, the two monikers cancel each other; this operation is often useful when maintaining composite monikers.

Pointer Monikers

Pointer monikers simply bind to COM objects that are already running. This type of moniker is useful when a moniker is required, but the COM object isn't persistent and can't be passed in an inactive state. In such a case, you can instantiate the object, and create a pointer moniker.

Class Monikers

Class monikers are used to bind to instances of class objects. A class object is a COM object used to create instances of COM objects. You typically use a class moniker as part of a composite moniker.

Asynchronous Monikers

Asynchronous monikers carry out the BindToObject operation asynchronously. Most other monikers bind synchronously, but in a network or Internet setting, these operations can take a while to complete. Asynchronous monikers enable binding operations to take place more efficiently in these settings.

URL Monikers

A URL moniker is an asynchronous moniker that enables binding to a file on the Internet or corporate intranet.

Composite Monikers

A composite moniker is an ordered collection of monikers. Taken as a whole, a composite moniker refers to a specific COM object. Each component of a composite moniker is resolved in turn in order to bind to the desired object. For example, a composite moniker might refer to a particular chart located on a particular worksheet in an Excel document. However, it is not necessary for the root of a composite moniker to be a file moniker—you are limited only by your imagination when composing monikers.

MFC Encapsulation of Monikers

In the previous section on Structured storage, you learned that MFC has a class called `COleStreamFile`. The purpose of this class is to encapsulate the functionality of `IStream` to provide access to the streams of data in a compound file. Derived from `COleStreamFile` is `CMonikerFile`. `CMonikerFile` is a class that encapsulates the functionality of monikers provided in the `IMoniker` interface. This class gives the ability to gain access to `IStreams` named by `IMoniker`. It is important to note that this class does not encapsulate the entire `IMoniker` interface. It provides the ability to work with the streams of a compound file. So, if you wish to bind to storage or an object, you have to implement the `IMoniker` interface directly. This means you will not be able to use MFC directly to implement all the moniker types stated previously.

Uniform Data Transfer (UDT)

OLE applications use a technology known as *Uniform Data Transfer*, or *UDT*, to exchange data. Uniform data transfer is a much more flexible way of exchanging data than the traditional Windows clipboard techniques. The primary interface used with UDT is `IDataObject`, and it's used in three major areas:

- OLE Clipboard
- OLE drag and drop
- Linking and embedding

COM objects that are data transfer sources expose the `IDataObject` interface and are known as *data objects*. The `IDataObject` interface makes use of two data describing structures:

- `FORMATETC`, which describes the data to be transferred
- `STGMEDIUM`, which describes the current location of the data

24

OVERVIEW OF
COM AND ACTIVE
TECHNOLOGIES

OLE Clipboard

The system clipboard is a system-level service used for interprocess communications. Because it is a system-level service, all applications have access to it. The Windows clipboard works great when transferring small pieces of data, but it is inefficient when transferring large objects. When transferring large bitmaps or multimedia clips, these objects must be loaded from disk, copied to global memory for the clipboard, and transferred to the other program. In low memory conditions, the same data may exist in several places simultaneously:

- In the original source file
- In the global memory (possibly swapped to disk)
- In the receiving program, which may copy the data to disk, copy it to local memory, or both

This is a poor use of system resources and leads to very poor performance. In fact, as the system begins to run low on resources, the traditional clipboard mechanism breaks down even more, as global memory is swapped to and from the hard drive.

The OLE clipboard uses UDT as its underlying transport mechanism. The OLE clipboard allows you to describe the data to be transferred, rather than passing the data directly in a global memory handle.

With an IDataObject pointer, you can use the function OleSetClipboard() to take a cut or copied object and expose this object to all processes through the OLE clipboard. Likewise, when you want to paste data from the OLE clipboard, you can use your IDataObject pointer to use the OleGetClipboard() function. This is a very powerful mechanism because it maintains the integrity of the object as a whole, enabling you to move complex object data types between applications.

Visual C++ and MFC provide access to the OLE clipboard through the use of member functions in the classes CWnd and COleClientItem.

Drag and Drop

Drag and drop is a method by which the user can select and move objects within an application and between applications. UDT is used to perform drag and drop actions. On the selection of the object, the source application packages the object and uses an IDataObject pointer to call DoDragDrop(). The source uses the IDropSource interface, which yields a pointer to its implementation. This pointer is passed to DoDragDrop(). The source controls the mouse cursors and handles the object in case of a cancellation.

Once the user brings the dragged object to its new client location or target, the client application evokes the IDropTarget interface. With the pointer to the IDropTarget, the client application tracks the object in relation to itself with the functions available in the IDropTarget interface. One function called IDropTarget::Drop() is called when the object is dropped on the target. Drop() passes the IDataObject pointer of the source to the target. Now that the client has the IDataObject pointer, it is free to manipulate the object.

OLE drag and drop will be discussed in detail as it is implemented in Visual C++ and MFC in Chapters 25, "Active Documents;" 26, "Active Containers;" and 27, "Active Servers." Drag and drop support is encapsulated in the following MFC classes:

- COleDropSource
- COleDropTarget
- COleClientItem
- COleServerItem
- COleDataSource

Embedding and Linking

A *linked* object is an object that is not stored within an OLE document, but rather elsewhere external to the document. In the document, a moniker is stored that references the linked object. This OLE function uses UDT to move the data from the data object source to the container application so that the data can be rendered as appropriate. Linked objects are manipulated through the IOleLink interface. By linking an object instead of embedding it, you cut down on the size of the compound file. In addition, you expose the linked object so that multiple people can use it.

An *embedded* object is an object that is stored, through the OLE Structured Storage mechanism, as native data within an OLE document. Although this increases the size of the compound file, it provides a single file object that can contain multiple data types.

OLE Documents

OLE documents are nothing more than compound files that use Structured Storage to hold the objects that make up the document. These objects can be native data, or they can, through the use of monikers, link to data outside the document. In addition, an OLE document can contain objects created by other processes, embedded as if they were natively a part of the document. OLE documents are handled through interfaces just like any other OLE object. As you can see, OLE documents are a conglomeration

24

OVERVIEW OF COM AND ACTIVE TECHNOLOGIES

of several OLE services. Here are some of the interfaces used to implement OLE document interfaces:

- IOleItemContainer
- IPersistFile
- IClassFactory
- IOleInPlaceActiveFrame
- IOleInPlaceUIObject
- IOleInPlaceSite

COleDocument encapsulates the functionality of OLE documents and ActiveX documents in MFC. However, it is important to note that there are a series of classes in MFC that are used together to provide this functionality. You will explore these classes in detail in the later chapters.

In-Place Activation

OLE documents support *in-place activation* or what is commonly referred to as "visual editing." This enables you to edit embedded objects in a container application as if they were native. When you activate visual editing in the container, the user interface of the container morphs to support selected user-interface functions of the server application that created the object. There are a whole series of interfaces to enable you to implement and support in-place activation. These interfaces all begin with IOleInPlace. These are some of the interfaces you can use to implement and support in-place activation:

- IOleInPlaceObject
- IOleInPlaceActiveObject
- IOleInPlaceSite
- IOleInPlaceActiveFrame
- IOleInPlaceUIObject
- IOleInPlaceSite

Automation

Automation was originally called OLE Automation; during one of the original renaming purges orchestrated by Microsoft's marketing department, the OLE was dropped and the technology is now known simply as Automation. Automation basically enables you to manipulate the properties and methods of an application from within another application through the use of high-level macro languages and scripting languages such as VBScript and JavaScript. This enables you to customize objects and provide interoperability between applications.

In the world of Automation, there are *Automation Servers* and *Automation Controllers*. An Automation Server is a component or application that exposes properties and methods for use by other applications. Microsoft Excel is a good example of an Automation Server, because it exposes services that can create and manipulate worksheets, cells, and rows.

Descriptions of the properties and methods that are available through an Automation Server are available in an IDL file or can be made available as a type library. A type library is a binary representation of the information in an IDL file, although it has slightly lower fidelity.

In Visual C++ 6, there is a nice utility named OLE View that reads and graphically displays the contents of type libraries. You can use this utility to display the properties and methods exposed by Automation Servers. Figure 24.10 shows OLE View in action.

> **Note**
>
> OLE View is accessible in two ways: If you're inside Developer Studio, click the Visual C++ Tools menu and select OLE/COM Object Viewer. You can also start OLE View from the Windows Start Menu, in the Visual Studio 6.0 Tools folder.

FIGURE 24.10

The OLE/COM Viewer that comes with Visual C++ 6.0.

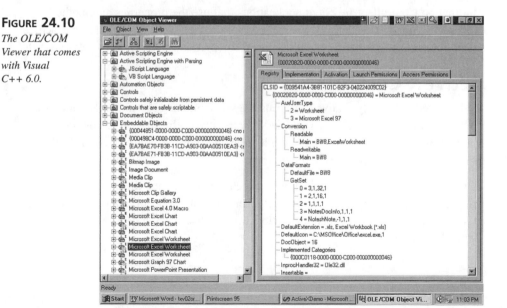

Notice that the Type Library Viewer screen shows the disassembled type library in
Interface Description Language (see Figure 24.11). It also displays the constants, properties, methods, and interfaces exposed by the Automation Server.

FIGURE 24.11

*OLE View's Type
Library Viewer.*

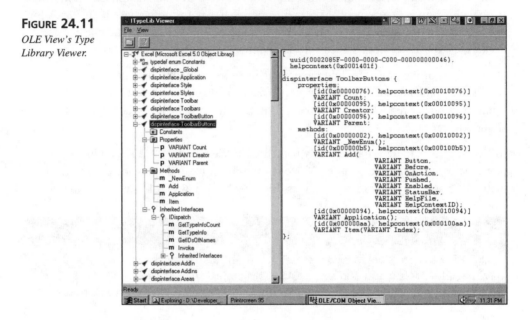

Automation Controllers are client applications that use the properties and methods
exposed by Automation Servers. Automation Controllers work through an interface
called IDispatch. All interfaces that support Automation are derived from IDispatch.

ActiveX Controls

As discussed previously, ActiveX controls are self-contained reusable components that
can be embedded in applications. ActiveX controls typically support Automation to
enable properties to be set at both compile time and runtime. ActiveX controls also have
methods that can perform certain operations.

They provide two-way communication between the control and the container. These
components have a very profound impact in the area of application development. These
reusable self-contained pockets of functionality are discussed in detail in Chapter 28,
"ActiveX Controls."

Evolving OLE with Active Technologies

The introduction of Active Technologies has extended many of the original OLE technologies beyond the bounds of the local machine to Enterprise Wide networks and the Internet. Specifically, the following Active Technologies have their roots in OLE:

- Active documents, an extension of OLE documents
- Active controls, an extension to OLE controls
- Internet monikers, which extend traditional monikers

This is not the total effect of the introduction of Active Technologies. Elements of OLE are also present in new Active technologies, as you will see in the next section, "New Active Technologies." For now, let's concentrate on the evolution of OLE into Active Technologies.

Active Documents

Active Technologies extends OLE documents so that they can be used in Internet and corporate intranet settings. This technology is a way for existing OLE documents, such as Microsoft Word, Microsoft Project, and Microsoft PowerPoint, to be activated by a Web browser and brought up through a viewer. Thus, you can have compound files with various data that can contain linked and embedded objects being accessed across the World Wide Web (WWW). Using the ActiveX Hyperlinks technology, you can extend OLE documents across the Web. ActiveX hyperlinks are discussed in the next section.

Asynchronous Storage

The ability to bring Active documents across the WWW gives rise to another new Active technology, asynchronous storage. Basically, this extends Structured Storage across the Web, allowing for the storage to happen asynchronously. Obviously, with the slow bandwidth of the Internet, if you allowed a storage operation to happen synchronously, nothing else could happen on the client or server until the transfer of data to or from Persistent Storage took place. Using ActiveX hyperlinks and the technology of asynchronous monikers, asynchronous storage is accomplished.

ActiveX Controls

ActiveX controls are simply OLE controls or OCXs that have been extended to make them easier to deploy and use, especially in a network setting. Microsoft has now replaced the term *OLE control* with *ActiveX control*. Remember, COM and OLE are extendible architectures; therefore, these reusable components cannot only be embedded in a Web page, but also in a non–Internet-enabled application.

ActiveX controls can be created in a variety of languages, including C, C++, Java, and Visual Basic. They can also be manipulated though scripting languages such as VBScript or JavaScript.

ActiveX controls are great components; they provide a virtual plethora of little pockets of prefabricated functionality of which you can take advantage. The possibilities for ActiveX controls are endless. Currently, ActiveX controls range from a Calendar control to a Picture control, which enables you to display static pictures.

COM is at the base of the ActiveX control technology. ActiveX controls are built on a series of OLE services, with COM as the base. The following list depicts the technologies that you may find in a typical ActiveX control:

- Component object model
- Connectable objects
- Uniform Data Transfer (UDT)
- OLE documents
- Property pages
- Persistent storage
- OLE automation

ActiveX Control: COM

Like the OLE controls previously discussed, ActiveX controls are COM objects. They are in-process COM servers activated from the inside out. Like every other COM object, they expose the IUnknown interface so that container applications can access their properties and methods through the pointers returned by the interface.

ActiveX Control: Connectable Objects

Using a mechanism known as *connection points*, ActiveX controls support two-way communication from the control to the client application. Objects that use connection points are known as *connectable objects*. It enables the control to notify the client of events or invoke a method or event. It also enables the client to communicate directly with the control.

ActiveX Control: Uniform Data Transfer

Controls can be dragged and dropped within their client application if that functionality is enabled in the client application.

ActiveX Control: Compound Documents

In the beginning of this chapter, you saw how an object from another application could be embedded in a host application. In addition, that object could be activated in-place for visual editing. Likewise, ActiveX controls are built on the concept of OLE documents and can be activated in-place.

ActiveX Control: Property Pages

ActiveX controls have property pages, like their predecessor OLE controls, that expose their properties and methods to the user. From the property pages, the properties can be set.

ActiveX Control: Automation

ActiveX controls are usually Automation servers. Their properties and methods can be set at compile time through the use of property pages, and at runtime through VBScript and JavaScript.

ActiveX Control: Persistent Storage

COM objects can use Persistent Storage in a variety of ways. ActiveX controls use Persistent Storage to store their state. This enables the control to be initialized to the state it was when you last used it.

COM

As you learned previously, COM is a binary standard for objects. Basically, COM operates the way it did before ActiveX, except that COM has been extended so that you can exchange and use objects across the Internet. This has given rise to Distributed COM.

Distributed COM (DCOM)

Distributed COM, also known as DCOM, is the basic extension of binary COM objects across LANs, WANs, and the Internet. Now you can instantiate and bind objects across a network.

24

OVERVIEW OF
COM AND ACTIVE
TECHNOLOGIES

Internet Monikers

With the advent of ActiveX and the extension of COM across the net, monikers were also extended and incorporated into this architecture. This gave rise to two new types of monikers:

- URL monikers
- Asynchronous monikers

URL Monikers

A *URL* is a *universal resource locator,* used for Web-based addressing of objects. As you learned earlier, monikers are an intelligent naming system, so that by using the `IMoniker` interface to a moniker object and the intelligent name, you can locate the object. This capability was simply extended to include URLs, because of the capability of passing objects across the Internet and intranets.

Asynchronous Monikers

Previously, monikers carried out their binding to the object synchronously. Nothing could happen until the binding was complete. On the high latency, slow-link communications network of the Internet, holding up operations while binding is accomplished is unacceptable. With asynchronous monikers, the interfaces to the object negotiate the transmission of the binding process, to perform it asynchronously. Right now, URL monikers are the only standard implementation of asynchronous monikers.

New Active Technologies

Active Technology includes many features that don't overlap or extend older OLE technologies. Many of these technologies facilitate the creation of interactive applications for the World Wide Web. These items are

- ActiveX hyperlinks
- NetShow, previously known as ActiveX Conferencing
- Code signing
- HTML extensions
- ActiveMovie

Active Hyperlinks

Active hyperlinks basically allow in-place activation from HTML files of non-HTML–based documents. Using an Active document container, you can access Microsoft Word, Microsoft Excel, Microsoft PowerPoint, Visio, and CorelDraw! documents from a hypertext link in an HTML document.

NetShow

The NetShow services are a suite of technologies that enable real-time, multiparty, multimedia communication over the Internet. This is much like video teleconferencing except you can do it on a PC. Just think what this does for programmers; we could all work at home and telecommute. This is a programmable interface opening up endless possibilities for innovation.

Active Scripting

Active scripts bring Automation to a wide range of areas, such as Web Servers, Network management, and even applications such as SQL Server. Any application that supports Active Scripting will accept scripts written in any scripting language supported by an Active scripting engine. Windows includes support for JavaScript and VBScript. Third-party scripting engines are available for Perl and LISP.

Code Signing

Code signing is a new technology that enables electronic signatures for code. This provides security from tampering of interactive applications across the net. Basically, the application vendors will provide a digital signature for their code that complies with the code signing specification. On the client side, when an application or component is downloaded from the net, it calls a Win32 API function called `WinVerifyTrust()`. This function checks the digital signature and verifies it.

HTML Extensions

Hypertext mark up language (HTML) is the language for all Web-based document production. In order to support ActiveX controls, extensions had to be made to the HTML language. In addition, Web browsers had to be modified to accommodate the new language extensions. Now you can add ActiveX controls to Web pages using the HTML `<OBJECT>` tag.

24

OVERVIEW OF
COM AND ACTIVE
TECHNOLOGIES

ActiveMovie

ActiveMovie is a new technology to replace the old Media Control Interface and Video for Windows. ActiveMovie is an audio- and video-streaming framework. With ActiveMovie, you will be able to play back MPEG, AVI, and Apple Quicktime movies.

Summary

In this chapter, you learned about Microsoft's component strategy, which consists of COM, OLE, and Active Technologies such as ActiveX.

COM is the Microsoft Component Object Model, which is the basic plumbing for all of Microsoft's component software strategy. COM includes features that enable components to be activated and used locally or remotely across a network. COM also provides for runtime discovery of a server's capabilities and lifetime management through the `IUnknown` interface.

OLE is the portion of Microsoft's component software strategy that enables applications to integrate document-like applications. Examples of applications that use OLE are Word, Excel, and Visio. OLE includes a number of technologies, such as drag and drop, embedding, and structured storage.

ActiveX controls are used in visual programming tools such as Visual C++ and Visual Basic, and enable programmers to create reusable software components that are easy to use. ActiveX controls can also be used to enhance Web pages when using browsers such as Internet Explorer.

Active Documents

*by Mark R. Wrenn
and Mickey Williams*

IN THIS CHAPTER

CHAPTER 25

Active documents are *Component Object Model* (*COM*) software components that present data and information to the user. Active documents enable users to view data in a variety of ways—perhaps as a graph, a spreadsheet, or text, depending on the purpose of the application. An Active document cannot work alone; it always requires an environment in which to work. The environment is called an *Active container.* Together, through an agreed-upon set of rules, the Active container and Active document work as one and give users the appearance of a single, homogeneous application.

If you look at an Active document running inside an Active container, you can visually identify each component. The Active document occupies the client area of the container and negotiates with the container for menu and toolbar space. The Active container is the frame that surrounds the client area. It shares its menu space and toolbar space with the document. Together, the Active container and Active document appear as a single application—but in fact, they are separate pieces of software that work together cooperatively. The only reason they work together is because each follows a well-documented set of rules or COM interfaces. COM is the foundation of all the *object linking and embedding* (OLE) and Active Technologies. This chapter requires at least an architectural understanding of COM and looks at some of the COM interfaces involved in writing an Active document, but certainly not all of the COM interfaces available. It is well worth your time to review COM and understand it. This chapter will help clarify and solidify your understanding of how Active documents work.

In addition to exploring the COM interfaces required to create an Active document, this chapter examines what has changed between OLE compound documents and Active documents, what MFCs have been added, and how you can use the Active Template Library to build an Active document. In passing, this chapter mentions Active document containers. For more information about Active document containers, see Chapter 26.

Just What Is an Active Document?

Active documents are an evolved form of OLE documents that originally were designed to enable users to view an OLE document inside a Web browser. In particular, Active documents are OLE embedded documents with the addition of four new COM interfaces: IOleDocument, IOleDocumentView, IOleCommandTarget, and IPrint. These new interfaces allow for a significant difference between OLE embedded documents and Active documents: Active documents occupy the entire client area of its container, whereas OLE embedded documents occupy a small, well-defined area. This ability to occupy the entire client area was added so that users browsing the Web with a tool such as Internet Explorer could click a hyperlink on a Web page and link directly to a Microsoft Word document, Microsoft Excel spreadsheet, or another application. To users, it appears as though the application data is just another Web page with perhaps more menu items and toolbars. This provides users with a positive and rich Internet experience.

Active documents first appeared with the release of Microsoft Office 95. Microsoft Office Binder is an Active container, and Microsoft Word and the other Office applications are Active documents. In fact, it is quite interesting to notice the following in the Visual C++ header DOCOBJ.H:

```
#define IMsoDocument            IOleDocument
#define IMsoView                IOleDocumentView
```

Clearly, the IOleDocument and IOleDocumentView interfaces began life as Microsoft Office (Mso) interfaces. Also, Active documents originally were referred to as *DocObjects*. You will notice API calls and interfaces that reference this name—for example, the MFC class CDocObjectServer.

Let's look a little more closely at the four new COM interfaces:

- IOleDocument is one of the new required interfaces. It allows the container to determine various attributes about the document, to enumerate the views that are supported, and to create specific views.

- IOleDocumentView is another required new interface. It is the interface the container uses to communicate with the view. Each view must support this interface in addition to existing OLE interfaces, such as IOleInPlaceObject and IOleInPlaceActiveObject.

- IOleCommandTarget is an optional interface. It allows the container to route commands that it doesn't handle to the document. The container also exposes this interface and allows the document to route commands to the container.

- IPrint is an optional interface. It allows the container to print the contents of the document and to specify to the document what to print and how to print it. This interface works with IContinueCallback which the container exposes. IContinueCallback allows the document to update the container on printing status and allows the container to cancel printing in progress.

Two MFC classes encapsulate the Active document interfaces: CDocObjectServer and CDocObjectServerItem. CDocObjectServer supports the IOleDocument, IOleDocumentView, IOleCommandTarget, and IPrint interfaces. CDocObjectServer is similar to what COleDocument does and replaces this class when you want to support Active documents. CDocObjectServerItem supports OLE server verbs required for Active documents. It derives from COleServerItem and overrides OnHide, OnOpen, and OnShow to implement Active document support. It replaces COleServerItem when you want to support Active documents.

Some Details About Active Documents

Active documents are the next step in OLE evolution; they are built on the foundation of OLE documents. In fact, an Active document can behave like an OLE document if the implementer chooses. Microsoft Word is a good example of this behavior. If you start Microsoft Excel, choose Insert Object, and insert Word into the spreadsheet, the Word document behaves like an embedded document server, as Figure 25.1 shows.

FIGURE 25.1

Microsoft Word as an embedded document inside Microsoft Excel.

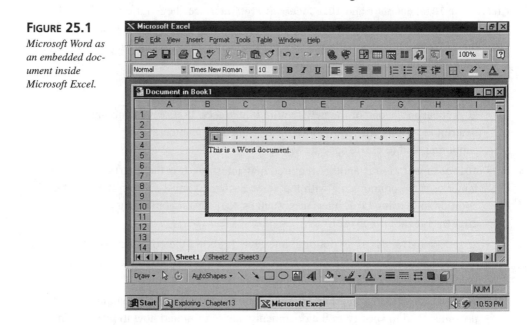

If you start Microsoft Binder and add a Word document to the Binder container, it behaves like an Active document. To determine whether a container supports the Active document specification, you can query it for support of the IOleDocumentSite interface. If the container supports this interface, the document server can behave like an Active document; otherwise, it should behave like an OLE document.

Because Active documents have an OLE heritage, this chapter spends some time discussing what it means to be an OLE document server. You can think of OLE document servers in two ways: as in-process servers or local servers and as miniservers or full servers. An in-process server can be a miniserver (usually) or a full server (with some care). A local server can be a miniserver (not very often) or a full server (usually).

An in-process server is essentially a *dynamic link library (DLL)*, which means that the OLE document server runs in the same address space as the container. Calls to the various OLE COM interfaces are no different than any other function calls within the container application. There is very little additional overhead when you call the OLE document server. For this reason, in-process servers are the most efficient and perform better than local servers.

A local server is essentially an executable. In this case, the OLE document server runs in another address space. Calls to the various OLE COM interfaces require special handling, called *marshaling*. Marshaling is the term for taking all the parameters to an OLE call, flattening them out, sending them over the process boundary, reassembling them on the other side, and calling the OLE interface in the server's address space. As you might imagine, this can be a rather tricky exercise. If you are passing a LONG as a parameter, it is fairly simple to move the data to another process. If you are moving a CMyObject* to another address space, though, how do you move the data successfully so that the OLE server in another address space can reference it? Fortunately, most of this is handled automatically by the COM remoting architecture. COM uses the Interface Definition Language (IDL) definitions to figure out how to marshal arguments—and, in fact, COM creates the necessary code to do all the work. The downside to this technique is that it is more expensive to make COM and OLE calls because of all the marshaling that takes place.

A miniserver is an OLE document server that only supports embedding. It cannot run as a standalone and depends on the container for its user interface and storage capabilities. A miniserver typically is implemented as an in-process server. Although there is no reason to create a miniserver as an EXE, because it is not meant to run as a standalone, it certainly is possible to do so.

A full server is an OLE document server that supports linking and embedding and can run as a standalone application. A full server typically is implemented as a local server. It is possible to write a full server as a DLL, but this would require another shell to load the DLL in standalone mode.

Active document servers are typically full servers. It is recommended that they run as standalone applications as well as Active document servers. If you create a new MFC OLE application, you will notice that on the wizard page used to specify OLE support, you can add Active document support only if the application is a full server (see Figure 25.2). It is possible to write an Active document server as an in-process server.

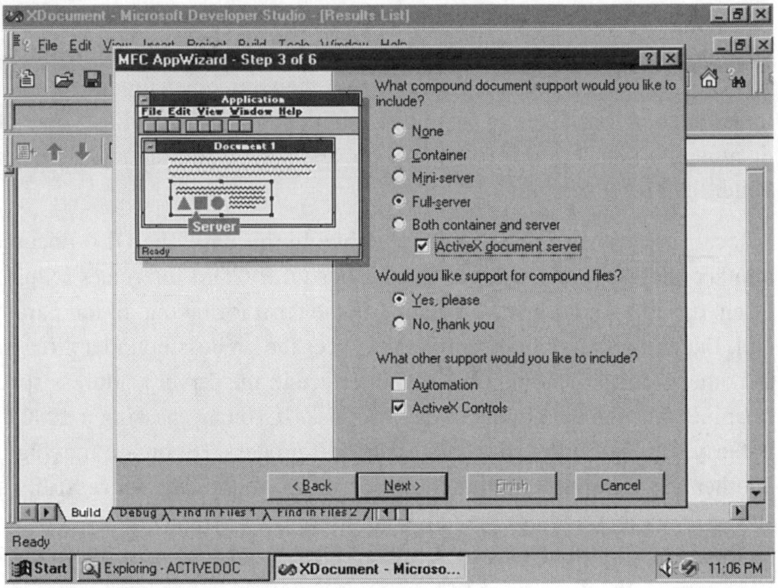

FIGURE 25.2

The MFC AppWizard dialog box for creating an Active document.

OLE document servers support linking, embedding, and in-place activation. Not all servers have to support these features. Active documents are both embedded and always in-place active. They do not support linking, though, so this chapter doesn't spend any time discussing OLE linking issues.

An embedded OLE document resides within part of a container and often exists with native container data, as well as other embedded documents. You can activate an embedded OLE document by double-clicking it or by right-clicking it and choosing Open from the context menu. OLE 1.0 specifies that when you open an embedded document, the native application starts and you can edit the document using the native tool. Figure 25.3 shows an embedded document open in its native application.

OLE 2.0 (now simply known as OLE) specifies that you also can open an embedded document within the context of the container. This action is called *in-place activation*. An Active document is always in-place active. In addition, it is the only embedded document in the container, and it occupies the entire client area.

OLE and Active document servers also have to support menu merging. When an OLE document is in-place active, it has the opportunity to merge any menus it has with the container's menus. This merging of menus is well-defined. OLE containers own and manage the File, Container, and Window menus. OLE documents own and manage the Edit, Object, and Help menus. Active documents must do some additional Help menu merging.

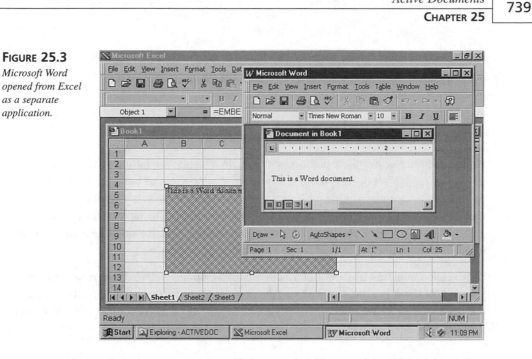

FIGURE 25.3

Microsoft Word opened from Excel as a separate application.

The drag-and-drop capability is supported optionally by OLE document servers. OLE drag-and-drop works through the use of `IDataObject`, `IDropSource`, and `IDropTarget`. `IDropSource` and `IDropTarget` track mouse movements and show appropriate user feedback. Ultimately, the target of a drop operation obtains the `IDataObject` pointer from the `IDropTarget` interface, and using Uniform Data Transfer, it obtains and manipulates the data through the `IDataObject` methods. The OLE Clipboard also is manipulated through the `IDataObject` methods.

OLE provides a means by which data from an OLE document server can be saved with data from the container and other OLE document servers into a single file. This technology is called *structured storage*. Through the use of the `IPersistStorage`, `IStorage`, and `IStream` interfaces, servers can store their data in a section of a single file. Structured storage makes a single file behave as if it were a file system, complete with hierarchical directories.

New to Active documents is the concept of *programmatic printing*. With the OLE document architecture, it is up to the container to print out its own data. A container can contain several embedded documents, none of which knows anything about the environment in which it is displayed—much less about other embedded documents that are also in the same container environment. It therefore would be impossible for an embedded document to control any aspect of printing. Only the container knows enough to control the printing. Active documents change this. Because the document occupies the entire client

25

ACTIVE DOCUMENTS

area, it knows about all the data and can have full control over how the data is printed. Active documents and containers do this by using the new IPrint and IContinueCallback interfaces.

The COM Interfaces

Active documents, like their predecessor OLE documents, are built on the foundation of COM. Through a set of well-defined interfaces, it is possible to build an Active document that can operate within any Active container without knowing anything more about the container than that it supports a set of COM interfaces. This architecture allows for a great deal of flexibility and enables you to combine these Active document components in ways perhaps not envisioned by the original programmers.

This section contains 10 COM interfaces that make up the Active document specification. Six of these interfaces are part of the original OLE document specification. Four of them are new to Active documents and are not found in OLE. Two of the new active document COM interfaces are optional: IPrint and IOleCommandTarget.

IOleObject

IOleObject is the largest of the interfaces used with OLE compound documents and Active documents. It provides the main interface for a container to communicate with an embedded object and is required if an object wants to support embedding. Table 25.1 describes the IOleObject interfaces.

TABLE 25.1   IOleObject Interfaces

Interface	Description
IUnknown Methods	
QueryInterface	Discovers required interfaces
AddRef	Adds a reference count to the object
Release	Decrements the reference count for the object and eventually deletes the object
IOleObject Methods	
SetClientSite	Provides a pointer to the container's client site object
GetClientSite	Obtains the pointer to the container's client site object
SetHostNames	Provides the names of the container application and container document
Close	Changes the state of the object from running to loaded
SetMoniker	Allows the container to tell the object about its moniker

GetMoniker	Obtains the object's moniker
InitFromData	Allows the object to initialize itself from an IDataObject interface
GetClipboardData	Obtains a current copy of the object in the form of an IDataObject interface
DoVerb	Requests an object to perform one of its actions
EnumVerbs	Enumerates the actions that an object supports
Update	Updates linked objects
IsUpToDate	Requests the object to check whether it is up to date
GetUserClassID	Returns the object's CLSID
GetUserType	Returns the object's displayable name
SetExtent	Allows the container to tell the object how much display space it has
GetExtent	Obtains the size of the object's display area
Advise	Creates a connection between the container and the document
Unadvise	Removes the connection between the container and the document
EnumAdvise	Enumerates the Advise connections
GetMiscStatus	Returns the status of the object
SetColorScheme	Tells the object what color scheme to use

IDataObject

IDataObject is the means by which data is transferred between COM and OLE objects. This technology is called *Uniform Data Transfer*. With IDataObject, data can be transferred using a particular format over a specific storage medium. It also is possible to advise others of changed data. Table 25.2 describes the IDataObject interfaces.

TABLE 25.2 IDataObject Interfaces

Interface	Description
	IUnknown *Methods*
QueryInterface	Discovers required interfaces
AddRef	Adds a reference count to the object
Release	Decrements the reference count for the object and eventually deletes the object

TABLE 25.2   continued

Interface	Description
	IDataObject *Methods*
GetData	Causes the source data object to render its data as described in a FORMATETC structure and transfers it through the STGMEDIUM structure
GetDataHere	Similar to GetData, except that it uses the storage structure allocated by the caller
QueryGetData	Asks the source data object whether it is capable of rendering its data as described in the FORMATETC structure
GetCanonicalFormatEtc	Returns a canonical FORMATETC based on an input FORMATETC
SetData	Sets the data of the object according to the FORMATETC and STGMEDIUM structures
EnumFormatEtc	Allows the caller to enumerate the data formats supported by the object
DAdvise	Allows the caller to be notified when data changes
DUnadvise	Removes a notification of data change
EnumDAdvise	Allows the caller to enumerate the advisory connection that has been set up

IPersistStorage

IPersistStorage provides a means for a container to pass a storage interface to an embedded object. The IPersistStorage interface uses structured storage and allows object data to be stored in its own area within the structured storage. Table 25.3 describes the IPersistStorage interfaces.

TABLE 25.3   IPersistStorage Interfaces

Interface	Description
	IUnknown *Methods*
QueryInterface	Discovers required interfaces
AddRef	Adds a reference count to the object
Release	Decrements the reference count for the object and eventually deletes the object
	IPersist *Method*
GetClassID	Returns the CLSID

Interface	Description
	IPersistStorage *Methods*
IsDirty	Allows the caller to determine whether the object has changed since it was last saved
InitNew	Initializes a new storage object and provides it with an IStorage interface
Load	Loads an object from storage
Save	Saves an object to storage
SaveCompleted	Notifies the object that it can write to its storage
HandsOffStorage	Notifies the object to release all storage objects

IPersistFile (Optional)

IPersistFile provides an interface that allows the object to store itself on the file system instead of in a structured storage object. Table 25.4 describes the IPersistFile interfaces.

TABLE 25.4   IPersistFile Interfaces

Interface	Description
	IUnknown *Methods*
QueryInterface	Discovers required interfaces
AddRef	Adds a reference count to the object
Release	Decrements the reference count for the object and eventually deletes the object
	IPersist *Method*
GetClassID	Returns the CLSID
	IPersistFile *Methods*
IsDirty	Allows the caller to determine whether the object has changed since it was last saved
Load	Loads an object from the specified file
Save	Saves the object to the specified file
SaveCompleted	Tells the object that the container has finished saving its data
GetCurFile	Obtains the name of the current file

IOleDocument

IOleDocument is one of the new COM interfaces that supports Active documents. It allows the container to discover what kind of views are supported by the document and to obtain pointers to those view interfaces. Table 25.5 describes the IOleDocument interfaces.

TABLE 25.5 IOleDocument Interfaces

Interface	Description
	IUnknown *Methods*
QueryInterface	Discovers required interfaces
AddRef	Adds a reference count to the object
Release	Decrements the reference count for the object and eventually deletes the object
	IOleDocument *Methods*
CreateView	Allows the container to request a view object from the document
GetDocMiscStatus	Returns miscellaneous status information about the document
EnumViews	Enumerates views that are supported by the document

IOleInPlaceObject

IOleInPlaceObject allows a container to activate and deactivate an in-place Active object. It also gives the container the opportunity to set the viewable area of the embedded object. Table 25.6 describes the IOleInPlaceObject interfaces.

TABLE 25.6 IOleInPlaceObject Interfaces

Interface	Description
	IUnknown *Methods*
QueryInterface	Discovers required interfaces
AddRef	Adds a reference count to the object
Release the object	Decrements the reference count for the object and eventually deletes
	IOleWindow *Methods*
GetWindow	Obtains a window handle
ContextSensitiveHelp	Determines whether context-sensitive help should be enabled

Interface	Description
	IOleInPlaceObject *Methods*
InPlaceDeactivate	Deactivates an in-place Active object
UIDeactivate	Deactivates and removes the user interface of the Active object
SetObjectRects	Indicates how much of the object is visible
ReactivateAndUndo	Reactivates the previously deactivated object

IOleInPlaceActiveObject

IOleInPlaceActiveObject provides a means for the embedded object to communicate with the container's frame and the container's document window. Table 25.7 describes the IOleInPlaceActiveObject interfaces.

TABLE 25.7   IOleInPlaceActiveObject Interfaces

Interface	Description
	IUnknown *Methods*
QueryInterface	Discovers required interfaces
AddRef	Adds a reference count to the object
Release	Decrements the reference count for the object and eventually deletes the object
	IOleWindow *Methods*
GetWindow	Obtains a window handle
ContextSensitiveHelp	Determines whether context-sensitive help should be enabled
	IOleInPlaceActiveObject *Methods*
TranslateAccelerator	Processes accelerator keys
OnFrameWindowActivate	Notifies the object when the container's top-level frame is activated
OnDocWindowActivate	Notifies the object when the container's document window is activated
ResizeBorder	Tells the object that it needs to resize its border space
EnableModeless	Enables or disables modeless dialog boxes

25

ACTIVE DOCUMENTS

IOleDocumentView

IOleDocumentView is another new COM interface that supports Active documents. It provides the means for a container to communicate with each of the Active document views. Table 25.8 describes the IOleDocumentView interfaces.

TABLE 25.8   IOleDocumentView Interfaces

Interface	Description
*IUnknown **Methods***	
QueryInterface	Discovers required interfaces
AddRef	Adds a reference count to the object
Release	Decrements the reference count for the object and eventually deletes the object
*IOleDocumentView **Methods***	
SetInPlaceSite	Gives the document a pointer to the container's view site
GetInPlaceSite	Gets the pointer to the document's view site
GetDocument	Gets the IUnknown pointer of the document
SetRect	Sets the rectangular coordinates of the view port
GetRect	Gets the rectangular coordinates of the view port
SetRectComplex	Sets the rectangular coordinates of the view port, scrollbars, and size box
Show	Asks the view to activate or deactivate itself
UIActivate	Asks the view to activate or deactivate its user interface
Open	Asks the view to open up in a separate window
Close	Asks the view to close itself
SaveViewState	Asks the view to save its state
ApplyViewState	Asks the view to initialize itself to a previously saved state
Clone	Asks the view to create a duplicate of itself

IPrint

IPrint is another new (and optional) Active document COM interface. It allows the container to communicate printing information to the document. Table 25.9 describes the IPrint interfaces.

TABLE 25.9   IPrint Interfaces

Interface	Description
	IUnknown *Methods*
QueryInterface	Discovers required interfaces
AddRef	Adds a reference count to the object
Release	Decrements the reference count for the object and eventually deletes the object
	IPrint *Methods*
SetInitialPageNum	Sets the page number of the first page
GetPageInfo	Gets the page number of the first page and the total number of pages
Print	Asks the document to print itself

IOleCommandTarget

IOleCommandTarget is an optional Active document COM interface. It provides a way for the container to pass on commands that it doesn't handle to the document. The reverse also is true; it provides a way for the document to pass on commands to the container. Table 25.10 describes the IOleCommandTarget interfaces.

TABLE 25.10   IOleCommandTarget Interfaces

Interface	Description
	IUnknown *Methods*
QueryInterface	Discovers required interfaces
AddRef	Adds a reference count to the object
Release	Decrements the reference count for the object and eventually deletes the object
	IOleCommandTarget *Methods*
QueryStatus	Asks the object for the status of one or more commands
Exec	Asks the object to execute a command

The Active Template Library

The *Active Template Library (ATL)* is a recent addition to the Visual C++ product. It came about primarily as a result of the explosive growth of the Internet and Microsoft's ActiveX strategy, which originally was developed to encourage the use of COM-based

components on the Internet and corporate intranets. In order for these controls to make sense in the Internet market, the controls have to be small and compact so that they can be downloaded from Web servers quickly. It certainly is possible to build these controls with MFC, but MFC applications are characteristically large and require large support DLLs. Another alternative to MFC was needed that could create smaller controls without the need for support DLLs. The ATL is the alternative Microsoft has provided.

ATL and MFC differ in their approaches. Both libraries rely on C++ capabilities, but that is where their similarities end. MFC is built on the concept of a class hierarchy. Most of the MFC classes derive from other classes, which eventually derive from CObject. This hierarchy allows classes to inherit many behaviors from their ancestors. As an example, consider the CButton class. It implements a handful of new methods but inherits a tremendous amount of behavior from the CWnd class. CWnd, in turn, inherits from CCmdTarget, which inherits from CObject. A strategy like this has a few interesting characteristics:

- The class hierarchy tends to be deep and therefore requires a lot of study to grasp.
- Application behavior is accomplished by inheriting from certain classes and overriding methods. This behavior creates a white-box effect and again requires a lot of study to understand how to integrate changes into any new derived classes.
- After you master the learning curve, you can quickly implement applications because so much behavior can be inherited.

> **Note**
>
> *White box* is an object-oriented design term that means you are able to see, and many times are required to see, the details of method implementations of classes that you inherit from. If you want to override the Add() methods of a linked list class, for example, you most likely will have to know how the linked list class implemented its internal structures in order to override the Add() method.
>
> *Black box* is just the opposite. The classes you use are completely opaque to you. You don't know how they are implemented and are able to manipulate the class only through its well-defined interfaces. COM interfaces fall into this category. COM exposes interfaces only and does not expose any internal implementation details.

ATL takes a different approach than MFC. It is based on the concept of a template. A template is a way of capturing an algorithm in the form of a pattern. For example, if you have a mathematical formula such as x + y + z that you want to implement for integers and floating-point numbers, you could create two classes:

```
class HighTechInteger
{
public:
   HighTechInteger();
   ~HighTechInteger();
   integer Calculate( int x, int y, int z ) { return( x+y+z ); }
};

class HighTechFloat
{
public:
   HighTechFloat();
   ~HighTechFloat();
   float Calculate( float x, float y, float z ) { return( x+y+z ); }
};
```

Notice how both implementations have identical algorithms for their `Calculate` methods. Given these classes, however, you could never use the `HighTechInteger` class to handle floating-point numbers. You must maintain two separate classes. This creates opportunities for bugs to be introduced if both classes are not kept in sync. The alternative is to create a template:

```
template <Type> class HighTech
{
public:
   HighTech();
   ~HighTech();
   Type Calculate( Type x, Type y, Type z ) { return( x+y+z ); }
};

HighTech<int>    htInteger;
HighTech<float>  htFloat;
```

Notice how this unifies the source code base and increases code reliability because the algorithm is implemented only once.

Another feature of C++ that ATL uses is multiple inheritance. C++ allows one class to inherit from several parent classes. Grady Booch, in his book *Object-Oriented Analysis and Design with Applications* (Addison-Wesley, 1998), describes special lightweight classes designed for multiple inheritance as *mixin classes*. C++ multiple inheritance can be used in many ways, but classes designed for the mixin approach typically are thin, focused, and easily reusable. Let's consider a mixin scenario:

25

ACTIVE
DOCUMENTS

```
class subtractMixin
{
public:
    int Sub( int x, int y );
};

class MyCoolClass : public CoolBaseClass
{
public:
    int Add( int x, int y );
};
class MyFriendsClass : public CoolBaseClass
{
public:
    int Mult( int x, int y );
}
```

Suppose that the subtractMixin class is a useful, reusable algorithm that can be used in a variety of situations—it can be mixed in with many different classes. One way to implement this kind of feature would be as a separate class that could be inherited from to obtain the desired behavior. This class would be considered a mixin class. Mixin classes do not necessarily provide usefulness by themselves but are useful as additive behaviors. Now suppose that you want your MyCoolClass to have the capability to sub-tract as well as add. You could define another method in the MyCoolClass class or just inherit the behavior from subtractMixin:

```
class MyCoolClass : public CoolBaseClass, public subtractMixin
{
public:
    int Add( int x, int y );
};
```

In addition, you could add subtract behavior to MyFriendsClass or any other class by inheriting from subtractMixin. It is not very useful to create an instance of subtractMixin by itself, however.

ATL uses both the template concept and the mixin concept. Because many of the COM interfaces are small and clean, they lend themselves to being used as mixin classes. The ATL strategy has these characteristics:

- There is no large class hierarchy to learn, but there are a number of mixin classes to learn.

- Application behavior is accomplished by inheriting from the required number of mixin classes. This approach tends to be more *black box,* although not necessarily.

- It takes more effort to implement the application. Unlike MFC applications, which inherit a great deal of behavior, ATL applications inherit only the necessities and must implement the rest manually.

- ATL applications are smaller than MFC applications as a result of shallow class hierarchies.

ATL is discussed in more detail in Part VII, "Using the Active Template Library."

ATL Classes Required for Active Document Support

The following list provides an overview of some of the ATL classes you will see in the ACTIVEDOC sample program:

- `CComObjectRoot` is a typedef of `CComObjectRootEx`. All ATL classes must inherit from this class. This class provides support for all the `IUnknown` interfaces and maintains the COM object's reference counts. It also determines whether the object supports single or multiple threading.

- `CComCoClass` is used to obtain CLSID and error information, and determines the default class factory. All classes that must be visible externally should inherit from this class.

- `CComControl` provides a number of useful functions for implementing ActiveX controls.

- `IDispatchImpl` provides an implementation of `IDispatch`.

- `IProvideClassInfo2Impl` provides type library information.

- `IPersistStreamInitImpl` provides a means of storing application data in a single storage stream.

- `IPersistStorageImpl` provides a means of asking the object to save and load itself from a storage object.

- `IQuickActivateImpl` provides a means for a container to ask for all the interfaces an object supports all at once.

- `IOleControlImpl` provides an implementation of `IOleControl`.

- `IOleObjectImpl` provides an implementation of `IOleObject`.

- `IOleInPlaceActiveObjectImpl` provides an implementation of `IOleInPlaceActiveObject`.

- `IViewObjectExImpl` provides implementations of `IViewObject`, `IViewObject2`, and `IViewObjectEx`.

- `IOleInPlaceObjectWindowlessImpl` provides an implementation of `IOleInPlaceObject` and `IOleInPlaceObjectWindowless`.

- `IDataObjectImpl` provides an implementation of `IDataObject`.

- `ISupportErrorInfo` defines a means by which the application can return error information to the container.

The ACTIVEDOC Program

Let's look at some code to understand how ATL can be used to create an Active document. You will be looking at a sample program called ACTIVEDOC located on the MSDN CD-ROM included with Visual C++ 6. To install the ACTIVEDOC sample on your hard drive, search for the ACTIVEDOC sample and follow the instructions on the sample page. We will focus on specific areas of this sample code to see how an ATL application is built.

This example builds an in-process Active document around the `RichEdit` control. The majority of the code is actually in the `RichEdit` control. The ACTIVEDOC program wraps an Active document layer around the control and provides a unique opportunity to focus on ATL issues without being distracted by all the other issues an application normally has to worry about. In particular, you will look closely at the declaration of the `CActiveDoc` class and will notice how COM support easily is added through the mixin concept. You also will look at how to add support for the new `IOleDocument` and `IOleDocumentView` COM interfaces. After this example is built, it can be run inside Microsoft Binder or Microsoft Internet Explorer. Figure 25.4 illustrates the ACTIVE-DOC program inside Microsoft Binder.

FIGURE 25.4

The ACTIVEDOC program inside Microsoft Binder.

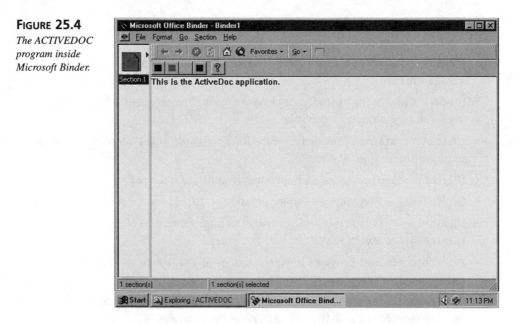

Nineteen files are located in the ACTIVEDOC directory. Table 25.11 briefly describes these files.

TABLE 25.11 Files Located in the ACTIVEDOC Directory

Filename	*Description*
toolbar.bmp	Bitmap used for the (guess what?) toolbar.
activedoc.mak	The Visual C++ makefile.
activectl.cpp	Some implementation code for CActiveDoc.
activedoc.cpp	Contains all the DLL entry points.
stdafx.cpp	Contains the precompiled headers.
activedoc.def	DEF table for the DLL exports.
activectl.h	Defines the CActiveDoc interfaces and most of the implementation.
menu.h	Defines the CMenu class and its implementation. This class is used to negotiate menus with the container.
oledocument.h	Defines two new template classes: IOleDocumentImpl and IOleDocumentViewImpl.
resource.h	Standard Visual C++ resource defines.
stdafx.h	Precompiled header file.
toolbar.h	Defines the CToolbar class and its implementation. This class is used to negotiate toolbars with the container.
activedoc.idl	IDL source for the ActiveDoc class.
activedoc.htm	Web page that demonstrates this Active document used with Internet Explorer.
activedoc.dsp	A Visual C++ 6.0 project file.
activedoc.dsw	A Visual C++ 6.0 workspace file.
activedoc.rc	Definition of the resources.
activedoc.rgs	Registry script file for ACTIVEDOC.
activedoc.txt	Description of the project.

We will focus on two key files in this project: activectl.h and oledocument.h. These files contain the majority of the code that we will be interested in. We also will review some other files as we encounter them.

25

ACTIVE DOCUMENTS

activectl.h

This file contains the definition of the CActiveDoc class and most of the implementation code. CActiveDoc is the class that implements all the support for Active documents. As we step through this header, we will discuss the important features of the CActiveDoc class.

The following code is from the beginning of activectl.h and shows the include files required by CActiveDoc. The first file, resource.h, is the standard header file that is generated by Visual C++ when dialog boxes or other resources are added to the project. It contains all the defines necessary for these resources. OleDocument.h is the header file that defines and implements two new classes: IOleDocumentImpl and IOleDocumentViewImpl. You will look more closely at this file later. Menu.h and toolbar.h provide definitions for CMenu and CToolbar. RichEdit.h is the standard header file that describes the RichEdit control.

```
// ActiveCtl.h : Declaration of the CActiveDoc class

#include "resource.h"        // main symbols
#include "OleDocument.h"
#include "Menu.h"
#include "ToolBar.h"
#include <RichEdit.h>
```

Next is the definition of the CActiveDoc class interface. Let's look at the inheritance that the class uses. Notice, as mentioned earlier, that CActiveDoc is defined through multiple inheritance, or mixins. If you want to add or remove functionality from CActiveDoc, you add or remove a class from which it inherits. Most of the classes that CActiveDoc inherits from are in fact OLE interfaces. Other required classes that CActiveDoc inherits from are CComObjectRoot and CComCoClass. Both these classes are required. Finally, CActiveDoc inherits from two new classes: IOleDocumentImpl and IOleDocumentViewImpl. These new classes are not part of the ATL library but are defined in the oledocument.h file.

For your information, CLSID_CActiveDoc is the unique COM identifier for CActiveDoc. It is defined in activedoc.h. IID_IActiveDoc is the unique COM interface identifier for ActiveDoc. It also is defined in activedoc.h. Most of the implementation templates—those that have Impl at the end of their name—use CActiveDoc as the parameter to the template. This provides a connection between the template classes and the Active document class that you are building. This declaration of CActiveDoc indicates that CActiveDoc supports all the COM interfaces in the inheritance list.

```
///////////////////////////////////////////////////////////////////////////
// CActiveDoc
class CActiveDoc :
      public CComObjectRoot,
      public CComCoClass<CActiveDoc, &CLSID_CActiveDoc>,
      public CComControl<CActiveDoc>,
      public IDispatchImpl<IActiveDoc, &IID_IActiveDoc, &LIBID_ACTIVEDOCLib>,
      public IProvideClassInfo2Impl<&CLSID_CActiveDoc, NULL,
                                    &LIBID_ACTIVEDOCLib>,
      public IPersistStreamInitImpl<CActiveDoc>,
      public IPersistStorageImpl<CActiveDoc>,
      public IQuickActivateImpl<CActiveDoc>,
      public IOleControlImpl<CActiveDoc>,
      public IOleObjectImpl<CActiveDoc>,
      public IOleInPlaceActiveObjectImpl<CActiveDoc>,
      public IViewObjectExImpl<CActiveDoc>,
      public IOleInPlaceObjectWindowlessImpl<CActiveDoc>,
      public IDataObjectImpl<CActiveDoc>,
      public ISupportErrorInfo,
      public IOleDocumentImpl<CActiveDoc>,
      public IOleDocumentViewImpl<CActiveDoc>,
      public CMenu<CActiveDoc>,
      public CToolbar<CActiveDoc>
```

Take a look at the next section of the CActiveDoc declaration and implementation:

```
{
public:
    CActiveDoc() : m_wndRTF(_T("RichEdit"), this, 1)
    {
        m_wndRTF.m_hWnd = NULL;
        m_bWindowOnly = TRUE;
    }
```

The class declaration begins with the constructor CActiveDoc(), a part of which is an initialization of m_wndRTF. If you look at the very end of the class declaration, you will notice that m_wndRTF is declared as CContainedWindow. CContainedWindow allows you to either superclass or subclass an existing control. In addition, it connects the existing control to the class that contains it. In our example, CActiveDoc is being declared as a superclass of a RichEdit control. m_wndRTF will provide the connection between the RichEdit control and CActiveDoc. All the message handling for the control will be routed through the CActiveDoc class message maps.

In the next section, you encounter the DECLARE_REGISTRY_RESOURCEID macro:

```
DECLARE_REGISTRY_RESOURCEID(IDR_ActiveDoc)
```

This macro is defined in atlcom.h:

```
#define DECLARE_REGISTRY_RESOURCEID(x)\
```

25

ACTIVE DOCUMENTS

```
static HRESULT WINAPI UpdateRegistry(BOOL bRegister)\
{\
return _Module.UpdateRegistryFromResource(x, bRegister);\
}
```

This macro declares a static method called `UpdateRegistry`. The purpose of this method is to add or remove the required Registry entries for the Active document. The ATL Object Wizard generates a *Registry script* (*RGS*) file. The RGS file is a specially encoded file that describes, in Backus-Nauer form, the required Registry entries to operate the Active document. The RGS file for this project follows:

```
HKCR
{
    ActiveDoc.ActiveDoc.1 = s 'ActiveDoc Class'
    {
        CLSID = s '{93901785-436B-11D0-B965-000000000000}'
    }
    ActiveDoc.ActiveDoc = s 'ActiveDoc Class'
    {

        CurVer = s 'ActiveDoc.ActiveDoc.1'
    }
    NoRemove CLSID
    {
        ForceRemove {93901785-436B-11D0-B965-000000000000} =
➡s 'ActiveDoc Class'
        {
            ProgID = s 'ActiveDoc.ActiveDoc.1'
            VersionIndependentProgID = s 'ActiveDoc.ActiveDoc'
            InprocServer32 = s '%MODULE%'
            {
                val ThreadingModel = s 'Apartment'
            }
            ForceRemove 'Control'
            'DocObject' = s '8'
            ForceRemove 'Programmable'
            ForceRemove 'Insertable'
            ForceRemove 'ToolboxBitmap32' = s '%MODULE%, 1'
            'MiscStatus' = s '0'
            {
                '1' = s '131473'
            }
            'TypeLib' = s '{93901783-436B-11D0-B965-000000000000}'
            'Version' = s '1.0'
        }
    }
}
```

We won't discuss the syntax of the RGS file in this chapter, but you might recognize some familiar text that is part of this file. The name of the Active document is `ActiveDoc`

Class, for example. You can see what its CLSID is. Notice the familiar Registry keywords, such as ProgID, InprocServer32, and Insertable. Fortunately, you don't have to write any code to read this file. A special routine is included as part of the ATL that knows how to read this file and make the appropriate Registry entries. This special routine is invoked when UpdateRegistry is called.

Following the DECLARE_REGISTRY_RESOURCEID macro are several macros enclosed by BEGIN_COM_MAP and END_COM_MAP.

```
BEGIN_COM_MAP(CActiveDoc)

    COM_INTERFACE_ENTRY(IActiveDoc)
    COM_INTERFACE_ENTRY(IDispatch)
    COM_INTERFACE_ENTRY_IMPL(IViewObjectEx)
    COM_INTERFACE_ENTRY_IMPL_IID(IID_IViewObject2, IViewObjectEx)
    COM_INTERFACE_ENTRY_IMPL_IID(IID_IViewObject, IViewObjectEx)
    COM_INTERFACE_ENTRY_IMPL(IOleInPlaceObjectWindowless)
    COM_INTERFACE_ENTRY_IMPL_IID(IID_IOleInPlaceObject,
                                 IOleInPlaceObjectWindowless)
    COM_INTERFACE_ENTRY_IMPL_IID(IID_IOleWindow,
                                 IOleInPlaceObjectWindowless)
    COM_INTERFACE_ENTRY_IMPL(IOleInPlaceActiveObject)
    COM_INTERFACE_ENTRY_IMPL(IOleControl)
    COM_INTERFACE_ENTRY_IMPL(IOleObject)
    COM_INTERFACE_ENTRY_IMPL(IQuickActivate)
    COM_INTERFACE_ENTRY_IMPL(IPersistStorage)
    COM_INTERFACE_ENTRY_IMPL(IPersistStreamInit)
    COM_INTERFACE_ENTRY_IMPL(IDataObject)
    COM_INTERFACE_ENTRY_IMPL(IOleDocument)
    COM_INTERFACE_ENTRY_IMPL(IOleDocumentView)
    COM_INTERFACE_ENTRY(IProvideClassInfo)
    COM_INTERFACE_ENTRY(IProvideClassInfo2)
    COM_INTERFACE_ENTRY(ISupportErrorInfo)
END_COM_MAP()
```

These macros create a COM interface map similar to the message maps used in MFC. The macros create a way for the QueryInterface call to determine whether this COM object supports a specific COM interface, and they provide a mapping to the classes that implement the specified interface. The macros used in the COM interface map are located in atlcom.h and are defined as the following:

```
#define COM_INTERFACE_ENTRY(x)\
    {&IID_##x, \
    offsetofclass(x, _ComMapClass), \
    _ATL_SIMPLEMAPENTRY},

#define COM_INTERFACE_ENTRY_IID(iid, x)\
    {&iid,\
```

25

ACTIVE DOCUMENTS

```
    offsetofclass(x, _ComMapClass),\
    _ATL_SIMPLEMAPENTRY},

#define COM_INTERFACE_ENTRY_IMPL(x)\
    COM_INTERFACE_ENTRY_IID(IID_##x, x##Impl<_ComMapClass>)

#define COM_INTERFACE_ENTRY_IMPL_IID(iid, x)\
    COM_INTERFACE_ENTRY_IID(iid, x##Impl<_ComMapClass>)
```

These macros provide two ways of mapping an interface ID (IID) to a class method.
COM_INTERFACE_ENTRY generates the IID for you by concatenating the string IID_ with
the parameter that you supply. COM_INTERFACE_ENTRY_IID allows you to specify the IID
yourself. COM_INTERFACE_ENTRY_IMPL and COM_INTERFACE_ENTRY_IMPL_IID are similar
but map to templatized versions of interfaces.

The next section of activectl.h contains the macros BEGIN_PROPERTY_MAP and
END_PROPERTY_MAP. These macros are used to define properties for Active controls.

```
BEGIN_PROPERTY_MAP(CActiveDoc)
    // PROP_ENTRY("Description", dispid, clsid)
END_PROPERTY_MAP()
```

Next is a section that begins with BEGIN_MSG_MAP and END_MSG_MAP:

```
BEGIN_MSG_MAP(CActiveDoc)
    MESSAGE_HANDLER(WM_PAINT, OnPaint)
    MESSAGE_HANDLER(WM_GETDLGCODE, OnGetDlgCode)
    MESSAGE_HANDLER(WM_SETFOCUS, OnSetFocus)
    MESSAGE_HANDLER(WM_KILLFOCUS, OnKillFocus)
    MESSAGE_HANDLER(WM_CREATE, OnCreate)
    MESSAGE_HANDLER(WM_DESTROY, OnDestroy)
    MESSAGE_HANDLER(WM_ERASEBKGND, OnEraseBackgnd)
    COMMAND_RANGE_HANDLER(ID_BLACK, ID_BLUE, OnColorChange)
    COMMAND_ID_HANDLER(ID_HELP_ABOUT, OnHelpAbout)
    NOTIFY_CODE_HANDLER(TTN_NEEDTEXT, OnToolbarNeedText)

    ALT_MSG_MAP(1)
//    MESSAGE_HANDLER(WM_CHAR, OnChar)
//    END_MSG_MAP()
END_MSG_MAP()
```

These macros are very similar to the message maps in MFC. They create a mapping
between a Windows message and a method that supports the message.

Next are some macros that define the toolbar that is part of this Active document:

```
BEGIN_TOOLBAR_MAP(CActiveDoc)
    TOOLBAR_BUTTON(ID_BLACK)
    TOOLBAR_BUTTON(ID_RED)
    TOOLBAR_BUTTON(ID_GREEN)
```

```
    TOOLBAR_BUTTON(ID_BLUE)
    TOOLBAR_SEPARATOR()
    TOOLBAR_BUTTON(ID_HELP_ABOUT)
END_TOOLBAR_MAP()
```

As official-looking as these macros are, they are not part of ATL. The definition of these macros is located in toolbar.h:

```
#define BEGIN_TOOLBAR_MAP(x) public: \
    const static int* _GetToolbarEntries(int& nButtons) { \
    static const int _entries[] = {
#define TOOLBAR_BUTTON(x) x,
#define TOOLBAR_SEPARATOR()     ID_SEP,
#define END_TOOLBAR_MAP() }; nButtons =
➥sizeof(_entries)/sizeof(int); return _entries; }
```

These macros create an array of toolbar IDs and a method called GetToolbarEntries, which returns the number of buttons and a pointer to the entry array.

The rest of activectl.h deals with the implementation of specific COM methods. As you examine this code, you will notice that each COM method uses the STDMETHOD macro. This macro is used to describe the standard calling conventions that all COM interfaces must follow. STDMETHOD is defined as the following, where STDMETHODCALLTYPE is defined as _stdcall:

```
#define STDMETHOD(method) virtual HRESULT STDMETHODCALLTYPE method
```

The rest of activectl.h provides an inline implementation of the code. Only five inherited methods are overridden: IOleInPlaceActiveObjectImpl::OnDocWindowActive, IPersistStorageImpl::IsDirty, IPersistStreamInitImp::Save, IPersistStreamInitImp::Load, and IOleInPlaceObjectWindowlessImpl::SetObjectRects. We will not discuss the details of these methods. However, note that because only five methods have been overridden, the rest of the COM support is inherited as-is from the ATL base classes.

To summarize, several pieces of code in activectl.h provide the framework for Active document support. First, the CActiveDoc class inherits from a number of required COM interface classes. Second, the Registry must be configured with correct entries so that Active document containers will know how to load and run the Active document. Third, the Active document interfaces have to be exposed through the QueryInterface method. Much of this is done by using the various COM INTERFACE macros to map an interface with an implementation of the interface. Again, many of these interfaces are inherited from base classes. Fourth, methods that require changing or enhancing have to be overridden.

oledocument.h

This file contains a templatized form of the definitions and implementations of the
IOleDocument and IOleDocumentView COM interfaces. Support for these interfaces is
not provided as part of the ATL. You could use this header file in your own application to
provide support for the IOleDocument and IOleDocumentView interfaces. The implementation of these interfaces supports only one view object, however. If your project requires
more than one view, you will need to enhance these classes.

IOleDocumentImpl implements the IOleDocument methods CreateView,
GetDocMiscStatus, and EnumViews.

LISTING 25.1   IOleDocumentImpl

```
#include <docobj.h>

///////////////////////////////////////////////////////////////////////////////
// IOleDocumentImpl
template <class T>
class ATL_NO_VTABLE IOleDocumentImpl
{
public:
    // IUnknown
    //
    STDMETHOD(QueryInterface)(REFIID riid, void ** ppvObject) = 0;
    _ATL_DEBUG_ADDREF_RELEASE_IMPL(IOleControlImpl)

    // IOleDocument methods
    //
    STDMETHOD(CreateView)(IOleInPlaceSite *pIPSite, IStream *pstm, DWORD /*
dwReserved */,
        IOleDocumentView **ppView)
    {
        ATLTRACE(_T("IOleDocument::CreateView\n"));
        T* pT = static_cast<T*>(this);

        if (ppView == NULL)
            return E_POINTER;

        // If we've already created a view then we can't create another as we
        // currently only support the ability to create one view
        if (pT->m_spInPlaceSite != NULL)
            return E_FAIL;

        IOleDocumentView* pView;
        pT->_InternalQueryInterface(IID_IOleDocumentView, (void**)&pView);
        // If we support IOleDocument we should support IOleDocumentView
        _ASSERTE(pView != NULL);
```

```
        // If they've given us a site then use it
        if (pIPSite != NULL)
            pView->SetInPlaceSite(pIPSite);

        // If they have given us an IStream pointer then use it to initialize
the view
        if (pstm != NULL)
        {
            pView->ApplyViewState(pstm);
        }

        // Return the view
        *ppView = pView;

        return S_OK;
    }
    STDMETHOD(GetDocMiscStatus)(DWORD *pdwStatus)
    {
        ATLTRACE(_T("IOleDocument::GetDocMiscStatus\n"));
        *pdwStatus = DOCMISC_NOFILESUPPORT;
        return S_OK;
    }
    STDMETHOD(EnumViews)(IEnumOleDocumentViews** /*ppEnum*/, IOleDocumentView
➥ppView)
    {
        ATLTRACE(_T("IOleDocument::EnumViews\n"));
        T* pT = static_cast<T*>(this);

        if (ppView == NULL)
            return E_POINTER;

        // We only support one view
        pT->_InternalQueryInterface(IID_IOleDocumentView, (void**)ppView);
        return S_OK;
    }
};
```

Notice that the preceding implementation of EnumViews has only one pointer to a view interface: ppView. As a result, this implementation of IOleDocument supports only one instance of a view. It certainly is possible to support more than one, but to do this, you have to extend these template classes.

Besides doing some error checking, CreateView does two basic things: It accepts an IOleInPlaceSite pointer if one is provided, and it returns a pointer to its only view. To obtain the view interface pointer, it calls its own InternalQueryInterface routine.

GetDocMiscStatus is called by the container to determine what kind of support is provided by the object. This implementation of IOleDocument returns DOCMISC_NOFILESUPPORT. This tells the container that this object does not support reading and writing to files. Table 25.12 lists other possible status values.

TABLE 25.12 DOCMISC Status Values

Name	This Object...
DOCMISC_CANCREATEMULTIPLEVIEWS	Can support more than one view.
DOCMISC_SUPPORTCOMPLEXRECTANGLES	Can support complex rectangles and requires the object to support IOleDocumentView::SetRectComplex.
DOCMISC_CANTOPENEDIT	Supports activation in a separate window.
DOCMISC_NOFILESUPPORT	Does not support reading and writing to a file.

Because this object supports only one view, EnumViews returns a pointer to its IOleDocumentView interface.

IOleDocumentViewImpl implements the IOleDocumentView methods: SetInPlaceSite, GetInPlaceSite, GetDocument, SetRect, GetRect, SetRectComplex, Show, UIActivate, Open, CloseView, SaveViewState, ApplyViewState, and Clone.

SetRectComplex, Open, SaveViewState, ApplyViewState, and Clone are not implemented by this version of the IOleDocumentView interface. The rest of the methods are fairly straightforward, with the exception of ActiveXDocActive, which is a helper method of this class that does most of the work of activating the Active document. The tasks that ActiveXDocActive performs are the standard sequence of events that any Active document must follow in order to activate itself inside an Active container. Let's look more closely at this method.

The first item this method takes care of is to make sure that the Active document is in-place active:

```
if (!pT->m_bInPlaceActive)
{
    BOOL bNoRedraw = FALSE;
    hr = pT->m_spInPlaceSite->CanInPlaceActivate();
    if (FAILED(hr))
        return hr;
    pT->m_spInPlaceSite->OnInPlaceActivate();
}
pT->m_bInPlaceActive = TRUE;
```

Next, this method obtains the location of the in-place active window inside the container. It ensures that the Active document window is visible—creating itself, if necessary—and remembers the rectangles by calling the `SetObjectRects` method.

```
if (pT->m_spInPlaceSite->GetWindow(&hwndParent) == S_OK)
{
    pT->m_spInPlaceSite->GetWindowContext(&spInPlaceFrame,
        &spInPlaceUIWindow, &rcPos, &rcClip, &frameInfo);

    if (!pT->m_bWndLess)
    {
        if (pT->m_hWnd)
        {
            ::ShowWindow(pT->m_hWnd, SW_SHOW);
            pT->SetFocus();
        }
        else
            pT->m_hWnd = pT->Create(hwndParent, rcPos);
    }
    pT->SetObjectRects(&rcPos, &rcClip);
}
```

After making itself visible, the method goes on to make itself `UIActive` by calling the `IOleInPlaceSite`'s `OnUIActivate()` method. After that, it synchronizes the `IOleInPlaceFrame` and `IOleInPlaceUIWindow` interfaces by calling their `SetActiveObject()` and `SetBorderSpace()` methods.

```
CComPtr<IOleInPlaceActiveObject> spActiveObject;
QueryInterface(IID_IOleInPlaceActiveObject, (void**)&spActiveObject);

// Gone active by now, take care of UIACTIVATE
if (pT->DoesVerbUIActivate(iVerb))
{
    if (!pT->m_bUIActive)
    {
        pT->m_bUIActive = TRUE;
        hr = pT->m_spInPlaceSite->OnUIActivate();
        if (FAILED(hr))
            return hr;

        pT->SetControlFocus(TRUE);
        // set ourselves up in the host.
        //
        if (spActiveObject)
        {
            if (spInPlaceFrame)
                spInPlaceFrame->SetActiveObject(spActiveObject, NULL);
            if (spInPlaceUIWindow)
                spInPlaceUIWindow->SetActiveObject(spActiveObject, NULL);
        }
```

25

ACTIVE DOCUMENTS

```
        if (spInPlaceFrame)
            spInPlaceFrame->SetBorderSpace(NULL);
        if (spInPlaceUIWindow)
            spInPlaceUIWindow->SetBorderSpace(NULL);
    }
}
```

Finally, the method merges its own menus with the container's menus and tells the container to position the Active document so that it is viewable to the user by calling the `ShowObject()` method of the `IOleClientSite` interface.

```
// Merge the menus
pT->InPlaceMenuCreate(spInPlaceFrame);
pT->m_spClientSite->ShowObject();
return S_OK;
```

In summary, `activectl.h` and `oledocument.h` provide most of the support for Active documents. The `CActiveDoc` class inherits most of its behavior, whereas `oledocument.h` was written specifically for the ACTIVEDOC sample from scratch and provides support for `IOleDocument` and `IOleDocumentView`. When you write your own Active document using the ATL, you need to implement code that is very similar to the `CActiveDoc` class. You also might want to borrow and enhance the `IOleDocument` and `IOleDocumentView` support found in `oledocument.h`.

activedoc.htm

The final file this chapter discusses is `activedoc.htm`. This file deserves an honorary mention, even though it is very straightforward. This file is an HTML file that (with some minor editing) enables users to view an Active document inside Internet Explorer. If you have Internet Explorer installed on your machine and you double-click this file, you will see the window shown in Figure 25.5.

This HTML file demonstrates how you can implement a very lightweight Active document object and include it in your Web pages. The key to activating the Active document object is the `OBJECT` HTML keyword. Using the CLSID supplied as part of this keyword, Internet Explorer can look up the object in the Registry. Having found the object in the Registry, Internet Explorer can discover that the object supports the Active document interface and interact with it as an Active container. Edit the `activedoc.htm` file so that it contains the source code shown in Listing 25.2.

FIGURE 25.5

The sample ACTIVEDOC program inside Internet Explorer.

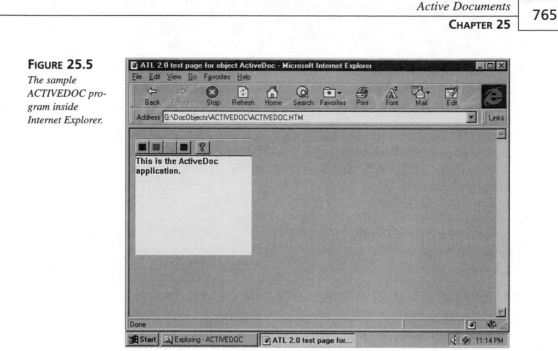

LISTING 25.2   A Test Page for the ACTIVEDOC Project

```
<HTML>
<HEAD>
<TITLE>ATL 2.0 test page for object ActiveDoc</TITLE>
</HEAD>
<BODY>
<OBJECT ID="ActiveDoc" <
 CLASSID="CLSID:93901785-436B-11D0-B965-000000000000">
>
</OBJECT>
</BODY>
</HTML>
```

Summary

In this chapter, you began to explore Active documents. Active documents owe much to their OLE document heritage. They share many of the same COM interfaces and add a few new ones of their own.

You can implement an Active document in a number of ways. You can use native COM APIs and do most of the work yourself. You can use MFC. This, in fact, is the easiest tool to use. However, MFC applications tend to be large and for that reason are not suited to downloading over the Internet. Finally, you can use the recent ATL, as you saw in the Microsoft sample program ACTIVEDOC. With ATL, you can build smaller executables, but you will have to do a little more work.

25

ACTIVE
DOCUMENTS

Active Containers

by Mark R. Wrenn
and Mickey Williams

CHAPTER 26

Active document containers are the environment through which the end user controls and manipulates the appearance of data. Containers, through their menus, provide a means for the user to view data differently, change data formats, insert new data, and so on. Containers also allow the user to change the viewable size of the data by manipulating the frame and add toolbars and other "decorations" to the window frame.

This control and manipulation of the data does not usually take place unilaterally on the part of the container. Typically, it requires an interaction between the container and the active document server responsible for the data.

This chapter specifically explores the active document container side of the interaction, although it will be impossible to ignore the active document server side. You'll learn what has changed between OLE containers and active document containers, which COM interfaces have to be supported, and how to use MFC classes to easily create active document containers. You can find more details about active documents in Chapter 25, "Active Documents."

Just What Is an Active Document Container?

What an exciting industry to work in! Just when you think you have it all figured out, it seems as though everything changes. It wasn't that long ago when Microsoft was all jazzed about compound documents—the capability for the user to combine graphics, text, and data in one document. Now, with ActiveX and other Active technologies, it appears as though this has all gone away and everything is suddenly enabled for the Internet and intranets! Not to worry: Everything you know about OLE technology still applies. It's just been extended to cover new opportunities. As this chapter unfolds, you will see how existing OLE container support has been enhanced with new COM interfaces and how MFCs have been extended to support these interfaces. If you're new to COM, OLE, and ActiveX, you're in the right place. You'll find all the information you need to understand how active document containers work.

So what is an active document container? The short answer is that an active document container is an OLE container with some new COM interfaces—in particular, `IOleCommandTarget`, `IOleDocumentSite`, and `IContinueCallback`. These new interfaces have been added to support corresponding new interfaces in active documents. These interfaces first appeared in the Microsoft Office Binder application. Binder, as well as Internet Explorer, are active document containers. Active documents differ from OLE embedded documents in that they occupy the entire client area of the container and control more of the menu. To the user, the active document container appears to be the native application frame window. If you create a new Binder document and insert a Word document, an Excel spreadsheet, or a PowerPoint presentation, you notice that as you click each component of the binder that the user interface changes and the menus and toolbars appear as they would in the native application. This capability of the container to take on the appearance of any native application is what active document containers are all about. They allow the Binder application to bind together several applications into one file, and they enable Internet Explorer to download and display any active document data from a Web server.

Let's explore these new interfaces further. The `IOleCommandTarget` interface allows menu commands or other actions to be routed from the active document to the active document container. A corresponding `IOleCommandTarget` interface is defined for the active document. This corresponding interface allows the container to route menu commands and other actions to the document. This allows a bi-directional communication of commands to flow cooperatively between container and document. The effect to the user is that the container and document behave as a unified application. The user is unable to tell which piece of software supplies support for which menu item. Supporting the `IOleCommandTarget` interface is optional.

> **Note**
>
> With all the various COM interfaces, it is easy to get confused about the purpose of each interface. Remember that a COM server supplies an interface for someone else to use. It is a means of manipulating the COM server. For example, the container exposes the `IOleCommandTarget` interface so that other software can route menu commands and the like to the container.

The `IOleDocumentSite` COM interface provides one method: `ActivateMe`, which allows the document server to ask the container to activate the document as a full active document instead of an OLE in-place embedded object.

The `IContinueCallback` COM interface provides printing support. It is used with the `IPrint` COM interface that the active document server exposes. The document server uses this interface to provide progress information to the container and to give the container the opportunity to cancel the printing operation.

Some Details About Active Document Containers

Active document containers have a rich history. Their roots go back to the first release of OLE, when OLE meant *object linking and embedding.* The original intent of OLE 1.0 was to allow the user to view different types of data in a single interface. Before OLE 1.0, applications were strictly monolithic. If you wanted to write a document, you would use a word processor. If you wanted to edit financial data, you would use a spreadsheet. OLE 1.0 changed that and allowed the user to view the document, spreadsheets, and charts side by side in a single application. Admittedly, this was a little awkward, because to edit a piece of data, you had to double-click the data and bring up a separate application to change it. But it was an improvement.

OLE 2.0 came along and added the concept of in-place activation. This meant the user could double-click a piece of data and, instead of launching a completely separate document, could edit the data inside the hosting application. This was a great step forward but still a little awkward. First you had to double-click the data to activate it. This was counterintuitive. Users were familiar with single-clicking something when they wanted to focus on it. Yet, despite this awkwardness, it was better than OLE 1.0.

Active documents add yet another layer to OLE. Instead of appearing inside another document, active documents occupy the entire client area of the container. It appears as though the container is the native application. This concept is very useful, particularly when you think of the Internet. A container application that can adapt itself to any document it receives is a powerful tool. This is exactly what browsing the Web is all about: exploring lots of different things and downloading lots of different documents into your browser. Internet Explorer is an example of an active document container that does just that.

Figure 26.1 illustrates the OLE architecture. Notice how the upper layers in the architecture depend, to some degree, on the lower layers. This diagram is like a historical summary of how OLE has changed. Each time the OLE specification changes, another building block is added to the existing foundation.

FIGURE 26.1
OLE architecture.

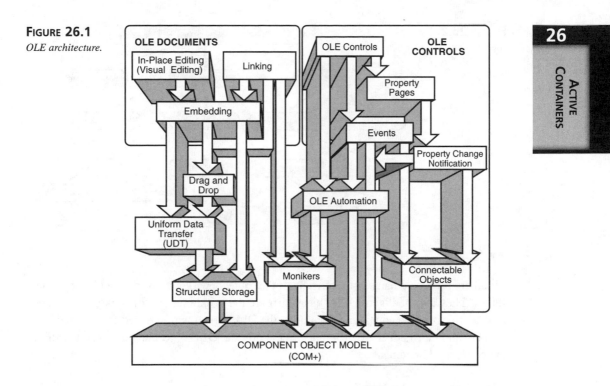

In this section, you will examine the various parts of the OLE architecture.

Structured Storage

Structured storage is a very interesting concept. It came about as a result of the implementation of compound documents. Not only should the user be able to view and edit dissimilar data within the same application, but the user also should be able to save all the changes to the same file. This requirement drove the need for structured storage.

Structured storage is similar to a file system. Data is stored in storage objects, which in turn can be stored in other storage objects. Storage streams that contain the real data can be stored in storage objects. This is analogous to files that reside in directories that reside in other directories.

This capability to segregate portions of one file into hierarchical partitions is very useful for documents that contain other embedded objects. Each object can be assigned its own storage area inside the file, and the embedded object can put anything it wants in its own storage area. Figure 26.2 illustrates the hierarchical nature of structured storage.

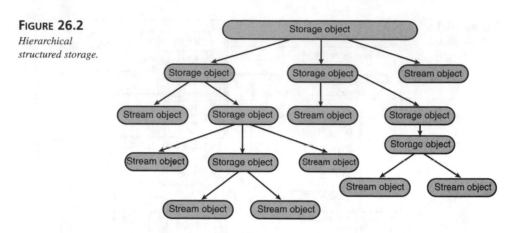

FIGURE 26.2

Hierarchical structured storage.

Monikers

Monikers provide a means of referencing other objects without storing the objects themselves. They are intelligent OLE objects that are the backbone of OLE linking. When you link an object into a compound document, the OLE object is referenced by a moniker. By activating a moniker, you can retrieve the original OLE object and activate it within the compound document.

Uniform Data Transfer

Uniform Data Transfer (UDT) provides a means of obtaining data from another object without being restricted to a particular transfer medium. The standard Windows Clipboard allows the transfer of data between applications using several formats. Each of these formats has to be transmitted through the Clipboard memory, however. Although appropriate for some kinds of data, UDT becomes impractical for large data sets.

Uniform Data Transfer allows several formats to be transferred between applications using several mediums. The medium could be memory, as with the Clipboard. It also could be a disk or the OLE IStorage and IStream interfaces.

Embedded Objects

Embedded objects are OLE objects that allow themselves to be embedded inside a container. Embedded objects store their data in the structured storage of the container. Microsoft Word is an example of an embedded object as well as an active document.

Linked Objects

Linked objects are OLE objects that allow themselves to be linked inside a container. Unlike an embedded object, a linked object is not stored in the structured storage of the container. Instead, a linked object contains a reference to the location of the real object. Typically, the linked object provides an iconic representation of itself inside the container. After you double-click this icon, the native application appears for editing.

Drag-and-Drop

OLE drag-and-drop provides a way for different applications to move data among themselves. Without OLE drag-and-drop, each application would have to define its own protocol by transferring data between itself and another application. OLE drag-and-drop, in combination with Uniform Data Transfer, provides a more system-wide protocol for exchanging data using the mouse.

In-Place Activation

In-place activation is a key feature introduced as part of OLE 2.0. It enables you to edit documents inside a container's client area without launching the native application. In-place activation also is called *visual editing*. Typically, an object that is in-place activated has some kind of hashed border around it. This indicates that the highlighted object is being worked on. Figure 26.3 shows Microsoft Word as an in-place activated object.

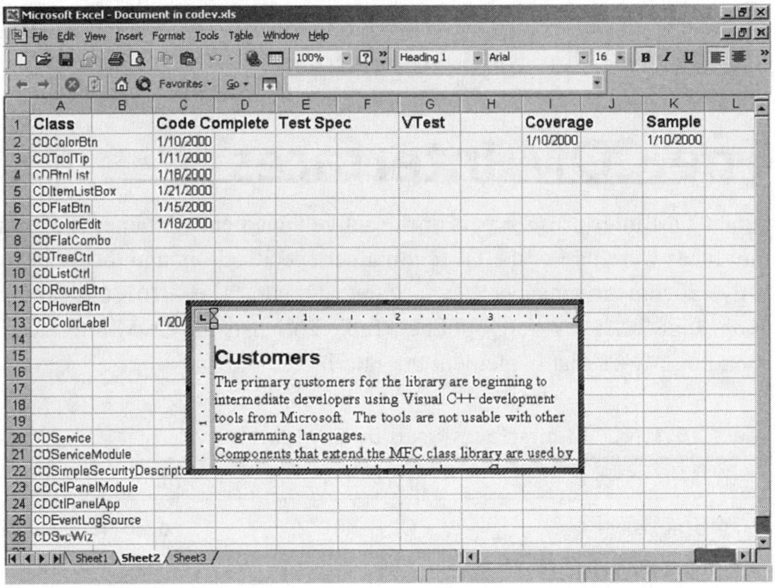

FIGURE 26.3

Microsoft Word as an in-place activated object inside Excel.

Active Documents

Active documents are in many ways just like in-place activated documents. The exception is that when you place an active document in an active document container, it takes up the entire client area of the container. Gone are the hash marks that identify an in-place activated object. You do not have to double-click the active document to activate it. It comes up active and appears to be a native application. Figure 26.4 shows Microsoft Word as an active document. Notice how the active document container appears very similar to the native Microsoft Word application.

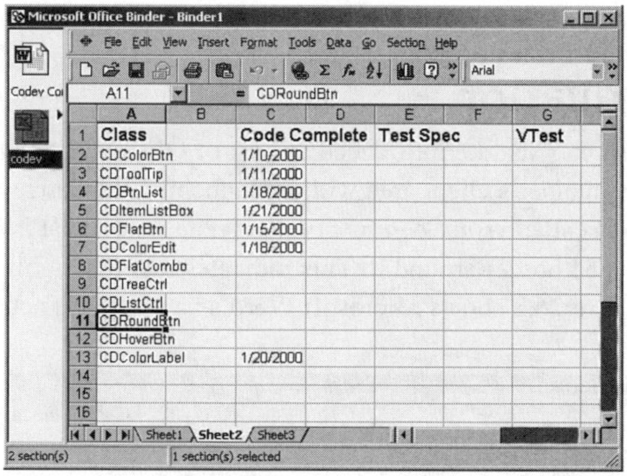

FIGURE 26.4

Microsoft Word as an ActiveX document inside Microsoft Binder, an active document container.

The COM Interfaces

Nine COM interfaces are part of the active document container specification. Six of these interfaces were part of the OLE container specification, and the other three are new to active document containers. Two of the new interfaces—IOleCommandTarget and IContinueCallback—are optional. Table 26.1 lists the COM interfaces with the corresponding MFCs that implement the interface.

TABLE 26.1   COM Interfaces Used By Containers

COM Interface	Type	MFC
IOleInPlaceFrame	OLE 2.0	COleControlContainer
IOleCommandTarget	New, optional	None
IOleInPlaceUIWindow	OLE 2.0	COleControlContainer
IOleContainer	OLE 2.0	COleControlContainer
IOleClientSite	OLE 2.0	COleClientItem

COM Interface	Type	MFC
IAdviseSink	OLE 2.0	COleClientItem
IOleDocumentSite	New, required	None
IOleInPlaceSite	OLE 2.0	COleClientItem
IContinueCallback	New, optional	None

This section discusses these interfaces in more detail.

IOleInPlaceFrame

IOleInPlaceFrame is a COM interface derived from three other COM interfaces: IOleInPlaceUIWindow, IOleWindow, and IUnknown. IOleInPlaceFrame controls the top-level frame window of the container. With this interface, it is possible to add and remove items from the composite menu, set status text, manage modeless dialog boxes, and translate accelerator keys. Each of the interfaces that IOleInPlaceFrame derives from contributes required methods. Table 26.2 describes these interfaces.

TABLE 26.2   IOleInPlaceFrame Interfaces

Interface	Description
	IUnknown *Methods*
AddRef	Adds a reference count to the object
QueryInterface	Discovers required interfaces
Release	Decrements the reference count for the object and eventually deletes the object
	IOleWindow *Methods*
ContextSensitiveHelp	Gives the container the opportunity to handle context-sensitive help
GetWindow	Gets the window handle to the frame, document, parent, or in-place object
	IOleInPlaceUIWindow *Methods*
GetBorder	Returns the rectangle where ActiveX documents can put their toolbars and other controls
RequestBorderSpace	Asks the container for space for toolbars and other controls
SetBorderSpace	Tells the container to allocate the space for toolbars and other controls

TABLE 26.2   continued

Interface	Description
IOleInPlaceUIWindow *Methods*	
SetActiveObject	Called by the ActiveX document to create a link between itself and the active document container
IOleInPlaceFrame *Methods*	
EnableModeless	Enables or disables modeless dialog boxes at the frame level
InsertMenus	Allows the container to insert its menu items into the shared menu
RemoveMenus	Allows the container to remove its menu items
SetMenu	Allows the ActiveX document to install the merged container/document menu
SetStatusText	Displays status text in the static area
TranslateAccelerator	Translates accelerator keystrokes intended for the container

IOleCommandTarget

IOleCommandTarget allows client and server to dispatch commands to each other. With the active document container, IOleCommandTarget allows the active document to route commands that it generates to the container. Table 26.3 describes the interfaces.

TABLE 26.3   IOleCommandTarget Interfaces

Interface	Description
IUnknown *Methods*	
AddRef	Adds a reference count to the object
QueryInterface	Discovers required interfaces
Release	Decrements the reference count for the object and eventually deletes the object
IOleCommandTarget *Methods*	
Exec	Executes the requested command
QueryStatus	Asks the object whether it supports a particular type of command

IOleInPlaceUIWindow

IOleInPlaceUIWindow allows active documents to negotiate border space in the frame window. The interface manages the allocation of border space and the interaction between the document and the frame. IOleInPlaceUIWindow derives from IOleWindow. Table 26.4 describes the interfaces.

TABLE 26.4   IOleInPlaceUIWindow Interfaces

Interface	Description
IUnknown *Interfaces*	
AddRef	Adds a reference count to the object
QueryInterface	Discovers required interfaces
Release	Decrements the reference count for the object and eventually deletes the object
IOleWindow *Interfaces*	
ContextSensitiveHelp	Gives the container the opportunity to handle context-sensitive help
GetWindow	Gets the window handle to the frame, document, parent, or in-place object
IOleInPlaceUIWindow *Methods*	
GetBorder	Returns the rectangle where ActiveX documents can put their toolbars and other controls
RequestBorderSpace	Asks the container for space for toolbars and other controls
SetActiveObject	Called by the ActiveX document to create a link between itself and the active document container
SetBorderSpace	Tells the container to allocate the space for toolbars and other controls

IOleContainer

IOleContainer queries objects in a compound document or locks the container in the running state. This interface is useful only when the container supports linked objects and requires both the container and the document to implement it. Table 26.5 describes the interfaces.

TABLE 26.5 IOleContainer Interfaces

Interface	Description
IUnknown *Interfaces*	
AddRef	Adds a reference count to the object
QueryInterface	Discovers required interfaces
Release	Decrements the reference count for the object and eventually deletes the object
IParseDisplayName *Methods*	
ParseDisplayName	Parses a display name into something usable by a moniker
IOleContainer *Methods*	
EnumObjects	Enumerates objects in the container
LockContainer	Keeps the container locked in running mode until it is explicitly released

IOleClientSite

IOleClientSite helps an active document get information about its container environment. It can get information about its display area as well as other user interface information from the container. Table 26.6 describes the interfaces.

TABLE 26.6 IOleClientSite Interfaces

Interface	Description
IUnknown *Interfaces*	
AddRef	Adds a reference count to the object
QueryInterface	Discovers required interfaces
Release	Decrements the reference count for the object and eventually deletes the object
IOleClientSite *Methods*	
GetContainer	Returns a pointer to the container's IOleContainer interface
GetMoniker	Creates a moniker to access the embedded active document
OnShowWindow	Notifies the container when an object is about to become visible or invisible; does not apply to active documents or other in-place activated objects

Interface	Description
	IOleClientSite *Methods*
RequestNewObjectLayout	Asks the container to provide more or less space for displaying the active document
SaveObject	Saves the active document associated with this site
ShowObject	Positions the active document so that it is visible to the user; makes sure the container itself is visible to the user

IAdviseSink

IAdviseSink provides a way for active documents to notify their containers when their data or states change. Table 26.7 describes the interfaces.

TABLE 26.7 IAdviseSink Interfaces

Interface	Description
	IUnknown *Interfaces*
AddRef	Adds a reference count to the object
QueryInterface	Discovers required interfaces
Release	Decrements the reference count for the object and eventually deletes the object
	IAdviseSink *Methods*
OnClose	Called when the active document has been closed
OnDataChange	Called when the data has changed
OnRename	Called when the name has changed
OnSave	Called when the active document has been saved to disk
OnViewChange	Called when the view has changed

IOleDocumentSite

IOleDocumentSite allows an active document to bypass the normal activation sequence for an in-place object and activate directly as a document object. Table 26.8 describes the interfaces.

TABLE 26.8   IOleDocumentSite Interfaces

Interface	Description
	IUnknown *Interfaces*
AddRef	Adds a reference count to the object
QueryInterface	Discovers required interfaces
Release	Decrements the reference count for the object and eventually deletes the object
	IOleDocumentSite *Methods*
ActivateMe	Actives the active document as a document object instead of an in-place object

IOleInPlaceSite

IOleInPlaceSite works with IOleDocumentSite. For each view an active document instantiates, an IOleInPlaceSite object must exist. IOleDocumentSite manages one or more IOleInPlaceSite objects. The IOleInPlaceSite interface provides methods that manage the active document. Table 26.9 describes the interfaces.

TABLE 26.9   IOleInPlaceSite Interfaces

Interface	Description
	IUnknown *Interfaces*
AddRef	Adds a reference count to the object
QueryInterface	Discovers required interfaces
Release	Decrements the reference count for the object and eventually deletes the object
	IOleWindow *Methods*
ContextSensitiveHelp	Gives the container the opportunity to handle context-sensitive help
GetWindow	Gets the window handle to the frame, document, parent, or in-place object
	IOleInPlaceSite *Methods*
CanInPlaceActivate	Gives the object permission to in-place activate
DeactivateAndUndo	Tells the container to end the in-place active session and return to its Undo state
DiscardUndoState	Tells the container to discard its Undo state

Interface	Description
	`IOleInPlaceSite` *Methods*
`GetWindowContext`	Provides window hierarchy information
`OnInPlaceActivate`	Notifies the container that the ActiveX document is about to in-place activate
`OnInPlaceDeactivate`	Tells the container that the ActiveX document is no longer in-place active
`OnPosRectChange`	Used by the active document to tell the container that its size has changed
`OnUIActivate`	Called when the active document is about to in-place activate and replace the menu with a composite menu
`OnUIDeactivate`	Tells the container that the ActiveX document is going away and that the container should restore its user interface
`Scroll`	Tells the container how to scroll the object

IContinueCallback

`IContinueCallback` helps the active document ask the container whether it should continue an interruptible process. This feature is used with the active document's `IPrint` interface. Table 26.10 describes the interfaces.

TABLE 26.10   `IContinueCallback` Interfaces

Interface	Description
	`IUnknown` *Interfaces*
`AddRef`	Adds a reference count to the object
`QueryInterface`	Discovers required interfaces
`Release`	Decrements the reference count for the object and eventually deletes the object
	`IContinueCallback` *Methods*
`FContinue`	Used by printing tasks to determine whether printing should continue
`FContinuePrinting`	Used by the printing tasks to determine whether the task should continue; also provides some progress information

You can find more information about these COM interfaces in the Visual C++ Help system. The system also provides good background information on the world of COM, OLE, and other Active technologies. Another interesting exercise is to search through the MFC source code to see where Microsoft has implemented these and other COM interfaces in the MFC Library. The MFC source code is located in the \Vc98\Mfc subdirectory.

Building an Active Document Container

You can build an active document container in several ways. The most educational method is to use the native COM interfaces. Building a container this way takes longer but would greatly increase your understanding of the intricacies of COM. In this chapter, however, you will not build a container using this method.

Another way to build an active document container is to use the new *Active Template Library* (ATL). This library is an alternative approach to using the MFC Library. These libraries are fundamentally different from each other. ATL is based on the idea of a template. Templates are ways of implementing code without knowing what kind of data you are working with.

Suppose that you have a class that adds two integers together and another class that adds two floating-point numbers. The code for both these classes would be remarkably similar—perhaps something like c = a + b. The only difference between the two implementations is the type of data used in the calculation. This is the perfect situation for a template class. The code for the template looks the same (c = a + b), but the types of a, b, and c are not resolved until the template class is declared in the code.

If you are interested in learning more about templates, take a closer look at some of the MFC collection classes, the Standard Template Library, or ATL. The key benefit to this approach is the small size of programs built with ATL.

MFC is based on the idea of a hierarchical class library. Programmers are encouraged to build layers of classes that can inherit behaviors from their parent classes. This approach tends to make it very easy to implement functionality, because in most cases, you can just inherit it. Hierarchical classes tend to grow large, however, both in terms of the size of programs generated and the number of classes to learn and understand. The programming language SmallTalk is built on the idea of inheriting functionality and overriding the behaviors you want to change. The key characteristic of a SmallTalk project is that it takes a person new to SmallTalk a long time to learn the SmallTalk hierarchy. But someone who knows SmallTalk can implement new functionality quickly. SmallTalk programs also tend to be large. MFC programs share these characteristics.

For the purpose of this chapter, you will use MFC to build a container program. You will do this because you can inherit a great deal of active document container behavior without writing any code.

Active Document Container Support in MFC

In earlier versions of Visual C++ and MFC, OLE container support was provided through the COleClientItem class. This class still is used when containers want to support embedded OLE objects without offering support for containing active documents.

With the release of Visual C++ 6, the COleDocObjectItem class represents a contained active document object. Beginning with Visual C++ 6, COleDocument stores COleDocObjectItem instances as well as COleClientItem instances.

The COleDocObjectItem class is derived from COleClientItem and provides the following additional functions:

- GetActiveView does not return a pointer to an MFC CView instance. It returns a pointer to the currently active IOleDocumentView interface exposed by an embedded object. If no view is active, NULL is returned. Take care when using this function: It violates a basic COM development rule and fails to increment the reference count on the returned interface pointer. If you intend to use this pointer, you must increment the reference count manually by calling AddRef. Additionally, you must never call Release through the interface pointer unless you have called AddRef first.

- OnPreparePrinting is called by the MFC framework before the active document object is printed.

- OnPrint is called by the MFC framework when the active document object is to be printed.

- GetPageCount provides page count information about the document, including the initial page number and the total number of pages in the document.

- ExecCommand is a wrapper around the IOleCommandTarget::Exec method that enables commands to be routed to the document.

If you are using MFC AppWizard to create a container application, COleDocObjectItem or COleClientItem is used as a base class in your project. A class derived from COleDocObjectItem is added automatically to your project if you select the Active Document Container check box in AppWizard Step 3. If you don't select the Active document checkbox, COleClientItem is used as a base class.

The Pocket Project

As an example of an application that acts as an active document container, the CD-ROM that accompanies this book includes Pocket, an MFC-based application that is similar to the Office Binder application. Pocket also is similar to the MFCBind example program included with MSDN, with the following changes:

- Icons for embedded documents are displayed in a list view control.
- Printing is not supported.
- The MFCBind example has a number of partially implemented features, which tend to clutter the example.

The source code presented in this chapter highlights the portions of the Pocket project that deal with active documents. The entire Pocket project, including all of the source code, is included on the CD-ROM.

Creating the Pocket Project

The Pocket container application enables you to embed a number of active document objects into a single file. The Pocket application is similar in appearance to the MFCBind and Microsoft Office Binder applications. The client area is divided by a splitter bar. A list view on the left side of the client area contains a list of documents in the container. The view on the right side of the splitter displays one of the activated documents.

Each active document in the container is represented by an instance of CPocketCntrItem, which is derived from COleDocObjectItem. Each instance of CPocketCntrItem is represented by an icon in the list view. To activate a document, you click on the icon associated with the document you want to activate.

Using MFC AppWizard to Create the Project

The Pocket application was built using MFC AppWizard. The project is a *single-document interface* (SDI) application and uses the default settings for all options—except for the compound document support options on AppWizard Step 3. The following options were selected for the Pocket project:

- **Container Compound Document Support.** This selection causes AppWizard to create a project that supports embedding OLE documents.
- **Active Document Container Selected.** Enabling this check box causes AppWizard to create a container that supports active documents; specifically, AppWizard uses COleDocObjectItem instead of COleClientItem.

All other options were set to their default values.

The initial Pocket project created by the wizard consisted of the CPP and H files shown in Table 26.11.

TABLE 26.11   Generated Files and Their Descriptions

CPP/Header Name	Purpose
CntrItem	These files contain the CPocketCntrItem class. This class is derived from COleDocObjectItem and supplies most of the active document support for the container.
MainFrm	These files contain the class derived from CFrameWnd.
Pocket	These files contain the class derived from CWinApp.
PocketDoc	These files contain the class derived from COleDocument.
PocketView	These files contain the class derived from CView.
StdAfx	Precompiled header support.

In addition to the files created by AppWizard, the Pocket project includes the ItemListView.h and ItemListView.cpp files. These files implement the CItemListView class, which is derived from CListView and displays the documents currently embedded in the container.

The CItemListView class was added to the project using the Insert Class dialog box. To open the Insert Class dialog box, choose New Class from the Insert menu. The values from Table 26.12 were used with the Insert Class dialog box to create the CItemListView class.

TABLE 26.12   Generated Files and Their Descriptions

Parameter	Value
Class type	MFC Class
Name	CItemListView
Base class	CListView

After using the Insert Class dialog box with the parameters from Table 26.12, the ItemListView.cpp and ItemListview.h files are added automatically to the Pocket project.

Adding a Splitter to the Pocket Project

The Pocket application is an SDI application, with the main view divided vertically by a splitter. The CMainFrame class has a member variable named m_wndSplitter, which is an instance of `CSplitterWnd`. The code shown in Listing 26.1 initializes the splitter window and creates the two contained views.

LISTING 26.1   Creating a Splitter Window That Contains the Views

```
BOOL CMainFrame::OnCreateClient(LPCREATESTRUCT lpcs,
                                CCreateContext* pContext)
{
    ASSERT(RUNTIME_CLASS(CPocketView)==pContext->m_pNewViewClass);
    // Create splitter window, with list view on the left and main
    // view on the right. The width is set to a default width that
    // can be adjusted by the user.
    int cxListWidth = ::GetSystemMetrics(SM_CXICON) * 2;

    CRect rc;
    GetClientRect(rc);
    CSize sizView(rc.Width() - cxListWidth, 50);
    CSize sizList(cxListWidth, 0);

    // Create splitter
    if(m_wndSplitter.CreateStatic(this, 1, 2) == FALSE)
    {
        TRACE0("Could not create splitter\n");
        return FALSE;
    }

    // Create main view
    BOOL fCreated = m_wndSplitter.CreateView(0, // row
                                    1, // column
                                    pContext->m_pNewViewClass,
                                    sizView,
                                    pContext);
    if(fCreated == FALSE)
    {
        TRACE0("Could not create main view\n");
        return FALSE;
    }

    // Create list view
    fCreated = m_wndSplitter.CreateView(0,
                                    0,
                                    RUNTIME_CLASS(CItemListView),
                                    sizList,
                                    pContext);
    if(fCreated == FALSE)
    {
        TRACE0("could not create list view\n");
        return FALSE;
    }
```

```
// Make the main view active
CView* pView;
// Downcast the CWnd* to a CView*
pView = reinterpret_cast<CView*>(m_wndSplitter.GetPane(0, 1));
SetActiveView(pView);
return TRUE;
}
```

The OnCreateClient function shown in Listing 26.1 is called by the MFC framework to create the client area of an MFC application. In the version implemented in the Pocket project, a splitter window is created, and then two views are inserted into the splitter panes. The first view created inside a splitter pane is the main view for the project. This view, CPocketView, is the view class that is associated with CPocketDoc, the document class used in Pocket. Next, an instance of CItemListView is created inside the other splitter pane. If both views are created successfully, the CPocketView instance is set as the active view.

Although the Pocket application includes two view classes, the CPocketDoc class is associated only with one view class—CPocketView. The CMainFrame class is responsible for caching pointers to both view classes so that other parts of the application have access to both views. Listing 26.2 shows the CMainFrame functions that provide access to pointers to each view.

LISTING 26.2   The CMainFrame Class Provides Access to View Pointers in the Pocket Application

```
CItemListView* CMainFrame::GetItemListView()
{
    return static_cast<CItemListView*>(m_wndSplitter.GetPane(0, 0));
}

CPocketView* CMainFrame::GetPocketView()
{
    return static_cast<CPocketView*>(m_wndSplitter.GetPane(0, 1));
}
```

Creating New Active Documents

You can embed new active documents into a Pocket document by choosing Add from Pocket's Section menu. Choosing this menu item displays the Insert Object dialog box, as shown in Figure 26.5.

FIGURE 26.5

*The Insert Object
dialog box.*

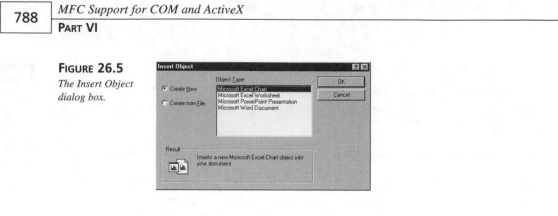

After you select the type of active document object to be embedded, a document of the selected type opens in the main view, and an icon representing the new item is added to the list view.

The CPocketDoc class is responsible for handling the insertion of a new active document. Listing 26.3 shows the code used for this processing.

LISTING 26.3   Adding a New Active Document in the Pocket Project

```cpp
void CPocketDoc::OnSectionAdd()
{
    CMainFrame* pFrame = (CMainFrame*) AfxGetApp()->m_pMainWnd;
    ASSERT_POINTER(pFrame, CMainFrame);

    CPocketView* pView = (CPocketView*)pFrame->GetPocketView();
    ASSERT_POINTER(pView, CPocketView);

    CPocketCntrItem* pItem = NULL;
    pView->BeginWaitCursor();
    // Use the standard OLE Insert Object dialog box.
    COleInsertDialog dlg;
    if (dlg.DoModal(COleInsertDialog::DocObjectsOnly) != IDOK)
    {
        pView->EndWaitCursor();
        return;
    }

    try{
        // Create a new instance of the container item to track
        // the new object, then pass the new instance to the OLE
        // insert dialog, which will create the object.
        pItem = new CPocketCntrItem(this);
        ASSERT_VALID(pItem);

        if (!dlg.CreateItem(pItem))
        {
            delete pItem;
            pView->EndWaitCursor();
```

```
            return;
        }
        ASSERT_VALID(pItem);

        // If there's already an active item, deactivate it before
        // making the new item active.
        COleClientItem* pActiveItem = GetInPlaceActiveItem(pView);
        if(pActiveItem)
            pActiveItem->Deactivate();

        pItem->Activate(OLEIVERB_SHOW, pView);
        ASSERT_VALID(pItem);

        // Set the selection to the most recently inserted item
        pView->m_pSelection = (CPocketCntrItem*)pItem;
        UpdateAllViews(NULL);
    }
    catch(CException* pe)
    {
        if(pItem != NULL)
        {
            ASSERT_VALID(pItem);
            pItem->Delete();

            CMainFrame *pFrame = (CMainFrame*) AfxGetApp()->m_pMainWnd;
            pFrame->GetItemListView()->RemoveItem(pItem);
        }
        AfxMessageBox(IDP_FAILED_TO_CREATE);
        // Not using the MFC exception macros, so the exception
        // must be cleaned up manually.
        pe->Delete();
    }
    pView->EndWaitCursor();
}
```

In Listing 26.3, the OnSectionAdd function begins by using the COleInsertDialog class to collect the type of OLE object to be inserted. The list of available objects is restricted to active documents by passing the COleInsertDialog::DocObjectsOnly value as a parameter when calling DoModal.

If you select an item to be embedded, an instance of CPocketCntrItem is created. As discussed earlier in this chapter, the CPocketCntrItem class is derived from COleDocObjectItem. Every active document object that is embedded into a Pocket document is represented by one instance of CPocketCntrItem. After the new instance of CPocketCntrItem is initialized, it's activated in the main view. Before the new item is activated, any currently activated item is deactivated.

When the instance of `CPocketCntrItem` is created, the MFC framework calls an undocumented function named `FinishCreate`. This function, shown in Listing 26.4, notifies you of the results after the framework and the operating system attempt to create the new item. If the `SCODE` indicates a failure, the item could not be inserted. If the `SCODE` indicates success, the item was inserted, and the item is added to the list view.

LISTING 26.4   Implementing the Undocumented `FinishCreate` Function

```
BOOL CPocketCntrItem::FinishCreate(SCODE sc)
{
    // Undocumented virtual function, see MFCBind example.
    // If we receive a failed result, the item couldn't be
    // created. Otherwise, we delegate to the base class, and
    // call our own processing function.
    ASSERT(SUCCEEDED(sc));
    BOOL fReturn = FALSE;
    if(SUCCEEDED(sc))
    {
        fReturn = COleDocObjectItem::FinishCreate(sc);
        if(fReturn)
            AddItemToListView();
    }
    else
    {
        AfxMessageBox(_T("Could not create new section"));
    }
    return fReturn;
}
```

The `FinishCreate` function in Listing 26.4 calls `AddItemToListView` to handle the work required to place an icon and description for the new item in the list view. Listing 26.5 shows the `AddItemToListView` function.

LISTING 26.5   Adding a New Item into Pocket

```
void CPocketCntrItem::AddItemToListView()
{
    // Uses the ATL/MFC string conversion macros.
    USES_CONVERSION;
    ASSERT_POINTER(m_lpObject, IOleObject);
    if (!m_lpObject)
        return;
    // Request the short form of the class type
    CString    strType;
    GetUserType(USERCLASSTYPE_SHORT, strType);
    // Get the Class ID, and store it as strClassId
    CLSID      clsid;
```

```
GetClassID(&clsid);
LPOLESTR  lpOleStr = NULL;
StringFromCLSID(clsid, &lpOleStr);
CString strClassId(OLE2T(lpOleStr));
CoTaskMemFree(lpOleStr);

// Call base class function to pull icon from the registry.
HICON hIcon = GetIconFromRegistry();
if(hIcon != NULL)
{
    // Walk through the framework, and get the pointer to
    // the main frame window.
    CWnd* pWndMain = AfxGetApp()->m_pMainWnd;
    ASSERT_POINTER(pWndMain, CWnd);
    CMainFrame* pFrame = DYNAMIC_DOWNCAST(CMainFrame, pWndMain);
    ASSERT_POINTER(pFrame, CMainFrame);
    // Get the pointer to the list view.
    CItemListView *pListView = pFrame->GetItemListView();
    if(pListView == NULL)
        return;

    pListView->AddItem(this,
                       hIcon,
                       strType,
                       strClassId);
}
}
```

The `AddItemToListView` function collects information about the new active document item, including

- The short version of the OLE class type. This name is used as a label to identify the item in the list view.

- A `CString` containing the `CLSID` for the new item. Converting this information into a `CString` requires several steps, including a call to `CoTaskMemFree` to release the memory allocated for the original string.

- A handle to the icon associated with the OLE class. The icon is retrieved by calling `GetIconFromRegistry`, a function that is part of the `COleClientItem` base class.

The preceding items, as well as a pointer to this instance of `CPocketCntrItem`, are passed to the list view's `AddItem` function, which Listing 26.6 shows.

LISTING 26.6   Adding a New Item to the List View

```
BOOL CItemListView::AddItem(COleClientItem* pItem,
                            HICON hIcon, CString strType,
```

LISTING 26.6   continued

```
                    CString strClassId)
{
    ASSERT_POINTER(pItem, COleClientItem);
    ASSERT(hIcon);
    ASSERT(strType.IsEmpty() == FALSE);
    ASSERT(strClassId.IsEmpty() == FALSE);

    CPocketItem* pListItem = new CPocketItem(pItem,
                                             hIcon,
                                             strType,
                                             strClassId);

    if(!pListItem) return FALSE;

    CListCtrl& ctrl = GetListCtrl();
    int nItemCount = ctrl.GetItemCount();

    int ndxImage = m_imgList.Add(hIcon);
    ASSERT(ndxImage != -1);

    UINT fuMask = LVIF_TEXT|LVIF_PARAM|LVIF_IMAGE;
    int ndxNewItem = ctrl.InsertItem(fuMask,
                                     nItemCount,
                                     strType,
                                     0,
                                     0,
                                     ndxImage,
                                     (long)pListItem);
    ASSERT(ndxNewItem == nItemCount);

    return TRUE;
}
```

The AddItem function in Listing 26.6 creates an instance of a CPocketItem structure that serves as a wrapper for the parameter data. The icon associated with the new item is added to the list view's image list, and then the new item is added to the list view control. The type name is used as a label for the item, and the CPocketItem pointer is stored in the list view for later use.

Switching Between Active Documents

You can switch between documents by clicking on an icon in the list view. The currently active document is replaced by the document represented by the icon you selected. The code responsible for handling this work is the OnClick function in the CItemListView class, which is provided in Listing 26.7.

LISTING 26.7   Selecting an Active Document

```cpp
void CItemListView::OnClick(NMHDR* pNMHDR, LRESULT* pResult)
{
    CMainFrame *pFrame = (CMainFrame*)AfxGetApp()->m_pMainWnd;
    ASSERT_POINTER(pFrame, CMainFrame);

    COleDocument *pDoc = (COleDocument*)pFrame->GetActiveDocument();
    ASSERT_POINTER(pDoc, COleDocument);

    CPocketView *pView = (CPocketView*)pFrame->GetPocketView();
    ASSERT_POINTER(pView, CPocketView);

    // This pointer may be NULL if no item is currently
    // activated in-place.
    COleClientItem *pActiveItem = NULL;
    pActiveItem = pDoc->GetInPlaceActiveItem(pView);
    ASSERT_NULL_OR_POINTER(pActiveItem, COleClientItem);

    CListCtrl& ctrl = GetListCtrl();
    int nSelected = ctrl.GetNextItem(-1, LVNI_SELECTED);
    if(nSelected == -1) return;

    DWORD dwData = ctrl.GetItemData(nSelected);
    CPocketItem* pItem = (CPocketItem*)dwData;
    ASSERT_POINTER(pItem, CPocketItem);

    if(pItem->m_pOleItem == pActiveItem)
    {
        CWnd* pWnd = pActiveItem->GetInPlaceWindow();
        ASSERT_NULL_OR_POINTER(pWnd, CWnd);
        if(pWnd)
            pWnd->SetFocus();
        pView->m_pSelection = pActiveItem;
        return;
    }
    else if(pActiveItem)
    {
        pActiveItem->Deactivate();
    }
    pActiveItem = pItem->m_pOleItem;
    pActiveItem->Activate(OLEIVERB_SHOW, pView);
    CWnd* pWnd = pActiveItem->GetInPlaceWindow()->SetFocus();
    ASSERT_NULL_OR_POINTER(pWnd, CWnd);
    if(pWnd)
        pWnd->SetFocus();
    pView->m_pSelection = pActiveItem;

    *pResult = 0;
}
```

The OnClick function begins by retrieving pointers to the application's frame, document, and view classes. Next, the CPocketItem pointer that is currently active is compared to the CPocketItem pointer for the item selected by the user. If the pointers are equal, the user has reselected the same item, and input focus is returned to the main view. If the items differ, the currently active item (if any) is deactivated, and the newly selected item is activated.

Destroying an Active Document

To delete an item from a Pocket document, choose Remove from the Section menu, and the currently selected item is removed from the document. The OnSectionRemove function in the CPocketDoc class is responsible for carrying out this work (see Listing 26.8).

LISTING 26.8   Handling the Section Remove Menu Command

```
void CPocketDoc::OnSectionRemove()
{
    CMainFrame* pFrame = (CMainFrame*) AfxGetApp()->m_pMainWnd;
    ASSERT_VALID(pFrame);

    CPocketView* pView = (CPocketView*)pFrame->GetPocketView();
    ASSERT_VALID(pView);

    COleClientItem* pItem = GetPrimarySelectedItem(pView);
    if(pItem)
    {
        CItemListView* pItemView = pFrame->GetItemListView();
        ASSERT_VALID(pItemView);

        pItem->Delete();
        pItemView->RemoveItem(pItem);
    }
    else
    {
        AfxMessageBox(_T("Select a section to be deleted."));
    }
}
```

The OnSectionRemove function in Listing 26.8 begins by retrieving a COleClientItem pointer that represents the currently active item in the main view. The Delete function is called through this pointer, which causes the underlying OLE object and the associated C++ instance to be released. Next, the item is removed from the list view by calling the CItemListView::RemoveItem function, which Listing 26.9 shows.

LISTING 26.9 Removing an Item from Pocket

```cpp
BOOL CItemListView::RemoveItem(COleClientItem *pRemove)
{
    BOOL fReturn = FALSE;
    CMainFrame *pFrame = (CMainFrame*)AfxGetApp()->m_pMainWnd;
    ASSERT_POINTER(pFrame, CMainFrame);

    CPocketView *pView = (CPocketView*)pFrame->GetPocketView();
    ASSERT_POINTER(pView, CPocketView);
    CPocketItem* pItem = NULL;

    CListCtrl& ctrl = GetListCtrl();
    int nItemCount = ctrl.GetItemCount();

    for(int n = 0; n < nItemCount; n++)
    {
        DWORD dwData = ctrl.GetItemData(n);
        CPocketItem* pItem = (CPocketItem*)dwData;
        ASSERT_POINTER(pItem, CPocketItem);
        if(pItem->m_pOleItem == pRemove)
        {
            ctrl.DeleteItem(n);
            break;
        }
    }
    if(ctrl.GetItemCount() == 0)
        return TRUE;

    // Activate one of the remaining items - we'll just pick the
    // first item in the list.
    DWORD dwData = ctrl.GetItemData(0);
    pItem = (CPocketItem*)dwData;
    ASSERT_POINTER(pItem, CPocketItem);
    ASSERT_POINTER(pItem->m_pOleItem, COleClientItem);
    pItem->m_pOleItem->Activate(OLEIVERB_SHOW, pView);

    CWnd* pWnd = pItem->m_pOleItem->GetInPlaceWindow();
    ASSERT_NULL_OR_POINTER(pWnd, CWnd);
    if(pWnd)
        pWnd->SetFocus();
    pView->m_pSelection = pItem->m_pOleItem;

    ctrl.SetItemState(0, LVIS_SELECTED, LVIS_SELECTED);
    VERIFY(ctrl.Arrange(LVA_DEFAULT));
    return TRUE;
}
```

The RemoveItem function has two sections. In the first section, the item to be removed is searched for, and if found, it is removed from the list view. In the second part of the function, another item from the list view is selected and made active.

Using the Pocket Application

To add a new item to a Pocket document, choose Add from the Section menu, and choose one of the displayed active document types. To remove an item, choose Remove from the Section menu. Figure 26.6 shows the Pocket container with several embedded documents.

FIGURE 26.6

The Pocket application with several embedded documents.

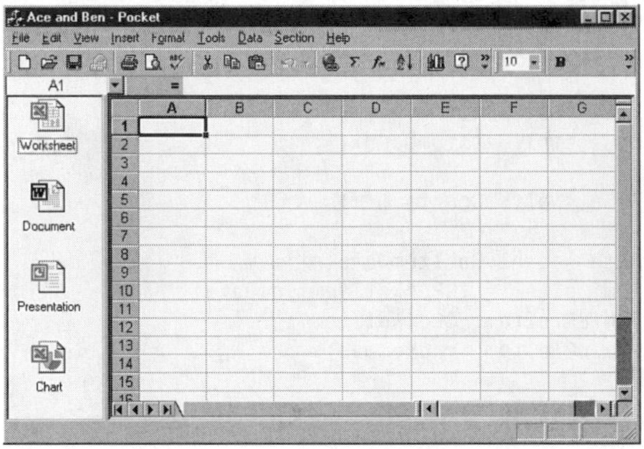

Summary

This chapter began to explore the world of active document containers. ActiveX represents Microsoft's continuing evolution of the OLE and COM technologies. It is a credit to the COM architecture that the OLE technologies can effectively change over time without becoming obsolete.

This chapter reviewed portions of the OLE and COM architectures that are relevant to active document container technology. In Visual C++ 6, the MFC Library was enhanced to include support for active document containers.

Other methods are available to implement active document containers, in addition to using MFC. Containers could be implemented using the native COM interfaces or with the more recent ATL. Using MFC is completely appropriate in this case, though, because containers don't have the same constraints on them as other Internet-oriented COM objects.

Active Servers

*by Ted Neustaedter
and Mickey Willaims*

IN THIS CHAPTER

In this chapter, you'll take an in-depth look at the different types of COM, OLE, and Active servers, including embeddable servers and Automation servers. You'll also look at examples that will give you a good understanding of the concepts discussed in this chapter.

After finishing this chapter, you should have a clear understanding of the purpose of each type of Active document server, as well as a good base for building your own. Hopefully, some of you might even decide to enhance and extend the OpenGL server example I've included.

For those of you looking for some tips and tricks, check out the GLServer example. This little gem is embeddable and returns a bitmap to the container through the metafile device context.

Active Servers Introduction

This chapter discusses the three types of COM, OLE, and Active servers.

First is the *full server.* A full server is both an OLE or Active document server and a fully functioning application. In Microsoft Word, for example, you can run the application (as I am doing while writing these words), create a document or brochure, and then save the contents to a .DOC file. Or, you can open an application such as WordPad and actually embed or link to content that you've created using Microsoft Word.

The second type of server is known as a *miniserver.* What this means is that the server can be used only to supply content for a container application. As an example, Microsoft Word comes with myriad applets that can help you produce professional-looking documents. One of these applets is Microsoft WordArt. If you attempt to run the WordArt program, you'll get a message telling you that the application can be run only when launched from inside another application.

Now, we'll veer off in a totally different direction and talk about the third type of server. This is where things get a bit confusing for some folks. The third type of server—*automation server*—doesn't necessarily act or appear to be anything like the full server or miniserver. In fact, a simple automation server doesn't support OLE or Active document embedding at all. Instead, this type of server exposes special objects, methods, and properties to enable you to tell it what to do. For example, suppose that I want to take a mail-merge document that I created in Microsoft Word and merge it with a mailing list stored in a Microsoft Access database. Sure, I could open up Microsoft Word and select the mail merge menu item (along with performing about half a dozen other steps) and manually achieve my goal. Or, I could write an application in Visual C++ (or any other language that supports automation) and remotely control Microsoft Word. That way, I could set up the program so that it runs every day at 4 a.m., unattended, for example.

There are two flavors of automation servers: in-process and out-of-process.

In a nutshell, an *in-process server* is created from a class stored in a DLL, which is loaded and runs in the same process space as the application that created it. All instances share the same code; however, each has its own independent data area.

An *out-of-process server* runs in its own address space. This type of server is built as an EXE application (such as for Microsoft Word and Excel) and can either manage multiple instances or launch a new copy of the EXE each time a server object is created.

Okay, I know, it's a lot to grasp right now. Don't worry, though, because by the time you get through this chapter, I'm sure you'll have a much better grasp of how these different types of servers work.

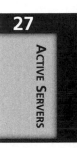

Three-Tier Development Using Server Components

Traditionally, when we refer to the term *client/server,* we are talking about an application that runs on a PC and connects to a database running on a server somewhere. This is fine for small- to medium-size businesses with anywhere from 5 to 50 users. However, it really becomes a hassle when you have 500 or more users. Every time a fix is made to an existing application, you need to distribute the new application to every desktop and ensure that it is installed properly. This process is both time-consuming and costly as far as ensuring software and component compatibility on all desktops.

What about Internet and intranet applications? These need to be browser-based applications, but if you attempt to service thousands of users with simple *common gateway interface* (CGI) scripts, you end up spending a lot of time making sure that you're not getting deadlocks on files or databases.

> **Note**
>
> So how do we handle large numbers of users? The term *scalability* is used to refer to the process of increasing the number of users from one user to hundreds of thousands of users.

The first network-aware COM or OLE technology introduced by Microsoft was called *remote automation.* Basically, remote automation permits an application running on PC 1 to connect to and create automation objects on PC 2.

The big problem with remote automation was that as a Visual Basic–centric technology, it didn't have any security, it didn't have any sort of pooling strategy to manage resources or database connections, and it was never designed to be used with the Internet or intranets.

Microsoft later released *distributed COM (DCOM)*, which improves on the distributed aspect of COM objects, including support for Internet and intranet applications, and has a fully defined security model.

The next major distributed technology milestone for Microsoft was the release of the *Microsoft Transaction Server (MTS)*. Not only does MTS address all of the problems mentioned earlier, but it also supports transaction processing.

Let's look at an example of how MTS could be useful. Given a bank account number, you could build two MTS components: one that performs a debit and the second that performs a credit. Now all you need to do is tell MTS about these two components (ingrain that word *components* into your brain) by installing them on the server that is running MTS instead of on the client workstation.

You now need to do little more than write a small applet that is integrated with the MTS server and starts a transaction, calls the debit component, calls the credit component, and completes. It is now MTS's responsibility to commit the processing steps these two components performed. If either of the components fails, MTS rolls back the transaction. Windows 2000 integrates the features of MTS into the operating system as part of COM+. COM+ and MTS are discussed in more detail in Chapter 32, "Using ATL to Create MTS and COM+ Components."

The point is, we're moving away from the client/server (two-tier) way of thinking. Instead, we're moving to a three-tier model, where the client application is very thin (commonly called a *thin client),* because it only has the minimal functionality of calling these automation servers and displaying results for the user (which can be done by a thin-client application or through a Web browser). The second tier is where the bulk of the work is done. It's an application server with hundreds—even thousands—of these tiny components installed. The third tier is the database tier.

MFC Versus Active Template Libraries

Before we get into the meat and potatoes of actually coding some of these servers, it's important to understand at least a few of the reasons why Microsoft has released a set of templates for developing active components (which includes automation servers, full servers and miniservers, containers, and controls).

MFC is a great class hierarchy, but it can be too large for some types of applications. This is especially true when you're creating small active components that you want to display on your Web site. It's a real annoyance spending 20 minutes downloading support DLLs that don't need to be there. If you decide to statically link an MFC control or component, the result is a very large DLL, EXE, or OCX.

So, after much debate, it was decided that a newer, leaner class library would be created. This class library initially was released with Microsoft Visual C++ 4.2 and is called the *Active Template Library* (*ATL*).

Now, for those of you who have ever done any programming with templates from the standard C++ library, you'll appreciate the beauty of this class library. It's a great solution for creating tight DLL or EXE components, because it doesn't use MFC at all (unless you specially include it). ATL is discussed in more detail in Part VII, "Using the Active Template Library."

Designing an MFC Miniserver

To demonstrate the building of an embeddable server, we will be implementing a fairly simple server with a slight twist. Instead of a simple Hello World example, we'll design an OpenGL-embedding server that embeds a three-dimensional cube object into the container.

AppWizard: Step-by-Step

Begin by choosing File | New from the Developer Studio menu and taking a quick peek at the list of projects you can create (see Figure 27.1).

Of particular interest to us are the two types of projects we're going to build:

- MFC AppWizard (dll)
- MFC AppWizard (exe)

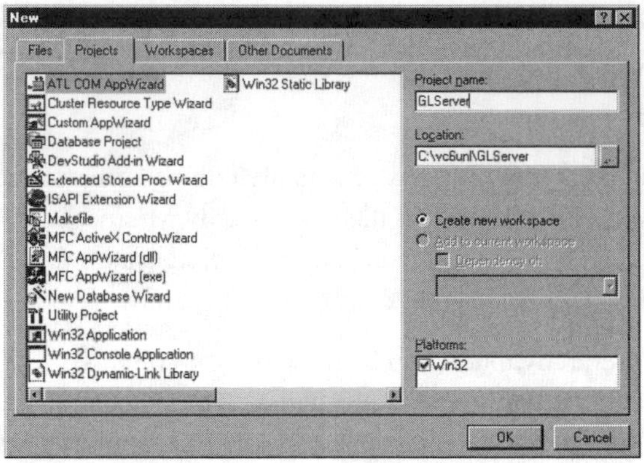

FIGURE 27.1

A list of new project types.

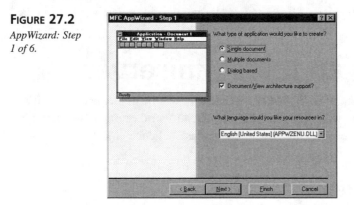

The first project will be an active document miniserver, which we will build as an EXE application. To begin, choose MFC AppWizard (exe). In the Project Name edit box, type `GLServer`.

Step 1 of 6

Figure 27.2 shows the first step in creating a miniserver. For our example, we'll create a *single-document interface (SDI)* application.

FIGURE 27.2

AppWizard: Step 1 of 6.

Step 2 of 6

Here, we have the option of including database support, but we'll simply choose None for our example.

Step 3 of 6

Now things get a little more interesting. Figure 27.3 shows the required parameters. You won't require automation, because you'll tackle that in the MFCAuto example later. Enable the Active Document Server check box.

You don't need support for ActiveX controls. For the GLServer project, this option isn't selected. On the other hand, this could be desirable for a full server to enhance the appearance of the application and provide more functionality to the user.

FIGURE 27.3

AppWizard: Step 3 of 6.

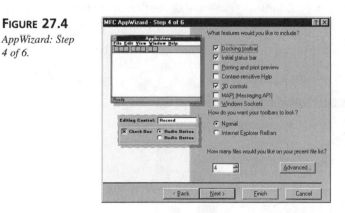

Step 4 of 6

The only thing to change here is to disable the Printing and Print Preview check box, because a miniserver does not need to support printing itself—this usually is left up to the container application. Figure 27.4 shows MFC AppWizard Step 4 for the GLServer project.

FIGURE 27.4

AppWizard: Step 4 of 6.

Before moving on to step 5, you must define a file extension for GLServer. If you attempt to move on, MFC AppWizard displays a dialog box as a reminder. Technically, the project doesn't use the file extension, because the server doesn't persist any data to a compound file, but MFC AppWizard will insist. Figure 27.5 shows the Advanced

Options dialog box for the GLServer project. The file extension GLS is used for this project.

FIGURE 27.5

The AppWizard Advanced Options dialog box.

Step 5 of 6

Don't change any options in step 5. It is better to use MFC in a DLL instead of statically linking the libraries, because it conserves disk space.

Step 6 of 6

You've reached the final step in the wizard. Notice that there are a couple of new classes that you may not have seen before: `CInPlaceFrame` and `CGLServerSrvrItem` (see Figure 27.6). These new classes are required to provide functionality for the server.

Also, note the base class for `CGLServerDoc`; it's no longer `CDocument` but rather `COleServerDoc` (which is a subclass of `CDocument`).

FIGURE 27.6

AppWizard: Step 6 of 6.

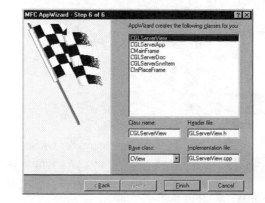

A Closer Look at the `GLServer` Classes

Now, let's open up the GLServer project and take a closer look at the classes AppWizard generated.

CGLServerApp

Notice that in the declaration section for the `CGLServerApp` class, a new variable has been declared (see Listing 27.1).

LISTING 27.1 New Data Member for `CGLServerApp`

```
// Implementation
 COleTemplateServer m_server;
```

This is probably the most important object your project will create. This object is the basis for in-place editing/activation (which is explained in detail later in this chapter in the section "`CInPlaceFrame`") and provides the functionality used by full servers, mini-servers, and automation servers.

Now, let's take a look at the implementation of the `CGLServerApp` class.

Listing 27.2 looks at the `CLSID`, or `ClassID`. When information about the GLServer COM class is added to the Windows Registry, the value is used to uniquely identify this class from other COM classes. If you create the project from scratch, your `CLSID` will be different from the one shown here.

LISTING 27.2 CLSID Source for This Application

```
// {469849A5-7272-11D3-B515-CC43834E4167}
static const CLSID clsid =
{0x469849a5, 0x7272, 0x11d3,{ 0xb5, 0x15, 0xcc, 0x43, 0x83, 0x4e, 0x41, 0x67}};
```

The `InitInstance()` method shown in Listing 27.3 is really the only method that is significantly different than in non–OLE server SDI projects. Comments and white space in the listing have been edited for space. The first thing to note is that we call `AfxOleInit()` to initialize the OLE libraries.

The document template is the same as with non–OLE server projects, except that the `CGLServerDoc` class now is derived from `COleServerDoc` instead of `CDocument`.

Notice the call to `SetServerInfo()` immediately after the document template is created, which lets the framework know what type of activation is available when the user requests to edit the data. Our server will provide in-place activation.

27

ACTIVE SERVERS

Lastly, notice that we check to see whether we are in embedding mode; if so, we call RegisterAll(), which actually creates the object the container will use. Notice also that we do not support standalone execution. (Remember, this is a miniserver that must be embedded in a container application.) If the user attempts to start the application as a standalone, a message box explains that the application must be launched by inserting an object into a container.

LISTING 27.3   Source Code for `CGLServerApp::InitInstance`

```
BOOL CGLServerApp::InitInstance()
{
    // Initialize OLE libraries
    if (!AfxOleInit())
    {
        AfxMessageBox(IDP_OLE_INIT_FAILED);
        return FALSE;
    }
#ifdef _AFXDLL
    Enable3dControls();
#else
    Enable3dControlsStatic();
#endif
    // Change the registry key under which our settings are stored.
    SetRegistryKey(_T("Local AppWizard-Generated Applications"));
    LoadStdProfileSettings();

    CSingleDocTemplate* pDocTemplate;
    pDocTemplate = new CSingleDocTemplate(
        IDR_MAINFRAME,
        RUNTIME_CLASS(CGLServerDoc),
        RUNTIME_CLASS(CMainFrame),         // main SDI frame window
        RUNTIME_CLASS(CGLServerView));
    pDocTemplate->SetServerInfo(
        IDR_SRVR_EMBEDDED, IDR_SRVR_INPLACE,
        RUNTIME_CLASS(CInPlaceFrame));
    AddDocTemplate(pDocTemplate);

    // Connect the COleTemplateServer to the document template.
    //  The COleTemplateServer creates new documents on behalf
    //  of requesting OLE containers by using information
    //  specified in the document template.
    m_server.ConnectTemplate(clsid, pDocTemplate, TRUE);
    // Note: SDI applications register server objects only if
    //     /Embedding or /Automation
    // is present on the command line.

    CCommandLineInfo cmdInfo;
    ParseCommandLine(cmdInfo);
    // Check to see if launched as OLE server
```

```
if (cmdInfo.m_bRunEmbedded || cmdInfo.m_bRunAutomated)
{
    // Register all OLE server (factories) as running.
    COleTemplateServer::RegisterAll();
    // Application was run with /Embedding or /Automation.
    // Don't show the main window in this case.
    return TRUE;
}

// When a server application is launched standalone, it
// is a good idea to update the system registry in case
// it has been damaged.
m_server.UpdateRegistry(OAT_DOC_OBJECT_SERVER);

// When a mini-server is run standalone the registry
// is updated and the user is instructed to use the
// Insert Object dialog in a container to use the server.
// Mini-servers do not have standalone user interfaces.
AfxMessageBox(IDP_USE_INSERT_OBJECT);
return FALSE;
}
```

CGLServerDoc

The `COleServerDoc` document class is the heart of the embeddable server and is ready to roll without any modifications. (You'll want to add some customization to make it useful.)

Although not necessary for our particular application, to enable compound files for storage and data display, we simply call the `EnableCompoundFile()` method during the construction of this document, as shown in Listing 27.4.

LISTING 27.4   `CGLServerDoc` Constructor

```
CGLServerDoc::CGLServerDoc()
{
    // Use OLE compound files
    EnableCompoundFile();
}
```

The `OnGetEmbeddedItem()` notification is called by the class factory to create a new `CGLServerSrvrItem` item. The `CGLServerDoc` class also includes the `Serialize()` method, which can be enhanced to automatically serialize data to the container's persistent storage, as required, to save the state of this server.

For example, if your server has special options that were configured, such as font size and color, you easily could add serialization code so that this information is saved to persistent storage when the user chooses Save As in the container application. The data then is serialized with the container's data, not in a separate file, so that when the container is opened in a future editing session and the server is invoked, it can serialize its data and continue where it left off.

CGLServerSrvrItem

When a GLServer item is embedded in a container (such as WordPad or MS Word), a new instance of CGLServerSrvrItem is created and passed to the container. The OnGetExtent() method is called by the container to determine the size of the object being embedded. The default implementation created by the AppWizard uses a hard-coded 3000×3000 HIMETRIC units extent (see Listing 27.5).

LISTING 27.5   OnGetExtent() Implementation Code

```
BOOL CGLServerSrvrItem::OnGetExtent(DVASPECT dwDrawAspect, CSize& rSize)
{

    if (dwDrawAspect != DVASPECT_CONTENT)
     return COleServerItem::OnGetExtent(dwDrawAspect, rSize);

    // CGLServerSrvrItem::OnGetExtent is called to get the extent in
    //  HIMETRIC units of the entire item.  The default implementation
    //  here simply returns a hard-coded number of units.

    CGLServerDoc* pDoc = GetDocument();
    ASSERT_VALID(pDoc);

    rSize = CSize(3000, 3000);    // 3000 x 3000 HIMETRIC units

    return TRUE;
}
```

GLServer also paints into a special device context provided by the container called a *metafile device context* (which can contain any GDI objects, including bitmaps and brushes) when the container calls the OnDraw() member function shown in Listing 27.6.

The container uses this metafile representation to display the item when the server is not active. This way, the container doesn't need to start the GLServer application to see this embedded data. The GLServer application will not be loaded unless the user specifically requests it.

By default, the AppWizard does not provide any painting, so if you build this project as-is, the embedded object will not contain any visual representation whatsoever.

LISTING 27.6 OnDraw() Implementation Code

```cpp
BOOL CGLServerSrvrItem::OnDraw(CDC* pDC, CSize& rSize)
{
 // Remove this if you use rSize
 UNREFERENCED_PARAMETER(rSize);

 CGLServerDoc* pDoc = GetDocument();
 ASSERT_VALID(pDoc);

 // TODO: set mapping mode and extent
 //  (The extent is usually the same as the size returned from OnGetExtent)
 pDC->SetMapMode(MM_ANISOTROPIC);
 pDC->SetWindowOrg(0,0);
 pDC->SetWindowExt(3000, 3000);

 // TODO: add drawing code here.  Optionally, fill in the HIMETRIC extent.
 //  All drawing takes place in the metafile device context (pDC).

 return TRUE;
}
```

When the container wants to store a document with a GLServer-embedded item, it calls `Serialize()` to save any modifications. The basic implementation simply calls the `CGLServerDoc`'s default implementation of `Serialize()` (see Listing 27.7). The data is not serialized to a file but to a persistent storage object provided by the container.

In some cases, calling the default implementation isn't the correct way to handle storage. For example, suppose that you don't want to save the data to the container's storage but would rather store it to a separate file and link that file to the container. Microsoft Word has this option. Instead of saving a picture inside the document, you can link to a separate file, thus saving document storage and retrieval time.

LISTING 27.7 Serialize() Implementation Code

```cpp
void CGLServerSrvrItem::Serialize(CArchive& ar)
{

    if (!IsLinkedItem())
    {
        CGLServerDoc* pDoc = GetDocument();
        ASSERT_VALID(pDoc);
        pDoc->Serialize(ar);
    }
}
```

27

ACTIVE SERVERS

CInPlaceFrame

This class requires a bit more explanation than the others did. First, let me explain the term *in-place activation*. Basically, in-place activation means that when the user invokes an embedded server by double-clicking the object in the container, instead of bringing up a separate window for editing the server data, the server actually uses the container's window. Figures 27.7 and 27.8 provide examples of in-place activation.

Figure 27.7 shows a WordPad application with an embedded bitmap in it. Currently, the WordPad application is active, allowing you to change the WordPad text.

FIGURE 27.7

WordPad with an embedded bitmap.

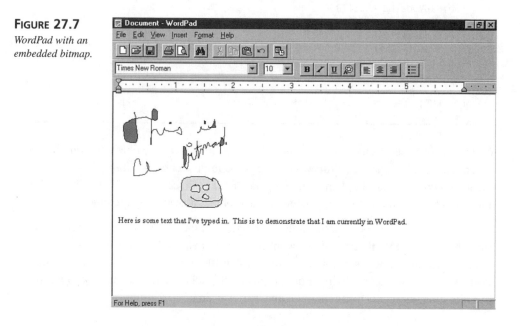

By double-clicking the bitmap image (remember that this is an embedded Paintbrush bitmap), the Paintbrush program is activated in-place. This means that it takes over the client area of the WordPad application. Notice that in Figure 27.8, the toolbars on the top have disappeared and have been replaced by the Paintbrush toolbar on the left side. Not visible here is the fact that the menus also have changed.

Remember, though, that in-place activation is not the only way to edit embedded objects. You also can use out-of-place activation if you embed an icon representation of the image instead of the image itself. You can do this either when you first insert the object by enabling the Display as Icon check box, or by right-clicking the object inside WordPad, choosing Object Properties, selecting the View tab, and selecting the Display as Icon radio button (see Figure 27.9).

FIGURE 27.8

Paintbrush in-place activation inside WordPad.

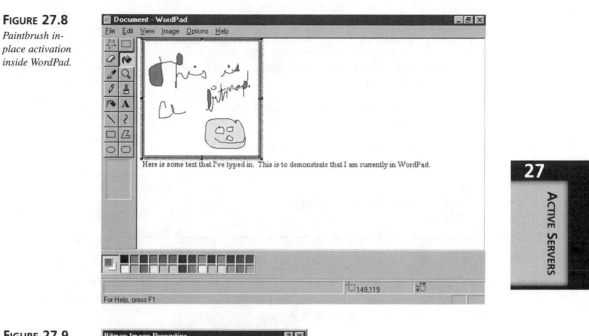

FIGURE 27.9

Setting the server item to out-of-place activation inside WordPad.

If you look carefully at the in-place activation session, you'll notice a funny rectangle around the object with sizers around the edges. This is called the *resizer bar.* You can use this bar to resize the embedded object during in-place activation. Listing 27.8 includes the default implementation for this resizer bar.

Drag-and-drop support is registered, although the default implementation does nothing.

LISTING 27.8 OnCreate() Member Function

```
int CInPlaceFrame::OnCreate(LPCREATESTRUCT lpCreateStruct)
{
    if (COleIPFrameWnd::OnCreate(lpCreateStruct) == -1)
        return -1;

    // CResizeBar implements in-place resizing.
    if (!m_wndResizeBar.Create(this))
    {
        TRACE0("Failed to create resize bar\n");
        return -1;       // fail to create
    }

    m_dropTarget.Register(this);
    return 0;
}
```

The AppWizard generates a toolbar that appears during in-place activation and temporarily replaces the container's toolbars. Listing 27.9 shows the code used to register the toolbars. Although this is an embedded toolbar, it still can have all the properties of a regular toolbar, including the dockable characteristic.

LISTING 27.9 OnCreateControlBars() Member Function

```
BOOL CInPlaceFrame::OnCreateControlBars(CFrameWnd* pWndFrame,
➡ CFrameWnd* pWndDoc)
{
    // Remove this if you use pWndDoc
    UNREFERENCED_PARAMETER(pWndDoc);

    m_wndToolBar.SetOwner(this);

    // Create toolbar on client's frame window
    if (!m_wndToolBar.Create(pWndFrame) ||
        !m_wndToolBar.LoadToolBar(IDR_SRVR_INPLACE))
    {
        TRACE0("Failed to create toolbar\n");
        return FALSE;
    }

    // TODO: Remove this if you don't want tool tips or a resizeable toolbar
    m_wndToolBar.SetBarStyle(m_wndToolBar.GetBarStyle() |
        CBRS_TOOLTIPS | CBRS_FLYBY | CBRS_SIZE_DYNAMIC);

    // TODO: Delete these three lines if you don't want the toolbar to
```

```
//  be dockable
m_wndToolBar.EnableDocking(CBRS_ALIGN_ANY);
pWndFrame->EnableDocking(CBRS_ALIGN_ANY);
pWndFrame->DockControlBar(&m_wndToolBar);

    return TRUE;
}
```

CGLServerView

Last but not least is the view class. The only real difference between this view class and view classes in non–OLE server projects is the addition of a special notification to cancel the embedded session, as shown in Listing 27.10. This is required for keyboard processing only (such as the use of the Esc key), because the mouse handler goes to the container instead of the server (by clicking outside the embedded server area).

LISTING 27.10   OnCancelEditSrvr() Member Function

```
void CGLServerView::OnCancelEditSrvr()
{
    GetDocument()->OnDeactivateUI(FALSE);
}
```

Combining Container and Server Menus During Activation

As you might have noticed in Figures 27.8 and 27.9, when you start in-place activation, the server's menus are combined with the container's menus.

You won't be modifying this functionality in the example, but I want to give you an understanding of just how these two menus are combined.

Both the container and the server provide partial menus. When the server is activated, the two sets of menus are merged to form the new in-place activation menus. Figure 27.10 shows the partial menu used by GLServer. The container menus can be merged with this menu before Edit, between View and Help (the two separator bars help to determine this) or after Help.

FIGURE 27.10

The GLServer in-place activation partial menus.

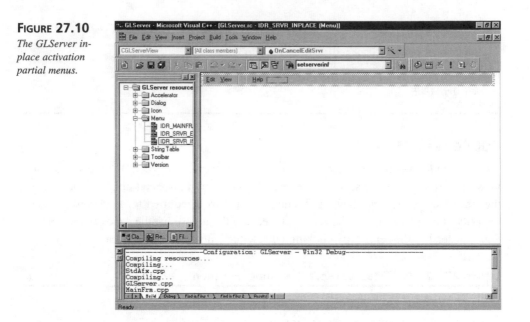

Testing Out the GLServer Skeleton

Before adding customization, try compiling the GLServer example the way it is right now and use WordPad to embed it. It won't do much, but you should be able to embed the server and see an empty window inside the sizer bar (see Figure 27.11). To register this example, you'll have to run the application. You should get a message from GLServer telling you that the application can be run only from a container. Just click OK. Your GLServer now is registered, and you can insert it into WordPad.

Adding Customization to the GLServer Skeleton

Now, let's start adding some customized methods, data members, and so on, to make this server sing.

Customizing CGLServerDoc

Our document class will hold the methods and data members used for this example. Therefore, most of the code that actually draws the OpenGL shape will be stored in this class, and rightly so. Change the CGLServerDoc declaration, as indicated by the bold text in Listing 27.11.

FIGURE 27.11

The GLServer skeleton.

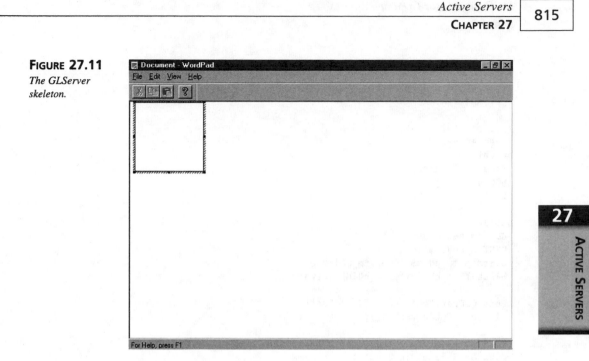

LISTING 27.11   Modifications to the `CGLServerDoc` Class

```
class CGLServerDoc : public COleServerDoc
{
public:
 // private member vars

protected: // create from serialization only
 CGLServerDoc();
 DECLARE_DYNCREATE(CGLServerDoc)

// Attributes
public:
 CGLServerSrvrItem* GetEmbeddedItem()
  { return (CGLServerSrvrItem*)COleServerDoc::GetEmbeddedItem(); }

// Operations
public:

// Overrides
 // ClassWizard generated virtual function overrides
 //{{AFX_VIRTUAL(CGLServerDoc)
 protected:
 virtual COleServerItem* OnGetEmbeddedItem();
 public:
 virtual BOOL OnNewDocument();
```

27

LISTING 27.11   continued

```
 virtual void Serialize(CArchive& ar);
 //}}AFX_VIRTUAL

// Implementation
//member vars
private:
 float m_fRadius;
 HGLRC m_hrc;
 LOGPALETTE *m_pPalette;

public:
 CDC *m_pMemoryDC;
 RECT m_rcViewRect;
 CBitmap *m_pOldBitmap, *m_pBitmap;
 HPALETTE m_hPalette, m_hOldPalette;

 void GLDraw(CDC* pDC, RECT *pRect);
 virtual ~CGLServerDoc();

 void CreateGLContext(HDC hdc, RECT& rc);
 BOOL SetGLPixels(HDC hdc);
 unsigned char GetPaletteIndex(int nIndex, UINT nBits, UINT nShift);
 void CreateGLPalette(HDC hdc);

#ifdef _DEBUG
 virtual void AssertValid() const;
 virtual void Dump(CDumpContext& dc) const;
#endif

protected:

// Generated message map functions
protected:
 //{{AFX_MSG(CGLServerDoc)
  // NOTE - the ClassWizard will add and remove member functions here.
  //    DO NOT EDIT what you see in these blocks of generated code !
 //}}AFX_MSG
 DECLARE_MESSAGE_MAP()

};
```

Now change the CGLServerDoc implementation as shown in Listing 27.12.

LISTING 27.12   Modifications to the CGLServerDoc Implementation

```cpp
// GLServerDoc.cpp : implementation of the CGLServerDoc class
//

#include "stdafx.h"
#include "gl\glaux.h"

#include "GLServer.h"

#include "GLServerDoc.h"
#include "SrvrItem.h"

#ifdef _DEBUG
#define new DEBUG_NEW
#undef THIS_FILE
static char THIS_FILE[] = __FILE__;
#endif

unsigned char cShift1[2] = { 0, 255 };
unsigned char cShift3[4] = { 0, 0x55, 0xaa, 0xff };
unsigned char cShift7[8] = { 0, 0111 >> 1, 0222 >> 1, 0333 >> 1,
        0444 >> 1, 0555 >> 1, 0666 >> 1, 0377 };
static int nPalColors[13] = { 0, 3, 24, 27, 64, 67, 88, 173,
        181, 236, 247, 164, 91 };
static PALETTEENTRY defPalette[20] =
{
 { 0,    0,    0,    0 }, { 0x80,0,   0,    0 }, { 0,    0x80,0,    0 },
 { 0x80,0x80,0,     0 }, { 0,    0,    0x80, 0 }, { 0x80,0,    0x80, 0 },
 { 0,    0x80,0x80, 0 }, { 0xC0,0xC0,0xC0, 0 }, { 192, 220, 192,  0 },
 { 166, 202, 240,   0 }, { 255, 251, 240,  0 }, { 160, 160, 164,  0 },
 { 0x80,0x80,0x80, 0 }, { 0xFF,0,    0,    0 }, { 0,    0xFF,0,    0 },
 { 0xFF,0xFF,0,     0 }, { 0,    0,    0xFF, 0 }, { 0xFF,0,    0xFF, 0 },
 { 0,    0xFF,0xFF, 0 }, { 0xFF,0xFF,0xFF, 0 }
};

///////////////////////////////////////////////////////////////////////////
// CGLServerDoc

IMPLEMENT_DYNCREATE(CGLServerDoc, COleServerDoc)

BEGIN_MESSAGE_MAP(CGLServerDoc, COleServerDoc)
 //{{AFX_MSG_MAP(CGLServerDoc)
  // NOTE - the ClassWizard will add and remove mapping macros here.
  //     DO NOT EDIT what you see in these blocks of generated code!
 //}}AFX_MSG_MAP
END_MESSAGE_MAP()

///////////////////////////////////////////////////////////////////////////
// CGLServerDoc construction/destruction

CGLServerDoc::CGLServerDoc()
{
```

LISTING 27.12   continued

```
// Use OLE compound files
EnableCompoundFile();

// set defaults
m_pPalette = NULL;
m_hPalette, m_hOldPalette = NULL;
m_hrc = NULL;
m_pMemoryDC = NULL;
m_pBitmap = m_pOldBitmap = NULL;
}

CGLServerDoc::~CGLServerDoc()
{
}

BOOL CGLServerDoc::OnNewDocument()
{
 if (!COleServerDoc::OnNewDocument())
  return FALSE;

 // TODO: add reinitialization code here
 // (SDI documents will reuse this document)

 return TRUE;
}

/////////////////////////////////////////////////////////////////////////////
// CGLServerDoc server implementation

COleServerItem* CGLServerDoc::OnGetEmbeddedItem()
{
 // OnGetEmbeddedItem is called by the framework to get the COleServerItem
 //  that is associated with the document.  It is only called when necessary.

 CGLServerSrvrItem* pItem = new CGLServerSrvrItem(this);
 ASSERT_VALID(pItem);
 return pItem;
}

/////////////////////////////////////////////////////////////////////////////
// CGLServerDoc serialization

void CGLServerDoc::Serialize(CArchive& ar)
{
 if (ar.IsStoring())
 {
  // TODO: add storing code here
 }
 else
 {
```

```
  // TODO: add loading code here
 }
}


/////////////////////////////////////////////////////////////////////////////
// CGLServerDoc diagnostics

#ifdef _DEBUG
void CGLServerDoc::AssertValid() const
{
 COleServerDoc::AssertValid();
}

void CGLServerDoc::Dump(CDumpContext& dc) const
{
 COleServerDoc::Dump(dc);
}
#endif //_DEBUG

/////////////////////////////////////////////////////////////////////////////
// CGLServerDoc commands

void CGLServerDoc::GLDraw(CDC *pDC, RECT *pRect)
{
 // setup
 HDC hdc = pDC->GetSafeHdc();
 CreateGLContext(hdc, *pRect);

 // clear buffers and colors
    glClearColor(0.0f, 0.0f, 0.0f, 10.0f);
    glClear(GL_COLOR_BUFFER_BIT | GL_DEPTH_BUFFER_BIT);

 // push matrix
    glPushMatrix();

 // set up geometric rotation scenario
    glTranslatef(0.0f, 0.0f, -m_fRadius);

 // FRONTSIDE
 // draw a side
 glBegin(GL_QUAD_STRIP);
  glColor3f(1.0f, 0.0f, 0.0f); glVertex3f(-1.25f,  0.0f, -0.5f);
  glColor3f(0.5f, 0.0f, 0.0f); glVertex3f(-1.25f, -1.0f, -0.5f);
  glColor3f(1.0f, 0.0f, 0.0f); glVertex3f(-0.75f,  0.0f, -0.5f);
  glColor3f(0.5f, 0.0f, 0.0f); glVertex3f(-0.75f, -1.0f, -0.5f);
 glEnd();

 // draw a side
 glBegin(GL_QUAD_STRIP);
  glColor3f(0.0f, 0.5f, 0.0f); glVertex3f(-0.75f,  0.0f, -0.5f);
  glColor3f(0.0f, 1.0f, 0.0f); glVertex3f(-0.75f, -1.0f, -0.5f);
```

27

ACTIVE SERVERS

LISTING 27.12   continued

```
 glColor3f(0.0f, 0.5f, 0.0f); glVertex3f(-0.25f,  0.5f,  0.0f);
 glColor3f(0.0f, 1.0f, 0.0f); glVertex3f(-0.25f, -0.5f,  0.0f);
glEnd();

// draw a side
glBegin(GL_QUAD_STRIP);
 glColor3f(0.0f, 0.5f, 1.0f); glVertex3f(-0.25f,  0.5f,  0.0f);
 glColor3f(0.0f, 1.0f, 0.5f); glVertex3f(-0.25f, -0.5f,  0.0f);
 glColor3f(0.0f, 0.5f, 1.0f); glVertex3f( 0.25f,  0.5f,  0.0f);
 glColor3f(0.0f, 1.0f, 0.5f); glVertex3f( 0.25f, -0.5f,  0.0f);
glEnd();

// draw a side
glBegin(GL_QUAD_STRIP);
 glColor3f(0.0f, 0.5f, 0.0f); glVertex3f( 0.25f,  0.5f,  0.0f);
 glColor3f(0.0f, 1.0f, 0.0f); glVertex3f( 0.25f, -0.5f,  0.0f);
 glColor3f(0.0f, 0.5f, 0.0f); glVertex3f( 0.75f,  0.0f, -0.5f);
 glColor3f(0.0f, 1.0f, 0.0f); glVertex3f( 0.75f, -1.0f, -0.5f);
glEnd();

// draw a side
glBegin(GL_QUAD_STRIP);
 glColor3f(0.5f, 0.0f, 0.0f); glVertex3f( 0.75f,  0.0f, -0.5f);
 glColor3f(1.0f, 0.0f, 0.0f); glVertex3f( 0.75f, -1.0f, -0.5f);
 glColor3f(0.5f, 0.0f, 0.0f); glVertex3f( 1.25f,  0.0f, -0.5f);
 glColor3f(1.0f, 0.0f, 0.0f); glVertex3f( 1.25f, -1.0f, -0.5f);
glEnd();

// BACKSIDE
// draw a side
glBegin(GL_QUAD_STRIP);
 glColor3f(0.5f, 1.0f, 0.0f); glVertex3f(-1.25f,  0.0f, -0.5f);
 glColor3f(1.0f, 0.5f, 0.0f); glVertex3f(-1.25f, -1.0f, -0.5f);
 glColor3f(0.5f, 1.0f, 0.0f); glVertex3f(-0.50f,  1.0f,  0.5f);
 glColor3f(1.0f, 0.5f, 0.0f); glVertex3f(-0.50f,  0.0f,  0.5f);
glEnd();

// draw a side
glBegin(GL_QUAD_STRIP);
 glColor3f(0.5f, 0.0f, 1.0f); glVertex3f(-0.50f,  1.0f,  0.5f);
 glColor3f(1.0f, 0.0f, 0.5f); glVertex3f(-0.50f,  0.0f,  0.5f);
 glColor3f(0.5f, 0.0f, 1.0f); glVertex3f( 0.50f,  1.0f,  0.5f);
 glColor3f(1.0f, 0.0f, 0.5f); glVertex3f( 0.50f,  0.0f,  0.5f);
glEnd();

// draw a side
glBegin(GL_QUAD_STRIP);
 glColor3f(0.5f, 1.0f, 0.0f); glVertex3f( 1.25f,  0.0f, -0.5f);
 glColor3f(1.0f, 0.5f, 0.0f); glVertex3f( 1.25f, -1.0f, -0.5f);
 glColor3f(0.5f, 1.0f, 0.0f); glVertex3f( 0.50f,  1.0f,  0.5f);
```

```
    glColor3f(1.0f, 0.5f, 0.0f); glVertex3f( 0.50f,  0.0f,  0.5f);
  glEnd();

  // TOPFACE
  glBegin(GL_QUAD_STRIP);
   glColor3f(0.0f, 0.0f, 0.5f); glVertex3f(-1.25f,  0.0f, -0.5f);
   glColor3f(0.0f, 0.0f, 1.0f); glVertex3f(-0.75f,  0.0f, -0.5f);
   glColor3f(0.0f, 0.0f, 0.5f); glVertex3f(-0.50f,  1.0f,  0.5f);
   glColor3f(0.0f, 0.0f, 1.0f); glVertex3f(-0.25f,  0.5f,  0.0f);
   glColor3f(0.0f, 0.0f, 0.5f); glVertex3f( 0.50f,  1.0f,  0.5f);
   glColor3f(0.0f, 0.0f, 1.0f); glVertex3f( 0.25f,  0.5f,  0.0f);
   glColor3f(0.0f, 0.0f, 0.5f); glVertex3f( 1.25f,  0.0f, -0.5f);
   glColor3f(0.0f, 0.0f, 1.0f); glVertex3f( 0.75f,  0.0f, -0.5f);
  glEnd();

  // BOTTOMFACE
  glBegin(GL_QUAD_STRIP);
   glColor3f(0.0f, 0.0f, 0.5f); glVertex3f(-1.25f, -1.0f, -0.5f);
   glColor3f(0.0f, 0.0f, 1.0f); glVertex3f(-0.75f, -1.0f, -0.5f);
   glColor3f(0.0f, 0.0f, 0.5f); glVertex3f(-0.50f,  0.0f,  0.5f);
   glColor3f(0.0f, 0.0f, 1.0f); glVertex3f(-0.25f, -0.5f,  0.0f);
   glColor3f(0.0f, 0.0f, 0.5f); glVertex3f( 0.50f,  0.0f,  0.5f);
   glColor3f(0.0f, 0.0f, 1.0f); glVertex3f( 0.25f, -0.5f,  0.0f);
   glColor3f(0.0f, 0.0f, 0.5f); glVertex3f( 1.25f, -1.0f, -0.5f);
   glColor3f(0.0f, 0.0f, 1.0f); glVertex3f( 0.75f, -1.0f, -0.5f);
  glEnd();


    glPopMatrix();

  // all done drawing, finish up and swap buffers
    glFinish();
    SwapBuffers(wglGetCurrentDC());
  SetBkMode(hdc, TRANSPARENT);

  // cleanup
    ::wglMakeCurrent(NULL,  NULL);

  // delete GL context
    if (m_hrc)
  {
        ::wglDeleteContext(m_hrc);
   m_hrc = NULL;
  }
}


void CGLServerDoc::CreateGLContext(HDC hdc, RECT& rc)
{
    PIXELFORMATDESCRIPTOR pfdPixels;

  // set up the pixel format
    if (SetGLPixels(hdc) == FALSE)
  {
```

LISTING 27.12 continued

```
        return;
    }

    // create our GL palette
    CreateGLPalette(hdc);

    // realize palette
    ::SelectPalette(hdc, m_hPalette, FALSE);
    ::RealizePalette(hdc);

    // set up pixel format
    ::DescribePixelFormat(hdc, ::GetPixelFormat(hdc), sizeof(pfdPixels),
&pfdPixels);

    // create gl context
    m_hrc = wglCreateContext(hdc);
    wglMakeCurrent(hdc, m_hrc);
    glClearDepth(10.0f);
    glEnable(GL_DEPTH_TEST);
    glMatrixMode(GL_PROJECTION);
    glLoadIdentity();

    // check for divide by zero
    if (rc.bottom != 0)
        gluPerspective(30.0f, (GLfloat)rc.right/rc.bottom, 3.0f, 20.0f);
    else
        gluPerspective(30.0f, 1.0f, 3.0f, 20.0f);

    glMatrixMode(GL_MODELVIEW);
    m_fRadius = 3.0f + 3.0f / 2.0f;
}

BOOL CGLServerDoc::SetGLPixels(HDC hdc)
{
    int nPixFmt;
    static PIXELFORMATDESCRIPTOR pfdPixels =
    {
        sizeof(PIXELFORMATDESCRIPTOR), 1,
     PFD_DOUBLEBUFFER | PFD_DRAW_TO_WINDOW | PFD_SUPPORT_OPENGL,
        PFD_TYPE_RGBA, 24, 0, 0, 0, 0, 0, 0, 0, 0, 0, 0, 0, 0, 0,
        32, 0, 0, PFD_MAIN_PLANE, 0, 0, 0, 0
    };

    if ((nPixFmt = ChoosePixelFormat(hdc, &pfdPixels)) == 0)
    {
        _ASSERTE(FALSE);
        return FALSE;
    }

    if (SetPixelFormat(hdc, nPixFmt, &pfdPixels) == FALSE)
    {
```

```
        _ASSERTE(FALSE);
        return FALSE;
    }

    return TRUE;
}

unsigned char CGLServerDoc::GetPaletteIndex(int nIndex, UINT nBits, UINT nShift)
{
    if (nBits == 1)
  return cShift1[(unsigned char) (nIndex >> nShift) & 0x1];

 else if (nBits == 2)
  return cShift3[(unsigned char) (nIndex >> nShift) & 0x3];

 else if (nBits == 3)
  return cShift7[(unsigned char) (nIndex >> nShift) & 0x7];

 else
  return 0;
}

void CGLServerDoc::CreateGLPalette(HDC hdc)
{
    PIXELFORMATDESCRIPTOR pfdPixels;
    int nPixelFormat, nCounter;

 // only do first time in
 if (m_pPalette)
  return;

 // calculate pixel format
    nPixelFormat = ::GetPixelFormat(hdc);
    ::DescribePixelFormat(hdc, nPixelFormat, sizeof(pfdPixels), &pfdPixels);

 // change palette if necessary
    if (pfdPixels.dwFlags & PFD_NEED_PALETTE)
    {
        nPixelFormat = 1 << pfdPixels.cColorBits;
        m_pPalette = (PLOGPALETTE) new char[sizeof(LOGPALETTE) +
    nPixelFormat * sizeof(PALETTEENTRY)];

        _ASSERTE(m_pPalette != NULL);

        m_pPalette->palVersion = 0x300;
        m_pPalette->palNumEntries = nPixelFormat;

  // loop through pixel set and set palette colors
        for (nCounter=0; nCounter < nPixelFormat; nCounter++)
        {
            m_pPalette->palPalEntry[nCounter].peRed = GetPaletteIndex(
```

LISTING 27.12   continued

```
            nCounter, pfdPixels.cRedBits, pfdPixels.cRedShift);
                m_pPalette->palPalEntry[nCounter].peGreen = GetPaletteIndex(
            nCounter, pfdPixels.cGreenBits, pfdPixels.cGreenShift);
                m_pPalette->palPalEntry[nCounter].peBlue = GetPaletteIndex(
            nCounter, pfdPixels.cBlueBits, pfdPixels.cBlueShift);
                m_pPalette->palPalEntry[nCounter].peFlags = 0;
          }

          if ((pfdPixels.cColorBits == 8) &&
              (pfdPixels.cRedBits    == 3) && (pfdPixels.cRedShift   == 0) &&
              (pfdPixels.cGreenBits  == 3) && (pfdPixels.cGreenShift == 3) &&
              (pfdPixels.cBlueBits   == 2) && (pfdPixels.cBlueShift  == 6))
          {
      for (nCounter = 1 ; nCounter <= 12 ; nCounter++)
                    m_pPalette->palPalEntry[nPalColors[nCounter]] =
    defPalette[nCounter];
          }

      // create GL palette
      m_hPalette = ::CreatePalette((LPLOGPALETTE)m_pPalette);

      // realize palette
          ::SelectPalette(hdc, m_hPalette, FALSE);
          ::RealizePalette(hdc);
      }
    }
```

I know a lot of additions are here, but trust me, the result is worth the effort—especially if you decide to add your own enhancements later (such as choice of shapes, colors, lighting, textures, and so on), but I'll leave that up to your imagination.

I'm not going to spend a lot time explaining how OpenGL works, but I will tell you that the only method you will need to call is the GLDraw() method. Pass it a device context to draw in and a rectangle for the size.

> **Note**
>
> OpenGL can only draw directly to overlapped child windows, so don't try passing it a metafile device context or a memory device context. The call to SetPixelFormat() always returns FALSE.

Customizing CGLServerView

During in-place activation, you'll want the shape to appear in the view window that the server creates; therefore, you'll need to override the OnDraw() method of the view class. Please add the changes shown in Listing 27.13 to your code.

Because the `OpenGL` can draw only to an overlapped window, I've fooled the system a little bit here. After calling the `GLDraw()` method with the view window's `HDC`, I copied its contents (using the palette that `GLDraw()` created) into a memory device context (in the `CGLServerSrvrItem::OnDraw()` method). That way, the server item will be able to copy the image to the metafile device context.

Notice the call to `UpdateAllItems()`. This tells the document to inform all server items that they need to redraw themselves. (A call to `CGLServerSrvrItem::OnDraw()` is made.)

To ensure that you always have the correct window size, each time you perform a draw, delete the previous memory DC and bitmap, and rc-crcatc thc bitmap based on the new window size.

It's really important to remember to realize the palette into the memory DC; otherwise, you'll get an ugly-looking shape.

LISTING 27.13   Modifications to the `CGLServerView` Implementation

```
void CGLServerView::OnDraw(CDC* pDC)
{
 CGLServerDoc* pDoc = GetDocument();
 ASSERT_VALID(pDoc);

 // check if memory DC is there, if so, copy contents to it
 if (pDoc->m_pMemoryDC != NULL)
 {
   // restore old palette and bitmap
   ::SelectPalette(pDoc->m_pMemoryDC->GetSafeHdc(), pDoc->m_hOldPalette, FALSE);
   pDoc->m_pMemoryDC->SelectObject(pDoc->m_pOldBitmap);

   // clean up previous device context stuff
   pDoc->m_pMemoryDC->DeleteDC();
   delete pDoc->m_pBitmap;
   delete pDoc->m_pMemoryDC;
 }

 // Get the window size
 GetClientRect(&pDoc->m_rcViewRect);

 // prepare memorydc and bitmap
 pDoc->m_pMemoryDC = new CDC();
 pDoc->m_pBitmap = new CBitmap();

 // create a compatible dc and bitmap
 pDoc->m_pMemoryDC->CreateCompatibleDC(pDC);
 pDoc->m_pBitmap->CreateCompatibleBitmap(pDC,
```

27

ACTIVE SERVERS

LISTING 27.13 continued

```
  pDoc->m_rcViewRect.right, pDoc->m_rcViewRect.bottom);
pDoc->m_pOldBitmap = pDoc->m_pMemoryDC->SelectObject(pDoc->m_pBitmap);

// draw the shape(s)
pDoc->GLDraw(pDC, &pDoc->m_rcViewRect);

// realize palette into memory dc
pDoc->m_hOldPalette = ::SelectPalette(pDoc->m_pMemoryDC->GetSafeHdc(),
          pDoc->m_hPalette, FALSE);
::RealizePalette(pDoc->m_pMemoryDC->GetSafeHdc());

// BitBlt to metafile dc
pDoc->m_pMemoryDC->BitBlt(0, 0, pDoc->m_rcViewRect.right,
  pDoc->m_rcViewRect.bottom, pDC, 0, 0, SRCCOPY);

// update the server item as well
pDoc->UpdateAllItems(NULL);
}
```

Customizing `CGLServerSrvrItem`

As I stated earlier, the `OnDraw()` for this class draws to a metafile device context that the container uses to display the server data when the server is not activated.

Use the memory DC created in the `CGLServerView` class and copy it to the metafile DC. Here, we'll also need to *realize the palette* (the process of selecting the palette into the device context).

Listing 27.14 contains the required modifications to `OnDraw()`.

LISTING 27.14 Modifications to the `CGLServerSrvrItem` Implementation

```
BOOL CGLServerSrvrItem::OnDraw(CDC* pDC, CSize& rSize)
{
 CGLServerDoc* pDoc = GetDocument();
 ASSERT_VALID(pDoc);

 // TODO: set mapping mode and extent
 //   (The extent is usually the same as the size returned from OnGetExtent)
 pDC->SetMapMode(MM_ANISOTROPIC);
 pDC->SetWindowOrg(0,0);
 pDC->SetWindowExt(3000, 3000);

 // calculate drawing rectangle
 CRect rect;
```

```
rect.TopLeft() = pDC->GetWindowOrg();
rect.BottomRight() = rect.TopLeft() + pDC->GetWindowExt();

// BitBlt memory DC to metafile DC
if (pDoc->m_pMemoryDC != NULL)
{
 // realize palette into memory dc
 HPALETTE hOldPalette = ::SelectPalette(pDC->GetSafeHdc(),
         pDoc->m_hPalette, FALSE);
 ::RealizePalette(pDC->GetSafeHdc());

 // BitBlt to metafile dc
 if (pDC->StretchBlt(rect.left, rect.top,
    rect.right - rect.left,
    rect.bottom - rect.top,
    pDoc->m_pMemoryDC, 0, 0,
    pDoc->m_rcViewRect.right,
    pDoc->m_rcViewRect.bottom, SRCCOPY) == FALSE)
 {
  return FALSE;
 }

 // restore old palette
 ::SelectPalette(pDC->GetSafeHdc(), hOldPalette, FALSE);
}

 return TRUE;
}
```

Testing the GLServer Example

Compile the GLServer example and embed it in WordPad as before. (If you don't already have the OpenGL DLLs GLU32.DLL and OPENGL32.DLL, you'll need to copy them from the CD-ROM included with this book.) You should see a three-dimensional arch-shaped object inside the sizer bar (see Figure 27.12). Now click the container, and the exact same image should be inside the container as a metafile bitmap.

You will get slightly different results if you test GLServer using an active container, such as a default active document container built using MFC AppWizard. For testing purposes, the CD-ROM that accompanies this book includes a project named DefCon that can be used to provide basic active document containment. Figure 27.13 shows an instance of GLServer running inside DefCon. Note that the image provided by GLServer completely fills the client area.

FIGURE 27.12

The GLServer
example in action.

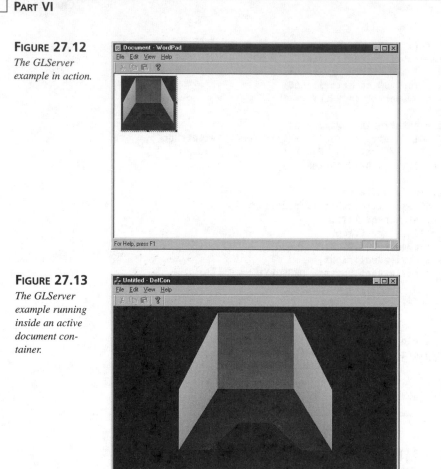

FIGURE 27.13

The GLServer
example running
inside an active
document con-
tainer.

Designing an MFC Automation Server

This section shows you how to create your own automation server with MFC. You'll use MFC AppWizard and ClassWizard to quickly and easily create the necessary class and methods for the demonstration.

The example is an in-process DLL server that exposes a class called SimpleMFC. You'll create four methods—Add, Subtract, Multiply, and Divide—to see how an automation server built with MFC works. The first three methods accept two long numbers and return a long (the result of the calculation). The fourth method also accepts two long values but instead returns a double precision number.

Using MFC AppWizard to Create Automation Servers

Choose File | New from the Developer Studio menu, and then choose MFC AppWizard (DLL). In the Project Name edit box, type MFCAuto.

AppWizard presents a single-step process to create the server. Enable the Automation check box and click Finish (see Figure 27.14).

FIGURE 27.14

Step 1 of 1.

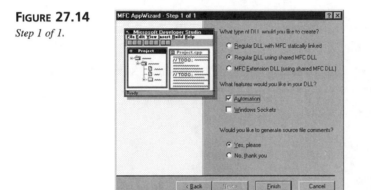

A Closer Look at the MFCAuto Classes

The AppWizard used to generate this project is very simple. The only code it generated is the required CLSID (because you enabled the Automation check box) and the registration of the DLL in the InitInstance() method, as Listing 27.15 shows.

LISTING 27.15 Registration Code for the Automation Server

```
BOOL CMFCAutoApp::InitInstance()
{
 // Register all OLE server (factories) as running.  This enables the
 //  OLE libraries to create objects from other applications.
 COleObjectFactory::RegisterAll();

 return TRUE;
}
```

Adding Customization to the MFCAuto Sample Skeleton

To make the server useable, you'll need to create a class derived from CCmdTarget. This is the root automation class provided by MFC.

Now do the following:

1. In the workspace window, select the MFCAuto project, right-click, and choose New Class.

2. In the Name text box, type CSimpleMFC.

3. In the Base Class combo box, select CCmdTarget.

4. For automation type, select Createable by Type ID and make sure that the text in the text box says MFCAuto.SimpleMFC.

Figure 27.15 shows the values for the new class.

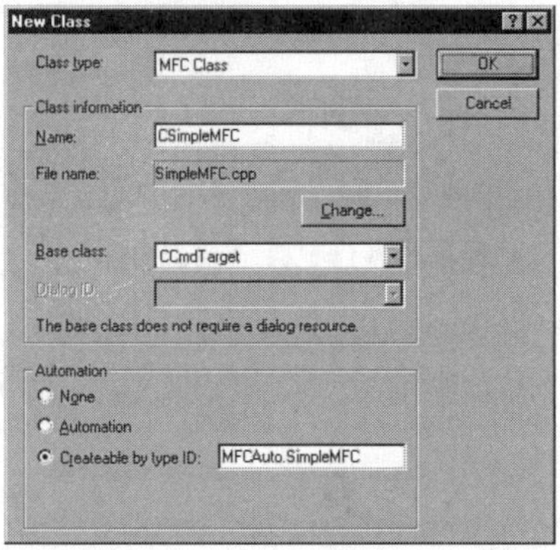

FIGURE 27.15

Adding the CSimpleMFC *class.*

Notice the addition of a new entry in the workspace window. The CSimpleMFC node is the C++ class you just created. The project's *Object Definition Language (ODL)* file also has been modified to include information about the new SimpleMFC COM class. The ODL file will be used to create a type library to expose a SimpleMFC class to other applications. To see this ODL file (shown in Listing 27.16), double-click the MFCAuto.ODL icon on the workspace File tab. Included in this file is the UUID for the class. After we finish coding this example, it will include our user-defined methods Add, Subtract, Multiply, and Divide.

LISTING 27.16 Object Definition Language (ODL) for MFCAuto

```
// MFCAuto.odl : type library source for MFCAuto.dll
// This file will be processed by the MIDL compiler to produce the
// type library (MFCAuto.tlb).

[ uuid(CF5B9E04-72A3-11D3-B515-CC43834E4167), version(1.0) ]
library MFCAuto
{
    importlib("stdole32.tlb");
    importlib("stdole2.tlb");

    //  Primary dispatch interface for CSimpleMFC

    [ uuid(CF5B9E11-72A3-11D3-B515-CC43834E4167) ]
    dispinterface ISimpleMFC
    {
        properties:
            // NOTE - ClassWizard will maintain property information here.
            //    Use extreme caution when editing this section.
            //{{AFX_ODL_PROP(CSimpleMFC)
            //}}AFX_ODL_PROP

        methods:
            // NOTE - ClassWizard will maintain method information here.
            //    Use extreme caution when editing this section.
            //{{AFX_ODL_METHOD(CSimpleMFC)
            //}}AFX_ODL_METHOD
    };

    //  Class information for CSimpleMFC
    [ uuid(CF5B9E12-72A3-11D3-B515-CC43834E4167) ]
    coclass SimpleMFC
    {
        [default] dispinterface ISimpleMFC;
    };

    //{{AFX_APPEND_ODL}}
    //}}AFX_APPEND_ODL}}
};
```

The CSimpleMFC class that was generated is fairly simple; however, note the
OnFinalRelease() method generated as a result of choosing automation support. As the
code documentation states, this notification is called when the last instance of this class
is deleted. You can optionally implement this code to perform special cleanup.

27

ACTIVE SERVERS

Adding Methods to the `MFCAuto` Example

Listing 27.17 shows the prototypes for the four methods you will be adding. This will come in handy in just a moment.

LISTING 27.17   CSimpleMFC Instance Method Prototypes

```
long Add(long First, long Second);
long Subtract(long First, long Second);
long Multiply(long First, long Second);
double Divide(long First, long Second);
```

Now, add these prototypes with these steps:

1. Open ClassWizard by choosing View | ClassWizard, or by pressing Ctrl+W.
2. Select the Automation tab in the MFC ClassWizard dialog box. In the Class Name combo box, select CSimpleMFC.
3. Click the Add Method button.
4. In the External Name combo box, type Add (the Internal Name text box is filled in automatically).
5. In the Return Type combo box, select Long.
6. Add the first and second methods in the Parameter List list box, using Long as the type for each.

Repeat these steps for each of the four methods and select Double as the return type for the `Divide` method. You can use Figure 27.16 as a guideline.

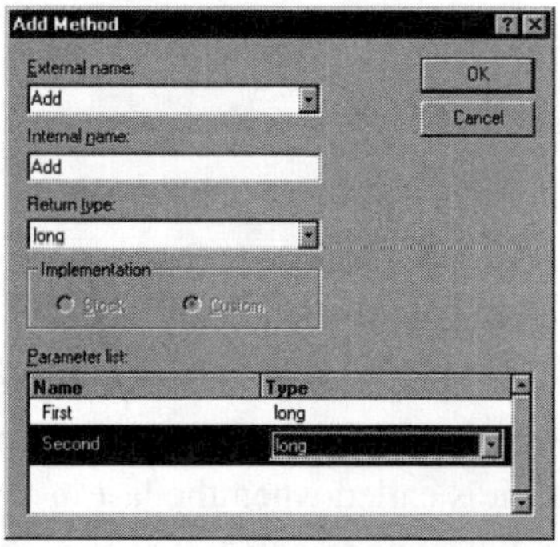

FIGURE 27.16

Using ClassWizard to add methods to MFCAuto.

> **Note**
>
> The MFCAuto example does not use any properties—but as you might have already guessed, if you need to add one or more properties, you can add them with ClassWizard by using Add Property on the Automation tab.

Now, change the implementation code for these methods, as Listing 27.18 shows.

LISTING 27.18   Implementing the CSimpleMFC Instance Methods

```
/////////////////////////////////////////////////////////////////////////////
// CSimpleMFC message handlers

long CSimpleMFC::Add(long First, long Second)
{
 return First + Second;
}

long CSimpleMFC::Subtract(long First, long Second)
{
 return First - Second;
}

long CSimpleMFC::Multiply(long First, long Second)
{
 return First * Second;
}

double CSimpleMFC::Divide(long First, long Second)
{
 return (double)First / (double)Second;
}
```

Take another look at the declaration for the CSimpleMFC class shown in Listing 27.19. ClassWizard has added prototypes for the methods to the ODL file. When this class is registered, the methods automatically are visible as part of the SimpleMFC COM class.

LISTING 27.19   ClassWizard Changes to the ODL File for New Methods

```
methods:
  // NOTE - ClassWizard will maintain method information here.
  //    Use extreme caution when editing this section.
  //{{AFX_ODL_METHOD(CSimpleMFC)
  [id(1)] long Add(long First, long Second);
  [id(2)] long Subtract(long First, long Second);
```

LISTING 27.19   continued

```
[id(3)] long Multiply(long First, long Second);
[id(4)] double Divide(long First, long Second);
//}}AFX_ODL_METHOD
```

Testing the `MFCAuto` Example

Compile the server example and then choose Tools | Register Control to register this automation server with the operating system. You can test the example using any application that can create automation servers.

For the test, I've included a file that VBScript tests that can be run against the `MFCAuto` example. This script, `Test.vbs`, runs under the Windows scripting host and calls the automation interfaces in the `MFCAuto` server. Listing 27.20 provides the contents of `Test.vbs`.

LISTING 27.20   An Automation Test File Written in VBScript

```
' Test.vbs
' VBScript example of an Automation test file.
' This file tests the MFCAuto example.

' The scripting host shell object is used to supply
' interaction with the user.

dim Result, AutoObj, WshShell

Set WshShell = Wscript.CreateObject("Wscript.Shell")
Set AutoObj = CreateObject("MFCAuto.SimpleMFC")

Result = AutoObj.Add(1, 2)
WshShell.Popup "1 + 2 = " + cstr(Result)

Result = AutoObj.Subtract(10, 5)
WshShell.Popup "10 - 5 = " + cstr(Result)

Result = AutoObj.Multiply(23, 47)
WshShell.Popup "23 x 47 = " + cstr(Result)

Result = AutoObj.Divide(10, 3)
WshShell.Popup "10 / 3 = " + cstr(Result)
```

The `Test.vbs` script file is located in the same directory as the `MFCAuto` project. To run the script file, double-click the file's icon using Windows Explorer. If the `MFCAuto` project is registered properly, the script displays a series of dialog boxes containing calculation results.

Summary

There are many more things I would like to be able to tell you about automation servers and many more examples I would like to give you, but unfortunately, there is a limit to the size this chapter can be. Therefore, let's quickly recap what you've learned in this chapter and move on.

Active servers come in three flavors:

- A *full server* is an EXE that can run as both an application and an embedded server. (Optional support can be added for both automation and ActiveX controls.)
- The *miniserver* is an EXE that can be run in embedded mode only. (Optional support can be added for both automation and ActiveX controls.)
- The *automation server* (EXE or DLL) exposes classes with methods and properties to allow an external application to control it.

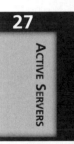

The embedded server can be activated in-place or out-of-place, depending on its implementation and eventual use. It can support persistent storage by serializing data to either the container's storage or a separate file. The server provides a mechanism to display its data on activation (by directly painting the server's view) and while inactive by providing the container with a metafile representation of its data.

The automation server can run in-process (meaning that it runs in the same process space as the application that created it) or out-of-process (meaning that it runs in its own process space).

ActiveX Controls

by Vincent W. Mayfield
and Mickey Williams

IN THIS CHAPTER

CHAPTER 28

This chapter discusses ActiveX controls. ActiveX controls are an evolved form of *object linking and embedding (OLE)* controls, which commonly are referred to as *OLE control extensions (OCXs)*. The ActiveX control specification contains enhancements that make ActiveX controls more useful in Internet applications.

You can think of ActiveX controls as functional pieces of code packaged into reusable components. Every ActiveX control offers guarantees about how it interacts with its environment through the interfaces it chooses to export. Although many ActiveX controls are user-interface components, these controls do not have to be visible.

A Short History

The term *control,* or *custom control,* has been around since Windows 3.0, when it was first defined. In fact, a custom control is nothing more than a *dynamic link library (DLL)* that exports a defined set of functions. Unlike a DLL, a custom control can manipulate properties and handle the firing of events in response to user or programmatic input. Custom controls were written in the C programming language and were used primarily by programmers writing their applications using C.

Shortly after C developers began using custom controls, the Visual Basic development environment caught on in the development community. Custom controls were necessary because developers found they needed better ways to express the user interface of their applications. Many times, there was simply no way to perform a complex operation in Visual Basic and reflect it in a meaningful way to the end user. As a result, the custom control came to be used in Visual Basic. Unfortunately—or fortunately, depending on your perspective—these C DLLs had no way of allowing Visual Basic to query the control for information on the properties and methods supported by the control. This inability made custom controls difficult to use in the Visual Basic development environment. Developers experienced great difficulty exporting the functions of the custom control to Visual Basic.

In 1991, Microsoft unveiled the *Visual Basic Extension (VBX)*. The idea was that these reusable software components could be embedded in their container applications. To everyone's surprise, VBXs took off like wildfire. Companies cropped up all over the place developing these little reusable software components. VBXs provided a wide range of functionality, from a simple text label to a complex multimedia or communications control. VBXs were written in C and C++ and provided a wide variety of capabilities that would not have been possible in a Visual Basic application otherwise. VBXs became extremely popular.

Demand for VBXs grew within the developer market. Soon, Windows NT was released, and developers wanted VBXs for 32-bit applications and even non-Intel platforms, such as the DEC Alpha, RISC, Power PC, and MIPS. Developers wanted to extend VBXs by using Visual Basic for Applications to connect VBXs with applications such as Access, PowerPoint, Excel, Project, and Word.

Unfortunately, VBXs were severely restricted. They were built on a 16-bit architecture that is not designed as an open interface. They were primarily designed to accommodate the Visual Basic environment. This design made VBXs almost impossible to port to a 32-bit environment.

In 1993, OLE 2.0 was released. Shortly after the release of OLE 2.0, Microsoft extended the OLE architecture to include OLE controls. OLE controls, unlike their predecessors, the VBX and the custom control, are founded on a binary standard called the *Component Object Model (COM)*. In addition, OLE controls support both 16- and 32-bit architectures.

> **Note**
>
> Kraig Brockschmidt wrote what sometimes is considered the bible for all OLE programmers. The book is *Inside OLE,* published by Microsoft Press. The original title of the book was *Inside OLE 2.0,* but for the second edition, the 2.0 version number was dropped. This book is an excellent reference. *Inside OLE* thoroughly explores the OLE standard from the API level.

Instead of creating an extended architecture for VBXs, Microsoft decided to develop OLE controls to offer the benefits of component architecture to a wider variety of development environments and development tools. The COM and OLE are open architectures, giving them a wider variety of input from the industry. Like their predecessor the VBX, OLE controls also are known by their file extension, OCX, and they likewise took the market by storm.

From 1993 to 1995, OLE controls flourished. Many *independent software vendors (ISVs)* converted their VBXs to OLE controls and in some cases maintained three versions: VBX, 16-bit OCX, and 32-bit OCX. The makers of Visual C++ and MFC created the OLE Control Developer's Kit and even incorporated it into Visual C++ 2.0 and 1.5, further adding to the success of OLE custom controls.

From 1995 to 1996, the Internet took the world by storm, causing Internet mania. Everyone had to become Web enabled. Companies began creating Web sites because they saw the Internet as the great advertisement media for the year 2000 and beyond. Since then, this trend has continued. Unfortunately, in previous years, the Internet had been a relatively static environment—due in part to the Internet's roots with the big-iron diehards who grew up with the IBM mainframes, VAXs, and UNIX boxes (the "dummy terminal" era). However, PC computers have become household devices for almost everyone. Users have become accustomed to graphical interaction with their machines, thanks to the Macintosh, Microsoft Windows, and X-Windows/Motif. In addition, thanks to Sun Microsystems and its invention of the Java programming language and the Java applet, the Internet is no longer a static environment. The days of static Web pages are gone. Now, Web pages have exploded to life with multimedia, sound, and dynamic interaction.

Realizing the potential and the hype surrounding the Internet explosion, Microsoft decided it needed to get with the program and take on a leadership role in this emerging environment. Microsoft boldly announced that it was going to "activate" the Internet in 1996 with ActiveX technologies (a little late, but better late than never). Thus, from these ActiveX technologies, the ActiveX controls were born. ActiveX controls were nothing really new—just an extension of their mother, the OLE control. ActiveX controls are simply OLE controls optimized for use across the Internet.

What Is an ActiveX Control?

Now that you know a little of the history behind ActiveX controls, this section explores just what an ActiveX control is. An ActiveX control is an embeddable COM object that is implemented as an in-process server DLL. It supports in-place activation as an *inside-out* activated object. Objects that are activated inside-out become user interface active with a single mouse click, instead of the double-click required for OLE or Active document embedded objects.

As an in-process object, an ActiveX control is loaded into the address space of its container. As you probably are aware, most Win32 processes have a virtual 4GB address space. (The Datacenter version of Windows 2000 has a much larger address space.)

> **Note**
>
> A *Win32 process* is a running instance of an application loaded into memory.

The lower 2GB is where the application is loaded, and the upper 2GB is reserved for use by the operating system. An ActiveX control is loaded in the lower 2GB with the application. Therefore, the control shares the same resources with the application; hence the term *in-process*.

An ActiveX control is also a server that establishes two-way communication between the control and its container. It also can respond to user-initiated events, such as mouse movements, keyboard input, and programmatic scripting input—and it can pass that input to the container application for action.

ActiveX controls also are in-place activated. This means they can be placed in the active state by the user or the container and edited or manipulated. This is a functionality ActiveX controls inherit from OLE documents. Like a DLL, the ActiveX control is a library of functions. In fact, an ActiveX control can be considered a "super DLL." More than just a "super DLL," an ActiveX control is a detached object that can fire and respond to events, process messages, contain unique properties, and possess multi-threaded capabilities. ActiveX controls also are known as OCXs because of their most common file extension, but they are actually DLLs. OCXs can contain several controls.

An ActiveX control can have its own data set and can act as an automation server, enabling you to manipulate its properties and methods. ActiveX controls can be 16 and 32 bit as well as Unicode. ActiveX controls can have properties set at both compile time and runtime, and ActiveX controls have methods that can perform certain operations.

ActiveX controls cannot be executed without an ActiveX container. You can use ActiveX controls in a wide variety of development tools, such as Delphi, Visual C++, Borland C++, Visual Basic, and PowerBuilder. You also can use ActiveX controls in a variety of environments not traditionally associated with programming, such as Microsoft Word, Microsoft Excel, Lotus, *Hypertext Markup Language (HTML)*, and Internet Explorer.

ActiveX Control Architecture

The beauty of ActiveX controls is that they are programmable and reusable. They expose themselves to the outside world and can be used in a variety of environments. ActiveX controls are similar to embedded object servers, in that they are embedded in a container and are responsible for providing a user interface. ActiveX controls also are expected to expose functionality through interfaces, which often are derived from `IDispatch` to take advantage of automation. ActiveX controls take advantage of the capability to send events to their container; this capability to send events separates ActiveX controls from other in-process OLE servers.

ActiveX controls communicate with the outside world in three ways:

- Properties
- Methods
- Events

28

ACTIVEX
CONTROLS

Properties

Properties are named attributes or characteristics of an ActiveX control. Properties may be marked as read-only, but typically these properties can be set or queried. Some examples of properties are color, font, and number.

Usually, ActiveX controls provide access to their properties through *property sheets*. Property sheets are exposed via automation. Property sheets are not limited to design/compile time but can be displayed at runtime to allow the user to manipulate the control's properties, events, or methods. Property sheets are user-interface components that basically are tabbed dialog boxes. Automation provides the mechanism by which ActiveX controls communicate with their property sheets.

ActiveX controls have access to what are called *stock properties*. These are properties common to all ActiveX controls. MFC enables you to take advantage of these stock properties because they already are built in. Table 28.1 lists all the stock properties supported by MFC.

TABLE 28.1 Stock Properties for ActiveX Controls Supported by MFC

Stock Property	*Get/Set Stock Method*	*Enables You To...*
Appearance	void SetAppearance (short sAppear) short GetAppearance( )	Set the appearance of an ActiveX control to flat or 3D.
BackColor	OLE_COLOR GetBackColor ( ) void SetBackColor (OLE_COLOR dwBkColor)	Set the background colors of the control.
Border Style	short GetBorderStyle ( ) void SetBorderStyle(short sBorderStyle)	Set the border style of the control to normal or none.
Caption	BSTR GetText( ) void SetText(LPCTSTR pszText)	Set the caption of the ActiveX control.
Enabled	BOOL GetEnabled( ) void SetEnabled(BOOL bEnabled)	Enable or disable the control.
Font	LPFONTDISP GetFont( ) void SetFont (LPFONTDISP pFontDisp)	Set the font properties used by the control.

Stock Property	Get/Set Stock Method	Enables You To...
Fore Color	OLE_COLOR GetForeColor( ) void SetForeColor (OLE_COLOR dwForeColor)	Set the forecolors of the control.
hWnd	OLE_HANDLE GetHwnd( )	Hold the control's window handle.
Ready State	long GetReadyState( )	Get or set the ready state of the control with the following values: READYSTATE_UNINITIALIZED READYSTATE_LOADING READYSTATE_LOADED READYSTATE_INTERACTIVE READYSTATE_COMPLETE
Text	const CString& InternalGetText( )	Get and set the control's text. This property is the same as `Caption`.

You can include the stock properties in your ActiveX controls by using the ClassWizard. Choose View, ClassWizard or press Ctrl+W. After the ClassWizard appears, select the Automation tab (see Figure 28.1).

FIGURE 28.1
Using the ClassWizard to access stock properties.

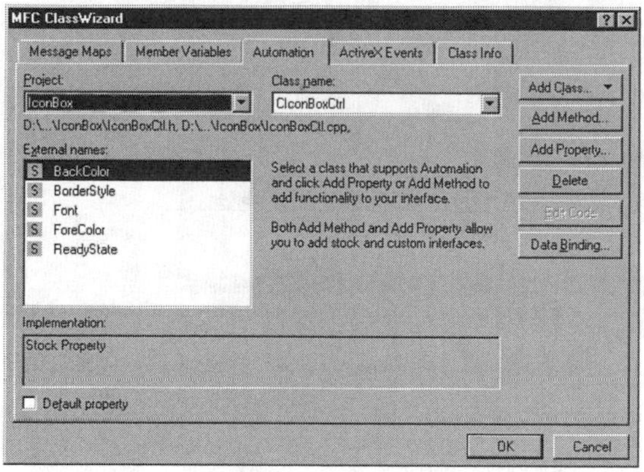

Click the Add Property button to invoke the Add Property dialog box. If you use the External Name combo box, you can select which stock properties you want your control to have (see Figure 28.2).

28

ACTIVEX CONTROLS

FIGURE 28.2

*You can select
stock properties to
support by using
the External
Name combo box.*

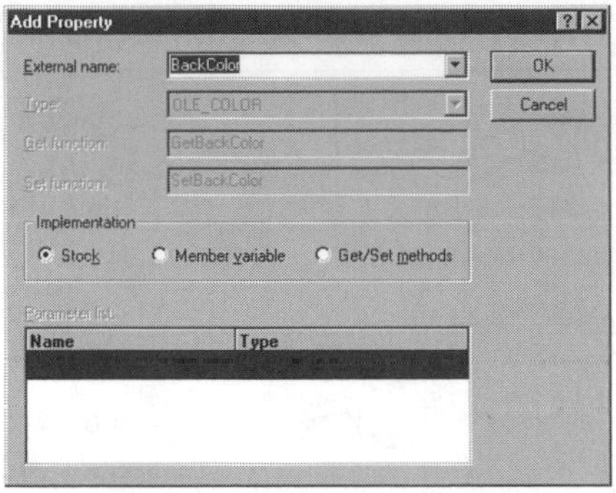

MFC and Visual C++ 6.0 also provide stock property sheets to add to our user interface
so that users can set stock properties. These are General (see Figure 28.3), Fonts (see
Figure 28.4), Colors (see Figure 28.5), and Pictures properties.

> **Note**
>
> Although the General property page is added to your control by default, it
> doesn't contain any controls. You must add the controls for this page yourself.

FIGURE 28.3

*The default
General
Properties page.*

FIGURE 28.4

*The stock Fonts
Properties page.*

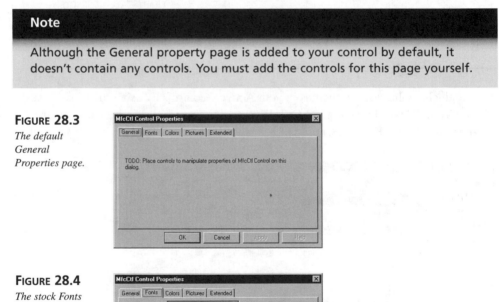

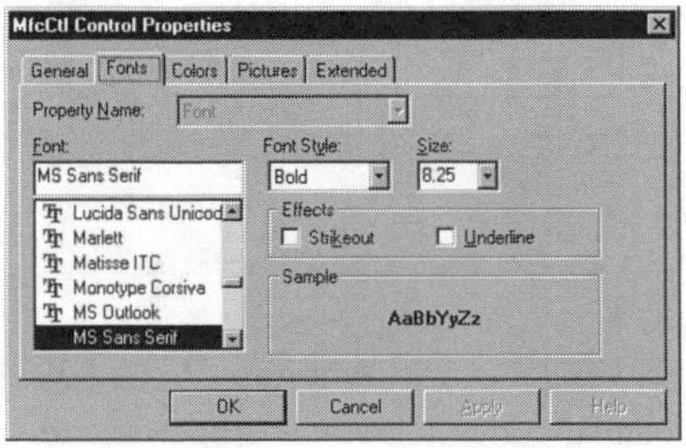

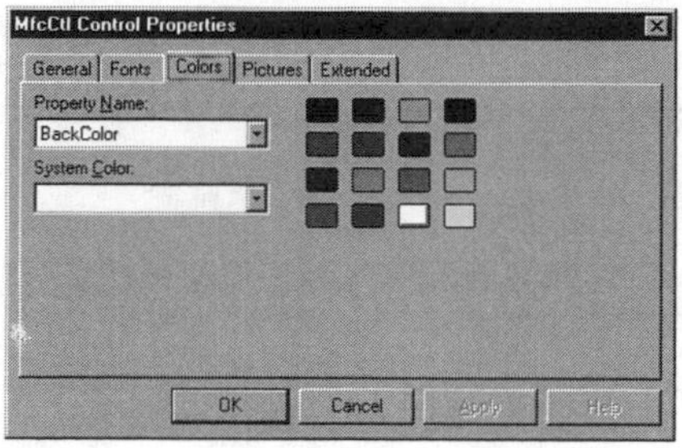

Figure 28.5

The stock Colors Properties page.

The human-readable class IDs for these Properties pages follow:

- CLSID_CColorPropPage

- CLSID_CFontPropPage

- CLSID_CPicturePropPage

When you use the MFC ActiveX ControlWizard to generate an ActiveX control, it generates a class derived from COleControl. In that class's .cpp file, the wizard includes support for a Properties page so that your control can have a user interface to set the control properties. This Properties page is derived from COlePropertyPage, and MFC has a macro for declaring the Properties pages in the control. Listing 28.1 shows the macros BEGIN_PROPPAGEIDS and END_PROPPAGEIDS. This code fragment is located in the .cpp file for the COleControl-derived class.

Listing 28.1 Using the BEGIN_PROPPAGEIDS and END_PROPPAGEIDS to Declare the COlePropertyPage for Your Control

```
1: BEGIN_PROPPAGEIDS( CMySampleCtrl, 1 )
2:    PROPPAGEID( CMyPropPage::guid )
3: END_PROPPAGEIDS(CSampleCtrl)
```

Notice on line 2 that PROPPAGEID is passed the *globally unique identifier (GUID—*pronounced *gwid,* as in *squid),* and also calls a *class ID (CLSID)* of the Properties page. The GUID for the Properties page is declared in the .cpp of the class created by the ControlWizard derived from ColePropertyPage.

If you want to implement the stock Properties pages that MFC provides, you have to pass the CSLID of the stock Properties pages. Listing 28.2 demonstrates this process.

LISTING 28.2   Adding Declarations for the Stock Fonts Properties Page, Colors
Properties Page, and Pictures Properties Page

```
1: BEGIN_PROPPAGEIDS( CMySampleCtrl, 4 )
2:    PROPPAGEID( CMyPropPage::guid )
3:    PROPPAGEID( CLSID_CFontPropPage )
4:    PROPPAGEID( CLSID_CColorPropPage )
5:    PROPPAGEID( CLSID_CPicturePropPage )
6: END_PROPPAGEIDS(CSampleCtrl)
```

Notice in line 1 that the second parameter is now 4. This second parameter represents the
number of Properties pages.

> **Warning**
>
> Don't forget to increment the number of Properties pages in the code when
> you add them. If you don't, the source file will compile fine; but when you try
> to use the ActiveX control, an assertion failure will occur in debug mode. When
> you use the control in release mode, it will show only the number of pages set
> in the second parameter of the BEGIN_PROPPAGEIDS macro.

ActiveX controls also have persistent properties. These properties are stored in the container and are set at design time or compile time. Controls also have the capability to
save persistent information about their properties at runtime, and thus, in effect, can save
their state. This means that the controls can load their persistent properties at initial load
time.

Events

Events are notifications generated by the control to provide some sort of notification to
the container. Usually, this is input by the user, such as a mouse click or keyboard input.
However, it also may be generated entirely within the control, such as when a timer
expires. The event then is communicated to the control's container by the control. This is
done through a communications mechanism known as a *Lightweight Remote Procedure
Call (LRPC)*. LRPCs are the scaled-down little brothers of the *Remote Procedure Call
(RPC)*.

RPCs are an interprocess communications mechanism used to provide two-way communications between applications. These applications can be on the same computer or on
computers across a network. RPC is the mechanism that *Distributed COM (DCOM)* uses
to exchange objects across process and computer boundaries. RPC is much more than

just a communications method. It allows a function in a process on one computer to evoke a function in a process on another computer. This computer can even be a computer across an enterprise-wide network or the Internet.

Unlike their big brother, the RPC, LRPCs are only for communications between processes or within processes on a single computer. LRPCs are the mechanism by which an ActiveX control dispatches control notifications to the container and from the container to the control. This communication is based on posting messages or events to window handles to transfer data between processes. It is known as *marshaling.*

The Microsoft Foundation Classes provide support for several stock events; Table 28.2 lists these events.

TABLE 28.2   Stock Events Supported in MFC and Visual C++ and Their Event Map Entries

Stock Event	*Function*	*Event Map Entry*
Click	void FireClick()	EVENT_STOCK_CLICK()
DblClick	void FireDblClick()	EVENT_STOCK_DBLCLICK()
Error	void FireError(SCODE scode, LPCSTR lpszDescription, UINT nHelpID = 0)	EVENT_STOCK_ERROR()
KeyDown	void FireKeyDown(short nChar, short nShiftState)	EVENT_STOCK_KEYDOWN()
KeyPress	void FireKeyPress(short* pnChar)	EVENT_STOCK_KEYPRESS()
KeyUp	void FireKeyUp(short nChar, short nShiftState)	EVENT_STOCK_KEYUP()
MouseDown	void FireMouseDown(short nButton, short nShiftState, float x, float y)	EVENT_STOCK_MOUSEDOWN()
MouseMove	void FireMouseMove(short nButton, short nShiftState, float x, float y)	EVENT_STOCK_MOUSEMOVE()
MouseUp	void FireMouseUp(short nButton, short nShiftState, float x, float y)	EVENT_STOCK_MOUSEUP()

28

ActiveX Controls

I think you will find that handling events is very easy. One of the great things about the folks at Microsoft who developed Visual C++ and MFC is that they have been extremely developer oriented. They set up a system to handle events very similar to the message maps. They have what is called an *event map*. The event map has two macros to define the beginning and the end of the event map, as shown in Listing 28.3 in lines 1 and 5, respectively. Notice in line 3 the stock event for the mouse move event, as shown in Table 28.2.

LISTING 28.3   The Event Map of an ActiveX Control

```
1: BEGIN_EVENT_MAP(CMySampleCtrl, COleControl)
2: //{{AFX_EVENT_MAP(CMySampleCtrl)
3:     EVENT_STOCK_MOUSEMOVE( )
4: //}}AFX_EVENT_MAP
5: END_EVENT_MAP()
```

The Visual C++ ClassWizard handles putting the event map entries in for you. You can put them in by hand, but I don't recommend it. Let the tool do it for you; there is less chance for error. As with message maps, if you do add entries by hand, make sure that you don't make any changes between the comment lines that mark the area reserved by ClassWizard.

To add a stock or custom event, choose View|ClassWizard or press Ctrl+W. After the ClassWizard appears, select the ActiveX Events tab (see Figure 28.6).

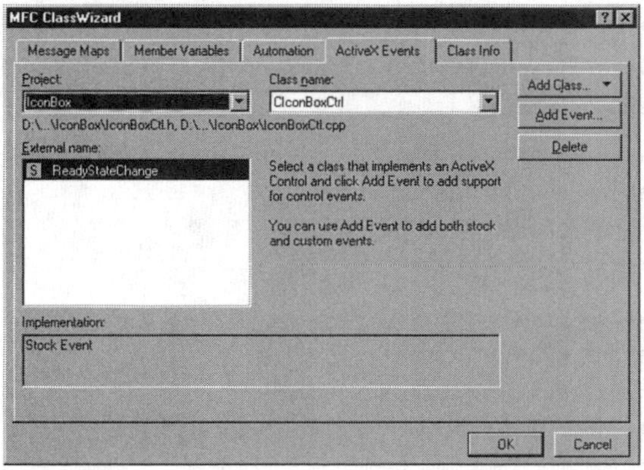

FIGURE 28.6

Using ClassWizard to add stock events to a control.

Click the Add Event button, which brings up the Add Event dialog box. If you use the External Name combo box, you can select which stock events you want to use in your control (see Figure 28.7).

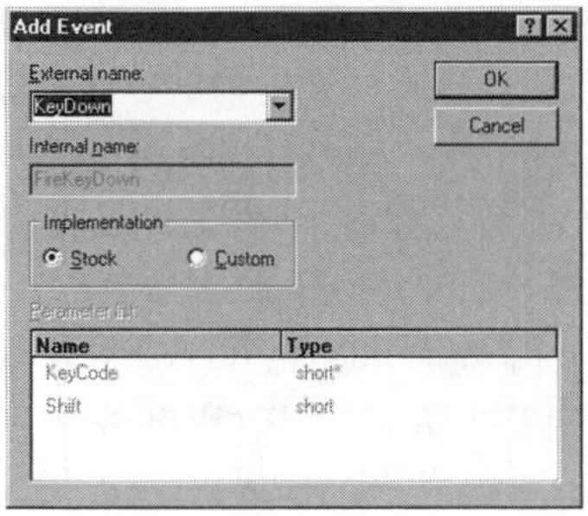

FIGURE 28.7

*You can select
stock events to
support using the
External Name
combo box.*

Methods

Methods are functions performed by the control to access the control's functionality.
These functions enable an external source to manipulate the appearance, behavior, or
properties of the control. These functions include actions such as GetColor, SetColor,
CutToClipBoard, PasteFromClipboard, and so on. A method is the interface an application or a programmer can use to set values for or receive values from an ActiveX control.

Methods are a lot like member functions in C++. They provide accessor functions that
provide and grant access to an ActiveX control's properties and data. An ActiveX control's properties are like a C++ class's member variables. Like properties, methods come
it two flavors: *stock* and *custom*. Stock methods provide access to stock properties, such
as color, font, and picture. Likewise, custom methods provide access to custom properties. With methods, you can change a control's appearance or initialize it with a value.

Like events, MFC provides two stock methods and handles the dispatch of all custom
and stock methods, much like the message map and event map. Again, two macros
define the beginning and end of the dispatch map: BEGIN_DISPATCH_MAP and
END_DISPATCH_MAP (see lines 1 and 5 of Listing 28.4).

LISTING 28.4   The Dispatch Map That Maps the Methods Handled by an ActiveX
Control

```
1: BEGIN_DISPATCH_MAP(CMySampleCtrl, COleControl)
2:     //{{AFX_DISPATCH_MAP(CSampleCtrl)
3:     DISP_STOCKPROP_REFRESH( )
4:     //}}AFX_DISPATCH_MAP
5: END_DISPATCH_MAP()
```

Notice also line 3. Line 3 has the DISP_STOCKPROP_REFRESH stock method. This is one of two stock methods supported by MFC. The other is DISP_STOCKPROP_DOCLICK. These methods also are known as the DoClick and Refresh methods. The DoClick method fires a click event to the container. The Refresh method is used by the container to force an update to the control's appearance.

Interfaces that expose properties, events, and methods for an ActiveX control often are derived from the IDispatch interface. Technically, an ActiveX control isn't required to derive its interfaces from IDispatch, but MFC enforces this restriction. Also, if you're using a scripting language, such as VBScript or JavaScript, your interfaces must be derived from IDispatch.

The IDispatch interface enables a client to call dispatch methods by name, instead of directly accessing the functions via a pointer. However, this is a multistep process that requires each method's name to be resolved before the method is actually called via the IDispatch::Invoke method. Because of the additional overhead, automation interfaces often are much slower than non-automation interfaces.

To create custom methods or add stock methods to your control in Visual C++ by using the ClassWizard, choose View|ClassWizard or press Ctrl+W. After the ClassWizard appears, select the Automation tab (see Figure 28.8).

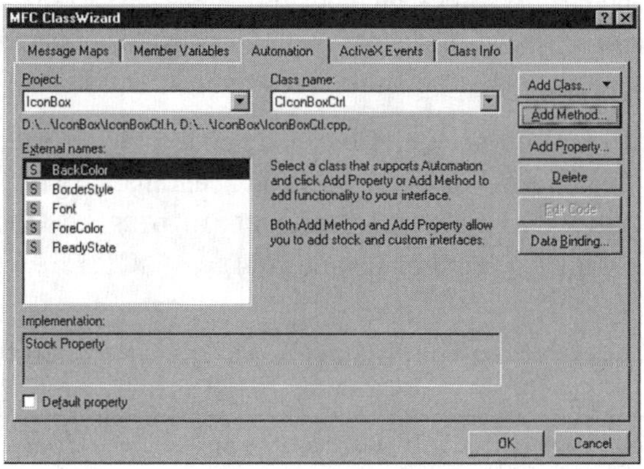

FIGURE 28.8

Using the ClassWizard to invoke stock or custom methods.

Click the Add Method button, which invokes the Add Method dialog box. If you use the External Name combo box, you can select which stock methods you want your control to have, or you can create a new method by typing its name in the External Name combo box (see Figure 28.9).

Add Method

| External name: | OK |
| DoClick | Cancel |

Internal name:
DoClick

Return type:
void

Implementation
◉ Stock ○ Custom

Parameter list:

Name	Type

ActiveX Control Interfaces

Like all other COM objects, including the OLE controls before them, ActiveX controls are manipulated through interfaces. In the original OLE control and OLE container specification, OLE controls were required to support certain interfaces, whether or not they needed or used them. This requirement left some controls bloated with code and overhead they didn't need.

Currently, the only interface a simple COM object is required to implement is IUnknown. To be considered an ActiveX control, though, a COM object still must implement the interfaces required so that programming tools such as Visual C++ or Visual Basic can use it, but all other interfaces are optional. The capability to be hosted inside a development environment is what separates ActiveX controls from simpler COM objects.

It wasn't always this way, however. In December 1995, Microsoft published the *OLE Controls and OLE Container Guidelines Version 2.0.* This was an extension of Version 1.1. With the advent of ActiveX controls, the standard was changed to the 1996 standard for ActiveX controls and ActiveX containers, and is again an extension to the previous standard. The next section discusses the specifics of an ActiveX control.

An ActiveX control exposes interfaces. Likewise, a container exposes interfaces to the ActiveX control. ActiveX controls and ActiveX containers link through interfaces. Approximately 26 interfaces exist for ActiveX controls and their containers. The next section, "ActiveX Controls," discusses the new interfaces. This is not considered an all-inclusive list, because a few other interfaces are used, but these represent the main interfaces.

In Table 28.3, notice that each object supports the IUnknown interface. This is now the only interface that a container can assume is implemented by every COM object. If you implement only the IUnknown interface, however, you will have a COM object that does

28

ACTIVEX CONTROLS

pretty much nothing. The idea is to implement only the interfaces needed to support the control.

When you write the code for your control, you must know which interfaces the control supports, and you also must realize that all containers do not support all interfaces. In order for your control to be compatible with as many containers as possible, you must check for the support of your interfaces by the container and degrade your control's functionality gracefully in the event an interface is not supported. This process is comparable to error checking—except that you still want your control to function, but with degraded capability or through an alternative interface.

The most important interfaces used by ActiveX controls are IOleControl and IDispatch. As discussed earlier, IDispatch is the mechanism through which ActiveX controls built with MFC communicate. IOleControl encapsulates the basic functionality of an ActiveX control. Table 28.3 shows the COM interfaces an ActiveX control or an ActiveX container can support to facilitate the operations between them. With MFC, most of the interfaces are hidden from you. You will use them, but you might not realize it. You can always explicitly use an interface if you want, but MFC has encapsulated most of the interfaces to make them easier for you to use.

TABLE 28.3 COM Interfaces for Facilitating Operations Between Controls and Containers

ActiveX Control	*Control Site*	*Client Site*	*Container*
IClassFactory2	IOleControlSite	IOleClientSite	IOleInPlaceUIWindow
IOleObject	IUnknown	IOleInPlaceSite	IOleInPlaceFrame
IDataObject	IAdviseSink	IUnknown	
IViewObject	IDispatch		
IPersistStorage	IUnknown		
IOleInPlaceActiveObject			
IOleCache			
IPersistStreamInit			
IOleControl			
IConnectionPointContainer			
IConnectionPoint			
IProvideClassInfo			
IProperNotifySink			
ISpecifyPropertyPages			

ActiveX Control	Control Site	Client Site	Container
IPerPropertyBrowsing			
ISimpleFrameSite			
IDispatch			
IUnknown			

The important thing to remember is that the interfaces a control supports define that control. However, you should implement only the interfaces your control requires to function. This idea will become more apparent in the following section on ActiveX controls.

ActiveX Controls

As discussed earlier, ActiveX controls originally were conceived as OLE controls that were optimized for use with the Internet and corporate intranets. This does not mean that ActiveX controls can be used only in the Internet environment; quite the contrary—they can be used in any container that can support their interfaces. ActiveX controls still must be embedded in a container application. When you are using a Web browser that supports downloading ActiveX controls, for example, and you encounter a page with an ActiveX control, the control is downloaded to the client if it is not loaded on the local machine. The two most prevalent browsers that support ActiveX controls are Microsoft Internet Explorer and Netscape, with the help of the NCompass plug-in.

The major difference between the older OLE control specification and the newer ActiveX control specification is that many interfaces now are optional. An ActiveX control is expected to support the interfaces required for hosting inside "visual" development tools and must be self registering. Other than these requirements, the control is free to implement interfaces as it sees fit. In contrast, in the previous standard, an OLE control was required to support an armada of COM interfaces, whether or not the control needed them. This made some controls bloated with code that was not used or needed. In the world of Internet development, code bloat is unacceptable.

Supporting the IUnknown Interface

As discussed earlier, all COM objects support the IUnknown interface. As discussed in Chapter 24, "Overview of COM and Active Technologies," IUnknown is an interface that supports three methods: QueryInterface, AddRef, and Release.

28

ACTIVEX
CONTROLS

All COM interfaces are inherited either directly or indirectly from IUnknown; hence, all other interfaces have these three functions also. With a pointer to IUnknown, a client can get a pointer to other interfaces the object supports through QueryInterface. In short, an object can use QueryInterface to find out the capabilities of another object. If the object supports the interface, it returns a pointer to the interface. If the object does not support the interface, E_NOINTERFACE is returned. Listing 28.5 demonstrates the use of the pointer to a control's IUnknown interface and QueryInterface to find out the class information using MFC.

LISTING 28.5 Using a Pointer to IUnknown and QueryInterface to Retrieve Class Information

```
1:   // Function to get a pointer to a control's IUnknown and use
2:   // QueryInterface to see if it supports the interface.
3:   int MyClass::DoControlWork()
4:   {
5:       LPUNKNOWN lpUnknown;
6:       LPPPROVIDECLASSINFO lpClassInfo;
7:
8:       lpUnknown = GetControlUnknown();
9:
10:      if(lpUnknown == NULL)
11:      {
12:          // return the common error code for bad pointers
13:          return E_POINTER;
14:      }
15:      else
16:      {
17:          if(SUCCEEDED(lpUnknown->QueryInterface(IID_IProvideClassInfo,
18:                                          (void**) &lpClassInfo)))
19:          {
20:              // QueryInterface Returned a Succeeded so this
21:              // Interface is Supported
22:              // {
23:              //          Perform some function with lpClassInfo such
24:              // as getting the class info and examining the class
                ➥attributes
25:              // {
26:
27:              lpClassInfo->Release();
28:          }
29:          else
30:          {
31:              // Control Does Not Support Interface
32:              return E_NOINTERFACE;
33:          }
34:      }
35:      return NO_ERROR;
36: }
```

In addition, the object can manage its own lifetime through the `AddRef` and `Release` functions. If an object obtains a pointer to an object, `AddRef` is called, incrementing the object's reference count. After an object no longer needs the pointer to the interface, `Release` is called, decrementing the object's reference count. When the reference count reaches zero, an object created on the heap can safely destroy itself.

Although the `IUnknown` interface is required for all COM objects, you also should take a look at the other interfaces an ActiveX control may choose to implement, as shown in Table 28.4.

In addition, the control may implement its own custom interfaces. By implementing only the interfaces it needs, the ActiveX control can be as lean as possible.

TABLE 28.4   Potential COM Interfaces for an ActiveX Control

Interface	*Purpose*
`IOleObject`	Principal mechanism by which a control communicates with its container.
`IOleInPlaceObject`	Manages activation and deactivation of an object.
`IOleInPlaceActiveObject`	Provides communications between an in-place active object and the outermost windows of the container.
`IOleControl`	Allows support for keyboard mnemonics, properties, and events.
`IDataObject`	Allows for the transfer of data and the communication of changes in the data.
`IViewObject`	Allows the object to display itself.
`IViewObject2`	Allows you to find the size of the object in a given view. An extension of the `IViewObject` interface.
`IDispatch`	Enables you to call virtually any other COM interface. Used in OLE automation to evoke late binding to properties and methods of COM objects.
`IConnectionPoint Container`	Supports connection points for connectable objects.
`IProvideClassInfo`	Encapsulates a single method by which to get all the information about an object's co-class entry in its type library.
`IProvideClassInfo2`	Provides quick access to an object's Interface ID (IID) for its event set. An extension to `IProvideClassInfo`.
`ISpecifyPropertyPages`	Denotes an object as supporting property pages.
`IPerPropertyBrowsing`	Supports methods to get access to the information in the Properties pages supported by an object.

28

ACTIVEX CONTROLS

TABLE 28.4 continued

Interface	Purpose
IPersistStream	Provides methods for loading and storing simple streams.
IPersistStreamInit	Adds an initialization method, InitNew. Designed as a replacement for IPersistStream.
IPersistMemory	Allows the method to access a fixed-sized memory block for an IPersistStream object.
IPersistStorage	Supports the manipulation of storage objects to include loading, saving, and exchanging.
IPersistMoniker	Exposes to asynchronous objects the capability to manipulate the way they bind data to the object.
IPersistPropertyBag	Allows the storage of persistent properties.
IOleCache	Controls access to the cache inside an object.
IOleCache2	Allows the selective update of an object's cache.
IExternalConnection	Allows the tracking of external locking on an embedded object.
IRunnableObject	Enables a container to control its executable objects.

A Control Must Be Self-Registering

Before you can use an ActiveX control or any other COM object, it must be registered in the System Registry. The System Registry is a database of configuration information divided into a hierarchical tree. This tree consists of three levels of information: hives, keys, and values. The System Registry is a centralized place where you can go to get information about an object (see Figure 28.10).

> **Note**
>
> You can view the System Registry in Windows 95 through a program called regedit.exe. If you are using Windows NT or Windows 2000, you can view the System Registry with a program called regedt32.exe, which is located in \WINNT\SYSTEM32, and is preferred over regedit.exe.

If the control is not registered in the Registry, it is unknown and therefore unusable by the system. If it's not in the Registry, the rest of the system doesn't know it's there.

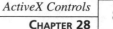
FIGURE 28.10

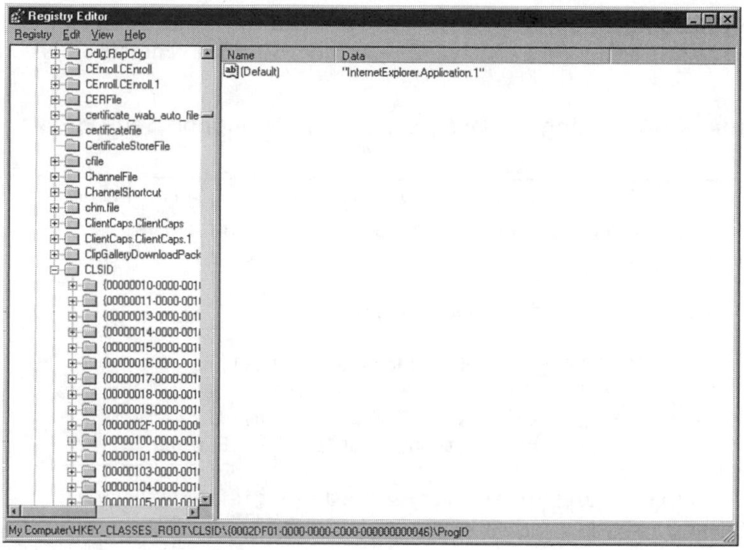

The Windows 98 System Registry as seen through the Regedit program.

Thus, it is a requirement for ActiveX controls to be self-registering. This means an ActiveX control must implement and export the functions `DllRegisterServer` and `DllUnregisterServer`. In addition, it is a requirement for ActiveX controls to register all the standard Registry entries for automation servers and embeddable objects. Listing 28.6 demonstrates the use of `DllRegisterServer` to support self-registration of the control using MFC. Visual C++'s AppWizard generates this code for you.

LISTING 28.6   Using the `DllRegisterServer` to Support Self-Registration of the Control

```
1:   /////////////////////////////////////////////////////////////
2:   // DllRegisterServer - Adds entries to the system registry
3:
4:   STDAPI DllRegisterServer(void)
5:   {
6:       AFX_MANAGE_STATE(_afxModuleAddrThis);
7:
8:      if (!AfxOleRegisterTypeLib(AfxGetInstanceHandle(), _tlid))
9:          return ResultFromScode(SELFREG_E_TYPELIB);
10:
11:     if (!COleObjectFactoryEx::UpdateRegistryAll(TRUE))
12:          return ResultFromScode(SELFREG_E_CLASS);
13:
14:      return NOERROR;
15:   }
```

Listing 28.7 demonstrates the use of `DllUnregisterServer` to support self-unregistration of a control using MFC. Visual C++'s ControlWizard generates this code for you.

LISTING 28.7 Using `DllUnregisterServer` to Support Self-Unregistration of a Control

```
1:   //////////////////////////////////////////////////////
2:   // DllUnregisterServer - Removes entries from the
system registry
3:
4:   STDAPI DllUnregisterServer(void)
5:   {
6:       AFX_MANAGE_STATE(_afxModuleAddrThis);
7:
8:       if (!AfxOleUnregisterTypeLib(_tlid))
9:           return ResultFromScode(SELFREG_E_TYPELIB);
10:
11:      if (!COleObjectFactoryEx::UpdateRegistryAll(FALSE))
12:          return ResultFromScode(SELFREG_E_CLASS);
13:
14:      return NOERROR;
15:  }
```

Listings 28.6 and 28.7 show how you support registration and unregistration, and Listing 28.8 shows how you register your control and its capabilities. Notice in line 15 of Listing 28.8 the variable dwMyControlOleMisc. It contains the status bits of your control. This is very important because it contains the capabilities of your control. These capabilities can be looked up in the System Registry to find out what capabilities your control contains without instantiating the object.

LISTING 28.8 Registering Your Control and Your Control's Capabilities in MFC

```
1:   //////////////////////////////////////////////////////////////
2:   // CMyCtrl::CMyCtrlFactory::UpdateRegistry -
3:   // Adds or removes system registry entries for CMyCtrl
4:   BOOL CMyCtrl::CMyCtrlFactory::UpdateRegistry(BOOL bRegister)
5:   {
6:       if (bRegister)
7:           return AfxOleRegisterControlClass(
8:               AfxGetInstanceHandle(),
9:               m_clsid,         // Records the Object's CLSID
10:              m_lpszProgID,    // Records a Unique Program ID for MyControl
11:              IDS_MYCONTROL,   // Records a Human Readable Name of MyControl
12:              IDB_MYCONTROL,   // Records the Bitmap to Represent MyControl
13:              TRUE,            // Records that MyControl can be insertable
14:                               // in a Container's Insert Object Dialog
15:              dwMyControlOleMisc, // Records the Status bits of MyControl
```

```
16:               tlid,          // Records the Unique ID of the MyControls
17:                              // Control Class
18:               wVerMajor,     // Records the Major Version of MyControl
19:               wVerMinor);    // Records the Minor Version of MyControl
20:    else
21:         return AfxOleUnregisterClass(m_clsid, m_lpszProgID);
22:  }
```

Table 28.5 lists the possible status bits that can be set for a control. These bits identify the capabilities of the control.

TABLE 28.5 The OLE Miscellaneous Status Bits Symbolic Constants and What They Mean to Controls and Objects

Symbolic Constant	Meaning
OLEMISC_RECOMPOSEONRESIZE	Identifies an object that, upon resizing by the container, will rescale its presentation data.
OLEMISC_ONLYICONIC	Identifies an object that only exists in the iconic state.
OLEMISC_INSERTNOTREPLACE	Identifies an object that initializes itself from the currently selected container data.
OLEMISC_STATIC	Identifies that an object is static and contains no native data—only presentation data.
OLEMISC_CANTLINKINSIDE	Identifies items such as OLE 1.0 objects, static objects, and links. These are objects that cannot be a linked source object. In addition, when the object is bound, it cannot run another object.
OLEMISC_CANLINKBYOLE1	Identifies that an object can be linked by the containers that conform to the OLE 1.0 specification.
OLEMISC_ISLINKOBJECT	Identifies that an object is a linked object. This is only important for OLE 1.0 objects.
OLEMISC_INSIDEOUT	Identifies that an object can be in-place activated without the need for toolbars or menus.
OLEMISC_ACTIVATEWHENVISIBLE	Identifies that an object can be activated only in the visible state. The OLEMISC_INSIDEOUT flag also must be set.
OLEMISC_RENDERINGISDEVICEINDEPENDENT	Identifies that the object's presentation data will remain the same, regardless of the target container.

28

ACTIVEX CONTROLS

TABLE 28.5   continued

Symbolic Constant	Meaning
OLEMISC_INVISIBLEATRUNTIME	Identifies controls that are invisible at runtime, such as Internet Explorer's Timer control or Internet Explorer's PreLoader control.
OLEMISC_ALWAYSRUN	Tells a control that a control should be set in the running state even when not visible.
OLEMISC_ACTSLIKEBUTTON	Identifies controls that can act like buttons.
OLEMISC_ACTSLIKELABEL	Identifies controls that can change the label provided by the container.
OLEMISC_NOUIACTIVATE	Identifies whether a control supports user-interface activation.
OLEMISC_ALIGNABLE	Identifies that a control can be aligned with other controls for containers that support control alignment.
OLEMISC_SIMPLEFRAME	Identifies that the control supports the ISimpleFrameSite interface.
OLEMISC_SETCLIENTSITEFIRST	In the new OLE container specification, identifies controls that support the SetClientSide function being called after the control is created but before it is displayed.
OLEMISC_IMEMODE	In the *Double Byte Character Set (DBCS)* versions of Windows, identifies that the control supports the Input Method Editor mode for internationalized controls.

These miscellaneous status bits are especially important when used with component categories as an accurate picture of what your control can or cannot do. You can obtain this picture of what the control can do from the System Registry.

Component Categories

Previously, in order to be registered on the system, an ActiveX control was registered through entries in the Registry with the Control keyword. To your benefit, controls can be used for multiple purposes. Therefore, a way was needed to identify a control's functionality as opposed to just listing the interfaces it supports. This is where component categories come in.

Component categories are a way of describing what a control does. They provide a better method for containers to find out what a control does without creating it and having to query for its methods using an `IUnknown` pointer and `QueryInterface`. Creating a control object involves a great deal of overhead. A container would not want to create a control if the container itself does not support the functionality the control requires.

Component categories are not specific to ActiveX but are an extension of the COM architecture. Each component category has its own GUID and a human-readable name stored in a well-known place in the System Registry. When a control registers itself, it does so using its component category ID. In addition, it registers the component categories it supports and the component categories it requires its container to support.

For backward compatibility, the control also should register itself with the `Control` keyword for containers that do not support the new component categories. The control also should register the key `ToolBoxBitmap32`. This key identifies the module name and resource ID for a 16×15 bitmap. `ToolBoxBitmap32` provides a bitmap to use for the face of a toolbar or toolbox button in the container application. If a control can be inserted in a compound document, it also should register the `Insertable` key.

Component categories can be mixed and matched depending on their type. Microsoft maintains a list of component categories. Any categories that are new should be submitted to Microsoft for inclusion in the list. This promotes interoperability. The following component categories have been identified:

- Simple Frame Site Containment
- Simple Data Binding
- Advanced Data Binding
- Visual Basic Private Interfaces
- Internet-Aware Controls
- Windowless Controls

This list is not all-inclusive. The following sections give you more information on these component categories.

Simple Frame Site Containment

A simple frame site container control contains other controls—for example, a 3D group box that contains a group of check boxes. The GUID for this component category is

```
CATID - {157083E0-2368-11cf-87B9-00AA006C8166} CATID_SimpleFrameControl
```

28

ACTIVEX
CONTROLS

To support a simple frame site container, the container application must implement the ISimpleFrameSite interface, and the control must have its status bit set to OLEMISC_SIMPLEFRAME.

Simple Data Binding

A control or container that supports simple data binding supports the IPropertyNotifySink interface. Data binding is how controls affiliate their persistent properties and how containers exchange property changes from their user interface to the control's persistent properties. This capability allows the persistent storage of their properties and at runtime binds the data to the control synchronizing property changes between the control and the container. The GUID for this component category is

```
CATID - {157083E1-2368-11cf-87B9-00AA006C8166} CATID_PropertyNotifyControl
```

> **Note**
>
> Although a control that supports simple data binding is meant to provide binding to a data source, such binding should not be required for the functionality of the control. Even though a lot of the functionality of the control is lost, the control should degrade gracefully and still be able to function, although potentially limited, independent of any data binding.

Advanced Data Binding

Advanced data binding is similar to simple data binding except that it supports more advanced binding techniques, such as asynchronous binding and Visual Basic data binding. The GUID for this component category is

```
CATID - {157083E2-2368-11cf-87B9-00AA006C8166} CATID_VBDataBound
```

Visual Basic Private Interfaces

These component categories are for components that specifically support the Visual Basic environment. Controls or containers that use these categories can support alternative methods. This capability is useful if a container encounters a control—or a control encounters a container—that does not support the Visual Basic private interface categories. The GUID for this component category is

```
CATID - {02496840-3AC4-11cf-87B9-00AA006C8166} CATID_VBFormat
```

if the container implements the IVBFormat interface for data formatting to specifically integrate with Visual Basic, or

```
CATID - {02496841-3AC4-11cf-87B9-00AA006C8166} CATID_VBGetControl
```

if the container implements IVBGetControl so that controls can enumerate other controls on a Visual Basic form.

Internet-Aware Controls

Internet-aware controls implement one or more persistent interfaces to support operation across the Internet. All these categories provide persistent storage operations. The following are GUIDs for components that fall into this category:

```
CATID - {0de86a50-2baa-11cf-a229-00aa003d7352} CATID_RequiresDataPathHost

CATID - {0de86a51-2baa-11cf-a229-00aa003d7352} CATID_PersistsToMoniker

CATID - {0de86a52-2baa-11cf-a229-00aa003d7352} CATID_PersistsToStorage

CATID - {0de86a53-2baa-11cf-a229-00aa003d7352} CATID_PersistsToStreamInit

CATID - {0de86a54-2baa-11cf-a229-00aa003d7352} CATID_PersistsToStream

CATID - {0de86a55-2baa-11cf-a229-00aa003d7352} CATID_PersistsToMemory

CATID - {0de86a56-2baa-11cf-a229-00aa003d7352} CATID_PersistsToFile

CATID - {0de86a57-2baa-11cf-a229-00aa003d7352} CATID_PersistsToPropertyBag
```

The RequiresDataPathHost category means that the object requires the container to support the IBindHost interface, because the object requires the capability to save data to one or more paths.

All the rest of the categories listed are mutually exclusive. They are used when an object supports only a single persistence method. If a container does not support a persistence method that a control supports, the container should not allow itself to create controls of that type.

Windowless Controls

Windowless controls are controls that do not implement their own window and rely on the use of their container's window when drawing themselves. These types of controls include nonrectangular controls, such as arrow buttons, gauges, and other items modeled after real-world objects. In addition, this category includes transparent controls. The GUID for this component category is

```
CATID - {1D06B600-3AE3-11cf-87B9-00AA006C8166} CATID_WindowlessObject
```

28

ACTIVEX CONTROLS

Component Categories and Interoperability

Components that do not support a category should degrade gracefully. In the case where a control or container is unable to support an interface, the control should either clearly document that a particular interface is required for the proper operation of the component or at runtime notify the user of the component's degraded capability.

By using self-registration, components can be self-contained. By using `DllRegisterServer` and `DllUnregisterServer` and the component category's API functions to register itself and the component categories it supports, a control can further its interoperability in a variety of environments.

Code Signing

In the Internet environment, users must download the components to their local machine and use them. Allowing the implementation of this foreign code poses an extreme hazard to the local machine.

This is where a security measure called *code signing* comes in. Browsers typically warn users that they are downloading a potentially unsafe object; however, the browser does not physically check the code for authenticity to ensure that it has not been tampered with, nor does it verify its source.

Microsoft has implemented *Authenticode,* which embodies the Crypto API. This feature enables developers to digitally sign their code so that it can be checked and verified at runtime. This function is built into the browser and displays a certificate of authenticity if the control is verified (see Figure 28.11).

FIGURE 28.11

The certificate the user sees at runtime after the code is authenticated.

Currently, the code-signing specification and the certification process are being reviewed by the *World Wide Web Consortium* (*W3 Consortium*), and the current specifications are subject to change. Internet Explorer and all Microsoft controls naturally support code signing and Authenticode, but Netscape supports a different type of code-signing technology, known as *object signing*.

Code signing works with DLLs, EXEs, Cabinet (CAB) files, and ActiveX controls. A developer who creates these items attains a digital certificate from an independent certification authority. The developer then runs a one-way hash on the code and produces a digest that has a fixed length. Next, the developer encrypts the digest using a private key. This combination of an encrypted digest coupled with the developer's certificate and credentials is a signature block unique for the item and the developer. This signature block is embedded in the executable program.

Here's the way code signing works on the client machine. When a user downloads a control from the Internet, the browser application, such as Internet Explorer or Netscape, calls a Win32 API function called `WinVerifyTrust`.

`WinVerifyTrust` then reads the signature block. With the signature block, the `WinVerifyTrust` can authenticate the certificate and decrypt the digest using the developer's public key. Using the public key, the function then rehashes the code with the hash function stored in the signature block and creates a second digest. This digest then is compared with the original. If the digests do not match, this indicates tampering and the user is warned.

The code-signing mechanism provides some security for end users and developers alike. It is a deterrent to malicious tampering with executable code for the intent of information warfare, such as viruses, and it is also a deterrent for those who can pirate code developed by others. Please be aware again that this is a proposed standard and has not yet been accepted officially, although there is nothing I can see at this time that can compete with it. It is safe to say that no matter what, Microsoft will continue to support and refine this standard. The bottom line is that you will need to continue to monitor the standard.

Performance Considerations

ActiveX controls are designed to work across the Internet. As such, they are Internet-aware. Unfortunately, the Internet is low bandwidth and highly subject to server latency. This means that ActiveX controls must be lean and mean, or to put it more plainly, highly optimized. Because ActiveX controls implement only the interfaces they need,

28

ACTIVEX
CONTROLS

they already are partially optimized. ActiveX controls are optimized to perform specific tasks. However, you can do several things to help optimize your controls:

- Optimize control drawing.
- Don't always activate your control when it is visible.
- Provide flicker-free activation.
- Optimize persistence and initialization.
- Use windowless controls.
- Use a device context that is unclipped.
- While a control is inactive, provide mouse interaction.

Tip

These performance considerations and optimizing techniques apply to older OLE controls as well as ActiveX controls. Even if you have already developed OLE controls with the old standard, you still can apply most of these principles to those controls.

Optimize Control Drawing

When you draw items, you have to select items such as pens, brushes, and fonts into the device context to render an object onscreen. Selecting these items into the device context requires time and is a waste of resources when the container has multiple controls that are selecting and deselecting the same resources every time they paint. The container can support optimized drawing. This means that the container handles the restoration of the original objects after all the items have been drawn. IViewObject::Draw supports optimized drawing by using the DVASPECTINFOFLAG flags set in the DVASPECTINFO structure. You must use this structure to determine whether your container supports optimized drawing when implementing API functions. MFC encapsulates this check for you in the COleControl::IsOptimizedDraw function. You then can optimize how you draw your code by storing your GDI objects as member variables instead of local variables. This method prevents your objects from being destroyed when the drawing function finishes. Then, if the container supports optimized drawing, you do not need to select the objects back, because the container has taken care of this for you.

Don't Always Activate Your Control When It Is Visible

If your control has a window, it might not need to be activated when visible. Creating a window is a control's single biggest operation and should not be done until it is absolutely necessary. Therefore, if there is no reason for your control to be activated when visible, turn off the OLEMISC_ACTIVATEWHENVISIBLE miscellaneous status bit.

Provide Flicker-Free Activation

When your control has a window, it sometimes must transition from the active to the inactive state. A visual flicker occurs when the control redraws from the active to the inactive state. Two methods—drawing off-screen and then copying to the screen in one big chunk, and drawing front to back—can eliminate flicker. The IViewObjectEx API function provides the necessary functions to use either method or a combination of both. With MFC, the implementation is much simpler—simply do what is shown in Listing 28.9.

LISTING 28.9   Setting the noFlickerActive Flag in MFC

```
1:  DWORD CMyControl::GetControlFlags()
2:  {
3:      return COleControl::GetControlFlags() | noFlickerActivate;
4:  }
```

Optimize Persistence and Initialization

Optimizing persistence and initialization means basically one thing: Keep your code as lean as possible. Because of the cheapness of hard drive space and memory, some programmers have gotten lazy when creating this code and have allowed it to become bloated and slow. With Internet applications, this is a death sentence. Most people access the Internet with dial-up modems. One megabyte of data takes almost nine minutes to transfer over a 14.4 Kbps modem. Users become impatient if they have to wait long periods of time. You can do several things to solve this problem.

First of all, make sure you do not leave any unused blocks of code or variables. You also should take any debugging or testing blocks out of your code. Suppose that you have written your code so a message box displays when you reach a certain segment of code. Take it out! It only adds to your code size. However, if you delimit your debugging blocks of code using the preprocessor #ifdef _DEBUG and #endif, you will not have to worry about the code being included in the release builds, because the debugging blocks of code will be left out of the compile.

Second, today's compilers have optimizing options on them. In the past, these optimizing compilers were not very efficient and sometimes introduced bugs into an application that already had been tested. But compilers have gotten much better. Use them! Let the compiler do some of the work for you. You might have to tweak and play with the optimizations to find the best combination of options.

28

ACTIVEX
CONTROLS

> **Warning**
>
> Make sure you perform your compiler optimizations before you send your code to testing. Any time you touch the code, however, it should go back through testing. Therefore, if you have to tweak the compiler optimizations after your code has been through testing, make sure you send it back through testing! This precaution can help prevent you from discovering a bug after release.

You also should turn off the incremental linking option on your compiler when you do a release build. Incremental linking can add serious bloat to your code.

> **Note**
>
> An excellent article on keeping your code small is "Removing Fatty Deposits from Your Applications Using Our 32-Bit Liposuction Tools," by Matt Pietrek, in *Microsoft Systems Journal,* October 1996, Vol 11, No 10. Matt Pietrek has many useful suggestions and even provides a nice tool to assist you.

The final thing you should consider is using asynchronous operations to perform initialization and persistence operations. Asynchronous downloading gives users the illusion that things are occurring faster than they are. In addition, you might want to give users other visual cues that progress is being made, such as a progress indicator or a message box. However, you will have to weigh the performance issues associated with those additions.

Use Windowless Controls

You should consider making your control a windowless control if appropriate. Creating a window is a control's single biggest operation, taking almost two-thirds of its creation time. This is a lot of unnecessary overhead for the control. Most of the time, a control does not need a window and can use its container's window and allow the container to take on the overhead of maintaining that window. Using windowless controls enables you to model your controls on real-world objects, such as gauges, knobs, and other non-rectangular items.

By using the API function `IOleInPlaceSiteEx::OnInPlaceActivateEx` and setting the `ACTIVATE_WINDOWLESS` flag, you can have your control be in windowless mode. Listing 28.10 demonstrates how you can do this with MFC.

LISTING 28.10   Setting the Windowless Flag in MFC

```
1:  DWORD CMyControl::GetControlFlags()
2:  {
3:      return COleControl::GetControlFlags() | windowlessActivate;
4:  }
```

In addition, a whole series of API functions allows you to manipulate windowless controls. MFC also has encapsulated many of these functions for you. The MSDN Library included with Visual C++ has a complete reference for these functions. In addition, the Win32 API references have the API-level functions. For more information, launch the MSDN Library by selecting Help|Search from the Developer Studio menu, then search for "windowless controls".

Use a Device Context That Is Unclipped

If you have a window and you are sure your control does not draw outside of that window, you can disable the clipping in your drawing of the control. You can yield a small performance gain by not clipping the device context. With MFC, you can do what is shown in Listing 28.11 to remove the clipPaintDC flag.

LISTING 28.11   Setting the clipPaintDC Flag in MFC

```
1:  DWORD CMyControl::GetControlFlags()
2:  {
3:      return COleControl::GetControlFlags() & ~clipPaintDC;
4:  }
```

> **Note**
>
> The clipPaintDC flag has no effect if you have set your control to be a windowless control.

With the API functions in the Platform Software Development Kit, you can implement the IViewObject, IViewObject2, and IViewObjectEx interfaces to optimize your drawing code so that you do not clip the device context.

While a Control Is Inactive, Provide Mouse Interaction

You can set your control to inactive because it does not always need to be activated when visible. You still might want your control to process mouse messages such as WM_MOUSEMOVE and WM_SETCURSOR, though. You will need to implement the

IPointerInactive interface to allow you to process the mouse messages. If you are using MFC, you just need to implement the following function, and the framework handles the rest for you. Listing 28.12 shows you how to notify the framework that your control is interested in receiving mouse messages while inactive.

LISTING 28.12   Setting the Pointer Inactive Flag in MFC

```
1:  DWORD CMyControl::GetControlFlags()
2:  {
3:       return COleControl::GetControlFlags() | pointerInactive;
4:  }
```

However, you will need to override the OLEMISC_ACTIVATEWHENVISIBLE miscellaneous status bit with OLEMISC_IGNOREACTIVATEWHENVISIBLE. This is because OLEMISC_ACTIVATEWHENVISIBLE forces the control to always be activated when visible. You have to do this to prevent the flag from taking effect for containers that do not support the IPointerInactive interface.

Reinventing the Wheel

In today's software development environment, software engineers not only are designers and programmers, but increasingly, software engineers are taking on the role of component integrators. End users demand that their software be developed quickly, be rich in features, and integrate with the rest of the software they use. With the advent of COM, *Common Object Request Broker Architecture (CORBA)*, and JavaBeans, you now have hundreds of thousands of reusable components and objects to choose from. An abundance of DLLs, controls, automation components, and document objects are at your fingertips. ActiveX controls especially provide an off-the-shelf, self-contained, reusable package of functionality created by someone else. ActiveX controls provide functionality of all types, such as multimedia, communications, user-interface components, report writing, and computational.

The functionality offered by available ActiveX controls is functionality you do not have to create. The key to component integration is to be able to integrate all the components with a custom application so that they work in single harmonious union, as if they were native to the application.

Before you embark on creating this application, however, you should take care not to reinvent the wheel. ActiveX controls, the COM, and the object-oriented paradigm present a unique opportunity for you to truly have code reuse. To achieve this nirvana of code reuse, you should evaluate what components are already out there. Likewise, before you decide to write your own ActiveX controls, you should take a look at what is already out there and see whether you can use what is already available.

When you choose to use off-the-shelf components, you should consider a few things. You should ask the following questions:

- Does the manufacturer supply the source code with the component, or does it offer a code-escrow service? The source code would come in handy if the manufacturer goes out of business or has a bug in its component that it is not going to fix.
- What are the licensing fees and distribution costs?
- Is the control Web-enabled?
- What kind of support and money-back guarantee does the manufacturer provide?
- What tools will the component be supported in?
- What kind of documentation, such as programmer manuals, help files, and installation guides, does the control come with?

These questions can save you a lot of heartache later. Integration of these off-the-shelf components sometimes is tricky. Make sure you thoroughly research the components you choose. To find some of these available off-the-shelf components, look in some of the computer industry trade magazines.

Visual C++ ActiveX Controls

Visual C++ 6.0 comes with a plethora of ActiveX controls. Therefore, before you take the time to create your own control, take a look around and see what is available. Take a look at all the ActiveX controls available to you from the Components and Controls Gallery in Visual C++. Choose Project, Add to Project, Components and Controls to invoke the Components and Controls Gallery dialog box, as shown in Figure 28.12.

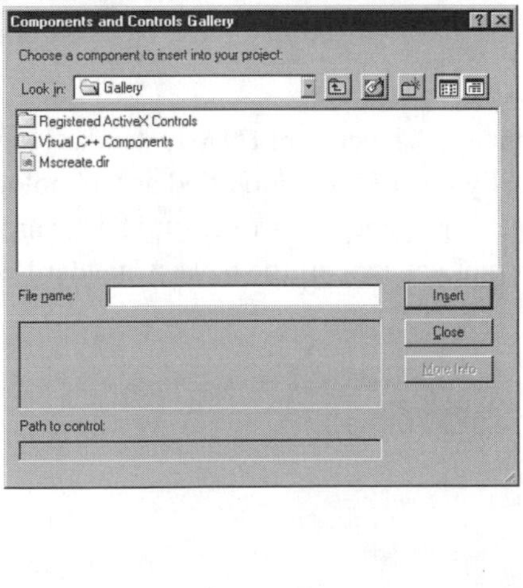

FIGURE 28.12

The Components and Controls Gallery dialog box.

28

ACTIVEX
CONTROLS

Click the Registered ActiveX Controls folder. Take a look at all of the ActiveX controls available, as shown in Figure 28.13.

Testing an ActiveX Control

To ensure that your ActiveX control works properly, you should test it in as many environments as possible. At a minimum, you should test your ActiveX controls in the following environments:

- A Web page, if your control is intended for use in a browser
- The ActiveX control container
- Visual C++, Visual Basic, or any other environments you're targeting

Displaying a Control on a Web Page

To "activate the Internet" with ActiveX controls, as the Microsoft marketing folks are fond of saying, you have to have a way of embedding those ActiveX controls in an HTML file.

The W3C controls the HTML standard. The current HTML standard is version 4.01. Like most standards, it is continually updated and modified as technology progresses. As the standard progresses, the controlling agency tries to ensure backward compatibility so that any HTML browser that does not yet support the newest standard will degrade gracefully and allow the HTML to be viewed.

The <OBJECT> HTML tag allows the insertion of dynamic content on the Web page, such as ActiveX controls. The tag is just a way of identifying such dynamic elements. It is up to the browser to parse the HTML tags and perform the appropriate action based on the meaning of the tag. In Listing 28.13, you can see the HTML syntax for the <OBJECT> tag. This syntax comes directly from the W3C, which controls the HTML standard. In this case, it is HTML standard Version 4.01.

LISTING 28.13   HTML Syntax for the <OBJECT> Tag

```
 1:  <OBJECT
 2:     ALIGN= alignment type
 3:     BORDER= number
 4:     CLASSID= universal resource locator
 5:     CODEBASE= universal resource locator
 6:     CODETYPE= codetype
 7:     DATA= universal resource locator
 8:     DECLARE
 9:     HEIGHT= number
10:     HSPACE= value
11:     NAME= universal resource locator
12:      SHAPES
13:      STANDDY= message
14:      TYPE= type
15:      USEMAP= universal resource locator
16:      VSPACE= number
17:      WIDTH= number
18:  </OBJECT>
```

28

ACTIVEX CONTROLS

By using the <OBJECT> tag, you can insert an object such as an image, document, applet, or control into the HTML document.

Table 28.6 shows the acceptable range of values to be used by the parameters of the <OBJECT> tag.

TABLE 28.6   Values for the Parameters of the `<OBJECT>` Tag

Parameter	Values
`ALIGN=` *alignment type*	Sets the alignment for the object. The alignment type is one of the following values: `BASELINE`, `LEFT`, `MIDDLE`, `CENTER`, `RIGHT`, `TEXTMIDDLE`, `TEXTTOP`, and `TEXTBOTTOM`.
`BORDER=` *number*	Specifies the width of the border if the object is defined to be a hyperlink.
`CLASSID=` *universal resource locator*	Identifies the object implementation. The syntax of the *universal resource locator (URL)* depends on the object type. For example, for registered ActiveX controls, the syntax is `CLSID:class-identifier`.
`CODEBASE=` *universal resource locator*	Identifies the codebase for the object. The syntax of the URL depends on the object.
`CODETYPE=` *codetype*	Specifies the Internet media type for code.
`DATA=` *universal resource locator*	Identifies data for the object. The syntax of the URL depends on the object.
`DECLARE`	Declares the object without instantiating it. Use this when creating cross-references to the object later in the document or when using the object as a parameter in another object.
`HEIGHT=` *number*	Specifies the height for the object.
`HSPACE=` *number*	Specifies the horizontal gutter. This is the extra empty space between the object and any text or images to the left or right of the object.
`NAME=` *universal resource locator*	Sets the name of the object when submitted as part of a form.
`SHAPES`	Specifies that the object has shaped and shared hyperlinks.
`STANDBY=` *message*	Sets a message to be displayed while an object is loaded.
`TYPE=` *type*	Specifies the Internet media type for data.
`USEMAP=` *universal resource locator*	Specifies the imagemap to use with the object.
`VSPACE=` *number*	Specifies a vertical gutter. This is the extra white space between the object and any text or images above or below the object.
`WIDTH=` *number*	Specifies the width for the object.

In Listing 28.14, you can see HTML document source code with an embedded ActiveX object in it. In addition, note the `<PARAM NAME= value>` tag. This tag was used to set any properties your ActiveX control can have.

LISTING 28.14   The HTML Page with an Embedded `<OBJECT>` Tag Showing an
`ActiveMovie` ActiveX Control Embedded in the Page

```
1:  <HTML>
2:  <HEAD>
3:  <TITLE>AN EMBEDDED ActiveX Control</TITLE>
4:  </HEAD>
5:  <BODY>
6:
7:  <p align=center><font size=6><em><strong><u>An EMBEDDED ActiveX Control
    ➥</u></strong></em></font></p>
8:  <OBJECT
9:  ID="ActiveMovie1"
10: WIDTH=347
11: HEIGHT=324
12: ALIGN=center
13: CLASSID="CLSID:05589FA1-C356-11CE-BF01-00AA0055595A"
14: CODEBASE="http://www.microsoft.com/ie/download/activex/amovie.ocx#
    ➥Version=4,70,0,1086">
15:   <PARAM NAME="_ExtentX" VALUE="9155">
16:   <PARAM NAME="_ExtentY" VALUE="8573">
17:   <PARAM NAME="MovieWindowSize" VALUE="2">
18:   <PARAM NAME="MovieWindowWidth" VALUE="342">
19:   <PARAM NAME="MovieWindowHeight" VALUE="243">
20:   <PARAM NAME="FileName" VALUE="E:\vinman\dstuds.avi">
21:   <PARAM NAME="Auto Start" VALUE="TRUE">
22: </OBJECT>
23:
24: </BODY>
25: </HTML>
```

When a browser such as Internet Explorer encounters this page, it begins to parse the HTML source code. When it finds `<OBJECT>` in line 8, it realizes it has encountered a dynamic object. The browser then takes lines 10 to 12—the `WIDTH`, `HEIGHT`, and `ALIGN` attributes, which in this case are `347`, `324`, and `center`, respectively—and sets up a place-holder for the object on the rendered page. It then takes the `ID` `"ActiveMovie1"` in line 9 and the CLASSID `"CLSID:05589FA1-C356-11CE-BF01-00AA0055595A"` in line 13 and checks to see whether this control has been registered in the Registry. If the control object has never been registered, it uses the `CODEBASE` attribute to locate the ActiveX control on the server machine and downloads the object into a local directory. The browser then registers `AMOVIE.OCX` by calling `DllRegisterServer` to register the control on the local machine. Now, with the control properly registered, the browser can get the `CLSID`

28

ACTIVEX
CONTROLS

for the object from the Registry. To use the control, the browser passes the CSLID to CoCreateInstance to create the object, and this returns the pointer to the control's IUnknown. The browser can use this pointer and the property information in lines 15 to 22 to actually render the object on the page.

Now, you can see that embedding controls to enhance a Web page with dynamic content is fairly easy. It is important that you, as an ActiveX control designer, understand how these controls are rendered.

ActiveX Control Pad

The ActiveX Control Pad provides a method of generating the HTML code, discussed earlier, to embed ActiveX and other dynamic objects into HTML source code (see Figure 28.14). This is a free tool provided by Microsoft to aid in the production of Internet-enabled applications.

FIGURE 28.14

The ActiveX Control Pad with the ActiveMovie *control properties being edited.*

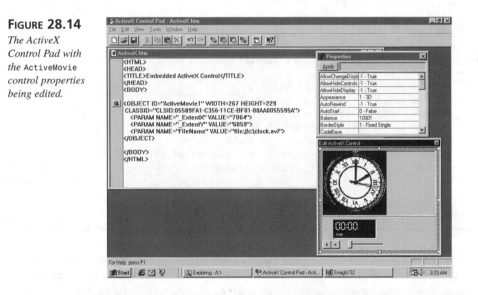

> **Note**
>
> You can download the ActiveX Control Pad from Microsoft from the following Internet URL:
>
> http://msdn.microsoft.com/workshop/misc/cpad/default.asp
>
> The ActiveX Control Pad also is included in the Microsoft Developer's Network (MSDN) subscription. To install the Control Pad, search for setuppad.exe in the MSDN Library.

You can use this tool to quickly embed your control in a page so that you can test its functionality. The ActiveX Control Pad can be a great time-saver, freeing you from having to remember how to write HTML source code. It even allows you to test the control using VBScript (see Figure 28.15).

FIGURE 28.15

The ActiveX Script Wizard helps you create scripts to further activate your controls.

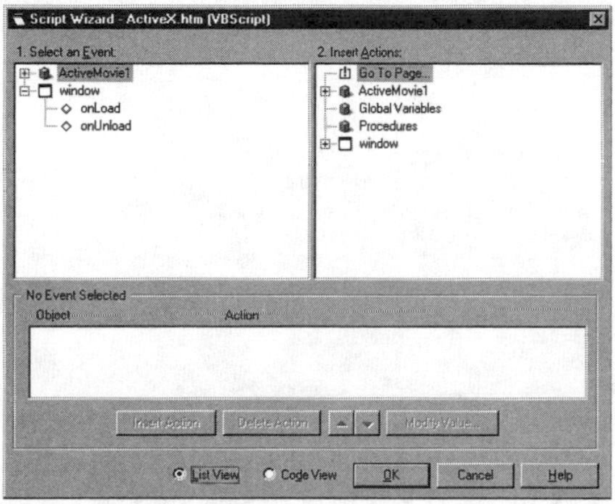

In addition, the ActiveX Control Pad comes with a suite of ActiveX controls for you to use in the development of your Web pages and your ActiveX-enabled applications. Some of these controls are the same controls that come with Internet Explorer; however, there are a few new ones to add to your bag of ActiveX controls.

ActiveX Control Test Container

The ActiveX Control Test Container is provided with Visual C++ to allow you to fully test your ActiveX control. This tool enables you to test your control's registration, events, properties, and methods. To invoke the ActiveX Control Test Container, choose Tools, ActiveX Control Test Container. The ActiveX Control Test Container appears, as shown in Figure 28.16.

In addition to the ActiveX Control Test Container, you might want to consider using Rational Software's Visual Test. This tool previously was known as the Microsoft Visual Test.

ActiveX Controls in Development Tools

One last way to test your ActiveX controls is with your development tools: Visual C++, Borland C++, Visual Basic, Delphi, PowerBuilder, Access, and almost any other mainstream Windows or Internet development suite. Become familiar with these development tools and ensure that they work in all environments. In addition, most of these tools

28

ACTIVEX CONTROLS

come with ActiveX controls. So use and take advantage of the components provided for you. This approach will make your job much easier and your users much happier.

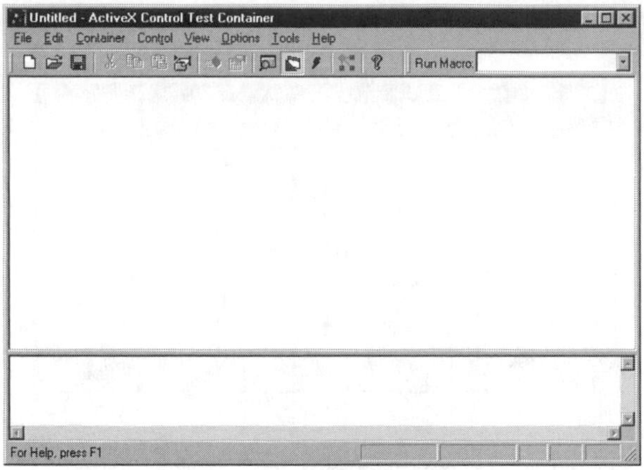

FIGURE 28.16

The ActiveX Control Test Container is a tool to help you test your controls.

Methods of Creating ActiveX Controls

Currently, you can create ActiveX controls with Visual C++ in two ways:

- Visual C++ and *Microsoft Foundation Classes (MFC)*
- *Active Template Library (ATL)*

Creating an ActiveX Control with Visual C++ and MFC

Previous versions of Visual C++ and MFC enabled development of ActiveX controls for the 16-bit versions of Windows. Microsoft recently stopped providing the Visual C++ 1.52c compiler to registered users of its 32-bit C++ compiler, so this section concentrates on the 32-bit environment only. Building 16-bit OLE controls is possible with Visual C++ 1.52c (if you currently have a copy), but 16-bit development is rapidly being left behind.

Using Visual C++ and MFC for ActiveX Controls

Before the ActiveX control specification was released, OLE controls had to have certain interfaces implemented whether or not they needed them. This meant that controls were larger than they needed to be. This is fine if you are using your controls on a local machine, but with ActiveX controls that may need to be downloaded and installed across a low-bandwidth, high-latency network, any excess baggage is less efficient in achieving this end. For your controls to be useful in a network setting, your ActiveX controls need to be lean, mean, and efficient downloading machines.

Visual C++ comes with the MFC ActiveX ControlWizard to help you create controls. This wizard is one of the fastest ways to create a control. In fact, if you are a newcomer to creating controls, it is the best way to learn, because it creates a framework for you. You can be up and running very quickly. However, you need to be aware of a few drawbacks.

To use a control created with Visual C++ and based on MFC, the MFC DLL must reside on the client machine. This file is about 1.2MB and must be downloaded to the client machine. This file must be downloaded only if the DLL hasn't been downloaded to the client machine already, however. So you take a small performance hit the first time your control is used. Furthermore, MFC-based controls tend to be larger than the controls created using ATL or the Platform SDK directly.

You need to weigh your options carefully, considering performance, programmer skill, timetable, and environment. This is not to say that MFC-based controls are not suitable for use in the ActiveX environment, but simply to make you aware of the factors associated with choosing this method. If you are building controls for a high-bandwidth and potentially low-latency intranet, the size of the control and the associated DLL are not major factors. Speed of development, less complexity, and rich features can be more important. In fact, a basic ActiveX control created with the MFC ActiveX ControlWizard is only 23KB. Even on the sluggish Internet, 23KB is not extremely large, especially in comparison to some of the large graphics files and Microsoft Video (AVI) files embedded in Web pages.

MFC Encapsulation of ActiveX and ActiveX Controls

MFC encapsulates the ActiveX control functionality in a class called `COleControl` (see Figure 28.17). `COleControl` is derived from `CWnd` and, in turn, from `CCmdTarget` and `CObject`.

`COleControl` is the base class from which you derive to create any ActiveX control you want. What's nice is that your control inherits all the functionality of the base class `COleControl`. You then can customize the control to include the capabilities you want in it. With MFC, the complexities of dealing with the COM interfaces are abstracted into an easy-to-use class. In addition, MFC provides a framework for your control so you can

28

**ACTIVEX
CONTROLS**

worry about the details of what you want your control to do instead of re-creating functionality that all controls have to contain in order to work.

FIGURE 28.17

The class hierarchy for COleControl.

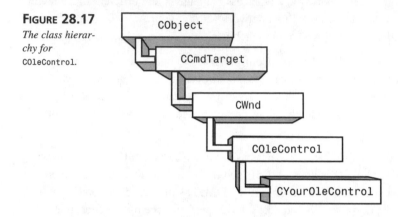

MFC itself provides a range of capabilities already created for you when you use it. It also includes functionality to perform messaging and automated data exchange.

The MFC ActiveX ControlWizard

The beauty of Visual C++ and MFC is that they perform the mundane task of creating the framework for your control, leaving you the task of making your control perform the functionality you want it to create. At the center of this is the MFC ActiveX ControlWizard, which you use to create ActiveX controls. In this section, you examine each feature of the ControlWizard and create your first ActiveX MFC control.

You first need to launch Visual C++. After you have Visual C++ up and running, choose File, New. You then see the New dialog box (see Figure 28.18).

FIGURE 28.18

The New dialog box in Visual C++.

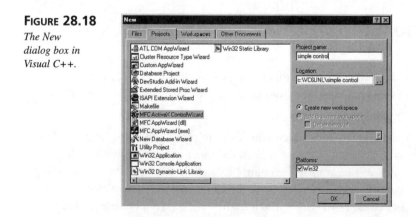

Select the Projects tab, and select MFC ActiveX ControlWizard as the project type. You also need to give your control a title and a location. In this case, call it `simple control` and accept the default location.

You now are looking at the first page of the MFC ActiveX ControlWizard (see Figure 28.19). Here, the wizard asks you a series of questions about what you want in your control:

- How many controls do you want in the project?
- Do you want a runtime license for your controls?
- Would you like the wizard to document your controls with source file comments?
- Would you like a help file generated for your control?

FIGURE 28.19

Step 1 of the MFC ActiveX ControlWizard in Visual C++.

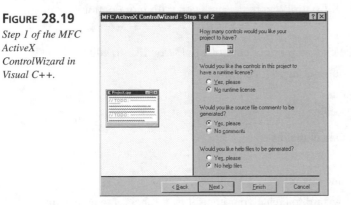

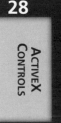

In this case, you are going to create only one control, so select one control for this project. As you already learned, one DLL hosting ActiveX controls can contain several controls.

Also, select the choice for the wizard to include licensing support for this control. In addition, ask the wizard to document the code it is going to write for you in the control framework with comments.

Lastly, ask the wizard to generate a basic help file so that you can provide online help for the programmers who will be using this control. It is extremely important that this control be well-documented. Then, click the Next button and go to page 2 of the ActiveX ControlWizard (see Figure 28.20).

FIGURE 28.20

Step 2 of the MFC ActiveX ControlWizard in Visual C++.

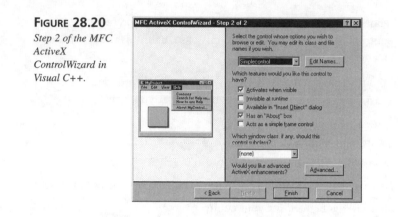

Step 2 of the MFC ActiveX ControlWizard presents you with more options for this ActiveX control:

- Which names of the classes for your control would you like to edit?
- What features do you want in your control?

    Activates when visible

    Invisible at runtime

    Available in Insert Object dialog

    Has an About box

    Acts as a simple frame control

- Would you like the wizard to create your control as a subclass to an existing control?
- Would you like advanced ActiveX enhancements for your control?

The MFC ActiveX ControlWizard enables you to control the naming of each of the controls in your project to include the class names, source filenames, and property sheet names (refer to Figure 28.19). If you click the Edit Names button (refer to Figure 28.20), you will see the Edit Names dialog box (see Figure 28.21). The ControlWizard does provide a default naming convention; in this case, accept the defaults provided.

Next are questions regarding what features you want to have in this control. You need to keep in mind the previous section on optimizations. Does the control need to be active when visible, or is it invisible at runtime like a timer control or a communications control? This control will need to be active and visible. You want this control to be available in the Insert Object dialog box, so you will choose this option. No doubt you are proud of the controls you create, so you can include an About dialog box to post your name or your company's name. Lastly, do you want this control to be a simple frame control and support the `ISimpleFrameSite` interface? This is so the control can act as a frame for other controls. For this example's purposes, do not choose this option.

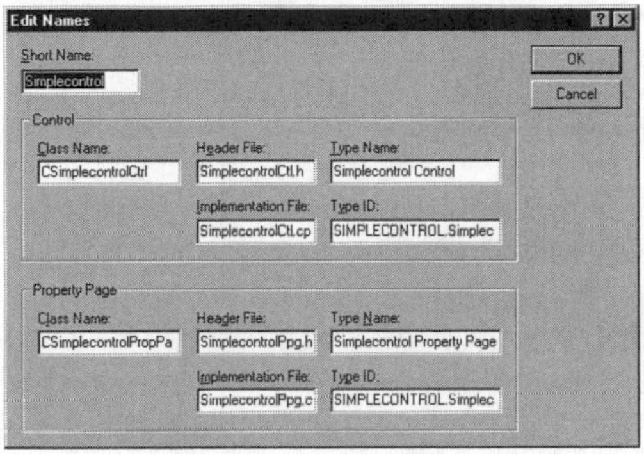

FIGURE 28.21

The Edit Names dialog box in step 2 of the MFC ActiveX ControlWizard in Visual C++.

You now need to take a look and select the advanced options that support ActiveX enhancements. Click the Advanced button and go to the Advanced ActiveX Features dialog box (see Figure 28.22).

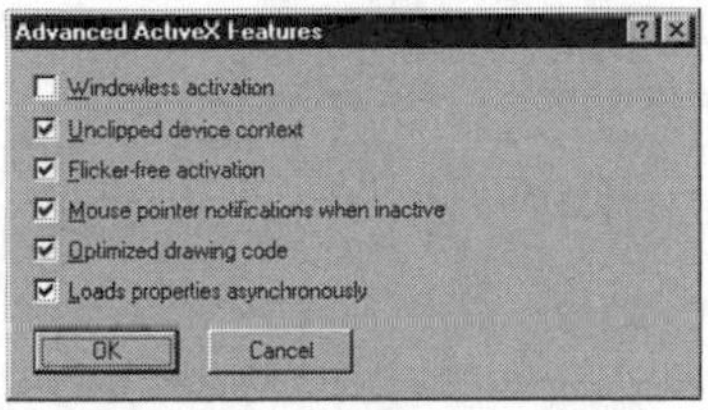

FIGURE 28.22

The Advanced ActiveX Features dialog box of step 2 of the MFC ActiveX ControlWizard in Visual C++.

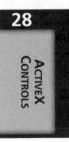

28

ACTIVEX CONTROLS

In the Advanced ActiveX Features dialog box, you can choose one of six options. Keep in mind the previous information you covered on these options.

- Windowless activation
- Unclipped device context
- Flicker-free activation
- Mouse pointer notifications when inactive
- Optimized drawing code
- Loads properties asynchronously

Choose all but Windowless Activation, and click OK. Then, click Finish. You then see a summary of the features the wizard will create for you in the New Project Information dialog box (see Figure 28.23).

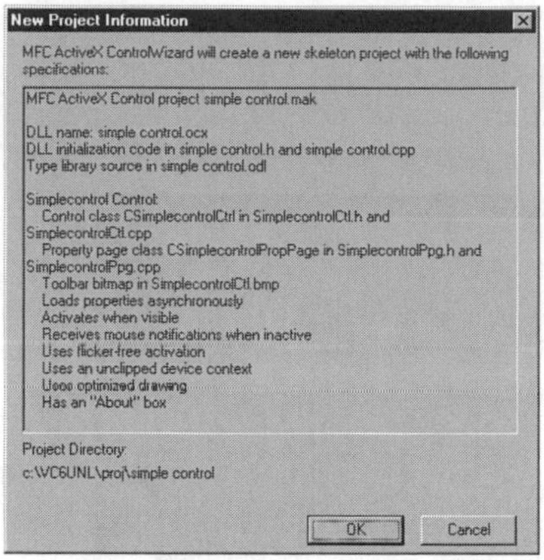

FIGURE 28.23

*The New Project
Information dia-
log box of the
ActiveX
ControlWizard in
Visual C++.*

Click OK in the New Project Information dialog box, and the wizard creates a basic control for you and implements all the features you selected in it. This control just needs to be compiled before it is up and running. The wizard even added an ellipse in this control's drawing code so that it will have something to display. You now have the framework to start customizing this control. The nice thing is that most of that functionality already is encapsulated in MFC. To assist you in this endeavor, Visual C++ provides you with the ClassWizard. The sky is the limit on what types of creations are possible now that you have the framework built for you.

Summary

This chapter has discussed ActiveX controls, which are an evolution of OLE custom controls. When compared to OLE custom controls, ActiveX controls can be smaller, faster, and offer features that improve performance.

This chapter discussed two ways that Developer Studio simplifies the task of writing ActiveX controls. The MFC ActiveX control wizard automates the process of creating your control. With a few mouse clicks, you can be well on your way to creating an ActiveX control. In addition, the MFC class library includes a great deal of functionality that you can easily leverage into your own controls. Support for property sheets, commonly used interfaces, and data binding are all built into the MFC library.

This chapter also included information on testing your ActiveX controls. Developer Studio includes the ActiveX Test Container, which is a great place to start testing your controls. You can also use your controls in Visual C++ or in a Web page, as discussed in this chapter.

Using the Active Template Library

PART VII

ATL Architecture

by Mickey Williams

CHAPTER 29

The *Active Template Library (ATL)* is a template-based class library used to create high-performance *Component Object Model (COM)* applications. This chapter discusses the major components of the ATL architecture. An example that uses ATL in a client program demonstrates how ATL simplifies COM programming.

This chapter also discusses the *Interface Definition Language (IDL)*. IDL is the standard language used to define interfaces in COM. The basic structure of an IDL file is described in this chapter, and an example IDL file is presented.

The History of ATL

The Active Template Library was introduced between Visual C++ 4.2 and Visual C++ 5.0. Initially, the library provided support for creating simple COM objects. Known at the time as the *ActiveX Template Library,* ATL 1.0 made it possible to create small, fast components with a minimal amount of code. The major features of ATL 1.0 follow:

- Capability to create components that take advantage of COM features not available in MFC
- Capability to create components that do not rely on the C runtime library
- CComPtr smart pointer class
- Prebuilt default implementations of standard interfaces

ATL 1.1 includes support for Registry handling via Registry scripts. This release also included a simple ATL AppWizard. The ATL 1.1 release was available from the Microsoft Visual C++ Web site.

Version 1.1 of ATL does not provide any support for Visual components. Support for creating components with a user interface is provided in ATL 2.0, which was released prior to Visual C++ 5.0. Visual C++ 5.0 shipped with ATL 2.1, which added improved integration with the Visual C++ environment, including GUI-based editing of IDL files.

Visual C++ 6.0 includes ATL 3.0, which adds support for components that are OLE-DB providers and consumers. ATL 3.0 also included support for writing Microsoft Management Console (MMC) snap-ins and Dynamic HTML (DHTML) controls. ATL 3.0 also included an improved interface wizard.

Recently released as part of the Windows 2000 version of the Platform SDK is the *Windows Template Library (WTL)*. WTL adds support for building high-performance GUI applications.

ATL's Advanced Use of Templates

The primary design goal for ATL is performance. To provide the maximum possible performance, ATL uses some advanced template idioms that you might not have seen elsewhere.

Many developers of lightweight components would like to avoid the overhead associated with virtual functions, for example. ATL declares abstract classes using the _declspec(novtable) compiler extension. This declaration prevents the compiler from emitting code to initialize the virtual function table for the abstract base class. When linked, the linker is able to perform further optimizations, reducing the size of the component.

ATL also avoids virtual functions whenever possible in favor of static linking. For an example of how ATL avoids the cost of virtual functions, consider the code shown in Listing 29.1, a typical example of how virtual functions are used in C++ programs.

LISTING 29.1   Using Virtual Functions in C++

```cpp
#include <iostream>
using namespace std;
class CBase
{
public:
    void CallVirtualFunc()
    {
        VirtualFunc();
    }
    virtual void VirtualFunc()
    {
        cout << "CBase::VirtualFunc called" << endl;
    }
};

class CDerived: public CBase
{
    void VirtualFunc()
    {
        cout << "CDerived::VirtualFunc called" << endl;
    }
};

int main()
{

    CBase* pb = new CDerived;
    pb->CallVirtualFunc();

    return 0;
}
```

29

ATL
ARCHITECTURE

In Listing 29.1, the CDerived class implements a virtual function that is called via a pointer to CBase. Calling functions implemented in a derived class is a key abstraction in C++ and is very powerful. Many class libraries, including MFC, are built on this abstraction.

Unfortunately, the use of virtual functions in Listing 29.1 does not come without a price. In addition to the cost of building and initializing the virtual-function table, each function call made through the virtual-function table incurs a performance penalty of several instructions. In some applications, particularly in lightweight server-side components, this runtime cost can be a noticeable drag on the component's overall performance.

To avoid this performance cost, ATL uses static, compile-time binding instead of runtime binding whenever possible. Listing 29.2 illustrates this practice.

Listing 29.2   Using Static Binding Instead of Virtual Functions

```
#include <iostream>
using namespace std;
template<typename T>
class _declspec(novtable) CBase
{
public:

    void CallVirtualFunc()
    {
        // Call the most derived version of the function directly.
        static_cast<T*>(this)->VirtualFunc();
    }
    virtual void VirtualFunc()
    {
        cout << "CBase::VirtualFunc called" << endl;
    }
};

class CDerived: public CBase<CDerived>
{
public:
    void VirtualFunc()
    {
        cout << "CDerived::VirtualFunc called" << endl;
    }
};

int main()
{

    CBase<CDerived>* pb = new CDerived;
    pb->CallVirtualFunc();

    return 0;
}
```

In Listing 29.2, the derived class type is passed as a template parameter. When the template is instantiated, code necessary to call the proper functions in the derived class is created, without the costs associated with virtual functions.

Commonly Used ATL Classes

The ATL class library includes a number of classes that are used to simplify COM programming. ATL classes can be separated into two categories:

- High-level classes that provide module-level or COM class-level services. These classes include CComObject and related classes, as well as classes used to implement executable modules, such as CComModule.

- Helper classes that simplify the use of commonly used COM interfaces, components, and structures, such as BSTRs, interface pointers, and variants.

High-Level ATL Classes

Here are some of the most commonly used high-level classes:

- CComModule   Provides the implementation for a COM server suitable for an EXE or DLL. CComModule manages the class factory, class objects, and component registration.

- CComObject   Implements the IUnknown interface for instances of your COM class. ATL also includes specialized versions of this class, such as CComObjectStack, which can be used if your COM objects will live on the stack, and CComAggObject for aggregated COM objects. The CComObject class defined for your COM class uses multiple inheritance to derive from all interfaces supported by the COM class it represents.

- CComObjectRoot   A typedef made for each project that consists of CComObjectRootEx parameterized with an appropriate threading class.

- CComObjectRootEx   A template that includes the basic IUnknown interface functionality used by CComObject. This template is instantiated using a threading model class as a parameter. The threading model contains functions that are implemented differently, depending on the threading model, such as AddRef and Release.

ATL Helper Classes

The AtlBase.h header file includes a number of helper classes that simplify the use of frequently used objects. The most commonly used helper classes follow:

- CComBstr   Wraps the COM BSTR string type
- CRegKey   Simplifies working with the System Registry

29

ATL
ARCHITECTURE

- CComVariant   Provides a wrapper around the COM VARIANT type
- CComPtr   Provides a smart pointer wrapper around COM interface pointers
- CComQIPtr   Adds the capability to automatically query for the desired interface; Similar to CComPtr

Using CRegKey to Access the Registry

The CRegKey class is used to encapsulate access to the System Registry. CRegKey properly manages any HKEY handles that are used to access Registry locations. The most commonly used CRegKey member functions follow:

- Open   Opens a specified key in the Registry, setting the internal HKEY to the handle of the requested key.
- Create   Creates a specified key in the Registry, or opens the key if it already exists. The internal HKEY is set to the handle of the requested key.
- Close   Closes the open Registry key held by the CRegKey object and sets the internal HKEY value to NULL.
- QueryValue   Retrieves the contents of a value field in the Registry. The name of the value is passed as a parameter.
- SetValue   Sets the contents of a value field in the Registry.

Listing 29.3 shows an example of using CRegKey.

LISTING 29.3   Using CRegKey to Read a Location from the System Registry

```
CRegKey regKey;
TCHAR   szBuff[1024];
DWORD   dwSize = sizeof(szBuff)/sizeof(szBuff[0]);
TCHAR   szPath[] = _T("SYSTEM\\CurrentControlSet\\Services\\"
                      "codevtestsvc\\parameters\\");
LONG err = regKey.Create(HKEY_LOCAL_MACHINE, szPath);
if(!err)
{
    regKey.QueryValue(szBuff, _T("PingCounter"), &dwSize);
}
```

In Listing 29.3, CRegKey is used to open a Registry key and then extract the PingCounter value. Note that the size of the string buffer is passed to QueryValue as a pointer to a DWORD. When QueryValue returns, the number of bytes copied into the buffer is stored in this variable.

Using `CComBstr` to Manage COM Strings

The `CComBstr` class is used to manage COM's string objects, which are known as `BSTR`s. When designing interfaces, you are free to use either the `BSTR` or `LPOLESTR` types to pass strings between components. If you want to interact with Visual Basic or VBScript users, however, you must expose your strings as the `BSTR` type.

A `BSTR` is similar but not identical to the `LPOLESTR` type. Both types are used to represent wide (16-bit) strings; in fact, a `typedef` in the `wtypes.h` header file causes a compiler to treat the two types identically:

```
typedef OLECHAR __RPC_FAR *BSTR;
```

Unfortunately, the two types are not equivalent—the `BSTR` type is actually a pointer to a wide string, with 16 bits reserved before the beginning of the string that contain the string's length. Visual Basic and other languages use the length to optimize string handling.

Because of the `typedef` in `wtypes.h`, it's impossible for your compiler to warn you when you interchange `LPOLESTR` and `BSTR`. For this reason, it's a good idea to pick one method of representing your strings and to use that method exclusively. The `CComBstr` class is an easy way to standardize your code toward using the COM `BSTR` type.

`CComBstr` has many of the same operators found in other commonly used string classes, such as the standard C++ library `string` or the MFC `CString`. `CComBstr` instances can be initialized from narrow or wide character arrays:

```
CComBstr bstrName("Mickey");
CComBstr bstrCar(L"Rover");
```

Using the `CComVariant` Class

COM uses the `VARIANT` structure to provide a generic wrapper around commonly used types. Internally, the `VARIANT` is a union, with a discriminator member variable that describes the particular value contained in the union.

Listing 29.4 provides a simplified and significantly shortened version of the `VARIANT` declaration. The full declaration of the `VARIANT` structure is located in the `OAIdl.h` header file.

LISTING 29.4   A Simplified Declaration of the COM `VARIANT` Structure

```
typedef struct tagVARIANT VARIANT;
struct tagVARIANT
{
    union
    {
```

LISTING 29.4 continued

```c
struct __tagVARIANT
{
    VARTYPE vt;
    union
    {
        ULONGLONG      ullVal;
        LONGLONG       llVal;
        LONG           lVal;
        BYTE           bVal;
        SHORT          iVal;
        FLOAT          fltVal;
        DOUBLE         dblVal;
        .
        .
        .
        // Some declarations omitted for clarity
        .
        .
        .
    };
    };
    DECIMAL decVal;
};
};
```

VARIANT structures originally were designed to be used with Visual Basic 3.0 and OLE Automation. Because Visual Basic 3.0 had a weak type system, the VARIANT structure and the IDispatch Automation interface were used for COM interaction with Visual Basic. Today the only COM clients that require Automation interfaces and VARIANT arguments are scripting clients such as VBScript.

Because of the many types of data that can be held in a VARIANT, proper handling of the structure can be difficult. Consider the (relatively) simple act of clearing the data stored in a variant. If the variant contains a simple type, such as a long or a short, the contents of the VARIANT can simply be set to zero. If the VARIANT contains an interface pointer, however, the Release method must be called before the pointer is destroyed, or the reference count for the interface will never reach zero, and the interface might never be released. Other complex types, such as BSTR, have similar requirements.

To simplify working with VARIANT structures, a number of SDK functions are designed to safely initialize, clear, copy, and convert VARIANT structures. Unfortunately, this requires the programmer to be constantly vigilant, avoiding code such as the following:

```c
HRESULT WrongWayToCopyVariants(VARIANT* pvTarget, VARIANT* pvSource)
{
    if(!pvTarget || !pvSource)
```

```
        return E_INVALIDARG;
    *pvTarget = *pvSource;
    return S_OK;
}
```

The preferred way to copy a variant is to use the `VariantCopy` function:

```
HRESULT MyCopyVariantFunc(VARIANT* pvTarget, VARIANT* pvSource)
{
    if(!pvTarget || !pvSource)
        return E_INVALIDARG;
    return VariantCopy(pvTarget, pvSource);
}
```

In fact, even the preceding code isn't safe because it assumes the code that calls the `MyCopyVariantFunc` function has properly initialized the `VARIANT` structure with a call to `VariantInit`:

```
VARIANT v;
VariantInit(&v);
```

A `VARIANT` that has not been initialized properly by calling `VariantInit` is not safe to use and can easily lead to bugs that are difficult to trace.

Because of the rigid handling required for the `VARIANT` type, the `CComVariant` class was a welcome addition to ATL. The `CComVariant` class ensures that its internal `VARIANT` is properly initialized and maintained, even during copies and assignments. Further, the class properly releases data stored in the `VARIANT` when an instance of the class is destroyed.

Using Smart Pointers

The `CComPtr` and `CComQIPtr` classes are used to provide smart pointer wrappers around COM interface pointers. In this context, a smart pointer is a pointer that properly releases its reference counts toward COM interfaces when it goes out of scope. The COM smart pointer classes also work correctly when used with C++ exception handling (although the classes do not use exception handling).

Like most other (non-COM) smart pointer classes, `CComPtr` and `CComQIPtr` override C++ operators to make the smart pointer class act like a normal C++ pointer. `CComPtr` and `CComQIPtr` overload the following operators:

- `operator->` Returns the wrapped interface pointer, protected from misuse.
- `operator&` Returns the address of the wrapped interface pointer. Asserts in debug builds if the internal pointer is NULL.
- `operator!` Returns true if the wrapped interface pointer is NULL.

- operator*   De-references the wrapped interface pointer and returns the interface. Asserts in debug builds if the internal pointer is NULL.

- operator T*   Returns a pointer to the wrapped interface pointer.

- operator=   Assigns the smart pointer to a new interface pointer, calling AddRef and Release automatically as required.

- operator==   Tests the wrapped interface pointer for equality against another interface pointer. This operator does not check to see whether the two interfaces belong to the same COM object.

- operator<   Tests the wrapped interface pointer against another interface pointer.

To use CComPtr, you instantiate it with the interface type that you'll be accessing:

```
CComPtr<IShellLink>  pShellLink;
```

As discussed earlier, the CComPtr and CComQIPtr classes manage the calls to AddRef and Release automatically. The classes use an interesting template trick to prevent a client from accidentally calling these functions through operator->. Instead of returning a raw pointer to the internal interface pointer, the following code is used:

```
_NoAddRefReleaseOnCComPtr<T>* operator->() const
{
    ATLASSERT(p!=NULL);
    return (_NoAddRefReleaseOnCComPtr<T>*)p;
}
```

The implementation of the _NoAddRefReleaseOnComPtr class makes the AddRef and Release member functions private, preventing a client from writing code like this:

```
CComPtr<IShellLink>  pShellLink;
HRESULT hr = pShellLink.CoCreateInstance(CLSID_ShellLink);
pShellLink->Release(); // Error, won't compile!
```

If you find the need to decrement the reference count for an interface wrapped with CComPtr or CComQIPtr, use the smart pointer's Release member function:

```
CComPtr<IShellLink>  pShellLink;
HRESULT hr = pShellLink.CoCreateInstance(CLSID_ShellLink);
pShellLink.Release(); // Explicit call to smart pointer class, okay
```

As discussed in the preceding list, operator== tests two interfaces to see whether they are equivalent. This operator only tests the interfaces, not the underlying objects. If you need to test two interfaces to determine whether they refer to the same object, use the smart pointer's IsEqualObject member function, which compares IUnknown interface pointers, performing QueryInterface if necessary.

You can assign an interface pointer to your smart pointer in four ways:

- Call the smart pointer's CoCreateInstance member function.

- Pass the interface's raw interface pointer to CoCreateInstance.

- Call the smart pointer's `Attach` member function to assign a previously created interface pointer to the smart pointer. This does not cause the smart pointer to call `AddRef` through the new interface pointer.

- Simple assignment through the smart pointer's assignment operator causes the smart pointer to call `AddRef` through the new interface pointer.

Calling the smart pointer's `CoCreateInstance` member function is the simplest way to create a new interface pointer, but the member function uses the `__uuidof()` compiler extension, which requires that the interface type have a GUID defined with `__declspec(uuid)` as part of the interface declaration. Most standard Windows COM interfaces do have declarations, which can be added to your project by including the `comdefs.h` header file. Be aware that some interfaces that exist in the standard Windows headers (such as some Active Directory interfaces) cannot be created using the smart pointer's `CoCreateInstance` method unless you create the appropriate `__declspec` declaration yourself.

For interfaces that do have a GUID defined, using the smart pointer's `CoCreateInstance` function is straightforward and the simplest way to create a new interface pointer:

```
CComPtr<IShellLink>    pShellLink;
HRESULT hr = pShellLink.CoCreateInstance(CLSID_ShellLink);
```

To set a smart pointer to the value of a pointer returned from a function, you also can use the `&` operator, which works just like the non-smart pointer case:

```
CComPtr<IShellLink> pShellLink;
HRESULT hr = CoCreateInstance(CLSID_ShellLink,
                              NULL,
                              CLSCTX_ALL,
                              IID_IShellLink,
                              reinterpret_cast<void**>(&pShellLink));
```

In the preceding case, the smart pointer automatically calls `Release` through the interface pointer when the `pShellLink` destructor is called.

Using the smart pointer's `Attach` method is appropriate in cases where you already have an interface pointer that has been `AddRef`'d, and you want to use the smart pointer to manage the interface's lifetime:

```
CComPtr<IShellLink> pShellLink;
IShellLink psl = GetShellPointer();
pShellLink.Attach(psl);
```

The final way to set the value of a smart pointer is to simply use the assignment operator, just as when assigning any built-in C++ type:

```
CComPtr<IShellLink>    pShellLink;
CComPtr<IShellLink>    pOtherShellLink;
HRESULT hr = pShellLink.CoCreateInstance(CLSID_ShellLink);
pOtherShellLink = pShellLink;
```

29

ATL ARCHITECTURE

Listing 29.5 shows how the CComPtr and CComQIPtr classes are used to simplify client-side COM code.

LISTING 29.5   Using ATL Smart Pointer Classes to Manage Interfaces

```
#define _UNICODE
#define UNICODE
#include <atlbase.h>
#include <shlobj.h>
#include <comdef.h>
HRESULT BuildShortcutLink(LPCTSTR pszTargetPath, LPCTSTR pszLinkPath, LPCTSTR
pszDesc);

// Demonstrates using ATL smart pointers for interface management.
// Call as:
// SmartPtr <target path> <shortcut path> <description>
int wmain(int argc, wchar_t* argv[])
{

    if(argc != 4)
        return 1;

    HRESULT hr = CoInitialize(NULL);
    if(FAILED(hr))
        wprintf(L"CoInitialize failed with HRESULT %X\n", hr);
    hr = BuildShortcutLink(argv[1], argv[2], argv[3]);
    if(FAILED(hr))
        wprintf(L"Failed with HRESULT %X\n", hr);
    else
        wprintf(L"Link to %s created at %s", argv[1], argv[2]);
    CoUninitialize();

    return 0;
}

HRESULT BuildShortcutLink(LPCTSTR pszTargetPath,
                          LPCTSTR pszLinkPath,
                          LPCTSTR pszDesc)
{
    CComPtr<IShellLink>  pShellLink;
    HRESULT hr = pShellLink.CoCreateInstance(CLSID_ShellLink);

    if(FAILED(hr))
        return hr;

    // Set the path to the link's target - this is not the
    // location of the shortcut, it's the file or location the
    // link refers to.
    hr = pShellLink->SetPath(pszTargetPath);
```

```
    if(FAILED(hr))
        return hr;

    // Set the description property for the link.
    hr = pShellLink->SetDescription(pszDesc);
    if(FAILED(hr))
        return hr;

    // Create a new pointer for the IPersistFile interface,
    // and query through pShellLink for that interface.
    CComQIPtr<IPersistFile> pFile = pShellLink;
    if(!pFile)
        return E_NOINTERFACE;

    // Persist the shortcut at the link's desired location.
    hr = pFile->Save(pszLinkPath, TRUE);

    return hr;
}
```

In Listing 29.5, the `CComPtr` and `CComQIPtr` classes are used to manage the program's interface pointers. No explicit management of the interface pointer is required—the smart pointer destructors automatically release their references to COM objects when the pointers are destroyed.

Using the Interface Definition Language

As discussed in earlier chapters, COM is a language-neutral specification that defines how objects interact on a binary level. Although some languages are more COM-friendly than others, COM makes no demands on languages except the following:

- The language runtime must provide some way to call a function or method indirectly through an interface function table. This indirection is commonly known as a *virtual-function table,* or *vtable* in C++. Some languages that support COM, such as Visual Basic, hide this capability from the programmer and treat it as a language implementation detail.

- The language, or at least its runtime, must be capable of reference count maintenance for COM interfaces. Some languages, such as C and C++, require the programmer to explicitly manage reference counts. Other languages, such as Visual Basic, hide this complexity from the programmer.

Given these relatively small requirements, most procedural languages can be made to work with COM.

This openness causes a problem with respect to defining interfaces for COM classes. How should an interface be defined in order to be used by any modern language? There are nearly as many ways to define interfaces as there are computer languages.

All COM interfaces are defined using the *Interface Definition Language* (*IDL*). IDL is similar to C and C++ header files, with new syntax elements specific to distributed computing added. IDL files are compiled to create source files and binary type libraries that can be used by practically all programming environments.

IDL was not created for COM—it has been used for years to define the interactions between systems that use *Remote Procedure Call* (*RPC*) interfaces.

Microsoft uses a version of IDL known as *Microsoft Interface Definition Language* (*MIDL*). MIDL is very much like IDL, with a few extra syntax features used to help define COM classes and interfaces. Listing 29.6 shows a typical MIDL code fragment.

LISTING 29.6   A Typical MIDL Source File

```
import "oaidl.idl";
import "ocidl.idl";
    [
        object,
        uuid(78EDC064-9077-4CE5-AA93-A096B9766DBD),
        dual,
        helpstring("ILatte Interface"),
        pointer_default(unique)
    ]
    interface ILatte : IDispatch
    {
        [id(1), HRESULT AddFoam([in] short nDepth);
        [id(2), HRESULT GetFoamDepth([out] short* pnDepth);
        [id(3), HRESULT AddVanillaShot([in] short nShots);
    };

    [
        uuid(063FDFB3-8ACA-4A64-BFE3-3795F81388CA),
        version(1.0),
        helpstring("JensCoffee 1.0 Type Library")
    ]
    library JensCoffeeLib
    {
        importlib("stdole32.tlb");
        importlib("stdole2.tlb");

        [
```

```
        uuid(2AE38564-6EB0-44EE-8063-4064A40143A7),
        helpstring("Latte Class")
    ]
    coclass Latte
    {
        [default] interface ILatte;
    };
};
```

The MIDL source provided in Listing 29.6 has three main sections (the first line of each section is shown in bold):

- The declaration of the ILatte interface. This section describes the attributes of the interface and specifies the signature for each function in the interface.

- The declaration of JensCoffeeLib, which is used to generate a type library. A *type library* is a binary representation of the IDL and is discussed in Chapter 30, "Creating COM Objects Using ATL."

- The declaration of the Latte coclass. The COM class, or coclass, is declared inside the library declaration. It lists the interfaces (and other objects) that are part of the Latte COM class.

Each of these objects begins with a list of descriptive attributes enclosed in brackets, like this:

```
[object]
```

Attributes are discussed in the next section.

In addition to interfaces and COM classes, here are some other objects you might find frequently in a MIDL file:

dispinterface	Marks an Automation-compatible interface as being derived from IDispatch
enum	Creates an enumerated type, just as in C and C++
struct	Creates an aggregated type, just as in C and C++
union	Creates an aggregated type that contains one of several possible types, just as in C and C++

This is only a partial list. The MIDL documentation included on your MSDN CD-ROM contains a complete MIDL reference.

When you create a COM class using ATL and the associated Visual C++ wizards, the IDL for the ATL class is created for you automatically. Simple controls and ATL classes often can use the auto-generated IDL file without further modification. More complex COM components often require a manual edit of the IDL source, however.

29

ATL ARCHITECTURE

In practice, you will need to know how to manipulate the IDL file manually—the more you know about IDL, the more effective you will be as a COM developer. Using IDL with the ATL class library is discussed in more detail in Chapter 30.

ATL Wizards

Two wizards are supplied by Visual C++ to simplify the building of custom COM objects with ATL:

- The ATL COM AppWizard helps you create a project that builds a module—a DLL, EXE, or service—that hosts COM classes.
- The ATL Object Wizard helps you add a COM object to your project.

These wizards are discussed in the next two sections.

Using the ATL COM AppWizard

The easiest way to create an ATL project is to use the ATL COM AppWizard. This wizard creates a skeleton project for you based on the type of project you select (see Figure 29.1).

FIGURE 29.1
The ATL COM AppWizard.

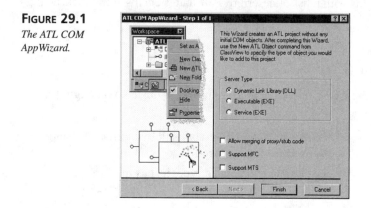

You can build three types of projects using the ATL COM AppWizard:

- **DLL**   The module will be built as an in-process DLL. As discussed in previous chapters, this is the most efficient type of COM module.
- **EXE**   The module will be built as an out-of-process server. As discussed in earlier chapters, this type of module is more robust than a DLL.
- **Service**   The module will be built as a Windows NT or Windows 2000 service.

If you chose to build your project as a DLL, you have three additional options that are enabled in the lower half of the wizard page:

- **Allow merging of proxy/stub code.** Enables you to include the proxy/stub marshaling code in your DLL, thus reducing the effort required to deploy the DLL on other machines. If you do not enable this check box, you will need to distribute a separate proxy/stub DLL with the DLL that contains your COM server.
- **Support MFC.** Enables MFC support in your ATL project. If you absolutely cannot live without MFC, enable this check box.
- **Support MTS.** Adds the necessary MTS libraries to your project.

Given a project named `JensCoffee`, the ATL COM AppWizard will create the following files for your ATL project:

`stdafx.h`	Just as in an MFC project, `stdafx.h` has all the standard `#include` directives that will be built into a precompiled header.
`stdafx.cpp`	Just as in an MFC project, `stdafx.cpp` is used to create the precompiled header.
`JensCoffee.dsp`	The Visual C++ project file.
`JensCoffee.dsw`	The Visual C++ workspace file.
`JensCoffee.opt`	The Visual C++ workspace options file.
`JensCoffee.ncb`	A binary file used by the Visual C++ ClassWizard.
`JensCoffee.rc`	The project resource file, which initially contains version information for the project.
`Resource.h`	The project resource header file.
`JensCoffee.idl`	Contains MIDL definitions for the project.
`JensCoffee.cpp`	Contains basic functions necessary for the module to interact with COM. DLL projects have a number of `DllXxxx` functions. EXE projects have `CExeModule` member functions.
`JensCoffee.h`	This file is empty initially, but it is replaced by a more meaningful file after the MIDL compiler is run against the project's `*.idl` file.
`JensCoffeeps.mk`	The makefile used to build the proxy/stub DLL if required for custom marshaling support.
`JensCoffeeps.def`	The module definition file for the proxy/stub DLL.

29

ATL ARCHITECTURE

If you create a DLL project that allows the proxy/stub code to be merged, the following files are created:

`dlldata.c`	A source file that must be added to the project in order to merge proxy/stub code into the DLL.
`dlldata.h`	The header file for `dlldata.c`.

The files are not automatically added to your project—you must follow the steps outlined later in the section "Merging the Proxy/Stub Code with Your DLL."

This file is created for all DLL-based projects:

`JensCoffee.def`   The module definition file for the project.

Finally, the following file is created for all EXE and service projects:

`JensCoffee.rgs`   The script file used to insert information into the System Registry.

Using the ATL Object Wizard

As discussed earlier, you use the ATL Object Wizard to add an ATL COM class to your project. You launch the ATL Object Wizard by choosing Insert, New ATL Object from the Visual C++ menu. The ATL Object Wizard appears, as shown in Figure 29.2.

FIGURE 29.2

The ATL Object Wizard.

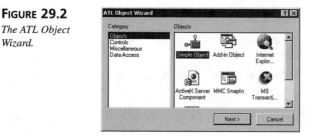

You can choose from four categories of ATL classes to insert into your project:

- **Objects**   Contains *Active Server Page (ASP)* components, *Microsoft Management Console (MMC)* snap-ins, *Microsoft Transaction Server (MTS)* components, and other basic COM components.
- **Controls**   Contains controls suitable for embedding in ActiveX containers. These controls are discussed in Chapter 31, "Creating ActiveX Controls Using ATL."
- **Miscellaneous**   Contains a dialog box that can be added to your project.
- **Data Access**   Contains data provider and consumer classes.

Seven types of classes are offered in the Objects category:

- **Simple Object**   Generates a simple COM class for the project.
- **Add-In Object**   Creates a COM class that can extend the Visual C++ IDE.
- **Internet Explorer Object**   Creates a non-visual COM class that can be hosted inside Internet Explorer.
- **ActiveX Server Component**   Creates a COM class that can be used with Active Server Pages in IIS.
- **MMC SnapIn**   Creates a class that can be used with Microsoft Management Console.
- **MS Transaction Server Component**   Creates a COM server that can be used with MTS.
- **Component Registrar Object**   Creates a class that enables you to register individual components in a DLL instead of registering all components at once.

After a component type has been selected, a property sheet is displayed that enables you to define attributes for the component. Some component types display specialized property pages specific to their object type. The MTS component includes an MTS page used only for that particular type of component, for example. All component types present a Names property page, as shown in Figure 29.3.

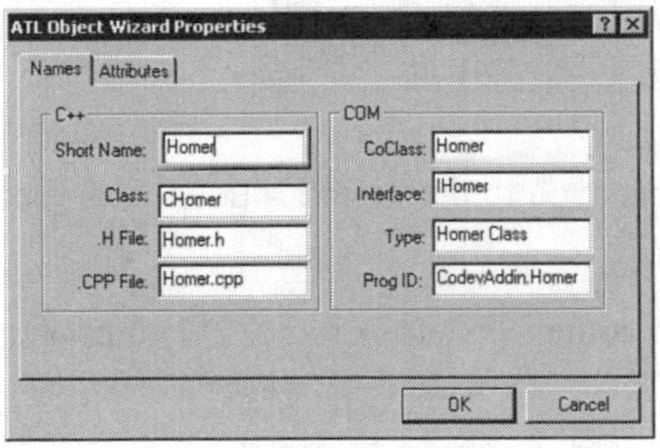

FIGURE 29.3

The Names property page contains naming attributes for ATL components.

29

ATL ARCHITECTURE

Eight items are displayed on the Names property page:

- **Short Name**   The name of the COM component.
- **Class**   The name of the C++ class that implements the component. By default, this is the name of the component prefixed with a C.
- **.H File**   The name of the header file for the component. By default, this is the name of the component with an .H extension.
- **.CPP File**   The name of the implementation file for the component. By default, this is the name of the component with a .CPP extension.

- **CoClass**   The name of the component's coclass. By default, this is the name of the component.

- **Interface**   The name of the interface exposed by the component. By default, this is the name of the component prefixed with I.

- **Type**   A description string stored in the System Registry under the component's Prog ID. By default, this is the name of the component, followed by Class.

- **Prog ID**   The program ID for the component. By default, this is `<project name>.<component name>`. A project named JensCoffee that has a component named Latte, for example, would have a Prog ID of JensCoffee. Latte.

The second tab for most component types is the Attributes property page, which is used to collect information about the component, such as its threading model (see Figure 29.4).

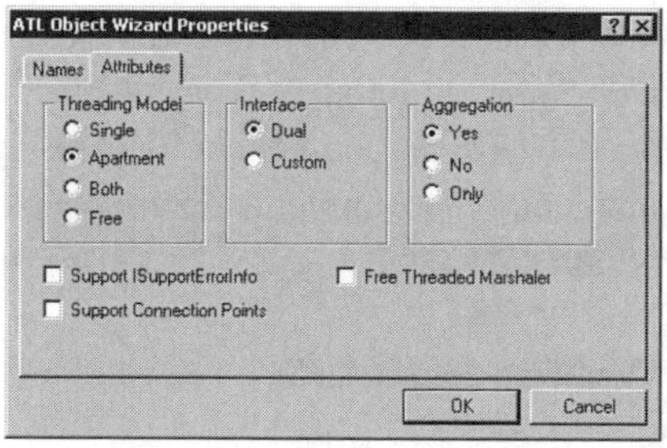

FIGURE 29.4

The Attributes property page contains characteristics for ATL components.

The Attributes property page enables you to define the following properties for the component:

- **Threading Model**   The threading model for the COM component. The options for this property follow:

  Single   The component will always be created in the first STA (also known as the main STA) of the process.

  Apartment   The component will be created in an STA.

  Both   The component will be created in either an STA or the MTA, depending on the apartment of the caller.

  Free   The component will be created in MTA of the process.

- **Interface**   Select Dual for an Automation-compatible interface or Custom for a COM vtable interface.

- **Aggregation**   The type of aggregation supported by the component. The options for this property follow:

  Yes   The component can be aggregated by another component.

  No   The component can not be aggregated by another component.

  Only   The component must be aggregated by another component

- **Support ISupportErrorInfo**   Adds support for the `ISupportErrorInfo` interface to your COM component.

- **Support Connection Points**   Adds support for connection points to your component. Using connection points is discussed in Chapter 30.

- **Free Threaded Marshaler**   Adds support for simplified marshaling of interface pointers between apartments (under some circumstances).

Given a component named `Latte`, the ATL Object Wizard creates the following files:

`Latte.cpp`   Contains the implementation of the `CLatte` class. Initially, this file is empty.

`Latte.h`   Contains the header file for the `CLatte` class.

`Latte.rgs`   The script file used to insert information about `CLatte` into the Registry.

The ATL Object Wizard also modifies the following files:

`JensCoffee.cpp`   Modified to add `CLSID_Latte` to the module's object map.

`JensCoffee.idl`   Modified to add the new `ILatte` interface.

Merging the Proxy/Stub Code with Your DLL

If your component uses custom interfaces, you must supply a DLL that contains a marshaling proxy and stub code. Normally, you compile a separate proxy/stub DLL that must be distributed and registered with your component. This DLL is created using the proxy/stub makefile that is created as part of the initial project. This file has the name `<project>ps.mk`. The `JensCoffee` project, for example, has a makefile named `JensCoffeeps.mk` that is used to create the proxy/stub DLL.

As discussed earlier in this chapter, the ATL COM AppWizard provides an option to allow proxy/stub DLL to be merged into the component's server DLL. If you select this option, the `dlldatax.c` and `dlldatax.h` files are added to your project. They will not be included in the build, however.

If you want to merge the proxy/stub into your DLL, you must follow these steps:

1. Go to the FileView tab in the Project Workspace and right-click on the `dlldatax.c` file. Choose Settings from the pop-up menu. The Project Settings dialog box appears.

2. On the General tab in the Project Settings dialog box, clear the Exclude File from Build check box. Keep the dialog box open.

3. Repeat this procedure for the `dlldatax.h` header file.

4. Click on the `dlldatax.c` file icon in the Project Workspace.

5. Keep the dialog box open and select the C++ tab.

6. Choose the Precompiled Headers category from the drop-down list, and select the Not Using Precompiled Headers radio button.

7. Choose the Preprocessor category, and add `_MERGE_PROXYSTUB` as a preprocessor definition. Make sure the new symbol is separated from the previous symbol by a comma.

8. Click OK to close the dialog box.

After the project has been built, the DLL that contains the component also will contain the code required for proxy/stub marshaling.

Summary

This chapter discussed the major architectural points of the ATL class library. You examined the architectural highlights of the class library, and you looked at the wizards that help you create projects that use ATL. A small example demonstrated how to use ATL in a client program.

You also learned about IDL and how to use it to describe interfaces in COM. You examined the Microsoft extensions to IDL and the MIDL compiler. You then looked at an example of an IDL file. You'll find more information on ATL and IDL in the following chapters.

CHAPTER 30

Creating COM Objects Using ATL

by Mickey Williams

IN THIS CHAPTER

In this chapter, you'll look at creating custom COM objects using the *Active Template Library* (ATL). You'll learn how to use the *Interface Definition Language* (IDL) to define interfaces that go beyond the basic types supported by IDispatch. You'll examine how structures, enumerations, and unions can be passed over COM interfaces. And finally, you'll see an example of a COM client and server that pass structures and enumerations through a custom interface.

Using IDL to Describe Custom COM Objects

As discussed in Chapter 29, "ATL Architecture," you define COM interfaces by using the *Interface Definition Language* (IDL). In that chapter, the IDL example extended IDispatch—the Automation interface used by scripting clients. You can use IDL to create custom interfaces that do not derive from IDispatch, however. These interfaces can use a wide variety of types, including structures and enumerations.

Understanding MIDL Attributes

An important part of an IDL source file is the attributes that tag elements in the source. As discussed in Chapter 29, elements in an IDL source file can be tagged with attributes enclosed in braces. Some of these attributes are optional; you may see the attributes on one interface but not another. Other attributes are required for all COM interfaces, such as these:

object	Specifies to the *Microsoft Interface Definition Language* (MIDL) compiler that this is a COM interface instead of a *Remote Procedure Call* (RPC) interface.
uuid	Contains the unique identifier for the interface, which will become its COM *Interface ID* (also known as its IID).

Every COM interface will have the preceding two attributes. Other commonly used attributes for COM interfaces follow:

dual	Specifies that the interface may be called through an Automation interface or its function table.
helpstring	Contains a description of the interface. The description is embedded into the type library; some development tools display this string as an aid to developers using the interface.
pointer_default	Defines the default behavior for pointers in the interface. More information about MIDL pointer notation is provided in the section "Pointers in IDL," later in this chapter.

Other attributes follow:

hidden	Prevents the interface, coclass, or library from being displayed in a browser.
size_is	Specifies the size of a dynamic array using another parameter as an argument, as in size_is(nSize).
max_is	Specifies the maximum index for a dynamic array using another parameter as an argument, as in max_is(nSize).
iid_is	Specifies the COM interface ID for an interface pointer passed as a parameter using another parameter as an argument, as in iid_is(riid).

Methods in an Automation-compatible interface are prefixed with a *dispatch ID*. The dispatch ID is basically a required index when using the IDispatch interface or any interface derived from IDispatch. The dispatch ID is used by Automation to identify the particular interface that is to be invoked. Here is the syntax for an interface method with a dispatch ID:

```
[id(1)] HRESULT DrinkLatte();
```

Two other attributes are commonly used with interface methods:

propput	Specifies a method used to set the value of a property exposed by the interface. The last parameter passed to the method must be an [in] parameter that will be used to set the property's value. The property must have the same name as the method.
propget	Specifies a method used to retrieve the value of a property exposed by the interface. The last parameter passed to the method must be an [out, retval] parameter that will be used to retrieve the property's value. The property must have the same name as the method.

Each property can have one propput and one propget method.

Compiling an IDL Source File with MIDL

IDL source files are compiled by invoking the MIDL compiler via this command line:

```
MIDL latte.idl
```

If you use Visual C++ and the ATL COM Wizard to create your project, the MIDL compiler is invoked automatically as part of the project build activity.

30

CREATING COM
OBJECTS USING
ATL

Given a source file named Latte.idl, the MIDL compiler generates five output files:

dlldata.c	Contains the functions required for the proxy/stub DLL.
Latte.h	Contains C and C++ versions of the interface definitions.
Latte_i.c	Contains definitions of the CLSIDs and IIDs used by the interfaces, type libraries, and coclasses found in Latte.idl.
Latte_p.c	Contains proxy/stub marshaling code.
Latte.tlb	Contains the *type library* for Latte.idl. The type library is a binary version of the IDL file and is used by programming languages such as Visual Basic that cannot read IDL files. Type libraries also are used by Automation controllers written in other languages to discover properties and methods exposed by a COM object.

The latte_i.c file typically would be included in one of the files used by C or C++ clients of interfaces defined in Latte.idl. Alternatively, the file could be linked into the program separately. This file contains definitions of the GUIDs used by all components in the IDL file.

The files latte_i.c, latte_p.c, latte.h, and dlldata.c can be compiled to create a proxy/stub DLL. This DLL is required if you're marshaling non–Automation-compatible interfaces across apartment boundaries. More information about creating a proxy/stub DLL is provided in the section "Compiling and Registering the Standard Proxy/Stub DLL," later in this chapter.

If you're targeting Windows NT 4.0 or Windows 2000, consider using the /Oicf compiler switch when invoking the MIDL compiler. This compiler switch notifies the compiler to generate code that uses interpretive marshaling features available only in Windows NT 4.0 and Windows 2000. Interpretive marshaling can greatly reduce the size of the marshaling code used in an interface. If you need to support Windows 95 or Windows 98, the /Oic compiler switch provides a somewhat less-optimized proxy.

Using Type Libraries

IDL files originally were created with the C and C++ RPC programmer in mind. Many languages cannot use IDL source files or the C and C++ source files generated by the MIDL compiler. For this reason, the MIDL compiler emits a type library, which is a binary representation of the IDL source.

Languages such as Java and Visual Basic extract information from type libraries instead of using the IDL source. This method allows these tools to provide a user interface that displays information about the COM interfaces in the type library.

When programming in C or C++, the LoadTypeLib or LoadRegTypeLib function is used to load the type library; these functions return a pointer to the ITypeLib interface. A related interface, ITypeLib2, is derived from ITypeLib and also returns type library attributes. The ITypeInfo and ITypeInfo2 interfaces are used to describe objects in the type library and are returned by ITypeLib methods.

Using Structures in IDL

Custom structures are defined in IDL much as they are in C and C++. Typically, the structure is defined as a typedef. The following code fragment defines a structure type named MyRect:

```
typedef struct tagMyRect
{
    int left;
    int right;
    int top;
    int bottom;
}MyRect;
```

After the MyRect structure is defined in the IDL file, it can be used just like any other type as a parameter:

```
HRESULT GetOurRect([out]MyRect* pRect);
HRESULT DrawOurRect([in]MyRect* pRect);
```

Structures such as MyRect are not Automation compatible. If you define and use a custom structure in your IDL, you must use custom interfaces, and you must build and register a proxy/stub DLL. This isn't difficult, but it does require an extra step when building your project. The steps required to build and register a proxy/stub DLL are discussed in the section "Compiling and Registering the Standard Proxy/Stub DLL," later in this chapter.

Using Enumerations in IDL

Like structures, enumerations are defined in IDL just as they are in C and C++. The following fragment defines an enumeration type named BaseballClubs that contains a few Major League Baseball teams:

```
typedef enum tagBaseballClubs
{
    Padres = 0,
    Braves,
    Yankees,
    Astros,
    Indians,
    Dodgers
}BaseballClubs;
```

After the enumeration is defined, it can be used like any other type:

```
HRESULT PlayBall([in]BasballClubs* pClub);
HRESULT GetWorldChamps([out]BasballClubs* pClub);
```

Later in this chapter, an example will use an enumerated type to return the operating system name to the client.

Pointers in IDL

If you're one of those people who thought pointers were a difficult topic when learning C or C++, you may need to study a few examples of how pointers work in a distributed system.

Consider what happens when a pointer value is transmitted between two distributed components. If you're writing the IDL for interfaces supported by distributed COM objects, your clients may be in the same process, they may be executing in separate processes, or they may even be executing on separate machines across a network, as Figure 30.1 shows.

FIGURE 30.1

An interface defines the contract, not the location of the client or server.

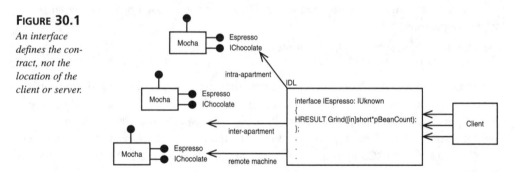

COM objects are placed into apartments that define their threading model. A component's apartment type controls the quantity and types of threads that are allowed to execute the component's methods. Three types of apartments exist:

- The *single-thread apartment* (STA) guarantees that only one thread is allowed to execute components in the apartment. There may be multiple STAs in a process. The first STA in a process is known as the *main STA* and is used to house legacy COM components that do not specifically declare a threading model.

- The *multiple-thread apartment* (MTA) allows multiple threads to execute components in the apartment. Although the MTA may potentially be more efficient, it demands that any component in the apartment be thread-safe. A process may contain at most one MTA.

- The *thread-neutral apartment* (TNA) was introduced in Windows 2000. COM objects in the TNA may be visited by threads that live in any other apartment; calling an object in a TNA never requires marshaling due to incompatible apartments. A process may contain at most one TNA.

A component running in the STA can assume thread affinity. COM will create a message loop that is used to pump messages to an STA component. For this reason, all components that provide a user interface must run in the STA to avoid deadlock.

When a client is in the same process as the server, pointers may be passed directly between the client and server, as Figure 30.2 shows.

FIGURE 30.2

No marshaling is needed for pointers inside a process.

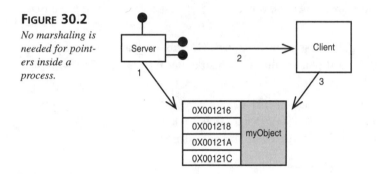

When a client and server are located in different processes, a pointer to the address in the client's process is meaningless in the address space of the server. In order for the pointer to be useful in both processes, it must be marshaled. As Figure 30.3 shows, an address in the address space of the current process is provided to the client or server.

FIGURE 30.3

When pointers are marshaled between processes, the pointers are managed by the COM runtime library.

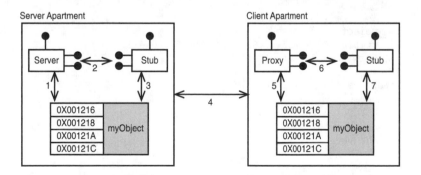

The previous examples demonstrate that marshaling of pointers is required between processes. Because interface pointers are bound to a single apartment, they are marshaled when passed between apartments, even when the apartments are part of the same process.

30

CREATING COM OBJECTS USING ATL

A similar pointer marshaling mechanism is required when the client and server are located on separate machines. The important point in this discussion is that the COM library and the operating system work together to marshal data properly using the proxy/stub DLL built from information in the IDL file.

When necessary, data is reconstituted across the network to provide the appearance of pointer transparency in the network. A great deal of work may be required when a pointer is shared between machines. You specify the work required for your pointers by using IDL attributes.

Three types of pointers are supported by COM:

- The *full* pointer is the most expensive pointer type. It is specified by using the `ptr` attribute.

- The *unique* pointer requires less work from the COM library than a full pointer, because it does not support pointer aliasing. This pointer type is specified with the `unique` attribute.

- The *reference* pointer is the least expensive pointer type, and it does not support aliasing or `NULL` values. It must always be possible to dereference this type of pointer. This pointer type is specified with the `ref` attribute.

You can define a different pointer type attribute for each pointer by specifying one of the three pointer attributes immediately before the parameter:

```
HRESULT Snore([in, ref] short* pDecibels);
```

Typically, you'll define a single pointer type for most of your pointers. You can define a default pointer type that will be used for all pointers in an interface with the `pointer_default` attribute:

```
[
    object,
    uuid(F8C53F2E-8744-4681-8D64-D5843DA46162),
    pointer_default(unique)
]
interface ICat : ISleepyAnimal
{
    HRESULT Sleep();
    HRESULT Eat();
    HRESULT Hide();
};
```

Top-level pointers will be set to `ref` if you don't supply a default pointer type. Pointers that are not top level—that is, pointers to pointers—and pointers embedded in structures will be set to `unique` if you don't supply a default type.

The full pointer type allows pointer *aliasing:* multiple pointers in a function call may refer to the same address. In return for this capability, you incur the cost required when the interface is marshaled; each pointer must be stored in a dictionary that is consulted to preserve the proper behavior after marshaling.

The full and unique pointer types also permit NULL values, so the marshaling code must test to ensure that invalid pointers aren't dereferenced. This gives you some flexibility when using your interface, but it increases the work done at runtime.

Using Direction Attributes in IDL

Every parameter in an IDL source file has an attribute that includes the parameter's direction. This attribute enables the MIDL compiler to generate the proper marshaling code for the interface. This attribute also defines the ownership of data passed via pointers. Three options are available:

[in]	Specifies a parameter sent from the client to the server. If the server has a use for the data after the function call completes, it must make a local copy of the data, because the data belongs to the caller.
[out]	Specifies a parameter, which must be a pointer, that carries data from the server to the client. The client allocates the top-level pointer, but any dynamic allocations other than the top-level pointer are made by the server and become the client's responsibility.
[in, out]	Specifies that data is allocated by the client and passed to the server, which may optionally free the data and allocate new data for the client. This parameter must be a pointer. The newly allocated data, if any, becomes the responsibility of the client.

A Custom COM Class Example

As an example of how custom COM classes are created with IDL and the Active Template Library, the CD-ROM that accompanies this book includes OsVersionInfo, a custom COM class that is a wrapper around the Win32 GetVersionEx function.

The OsVersionInfo project creates an EXE module that includes a COM class named OsVersion created using the ATL Object Wizard. Table 30.1 lists the values used in the Names property sheet for the OsVersion ATL class.

TABLE 30.1 Names Property Sheet Values for OsVersion

Field	Name
Short Name	OsVersion
Class	COsVersion
.H File	OsVersion.h
.CPP File	OsVersion.cpp
CoClass	OsVersion
Interface	IOsVersion
Type	OsVersion Class
Prog ID	OsVersionInfo.OsVersion

Table 30.2 lists the values used on the Attributes property page for OsVersion.

TABLE 30.2 Attributes Property Sheet Values for OsVersion

Field	Name
Threading Model	Both
Interface	Custom
Aggregation	Yes
ISupportErrorInfo	Unchecked
Connection Points	Unchecked
Free Threaded Marshaler	Unchecked

Defining the IOsVersion Interface

The IOsVersion interface has a number of methods, as shown in the IDL provided in Listing 30.1. Lines that were added to the original code generated by the wizard are shown in bold.

LISTING 30.1 OsVersionInfo IDL File

```
import "oaidl.idl";
import "ocidl.idl";

typedef enum tagOsType
{
```

```
    OsUnknown = 0,
    OsWin32s,
    OsWin95,
    OsWin98,
    OsWinNt,
}OsType;

typedef struct tagOsVerNum
{
    long Major;
    long Minor;
}OsVerNum;

    [
        object,
        uuid(414AE921-EAFA-11D3-8E67-00C04F8DC7A5),

        helpstring("IOsVersion Interface"),
        pointer_default(unique)
    ]
    interface IOsVersion : IUnknown
    {
        HRESULT GetVersionInfoString([out,retval]BSTR* pBstrInfo);
        HRESULT GetVersion([out]OsVerNum *pVerNum);
        HRESULT GetBuildNumber([out]long* pBuild);
        HRESULT GetOsType([out]OsType* pType);
    };

[
    uuid(414AE913-EAFA-11D3-8E67-00C04F8DC7A5),
    version(1.0),
    helpstring("OsVersionInfo 1.0 Type Library")
]
library OSVERSIONINFOLib
{
    importlib("stdole32.tlb");
    importlib("stdole2.tlb");

    struct OsVerNum;
    enum OsType;

    [
        uuid(414AE922-EAFA-11D3-8E67-00C04F8DC7A5),
        helpstring("OsVersion Class")
    ]
    coclass OsVersion
    {
        [default] interface IOsVersion;
    };
};
```

Listing 30.1. contains two typedefs:

- The OsType enumeration contains values that represent different flavors of Windows operating systems.
- The OsVerNum structure is a simple container for the major and minor version numbers for an operating system release.

The OsType and OsVerNum types are referenced in the library section of the IDL file. This causes the MIDL compiler to include these two types in the type library when the IDL is compiled.

Modifications to the COsVersion Declaration

The definition for the COsVersion class is located in the OsVersion.h header file, portions of which are shown in Listing 30.2. Modifications to the wizard-generated source are shown in bold.

LISTING 30.2   Definition of the COsVersion Class

```
class ATL_NO_VTABLE COsVersion :
    public CComObjectRootEx<CComMultiThreadModel>,
    public CComCoClass<COsVersion, &CLSID_OsVersion>,
    public IOsVersion
{
public:
    COsVersion()
    {
    }

DECLARE_REGISTRY_RESOURCEID(IDR_OSVERSION)

DECLARE_PROTECT_FINAL_CONSTRUCT()

BEGIN_COM_MAP(COsVersion)
    COM_INTERFACE_ENTRY(IOsVersion)
END_COM_MAP()

    HRESULT FinalConstruct();

// IOsVersion
public:
    STDMETHOD(GetOsType)(OsType* pType);
    STDMETHOD(GetBuildNumber)(long* pBuild);
    STDMETHOD(GetVersion)(OsVerNum* pVerNum);
    STDMETHOD(GetVersionInfoString)(/BSTR* pBstrInfo);
protected:
    OSVERSIONINFO m_info;
};
```

The `FinalConstruct` method declared in Listing 30.2 is called by the framework after the COM object is constructed. This enables you to perform initialization work, such as calling a virtual function that isn't safe in a constructor. It also allows you to bypass the constructor completely—a technique used when omitting the C runtime library from your component.

Implementing the `COsVersion` Class

The implementation of the `COsVersion` class is located in the `OsVersion.cpp` source file. A partial listing of this file is provided in Listing 30.3. The accompanying CD-ROM includes the complete source for this file.

LISTING 30.3   Implementation of the `COsVersion` Class

```
HRESULT COsVersion::FinalConstruct()
{
    ZeroMemory(&m_info, sizeof(OSVERSIONINFO));
    m_info.dwOSVersionInfoSize = sizeof(OSVERSIONINFO);
    GetVersionEx(&m_info);
    return S_OK;
}

STDMETHODIMP COsVersion::GetVersionInfoString(BSTR *pBstrInfo)
{
    CComBSTR bstrTemp(m_info.szCSDVersion);
    if(!bstrTemp)
        return E_OUTOFMEMORY;
    *pBstrInfo = bstrTemp.Detach();
    return S_OK;
}

STDMETHODIMP COsVersion::GetVersion(OsVerNum *pVerNum)
{
    pVerNum->Major = m_info.dwMajorVersion;
    pVerNum->Minor = m_info.dwMinorVersion;
    return S_OK;
}

STDMETHODIMP COsVersion::GetBuildNumber(long *pBuild)
{
    // If the OS is Windows 9x, the build is in the lower
    // word of dwBuildNumber. If the OS is Windows NT/2000
    // the build is the entire DWORD. For Win32s, the build
    // number is cleared.
    if(m_info.dwPlatformId == VER_PLATFORM_WIN32_NT)
        *pBuild = m_info.dwBuildNumber;
    else if(m_info.dwPlatformId == VER_PLATFORM_WIN32_WINDOWS)
        *pBuild = LOWORD(m_info.dwBuildNumber);
```

30

CREATING COM
OBJECTS USING
ATL

LISTING 30.3 continued

```
    else
        *pBuild = 0;
    return S_OK;
}

STDMETHODIMP COsVersion::GetOsType(OsType *pType)
{
    switch(m_info.dwPlatformId)
    {
        case VER_PLATFORM_WIN32s:
            *pType = OsWin32s;
            break;

        case VER_PLATFORM_WIN32_WINDOWS:
            if(m_info.dwMinorVersion == 0)
                *pType = OsWin95;
            else
                *pType = OsWin98;
            break;

        case VER_PLATFORM_WIN32_NT:
            *pType = OsWinNt;
            break;

        default:
            *pType = OsUnknown;
            break;
    }
    return S_OK;
}
```

When a COM object is constructed, the ATL framework calls the FinalConstruct method. Inside COsVersion::FinalConstruct, the Win32 GetVersionEx function is called to collect version information from the operating system and store it in the m_info member variable. Other method calls return information to the client based on the contents of m_info.

Build the OsVersionInfo project. After the OsVersionInfo module is compiled successfully, the project takes steps to register the component on your system. You won't be able to use the component from a client, however, until you build and register the proxy/stub DLL, as described in the next section.

Compiling and Registering the Standard Proxy/Stub DLL

ATL projects include a command-line makefile used to build the proxy/stub DLL for each ATL project. This makefile is the only file in the project directory with an `.mk` filename extension. For the `OsVersionInfo` project, the name of the makefile is `OsVersionInfoPs.mk`. To build the DLL, use the NMAKE utility, like this:

```
nmake OsVersionInfoPs.mk
```

After the proxy/stub DLL is built successfully, you can register the DLL using the RegSvr32 utility:

```
regsvr32 OsVersionInfoPs
```

You should run both of these commands in a DOS command window from the project directory. In order to compile the proxy/stub DLL from a command window, you may need to run the vcvars32.bat file located in the Visual C++ bin directory. The default path to this file is:

```
\Program Files\Microsoft Visual Studio\VC98\bin\vcvars32.bat
```

If the DLL is registered successfully, a message box appears, as shown in Figure 30.4.

FIGURE 30.4

The RegSevr32 utility is used to register the proxy/stub DLL.

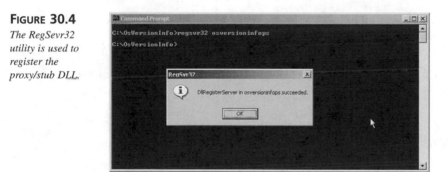

Creating Test Clients for `OsVersionInfo`

To facilitate testing of the `OsVersionInfo` COM object, the CD-ROM that accompanies this book includes `OsInfoClient`, a console-mode test driver. `OsInfoClient` calls each of the `IOsVersion` interface functions and displays the results to the console window.

The `OsInfoClient` project was built as a Win32 console application. Unicode compatibility macros are used to enable the project to be built as either a Unicode or ANSI

project. The project uses the osversioninfo_i.c and osversioninfo.h files from the OsVersionInfo project directory. The MIDL compiler generates these two files when the IDL file is compiled; they contain information about the GUIDs and interface declarations used by the OsVersionInfo COM object.

The OsInfoClient project contains the main.cpp source file, portions of which are provided in Listing 30.4. The accompanying CD-ROM includes the complete source for this project.

LISTING 30.4   OsInfoClient Test Driver

```
#define _WIN32_DCOM

#include <windows.h>
#include <tchar.h>
#ifndef UNICODE
    #include <stdio.h>
#endif
#include <atlbase.h>
#include "osversioninfo_i.c"
#include "osversioninfo.h"

// Display a dialog box that contains an error message
void HandleError(LPCTSTR pszTitle, HRESULT hr);

// Macro that tests an HRESULT - if an error exists, a dialog box
// with the error message is displayed, and zero is returned.
#define TESTHR(hr,str) if(FAILED(hr)){HandleError(str,hr);return 0;}

// Utility class that ensures that CoInitialize and CoUninitialize are
// called at the appropriate times.
struct CComInit
{
    HRESULT hr;
    CComInit(DWORD dwInit)
    {
        hr = CoInitializeEx(NULL, COINIT_MULTITHREADED);
    }
    ~CComInit()
    {
        CoUninitialize();
    }
};

CComInit init(COINIT_MULTITHREADED);

int _tmain()
{
    // Uses the AFX string conversion macros to convert between
    // OLE/BSTR strings and T strings.
```

```
USES_CONVERSION;
CComQIPtr<IOsVersion> pVersion;

HRESULT hr = pVersion.CoCreateInstance(CLSID_OsVersion);
TESTHR(hr, _T("CoCreateInstance"));

OsVerNum ver;
hr = pVersion->GetVersion(&ver);
TESTHR(hr, _T("GetVersion"));

// Get the OS type, and convert the enumerated type into a
// string.
OsType ost;
hr = pVersion->GetOsType(&ost);
TESTHR(hr, _T("GetOsType"));

CComBSTR bstrOsType;
switch(ost)
{
    case OsWin32s:
        bstrOsType = _T("Win32s");
        break;
    case OsWin95:
        bstrOsType = _T("Windows 95");
        break;
    case OsWin98:
        bstrOsType = _T("Windows 98");
        break;
    case OsWinNt:
        bstrOsType = _T("Windows NT/2000");
        break;
    default:
        bstrOsType = _T("Unknown");
}

long build;
hr = pVersion->GetBuildNumber(&build);
TESTHR(hr, _T("GetBuildNumber"));

CComBSTR bstrVersionInfo;
hr = pVersion->GetVersionInfoString(&bstrVersionInfo);
TESTHR(hr, _T("GetVersionInfoString"));

// Display results to the console - use W2T to convert from
// wide strings to T strings.
_tprintf(_T("Windows OS Type: %s\n")
         _T("Version        : %d.%d\n")
         _T("Build Number   : %d\n")
         _T("Version Info   : %s\n"),
         W2T(bstrOsType),
         ver.Major,
```

30

CREATING COM
OBJECTS USING
ATL

LISTING 30.4   continued

```
            ver.Minor,
            build,
            W2T(bstrVersionInfo));

    return 0;
}
```

Listing 30.4 includes the CComInit class, which guarantees that CoInitialize and CoUninitialize are called at the appropriate times. By declaring a global variable of CComInit, you can be sure that CoInitialize is called before any smart pointers have been initialized, and CoUninitialize is called after all of the COM smart pointer instances are destroyed.

Build the OsInfoClient project. After OsInfoClient is run from the command line, it displays information about the version of the operating system, as Figure 30.5 shows.

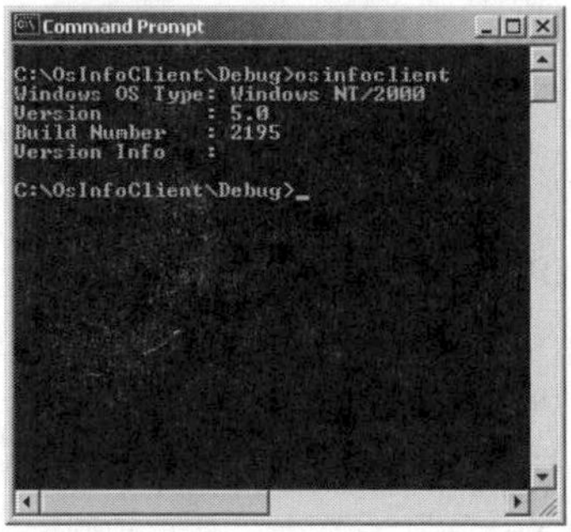

FIGURE 30.5

The OsInfoClient *project uses* OsVersionInfo *to collect version information about the operating system.*

Summary

This chapter introduced you to some of the issues involved in creating custom COM objects using the Active Template Library. This chapter discussed the different options for passing pointers to and from COM objects. Also discussed were how complex data types, such as structures, enumerations, and unions can be declared and used in IDL. Proper declaration of pointers, structures, and other types is essential if you want to be able to efficiently use your COM objects with a wide variety of programming tools.

You looked at an example of a custom COM object being created, along with a sample client that tests the COM object. This custom COM object used enumerations and structures in its interface, and demonstrated how complex types can be sent through a COM interface.

Using complex types, as was done in the OsVersionInfo project, is useful when large amounts of data must be passed through a COM interface. Rather than passing hard-coded flags, it's more flexible to use enumerations. Rather than passing large numbers of parameters, it's often more efficient to pass a structure.

Creating ActiveX Controls Using ATL

by Mickey Williams

IN THIS CHAPTER

CHAPTER 31

Chapter 29, "ATL Architecture," discussed using MFC to build ActiveX controls. Although these controls are very useful when used with traditional clients such as Visual Basic, they tend to be quite large and often have dependencies on MFC42.DLL.

In this chapter, you'll learn how to use the *Active Template Library* (ATL) to create ActiveX controls that are lightweight, have few dependencies, and are safely usable by scripting clients. You'll look at the major classes used by ATL for ActiveX controls. You'll also examine connection points, object safety, and persistence for components used by scripting clients.

ATL Control Classes

The *Active Template Library* (ATL) offers advantages over MFC when building ActiveX controls when size or performance is a consideration. A control built with ATL is always smaller than an equivalent control built using MFC. In addition, you can build an ATL control that has no external dependencies—simplifying distribution, especially to network clients.

The classes used primarily for ActiveX controls follow:

CWindow	Similar to the MFC CWnd class, but much lighter in weight. This class provides easy access to a number of commonly used functions.
CWindowImpl	Derived from CWindow and used by the control class to subclass or superclass an existing window class. It implements the ATL message map.
CDialogImpl	Derived from CWindow and used to implement dialog boxes.
CContainedWindow	Derived from CWindow and used to model a window contained in another object. If you superclass or subclass an existing window, an instance of CContainedWindow will represent the original window.

In addition to these classes, ATL provides support for adding properties, events, and connection points to your ActiveX control. The following sections discuss these features.

Implementing Stock Properties Using ATL

The easiest way to add a stock property to a control built with ATL is with the ATL Object Wizard. The Stock Properties tab enables you to select stock properties to be added to your control by moving the property name between two lists (see Figure 31.1).

Creating ActiveX Controls Using ATL

CHAPTER 31

931

31

CREATING ACTIVEX
CONTROLS USING
ATL

FIGURE 31.1

The ATL Object Wizard's Stock Properties tab.

The ATL Object Wizard creates a property map in your ATL control's class header that manages the properties exposed by the control. The property map begins with the BEGIN_PROP_MAP macro and ends with the END_PROP_MAP macro. Inside the property map are a series of macros, each specifying a property supported by the control (see Listing 31.1).

LISTING 31.1   An ATL Property Map

```
BEGIN_PROP_MAP(CShapedButton)
    PROP_DATA_ENTRY("_cx", m_sizeExtent.cx, VT_UI4)
    PROP_DATA_ENTRY("_cy", m_sizeExtent.cy, VT_UI4)
    PROP_ENTRY("Caption", DISPID_CAPTION, CLSID_NULL)
END_PROP_MAP()
```

Stock properties are implemented using the PROP_ENTRY macro. PROP_ENTRY has three parameters:

- The description of the stock property
- The dispatch identifier (DISPID) for the stock property
- The class ID (CLSID) of the property page used for entering the property (or CLSID_NULL if no property page is used)

Each stock property has a specific DISPID that refers to the property. DISPID_CAPTION is the dispatch ID for the control's label, for example. The ATL Object Wizard knows all about these names. If you're adding a stock property by hand, you have two choices:

- Create a dummy project and add the stock property using the ATL Object Wizard. You can add the stock property to your project using the DISPID used by the wizard in the dummy project.
- Look in the OLECTL.H header file in the Visual C++ include directory. This file contains all the standard dispatch identifiers used for stock properties, as well as other standard Automation identifiers. Search for DISPID_AUTOSIZE, which is at the start of the list.

In addition to adding an entry to the property map, the ATL Object Wizard adds a member variable to your class declaration for every property exposed by your control. The wizard doesn't add any code that explicitly maps the variable name to the property, however; it's not needed.

The mapping between variable names and properties is done in the ATL class library. Every stock property is mapped to a particular member of an anonymous union declared in the ATL CComControlBase class. ATL Object Wizard uses a name from this union when adding member variables for properties to your control. If you're adding a property by hand, you again have two choices:

- Create a dummy project, as described earlier, and use the variable name selected by the ATL Object Wizard.
- Look in the anonymous union declared in the CComControlBase class, and select the proper variable name yourself.

Whichever method you choose for selecting the variable name, make sure you name the variable correctly. If you declare a variable with a different name, your project will compile, but your property value won't be updated properly.

Implementing Custom Properties Using ATL

Implementing custom properties is similar to implementing stock properties. One obvious difference between stock and custom properties is that you must name the custom properties yourself. You add custom properties by right-clicking the IDL icon in the ClassView window and choosing the Add Properties item from the pop-up menu. A dialog box appears, as shown in Figure 31.2.

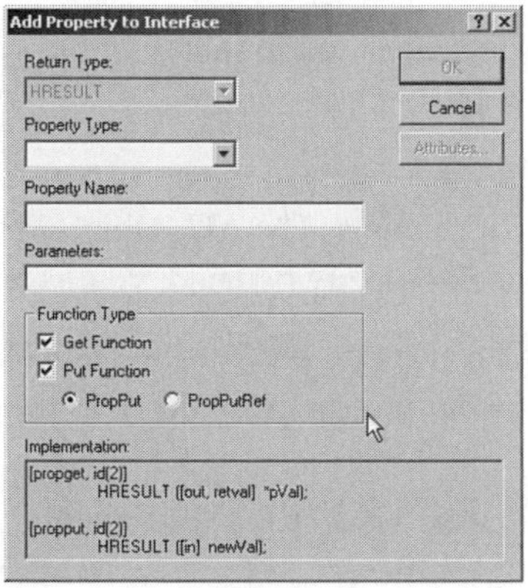

FIGURE 31.2

Adding a property to an ATL object.

Creating ActiveX Controls Using ATL

CHAPTER 31

933

31

CREATING ACTIVEX
CONTROLS USING
ATL

You use the Add Property to Interface dialog box to add the named property, the IDL statements, and the glue code necessary in your class so that the property can be exposed to the outside world.

You must provide the following values:

Property Type	The Automation-compatible type that contains the property.
Property Name	The name of the property as it will be exposed to the outside world. This is the name Visual Basic or Visual InterDev displays in property pages for your control, for example.
Parameters	Any additional parameters you want to apply to the property.
Get Function	If you enable this check box, the option generates a function to retrieve the property value from the control. If you disable this option, the property cannot be read.
Put Function	If you enable this check box, the option generates a function to set the control's property. If you disable this option, the property is read-only.
PropPut/PropPutRef	If you select the PropPutRef radio button, the property is set by reference, which is more efficient for large objects. If you select PropPut, the property is set with a parameter that is passed by value.

You can click the Attributes button to set IDL attributes, such as `hidden` or `call_as`, for the property.

Consider a project named `TestBtn` that exposes a `BevelSize` property, for example. To enable this property, you fill in the Add Property to Interface dialog box with the values shown in Table 31.1.

TABLE 31.1 Sample Values for the Add Property to Interface Dialog Box

Control	*Value*
Property Type	long
Property Name	BevelSize
Parameters	(none)
Get Function	Checked
Put Function	Checked
PropPut	Selected

Given these values, Visual C++ creates the following IDL for the new property:

```
interface ITestButton : IDispatch
{
    [propget, id(1), helpstring("property BevelSize")]
    HRESULT BevelSize([out, retval] long *pVal);
    [propput, id(1), helpstring("property BevelSize")]
    HRESULT BevelSize([in] long newVal);
};
```

Visual C++ also will create class member functions to implement the necessary interface methods declared by the IDL fragment. What Visual C++ will not do is declare a member variable for you. You must add a member variable (if needed) and fill in the skeleton member functions provided by Visual C++, as Listing 31.2 shows.

Listing 31.2   Using Member Functions to Provide Access to Custom Properties

```
STDMETHODIMP CTestButton::get_BevelSize(long *pVal)
{
    *pVal = m_nBevelSize;
    return S_OK;
}

STDMETHODIMP CTestButton::put_BevelSize(long newVal)
{
    m_nBevelSize = newVal;
    return S_OK;
}
```

Visual C++ will not automatically add the custom property to the property map, so the property will not be persisted automatically. If you want the property to be persistent, you must add an entry to the property map using the PROP_DATA_ENTRY macro, as Listing 31.3 shows.

Listing 31.3   Adding a Custom Property to the Property Map

```
BEGIN_PROP_MAP(CSlaskPop)
    PROP_DATA_ENTRY("_cx", m_sizeExtent.cx, VT_UI4)
    PROP_DATA_ENTRY("_cy", m_sizeExtent.cy, VT_UI4)
    PROP_DATA_ENTRY("BevelSize", m_nBevelSize, VT_I4)
    PROP_ENTRY("Caption", DISPID_CAPTION, CLSID_NULL)
END_PROP_MAP()
```

The PROP_DATA_ENTRY macro has three parameters:

- The description of the property
- The member variable that contains the property's value
- The Automation tag that suits the variable's type

Creating ActiveX Controls Using ATL

CHAPTER 31

935

31

CREATING ACTIVEX
CONTROLS USING
ATL

A complete list of valid Automation tags is located in the Visual C++ online documentation in the COM and ActiveX folder. You will find one good source by searching for the document titled "VARIANT and VARIANTARG."

Using Ambient Properties with ATL

You can retrieve ambient properties by calling functions implemented in the `CComControlBase` class. Table 31.2 lists three of the most commonly used ambient properties and the functions you use to access them.

TABLE 31.2   Commonly Used Ambient Properties and Access Functions

Property	*Function*
Background Color	`GetAmbientBackColor`
Foreground Color	`GetAmbientForecolor`
Font	`GetAmbientFont`

The online documentation for Visual C++ has more examples of ambient property functions. Go to the index and search for topics that begin with `GetAmbient`. `CComControlBase` also has a catchall member function named `GetAmbientProperty` that will return the value of any ambient property, given its `DISPID`.

Adding Message and Event Handlers

You can add handlers for messages and events to an ATL project in two ways. The graphical way is to right-click the ATL object's C++ class icon in `ClassView` and choose Add Windows Message Handler from the pop-up menu. A dialog box appears, as Figure 31.3 shows.

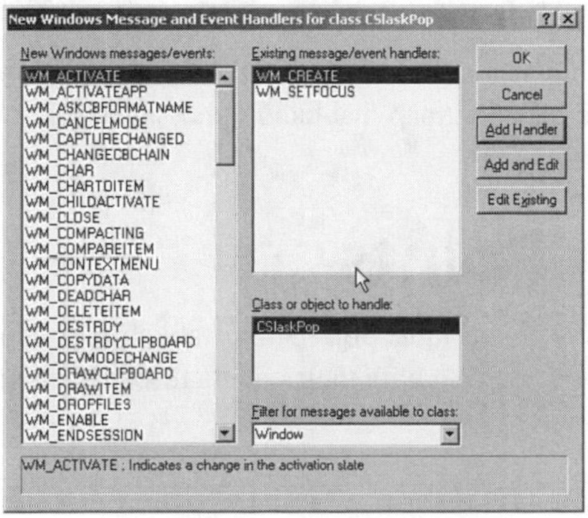

FIGURE 31.3

The New Windows Message and Event Handlers dialog box.

You can easily add handlers for Windows messages by selecting a message from the left column and clicking the Add Handler button.

Another option is to manually add the handlers to the class message map using the MESSAGE_HANDLER macro:

MESSAGE_HANDLER(WM_ERASEBKGND, OnEraseBkgnd)

The MESSAGE_HANDLER macro has two parameters:

- The Windows message to be handled
- The name of the member function that will handle the message

If you're handling events from a WM_COMMAND message, you must use the COMMAND_CODE_HANDLER macro:

COMMAND_CODE_HANDLER(LBN_DBLCLICK, OnLbDblClicked)

The COMMAND_CODE_HANDLER macro has two parameters:

- The notification message sent in WM_COMMAND
- The name of the member function that will handle the message

You can use either of these macros inside the message map, which begins with the BEGIN_MSG_MAP macro and ends with the END_MSG_MAP macro (see Listing 31.4).

LISTING 31.4 A Typical ATL Message Map

```
BEGIN_MSG_MAP(CMyButton)
    MESSAGE_HANDLER(WM_CREATE, OnCreate)
    MESSAGE_HANDLER(WM_ERASEBKGND, OnEraseBkgnd)
    COMMAND_CODE_HANDLER(BN_CLICKED, OnClicked)
ALT_MSG_MAP(1)
    // Alternate window message handling
END_MSG_MAP()
```

Note that the message map in Listing 31.4 also contains an ALT_MAP macro. This marks the beginning of an alternate message map that handle messages from another window within a single message map.

Connection Points

Connection points are used by connectable objects to establish bidirectional communication. Connectable objects communicate with their clients through *connection-point*

Creating ActiveX Controls Using ATL

CHAPTER 31

937

31

CREATING ACTIVEX
CONTROLS USING
ATL

interfaces—back-channel interfaces that allow a COM server to notify its clients of events. Two interfaces are implemented by a connectable object:

- IConnectionPoint is implemented by a control or other COM object and allows a container or client of the COM object to request event notifications.

- IConnectionPointContainer is used by a client to query a COM object about IConnectionPoint interfaces supported by the object. This interface includes functions that return a pointer to a known IConnectionPoint interface or enumerate IConnectionPoint interfaces supported by a control.

Most ActiveX controls are connectable objects. Other types of COM objects can implement the IConnectionPointContainer and IConnectionPoint interfaces, however, and thus become connectable objects. Figure 31.4 illustrates the coupling between a connectable client and server.

FIGURE 31.4
The interfaces used to implement connectable objects.

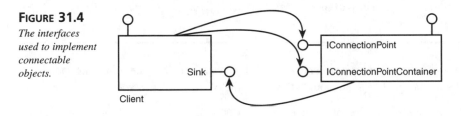

A client interested in a specific IConnectionPoint interface first invokes QueryInterface, requesting the IConnectionPointContainer interface from the server. If an interface pointer is returned, the particular IConnectionPoint interface is requested through IConnectionPointContainer. If the request is successful, the client passes a pointer to its notification sink to the server through the IConnectionPoint interface. The server transmits event notifications to the client using the pointer to the notification sink.

The simplest way to support connection points in a project built by using ATL is to select the Support Connection Points option when using the ATL Object Wizard. A definition of an outgoing interface will be added to the project IDL file. Listing 31.5 is a fragment of an IDL file with an example of an outgoing interface for a COM class named Bothway.

LISTING 31.5   Defining an Outgoing Interface for a Connectable Object

```
library CONNECTEXAMPLELib
{
    importlib("stdole31.tlb");
    importlib("stdole2.tlb");

    [
        uuid(FCB636B8-FD81-4AB2-B455-9F2BEDA22FBF),
```

LISTING 31.5   continued

```
        helpstring("_IBothwayEvents Interface")
    ]
    dispinterface _IBothwayEvents
    {
        properties:
        methods:
    };

    [
        uuid(F7706E85-129F-4B2D-A694-90EF33F3357D),
        helpstring("Bothway Class")
    ]
    coclass Bothway
    {
        [default] interface IBothway;

        [default, source] dispinterface _IBothwayEvents;
    };
};
```

Note that the outgoing interface is named _IBothwayEvents. The outgoing interface is prefixed with _I and has Events added to the name of the COM class.

To implement connection-point methods for your COM class, you must follow these steps:

1. Add methods and properties to the IDL definition for the outgoing interface.

2. Compile the IDL using the MIDL compiler to create a type library containing the connection-point information. The easiest way to do this is to build the ATL project.

3. After the build is complete, right-click the ATL class in the Class View window, and select Implement Connection Points from the pop-up menu. A dialog box appears, as Figure 31.5 shows.

   The Implement Connection Point dialog box contains a list of interfaces you can use to implement connection points. In most cases, this dialog box contains only one entry.

4. Check the outgoing interface and click OK.

The connection-point class is created with a name generated by prefixing CProxy to the interface name. For the _IBothwayEvents example, the generated class is named CProxy_IBothwayEvents. The connection-point class contains member functions that can be used to generate events that are sent out to the client. These functions are named by

Creating ActiveX Controls Using ATL

CHAPTER 31

939

31

CREATING ACTIVEX
CONTROLS USING
ATL

prefixing Fire_ to the name of the outgoing interface method defined in IDL. For an outgoing method defined as SayHey in IDL, the connection-point class contains a function with the following name:

```
Fire_SayHey()
```

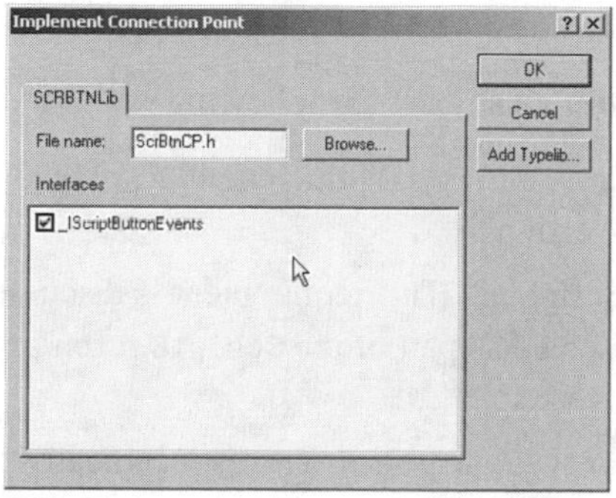

FIGURE 31.5

*Implementing
connection points
for a COM server.*

The new connection-point class is added to the multiple inheritance list for the control. You then can fire any event directly. Here's an example:

```
if(eyesShut && snoringLoudly)
    Fire_DadIsSleeping();
```

Connection points were developed for use in ActiveX controls. ActiveX controls use connection points to coordinate the interfaces used between controls and their containers.

> **Note**
>
> You don't need to implement IConnectionPoint or IConnectionPoint container to exchange interface pointers between COM objects. The connection-point mechanism allows a client and server to negotiate available outgoing interfaces that are unknown at compile time.
>
> If you're specifying a fixed set of interfaces for bidirectional communication, you have no need for connection points.

Creating Scriptable Controls

A *scriptable* ActiveX control is a control that is constructed so that it is appropriate for use by scripting clients. Scriptable controls are designed to be safe when used in a Web browser, such as Internet Explorer, or by scripts written for the *Windows Scripting Host*

(WSH). Scriptable controls also support mechanisms to simplify passing parameters to the control via a scripting language.

By default, ActiveX controls are not considered safe for scriptable clients. If you have an ActiveX control that could be useful by scripting clients, taking a few simple steps can expand the usefulness of your control. If you're using ATL, these changes typically take just a few minutes.

To be scriptable, an ActiveX control must meet the following requirements:

- Be safe when executed by an arbitrary scripting client. This requirement is discussed in detail in the next section.

- Be registered as "Safe for Scripting." This requirement is discussed in the next section, and an example is presented as part of the ScriptButton project later in this chapter.

- Support the IPersistPropertyBag interface. This is technically not a requirement, but it simplifies the task of passing parameters to the control. The IPersistPropertyBag interface is discussed in the section "Persistence for ActiveX Controls," later in this chapter.

Requirements for Scriptable Controls

Microsoft has published a document that describes all aspects of component object safety with regard to scripting ActiveX controls. The document, "Designing Safe ActiveX Controls," is located in the MSDN Library included with Visual C++.

Before registering your control as safe for scripting, you must ensure that your control does not take any actions that may be unsafe when used by a scripting client. Unsafe actions include exposing information normally kept private, such as passwords and other sensitive information, executing files, and making dangerous system calls.

Another type of object safety concerns the use of parameters and properties with the control. When used with a scripting client, a safe control must ensure that the control can continue to function with any possible combination of properties defined by the user.

Later in this chapter, you'll look at an example of a control that is safe for scripting.

Persistence for ActiveX Controls

By default, ActiveX controls built with ATL support the IPersistStream interface for object persistence. Persisting data via a binary stream is an efficient way to transfer data to and from a control, and this method is preferable for most containers.

Creating ActiveX Controls Using ATL

CHAPTER 31

941

31

CREATING ACTIVEX
CONTROLS USING
ATL

The native form for parameter information for scripting clients is a text string, however, and attempting to persist binary parameter information in a scripting language such as VBScript is painful (although not impossible). For this reason, most scriptable controls support the `IPersistPropertyBag` interface, which allows properties to be persisted as pairs of property names and property values. Instead of passing a binary stream to an ActiveX control, a client simply can pass pairs of parameter names and values to initialize a control.

A Scriptable ActiveX Control

This book's CD-ROM includes ScriptButton, an ATL-based ActiveX control that superclasses the standard Windows pushbutton. ScriptButton is a scriptable control; sample programs presented later in this chapter demonstrate how ScriptButton is used with Internet Explorer.

ScriptButton is similar to the standard Windows pushbutton, except that it appears to be a label until the mouse pointer is placed over the control. When the pointer is over the control, the control is redrawn with beveled edges so that it looks like a standard button.

The Basic Design of ScriptButton

As you learned in the preceding section, ScriptButton is similar to the standard Windows pushbutton control, except that it only has a 3D appearance when the mouse pointer is moved over the control. For the control to be drawn properly, the control must be able to perform the following tasks:

- Track the current state of the button (raised, flat, clicked)
- Detect when the mouse pointer is over the control
- Detect when the mouse pointer is clicked over the control
- Track the current focus state of the control so that the focus rectangle can be drawn correctly

In addition, ScriptButton must use a set of stock properties that a user of a button control may want to adjust:

- Background Color
- Foreground Color
- Tab Stop
- Caption

Two events are sent from the ScriptButton control to its container:

- OnClicked is sent after the control is clicked. This event is sent if the user clicks the button with the mouse or selects the button using the keyboard.
- OnHover is sent when the control enters a raised, or *hover,* state. This event notifies the container that the mouse is hovering over the control and allows the container to update a status bar or provide some other sort of feedback.

Messages Handled by ScriptButton

ScriptButton handles messages sent by the operating system, as well as one message sent by the underlying button control. The control must handle the following messages:

- WM_MOUSEMOVE is sent as the mouse pointer passes over the control.
- WM_SETFOCUS is sent just before the control receives input focus.
- WM_KILLFOCUS is sent just before the control loses input focus.
- WM_LBUTTONDOWN is sent after the user presses the primary mouse button (usually the left button) while the pointer is over the control.
- WM_LBUTTONUP is sent after the user releases the primary mouse button while the pointer is over the control.
- WM_ERASEBKGND is sent just before the control is repainted by Windows.
- WM_MOUSELEAVE is sent when the mouse moves away from the control's window.

In addition, the control handles one notification message sent by the pushbutton control:

BN_CLICKED is sent after the user successfully clicks the button control.

The BN_CLICKED message is sent after the user clicks the button with the mouse or selects the button using the keyboard. After this message is received from the underlying control, ScriptButton fires an OnClicked event to its container.

Handling Raised-Button and Flat-Button States

The WM_MOUSEMOVE and WM_MOUSELEAVE messages are used together to control the raised appearance of the control. As discussed earlier, the button initially is drawn in a flat state. After a WM_MOUSEMOVE message is received by the control, the control redraws itself in the raised state.

While the button is in the raised state, it must handle two cases:

- The user clicks on the control.
- The user moves the mouse away from the control rectangle.

Creating ActiveX Controls Using ATL

CHAPTER 31

943

31

CREATING ACTIVEX
CONTROLS USING
ATL

The first case is handled easily and is discussed in the next section. If the mouse is moved away from the control rectangle, however, no event is sent to the control's window. To detect the departure of the mouse, the Win32 _TrackMouseEvent function is called when the mouse initially moves over the control. This function registers the control window as requesting additional information about mouse events. When the mouse is moved away from the control, a WM_MOUSELEAVE message is sent to the control's window, and the button is redrawn in its flat state.

Handling Button Clicks

Three messages are used to draw the control and report events after the user clicks the ScriptButton control. WM_LBUTTONDOWN and WM_LBUTTONUP are sent from the operating system as the user presses and releases the primary mouse button while the pointer is over the control. In response to these messages, the control is drawn in either the down state (for WM_LBUTTONDOWN) or the raised state (for WM_LBUTTONUP).

After the user clicks the ScriptButton control, the underlying button generates a BN_CLICKED notification message. This message is used to create an OnClicked event that is sent to the control's container.

Handling the Focus Rectangle

One important visual indicator supplied by user interface components is the focus rectangle. If the focus rectangle isn't drawn correctly, the user may be confused about the input state of the control.

Two messages are used to draw the focus rectangle. The WM_SETFOCUS message is sent just before the control receives input focus; it causes the familiar dotted rectangle to be drawn around the control. The WM_KILLFOCUS message is sent just before focus is lost; it causes the focus rectangle to be removed.

It's so important that the focus rectangle be drawn correctly that Windows offers an API function to handle it all for you:

```
DrawFocusRect(hdc, lprc);
```

You call DrawFocusRect with two parameters: the device context that you're drawing into, and the rectangle that describes the boundary of the focus rectangle. This function also is used to remove the focus rectangle: If you call it a second time with the same rectangle, the focus rectangle is removed.

Creating the ScrBtn Project

The ScrBtn project is used to create the ScriptButton control, which is created using the Visual C++ ATL COM AppWizard. The control begins as a DLL project, as Figure 31.6 shows.

FIGURE **31.6**

Using the ATL COM AppWizard to create the ScrBtn project.

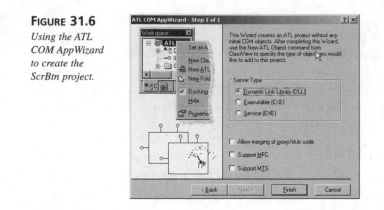

The ScrBtn project does not use any of the optional features offered by the ATL COM AppWizard, such as MFC or MTS support or the capability to merge proxy/stub code.

Adding the `ScriptButton` Control Class to the Project

The ActiveX control component in the ScrBtn project is implemented by adding a new COM class into the project with the ATL Object Wizard. Start by choosing New ATL Object from the Visual C++ Insert menu. The ATL Object Wizard appears, as shown in Figure 31.7.

FIGURE **31.7**

The ATL Object Wizard.

The ScrBtn project will implement a full control named `ScriptButton`. Select Controls from the wizard's Category list box, and then select Full Control as the control type. Click Next to begin adding `ScriptButton` to the project.

The ATL Object Wizard Properties dialog box appears so that you can define your control's properties (see Figure 31.8). For full controls, such as `ScriptButton`, the dialog box offers four tabs.

The Names tab is just like the Names tab used in custom COM objects in Chapter 29. You only need to fill in the Short Name property for `ScriptButton`—the other fields are filled in automatically and should contain the values shown in Table 31.3.

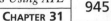

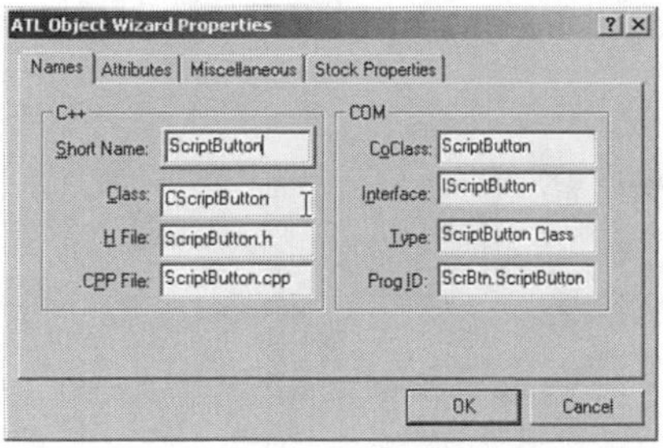

FIGURE 31.8
*The ATL Object
Wizard Properties
dialog box.*

TABLE 31.3 Contents of the Names Tab for the `ScriptButton` Control

Property	Name
Short Name	`ScriptButton`
Class	`CScriptButton`
.H File	`ScriptButton.h`
.CPP File	`ScriptButton.cpp`
CoClass	`ScriptButton`
Interface	`IScriptButton`
Type	`ScriptButton Class`
Prog ID	`ScrBtn.ScriptButton`

The second tab is the Attributes tab; again, it is identical to the Attributes tab discussed in Chapter 29. Table 31.4 shows the values used for `ScriptButton` on the Attributes tab. All these values are the default options, except that `ScriptButton` supports connection points. (This property appears in bold in Table 31.4, because it is not a default setting.) As discussed earlier in the chapter, connection points are used to supply events to a control's container.

TABLE 31.4 Contents of the Attributes Tab for the `ScriptButton` Control

Property	Name
Threading Model	Apartment
Interface	Dual
Aggregation	Yes
Support `ISupportErrorInfo`	Unchecked
Support Connection Points	**Checked**
Free Threaded Marshaler	Unchecked

The third tab is the Miscellaneous tab (see Figure 31.9). It contains attributes specific to ActiveX controls.

FIGURE 31.9

Miscellaneous tab values for the ScriptButton *control.*

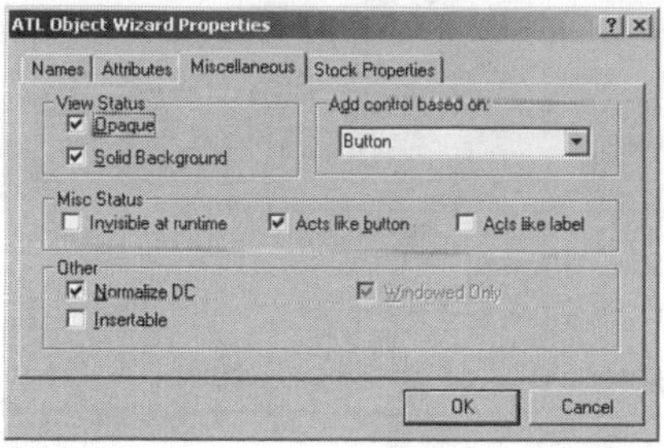

Table 31.5 shows the values for the ScriptButton control; nondefault values appear in bold type.

TABLE 31.5   Contents of the Miscellaneous Tab for the ScriptButton Control

Property	Name
Opaque	Checked
Solid Background	Checked
Add Control Based On	**Button**
Invisible at Runtime	Unchecked
Acts Like Button	**Checked**
Acts Like Label	Unchecked
Normalize DC	Checked
Windowed Only	(Disabled)
Insertable	Unchecked

The final tab in the dialog box is Stock Properties. It contains a list of all stock properties that can be implemented by an ActiveX control (see Figure 31.10).

The ScriptButton control uses these stock properties:

- Background Color
- Caption
- Foreground Color
- Tab Stop

After you select the stock properties listed here, click OK to close the dialog box. The ATL New Object Wizard then generates the necessary code and adds it to your project.

FIGURE 31.10

*The Stock
Properties tab
values for the*
ScriptButton *con-
trol.*

Adding Outgoing Events

As discussed earlier, the ScriptButton control provides two events to its containers:

- OnClick is sent after the button is clicked.
- OnHover is sent after the button is raised.

Open the ScrBtn.idl file and add the two lines shown in bold in Listing 31.6 to the
_IScriptButtonEvents interface. Alternatively, you can add the events by right-clicking
the _IScriptButtonEvents icon in ClassView and choosing Add Method from the pop-
up menu.

LISTING 31.6   Changing the ScrBtn IDL File to Add Outgoing Events

```
library SCRBTNLib
{
    importlib("stdole31.tlb");
    importlib("stdole2.tlb");

    [
        uuid(416D4C0E-A2C9-49AA-887F-0E1D8BCE280F),
        helpstring("_IScriptButtonEvents Interface")
    ]
    dispinterface _IScriptButtonEvents
    {
        properties:
        methods:
        [id(1), helpstring("OnClick event")] HRESULT OnClick();
        [id(2), helpstring("OnHover event")] HRESULT OnHover();
    };

    [
        uuid(B584CB87-D818-4E6B-9DC5-F0063CF64E22),
        helpstring("ScriptButton Class")
    ]
    coclass ScriptButton
    {
```

LISTING 31.6   continued

```
        [default] interface IScriptButton;
        [default, source] dispinterface _IScriptButtonEvents;
    };
};
```

Before proceeding, compile the skeleton project. This project compiles the type library and makes it possible to add the event connection point for the control.

After the project is compiled, add the connection point to the project by right-clicking the `CScriptButton` icon in `ClassView` and choosing Implement Connection Point from the pop-up menu. The Implement Connection Point dialog box appears. Enable the check box next to `_IScriptButtonEvents` and click OK. The `CProxy_IScriptButtonEvents` class then is generated and added to the project.

Modifying the Message Map

Seven messages must be added to the `CScriptButton` message map. Six of the messages are generated by the operating system, and one message is generated by the superclass pushbutton control.

As discussed earlier, you can open the dialog box that adds message-handling functions by right-clicking the `CScriptButton` icon in `ClassView` and choosing Add Windows Message Handler from the pop-up menu. Add handlers for these messages:

- `WM_ERASEBKGND`
- `WM_KILLFOCUS`
- `WM_LBUTTONDOWN`
- `WM_LBUTTONUP`
- `WM_MOUSEMOVE`

You must manually add message-handling macros for the `BN_CLICKED` and `WM_TRACK-MOUSEMESSAGE` messages to the message map. Listing 31.7 shows the finished message map; the manually added macros appear in bold. Note that all the message handlers are in the main part of the message map. Make sure your message map doesn't have any macro entries in the alternate message map.

LISTING 31.7   The Message Map for `ScriptButton`

```
BEGIN_MSG_MAP(CScriptButton)
    MESSAGE_HANDLER(WM_CREATE, OnCreate)
    MESSAGE_HANDLER(WM_SETFOCUS, OnSetFocus)
```

```
    MESSAGE_HANDLER(WM_ERASEBKGND, OnEraseBkgnd)
    MESSAGE_HANDLER(WM_KILLFOCUS, OnKillFocus)
    MESSAGE_HANDLER(WM_LBUTTONDOWN, OnLButtonDown)
    MESSAGE_HANDLER(WM_LBUTTONUP, OnLButtonUP)
    MESSAGE_HANDLER(WM_MOUSEMOVE, OnMouseMove)
    MESSAGE_HANDLER(WM_MOUSELEAVE, OnMouseLeave)
    COMMAND_CODE_HANDLER(BN_CLICKED, OnClicked)
    CHAIN_MSG_MAP(CComControl<CScriptButton>)
ALT_MSG_MAP(1)
    // Replace this with message map entries for superclassed Button
END_MSG_MAP()
```

Initializing the `CScriptButton` Object

Before adding the code needed to initialize an instance of the `CScriptButton` class, add
an enumeration used to track button states to the `ScriptButton.h` header file. Insert the
contents of Listing 31.8 just above the declaration of the `CScriptButton` class.

LISTING 31.8   The `BtnState` Enumeration

```
enum BtnState { bsFlat, bsDown, bsHover };
```

Earlier in this chapter, when the stock properties were added to the `ScriptButton` control, the ATL Object Wizard inserted member variables into the `ScriptButton.h` header
file. These variables, shown in Listing 31.9, are used to hold the values of the stock properties supported by the control. Add the member variables shown in bold to the class declaration; these variables are used to implement various control features that will be
discussed throughout the remainder of this chapter.

LISTING 31.9   Additional Member Variables Used by `CScriptButton`

```
public:
    OLE_COLOR           m_clrBackColor;
    CComBSTR            m_bstrCaption;
    OLE_COLOR           m_clrForeColor;
    BOOL                m_bTabStop;
    CComPtr<IFontDisp>  m_pFont;      // Contains ambient font
    BtnState            m_btnState;   // Tracks button state
    bool                m_fHasFocus;  // TRUE if button has focus
```

Add the lines shown in bold in Listing 31.10 to the `CScriptButton` constructor. Note that
you must add a comma to the first line of the constructor initializer list.

LISTING 31.10 The Constructor for the `CScriptButton` Class

```
CScriptButton() :
    m_ctlButton(_T("Button"), this, 1), // add comma to this line
    m_btnState(bsFlat),
    m_fHasFocus(false),
{
    m_bWindowOnly = TRUE;
}
```

The default handler for `OnCreate` will superclass a default instance of the Windows `BUTTON` class. The `ScriptButton` control must superclass a `BUTTON` with pushbutton attributes, so modify the `OnCreate` member function, as shown in Listing 31.11, by changing the lines shown in bold.

LISTING 31.11 Changes to the `OnCreate` Member Function

```
LRESULT OnCreate(UINT, WPARAM, LPARAM, BOOL&)
{
    RECT rc;
    GetWindowRect(&rc);
    rc.right -= rc.left;
    rc.bottom -= rc.top;
    rc.top = rc.left = 0;
    m_ctlButton.Create(m_hWnd,
                       rc,
                       _T("BUTTON"),
                       WS_CHILD|BS_PUSHBUTTON);
    return 0;
}
```

Retrieving Ambient Properties

When the control is initially loaded, it collects the current foreground color, background color, and font from its container. A good time to collect ambient properties is when the control and its container negotiate the client site. Add the source code in Listing 31.12 to the `ScriptButton.cpp` source file. This function overrides the base class implementation of `SetClientSite` and stores the ambient values of these three properties.

LISTING 31.12 A New Version of `SetClientSite` That Collects Ambient Properties from the Container

```
STDMETHODIMP CScriptButton::SetClientSite(LPOLECLIENTSITE pSite)
{
    HRESULT hr = CComControlBase::IOleObject_SetClientSite(pSite);
    if(!m_pFont && pSite)
    {
        hr = GetAmbientFontDisp(&m_pFont);
    }
```

Creating ActiveX Controls Using ATL

CHAPTER 31

951

31

CREATING ACTIVEX
CONTROLS USING
ATL

```
GetAmbientBackColor(m_clrBackColor);
GetAmbientForeColor(m_clrForeColor);
return hr;
}
```

Add the following member function declaration to the `CScriptButton` class:

```
STDMETHOD(SetClientSite)(LPOLECLIENTSITE pSite);
```

A good place for this declaration is just after all the member variables used to track properties.

Handling Focus Events for the Control

When a focus event is received by the control, the focus member variable is set with the new input focus state, and the control's window is invalidated. The control's container also is notified that the control is changing its view.

Listing 31.13 contains the `OnSetFocus` and `OnKillFocus` member functions, which handle the `WM_SETFOCUS` and `WM_KILLFOCUS` messages, respectively. Add the lines shown in bold to the member functions.

LISTING 31.13 The `OnSetFocus` and `OnKillFocus` Member Functions for the `CScriptButton` Class

```
LRESULT OnSetFocus(UINT uMsg, WPARAM wParam, LPARAM lParam,
                                        BOOL& bHandled)
{
    LRESULT lRes = CComControl<CScriptButton>::OnSetFocus(uMsg,
                                                     wParam,
                                                     lParam,
                                                     bHandled);

    if (m_bInPlaceActive)
    {
        DoVerbUIActivate(&m_rcPos,  NULL);
        if(!IsChild(::GetFocus()))
            m_ctlButton.SetFocus();
    }
    m_fHasFocus = true;
    FireViewChange();
    return lRes;
}

LRESULT OnKillFocus(UINT uMsg, WPARAM wParam, LPARAM lParam,
                                        BOOL& bHandled)
{
    m_fHasFocus = false;
    FireViewChange();
    return 0;
}
```

Handling Mouse Events for the Control

The following four message handlers control mouse and click events for the
CScriptButton class:

- OnLButtonDown updates the button state variable and invalidates the control's rectangle so that it will be redrawn.

- OnLButtonUp updates the button state variable and invalidates the control's rectangle so that it can be redrawn. If the mouse pointer is currently over the control, the new button state is bsHover; if the mouse pointer is not over the control, the new button state is bsFlat.

- OnMouseMove updates the button state if the current button state is bsFlat. If the button state is moving from bsFlat to bsHover, the control's rectangle is invalidated so that it can be redrawn. In addition, the OnHover event is fired to the control's container.

- OnClick is sent to the CScriptButton class when the underlying button control generates a click event. In response, the OnClick member function fires an OnClick event to the container.

To implement these member functions, add the lines shown in bold in Listing 31.14 to
the member functions in the CScriptButton class.

LISTING 31.14   Event-Handling Member Functions in the CScriptButton Class

```
LRESULT OnLButtonDown(UINT uMsg, WPARAM wParam, LPARAM lParam,
                                            BOOL& bHandled)
{
    // Change the state to bsDown, and redraw the control
    m_btnState = bsDown;
    FireViewChange();
    m_ctlButton.DefWindowProc(uMsg, wParam, lParam);
    return 0;
}

LRESULT OnLButtonUP(UINT uMsg, WPARAM wParam, LPARAM lParam,
                                            BOOL& bHandled)
{
    if(MouseOverCtl())
        m_btnState = bsHover;
    else
        m_btnState = bsFlat;
    FireViewChange();
```

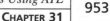

```
    m_ctlButton.DefWindowProc(uMsg, wParam, lParam);
    return 0;
}

LRESULT OnMouseMove(UINT uMsg, WPARAM wParam, LPARAM lParam,
                                        BOOL& bHandled)
{
    if(m_btnState == bsFlat)
    {
        // Moving from flat to hover...
        Fire_OnHover();
        m_btnState = bsHover;
        FireViewChange();

        TRACKMOUSEEVENT tme;
        ZeroMemory(&tme, sizeof(tme));
        tme.cbSize = sizeof(tme);
        tme.dwFlags = TME_LEAVE;
        tme.hwndTrack = m_hWnd;
        TrackMouseEvent(&tme);
    }
    m_ctlButton.DefWindowProc(uMsg, wParam, lParam);
    return 0;
}

// BN_CLICKED
LRESULT OnClicked(WORD wNotifyCode, WORD wID, HWND hWndCtl,
                                        BOOL& bHandled)
{
    Fire_OnClick();
    m_btnState = bsFlat;
    FireViewChange();
    bHandled = TRUE;
    return 0;
}
```

Note that when the mouse pointer is initially moved over the control, the
TrackMouseEvent function is called to request a notification when the pointer leaves the
control's window. When the pointer leaves the control window, the operating system
sends the control a WM_MOUSELEAVE message. Add the message-handling function for
WM_MOUSELEAVE provided in Listing 31.15 to the ScriptButton.h header file, inside the
CScriptButton class declaration.

LISTING 31.15   Handling the WM_MOUSELEAVE Message

```
LRESULT OnMouseLeave(UINT uMsg, WPARAM wParam, LPARAM lParam,
                                              BOOL& bHandled)
{
    m_btnState = bsFlat;
    FireViewChange();
    bHandled = TRUE;
    return 0;
}
```

Several of the functions in CScriptButton need to determine whether the mouse pointer is over the control. The MouseOverCtl function provided in Listing 31.16 returns TRUE if the pointer is over the control; otherwise, it returns FALSE. Add this function to the ScriptButton.h header file, inside the CScriptButton class declaration.

LISTING 31.16   Handling the WM_MOUSELEAVE Message

```
BOOL MouseOverCtl()
{
    RECT   rc;
    POINT pt;

    GetWindowRect(&rc);
    GetCursorPos(&pt);

    return PtInRect(&rc, pt);
}
```

Drawing the Control

The most complex part of the ScriptButton control involves drawing the control. Before getting into the actual drawing code, there are two functions that make it easy to determine which state the button is in. Listing 31.17 contains the IsSelected and IsRaised member functions, which are used by the CScriptButton class when drawing the control. These functions can be found in the ScriptButton.h file.

LISTING 31.17   The IsSelected and IsRaised Member Functions

```
BOOL IsSelected()
{
    return m_btnState == bsDown;
}

BOOL IsRaised()
{
    return m_btnState == bsHover;
}
```

Creating ActiveX Controls Using ATL

CHAPTER 31

955

31

CREATING ACTIVEX
CONTROLS USING
ATL

The source code provided in Listing 31.18 contains OnDraw, the function primarily responsible for drawing the control. The complete drawing code for the control is not shown here, but you can find the full source code on the CD-ROM that accompanies this book.

LISTING 31.18 The CScriptButton::OnDraw Function

```
HRESULT OnDraw(ATL_DRAWINFO& di)
{
    RECT& rc  = *(RECT*)di.prcBounds;
    HDC   hdc = di.hdcDraw;

    COLORREF clrFore, clrBack;
    OleTranslateColor(m_clrForeColor, NULL, &clrFore);
    OleTranslateColor(m_clrBackColor, NULL, &clrBack);
    SetTextColor(hdc, m_clrForeColor);
    HBRUSH hbrBtn = CreateSolidBrush(m_clrBackColor);

    FillRect(hdc, &rc, hbrBtn);
    DrawEdges(hdc, &rc);
    DrawButtonText(hdc, &rc, m_bstrCaption);

    if(m_fHasFocus)
    {
        InflateRect(&rc, -2, -2);
        DrawFocusRect(hdc, &rc);
    }

    DeleteObject(hbrBtn);
    return 0;
}
```

Implementing `IPersistPropertyBag`

To simplify the use of ScriptButton in a scripting client, such as Internet Explorer, the control must support the IPersistPropertyBag interface. The ATL class library includes a class, IPersistPropertyBagImpl, that provides a default implementation of IPersistPropertyBag that is sufficient in most cases. IPersistPropertyBagImpl is a parameterized class that takes one argument—the name of the class to be persisted:

```
IPersistPropertyBagImpl<CLatte>
```

To add support for IPersistPropertyBagImpl to CScriptButton, make the changes shown in Listing 31.19 to the declaration of the CScriptButton class. These changes, shown in bold, add IPersistPropertyBagImpl to the classes that CScriptButton is derived from.

LISTING 31.19   Deriving `CScriptButton` From `IPersistPropertyBagImpl`

```
class ATL_NO_VTABLE CScriptButton :
    public CComObjectRootEx<CComSingleThreadModel>,
    public CStockPropImpl<CScriptButton,IScriptButton,
                          &IID_IScriptButton, &LIBID_SCRBTNLib>,
    public CComControl<CScriptButton>,
    public IPersistStreamInitImpl<CScriptButton>,
    public IPersistPropertyBagImpl<CScriptButton>,
    public IOleControlImpl<CScriptButton>,
    public IOleObjectImpl<CScriptButton>,
    public IOleInPlaceActiveObjectImpl<CScriptButton>,
    public IViewObjectExImpl<CScriptButton>,
    public IOleInPlaceObjectWindowlessImpl<CScriptButton>,
    public IConnectionPointContainerImpl<CScriptButton>,
    public IPersistStorageImpl<CScriptButton>,
    public ISpecifyPropertyPagesImpl<CScriptButton>,
    public IQuickActivateImpl<CScriptButton>,
    public IDataObjectImpl<CScriptButton>,
    public IProvideClassInfo2Impl<&CLSID_ScriptButton,
                &DIID__IScriptButtonEvents, &LIBID_SCRBTNLib>,
    public IPropertyNotifySinkCP<CScriptButton>,
    public CComCoClass<CScriptButton, &CLSID_ScriptButton>,
    public CProxy_IScriptButtonEvents< CScriptButton >
```

You also must add `IPersistPropertyBagImpl` to the `COM_MAP` macro by making the changes shown in bold in Listing 31.20.

LISTING 31.20   Adding `IPersistPropertyBagImpl` to the `COM_MAP`

```
BEGIN_COM_MAP(CScriptButton)
    COM_INTERFACE_ENTRY(IScriptButton)
    COM_INTERFACE_ENTRY(IDispatch)
    COM_INTERFACE_ENTRY(IViewObjectEx)
    COM_INTERFACE_ENTRY(IViewObject2)
    COM_INTERFACE_ENTRY(IViewObject)
    COM_INTERFACE_ENTRY(IOleInPlaceObjectWindowless)
    COM_INTERFACE_ENTRY(IOleInPlaceObject)
    COM_INTERFACE_ENTRY2(IOleWindow, IOleInPlaceObjectWindowless)
    COM_INTERFACE_ENTRY(IOleInPlaceActiveObject)
    COM_INTERFACE_ENTRY(IOleControl)
    COM_INTERFACE_ENTRY(IOleObject)
    COM_INTERFACE_ENTRY(IPersistStreamInit)
    COM_INTERFACE_ENTRY(IPersistPropertyBag)
    COM_INTERFACE_ENTRY2(IPersist, IPersistStreamInit)
    COM_INTERFACE_ENTRY(IConnectionPointContainer)
    COM_INTERFACE_ENTRY(ISpecifyPropertyPages)
    COM_INTERFACE_ENTRY(IQuickActivate)
    COM_INTERFACE_ENTRY(IPersistStorage)
```

```
    COM_INTERFACE_ENTRY(IDataObject)
    COM_INTERFACE_ENTRY(IProvideClassInfo)
    COM_INTERFACE_ENTRY(IProvideClassInfo2)
    COM_INTERFACE_ENTRY_IMPL(IConnectionPointContainer)
END_COM_MAP()
```

With these changes, a container that supports scripting can obtain a pointer to the control's `IPersistPropertyBag` interface, and will use that interface for persisting data instead of `IPersistStreamInit`. Containers that prefer to persist data with binary streams still will query for `IPersistStream` or `IPersistStreamInit`.

Marking the Control as Safe for Scriptable Clients

You can use two methods to mark a control as safe for scripting clients:

- Make appropriate entries directly in the System Registry.
- Implement the `IObjectSafety` interface.

Microsoft recommends that you use new controls to implement the `IObjectSafety` interface instead of making Registry entries. `IObjectSafety` enables the control to apply much finer-grained safety policies than possible using the Registry.

ATL provides a default implementation of `IObjectSafety` that you easily can take advantage of by deriving your class from the `IObjectSafetyImpl` class. To add this class to `CScriptButton`, add the code shown in bold in Listing 31.21 to the declaration of `CScriptButton`.

LISTING 31.21   Deriving `CScriptButton` from `IObjectSafetyImpl`

```
class ATL_NO_VTABLE CScriptButton :
    .
    .
    .
    public IPersistPropertyBagImpl<CScriptButton>,//
    public IObjectSafetyImpl<CScriptButton,
                        INTERFACESAFE_FOR_UNTRUSTED_CALLER|
                        INTERFACESAFE_FOR_UNTRUSTED_DATA>,
    public IOleControlImpl<CScriptButton>,
    .
    .
    .
```

Two template arguments are passed to `IObjectSafetyImpl`:

- The name of the class deriving from `IObjectSafetyImpl`
- The type of safety to be applied to the control

Two values may be passed for the safety options:

- `INTERFACESAFE_FOR_UNTRUSTED_CALLER` specifies that your control can be used safely by a scripting client and does not violate any of Microsoft's security or safety guidelines.

- `INTERFACESAFE_FOR_UNTRUSTED_DATA` specifies that your control will work (or at least degrade gracefully) in the presence of any possible set of parameters passed by a client, including invalid or conflicting parameters.

You can combine either or both of these values as appropriate for your control.

You also must add `IObjectSafetyImpl` to the `COM_MAP` macro by making the changes shown in bold in Listing 31.22.

LISTING 31.22 Adding `IObjectSafetyImpl` to the `COM_MAP`

```
BEGIN_COM_MAP(CScriptButton)
 .
 .
 .
    COM_INTERFACE_ENTRY(IPersistPropertyBag)
    COM_INTERFACE_ENTRY(IObjectSafety)
    COM_INTERFACE_ENTRY2(IPersist, IPersistStreamInit)
 .
 .
 .
END_COM_MAP()
```

Testing ScriptButton with Internet Explorer

Compile the `CScriptButton` project. You can test the control in a variety of control containers, including Visual Basic and `TstCon31.exe`—the test container included with Visual C++. Because the `ScriptButton` control is scriptable, you also can use the control on an HTML page with Internet Explorer.

The `ScriptButton` control can be inserted on an HTML page using the `OBJECT` tag, as Listing 31.23 shows. The complete source for an HTML file used to test `ScriptButton` is located in the `ScriptButton` project directory as `IETest.htm`.

LISTING 31.23 Inserting `ScriptButton` in an HTML File

```
<OBJECT classid=clsid:B584CB87-D818-4E6B-9DC5-F0063CF64E22
        id=ScriptButton1
        style="HEIGHT: 39px; WIDTH: 192px"VIEWASTEXT>
        <PARAM NAME="_cx" VALUE="5080">
        <PARAM NAME="_cy" VALUE="1032">
```

```
            <PARAM NAME="BackColor" VALUE="8438015">
            <PARAM NAME="Caption" VALUE="Click Me!">
            <PARAM NAME="TabStop" VALUE="-1">
</OBJECT>
```

When the IETest.htm file runs in Internet Explorer, the ScriptButton control is displayed, as shown in Figure 31.11. When the mouse pointer moves over the control, the button raises up and changes its caption. After the button is clicked, the caption also changes.

FIGURE 31.11
The ScriptButton
control running in
Internet Explorer.

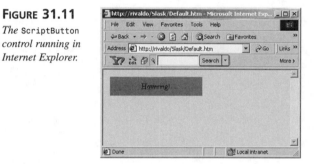

Summary

In this chapter, you looked at creating scriptable ActiveX controls with the Active Template Library. You first learned about the ATL classes used specifically for ActiveX controls. You then focused on the steps required to add properties and methods to a control built with ATL.

Connection points originally were developed to make it possible for ActiveX controls to interact with their containers. You learned about connection points and how you can add support for connection points to an ATL project.

For a control to be scriptable, it must follow Microsoft's object safety guidelines and be marked as safe for scripting. In this chapter, you examined the IObjectSafety interface and learned how a control built using ATL can take advantage of IObjectSafety. An example of a safely scriptable ActiveX control helped you explore this topic.

CHAPTER 32

Using ATL to Create MTS and COM+ Components

by Mickey Williams

In This Chapter

This chapter discusses how you can use the *Active Template Library* (ATL) to build components that can be used with *Microsoft Transaction Server* (MTS) and COM+. Components used in MTS and COM+ must be small, lightweight, and scale well in environments where dozens, or perhaps hundreds, of instances of each component may be running at any given time. Visual C++ and ATL are tools that are well-suited to this task.

This chapter focuses on the basics of transactions, as well as the major features introduced with COM+ in Windows 2000. Code examples in this chapter will work for both MTS and COM+ but are demonstrated using COM+ and Windows 2000.

Understanding Transactions

Microsoft Transaction Server (MTS) was introduced shortly after the release of Windows NT 4.0. MTS extended COM to simplify the process of creating multitier applications that support transactions.

In computing terms, a *transaction* is a set of functions that must succeed as a group or fail as a group. Banking operations are typically used as examples of transactions. Consider the case of a money transfer, where money is transferred from account A to account B. The transfer consists of two functions:

- Money is debited from account A.
- Money is credited to account B.

If either of these functions fails, the entire transaction must fail. It is not permissible to debit money from account A and fail to credit account B. Likewise, it is not acceptable to credit account B without debiting account A.

COM+ and MTS Features

MTS introduced basic support for creating multitier applications with transaction support. MTS 1.0 was really an application that was layered on top of the Windows NT 4.0 operating system, and many features that are expected in a transaction support system weren't present.

COM+ is more tightly integrated than MTS and takes advantage of that integration to provide a wide range of features that simply weren't possible in MTS.

Understanding Contexts

The *context* is a new concept introduced with COM+ in Windows 2000. All COM and COM+ components execute in contexts, which are sets of execution attributes that define transaction, synchronization, and other characteristics for components. Each process is partitioned into one or more contexts, much as processes previously were portioned into apartments.

Today in Windows 2000, the apartment is now just one part of an object's context. Two components that are identical except for their apartment membership will live in separate contexts. In a similar way, components with different transaction support will execute in separate contexts.

Direct communication between contexts is not allowed. Instead, lightweight interception proxies are used as communication channels between components in separate contexts. These interception proxies work very much like the proxies used to marshal data between apartments prior to the introduction to COM+.

Interception proxies are not invoked explicitly. Instead, the operating system detects that components in incompatible contexts are attempting to communicate and marshals the communication via an interception proxy.

Concurrency in COM+

In COM, concurrency and synchronization were enforced using apartments. In reality, the apartment actually controlled thread affinity rather than concurrency; synchronization was a side effect of the thread-affinity restriction. In a single-threaded apartment (STA), only one thread is permitted to visit an apartment; therefore, it is not possible to have thread-synchronization issues. In a multi-threaded apartment (MTA), any thread in the apartment may visit a component, so thread-synchronization issues must be addressed by the component.

The problem with using apartments for synchronization is that the concept of an apartment is not fine-grained. In COM+, the apartment is still used, but it now is used for thread-affinity purposes. For synchronization, COM+ introduces the *activity*. An activity is a collection of one or more components grouped together. Only one call is permitted in a single activity at any given time. This method allows for fine-grained control over component synchronization, because it separates thread affinity from concurrency. In COM+, it is possible to have components that exist in an MTA and can be visited by multiple threads, while relying on the operating system for synchronization.

Just-In-Time Activation

One of the key features offered by MTS and COM+ is *just-in-time* (JIT) activation. With JIT activation, references to objects are created when a client creates an instance of a configured component. The COM+ (or MTS) runtime does not automatically create a real instance of the component, however, and waits until the client makes a method call toward the component. After the method call, the component is deactivated and returned to a pool of components available for the next method call.

Just-in-time activation enables many clients to share small pools of components in an efficient manner. Just-in-time activation is enabled automatically for components that support or require transactions. If you enable JIT activation, your component also is configured automatically to require synchronization.

What Is Object Pooling?

Object pooling is similar to JIT activation. In object pooling, the operating system preallocates a pool of components that are ready to be used by clients. Object pooling is useful when clients are sensitive to the initial startup costs of activating components. When providing components for Web servers, for example, you will get better performance by taking advantage of object pooling.

Registering a COM+ Application

COM+ components are grouped into COM+ applications. The first step in registering one or more COM+ components is to create a COM+ application that contains the component(s).

To register a COM+ component, launch the COM+ MMC snap-in, and expand the tree below Component Services until you reach the COM+ applications node. Figure 32.1 shows the COM+ MMC snap-in with the Component Services tree expanded to show currently configured COM+ applications. New COM+ applications are added to this portion of the tree.

FIGURE 32.1

The COM+ MMC snap-in.

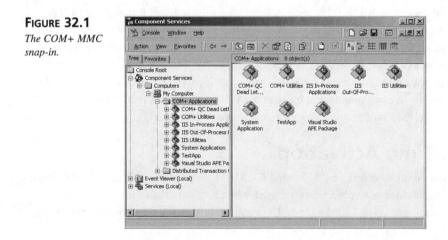

You add new applications by right-clicking on the COM+ Applications icon. Choose New, Application from the context menu. The COM Application Install Wizard appears. Initially, a welcome message is displayed. If you click Next, you move to the second wizard page, shown in Figure 32.2.

FIGURE 32.2

Installing a COM+ application.

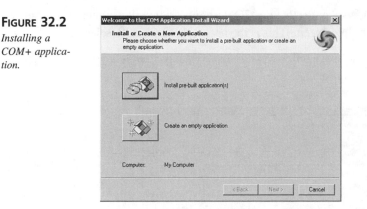

The page in Figure 32.2 offers two options:

- Install an application that is supplied to you as a prebuilt application. You can use this option to install applications that are exported from an existing installation.

- Install an empty application. This option creates an empty application that contains no COM+ components.

This chapter does not cover redistributing and installing prebuilt COM+ applications. To create a new application, click the Create an Empty Application button. The next wizard page appears, as shown in Figure 32.3.

FIGURE 32.3

Defining the name and activation type.

32

USING ATL

You use this wizard page to enter the name of the COM+ application. You also can specify the type of activation to be used for the new application:

- Library Application specifies that the COM+ application will run in the process of the client. This option is rather limited and is rarely used.

- Server Application specifies that the COM+ application will run in a process managed by the operating system. This is the option that is usually selected.

After filling in this wizard page, click Next to display a page that lets you set the application identity (see Figure 32.4).

FIGURE 32.4

Defining the name and application type.

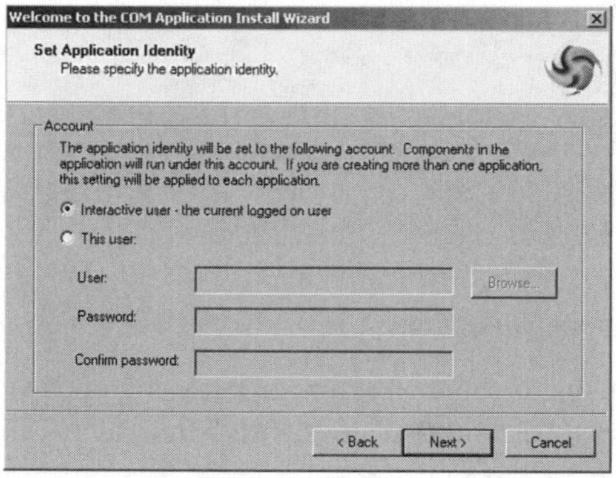

You use this wizard page to specify the security principal that will be used to execute the COM+ application. For debugging and testing purposes, the easiest approach is to choose the interactive user option. For a COM+ application deployed in a production environment, you should specify a security context to be used to execute the application.

This is the last wizard page. Click Next to display a thank-you message.

Configuring Properties for a COM+ Application

After a COM+ application is installed, you can access the application's properties by right-clicking the COM+ application's icon and choosing Properties from the context menu. The application's properties sheet appears, as shown in Figure 32.5.

You use the first tab on the properties sheet, the General tab, to specify the name and description of the application. The GUID associated with the application also is displayed.

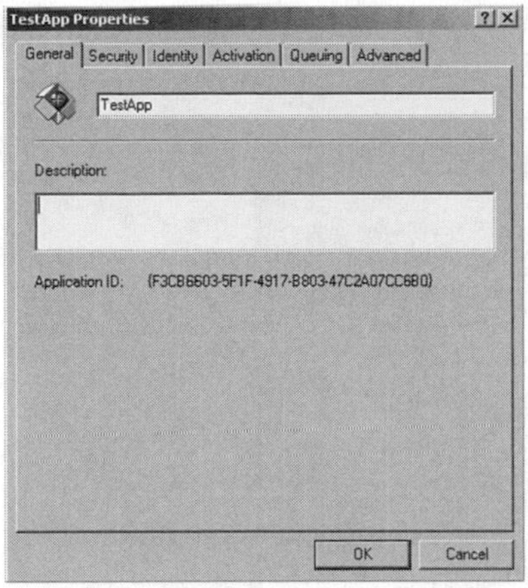

FIGURE 32.5

The COM+ application properties sheet.

You use the Security tab, shown in Figure 32.6, to specify security attributes for the application, including these:

- **Enforce Access Checks for This Application.** You select this option to enable role-based security checking.

- **Security Level.** By default, security access checks are performed at the component and process level. You also can elect to perform checks at only the process level.

- **Authentication Level for Calls.** You use this combo box to specify the security level that is used when information is passed to or from a COM+ application.

- **Impersonation Level.** You use this combo box to specify the type of impersonation available to a COM+ application.

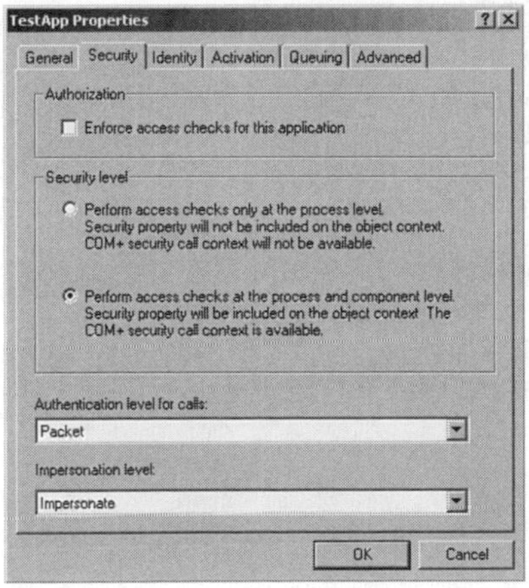

FIGURE 32.6

The Security tab.

32

USING ATL

You use the Identity tab, shown in Figure 32.7, to specify the security principal that will be used to execute the COM+ application.

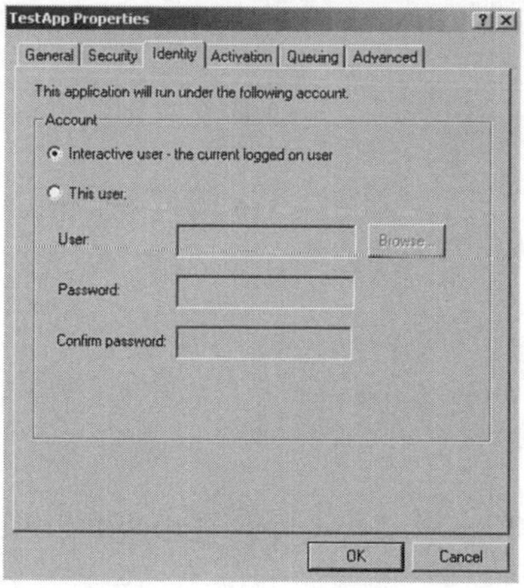

FIGURE 32.7

The Identity tab.

FIGURE 32.7

The Identity tab.

The Activation tab specifies how the application will be activated (see Figure 32.8). You have the same options you had when the application was created: The application may be activated in the client's process, a library application, or a process managed by COM+—a server application.

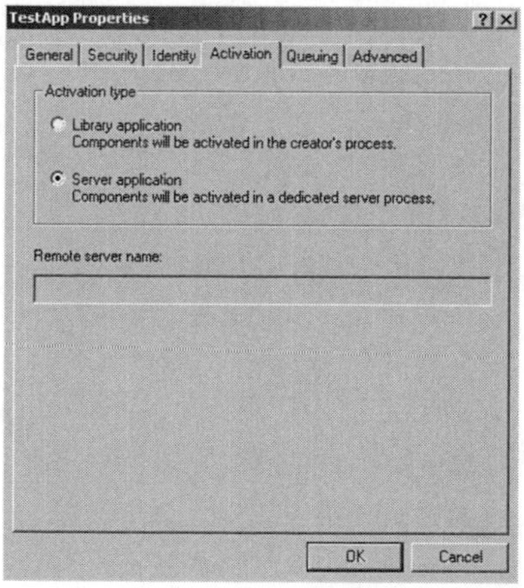

FIGURE 32.8

The Activation tab.

FIGURE 32.8

The Activation tab.

The Queuing tab specifies characteristics for queued components (see Figure 32.9). You can choose from two check boxes:

- Enable Queued if the COM+ application can receive messages from message queues.
- Enable Listen if the Queued option is selected. If you select this option, the application listens for messages that arrive from the message queue.

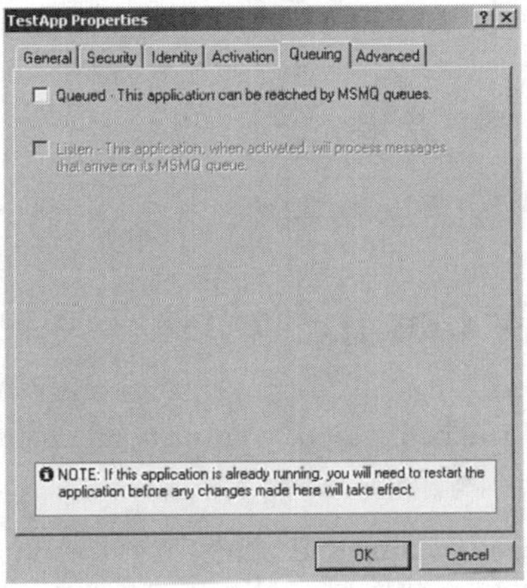

FIGURE 32.9
The Queuing tab.

You use the Advanced tab, shown in Figure 32.10, to specify various advanced options for the COM+ application:

- **Server Process Shutdown.** This area specifies whether and when the application should be shut down. You can specify that the application should never be shut down, or that it should shut down after being idle for a specified period of time.
- **Permission.** You can use these options to specify that client applications cannot change or delete the COM+ application.
- **Debugging.** You choose this to enable the application to be launched in a specific debugger.
- **Enable Compensating Resource Managers.** You use compensating resource managers when using resources that do not directly support transactions.
- **Enable 3GB Support.** This option enables the application to access up to 3 gigabytes of memory when using Windows 2000 Advanced Server.

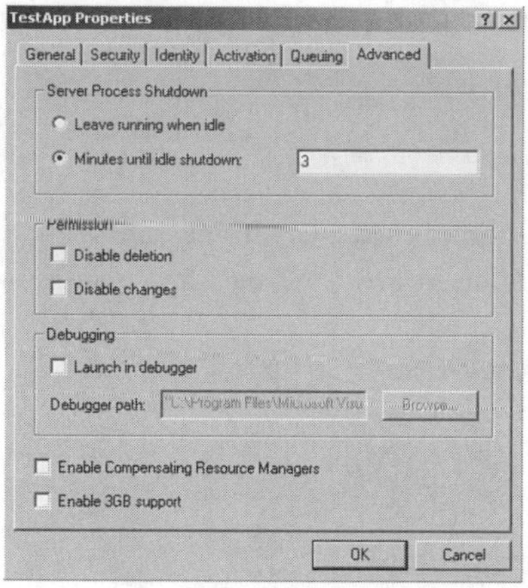

FIGURE 32.10

The Advanced tab.

Registering a COM+ Component

When a COM+ application is created, it has no components associated with it. After your COM+ application is installed and configured, your next step is to add one or more components to the COM+ application.

To install a COM+ component, expand the tree under the COM+ application node in the COM+ MMC snap-in. Right-click on the Components folder, and then choose New, Component from the context menu. The COM+ Component Install Wizard appears. Click Next to move from the welcome page and begin working with the wizard (see Figure 32.11).

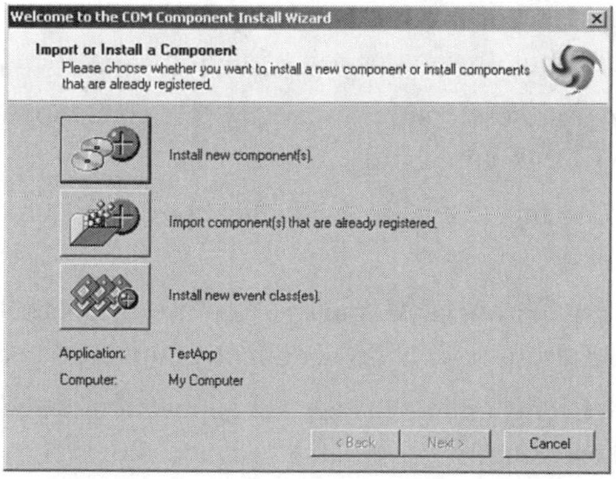

FIGURE 32.11

The COM+ Component Install Wizard.

This wizard page has three options:

- **Install New Component(s).** Installs a new component that had not been registered previously.

- **Import Component(s) That Are Already Registered.** Registers a COM+ component that was registered previously as a nonconfigured COM component.

- **Install New Event Class(es).** Installs classes that will be used with COM+ events.

In most cases, you will add new components to your COM+ application by clicking the Install New Components button.

After clicking one of the options on the wizard page just described, the File Open dialog box appears. Navigate to the DLL that houses your COM+ component, and click the Open button. The wizard page shown in Figure 32.12 appears.

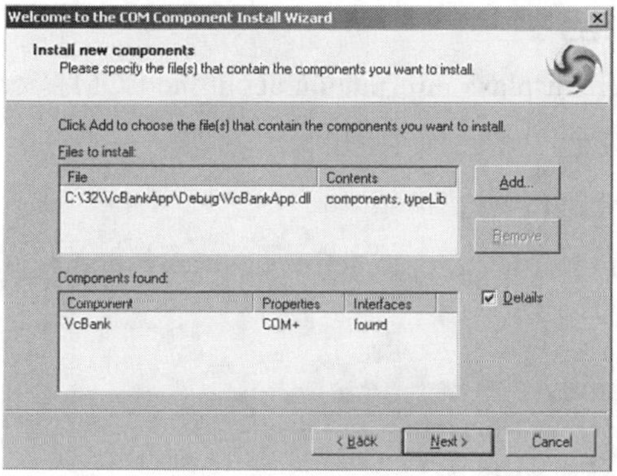

FIGURE 32.12
*The COM+
Component
Install Wizard.*

This wizard page displays the components found in the selected module. This is the last wizard page; to move to the thank-you page, click Next. Click Finish on the thank-you page to dismiss the wizard.

Configuring Properties for a COM+ Component

After registration, you can configure a COM+ component via its properties sheet, which you can display by right-clicking on the component in the COM+ Explorer snap-in and choosing Properties from the context menu. The properties sheet includes six properties pages you can use to configure the component (see Figure 32.13).

FIGURE 32.13

The Object Properties dialog box.

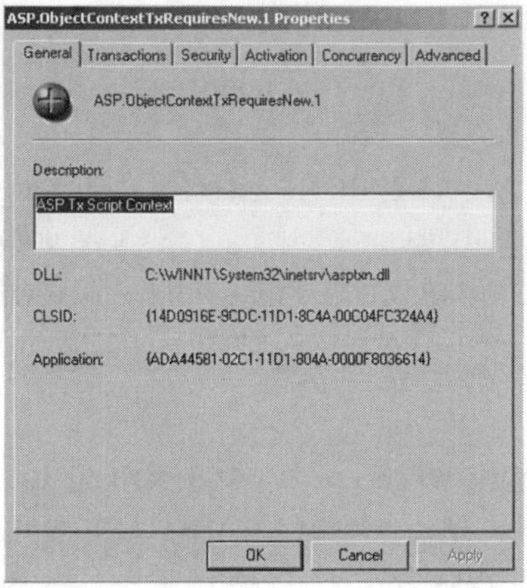

General Properties

The General Properties page displays information about the COM+ component, such as its description, class ID, location, and application GUID.

Transactions Properties

You use the Transactions Properties page to define the transaction requirements for a COM+ object (see Figure 32.14).

FIGURE 32.14

The Transactions Properties page.

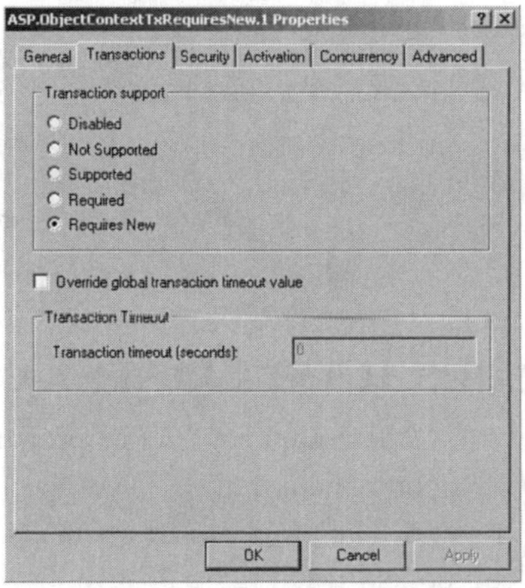

The transaction support required for the COM+ object may be one of the following values:

- **Disabled.** This option eliminates all transaction-related overhead when executing the COM+ component.

- **Not Supported.** The component does not participate in transactions.

- **Supported.** The component participates in a transaction if it is called in the context of an existing transaction. The component does not create a new transaction if it is called in a nontransaction context, however.

- **Required.** The component must run in a transaction context. The component creates a new transaction, if necessary, but also participates in an existing transaction if it is called in a transaction context.

- **Requires New.** The component must run in a new transaction context, creating a new, nested transaction if necessary.

If you select the Required or Requires New option for transaction support, you can override the default transaction timeout by enabling the Override Global Transaction Timeout Value check box. Checking this box enables the edit control that collects the new transaction timeout value.

Security Properties

You use the Security Properties page to define the security attributes for a COM+ component (see Figure 32.15).

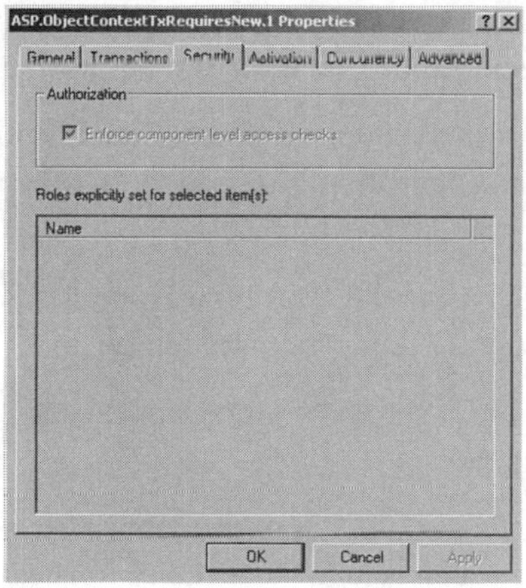

FIGURE 32.15

The Security Properties page.

To take advantage of component-level security, you must enable the Enforce Component Level Access Checks check box. In addition, component and process-level access checking must have been enabled for the COM+ application.

32

USING ATL

Roles defined for the application are listed in the lower half of the Properties page. Each role that is explicitly granted access to this component has a check next to its name.

Activation Properties

You use the Activation Properties page to define the activation semantics for a COM+ component (see Figure 32.16).

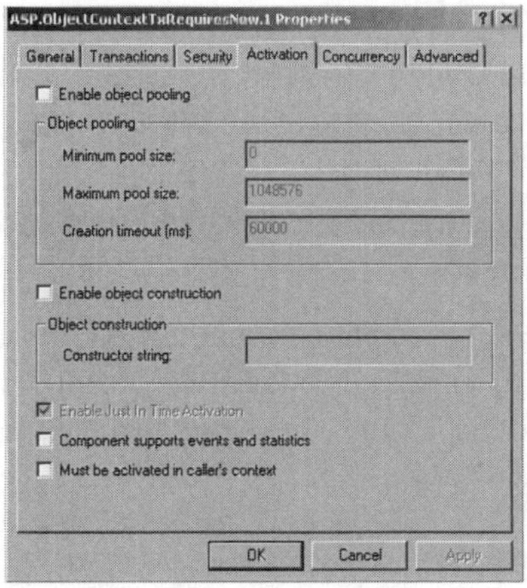

FIGURE 32.16

The Activation Properties page.

You can enable object pooling by enabling the Enable Object Pooling check box. If this option is enabled, you may optionally specify the minimum and maximum size of the object pool, as well as the amount of time allowed for object creation. If no object can be provided to a caller before this timeout expires, an error is returned to the caller.

You can enable object construction with the Support Object Construction check box. When this option is enabled, a construction string is passed to the component if the component supports the `IObjectConstruction` interface.

You can enable just-in-time activation using the Activation Properties page. This option is required for components that support or require transaction support.

To view event and statistic information about your component, enable the Component Supports Events and Statistics check box.

The last check box, Must Be Activated in Caller's Context, prevents a component from being created via a proxy. If a caller attempts to activate the component from an incompatible context, the call will fail instead of activating the component through a proxy.

Concurrency Properties

You use the Concurrency Properties page to define the concurrency and synchronization semantics for a COM+ component (see Figure 32.17).

FIGURE 32.17

The Concurrency Properties page.

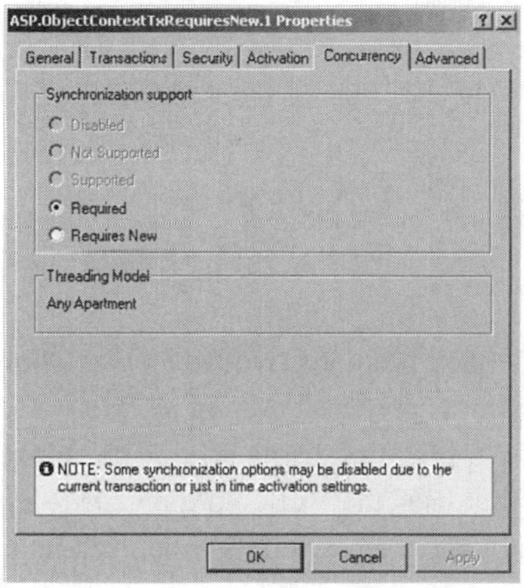

You cannot change the threading model for the COM+ object by using this Properties page; the threading model is displayed for informational purposes only.

The synchronization support required for the COM+ object may be one of the following values:

- **Disabled.** This option eliminates all synchronization-related overhead when using the component.

- **Not Supported.** The component never executes with synchronization support.

- **Supported.** The component directly participates in a context that requires synchronization without requiring a proxy. The component does not create a new synchronization activity if called in a nonsynchronization context, however.

- **Required.** The component must run in a context that supports synchronization. The component creates a new synchronization activity, if necessary, but also participates in an existing activity if called in a context that requires synchronization.

- **Requires New.** The component must run in a new synchronization activity context, creating a new activity if necessary.

If just-in-time activation is enabled for the component, only the Required and Requires New options are available.

Advanced Properties

You can use the Advanced Properties page to define the exception component class to be used for queued components. If defined, this class is used instead of sending messages to the dead letter queue. The exception class is expected to support the same queued interfaces as the original class.

The Advanced Properties page has no effect for non-queued components.

An Example of a COM+ Application

The CD-ROM that accompanies this book includes two projects to show you how an application that supports transactions runs under COM+ in Windows 2000. The VcBankApp project creates a COM+ application using ATL. The BankClient project creates a dialog box-based application that uses the VcBankApp COM+ application to deposit, withdraw, and transfer money between accounts in an Access database.

The VcBank Database

The database used for the VcBankApp application is included on the accompanying CD-ROM. The database is named VcBank.mdb and consists of a single table named AccountTab. Table 32.1 describes the AccountTab table.

TABLE 32.1   Fields in the AccountTab Table

Field	Type
Account	long
Balance	long

This database tracks the current balance for bank accounts.

Before using the database in the COM+ application, you'll need to register a new data source on your machine that refers to the VcBank database.

Run the Data Sources applet, which you can find in the Control Panel. The Data Sources applet icon is located in the Control Panel's Administrative Tools folder. Click on the Administrative Tools icon to display the Administrative Tools folder, then click on the Data Sources icon to open the Data Sources applet.

As Figure 32.18 shows, the Data Sources applet includes seven tabs. For the COM+ application, you'll want to create a system DSN—a data source that can be accessed by any user on your machine.

FIGURE 32.18

Use the Data Sources applet to define data source names.

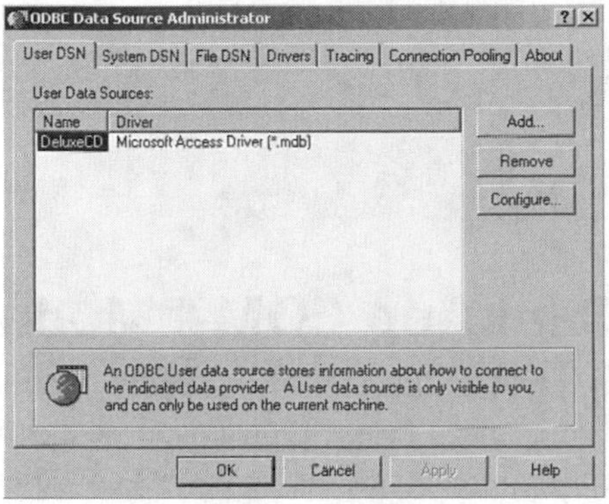

Click the System DSN tab to display the System DSN page, as shown in Figure 32.19.

FIGURE 32.19

Use the System DSN page to define data sources accessible by any user.

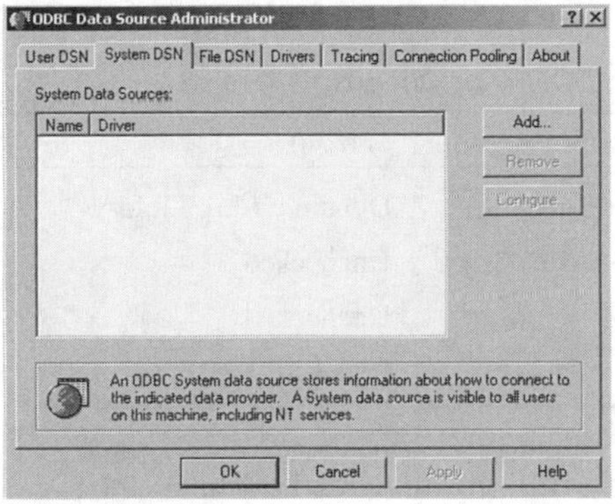

Click Add to display the Create New Data Source dialog box. You use this dialog box to select the driver to be used to access the data source. Select Microsoft Access Driver (*.mdb) and click Finish to continue. The ODBC Microsoft Access Setup dialog box appears, as shown in Figure 32.20.

Enter a name for the data source; the VcBank application requires the name to be Vc Bank Data. Feel free to enter a description for the data source, although it is not required for this example.

To specify the path to the database, click Select. The database must be located on your hard drive instead of on the book's CD-ROM. Click OK to dismiss the dialog box and create the data source.

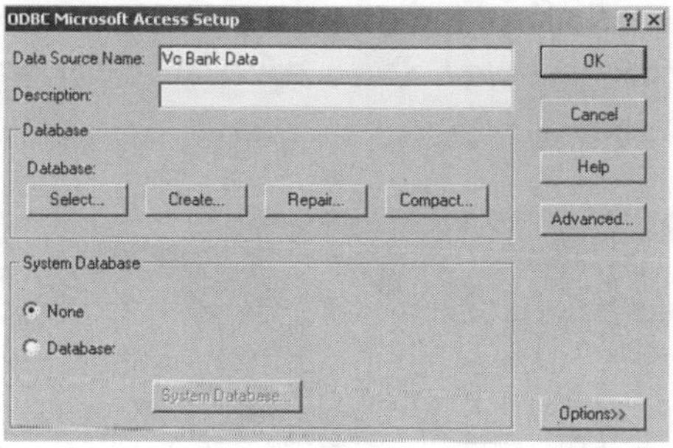

FIGURE 32.20

The ODBC Microsoft Access Setup dialog box.

Creating the VCBankApp COM+ Module

The VCBank COM+ component is housed in an in-process server created using an ATL named VCBankApp. The complete source for the project is located on the CD-ROM that accompanies this book; the steps required to create the project are described in the following sections.

To begin building the project, create an ATL project named VcBankApp using the ATL COM AppWizard. Use the settings provided in Table 32.2 to fill in the first wizard page.

TABLE 32.2   VcBankApp ATL COM AppWizard Values

Option	Setting
Server Type	Dynamic Link Library
Allow Merging of Proxy/Stub Code	Unchecked
Support MFC	Unchecked
Support MTS	Checked

To create the project and dismiss the wizard, click Finish.

Inserting the VcBank COM+ Component

The next step is to add the VcBank component to the project. Choose New ATL Object from the Insert menu. The ATL Object Wizard appears, as shown in Figure 32.21.

Select the MS Transaction Server Component object type, and click Next. The ATL Object Properties dialog box appears, as shown in Figure 32.22.

FIGURE 32.21

Using the ATL Object Wizard to insert a component that supports transactions.

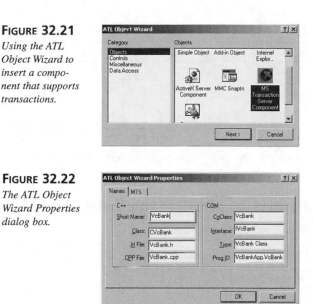

FIGURE 32.22

The ATL Object Wizard Properties dialog box.

32

USING ATL

Fill in this dialog box using the properties provided in Table 32.3. You should only need to provide the short name for the component—the other values are filled in automatically.

TABLE 32.3 Name Properties for the VcBank Components

Option	Value
Short Name	VcBank
Class	CVcBank
.H File	VcBank.h
.CPP File	VcBank.cpp
CoClass	VcBank
Interface	IVcBank
Type	VcBank Class
Prog ID	VcBankApp.VcBank

The options in Table 32.3 are identical to the parameters used in all COM objects built using ATL. The purpose of these properties is to define the names and symbols that will be used by the new object.

Select the MTS tab, and select the properties shown in Table 32.4.

TABLE 32.4   Name Properties for the VcBank Components

Option	Setting
Interface	Dual
Support IObjectControl	Checked
Can Be Pooled	Checked

Click OK to insert the VcBank component into the VcBankApp project. The files and classes associated with the component are added to the project workspace window.

Adding Interface Methods to the VcBank Component

Four methods must be added to the VcBank component:

- Balance returns the current balance for an account.
- Withdraw removes money from an account.
- Deposit adds money to an account.
- Transfer moves money from one account to another.

To add these methods, right-click on the IVcBank icon in the project workspace class view, and choose Add Method from the context menu. The Add Method dialog box appears and requires two pieces of information: the method's name and the method's parameters. After providing these two properties, click OK to add the method to the component. Use the values in Table 32.5 to add the four new methods to the VcBank component.

TABLE 32.5   Name Properties for the VcBank Component

Method	Parameters
Balance	[in]long account, [out]long* balance
Withdraw	[in]long account, [in]long amount
Deposit	[in]long account, [in]long amount
Transfer	[in]long source, [in]long dest, [in]long amt

Changes to StdAfx.h

The VcBank component will use *ActiveX Data Objects* (ADO) to interact with the bank database. Add the code provided in Listing 32.1 to the project's StdAfx.h header file. Insert this code after the #include directive for atlcom.h.

LISTING 32.1 The #import Directive for ADO for the VcBankApp Project

```
#import "c:\program files\common files\system\ado\msado15.dll" \
                    no_namespace rename("EOF", "adoEOF")
```

The #import directive in Listing 32.1 causes the compiler to generate a header file that contains smart pointers and other types that may be used to simplify programming with ADO.

Changes to `VcBank.h`

In order for a COM+ component to be pooled, it must support aggregation. In order for the VcBank component to support aggregation, you need to make one minor change to the VcBank.h header file. By default, Visual C++ inserts the DECLARE_NOT_AGGREGATABLE macro into your component's header file. This macro must be changed to a DECLARE_AGGREGATABLE macro, like this:

```
DECLARE_AGGREGATABLE(CVcBank)
```

This is the only change required to the VcBank.h header file.

Adding Helper Functions to `VcBank.cpp`

The interface methods used in the VcBank component will use two helper functions. The AccountToCmdString method takes an account number as a parameter and returns a _bstr_t that contains the SQL query string that selects the relevant record in the database. The UpdateBalance function has two parameters: the account number and a new balance for the account. Listing 32.2 provides the source code for these two functions. Add these functions to the VcBank.cpp source file before any other functions in the file.

LISTING 32.2 Helper Functions Used in VcBank.cpp

```
// Given an account number, create a SQL command string that
// selects the account number from the database.
_bstr_t AccountToCmdString(long account)
{
    char szAccount[256];
    wsprintf(szAccount, "%d", account);

    _bstr_t bstrCmd = L"SELECT * FROM AccountTab WHERE Account = ";
    bstrCmd += szAccount;

    return bstrCmd;
}

// Given an account number, update the account balance.
HRESULT UpdateBalance(long account, long amount)
{
```

LISTING 32.2   continued

```
_RecordsetPtr rs = NULL;
_bstr_t bstrAccount = AccountToCmdString(account);
try
{
    _variant_t vBalance;

    rs.CreateInstance(__uuidof(Recordset));
    rs->Open(bstrAccount,
             "DSN=VC Bank Data;",
             adOpenForwardOnly,
             adLockOptimistic,
             adCmdText);
    rs->PutCollect(L"Balance", amount);
    rs->Update();
    rs->Close();
}
catch(_com_error& e)
{
    return e.Error();
}
return S_OK;
}
```

The `AccountToCmdString` function simply concatenates the account number to a SQL query string. The `UpdateBalance` function is more complicated, however. The function begins by calling `AccountToCmdString` to create the appropriate query string toward the database. An ADO recordset object is created and is opened using the query string. The recordset then is updated using the new account balance.

Note that the `UpdateBalance` function uses C++ exception handling. In order for this component to work properly, you must enable C++ exception handling for the VcBankApp project by following these steps:

1. Open the Project Settings dialog box by choosing Settings from the Project menu.
2. Select the C++ tab.
3. Select All Configurations from the Settings combo box. Selecting All Configurations will apply these changes to Release and Debug builds of the project.
4. Select C++ Language from the Category combo box.
5. Enable the Enable Exception Handling check box.
6. Click OK to close the dialog box.

Additionally, you must remove the _ATL_MIN_CRT preprocessor macro that is included by default in all ATL release builds. This macro definition prevents the C runtime library from being linked with the project, resulting in smaller, faster code with fewer dependencies. Since this project uses exception handling, the C runtime is required. Remove the _ATL_MIN_CRT macro by following these steps:

1. Open the Project Settings dialog box by choosing Settings from the Project menu.

2. Select the C++ tab.

3. Select Multiple Configurations from the Settings combo box, which will display a dialog box containing all build configurations for the project. Check all Release builds, and close the dialog box by clicking OK.

4. Select Preprocessor from the Category combo box.

5. Remove the _ATL_MIN_CRT macro from the Preprocessor definitions edit control.

6. Click OK to close the dialog box.

Implementing the VcBank Interface Methods

The function bodies for each of the four VcBank interface methods have been created in VcBank.cpp. Modify these functions by adding the source code shown in bold in Listing 32.3.

LISTING 32.3   The VcBank Interface Methods

```
STDMETHODIMP CVcBank::Balance(long account, long *balance)
{
    _RecordsetPtr rs = NULL;
    _bstr_t bstrAccount = AccountToCmdString(account);
    try
    {
        _variant_t vBalance;

        rs.CreateInstance(__uuidof(Recordset));
        rs->Open(bstrAccount,
                "DSN=VC Bank Data;",
                adOpenForwardOnly,
                adLockReadOnly,
                adCmdText);
        vBalance = rs->Fields->GetItem("Balance")->Value;
        *balance = vBalance;
        rs->Close();
        m_spObjectContext->SetComplete();
    }
    catch(_com_error& e)
    {
```

LISTING 32.3 continued

```
        m_spObjectContext->SetAbort();
        return e.Error();
    }
    return S_OK;
}

STDMETHODIMP CVcBank::Withdraw(long account, long amount)
{
    long balance = 0;
    HRESULT hr = Balance(account, &balance);
    if(SUCCEEDED(hr))
    {
        if(balance < amount)
        {
            m_spObjectContext->SetAbort();
            return E_FAIL;
        }
        balance -= amount;
        hr = UpdateBalance(account, balance);
    }
    if(FAILED(hr))
        m_spObjectContext->SetAbort();
    else
        m_spObjectContext->SetComplete();
    return hr;
}

STDMETHODIMP CVcBank::Deposit(long account, long amount)
{
    long balance = 0;
    HRESULT hr = Balance(account, &balance);
    if(SUCCEEDED(hr))
    {
        balance += amount;
        hr = UpdateBalance(account, balance);
    }
    if(FAILED(hr))
        m_spObjectContext->SetAbort();
    else
        m_spObjectContext->SetComplete();
    return hr;
}

STDMETHODIMP CVcBank::Transfer(long source, long dest, long amt)
{
    long balance = 0;
    HRESULT hr = Balance(source, &balance);
    if(SUCCEEDED(hr))
    {
```

```
        if(balance < amt)
            return E_FAIL;
        long newBalance = balance - amt;
        hr = UpdateBalance(source, newBalance);
        if(SUCCEEDED(hr))
        {
            hr = Balance(dest, &balance);
            if(SUCCEEDED(hr))
            {
                newBalance = balance + amt;
                hr = UpdateBalance(dest, newBalance);
            }
        }
    }
    if(FAILED(hr))
        m_spObjectContext->SetAbort();
    else
        m_spObjectContext->SetComplete();
    return hr;
}
```

The functions in Listing 32.3 use some basic ADO code to interact with the VcBank database. Each of these functions calls SetAbort or SetComplete, depending on the function's success or failure. This is especially useful when performing a money transfer. The transfer of money consists of two operations:

- The removal of money from the first account
- The addition of money to the second account

If the first operation succeeds but the second fails, SetAbort is called, causing the first operation to be rolled back. This type of mechanism is especially useful when a transaction consists of operations performed by multiple components. If any component calls SetAbort, the entire transaction rolls back.

Registering the VcBank COM+ Application

Open the COM+ MMC snap-in and select the COM+ applications node. Create a new COM+ application by following these steps:

1. Right-click on the COM+ applications node; then choose New, Application from the context menu. The COM Application Install Wizard appears.

2. Click Next to move past the welcome page.

3. Click the icon to create an empty application.

4. For the application name, enter **Visual C++ Bank**. Leave the application type set to the default value of Server application, and click Next.

5. Leave the application identity set to the default value of the interactive user. Click Next.

6. Click Finish to complete the application creation procedure.

The next step is to add the VcBank component to the COM+ application. Expand the tree node associated with the Visual C++ Bank and the component by following these steps:

1. Right-click on the Components node; then choose New, Component from the context menu. The COM Component Install Wizard appears.

2. Click Next to move past the welcome page.

3. Click the icon to install a new component. A File Open dialog box appears.

4. Navigate to the directory that contains VcBankApp.dll, select the file, and click Open.

5. The VcBank component is listed as a component found in the DLL. Click Next to continue.

6. Click Finish to complete the component installation.

The component now is registered in the COM+ catalog. Some changes must be made to the component before you use it in this example, however. Finish configuring the component by following these steps:

1. Right-click on the VcBank component, and choose Properties from the context menu.

2. Select the Transactions tab, and click the Transactions Required radio button.

3. Select the Activation tab, and enable object pooling.

4. Click OK to complete the configuration changes.

The Visual C++ Bank COM+ application now is registered and ready to use. The next several sections create a client application that will use the component.

A Client Application for VcBank

You can access a COM+ application in a number of ways. Visual Basic, the *Windows Scripting Host* (WSH), and *Active Server Pages* (ASP) are three of the more popular ways to use COM+ applications. Because this is a Visual C++ book, this chapter creates an MFC application that serves as a client to the VcBank component.

Begin by using MFC AppWizard to create a dialog-based application named BankClient. Accept all the default properties for a dialog box–based application.

Adding Dialog Boxes to the BankClient Project

The BankClient project consists of several dialog boxes. In addition to the dialog boxes created by AppWizard, you must add three new dialog boxes to the BankClient project:

- A dialog box to handle withdrawals from an account
- A dialog box to handle deposits to an account
- A dialog box to handle money transfers between accounts

Begin by adding three new dialog box resources to the BankClient project:

1. Open the project workspace Resources tab.
2. Right-click on the dialog box icon, and choose Insert Dialog from the context menu.
3. Repeat Step 2 twice to create three dialog boxes.

Use the information in Table 32.6 to set the properties for each dialog box.

TABLE 32.6 New Dialog Boxes for the BankClient Project

Resource ID	Caption
IDD_DEPOSIT	Deposit to account
IDD_WITHDRAW	Withdraw from account
IDD_TRANSFER	Transfer money to another account

Figure 32.23 shows the IDD_DEPOSIT dialog box. Add two edit controls and two static text labels to the dialog box.

Use the values from Table 32.7 to define the properties for the new controls.

TABLE 32.7 Control Properties for the Deposit Dialog Box

Control	Resource ID	Caption
Account edit	IDC_ACCOUNT	None
Amount edit	IDC_AMOUNT	None
Account label	IDC_STATIC	Account
Amount label	IDC_STATIC	Amount

In addition to the properties listed in Table 32.7, the IDC_ACCOUNT edit control has the read-only property.

FIGURE 32.23

*The BankClient
Deposit dialog box.*

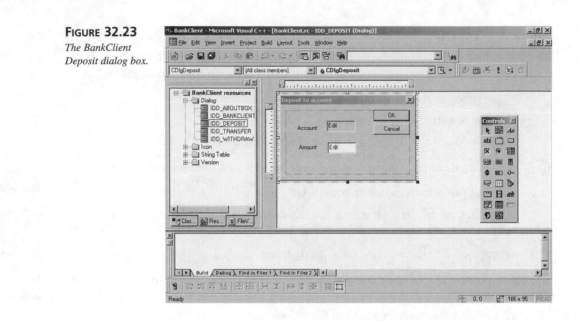

Use the ClassWizard to associate a new class with the dialog box. Open ClassWizard by pressing Ctrl+W. As the ClassWizard opens, you are asked whether a new class should be created or an existing class reused. Select the default option, which is to create a new class to manage the dialog box, and click OK. The New Class dialog box appears.

Use the values in Table 32.8 to fill in the New Class dialog box.

TABLE 32.8 New Class Dialog Box Properties for the Deposit Dialog Box

Property	Value
Class Name	CDlgDeposit
Base Class	CDialog
Dialog ID	IDD_DEPOSIT
Automation	None

Click OK to add the CDlgDeposit class to the project, and then use the values in Table 32.9 to associate two CDlgDeposit member variables with dialog box controls.

TABLE 32.9 New Class Dialog Box Properties for the Deposit Dialog Box

Control ID	Variable Name	Category	Type
IDC_ACCOUNT	m_nAccount	Value	long
IDC_AMOUNT	m_nAmount	Value	long

Click OK to dismiss the ClassWizard, and add the new member variables to the project.

The IDD_WITHDRAW dialog box is similar to the IDD_DEPOSIT dialog box (see Figure 32.24). Add two edit controls and two static text labels to the dialog box.

FIGURE 32.24

The BankClient Withdraw dialog box.

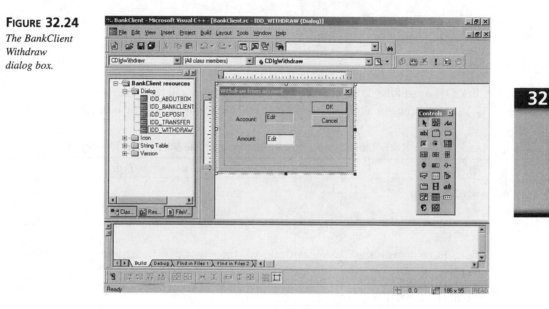

Use the values in Table 32.10 to define the properties for the new controls.

TABLE 32.10 Control Properties for the Withdraw Dialog Box

Control	Resource ID	Caption
Account edit	IDC_ACCOUNT	None
Amount edit	IDC_AMOUNT	None
Account label	IDC_STATIC	Account
Amount label	IDC_STATIC	Amount

In addition to the properties listed in Table 32.10, the IDC_ACCOUNT edit control has the read-only property.

Use the ClassWizard to associate a new class with the Withdraw dialog box. Open the ClassWizard by pressing Ctrl+W, and elect to create a new class to manage the dialog box. The New Class dialog box appears.

Use the values in Table 32.11 to fill in the New Class dialog box.

TABLE 32.11   New Class Dialog Box Properties for the Withdraw Dialog Box

Property	Value
Class Name	CDlgWithdraw
Base Class	CDialog
Dialog ID	IDD_WITHDRAW
Automation	None

Click OK to add the CDlgWithdraw class to the project, and then use the values in Table 32.12 to associate two CDlgWithdraw member variables with dialog box controls.

TABLE 32.12   New Class Dialog Box Properties for the Withdraw Dialog Box

Control ID	Variable Name	Category	Type
IDC_ACCOUNT	m_nAccount	Value	long
IDC_AMOUNT	m_nAmount	Value	long

Click OK to dismiss the ClassWizard and add the new member variables to the project.

Figure 32.25 shows the IDD_TRANSFER dialog box. Add three edit controls and three static text labels to the dialog box.

FIGURE 32.25

The BankClient Transfer dialog box.

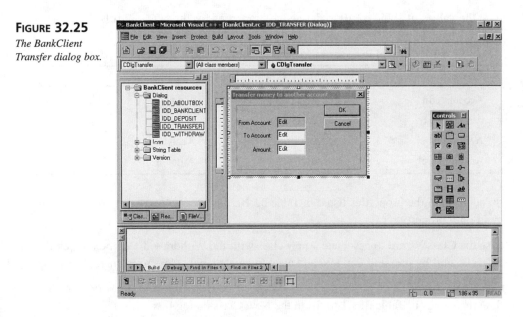

Use the values in Table 32.13 to define the properties for the new controls.

TABLE 32.13   New Dialog Boxes for the BankClient Project

Control	Resource ID	Caption
From account edit	IDC_ACCOUNT	None
To account edit	IDC_TO_ACCOUNT	None
Amount edit	IDC_AMOUNT	None
From account label	IDC_STATIC	From Account
To account label	IDC_STATIC	To Account
Amount label	IDC_STATIC	Amount

In addition to the properties listed in Table 32.13, the IDC_ACCOUNT edit control has the read-only property.

As with the previous dialog boxes, use the ClassWizard to associate a new class with the dialog box. Use the values from Table 32.14 to fill in the New Class dialog box.

TABLE 32.14   New Class Dialog Box Properties for the Transfer Dialog Box

Property	Value
Class Name	CDlgTransfer
Base Class	CDialog
Dialog ID	IDD_TRANSFER
Automation	None

Click OK to add the CDlgTransfer class to the project, and then use the values in Table 32.15 to associate three CDlgTransfer member variables with dialog box controls.

TABLE 32.15   New Class Dialog Box Properties for the Transfer Dialog Box

Control ID	Variable Name	Category	Type
IDC_ACCOUNT	m_nAccount	Value	long
IDC_AMOUNT	m_nAmount	Value	long
IDC_TO_ACCOUNT	m_nDestination	Value	long

Click OK to dismiss the ClassWizard and add the new member variables to the project.

Modifying the Main Dialog Box for BankClient

Figure 32.26 shows the main dialog box for the BankClient application. Add one edit control, three static text labels, and four pushbutton controls to the dialog box. The IDC_BALANCE_LABEL static control is located directly under the edit control, but isn't shown in the figure because it has no caption.

FIGURE 32.26

The main dialog box for BankClient.

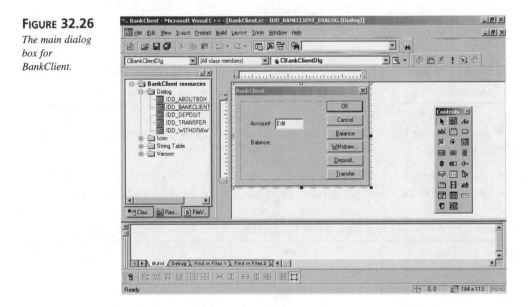

Use the values in Table 32.16 to define the properties for the new controls.

TABLE 32.16   Control Properties for the Withdraw Dialog Box

Control	Resource ID	Caption
Account edit	IDC_ACCOUNT	None
Balance value	IDC_BALANCE_LABEL	None
Account label	IDC_STATIC	Account
Balance label	IDC_STATIC	Balance
Balance button	IDC_BALANCE	&Balance
Withdraw button	IDC_WITHDRAW	&Withdraw
Deposit button	IDC_DEPOSIT	&Deposit
Transfer button	IDC_TRANSFER	&Transfer

Use the values in Table 32.17 to associate a `CBankClientDlg` member variable with the dialog box control.

TABLE 32.17 Control Properties for the Main Dialog Box

Control ID	Variable Name	Category	Type
IDC_ACCOUNT	m_strAccount	Value	CString

Use the values in Table 32.18 to add four message-handling functions to the `CBankClientDlg` class. These functions will handle messages generated when the pushbuttons in the main dialog box are clicked.

TABLE 32.18 Message-Handling Functions for the Main Dialog Box

Object ID	Message	Function
IDC_BALANCE	BN_CLICKED	OnBalance
IDC_WITHDRAW	BN_CLICKED	OnWithdraw
IDC_DEPOSIT	BN_CLICKED	OnDeposit
IDC_TRANSFER	BN_CLICKED	OnTransfer

Click OK to dismiss the ClassWizard.

Accessing the COM+ Application

For maximum efficiency, COM+ clients typically acquire references to COM+ objects as early as possible and release them as late as possible. The BankClient application will hold on to a single `IVcBank` interface pointer for as long as the application is running. The COM+ application will use just-in-time activation and object pooling to make the application as efficient as possible.

To include definitions for the symbols used in the VcBankApp module, copy the `VcBankApp.h` and `VcBankApp_i.c` files from the VcBankApp project directory to the BankClient project directory.

Add the following `#include` directive to the `StdAfx.h` header file after the existing `#include` directives.

```
#include "vcbankapp.h"
```

Add the following `#include` directive to the `BankClientDlg.cpp` source file. This file contains definitions for the `CLSID` and other symbols from VcBankApp.

```
#include "vcbankapp_i.c"
```

32

USING ATL

Add a new member variable to the CBankClientDlg class. The new member variable is an ATL smart pointer that will store a pointer to the IVcBank interface. In Listing 32.4, the modification to the CBankClientDlg class is shown in bold, with most existing lines in the class removed to conserve space.

LISTING 32.4 Modifications (in bold) to the CBankClientDlg Declaration

```
class CBankClientDlg : public CDialog
{


// Implementation
protected:
    HICON m_hIcon;
    CComQIPtr<IVcBank> m_pBank;




};
```

The m_pBank interface pointer is set when the dialog box is initialized. The initialization code is provided in Listing 32.5 and is located in the CBankClientDlg::OnInitDialog function. As with the preceding listing, the new code is shown in bold, and many existing lines have been removed for clarity and to conserve space.

LISTING 32.5 Modifications (in bold) to the CBankClientDlg::OnInitDialog Function

```
BOOL CBankClientDlg::OnInitDialog()
{



    // TODO: Add extra initialization here
    CoInitializeEx(NULL, COINIT_MULTITHREADED);
    HRESULT hr = m_pBank.CoCreateInstance(CLSID_VcBank);
    if(FAILED(hr))
    {
        ErrorHandling(hr);
    }
    return TRUE;
}
```

The m_pBank member variable is an ATL smart pointer. In order to use this type of variable, you must include one of the ATL header files into the project. Add the following #include directive to the StdAfx.h header file after the existing #include directives.

```
#include "atlbase.h"
```

Also, in order to use multithreaded COM features, you must add the following pre-processor directive to the top of the StdAfx.h header file before any existing #include directives.

```
#define _WIN32_WINNT 0x0400
```

Retrieving an Account Balance

Listing 32.6 provides the code required to retrieve an account balance. Add this code to the CBankClientDlg::OnBalance member function.

LISTING 32.6   Retrieving an Account Balance in BankClient

```
void CBankClientDlg::OnBalance()
{
    long nBalance = 0;
    BOOL fValid = FALSE;
    int nAccount = GetDlgItemInt(IDC_ACCOUNT, &fValid);
    if(!fValid)
    {
        AfxMessageBox("Please enter an account number");
        return;
    }
    ASSERT(m_pBank);
    HRESULT hr = m_pBank->Balance(nAccount, &nBalance);
    if(SUCCEEDED(hr))
        SetDlgItemInt(IDC_BALANCE_LABEL, nBalance);
}
```

The OnBalance function begins by retrieving the account ID from the account edit control. The account number and a pointer to a variable that will store the account balance then are passed the IVcBank::Balance function. If the function succeeds, the balance label is updated with the account balance.

Making a Deposit

Listing 32.7 provides the code used to deposit additional money into an account. Add this code to the CBankClientDlg::OnDeposit member function.

LISTING 32.7   Depositing Money into an Account in BankClient

```
void CBankClientDlg::OnDeposit()
{
    CDlgDeposit dlg;

    BOOL fValid = FALSE;
    int nAccount = GetDlgItemInt(IDC_ACCOUNT, &fValid);
```

32

USING ATL

LISTING 32.7   continued

```
    if(!fValid)
    {
        AfxMessageBox("Please enter an account number");
        return;
    }

    dlg.m_nAccount = nAccount;

    if(!dlg.DoModal())
    {
        return;
    }
    ASSERT(m_pBank);
    HRESULT hr = m_pBank->Deposit(nAccount, dlg.m_nAmount);
    if(FAILED(hr))
        AfxMessageBox("Could not deposit to account");

    long nBalance = 0;
    hr = m_pBank->Balance(nAccount, &nBalance);
    if(SUCCEEDED(hr))
        SetDlgItemInt(IDC_BALANCE_LABEL, nBalance);
}
```

Like the `OnBalance` function, the `OnDeposit` function begins by retrieving the account ID from the account edit control. The `CDlgDeposit` class is used to collect the amount of money to be added to the account. The account number and the amount of money to be deposited are passed the `IVcBank::Withdraw` function. If the function succeeds, the balance label is updated with the account balance.

The `OnDeposit` function uses the `CDlgDeposit` class to collect information about the deposit from the user. Add the following #include directive below the existing #include directives in the `BankClientDlg.cpp` file:

```
#include "dlgdeposit.h"
```

Making a Withdrawal

Listing 32.8 shows the code used to make a withdrawal from an account. Add this code to the `CBankClientDlg::OnWithdraw` member function.

LISTING 32.8   Withdrawing Money from an Account in BankClient

```
void CBankClientDlg::OnWithdraw()
{
    CDlgWithdraw dlg;

    BOOL fValid = FALSE;
    int nAccount = GetDlgItemInt(IDC_ACCOUNT, &fValid);
    if(!fValid)
    {
        AfxMessageBox("Please enter an account number");
        return;
    }

    dlg.m_nAccount = nAccount;
    if(!dlg.DoModal())
    {
        // User cancelled dialog box.
        return;
    }

    ASSERT(m_pBank);
    HRESULT hr = m_pBank->Withdraw(nAccount, dlg.m_nAmount);
    if(FAILED(hr))
        AfxMessageBox("Could not withdraw from account");

    long nBalance = 0;
    hr = m_pBank->Balance(nAccount, &nBalance);
    if(SUCCEEDED(hr))
        SetDlgItemInt(IDC_BALANCE_LABEL, nBalance);
}
```

The OnWithdraw function works very much like the OnDeposit function. The OnWithdraw function begins by retrieving the account ID from the account edit control. The CDlgWithdraw class is used to collect the amount of money to be withdrawn from the account. The account number and the amount of money to be withdrawn are passed the IVcBank::Withdraw function. If the function succeeds, the balance label is updated with the account balance.

The OnWithdraw function uses the CDlgWithdraw class to collect information about the deposit from the user. Add the following #include directive below the existing #include directives in the BankClientDlg.cpp file:

```
#include "dlgwithdraw.h"
```

32

USING ATL

Transferring Money Between Accounts

Money is transferred between accounts using the code provided in Listing 32.9. Add this code to the `CBankClientDlg::OnTransfer` member function.

LISTING 32.9 Transferring Money Between Accounts in BankClient

```
void CBankClientDlg::OnTransfer()
{
    CDlgTransfer dlg;

    BOOL fValid = FALSE;
    int nAccount = GetDlgItemInt(IDC_ACCOUNT, &fValid);
    if(!fValid)
    {
        AfxMessageBox("Please enter an account number");
        return;
    }

    dlg.m_nAccount = nAccount;
    if(!dlg.DoModal())
    {
        // User cancelled dialog box.
        return;
    }

    ASSERT(m_pBank);
    HRESULT hr = m_pBank->Transfer(nAccount, dlg.m_nDestination, dlg.m_nAmount);
    if(FAILED(hr))
        AfxMessageBox("Could not transfer from account");

    long nBalance = 0;
    hr = m_pBank->Balance(nAccount, &nBalance);
    if(SUCCEEDED(hr))
        SetDlgItemInt(IDC_BALANCE_LABEL, nBalance);
}
```

The `OnTransfer` function works like the previous two functions. The account number is retrieved from the account edit control, and the `CDlgTransfer` class is used to retrieve the destination account and transfer amount. The account number, destination account, and amount of money to be transferred are passed the `IVcBank::Transfer` function. If the function succeeds, the balance label is updated with the account balance.

The `OnTransfer` function uses the `CDlgTransfer` class to collect information about the money transfer from the user. Add the following `#include` directive below the existing `#include` directives in the `BankClientDlg.cpp` file:

```
#include "dlgtransfer.h"
```

Using BankClient

Compile and run the BankClient project. The database supplied with the CD-ROM has two account numbers: 1111 and 1234. Use the BankClient application to retrieve the account balances, make deposits, and transfer money between the accounts.

You may notice a delay when the COM+ component is executed for the first time. This is normal, and the call time is typically much faster for additional method calls.

Summary

This chapter discussed how you can use MTS and COM+ to build applications that take advantage of transactions, object pooling, and just-in-time activation to build scalable server applications. Visual C++ and ATL are tools that are well-suited to building light-weight components that work well with MTS and COM+.

You looked at an example of an application that uses COM+ and was built with ATL, and you examined a simple client application that was built with MFC. These applications simulated a banking application and used transactions to ensure that operations were performed correctly.

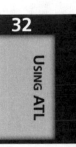

32

USING ATL

Finishing Touches

PART

VIII

IN THIS PART

CHAPTER 33

Adding Windows Help

*by Vincent Mayfield
and Mickey Williams*

IN THIS CHAPTER

Perhaps one of the most important features of a user-friendly Windows application is a good help system. This is especially important when you consider how many people never take the time to read a manual before diving right in to your application. In a way, this is a good sign; if your application interface is similar to other applications, users will feel right at home. However, eventually, users will want a bit more information about what a particular widget does or how to create a certain type of gizmo.

This is where online help comes in handy. If properly implemented, your help system can quickly and easily tell the user what he wants to know. Fortunately, Windows has standardized the user interface to Windows help. In this chapter, you will see how to implement Windows help in your applications, including how to add context-sensitive help to give your users the easiest access to relevant help topics.

Recently, Microsoft has released HTML Help, which enables you to provide much richer content in your help files by leveraging Dynamic HTML and other Internet Explorer technologies.

Windows Help Basics

Microsoft has already done most of the work for you when it comes to implementing help for your application. It has taken care of handling the user-interface framework that is presented to the user. You need to add the specific content for your project, and add code to your application to start up the Windows help facility. You will see how to implement your own help later in this chapter, but let's start with the basics of how Windows help works.

There are two different types of online help provided by Windows applications:

- Windows Help, also known as WinHelp, is the traditional online form of help found in many older Windows applications.
- HTML Help, the newer form of online help that's based on compiled HTML scripts. This is the type of online help used by Visual C++.

Understanding WinHelp

The older, traditional form of Windows help is handled by a separate program named `WinHelp.exe`, or WinHelp for short. This program presents the standard help dialog to the user, displaying the contents of your help project, as shown in Figure 33.1.

You can quickly tryout this yourself by entering a command line like the following:

```
WinHelp MyHelp.hlp
```

FIGURE 33.1

The WinHelp dialog.

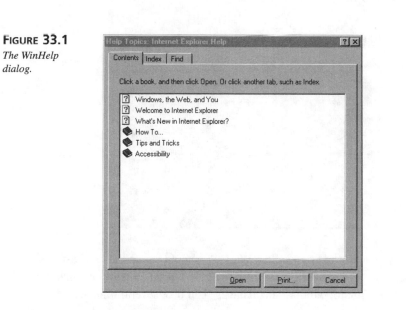

By default, the WinHelp dialog provides three tabs, although you may add your own custom tabs if you like. The Contents tab will display the table of contents for your help file, as shown in Figure 33.1.

The Index tab will display a list of the topics contained in your help file, and allows the user to search the list to find the subject she is interested in, as shown in Figure 33.2.

FIGURE 33.2

The WinHelp Index tab.

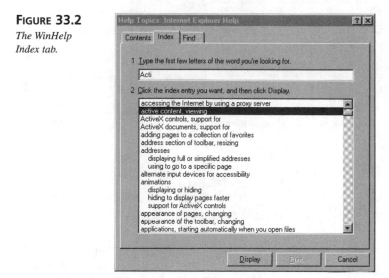

In addition, WinHelp allows the user to do a full-text search through the help file by using the Find tab. However, before the user can access the Find tab, the user will see the Find Setup Wizard dialog shown in Figure 33.3.

FIGURE 33.3

The Find Setup Wizard.

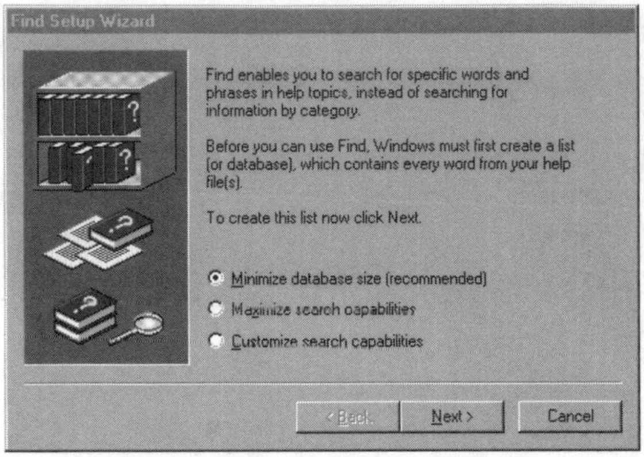

This dialog allows the user to specify how WinHelp should create the database file (.FTS) that is used to help perform the full-text search. For large help files, like those used with Developer Studio, building this database can take several minutes.

After the database has been created, the user is presented with the Find tab, as shown in Figure 33.4.

FIGURE 33.4

The WinHelp Find tab.

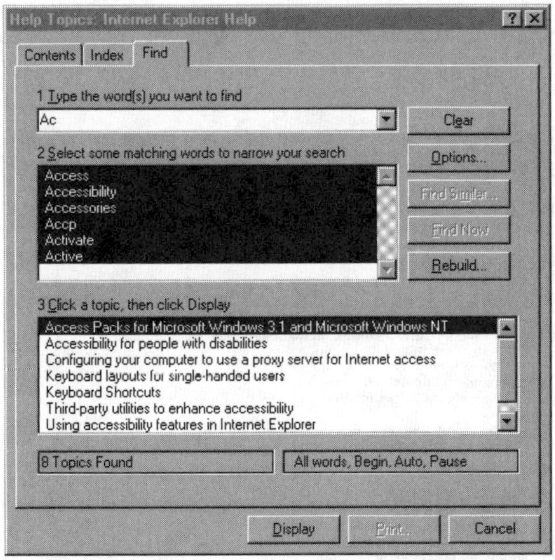

This dialog allows the user to search the list of words contained in the help file, or begin typing a keyword or phrase in the top edit box. Whenever a word or phrase is selected, the user will see the list of topics containing that word in the bottom list box. Double-clicking one of these topics or clicking the Display button will bring up the help text for the selected topic.

Most users of Windows applications are familiar with how to use this interface to retrieve the help information that they want. All you have to do is make sure that your help file contains this information and that it is structured to allow easy access.

Understanding HTML Help

HTML Help is similar in many ways to the older WinHelp online help system discussed in the previous section. HTML Help is widely used in Microsoft products—it's used to create the MSDN Library used for online help with Visual C++.

To the end-user, the HTML Help user interface appears similar to the WinHelp user interface. By default, the user interface is divided into two sections. On the left side, navigation tabs enable a user to choose a method to find a particular help topic. By default there are three tabs:

- Contents
- Index
- Search

It's also common to add an additional Favorites tab, as found with the MSDN Library.

The Contents tab lists available help topics in a hierarchical view, as shown in Figure 33.5.

FIGURE 33.5

An example of a basic HTML Help Contents page.

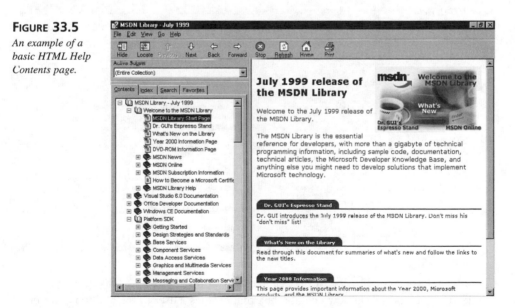

The Index tab, shown in Figure 33.6, lists topics in alphabetical order.

FIGURE 33.6

*An example of a
basic HTML Help
Index page.*

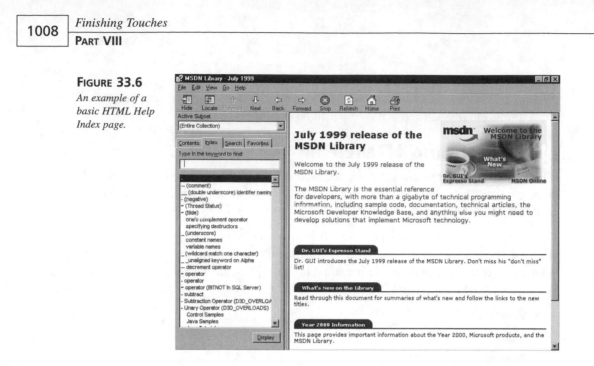

The Search tab, shown in Figure 33.7, lists topic keywords in alphabetical order.

FIGURE 33.7

*An example of a
basic HTML Help
Search page.*

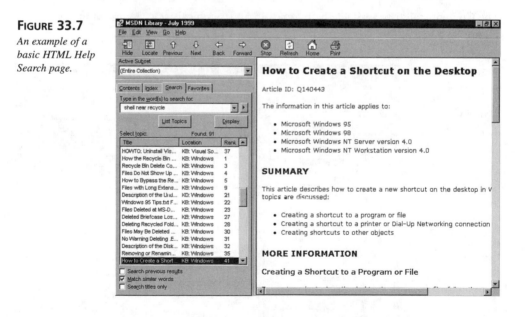

The user interface used by the MSDN Library, shown in Figure 33.8, has been customized to include a drop-down combo box that enables a user to select library subsets
for browsing, as well as store a list of topics in the Favorites page.

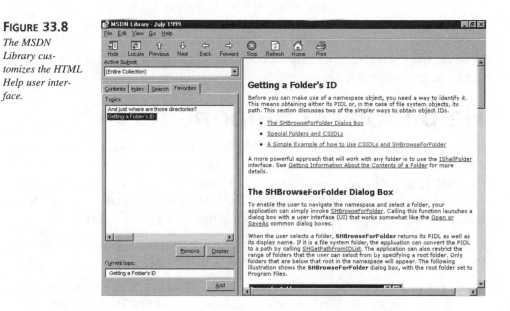

FIGURE 33.8

The MSDN Library customizes the HTML Help user interface.

Help Options in AppWizard

When creating applications with AppWizard, you might have already noticed that the AppWizard gives you the option to automatically add context-sensitive help to your applications. This option is available for any application that you create with the MFC AppWizard, whether it is a dialog-based single document or a multiple document application. If you choose to add context-sensitive help, the AppWizard will set up the basic framework that you will need to add effective help to your application, including some basic help information on the standard menu items.

For a document-based application, selecting the context-sensitive help option will create a `Help Topics` menu item to the `Help` menu, which would otherwise only contain the `About` menu choice. The `Help Topics` command is set up for you to open the Contents page of your help file. Strictly speaking, this isn't context-sensitive help, but if you don't select the context-sensitive help option in AppWizard, only the About box will be created for you.

For real context-sensitive help, your new application will include support for the Shift+F1 keystroke, which will put the application in Help mode. The user can then click any particular control to see help text for the particular button, edit box, and so on. In addition, the default toolbar will contain a Context Help button, which has the same effect as pressing Shift+F1. You will see just how the code generated by the AppWizard implements these features later on in this chapter.

If you have chosen the context-sensitive help option for a dialog-based application, a Help button will be added to your application that will open the index for your help file. However, true context-sensitive help isn't implemented for you, so Shift+F1 won't be functional in your project.

Help Project Components

If you have chosen to create a project with AppWizard using context-sensitive help, you will notice that quite a few new files have been added to your project directory. Most of these will reside in the hlp subdirectory of your project. You can view these files from Developer Studio by opening the Help Files folder in the FileView tab of the Workspace window. (The help project file (.hpj) is shown in the Source Files folder.)

Depending on your particular application, the help project will consist of one or more of the following sorts of files:

- .rtf files: These are specially formatted rich-text format (RTF) files that make up the body of your help text, including additional information like hyperlinks.

- .bmp files: Bitmap files may be added to your help project. These are added as illustrations in the help text to represent particular items in the user interface. The projects created by AppWizard will include a bitmap for each of the toolbar buttons on the standard toolbar.

- .cnt file: Each help project will contain a single file that holds the information used to present a table of contents for the help file.

- .hpj file: The help project file is used to control how all of the individual components of your help project are put together to build the .hlp file that is used by your application.

- MakeHelp.bat: To help with building your help project, AppWizard creates a batch file named MakeHelp.bat that will handle the task of building your help project. This batch file is called when your application project is built.

- .hm files: In addition, if you have built your project, you will notice one or more help map files. These files are used to map resource identifiers to the help context values that are used in working with the .hlp file. These are generated by the help map utility, makehm.exe, which is called from within MakeHelp.bat.

The next few sections discuss each of these file types in more detail.

Authoring Help Topics Using WinHelp

The actual text of all of your WinHelp help topics is created in rich-text format (RTF) files. Rich-text format allows you to create files that use only the ASCII character set, but can also include additional formatting information, as well as special information about links.

For some reason, Microsoft has never felt that it needed to include the ability to edit RTF files from within Developer Studio. Their recommendation is to use an additional editor, such as Microsoft Word, which can save files in an RTF format. However, because RTF files only use the standard ASCII character set, you may use any plain ASCII editor to work with the .rtf files, although the files are much more difficult to work with in plain ASCII.

> **Tip**
>
> Actually, if you are developing full-scale help files, I *highly* recommend that you use a third-party tool. I use RoboHelp, by Blue Sky Software, and have been very happy with it. RoboHelp, and other available tools (both free and commercial), can make the creation of help files much, much easier on you. RoboHelp can be used to author WinHelp and HTML Help projects.

For example, see Figure 33.9 for the simple .rtf file as shown in Microsoft Word.

The same file would look like the one in Figure 33.10 in a native ASCII text editor, such as Notepad.

> **Tip**
>
> When using an RTF editor, such as Word, you should display all hidden text and footnotes because these have special meaning when creating help files. In Word, you can turn on hidden text by choosing Tools, Options, View. You can display footnote text with the View, Footnotes menu command.

FIGURE 33.9

RTF in Microsoft Word.

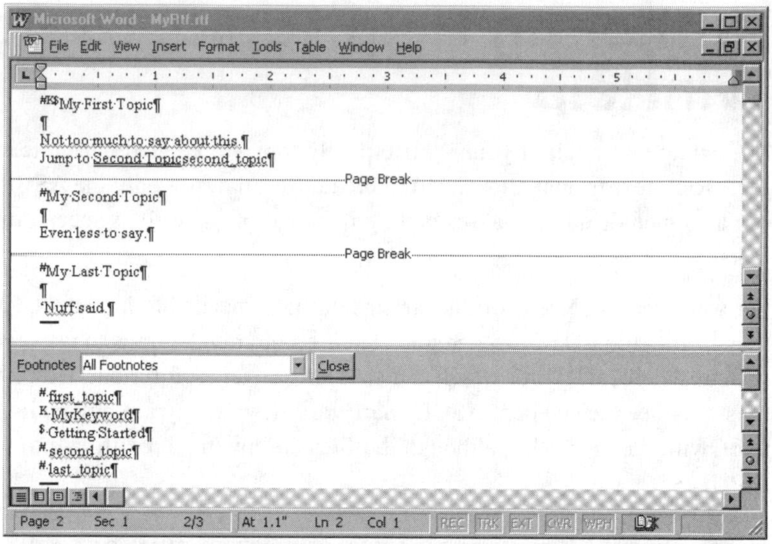

FIGURE 33.10

RTF in Notepad.

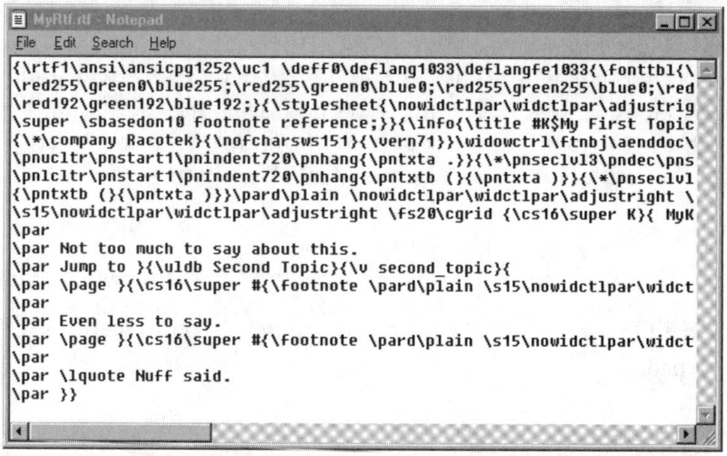

Creating Help Topics

Individual topics in your RTF files are separated by a hard page break. These are used to separate the RTF text into the individual pages that will be displayed by WinHelp. In addition, each topic may contain several special footnotes.

To start with, most of your topics should include a footnote using the special character (#), which is used to assign a context name to the topic. This context name given in the footnote text is used for referencing this topic as the destination of a hypertext link or directly from your application.

Secondly, you might want to add a footnote using the special character (K). The text for this footnote lists keywords that may be used in searches to find this particular topic. These keywords appear to the user in the Index tab of the WinHelp dialog.

In addition, you may specify a footnote with the ($) character, which assigns a topic name. Topic names assigned with this footnote will appear to the user in the Find tab of the WinHelp dialog.

> **Tip**
>
> By using an RTF editor such as Microsoft Word, you may add different fonts and formatting to your help files, just as you would with any other Word document.

Adding Hot Spots

I'm sure that by now you are familiar with using help files that allow you to click certain keywords or phrases to move to a new topic. These are known as *hot spots,* or hypertext links. To implement these hot spots in your help files, you will need to add a few special things to your RTF file.

The displayed text that you want to make a hot spot should be formatted with double underlining. Immediately following the double underlined text, add a context name, which should be formatted as hidden text. This hidden text gives the context name for a topic somewhere in your help file. Remember that the context name for a topic is assigned using the # footnote.

This is all you need to do to add hypertext links to your help files. However, you might also want to use tables to format groups of links, as you will see in the .rtf files generated by AppWizard.

Including Graphics in Help Files

As you will see in the .rtf files that are created by AppWizard, you can also add graphics to your help files. You can include bitmap files anywhere in your help file by adding a directive to your .rtf file in the location where you intend to display the bitmap. The format of the directive looks like this:

```
{bmc MyPic.bmp}
```

The directive is enclosed in curly braces and uses the bmc command to indicate that the filename of a bitmap file will follow.

> **Note**
>
> When compiling a help project that includes bitmaps, you will need to make sure that the `.bmp` files are in the bitmap file path, as specified in the BMROOT setting in the [OPTIONS] section of the `.hpj` file.

Managing Help Projects

As mentioned previously, Microsoft doesn't provide any integrated tools for developing your own RTF files that go into a help project. However, Visual C++ 6.0 does include a tool that is very useful for managing all the other tasks involved in developing help projects. This tool is the Help Workshop.

You won't find the Help Workshop in any of the menus in Developer Studio, although you can add it to your Tools menu as you saw in Chapter 1. The executable for Help Workshop is found in `...\vc\bin\hcw.exe` under whichever directory you have installed Developer Studio.

Help Workshop allows you to do many different things associated with help project development, including the following:

- Create and edit help project (`.hpj`) files
- Edit contents (`.cnt`) files
- Compile your help project
- Test your help project

The next few sections cover each of these items.

Help Project Files

The help project (`.hpj`) file controls how the various pieces of your help project are assembled to create the `.hlp` file that is actually used by your applications. This file contains several sections, similar to those that you might have seen in `.ini` files. You may edit the `.hpj` file for your project with any text editor or you can edit it from within the Help Workshop, as shown in Figure 33.11.

Help project files contain the following sections:

- [OPTIONS]: This section contains several different option settings that affect how the help project is built, including the title of the project, the context name for the contents page, and the directories that are searched for component files.

- [ГILES]: This section lists all the .rtf files that are to be used in creating the help file.

- [ALIAS]: This section maps numeric constants to context names, which are used for context-sensitive help.

- [MAP]: This section contains the mappings that assign numeric values to the context constants, in much the same way that #define is used in C/C++ files. In most cases, this section simply #include's one or more .hm files that contain the actual mappings.

FIGURE 33.11

Help Project Files in Help Workshop.

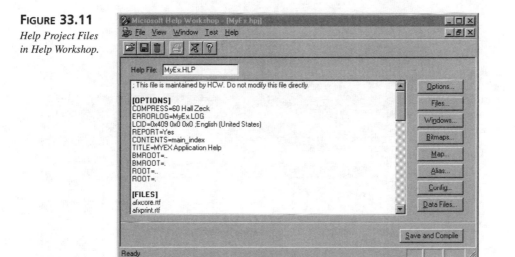

You may edit the help project file directly, using a text editor, although it is generally easier to use Help Workshop, which provides a nice graphical interface for filling in all the relevant settings, including additional help on what each of the settings means. For example, a portion of the dialog for setting project options is shown in Figure 33.12.

Contents Files

The contents (.cnt) file specifies the help page that will be displayed to the user when he or she chooses the Contents tab of WinHelp. Once again, you can edit the .cnt file directly with a text editor, although it is easier to use the graphical interface provided by Help Workshop. To do this, simply open your .cnt file in Help Workshop, which will present a dialog like the one shown in Figure 33.13.

33

ADDING WINDOWS HELP

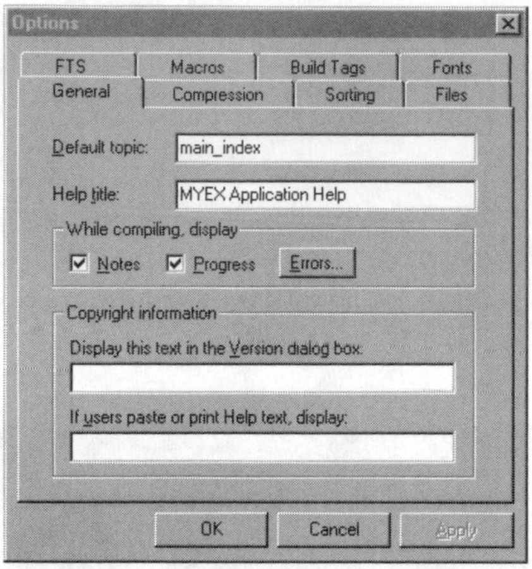

FIGURE 33.12

Help Workshop Options settings.

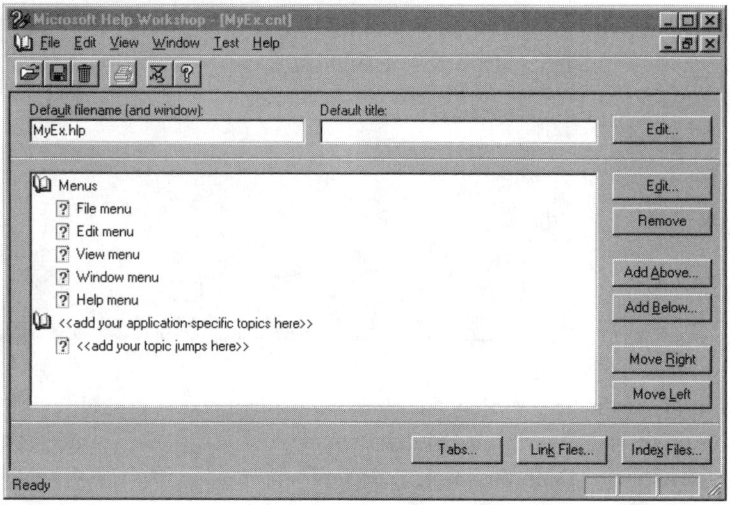

FIGURE 33.13

Editing Contents files.

This dialog allows you to use the buttons on the left to edit or remove existing entries, as well as add new entries to your table of contents.

Compiling Help Projects

Before your applications can make use of your help projects, all the components previously discussed must be compiled to create a single Windows help file, which is given an `.hlp` extension. You may compile your help project from within Help Workshop by selecting the Compile command from the File menu. This is useful for when you are developing your help project.

However, if you created your application with AppWizard, you will notice that a batch file named MakeHelp.bat has been added to your project directory. This file is called whenever you build your Visual C++ project and is responsible for creating the help file for your project. An example of MakeHelp.bat is shown here:

```
@echo off
REM -- First make map file from Microsoft Visual C++ generated resource.h
echo // MAKEHELP.BAT generated Help Map file.  Used by HELPSDI.HPJ.
➥>"hlp\HelpSdi.hm"
echo. >>"hlp\HelpSdi.hm"
echo // Commands (ID_* and IDM_*) >>"hlp\HelpSdi.hm"
makehm ID_,HID_,0x10000 IDM_,HIDM_,0x10000 resource.h >>"hlp\HelpSdi.hm"
echo. >>"hlp\HelpSdi.hm"
echo // Prompts (IDP_*) >>"hlp\HelpSdi.hm"
makehm IDP_,HIDP_,0x30000 resource.h >>"hlp\HelpSdi.hm"
echo. >>"hlp\HelpSdi.hm"
echo // Resources (IDR_*) >>"hlp\HelpSdi.hm"
makehm IDR_,HIDR_,0x20000 resource.h >>"hlp\HelpSdi.hm"
echo. >>"hlp\HelpSdi.hm"
echo // Dialogs (IDD_*) >>"hlp\HelpSdi.hm"
makehm IDD_,HIDD_,0x20000 resource.h >>"hlp\HelpSdi.hm"
echo. >>"hlp\HelpSdi.hm"
echo // Frame Controls (IDW_*) >>"hlp\HelpSdi.hm"
makehm IDW_,HIDW_,0x50000 resource.h >>"hlp\HelpSdi.hm"
REM -- Make help for Project HELPSDI


echo Building Win32 Help files
start /wait hcw /C /E /M "hlp\HelpSdi.hpj"
if errorlevel 1 goto :Error
if not exist "hlp\HelpSdi.hlp" goto :Error
if not exist "hlp\HelpSdi.cnt" goto :Error
echo.
if exist Debug\nul copy "hlp\HelpSdi.hlp" Debug
if exist Debug\nul copy "hlp\HelpSdi.cnt" Debug
if exist Release\nul copy "hlp\HelpSdi.hlp" Release
if exist Release\nul copy "hlp\HelpSdi.cnt" Release
echo.
goto :done

:Error
echo hlp\HelpSdi.hpj(1) : error: Problem encountered creating help file

:done
echo.
```

33

ADDING
WINDOWS HELP

The first half of MakeHelp.bat is devoted to generating the help mapping (.hm) file that is used to associate help contexts with the resource identifiers used within your C++ project. You will look at help mapping files and the makehm utility in more detail later.

The most important part of MakeHelp.bat is the line that actually compiles your help project. This is done by calling hcw.exe, as in the following line:

```
start /wait hcw /C /E /M "hlp\HelpSdi.hpj"
```

The /C switch tells hcw to compile the help project file that is specified, and the /E switch tells hcw to exit when it finishes. The /M option is used to minimize the window for hcw so that it is out of the way while it is compiling.

Tip

When compiling your help project from the command line or from within Developer Studio, you see only basic error messages, like the one shown here:

```
hlp\HelpSdi.hpj(1) : error: Problem encountered creating help file
```

Obviously, this doesn't give you much help on what went wrong. You can see more detailed error messages if you try to compile the help project from within the Help Workshop GUI.

If your help project compiles successfully, you will be the proud owner of a bouncing baby help file with a .hlp extension. The remainder of MakeHelp.bat simply copies this file (and your contents file) to the appropriate target directories. Be sure that you distribute these files with your application.

Testing Help Projects

The next section shows how to call on the Windows help system from your applications. However, it is often useful to be sure that your help file is behaving as expected before you integrate it with your application.

Help Workshop can be a great help when you test your help file, and you don't need to change the source code in your application and rebuild each time.

From the Test menu of the Help Workshop, you can test the contents file for your help project, send a macro to WinHelp, or use a graphical interface to make calls to the WinHelp API directly. In addition, you can close all of the help windows that are left hanging around with a single menu command.

Calling WinHelp from Your Applications

Now that you have created a working help file, you need to be able to access the help file from within your application. This is done by using the `::WinHelp()` function, although you will also take a look at some of the MFC functions that simplify calling `::WinHelp()`.

`::WinHelp()`

The Win32 API provides access to many different features of the WinHelp system via a single function call, `::WinHelp()`. The prototype for `::WinHelp()` is shown here:

```
BOOL WinHelp( HWND hWndMain, LPCTSTR lpszHelp,
            UINT uCommand, DWORD dwData );
```

The `hWndMain` parameter should be passed as a handle of the window that is requesting help, and the `lpszHelp` parameter should contain the path to the help file that is to be used.

The `uCommand` parameter is used to specify the operation that will be performed, and `dwData` is used in different ways depending on the value of `uCommand`. Some of the most commonly used values of `uCommand` are shown here:

- `HELP_FINDER`: Displays the Help Topics dialog box, containing the table of contents for the help file.
- `HELP_HELPONHELP`: Displays help information on using WinHelp. The file `winhlp32.hlp` must be available for this.
- `HELP_CONTEXT`: Displays a topic identified by a context ID that appears in the `[MAP]` section of the `.hpj` file. `dwData` should contain the context ID.
- `HELP_CONTEXTPOPUP`: This is similar to `HELP_CONTEXT`, but the help topic is displayed as a pop-up window. `dwData` should contain the context ID.
- `HELP_QUIT`: This tells WinHelp to close all WinHelp windows. `dwData` is ignored.

For more on additional commands for use with `::WinHelp()`, see the online help in Developer Studio.

Using Help with MFC

The Microsoft Foundation Classes provide easy access to the WinHelp system, particularly if you have created your application with AppWizard.

CWinApp::WinHelp()

The CWinApp class supports a WinHelp() method that can simplify the process of displaying help. The prototype for CWinApp::WinHelp() is shown here:

```
virtual void WinHelp( DWORD dwData, UINT nCmd = HELP_CONTEXT );
```

Basically, this function simply wraps the Win32 API ::WinHelp() function, although MFC will keep track of the window handle and help file path for you. The values of dwData and nCmd should be the same as the values of dwData and uCommand shown previously for ::WinHelp().

MFC Help Handlers

If you have created your MFC application with AppWizard and selected the context-sensitive help option, you will notice that several handlers have been added to the message map for your applications. These are used to handle the messages that are generated by the commands on the Help menu that AppWizard generates. An example of these message map entries is shown here:

```
ON_COMMAND(ID_HELP_FINDER, CFrameWnd::OnHelpFinder)
ON_COMMAND(ID_HELP, CFrameWnd::OnHelp)
ON_COMMAND(ID_CONTEXT_HELP, CFrameWnd::OnContextHelp)
ON_COMMAND(ID_DEFAULT_HELP, CFrameWnd::OnHelpFinder)
```

The ID_HELP_FINDER message is sent by the Help Topics command on the Help menu. The handler function, OnHelpFinder(), simply calls CWinApp::WinHelp(), as shown here:

```
AfxGetApp()->WinHelp(0L, HELP_FINDER);
```

The ID_HELP message is sent when the user presses F1. The OnHelp() function will attempt to display a help topic that is relevant to the current window. If none is found, the default help topic will be displayed.

The ID_CONTEXT_HELP message is sent when the user enters help mode by pressing shift+F1 or clicks the Help mode tool. The OnContextHelp() handler places the application in Help mode. Once in Help mode, user input is handled differently. MFC will try to display help for any controls clicked, rather than send the command message for the control.

When no help topics are found for a particular context, the ID_DEFAULT_HELP message is sent. MFC handles this by displaying the table of contents for the help file.

In addition, the CWinApp class supports the OnHelpUsing() method, which will display help on using the WinHelp interface. You can easily add support for this to your application by adding a menu item with the ID of ID_HELP_USING and adding the following message map entry:

```
ON_COMMAND( ID_HELP_USING, OnHelpUsing )
```

In most cases, it is easiest to use the predefined command IDs for requesting help and simply use the message map entries to call the appropriate handlers in the CWinApp class. However, you might want to call CWinApp::WinHelp() directly from your application in some cases.

Adding Context-Sensitive Help

You can make your applications much more user-friendly by presenting help for a particular dialog or menu command that the user has selected when he presses F1. This is much easier to use than searching through the whole help file for the information.

Using the MFC help framework, adding context-sensitive help is rather simple. To show how to do this, we will add a new menu command to an application and add context-sensitive help for it.

You will need to add the menu to your application, adding a command handler for it as you normally would. For the sake of this example, assume that the new command is given the ID of ID_MY_COMMAND.

Next, you will need to add a help topic for this command, as shown earlier. For this example, make sure to use the (#) footnote to assign a context name of my_command.

Now, you will need to add an entry to the [ALIAS] section of the project's .hpj file, like the following:

```
HID_MY_COMMAND = my_command
```

Now when you build your application, Developer Studio will call on MakeHelp.bat. One of the first things that this batch file will do is call on the makehm utility to map help context IDs for the resource IDs that are used in your application. This mapping is written to a .hm file, which would contain a line like the following:

```
HID_MYCOMMAND                           0x18003
```

This .hm file is included in the [MAP] section of the help project (.hpj) file. This mapping, when combined with the entry in the [ALIAS] section, will tell WinHelp to bring up the my_command help topic whenever the user highlights the new menu command and presses F1.

Using HTML Help with Visual C++

HTML Help doesn't use HTML source files directly. Rather, the files are compiled into files with the .CHM extension. This is because HTML Help requires information that isn't part of a typical IITML document. An HTML Help file also includes the topic and index information that is expected by Windows users.

HTML Help requires Internet Explorer 3.01 or later. If you use Internet Explorer 4.0 or later, you can take advantage of many of the IE 4.0 features, such as DHTML and cascading style sheets.

On the negative side, using HTML Help requires more work on the developer's part than using WinHelp. MFC AppWizard easily adds WinHelp to your MFC project with a simple click of a check box. HTML Help requires you to make a few extra steps.

Creating an HTML Help Project

You may find it fairly simple to create an HTML Help project when compared to a WinHelp project. If nothing else, it's certainly less expensive for an amateur programmer. There's no need to purchase Microsoft Word to edit your source files for one thing. And although you may want to purchase RoboHelp or another third-party tool to help create your HTML Help project, the tools supplied by Microsoft are quite serviceable.

Before beginning an HTML Help project, you must install the latest version of the HTML Help Workshop. This tool is included in the MSDN Library included with Visual C++. Search for the topic titled, "Microsoft HTML Help Download." This MSDN Library topic contains information about installing HTML Help workshop on your computer.

When HTML Help Workshop is installed, an HTML Help Workshop folder is placed in your Programs group. Clicking on the HTML Help Workshop icon launches HTML Help Workshop, as shown in Figure 33.14.

Creating an HTML Help file consists of the following steps:

1. Create an HTML Help project.
2. Create one or more HTML help topics, using HTML Help Workshop or any other HTML editor.
3. Create an index file for your help topics.
4. Create an alias file to map your application's help constants to the relevant help topics.

5. Create a table of contents.

6. Use HTML Help Workshop to compile the content into a Compiled Help Module (CHM) file.

FIGURE 33.14

HTML Help Workshop,

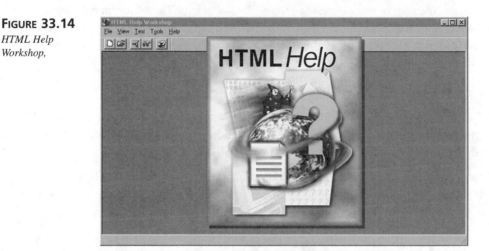

Using HTML Help Workshop to Create a Project

HTML Help Workshop includes a wizard that is used to create a new help project. Simply select File, New from the menu, and select Project from the dialog box. You will be presented with the wizard shown in Figure 33.15.

FIGURE 33.15

The HTML Help Workshop Project Wizard.

The wizard can be used to create an HTML help project from an existing WinHelp project, or to create new HTML help projects from scratch.

Creating Topic Pages

Each help topic in an HTML Help project is a separate HTML page. You can use any tool capable of creating an HTML page to create your topics—anything from basic tools such as Notepad, to more expensive tools like RoboHelp. The editor included with HTML Help Workshop is very much like Notepad—it requires you to have some basic knowledge of HTML, although it does automatically generate the HTML skeleton for your document automatically.

Create an Index File for Help Topics

The index for an HTML Help file is one of two ways that a user navigates through help topics. (The other method is the Table of Contents.) An index is an HTML file with an HHK extension, and is easily created using HTML Help Workshop.

To open an index file for an open project, click on the Index tab in HTML Help Workshop. If no index file is associated with the help project, the dialog box shown in Figure 33.16 will be displayed.

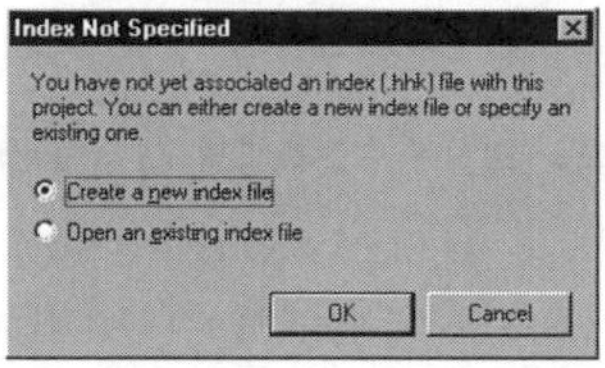

FIGURE 33.16

This dialog box displays when no index file is associated with your help project.

The dialog box shown in Figure 33.16 prompts you to select from two options:

- You can specify an existing index file; this index file will be added to your HTML help project.
- You can elect to have a blank index file added to your project.

The form view used to create an index is shown in Figure 33.17. In Figure 33.17, several index entries have been added to the index file.

The form shown in Figure 33.17 includes a toolbar that enables you to perform common operations on the index file:

- Configure properties for the index file
- Create a new keyword entry for the index
- Edit a selected keyword entry in the index
- Delete an entry from the index

- Move the keyword up or down in the index
- Change the indentation for a keyword in the index
- Sort keywords in the index
- View the HTML source for a particular topic file
- Save the index file to disk

FIGURE 33.17

The index dialog box used from HTML Help Workshop.

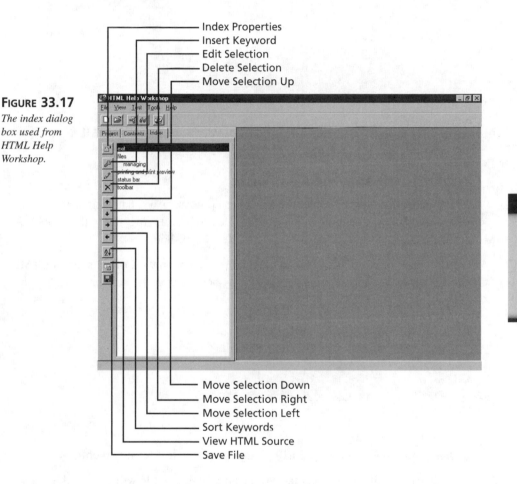

Index Properties
Insert Keyword
Edit Selection
Delete Selection
Move Selection Up

Move Selection Down
Move Selection Right
Move Selection Left
Sort Keywords
View HTML Source
Save File

To add a new keyword to the index, click the Insert A Keyword icon. The Index Entry dialog box will be displayed, as shown in Figure 33.18.

A new keyword is added by typing the keyword name into the keyword edit control. You must then click the Add button to select an HTML help topic file. The Add button may be used to associate multiple help topics with a single keyword.

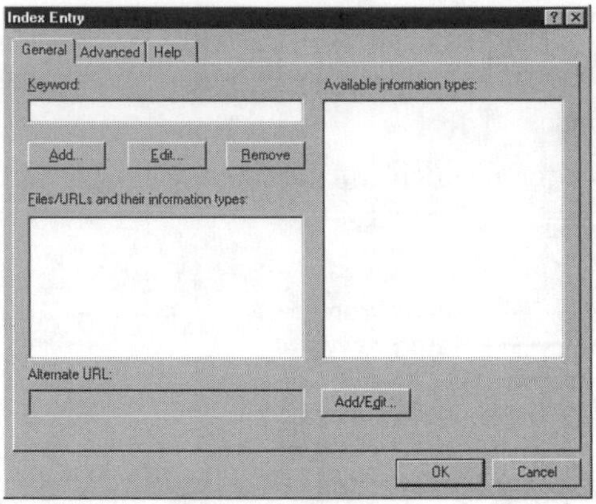

FIGURE 33.18

The Index Entry dialog box is used to add new index keywords.

Another way to access the index file is to select File, New from the HTML Help Workshop menu. A new, untitled index file will be opened for you to edit.

Creating a Table of Contents

Like the index, the table of contents is one of the primary ways that users navigate through online help. The table of contents source file is an HTML file with an .HHC extension, and is easily created using HTML Help Workshop.

To open a table of contents file for an open project, click on the Contents tab in HTML Help Workshop. If no table of contents file is associated with the help project, the dialog box shown in Figure 33.19 will be displayed.

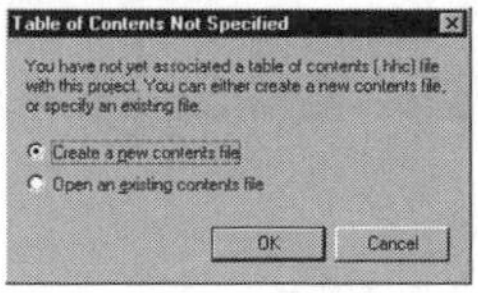

FIGURE 33.19

This dialog box displays when no table of contents file is associated with your help project.

The dialog box shown in Figure 33.19 prompts you to select from two options:

- You can specify an existing table of contents file; this file will be added to your HTML help project.
- You can elect to have a blank table of contents file added to your project.

The form view used to create a table of contents is nearly identical to the dialog box used to create an index shown earlier, and is shown in Figure 33.20.

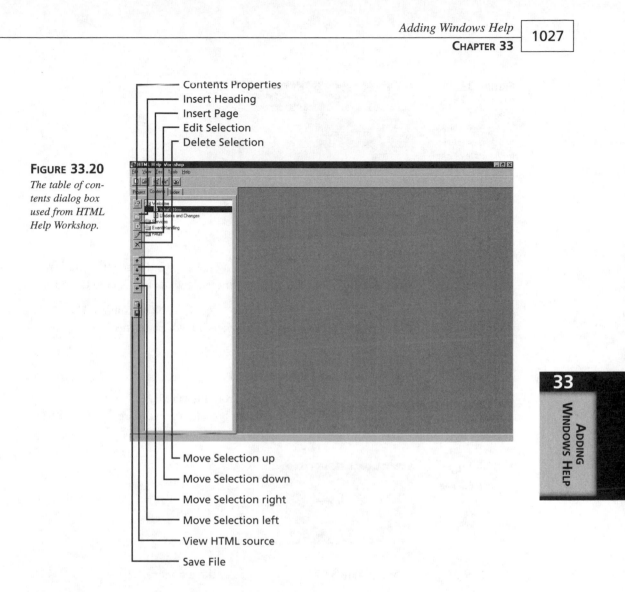

Contents Properties
Insert Heading
Insert Page
Edit Selection
Delete Selection

FIGURE 33.20

The table of contents dialog box used from HTML Help Workshop.

Move Selection up
Move Selection down
Move Selection right
Move Selection left
View HTML source
Save File

The toolbar included with the form shown in Figure 33.20 enables you to perform common operations on the table of contents file. This toolbar differs from the toolbar used in the index dialog box in two ways:

- Two types of icons—headings or pages, can be associated with entries.
- Entries can't be sorted alphabetically.

To add a new entry to the table of contents, click the Insert A Heading or Insert A Page icons. The Table of Contents Entry dialog box will be displayed, as shown in Figure 33.21.

FIGURE 33.21

The Table of Contents Entry dialog box is used to add new entries to the table of contents.

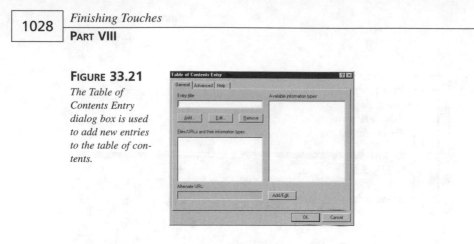

A new entry is added to the table of contents by typing the keyword name into the Entry Title edit control. You must then click the Add button to select an HTML help topic file.

Another way to access the table of contents file is to select File, New from the HTML Help Workshop menu. A new, untitled table of contents file will be opened for you to edit.

Compiling an HTML Help Project

To compile your help project, select File, Compile from the HTML Help Compiler menu, or click the Compile toolbar icon. The dialog box shown in Figure 33.22 will be displayed.

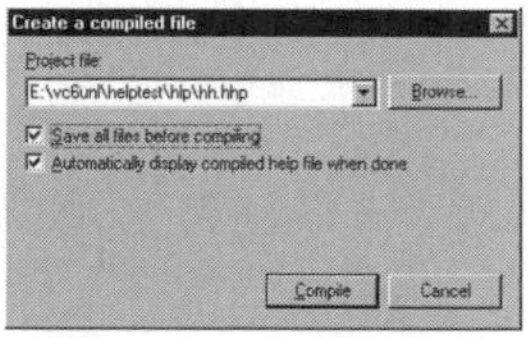

FIGURE 33.22

The Index dialog box used from HTML Help Workshop.

The dialog box shown in Figure 33.22 lets you specify three options:

- The location of the HTML help project to be compiled
- Whether open HTML files should be saved before compiling
- Whether the HTML help file should be displayed after the compile is completed

To compile the project, click the Compile button. At this point, you have a fully compiled HTML help file. The next section discusses the steps required to integrate the help file into a Visual C++ project.

Integrating HTML into a Visual C++ Project

In order to use HTML Help, you must make a few minor changes to your Visual C++ project and compiler settings, as well as a few changes to your HTML help project These changes make it possible for you to call the HTML Help functions exposed by the operating system.

Modifications Required in the HTML Help Project

The first step in integrating HTML help with a Visual C++ project is to add ALIAS and MAP sections to the HTML help project file. These two sections serve a similar purpose as the MAP and ALIAS sections used in WinHelp project files.

The ALIAS section is used to establish a relationship between symbolic constants and HTML help files. An example of an ALIAS section is shown here:

```
[ALIAS]
IDH_LATTE      =    html\latte.htm
IDH_MOCHA      =    html\mocha.htm
IDH_ESPRESSO   =    html\espresso.htm
IDH_DECAF      =    html\decaf.htm
```

Each entry in the ALIAS section associates an HTML help topic file with a symbol that's defined in the MAP section. Any symbols found in the ALIAS section must have a corresponding entry in the ALIAS section. A typical ALIAS section is shown below:

```
[MAP]
#define IDH_LATTE      101
#define IDH_MOCHA      102
#define IDH_ESPRESSO   103
#define IDH_DECAF      104
```

Alternatively, you can include a header file that defines the values for the HTML help symbols:

```
 [MAP]
#include "coffee.h"
```

Unfortunately, HTML Help Workshop doesn't provide any way to add ALIAS and MAP sections. You must open the help project file using Notepad or another editor, and add the sections manually.

33

ADDING
WINDOWS HELP

Modifications Required in the Visual C++ Project

In order to use the HTML help API, you must perform the following steps:

- Include `htmlhelp.h` in any source files that call the HTML help API.
- Put the `htmlhelp.h` include file in the compiler's search path. You alter the Developer Studio directory options to search the HTML Help Workshop's include directory by selecting Tools, Options from the Developer Studio menu, and using the Directories tab on the Options dialog box.
- Add `htmlhelp.lib` to the Visual C++ project by selecting Project, Settings from the Developer Studio menu, and clicking the Link tab in the Project Settings dialog box. Select General from the category list, and enter **htmlhelp.lib** in the Object/library modules edit control.
- Put the `htmlhelp.lib` library file in the compiler's search path. You alter the Developer Studio directory options to search the HTML Help Workshop's lib directory by selecting Tools, Options from the Developer Studio menu, and using Directories tab on the Options dialog box.

These steps make it possible for you to use the `HTMLHelp` function, which is typically called like this:

```
HtmlHelp(m_hWnd, "htest.chm", HH_HELP_CONTEXT, IDH_TELETUBBY_PO);
```

The `HTMLHelp` function has four parameters:

- A window handle for the calling application, or `NULL`.
- The name of the compiled HTML help file to be used to display the help topic. If no path is specified, the help file must be in the project directory.
- The action to be performed, either `HH_HELP_CONTEXT` for context-sensitive help, or `HH_HELP_TOPIC` to display a specific topic.
- A context ID for the help topic to be displayed.

You can use HTML Help in addition to any support your application currently has for WinHelp. If you want to replace WinHelp entirely, you can override `CWinApp::WinHelp` function in your CWinApp-derived class, and call `HtmlHelp` instead of `WinHelp`.

Summary

One of the most important attributes of a good Windows application is ease of use. Adding online help to your application certainly goes a long way toward making your application easier to use.

In this chapter, you learned

- How the Windows help system can be used to provide your users with easy access to the information that they will need when using your application.

- How to author your own rich-text format help topic files, and how these are compiled along with help project, contents, and help mapping files to create a Windows help file (.hlp) that can be used with your applications.

- HTML Help is a new type of online help that is used in new products from Microsoft, such as Visual C++ and Office 2000.

- How you can use HTML Help Workshop to create HTML help files that can be used in your applications.

- How to call on the services of WinHelp or HTML help from your application, both with and without the aid of the Microsoft Foundation Classes.

33

ADDING WINDOWS HELP

Appendix

Additional Resources

by Mickey Williams

As you probably know, the documentation provided with Visual C++ is superb, and the MSDN Library included with Visual C++ provides fingertip access to a wealth of information. One of the great things about Visual C++ and MFC is the plethora of Microsoft and third-party resources available to you as a programmer. This chapter provides you with sources of information to aid you in your development activities. Remember, knowledge is power. That power can help you develop killer professional, commercial-grade applications.

Visual C++ Resources

As you enter the cutthroat world of applications development and create your own Visual C++ applications, you should be armed with the knowledge that you have a multitude of available sources to assist you in your programming endeavors. Chances are that the problem you are having or your area of inquiry has been explored by another programmer. Why reinvent the wheel? Visual C++, MFC, and Microsoft Windows programming in general have an abundance of resources, such as Software Developer's Kits, magazines, Internet sites, books, and—most important—the *Microsoft Developer's Network* (MSDN) Library subscription.

Microsoft Developer's Network

The MSDN Library is one of the greatest assets in my set of development tools. Many times it has saved me countless hours of development time and frustration. I cannot imagine doing without it.

What is this great tool? How can you get it? There are actually three ways:

- Access the free online version of the MSDN Library at

  `http://msdn.microsoft.com`

- For a limited time, Microsoft is offering a free subscription to the MSDN Library to developers who purchase Visual C++ or other Visual Studio tools. You can get more information on this offer at

  `http://msdn.microsoft.com/subscriptions/offer/default.asp`

- And finally, you can order a subscription to the MSDN Library from Microsoft or an approved reseller.

> **Note**
>
> You can get information about a subscription to the Microsoft Developer's Network at
>
> `http://msdn.microsoft.com`

The Microsoft Developer's Network offers multiple subscription levels. The MSDN Library is just one of your options. Three levels of subscription are available:

- Library
- Professional
- Universal

The subscription is for one year and is updated every month (the Library is updated quarterly). Each of these levels offers goodies to aid you in the development process. The Library subscription is the basic level; the top level is the Universal subscription. At each level, you get the previous level's items. The following sections explain the components of each level.

Library Subscription

The MSDN Library is the centerpiece of all levels. The MSDN Library is a DVD or a set of CD-ROMs that is updated quarterly. The Library contains gigabytes of developer product documentation, technical articles from Microsoft and other third-party sources, thousands of reusable code samples, and the Developer Knowledge Base. This is more than 150,000 pages of essential information on programming for Windows. Each quarter, this information is enhanced and updated with the latest in Windows programming information. The MSDN Library is based on Microsoft's HTML Help Engine. The MSDN Library enables you to perform full text searches and includes an extensive cross-referenced index.

With an MSDN subscription, you also get a subscription to *The Developer Network News*. It contains up-to-the-minute information on the hottest Microsoft technology. Articles consist of information on developing software for the Windows family of operating systems from the people who make the operating systems.

As a member of MSDN, you get a 20% discount on all Microsoft Press books—and several of the hottest books are on the MSDN Library CD-ROM.

Professional Subscription

The MSDN Professional subscription contains all the benefits of the Library subscription plus the Development Platform. The Development Platform contains all the *Software Developer's Kits* (SDKs), *Device Driver Kits* (DDKs), and Microsoft operating systems on a set of CD-ROMs or DVDs that is updated quarterly. This optionally includes the international versions; as an MSDN member, you will receive the beta releases of these items. An SDK is a companion CD-ROM that contains a development toolkit, examples, redistributables, and API documentation. There are SDKs for ODBC, MAPI, WIN32, TAPI, DirectX, and BackOffice, to name a few. DDKs are similar kits for developers of device drivers (such as printers and video cards). These SDKs and DDKs are invaluable sources of information. Most of the SDKs and their components are not available anywhere else.

In addition, you get two phone support calls to help you with the setup of the Development Platform or the MSDN Library.

Any serious Windows developer should consider purchasing at least the MSDN Professional subscription. Now that I have it, I don't know how I ever got along without it.

Universal Subscription

As an MSDN Universal subscriber, you receive all the benefits of the Professional subscription plus the BackOffice Test Platform. The BackOffice Test Platform is a set of CD-ROMs with the latest released versions of the server components of Microsoft BackOffice:

- Windows NT Server
- Microsoft SQL Server
- Microsoft SNA Server
- Microsoft Systems Management Server
- Microsoft Exchange Server

Also included in the Universal subscription is a one-year subscription to the following development tools:

- Microsoft Visual Basic Enterprise Edition
- Visual SourceSafe
- Visual C++ Enterprise Edition
- Visual FoxPro Professional Edition
- Microsoft Project
- Microsoft Office Developer
- Microsoft Access Developer's Kit
- Visual J++ Enterprise Edition

Hard-Copy Visual C++ Documentation

Some developers prefer hard-copy documentation. You can order printed copies of Visual C++ documentation from Microsoft Press.

> **Note**
>
> You can reach Microsoft Press at 800-MSPRESS. You can visit the online book-store at
>
> `http://mspress.microsoft.com`

All the hard-copy references are available from the MSDN Library CD-ROMs that come with your Visual C++ CD-ROM. These books are viewable with the MSDN Library and are capable of a full text search. If you prefer the hard-copy editions, here are the titles:

- *Microsoft Visual C++ 6.0 Language Reference*
- *Microsoft Visual C++ 6.0 MFC Library Reference, Part I*
- *Microsoft Visual C++ 6.0 MFC Library Reference, Part II*
- *Microsoft Visual C++ 6.0 Run-Time Library Reference*
- *Microsoft Visual C++ 6.0 Template Libraries Reference*

Magazines and Journals

You can go broke with all the magazine subscriptions available that deal with computers and computer programming. The following are some of the really good magazines for developers. All these magazines are excellent, but I have found *Microsoft Systems Journal* and *Windows Tech Journal* to be especially helpful.

C/C++ Users Journal
1601 W. 23rd Street
Suite 200
Lawrence, KS 66046-2700
785-841-1631
`http://www.cuj.com`

Dr. Dobb's Journal
P.O. 56188
Boulder, CO 80322-6188
800-456-1215
`http://www.ddj.com`

MSDN Magazine
Miller Freeman
P.O. 56621
Boulder, CO 80322-6621
800-666-1084
`http://msdn.microsoft.com/msdnmag`

Software Development
600 Harrison Street
San Francisco, CA 94107
415-905-2200
http://www.sdmagazine.com

Windows Developer's Journal
P.O. 56565
Boulder, CO 80322-6565
800-365-1425
http://www.wdj.com

Conferences

Several excellent developers conferences are offered. Until March 1996, I had never been to a development conference. I was able to talk my boss into going—and taking me and two of my developers—to Software Development 96 in San Francisco at the Moscone Center. My boss was so impressed she has championed the effort to send many more of my company's developers and managers next year.

I garnered so much information, it took me months to assimilate it all. I got training from renowned industry professional trainers such as Richard Hale Shaw and Bruce Eckel. I actually got to meet Jeff Prosise (Microsoft engineer and columnist for *MSJ),* Charles Petzold (father of Microsoft Windows), Jim McCarthy (former senior developer and project manager of Visual C++), and Bjarne Stroustrup (inventor of C++). There were product demos, seminars, and freebies galore.

I highly recommend that you attend one of the professional developers conferences. Although I have attended only SD 96, several of my friends have recommended the following:

COMDEX

http://www.comdex.com

Software Development Conference

http://www.sdexpo.com

VBITS

http://www.vbits.net

Visual C++ Developers Conference

http://www.vcdc.com

Win-Dev

http://www.butrain.com/Windev/

In addition, Microsoft dedicates a Web page to upcoming events, including TechEd, the Professional Developers Conference, TechNet Briefings, and even third-party conferences and events:

Microsoft Events

`http://events.microsoft.com`

The information and experience you receive are well worth the time and investment of attending. I was excited and motivated when I was able to meet and talk with my peers in the industry, as well as leaders and legends. Take the time to attend. If your boss won't pay for it, get the boss to go with you. You won't be sorry!

Software

Many third-party add-ons and programs are available to enhance and integrate with your application. In addition, several multimedia CD-ROM titles may be of use to you in enhancing your software development skills. Here are a few of them:

- **Crystal Reports**   Crystal Reports is report writer software. The standard edition comes with Visual C++ Professional. Crystal Reports Professional has many more features, including an intuitive interface and an easy-to-use report designer. It offers support for almost every database known to the modern programmer. It also integrates into Microsoft Developer Studio. For more information, contact Seagate Software at

  `http://www.seagatesoftware.com`

- **Install Shield**   For all your installation needs, Install Shield is the tool. A scaled-down SDK version comes with Visual C++; however, I highly recommend that you purchase the Professional version. Most major software vendors use Install Shield, and users have become accustomed to the Install Shield setup interface, which is very easy to use. You can find information on Install Shield at Install Shield Corporation's home page:

  `http://www.installshield.com`

Caution

If you build your setup utility with the Install Shield SDK that comes with Visual C++, and you upgrade to the Professional version of Install Shield, you have to re-create your setup utility. No tool is available to convert your setup utility from the SDK version to work in the Professional version.

- **Mastering MFC Development Using Visual C++ 6.0**   This is a multimedia training application from Microsoft Press. This CD-ROM contains a well-laid-out tutorial on Visual C++ and is part of the Microsoft Certified Professional curriculum. You can reach Microsoft Press at 800-MSPRESS, or you can visit the online bookstore at

  http://mspress.microsoft.com

- **Microsoft Visual SourceSafe**   Visual SourceSafe provides source code and distributable control. It tracks your changes and keeps a record of who made those changes. It is an invaluable tool for use in software configuration management. Visual SourceSafe comes with the Enterprise Edition of Visual C++. You can purchase it separately, however, if you have only the Standard or Professional Edition. The nice thing about Visual SourceSafe is that it integrates with the Visual C++ IDE. If you try to edit a file without checking it out, SourceSafe prompts you to do so. Visual SourceSafe is available from Microsoft, and you can get information on it at

  http://msdn.microsoft.com/ssafe

- **Microsoft Visual Test**   Visual Test is a great tool to automate the testing of your software. It integrates with all of Microsoft's development tools. Microsoft recently sold Visual Test to Rational Software. You can get information on Visual Test from Rational Corporation's home page:

  http://www.rational.com/vtest

- **NuMega Bounds Checker**   NuMega Bounds Checker is a must for Visual C++ developers. It is a tool to help you detect and eliminate those pesky memory leaks. It also has the capability to spy into DLLs and low-level operating system calls. I once used it to find out that an ODBC driver (not my software) was causing my memory leak. It is an excellent enhanced debugger. You can get information on NuMega at

  http://www.numega.com

Books on Visual C++, MFC, and Windows Programming

A wealth of books is available on Visual C++, MFC, and Windows programming. A good professional library is a must for every developer. Many of these books have saved my bacon when I needed assistance. I hope you will find them equally useful.

Don Box, *Essential COM* (Addison Wesley, 1998).

Davis Chapman, *Teach Yourself Visual C++ 6 in 21 Days* (Sams Publishing, 1998).

David Chappell, *Understanding ActiveX and OLE* (Microsoft Press, 1996).

Adam Denning, *OLE Controls—Inside Out,* 3rd ed. (Microsoft Press, 1997).

Dino Esposito, *Visual C++ Windows Shell Programming* (Wrox Press, 1998).

James D. Murray, *Windows NT Event Logging* (O'Reilly & Associates, 1998).

Charles Petzold, *Programming Windows* (Microsoft Press, 1998).

Jeff Prosise, *Programming Windows with MFC* (Microsoft Press, 1999).

John Robbins, *Debugging Applications* (Microsoft Press, 2000).

Lyn Robison, *Teach Yourself Database Programming with Visual C++ 6 in 21 Days* (Sams Publishing, 1998).

Rick Sawtell and Richard Waymire, *Teach Yourself SQL Server in 21 Days* (Sams Publishing, 1999).

Mickey Williams, *Programming Windows 2000 Unleashed* (Sams Publishing, 1999).

Mickey Williams, *Teach Yourself Visual C++ in 24 Hours* (Sams Publishing, 1998).

Scott Wingo and George Sheppard, *MFC Internals* (Addision Wesley, 1996).

Internet

The Internet has brought an information explosion. Thousands of sites crop up every day. Here are some Internet sites I have found helpful in my development efforts:

ActiveX Resource Center
`http://www.active-x.com`

Code Guru
`http://www.codcguru.com/`

Code Project
`http://www.codeproject.com/`

Codev Technologies
`http://www.codevtech.com/`

DevelopMentor
`http://www.develop.com/`

Dundas Software
`http://www.dundas.com/`

Interface Technologies
`http://www.iftech.com/`

Microsoft Corporation
`http://www.microsoft.com/`

Microsoft Developer's Network
`http://msdn.microsoft.com`

NuMega Technologies
`http://www.numega.com/`

Rogue Wave Software
`http://www.roguewave.com/`

Visual C++ Developer's Journal
`http://www.vcdj.com/`

The World Wide Web Consortium (W3C)
`http://www.w3.org`

ZD Net Developer
`http://www.zdnet.com/devhead/`

Newsgroups and FAQs

With newsgroups, you can post questions to fellow developers in the hope that someone out there has the answer. Many times, developers from Microsoft browse the newsgroups and answer questions. Here are a few newsgroups that cover everything from MFC to OLE to C++:

```
comp.lang.c++

comp.os.ms-windows.programmer.misc

comp.os.ms-windows.programmer.ole

comp.os.ms-windows.programmer.tools

comp.os.ms-windows.programmer.tools.mfc

comp.os.ms-windows.programmer.win32

microsoft.public.vc.database

microsoft.public.vc.debugger

microsoft.public.vc.events

microsoft.public.vc.language

microsoft.public.vc.mfc

microsoft.public.vc.database

microsoft.public.vc.mfc.docview

microsoft.public.vc.mfc.macintosh

microsoft.public.vc.mfcole

microsoft.public.vc.utilities
```

Summary

As you can see, a great deal of information and support is available to aid you in the development of your Windows-based applications. Gone are the days of cryptic command-line help systems, poor support, and lousy documentation. This type of support available through MSDN, the Internet, books, newsgroups, and FAQs is unparalleled in any other development environment. I remember the days of clunking around on a VAX or a UNIX box, and I don't ever want to go back. Although development is still a dynamic and complicated process, the tools and information are available to allow software engineers to concentrate on solving problems, not searching for information.

INDEX

FROM KNOWLEDGE TO MASTERY

Unleashed *takes you beyond the average technology discussions. It's the best resource for practical advice from experts and the most in-depth coverage of the latest information.* **Unleashed**—*the necessary tool for serious users.*

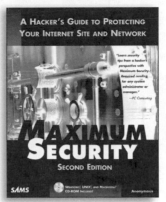

Maximum Security, Second Edition

Anonymous
0-672-31341-3
$49.99 USA/$70.95 CAN

Other Unleashed Titles

Windows 2000 API SuperBible
Richard Simon
0-672-31933-0
$64.99 USA/$96.95 CAN

Sams Teach Yourself SQL in 10 Minutes
Ben Forta
0-672-31664-1
$12.99 USA/$19.95 CAN

Creating Lightweight Components with ATL
Jonathan Bates
0-672-31535-1
$49.99 USA/$74.95 CAN

Sams Teach Yourself SQL Server 7.0 in 21 Days
Rick Sawtell and Richard Waymire
0-672-31290-5
$39.99 USA/$57.95 CAN

Building Enterprise Solutions with Visual Studio 6
G.A.Sullivan
0-672-31489-4
$49.99 US/$71.95 CAN

Sams Teach Yourself CGI in 24 Hours
Rafe Colburn
0-672-31880-6
$24.99 USA/$37.95 CAN

Microsoft SQL Server 7 DBA Survival Guide
Mark Spenik; Orryn Sledge
0-672-31226-3
$49.99 USA/$74.95 CAN

F. Scott Barker's Microsoft Access 2000 Power Programming
F. Scott Barker
0-672-31506-8
$49.99 USA/$74.95 CAN

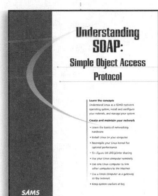

Understanding SOAP

Kennard Scribner
0-672-31922-5
$29.99 US/$44.95 CAN

Active Directory Programming

Gil Kirkpatrick
0-672-31587-4
$39.99 US/$59.95 CAN

SAMS

www.samspublishing.com

All prices are subject to change.

Please Read This Before Opening Package

Note

This CD-ROM uses long and mixed-case filenames requiring the use of a protected-mode CD-ROM Driver.

What's on the Disc

The companion CD-ROM contains all of the authors' source code and samples from the book and some third-party software products.

Windows 95, Windows 98, Windows NT 4, and Windows 2000 Installation Instructions

1. Insert the CD-ROM disc into your CD-ROM drive.

2. From the desktop, double-click on the My Computer icon.

3. Double-click on the icon representing your CD-ROM drive.

4. Double-click on the icon titled START.EXE to run the installation program.

5. Follow the onscreen instructions to finish the installation.

> **Note**
>
> If Windows 95, Windows 98, Windows NT 4, or Windows 2000 is installed on your computer and you have the AutoPlay feature enabled, the START.EXE program starts automatically whenever you insert the disc into your CD-ROM drive.